INDIAN PHILOSOPHY

INDIAN PHILOSOPHY

BY

S. RADHAKRISHNAN

VOLUME II

OXFORD
UNIVERSITY PRESS

OXFORD
UNIVERSITY PRESS

YMCA Library Building, Jai Singh Road, New Delhi 110 001

Oxford University Press is a department of the University of Oxford. It furthers the University's objective of excellence in research, scholarship, and education by publishing worldwide in

Oxford New York

Auckland Bangkok Buenos Aires Cape Town Chennai Dar es Salaam Delhi Hong Kong Istanbul Karachi Kolkata Kuala Lumpur Madrid Melbourne Mexico City Mumbai Nairobi São Paulo Shanghai Singapore Taipei Tokyo Toronto

with an associated company in Berlin

Published in India
By Oxford University Press, New Delhi

First published 1923
Revised edition 1929, Indian edition 1940
Published by George Allen & Unwin Ltd.
This edition published in India 1989
By arrangement with the original publisher
Seventh impression 1994
Oxford India Paperbacks 1996
Ninth impression 2002

ISBN 019 563820 4

Printed by Sai Printopack Pvt Ltd, New Delhi 110 020
Published by Manzar Khan, Oxford University Press
YMCA Library Building, Jai Singh Road, New Delhi 110 001

PREFACE TO THE SECOND EDITION

I HAVE utilised the opportunity offered by the Second Edition to correct a number of minor errors and misprints, and to extract in a few doubtful and difficult cases the Sanskrit originals so as to enable the reader to compare the interpretations with the text. These latter are found in the Notes at the end of the book, which also include material intended to clear up difficulties or bring the book up-to-date.

The English renderings of Sanskrit texts are generally based on standard translations where available, and these are mentioned in the bibliographical references. These latter are intended mainly as a guide to the literature available in English, though they indirectly point the way to the whole literature on the subject.

I have to thank many friends and critics for their valuable suggestions. I am specially indebted to Professor M. Hiriyanna of Mysore. Among others who helped me with valuable advice are Mahāmahopādhyāya S. Kuppuswāmi Śāstri of Madras and Mahāmahopādhyāya N.S. Anantakrishna Śāstri of Calcutta. My friend and colleague, Mr. K. C. Chatterji, checked the references, and my thanks are due to him.

September 1930

PREFACE TO THE FIRST EDITION

In this volume, which is devoted to the discussion of the six Brahmanical systems, I have adopted the same plan and method of treatment as in the first. I have tried to adopt, what is acknowledged to be, the true spirit of philosophical interpretation, *viz.*, to interpret the ancient writers and their thoughts at their best and relate them to the living issues of philosophy and religion. Vācaspati Miśra, who commented on almost all the systems of Hindu thought, wrote on each, as if he believed in its doctrines. In presenting intelligently tendencies of thought matured long ago and embodied in a number of difficult works, it has been necessary to select, emphasise and even criticise particular aspects, which naturally betrays the direction in which my own thinking runs. Involving as the work does so many decisions on points of detail, it is, perhaps, too much to hope that the book is free from errors of judgment; but I have endeavoured to give an objective treatment and avoid playing tricks with the evidence.

I should repeat here that my discussion is not to be regarded as complete in any sense of the term, for almost every chapter deals with a subject to which a fully equipped specialist devotes a lifetime of study. Detailed discussions of particular systems require separate monographs. My task is the limited one, of sketching in broad outlines the different movements of thought, their motives and their results. I have made practically no attempt to deal with secondary variations of opinion among the less important writers of the various schools. My treatment of the Śaiva, the Śākta and the later Vaiṣṇava systems, which belong more to the religious history than to the philosophical development of India, has been brief and summary. I shall be thoroughly satisfied if I succeed in conveying an idea, however inadequate, of the real spirit of the several phases of Indian speculative thought.

If this volume is slightly more difficult than the previous one, I hope it will be felt that the difficulty is not entirely of my making, but is to some extent inherent in the subject and in the close thinking which its study involves. To condense a mass of facts into a clear narrative which can be followed by the reader without bewilderment or boredom is a task which I felt to be more than what I could compass. It is for the reader to judge how far I have succeeded in my attempt to steer a middle course between looseness and pedantry. To help the general reader, the more technical and textual discussions are printed in small type.

In the preparation of this volume I have found, not only the Sanskrit texts of the different schools, but also the writings of Deussen and Keith, Thibaut and Garbe, Gaṅgānāth Jhā and Vidyābhūṣaṇ, very helpful. I am greatly indebted to my friends, Mr. V. Subrahmanya Aiyar and Professor J. S. Mackenzie, for their kindness in reading considerable parts of the MS. and the proofs, and making many valuable suggestions. Professor A. Berriedale Keith was good enough to read the proofs, and the book has profited much by his critical comments. My deepest thanks, however, are due, as in the case of the first volume, to the General Editor, Professor J. H. Muirhead, who gave to the work much of his time and thought. But for his generous assistance, the defects of the book—whatever they may be—would have been very much greater. The printing of the work involved considerable trouble, and I am glad that it has been extraordinarily well done.

December 1926

CONTENTS

PAGE

PREFACE TO THE SECOND EDITION 5

PREFACE TO THE FIRST EDITION 7

PART III

THE SIX BRAHMANICAL SYSTEMS

CHAPTER I

INTRODUCTION 17

The spirit of the age—The Darśanas—Āstika and Nāstika—Sūtra literature—Date—Common ideas—The six systems.

CHAPTER II

THE LOGICAL REALISM OF THE NYĀYA 29

The Nyāya and the Vaiśeṣika—The beginnings of the Nyāya—Literature and history—Aim and scope—The nature of definition—Perception—Its analysis and kinds—Inference—Syllogism—Induction—Causation—Plurality of causes—Asatkāryavāda—Criticism of the Nyāya view of causation—Comparison—Verbal knowledge—Authoritativeness of the Vedas—Other forms of knowledge—Aitihya and Arthāpatti, Saṁbhava and Abhāva—Tarka, Vāda, Nigrahasthāna—Memory—Doubt—Fallacies—Truth, its nature and criterion—Theories of error—The Nyāya theory of knowledge examined—The world of nature—The individual soul—Saṁsāra—Mokṣa—Criticism of the Nyāya theory of soul and its relation to consciousness—Ethics—Proofs for the existence of God—Conclusion.

CHAPTER III

THE ATOMISTIC PLURALISM OF THE VAIŚEṢIKA . . . 176

The Vaiśeṣika—Date and literature—Theory of knowledge—Categories—Substance—Soul—Manas—Space—Time—Ākāśa—Earth, water, light and air—The atomic theory—Quality—Activity—Generality—Particularity—Inherence—Non-existence—Ethics—Theology—General estimate.

INDIAN PHILOSOPHY

CHAPTER IV

PAGE

THE SĀṀKHYA SYSTEM 248

Introduction—Antecedents—Literature — Causality — Prakṛti—Guṇas—Cosmic evolution—Puruṣa—The relation between Puruṣa and Prakṛti—The problem of knowledge—Jīva—Ethics—Release—God—Is Sāṁkhya atheistic?—General estimate.

CHAPTER V

THE YOGA SYSTEM OF PATAÑJALI 336

Introduction—Antecedents of the Yoga system—Date and literature—The Sāṁkhya and the Yoga—Psychology—The means of knowledge—The art of Yoga—Ethical preparation—The discipline of the body—Regulation of breath—Sense-control—Contemplation—Concentration—Freedom—Karma—Supernormal powers—Theism of the Yoga—Conclusion.

CHAPTER VI

THE PŪRVA MĪMĀṀSĀ 374

Introduction—Date and literature—The sources of knowledge—Perception—Inference—Scriptural testimony—Comparison—Implication—Non-apprehension—Theory of knowledge: Prabhākara, Kumārila—The self: Prabhākara, Kumārila—Nature of reality—Ethics—Apūrva—Mokṣa—God—Conclusion.

CHAPTER VII

THE VEDĀNTA SŪTRA 430

The Vedānta and its interpretations—Authorship and date of the *Sūtra*—Relation to other schools—Brahman—The world—The individual self—Mokṣa—Conclusion.

CHAPTER VIII

THE ADVAITA VEDĀNTA OF ŚAṀKARA 445

Introduction—Date—Life and personality of Śaṁkara—Literature—Gauḍapāda's *Kārikā*—Buddhist influence—Analysis of experience—Causation—Creation—Ethics and religion—Relation to Buddhism—General estimate of Gauḍapāda's position—Bhartṛhari—Bhartṛprapañca—Śaṁkara's relation to the Upaniṣads and the *Brahma Sūtra*—Relation to Buddhism and other systems of philosophy—The reality of Ātman—Its nature—Theory of knowledge—Mechanism of knowledge—Perception, its nature and varieties—Inference—Scriptural testimony—Refutation of subjectivism—Criterion of truth—Inadequacy of logical knowledge—Self-consciousness—Adhyāsa—Anubhava—

CONTENTS

PAGE

Scriptural authority—Higher wisdom and lower knowledge—Śaṁkara and Kant, Bergson and Bradley—The objective approach—Reality and existence—Space, time and cause—The world of phenomena—Brahman—Saguṇa and Nirguṇa—Īśvara—Proofs for the existence of God—Brahman and Īśvara—Personality—Creation—The phenomenal character of Īśvara—Being, not-being and becoming—The phenomenality of the world—The doctrine of māyā—Avidyā—Is the world an illusion?—Avidyā and māyā—The world of nature—The individual self—Sākṣin and jīva—Brahman and jīva—Avacchedavāda—Bimbapratibimbavāda—Īśvara and jīva—Ekajīvavāda and Anekajīvavāda—Ethics—Charges of intellectualism and asceticism considered—Jñāna and Karma—Karma and freedom—Mokṣa—Future life—Religion—Conclusion.

CHAPTER IX

The Theism of Rāmānuja 659

Introduction—The Purāṇas—Life—History and literature—Bhāskara — Yādavaprakāśa — The Pramāṇas — Implications of Rāmānuja's theory of knowledge—God—The individual soul—Matter—Creation—Ethics and religion—Mokṣa—General estimate.

CHAPTER X

The Śaiva, the Śākta, and the Later Vaiṣṇava Theism 722

Śaiva Siddhānta—Literature—Metaphysics, ethics and religion The Pratyabhijñā system of Kashmir—Śāktaism—The dualism of Madhva—Life and literature—Theory of knowledge—God—Soul—Nature—God and the world—Ethics and religion—General estimate—Nimbārka and Keśava—Vallabha—Caitanya, Jīva Gosvāmi and Baladeva.

CHAPTER XI

Conclusion 766

The course of Hindu philosophic development—The unity of the different systems—The decline of the philosophic spirit in recent times—Contact with the West—The present situation—Conservatism and radicalism—The future.

Notes 783

Index 793

LIST OF ABBREVIATIONS

B.G. . . .	Bhagavadgītā.
B.S. . . .	Brahma Sūtra.
D.S.V. . . .	Deussen's System of the Vedānta—E.T.
I.P.	Indian Philosophy, Vol. I.
N.B. . . .	Nyāya Bhāṣya.
N.S.	Nyāya Sūtra.
N.V. . . .	Nyāyavārttika.
N.V.T.T. . .	Nyāyavārttikatātparyaṭīkā.
P.P.	Padārthadharmasaṁgraha of Praśastapāda.
M.S.	Mīmāṁsā Sūtra.
R.B. . . .	Rāmānuja's Bhāṣya on the Brahma Sūtra.
R.B.G. . . .	Rāmānuja's Bhāṣya on the Bhagavadgītā.
S.B. . .	Śaṁkara's Bhāṣya, or the Brahma Sūtra.
S.B.G. . . .	Śaṁkara's Bhāṣya on the Bhagavadgītā.
S.K.	Sāṁkhya Kārikā.
S.L.S. . . .	Siddhāntaleśasaṁgraha.
S.P.B. . . .	Sāṁkhyapravacana Bhāṣya.
S.P.S. . . .	Sāṁkhyapravacana Sūtra.
S.D.S. . . .	Sarvadarśanasaṁgraha.
S.S.S.S. . .	Sarvasiddhāntasārasaṁgraha.
S.V. . . .	Ślokavārttika.
V.S. . . .	Vaiśeṣika Sūtra.
Y.B. . . .	Yoga Bhāṣya.
Y.S.	Yoga Sūtra.

PART III

THE SIX BRAHMANICAL SYSTEMS

CHAPTER I

INTRODUCTION

The spirit of the age—The Darśanas—Āstika and Nāstika—Sūtra literature—Date—Common ideas—The six systems.

I

THE RISE OF THE SYSTEMS

THE age of Buddha represents the great springtide of philosophic spirit in India. The progress of philosophy is generally due to a powerful attack on a historical tradition when men feel themselves compelled to go back on their steps and raise once more the fundamental questions which their fathers had disposed of by the older schemes. The revolt of Buddhism and Jainism, even such as it was, forms an era in the history of Indian thought, since it finally exploded the method of dogmatism and helped to bring about a critical point of view. For the great Buddhist thinkers, logic was the main arsenal where were forged the weapons of universal destructive criticism. Buddhism served as a cathartic in clearing the mind of the cramping effects of ancient obstructions. Scepticism, when it is honest, helps to reorganise belief on its natural foundations. The need for laying the foundations deeper resulted in the great movement of philosophy which produced the six systems of thought, where cold criticism and analysis take the place of poetry and religion. The conservative schools were compelled to codify their views and set forth logical defences of them. The critical side of philosophy became as important as the speculative. The philosophical views of the presystematic period set forth some general reflections regarding the nature of the universe as a whole, but did not realise that a critical theory of knowledge is the necessary basis of any fruitful speculation. Critics forced their opponents to employ the natural methods relevant to life and experience, and not some supernatural revelation, in the defence of their speculative schemes. We should not lower our standards to let in the beliefs we wish to secure. Ātmavidyā or philosophy is now supported by Ānvīkṣikī or the science of inquiry.[1] A rationalistic defence of philosophic systems could not have been very congenial to the conservative mind.[2] To the devout it must have appeared that the breath of life had departed since intuition had given place to critical reason. The force of thought which springs straight from life and experience as we have it in the Upaniṣads, or the epic greatness of soul which sees and chants the God-vision as in the *Bhagavadgītā* give place to more strict philosophising. Again, when an appeal to reason is admitted, one cannot be sure of the results of thought. A critical philosophy need not always be in conformity with cherished traditions. But the spirit of the times required that every system of thought based on reason should be recognised as a darśana. All logical attempts to gather the floating conceptions of the world into some great general ideas were regarded as darśanas.[3] They all help us to see some aspect of the truth. This conception led to the view that the apparently isolated and independent systems were really

[1] N.B., i. 1. 1.; *Manu*, vii. 43. Kauṭilya (about 300 B.C.) asserts that Ānvīkṣikī is a distinct branch of study over and above the other three, Trayī or the Vedas, Vārtā or commerce, and Daṇḍanīti or polity (i. 2). The sixth century B.C., when it was recognised as a special study, marks the beginning of systematic philosophy in India, and by the first century B.C. the term Ānvīkṣikī is replaced by "darśana" (see M.B., Śāntiparva, 10. 45; *Bhāgavata Purāṇa*, viii. 14. 10). Every inquiry starts in doubt and fulfils a need. Cp. Jijñāsayā saṁdehaprayojane sūcayati (*Bhāmatī*, i. 1. 1).

[2] In the Rāmāyaṇa, Ānvīkṣikī is censured as leading men away from the injunctions of the dharmaśāstras (ii. 100. 36) (M.B., Śānti, 180. 47–49; 246–8). Manu holds that those who misled by logic (hetuśāstra) disregard the Vedas and the Dharma Sūtras deserve excommunication (ii. 11); yet both Gautama in his Dharma Sūtra (xi) and Manu (vii. 43) prescribe a course of Ānvīkṣikī for kings. Logicians were included in the legislative assemblies. When logic supports scripture, it is commended. By means of Ānvīkṣikī, Vyāsa claims to have arranged the Vedas (*Nyāyasūtravṛtti*, i. 1. 1).

[3] Mādhava: S.D.S.

members of a larger historical plan. Their nature could not be completely understood so long as they were viewed as self-dependent, without regard to their place in the historic interconnection.

II

Relation to the Vedas

The adoption of the critical method served to moderate the impetuosity of the speculative imagination and helped to show that the pretended philosophies were not so firmly held as their professors supposed. But the iconoclastic fervour of the materialists, the sceptics and some followers of Buddhism destroyed all grounds of certitude. The Hindu mind did not contemplate this negative result with equanimity. Man cannot live on doubt. Intellectual pugilism is not sufficient by itself. The zest of combat cannot feed the spirit of man. If we cannot establish through logic the truth of anything, so much the worse for logic. It cannot be that the hopes and aspirations of sincere souls like the ṛṣis of the Upaniṣads are irrevocably doomed. It cannot be that centuries of struggle and thought have not brought the mind one step nearer to the solution. Despair is not the only alternative. Reason assailed could find refuge in faith. The seers of the Upaniṣads are the great teachers in the school of sacred wisdom. They speak to us of the knowledge of God and spiritual life. If the unassisted reason of man cannot attain any hold on reality by means of mere speculation, help may be sought from the great writings of the seers who claim to have attained spiritual certainty. Thus strenuous attempts were made to justify by reason what faith implicitly accepts. This is not an irrational attitude, since philosophy is only an endeavour to interpret the widening experience of humanity. The one danger that we have to avoid is lest faith should furnish the conclusions for philosophy.

Of the systems of thought or darśanas, six became more famous than others, *viz.*, Gautama's Nyāya, Kaṇāda's Vaiśeṣika, Kapila's Sāṁkhya, Patañjali's Yoga, Jaimini's Pūrva Mīmāṁsā and Bādarāyaṇa's Uttara Mīmāṁsā or the Vedānta.[1] They are the Brahmanical systems, since they all accept the authority of the Vedas. The systems of thought which admit the validity of the Vedas are called āstika, and those which repudiate it nāstika. The āstika, or nāstika character of a system does not depend on its positive or negative conclusions regarding the nature of the supreme spirit, but on the acceptance or non-acceptance of the authority of the Vedas.[2] Even the schools of Buddhism have their origin in the Upaniṣads; though they are not regarded as orthodox, since they do not accept the authority of the Vedas. Kumārila, a great authority on these questions, admits that the Buddhist systems owe their inspiration to the Upaniṣads, argues that they were put forth with the purpose of checking the excessive attachment to sensuous objects, and declares that they are all authoritative systems of thought.[3]

The acceptance of the Veda is a practical admission that spiritual experience is a greater light in these matters than intellectual reason. It does not mean either full agreement with all the doctrines of the Veda or admission of any belief in the existence of God. It means only a serious attempt to solve the ultimate mystery of existence; for even the infallibility of the Veda is not admitted by the schools in the same sense. As we shall see, the Vaiśeṣika and the Nyāya accept God as the result of inference. The Sāṁkhya is not a theism. The Yoga is practically independent of the Veda. The two Mīmāṁsās are more directly dependent on the Vedas. The Pūrva Mīmāṁsā derives the general conception of deity from the Vedas, but is not anxious about the supreme spirit. The Uttara Mīmāṁsā accepts God on the basis of śruti assisted by inference, while realisation of God can be had through meditation and jñāna. Theistically minded thinkers of a later day declined to include the Sāṁkhya under orthodox darśanas.[4]

[1] Haribhadra, in his *Ṣaḍdarśanasamuccaya*, discusses the Buddhist, the Naiyāyika, and the Sāṁkhya, the Jaina, the Vaiśeṣika, and the Jaiminīya systems (i. 3). Jinadatta and Rājaśekhara agree with this view.

[2] Prāmāṇyabuddhir vedeṣu. Manu says that a nāstika is he who despises the Vedas. Nāstiko vedanindakaḥ (ii. 11). See M.B., xii. 270. 67.

[3] *Tantravārttika*, i. 3. 2, p. 81.

[4] In Bhīmācārya's *Nyāyakośa* the āstika is said to be paralokādyastitvavādi and nāstika as vedamārgam ananurundhānaḥ. He includes Sāṁkhya and the Advaita Vedānta under the latter. "Māyāvādivedānty api nāstika

The philosophical character of the systems is not much compromised by the acceptance of the Veda.[1] The distinction between śruti and smṛti is well known, and where the two conflict, the former is to prevail. The śruti itself is divided into the karmakāṇḍa (the Saṁhitās and the Brāhmaṇas and the jñānakāṇḍa (the Upaniṣads). The latter is of higher value, though much of it is set aside as mere arthavāda or non-essential statements. All these distinctions enable one to treat the Vedic testimony in a very liberal spirit. The interpretations of the Vedic texts depend on the philosophical predilections of the authors. While employing logical methods and arriving at truths agreeable to reason, they were yet anxious to preserve their continuity with the ancient texts. They did not wish it to be thought that they were enunciating something completely new. While this may involve a certain want of frankness with themselves, it helped the spread of what they regarded as the truth.[2] Critics and commentators of different schools claim for their views the sanction of the Veda and exercise their ingenuity in forcing that sanction when it is not spontaneously yielded. In the light of the controversies of subsequent times, they read into the language of the Vedas opinions on questions of which they knew little or nothing. The general conceptions of the Vedas were neither definite nor detailed, and so allowed themselves to be handled and fashioned in different ways by different schools of thought. Besides, the very vastness of the Vedas, from

eva paryavasāne saṁpadyate." Kumārila regards the Sāṁkhya, the Yoga, the Pañcarātra and the Pāśupata systems as being opposed to the Veda as much as Buddhism (*Tantravārttika*, i. 3. 4).

[1] What Keith says of the Nyāya and the Vaiśeṣika is true of the other systems as well. "The systems are indeed orthodox and admit the authority of the sacred scriptures, but they attack the problems of existence with human means, and scripture serves for all practical purposes but to lend sanctity to results which are achieved not only without its aid, but often in very dubious harmony with its tenets" (I.L.A., p. 3).

[2] Cp. Goethe: "Some very intelligent and brilliant men appeared, in this respect, like butterflies which, quite oblivious of their chrysalis state, threw away the covering in which they had grown to their organic maturity. Others, more faithful and more modest, could be compared with flowers, which, though developing into beautiful blossoms, do not leave the root nor separate themselves from the mother stem, but rather through this connection bring the hoped-for fruit to ripeness" (quoted in Merz: *European Thought in the Nineteenth Century*, vol. iv, p. 134, fn. 1).

which the authors could select out of free conviction any portion for their authority, allowed room for original thought.

The religious motive of philosophical speculations accounts for the apparently miscellaneous character of the contents of the systems. The eternity of sound doctrine is more a theological than a philosophical problem, related as it is to the doctrine of Vedic infallibility. Every system is an admixture of logic and psychology, metaphysics and religion.

III

The Sūtras

When the Vedic literature became unwieldy and the Vedic thinkers were obliged to systematise their views, the Sūtra literature arose. The principal tenets of the darśanas are stated in the form of sūtras or short aphorisms. They are intended to be as short as possible, free from doubt, able to bring out the essential meaning and put an end to many doubts; and they must not contain anything superfluous or erroneous.[1] They try to avoid all unnecessary repetition and employ great economy of words.[2] The ancient writers had no temptation to be diffuse, since they had to rely more on memory than on printed books. This extreme conciseness makes it difficult to understand the Sūtras without a commentary.

The different systems developed in different centres of philosophical activity. The views had been growing up through many generations even before they were summed up in the Sūtras. They are not the work of one thinker or of one age but of a succession of thinkers spread over a number of generations. As the Sūtras presuppose a period of gestation and of formation, it is difficult for us to trace their origin. There are no absolute beginnings for spiritual possessions.

[1] Alpākṣaram asaṁdigdhaṁ sāravad viśvatomukham
Astobham anavadyaṁ ca sūtraṁ sūtravido viduḥ

(Madhva on B.S., i. 1. 1). See Jayatīrtha's *Nyāyasudhā*, i. 1. 1; *Bhāmatī*, i. 1. 1.

[2] The remark that "a grammarian rejoices in the economising of half a short vowel as much as he does on the birth of a son" points to the ideal of the rigid economy of words.

The Sūtras are the outcome of a series of past efforts and "occupy a strictly central position summarising, on the one hand, a series of early literary essays extending over many generations, and forming, on the other hand, the headspring of an ever-broadening activity of commentators as well as virtually independent writers, which reaches down to our days and may yet have some future before itself."[1] The systems must have evolved at a much earlier period than that in which the Sūtras were formulated. The whole tone and manner of the philosophical Sūtras suggests that they belong approximately to the same period.[2] The authors of the Sūtras are not the founders or originators of the systems but only their compilers or formulators. This fact accounts for the cross references in the philosophical Sūtras, and it must be noted that the various systems had been growing side by side with one another during the period which preceded the formation of the Sūtras. To the early centuries after Buddha and before the Christian era belongs the crystallisation of the different systems out of the complex solution. Oral tradition and not books were the repositories of the philosophical views. It may be that, through lapse of oral tradition, several important works perished, and many of those that have reached us are not even pure. Some of the earlier important Sūtras, as the Bṛhaspati Sūtras, Vaikhānasa Sūtras and Bhikṣu Sūtras, as well as large quantities of philosophical literature, are lost to us, and with them also much useful information about the chronological relations of the different systems. Max Müller assigns the gradual formation of the Sūtras to the period from Buddha to Aśoka, though he admits that, in the cases of the Vedānta, the Sāṁkhya and the Yoga, a long previous development has to be allowed. This view is confirmed by the evidence of Kauṭilya's *Arthaśāstra*. Up till then, the orthodox Ānvīkṣiki or logical systems were divided mainly into two schools, the Pūrva Mīmāṁsā and the Sāṁkhya. Though the references in Buddhist texts are very

[1] Thibaut: Introduction to S.B., p. xii.

[2] In some form the different systems must have existed before the Christian era. The early sacred literature of the Jainas mentions the systems of Vaiśeṣika, Buddhism, Sāṁkhya, Lokāyata and Ṣaṣṭitantra (Weber's *Sanskrii Literature*, p. 236, n. 249) See also *Lalitavistara*, xii; *Carakasaṁhitā*; M.B., Nārāyaṇīya section.

vague, it may be said that the Buddhist Sūtras assume a knowledge of the six systems. The vivid intellectual life of the early centuries after Buddha flowed in many streams parallel to one another, though the impulse to codify them was due to the reaction against the systems of revolt. These systems of thought undergo modifications at the hands of later interpreters, though the resultant system is still fathered on the original systematiser. The philosophy of the Vedānta is called Vyāsa's, though Śaṁkara, Rāmānuja and a host of others introduced vital changes of doctrine. The greatest thinkers of India profess to be simply scholiasts; but in their attempts to expound the texts, they improve on them. Each system has grown in relation to others which it keeps always in view. The development of the six systems has been in progress till the present day, the successive interpreters defending the tradition against the attacks of its opponents.

In the case of every darśana, we have first of all a period of philosophic fermentation, which at a particular stage is reduced to sūtras or aphorisms. This is succeeded by the writing of commentaries on the aphorisms, which are followed by glosses, expositions and explanatory compendia, in which the original doctrines undergo modifications, corrections and amplifications. The commentaries use the form of the dialogue, which has come down from the time of the Upaniṣads as the only adequate form for the exposition of a complex theme. The commentator by means of the dialogue is enabled to show the relation of the view he is expounding to the diverse trains of thought suggested by the rival interlocutors. The ideas are restated and their superiority to other conceptions established.

IV

Common Ideas

The six systems agree on certain essentials.[1] The accept-

[1] "The longer I have studied the various systems, the more have I become impressed with the truth of the view taken by Vijñānabhikṣu and others that there is behind the variety of the six systems a common fund of what may be called national or popular philosophy, a large mānasa lake of philosophical thought and language far away in the distant North and in the distant past, from which each thinker was allowed to draw for his own purposes" (Max Müller: S.S., p. xvii).

ance of the Veda implies that all the systems have drawn from a common reservoir of thought. The Hindu teachers were obliged to use the heritage they received from the past, in order to make their views readily understood. While the use of the terms avidyā, māyā, puruṣa, jīva shows that the dialect of speculation is common to the different systems, it is to be noted that the systems are distinguished by the different significations assigned to those terms in the different schools. It frequently happens in the history of thought that the same terms and phrases are used by different schools in senses which are essentially distinct. Each system sets forth its special doctrine by using, with necessary modifications, the current language of the highest religious speculation. In the systems, philosophy becomes self-conscious. The spiritual experiences recorded in the Vedas are subjected to a logical criticism. The question of the validity and means of knowledge forms an important chapter of each system. Each philosophical scheme has its own theory of knowledge, which is an integral part or a necessary consequence of its metaphysics. Intuition, inference and the Veda are accepted by the systems. Reason is subordinated to intuition. Life cannot be comprehended in its fulness by logical reason. Self-consciousness is not the ultimate category of the universe. There is something transcending the consciousness of self, to which many names are given—Intuition, Revelation, Cosmic Consciousness, and God-vision. We cannot describe it adequately, so we call it the super-consciousness. When we now and then have glimpses of this higher form, we feel that it involves a purer illumination and a wider compass. As the difference between mere consciousness and self-consciousness constitutes the wide gulf separating the animal from man, so the difference between self-consciousness and super-consciousness constitutes all the difference between man as he is and man as he ought to be. The philosophy of India takes its stand on the spirit which is above mere logic, and holds that culture based on mere logic or science may be efficient, but cannot be inspiring.

All the systems protest against the scepticism of the Buddhists, and erect a standard of objective reality and truth as opposed to an eternal, unstable flux. The stream of the world has been flowing on from eternity, and this flow is not merely mental, but is objective; and it is traced to the eternal prakṛti or māyā or atoms. "That in which the world resides, when divested of name and form, some call prakṛti, others māyā, others atoms."[1] It is assumed that whatever has a beginning has an end. Everything that is made up of parts can be neither eternal nor self-subsistent. The true individual is indivisible. The real is not the universe extended in space and time; for its nature is becoming and not being. There is something deeper than this—atoms and souls, or puruṣa and prakṛti, or Brahman.

All the systems accept the view of the great world rhythm. Vast periods of creation, maintenance and dissolution follow each other in endless succession. This theory is not inconsistent with belief in progress; for it is not a question of the movement of the world reaching its goal times without number, and being again forced back to its starting-point. Creations and dissolutions do not mean the fresh rise and the total destruction of the cosmos. The new universe forms the next stage of the history of the cosmos, where the unexhausted potencies of good and evil are provided with the opportunities of fulfilment. It means that the race of man enters upon and retravels its ascending path of realisation. This interminable succession of world ages has no beginning.

Except perhaps the Pūrva Mīmāṁsā, all the systems aim at the practical end of salvation. The systems mean by release (mokṣa) the recovery by the soul of its natural integrity, from which sin and error drive it. All the systems have for their ideal complete mental poise and freedom from the discords and uncertainties, sorrows and sufferings of life, "a repose that ever is the same," which no doubts disturb and no rebirths break into. The conception of jīvanmukti, or liberation in life, is admitted in many schools.

It is a fundamental belief of the Hindus that the universe is law-abiding to the core, and yet that man is free to shape his own destiny in it.

> Our actions still pursue us from afar,
> And what we have been makes us what we are.

---

[1] Vijñānabhikṣu quotes from *Bṛhadvāśiṣṭha* in his *Yogavārttika*:
Nāmarūpavinirmuktaṁ yasmin saṁtiṣṭhate jagat
Tam āhuḥ prakṛtiṁ kecin māyām anye pare tv aṇūn

The systems believe in rebirth and preexistence. Our life is a step on a road, the direction and goal of which are lost in the infinite. On this road, death is never an end or an obstacle but at most the beginning of new steps. The development of the soul is a continuous process, though it is broken into stages by the recurring baptism of death.

Philosophy carries us to the gates of the promised land, but cannot let us in ; for that, insight or realisation is necessary. We are like children stranded in the darkness of saṁsāra, with no idea of our true nature, and inclined to imagine fears and to cling to hopes in the gloom that surrounds us. Hence arises the need for light, which will free us from the dominion of passions and show us the real, which we unwittingly are, and the unreal in which we ignorantly live. Such a kind of insight is admitted as the sole means to salvation, though there are differences regarding the object of insight.[1] The cause of bondage is ignorance, and so release can be had through insight into the truth. The ideal of the systems is practically to transcend the merely ethical level. The holy man is compared to the fair lotus unsullied by the mire in which it grows. In his case the good is no more a goal to be striven after, but is an accomplished fact. While virtue and vice may lead to a good or bad life within the circle of saṁsāra, we can escape from saṁsāra through the transcending of the moralistic individualism. All systems recognise as obligatory unselfish love and disinterested activity, and insist on cittaśuddhi (cleansing of the heart) as essential to all moral culture. In different degrees they adhere to the rules of caste (varṇa) and stages of life (āśrama).

A history of Indian philosophy, as we noted in the Introduction,[2] is beset with innumerable difficulties. The dates of the principal writers and their works are not free from doubt ; and in some cases the historicity of well-known authors is contested While many of the relevant works are not available, even the few that are published have not all been critically studied. A historical treatment of Indian philosophy

[1] Even the Buddhist thinker Dharmakīrti opens his *Nyāyabindu* with the remark that all fulfilment of human desires is preceded by right knowledge. Samyagjñānapūrvikā sarvapuruṣārthasiddhiḥ (i)

[2] I P.. vol. i.

has not been taken up by the great Indian thinkers themselves. Mādhava in his *Sarvadarśanasaṁgraha* treats of sixteen different darśanas. In the first volume we dealt with the materialist, the Buddhist and the Jaina views. In this we propose to deal with the Nyāya, the Vaiśeṣika, the Sāṁkhya, the Yoga, the Pūrva Mīmāṁsā and the Vedānta darśanas. The four schools of Śaivism and those of Rāmānuja, the Pūrṇaprajña are founded on the Vedānta Sūtra and attempt to interpret it in different ways. Pāṇini's system is of little philosophical significance. It accepts the Mīmāṁsā view of the eternity of sound and develops the theory of sphoṭa or the indivisible unitary factor latent in every word as the vehicle of its significance. Of these six systems, the Vaiśeṣika is not very much in honour, while the Nyāya on its logical side is popular and finds many devotees, especially in Bengal. The Yoga in its practical form is practised by a few, while the Pūrva Mīmāṁsā is closely related to Hindu law. The Sāṁkhya is not a living faith, while the Vedānta in its different forms pervades the whole atmosphere. In dealing with the six systems of Hindu thought, we shall confine our attention to the great classics, the Sūtras as well as their chief commentators. With regard to almost all the thinkers of recent times—of course there are exceptions—their metaphysical contributions do not seem to be sufficiently impressive. Their learning is prodigious; but they belong to the period of decadence, where the tendency to comment and recast ceaselessly takes the place of creation and construction. There are too many concessions to dogma, too much attachment to the mystifying elaboration of the obvious and, by reason of the warping theological bias and metaphysical sterility, do not deserve any great attention.

In obedience to custom, which it would be vain to try to unsettle, we shall start with the Nyāya and the Vaiśeṣika theories, which give us an analysis of the world of experience, and pass on to the Sāṁkhya and the Yoga, which try to explain experience by bold speculative ventures; and we shall conclude with a discussion of the Mīmāṁsās, which attempt to show that the revelations of śruti are in harmony with the conclusions of philosophy. Such a treatment has at least the support of sound logic though not of sound chronology.

CHAPTER II

THE LOGICAL REALISM OF THE NYĀYA

The Nyāya and the Vaiśeṣika—The beginnings of the Nyāya—Literature and history—Aim and scope—The nature of definition—Perception—Its analysis and kinds—Inference—Syllogism—Induction—Causation—Plurality of causes—Asatkāryavāda—Criticism of the Nyāya view of causation—Comparison—Verbal knowledge—Authoritativeness of the Vedas—Other forms of knowledge—Aitihya and Arthāpatti, Saṁbhava and Abhāva—Tarka, Vāda, Nigrahasthāna—Memory—Doubt—Fallacies—Truth, its nature and criterion—Theories of error—The Nyāya theory of knowledge examined—The world of nature—The individual soul—Saṁsāra—Mokṣa—Criticism of the Nyāya theory of soul and its relation to consciousness—Ethics—Proofs for the existence of God—Conclusion.

I

The Nyāya and the Vaiśeṣika

While the other systems of Indian thought are mainly speculative, in the sense that they deal with the universe as a whole, the Nyāya and the Vaiśeṣika represent the analytic type of philosophy, and uphold common sense and science, instead of dismissing them as "moonbeams from the larger lunacy." What is distinctive of these schools, is the application of a method, which their adherents regard as that of science, to material which has hitherto been treated in quite a different way. Applying the methods of logical inquiry and criticism, they endeavour to show that these do not warrant the conclusions which the Buddhist thinkers derived from them, and that logic does not compel us to disperse the unity and pattern of life into its fleeting moments. They are interested mainly in averting the sceptical consequences of the Buddhist phenomenalism, which merged external reality in the ideas of mind. They seek to restore the traditional substances, the soul within and nature without, but not on the basis of mere authority. The general scepticism which set in like a flood, could not be checked by a mere resort to faith, when its citadel was attacked by the heretical thinkers who presumably took their stand on the evidence of the senses and the conclusions of reason. Only by a thorough examination of the modes and sources of correct knowledge can the ends of life and religion be truly met. What is supplied to us by scripture or the evidence of the senses must be submitted to a critical inquiry, as the etymological meaning of the word ānvīkṣikī suggests.[1] The Naiyāyika is willing to admit as true whatever is established by reason.[2] Vātsyāyana and Uddyotakara urge that if the Nyāya philosophy dealt only with the nature of the soul and its released condition, there would not be much to distinguish the Nyāya from the Upaniṣads which also treat of these problems. That which gives distinction to the Nyāya is its critical treatment of metaphysical problems. Vācaspati defines the purpose of the Nyāya as a critical examination of the objects of knowledge by means of the canons of logical proof.[3]

The Nyāya and the Vaiśeṣika take up the ordinary stock notions of traditional philosophy, as space, time, cause, matter, mind, soul and knowledge, explore their significance for experience, and set forth the results in the form of a theory of the universe. The logical and the physical departments become the predominant features in these traditions. The Nyāya and the Vaiśeṣika take up respectively the world within and the world without. The Nyāya describes at great length the mechanism of knowledge and argues vigorously against the scepticism which declares that nothing is certain. The Vaiśeṣika has for its main objective the analysis of experience. It formulates general conceptions which apply to things known, whether by the senses or by inference or by authority. Adopting such an attitude, it is no wonder that

[1] Pratyakṣāgamābhyām ākṣiptasya anvīkṣā tayā vartata ity ānvīkṣikī (N.B., i. 1. 1). Again: "It is called anvīkṣā or investigation, since it consists in the reviewing (anu-īkṣaṇa) of a thing previously apprehended (īkṣita) by perception and verbal testimony" (N.B., i. 1. 1). Logic is the science of second intentions, as Aristotle would say It is essentially the reflection of knowledge on itself.

[2] Buddhyā yad upapannaṁ tat sarvaṁ nyāyamatam.

[3] Cf. Pramāṇair arthaparīkṣaṇam (N. B. and N.V.T.T., i. 1. 1).

the Nyāya and the Vaiśeṣika systems advocate belief in individual souls as substantial beings, interacting with a whole environing system of things.

The two systems had been for long treated as parts of one whole. It is sometimes suggested that they branched off as independent streams from the same original source, which treated of things known and the means of knowledge. It is, however, difficult to be certain on this point. The later works regard these systems as forming parts of one discipline.[1] Even in the *Nyāya Bhāṣya* of Vātsyāyana, the two are not kept distinct. The Vaiśeṣika is used as a supplement to the Nyāya.[2] Uddyotakara's *Nyāyavārttika* uses the Vaiśeṣika doctrines. Jacobi observes that "the fusion of these two schools began early and seems to have been complete at the time when the *Nyāyavārttika* was written."[3] Many of the Nyāya sūtras presuppose the tenets of the Vaiśeṣika. They are called samānatantra or allied systems, since they both believe in a plurality of souls, a personal God, an atomic universe, and use many arguments in common. While there is no doubt that the two systems coalesced very early, a difference in the distribution of emphasis on the logical and the physical sides distinguishes the one from the other.[4] While the Nyāya gives us an account of the processes and methods of a reasoned knowledge of objects, the Vaiśeṣika develops the atomic constitution of things which the Nyāya accepts without much argument.[5]

[1] See Varadarāja's *Tārkikarakṣā*, Keśava Miśra's *Tarkabhāṣā*, Śivāditya's *Saptapadārthī*, Viśvanātha's *Bhāṣāpariccheda* and *Siddhāntamuktāvali*, Annam Bhaṭṭa's *Tarkasaṅgraha* and *Dīpikā*, Jagadīśa's *Tarkāmṛta*, and Laugākṣi Bhāskara's *Tarkakaumudī* The Buddhist thinkers Āryadeva and Harivarman did not look upon the Nyāya as a system independent of the Vaiśeṣika (Ui : *Vaiśeṣika Philosophy*, pp. 54 and 56).

[2] N.B., i. 1. 4. Vātsyāyana quotes V.S., iii. 1. 16 in N.B., ii. 2. 34; V.S., iv. 1. 6 in N.B., iii. 1. 33 and iii. 1. 67.

[3] E.R.E., vol. ii, p. 201 *b*.

[4] Uddyotakara says that "the other sciences are not meant to deal with the subjects (of pramāṇas), though they deal with things made known by them (N.V., i. 1. 1).

[5] Garbe looks upon the Vaiśeṣika as prior to the Nyāya (E.R.E., vol. xii, p. 569 ; see also *Philosophy of Ancient India*, p. 20 ; Jacobi : J.A.O.S., xxxi), while Goldstucker regards the Vaiśeṣika as a branch of the Nyāya. Keith inclines to the former view (I.L.A., pp. 21–22). It is more logical, since critical investigations generally follow dogmatic metaphysics. The more systematic character of the N.S., the greater attention paid to the problems

The Nyāya philosophy has been held in great reverence for a very long time past. Manu includes it under śruti. Yājñavalkya regards it as one of the four limbs of the Veda.[1] The classical studies of the Hindus comprise the five subjects of Kāvya (literature), Nāṭaka (drama), Alaṁkāra (rhetoric), Tarka (logic), and Vyākaraṇa (grammar). Whatever other specialised studies a student may take up later, the preliminary course includes logic, which is the basis of all studies. Every system of Hindu thought accepts the fundamental principles of the Nyāya logic, and even in criticising the Nyāya system, uses the Nyāya terminology and logic. The Nyāya serves as an introduction to all systematic philosophy.[2]

II

THE BEGINNNGS OF THE NYĀYA

Ānvīkṣikī, as we have seen, is the treatment in a consciously critical manner of the ultimate problems of spirit; and it has been used in a comprehensive sense, so as to include all systematic attempts to solve the problems of philosophy, the Sāṁkhya, the Yoga and the Lokāyata. Soon attention was directed to the nature of logical procedure and criticism, used in common by these different systems of thought. Every science is a nyāya, which means literally going into a subject

of the eternity of sound, the nature of the self and the process of inference support Keith's view. The explicit reference to Īśvara in N.S., iv. 1. 19, is more than what the Vaiśeṣika has to say on this question. The argument for the existence of the self from bodily activities is cruder than the Nyāya view of self as the basis of mental phenomena. The absence of any direct reference to the Nyāya in the B.S., which criticises the Vaiśeṣika theory (ii. 2. 12–17), supports the view of the greater antiquity of the latter. This position will be considerably strengthened if the Nyāya reference to pratitantrasiddhānta is taken as an allusion to the Vaiśeṣika. The more elaborate account of the grounds of inference and the simpler scheme of fallacies in the V.S. are not of great value on the question of date. We find a number of coincidences between the N.S. and the V.S. Cp. N.S., iii. 1. 36; ii. 1. 54; i. 1. 10; iii. 1. 28; iii 1. 35; iii 1. 63; iii. 1. 71; iii. 2. 63, with V.S., iv. 1. 8; vii. 2. 20; iii. 2. 4; iv. 2. 3; iv. 1 6–13; vii. 2. 4–5; viii. 2. 5; vii. 1. 23, respectively. If some of the V.S. seem to be elaborations of the Nyāya views, it only shows that those sūtras were compiled later than the N.S. The priority of the bulk of V.S. is not affected thereby.

[1] *Yājñavalkya Smṛti*, i. 3. Cp. *Ātmopaniṣad*, ii, and *Viṣṇu Purāṇa*, iii. 6.

[2] Cp. Kauṭilya (i. 2), quoted in N.B., i. 1. 1.

or analytic investigation. The system of Nyāya, which studies the general plan and method of critical inquiries, may be called the science of sciences. Such purely logical studies were encouraged by the Mīmāṁsakas, who were not merely exegetes but also logicians. It may well be that logic arose out of the necessities of the sacrificial religion, especially out of the need that existed for interpreting correctly the Vedic texts regarding sacrificial rites, rules and results; and that hence the thinkers who founded and developed the Mīmāṁsā helped the growth of logic.[1] When Gautama expounded the logical side more carefully than other thinkers, his view became identified with the Ānvīkṣikī. Thus a term which was used for long in the general sense of systematic philosophy became narrowed down in signification.[2]

In the long chain of antecedents out of which the Nyāya evolved, an important place will have to be assigned to dialectical discussions.[3] The Nyāya is called sometimes Tarka-vidyā or the science of debate, Vādavidyā, or the science of discussion. Discussion or vāda is the breath of intellectual life. We are obliged to use it in the search for truth, which is complex in character and yields only to the co-operation of many minds.[4] The Upaniṣads speak of learned assemblies

[1] From the names of the Mīmāṁsā works, like Mādhava's *Nyāyamālavistara*, Pārthasārathi Miśra's *Nyāyaratnākara*, and Āpadeva's *Nyāyaprakāśa*, it is evident that the term Nyāya was used as a synonym for Mīmāṁsā. See also Āpastamba's *Dharma Sūtra*, ii. 4. 8. 23; ii. 6. 14. 3.

[2] See also *Manu*, vii. 43; Gautama's *Dharma Sūtra*, xi; *Rāmāyaṇa*, Ayodhyākāṇḍa, 100. 36; M.B., Śāntiparva, 180. 47.

[3] The first sūtra enumerates the topics considered in the system, which are: (1) pramāṇa, the means of knowledge; (2) prameya, the objects of knowledge; (3) saṁśaya, doubt; (4) prayojana, purpose; (5) dṛṣṭānta, example; (6) siddhānta, accepted truth; (7) avayava, members of the syllogism; (8) tarka, indirect proof; (9) nirṇaya, determination of the truth; (10) vāda, discussion; (11) jalpa, wrangling; (12) vitaṇḍā, cavil or destructive criticism; (13) hetvābhāsa, fallacious reasons; (14) chala, quibbling; (15) jāti, futile objections; and (16) nigrahasthāna, occasions for reproof. The first nine are more strictly logical than the last seven, which have the negative function of preventing erroneous knowledge. They are more weapons for the destroying of error than for the building up of truth.

[4] Socrates practised it. Plato's works illustrate its value for the attainment of truth. Aristotle says: "Some see one side of a matter and others another, but all together can see all sides" (*Politics*). Milton's *Areopagitica* and Mill's *Essay on Liberty* praise the method of free discussion

or pariṣads where philosophical disputations were carried on.[1] Greek logic owed much to the Sophistic movement, which adopted the mode of disputation called Dialectic, the game of question and answer. In the practice of the art of discussion, the Sophists not only discovered the true principles of reasoning but also invented tricks of argument and sophisms. From the *Dialogues* of Plato we learn that Socrates used the art of debate for the purpose of eliciting the truth. Aristotle devoted two of his logical treatises, the *Topics* and the *Sophistical Refutations* to the guidance of disputants, questioners as well as respondents, though he distinguished logic from rhetoric, the principles of reasoning from the rules of debate. There is no doubt that Gautama's logic sprang from the dialectical tournaments, the sound of which filled the durbars of kings and the schools of philosophers. The attempt to regulate the use of debates led to the development of logical theory. Gautama, like Aristotle, systematised the principles of reasoning, distinguished the true from the false, and gave an elaborate account of the various forms of sophisms and argumentative tricks. The sixteen topics mentioned in the first sūtra may be regarded as representing stages in dialectical controversy intended to lead up to knowledge.[2] Many of the later works on logic discuss the rules of debate,[3] while all of them refer to dialectical problems.[4]

Jayanta asserts that, though Gautama's work provides the most satisfactory account of the subject, there was logic before Gautama, even as Mīmāṁsā was before Jaimini and grammar before Pāṇini.[5]

---

[1] See Chān. Up., v. 3. 1; Bṛh. Up., vi. 2. 1; *Praśna*, i. 6. See also *Manu*, vi 50; viii. 269; xii. 106; M.B., Śāntiparva, 180. 47; 246. 18. In *Manu*, xii. 110–111, *Parāśara*, viii. 19, and *Yājñavalkya*, i. 9, *Parivāra* of the Vinaya Piṭaka, details regarding the pariṣads are mentioned.

[2] See also N.B., i. 1. 1.

[3] *Tārkikarakṣā*.

[4] Kauṭilya mentions thirty-two technical terms called Tantrayukti, and this list is also found in *Carakasaṁhitā*, Siddhisthāna, xii, and *Suśrutasaṁhitā*, Uttaratantra, lxv. The ānvīkṣikī portion of Caraka's work deals extensively with the rules of debate (Vimānasthāna, viii).

[5] Dr. Vidyābhūṣaṇ is of opinion that a number of writers made contributions to Indian logic before the author of the Sūtra. He mentions the names of Dattātreya, Punarvasu Ātreya, Sulabhā the lady ascetic, and Aṣṭāvakra (*History of Indian Logic*, pp. 9–17).

The *Chāndogya Upaniṣad* refers to Vākovākya,[1] which Śaṁkara interprets as *Tarkaśāstra*.[2] The *Mahābhārata* refers to Tarkaśāstra and Ānvīkṣikī,[3] and states that Nārada was familiar with the Nyāya syllogism as well as the Vaiśeṣika principles of conjunction and inherence. Viśvanātha quotes from some Purāṇa a passage to the effect that the Nyāya is counted among the subsidiary parts (upāṅgas) of the Veda.[4] Though Buddha's system was eminently rational, we do not come across any systematic treatment of logical theory in the early canonical works. There are, however, references to men skilled in logic. The *Brahmajāla Sutta* refers to Takki (sophist), and Vīmaṁsi (casuist).[5] The name *Anumāna Sutta* of Majjhima Nikāya perhaps indicates the use of the word "anumāna" in the sense of inference. *Kathāvattu* uses the terms patiññā, upanaya, niggaha in their technical signification.[6] The *Yamaka* knows of the distribution of terms and the rules of conversion. The *Paṭisaṁbhidāmagga* refers to the analysis of words and things. *Nettipakaraṇa* shows a great appreciation of logical theory. In the *Questions of Milinda* the Nyāya system is perhaps referred to under the name Nīti.[7] *Lalitavistara* mentions logic under the name of Hetuvidyā. The Jaina Āgamas testify to the antiquity of Indian logic. *Anuyogadvāra* composed by Āryarakṣita who lived about the first century A.D. has the same division of anumāna into pūrvavat, śeṣavat and sāmānyatodṛṣṭa as the Sūtra of Gautama. Āryarakṣita seems to have been only a redactor of an earlier work referred to in the *Bhagavatī Sūtra*, one of the aṅgas of the Jaina canon settled at the Pataliputra Council in the beginning of the third century B.C. Probably the doctrine of the three kinds of inference is earlier than the third century B.C.

---

[1] vii. 1. 2.

[2] See also *Subāla Up.*, ii. Some of the later Upaniṣads use the term pramāṇa in the technical sense. See *Maitrī Up.*, 6. 6, 24; *Nṛsiṁhottaratāpaṇi*, 8; *Sarvopaniṣatsāra*, 4; *Kālāgnirudropaniṣad*, 7; *Muktikopaniṣad*, 2. The *Taittirīya Āraṇyaka* refers to smṛti or scripture, pratyakṣa or perception, aitihya or tradition, and anumāna or inference as the four sources of knowledge. See also *Rāmāyaṇa*, v. 87–23; *Manu*, xii. 105. Many Nyāya terms, such as Tarka or reasoning (*Kaṭha Up.*, ii. 9; *Manu*, xii. 106; *M.B.*, ii. 153), Vāda or discussion (*Manu*, vi. 50; *Rāmāyaṇa*, i. 13–23; vii. 53–60), Yukti or continuous argument (*Aitareya Brāhmaṇa*, vi. 23; *Rāmāyaṇa*, ii. 1. 13), Jalpa or wrangling (*M.B.*, xiii. 4322), Vitaṇḍā or cavilling (*M.B.*, ii. 1310; vii. 3022; and *Pāṇini*, iv. 4. 102), Chala or quibbling (*Manu*, viii. 49; *Rāmāyaṇa*, iv. 57. 10), Nirṇaya or ascertainment (*M.B.*, xiii. 7553, 7535), Prayojana or purpose (*Manu*, vii. 100; *M.B.*, i. 5805), Pramāṇa or proof (*Manu*, ii. 13; *Rāmāyaṇa*, ii. 37. 21; *M.B.*, xiii. 5572), Prameya, the object of knowledge (*Rāmāyaṇa*, i. 52. 13; *M.B.*, i. 157; vii. 1419), are to be met with in earlier works. See Vidyābhūṣaṇ's *History of Indian Logic*, p. 23.

[3] M.B., i. 70. 42; xii. 210. 22.

[4] *Nyāyasūtravṛtti*, i. 1. 1.

[5] See also *Udāna*, vi. 10.

[6] See also *Vibhaṅga*, pp. 293 ff.

[7] S.B.E., pp. 6–7.

The beginnings of the Nyāya belong to the pre-Buddhistic period, though a scientific treatment of it was undertaken some time about the period of early Buddhism, and the main principles were well established before the third century B.C. We know little about the historical development of the Nyāya prior to the composition of the Sūtra.

III

Literature and History

The history of the Nyāya literature extends over twenty centuries. The *Nyāya Sūtra* of Gautama, divided into five books, each containing two sections, forms the first textbook of the Nyāya. According to Vatsyāyana, this treatise follows the method of enunciation, definition and critical examination. The first book states in general terms the sixteen topics to be considered in the other four. The second book deals with the nature of doubt, the means of proof and their validity. The third book discusses the nature of self, body, senses, their objects, cognition and mind. The fourth treats of volition, sorrow, suffering and liberation. Incidentally, it refers to the theory of error and the relation of whole and parts. The last book discusses jāti or unreal objections and nigrahasthāna or occasions for rebuke. The *Nyāya Sūtra* attempts to combine the results of Brahmanical thought in the department of logic with their religious and philosophical dogmas; and we have, as a result, a logical defence of theistic realism. The Sūtras of Gautama, at any rate the earlier of them, belong to the third century B.C., the age of the Āhnikas, or daily lessons like the Navāhnikas of Patañjali's *Vyākaraṇa Mahābhāṣya*, though some of the contents of the *Nyāya Sūtra* are certainly of a post-Christian era.[1]

[1] Jacobi believes that the N.S. and N.B. belong to about the same time, perhaps separated by a generation. He places them between the second century A.D., when the Śūnyavāda developed, and the fifth century A.D., when the Vijñānavāda became systematised (see J.A.O.S., xxxi. 1911, pp. 2, 13). He thinks that the Buddhist views criticised in the N.S. are those of Śūnyavāda advocated by Nāgārjuna, who is placed about the third century A.D., and not Vijñānavāda of Asaṅga and Vasubandhu, who are assigned to the middle of the fourth century A.D. It is, however, difficult to accept this view. Both Vātsyāyana and Vācaspati hold that N.S., iv. 2. 26, is directed against the Vijñānavāda. We need not deny that the Śūnyavāda is attacked in the N.S. (cp. N.S., iv. 1. 40; iv. 1. 48, with the *Mādhyamika Kārikā*, xv. 6, and vii. 20, respectively, and also N.S., iv. 1. 34–35, with Candrakīrti's *Vṛtti*, pp. 64–71). But Śūnyavāda is earlier than Nāgārjuna, who is familiar with the Nyāya terminology and denies the doctrine of atoms (cp. N.S., iv. 2. 18–24, 31–32, with the *Mādhyamika Kārikā*, vii. 34, and N.S., iii. 2. 11 and iv. 1. 64). All that we can say is that the N.S. is of an earlier date than Nāgārjuna, though later than the Mādhyamika tradition (see also *I.P.*, vol. i, p. 643 n.; Ui: *Vaiśeṣika Philosophy*, p. 85). The *Lankāvatāra Sūtra* refers to Tārkikas and Naiyāyikas, and if we remember

Vātsyāyana's *Nyāya Bhāṣya* is the classic commentary on the *Nyāya Sūtra.* Evidently, Vātsyāyana is not the immediate successor of Gautama, since his work contains passages of the character of vārttikas, which state in a condensed form the results of discussions

---

that some of the cosmological views refuted in the N.S. are as old as early Buddhism, Jacobi's date, which is supported by Suali, who refers the N.S. to A.D. 300 or 350, seems to be much too late (see also Ui: *Vaiśeṣika Philosophy*, p. 16). Garbe inclines to the view that the N.S. belongs to the first century A.D., since they were known to Pañcaśikha, whom he believes to have been a contemporary of Śabara, who lived some time between A.D. 100 and 300. Gautama is familiar with the terminology of the B.S. (cp. N.S., iii. 2. 14–16, with B.S., ii. 1. 24) and the Pūrva Mīmāṁsā of Jaimini (see N.S., ii. 1. 61, 67; Bodas: Introduction to *Tarkasaṁgraha*). Bodas believes that the V.S., iv. 1. 4–5, have in view Bādarāyaṇa's criticism of the theory of atoms, and V.S., iii. 2. 9 (cp. also N.S., iii. 1. 28–30), is aimed at the Vedānta view that the self is known only through the śruti. Similarly, V.S., iv. 2. 2–3, controvert the view of B.S., ii. 2. 21–22, that the body is the result of the union of five or three elements. Gautama propounds views very similar to those of Bādarāyaṇa in several places. See N.S., iv. 1. 64, and iii. 2. 14–16. The absence of any direct reference to the Nyāya in the B.S. and the M.S. is sometimes emphasised. It may be that Vyāsa, reputed to be a disciple of Gautama, did not care to criticise the Nyāya view, especially as it was agreeable to the admission of Īśvara. Again, it is sometimes held that the B.S., ii. 1 11–13, attempt to disprove the Nyāya view of establishing God by reasoning. The doctrines of atomism and asatkāryavāda are examined in B.S., ii. 2. 10–16, and ii. 1. 15–20. Early Buddhist works do not contain information for assigning the date of the N.S. Kātyāyana (fourth century B.C.) and Patañjali (whose great work was written about 140 B.C.) knew the Nyāya system. See Goldstucker's *Pāṇini*. Śabara's quotations from Bhagavān Upavarṣa, who is said to have written commentaries on both the Mīmāṁsās, indicate Upavarṣa's familiarity with the Nyāya views. Harivarman (A.D. 260) knows about the sixteen topics of the Nyāya. Aśvaghoṣa uses the five-membered syllogism. See Ui: *Vaiśeṣika Philosophy*, pp. 56 and 81. We may therefore conclude that the N.S. existed in the fourth century B.C., though not in the present form. M. M. Haraprasād Śāstri says: "I am not sure if the work N.S. had not gone through several redactions before it assumed its present shape" (J.A.S. of Bengal, 1905, p. 178; see also pp. 245 ff.). Vācaspati made two attempts to collect the Sūtras in his *Nyāyasūcī* and *Nyāyasūtroddhāra*, thus suggesting doubts about the authenticity of the N.S. Dr. Vidyābhūṣaṇ believes that Gautama wrote only the first chapter of the work, and he was a contemporary of the Buddha, the same as the author of the *Dharma Sūtra*, who lived in Mithilā in the sixth century B.C. (see S.B.H: N.S., pp. v–viii, and Bhāndārkar Commemoration volume, pp. 161–162). He suggests that Gautama's original views are those contained in the *Caraka Saṁhitā* (Vimānasthāna, viii). The N.S. and *Caraka Saṁhitā* have much in common; but it is said, "Caraka's references to the Nyāya principles and the Vaiśeṣika categories are of little value in fixing the date of the N.S., since the work has suffered considerable re-fashioning, and its date is also uncertain" (I.L.A., p. 13).

There are doubts expressed even about Gautama's authorship of the N.S. Vātsyāyana, Uddyotakara and Mādhava credit Akṣapāda with the author-

carried on in the school of Gautama. Vātsyāyana offers different explanations of some sūtras, indicating thereby that there were earlier commentators who did not all agree on the interpretations of the sūtras.[1] Besides, Vātsyāyana refers to Gautama as a sage of the remote past, and quotes from Patañjali's *Mahābhāṣya* and Kauṭilya's *Arthaśāstra*,[2] and also from the *Vaiśeṣika Sūtra*.[3] Nāgārjuna, the author of *Upāyakausalya* and *Vigrahavyāvartanī*, is certainly earlier than Vātsyāyana, who attempts to combat the views of Nāgārjuna. Dignāga criticised Vātsyāyana's interpretation from the Buddhist point of view. From all this, we may infer that Vātsyāyana lived some time before A.D. 400.[4]

---

ship of the N.S., a view which is supported by Vācaspati and Jayanta. According to *Padma Purāṇa* (Uttarakhaṇḍa, 263) and *Skanda Purāṇa* (Kālikā Khaṇḍa, xvii), Gautama is the author of the N.S., and Viśvanātha is of this opinion. Hindu tradition identifies the two and holds that Gautama is called Akṣapāda, or one who has eyes in his feet. The story runs that when Gautama was absorbed in meditation and fell into a well, God in his mercy bestowed on his feet the power of vision to prevent further mishaps. Dr. Vidyābhūṣaṇ goes against a well-established tradition when he observes that "Gautama and Akṣapāda seem both to have contributed to the production of the work. The *Nyāya Sūtra* treats mainly of five subjects, viz. (1) pramāṇa, the means of right knowledge; (2) prameya, the object of right knowledge; (3) vāda, debate or discussion; (4) avayava, the members of the syllogism; and (5) anyamataparīkṣā, an examination of contemporary philosophical doctrines. The second and the third subjects, and possibly also the first subject in its crude form, ample references to which are met with in the old Brāhmanic, Buddhistic and Jaina books, were in all probability handled by Gautama, whose Ānvīkṣikīvidyā was constituted by them. The fourth and the fifth subjects, and possibly also the first subject in its systematic form, were introduced by Akṣapāda into the Ānvīkṣikī-vidyā, which in its final form was styled the N.S. Akṣapāda was therefore the real author of the N.S., which derived a considerable part of its materials from the Ānvīkṣikī-vidyā of Gautama" (*History of Indian Logic*, pp. 49–50). This view is but a conjecture which it is impossible either to defend or refute. Not only is Gautama identified with the author of the *Dharma Sūtra*, but is also regarded as the same as the sage of that name mentioned in Vālmīki's *Rāmāyana* in connection with the episode of Ahalyā. According to the M.B. (Śāntiparva, 265. 45), Medhātithi is another name for Gautama. Bhāsa, in his *Pratimānāṭaka*, refers to Medhātithi as the founder of the Nyāya system: "Mānavīyaṁ dharmaśāstram, māheśvaraṁ yogaśāstram, bārhaspatyam arthaśāstram, medhātither nyāyaśāstram" (Act V). See also *History of Indian Logic*, p. 766.

[1] See N.B., i. 1. 5, i. 2. 9. Vātsyāyana refers to other interpreters in i. 1. 32 in the usual style: eke, some; kecit, certain; anye, others. See M.B., Ādiparva, 42–44.

[2] N.B., i. 1. 1, and *Arthaśāstra*, 11; N.B., v. 1. 10, and *Mahābhāṣya*, i. 1. 3.

[3] Cp. V.S., iv. 1. 6, and N.B., iii. 1. 33, iii. 1. 67; V.S., iii. 1. 16, and N.B., ii. 2. 34.

[4] Dr. Vidyābhūṣaṇ believes that Vātsyāyana was a native of South India of the middle of the fourth century A.D. (*History of India Logic*,

Dignāga's works, which are preserved in Tibetan translations, are *Pramāṇasamuccaya*, with a commentary by the author himself, *Nyāyapraveśa*, *Hetucakrahamaru*, *Ālambanaparīkṣā* and *Pramāṇaśāstrapraveśa*, and they are said to be popular in Japan.[1] Dignāga belongs to the fifth century A.D.[2] Many of the important changes introduced in logical doctrine by Praśastapāda are traced to Dignāga, whose originality will suffer a good deal, if Praśastapāda is found to be his predecessor.

Uddyotakara's *Nyāyavārttika* (sixth century A.D.)[3] is a defence of Vātsyāyana against the attacks of Dignāga. Dharmakīrti's *Nyāyabindu* is a defence of Dignāga against the criticisms of Uddyotakara. If we assume that the *Vādavidhi* referred to by Uddyotakara[4] is another name for Dharmakīrti's *Vādanyāya*, and that the śāstra referred to by Dharmakīrti in his *Nyāyabindu*[5] is the *Vārttika* of Uddyotakara, then these two writers may be supposed to belong to the same period. The latest date, however, for Dharmakīrti is the beginning of the seventh century.[6] In the ninth century Dharmottara followed on the lines of Dignāga and Dharmakīrti, in his *Nyāyabinduṭīkā*.

Towards the first half of the ninth century, Vācaspati re-established

---

pp. 42, 116–117; A., 1915, Art. on *Vātsyāyana*). While Keith (I.L.A., p. 28) and Bodas (Introduction to *Tarkasaṁgraha*) agree with this view, Jacobi and Suali are inclined to place him about the beginning of the sixth century A.D., or a little earlier. Haraprasād Śāstri makes Vātsyāyana a successor of Nāgārjuna and Āryadeva, since he is familiar with the Mahāyānist doctrines of momentariness, śūnyavāda, individuality, etc. See J.A.S. of Bengal, 1905, pp. 178–179.

[1] Some idea of their contents may be gathered from Vidyābhūṣan's *History of Indian Logic*, pp. 276–299, and Uddyotakara's references to Dignāga's views in his N.V.

[2] Tāranātha's *History of Buddhism* says that Dignāga was the son of a Brāhmin of Conjeevaram, who soon became proficient in the teachings of the Hīnayāna, though he later acquired from Vasubandhu Mahāyāna teachings. According to the evidence of Yuan Chwang, Vasubandhu, before he became a Buddhist, was well versed not only in the eighteen schools of Buddhism, but also in the six systems of the Hindus. Vasubandhu is now assigned to the first half of the fourth century A.D., and Dignāga may have flourished some time before A.D. 400. Kālidāsa's suggested reference to Dignāga in his *Meghadūta* confirms this view, since Kālidāsa belongs to the same period (see Keith: *Classical Sanskrit Literature*, pp. 31–32, and I.P., p. 624 n.).

[3] Subandhu's *Vāsavadattā* refers to Uddyotakara as the rescuer of the Nyāya (see Hall's edition, p. 235). Bāṇa's *Harṣacarita*, written during the time of King Harṣa, who reigned in Thanesvar, at any rate during the years from A.D. 629–644, when the Chinese pilgrim Yuan Chwang travelled through India, mentions *Vāsavadattā* (i), which refers to Uddyotakara. It is therefore safe to assume that he belonged to the sixth century A.D. Uddyotakara is a Bhāradvāja by gotra and a Pāśupata by sect.

[4] N.V., i. 33.

[5] *Nyāyabindu*, iii, Peterson's edition, pp. 110–111.

[6] I-tsing refers to him. See Takakusu: *I-tsing*, p. lviii.

the orthodox view of the Nyāya in his *Nyāyavārttikatātparyaṭīkā*. He also wrote smaller works on the Nyāya like *Nyāyaṣūcīnibandha*. *Nyāyasūtroddhāra* is also attributed to him.[1] He is a versatile genius, and has written authoritative works on other systems of thought, as the *Bhāmatī* on the Advaita Vedānta and the *Sāṁkhyatattvakaumudī* on the Sāṁkhya. He is therefore styled Sarvatantrasvatantra or Ṣaḍdarśanīvallabha. Udayana's (A.D. 984) *Tātparyapariśuddhi* is a valuable commentary on Vācaspati's work. His *Ātmatattvaviveka* is a defence of the permanent soul theory and a criticism of the Buddhist thinkers Āryakīrti and others. His *Kusumāñjali* is the first systematic account of the theism of the Nyāya.[2] His other works are *Kiraṇāvali* and *Nyāyapariśiṣṭa*. Jayanta's *Nyāyamañjari* is an independent commentary on the *Nyāya Sūtra*. Jayanta, who quotes Vācaspati, and is quoted by Ratnaprabhā and Devasūri, belongs to the tenth century.[3] Bhāsarvajña's *Nyāyasāra* is, as its name implies, a survey of the Nyāya philosophy. He admits the three proofs of perception, inference and verbal testimony, and rejects comparison as an independent means of proof. He is a Śaivite, perhaps of the Kashmir sect, and belongs to the tenth century A.D. Vardhamāna's *Nyāyanibandhaprakāśa* (A.D. 1225) is a commentary on Udayana's *Nyāyatātparyapariśuddhi*, though it incorporates the views of Gaṅgeśa, the father of Vardhamāna and the founder of the modern school. Rucidatta's *Makaranda* (A.D. 1275) develops Vardhamāna's views.[4]

The later works on the Nyāya openly accept the Vaiśeṣika categories, which they bring under prameya or objects of knowledge, or under artha, which is one of the twelve kinds of prameya. Varadarāja's *Tārkikarakṣā* (twelfth century A.D.) is an important treatise of the syncretist school. He brings under prameya the twelve objects of the Nyāya as well as the six categories of the Vaiśeṣika. Keśava Miśra's *Tarkabhāṣā* (end of the thirteenth century) combines the Nyāya and the Vaiśeṣika views.[5]

The important Jaina logical works are Bhadrabāhu's *Daśavaikālikaniryukti* (357 B.C. *circa*), Siddhasena Divākara's *Nyāyāvatāra* (sixth

---

[1] The author of the *Nyāyasūtroddhāra* is different from the writer here referred to, and lived in the fifteenth century A.D. Vācaspati says that his *Nyāyasūcī* was composed in the year 898, which most probably refers to the Vikrama era and corresponds to our A.D. 841. There is no doubt that he preceded Ratnakīrti, the Buddhist logician (A.D. 1000).

[2] When he felt that God did not show any mercy towards him in consideration of his services for theism, he is reported to have addressed the Supreme in the words, "Proud of thy prowess thou despisest me upon whom thy existence depended when the Buddhists reigned supreme."

Aiśvaryamadamatto 'śi mām avajñāya vartase
Parākrānteṣu bauddheṣu madadhīnā tava sthitiḥ.

[3] See *History of Indian Logic*, p. 147, and I.L.A., p. 33.

[4] It is a commentary on Vardhamāna's Prakāśa or Udayana's Kusumāñjali.

[5] It is translated by Dr. Jhā in *Indian Thought*, vol. ii.

century A.D.), Māṇikyanandi's *Parīkṣāmukhasūtra* (A.D. 800), Devasūri's *Pramāṇanayatattvālokālaṁkāra* (twelfth century A.D.) and Prabhācandra's *Prameyakamalamārtāṇḍa*. The Jaina thinkers and the Buddhist logicians differentiated logical inquiries from those of religion and metaphysics, with which they were mixed up in the discussions of the Hindu writers. The Nyāya works of the latter treat of atoms and their properties, souls and rebirth, God and the world, as well as logical problems of the nature and limits of knowledge. The Buddhist and the Jaina thinkers showed no interest in the metaphysical implications of the ancient Nyāya, but laid great stress on the purely logical aspects, and thus prepared the way for the modern Nyāya, which is pure logic and dialectic.

Gaṅgeśa's *Tattvacintāmaṇi* is the standard text of the modern school.[1] Vardhamāna, the son of Gaṅgeśa, continued the tradition in his works. Jayadeva wrote a commentary on *Tattvacintāmaṇi* called the *Āloka* (thirteenth century). Vāsudeva Sārvabhauma's *Tattvacintāmaṇivyākhyā*[2] may be regarded as the first great work of the Navadvīpa (Nuddea) school, and it belongs to the end of the fifteenth or the beginning of the sixteenth century. He was fortunate in his disciples, the chief of them being Caitanya, the famous Vaiṣṇava reformer, Raghunātha, the renowned logician and the author of *Dīdhiti* and *Padārthakhaṇḍana*,[3] Raghunandana, the famous jurist, and Kṛṣṇānanda, the great authority on Tāntrik rites. Though Gaṅgeśa wrote only on the four pramāṇas, and did not concern himself directly with the metaphysical implications, Raghunātha, like some other writers of this school, showed much interest in metaphysics also. Jagadīśa (end of the sixteenth century) and Gadādhara (seventeenth century) are well-known logicians of this school. Annaṁ Bhaṭṭa[4] (seventeenth century), a Brahmin of Andhra, tried to evolve a consistent system from out of the ancient and the modern Nyāya and the Vaiśeṣika philosophy, though his views leaned towards the ancient Nyāya. His *Tarkasaṁgraha* and *Dīpikā* are popular manuals of the Nyāya-Vaiśeṣika school. Vallabha's *Nyāyalīlāvati*, Viśvanātha's *Nyāyasūtravṛtti* (seventeenth century) are other works of some importance.[5]

It is possible to distinguish different stages in the development of logical studies in India. We have first of all

[1] A summary of this work is given in Vidyābhūṣan's *History of Indian Logic*, pp. 407–453. Gaṅgeśa lived at Mithilā in the last quarter of the twelfth century, as is evident from his familiarity with Udayana's works and quotations from Śivāditya and Harṣa. In *Tattvacintāmani* (ii. p. 233) Śrī Harṣa's views are criticised.

[2] *Sārāvali* is the name of it, and I am told that the MS. of it is in the Benares Government Sanskrit College Library.

[3] This criticism of the Vaiśeṣika system is published in the *Pandit* (xxiv and xxv) under the title "Padārthatattvanirūpaṇa."

[4] *History of Indian Logic*, p. 388.

[5] For the History of Hindu logic in China and Japan, see Suguira: *Hindu Logic as Preserved in China and Japan*.

Ānvīkṣikī, which is given a separate place along with the Nyāya in the Mahābhārata. It soon becomes blended with the Nyāya, and in the classical texts of the ancient school we have in addition to logical theory a metaphysical view of the universe as a whole. As Vātsyāyana says, "The highest good is attained only when one has rightly understood the real nature of (1) that which is fit to be discarded (i.e. suffering along with its causes in the shape of avidyā and its effects), (2) that which puts an end to suffering, in other words, jñāna (knowledge), (3) the means by which the destruction of suffering is accomplished, i.e. philosophical treatises, and (4) the goal to be attained or the highest good."[1] Ancient Nyāya discussed logical questions, though not for their own sake. The contributions of the Jaina and the Buddhist thinkers bring about a change in the outlook. The modern Nyāya, with its exclusive interest in the theory of knowledge, forgets the intimate relation between logic and life. The ancient Naiyāyika had a more adequate idea of the relation of logic and metaphysics. Logic can ascertain the normative forms of thought only in relation to the content of thought. The modern Naiyāyika devotes great attention to pramāṇa or the means of knowledge and the theory of definition,[2] and discards altogether the question of prameyas or the objects of knowledge. The scholastic subtleties, the logical legerdemain, the fine hair-splitting in which the works of the successors of Gaṅgeśa indulge, terrify many, and even those who have grappled with them cannot be sure that they have comprehended their ideas. Many of those who have waded through these works are impressed by their brilliant dialectical feats, but find them often more confusing than enlightening. Plain issues are obscured by over-subtlety. The fondness of the logical mind for drawing distinctions often degenerates into a love of formulas, and leaves on the mind the impression of a formalism rather poor in content. Elaboration of terminology takes the place of inquiry into subject-matter. Terms which ought to define distinctions are sometimes employed to circumvent difficulties. Of some at least of these works it may be said that they merely succeed in showing how learned one can be

[1] N.B., i. 1. 1.
[2] Lakṣaṇapramāṇābhyāṁ vastusiddhiḥ.

about one knows not what. Even those who believe that the mill of their intellect grinds exceeding small cannot help admitting that it is not always fed with a sufficiency of grain.[1] The value of Navya Nyāya as a training-ground for the intellect can hardly be overestimated.

IV

The Scope of the Nyāya

The term Nyāya means literally that by means of which the mind is led to a conclusion.[2] "Nyāya" becomes equivalent to an argument, and the system which treats of arguments more thoroughly than others comes to be known as the Nyāya system. Arguments are either valid or invalid. The term "nyāya" means in popular usage right or just, and so the Nyāya becomes the science of right reasoning. "Nyāya" in the narrow sense stands for syllogistic reasoning,[3] while in the wider sense it signifies the examination of objects by evidences. It thus becomes a science of demonstration or of correct knowledge, pramāṇaśāstra. All knowledge implies four conditions: (1) The subject or the pramātṛ, the cogniser or the substantive ground of the cognitions; (2) the object, or the prameya to which the process of cognition is directed; (3) the resulting state of cognition, or the pramiti; and (4) the means of knowledge, or the pramāṇa.[4] Every cognitive act, valid or invalid, has the three factors of a cognising subject, a content or a what of which the subject is aware, and a

[1] Cp. Bodas: *Tarkasaṁgraha*, p. xiii; Keith: I.L.A., p. 35. Dr. Vidyābhuṣan divides the history of the Nyāya philosophy into three periods: Ancient (650 B.C. to A.D. 100), Mediæval (up to A.D. 1200), and Modern (from A.D. 900). See his *History of Indian Logic*, p. xiii. For an idea of the character of Modern Nyāya, see Dr. Śaileśvar Sen's *A Study of Mathurānātha's Tattva-cintāmaṇi-rahasya*, 1924.

[2] Nīyate anena iti nyāyaḥ.

[3] N.B., i. 1. 1. Vātsyāyana uses the expression paramanyāya for the syllogism which combines in itself the five parts. Dignāga calls the members of a syllogism nyāyāvayava. See also N.V., iv. 1. 14. In Vācaspati's *Nyāyasūcī* the section on the syllogism (i. 1. 32–39) is spoken of as the Nyāyaprakaraṇa. Viśvanātha means by Nyāyasvarūpa the essential structure of the syllogism. See his *Nyāyasūtravṛtti*, i. 1. 25; i. 1. 31; i. 1. 38; i. 1. 40. Mādhava (S.D.S., xi) uses the word nyāya in the sense of inference for the sake of others.

[4] Pramākaraṇam pramāṇam. See also *Vedāntaparibhāṣā*, i.

relation of knowledge between the two, which are distinguishable though not separable. The nature of knowledge, as valid or invalid, depends upon the fourth factor of pramāṇa. It is the operative cause of valid knowledge in normal circumstances.[1]

While Vātsyāyana defines pramāṇa as an instrument of knowledge or "that by which the knowing subject knows the object,"[2] Uddyotakara calls it the cause of knowledge (upalabdhihetu).[3] He admits that this definition is rather wide, since the cogniser and the object cognised are also causes of cognition, but justifies it on the ground that "The cogniser and the cognised have their function fulfilled elsewhere, i.e. the function of the cognising subject and the cognised object lies in, and is only fulfilled by the inciting of the pramāṇa into activity; pramāṇa, on the other hand, does not have its function fulfilled (except by the bringing about of the cognition); so it is the pramāṇa that is to be regarded as the real cause of the cognition." Wherever the pramāṇa is present, cognition arises; wherever it is absent, whatever else may be present, cognition does not arise. Pramāṇa is thus the most efficient cause of cognition and the last to appear before the cognition arises.[4] Śivāditya brings out the logical implication when he defines pramāṇa as that which produces pramā or knowledge in accord with reality.[5] Jayanta makes pramāṇa the cause which produces non-erroneous, certain knowledge of objects.[6]

The specific form of knowledge depends on the pramāṇa. The other factors of subject and object may be the same in perception or inference. Similarly, the contact of the manas with the soul is the common mediate cause of all forms of knowledge. Only contact (saṁyoga) takes different forms in the different kinds of knowledge. Though the Nyāya deals with know-

[1] N.V., i. 1. 1.

[2] N.B., i. 1. 1.

[3] See also N.V.T.T., i. 1. 1.

[4] N.V., i. 1. 1. Another objection, viz., that if the pramāṇa is brought into existence by the cognising subject and the cognised object, then these two must exist prior to the pramāṇa, though as a matter of fact, until the pramāṇa is there, we cannot recognise subject or object, which have a meaning only in relation to the thought activity called the pramāṇa, is considered. Uddyotakara admits all this, but says: "These words are not dependent on their relation to present action only." A cook is a cook whether he is actually cooking or not. "The reason for such usage lies in the (expressive) potency of the word itself; and this potency is present at all times; in the same manner, there need be no incongruity in the assertion that the pramāṇa is brought into existence by the cognising subject and the cognised object."

[5] *Saptapadārthī*, sec. 144. See also S.D.S., xi.

[6] Avyabhicāriṇīm asaṁdigdhām arthopalabdhim. *Nyāyamañjari*, p. 12.

ledge, it deals more especially with the supreme condition of knowledge called the pramāṇa, and so it is called pramāṇaśāstra.[1] Before we investigate the nature of objects, we must know the capacity of the instruments of knowledge; for "knowledge of the thing to be measured depends on the knowledge of the measure."[2] Pramāṇaśāstra not only helps us to a right apprehension of objects, but also enables us to test the validity of knowledge.[3] It is both formal and material, and is interested in consistency as well as in truth. The Nyāya starts with the assumption that the account of the world which our minds afford us is in the main a trustworthy account. All knowledge is revelatory of reality (arthaprakāśa). We are so constituted as to perceive objects, notice their resemblances and draw inferences. These operations are performed by all thinking men, though with different degrees of care and exactness. Whenever we have mental activity, controlled by the purpose of acquiring a knowledge of reality, we have a topic for logical inquiry. Truth-seeking is already present in human action. Logical theory does not create it. It only tries to interpret this element and express its nature in general principles. Its problem is not much different from that of any positive science. Just as a physiologist investigates the processes by which life is sustained in the individual, the logician states the laws governing the process of knowledge. He is no more responsible for it than the physiologist is for the working of the bodily mechanism.

The Nyāya system does not assume that value and fact are wholly disparate and require altogether different methods of treatment. Values attach to facts and can be studied only in relation to them. We do not start with empty minds; we possess information about the nature of the world through experience and tradition. A complex system of knowledge is handed down through the scriptures. Adopting the inductive method of science, the Nyāya classifies the different ways in which our knowledge is acquired. The four pramāṇas through

[1] The importance attached by the Hindu thinkers to the investigation of pramāṇas is evident from Viśvanātha's reference that pramāṇa is one of the names of Viṣṇu.

[2] Mānādhīnā meyasiddhiḥ. Citsukhī, ii. 18.

[3] Cp. W. E. Johnson's definition of logic as "the analysis and criticism of thought" (*Logic*, vol. i, p. xiii).

which correct knowledge is acquired are pratyakṣa or intuition,[1] anumāna or inference,[2] upamāna or comparison and śabda or verbal testimony.[3] Western treatises on logic do not generally treat of perception,[4] but the Nyāya regards it as one of the important sources of knowledge. Inference is a central topic of the Nyāya system, which is sometimes called Hetuvidyā, or the science of reason on which the validity of an inferential argument depends.[5] According to this view logic is the theory of inference or anumānavāda. Intuitive or immediate knowledge is beyond the scope of logic as thus understood. The Nyāya does not justify this narrow usage. The inclusion of verbal testimony, which covers the problem of Revealed Theology, shows the religious interest of the system. The Nyāya gives us a psychological account of these four sources of knowledge. It affirms that logical inquiry cannot be carried on without regard to the psychological processes by which knowledge as mental content is gained. It treats at length the ways by which the mind is carried forward and impelled to produce fresh results. In doing so, it also points out the pitfalls which are incidental to the employment of these means. The problem of logic is not a purely inductive one. The mere generalisation, that all our knowledge is gained through one or other of the four sources of knowledge, does not explain the problem of knowledge. Generalisation is not explanation.

The Nyāya not only inquires into the ways and means by which the human mind assimilates and develops knowledge, it also interprets the logical facts and expresses them in logical formulas which assume the form of standards or norms in all cases of the divergence of thought from its normal course of truth-seeking. Pramāṇas thus become the measures or canons

[1] Sense-perception is only a variety of intuition or direct apprehension.

[2] Anumāna means literally the knowledge of one thing after, or through that of, another.

[3] N.S., i. 1. 3. Caraka gives āptopadeśa or reliable assertion, pratyakṣa, anumāna and yukti or continuous reasoning. See also *Sthānāṅga Sūtra.*

[4] Cp., however, J. S. Mill : " Truth is known to us in two ways, intuition and inference " (*System of Logic,* Introduction, p. 4).

[5] The term " hetuvidyā " occurs in *Milinda* (S.B.E., vol. xxxv, pp. 6–7), *Lalitavistara* (xii). Though " hetu " means only reason or ground, the Jaina thinkers use it in a wider sense. See also *Manu,* ii. 11 ; M.B., Ādiparva, 1–67 ; Śāntiparva, 210. 22 ; Aśvamedhaparva, 85. 27. The earlier grammarians, Pāṇini, Kātyāyana and Patañjali accept this view. See also N.V., iv 1. 14 ; I.L.A., p. 11.

of knowledge by means of which we can check and evaluate the knowledge already existing in us. Logic is thus the science of proof or the estimation of evidence. It discusses the validity of knowledge by showing its dependence on given grounds or compatibility with reality. The problem of truth has important bearings on metaphysical theory. The Nyāya is a metaphysics of reality (tattvaśāstra),[1] as well as a theory of knowledge. Thus it is not merely formal logic but a full epistemology, combining discussions of psychology and logic, metaphysics and theology.

V

The Nature of Definition

The several topics discussed in the *Nyāya Sūtra* are first enunciated, then defined, and lastly examined.[2] Definition states the essential nature (svarūpa) of a thing so as to differentiate it from others. The function of a definition is to distinguish the thing defined from all things different from itself, with which it is likely to be confused.[3] We can distinguish things without stating their respective essences. An asādhāraṇa dharma or a peculiar attribute also helps us to distinguish. The fallacies incident to definition are of three kinds: Ativyāpti, or the extension of the attribute to objects beyond the class defined, occurs in definitions which are too wide, as when we define a cow as a horned animal; Avyāpti, or limitation of the attributes to only a portion of the class defined, which occurs in definitions which are too narrow, as when we define a cow as a tawny animal; Asambhava, or the fallacy committed when the definition states an attribute which is not found in any of the objects defined, as when we define a cow as an animal with uncloven hoofs. Definition states " a characteristic mark which applies to all things denoted by the term defined, neither more nor less." [4] To secure this, we may start with the genus and subsequently narrow its denotation by the express exclusion of superfluous objects, by

[1] N.B., i. 1. 1.

[2] Uddeśa, lakṣaṇa and parīkṣā, N.B., i. 1. 3.

[3] N.B., i. 1. 3.

[4] Lakṣyatāvacchedakasamaniyatatvam.

the use of words like other than (itara), different from (bhinna).[1] This is definition by genus and difference.

VI

Pratyakṣa or Intuition

Of the different sources of knowledge, pratyakṣa or intuition is the most important. Vātsyāyana says, " when a man seeks the knowledge of a certain thing, if he is told of it by a trustworthy person and has the verbal cognition of the thing, there is still a desire in his mind to ratify his information by means of inference through particular indicative features; and even after he has been able to get at the inferential knowledge of the thing, he is still desirous of actually seeing the thing with his eyes; but when he has once perceived the thing directly, his desires are at rest and he does not seek for any other kind of knowledge." [2] The word " pratyakṣa " is ambiguous, as it is used for both the result, the apprehension of the truth and the process or the operation which leads to that result. Though " pratyakṣa " originally meant sense-perception, it soon came to cover all immediate apprehension whether through the aid of the senses or not.[3] Gaṅgeśa defines pratyakṣa as direct apprehension.[4] It is knowledge whose instrumental cause is not knowledge.[5] In inference, comparison and verbal testimony, we have as our data knowledge of premises or of similarity or of convention. In memory

[1] Cp. the definition of earth as jalādy aṣṭadravya bhinnam dravyam pṛthivī.

[2] N.B., i. 1. 3. It is clear that one and the same object may be cognised by more than one pramāṇa. The existence of the soul may be known from scripture, inference or mental perception. The existence of fire may be known through information conveyed by another or actual perception or inference. There are also cases where only one pramāṇa can function. That the performance of the agnihotra ceremony leads to heaven is known only through scriptural evidence. Uddyotakara holds that " when the same object is cognised through different pramāṇas it is cognised in its different aspects " (N.V., Introduction).

[3] *Nyāyabinduṭīkā*, p. 7; I.P., pp. 295–296

[4] Pratyakṣasya sākṣātkāritvaṁ lakṣaṇam. *Tattvacintamaṇi*, p. 552.

[5] Jñānākaraṇakaṁ jñānaṁ pratyakṣam. Cp. McTaggart: " A belief which is directly based on a perception . . . is properly called ultimate, since, although it is based on something—the perception—it is not based on any other *belief* ". (*The Nature of Existence*, pp. 42–43).

we have knowledge of what we have previously apprehended. In pratyakṣa, knowledge is not an antecedent condition. God's knowledge is direct, immediate and entire, and is not instrumented by any other cognition.

Gautama defines sense-perception as "that knowledge which arises from the 'contact' of a sense-organ with its object, inexpressible by words, unerring and well defined."[1] This definition mentions the different factors involved in the act of perception: (1) the senses (indriyas), (2) their objects (artha), (3) the contact of the senses with their objects (sannikarṣa), and (4) cognition produced by this contact (jñānam). It is a matter of inference that there are sense-organs. The cognition of colour is not possible, if there is not a visual organ.[2] The senses are said to be five, corresponding to the five characters of knowledge (buddhilakṣaṇa) visual, auditory, olfactory, gustatory and tactual.[3] They occupy different sites (adhisṭhāna), the eyeball, the earhole, the nose, the tongue and the skin. From the varied nature of the processes (gati), forms (ākṛti) and constituents (jāti), of which they are made, it is evident that the senses are five in number. The five sense-organs, eye, ear, nose, tongue and skin, are said to be of the same nature as the five elements, light, ether, earth, water and air, whose special qualities of colour, sound, smell, taste and tangibility are manifested by them.[4]

A view similar to that of Democritus, that all the senses are only modifications of touch,[5] is refuted on the ground that a blind man

---

[1] i. 1. 4. Cp. Caraka's definition of perception as the knowledge which is produced by a union of the soul with the mind (manas), the senses and their objects. Gaṅgeśa criticises Gautama's definition on several grounds; it is too wide, since every cognition is produced by the contact of the object with the manas, which is also a sense. Again, it does not apply to the intuitive apprehension of all things that God has without any sense-mediation. What is a sense organ can be determined only by perception, and the use of the term sense in the definition involves the fallacy of circular reasoning.

[2] Since the senses consist of elements endowed with special qualities, they are able to perceive their respective objects and not themselves. An eye sees an external object, but not itself The only exception is sound (N.S., iii. 1. 68–69, 71).

[3] N.S., iii. 1. 54.

[4] Nothing can offer resistance to a non-material all-pervading substance. Since the eye receives obstruction from material things like walls, it is itself material.

[5] This view is attributed to the Sāṁkhya by *Ratnaprabhā* and *Bhāmatī* (ii. 2. 10).

cannot see colour.[1] If the special parts of touch partake of the nature of the senses, then the senses are many; if they do not, then we have to admit that colour, sound and the like are not cognisable by the senses.[2] If there is only one sense, the different functions of seeing, hearing, smelling can be produced simultaneously. Besides, touch can perceive only objects which are near, whereas sight and sound perceive objects which are far off. While the Nyāya rejects the theory of the unity of sense-organs, it recognises the distinctive character of tvak or touch. Relative consciousness is possible only when there is contact between manas and tvak, and when manas happens to be within the purītat, beyond the sphere of tvak, as it is in suṣupti or dreamless sleep, there is abeyance of conscious life altogether.[3]

Manas (or mind) is a condition of perception. When we are deeply absorbed in some study we do not hear the sound of the wind, though the sound affects the organ of hearing and the self is in connection with it, being all-pervading. Again, "even when the contact of more than one sense-organ with their respective objects is present, there is no simultaneous perception of all these objects—which is due to the fact that while there is proximity or contact of the manas (with one object) there is no such contact of it (with the other objects), which shows that the operation of the manas is necessary in every act of perception."[4] Manas mediates between the self and the senses. It accounts for the non-simultaneity of the acts of knowledge.[5] The quick succession of impressions gives sometimes the appearance of simultaneity. When we run a pin through a number of sheets we imagine that the piercing is simultaneous, while it is really successive.[6] It follows that if the manas is in contact with one sense-organ, it cannot be so with another. It is therefore said to be atomic in dimension. If the manas were all-pervading (vibhu), then we cannot account for the successive character of our sense-experiences. As soon as the sense is in contact with the object, the manas comes with lightning speed to reach the sense. Besides, contact between two all-pervading substances is inconceivable. "Remembrance, inference, verbal cognition, doubt, intuition

[1] N.S., iii. 1. 51–52.
[2] See N.S., iii. 1. 53.
[3] See Brh. Up., iv 1. 19; *Tarkasaṁgrahadīpikā*, 18.
[4] N.B., i. 1. 4.
[5] i. 1. 16; ii. 1. 24; iii. 2. 6–7; N.V., i. 1. 16.
[6] N.B., iii 2. 58.

(pratibhā), dream, imagination (ūha), as also perception of pleasure and the rest are indicative of the existence of manas." [1] The cognitions which the soul has, except anuvyavasāya, are not self-luminous.[2] We become aware of them as we become aware of feelings and desires through the manas.

Vātṣyāyana includes manas under the senses. He calls it the inner sense by which we apprehend the inner states of feelings, desires and cognitions. While the sun in the sky and the inkstand on the table are experienced immediately as belonging to a world other than myself, feelings of pleasure and pain, emotions of joy and sorrow, and acts of wishing and desiring are experienced immediately as qualities of the soul. The self perceives the inner states through the instrumentality of the manas, while the co-operation of the senses is necessary for the apprehension of outer non-subjective states.[3] The distinction between inner and outer is not coincident with that between subjective and objective, since the desire to write on paper is as much an object of direct apprehension as the paper itself. The relation of knowledge is exactly the same whether the object is an external one like the paper or an internal one like desire. The object is as directly and immediately known in the one case as in the other.[4]

Vātsyāyana holds that manas is as good a sense-organ as the eye and the like, though there are certain marked differences. The outer senses are composed of material or elemental substances, are effective on only a few specific objects, and are capable of acting as organs

---

[1] N.B., i. 1. 16.

[2] Even the Naiyāyikas regard anuvyavasāya as self-luminous.

[3] Cp. with this Locke's distinction between sensation and reflection, the outer sense which gives us knowledge of the external world and the inner sense which gives us knowledge of the activity of our own minds (*Essay on the Human Understanding*, ii. 1. 4). Uddyotakara makes a distinction between pleasure and the cognition of pleasure. Pleasure is the object perceived, and the cognition of pleasure arises when the manas is brought into contact with the feeling. The agreeable feeling of coolness is produced by the contact of the skin with the cool wind, and when the manas comes into contact with it the cognition of agreeableness arises.

[4] Manas, however, cannot be regarded as the instrument of its own cognition. When the cognition of non-simultaneity, which indicates the existence of manas, is brought about by means of the manas, the cognition of manas thus obtained is due to the presence of the manas. It is not a case of manas operating on itself, for manas is not the instrument in the existence or cognition of itself. In the cognition of manas, the instrument consists of the manas along with the cognition of its indicative. The manas thus qualified is not the manas by itself. See N.V.T.T., iii. 1. 17. Uddyotakara holds that manas can be directly perceived through yogic practices (N.V., iii. 1. 17).

only, as endowed with specific qualities which they apprehend, whereas manas is immaterial, effective on all objects, and is capable of acting as an organ, without being endowed with any specific quality.[1] Uddyotakara does not altogether support this view. The question of materiality or its opposite applies only to produced things, while manas is not a product at all. He admits that manas operates on all things while the senses function only in limited areas. Manas, according to this writer, resembles the self in being the substratum of the contact which is the cause of remembrance, as also of that contact which brings about the cognition of pleasure.[2] Each self has its own manas, which is eternal, though subtle and devoid of magnitude. The manas in each self is one and not many, for if there were many in a single self, there would be simultaneous appearance of many cognitions, many desires in the same self, which is not the case.[3]

Since perception is a kind of knowledge or jñana, it belongs to the self. Though the contact between the self and the manas is eternal in a certain sense, it may be said to be renewed with each fresh mental act. The Nyāya assumes a naturalistic relation between the self and the object. The outward object is conceived as making an impression on the self, even as the seal does on the wax. The Nyāya theory of perception does not solve the central problem of physiological psychology as to how the stimulus of an external object on the sense-organ which is resolved into a form of mechanical contact becomes transformed into a psychical state. Even to-day the problem remains a mystery, in spite of the great advance of scientific knowledge.

For a perception to arise there must be objects external to the percipient. By this realistic assumption, the Nyāya is saved from subjectivism, which holds that we have only momentary feelings and that the belief in external reality is the fancy of the unlearned. The contact of sense with its appropriate object leads to the direct presentation of that object to consciousness. The relation between the object which is the stimulus and the conscious effect which is the perception is studied and suggestions of *minima sensibilia*, etc., are not wanting, though accurate results on these questions were not possible in the absence of fine apparatus.

The definition of perception assumes the contact of self and manas which is present in all cognitions and the contact

[1] N.B., i. 1. 4. [2] N.V., i. 1 4. [3] N.V., iii. 2. 56.

of manas and the senses, and specifies "sense-object contact" as its distinguishing feature.[1] Perception follows upon or accompanies the modification of the self produced by the contact of the senses with their objects. "If the sense-organs were operative without actually getting at the objects, then they could perceive things behind the wall also," [2] which is not normally the case. Sannikarṣa does not mean, according to Uddyotakara, conjunction, but only "becoming" an object of sense or standing in a definite relation to the sense-organ.

Objects are of different kinds. A blade of grass is a substance, its greenness is a quality, and since qualities inhere in substances, they cannot be perceived apart from the latter.[3] Substances and qualities as genera do not have independent existence, and are perceived only through the perception of their substrata. The contact between a sense-organ and a substance is one of conjunction or saṁyoga, while the relation between a substance and its quality or genus and individual is one of inherence or samavāya. The eye, for example, comes directly into conjunction with substance, but only "indirectly" with colour which inheres in that substance, and still more "indirectly" with the class concept which inheres in colour which resides in the object with which the eye is in conjunction.

The sense-object contact is said to be of six different kinds. The first is mere conjunction (saṁyoga), as when we perceive a substance jar. The second is inherence in that which is in conjunction (saṁyukta-samavāya), as when we perceive the quality or the genus of a substance, as the colour of the jar. The third is inherence in that which inheres in that which is in conjunction (saṁyukta-samaveta-samavāya), as when we perceive the genus of the quality of a substance or the genus of the colour of the jar. The fourth is inherence (samavāya), as when we cognise the quality of sound where the relation between the ear and the sound is one of inherence.[4] The fifth is inherence in that which inheres (samavetasamavāya), as when we cognise the genus of a quality independent of the substance, as the genus of the quality of sound. The last is (viśeṣaṇatā), or the relation of the qualification

---

[1] ii. 1. 29

[2] *Nyāyakandalī*, p. 23; N.B., ii. 1. 19.

[3] Except in the case of sound, which, though a quality, is perceived by itself.

[4] The organ of hearing is the ākāśa confined within the cavity of the ear, and śabda or sound is the property of ākāśa

and the qualified. When we perceive the absence of the jar we have an illustration of this, since there is union of our eye with the floor in which abides the qualification of the non-existence of the jar. The contact may be expressed in two forms, either as "the ground is qualified by the absence of the jar" (ghaṭābhāvavad bhūtalam), the ground serving as the subject and the absence of the jar as the qualification, or as, "there is the absence of a jar on the ground" (bhūtale ghaṭābhāvo'sti), in which case the relations are reversed. In the first case, the negation forms the qualification of that which is in contact (saṁyukta-viśeṣaṇatā), namely, the ground with the eye; in the second case, the negation is to be qualified by that which is in contact (saṁyukta-viśeṣyatā).[1] These distinctions are based on the metaphysical assumptions of the Nyāya regarding the nature of reality, that things, qualities and relations belong to the object-world. The Nyāya assumes, with the Vaiśeṣika, that there are substances, qualities, actions, generality, particularity, inherence and non-existence. A substance having magnitude is perceived by sight provided it has manifest colour.[2] The form of contact is conjunction, the eye and the object are said to come into actual contact. According to modern Nyāya, touch also apprehends substances, if the latter are tangible. Qualities and motion are perceived by the second form of contact. Generality is perceived by the second or the third kind, according as it is the generality of substance, quality or motion. The Nyāya holds that samavāya or inherence is itself a matter of perception, while the Vaiśeṣika regards it as an object of inherence. Non-existence is covered by the sixth mode.

Kumārila and the followers of the Vedānta adopt the view that non-cognition (anupalabdhi) is an independent means of knowledge. According to Kumārila, when we apprehend the non-existence of the jar, we have two different cognitions, a positive of the ground and a negative of the absence of the jar. The Naiyāyika believes that the non-existence of the jar qualifies the vacant ground, and the ground thus qualified is perceived. If it is said that we can perceive only things which are in contact with sense-organs and there can be no contact between the absence of things and the sense-organs, the Naiyāyika replies, that the critics wrongly assume that conjunction and inherence are the only relations. Neither of them is possible in the case of non-existence, since conjunction holds good only between two substances, and non-existence is not a substance, and inherence is not possible, since non-existence is not inseparably related with anything.[3]

---

[1] Keith: I.L.A., p. 77.

[2] V.S., iv. 1. 6.

[3] The Nyāya view of the relation of the qualification and the qualified is criticised on the ground that it is not strictly a relation, since it is not one subsisting in two things distinct from itself. A relation is distinct from the two things related, and one only while subsisting in both of them. Conjunction is different from the drum and the stick, and is one as sub-

According to the Buddhists, the perception of negation does not mean the existence of negation, but only the existence of "*something*" which is the basis of negation. The positive perception of the ground without the jar is confused with the perception of the negation of the jar. But the Nyāya holds that the perception of positive existents is as much a fact as the perception of the negative ones. If it is said that the non-perception of the jar on the ground is the perception of the ground without the jar, the question may be asked, is this being without the jar identical with the ground or different from it? The two cannot be identical. If there is a difference between the ground with the jar and the ground without it, one is apprehended by perception as much as the other.[1]

The Buddhist logicians make out that the visual and the auditory organs do not come into direct contact with their objects, but apprehend objects at a distance as well. They are capable of apprehending objects without coming into contact with them (aprāpyakāri). The Naiyāyika argues that the visual organ is not the eyeball or the pupil of the eye, which is only the seat (adhiṣṭhāna) of the visual organ, which is of the nature of light (tejas), and the ray of light goes out of the pupil to the object at a distance and comes into direct contact with it. That is why we have a direct visual perception of direction, distance and position.[2]

---

sisting in both of them. The relation between the qualification and the qualified is not of this character. In the case of a man carrying a stick, the character of qualification belonging to the stick is not distinct from itself, nor is the qualifiedness of the man distinct from the man. The qualification and the qualified are identical with the things themselves. In the case of non-existence, it must be both the qualification and the qualified, since it is not possible for any substance, quality or action to subsist in non-existence. So the character of a qualification as belonging to non-existence must consist in its own form as capable of bringing about a cognition tainted with itself. So it is said that non-existence which is incapable of any relation cannot be perceived by the senses. Gangeśa adopts the view that the same instrument helps us to perceive the object as well as its absence. Non-existence is not the result of inference from non-perception, but is an object of perception.

[1] *Nyāyabindu*, p. 11, and *Nyāyamañjari*, pp. 53–57.

[2] N.V., i. 1. 4. An interesting question about the visual organ, whether it is single or double, is considered. Vātsyāyana assumes that the organs are two, and when we see a thing first with one eye and then with the other we have recognition of the thing as being the same as that seen on a previous occasion, which only shows that there is a common perceiver. Uddyotakara does not accept this view (see N.B. and N.V. on iii. 1. 7, 11). Descartes was much exercised with the problem how and why two separate impressions such as are given by our two eyes or our two ears unite to give a single sensation to the mind. He thought it was accounted for by the single narrow passage at the pineal gland which gave the movements in the animal spirits admission to the brain. The rays do not possess the quality of obviousness, since, on that view, they would have obstructed our vision by standing as a screen between the eye and their object. Though unperceived, the rays of the eye reach the object through the aid of external light (see N.B., iii. 1. 38–49).

The Buddhist logician objects to the Nyāya view on the following grounds: (1) The visual organ is the pupil of the eye through which we see the objects, and the pupil cannot go out of itself and come into contact with the object at a distance. (2) The visual organ apprehends objects much larger than itself, like mountains, etc., which it cannot do if it were to come into direct contact with the objects to apprehend them. (3) The fact that the visual organ takes the same time to apprehend the top of a tree or the moon, shows that the eye need not go out to the object. (4) The eye cannot go out to its object, since then it would not be able to apprehend objects behind glass, mica and the like. The visual perception of distance and direction is not direct but acquired.[1] Udayana in his *Kiraṇāvali*[2] attempts to answer these objections. (1) Whatever apprehends or manifests an object must come into contact with it. A lamp illuminates an object with which it comes into contact. So also the visual organ, which is of the nature of light, goes out of the pupil to reach the object. (2) The light issuing out of the pupil spreads out and covers the object and it becomes coextensive with the field of vision. (3) There is a difference in the time intervals required in the apprehension of near and distant objects, though it is not felt by us. The distant moon is seen on opening the eye, since the motion of light is inconceivably swift. The suggestion that the light of the eye issuing out of the pupil becomes blended with the external light and comes into contact with near and distant objects simultaneously is set aside on the ground that on such a theory we must be able to apprehend objects hidden from our view, even those at our back. (4) Glass, mica and the like are transparent in nature, and so do not obstruct the passage of light. The Pūrva Mīmāṁsā supports the Nyāya view that all sense-organs are prāpyakāri, i.e. come into contact with objects they apprehend. In the case of auditory perception, the sound that starts at a certain place travels through air by a series of sound-waves, and the auditory sense and last sound meet. Sound is propagated from its original source in a series comparable to the motion of waves or the shooting out of the filaments in all directions from the plant.[3] We get the sense of direction from the sound since the diversity of the sources qualifies the sound and particular parts of the auditory organ are roused to action. In the case of smell, small particles of the object are carried by the air to the nose. Mere contact of object with sense is enough to provoke perception, as when a sleeping person hears the thunderclap.[4]

---

[1] N.V., i. 1. 4.; see also Vivaranaprameyasaṁgraha, pp. 187 ff.

[2] Bibl. Ind. ed., pp. 286 ff.

[3] See *Vivṛti* of Jayanārāyaṇa, ii. 2. 37. Kumārila disputes this view on the ground that, since the ākāśa is one and invisible, all ears should be equally affected and every sound heard by all; or again, if one is deaf, all should be deaf. Again, sounds travelling with the wind are heard at a greater distance than those travelling against it, which cannot be accounted for, as the propagation of waves takes place in ākāśa which is unaffected by sound.

[4] N.B., ii. 1. 26. It is involuntary, as it is not due to the effort (prayatna) of the self, and so is traced to adṛṣṭa or unseen destiny (N.B., ii. 1. 29).

The first characteristic of the nature of perceptual knowledge mentioned by Gautama is that it is inexpressible (avyapadeśyam). A thing is not necessarily perceived as bearing a name. The name has value for social intercourse, but is not necessarily operative at the time when the object is perceived. According to a famous teacher mentioned by Jayanta, perception excludes all cognitions of things where names enter as integral factors. If a man sees a fruit and experiences its nature, it is a perception; but if he hears from somebody its name as jack-fruit, then it is not perception but verbal cognition.[1] Vātsyāyana holds that an object may be perceived with or without the apprehension of its name. In the former case we have determinate perception, in the latter indeterminate perception.[2] The distinction between inexpressible (avyapadeśya) and well defined (vyavasāyātmaka) is equated with indeterminate (nirvikalpaka) and determinate (savikalpaka).

Vātsyāyana and Uddyotakara do not refer to this distinction, and Vācaspati, who mentions it, attributes it to his teacher Trilocana.[3] All the later logicians, such as Bhāsarvajña, Keśava Miśra, Annaṁ

[1] The Śābdikas hold that the object of all perception is the word denoting the object (vāgrūpaṁ tattvam). Jayanta criticises this (*Nyāyamañjari*, p. 99), and Vācaspati asks, if objects are identical with names, are they identical with eternal sounds or conventional sounds? Perceived objects cannot be identical with unperceived sounds; nor are they identical with names, since children perceive objects without knowing their names. So those who do not know the meanings of words have indeterminate perceptions, and even those who know them have first indeterminate perception, which revives the subconscious impression of the name perceived in the past, and then the indeterminate perception becomes determinate (N.V.T.T., i. 1. 4).

[2] N.B., i. 1. 4. See also *Nyāyamañjari*, p. 99. Jayanta says that indeterminate perception cannot apprehend the word or name denoting the object. The word is not an object of visual perception, and there can be no comprehension of the word if the relation between the sign and the thing signified is not apprehended and the residual trace is not revived. Determinate perception is mixed up with verbal images, while indeterminate perception is not, and in the matter of the apprehension of generality, quality, etc., there is no difference between the two. Bhartṛhari believes that there can be no thought without language, and so indeterminate perception, which is supposed to be independent of all language, is for him an impossibility (N.V.T.T., i. 1. 4).

[3] Ratnakīrti refers to this writer in his *Apohasiddhi* and *Kṣaṇabhaṅgasiddhi*. See *Six Buddhist Nyāya Tracts*, edited by M. M. Haraprasād Śāstri. Viśvanātha mentions the distinction of indeterminate and determinate as an alternative explanation. See his *N.S. Vṛtti*, i. 1. 4.

Bhaṭṭa, and the followers of the Sāṁkhya and the Vaiśeṣika and Kumārila accept it. Gautama's definition seems to regard all perceptual knowledge as determinate. If we are in doubt whether the object at a distance is a man or a post, dust or smoke, we do not have perception. The Jainas, who hold that in all perception we are conscious of the subject which perceives as well as the object that is perceived, deny the possibility of indeterminate perception.

Savikalpaka or determinate perception implies a knowledge of the genus to which the perceived object belongs, of the specific qualities which distinguish the individual object from the other members of the same class and of the union of the two. This distinct knowledge of the genus, the differentia and their union, is absent in indeterminate perception.[1] The distinction between indeterminate and determinate perception answers roughly to that between acquaintance with and knowledge about an object, simple apprehension and perceptual judgment.

According to the earlier Vaiśeṣikas, indeterminate perception is an immediate cognition of the generic and specific characters of its object without a knowledge of the difference between them. In determinate perception the distinction between the two sets of properties is apprehended and the object is perceived as belonging to a determinate class.[2] Vācaspati thinks that in indeterminate perception we perceive the properties of the object, though we do not relate them with the object in the subject-predicate relation (viśeṣaṇa-viśeṣyabhāva), which we do in determinate perception. Śrīdhara is of this opinion. Prabhākara agrees with the earlier Vaiśeṣikas, who hold that in indeterminate perception we apprehend the mere form of the object (svarūpamātra). Though we perceive the generic and the specific features, there is no discriminative apprehension of the two, as we have in determinate perception. Gaṅgeśa defines indeterminate perception as that of an object and its generic nature as unrelated to each other. Immediately after the contact of an object with the sense-organ, say a jar with the eye, the jar is not perceived as belonging to the class of jars.[3] When the relation between the object and the class to which it belongs is also apprehended, we have determinate

[1] According to the *Tarkabhāṣā*, in indeterminate perception, though the self is in contact with the manas, manas with the sense, and the sense with the object, still the last factor of the object is secondary, while it becomes primary in the case of determinate perception.

[2] *Nyāyakandalī*, p. 190. Prabhākara and Pārthasārathi Miśra, who hold that determinate perception is a complex of sense-presentation and memory image, support this view.

[3] Prathamato ghaṭaghaṭatvayor viśiṣṭānavagāhy eva jñānaṁ jāyate, tad eva nirvikalpam. See *Siddhāntamuktāvali*, p. 58.

perception. Indeterminate perception, according to Annaṁ Bhaṭṭa, is the perception of an object without its qualifications, while determinate perception comprehends the relation of the qualified and the qualifications such as name and class.[1]

This analysis of determinate perception brings out the elements of conception and judgment involved in the act of perception. The fallacy of the psychical staircase theory, that we have first perception, then conception and then judgment, is avoided.

A different view of indeterminate perception, which is rather unsatisfactory, makes itself felt in the later Nyāya. It is said that what is present to consciousness is determinate perception, from which we infer the existence of the indeterminate. The determinate perception of an object as qualified by some properties presupposes an indeterminate perception of the properties, without which determinate perception is not possible. If the perception of the properties were also determinate, then it would imply the perception of the properties of the properties and so on *ad infinitum*. To avoid it we assume indeterminate perception.[2]

Some Naiyāyikas do not regard indeterminate perception as a matter of inference, but look upon it as a state of consciousness, which gives us mere existence.[3] Those who regard it as a fact of consciousness mean by it vague apprehension, while those who take it as an

---

[1] He also makes indeterminate perception niṣprakārakam, while determinate perception is saprakārakam, where prakāratā means the property of a particular cognition, which distinguishes it as the cognition of a particular object from other cognitions.

[2] I.L.A., pp. 72–73. Annaṁ Bhaṭṭa, in *Dīpikā* (42), says: " Viśiṣṭajñānam viseṣaṇajñānajanyam, viśiṣṭajñānatvāt, daṇḍīti jñānavat. Viśeṣaṇajñānasyāpi, savikalpakatve, anavasthāprasaṅgān nirvikalpakasiddhiḥ." See also *Siddhāntamuktāvali*, 58. Viśiṣṭajñāna is judgment or knowledge of a subject (viśeṣya) as qualified by an attribute (viśeṣaṇa). The Nyāya holds that for such knowledge (ghaṭo 'yam) we require not only contact of the sense-organ with the viśeṣya (ghaṭa) jar, but also a previous knowledge of the viśeṣaṇa or jarness (ghaṭatva). This previous knowledge is technically called nirvikalpaka or indeterminate, and is inferred and not directly known (atīndriyam). The Pūrva Mīmāṁsā and the Vedānta deny the necessity of a previous knowledge of the attribute, and hold that the senses come into contact with both the attribute and its subject. This view that we have indeterminate knowledge of the mere jarness first is not supported by psychology. Universal ideas are not the first to appear in consciousness. Knowledge progresses from the indefinite to the definite. The concept of jar is logically and not chronologically prior to the perceptive judgment.

[3] Vastusvarūpamātra: *Nyāyasāra*, pp. 3, 4, 84–86.

abstraction from determinate consciousness equate it with the awareness of abstract qualities, which is, however, called indeterminate, since there is not self-appropriation (anuvyavasāya).

The main tendency, however, of the Nyāya is to regard indeterminate perception as the starting-point of all knowledge, though it is not itself knowledge. It is immediate apprehension of an object which is not in the strict sense cognitive. It is a state of undifferentiated, non-relational consciousness, free from the work of assimilation and discrimination, analysis and synthesis. It may be regarded as dumb and inarticulate and free from verbal images. Determinate perception is a mediate, differentiated, relational mode of consciousness involving the results of assimilation and discrimination. It is articulate, concrete and determinate. In indeterminate perception, the class characters and relations are implicitly present, though they are brought into relief in determinate perception. This view is supported by Pārthasārathi Miśra. Indeterminate perception or sense-experience and determinate perception or perceptual judgment are the rudimentary and the advanced types of a process which is essentially identical in nature. Since indeterminate perception does not transcend immediacy, is dumb and unanalysed, is what James calls "raw unverbalised experience," the distinction between true and false does not apply to it.[1] "The first time that we see light, in Condillac's phrase, we *are* it rather than *see* it."[2] There is therefore no possibility of error in simple apprehension. In perceptual judgment, where a predicate is ascribed to a subject, the logical issue arises, since our judgment may or may not conform to the objective order. When we say "That is a man," our knowledge in so far as it is called "that" is true, while in so far as it is described as "man," it may or may not be true.[3]

The Buddhist logicians contend that determinate perception is mediate knowledge which is not free from preconceptions, while indeterminate perception is free from preconceptions (kalpanāpoḍham).[4] The latter does not

[1] See Nīlakaṇṭha's *Tarkasaṁgrahadīpikāprakāśa*.

[2] James: *Principles of Psychology*, vol. ii, p. 4. See also N.B., iv. 2. 37.

[3] N.B., iii. 2. 37.

[4] Kalpanā, according to Dharmakīrti, is the activity of thought by which a name is given to the object. Abhilāpasaṁsargayogyapratibhāsapratītiḥ

apprehend the qualifications of the object, such as generality, substantiality, quality, action, name, but simply grasps the specific individuality of the object, its svalakṣaṇa.[1] The real with which we come into contact is inexpressible, and what we express has for its province concepts. Dharmakīrti says, "the object of perception is like itself (svalakṣaṇa), while that of mediate knowledge is like one of its class (sāmānyalakṣaṇa). The given is the unique, the particular and the momentary; the known is the typical, the universal and the lasting.[2] The moment we say something about the felt real, we bring it into relation to something else, and the real thus loses its nature, becoming overlaid with the inventions of the intellect. We hear the humming which alone is true, but that it is due to the fly or the distant steam-whistle is our imagination. Dharmottara argues that even the cognition of the mother's breast by the infant the second time is determined by its past experience, and is not therefore pure or undetermined. All relations, as Kant would say, are the forms which our mind imposes on the given elements to make them into objects of knowledge. In determinate perception we twist the real out of its shape, and so it is said to be invalid.[3] Dignāga dismisses

kalpanā. It is the knowledge which is capable of connection with words. Jayanta holds that kalpanā signifies the connection of an object with its adjuncts as genus (jāti), quality (guṇa), action (kriyā), name (nāma), and substance (dravya) (*Nyāyamañjari*, p. 97). According to the Buddhist view there is no difference between the individual and the genus, the particular and the universal, substance and quality, and our determinate perception attributes differences where they do not exist. We do not perceive the genus of the cow apart from the cow, or the substance cow apart from its qualities. Nor is motion different from that which moves. When we give a name to an object, we identify things which are different. When we say "This is Caitra," "this" refers to an object and "Caitra" to a word, and our judgment identifies the two. Similarly, the category of substance ascribes identity or coinherence to objects that are essentially different. In the case of "This is the man with a stick," "man" and "stick," which are different from each other, are said to inhere in the same substratum. So it is argued that these categories are ideal constructions. (*Ibid.*)

[1] Sajātīyavijātīyaparāvṛttaṁ svalakṣaṇam (*Nyāyamañjari*, p. 97).

[2] *Śāstradīpikā* describes the view that the universals are unreal products of fancy: "Vikalpākāramātraṁ sāmānyam, alīkaṁ vā" (p. 278).

[3] Kant, however, denies the possibility of indeterminate perception by which, the Buddhist imagines, the bare difference is intuited. Cp. his famous statement, "Perceptions without notions are blind and notions without perceptions are empty," though this conflicts with the earlier view of the *Prolegomena* (18), with its distinction of judgments of perception and judgments of experience.

all knowledge of substances, qualities and actions as false.[1] The outer objects are momentary and so cannot be known.[2] Constructive imagination works up the momentary stage into a series penetrated by the past and projecting into the future. The unreal (an-artha) is the world of thought. The absolutely real (paramārthasat) is the felt sensation.[3] The whole view is determined by the metaphysical presuppositions of these thinkers. Dignāga is a subjectivist who looks upon all knowledge as purely mental. The question of the nature of the real is left undecided by him, though the facts of perception compel him to concede that we come into contact with some reality, however momentary it may be. Dharmakīrti, with his Sautrāntika leanings, admits extra-mental reals to account for the variation in perception, though their momentary character renders knowledge of them impossible. He makes sensations individual and their objective reference inferential.

The Naiyāyikas subject the Buddhist view to severe criticism. Uddyotakara argues that pure sense knowledge specific in itself and cognised by itself, without any admixture of name or genus, is an impossibility. Our cognition of an object invariably assumes the generic form.[4] The Buddhist view that all universals are imagined, since specific individuals alone exist, is rejected by the Naiyāyikas, who hold that the universals are as real as the individuals in which they subsist by the relation of inherence (samavāya). This relation is either directly perceived or inferred from the fact that we are conscious of individuals as forming real kinds. The ultimate appeal is to the nature of things which manifests itself in and determines our consciousness. The relations are not superinduced on the given but are observed within the nature of the real. All that our understanding does is to discover the relation in the fulness of the real. If the *real* excludes relations and the object of knowledge is relational, then we are committed to the false antithesis of the noumenon and the phenomenon. The object known is not the object as it is in

[1] See Ui: *Vaiśeṣika Philosophy*, p. 67.
[2] Kṣaṇasya (jñānena) prāpayitum aśakyatvāt (*Nyāyabinduṭīkā*, p. 16).
[3] *Nyāyabindu*, p. 103.
[4] N.V., i. 1. 4.

itself but an intermediary, a *tertium quid* interposed between the cognising subject and the stimulating object. But, as we have seen, the Nyāya regards indeterminate perception as identical in essence with determinate perception. The relations do not suddenly emerge out of nothing. They are present in indeterminate perception, though we become conscious of their presence in determinate perception. The object of determinate perception, Jayanta argues, is not unreal since it is apprehended by indeterminate perception also. The mere presence of ideal factors or remembered elements does not interrupt sense-activity. The complexity of determinate perception is not a logical defect. The exercise of thought involved in it strengthens the case for its validity. If determinate perception apprehends what is already apprehended in indeterminate perception, that is no reason why it should not be true. Novelty is not the test of truth. The ideal elements are not mere fancies (vikalpas). The universal which is an object of direct perception is not a mere name, since it is apprehended even in the absence of a name. When a visitor from the Deccan sees camels in North India, he notices their universality though he may not know the name. When we perceive our four fingers we notice their general features as well as their distinctive properties. If we simply take in the special individuality of the object, we should not be able to relate the second instance with the first. If it is argued that the first case is remembered when the second is perceived, Jayanta holds that nothing is to be gained from remembering the first since it is unrelated to the second. If it means that the perception of the second suggests the first, since the two belong to the same class, then it is clear that in the case of the first perception also there was a cognition of its universality as well as individuality. There is apprehension of the universal and the particular, indistinctly in indeterminate perception and distinctly in determinate perception. Even the Buddhists do not deny that we have a notion of universality (anuvṛttijñāna) when we perceive an individual, and the question arises as to the basis of this knowledge (anuvṛttijñānotpādikā śaktiḥ) whether it is the individual or something different from it, eternal or non-eternal, perceptible or non-perceptible, for if there is a peculiarity in the cognition, there must be an answering peculiarity in the object of cognition.[1] The universal is therefore different from the individual, eternal since it is universal, while the individuals die and are born, and real whether perceptible or inferrible.[2] The argument that determinate perception depends on the recollection of the word denoting its object and not on the direct contact of the object with the sense-organ is criticised on the ground that though determinate perception is a complex of sense-presentation and the memory image, the principal factor is the sense-contact, while the recollection of the name is auxiliary. Whether a cognition is perceptual or not depends on the presence or absence of peripheral excitement.[3]

We reach here a fundamental divergence between the conceptions of reality advocated by the Buddhists and the Naiyāyikas. The former assume that the real is the simple *this*, the momentary individual shut up within its quality,

[1] Viṣayātiśaya vyatirekeṇa, pratyayātiśayānupapatteḥ (*Nyāyamañjari*, p. 314).

[2] See *Nyāyamañjari*, pp. 309–311, 313–314. Cp. the Nyāya view with that of Saint Thomas that the primary object of man's knowledge is a synthetic unity in which both the senses and the understanding play their indispensable part. The individuation or the quantitative specification is derived from the sense, while the qualitative unity is from the understanding. The object of knowledge contains within itself the intuition of essence and the sense-knowledge of particulars. It is neither the essence alone, as Descartes thought, nor the sense-datum alone, as the empiricists believed. We know things, and things are neither disembodied essences nor subjective images. To separate universals from individuals is to miss the unity of the two in things.

[3] *Nyāyakandalī*, p. 193. Pārthasārathi Miśra says, "savikalpam api, anuparatendriyavyāpārasya, jāyamānam aparokṣāvabhāsatvāt, pratyakṣam eva" (*Śāstradīpikā*, pp. 103–4). The Buddhists argue that determinate perception is not direct (aparokṣa) or distinct (viśada), though it seems to be so, from its connection with the immediately preceding indeterminate perception. But this is a conjecture. Prabhācandra also criticises the Buddhist view. Indistinctness is not peculiar to determinate perceptions. Perceptions of objects at a distance hidden by glass or mica are indistinct, be they determinate or indeterminate. If determinate perception is invalid on the ground that it perceives what is already apprehended, then inference also is invalid, since it apprehends what has already been apprehended in the cognition of universal concomitance. On the Buddhist view all objects are momentary, and so no perception is possible. Even in inference we do not grasp the specific individuality of the object, but that does not make inferential knowledge invalid. The presence of word or ideal relations has nothing to do with validity. Liability to error is common to, and practical efficiency is present in both determinate and indeterminate perception.

without either continuance in time or extension in space—"sarvam pṛthak." All relations are an arbitrary network spread from the outside by imagination. The Naiyāyika, on the other hand, contends that what exists is not the momentary quality but the individual with an internal diversity of content. In spite of the manyness it remains one. It is the one in the many. So far as it is one against other individuals, it is a particular; so far as it is the same throughout its diversity, it is universal, and this sameness makes it also a member of a class. Every individual has these two sides or aspects. The atomic particular which excludes all differences, as well as a mere relation which has no terminal points, is a superstition which cannot be verified in experience. Identity and difference are distinguishable moments within a whole, which become false when they get hardened into units that stand by themselves. Modern psychology confirms the Nyāya view that the content of the given has the two sides of sensible qualities and relations.

A superficial view leads us to think that crude sense-impressions which are the raw material of knowledge are the highest reality. But it is difficult to accept the position that man's scrappy impressions are the truth of things. Chaotic masses of stone, brick and wood are not a house. The felt impressions are not knowledge. Solipsism confined to the present moment leads us straight to intellectual suicide, by reducing the life of thought to a tale of fancy. The Buddhists identify passive awareness with a feeling of reality. They ask us to free ourselves from the sin of reflection. But their passion for immediacy is a sheer prejudice. Loyalty to fact does not mean freedom from reflection. I do not wantonly indulge in the folly of reflection when I say that that which I see before me is an orange. Apperception is a normal function of the human mind. The mind of man is not an empty room into which sensations simply walk. Every perception is the result of an active reaction to a stimulus. We are born thinkers, and cannot help interpreting what we receive. Sensations do not come to us detached. They come to us with a sense of objectivity. They are presented, surrounded by a complex mass of other elements. The atomic "now" has no existence. Every particular point in space has other points round it, as every instant of time flows ceaselessly into another. The Buddhist view divorces "sense" from "understanding" and makes them two totally disparate functions. The sense-data combine in various ways and build up the world of knowledge. They possess relations which our knowledge disentangles. We do not alter or make reality in knowledge. What is vaguely perceived at the sense-level is clearly grasped when we rise to the level of understanding. The real is the related and the rational. The full nature of reality yields itself neither to the senses nor to the understanding, but to the complete spirit.

Dharmakīrti recognises four kinds of perceptions: sense-perception, mental perception (manovijñāna), self-consciousness and yogic intuition. Sense-perception is mediated by the senses. Mental perception (manovijñāna) is said to be similar to sense-perception as belonging to the same series (ekasaṁtāna) and arising at the next moment to sense-perception. It seems to be somewhat of an after-image, for Dharmottara says, "Mental perception cannot arise unless and until the eye has ceased to function for the time being. For if the eye remains active, we continue to have the perceptions of form, visual or sensuous perceptions."[1] The internal perception of pleasures and pains is brought under the third variety, *svasaṁvedanā* or self-consciousness. We perceive the self through the perception of its states as pleasure or pain. It is direct intuition by which the self is revealed (ātmanah sākṣātkāri), free from intellectual interference and therefore from error. It is said to accompany all mental phenomena. Dharmottara identifies this self-consciousness with the feeling of intimacy and emotional warmth

[1] Etac ca manovijñānam uparatavyāpāre cakṣusi pratyakṣam iṣyate, vyāpāravati tu cakṣuṣi yad rūpajñānaṁ tat sarvaṁ cakṣurāśritam eva (*Nyāyabinduṭīkā*, p. 13). Cp. Richard Semon's view that we experience sensations in two forms, either as original or as mnemic. The original sensation is synchronous with the excitation, and in this form the sensation perishes when the excitation ceases, but, like the storm at sea, which, when it ceases, is followed by the gradual dying down of the waves it has raised, so the sensation dies down after the excitation has ceased. It is the after-image effect which Semon names the *akoluthic* stage of the original sensation. Semon says that the original sensation leaves behind an engram which on occasion and subject to conditions may give rise to a sensation called mnemic and not original. See Semon's *Mnemic Psychology*.

which accompanies all perception. Later Nyāya makes it a secondary product supervening on consciousness. According to Gaṅgeśa, it occurs when we say "I know this is a pot." Vyavasāya or determinate cognition gives us the cognition of an object, but the cognition that "I am aware of the object" is called anu-vyavasāya or after-cognition. "This is a jar" is a cognition; "I know that this is a jar"[1] is anu-vyavasāya, or what follows the cognition of the object. The Sāṁkhya and the Vedānta believe that every mode of consciousness reveals an object as well as itself, as involving a self.[2]

[1] Dīpikā, 34.

[2] The Nyāya-Vaiśeṣika view differs from that of Kumārila, who holds that a cognition is inferred from the cognisedness of the object. The Jainas, the Vedāntins, and some Buddhists believe that a cognition is cognised by itself. A cognition, according to the Nyāya-Vaiśeṣika, cannot turn on itself and make itself the object of cognition. A cognition manifests another (paraprakāśaka) and not itself (svaprakāśaka). It is manifested by another cognition, since it is an object of knowledge like a cloth (jñānaṁ jñānāntaravedyam prameyatvāt paṭādivat). The Jaina criticism of this view may be briefly stated: (1) As pleasure is cognised by itself and not by another, as the divine cognition is cognised by itself and not by another, so every cognition of the self must be regarded as self-cognised; otherwise one cognition has to be cognised by another, and that by still another, and this would lead to infinite regress. (2) A flimsy argument that in God there are two cognitions, one which apprehends the entire universe and the other that cognises this apprehension, is easily criticised. Is the second cognition perceived or not? If perceived, is it perceived by itself or by another? If by itself, then why should we not allow that capacity to the first? If by another, we are committed to an infinite regress. If we say that the second is apprehended by the first, then we are involved in circular reasoning. If the second is not perceived, then if it can perceive the first, without itself being perceived, then may not the first perceive the entire universe without itself being perceived? We must admit that the divine cognition is self-cognising. It apprehends itself in apprehending the entire universe. There is no distinction between the divine and the human cognition on this question. The character of manifesting itself and another (svaparaprakāśaka) belongs to the essence of consciousness, human or divine, while omniscience is not a general characteristic, since it belongs to divine consciousness alone. (3) There is no proof of after-cognition (anuvyavasāya) by means of perception or inference. The Nyāya view that the self is in contact with manas in anuvyavasāya is not accepted, since the existence of manas is unproved (4) If a cognition is perceived by another, the second cannot arise when the first continues to exist, since cognitions are successive. It cannot arise when the first is destroyed, since there is nothing to be cognised. If it cognises the non-existent first cognition, then it is illusory, like the cognition of the double moon. (5) If the second cognition is perceived, it must be by another, which leads to infinite regress. If the second is not perceived, then how can an unperceived cognition perceive the first? This would mean that my cognition can be perceived by another's unknown to me.

According to Dharmakīrti, we perceive the four truths of Buddhism which are beyond the ordinary means of knowledge by means of yogic intuition, which is free from all error and intellectual taint,[1] albeit indeterminate in character. There are various degrees of the power of perception. Cats can see objects in utter darkness and vultures can descry their prey from a great distance. By constant practice of meditation a man may acquire supersensuous vision, and can apprehend all objects near and far, past and future, remote and hidden.[2] This highest kind of insight has the immediacy of intuition. What is a miracle for us is a natural power of the seers. What seems to our bewildered eyes immeasurably complicated and subtle is revealed to the seers *sub specie simplicitatis*. Everything is there transfigured. We have at the lowest level the simplicity of sense-perception of concrete objects, and at the highest yogic intuition. The former is the simplicity of the natural man, of the once-born type, the latter that of the spiritual man, of the twice-born type. The one comes before the great struggle of self-discovery begins, the other when it ends. The latter is an achievement issuing out of much knowledge and inward agony. Yogic intuition apprehends reality as it is in its fulness and harmony.[3] Yogic intuition differs from divine omniscience in that it is produced, while the latter is eternal.[4]

Gangeśa distinguishes ordinary (laukika) perception from transcendent (alaukika) perception. There are three varieties of transcendental perception produced by three kinds of transcendental contact

---

(6) The argument that as sense-organs are not perceived, though they produce the apprehension of objects, so the unperceived second cognition may produce the apprehension of the first cannot be seriously pressed, since it must then be allowed that the first cognition of an external object apprehends its object, though it is not itself perceived, a position which the Nyāya-Vaiśeṣika repudiates (*Prameyakamalamārtāṇḍa*, pp. 34 ff.).

[1] See also *Nyāyabinduṭīkā*, pp. 14–15. See V.S., ix. 1. 13; I.L.A., pp. 81 ff.

[2] *Nyāyamañjari*, p. 103. Bhāsarvajña holds that yogic powers may also be had by the grace of God.

[3] Ārṣajñāna, or the intuitive knowledge possessed by the sages through the force of meditation, is sometimes called pratibhā, though the latter term is more often applied to flashes of intuitive genius which ordinary men at times display (P.P., p. 258).

[4] Praśastapāda distinguishes two varieties of yogic intuition (P.P., p. 187). Nyāyakandalī, pp. 195 ff. See also *Upaskāra*, ix. 1. 11.

(alaukikasannikarṣa), viz., sāmānyalakṣaṇa, jñānalakṣaṇa and yogajatharma.[1] The last is yogic intuition. When we perceive the generic nature of individuals we have a case of sāmānyalakṣaṇa. The ancient school of Nyāya admits the perception of generality. In Gaṅgeśa we find a greater appreciation of the work of intellect in the apprehension of universals. Through the knowledge of the generic nature of an individual, we are able to know all other individuals at all times, and all places, possessed of the same generic nature. To the objection that such knowledge of all cases, say, of smoke, would appear to make us omniscient, Viśvanātha replies that we know only the general character of all individual instances and not their mutual differences. The apprehension of generality is said to be non-sensuous, since it can be had even when there is not a particular example of smoke perceived by us. Both the particular and the universals are out there, real and are directly apprehended. The universal is not a mental construction, but a real essence abiding in the particulars. This essence reminds us of all the particulars in which it is realised. The nature of the relation between the universal and the particular is said to be inseparable and organic (samavāya). The apprehension of the universal renders possible universal connections presupposed by inferential processes.[2] Jñānalakṣaṇa occurs when we only see the sandalwood but perceive its fragrance. When we only see it, the visual presentation recalls the fragrance with which manas comes into contact. It is indirect perception. It is called also smṛti jñāna, or memory knowledge.

The Jainas think that it is a mixed mode of consciousness (samūhālambanajñānam) in which the visual presentation of sandal and the idea of fragrance are integrated. The *Vedāntaparibhāṣā* holds that the single content of knowledge includes two elements, one immediate and the other mediate.[3] While the Jainas and the Advaitins do not admit transcendental contact (alaukikasannikarsa), the Naiyāyika believes in it. He does not admit mixed modes of consciousness. Every psychosis is single, and the atomic nature of manas makes two simultaneous psychoses impossible. So he regards the visual perception of fragrant sandal as a simple psychosis, though it is preceded by the visual presentation and the recollection of fragrance. Śrīdhara and Jayanta think that the visual perception is qualified by the revival of the previously perceived fragrance, and the present perception of the fragrant sandal is due more to the manas than to the visual organ.[4] Modern psychology accounts for this phenomenon by the doctrine of the association of ideas. Yogajadharmalakṣaṇa is that which is born of meditation.

The nature of the phenomenon of recognition (pratyabhijñā),

[1] See also Laugākṣi Bhāskara's *Tarkakaumudī*, p. 9, and Viśvanātha's *Bhāṣāpariccheda*, sec. 3.

[2] The *Vedāntaparibhāṣā* (i) holds that the admission of alaukikapratyakṣa renders inference and other pramāṇas unnecessary.

[3] Surabhicandanam ityādi jñānam api candanakhaṇḍāṁśe aparoksam saurabhāṁśe tu parokṣam (1).

[4] See *Nyāyamañjari*, p. 461, and Śrīdhara's *Nyāyakandalī*, p. 117.

such as that "this is the same jar that I saw," whether it is simple or complex, is discussed by the Nyāya thinkers. Is the state of recognition a confusion of two cognitions—one directly apprehended, the jar seen and the other remembered, the jar with which the present one is identified? Is it one cognition which is in part perception and in part memory, as Prābhākara believes, or pure remembrance (smṛti) or pure perception (anubhūti)? The Buddhists look upon it as a mechanical compound of presentative and representative mental states.[1] It is not a single psychosis of the nature of presentation or representation, since its cause is not a mere sense-impression, for there cannot be a sense-contact with a past object; and it is not a residual trace or saṁskāra; since there is a consciousness of "thisness" in the state of recognition. Nor is it a combination of these two, since the two operate separately and issue in different effects. Even if we allow that the phenomenon of recognition is a single unitary effect, what is the nature of its object? Not an event in the past, since in that case recognition is not different from recollection; not an event of the future, since recognition then would become one with constructive imagination; not merely the present object, since recognition identifies a present object with a past one. It is self-contradictory to hold that it apprehends an object as existing in the past, present and the future. The Naiyāyika therefore contends that recognition is a kind of qualified perception, giving us a knowledge of present objects as qualified by the past. We see an object and recognise it as having been perceived on a previous occasion.[2] The Mīmāṁsakas and the Vedāntins support this view, while the Jainas argue that the state of recognition though simple is of a character different from that of perception or of memory.[3] Every perception involves an element of inference. When we perceive a tree, we really perceive only a part of it (ekadeśa), a side of its surface. We synthesise the sense-impression with image or meaning and thus perceive the object.[4] The previous perception of the whole, and the

[1] See also *Khaṇḍana*, i. 14.

[2] See *Nyāyamañjari*, pp. 448–459. *Mitabhāṣiṇī* (Vizianagaram Sanskrit series, p. 25) says: "So 'yaṁ devadatta ity atītavartamānakālaviśiṣṭaviṣayakaṁ jñānam pratyabhijñā."

[3] *Prameyakamalamārtāṇḍa*, pp. 97–98.

[4] N.B., ii. 1. 30. See also N.B., ii. 1 31–32.

inference to that whole from the part which is now perceived, are involved in every act of perception. The elements of recollection and inference are auxiliary, while sense-presentation is the principal factor. Whatever mental state is produced by means of sense-contact is a perception, even though it may involve other elements, such as those of memory and inference.

Gautama's definition of perception includes the characteristic of freedom from error. Not all perceptions are valid. In normal perception we have: (1) the object of perception, (2) the external medium such as light in the case of the visual perception, (3) the sense-organ through which the object is perceived, (4) the manas or the central organ, without the help of which the sense-organs cannot operate on their objects, and (5) the self. If any of these fail to function properly, erroneous perceptions arise. The defects of the external objects may be due to either movement or to similarity; the shell is perceived as silver on account of similarity. If the light is dim we cannot see clearly. If our eyes are diseased or partially blind, then our perception is defective. If the manas is otherwise engaged, or if the self is emotionally excited, illusions arise.[1] The causes of illusions are generally classified under three heads: (1) doṣa, or defect in the sense-organ, such as a jaundiced eye; (2) saṁprayoga, or presentation of a part or an aspect instead of the whole object; (3) saṁskāra, or the disturbing influence of mental prejudice or habit producing irrelevant recollections. The illusion of the snake arises on the occasion of seeing the rope, since the recollection of the snake is aroused.[2]

Dreams are presentative in character, aroused by external and internal stimuli. They are produced by the revival of subconscious impressions caused by organic disturbances as well as past merit and demerit. Prophetic dreams, which even Aristotle recognised,[3] are said to be due to the influence of spirits.

Kaṇāda attributes dreams to the conjunction of the self with the central organ, manas, aided by the subconscious impressions of past experience.[4] Praśastapāda regards dreams as internal perceptions caused by manas, when the senses are subdued into sleep and cease to operate.[5]

---

1 *Nyāyamañjari*, pp. 88–89, 173.
2 *Nyāyabinduṭīkā*, p. 12.
3 Gomperz: *Greek Thinkers*, vol. iv, p. 185.
4 V.S., ix. 2, 6–7.
5 P.P., p. 183; *Upaskāra*, ix. 2. 7.

They are traced to the strength of residual impressions by previous cognitions, the disorders of bodily humours and unseen forces. Śrīdhara does not look upon dreams as mere reproductions of past experience, but holds that they are centrally excited.[1] Udayana is of a different opinion, and thinks that the peripheral organs do not cease to function in dream states. He admits that dreams sometimes come true.[2] Prabhākara, in conformity with his general standpoint, makes dreams reproductions of past experiences, which, owing to obscuration of memory (smṛtipramoṣa), appear to consciousness as immediate presentations. Pārthasārathi identifies dream states with recollection.[3] Praśastapāda distinguishes dream knowledge from that which lies near to sleep or dream, called svapnāntika, which recollects what is experienced in the dream itself. Illusions which are based on an objective element (adhiṣṭhāna) are distinguished from hallucinations, which are devoid of objective basis (niradhiṣṭhāna). Śrīdhara gives as an example of the latter the case of one who, infatuated with love for a woman, perceives the semblance of his beloved everywhere.[4]

VII

Anumāna or Inference

Anumāna means literally the measuring after something. It is knowledge which follows other knowledge. From the knowledge of the sign (liṅga) we get a knowledge of the object possessing it. Anumāna is usually translated by the word "inference," which, however, is to be taken in a comprehensive sense, as including both deduction and induction. Anumāna is sometimes defined as knowledge which is preceded by perception. Vātsyāyana holds that "no inference can follow in the absence of perception." Only when the observer has perceived fire and smoke to be related to each other is he able to infer the existence of the fire on the next occasion he perceives smoke.[5] Uddyotakara mentions some points of distinction between perceptual and inferential knowledge: (1) All perception is of one kind, if we exclude yogic intuition, while there are varieties of inference; (2) Perception is confined to objects of the present time and within the reach of the senses, while inference relates to the past, the present and the future; (3) Inference requires the remembrance of a vyāpti, or a universal relation, which is not the case with

[1] Manomātraprabhāvaṁ svapnajñānam.

[2] Svapnānubhavasyāpi kasyācit satyatvam. *Kusumāñjali*, p. 147.

[3] Smṛtir eva tāvat svapnajñānam iti niscīyate. Nyāyaratnākara on S.V., p. 243.

[4] *Nyāyakandalī*, p. 179.

[5] N.B., ii. 1. 31.

perception.[1] Where perception is available, inference has no place.[2] We need not reflect much to know objects present to our perception.[3] Inference operates "neither with regard to things unknown, nor with regard to those known definitely for certain; it functions only with regard to things that are doubtful."[4] It is employed to know that part of the real which does not fall within the directly perceived. What is perceived points to something else, not perceived, with which it is connected. Bhāsarvajña in his *Nyāyasāra* defines inference as the means of knowing a thing beyond the range of the senses through its "inseparable connection with another thing" which lies within their range. Gaṅgeśa,[5] following Śivāditya,[6] defines inferential knowledge as knowledge produced by other knowledge.

Gautama distinguishes inference into three kinds: pūrvavat, śeṣavat and sāmānyato dṛṣṭam[7]; and Vātsyāyana offers slightly different explanations of this division, which indicates that even before Vātsyāyana there were conflicting interpretations of the Nyāya aphorisms. In inference we pass from the perceived to the unperceived with which it is related; and this relation may be of three kinds, according as the element to be inferred is either the cause of the element perceived or its effect, or as the two are joint effects of something else. When we see the clouds and expect rain, we have a case of pūrvavat inference, where we perceive the antecedent and infer the consequent. It is, however, used to indicate not merely inference from a cause but also inference based on

1 N.V., ii. 1. 31.

2 Pratyakṣatvād anumānāpravṛtteḥ (Śaṁkara: D.S.V., p. 88 n.).

3 Ghaṭo 'yam iti vijñātuṁ niyamaḥ ko nv apekṣate.

4 N.B., i. 1. 1.

5 *Tattvacintāmaṇi*, ii. p. 2. Cp. Māṇikyanandi's definition of inference as sādhanāt sādhyavijñānam (*Parīkṣāmukha Sūtra*).

6 *Saptapadārthī*, 146.

7 Cp. P.M.S., i. 2. 19, 22, 23, 29; iii. 1. 2–3; iii. 2–1, where the words pūrva and śeṣa occur as referring to the logically prior and posterior parts of a sentence or a paragraph, and are sometimes used to refer to vidhi and arthavāda. Pūrva is the principal or the primary, and śeṣa is the secondary. Evidently in the P.M. an argument from śeṣa would be one from the subsidiary to the principal. Perhaps the Nyāya interpreted the relation of principal and secondary as one of cause and effect. See Professor Dhruva's article on "*Trividham Anumānam*" in the *Proceedings of the Oriental Conference*, Poona, p. 265.

former experience. When we see a river in flood and infer that there was rain. we have a case of śeṣavat inference, where we perceive the consequent and infer the antecedent. It is also used to cover the inference of one member of a pair of correlatives from the other, or inference from a part or from elimination. The inference of the nature of sound as quality is given to illustrate the principle of exclusion or elimination. We prove that sound is not generality, particularity or inherence, not even substance or action, and so conclude that it must be a quality. When we see a horned animal and infer that it has a tail, we have a case of sāmānyatodṛṣṭa inference. It is based, not so much on causation, as on uniformity of experience. Uddyotakara agrees with this and gives as an illustration the inference of the existence of water in a particular place from the appearance of cranes. It is also used to indicate inference of supersensible truths (sāmānyato' dṛṣṭa).[1] We perceive the different places of the sun, and infer that the sun must be moving, though we do not see it. Perceiving aversion, affection, etc., we infer the existence of a soul which we do not perceive.[2]

These illustrations are enough to bring out the necessity of a universal connection or vyāpti. Each vyāpti relates the two elements of a vyāpaka or the pervader and the vyāpya or the pervaded. Anumāna or inference derives a conclusion

[1] Keith thinks that this interpretation is an impossible one (I.L.A., p. 88 n.).

[2] Uddyotakara criticises Vātsyāyana's illustration of the inference of the motion of the sun from its appearance at different places in different times on the ground that we see only different portions of the solar orb and not the movement of the sun. It may be noted that Uddyotakara regards the distinction into pūrvavat, śeṣavat and sāmānyatodṛṣṭa not as three kinds of inference, but as three conditions of a valid inference: (1) pūrvavat means that the middle term (hetu) should be invariably accompanied by its antecedent (pūrva) or the sādhya or the major term; (2) śeṣavat means that the middle term must have been observed as invariably accompanied by the major term in other (śeṣa) cases; (3) sāmānyatodṛṣṭa is analysed into sāmānyataḥ and adṛṣṭa, and taken to mean that the middle term should not be common to the predicate and the absence of the predicate (P and not P, sādhya and sādhyābhāva), *i.e.* it must not be too wide, which is the fallacy of sādhāraṇa. To these, two other conditions supposed to be implied by *ca* at the end of the sūtra are added, namely, that the inference should not be opposed to perceptual and scriptural evidence. All these five conditions are to be fulfilled in a valid anvayavyatireki inference and four in Kevalānvayi and Kevalavyatireki.

from the ascertained fact of the subject possessing a property which is pervaded or constantly attended by another property. We ascertain that the mountain is on fire from the fact that the mountain has smoke, and smoke is universally attended by fire. By the contemplation of the sign, middle term, smoke, we infer that the object which has smoke has also fire. Inference, according to Uddyotakara, is the argument from sign as aided by remembrance,[1] or the knowledge which is preceded by the perception of the hetu (middle term) and remembrance of its invariable concomitance with the sādhya or the major term. The different factors of inferential reasoning are brought out in the form of the syllogism.

VIII

The Syllogism

The five members of the syllogism are : (1) pratijñā, or the proposition : the hill is on fire ; (2) hetu, or the reason : because it smokes ; (3) udāharaṇa, or the explanatory example : whatever shows fire shows smoke, *e.g.* a kitchen ; (4) upanaya, or the application : so is this hill ; (5) nigamana, or the statement of the conclusion : therefore the hill is on fire.[2]

Pratijñā, or the proposition, sets forth at the very beginning the thesis to be established. It fixes the problem and limits the inquiry. The suggestion to be established controls the process from the very start, and the act of inference tries to strengthen and reinforce the suggestion. The proposition is only a " suggestion or mere probability." [3] There can be no argument unless we are impelled to know more about (ākāṅkṣā) the suggestion or the hypothesis which is set forth in the pratijñā, or the proposition. The proposition has the two

[1] Smṛtyanugṛhīto liṅgaparāmarśo 'numānam (N.V., i. 1. 5).

[2] N.S., i. 1. 32. Cp. the names given by Praśastapāda (P.P., p. 233): pratijñā, apadeśa, nidarśana, anusaṁdhāna and pratyāmnāya. This difference in terminology suggests the independent growth of logical views in the Vaiśeṣika. Vātsyāyana points out that the syllogism contains elements contributed by the different pramāṇas. The first is verbal, the second inferential, the third perceptual, the fourth analogical, and the conclusion suggests that all these bear on the same problem (N.B., i. 1. 1).

[3] N.B., i. 1. 39.

factors of subject or what is observed, which is generally an individual or a class capable of being regarded as a single object,[1] and the predicate which is to be proved. In "the hill is on fire," the hill is the subject, the minor term, the pakṣa or the dharmin, and "on fire" is the predicate or the major term, the sādhya, the dharma or the anumeya, or that which is to be inferred. The subject calls our attention to a part of the real, and the predicate particularises the subject by suggesting its possession of a property P or its inclusion in the class of objects denoted by P. The syllogism is intended to prove that the subject presented in perception possesses the feature indicated in the predicate. The copula is an accident of language and not an essential part of the proposition.[2] The proposition should not be opposed to direct perception or the testimony of the scriptures. According to Dignāga, unintelligible, self-contradictory and self-evident propositions cannot serve as theses.[2] They should not contain any unfamiliar terms, should not be opposed to well-established truths, or one's own convictions.[3] To find out whether the proposition, S is P, is true, we attend to the minor term, analyse it into its elements and discover in it the presence of the middle term. In all reasoning, the analysis of the minor follows the statement of the thesis. The second member of the syllogism states the presence of the middle term called hetu, or ground, sādhana, or the means of proof, liṅga, or the sign, in the minor term. It gives the possession of the character which entitles its possessor to be the subject of the conclusion, or pakṣadharmatā. The hill is found to be smoky. Pakṣatā is a necessary condition of inference. Any hill is not the minor, or pakṣa, though it becomes one, the moment we perceive smoke in it and desire to infer that it has fire also. If we see the fire also, it is not a pakṣa. Pakṣa is defined by Annaṁ Bhaṭṭa as the subject in which the predicate or that which is to be proved is doubted.[4] Pakṣa is more a proposition than a term. We now have the three terms necessary for a

[1] N.S., ii. 2. 66.

[2] See *History of Indian Logic*, p. 290. See also P.P., p. 234, and V.S., iii. 1, 15.

[3] See also P.P., p. 234; V.S., iii. 1. 15.

[4] *Tarkasaṁgraha*, 49 and 51, Saṁdigdhasādhyavān pakṣaḥ.

syllogistic inference, namely, the minor term or the pakṣa, that about which something is inferred, the major term or the sādhya, that which is inferred about the minor term, the middle term, by which the major is inferred to be true of the minor.

The presence of the middle in the minor (pakṣadharmatā) cannot lead to a valid inference unless it is combined with a universal relation between the middle and the major terms. The third member, udāharaṇa, or example, " whatever is smoky has fire, like the kitchen," takes us to the basis of inference, the major premise. Gautama means by example a similar instance possessing the essential property of the major term. Vātsyāyana seems to be of the same opinion. There is little to suggest that these two thinkers regarded the example as an illustration of a general rule. It was perhaps their idea that all reasoning was from particulars to particulars. Certain individuals have a given attribute, an individual or individuals resemble the former in certain other attributes: therefore they resemble them also in the given attributes. It may be that the Nyāya syllogism is developed out of the argument by example which Aristotle recognises.[1] It was soon realised that, though it is the way in which we often do reason, it is not a logical inference, where the conclusion is warranted by the premises. The argument is invalid if the example is not indicative of a general rule. The similarity (sādharmya) suggests class nature (sāmānya). Praśastapāda is familiar with the conception of sāhacarya, or concomitance, and attributes it to Kaṇāda.[2] Later logic equates the third member with the statement of the general relation.[3] No inference is possible unless there is an invariable concomitance (vyāpti) between the mark and the character inferred. The *Vedāntaparibhāṣā* says: "The instrument of inference is the knowledge of the universal relation."[4] The mention of the example indicates that inference is both inductive and deductive. The generalisation is based on

[1] Cp. the war of Athens against Thebes was mischievous, because it was a war against neighbours, just as the war of Thebes against Phokis was.

[2] P.P., p. 205.

[3] Vyāptipratipādakaṁ udāharaṇam (*Tarkasaṁgraha dīpikā*), 46.

[4] Anumitikaraṇam ca vyāptijñānam, ii.

instances, and it helps us in deducing new truths. The auxiliary and non-essential character of the example was emphasised by Dignāga. Dharmakīrti holds that the example is unnecessary and inserted only to help the person spoken to. The example illustrates but does not establish the universality of the rule. The third member, according to Dr. Seal, "combines and harmonises Mill's view of the major premise as a brief memorandum of like instances already observed, fortified by a recommendation to extend its application to unobserved cases, with the Aristotelian view of it as a universal proposition which is the formal ground of the inference." [1] Examples may be of different kinds, homogeneous or affirmative (sādharmya) where the property to be proved (major) and the ground (middle) are present, as the kitchen, and heterogeneous or negative (vaidharmya), where the property to be proved and the ground are both absent, as the lake.[2] Dignāga adds to these two, analogical examples. He also mentions ten kinds of fallacies relating to examples, while Siddhasena Divākara gives six kinds of fallacies about homogeneous and six about heterogeneous examples.

Regarding the distribution of the middle term, it is said: (1) that the middle should cover the whole of the extension of the minor, as in the illustration, "sound is non-eternal because it is a product," where the middle term product includes all cases of sound (All S is M); (2) that all things denoted by the middle must be homogeneous with the things denoted by the major, as in the example, "all products are non-eternal" (All M is P), and (3) that none of the things heterogeneous from the major term must be included in the middle, "no non-eternal thing is a product" (No non P is M). Dignāga insists that the middle term must be universally and invariably connected with the major term. Uddyotakara argues that there must be a universal relation between the middle and the major, such that, wherever the major is, there must be the middle, and wherever the major is not, the middle must not be. Praśastapāda affirms the same view when he says that the liṅga, or the middle term, is "that which is related to the object to be inferred, and is known to exist in that which is connected with that object, and does not exist where it is not present." [3] Varadarāja mentions five characteristics of the middle

[1] *The Positive Sciences of the Ancient Hindus*, p. 252.

[2] N.B., i. 1. 36–37.

[3] P.P., p. 200.

Yad anumeyena saṁbaddhaṁ prasiddhaṁ ca tadanvite
Tadabhāve ca nāsty eva tal liṅgam anumāpakam.

term, which are: (1) pakṣadharmatā, or the presence of the middle in the minor, the smoke in the hill; (2) sapakṣasattva, or the presence of the middle in positive instances homogeneous with the proven, as smoke in the kitchen; (3) vipakṣasattva, or non-presence of the middle in negative instances heterogeneous from the proven, as no smoke in the lake; (4) abādhitaviṣayatva, or non-incompatibility with the minor; and (5) asatpratipakṣatva, or the absence of counteracting forces.[1] In the case of an exclusively affirmative or exclusively negative inference, the valid middle term fulfils only four requirements, since it cannot abide in negative or positive instances. Annaṁ Bhaṭṭa holds that the middle term is of three kinds corresponding to the three kinds of inference: (1) positive and negative (anvayavyatirekin), where the middle is invariably concomitant with the major, as smoke with fire, wherever there is smoke there is fire, as in the kitchen: where there is no fire, there is no smoke, as in a lake[2]; (2) merely positive (kevalānvayin), where we have only affirmative invariable concomitance, as in "what is knowable is nameable," where we cannot have a negative instance to illustrate the position "what cannot be named cannot be known"; and, (3) merely negative (kevalavyatirekin), where a positive instance is not possible. All beings that possess animal functions have souls, where we can prove only that chairs and tables have no animal functions, and therefore no souls, but cannot give positive instances, since souls and beings that possess animal functions are coextensive in their nature.[3] According to the *Vedāntaparibhāṣā*, inference from an affirmative universal is regarded as anumāna, while that from a negative universal is treated as arthāpatti, on the ground that there is not in the latter an application of a general principle to a particular case.[4] The Nyāya is, however, of the view that every

---

Dharmakīrti thinks that unless the middle term is present in those things in which the thing to be inferred exists, and is absent in all things in which it is not found, the inference is of doubtful validity. Siddhasena Divākara defines the middle term as "that which cannot occur otherwise than in connection with the major term." Smoke cannot arise from any other thing than fire.

[1] The first three are mentioned by Dharmakīrti and Dharmottara. See *Nyāyabindu*, p. 104, and also Laugākṣi Bhāskara's *Tarkakaumudī*, p. 12, Bombay ed.

[2] It is to be noted that the negation of the pervaded becomes the pervader in the negative vyāpti and the negation of the pervader becomes the pervaded. See S.V., Anumāna, p. 121.

[3] *Tarkasaṁgraha*, 48. This distinction is accepted by Uddyotakara and Gaṅgeśa. Cp. with this the classification of inference in the Jaina canonical works into: (1) This is, because that is. There is fire because there is smoke. (2) This is not, because that is. It is not cold, because there is a fire. (3) This is, because that is not. It is cold here, because there is no fire. (4) This is not, because that is not. There is no mango-tree here, because there are no trees at all.

[4] ii.

negation has a positive opposed to it, and so affirmative conclusions can be derived from negative universals.[1] The chief characteristic of the middle term is that it should be free from all conditions. We cannot argue that A is dark simply because he is B's son, like other children of B and unlike other men's children. The conclusion may or may not be true as a matter of fact, but it is logically defective, since there is not an unconditional relationship (anupādhikasaṁbandha) between B's sonship and dark complexion.

Application is the fourth member of the syllogism. It asserts the presence or absence of the ground suggested in the minor term. It is affirmative in the former case, as in the example, " so is this hill," *i.e.* smoky, and negative in the latter case, as in the example, " not so is this hill," *i.e.* not smoky.[2]

Conclusion restates the proposition as grounded : " therefore the hill is on fire." [3] What is tentatively put forth in the first member is established in the conclusion.

Vātsyāyana points out that some logicians regarded the syllogism as consisting of ten members. In addition to the five given above, the following are included : (1) jijñāsā, or the desire to know the exact truth of the proposition, whether the hill is on fire in all its parts or in only some ; (2) saṁśaya, or doubt about the reason, whether after all that which we regard as smoke is only vapour ; (3) śakyaprāpti, or the capacity of the example to warrant the conclusion whether smoke is always a concomitant of fire, since it is not present in a red-hot iron ball ; (4) prayojana, or purpose of drawing the conclusion ; and (5) saṁśaya-vyudāsa, or the removal of all doubts about the relation of the middle to the major and its presence in the minor.[4] These five

[1] Vyāpti, or universal, may be either affirmative (anvaya) or negative (vyatireka), and of the former there are two kinds : samavyāpti (equipollent concomitance), where M and P are coextensive, as in the case " all produced things are non-eternal " ; and viṣamavyāpti (non-equipollent concomitance), where the two are not coextensive. All cases of smoke are cases of fire, but not *vice versa*.

[2] N.S., i. 1. 38.

[3] N.S., i. 1. 39.

[4] N.B., i. 1. 32. This is an indication that the form of the syllogism developed out of the practices and traditions of the art of debate. Bhadrabāhu, the Jaina logician gives a different list of the ten members of the syllogism, *viz.* : (1) pratijñā, or the proposition ; (2) pratijñā-vibhakti, or the limitation of the proposition ; (3) hetu, or the reason ; (4) hetuvibhakti, or the limitation of reason ; (5) vipakṣa, or the counter-proposition ; (6) vipakṣapratiṣedha, or the denial of the counter-proposition ; (7) dṛṣṭānta, or example ; (8) ākāṅkṣā, or doubt about the validity of the example ; (9) ākāṅkṣāpratiṣedha, or the dispelling of the

additional members of the syllogism are, according to Vātsyāyana, unnecessary for proof, though they help to make our cognitions clear. They have in view the psychological process. Jijñāsā, or the desire to know, is undoubtedly the starting-point of all knowledge; but, as Uddyotakara observes, it is not an integral factor of reasoning or proof.[1]

It was soon realised that the conclusion repeats the first proposition, while the fourth member is a restatement of the second. Strictly speaking, every syllogism has only three members. Nāgārjuna is said to have started the view of the three-membered syllogism in his *Upāyakauśalya Sūtra*, where he urges that a conclusion can be established through a reason and an example, affirmative or negative.[2] Sometimes Dignāga is given the credit for it.[3] In his *Nyāyapraveśa* he mentions only three members of the syllogism, though the third states both an affirmative and a negative example; this hill is on fire, because it has smoke; all that has smoke has fire, like a kitchen, and whatever is not on fire has no smoke, like a lake. In Dignāga the third factor is a general law with suggestive illustrations. Dharmakīrti thinks that even the third member is unnecessary, since the general proposition is implied in the reason. It is enough to say the hill is on fire because it smokes. This form which corresponds to an enthymeme is found much in use in Hindu philosophical treatises as well. The Jaina logicians, Māṇikyanandi and Devasūri,[4] are of this view. The Mīmāṁsakas and the Vedāntins admit only the three-membered syllogism. The *Vedāntaparibhāṣa* allows the use of the first three or the last three members.[5]

Both Vātsyāyana and Uddyotakara argue against the attempt to dispense with the last two members of the syllogism.[6] They admit that the first member of the syllogism is restated in the conclusion,

---

doubt; (10) nigamana, or the conclusion (*Daśavaikālikaniryukti*, p. 74, Nirṇayasāgar edition). Bhadrabāhu here adopts the double method of proof. When a reasoning is put forward to prove the non-eternity of sound, the counter-proposition is asserted and denied by means of the statement. If sound were eternal, it would not be a product. This hypothetical reasoning lends support to the previous inference, though by itself it has not much value. Siddhasena Divākara reduces the syllogism to five members in his *Nyāyāvatāra*. Anantavīrya, commenting on the latter (13), says that the best form of the syllogism has ten members, the mediocre of five, and the worst of two.

[1] N.V., i. 1. 32.

[2] *History of Indian Logic*, p. 119.

[3] Suguira: *Hindu Logic as preserved in China and Japan*; Ui: *Vaiśeṣika Philosophy*, p. 82, n. 2.

[4] *Pramāṇanayatattvālokālaṁkāra*, p. iii.

[5] ii. Varadarāja, in his *Tārkikarakṣā* (pp. 82 ff.), refers to the Mīmāṁsā view of the three-membered syllogism and the Buddhist view of the two-membered. *Māṭharavṛtti* is aware of the three-membered syllogism of pakṣa, hetu and dṛṣṭānta.

[6] N.B., i. 1. 39; N.V., i. 1. 39.

while the fourth is a combination of the second and the third. Though they are unnecessary from the standpoint of logic, they are useful for purposes of debate, since they confirm the reason and reassert decisively the proposition tentatively set forth in the first member. A distinction was drawn between the five-membered syllogism, useful for convincing others (parārthānumāna), and the three-membered one, sufficient for convincing oneself (svārthānumāna). The latter deals with inference as a process of movement of thought, and so belongs to the science of discovery, while the former deals with proof. Gautama and Kaṇāda do not explicitly mention it, though later logicians admit it.[1] Praśastapāda distinguishes inference for oneself (svaniścitārtha) from inference for others (parārtha).[2] Inference for the sake of others (parārthānumāna) is rather a formal exposition. We see a hill, and are in doubt whether it has fire or not. Noticing smoke, we remember the connection between fire and smoke, and conclude that there must be fire on the hill. When we attempt to convey this information to others we use the five-membered form.[3]

In spite of differences in regard to the number of the parts of the syllogism, all logicians are agreed that the two essentials of a valid inference are vyāpti (universal relation), or the major premise, and pakṣadharmatā, or the minor premise. The former gives the universal connection of attributes, and the latter states that the subject possesses one member of the universal relation.[4] These answer to the two steps of J. S. Mill, ascertaining (1) what attributes are marks of what others, and (2) whether any given individuals possess these marks.

Neither the major by itself nor the minor by itself can warrant the conclusion. A synthesis of the two is necessary. Liṅgaparāmarśa or consideration of the sign, is the essential element of the inferential process. According to Gaṅgeśa, vyāpti by itself is the indirect cause of inferential knowledge, while liṅgaparāmarśa, or consideration of the sign, is the last cause (caramakāraṇa) or the chief cause (karaṇa).[5] It is the synoptic view of the fact that the middle related to the major

[1] Dignāga, Praśastapāda, Dharmakīrti, Siddhasena Divākara, Māṇikyanandi, Devasūri, Bhāsarvajña, and Gaṅgeśa, among others, adopt this distinction.

[2] P.P., p. 231. Cp. with this Dharmottara's distinction between jñānātmaka and śabdātmaka (*Nyāyabinduṭīkā*, p. 21) and Śivāditya's artharūpatva and śabdarūpatva (*Saptapadārthī*, 154).

[3] *Tarkasaṁgraha*, p. 45.

[4] *Tattvacintāmaṇi*, ii. p. 2; *Bhāṣāparicceheda* and *Siddhāntamuktāvali*, pp. 66 and 68.

[5] *Tattvacintāmaṇi*, ii. p. 2.

abides in the minor,[1] that leads to the conclusion. Inferential act is, however, an integral one.

The Advaita argues that there is no such thing as the reflection on the middle term. Knowledge of a universal relation is the instrumental cause; we remember it and derive the conclusion.[2] The objection seems to be directed against the view that we first have an act of perception, next an act of recollection, and lastly the act of inference. The Advaita tries to make out that the inferential act is not a putting together of two judgments, but one single process (vyāpāra), where the perceived element (the minor) operates along with the revived general principle, the major. These two elements are not substantive mental states, and are not operative as definite stages in the inferential process. The Naiyāyika, who is more of a logician than a psychologist, urges that the act of synthesis is necessary for inference.

Dignāga raises the interesting question about the nature of the thing that is inferred. We do not infer fire from smoke, since it is not a piece of new knowledge. We know already that smoke is connected with fire. We cannot be said to infer the relation between the fire and the hill, since relation implies two things, while in inference we have only one thing, the hill, as the fire is not perceived. What is inferred is neither the fire nor the hill, but the fiery hill.[3] The conclusion is a judgment.

The Naiyāyika did not attach much importance to the different positions in which the middle term might occur. He regarded Barbara as typical of all syllogistic reasoning. The use of positive and negative instances inclined him to view the affirmative and the negative general propositions as mutually involved. All inference, strictly speaking, is supported from both the sides.[4] Hindu logic has practically only

[1] Vyāptiviśiṣṭapakṣadharmatājñānam (*Tarkasaṁgraha*, p. 44). See *Bhāṣāpariccheda*, p. 66; *Tattvacintāmaṇi*, ii. 2; Jānakīnātha's *Nyāyasiddhāntamañjari*, pp. 86–87, *Paṇḍit* ed.

[2] *Vedāntaparibhāṣā*.

[3] Dignāga, quoted in N.V.T.T., N.S., i. 1. 5. *Vedāntaparibhāṣā* (ii), says that the hill is perceived and the fire is inferred.

[4] If A is, then B is. If B is not, then A is not. Dharmakīrti, while agreeing that all arguments can be expressed in the affirmative or negative form, when based on likeness (sādharmya) and unlikeness (vaidharmya), thinks that some arguments fall naturally into the latter form.

All objects existent here and now are perceived.
The jar is not perceived.
Therefore the jar is not existent here and now.
This is Camestres.

one figure and one mood. From the knowledge that the subject of the proposition possesses a characteristic, which is invariably accompanied by the property, the presence of which we wish to establish, we infer that the subject has the said property. The principle is expressed in terms of connotation. If it is translated into terms of classes, we get the *dictum de omni et nullo.* Whatever may be asserted of every individual in a class may be asserted of any individual belonging to the class. The detailed distinctions of figures and moods are not so necessary for purposes of correct thinking, though they afford a training-ground for subtle thinking.[1] Aristotle admitted that the last three figures could be reduced to the first. The Nyāya recognises even in the first figure only Barbara. Darii and Ferio are not used in the Nyāya, since the conclusion refers always to a limited object, and the distinction between the universal and the particular does not arise. This distinction is only relative, as what is universal with regard to a limited class is particular in a wider reference. The minor term in the Nyāya syllogism is always an individual object or a class, and so a universal and not a particular. A conclusion about " some " cases gives us no definite information about the individual case in question. Celarent is easily derived from Barbara. Aristotle admitted that all his moods could be reduced to the first two moods of Figure I, and these two are interchangeable if we know that all judgments are double-edged.

The analysis of the reasoning process resembles pretty closely the syllogistic analysis of Aristotle. Even the five-membered form has only three terms, and the three-membered syllogism has three propositions, which correspond to Aristotle's

[1] Gomperz says : " At an enormous expense of original thought, Aristotle investigated the forms of inference, distinguished them, and analysed their ramifications And, lo and behold ! in all his numerous works, covering the whole domain of knowledge which was then accessible, he makes practically no use of the ' kinds ' (moods) and ' figures ' of the syllogism. He does not even shrink from the admission that all this great wealth of forms might be reduced to a few fundamental ones without loss in practice. We may add that subsequent research, greatly as it has developed and refined its instruments, confirms him in this : that the figures and the moods have remained a collection of curiosities, preserved by the history of science, but never put to practical use by science itself " (*Greek Thinkers,* vol. iv, pp. 44–45). See also H. N. Randle : " A Note on the Indian Syllogism," October, *Mind,* 1924.

conclusion, the minor premise and the major premise. The attempt has been made to account for the striking similarity by theories of mutual influence. Dr. Vidyābhūṣaṇ says: "It is not inconceivable that the knowledge of Aristotle's logic found its way through Alexandria, Syria and other countries into Taxila. I am inclined to think that the syllogism did not actually evolve in Indian logic out of inference, and that the Hindu logician owed the idea of the syllogism to the influence of Aristotle."[1] The learned professor believes that the art of the syllogism is "borrowed," while the doctrine of inference is an indigenous growth. Professor Keith writes: "Of logical doctrine in its early stages there is no reason whatever to suspect a Greek origin: the syllogism of Gautama and Kaṇāda alike is obviously of natural growth, but of stunted development. It is with Dignāga only that the full doctrine of invariable concomitance as the basis of inference in lieu of reasoning by analogy appears; and it is not unreasonable to hazard the suggestion that in this case Greek influence may have been at work."[2] He supports this suggestion by referring to the knowledge of Greek astrology possessed by Āryadeva, a predecessor of Dignāga by nearly two centuries. This, coupled with the alleged influence of Aristotle on the Hindu theory of drama as found in the Bharata Śāstra, makes probable some sort of cultural intercourse between India and Greece. It is sometimes made out that Aristotle was much influenced by the Hindu theory, which was conveyed to him by Alexander, who is reported to have had conversations with the logicians of India. Little positive evidence of direct influence is available, and when we remember that syllogistic types of reasoning are to be met with even in pre-Aristotelian works of the Hindu and the Buddhist thinkers,[3] it is difficult to accept the theory of "borrowing" from Greece. The words of Max Müller can bear repetition, "that we must here also admit the existence of undesigned coincidences to a much larger extent than our predecessors were inclined to do. We must never forget that what has been possible in one country is possible in another

[1] *History of Indian Logic*, p. xv.
[2] I.L.A., p. 18.
[3] *History of Indian Logic*, p. 500, n. 1, and Appendix B.

also."[1] This view is strengthened when we realise that there are fundamental differences between the Greek and the Indian syllogisms. There is little in the analysis of reasoning in Greek logic answering to the example which the Hindu thinkers regarded as indispensable for the statement of the universal relation. It does not require much thought to grasp that the basis of the inference is the universal relation, for the example is just the suitable embodiment of that relation.

IX

Induction

Inference claims to be true of reality, and the claim cannot be sustained unless the two premises are true. The minor premise is the result of perception, and the major takes us to the problem of induction.

How are universal propositions arrived at? The Naiyāyika gives us different answers. He speaks of enumeration, intuition and indirect proof. The syllogism mentions an example along with the rule. While an example may be sufficient to illustrate a rule, it cannot by itself establish a universal relation. There may be invariable concomitance of the smoke in the kitchen with the fire in it, or of the smoke in the sacrificial ground with the fire in it, but from these we cannot infer fire in a hill, simply because we perceive smoke in it, unless we establish the invariable concomitance of all cases of smoke with cases of fire. If we observe smoke and fire in a number of instances, we are perhaps on better ground. Bhūyo darśana, or frequency of experience, without a single exception (avyabhicarita sāhacarya), helps us in framing a general rule. It is not enough if we observe smoke wherever there is fire; we should also notice that there is no smoke where there is no fire. Agreement in presence and agreement in absence are both necessary.[2] If uninterrupted agreement (niyatasāhacarya) is reinforced by absence of exceptions (avinābhāvarūpasaṁbandha), we have unconditional concomitances,

[1] S.S., pp. 385–386.
[2] Sāhacaryajñāna and Vyabhicārajñānaviraha (*Tarkasaṁgraha dīpikā*, 45).

which exclude upādhis, or adventitious conditions.[1] We do not have smoke wherever we have fire. A red-hot iron ball has no smoke in it. Only fire fed by wet fuel is concomitant with smoke. The relation of fire and smoke is a conditional one, while that between smoke and fire is an unconditional one. The principle "all cases of fire are cases of smoke" is inadmissible, while the other, "all cases of fire fed by wet fuel are cases of smoke," is admissible. A condition is not necessarily a defect, since it misleads only when it is not recognised. Whenever conditions are suspected, it is necessary for us to examine the accompanying circumstances and show that the concomitance holds even when the suspected condition is absent. The positive instances disprove the case for conditions, since they show that the middle and the major are present, while nothing else is constantly present: the negative instances support the case by showing that the middle and the major are absent even when no other material circumstance is constantly absent. Later logic laid the greatest stress on the negative instances and even defined vyāpti so as to bring out the exclusive adequacy of the sign to the thing signified.[2] The Naiyāyika demanded that the disciplined mind should control its fancies and bow beneath the hard yoke of facts. An accurate account of the experimental methods is possible only with the development of the experimental sciences; and, in the absence of the latter, the Indian logician's views about

[1] Udayana defines a condition or upādhi as a thing which imparts its own property to another object placed in its vicinity (upa samīpavartini, ādadhāti saṁkrāmayati, svīyaṁ dharmam ity upādhiḥ). The red flower which makes the crystal placed over it look like a ruby by imparting to it its own redness is an upādhi. Cp. Varadarāja's definition, sādhanavyāpakāḥ, sādhyasamavyāptā upādhayaḥ (*Tārkikarakṣā*, p. 66). A valid universal must be free from all conditions (nirupādhikaḥ) which are suspected by oneself (śaṁkita) or with which one is charged by one's opponent (samāropita). See also Vācaspati's N.V.T.T., i. 1. 1. In logic, according to Udayana, an upādhi is (1) that which constantly accompanies the middle term, and (2) is accompanied by it, and (3) which does not constantly accompany the major term. Four kinds of upādhis are recognised in *Tarkadīpikā*. See Athalye: *Tarkasaṁgraha*, p. 317.

[2] After reviewing several definitions of vyāpti, Gaṅgeśa concludes that "invariable concomitance is the co-presence of the middle term with the major term, which is not qualified by the nature of the counterpart of that absolute non-existence, which abides in the same locus with the middle term, but abides in a different locus in respect of that counterpart" (*Tattvacintāmaṇi*, ii) See *History of Indian Logic*, p. 424.

scientific method are not of great interest. The Naiyāyika was aware of the general problem of induction and the method of careful observation of the facts of nature by which universal propositions are arrived at.

Nature does not always supply us with positive and negative instances of the right kind to help us to establish or reject theories. The Naiyāyika says that we may employ the method of tarka or indirect proof to obtain the negative evidence. If the general proposition, where there is smoke there is fire, is not valid, then its contradictory that "sometimes smoke is not accompanied by fire" must be true. In other words, fire is not the invariable antecedent of smoke. But we cannot deny that fire is the cause of smoke. Thus tarka is employed to strengthen a universal proposition based on positive instances of uninterrupted agreement. It is also a way of establishing a hypothesis.[1] By pointing out the absurdities in which we are landed, if we deny a suggested hypothesis, indirect proof tends to confirm the hypothesis. It shows that no other hypothesis is able to account for the facts.[2]

Tarka is only an aid to the empirical method of induction, which cannot give us universal propositions. Even when we observe all possible cases and strengthen our conclusion by the method of indirect proof, still we do not reach absolute certainty about universal propositions. So long as they are based on limited observation, they do not possess any necessity. Enumerative universals are only probable, but not certain. While it is true that the experience of sensible particulars gives rise to the knowledge of the universals, it

[1] N.S., i. 1. 31.

[2] "A legitimate hypothesis must satisfy the following conditions: (1) The hypothesis must explain the facts. (2) Must not be in conflict with any observed facts or established generalisations. (3) No unobserved agent must be assumed where it is possible to explain the facts satisfactorily by observed agencies. (4) When two rival hypotheses are in the field, a crucial fact or test is necessary; the absence of such a test is fatal to the establishment of either. (5) Of two rival hypotheses, the simpler, *i.e.* that which assumes less, is to be preferred, *caeteris paribus*. (6) Of two rival hypotheses, that which is immediate or relevant to the subject-matter is to be preferred to that which is alien or remote. (7) A hypothesis that satisfies the above conditions must be capable of verification before it can be established as a theory" (Seal: *The Positive Sciences of the Ancient Hindus*, p. 288)

cannot be said that the apprehension of the universals is fully accounted for by the sensible particulars, since the universal goes beyond any or all of the particulars.

Even collective judgments presuppose a knowledge of the universal. We do not count up all instances, but only those which possess a generic quality which entitles them to a place in the group. So even the method of enumeration cannot operate without an apprehension of the universal. The ancient Nyāya asserts that we can discern universals by means of perception. Gaṅgeśa recognises the non-sensuous activity involved in the apprehension of the universals (sāmānyalakṣaṇa), when he makes it a variety of alaukika pratyakṣa, or non-sensuous intuition.[1] On either view it is not necessary for us to make an exhaustive survey of instances. Through the perception of the universal smokiness, we apprehend all cases of smoke. We apprehend the universals of fire and smoke by sāmānyalakṣaṇapratyāsatti, and realise their invariable relation. So by analysis of one instance we can discern the universal relation; and what is true of that instance can be rightly extended to all members of the class, since there is such a thing as identical nature. What is once true is always true. When we say "smoke," we do not have in our mind all cases of smoke; but the connotation of smoke is what is in our thought. The connotations of smoke and fire are related in the vyāpti as the vyāpya, the pervaded, and the vyāpaka, the pervader. A multiplicity of instances is necessary, not because we abstract the universal relation from these particulars, but because the relation is not clearly differentiated in a single case. Those with exceptional powers of discrimination can differentiate relations even from a few instances. The universal relation is a discovery and not a creation. Through an act of thought exercised on a single instance we can obtain a universal connection. If the universal relation is not presented to us in the judgment itself, a repetition of similar events cannot help us to it. It is given

[1] Cp. with this Aristotle's apprehension of the universal by *nous* following upon the perception of the relevant particulars. An enumeration of instances, even when exhaustive, cannot give rise to absolute certainty unless we transcend the contingency of matter (Aristotle: *An. Post.*, I. 5).

to the subject and not constructed by the understanding. What transcends sense-perception does not transcend experience. Methodical observation and experiment but confirm what is intuited sometimes from a single case. Every event of nature contains within itself the relation or law in accordance with which it has been brought about. It is intuition alone that helps us to distinguish the essential features of a given event from its accidental accompaniments. Universal propositions are connections of content. If all little-biled animals are long-lived, it is not because man, horse and mule, which are little-biled, are long-lived, but because there is a necessary connection between the contents of little-biled and long life. The significance of the Nyāya syllogism is best brought out if it is put in the hypothetico-categorical form. If A, then B. A, therefore B.

On this view, the problem how deductive reasoning can give us more in its conclusion than was contained in its premises appears in a new light. General principles are not enumerative judgments, and the relations which govern the particulars are as real as the particulars themselves. When we derive a particular truth from a universal judgment, the conclusion goes beyond the premise in one sense, though it is contained in it in another.

But if universal relations are real and require only to be intuited, how is it that lovers and lunatics miss the significance of those general principles which leap to the eye of scientists and philosophers? Nor is it easy to account for the fact that our generalisations sometimes fail to be true. The relations are not correctly apprehended in erroneous inductions. They are not properly differentiated from the unlimited fulness of the particulars. The complexity of reality makes discrimination of relations difficult. Under the influence of passion and prejudice, inertia and thoughtlessness, we accept propositions as true, though they are not so. In this sense, even particular perceptions may be wrong. The intuited inductive principles become more convincing when they are applied to fresh particulars, *i.e.* when we pass from the inductive to the deductive stage. As we shall see, the validity of the universal relations, like that of all other knowledge, is to be established by other forms of knowledge. The intuition unconfirmed by empirical verification is only a hypothesis. Mere intuition is not of much use. Exhaustion of empirical material is an unrealisable ideal. The two help each other. The general principle has some necessity about it, even though it is grasped by us only on the occasion of an empirical fact.

The Nyāya view of vyāpti assumes that universals are factors of reality[1] and universal relations are real.[2] The Cārvākas, who are materialists, deny the possibility of universal relations, and so dispute the validity of inference. The Buddhists regard universal propositions as ideal constructions and not real relations. The universal is but a name and the identity a fiction. In the Buddhist work, *Sāmānya-dūṣaṇadikprasāritā*, the theory that we perceive the universals as real is criticised. We see the five fingers of the hand and not a sixth universal, which is as unreal as a horn on one's head.[3] Though a strict interpretation of this view makes all inference impossible, still the Buddhists assume its validity for all practical purposes and distinguish different kinds of universal relations. The middle term may be related to the major by way of identity (svabhāva, tādātmya), causality (tadutpatti), or negation (anupalabdhi). It comes to this, that our inferences are either affirmative or negative, and the former may be analytical or synthetical.[4] We have an inference of the type of tādātmya, or analysis, identity, or co-existence, when we say that "this is a tree because it is a kind of pine." We have an inference of the type of tadutpatti, synthesis, causality or succession, when we say "there is fire because there is smoke." Inference by anupalabdhi, or non-perception, arises when we infer the non-existence of the jar from the non-perception of it. Universal relations are not derived from observation of facts, but are deduced from *a priori* notions of identity in essence and causal necessity. The Buddhists assume the universal validity of these principles of causality and identity, since it is impossible to live without accepting them. According to Dignāga, knowledge does not express real relations of objective existence. The relations of inherence and essence, quality and subject, from which we derive conclusions, are all imposed by thought.[5] Relations are only logical.

Vācaspati subjects the Buddhist view to a severe scrutiny. The law of causality, as the Buddhist conceives it, will be satisfied if we trace the smoke on the occasion of fire to the agency of an invisible

---

[1] Sāmānyasya vastubhūtatvāt (*Tarkabhāṣā*, p. 31, Poona ed.).

[2] Svabhāvikas tu sambandho vyāptiḥ (p. 35).

[3] Keith: *Buddhist Philosophy*, p. 233. Cp. Berkeley's view of abstract ideas in *Principles of Human Knowledge*, Introduction, p. 13.

[4] *Nyāyabindu*, III.

[5] See *Nyāyakandalī*, p. 207. Vācaspati quotes from Dignāga, "Sarvo 'yam anumānānumeyabhāvo buddhyārūḍhena, dharmadharmibhāvena na bahissadasattvam apekṣate" (N.V.T.T., i. 1. 5).

demon (piśāca). Nor is there any necessity why the same effect should have the same cause. If the cause is what precedes the effect, it is not simultaneous with it. From the perception of smoke we can infer, not the present but the past existence of fire. If two things are identical, then the perception of one means the perception of the other, and there is no need for inference. Vācaspati and Jayanta urge that the relation between the pine and the tree is not one of identity, since all trees are not pines.[1] The Buddhist does not tell us how his principles of causality and identity of essence are themselves derived. There are many cases of concomitance which have little to do with causality or identity. The Naiyāyika includes all reciprocal relations under vyāpti, and not merely those of causal successions and genus and species, but such others as "all horned animals have cloven hoofs."[2]

X

CAUSE

Like all general principles, the law of causation is for the Naiyāyika a self-evident axiom known intuitively as it were and corroborated by experience. Observed causal relations confirm the principle with which all investigation starts. A cause is that which invariably precedes the effect, and is not merely accessory to but is necessary for the production of the effect. It is the antecedent member of a sequence of phenomena, the unvaried event which throughout a number of cases has happened in time before something else. But mere antecedence is not enough.[3] It must be a necessary antecedent.

Anyathāsiddha is an antecedent which is not causally connected with the effect, though conjoined with it. Viśvanātha[4] mentions different kinds of such causal antecedents. We may point to the

---

[1] *Nyāyamañjarī*, p. 114, and N.V.T.T., i. 1. 5.

[2] Praśastapāda mentions that non-causal coexistences such as "the rise of the moon is indicative of the rise in the sea and of the blooming of the water-lily" are included under vyāpti (P.P., p. 205).

[3] GLENDOWER. At my nativity
The front of heaven was full of fiery shapes,
Of burning cressets; and at my birth
The frame and huge foundation of the earth
Shaked like a coward.

HOTSPUR. Why, so it would have done at the same season if your mother's cat had but kittened, though yourself had never been born (i., *Henry IV*, 3. 1 13).

[4] *Siddhāntamuktāvali*, pp. 19–22.

spatial position of an object by means of our finger. This pointing with the finger, though it may be invariably present, is not causally related with the perception of spatial position. The potter's stick is an unconditional antecedent, while the colour of that stick is an irrelevant one. The sound produced by its motion is a coeffect. Eternal and all-pervading substances, which cannot be introduced and withdrawn at pleasure, are not unconditional antecedents. The condition of the condition, as the father of the potter, has nothing to do with the production of the pot. We are concerned only with the immediate antecedents. The co-effects of the same cause are sometimes confounded as cause and effect. The common cause of gravity brings about the rise and fall of the balance. When these co-effects are successive, the danger of mistaking the antecedent co-effect for the cause of the succeeding one is great. Whatever is unnecessary for the production of the effect is not its unconditional antecedent. The cause should not be mixed up with the collateral, indirect and adventitious accompaniments.[1] It is admitted that the cause cannot issue in the effect if there are counteracting forces. Pratibandhakābhāva or non-existence of counteracting factors, is sometimes added to the definition of cause. Keśava Miśra defines a cause as that necessary antecedent which is not taken up in the bringing about of something else. The threads constitute the cause of the cloth and not their colour, since the latter brings about the colour of the cloth and not the cloth itself.

Two things cannot be said to be causally related unless there is the positive-negative (anvaya-vyatireki) relation between them, such that the presence of the cause means the presence of the effect, and the absence of the cause means the absence of the effect. Causal relations are reciprocal and reversible. They are not mysterious forces but are ascertained from empirical successions which are uniform and exceptionless.[2] Careful observation of facts is insisted on. Udayana says: "We must diligently strive for ourselves to fix the several limitations, by determining the constant limitations and separations."[3] Nature presents us with a complex tangle of details from which our understanding selects the succession A-B, setting aside the many irrelevant details constituting the flux of actual events. We must find out whether the disappearance of the effect is due to the disappearance of the suspected cause. In all this investigation,

[1] Anyathāsiddhaniyatapūrvavṛtti kāraṇam. See *Tarkasaṁgraha*, 38; *Tarkabhāṣā*, p. 11.

[2] *Bhāṣāpariccheda*, 16.

[3] *Kusumāñjali*, i. 6.

one must be careful that no other condition is changed. The unconditionality of the antecedent cannot be ascertained without the employment of the double method of difference used in the Buddhist doctrine of pañcakāraṇi.[1]

Causal relations are not derived either *a priori* or *a posteriori*. They are not presented facts, but intellectual constructions based on presented data. To say that A is the cause of B is to go beyond the particulars of sense and apprehend the law of succession. Causation is not mere phenomenal sequence but a connection of elements. While the elements are presented, the connection is not.

The whole endeavour after causal explanation becomes useless if we admit plurality of causes. If plurality of causes were scientifically true, then inference would not be a valid means of knowledge.[2] If we see a river swollen, we cannot infer that it is due to past rain. It may be due to partial embankment. If we see ants carrying off their eggs, it may be due to the damaging of their nests and not necessarily to the coming rain. What we regard as the scream of a peacock need not imply that clouds are gathering, for it may after all be the voice of somebody imitating the peacock's scream. The Nyāya believes that there is no plurality and there is only one cause for one effect. The appearance of plurality is due to defective analysis. Plurality disappears if the effect is sufficiently limited and specialised. The swelling of the river caused by rain is different from that which results from the embankment of a part of it. The former is attended by rapid currents, abundant foam, a mass of fruit and foliage. The manner in which ants carry off their eggs before rain is quite different from the way they do when their nests are damaged. The scream of the peacock can certainly be distinguished from a man's imitation of it. If we take the effect with its distinctiveness (kāryaviśeṣa), then it will be seen to have only one specific cause (kāraṇaviśeṣa). If we take the effect abstractly. let us take the cause also in the same way. Vācaspati and Jayanta ask us to consider the full complement of the causes when the appearance of plurality vanishes. Some logicians however, assume that the different

[1] I.P., p. 463.

[2] N.B., ii. 1. 37–38.

possible causes of the same effect possess a common power or efficiency (ātiriktaśakti). If we refuse to be scientific, we may accept plurality. In that case, as the later Nyāya tells us, since more than one causal aggregate can be supposed for any effect, the latter is a mark or sign, not of any one of the causal aggregates in particular, but of the one or the other of them. If we are to be certain of the absence of the effect, then we must be certain of the absence of not one such cause, but of each and every one of them. A cause, in this sense, is the one or the other of the possible alternative aggregates which, being given, the effect follows invariably and unconditionally. The defining mark of the cause (kāraṇatāvacchedaka) is the presence of the one or the other of the possible causal aggregates and nothing else.

Three different kinds of causes are distinguished.[1] (1) The material (upādāna) cause is the stuff from out of which the effect is produced, *e.g.* the threads are the material cause of the cloth or the clay of the jar.[2] (2) The non-material or the non-inherent (asamavāyi) cause is that which inheres in the material cause, and whose efficiency is well known. The conjunction (saṁyoga) of the threads is the non-material cause. The threads will remain a bundle, and not make a cloth unless they are conjoined. The colour of the threads is a non-material cause, since its efficiency in producing the colour of the cloth is well known. While the material cause is a substance, the non-material cause is a quality or an action.[3] The atomic theory of the Nyāya reduces all alteration and change in the

[1] V.S., x. 2. 1–7; *Tarkabhāṣā*, pp. 15–25; *Bhāṣāparicchecda*, 17–18; *Tarkasaṁgraha*, 40.

[2] According to the Nyāya, the destruction of the effect (kāryam) is due to the destruction of its material cause. When one thread is destroyed, the original piece of cloth is also held to be destroyed. The fact that a piece of cloth still remains, without the weaver and the shuttle, etc., being required to produce it anew, is explained by the assumption that the original material cause was not altogether destroyed, but continued to exist as a latent self-productive impression or habit (sthitisthāpakaḥ saṁskāraḥ) in the remaining threads, so that they forthwith produce a new piece of cloth.

[3] This second kind of cause is not admitted by the Sāṁkhya and the Vedānta, who regard the cause and the effect as bound by the relation of identity. No link is necessary to bind the two. The distinction between inherent and non-inherent causes is not tenable. Strictly speaking, only the efficient cause is non-inherent. While the Sāṁkhya and the Vedānta admit the material and efficient causes, the Buddhists do not admit even

physical world to the combination and the severance of parts. The ultimate constituents are practically the same, though the order of the plan into which they enter changes every moment. The efficient (nimitta) cause is distinct from the preceding ones. It refers to the motive power by which the effect originates or the means by which it is produced. The potter is the efficient cause of the jar, while his stick and wheel are regarded as accessory (sahakāri).[1] The three kinds of causes correspond to Aristotle's material, formal and efficient causes. The effect itself may be regarded as the final cause of Aristotle.

Sometimes the cause which immediately produces the effect is called karaṇa, and is defined as the peculiar cause.[2] It is, according to Keśava Miśra, the cause *par excellence*.[3] Of the assemblage of causes that which immediately produces the effect is the cause.[4] In the act of perception, knower and object of knowledge are both necessary, though the chief cause or karaṇa is sense-contact. Nīlakaṇṭha defines karaṇa as the cause without which the desired effect will never be produced.[5] The potter's stick is the instrumental cause of the jar. The stick in the forest is not the cause. It becomes the cause only when it is actually employed in producing the jar. So the qualification "vyāpāravad" is added. Modern Nyāya goes a step further and asserts that the karaṇa is not that in which the vyāpāra or activity subsists, but is the activity itself which is the proximate cause of the appropriate effect.[6]

In the later Nyāya, the effect is defined as "the counterentity of its antecedent negation."[7] It is the positive correlate of prior negation. To say that the effect has prior non-existence is to admit that it has a beginning. This is the view of asatkāryavāda, or the doctrine that the effect has no existence before it is brought into being, also known as ārambhavāda, or the theory of new beginnings. The effect does not pre-exist in the cause but originates freshly. It is the doctrine

---

this distinction. Every event is momentary, giving rise to another. Milk is changing every moment; only we call it at one stage milk and at another curds

[1] Among efficient causes, a distinction is made between the general and the special causes. Of the former there are eight: God, his knowledge, desire, and action, antecedent non-existence, space, time, merit and demerit, to which sometimes absence of counteracting influences is added (*Tarkasaṁgraha*, 207–208.)

[2] Asādhāraṇaṁ kāraṇaṁ karaṇam (*Tarkasaṁgraha*, 37).

[3] Prakṛṣṭaṁ kāraṇam.

[4] Avilambena kāryotpatti.

[5] *Tarkasaṁgraha*, 186.

[6] Phalāyogavyavacchinnaṁ kāraṇam.

[7] Prāgabhāvapratiyogi (*Tarkasaṁgraha*, 39).

of epigenesis, or the creative process of reality that goes on adding fresh aspects to itself.[1] Some Buddhists deny that an effect before its production can be described as existent, non-existent, or both. The Nyāya contends that the effect is non-existent before its production from its cause, and this view is in conformity with the Nyāya doctrine that the whole is something other than the parts from which it is made up.[2] The Sāṁkhya and the Vedānta urge that we have in the effect the actualisation of pre-existing potentialities. According to the Sāṁkhya, the efficient cause aids the process of manifestation. The Naiyāyika criticises this view. If the cloth already exists in the threads, how is it that we do not see it? The threads are not the cloth, and we cannot wear the threads. It is no argument to say that the cloth is not manifested, since the non-manifestation is just the problem. If the manifestation means "the absence of such form as would be perceptible and capable of effective action," then it amounts to the non-existence of the effect prior to causal operation. Something which did not exist in a particular form is brought into existence by the operation of the cause.[3] The effect differs from the cause in form, potency and position. Besides, if the Sāṁkhya theory of the non-difference of the effect from the cause is true, then it would follow that the whole world regarded as the product of the primordial prakṛti would be as imperceptible as the prakṛti itself. If the effect occupies the same extension in space as the cause, it is because the effect rests or has its basis in the cause. There is no reason to reject the view, suggested by the facts of nature, that things are freshly produced and destroyed.[4] The view that when milk changes into curds there is only transformation and no destruction is not tenable. "When we perceive a new substance being produced by a fresh reconstitution, we infer from it the cessation or the destruction of the previous substance."[5] The disruption of the component particles of the milk and their rearrangement bring into existence curds. The Naiyāyika concedes that a complete destruction of the previous substance will make the formation of the new impossible. It follows that the substance only relinquishes its former condition, though the Naiyāyika is not inclined to accept it openly.

The works of the Sāṁkhya and the Vedānta, which hold a different theory of causal relation, criticise the Nyāya view. One illustration may be given here from the *Sāṁkhya kārikā*.[6] That which does not exist can never be produced. However much we may try, we cannot

---

[1] Kaṇāda mentions a number of arguments to show that the cause and the effect are quite different: (1) They are objects of different ideas; (2) and of different words; (3) they produce different effects; and (4) occur in different instants of time; (5) there is a difference of form; (6) of number, as the threads are many and the cloth is one; (7) if cause and effect were identical, there would be no need for any effort to derive the effect from the cause. See also N.V.T.T., iii. 2. 17.

[2] N.S., iv. 1. 48–54. [3] N.V., iv. 1. 49. [4] N.B., iv. 1. 49.

[5] N.B., iii. 2. 16. [6] 9.

change blue into yellow. Again, the material cause is always found associated with the effect, as oil-seeds with oil. Since there can be no association with a non-existent thing, the effect must exist in the cause. It cannot be said that a cause might produce an effect, even though unconnected with it. For in that case, anything can be produced from anything, and there will be no necessity why a particular effect should be produced from a particular cause only.[1] If it is said that an unconnected cause produces the effect on account of some inherent potency in it,[2] then if the power is connected with the effect, it is as good as saying that the effect pre-exists in the cause; if it is not, then the difficulty as to why a particular effect is produced from a particular power is not solved. Besides, since the cause and the effect are of the same nature, if the one exists, the other must also exist. The Sāṁkhya and the Vedānta insist that, if the effect is totally distinct from the cause, there cannot be any determining principle to relate the two. The Naiyāyika says that, if the effect is not distinct from the cause, we cannot distinguish the two as cause and effect. Both views are justified, though from different standpoints.

Before we pass from this section, we may make a few critical observations regarding the Nyāya view of causation. The Naiyāyika lays stress on antecedence, which, strictly speaking, is logical and not chronological. The sun is the cause of light, and the two, the cause and the effect, are simultaneous. The real cause continues as long as the effect does, and the existence of the cause, before or after the effect is unnecessary. In the interests of practice, though not of truth, the Naiyāyika exaggerates the importance of antecedence (pūrvabhāva) for causality.[3] The Nyāya analysis into the antecedent conditions and the change which brings together the conditions and makes them into causes so as to result in the effect, is artificial. The moment the union of the conditions is brought about, the effect appears. If it does not, the cause might exist for ever and not begin to

[1] On that view, it is said that even impossible things like a hare's horn may be produced The Nyāya answers this objection by saying that it holds that whatever is produced is non-existent, and not that anything non-existent can be produced (*Nyāyamañjari*, p. 494).

[2] If the effect has no existence before it is produced, the activity of the agent must be supposed to operate elsewhere than on the effect. In other words, the agent's effort with reference to threads may give rise to jars. The Vaiśeṣika gets over this difficulty by contending that the activity applied to a certain cause gives rise to those effects only, the potentiality of which inheres in that cause.

[3] *Kusumāñjali*, i. 19.

produce its effect. No cause can exist without producing the effect. The process of change is itself the effect, and nothing else can be called the effect. The distinction into the elements by themselves, their union and the production of the effect, is purely ideal.[1] Śaṁkara rightly urges that we cannot insist on both antecedence and unconditionality or inseparability. If the cause and the effect are in inseparable union (ayutasiddha), then the cause need not always precede the effect. It is truer to say that the cause and the effect are two modes of one thing than that they are two separate things joined together inseparably.[2] This conclusion is strengthened by the Nyāya insistence on samavāya or inherence. If the cause and the effect are related by way of inherence, then it is simpler to regard them as related to each other by way of identity (tādātmya).

It cannot be said that the facts of nature contain the causal relations in such an obvious manner that one has only to open his eyes to see them. We say that A is the cause of B, or that A is necessary or B is contingent, and thus order our experience. Causality is a form of our thought, a mode of intellect. That the universe is governed by laws, is a postulate which we accept in logic, though it has to be established in metaphysics. In life we do not ask for the real cause or the explanation of an event, but are content with the knowledge of the things that we should secure to produce a desired effect. Clay is the cause of the jar, where nature provides the clay and the potter uses it for his purpose. We can never exhaust the conditions, and so all our causal predications are relative. We say, given such and such conditions, if they are not counteracted, such and such effects are bound

[1] "Causation is really the ideal reconstruction of a continuous process of change in time. Between the coming together of the separate conditions and the beginning of the process is no halt or interval. Cause and effect are not divided by time in the sense of duration or lapse or interspace, They are separated in time by an ideal line which we draw across the indivisible process. For if the cause remained for the fraction of a second, it might remain through an indefinite future" (Bradley: *Logic*, ii. p. 539 n.). "The thread of causation is an ideal unity which we discover and make within the phenomenal flux of the given. But it has no actual existence within that flux, but lives first within the world of universals" (*ibid.*, p. 540).

[2] S.B., ii. 2. 17.

to follow. The difficulties about the cause of the cause and the consequent regress, are dismissed by the Naiyāyika as purely dialectical. Both cause and effect are passing events and not permanent facts, though we tend to speak of them as substances maintaining an identity in spite of events. The atoms themselves, if they are causes, cannot be real. Cause has no meaning apart from change, and whatever changes is a passing phenomenon. Causality, when analysed, resolves itself into a mere sequence of events, one depending on another *ad infinitum*, and yet we are obliged to use it as if it were a valid concept. It is certainly useful within the limits of experience, but we cannot regard it as of absolute validity. Causality is only a form of experience.[1]

The conception of the non-existence of the effect in the cause, adopted by the Nyāya, has its source in the naturalistic bias which regards the real as the perceived.[2] We see actually the higher and more complex levels arising out of the lower and simpler ones, in which they were not found to exist previously. Many scientific thinkers of the present day accept this view of reality as a one-way series, proceeding from the simple to the complex, from the lower to the higher. They may differ from the Nyāya realists with regard to the nature of the ultimate simple unit, but their ideal of explanation is in essence the same. Whether we start with material atoms, as the Naiyāyika does, or with electrons as modern scientists do, or with neutral stuff, sense-data or space-time passing through various growing complexities, as some contemporary realists do, we shall be obliged to adopt an inadequate ideal of explanation. The first condition of philosophic intelligibility is that the less can be derived from the more and not the more from the less. The natural movement of thought leads us to the acceptance of such a principle. The stream cannot rise higher than its source. If *a priori* conditions of intelligibility are violated in any such view, the conditions, we are told, must be given up. But we cannot alter the constitution of our minds at the bidding of realism. Thought is obliged to posit the implicit or the potential, and hold that the effect is implicitly or potentially prefigured in the cause.

[1] Āropita or adhyastadharma.

[2] N.B., ii. 2, 18.

A strict realism will have to treat development as mere appearance. If it regards it as more than appearance, it is not loyal to itself. Realists like Alexander assume some other principle, besides space-time when they speak of a nisus and development of higher qualities or beings. If the realist regards the real as what is actual, and dismisses the potential as a meaningless expression, then causality becomes unintelligible. The Naiyāyika violates his own view when he admits the reality of atoms and souls which are not seen. Things which we see are produced and destroyed and so are non-eternal; eternal things are not seen by us and yet they are assumed. The realist is forced to exaggerate the importance of time. Guyau observes in his little book on *Time*, "Time is made by us moderns a sort of mysterious reality designed to replace the old idea of providence and made almost omnipotent."[1] On the hypothesis of the absoluteness of time, we can never be sure of the goal of the world, which is neither fixed nor stable. We live in a universe which changes and where anything can come out of anything. There is no place for God in such a scheme, unless we piously assume that things are tending in the upward direction and God is in the making. Professor Alexander assures us that deity is the next higher quality than mind. We must ask, after God, what next?

The Naiyāyika insists on the continuity between the cause and the effect. If we attempt to formulate the Nyāya view in terms of modern science, we may say that it regards all causation as expenditure of energy. It denies the existence of any transcendent power in the mechanism of nature, if we, for the moment, overlook its view of unseen merit or demerit (adṛṣṭa). Causation is a mere redistribution of energy. The cause is the totality of conditions (kāraṇasāmagri) and the effect is what issues from it.[2] In his anxiety

[1] Quoted in the *Philosophical Review*, September 1923, p. 466.

[2] As we shall see, the Vaiśeṣika admits that the qualities of the cause are the causes of the qualities of the effect. The black colour of the clay is the cause of the black colour of the pot, unless the counteracting force of heat changes the colour. The exception to this in the Vaiśeṣika is the production of the diads from aṇus and triads from diads, where the number of the constituent elements determines the parimāṇa, or dimension The Nyāya allows a change of qualities in compound substances.

to do justice to the dictates of common sense, that things are produced and destroyed, the Naiyāyika runs the risk of overlooking the continuity of nature. He attempts to reconcile the popular view, that nothing comes from nothing, with the notion that things begin to be. The flower comes from the plant, the fruit from the tree, but yet he realises that the plant and the flower and the fruit and the tree are all unreal. The Nyāya admits the substantial identity of the cause, and holds that the collocations differ, so as to give rise to new properties. The question for metaphysics is, whether these newly produced properties are real. That they are observed by us in the effect condition, and were not observed by us in the causal condition, is quite true. But can we on that ground infer that they are real? When the Naiyāyika allows that the changing states of the world are perishable, he admits that they are not absolutely real. The real is the unaltered, while the aggregates change form. We say popularly that things come into and go out of existence: in reality there are only integration and separation of distinct elements which can neither be produced nor be destroyed, neither be increased nor be decreased. The real abides while its states change. Even in the realm of matter the first principle of constancy is admitted. Atoms abide while their accidental aggregations pass into and out of existence. The paradoxical ring of the statement that from nothing comes something is lost when we remember that what is present in germ becomes actual. It is a misuse of language to identify one stage with something and its preceding stage with nothing.

XI

Upamāna or Comparison

Upamāna, or Comparison, is the means by which we gain the knowledge of a thing from its similarity to another thing previously well known. Hearing that a wild ox (gavaya) is like a cow, we infer that the animal which we find to be like the cow is the gavaya.[1] Two factors are involved in an

[1] Prasiddhavastusādharmyād aprasiddhasya sādhanam,
Upamānaṁ samākhyātaṁ yathā gaur gavayas tathā.
Haribhadra: *Ṣaḍdarśanasamuccaya*, 23. See also N.S., i. 1. 6.

argument by comparison which are (1) the knowledge of the object to be known, and (2) the perception of similarity. While the ancient Naiyāyikas regarded the former as the principal cause of the new knowledge, the modern Naiyāyikas attach more importance to the perception of similarity.[1] Mere resemblance, whether it be complete, considerable or partial, is not enough to justify an argument by comparison. In the first case of complete resemblance or identity, there is not any new knowledge. We do not say the cow is like a cow. In the second case of considerable resemblance, the inference need not be valid, for a buffalo is not a cow, though there are many points of resemblance between the two. If there is only partial resemblance, the case is worse. A mustard seed is not Mount Meru, simply because both share the attribute of existence. In a valid argument through comparison, we do not so much *count* the points of resemblance as *weigh* them.[2] The resemblance must be important or essential[3] and have relation to the causal tie.[4] Argument by comparison gives us a knowledge of the relation between an object and its name.[5] It relates to the problem of identification. We are told that the particular name "gavaya" is given to the object which resembles the cow, and we give the name when we find such an object. Later logicians are of opinion that this mediate identification takes place through the recognition not only of similarity but also of dissimilarity (vaidharmya), as when we identify a horse which is different from the cow since it has not cloven hoofs or the characteristic nature of the object (dharmamātra), as when we identify a camel from its peculiar properties of a long neck and the like.[6] Upamāna, in this sense, does not correspond to the modern argument by analogy.

As we shall see, the Nyāya theory assumes the pragmatist view of truth as that which leads to successful activation. While this test can be applied to the objects of our experience, truths regarding the supersensible are beyond it. The Naiyāyika attempts to overcome the difficulty by means of this

[1] Sādṛśyajñānam (*Tarkāsaṃgraha*, 58).
[2] N.B., ii. 1. 44.
[3] Prasiddhasādharmyāt, ii. 1. 45.
[4] Sādhyasādhanabhāva (N.B., ii. 1. 45).
[5] Saṃjñāsaṃjñibhāva.
[6] *Tārkikarakṣā*, 22.

method of comparison. If the theory of medicine propounded by the sages of old is tested and found true, then the science of spiritual freedom as expounded by them must also be true.

Since the perception of similarity plays an important part in upamāna, Dignāga regards it as a case of perception. The Vaiśeṣika includes it in inference, since the argument may be put in the form: "This object is gavaya, since it is like a cow, and whatever is like a cow is gavaya." [1] The Sāṁkhya argues that upamāna is not an independent means of knowledge, since the instruction of the forester is a case of verbal knowledge and the perception of similarity an instance of perceptual knowledge.[2] Even Bhāsarvajña brings it under verbal knowledge. Argument by comparison is a complex one involving an element of verbal knowledge derived from the forester that the gavaya is like the cow, one of perception in that we perceive the gavaya in the forest, one of memory since we remember the statement when we see the gavaya, one of inference, since we assume the general proposition that whatever is like the cow is a gavaya, and lastly, the knowledge characteristic of the argument that the name gavaya is applicable to an animal of this kind. The last is the distinctive contribution of the argument by comparison which should not be confused with the other modes of cognition, though it may have some features in common with them.[3]

XII

Śabda or Verbal Knowledge

One of the chief sources of knowledge is authority. We accept many things which we have not observed or thought about on the authority of others. We learn a good deal from popular testimony, historical tradition and scriptural revelation. The logical issues involved in this mode of acquiring knowledge are discussed under śabda, or verbal testimony.

We may refer briefly to the Nyāya views about the origin and nature of sounds, the import of words and the structure of sentences.

---

[1] *Upaskāra*, ix. 2. 5. [2] *Tattvakaumudī*, 5.

[3] *Siddhāntamuktāvali*, 79 and 80. The Pūrva Mīmāṁsā and the Vedānta admit the independence of the argument by comparison, though they define it in a different way. When we meet with a gavaya in the forest, we not only have a cognition of its likeness to the familiar cow, but also a cognition of the likeness of the cow to the gavaya. The latter is due to comparison, since the cow is not actually perceived while the gavaya is.

Ākāśa, which pervades all space and not air, is the substratum of sound.[1] Sound can be produced even in a vacuum, though we cannot hear it, since there is no air to convey it. The quality of sound does not depend on air though the loudness, etc., do.[2] It is, however, produced by the contact of two hard substances. One sound produces another which causes another, until the last sound ceases owing to some obstacle.[3] We cannot argue that sound is eternal simply because it has an intangible substratum.[4]

A word is a combination of letters signifying an object, by way of denotation (abhidhā) or implication (lakṣaṇa). Every word has a meaning, which is generally regarded as a

[1] "The sound series is perceived even at a time when there is no perception of anything possessing colour and other qualities, which shows that sound has for its substratum a substance which is intangible and all-pervading, and it does not subsist in the same substratum as the vibrations (kampa)" (N.B., ii. 2. 38).

[2] V.S., i. 1. 6

[3] N.B., ii. 2. 35–6.

[4] Several grounds are urged to establish its non-eternality (N.S., ii. 2. 13–38). (1) Sound has a beginning, since it arises from the concussion of two hard substances, say, an axe and a tree. It cannot be said that the concussion aids the manifestation of sound but does not produce it, for the concussion and the sound are not simultaneous. We hear the sound at a great distance even after the concussion which occasioned it has ceased. (2) Sound is not eternal, since it has a beginning and an end. If it were eternal, then it must always be heard, since it is close to the perceiving organ, which is not the case. We know also that the sound ceases on account of known causes. We stop the gong by the contact of our hand with the bell (ii. 2. 32–36; V.S., ii. 2. 26–37). Vātsyāyana says that in the case of every sound there is a series of sounds, and in this series the succeeding destroys the preceding. What destroys the final sound of the series is the conjunction or impact of an obstructing substance (N.B., ii. 2. 34). Later Naiyāyikas modify this account to suit the Vaiśeṣika theory that a quality cannot subsist in a quality and cannot have another quality conjunction. Vācaspati observes that what destroys the sound is the impact with the obstacle of, not sound, but the ākāśa, which is the material cause of the sound. The impact of ākāśa with a denser substance renders it incapable of functioning as the material cause of further sounds, and when the immaterial cause of the initial sound, namely, the contact of the stick with the drum, ceases, there is nothing to start the series afresh, and thus the final sound is destroyed. (3) Sound is cognised by one of our senses as advancing in a series. It belongs to the genus of soundness, and is therefore non-eternal (N.S., ii. 2. 16). (4) Sound is spoken of as possessing the properties of products. It is described as grave, acute, etc. (5) From the fact that we repeat the sounds taught by the teacher, we cannot argue that sounds are eternal. When they were inaudible they did not exist, and we now simply reproduce them. Even different sounds may be said to be repeated, as we are said to sacrifice twice or dance twice (N.S., ii. 2. 29). (6) From the intangibility of sound we cannot argue to its eternality Motion is intangible and yet non-eternal (N.S., ii. 2. 22–24).

relation between the word or the sign and the object which it signifies.[1]

The fact of meaning is explained by the grammarians on the theory of the sphoṭa.[2] According to it, any single letter, c, o, w, or all the letters, "cow," cannot produce the knowledge of a thing corresponding to the word, since each letter perishes as soon as it is produced. Even if the last letter is aided by the impressions left by the preceding ones, a number of letters cannot explain the cognition of a thing. There must be something over and above the letters by which the knowledge is produced, and that is the sphoṭa, or the essence of sound revealed by letter, word or sentence.[3] This sound-essence produces the cognition of the thing. A single letter, unless it is a complete word, cannot signify any thing. The advocates of padasphoṭa argue that only a pada, or a word, can signify a meaning, while those of vākyasphoṭa hold that only a vākya, or a sentence, can signify a complete meaning. According to the latter, a sentence is the beginning of speech, while words are parts of sentences, and letters parts of words. Sphoṭa, or sound-essence, is said to be eternal and self-existent, bearing a permanent relation to the thing signified by it. Letters, words and sentences manifest, but do not produce, the eternal meanings. The Naiyāyikas hold that whatever is significant is a word,[4] and we become cognisant of its signification when we hear the last letter of the word. On hearing the last letter "w," we recollect the previous ones, c, o, and grasp the whole word by the mind; and we cognise the object by means of the conventional association between the word and the object.[5]

The relation between the word and its meaning is not due to nature, but to convention, and this view is confirmed by our experience of the way in which we acquire a knowledge of the meanings of words. We get to know the meanings of words through popular usage, grammar, dictionaries; and

[1] Cp. Vijñānabhikṣu on S.S., v. 37. The grammarians Bhaṭṭoji Dīkṣita (*Vaiyākaraṇabhūṣaṇa*, p. 243) and Nāgeśa Bhaṭṭa (*Mañjūṣā*, pp. 23–26) regard this signifying power as residing exclusively in words, while the Sāṁkhya and the Vedānta maintain that it resides in objects also. *Pañcadaśī*, viii. 4–15; *Nyāyabinduṭīkā*, pp. 10–11.

[2] Pāṇini's reference to sphoṭāyana in vi. 1. 123 indicates that the theory prevailed in his times. See S.D.S., Pāṇinidarśana.

[3] Deussen identifies the sphoṭa with the notion. Thibaut regards it as a grammatical fiction, and is certain that it cannot be a notion, since it is distinctly called a vācaka or abhidhāyaka, and is said to be the cause of the conception of the sense of the word (Thibaut's E.T. of S.B., p. 204 n.) See also S.B., i. 3. 28.

[4] Śaktam padam (*Tarkasaṁgraha*, 59).

[5] N.V., ii. 2. 55.

the Vedānta mentions gesture as well.[1] The convention that such and such a word should mean such and such an object is established by God (Īśvarasaṁketaḥ).[2] Later Nyāya admits that men also establish conventions (icchāmātraṁ śaktiḥ),[3] though the latter are styled pāribhāṣika, since they vary with different people.

What is the import of words, an individual (vyakti), or form (ākṛti), or genus (jāti), or all these?[4] The individual is that which has a definite form (mūrti) and is the abode of particular qualities.[5] It is manifested and perceptible.[6] The form is the peculiar properties; the collocation of the dewlap is the form of the cow. The genus is the type or class, the general notion underlying the object of a class. It helps us to attain a comprehensive knowledge of things similar to the individual in question.[7] The Nyāya holds that a word denotes all the three, the individual, its form and its genus, though in different degrees.[8] In practice we refer to the form. When our interest is in distinction, the word refers to the individual; and, when we try to convey the general idea, we refer to the genus. The word suggests the form, denotes the individual and connotes the genus. There is no such thing as a pure indeterminate attribute. It is determined in some way (avacchinna). Again, form by itself is not enough. A clay model of the cow is not treated as a cow, though it has the form, since it is lacking in the generic qualities. Popular usage supports the theory that words denote individuals.[9]

[1] *Siddhāntamuktāvali*, 81; *Nyāyamañjari*, p. vi.

[2] N.B., ii. 1. 55. See also *Nyāyamañjari*, p. 243.

[3] *Tarkasaṁgraha*, 59. *Siddhāntamuktāvali*, 81.

[4] N.S., ii. 2. 56. [5] ii. 2. 64. [6] ii. 2. 65.

[7] Samānaprasavātmikā jātiḥ (N.B., ii. 2. 66). Since we have a definite conception of cowness apart from the idea of individual cows, there must be an objective basis for the former (N.B., ii. 2. 61 and 66). Uddyotakara holds that the class nature subsists in each individual by way of inherence, or samavāya. The question whether the genus subsists in its entirety or in parts in each individual is meaningless, since jāti is not a composite and the distinction of whole and part is inapplicable to it. Jāti, or the eternal essence, is said to be in a necessary relation of samavāya to the individuals whose essence it is and in indirect or temporal relation (kālikasaṁbandha) to the other individuals.

[8] ii. 2. 63. Jātiviśiṣṭavyakti. [9] ii. 2. 57.

Words, according to the Buddhist thinkers, do not represent positive objects, but simply exclude others erroneously recalled to mind. The word "cow" denotes the negation (apoha) of objects which are not cows, such as horses, etc. From this exclusion we infer that the word "cow" refers to the object "cow."[1] Uddyotakara criticises the apoha doctrine on the following grounds.[2] We cannot conceive of a negative denotation unless we have previously conceived of a positive one. All negation has a positive basis. Bare negation is meaningless, while every specific negation has a positive implication. Though in the case of two contradictory words the denotation of the one may exclude that of the other, such an exclusion is not possible in the case of a word like "all."[3] Every word denotes something positive which is not exhausted by its distinction from something else.[4]

It is objected that words cannot denote objects, since they do not co-exist with objects, and are present even when the objects are not present, as in a negative judgment "there is no jar here."[5] Vācaspati meets this objection by saying that a word denotes the universal, including all individuals dispersed in time and place, and so refers to individuals present as well as past.[6] Nor can it be said that the word is only an abstract idea, since it cannot signify the different features of the different individuals. The word refers to the distinctive features which are objective. We use words in experience and they lead to success in life. All this would be impossible if the word referred simply to mental images and not to outer objects.[7]

Sometimes, it is said, that we cannot conceive of the relation between the word and the object. The word is an attribute, and the object denoted by it is a substance, and between the two there cannot be the relation of saṁyoga (conjunction). Even if the object denoted be an attribute, this relation is impossible between two attributes.[8]

---

[1] See *Nyāyamañjari*, pp. 303, 306–8, and Pārthasārathi Miśra's *Nyāyaratnākara*. Early Buddhist works do not contain definite information about this view, though it appears in a modified form in the *Apohasiddhi* of Ratnakīrti. For him words denote neither positive objects nor negative ones. The positive meaning is not a consequence of the negation of other objects any more than the negative meaning is the consequence of the positive denotation. The essence of meaning consists in the simultaneous cognition of the positive and the negative sides. All determinate objects have a positive nature which excludes others. This theory is certainly more satisfactory, though it is not easily reconcilable with the general metaphysics of the Buddhists. Nor do the Hindu logicians accept it as the Buddhist view.

[2] N.V., ii. 2. 65.

[3] See Udayana's *Ātmatattvaviveka*.

[4] *Nyāyamañjari*, p. 311. See also *Nyāyakandalī*, pp. 317–321.

[5] *Prameyakamalamārtāṇḍa*, p. 124; V.S., vii. 2. 17.

[6] N.V.T.T., ii. 2. 63.

[7] *Prameyakamalamārtāṇḍa*, p. 136; Vidyānanda's *Aṣṭasahasrī*, p. 249.

[8] V.S., vii. 2. 14.

Words are inactive, and conjunction is based on the movement of one of the members of the relation. The word ākāśa and the object ākāśa are both inactive, and there can be no conjunction between them. Nor do we have between a word and its meaning the relation of inherence. Vātsyāyana admits that the relation between the word and its meaning is not of a productive character (prāptilakṣaṇa). The word "fire" does not produce the object of fire.[1] That is why verbal cognition is less distinct than sense-perception.[2] But it is none the less cognition.

A sentence (vākya) is a collection of significant sounds or words. We cognise the constituent words and then their meanings. The cognitions of the words leave behind traces (saṁskāras) which are remembered at the end of the sentence, and then the different meanings are related together in one context. While the ancient Naiyāyikas contend that the chief means (mukhya karaṇam) of verbal cognition is the recollection of objects due to verbal memory, the modern Naiyāyikas argue that the verbal memory is the chief means. The meaning of a sentence depends on (1) ākāṅkṣā, mutual need or interdependence, or the inability of a word to indicate the intended sense in the absence of another word, (2) yogyatā, or compatibility or fitness or the capacity to accord with the sense of the sentence and not render it futile and meaningless, (3) sannidhi, propinquity, juxtaposition or the utterance of words in quick succession without a long pause between one word and another. These insist on the syntactical, logical and phonetical connections of words. A collection of words devoid of interdependence, man, horse and colony, conveys no sense. A sentence like "moisten with fire" (agninā siñcet) conveys no intelligible meaning. Similarly, words uttered at long intervals do not convey any sense. A sentence is made up of words which are interdependent, capable of being construed together and in close juxtaposition. Gangeśa adds a fourth condition, namely, a knowledge of the intention of the speaker. A sentence like "saindhavam ānaya" may mean either "bring the horse" or "bring salt," and we can be sure of its meaning only if we know the mind

[1] N.B. and N.V.T.T., ii. 1. 50–51.

[2] *Prameyakamalamārtāṇḍa*, pp. 128–130; Kumārila's S.V., v. 11. 6–8 and 10.

of the speaker. Fitness of words to express a definite meaning covers this requirement also.[1] While fitness demands formal consistency, tātparyajñāna, or knowledge of the intention, may be said to imply material compatibility.[2]

Propositions are divided into three classes: command (vidhi), prohibition (niṣedha), explanation (arthavāda).[3] Śabda, when used as a source of knowledge, means āptopadeśa, or the assertion of a reliable person.[4] The āpta, or the reliable person is the specialist in a certain field, " one who, having had direct proof of a certain matter, desires to communicate it to others who thereby understand it." They may be of any caste or race, " ṛṣis, āryas or mlecchas."[5] When a young man is in doubt whether a particular river is fordable or not, the information of an old experienced man of the locality, that it is fordable, is to be trusted.

These trustworthy assertions relate to the visible world (dṛṣṭārtha) or the invisible (adṛṣṭārtha). That quinine cures fever is of the former kind, that we gain heaven by virtue is of the latter. The words of the ṛṣis deal with the latter.[6] Their statements are to be relied on, since their assertions about the verifiable world have been found to be true. The authors of the Vedas are āptas, or reliable persons, since they had an intuitive perception of the truths, love for humanity and the desire to communicate their knowledge.[7]

Later Naiyāyikas, like Udayana and Annaṁ Bhaṭṭa and the Vaiśeṣika thinkers, regard the supreme Īśvara as the eternal author of the Vedas. Udayana sets aside the view that the authoritativeness of the Vedas is to be inferred from their eternality, freedom from defects and acceptance by great saints. At the beginning of new world-epochs there can be no acceptance by saints. The Mīmāṁsaka argument of the eternality of the Vedas is controverted by Udayana, who argues that there is no continuous tradition to indicate eternality,

---

[1] *Bhāṣāpariccheda*. See also *Vedāntaparibhāṣā*, iv.

[2] While the Mīmāṁsakas and the grammarians hold that the words of a sentence centre round the verb, without which they convey no sense, the Naiyāyikas hold that a proposition is but a number of significant words (padasamūha) whose collective meaning is apprehended, whether or not there be a verb in the sentence (*Tarkasaṁgraha*, p. 59; Jhā: *Prabhākara School*, p. 63).

[3] N.S., ii. 1. 63, and *Tarkakaumudī*, p. 17.

[4] i. 1. 7.

[5] N.B., i. 1. 7.

[6] N.B., i. 1. 8.

[7] ii. 1. 68.

since such a tradition must have been interrupted at the dissolution of the world which preceded the existing creation. Vātsyāyana, however, accepts the continuity of tradition, in the sense that God at the beginning of every epoch recomposes the Vedas and keeps up the tradition.[1] If the Mīmāṁsakas adduce texts in support of their view, that the Vedas are eternal, and that the ṛṣis are not their authors but only their seers (mantradraṣṭāraḥ), other texts are quoted in support of the Nyāya view of the origin of the Vedas.[2] Besides, the Vedas contain sentences which imply an author.

Objections against the validity of the Vedas, such as those of untruth, contradiction and tautology, are rejected as untenable.[3] Their validity is defended on the ground that their contents form a coherent whole. Acceptance of the Vedas does not mean a resort to blind faith or revelation.

Dignāga contends that śabda is not an independent source of knowledge. When we speak of credible assertion, we mean either that the person who utters it is credible or that the fact that he utters is credible. If it is the former, we have a case of inference; if it is the latter, we have a case of perception.[4] Though śabda is like inference since it conveys the knowledge of an object through its sign, yet the sign here is different from what it is in inference, indicating as it does whether the words come from a reliable person or not.[5] The relation between the sign and the thing signified is natural in inference, while it is conventional in verbal knowledge.[6] If we argue that verbal cognition follows the remembrance of the meanings of words and therefore is inferential, then even doubtful cognition and knowledge by comparison should be regarded as inferential. If a reference to the three periods of time makes verbal cognition inferential, then other forms of reasoning, as tarka, will also be inferential. If it is urged that verbal cognition depends on positive and negative concomitance, to the effect that the word "jar" means the cognition of the object, and there is no cognition of the object where it is not pronounced, then even perception may be regarded as a case of inference, since it is present where the jar is present, and where the jar is absent there is no perception of the jar.[7] Knowledge derived through words is thus different from that gained through perception, inference and comparison.[8]

---

1 N.B., and N.V.T.T., ii. 1. 68.

2 Idaṁ sarvam asṛjata ṛco yajūṁṣi sāmāni, etc.

3 If we perform a sacrifice for the sake of getting a son, and do not get one, the fault may be in the action and not in the Vedic rule. Injunctions such as "offer the oblation after sunrise" or "before" need not be taken as contradicting each other, since they state alternative courses of conduct. There is no useless tautology (N.B., ii. 1. 58–59).

4 Dignāga, however, accepts the sayings of Buddha as authoritative, See Kumārila's *Tantravārttika*, pp. 169 ff.

5 N.B., ii. 1. 52.

6 N.B., ii. 1. 55.

7 N.V, ii. 1. 49–51.

8 N.B., ii. 1. 52; N.V., i. 1. 7.

XIII

Other Forms of Knowledge

To the four sources of knowledge admitted by the Nyāya, the Mīmāṁsakas add arthāpatti, or presumption, and the Bhāṭṭas and the Vedāntins abhāva, or non-existence. The Paurāṇikas regard tradition and probability also as valid sources of knowledge. The Naiyāyika believes that all forms of knowledge are comprehended by the four pramāṇas.[1]

Aitihya, or tradition, is brought under śabda.[2] If the rumour or tradition is started by a reliable person, then it is as valid as śabda. Arthāpatti, or implication, is getting at a new fact or presuming something (āpatti) on the basis of another fact (arthāt). It is assuming a thing not itself perceived, though implied by another thing perceived or inferred. The fat Devadatta does not eat in the day. The implication is that he eats in the night, since it is impossible for one to be fat if one does not eat at all. The Mīmāṁsakas, who regard it as an independent means of knowledge, view it as a disjunctive hypothetical syllogism.[3] According to Gaṅgeśa, it is an example of a negative inference which establishes the absence of the middle term through the absence of the major. According to the *Bhāṣāpariccheda*, arthāpatti is accomplished through the recognition of a negative relationship between the middle and the major (vyatirekavyāpti).[4] Saṁbhava, or subsumption, where we cognise a part from a whole of which it is a member, is a case of deductive inference. It is strictly numerical inclusion.

Abhāva, or negation, is sometimes mentioned as an inde-

[1] N.B., ii. 1. 19.

[2] ii. 2. 2.

[3] See also *Bhāṣāpariccheda*, p. 143.

[4] It may be expressed in two different stages :—

> He who does not eat at all is not fat.
> This man is fat.
> Therefore this man is not one who does not eat at all—*i.e.* he is one who eats.

This is Cesare. The next step is :—

> He who eats must do so either by day or by night.
> He does not eat by day.
> Therefore he eats by night.

pendent pramāṇa. Though the Nyāya-Vaiśeṣika system admits non-existence as an object of cognition, it does not believe that a special pramāṇa is necessary for its apprehension. We have already seen how existence is an object of perception which is connected with its adhikaraṇa, or locus, by the relation called viśeṣaṇatā (or qualified and qualification). The non-existent thing is of the same order of reality as its locus, which is perceived; otherwise the perception of its absence cannot be implied by the perception of its locus. Absolute negation is inconceivable. The negation which is the object of knowledge is relative.[1]

By means of inference, we can infer the non-existence of things. Abhāva means not mere negation but contrast. It is contrast as between what exists and what does not exist, as when the non-existent rain brings about the cognition of the existence of the connection of the clouds with high winds; since it is only when there is some such obstruction, as the connection of the clouds with high winds, that there is no fall of the raindrops, which would otherwise be there by reason of the force of gravity in the drops.[2] Of two contradictory things, the non-existence of one establishes the existence of the other. The Nyāya logic proceeds on the principle of dichotomous division. The distinction of homogeneous and heterogeneous examples rests on this assumption. Two contradictory judgments cannot both be false, nor can they both be true. A is either B or not B. One or the other of two contradictories must be true since no other course is possible.[3] If we infer the non-existence of a thing from the existence of another, it is only a case of inference.[4] Vātsyāyana says: "At the time the existent thing is cognised, the non-existent thing is not cognised, that is to say there is the non-cognition of the non-existent, only at the time that there is the cognition of the existent. When the lamp illumines and renders visible something that is visible, that which is not seen in the same manner as that visible thing is regarded as non-existent, the mental process being as follows: 'If the

[1] For a different view, see *Śāstradīpikā*, pp. 234 ff.; *Vedāntaparibhāṣā*, vi.
[2] N.B., ii. 2. 1.
[3] Parasparavirodhe hi na prakārāntarasthitiḥ (*Kusumāñjali*, iii. 8).
[4] N.B., ii. 2. 2.

thing existed, it would be seen : since it is not seen, it must be concluded that it does not exist.' "[1] Praśastapāda supports this view. "As the appearance of the effect is indicative of the existence of the cause, so is the non-appearance of the effect indicative of the non-existence of the cause."[2] Even by means of śabda, we can have cognition of non-existence.[3]

XIV

TARKA AND VĀDA

In tarka, or indirect proof, we start with a wrong assumption and show how it leads to absurdities. If the soul were not eternal, it would not be able to experience the fruits of its actions, undergo rebirth or attain release. It is therefore eternal. The admission of a false minor necessitates the admission of a false major.[4] Tarka is a type of inference distinct from other types, since it is not based on any perception. It leads indirectly to right knowledge.[5] Vātsyāyana thinks that it does not give us determinate knowledge, though it tells us that the opposite of a suggested premise is impossible.[6] Uddyotakara argues that the reasoning about the soul does not enable us to say that the soul is beginningless, but only that it should be so.[7] Tarka is not by itself a source of valid knowledge, though it is valuable as suggesting hypotheses.

The older Nyāya admits eleven kinds of tarka, which the modern reduces to five, of which the chief is what we have described, the *reductio ad absurdum*, called pramāṇabādhitārthaprasaṅga. The other four are ātmāśraya, or *ignoratio elenchi* ; anyonyāśraya, or mutual dependence ; cakrika, or circular reasoning ; and anavasthā, or infinite regress. Even the *reductio ad absurdum* is regarded as a case of fallacious reasoning, since it derives a conclusion which is absurd. But when we transcend the error, we arrive at definitive cognition (nirṇaya).[8]

---

[1] N.B., Introduction.

[2] P.P., p. 225. See also V.S., ix. 2. 5; *Nyāyakandalī*, pp. 225–226; and *Kusumāñjali*, iii. 20, 22 and 26.

[3] Jayanta mentions eleven kinds of anupalabdhi. See *Nyāyamañjari*, pp. 56–57.

[4] S.D.S., xi.

[5] Pramānugrāhakas tarkah (S.S.S.S., vi. 25). Tarkabhāsā.

[6] N.B., i. 1. 40.

[7] N.V., i. 1. 40.

[8] i. 1. 41.

Vāda, or discussion, proceeds by means of the free use of syllogisms and aims at the ascertainment of truth. But it often degenerates into mere wrangling (jalpa), which aims at effect or victory and cavil (vitaṇḍā), which delights in criticism for its own sake.[1] Such a futile discussion can be put an end to by convicting the opponent of his error and forcing him to accept defeat.[2]

XV

Memory

All knowledge is divided into presentative cognitions (anubhava), which are not reproductions of former states of consciousness, and representative cognition (smṛti), which recall previous experiences into consciousness.[3] If we exclude memory knowledge, the entire past will drop out of the field of certitude. Memory knowledge is based on residual traces (saṁskārajanya). Memory is defined as "due to a peculiar contact of the soul with the manas and the trace left by the previous experience."[4] It is sometimes said to be caused solely by the impression (saṁskāramātrajanya), and thus distinguished from recognition (pratyabhijñā). While the impression is the immediate cause of the recollection, the perception of the identity of the present object with something else is the cause of recognition. The Nyāya does not admit

[1] i. 2. 1–3.

[2] The points of defeat (nigrahasthāna) are of twenty-two different kinds: (1) pratijñāhāni, or surrendering the proposition to be established; (2) pratijñāntara, or shifting the argument by importing new considerations; (3) pratijñāvirodha, or self-contradiction; (4) pratijñāsamnyāsa, or disclaiming the proposition; (5) hetvantara, or shifting the reason; (6) arthāntara, or shifting the topic; (7) nirarthaka, or senseless talking; (8) avijñātārtha, or using unintelligible jargon; (9) apārthaka, or incoherent talk; (10) aprāptakāla, or overlooking the order of argumentation; (11) nyūna, or dropping essential steps of the argument; (12) adhka, or elaborating the obvious; (13) punarukta, or repeating oneself; (14) ananubhāṣaṇa, or keeping quiet; (15) ajñāna, or not understanding the proposition; (16) apratibhā, or wanting in resourceful replies; (17) vikṣepa, or evading the discussion by feigning illness, etc.; (18) matānujña, or admitting the defeat by pointing out that it is also present in the opponent's view; (19) paryanuyogyopekṣaṇa, or overlooking the censurable; (20) niranuyogyānuyoga, or censuring the non-censurable; (21) apasiddhānta, or deviating from an accepted tenet; and (22) hetvābhāsa, or semblance of a reason.

[3] *Tarkasaṁgraha*, 34.

[4] V.S., ix. 2. 6.

memory as a separate source of knowledge, since we have in it not any cognitive knowledge of objects, but only a reproduction of a past experience in the same form and order in which it once existed in the past and has now ceased to exist.[1] The validity of remembered knowledge depends on that of the previous experience which is reproduced. Some logicians include remembered knowledge under valid cognition when the latter is defined as knowledge which is not contradicted.[2] Recollections are not simultaneous, since attention (praṇidhāna), perception of the sign and the rest (liṅgādijñāna) are not present at one and the same time.[3]

XVI

Doubt

The state of doubt is said to arise from : (1) the recognition of properties common to many objects, as when we see a tall object in the twilight and are not sure whether it is a man or a post, since tallness is found in both ; (2) the recognition of properties not common to any of the objects, as when we find it difficult to decide whether sound is eternal or not, since it is not found in man or beast, which are non-eternal, or in atoms, which are eternal ; (3) conflicting testimony, as when two competent authorities differ about the nature of the soul ; (4) irregularity of perception, as when we see water and are not sure whether it is real, as in a tank, or unreal, as in a

[1] *N.S. Vṛtti*, i. 1. 3.

[2] *Tarkakaumudī*, p. 7.

[3] N.S., iii. 2. 33; N.B., iii. 2. 25–30; N.V., iii. 2. 25–26. Among the causes of recollection are mentioned: (1) praṇidhāna, or attention; (2) nibandha, or association; (3) abhyāsa, or repetition; (4) liṅga, or sign; (5) lakṣaṇa, or descriptive sign; (6) sādṛśya, or similarity; (7) parigraha, or ownership; (8) āśrayāśritasaṁbandha, or the relation of correlatives; (9) ānantarya, or immediate sequence ; (10) viyoga, or separation ; (11) ekakārya, or identity of function ; (12) virodha, or enmity ; (13) atiśaya, or superiority ; (14) prāpti, or acquisition ; (15) vyavadhāna, or intervention ; (16) sukhaduḥkha, or pleasure-pain ; (17) icchādveṣa, or desire and aversion ; (18) bhaya, or fear ; (19) arthitva, or need ; (20) kriyā, or action ; (21) rāga, or affection ; (22) dharma, or merit ; (23) adharma, or demerit. These, according to Vātsyāyana, are only suggestive and by no means exhaustive. Nidarśanaṁ cedaṁ smṛtihetūnāṁ na parisaṁkhyānam iti (N.B., iii. 2. 41). All the causes of the association and recall of ideas can be brought under these heads.

mirage, since it is perceived in both ; (5) irregularity of non-perception, which is the converse of the preceding.[1] According to Uddyotakara, the two last do not by themselves cause doubt, unless there is the perception of common inconclusive features. Since the element perceived is associated with more than one object, it revives simultaneously two chains of ideas, between which the mind oscillates and the state of doubt arises.[2] Neither idea is integrated with the percept, though both are alternately suggested.[3] The state of doubt is unpleasantly toned and it arrests all activity.[4]

If one of the alternatives is suppressed, and the mind is inclined towards another, we have a case of ūha, or conjecture, where we tentatively accept an alternative.[5] The suppression of one alternative is due to the strength of the other. If in a rice field we see a tall object, we conjecture that it is a tall man and not a tall post, since posts are not often met with in rice fields. While in the state of doubt, the two alternatives are equally probable ; in that of ūha, one becomes more probable than the other.

Another kind of doubtful state is mentioned, called anadhyavasāya, due to lapse of memory. We perceive a tree, but forget its name, and so ask " what may its name be ? "[6] According to Śivāditya, we have here also two alternative suggestions, though they are not present to consciousness. If we become conscious of them, we have a state of doubt. Praśastapāda, Śrīdhara and Udayana give a different account. It is said to be an indefinite perception of an object, either familiar or unfamiliar, due to absent-mindedness or desire for further knowledge. When a familiar object passes by

[1] *Tarkasaṁgraha*, 64. V.S., ii. 2. 17.

[2] Dolāyamānā pratītiḥ saṁśayaḥ (Guṇaratna's *Ṣaḍdarśanasamuccaya-vṛtti*).

[3] Laugākṣi Bhāskara defines the state of doubt as knowledge consisting in an alternation between various contradictory attributes. *Tarkakaumudī:* Ekasmin dharmiṇi viruddhanānākoṭikaṁ jñāmam, p. 7. Cp. also *Tarka-saṁgraha*, 64; *Bhāṣāpariccheda*, 129–130.

[4] Praśastapāda distinguishes two kinds of doubt, internal and external (P.P., p. 174).

[5] *Saptapadārthī*, 68.

[6] See *Saptapadārthī*, p. 69. Cp. *Mitabhāṣiṇī*, Vizianagram skt series, p. 26: kim saṁjñako 'yam ity atrāpi, cūtaḥ panaso vety, vikalpasphuraṇād anadhya-vasāyopi, saṁśaya eva.

and we fail to notice it owing to absent-mindedness or inattention, we have a case of anadhyavasāya, where we know that something passed, though we do not know what it is that passed. When the object is unfamiliar and we do not know its name, we have a state of imperfect knowledge, which is distinct from the state of ordinary doubt.[1]

Doubt is the impetus to investigation, for it creates a desire for what is not cognised. It precedes inference, though not perception or verbal knowledge. Doubt ends when our knowledge becomes precise. Doubt is not to be confused with error So long as we know that we do not know the nature of the object for certain, we have true knowledge or pratyaya. Doubt is incomplete knowledge, while error is false knowledge.

XVII

Fallacies

The logic of the Nyāya elaborates the principles by which we acquire knowledge. It adopts the standpoint of natural science, and its laws are not precepts of conduct, but general statements based on the observation of the means by which man satisfies his intellectual needs Normally, knowledge is valid; error is adventitious and arises when the conditions under which right cognition is produced fail. Fallacies occur when the normal working of the cognitive powers is interfered with. The Nyāya deals at great length with fallacies; and it is not surprising, if we remember that liability of thought to error calls logic into existence.

A good deal of attention is paid to jugglery with words, since logic aims at protecting us from the arts of the sophist. Three kinds of verbal quibbling (chala) are distinguished: (1) Vākchala. An ambiguous term is used and the person spoken to takes it in a sense different from that intended by the speaker. When one says, "This boy is a navakambala," possessed of a new blanket (or nine blankets), the quibbler replies, "No, he has not nine blankets, but only one." (2) Sāmānyachala. A statement made with reference to a particular is extended to the whole class. When one says, "this Brahmin has learning and conduct," the quibbler objects that not all Brahmins possess learning and conduct. (3) Upacārachala. Here a figurative

[1] P.P., pp. 182–183.

expression is taken literally. When one says, "the scaffolds cry out," the quibbler objects that inanimate objects like scaffolds cannot be expected to cry out.

Fallacies such as jāti and nigrahasthāna relate to dialectic more than to logic. Logical fallacies occur in connection with the different members of the syllogistic argument. The fallacies of the minor term, pakṣābhāsas, of the example, dṛṣṭāntābhāsas, are not so important as the hetvābhāsas, or fallacies of the middle term. Gautama[1] mentions five kinds of these: (1) Savyabhicāra, or the inconclusive, leading to more conclusions than one. From the ground of intangibility we may conclude either the eternality or the non-eternality of sound, since both eternal atoms and non-eternal cognitions are intangible. The middle term is not pervaded by the major. As the middle term is not uniformly concomitant with any one alternative, it is called anaikāntika in later logic. Three subdivisions of these are admitted, namely, (*a*) sādhāraṇa, or the common, where the middle term is too wide; (*b*) asādhāraṇa, or the uncommon, where the middle term is too narrow; (*c*) anupasaṁhārin, or the indefinite, where the middle term cannot be verified.[2] (2) Viruddha, or the contradictory, is the reason which contradicts the proposition to be established.[3] (3) Prakaraṇasama, or the equivalent to the proposition, leads to no conclusion, since it raises the question which it is intended to answer. It puts forward one of two contrary characters, both of which are equally unperceived.[4] Later logic brings it under satpratipakṣa. It is also taken as a reason which is available for both sides when it becomes identical with savyabhicāra.[5] (4) Sādhyasama gives a reason which is not different from what is to be proved and itself requires proof. It is a case of the unproved or the asiddha, of which different kinds are admitted: (*a*) svarūpāsiddhi, where the nature of the middle is absolutely unknown, as when we say sound is eternal because it is visible, where the visibility of sound is something absolutely unknown; (*b*) āśrayāsiddhi, where the middle has no basis, as in the example, "there is no God since he has no body," where bodylessness has no substratum if there were no God; (*c*) anyathāsiddhi, or that which is otherwise known.[6] (5) Kālātīta, or the mistimed, is the reason adduced when the time is past. The argument that "sound is durable

---

[1] i. 2. 4. See also V.S., iii. 1. 15. Praśastapāda mentions asiddha, or unproved; viruddha, or opposed; saṁdigdha, or doubtful; and anadhyavasita, or unascertained (P.P., pp. 239–240). Dignāga mentions fourteen kinds, and Bhāsarvajña six. See also *Tarkasaṁgraha*, 52.

[2] *Tarkasaṁgraha*, 53. See also Viśvanātha's *N.S. Vṛtti*, i. 2. 46.

[3] N.V., i. 2. 6. Vātsyāyana (i. 2. 6) gives an example from the *Yogabhāṣya* (iii. 13) to the effect that the two statements that (1) the world ceases from manifestation because it is not eternal, and (2) it continues to exist because it cannot be destroyed. See also *Tarkasaṁgraha*, 54.

[4] N.B. and N.V., i. 2. 7.

[5] *Tarkasaṁgraha*, 55.

[6] Vācaspati adds ekadeśāsiddhi, and Udayana adds vyāpyatvāsiddhi where the concomitance is not known to be invariable.

because it is manifested by union as a colour," is an example of this fallacy. The colour of the jar is manifested when the latter comes into union with a lamp, though it existed before the union took place, and will continue to exist after the union has ceased. To argue on the analogy of colour that sound existed before the union of the drum and the stick, and will continue to exist after the union has ceased, is fallacious. The reason adduced is said to be mistimed, since sound is produced immediately after the union of the drum and the stick, while colour is manifested simultaneously with the union of the jar and the lamp. This fallacy is also called bādhita, where the middle term asserts something the opposite of which is ascertained to be true by other evidence. In later logic the list of fallacies is considerably developed.

XVIII

Truth

The fact from which a theory of knowledge starts, is not that we have knowledge, but that we claim to have it. The task of the epistemologist is to investigate how far the claim can be sustained. In the theory of pramā, or truth, the Naiyāyika sets out to inquire how far the claim which we implicitly grant is justified. He tries to show that the content of knowledge we acquire by means of the four pramāṇas has validity or normative necessity.

The Nyāya theory of knowledge comes into conflict with the scepticism of the Mādhyamika doctrine, which holds that we do not know the essence of things, and our thought is so contradictory that it cannot be regarded as real. Against this, Vātsyāyana urges that if the Mādhyamika is certain that nothing exists, he allows the possibility of certainty to that extent at least and thus contradicts himself. If, however, there is no proof for the contention that nothing exists, if it is but an unwarranted assumption, then its opposite may be assumed. Again, he who denies the validity of the pramāṇas does so on the basis of some pramāṇa or on no basis. If the latter, the argument is useless; if the former, the validity of the pramāṇa is accepted. Radical scepticism is unworkable. Everyone admits the principles of knowledge the moment he begins to think. Again, he who admits the functioning of thought must admit also the world of reality, for thought and reality are interdependent. Vātsyāyana says: "If an analysis of things by thought is possible, then it is not true that the real nature of things is not apprehended ; if, on the other hand, the real nature of things is not apprehended, then there can be no analysis of things by thought. So that to allege that 'there is analysis of things by thought and the real nature of things is not apprehended' involves a contradiction in terms."[1] Uddyotakara paraphrases it thus : "If there can be analysis of things by thought, then things cannot be non-existent ; and if things are non-existent, then there can be no analysis of things by thought."[2] The Nyāya believes that knowledge is significant of reality (arthavat).[3]

Vātsyāyana attacks the Vijñānavada view, that the objects of experience are mere strings of presentations. Things seen in dreams are refuted as unreal, since they are not experienced in waking consciousness. If there were not a sensible world of experience, dream states could not exist. The diversity of dreams can be traced to the diversity of their causes.[4] If there were not an existent reality, the difference between truth and error would be negligible, and there would be no explanation for the obvious facts that we cannot control our perceptions and have them at our pleasure.[5] Nor is the Naiyāyika satisfied with the view that postulates objects, though of a momentary character. If the objects are the causes of our cognition, they must precede the effect. But, on the view of momentariness, the object which has produced the cognition has ceased to be in the next moment when it is

[1] N.B., iv. 2. 27. [2] N.V., iv. 2. 27.

[3] The impossibility of certain knowledge is based by the Mādhyamikas on the ground, among others, that perception can be neither prior to nor posterior to nor simultaneous with the objects of sense. If it is prior, then it cannot be the result of the contact of sense with its object ; if it is posterior, then it cannot be said that the object of sense is established by perception. If perception were simultaneous with its object, then there need not be any order of succession in our cognitions, since there is no such order in their corresponding objects. Colour and smell can be perceived at the same time, which the Nyāya does not admit. What is true of perception applies to the other pramāṇas and their relation to prameya, or objects of knowledge as well. So these means of knowledge are both invalid and impossible. This objection against perceptual knowledge is set aside on the ground that the means of knowledge may precede its object as a drum precedes its sound, succeed as an illumination succeeds the sun, or are simultaneous with it as smoke synchronises with fire (N.B., ii. 1. 8–19).

[4] N.B., iv. 2. 33–34 and 37. [5] N.B., iv. 2. 26–37.

perceived; and this cannot be allowed, since perception is only of what is immediately present. To argue that the disappearance of the object synchronises with the emergence of perception, is of no avail, since we perceive the object as present and not as past. Even inference would be impossible [1] Again, cause and effect, being related to each other as container and contained, must exist at the same time. The fundamental character of that which really is, as distinct from that which is only imagined to be, is found in its independence of all relation to the experience of a subject. What exists at all, exists equally whether it is experienced or not. Experience is a relation of one-sided dependence. For it to exist, things are necessary; but for things to exist, no experience is necessary. Thus the Naiyāyika concludes that our ideas submit to an objective standard of facts relatively independent of the subject's will and purpose.[2] The existence of things does not depend on pramāṇas, though their existence as objects of cognition depends entirely on the operation of the pramāṇas.

Pramāṇas are so called because they give us pramā.[3] Udayana in his *Tātparyapariśuddhi* says: "Cognition of the real nature of things is pramā, and the means of such knowledge is pramāṇa." [4] What is the real nature (tattvam) of things? "It is nothing else but being or existence in the case of that which is and non-being or non-existence in the case of that which is not.[5] That is to say, when something that is, is apprehended as being or existent, so that it is apprehended as what it really is (yathābhūtam) and not as something of a contrary nature (aviparītam), then, that which is thus apprehended constitutes the true nature of the thing: and analogously when a nonentity is apprehended as such, *i.e.* as what is not, as something of a contrary nature

[1] See N.V., i. 1. 37; iii. 2. 14. Uddyotakara observes: "In the syllogism, 'sound is non-eternal, because it is a product like a pot,' pot, the instance, must contain non-eternality and productibility, and the former is posterior non-existence, the latter prior non-existence. How can the two coexist in a pot, if it is but momentary?"

[2] N.B.; Viśvanātha: *N.S. Vṛtti*, iv. 2. 26 ff.

[3] Pra, valid; mā, knowledge (iv. 2. 29).

[4] Yathārthānubhavaḥ pramā, tatsādhanaṁ ca pramāṇam.

[5] Sataś ca sadbhāvo 'sataś cāsadbhāvaḥ. N.B., i. 1. 1.

—then, that which is thus apprehended constitues the true nature of the thing." [1] Apramā, bhrama, or mithyājñāna, is the knowledge of a thing as it is not. It is that in which the thing is apprehended as what it is not,[2] as when we mistake the shell for silver. It is not mere absence of knowledge but positive error.[3]

Interrogation, doubt and the like have a place in the mental history of the individual, though the question of truth and falsity does not arise with regard to them. Judgment or assertion of a content, regardless of the person asserting, is the object of logical evaluation. All knowledge is of the form of judgment where we have in the subject the viśeṣya, or the qualified and in the predicate, the viśeṣaṇa, or the qualification. In the Nyāya the judgment is analysed, not so much into subject and predicate as into substantive and adjective, the substantive being that which is characterised and the adjective that which characterises.[4] All knowledge consists in comprehending the nature and qualities of objects. The subject tells us that a certain thing exists and the predicate determines further the nature of the given by specifying its properties. Where the determinations agree with the nature of the object, we have truth, or yathārtha.[5] Every subject has some character in reality, and thought distinguishes the substantive and the adjective, and asserts that the two are found united in the world of reality.

1 N.B. and N.V., i. 1. 1.

2 N.B., i. 1. 4.

3 N.B., iv. 2 1 ; iv. 2. 35.

4 Cp. " We find that in every proposition we are determining in thought the character of an object presented to thought to be thus determined. In the most fundamental sense, then, we may speak of a determinandum and a determinans ; the determinandum is defined as what is presented to be determined or characterised by thought or cognition ; the determinans as what does characterise or determine in thought that which is given to be determined " (W. E. Johnson : *Logic*, i. p. 9).

5 Tadvati tatprakārako'nubhavo yathārthaḥ, tadabhāvavati tatprakarako'nubhavo, 'yathārthaḥ (*Tarkasaṁgraha*, 35). Prakāra is the name of the predicate, while the quality of the real denoted by the predicate is called viśeṣaṇa. Prakāra refers to the cognition and viśeṣaṇa to the object. Annaṁ Bhaṭṭa raises the difficulty whether in the judgment, "jarness is in the jar," jarness can be regarded as substantive and " jar " as an adjective, and answers it by saying that the predicate need not always be an attribute but should only be related to the subject. Tadvati means tatsaṁbandhavati. See also N.V., iii. 2. 42.

Pramāṇas are said to give us a knowledge of objects as they really are.[1]

The relation between the object, jar, and our knowledge of the object, is not one of inherence (samavāya); for the knowledge pertaining to the object "jar" (ghaṭaviṣayaka-jñāna) is a quality (guṇa) of the self and not of the jar. Nor is it one of conjunction (saṁyoga), for this relation holds only between substances, while knowledge is a quality. Yet there must be some relation between the object and the knowledge of the object, in order that the particular judgment and not any other should result. Hence the only possible determining cause (niyāmaka) of our judgment is the nature of the jar itself (ghaṭasvarūpa). This relation is called svarūpasaṁbandha, which is defined in Bhīmācārya's *Nyāyakośa* as "the relation which must be held to exist in a case where determinate knowledge or judgment (viśiṣṭajñāna) could not have been effected by any other relation (samavāya or saṁyoga)."[2] It is a relation *sui generis* between the object and the cognition.[3] The effect of knowledge, as distinct from the act or the process of knowledge, is neither the physical object in itself nor a merely mental state, it is the essence, or svarūpa, or character, the what of the object known.[4] If the object of knowledge in outer perception is the physical existent itself, then there can be no possibility of error. Everyone's account of the object must be true. It is at variance with the facts to hold that when we think of the North Pole, it actually gets into

[1] Pramāṇasya sakalapadārthavyavasthāpakatvam (Viśvanātha's *N.S. Vṛtti*, i. 1. 1).

[2] Saṁbandhāntareṇa viśiṣṭapratītijananāyogyatvam. The obvious objection to making the jar itself a saṁbandha, namely, that the distinction between the relation and the related thing is obliterated, is met by the fact that the jar as the jar is not the saṁbandha, but only the jar as the object of knowledge.

[3] Avacchedakatva is a case of svarūpasambandha. In some cases it is the essential constitutive attribute of the individual which is non-existent. In the case of ghatābhāva or absence of the jar, jarness is avacchedaka. Where there are both simple and complex attributes, the simpler attribute is the avacchedaka. Where the attribute is coextensive with the instances, we have a case of anatiriktavṛttitva. The relation between knowledge and the object known is viṣayatā.

[4] Cp. "Our data are simply character complexes, essences, logical entities, which are irresistibly taken to be the characters of the existents perceived or otherwise known" (*Essays in Critical Realism*, p. 5).

our consciousness. If it is a mere mental state, then subjectivism engulfs us. The object of knowledge is neither a physical existent nor a psychological existent, but the svarūpa or the character of the object. In all knowledge we have this "what," essence or character which claims to be real. Even in dreams we have the "what," but we discover that the dream objects have no existence. Their implicit affirmation of reality is not justified. All knowledge is of svarūpas, or character-complexes, together with an implicit attribution of existence. This implied belief is occasionally mistaken. Whether the content belongs to the object or not is not made known by the act of knowledge itself. The validity of knowledge is not self-established (svataḥprāmāṇya).[1] The Nyāya holds that the validity of knowledge is not self-established, but is proved by something else (parataḥ pramāṇa). While the Sāṁkhya thinks that validity and invalidity are inherent in the cognition itself, the Mīmāṁsakas believe that validity is due to the cognition itself,[2] while invalidity is due to external causes, so that a cognition must be taken as true until it is proved to be otherwise. The Buddhists hold that invalidity belongs to all cognitions, and validity will have to be established by some other means. Against all these, the Naiyāyika contends that validity and invalidity are established by something independent of the cognition itself. If every cognition were self-evident, there would be no possibility of doubt.[3] So validity is determined by an appeal to facts. Suppose we perceive an object, we cannot be immediately certain that the object we perceive is of the same size and shape as it seems

[1] Cp. Drake: "All cognitive experiences are knowledge of, not possession of, the existent known (if it is an existent); their validity must be tested by other means than the intuition of the moment" (*Critical Realism*, p. 32).

[2] For them the truth of the Vedas is self-evident, requiring no external sanction to prove their claim to obedience, while for the Naiyāyikas the authoritativeness of the Vedas depends on God's authorship of them.

[4] *Siddhāntamuktāvali*, 136. "If the validity of a cognition were self-apprehended, then there would be no doubt in regard to a cognition produced by practice. For if, in this case, the cognition and its validity are cognized, how can there be doubt? If, on the other hand, the cognition is not cognised, then, in the absence of the knowledge of something possessing a quality, how can there be doubt? Hence the validity of cognition is a matter of inference (anumeyam)."

to have. We perceive that the sun is moving while it does not. So perception or immediate knowledge of an object does not carry with it an assurance of its own validity. The validity of our knowledge can only be arrived at by a mediate process of reflection.[1] What is true of perception is also true of knowledge gained through other means.

The Nyāya considers a number of objections to this theory. How can a pramāṇa which gives us knowledge of an object, itself become an object of another pramāṇa? Just as a balance is an instrument when it weighs a thing but is an object when it is itself weighed in another balance, so also a means of knowledge is an instrument when it establishes an object, but an object when it is itself to be established. Vātsyāyana says: " buddhi, or apprehension, is pramāṇa, or the means of cognising things; it is prameya when it is itself cognised." [2] If it is said that a means of knowledge does not require another means of knowledge for its establishment, but is self-established, then even the object of knowledge may be thus self-established, and pramāṇas become superfluous. It is objected that if the validity of knowledge is apprehended by some other knowledge, and if the validity of the latter is proved by some other, then we are led to an infinite regress.[3] If we stop anywhere in the middle, the pramāṇa is not proved. The Naiyāyika does not regard this as a serious objection since it is purely theoretical. For all practical purposes, we assume the validity of

---

[1] *Tarkabhāṣa* says: " The cognition is apprehended by sense-perception . . . while its validity is apprehended by means of inference. A man seeking for water has the perception of water. The exertion he puts forth is either fruitful or not. From the fruitulness of the cognition its validity is inferred, for that which is not valid does not give rise to fruitful exertion."

[2] N.B., ii. 1. 16. Vātsyāyana uses the illustration of lamplight, which is said to illumine itself and other objects. " In the case of the lamplight, it is found that while it is itself visible it is also the means by which we see other visible things, and thus it comes to be called the object or the means of cognition according to circumstances " (N.B., ii. 1. 19). Nāgārjuna objects that a lamp cannot illumine itself, since there is no darkness in it. It illumines objects by removing the darkness that covers them (*Mādhyamika Karikā*, vii). Vātsyāyana's view is not to be confused with the Vedāntic position of the self-evident character of the pramāṇas. The same pramāṇa does not reveal the object as well as its own validity. Uddyotakara explains that the lamplight is pramāṇa in relation to objects, while it is itself established by another perception by means of its contact with the optic nerve, so that one pramāṇa may be established by another (N.V., ii. 1. 19). See also N.V.T.T., ii. 1. 19.

[3] This objection is identical with Nāgārjuna's in *Vigrahavyāvartanī Kārikā*. See *History of Indian Logic*, p. 257. See also N.B., ii. 1. 17–18. Śrī Harṣa quotes Dharmakīrti, the Buddhist logician, to the effect, " For him who does not accept the cognition as directly cognised by itself the cognition of the thing cannot be established." See *Khaṇḍana*, i. 3.

pramāṇas and need not go about validating one pramāṇa by another endlessly.[1] In the case of clear cognitions, as when we see a fruit in our hand, we have no doubt about the validity of the cognition. We have certain knowledge of the object through one cognition. In the case of doubtful cognitions we seek the aid of further cognitions to determine the validity of the present one, and when we come across a perfectly valid cognition, we cease to search. There are certain pramāṇas which require a knowledge of themselves to prove their objects and lead to practical action; and there are others which prove their objects without any knowledge of themselves. Smoke must be known before it can lead to a knowledge of fire, but sense-organs give us a knowledge of objects even when they are not themselves perceived or known. We may know sense-organs by other means, but that knowledge is unnecessary.

The Naiyāyika holds that we cannot straightaway know whether our cognitions correspond to reality or not. We have to infer this correspondence from its capacity to lead to successful action. All knowledge is an incitement to action. It tells us that the object is desirable or undesirable or neither. The self is not a purely passive spectator interested in the mere contemplation of things. It is anxious to attain desirable objects and avoid undesirable ones. Thinking is but an episode in the conduct of life. "Knowledge is apprehension exciting desire and leading to action."[2] The Naiyāyika agrees with the school of Pragmatists in his view that knowledge has its basis in the vital needs of human nature, and issues in a volitional reaction. The agreement of our ideas with objects can be ascertained through their capacity to lead to successful action (pravṛttisāmarthyam).[3] It is therefore obvious that the relation of ideas to objects is one of correspondence and not necessarily resemblance. The Naiyāyika makes the truth of our ideas depend on their relations to facts, and holds that the relation is one of agreement or correspondence, which we infer from the working of ideas.[4]

[1] N.V.T.T., ii. 1. 19.

[2] N.B., i. 1. 2.

[3] N.S., i. 1. 17 See also N.B. and N.V., i. 1 1, and *Kusumāñjali*, iii. 18.

[4] Cp. the distinction between resemblance and correspondence, the copy and the picture theories of truth, in McTaggart's *The Nature of Existence*, ii. It is interesting to notice that the Critical Realists, whose analysis of knowledge is similar to that of the Nyāya, adopt the same device to overcome this difficulty. The question whether we have any right to believe in the existence of physical objects is answered thus: "Our instinctive (and practically inevitable) belief in the existence of the physical world about

Strictly speaking, the idea is said to be true if it leads to the perceptions demanded by the idea, and enables us to act on the environment successfully. According to the Prāmāṇyavada of *Tattvacintāmaṇi*, the validity of cognitions is established through inference. When we see a horse, we have first of all a cognition of the form, " This is a horse," followed by a vague idea, " I have seen a horse " ; and it is when one goes near it and actually feels it, that he infers the validity of his cognition ; and if the expected perceptions do not arise, he infers that the cognition is mistaken. We see water and go near it, and if it answers our needs we call our perception of water valid, since what is not true does not induce successful activity.[1] When our desires are met, we become cognisant of the validity of our knowledge. Thus from consequences we infer causes. This theory of truth is an induction from positive instances of the successful leading of valid knowledge and negative instances of the unsuccessful leading of invalid knowledge.

This workability is only the test of truth and not its content. Some advocates of pragmatism are, however, of the opinion that the practical effects are the whole of truth, a view which has the support of Buddhist logicians. The latter hold that " right knowledge is uncontradicted knowledge. That which enables us to attain the object observed is uncontradicted knowledge." [2] To attain the object is to act successfully in regard to it and understand its nature.[3]

us is pragmatically justifiable. This realm of appearance (*i.e.* what appears, what is given) might conceivably be merely the visions of a mind in an empty world. But we instinctively feel these appearances to be the characters of real objects. We react to them as if they had an existence of their own, even when we are asleep or forgetting them. We find that this belief, those reactions *work* " (*Essays in Critical Realism*, p. 6).

[1] Pūrvotpannaṁ jalajñānam pramā, saphalapravṛttijanakatvāt ; yan naivaṁ tan naivaṁ yathā apramā (Annaṁ Bhaṭṭa's *Dīpikā*, 63).

[2] Dharmottara: *Nyāyabinduṭīkā*, i. " Avisaṁvādakaṁ jñānaṁ samyagjñānam . . . pradarśitam artham prāpayan saṁvādaka ucyate."

[3] Pravartakatvam eva prāpakatvam . . . pravartakatvam api pravṛttiviṣayapravartakatvam eva. Dharmottara thinks that the object attained is not identical with the object known, though they belong to the same series. Though the Buddhists cannot admit the Nyāya view of the relation of facts and ideas, they accept arthasiddhi, or attainment of the object, or practical efficiency (arthakriyāsāmarthyam) as the test of truth, and indulge in vague phrases of similarity of ideas to objects as arthasārūpyam asya pramāṇam (*Nyāyabindu*, i. 1).

For the Naiyāyika, truth is not mere workability, though it is known by it. Truth is prior to verification. A judgment is true, not because it is verified; but it is verified because it is true. Several objections to this theory are considered by the Naiyāyika. We cannot be sure that our desires are realised. Cases of illusory satisfaction are not unheard of. In dreams we have instances of apparent satisfaction, but that does not mean that dream states are to be regarded as valid. The Naiyāyika answers that what counts is not the mere feeling of successful activity, but the feeling of a normal healthy mind, which must support past experiences of successful activity. It is neither the vividness of the mental state nor the feeling of satisfaction, but conformity with experience as a whole. The objects of dreams cannot be fitted into the space-time framework of experience, and are therefore imaginary.

Prior to fruition, our knowledge cannot be ascertained to be valid. So we cannot have that confidence without which no endeavour is possible. A valid knowledge of objects is the precondition of successful activity, and prior to successful activity we cannot have true knowledge of objects.[1] Uddyotakara urges that this question of the relative priority of activity and knowledge is meaningless, in view of the beginninglessness of the world. Besides, knowledge of the object, and not of the validity of knowledge, is necessary for action. So far as familiar objects are concerned, the difficulty does not arise. In situations presenting novel features, where a mere application of precedents is insufficient, we experiment even with inadequate knowledge. We act, sometimes, to verify hypotheses. Life generally moves on the basis of assumptions, and it is not possible to weigh every suggested line of action in a fine balance of logic before acting on it. Pressure of practical necessities compels us to act on ideas even when their evidence is incomplete. Objects of religious belief determine our action, even though they lie beyond the range of reason. The Naiyāyika admits that there are cases where complete verification is not possible. Whether we shall attain heaven or not through the performance of agnihotra cannot be ascertained until we die. He that will act only when he can fully comprehend, must have either a very long head or a very short life.

---

[1] In this difficulty, Dharmottara makes a distinction between the right knowledge which is the immediate antecedent of attainment (arthakriyānirbhāsam) and that which leads to attainment through certain intermediate stages (arthakriyāsamarthe ca pravartakam). The first leads directly to action and cannot be an object of inquiry. See Uddyotakara and Vācaspati on i. 1. 1.

Later Naiyāyikas, like Vācaspati and Udayana, admit the self-evident character (svataḥprāmāṇyam) of some forms of valid knowledge. Inference free from all error and inconsistency and comparison (upamāna) based on essential resemblance are, according to Vācaspati, of self-evident validity, since there is rational necessity binding the cognition and the objects. In the case of sense-perception and verbal testimony, we cannot be equally certain.[1] Udayana admits Vācaspati's contention, and argues that besides inference and comparison, self-consciousness (anuvyavasāya) and internal as well as external perception of mere existence (dharmijñāna) possess self-evident validity.[2]

XIX

Error

Pramā, or valid knowledge, is distinguished from doubt (saṁśaya) and erroneous knowledge (viparyaya), where the ideas do not lead to successful action. Illusions and hallucinations fail to realise their ends, *i.e.* do not fulfil the expectations roused by them. We become conscious of error when the demands of our ideal past are not met by the present. We see a white object and take it to be silver, pick it up and find it to be a piece of shell. The new experience of the shell contradicts the expectation of silver. According to the Nyāya, all error is subjective. Vātsyāyana says: "What is set aside by true knowledge is the wrong apprehension, not the object."[3] Uddyotakara observes, taking the mirage as an instance, "the object all the while remains what it actually is: In regard to the flickering rays of the sun, when there arises the cognition of water, there is no error in the object: it is not that the rays are not rays, nor that the flickering is not flickering: the error lies in the cognition: as it is the cognition which instead of appearing as the cognition of the flickering rays, appears as the cognition of water, *i.e.* as the cognition of a thing as something which it is not."[4] Water is not absolutely non-existent, as a flower in the sky, but is not existent here and now, though it is imagined to exist. The rays are the cause of the illusion, though not the object of

[1] N.V.T.T., i. 1. 1.

[2] For a searching criticism of the Nyāya theory of truth, see *Khaṇḍana*, i. 13–14.

[3] N.B., iv. 2. 35.

[4] N.V., i. 1. 4.

the illusory perception of water. The realism of the Nyāya is here slightly modified, since it cannot account for the rise of illusions on the view that the world of experienced things with all their peculiar qualities exists independently of any relation to the experiencing subject. All erroneous cognition has some basis in reality. Vātsyāyana says: "No wrong apprehension is entirely baseless." [1] Error is the apprehension of an object as other than what it is. This view of anyathākhyāti is supported not only by the Nyāya but also by the Jaina logicians, and Kumārila.

The Naiyāyikas repudiate other theories of error,[2] which are more metaphysical than logical. The Sautrāntikas hold that in error there is a wrong superposition (āropa) of something which is a form of cognition (jñānākāra) on an external object. The Yogācāras do not admit extra-mental realities, yet for all practical purposes objects are admitted to be real, thanks to the tendencies of beginningless avidyā. Error consists in the superposition of the form of cognition on such objects.[3] We know that a cognition is erroneous, since it is sublated by another apprehension [4] and is devoid of practical efficiency (arthakriyākāritva). In the apprehension "this is silver," what is sublated is not silver but thisness (idantā), for, in the judgment a form of cognition "silver" is attributed to the "this"; in the sublative judgment "this is not silver," we sublate the "this" and not the "silver," for, to deny the latter is to deny its existence as a form of cognition. This is the view of Jñānākārakhyāti, according to which a form of cognition is wrongly referred to an external object. When the illusion is off, the external reference of silver is denied. This view is a corollary from the general metaphysical position of the Yogācāras, that there is no real difference between the self, the object of knowledge and knowledge. The Naiyāyika objects that, on the Yogācāra view, our cognitions should take the form of not "this is silver" but "I am silver," which is not the case. The Yogācāras cannot account for the distinction between truth and error. Subjectivism vitiates the whole position. Sweetness is in the honey and bitterness in the gall, and these qualities are not purely imaginary. The Nyāya formula, that error is the apprehension of a thing as what it is not, is applicable even on the Yogācāra view.[5] The Mādhyamikas hold the asatkhyāti view, that there is only non-being (asat), and that all perception of internal and external objects is erroneous. Non-existent silver manifests itself as existent, thanks to our cognitive mechanism. The

---

[1] N.B., iv. 2. 35.

[2] N.V.T.T., i. 1. 2.

[3] Anādyavidyāvāsanāropitamalīkam bāhyam, tatra jñānākārasyāropaḥ (*Bhāmatī*, i. 1. 1).

[4] *Bhāmatī*. Balavad bādhakapratyayavaśāt.

[5] Aniruddha on S.P.S, i. 42; *Nyāyamañjari*, p. 178

Naiyāyika objects that the incorrect apprehension of silver in a shell is produced not by nothing but by something in the piece of shell. If illusions are not excited by external stimuli and have no objective basis, we cannot distinguish one illusion from another. A non-existent thing cannot produce any effect. Erroneous cognitions cannot be traced to residual impressions which are not possible without real objects.[1] The Advaita adopts the anirvacanīyakhyāti. Whatever is manifested in a cognition is the object of that cognition. In the illusion of silver, silver appears to consciousness and is cognised; otherwise we shall have no reason to say that it is the illusion of silver and not of something else. But the silver so cognised is neither real nor unreal nor both real and unreal. If real, the cognition would be valid; if unreal, no activity will be induced; if both unreal and real, then two contradictory qualities will subsist in one and the same entity. Its nature is really indefinable or anirvacanīya. This inexplicable silver is produced through avidyā with the help of residual traces of the past cognitions of silver revived by the perception of the similarity of silver with the object with which the defective sense-organ is in contact. According to the Advaita, the illusion is a presentative cognition produced by an object actually present to consciousness. Silver is present at the time and place when and where the illusion is produced. Otherwise the illusion is not a presentation. This presented silver lasts as long as the illusion lasts. The Naiyāyika objects that, if the illusory object of silver is created in the absence of silver, then we could see anything of which we have an idea, and there could be no difference between image and percept. The Naiyāyika, however, congratulates himself on the fact that this view can be brought under his anyathākhyāti, since an indefinable object appears to consciousness as real.[2] Akhyāti (or vivekākhyāti), or non-discrimination, is the name given to Prābhākara's view of error. The difference between the piece of shell we see and the silver we imagine is not noticed, and we say "this is silver." The sublating cognition does not contradict the illusion, but simply recognises the distinction between the perceived and the remembered elements of the erroneous cognition. Against this view, the Nyāya urges that, as long as the illusion lasts, there is an actual presentation or perception of silver, and not a mere representation. We are conscious of silver as something presented to consciousness here and now, and not as something

---

[1] If illusions are not produced by external objects, then there is no difference between dreamless sleep and illusions except that in the latter we have consciousness and in the former not. *Prameyakamalamārtāṇḍa*, pp. 13 ff.; *Nyāyamañjari*, pp. 177–178.

[2] Rāmānuja, criticising the Advaita view, asks, What is the cause of the production of the indefinable silver at the time of the illusion? The cognition of silver cannot produce the object, since the latter is the cause of the former. It cannot be due to a defect in the sense-mechanism, since the sense-organs do not produce effects in the outward objects. Senses cause knowledge and not objects of knowledge.

perceived in the past and remembered now. Non-discrimination at the time of the illusion cannot induce action. The nature of obscuration of memory (smṛtipramoṣa) is not clearly stated. So it must be said that our immediate perceptual consciousness is itself infected with error.[1]

The Nyāya theory of anyathākhyāti is criticised by the other schools, notably the Advaita Vedānta.[2] Silver existing at some other time and place cannot be an object of perception, since it is not present to the senses. If it is said to be recalled to consciousness, then even in inference of fire from smoke, fire may be said to be recalled to consciousness, and there would be no need for inference at all. Again, to what does the otherwiseness (anyathātva) refer ? It cannot refer to the cognitive activity, where the substratum shell cannot impart its own form to a cognition which apprehends silver ; not to the result of the cognitive activity, since a presentation does not differ essentially whether it is valid or invalid ; not to the object of cognition which is the shell, which cannot identify itself with or transform itself into silver. If the shell is absolutely different from silver, then it cannot be identified with it ; if it is both different and not different, then even judgments like " the cow is shorthorned " would be illusory. If the shell actually transforms itself into silver, then the cognition of silver is not invalid and cannot be sublated. If it is said that it is a momentary transformation for the time the illusion lasts, then the perception of silver must be had even by those who do not suffer from any sense defects.[3]

XX

General Estimate of Nyaya Epistemology

The Nyāya view of knowledge as an attribute of the soul, which copies reality, seems to common sense too simple to need

[1] J.yasimhasūri mentions the theory of alaukikārthakhyāti, which Jayanta attributes to a Mīmāṁsaka. According to it, in the illusory cognition of silver, the object of the illusion is silver, which is different from the ordinary (laukika) silver. What serves our practical needs is laukika, and what does not is alaukika. Even alaukika silver induces some activity. The Naiyāyika asks whether we have any knowledge of alaukika silver and what becomes of it the moment we realise our mistake. Prabhācandra, in his *Prameyakamalamārtāṇḍa*, mentions prasiddhārthakhyāti as the view supported by Bhāskara and the followers of the Sāṁkhya. According to it, the object of illusory cognition is not a non-existent thing, but an existent object established by knowledge. Water is the object of the illusion of water, and when this illusory cognition is contradicted by the cognition of the rays of the sun, the latter cognition has for its object the rays of the sun. This view is not satisfactory, since it makes all cognitions valid (*Nyāyamañjari*, pp. 187–188 ; *Prameyakamalamārtāṇḍa*, i).

[2] See *Vedāntaparibhāṣā*, 1.

[3] *Vivaraṇaprameyasaṁgraha*, p. 33.

any justification ; yet this apparently innocent view involves assumptions that have been uncritically accepted. In its hostility to Buddhist subjectivism the Nyāya insists that things are the ground of logical truth, that the external world exists apart from our knowledge of it and determines that knowledge, that our ideas correspond to things. It divides the real into two compartments of subjects and objects, and thus transforms the ordinary assumptions of common sense into a metaphysical theory which is inadequate to the facts of consciousness as well as the demands of logic. The main assumptions which vitiate the epistemology of the Nyāya are : (1) that self and not-self are sharply separated from one another, (2) that consciousness is the result of the causal action of the not-self on the self, (3) that knowledge is a property of the self. In spite of these metaphysical prejudices, the Nyāya contains fruitful suggestions by which its defects may be overcome. So long as the Nyāya gives an account of what is immediately experienced in the act of knowledge, it is on secure ground ; but when it tries to offer a metaphysical explanation, in terms which take us behind the ultimate fact of knowledge, it is open to criticism. That we have a direct awareness of the world which is not a mere putting together of abstract particulars but a complex cosmos with terms and relations, particulars and universals, that our ideas have working value, are views warranted by experience. The fundamental mistake of the Nyāya is the mistake of Locke, and other empirical thinkers who regard the individual as one natural unit and the world as another. This mechanical view, however legitimate for the limited purposes of daily life and psychology, is not ultimately defensible. The problem for logic is not so much the genesis of knowledge as its nature. We cannot hope to determine the nature of knowledge by trying to go behind it and observe the manner of its coming to be. When the Naiyāyika regards consciousness as a product or a resultant, he is trying to get behind the process of knowing.

If the self and the not-self are sharply separated from one another, and if consciousness is but the result of the causal action of the not-self on the self, as Locke and Descartes, Hume and Kant thought, then all the contents of consciousness are purely subjective states of the knowing individual. Events of the world of not-self cannot form part of the knowledge which belongs to the self; and if knowledge reproduces reality, it can only contain copies of real events and not the events themselves. When we divide the subject from the object, the question of building the bridge from the one to the other becomes difficult. Either we have to hold that the object is the creation of the subject or that there is no object at all. Whether we say that the object is taken into consciousness, or is mirrored in it, or represented by a sketch or an outline, whatever view of the relation of knowledge to object we may adopt, it becomes impossible for us to be certain that the world is as we perceive it. So long as the two are external to each other, as one piece of matter is external to another, we can never be sure that our ideas correctly represent objects, or that they represent objects at all. We cannot compare our cognitions with reality, since the latter is external to thought. Nothing but thought itself is known directly, and we cannot compare the thought with the real, since only one of the terms is given, and the act of comparison implies that both the terms should be given. If anything can compare the idea on the one side and the object on the other, it must be consciousness[1]; but such a consciousness must include both the idea and the object.

If truth means agreement of ideas with reality, and if reality is defined as that which is external to thought, what is not and cannot be in thought or made up of thought, then truth-seeking is a wild-goose chase. Thought seeks an end which could never conceivably be attained, nay, an end of which no clear notion could be formed. The Naiyāyika faces the conclusion that the goal of thought, *i.e.* the attainment of truth, cannot be directly realised. He holds that for a finite mind the goal of thought is beyond attainment. We have to be content with the lower ideal of acquiring confidence in the working value of our ideas. Serviceability or

[1] Professor Alexander holds that consciousness and reality are independent things, and the relation between them is that of compresence. The two happen to be together, though they are separate in the world. But what is the nature of this consciousness? Consciousness is always of something, and it does not tell us about the existence of an object outside and independent of it.

practical efficiency generates this feeling of confidence. This workability does not, however, justify the Nyāya assumption that ideas work because they are in accord with reality.[1] The Buddhist logicians who adopt the same test of truth derive a different conclusion from it; and it must be said that the Buddhist view is more logical. The content of truth is not correspondence of knowledge with objects which are but ideal, but verification by experience.[2] Ideas prompt us to activity, and when we realise our desires their claim to truth is granted. Our dreams are declared to be illusory, since activities based on them fail to achieve the ends. Suppose we dream something, dig up our field and light on a treasure, then our dream is true, whether or not it accords with reality. It is clear that the best grounded and the most certain of our knowledge has a possibility of error. No belief of ours is so firmly grounded that there does not remain at least a bare chance of its being false. While it is possible to lead some sort of existence, depending on this pragmatic test, we cannot have complete satisfaction. What serves one need may not serve another; and we are interested in the vital logical need to know reality, which cannot be met The Nyāya, which is anxious to save us from Buddhist subjectivism, has not provided us with a more satisfactory view of reality. When the patent fact of our knowledge of the external world is not accounted for by the Nyāya theory, it must return upon its initial assumptions and examine them in the light of the analysis of the fact of knowledge itself.

While it is quite true that things may be real without being consciously present to my or your experience and do not begin to exist when you or I become aware of them, still it cannot be said that real existence is independent of all experience. The relation between knowledge and its object is called in Nyāya the svarūpa-sambandha. The object apprehended determines the knowing process. Cognition is

[1] Cp. Broad: "It does not in the least matter to science what is the *inner nature* of a term, provided it will do the work that is required of it If we can give a definition of points which will make them fulfil a certain pair of conditions, it will not matter though points themselves should turn out to be entities of a very different kind from what we had supposed them to be" (*Scientific Thought*, p. 39).

[2] *Nyāyabindu*, p. 103; and *Nyāyabinduṭīkā*, p. 6.

consciousness of an object.[1] Madhusūdana Sarasvatī[2] quotes from Udayana that "Cognitions by themselves formless are specified only by their objects. That is to say, the objects are the only specifications of cognitions." All cognitions are qualified or characterised by certain things as "This is an inkstand." "That is a tablecloth." If the object known is entirely outside the process, then the correspondence notion of truth will have to be adopted; but its svarūpa is said to be within the process, though the object-in-itself is not identical with the knowledge of it. According to this view, knowledge does not produce objects; nor does it correspond to them, but it apprehends them. It is therefore wrong to hold that the object lies outside the boundaries of knowledge, and what can be known of it is either its effect or its copy in the consciousness of the subject. Whether we perceive, conceive or remember an outer object or an inner state, what we perceive, conceive or remember is the object itself, which is independent of the knowledge process. The Nyāya theory of our immediate and direct awareness of reality is inconsistent with its other assumption, that subject and object are substances which are isolated from one another. Nothing stands between the cognising subject and the cognised object. The two, subject and object, are inseparably connected. One cannot be reduced to the other. The Nyāya is right in repudiating subjectivism, that the objects are the creations of the subject's fancy. The object is not brought into being by the subject's knowing process. Even universal relations are said to be given to and not created by the subject. Sense-data do not appear as disconnected particles, but as possessed of certain properties and qualities. Only, according to later Nyāya, the universal or the basis of identity is known through non-sensuous (alaukika) mental functioning. A large part of the experiences that enter into our knowledge is non-sensuous in character. The constraining power of reality is admitted by the Naiyāyika. The necessity of our experience is not imposed by the subject, but is due to the necessity of the world. The real is not intrinsically divided into the two, selves and the world. The prerequisite of all thinking is the undivided

[1] N.B., iv. 2. 29. [2] *Advaitasiddhi*, i. 20.

reality from which subject and object are derived by a process of abstraction. It is true that abstractions play a large part in our lives, but yet reality in itself, on which our theory of knowledge should take its stand, the primary ontological fact, is consciousness (caitanya). A metaphysical investigation of the nature and conditions of knowledge reveals to us the universality of consciousness. It is the basis and creator of all things, and it is risky to represent consciousness in a semi-materialised image. It is not a compound, though our world may be concrete enough. Our analysis into selves and objects is relative to our practical needs; but this complex cosmos is based on a reality which is intrinsically undivided. The real when thought out assumes this aspect. It is not possible for us to give an intellectual account of reality apart from intellectual discrimination; yet our ideas deal with a reality to which no one of our distinctions is essential. The only absolute, then, is the undivided reality of consciousness, which the Naiyāyika ignores in favour of a plurality of souls and material objects.

While reality is caitanya, or consciousness, truth, which logicians aim at, is something different, since logic assumes the distinction between subject and object, and its impulse can be satisfied only if the world of selves and objects is organised into a coherent whole. The Nyāya, in spite of its allegiance to the correspondence notion, grasps the more adequate character of the coherence theory. It regards all forms of knowledge as parts of one whole, each having its function through its place in the whole, and having no justification beyond what it can claim as part of that whole. The validity of any pramāṇa is established through other pramāṇas.[1] The different kinds of knowledge are interrelated. All knowledge has mediate necessity. When the Naiyāyika warns us against the feeling of satisfaction which dreamers and lunatics

[1] We perceive an object, and the validity of this perceptioni s established through inference and perception of the validity of the factors involved in it—sense-organs, objects, contact between the two, and the resulting act of cognition. The sense-organ is established by inference as the recipient of one class of external stimuli; objects are established by sense-perception; contact is inferred from the non-perception of distinctions; and the resulting act of cognition is perceived by the self through its contact with manas and intimate relation with the cognition (N B, ii. 1. 19).

have, and asks us to take into account the feeling of a normal healthy-minded individual, he is surrendering his theory of correspondence. The normal individual is not he who has the support of the majority. Some illusions may be normal in this sense, but they are not therefore true. The social factor simply distinguishes purely imaginary experiences from those which have more objectivity about them. By comparing our observations with those of others, we can get a working certainty, sufficient for all ordinary purposes. What others perceive no less than ourselves, what is perceived by us identically at different places and times, may be looked upon as true and real. The demands of science require us to check our ordinary perceptions. Though we perceive the movement of the sun across the sky, science tells us that the earth revolves round the sun. More elementary and disconnected experiences are to be interpreted in the light of more unified and systematised experiences. The standard is set by the latter. Truth depends not so much on the object as on its capacity to fit into the space-time scheme. The structure of reality must be capable of accommodating the truth. It is assumed that the space-time continuity has a systematic nature. The Naiyāyika who adopts the pragmatic test is bound to hold that our views of reality are relative to our purposes. Knowledge of an object is just its meaning for our present needs. In practical life we are not concerned about the essences of objects but only their meaning for us. To say that for all men stones are hard and fires are hot means that these objects have the same meaning for us. Practically justified correspondence is the Naiyāyika's meaning of truth, and ever so many illusions normal to all individuals and the race are true by this criterion. Nor is this test capable of use with regard to events in the past and the future. Though our truths are relative, they are not all of equal value. The highest truth is that which satisfies the vital logical need of understanding the world as a whole. The ideal experience which comprehends the nature of reality as it is, including both the finite subjects and the environment, is the absolute standard of truth. Not in the sense that many men have attained to it, but in the sense that when one attains the logical view, he will realise it as the truth. True normality cannot be ascertained by a counting of heads.[1] The mere fact that the large majority of men believe in the pluralistic view does not indicate anything else than the practical value of that conception. Truth and untruth are not questions to be decided by a plebiscite. If the majority of men have an attack of jaundice, the nature of truth does not alter. Truth is that which reveals itself to those who have sounded the depths of experience. The Naiyāyika admits the higher validity of ārṣajñāna, or the wisdom of the seers. He asks us to judge our experiences by the achievement of individuals who have better comprehended the nature of reality. Truth, like goodness and beauty, is an achievement of the individual mind, and in another sense it is a revelation to the human mind of a world unrealised as yet but awaiting realisation in and through a fuller experience. We do not so much construct truth as find it. Yet the Naiyāyika again and again slips into the point of view of the psychologist who assumes that souls and matter are conditions which bring about knowledge. The relativity of knowledge to our ends does not confirm the absolute division between subject and object which the Nyāya assumes. It implies faith in the demands of our nature and in the possibility of their satisfaction. That the nature of the real is adapted to the needs of human action, shows the essential interrelatedness of the two aspects of reality, minds and their environment. The manifest pluralism and the unrelatedness of things is only apparent. The conception of a plurality of reals externally related to one another must yield place to the idea of the essential unity of the world.

In accordance with the implications of the instrumental and relative character of all thought, the Naiyāyika should admit the relative nature of the ideal of truth itself. Logical truth, which is reality conceived as a system of interrelated

[1] Cp. " Does the truth of the fact that a blind man has missed the perfect development of what should be normal about his eyesight depend for its proof upon the fact that a larger number of men are not blind ? The very first creature which suddenly groped into the possession of its eyesight had the right to assert that light was a reality. In the human world there may be very few who have their spiritual eyes open, but in spite of the numerical preponderance of those who cannot see, their want of vision must not be cited as an evidence of the negation of light " (Rabindranath Tagore) See Foreword in Radhakrishnan's *Philosophy of the Upaniṣads*.

selves and objects, is relative to the logical interest, though it is very much more satisfactory than the view which regards the universe as a plurality of independent reals. Truth is reality taken as ideal, regarded as an intelligible system. Our judgments and inferences aim at the comprehension of the whole. According to the degree in which they succeed and fail in the endeavours, their place in the body of knowledge is determined. All logical truth is relative in the sense that the individual is a fragment of reality handling another fragment loosened from its context, and it is impossible, so long as one occupies the logical standpoint, to grasp reality in itself. Our thought is forced to distinguish and select, and we are obliged to use the pragmatic test. The widest thought is compelled to leave out the existence of itself, which in reality it must include. All knowledge is an abstraction from the real. It is an ideal reconstruction of the absolute.[1]

The Nyāya analysis of perception and its view of svarūpa-saṁbandha support the doctrine of the presence in knowledge of reality. The distinction of indeterminate and determinate perception suggests the view of the relativity of our knowledge to our interests. In some stages we have but an undiscriminating acquaintance with reality, and in others a closer grasp of its complexity. The acceptance of the pragmatic test of practical utility confirms the view of the relativity of our knowledge to our limited standpoints. While the conception of reality as made up of two unlike spheres may be legitimate and useful for the purposes of psychology, it has to be transcended when we arrive at the logical point of view. As we have shown, the Nyāya is aware that it is only the coherence conception of truth that can be adopted in logic. The natural conclusion from this whole doctrine of relativity is that even this logical ideal of a complex cosmos with interrelated members cannot be regarded as absolute. The Nyāya did not choose to face this ultimate problem. But its theory of knowledge, when consistently carried out, leads clearly to the position

[1] Cp. Bradley: "That the glory of this world in the end is appearance leaves the world more glorious, if we feel it is a show of some fuller splendour; but the sensuous curtain is a deception and a cheat, if it hides some colourless movement of atoms, some spectral woof of impalpable abstractions, or unearthly ballet of bloodless categories" (*Logic*, vol. ii, p. 591).

that the distinctions of subject and object arise within the fact of knowledge or experience, which alone is the absolute or the ultimate fact behind which we cannot go.

XXI

The World of Nature

The Nyāya accepts the metaphysics of the Vaiśeṣika, and regards the world of nature as a composite of eternal, unalterable, causeless atoms, existing independently of our thoughts. The physical conceptions of the Nyāya are almost the same as those of the Vaiśeṣika.

It will, however, be of interest to know the way in which the Nyāya answers the objections of the rival schools. The problem of time offers peculiar difficulties. Some Naiyāyikas hold that time is a form of experience and is perceived by the sense-organs as a qualification of objects of perception. For example, Rāmakṛṣṇādhvarin, the author of *Śikhāmaṇi*, says that since we cognise objects as existing at present, time also may be said to be perceived. In the perception of the jar as existing at present (idānīm ghaṭo vartate), present time also enters into the perception of the object. Every object is perceived as existing in time, though time is never perceived by itself.[1] Temporal relations are dependent on the terms related. There is no sooner or later, before or after, apart from events and actions. Time is perceived as a qualification of objects, and is therefore a substantive reality.[2]

The Mādhyamika theory, that there is no present time (vartamānakāla) apart from the past and the future, is examined by Vātsyāyana.[3] The past is defined as that which precedes the present, and the future as that which succeeds it. But the present has no meaning apart from the past and the future. Vātsyāyana replies that all this is due to a confusion between time and space. The objector argues that when the object falls, we have the time taken up by its traversing a certain distance and the time that will be taken up by it in traversing the remaining distance, and there is no intervening distance which the object can be said to traverse at the present time. Space traversed gives the idea of past time, space to be traversed that of the future, and there is no third space which could give rise to the present time.[4] But, says Vātsyāyana, " time, or kāla, is not manifested by space (adhvā) but by action (kriyā)." " We have the con-

---

[1] *Nyāyamañjari*, p. 130.
[2] *Ibid.*, p. 137.
[3] N.B., ii. 1. 39–ii. 1. 43. See I.P., p. 649.
[4] N.B., ii. 1. 39.

ception of time (as past) when the action of falling has ceased. . . . When the same action is going to happen, we have the conception of time as future ; and lastly, when the action of the thing is perceived as going on at the time, we have the conception of present time. In the circumstances, if a person were never to perceive the action as 'going on,' at the time, what could he conceive of as having ceased or as going to happen ? . . . At both the points of time (past and future) the object is devoid of action ; whereas, when we have the idea that the thing is falling down, the object is actually connected with the action ; so that what the present time apprehends is the actual existing connection of the object and the action, and thus it is only on the basis of this (existing connection and the time indicated by it) that we could have the conception of the other two points of time ; which latter, for this reason, would not be conceivable, if the present time did not exist."[1] Again, perceptions arise in connection with things which are present in time. There cannot be perception, if there is not present time. The present therefore is not a mere mathematical point but a tract of time with a certain duration, "a slab of time with temporal thickness."[2]

Vātsyāyana argues against several theories of the origin and nature of the world.[3] He criticises the idea of momentariness (kṣaṇikavāda) on the ground that we cannot be certain that an entity will be replaced by another after the lapse of a moment, and there must be a connecting link between the origination of an entity and its cessation. We may admit the truth of momentariness where it is perceived but not where it is not perceived, as in stones, etc.[4] From the successive cognitions we have of objects, their continued existence follows. The theory that all is non-being is rejected on the ground, that if everything is non-being, there cannot be any aggregates.[5] Nor can all things be said to be relative to one another. If long and short are interdependent, then neither of them can be established in the absence of the other. If neither of them is self-existent, it will be impossible to establish their interrelation.[6] The doctrine of impermanence (anityatā) is based on the facts of the production and destruction of things. The Naiyāyika argues that there are things like atoms, ākāśa, time and space, and some qualities of these which are neither produced nor destroyed.[7] The

---

1 N.B., ii. 1. 40.

2 Whitehead : *The Principle of Relativity*, p. 7.

3 N.B., iv. 2. 31–33, and iv. 2. 26–27.

4 N.B., iii. 2. 11. See also iii. 2. 12–13.

5 N.B., iv. 1. 37–40. See also iv. 2. 26–27, 31–33.

6 " If there is no such thing as the character (or individuality) of things, why do we not have the relative notions of length and shortness in regard to two equal atoms or any two objects of equal size ? . . . What relativity (apekṣā) means is that when we perceive two things it becomes possible for us to perceive the preponderance of one over the other " (N.B., iv. 1. 40).

7 N.B., iv. 1. 25–28.

opposite view that all things are permanent is equally defective, since some things we perceive are produced and destroyed. Composite substances are liable to production and destruction.[1] Vātsyāyana considers also the theory of the absolute diversity of things (sarvapṛthaktvavāda).[2] The Naiyāyika holds that a whole is not a mere aggregate of its parts, but is something over and above the parts to which it stands in the peculiar relation of samavāya (inherence). Vātsyāyana repudiates the Buddhist view[3] that the whole is nothing but the aggregate of parts, and that the relation is a myth.[4]

The world cannot be produced by abhāva, or non-existence. The supporters of the abhāva hypothesis argue that no effect arises until the cause is destroyed. For the sprout to arise, the seed must be destroyed. Vātsyāyana argues against this view that the cause which is said to destroy cannot come into existence after the destruction, and there is no production out of things destroyed. If the destruction, of the seed were the cause of the rise of the sprout, then the latter must appear at the very moment the seed is broken to pieces. As a matter of fact, the sprout appears only when the disruption of the seed is followed by a fresh composite formed out of its particles. So the sprout is due not to abhāva but a rearrangement of seed particles.[5] The view that the world is the result of chance is examined and rejected. The law of causality cannot be denied without stultifying all experience.[6]

XXII

The Individual Self and Its Destiny

According to the Nyāya, the universe has certain elements which are not corporeal. These are our cognitions, desires, aversions, volitions, and the feelings of pleasure and pain.[7] All these modes of consciousness are transitory, and so are not themselves to be identified with substances. They are viewed as qualities of the substance called the soul.

The soul is a real substantive being, having for its qualities desire, aversion, volition, pleasure, pain and cognition As a

[1] N.B., iv. 1. 29–33. [2] N.B., iv. 1. 34–36.

[3] See *Avayavanirākaraṇa* of the Buddhist Aśoka, who lived about the close of the ninth century A.D.

[4] Vātsyāyana's explanation of *Saṁkhyaikāntavāda* is not clear. It may possibly refer to some doctrine as Pythagoras's theory of numbers.

[5] N.B., iv. 1. 14–18. [6] N.B., iv. 1. 22–24.

[7] If pleasure, pain, desire and aversion are regarded as modes of feeling, we have the three modes of consciousness, knowledge, feeling and will.

rule the Naiyāyika proves the existence of the self by means of inference, though scriptural evidence is adduced in confirmation.[1] Uddyotakara holds that the reality of the self is apprehended by means of perception also. According to him the object of the notion of " I " is the soul.[2] The recognition of the different cognitions as mine proves the continued persistence of the soul.[3] " When a man is desirous of knowing or understanding (a certain thing) at first, he reflects as to what this may be and comes to know it " this is so-and-so." This knowing of the thing is by the same agent to whom belongs the previous desire to know and the subsequent reflection; so this knowledge becomes an indication of the presence of the common agent in the shape of the soul."[4] We remember things which we previously cognised.[5] When one perceives an object, is attracted by it, struggles to obtain it, it is one soul that is the basis of these different activities.[6] If our mental life has at each instant a unique qualitative character which constitutes it a moment in the concrete history of an individual subject, it is because it belongs to this self and not to another. Uddyotakara says: " For one who denies a soul, every cognition must be distinct with a distinct object of its own; and no cognition or recollection would ever be possible."[7] As a mere complex of sensational and affectional elements, no state of consciousness can be distinguished as mine or another's. The experience of another is not *my* experience, for my self is different from his self. All our mental states, such as remembrance, recognition, awareness of the relative persistence of the self, volition or

1 N.S., i. 1. 10.

2 N.V., iii. 1. 1. The Vaiśeṣika makes the self an object of yogic perception (V.S., ix. 1. 11; *Nyāyakandalī*, p. 196).

3 N.B. and N.V., i. 1. 10.

4 N.B., i. 1. 10.

5 N.B., iii. 1. 14; also iii. 1. 7–11.

6 Ekakartṛkatvaṁ jñānecchāpravṛttīnāṁ samānāśrayatvam (N.B., iii. 2. 34).

7 N.V., i. 1. 10. Vācaspati observes: " If in the absence of the soul the recollection and fusion of cognitions were possible under the hypothesis of every cognition setting up and forming a factor in a series of cognitions, then every cognition would recall and fuse with every other cognition of the same series." This statement of Vācaspati is a paraphrase of Vātsyāyana's remark that " the recognition of one cognition by another cognition would be as possible as the recognition by one body of the experiences of another body " (N.B., i. 1. 10).

the assertion of self, sympathy or consciousness of relation to other selves, all these imply the reality of a self.

The materialist view that consciousness is a property of the body is easily refuted. If it were a property of the body, it would exist in the various parts of the body and its material constituents.[1] If the latter were also conscious, then we have to regard the individual consciousness as the combination of several consciousnesses produced by the different constituents. If body has consciousness, then all matter must have it, since it is of the same nature as the body. If beyond the body there is no soul, then the moral law would seem to be without any significance.[2] Since the body is changing from moment to moment, no sin can pursue us in subsequent lives. If consciousness is the essential property of the body, then it can never lose its essence, and it should be impossible for us to find bodies devoid of consciousness, as we do in corpses. Consciousness is not found in states of trance. It is not a natural quality of the body, since it does not last as long as the body lasts, as colour and the like do.[3] If it were an accidental property of the body, then its cause is something else than the body itself. Again, consciousness cannot be the property of that of which one is conscious but of that which is conscious. If consciousness is a property of the body, then it must be capable of being perceived by others also.[4] Body is not even an auxiliary of consciousness in view of certain familiar experiences. At best it is an instrument or aid for the expression of consciousness. Body is defined as "the vehicle of actions, sense-organs and objects."[5] The soul exerts itself to gain or get rid of objects by means of the body, which is the seat of the senses, mind and sentiments. We cannot identify the body with either consciousness or the self which possesses it. Nor can we identify consciousness with the vital processes. Vitality is a name for a particular relation of the self to the body.[6]

The self is not the senses but what controls them, and

[1] See *Sāṁkhya Sūtra*, iii. 20–21, and Vijñānabhikṣu and Aniruddha on them.

[2] N.B., iii. 1. 4.

[3] N.B., iii. 2. 47.

[4] See I.P., vol. i, pp. 284–285. See also N.B., iii. 2. 53–55.

[5] N.S., i. 1. 11.

[6] *Nyāyakandalī*, p. 263

synthesises their contributions.[1] It is the soul that confers unity on the various kinds of apprehensions. The eye cannot hear sounds nor the ear see visions, and the consciousness that I who am seeing a thing now have also heard of it will not be possible if the soul were not different from and beyond the senses. As instruments, the senses imply an agent which uses them. Being only products of matter, they cannot have consciousness as their property. Even when the object seen and the eye are both destroyed, the knowledge that I have seen remains, and so this knowledge is not a quality of either the outer objects or the senses.[2] Nor is the soul to be identified with manas, which is only the instrument by the aid of which the soul thinks. Since the manas is atomic in nature, it can no more be the self than the body can. If intelligence is a quality of manas, then the simultaneous cognition of things such as yogis have would be inexplicable.[3] The self cannot be identified with the body, senses or manas, since it is present even when the body is lost, the senses are cut off and manas is quieted down.[4] All these belong to the object side, and can never be the subject while self is the subject.[5]

This permanent self is not buddhi or intellection, upalabdhi or apprehension, or jñāna or knowledge.[6] Buddhi is non-permanent, while the soul must be permanent.[7] Our consciousness is to be compared to a flowing stream, where one mental state vanishes as soon as another appears. Whatever be the nature of the object, fleeting like sound or relatively permanent like a jar, cognitions themselves are transitory.[8] The relative permanence of the object accounts for the relative distinctness of the cognition, but cannot make the cognition itself permanent.[9] The capacity for recognition cannot be attributed to buddhi.[10] Intellect (buddhi) according to the Naiyāyika is not a substance nor the cogniser, but a quality of the soul which is capable of being perceived. The self is the perceiver of all that brings about pain and pleasure

[1] N.B., iii. 1. 1. [2] N.B., iii. 2. 18. [3] N.B., iii. 2. 19.
[4] P.P., p. 69. See also *Bhāṣāpariccheda*, 47–49.
[5] N.V., iii. 2. 19. [6] N.S., i. 1–5. [7] N.V.T.T., i. 1. 10.
[8] N.B., iii. 2. 1–2; iii. 2. 18–41.
[9] N.B., iii. 2. 44. See also N.V., iii. 2. 45. [10] N.B., iii. 2. 3.

(sarvasya draṣṭā), the experiencer of all pains and pleasures (bhoktā) and the knower of all things (sarvānubhāvī).

The substance to which these qualities belong cannot be made up of parts, for it is an assumption of the Nyāya that compound substances are destructible while simple ones are eternal. Whatever has an origin is necessarily made up of parts, and when the parts fall asunder, the thing perishes. The soul is partless (niravayava) and eternal. It has no beginning and no end. If a soul once began to be, it will sometime cease to be. The soul cannot be of a limited size, since what is limited has parts and is destructible. The soul must be either atomic or infinite, and of no medium size (madhyamaparimāṇa) like compound substances. It cannot be atomic, since we cannot then perceive its qualities of intellection, will, etc. If it were atomic, it would be impossible to account for the cognition which extends all over the body.[1] If of intermediate size, it must be either larger or smaller than the body. Either way, it cannot occupy the body as it does and should do. If it is of the same size as the body, it will be too small for the body, as it grows from birth onwards. Nor can the difficulty of its changing dimension from birth to birth be avoided. So it is all-pervading, though it cannot cognise many things simultaneously, on account of the atomic nature of manas. It is manas that retains the impressions of acts done in the body, and each soul has normally only one manas which is regarded as eternal.[2]

The soul is unique in each individual.[3] There are an infinite number of souls; if not, then everybody would be conscious of the feelings and thoughts of everybody else.[4] If one soul were present in all bodies, then when one experiences pleasure or pain, all should possess the same experiences, which is not the case.

Consciousness is not an essential property of the soul. The series of cognitions can have an end. "As regards the final cognition, it is destroyed either when there are no causes for its continuance (in the form of merit or demerit) or by

[1] *Tarkasaṃgrahadīpikā*, 17.
[2] N.B., i. 1. 16; iii. 2. 56.
[3] N.V.T.T., i. 1. 10; N.B., iii. 1. 14.
[4] The possibility of one soul guiding different bodies is admitted as a supernormal phenomenon (N.B., iii. 2. 32).

reason of the peculiarities of time (which can put an end to the operation of merit and demerit), or by the appearance of impressions produced by the final cognition itself." [1] It follows that the soul which is the substratum of consciousness need not always be conscious. As a matter of fact, it is an unconscious (jaḍa) principle capable of being qualified by states of consciousness.[2] Consciousness cannot exist apart from self, even as the brilliance of the flame cannot live apart from the flame ; but the soul itself is not necessarily conscious. Consciousness is regarded as a quality of the soul produced in the waking state by the conjunction of the soul with manas. It is an intermittent quality of the self.[3]

The soul is an eternal entity which is from time to time connected with a body suitable to its desert. The body has its source in the acts done by the person, and is the basis of pleasure and pain.[4] The body is formed under the influence of the unseen force of destiny,[5] and is the result of the persistence of the effect of the previous acts.[6] Each man becomes endowed with a body fit for being the medium of the experiences which he has to undergo. The birth of a being is not a mere physiological process. Uddyotakara says: "The karma of the parents who have to enjoy the experiences resulting from the birth of the child, as well as the karma of the personality which has to undergo experiences in the world, both these conjointly bring about the birth of the body in the mother's womb." [7] The connection of the soul with the body is called its birth and its separation from it death.[8] At the

[1] N.V., iii. 2. 24.

[2] Udayana views it as a substance possessing knowledge, joy and other pure qualities, eternal, imperishable, unchangeable, not bigger than an atom in size though capable of pervading the body.

[3] N.B. and N.V. on i. 1. 10, and P.P., p. 99.

[4] N.B., iii. 1. 27. The body is composed mainly of earth, though the other elements help in its formation (iii. 1. 27–29). While the human body is mainly made of earth, the Nyāya admits aqueous bodies formed in the regions of Varuṇa, fiery in those of Sun, and aerial in those of Vāyu. There are not, however, ākāśic, or ethereal bodies

[5] N.B., iii. 2. 60–72.

[6] Pūrvakṛtaphalānubandhāt (N.B., iii. 2. 60).

[7] N.V., iii. 2. 63.

[8] iv. 1. 10. The question is asked whether birth and death, *i.e.* rotation in the wheel of saṁsāra, belong to the soul or the manas. Uddyotakara answers: "If by saṁsāra you mean the action (of entering and moving

beginning of creation, an activity is set up in the atoms by which they combine so as to form material objects. A similar activity arises in the minds of the souls, which brings about several other qualities consequent upon the past careers of the souls themselves. The concrete history of each soul embraces a number of lives. At any one moment its historically continuous existence is rooted in the past and embraces an outline of the future. Any one life is but a part of a historically conditioned series.

No serious attempt is made to prove the pre-existence theory, since it is generally accepted. Infants show signs of pleasure and pain in quite early stages; and we cannot reduce the smiles and cries of the baby to mere mechanical movements like the opening and the closing of the lotus flowers.[1] The human being is very much more than a mere flower. The newborn babe's desire for milk cannot be explained on the analogy of the attraction of the iron by the magnet, since the child is not a mere piece of metal.[2] The objection that children with desires may be produced, even as substances with qualities are produced, is not valid, since desires are not mere qualities but take their rise from previous experience.[3] We come into the world "not in entire forgetfulness, and not in utter nakedness," but with certain memories and habits acquired in the previous state of existence.[4] The argument for pre-existence as well as future life is strengthened by ethical considerations. If we do not assume a past and a future for our souls, then our ethical sense will be violated by loss of merited action (kṛtahāni) and gain of unmerited result (akṛtābhyāgama). There must be a future where we can experience the fruits of our deeds and a past to account for the differences in our lots in the present. When our desert is completely exhausted, our soul is freed from saṁsāra and

off from the bodies), then it belongs to the manas, as it is the manas that actually moves (saṁsarati); on the other hand, if by saṁsāra you mean experiencing (of pleasure and pain), then it belongs to the soul, since it is the soul that experiences pleasure and pain" (N.V., i. 1. 19).

[1] iii. 1. 19–21. [2] iii. 1. 22–24. [3] iii. 1. 25–26.

[4] It may well be said that desires and inclinations prove only the existence of the soul and not its previous existence. After all, the Nyāya theory of new beginnings does not require us to accept a past for our souls.

rebirth and attains release or emancipation (mokṣa).[1] According to Vātsyāyana, " the fruition of all one's acts comes about in the last birth preceding release." [2]

Release is freedom from pain.[3] " This condition of immortality, free from fear, imperishable, consisting in the attainment of bliss, is called Brahma." [4] Mokṣa is supreme felicity marked by perfect tranquillity and freedom from defilement. It is not the destruction of self, but only of bondage. It is defined negatively as the cessation of pain, and not as the enjoyment of positive pleasure. For pleasure is always tainted with pain. It is caused as much as pain. Uddyotakara urges that if the released soul is to have everlasting pleasure, it must also have an everlasting body, since experiencing is not possible without the bodily mechanism.[5]

When the scriptural texts speak of the essence of the soul as pleasure, they mean only perfect freedom from pain. The Naiyāyika proves that every idea of liberation includes this minimum of freedom from pain.[6] Freedom is, in the Nyāya, complete cessation of effort, activity, consciousness and absolute cessation of the soul from body, manas, etc. This state of pure existence to which the liberated souls attain is compared to the state of deep dreamless sleep.[7] This state of abstract existence, without knowledge and joy, is, however, said to be one of great glory, as the soul possesses the general qualities of vibhutva, or ubiquity, though not the specific ones (viśeṣaguṇa) of knowledge, desire and will. Vātsyāyana criticises the theory that freedom consists in the manifestation of the soul's happiness on the ground that there is neither evidence nor justification for it. If there is a cause for the manifestation of happiness, it must be either eternal or non-eternal. If the former, then there would be no difference between the soul released and the soul bound. If the cause be non-eternal, what can it be ? Not the contact of soul with manas, which by itself brings about nothing. Other aids like merit have to be admitted. But the product of non-eternal merit cannot be eternal. When the merit is exhausted, its product of pleasure must also cease.[8] It is a state absolutely free even from cognitions, which are, according to the Nyāya, evanescent and productive of activity and so bondage. The

---

[1] N.B., iii. 2. 67. [2] N.B., iv. 1. 64. [3] i. 1. 9.

[4] Tad abhayam, ajaram, amṛtyupadam, brahmaksemaprāptiḥ (N.B., i. 1. 22).

[5] N.V., i. 1. 22. See also N.B., iv. 1. 58. Pleasure is a quality and not a constituent of the soul, according to Vācaspati. See N.V.T.T., i. 1. 22

[6] S.D.S., xi.

[7] Suṣuptasya svapnādarśane kleśābhāvavad apavargaḥ (iv. 1. 63)

[8] N.B., i. 1. 22. See also *Nyāyakandalī*, pp. 286–287.

Sāṁkhya view, that freedom is a state of pure consciousness, is criticised on the ground that there must be some cause for the emergence of this consciousness; and whatever is caused is non-eternal. Besides, the Sāṁkhya view that the puruṣa is discriminated from prakṛti in mokṣa, so that the latter ceases to function and the former rests in its own nature, credits the unintelligent principle of prakṛti with too much wisdom.[1]

The critic feels that the mokṣa of the Naiyāyikas is a word without meaning. There is not very much to distinguish the Nyāya philosophy from materialism. It regards the individual as neither the soul nor the body, but the result of their union. When there is a separation between soul and body, "nothing whatever can happen to excite sensation," as Lucretius says, "not if earth shall be mingled with sea and sea with heaven." The peace of extinguished consciousness may be the peace of death. The sleep without dreams is a state of torpor, and we may as well say that a stone is enjoying supreme felicity in a sound sleep without any disturbing dreams. The state of painless, passionless existence, which the Nyāya idealises, seems to be a mere parody of what man dreams to be. To lose sensations, passions, interests, to be free from the conditions of space and time, is certainly different from being born anew in God. Men of a feeling heart shun such a monster as cast of brass, which may find a fit dwelling in a sanctuary filled with the statues of gods. The Vedāntin, to whatever school he belongs, argues that freedom consists in quitting this frail, perishable individuality to be taken up into the being of the infinite. Naiyāyikas are anxious to make out that the condition of freedom is one of bliss,[2] but they cannot do so until they revise their conception of the soul's relation to consciousness.

XXIII

Some Critical Considerations on the Nyāya Theory of the Soul and Its Relation to Consciousness

The Naiyāyika is not clear about the status of consciousness in his theory. He regards the soul by itself as unconscious, and argues that consciousness is produced by the reaction of

[1] N.S., iii. 2. 73–78. [2] *Nyāyasāra*, pp. 39–41. Cp. also N.B., i. 1. 22.

the self to organic nature. He assumes the reality of a soul substance to account for the unity of our consciousness. Our consciousness is not the same for two moments, and there are periods when it often lapses altogether. Yet there seems to be an identity which makes us remember things and say that we are the same in childhood and old age To explain this phenomenon, the Naiyāyika assumes an eternal self-substance, which remains the same, though conscious states supervene one upon another. But can the soul be unconscious and yet be able to recognise? If in sleep and such other states there is a complete breach of our conscious life, and if the soul were an unconscious substance, how can the phenomenon of recognition be accounted for? If the self assumed by the Naiyāyika were not an eternal consciousness witnessing the series of mental states, it cannot recognise or remember. As Śaṁkara says: "Even for him who maintains that consciousness fails in those states, it is not possible to speak of a failure not witnessed by consciousness."[1] The self must be an uninterrupted consciousness which never takes a holiday. The Naiyāyika is right in holding that, if consciousness means a succession of states of consciousness of something observed either by itself or from outside, then it is not the fundamental reality, the subject which is eternal and self-sufficient. But this latter principle need not be beyond consciousness. An unconscious soul registering the traces left by conscious states, is on the same level with the brain retaining the impressions of conscious occurrences. If the self is not to be viewed as a constant consciousness, then we need not assume it at all. The brain cells of the organism may serve as the basis of memory and recognition. But the Naiyāyika is not satisfied with such a solution, and therefore he has to admit a conscious subject or self. This seems to be the implication of his view of the self as an immaterial substance. It is said to be spiritual, and it is necessary to admit that it is conscious, though not in the empirical sense. The Naiyāyika is anxious that the eternal self should not be identified with fleeting cognitions. The spiritual reality of the self is not to be confused with the transitory mental states. The self is not always qualified by these passing mental phenomena. But if it is to serve the

[1] S.B., ii. 3. 18.

purpose for which it is assumed, then it must be of the nature of consciousness. The Sāṁkhya view is, on this point, a step in advance of the Nyāya.

Unless we assume the reality of self as consciousness, the explanation of consciousness becomes difficult. We cannot make consciousness a *tertium quid*, a sort of mechanical glow which arises when two unconscious substances, soul and matter, interact. If the soul by itself is not conscious, and if consciousness is induced in it by the action of the outer world on it, there is nothing to distinguish the Nyāya theory from materialism, say as it may that consciousness is not a mere by-product of the brain. Consciousness is furthest removed from materiality, and we cannot find any mechanical equivalent to it. It is inconceivable how material and non-material entities interact. When we pass from a material event to a psychical state, we step from one world into another incommensurable one. It is no explanation to say that conscious states are epiphenomena produced by the interaction of two unconscious substances, soul and manas. The soul is infinite and partless (niravayava), the manas is atomic and partless, and how can we conceive the interaction between the two ?[1] If consciousness is something originated in the infinitely extended self, is the substrate of this consciousness the self in its whole extent, or a part particularised by the body ? The former is not admissible, since then all things should present themselves to consciousness all at once. The latter is not admissible, since the self has no parts. It is no use taking shelter under the determining character of merit and demerit, for these can have little to do with the apprehension of the sea or the sky or the rivers or the mountains. Śaṁkara urges several objections. Since every soul is omnipresent, the manas connected with one soul must be connected with all souls, with the result that all souls should have the same experiences. Since all souls are all-pervading, they must be in all bodies as well. Many all-pervading souls must be regarded as occupying the same space.[2] If consciousness

[1] S.B., ii. 2. 17. In the state of pralaya, or destruction, the souls are not supposed to be in contact with atoms. How do they retain the traces of their past ? Does the manas retain them, and is the manas with the soul in the pralaya as well

[2] S.B., ii. 3. 50–53.

is traced to the action of the self on manas, which is material in nature, then the soul must be looked upon as sharing the character of consciousness, for two material bodies, when they come into contact with each other, can only produce a material phenomenon. If we wish to escape from the charge of materialism, which makes intelligence the unpurposed effect of a blind dance of atoms or electrons, we have to assume the independence of consciousness. The soul must be regarded as a spirit unceasingly active, though we may not be aware of its activity. Forgetfulness and falsehood require explanation, and not memory and knowledge.

If we distinguish soul and body, we have to rely upon the conception of adṛṣṭa or Descartes's *deus ex machina* to account for their interaction. According to the Nyāya, the soul as vibhu or all-pervading, is always in contact with manas, and cognitions arise when manas comes into contact with sense-organs. Manas is on the one side, joined to the sense-organs, and, on the other, to the soul. How it is able to do this is a mystery which the Naiyāyika solves by appealing to the power of God.

The Nyāya regards soul and body as not only distinct but as co-ordinately real. It adopts the theory of a separable soul inhabiting a body which is to be defined in terms of matter. In the human organism, soul and body cannot be regarded as of equal rank. Nor are they exclusive. The soul is not something added from outside to the machine of the body. The Naiyāyika believes in a more organic connection between the spiritual and the physical aspects of human nature.[1] According to the theory advocated by the Nyāya and the Vaiśeṣika, matter is the vehicle and instrument for the expression of ideal purposes. There is more of meaning and value in spirit than in matter, and therefore more of reality. The distinction between soul and body has to be viewed as one of higher and lower levels of experience.

The Naiyāyika is aware that consciousness is the basis and *prius* of all experience. It is not a fact among facts, like the sun or the earth, but the necessary ground of reference of all facts. Buddhi, instead of being a mere quality induced in the self by the action of the outer objects, is the necessary basis of all experience. Annaṁ Bhaṭṭa defines it as the

[1] N.B., iii. 2. 60.

"condition of all experience" (sarvavyavahārahetuḥ).[1] Śivāditya defines buddhi as "the illuminating principle belonging to the soul," [2] which the commentator Jinavardhaṅa explains more clearly as "of the nature of light, since it dispels the darkness of ignorance and illuminates all objects." [3] What is prior to all experience cannot be derived from experience. While the particular ideas and beliefs may be consequent upon environmental conditions, the latter by themselves cannot account for them apart from the basis of consciousness. Buddhi as defined by the Nyāya belongs to the subject side.[4] It is not a temporary phase, but the essential nature of the subject which can never become the object, the universal consciousness, apart from which neither finite individuals nor objects are possible.

If consciousness is the basis of all experience, the foundational reality within which the finite selves and the objects of which they are conscious fall, it is more than finite. The individual subject and the object are fragmentary phases of the infinite, which are ever changing. The self which the Nyāya assumes to account for the synthesis of the manifold experiences of life, is of the nature of consciousness which makes possible all experience. We cannot call it a substance, since that would be to apply to it conceptions valid only in the world of experience, seeing that it is in virtue of the presence of this constant consciousness that a world of experience is possible. If we include within this experience that which is superior to it and at the same time constitutes it, the self becomes a thinking *substance* with other things outside it.

A distinction will have to be made between the self as pure consciousness, common to all individuals, and the finite selves which have a historical existence. The self of the Naiyāyika is something which grows, is plastic and has a

[1] *Tarkasaṁgraha*, 43. Govardhana, in his *Nyāyabodhinī*, regards vyavahāra as equivalent to śabdaprayoga, or whatever can be expressed through words, though this view is too narrow.

[2] Ātmāśrayaḥ prakāśaḥ. *Saptapadārthī*, 93. Cp. Annaṁ Bhaṭṭa's definition of Ātman as jñānādhikaraṇam (*Tarkasaṁgraha*, 17).

[3] Ajñānāndhakāra - tiraskārakāraka - sakalapadārthasyārthaprakāśakaḥ pradīpa iva dedīpyamāno yaḥ prakāśaḥ sā buddhiḥ.

[4] N.V., iii. 2. 19.

history. The arguments that what has a beginning will have an end, what is put together is liable to dissolution and decay, and that the simple can in no manner be dissolved or destroyed, prove the eternal character of the pure self, and not that of the historical souls. The latter have ends and ideals which determine their reactions to the conditions of life. The susceptibility of the finite individual to particular emotions and the obstacles which impede its activity are due to historical circumstances. The kind of permanence which the growing individuals possess is not to be confused with the constancy of the pure self. The relatively fixed character of the nature of the finite selves is derived from external factors. The self-enclosed historical selves are infinite in number. A sure philosophic instinct guides the Naiyāyika when he regards the limits of individual and physical particularity as accidents of the self, which it will be freed from when it is delivered from the curse of mortality. The defining character of the self must persist, whether it is in a state of freedom or bondage. Since the nature of the self transcends our knowledge, we feel that what remains after eliminating the intellectual, emotional and volitional impulses, is a mere blank. The Naiyāyika is, however, convinced that the basis of the accidental properties is something real. It is the relation to the object that hides the truth of the self. The self in us is clouded by the passive element of matter. The Naiyāyika is right in his view that the spirit is immortal, though he is wrong in confusing it with the jīvātman, which has no recollection of the former life, any more than of the uninterrupted presence of consciousness. While the ātman in us is the universal spirit, the identical self, yet the faculty which receives impressions is, because of its receptivity, something dependent, passive, perishable, partaking more of the nature of matter. The ātman or the self in us which is regarded as immaterial cannot admit of any suspension of its activity. It is not subject to enfeeblement or corruption, while the manas, like the body which houses it and the associated organs, is of a different character. The facts experienced by each soul are different, since the souls are attached to different organs of thought. If the soul is freed from its association with manas, then all objects would reach consciousness simultaneously, and the contents of all souls which are omnipresent would be the same. This universal content is grasped by each finite soul from one peculiar point of view determined by the spatio-temporal order in which each soul is placed. The view which Viśvanātha assigns to the Vedāntin, that the self is knowledge, while all objects are but special forms of it determined by historical circumstances, is unavoidable.[1]

That the exclusiveness of the jīvātman is not its essential property comes out from the fact of knowledge itself. If each soul is a distinct spiritual unit with a peculiar manas, we cannot be sure that the worlds which they perceive are all one. If each unit makes a world for itself, a radical pluralism, where there are as many worlds as there are units, would result. The Nyāya is anxious to escape from subjectivism, and believes that we all know a common world. In other words, we are able to transcend the limits of the here and the now, rise above the contingent, the particular and the fragmentary, to the necessary, the universal and the infinite. All knowledge has an element of the necessary, something that must be. The knowing self cannot be finite. The relation of the finite subject to the world is not static. The finite consciousness is never complete, and is therefore ever at unrest with itself. The characteristic of finite thought is to be continuously self-transforming. Human thinking is dialectical in its procedure, always attempting to negate the relatively static character of what is external to it. All that seems external to consciousness is not really so. That we are discontented with what we are, is a claim to what we ought to be. To try to get beyond the merely empirical order of things and events is to aim at a more fundamental reality, which is nothing else than the supreme consciousness which regards nothing as alien to itself. The Naiyāyika distinguishes the pure self from the historical individuality dependent on the ideals and beliefs which give, so to say, a sort of concretion

[1] Nan vastu vijñānam eva ātmā tasya svataḥ prakāśarūpatvāc cetanatvam Jñānasukhādikaṁ tu tasyaivākāraviśeṣaḥ. Tasyāpi bhāvatvād eva kṣaṇikatvam pūrvapūrvavijñānasyottaravijñāne hetutvāt (*Siddhāntamuktāvali*, 49). The self is knowledge indeed. Its character as knowledge is proved by its self-manifestation. Knowledge of this or that object, happiness, etc., are special forms of it. Being simply objects, they are transitory, the preceding mental states causing the succeeding ones.

to the pure self. If we are able to distinguish at any moment the nature of the finite self, it is through its organic character and ideals, determined by its past history and environmental conditions. But these individualising conditions of the ideals, the organism and the environment, are admitted by the Naiyāyika to be different from the true self, though resting on it. The Naiyāyika has logically to admit that the doctrine of the plurality of selves is based on the accidental properties of the self, and it will have to be given up when the essential nature of the self is emphasised. The historical point of view which is not ultimate yields a pluralistic conception of the universe ; the metaphysical point of view which is ultimate transcends pluralism. The Nyāya argument, that the supreme self cannot be one, since on that view there will be a confusion of the different experiences of pleasure—pain, cannot be pressed, since the distinction of historical selves is not denied. The many minds determine the different souls, which in their turn are said to mould into shape the universe by their deeds. While the individual souls are not in touch with all aspects of the universe, Śrīdhara admits that there must be at least one soul which has the whole universe for its sphere of experience. This soul has not any general relation to all things, but has intimate relation with and control over all.[1] In essence all souls are one. The empirical differences which we notice among the souls are determined by the intimate and special relations into which the souls, which are in general touch with all things, enter.

To assume the fundamental reality of the universal consciousness or self is not to support the doctrine of subjectivism. To base the distinction of subject and object on the reality of the universal self is not to deny that the earth and the planets spun on their axes and waltzed round the sun æons before there was a living plant to respond to the light of the sun or a sentient eye to translate solar energy into light.

The Nyāya cannot account for experience so long as it regards consciousness as a mere property of the soul. Self, as universal consciousness, is to be admitted, if experience is to be rendered intelligible. The Nyāya is right when it says that environmental conditions lead to the development of

[1] *Nyāyakandalī*, p. 88.

certain ideas and beliefs, and the development constitutes the historicity of human nature. This human nature, however, is not the subject of all consciousness, but is a development within consciousness determined through an objective medium. The distinctness of the souls is due to the earthly life in which they partake. The finite beings, though rooted in matter, strive to flower in spirit. The perfected souls live within the spirit's fire when the smoke of their bodies passes away. Nor have we on this view the danger that the freed soul is empty-handed. The distinction of one and many has no meaning, so far as the freed condition of the souls is conceived. It is to some such view that we are led, if we try to carry out the central teaching of the Nyāya philosophy and rid it of its inconsistencies, though the Nyāya thinkers themselves were not clearly aware of it.

XXIV

Ethics

The Nyāya thinkers do not draw a hard and fast line of distinction between will and intellect. Intellect is no more a passive agent receiving or reflecting objects presented to it than will is a mysterious power which comes into operation after the intellect presents objects to it. All knowledge is purposive and even as we cognise objects we like or dislike them, try to obtain or avoid them. When we think an object, we at the same time value it and adopt a definite practical attitude to it. Ethics deals with the practical side of man's life, more especially with voluntary activities.

A psychological analysis of the nature of volition is given in some Nyāya treatises. Viśvanātha[1] mentions a number of conditions of icchā or desire. We do not desire impossible things. Only children cry for the moon. As a rule we desire things which seem to be within our reach.[2] Again, the objects willed are recognised to be desirable, as conductive to the good of the agent.[3] Even when we will to commit suicide, or drive a thorn into our flesh, it is because we believe in the value of these objects. Nothing has value except in relation to a subject, though the subject may look upon suicide and such other courses of conduct as conducive to his welfare, in an abnormal state

[1] *Siddhāntamuktāvali*, 146-150.
[2] Kṛtisādhyatājñāna.
[3] Iṣṭasādhanatājñāna.

of mind.[1] Whatever other judgment may be passed on it later, at the time of the volition the object must be regarded as desirable. In determining the desirability of a plan of action, we take into account all its consequences and make sure that its adoption will not be accompanied by greater evil.[2] When an object threatens to yield more harm, we do not care to pursue it. This condition involves a careful survey of the consequences of the proposed course of action.

Voluntary activities which are instinctive[3] and automatic, where the operation of will (svecchādhīnatva) is absent, are not, strictly speaking, the objects of moral judgment. The soul is not the victim of desires and aversions which flood upon it from outward sources. If the soul were by itself an unconscious entity, then its aversions and the preferences may be regarded as the destiny which drags the soul along in its train. The Nyāya assumes a power of initiative, selection and choice, implying thereby that the nature of the soul is spiritual freedom. Vātsyāyana combats the view which traces all events to the direct intervention of God, providing no room for human effort (puruṣakāra).[4] The human will is efficient enough, though it works under the control of God. Vātsyāyana refutes the notion that the will works without any cause.[5]

All acts have for their motive (prayojana)[6] the desire to obtain pleasure (sukhaprāpti) and avoid pain (duhkhaparihāra). Pain, the cause of uneasiness,[7] is the sign that the soul is not at rest with itself. The highest good is deliverance from pain and not the enjoyment of pleasure, for pleasure is always mixed up with pain.[8] Saṁsāra is of the nature of

[1] Rogadūṣitacittaḥ.

[2] Balavad aniṣṭānanubandhitvajñāna. This is ambiguous, and may mean either the consciousness of the absence of evil (aniṣṭa ajanakatvajñāna) or the absence of the consciousness of any evil (aniṣṭajanakatvajñānābhāva). Viśvanātha inclines to the latter view.

[3] Jīvanayonipūrvaka, 152.

[4] N.B., iv. 1. 19–21.

[5] N.B., iv. 1. 22–24.

[6] N.B. and N.V., i. 1. 24, on it; also N.B., iii. 2. 32–37.

[7] i. 1. 21.

[8] S.D.S., xi. Uddyotakara somewhat modifies the view. "If there were no pleasure, merit would be entirely useless. . . . Nor will it be right to regard the mere negation of pain as the result of merit, since then the result of merit will be a merely negative entity. In ordinary life we find a twofold activity among men. One acts with a view to obtain something

suffering, though it may seem on occasions to be pleasant. To escape from saṁsāra is to attain the highest good. "Pain, birth, activity, faults, false notions: on the successive annihilation of these in turn, there is the annihilation of the one next before it."[1] Pain (duḥkha) is the result of birth (janma), which is the result of activity (pravṛtti). All activity, good or bad, binds us to the chain of saṁsāra and leads to some kind of birth, high or low. The Naiyāyika blushes that he has a body, and declares with Novalis that "life is a disease of the spirit, an activity excited by passion." The activity is due to the defects of aversion (dveṣa), attachment (rāga) and stupidity (moha). Aversion includes anger, envy, malignity, hatred and implacability. Attachment includes lust, avarice, avidity and covetousness. Stupidity includes misapprehension, suspicion, conceit and carelessness. Stupidity is the worst since it breeds aversion and attachment.[2] Through these defects, we forget that there is nothing agreeable or disagreeable to the soul and come to like and dislike objects. The cause of these defects is false knowledge (mithyājñāna) about the nature of the soul, pain, pleasure, etc. To attain the timeless condition of freedom, which is the only real value, we must put an end to the chain which begins with false notions and ends with pain. When false knowledge disappears, faults pass away. With their disappearance, activity has no *raison d'être*, and so there is no chance of birth. Cessation of birth means abolition of pain, which is another name for final bliss.[3]

So long as we act, we are under the sway of attachment and aversion and cannot attain the highest good. The hatred of pain is still hatred and the attachment to pleasure is still

desirable, while another acts with a view to avoid the undesirable; and if there were nothing desirable, this twofold activity would not be possible. Again (if there were no pleasure), there could be no such advice, as that pleasure should be looked upon as pain; lastly, there could be no attachment, since no one is ever attached to pain" (N.V., i. 1. 21). Śrīdhara does not agree with the view that pleasure is the mere absence of pain in view of the positive experience of bliss and the twofold activities of men (*Nyāyakandalī*, p. 260).

[1] N.S., i. 1. 2; iv. 1. 68. Cp. with this the Buddhist chain of causation (*Visuddhimagga*, xix).

[2] iv. 1. 3–9.

[3] N.B., iii. 2. 67; iv. 1. 6; iv. 2. 1.

attachment and, so long as these are operative, the highest good is beyond our reach.

The Naiyāyika asks us to suppress all sense of separateness, for he allows that the activities of one whose defects are overcome do not tend to rebirth.[1] Those who are saved in this life go on performing work as long as they are in body, and this work does not bind them. So long as we cling to individuality and accumulate virtue to become Indra or Brahmā, we are bound to the circuit, for even the states of Indra and Brahmā have an end. The highest good consists in freedom from all sense of separateness.

The realisation of true knowledge does not mean an immediate escape from saṁsāra. The desert which is the basis of the connection between the soul and the body must be completely exhausted, thus destroying every chance of a revival of connection between the two.[2]

While the only good is thus freedom from individuality, all courses of conduct which tend to this are said to be good, and those which lead in the opposite direction bad. Activities are distinguished into those of speech, mind and body, and each of them is divided into good and bad.[3] The essence of moral evil lies in the conscious choice of the evil in preference to the good. Under the influence of strong passion (utkaṭarāga), we misconceive the painful effects of sin and fall a prey to the attractions of pleasure.

The adoption of virtuous activities will enable one to discriminate the soul from the body and the senses. True knowledge, so much insisted on, is not a matter of mere intellectual opinion, but a kind of general attitude. False knowledge and selfish attitude go together.[4] True knowledge and unselfishness are organically related. This true knowledge cannot be acquired from books, but only through meditation

[1] N.S., iv. 1 64. [2] N.S., iv. 1. 19–21.

[3] i. 1. 17. Charity, protection and service are good bodily activities, while murder, theft and adultery are bad. Speaking the true, the useful and the pleasant and study of sacred books are good activities relating to speech, while lying, using harsh language, and slandering and indulging in frivolous talk are bad. Compassion, generosity and devotion are good activities of the mind, while those of malice, covetousness and scepticism are bad.

[4] N.V., iv. 2. 2.

and increase of righteousness.[1] In addition to study and reflection,[2] yoga practices are enjoined.[3] Uddyotakara advises scriptural study, philosophic thought and meditation.[4] We are sometimes asked to refrain from worldly pleasures, renounce all desires, retire to a forest and make our souls the sacrificial fire in which oui physical actions are offered as oblations. Bhakti as a means of securing peace and happiness is permitted. Though God does not interfere, the act of devotion brings its own reward.[5]

Like the other systems of Hindu thought, the Nyāya accepts the principle of karma, and believes in the persistence of the results of our activity. Some of our activities produce their results immediately like, say, the act of cooking, while others take a longer time to mature, like the act of ploughing. Acts of piety and ceremonialism are of the latter kind, since attainment of heaven is not possible until after death.[6] In the interval the causes have not disappeared, but persist in the form of dharma and adharma. " Prior to the actual accomplishment of fruition, there would be something (in the shape of an intermediary) just as there is in the case of the fruit of the trees." [7] The adṛṣṭa, or the unseen quality, is not different from karma ; for, if so, " even after final release there would be a likelihood of a body being produced." [8] The bodies which the souls assume are determined by their past karma. The body gives the name to the soul, which, though neither man nor horse, is yet called man or horse according

[1] N.B., iv. 2. 38 and 41.

[2] N.B., iv. 2. 47.

[3] N.B., iv 2. 46. The Naiyāyikas are also called yogas. " Naiyāyikānāṁ yogaparābhidhānānām " (Guṇaratna's *Ṣaḍdarśanasamuccayavṛtti*) See also his *Tarkarahasyadīpikā*. Vātsyāyana mentions the Nyāya view under yoga in i. 1. 29.

[4] N.V., i. 1. 2.

[5] *Nyāyasāra*, pp. 38, 40–41 ; and S.S.S.S., vi. 10–21, and 40–44.

[6] Uddyotakara writes : " In cases where the action does not bring about the effect immediately, this is due to the obstruction caused by the peculiar circumstances attending the karmic residuum that is undergoing fruition or the obstruction caused by the fructifying karmic residuum of other living beings whose experiences are akin to those in question, or the acts being obstructed by the acts of those other living beings who may be sharers in the karma of the man in question, or because such auxiliary causes as merit and demerit are not present at the time " (N V., iii. 2. 60).

[7] N.B., iv. 1. 47. See iv. 1. 44–54

[8] N.B., iii. 2. 68.

to the body with which it is endowed.[1] The Nyāya-Vaiśeṣika system does not believe in any subtle body. The soul passes from one frame to another through the aid of manas, which is atomic and therefore supersensuous, and is not seen when it leaves the body on death. Since the souls are all-pervading, it is only the manas that can be said to proceed to the new abode of fruition in rebirth.

The real, according to the Nyāya-Vaiśeṣika, is a complex of souls and nature. The natural order is not the product of souls, but is the arrangement of a God, who so fashions the atoms as to make the natural order the medium for the souls' experiences. The harmony between souls and nature is due to divine design.

XXV

Theology

In the *Nyāya Sūtra*, we find only a casual mention of God, which justifies the suspicion that the ancient doctrine of the Nyāya was not theistic.[2] The theory of divine causality is referred to in the *Nyāya Sūtra*.[3] While Vātsyāyana, Uddyotakara and Viśvanātha regard it as the Nyāya view, Vācaspati, Udayana and Vardhamāṇa interpret is as a criticism of the Vedānta view, that God is the constituent cause of the universe. To the objection that man does not often reap fruits proportionate to his acts, and so everything seems to depend on God's will and not on human effort, the Nyāya says that human acts produce their results under the control and with the co-operation of God. Vātsyāyana supports theism when he declares that the self sees all, feels all and knows all. This description loses all meaning, if it is applied to the imperfect individual self.[4] Later Naiyāyikas as well as Vaiśeṣikas are frankly theistic and enter into a discussion of

[1] N B., iii. 1 26.

[2] "The fundamental textbooks of the two schools, the Vaiśeṣika and the Nyāya Sūtras, originally did not accept the existence of God; it was not till a subsequent period that the two systems changed to theism, although neither ever went so far as to assume a creator of matter" (Garbe: *Philosophy of Ancient India*, p. 23). Muir "is unable to say if the ancient doctrine of the Nyāya was theistic" (*Original Sanskrit Texts*, vol. iii, p. 133)

[3] iv. 1. 19–21.

[4] N.B., i. 1. 9; iv. 1. 21.

the nature of God in considering the theory of ātman. Annaṁ Bhaṭṭa classifies souls into two kinds, supreme and human. While the supreme is God, one, omniscient, the human souls are infinite in number, different in each body.[1] God is looked upon as a special soul, possessing the attributes of omnipotence and omniscience, by which he guides and regulates the universe. Since the human and the divine souls differ in many respects, it is difficult to believe that the original authors, Gautama and Kaṇāda, meant to bring together these two kinds of souls under one comprehensive class. The empirical tendency and the dialectical interests of the Nyāya are responsible for its practical indifference to the question of the reality of God.[2]

Udayana's *Kusumāñjali* is the classic statement of the Nyāya proofs for the existence of God. It sets out, in the first chapter, certain considerations which make for the reality of an unseen cause, adṛṣṭa, or the force which determines our happiness and misery.[3] Every effect depends on a cause, and so there must be a cause for our happiness and misery.[4] Every cause is an effect in relation to its preceding cause, which in its turn is the effect of some other cause. As the world has no beginning, this succession of cause and effect has also no beginning. So the cause of our happiness and misery cannot be traced back to its beginning.[5] Diversity of effects implies diversity of causes. Our varying lots cannot be traced to common causes like God or nature.[6] Our acts

[1] *Tarkasaṁgraha*, 17.

[2] Athalye writes: "Kaṇāda and Gautama might have at first purposely excluded God from their systems, not as being totally non-existent, but as being beyond and above the phenomenal world with which their systems were chiefly concerned. Possibly the aphorists confined themselves to a classification and discussion of sublunary things only, without minding the supernatural agency, while commentators, considering this to be a defect, supplied the omission by inserting God under the only category where it was possible to do so" (*Tarkasaṁgraha*, p. 137). "The Nyāya is so predominantly dialectical in interest that its excursions into metaphysics have an air of divagation from the work in hand, which forbids us to assume that silence on any topic means its exclusion" (Keith: I.L.A., p. 265).

[3] Sāpekṣatvād anāditvād vaicitryād viśvavṛttitaḥ.
Pratyātmaniyamād bhukter asti hetur alaukikaḥ (i. 4).

[4] i. 5.

[5] i. 6. Thus the question about the beginning of adṛṣṭa is avoided. See N.V., iv. 1. 21.

[6] i. 7.

disappear, leaving behind them traces capable of bringing about the fruits. "A thing long passed cannot produce its result without some continuant influence (karmātiśayam)." [1] The trace of a good action is called merit (puṇya) and that of an evil one demerit (pāpa), and the two together form the adṛṣṭa, or the desert which resides in the soul of the person who performs the acts, and not in the thing from which he derives happiness or misery. This adṛṣṭa causes happiness and misery when the suitable time, place and object occur. The persistence of merit and demerit is accounted for by the transcendent agency of adṛṣṭa. The connection of souls with organic bodies is not due to natural causes. The law of moral causation supervenes on the natural order. The different degrees of enjoyment which different souls receive are determined by the differences in their adṛṣṭa.

Udayana, thus far, is faithful to the ancient Naiyāyikas, who account for the creation of the universe by the hypothesis of an original activity among the atoms and adṛṣṭa among the souls. But he goes beyond them when he argues that a non-intelligent cause like adṛṣṭa cannot produce its effect without the guidance of an intelligent spirit. God is said to supervise the work of adṛṣṭa.[2] The world cannot be explained by the atoms or the force of karma. If atoms are active by nature, then their activity should be unceasing. If their activities are determined by the force of time, then this unconscious principle of time must be either always active or always inactive. The analogy of the flow of milk for the nourishment of the calf will not serve, since milk should flow out of the dead cow also, if it were active by itself. It follows that if an unconscious thing is active, it is so under the influence of a conscious agent. The individual soul cannot be the controller of adṛṣṭa, since then it would be able to avert unwished-for miseries, which it is not. So the unintelligent principle of adṛṣṭa, which governs the fate of beings, acts under the direction of God, who does not create it or alter its inevitable course, but renders possible its operation. God is thus the giver of the fruits of our deeds (karmaphalapradaḥ).

[1] i. 9. [2] i. 19.

The other arguments are summed up by Udayana in the following verse. "From effects, combination, support, etc., from traditional arts, from authoritativeness, from scriptures, from sentences thereof, and from particular numbers, an everlasting omniscient being is established."[1] The causal argument is considered first. The world is looked upon as a product, since it consists of component parts, and so it must have had a maker. For "that is not an effect which can attain its proper nature independently of any series of concurrent causes." The maker of the world is an intelligent being, "possessed of that combination of volition, desire to act, and knowledge of the proper means which sets in motion all other causes, but is itself set in motion by none." Combination (āyojana) is the action which produces the conjunction of two atoms, forming the binary compound at the beginning of creation. This action implies an intelligent agent. Support (dhṛti) signifies that this wonderful universe is supported by his will. The "etc" (ādi) is intended to make out that God is also the destroyer of the world. God makes, unmakes and remakes the world. The traditional arts imply an intelligent inventor. The authoritativeness of the Vedas is derived from a being who imparted that character to them. Udayana holds that the Vedas are non-eternal, like the other things of the world subject to creation and destruction. If they are yet sources of right knowledge, it is because God is their author.[2] Besides, śruti, or the scripture, speaks to us of the author of the world. Again, since the Vedas consist of sentences, they require an author who can only be God. The argument from number is based on the view that the magnitude of the dyad is produced not from the infinite minuteness (parimāṇḍalya) of the atoms, but from the number (two) of the atoms composing the binary. As we shall see, this conception of duality is dependent on understanding (buddhyapekṣā), so that to account for duality which produces the dyads at the beginning of creation, an intelligent being must be postulated. Udayana sets aside the objection against the existence of God based on non-perception. The non-perception of an object proves its non-existence, only if the object is one which is ordinarily open to perception. Things beyond the range of the senses are not non-existent. The utmost that we can say is that the existence of God cannot be established through perception.[3] Inference neither proves nor disproves the existence of God.[4] Comparison has nothing to do with the existence and non-existence of objects.[5] Śabda is in favour of theism.[6] Presumption (arthāpatti) and non-perception (anupalabdhi) are not independent means of knowledge.[7]

The God of the Naiyāyika is a personal being, possessing existence, knowledge and bliss. He is "endowed with such

[1] Kāryāyojanadhṛtyādeḥ padāt pratyayataḥ śruteḥ
Vākyāt saṁkhyāviśeṣāc ca sādhyo viśvavid avyayaḥ (v. 1).

[2] ii. 1.
[3] iii. 1.
[4] iii. 4–7.
[5] iii. 8–12.
[6] iii. 13–17.
[7] iii. 18–23.

qualities as absence of demerit (adharma), wrong knowledge (mithyājñāna) and negligence (pramāda), and presence of merit, knowledge and equanimity (dharmajñānasamādhisaṁpad). He is omnipotent in regard to his creation, though he is influenced by the results of acts done by the beings he creates. He has obtained all the results of his deeds (āptakarmaphala), and continues to act for the sake of his created beings. Just as the father acts for his children, so also does God act fatherlike for living beings."[1] God is omniscient since he possesses right knowledge, which is an independent apprehension of reality. He has eternal intelligence and, since his cognitions are everlasting, there is no need for memory and inferential knowledge. What in ordinary men is a sort of intermittent mystical perception, what in the yogis is an acquired power, is in God a steady mode of apprehension.[2] God is also endowed with desire.[3] God has pure unimpeded intelligence as well as eternal bliss.

The difficulties of creation are not ignored. All activity is brought under pain, and is said to be caused by faults (doṣa).[4] The question is raised whether God creates the world to realise any desire of his own, or for the sake of others. But God has all his desires fulfilled, and so creation cannot be the means of helping God to realise his desires. He who worries about other people is a mere busybody. Nor can we justify God's activity by tracing it to his love for humanity. The miserable nature of the world militates against this supposition. The Naiyāyika answers this criticism thus: "His action in creation is indeed solely caused by compassion, but the idea of creation which can consist only of happiness, is inconsistent with the nature of things, since there cannot but arise eventual differences from the different results which will ripen from the good or evil actions of the beings who are to be created. Nor need you object that this would interfere with God's own independence (as he would thus seem to

[1] N.B., iv. 1 21.

[2] Udayana raises the interesting question whether God's omniscience includes a knowledge of the illusory cognitions of finite beings together with their objects, and consequently whether God perceives things otherwise than they are, and answers it by saying that God's knowledge of human illusions is not illusory.

[3] N.N., iv. 1. 21; [4] i. 1. 18.

depend on others' actions). For there is the maxim, "one's own body does not hinder one; nay rather it helps to carry out one's aims."[1] Uddyotakara admits that God's activity is limited by other considerations, and yet these latter are only self-imposed limitations.[2] The end which God has in view is not so much the happiness of creatures as their spiritual development. The world is to be regarded as the sphere for the realisation of spiritual ends, as goodness through suffering and perfection through sacrifice.

The Naiyāyikas are Śaivas, while the Vaiśeṣikas are said to be Pāśupatas.[3] Jinadatta in his *Vivekavilāsa* (middle of the thirteenth century) says that Śiva is the deity of the Nyāya-Vaiśeṣika. Uddyotakara was a Pāśupata. Bhāsarvajña speaks of the direct vision of Maheśvara as the result of meditation.[4] Udayana equates the Supreme with Śiva.[5]

The Nyāya doctrine of theism has been the subject of great discussion in the history of Hindu thought. The critic observes that the Naiyāyika resorts to adṛṣṭa whenever natural explanation fails. The first stirrings in the primordial atoms, the upward motion of fire, even the attraction of the needle by the magnet, are assigned to it. Adṛṣṭa constitutes only a limit of explanation.[6] It is supposed to call for an intelligent controller, Īśvara, for the remarkable regularity with which events happen cannot be explained apart from God, who has jñāna (wisdom), icchā (desire) and prayatna (volitional effort). The souls lose their activity at the time of dissolution, and regain it at creation, and all this is inexplicable apart from divine guidance. The causal argument is made much of by Udayana and Śrīdhara.[7] By assuming

[1] S.D.S., xi

[2] N.V., iv. 1. 21.

[3] See Guṇaratna's *Ṣaḍdarśanasamuccayavṛtti*, pp. 49–51. See also Har bhadra's *Ṣaḍdarśanasamuccaya*:—

Akṣapādamate devaḥ sṛṣṭisaṁhārakṛc chivaḥ
Vibhur nityaikaḥ sarvajño nityabuddhisamāśrayaḥ (13).

Rājaśekhara's *Ṣaḍdarśanasamuccaya* of a slightly earlier date confirms this view. See Keith: I.L.A., pp. 262–263.

[4] *Nyāyasāra*, p. 39.

[5] *Kusumāñjali*, ii. 4.

[6] Jayanta, criticising the Cārvāka theory in his *Nyāyamañjari*, says that we put down a thing as svābhāvika, or natural, when we do not know its cause.

[7] *Nyāyakandalī*, pp. 54–57

that the world is an effect, the Naiyāyika takes for granted what is to be proved. Plants and animals are not self-sufficient, they are born, they grow and die. To say that individual things are products, is not to say that the world as a whole is a product. The Naiyāyika admits several eternal entities which are not products.[1] May not the world as a whole also be eternal? Again, should all effects have efficient causes as well? As we have already seen, the law of causality, as the Naiyāyika interprets it, has not universal validity. It has no other signification than uniform and concomitant variation. Since its evidence is derived from the phenomenal world, it is wrong to extend its scope beyond it. To know the cause of the world is not within the power of the human understanding. The impossibility of an infinite regress of infinite causes leads the Naiyāyika to assert the reality of a cause outside the series, an uncaused cause. Śaṁkara repudiates the causal argument and asks us to admit boldly that we know nothing except that the universe appears to us to exist. Whether it exists of itself or is but the effect of a remote cause cannot be understood by us. If we admit a remote cause, why should we not demand another remoter cause for it and so forth indefinitely to the verge of madness? If God is, who created him? According to the Sāṁkhya, it is as easy to believe that the universe made itself as to believe that the maker of the universe made himself. The question remains metaphysically irreducible, and the solution is worse than the riddle. The anthropomorphism of the Naiyāyika, moreover, creates other difficulties. It is asked, whether God, the maker of the world, has a body or not. If he has a body, then he is subject to adṛṣṭa, since bodies are all determined by it. Embodied beings are created, and are not capable of exercising control over subtle atoms and merit and demerit. We do not know what an eternal body is. The Naiyāyikas are not clear on this question. They sometimes say that God creates without the aid of any body, while it is also suggested that God becomes endowed with a body, on account of our adṛṣṭa. Sometimes the atoms are made the body of God, while ākāśa is assigned this status on other

[1] "Of the eternal thing there is no production; nor is there any cause of the eternal thing" (N.V., iv. 1. 32).

occasions. If in some inscrutable manner God is able to fashion the world out of atoms without a body, we may as well say that he can create the world without any pre-existing material.

Even if we grant the validity of the arguments employed to establish the reality of God, the Īśvara of the Nyāya philosophy is not the comprehensive spiritual reality of which we are the imperfect expressions. He is outside of us and the world too, however much he may be said to cause, govern and destroy it. Reality is composed of a great number of particulars, linked together by an external bond, even as a cord binds together a number of sticks. God is not the creator of atoms, but only their fashioner. His reason works on the elements of the universe from without, but does not operate as a power of life within. This conception of God as beyond the world, as outside the entire frame of space, as dwelling apart in eternal self-centred isolation, is arid and empty. We cannot maintain the dualism of an infinite creator on the one side and the infinite world on the other. The two limit each other. Things which are defined each against the other cannot but be finite. The souls obtain release some time or other. With the liberation of all, saṁsāra disappears. The lordship of Īśvara will also come to an end. What has an end has a beginning. The two must have come out of the void, and must disappear into the void. It is true that the creation of the world is assigned to the love of God ; but what is the meaning of creation on this hypothesis ? If atoms and souls are both eternal, and if the world is an interaction between the two types, then there is nothing for God to create. The Naiyāyika must either give up his notion of God as creator or admit that the atoms and the souls are the expressions of the eternal and constant causality of God, though this causality ought not to be conceived in a mechanical sense. This seems to be the implication of the Nyāya suggestion that the nature of things is the body of God, an analogy, worked out with great care and to high purpose, in Rāmānuja's system. Some such immamental conception of God is forced on us by a consideration of God's omniscience. According to the Nyāya, finite beings know only thought and the bare fact that the real is not a thought. Whether and how thought and reality are related to each other, only an infinite mind, conceived as identical with the finite minds, is capable of knowing. The souls and atoms are co-eternal with God, who is only *primus inter pares*. At first sight, it may perhaps appear that the Nyāya by insisting on devotion to Īśvara helps the religious life of mankind. But certainly the Nyāya cannot hold up the ideal of communion or identity with God, for by the nature of the hypothesis, God is outside man and the universe. The Vedānta in all its forms and the Yoga advocate the method of worship (upāsana), but it is with a view to enable the individual to attain the divine status. The Nyāya is bound to revise its conception of God, if it is to meet the highest religious instincts of humanity.

XXVI

Conclusion

The greatest contribution of the Nyāya to Hindu thought is in its organon of critical and scientific investigation. Its methodology is accepted by the other systems, though with slight modifications due to their metaphysical conceptions. It mapped out the world of knowledge in its essential features and gave to its main divisions the names which they still retain in Hindu thought, a clear proof of the immense advance which it won for the human intellect. The Nyāya list of fallacies has supplied the Indian thinkers through a long series of centuries with the means of discriminating, quickly and surely, between true and false inferences and affixing promptly to erroneous conclusions labels indicative of their unsoundness. In the Sanskrit philosophical works we frequently meet with silencing criticism, such as "this is a cakraka, or an argument in a circle"; "that is sādhyasama, or *petitio principii*"; "this is anyonyāśraya, or mutual dependence": "that leads to anavasthā, or infinite regress." The Nyāya theory of fallacies has served Indian thinkers as a ready-reckoner, "saving us," to use Börne's expressive words, "from the need of going to the ocean every time we want to wash our hands."

The strength, as well as the weakness of the Nyāya philosophy, is in its faith that the method of ordinary common sense and experience can be applied to the problems of religion and philosophy. A pluralistic universe based on the fundamental dualism between soul and matter is legitimate enough as a procedure and a method, but it cannot be transformed into a general philosophy. The average man has no hesitation in asserting the intrinsic reality of the outward visible world. He is also an animist, though his animism is more instinctive than reasoned, and so he admits the reality of his own and other spirits. He would not admit any degrees of reality, since such a conception would conflict with his rooted faith in dualistic realism ; but in the interests of logic he is hospitable to the idea of planes of objective being beyond the reach of the senses. In theology he raises the question of the cause of the universe. How does the universe come into being ? Such as it is now, he says, it has always been, since it began to be. Though, as a dualist, he fights shy of any transition between being and non-being, his empirical sense will not allow him to accept the static view of the universe. In this difficulty he turns to his own experience, where he finds that he makes several things, like tables and chairs, distinct from himself. As we are distinct from the things which we make, so is the divine spirit, the cause of all things distinct from his handiwork, the world. As we refashion existing material, so does God re-fashion the available elements of souls and atoms, which are co-eternal with him. Thus does the Nyāya attempt to do justice to the impressions of common sense and build a metaphysics of pluralistic realism.

In the course of this exposition we have pointed out that the Nyāya view is undoubtedly a natural and necessary stage in the evolution of thought, but is by no means final. The mechanical explanation of reality, which traces it back to its elements, eliminates the fact of development. The plausibility of the system is due to the insistence with which mere subjectivism is repudiated and the primal instincts of humanity satisfied. No system of Hindu thought, not even that of Śaṁkara, accepts the view of mere mentalism. But there is no inconsistency between metaphysical idealism and psychological realism.[1] The practical reality of things independent of finite minds is conceded by all systems of objective idealism. A metaphysical investigation of the nature and conditions of thought compels us to give up the view of self as a thing among other things. It will yield an idealism which does not so much upset the common-sense view as transcend it. Even metaphysical idealism allows us to admit, from the point of view of common sense and psychology, the distinction between thought and reality. The continuity and coherence of our experience means the reality of non-experienced entities. A deeper analysis of experience on the logical side was undertaken by the Sāṁkhya and the Vedānta. A more systematic co-ordination of the Nyāya ideas on the theological side is found in Rāmānuja.

REFERENCES.

ATHALYE : Tarkasaṁgraha of Annaṁ Bhaṭṭa, E.T.
COWELL : Udayana's Kusumāñjali, E.T.
COWELL and GOUGH : Sarvadarśanasaṁgraha, xi.
GANGĀNĀTH JHĀ : Nyāya Sūtras with Vātsyāyana's Bhāṣya and Uddyotakara's Vārttika, E.T.
KEITH : Indian Logic and Atomism.
SEAL : The Positive Sciences of the Ancient Hindus.
VIDYĀBHŪṢAṆ : History of Indian Logic.

---

[1] Cp. Green : "It is quite a tenable position to deny that an object is a state of consciousness and yet to hold that only for a thinking consciousness has it any reality" (*Works*, vol. i, p. 423).

CHAPTER III

THE ATOMISTIC PLURALISM OF THE VAIŚEṢIKA

The Vaiśeṣika—Date and literature—Theory of knowledge—Categories —Substance—Soul—Manas—Space—Time—Ākāśa—Earth, water, light and air—The atomic theory—Quality—Activity—Generality—Particularity — Inherence — Non-existence — Ethics — Theology — General estimate.

I

The Vaiśeṣika

The Vaiśeṣika system takes its name from viśeṣa, or particularity. It insists that it is in the particulars of the world, pre-eminently in the particular imperceptible souls and atoms that true individuality is to be found. Though the particular selves have cosmic and social relations, through which alone they can realise themselves, yet they retain their selfhood in spite of all these relations. The Vaiśeṣika is essentially a philosophy of distinctions, since it does not tolerate any attempt at dissipating the independence of selves and objects in a supposed more perfect individuality. Its standpoint is more scientific than speculative, more analytic than synthetic, though it is not able to set aside questions about the general character of the universe as a whole. Science sorts out, while philosophy sums up. The Vaiśeṣika is not interested in constructing an all-embracing synthesis within whose bounds there is room for all that is, bringing all the variety of the worlds of sense and of thought under a single comprehensive formula. In the spirit of science, it endeavours to formulate the most general characters of the things observed. It tickets different aspects of experience and assigns each to an appropriate pigeon-hole. The resulting philosophy comes to be of piecemeal character, and not an adequate and comprehensive one.

The impulse of the Vaiśeṣika system is derived from its hostility to Buddhistic phenomenalism. While the Vaiśeṣika accepts the Buddhist view of the sources of knowledge, perception and inference, it argues that souls and substances are solid facts, and cannot be dismissed as fancy pictures of a faery tale, supposed to be enacted behind the scenes. It does not concern itself with the problems of theology, and Śaṁkara's criticism even suggests that the dominant tendency of the system was in the direction of atheism.[1] The Vaiśeṣika in its early form, at any rate, was thought out in an age of excessive mental suppleness, when thought was full of the germs of scepticism.

Though mainly a system of physics and metaphysics, logical discussions are skilfully dovetailed into it in the later works. The Vaiśeṣika and the Nyāya agree in their essential principles, such as the nature and qualities of the self and the atomic theory of the universe, yet the classification and characterisation of the categories and the development of the atomic theory give to the Vaiśeṣika its distinctive interest and value.

II

Date and Literature

"The Vaiśeṣika system seems to be of much greater antiquity than the Nyāya."[2] This opinion of Garbe seems to be a reasonable one. In human knowledge the particular precedes the general. A theory of knowledge such as the one we have in the Nyāya is not possible until knowledge has made independent progress. Logic appears as a criticism and a corrective. The Sūtra of Kaṇāda does not show so much the influence of the Nyāya system, while the Sūtra of Gautama and the Bhāṣya of Vatsyāyana are considerably influenced by the Vaiśeṣika views.

It is urged that the Vaiśeṣika preceded Buddhism and Jainism. The Buddhist theory of nirvāṇa is traced to the asatkāryavāda of the Vaiśeṣika. The astikāyas of the Jainas, as well as their atomic theory,

[1] Saṁkara regards the followers of the Vaiśeṣika as ardhavaināśikas or semi-nihilists (S.B., ii. 2. 18). See however S.B., ii. 2. 37.

[2] Garbe: *The Philosophy of Ancient India*, p. 20.

are traced to the Vaiśeṣika, which is mentioned in many Jaina works as well as the *Lalitavistara*. The *Lankāvatāra Sūtra* alludes to the atomic views. One of the late Jaina works, *Āvaśyaka* [1] attributes the authorship of the Vaiśeṣika system to a Jain Rohagutta (A.D. 18), the chief teacher in the sixth schism of Jainism. Though its statement of the Vaiśeṣika view agrees with Kaṇāda's scheme,[2] the claim that the Vaiśeṣika is an offshoot of Jainism is hardly warranted. The point of similarity between the two, suggestive of such a claim, is the atomic theory; but even on this matter we find fundamental differences between the two views. According to the Jaina view, the atoms are qualitatively alike, each atom possessing colour, taste, smell and contact, as well as the capacity to produce sound though itself soundless. According to the Vaiśeṣika, atoms are qualitatively different, and possess one, two, three or four of the ordinary qualities according as they are atoms of air, fire, water, and earth, and they have no connection with sound. The atomic theory, the classification of substances and the acceptance of the two means of knowledge, strongly suggest that the Vaiśeṣika arose about the time of Buddha and Mahāvīra [3] (sixth-fifth century B.C.).

The first systematic exposition of the Vaiśeṣika philosophy is found in the *Vaiśeṣika Sūtra* of Kaṇāda (or Kaṇabhuj or Kaṇabhakṣa). The name, which signifies etymologically atomeater, seems to have been suggested by the character of the system,[4] which is also called Aulūkya Darśana.[5] The real name of the author of the Sūtra seems to have been Kāśyapa.[6] His work is divided into ten books. Book I discusses the five categories of substance, quality, action, generality and particularity. Book II deals with the different substances, excepting soul and mind, which, along with the objects of the senses and the nature of inference, are treated in Book III. The atomic structure of the universe is the central topic of Book IV. Book V is devoted to a discussion of the nature and kinds of action, while ethical

---

[1] S.B.E., vol. xlv, p. xxxviii.

[2] Dravya, guṇa, karma, samavāya are admitted, and slight variations are found as regards sāmānya and viśeṣa. The former is distinguished into: (1) mahāsāmānya, which answers to padārtha or abhidheyatva, or the possibility of being named, or jñeyatva, or the possibility of being known. All the categories are covered by it (see P.P., p. 16; V.S., i. 1. 8). Mahāsāmānya is pure sāmānya, and not a species of anything higher, while others are both sāmānya (general) and viśeṣa (particular); (2) sattāsāmānya, which corresponds to sattā or bhāva of the V.S. Praśastapāda ascribes existence (astitva) to all the six categories as a common quality (sādharmya); and (3) sāmānya-viśeṣa, which covers the other instances of generality. See Ui: *Vaiśeṣika Philosophy*, pp. 37–38.

[3] See Ui: *Vaiśeṣika Philosophy*, p. 33. Aśvaghoṣa, in his *Sūtrālaṁkāra*, assigns the Vaiśeṣika to the period before Buddha (*ibid.*, pp. 40–41).

[4] Though the atomic theory is found in some Buddhist and Jaina views, it is regarded as the central feature of the Vaiśeṣika. See B.S., ii. 2. 11, and Dharmottara's *Nyāyabinduṭīkā*, p. 86.

[5] Ui: *Vaiśesika Philosophy*.

[6] See P.P., p. 200.

problems are considered in Book VI. Book VII discusses the questions of quality, self and inherence. The last three books are mainly logical, and treat of the problems of perception, inference and causality. For reasons already stated, the *Vaiśeṣika Sūtra* seems to be of an earlier date than the *Nyāya Sūtra*, and is perhaps contemporaneous with the *Brahma Sūtra*.[1] Since Kauṭilya does not refer to the Vaiśeṣika under Ānvīkṣikī, it is said that the system was formulated later than 300 B.C.[2] Kaṇāda's Sūtra seems to have received additions from time to time.[3] Some of the sūtras now found in his treatise were not commented on by the scholiast, Praśastapāda, which indicates that at the time the latter commented on the Sūtra, they were not included in it. While

---

[1] Vātsyāyana quotes from the V.S., which is unaware of the Nyāya distinction of inference into pūrvavat and śeṣavat. In the V.S. there is a reference to time as the ultimate cause (ii. 2. 9; v. 2. 26), a view mentioned in the *Śvetāśvatara Up*. (i. 1. 2), and not adopted by any of the well-known systems. Even on the problem of self the Vaiśeṣika does not seek to establish its existence, but is more interested in discussing whether the self is an object of inference or of direct intuition. Bādarāyaṇa refers to the atomic theory in B.S., ii. 2. 11, and Kaṇāda uses Vedānta terms like avidyā and pratyagātman, and has in view the Vedānta theory when he asserts that the soul is not proved by scripture alone and the body is not compounded of three or five elements (V.S., iii. 2. 9; iv. 2. 2–3). If we trust the commentators, V.S. presupposes a knowledge of the Mīmāṁsā and the Sāṁkhya. See V.S., ii. 1. 20; iii. 1. 1–2; v. 2. 19–20; vii. 2. 3–8; vii. 2. 13; ix. 2. 3. The *Abhidharmamahāvibhāṣāśāstra* of Vasumitra refers to the five kinds of karma. Caraka's allusions to the Vaiśeṣika do not help us much. Nāgārjuna, in his *Prajñāpāramitāśāstra*, refers to the Vaiśeṣika theory of time as an unchangeable real existence relating to a cause (V.S., ii. 2. 7–9; v. 2. 26; vii. 1. 25). His references to space, atoms and self indicate that he was familiar with the V.S., and he practically quotes a number of them: iii. 2. 4, and viii. 1. 2, on the nature of self; iv. 1. 1, and vii. 1. 10, on the theory of atoms; and vi. 2. 13, and v. 2. 17–18, on atomic combination. Āryadeva is familiar with the V.S., and Harivarman knows the development of the Vaiśeṣika system after the formulation of the Sūtra. See Ui: *Vaiśeṣika Philosophy*, pp. 46–55.

[2] Dr. Das Gupta suggests that the Vaiśeṣika as expounded in the Sūtra of Kaṇāda represents an old school of the Mīmāṁsā (*History of Indian Philosophy*, pp. 280–285). The argument that the V.S. opens with the declared aim of explaining dharma and closes with the exhortation that Vedic works lead to prosperity through the force of adṛṣṭa, or unseen virtue, is not conclusive, since the discussion of and emphasis on dharma cannot be regarded as the monopoly of any system of thought. The attempt to explain away the points of distinction between the Vaiśeṣika and the Mīmāṁsā is hardly convincing. Kaṇāda believes that the Vedas are the work of ṛṣis, though not of Īśvara (ii. 1. 18; vi. 1. 1–2), while the Mīmāṁsā clings to the eternality of the Vedas, which cannot be said to be a later development. The two doctrines of the eternality of sound and that of the Vedas are closely allied. In spite of the occurrence of identical views and terms in the two systems, it is difficult to say that the Vaiśeṣika is a branch of the Mīmāṁsā.

[3] Faddegon: *The Vaiśeṣika System*, pp. 10–11.

Kaṇāda mentioned only three categories,[1] Praśastapāda added three more, and still later, the category of non-existence (abhāva) was introduced. Praśastapāda added seven qualities to the list mentioned by Kaṇāda.[2]

Praśastapāda's *Padārthadharmasaṁgraha* is not so much a commentary on the Sūtra as an important independent work on the subject. It is difficult to defend the position that Praśastapāda's mature views are simply the development of the suggestions contained in Kaṇāda's work.[3] Praśastapāda's account of the twenty-four qualities, the theory of the creation and the destruction of the world, the statement of fallacies and the nature of inference are distinct additions to Kaṇāda's work. He was much influenced by the Nyāya philosophy and was later than Vātsyāyana. He may be assigned to the end of the fourth century A.D.[4]

A Vaiśeṣika treatise based on Praśastapāda's work is Candra's *Daśapadārthaśāstra*, which is preserved in a Chinese version (A.D. 648). It did not, however, influence the development of thought in India.[5] *Rāvaṇabhāṣya* and *Bhāradvājavṛtti*,[6] which are said to be commen-

---

[1] V.S., viii. 2. 3. Artha iti dravyaguṇakarmasu, i. 1. 4, which mentions the six categories, is said to be a later addition.

[2] See also V.S., i. 1. 4; i. 1. 6; i. 2. 3.

[3] See Das Gupta: *History of Indian Philosophy*, vol. i. p. 351; I.L.A., pp. 25 and 93; Ui: *Vaiśeṣika Philosophy*, p. 17, n. 3. "Almost all the peculiar doctrines that distinguished the later Vaiśeṣikas from the Naiyāyikas and other schools are to be found in Praśastapāda's work, and are conspicuously absent in Kaṇāda's Sūtra. The doctrines about dvitva, pākajotpatti, vabhāgajavibhāga and several others, which are regarded as the peculiarities of the Vaiśeṣika system, are not even touched upon in Kaṇāda's aphorisms, although they are pretty fairly discussed in Praśastapāda's Bhāṣya" (Bodas: *Tarkasaṁgraha*, p. xxxvii).

[4] Keith makes out an elaborate case for the priority of Dignāga and Praśastapāda's indebtedness to him in several points of logical doctrine (I.L.A., pp. 93–110). For a different view, see Faddegon: *The Vaiśeṣika System*, pp. 319–323. Śaṁkara and Uddyotakara are familiar with the work of Praśastapāda. Even if Keith's view is accepted, he is earlier than Uddyotakara and later than Dignāga, and so belongs to the fifth century A.D. If Praśastapāda is credited with the authorship of the doctrine of the six categories, then he is earlier than, or at least of the same period as, Vātsyāyana. Dharmapāla (A.D. 535–570) and Paramārtha (A.D. 499–569) discuss Praśastapāda's views. See Ui: *Vaiśeṣika Philosophy*, p. 18.

[5] According to Ui, who has translated it into English, its author belongs to the sixth century A.D. As its name implies, the work mentions ten categories, the four additional being potentiality (śakti), non-potentiality (aśakti), commonness (sāmānyaviśeṣa), and non-existence (abhāva). There is no reference to Īśvara. The work has been widely commented on by Japanese writers.

[6] See *Ratnaprabhā*, ii. 2. 11; Bodas: *Tarkasaṁgraha*, p. 40. *Bhāradvājavṛttibhāṣya*, edited by Gaṅgādhara (Calcutta, 1869), is considerably influenced by the Sāṁkhya, and makes several important alterations. See Faddegon: *The Vaiśeṣika System*, pp. 35–40.

taries on the Vaiśeṣika, are not available. Four commentaries were written on Praśastapāda's work, which are Vyomaśekhara's *Vyomavatī*, Śrīdhara's *Nyāyakandalī*, Udayana's *Kiraṇāvali* (tenth century A.D.), and Śrīvatsa's [1] *Līlāvatī* (eleventh century A.D.). *Vyomavatī* is earlier than the other three.[2] Śrīdhara's *Nyāyakandalī* was written in A.D. 991, and the author is familiar with the views of Kumārila, Maṇḍana and Dharmottara. *Līlāvatī* and *Kiraṇāvali* came perhaps immediately after *Nyāyakandalī*. Both Śrīdhara and Udayana admit the existence of God and accept the category of non-existence. Śivāditya's *Saptapadārthī* belongs to this period.[3] It presents the Nyāya and the Vaiśeṣika principles as parts of one whole. It starts as an exposition of the categories and introduces the Nyāya logic under the quality of cognition. Laugākṣi Bhāskara's *Tarkakaumudī* is another syncretical work based on Praśastapāda's treatise. Śaṁkarā Miśra's *Upaskāra* on the *Vaiśeṣika Sūtra* is a work of some importance.[4] Viśvanātha (seventeenth century) treats of Kaṇāda's scheme in his *Bhāṣāpariccheda* and the commentary on it called *Siddhāntamuktāvali*. He was influenced considerably by the modern school of Nyāya. Annaṁ Bhaṭṭa's works, Jagadīśa's *Tarkāmṛta* (A.D. 1635) and Jayanārāyaṇa's *Vivṛti* (seventeenth century A.D.) are useful compendiums of the Vaiśeṣika principles. The *Vivṛti*, though based on the *Upaskāra*, differs from it on certain points.[5]

III

Theory of Knowledge

The logic of the Vaiśeṣika differs only slightly from the Nyāya logic. Knowledge, which is the problem of logic, assumes various forms, since its objects are endless.[6] Four kinds of valid knowledge are admitted, which are perception (pratyakṣa), inference (laiṅgika), remembrance (smṛti), and intuitive knowledge (ārṣajñāna). Perception enables us to apprehend substances, qualities and actions. Gross substances, which are made up of parts, are within the reach of perception, while atoms and diads are not. The Vaiśeṣika admits yogic perception, by which the perceptual

1 *Alias* Vallabha.

2 See Introduction to Ghate's edition of *Saptapadārthī*.

3 Śivāditya is later than Udayana and earlier than Gaṅgeśa, who is familiar with his views.

4 It refers to a Vṛtti (see i. 1. 2; i. 2. 4, 6; iii. 1. 17; iv. 1. 7; vi. 1. 5, 12; vii. 1. 3) which has not been traced.

5 See especially i. 1 4, 25; ii. 1. 1; ii. 2. 5; ix. 1. 8.

6 P.P., p. 172.

cognition of the soul (ātmapratyakṣa) arises.[1] The Vaiśeṣika brings comparison (upamāna), tradition (aitihya), and verbal knowledge (śabda) under inference.[2] The validity of scriptural statements is an inference from the authoritative character of the speakers.[3] Like the Nyāya, the Vaiśeṣika repudiates the Mīmāṁsā theory of the eternity of sound and the absolute authoritativeness of the Vedas.[4] While the Nyāya bases the validity of the Vedas on the ground of the direct communication from seers who had realised the eternal truths and laws, the Vaiśeṣika infers it from the unimpeachable veracity of the inspired seers. The scriptures give us real knowledge and not mere speculation. It is knowledge of things as they are, and in this sense has no beginning, though it is always directly known and realised by some beings in its entirety and by others in part. Abler minds realised the truths and communicated them to us. The Vedas, as collections of sentences, presuppose intelligent authors; and they must be possessors of complete and accurate knowledge of heaven and unseen destiny (adṛṣṭam). Gradually this authorship was assigned to God. "The authoritativeness of the Veda follows from its being the word of God." [5] The meanings of words and sentences must be understood before they give us knowledge. Since the understanding of meanings depends on the recognition of universal concomitance, verbal knowledge is a case of inference.[6] Ceṣṭā or gesture,[7] arthāpatti or implication,[8] saṁbhava or inclusion,[9] and abhāva or negation,[10] are all brought under inference. Smṛti, or remembrance, is given an independent place.[11] Ārṣajñāna is the insight of seers. If remembrance is ignored, since it only reproduces what has already been experienced, and if intuitive wisdom is brought under perception, we have, according to the Vaiśeṣika, only two sources of knowledge, intuition and inference.[12]

Four varieties of invalid knowledge are mentioned, which

[1] V.S., ix. 1. 11–15.
[2] P.P., pp. 212 ff.
[3] ix. 1. 3.
[4] V.S., ii. 2. 21–37; vi. 1. 1 ff.; N.S., ii. 2. 13–40.
[5] Tad vacanād āmnāyasya prāmāṇyam iti (x. 2. 9) See also *Nyāyakandalī*, p. 216, and V.S., vi. 1. 1–4.
[6] iii. 1. 7–15.
[7] P.P., p. 220.
[8] P.P., p. 223.
[9] P.P., p. 225; V.S., ix. 2. 5.
[10] *Ibid.*
[11] P.P., p. 256.
[12] S.S.S.S., v. 33.

are doubt (saṁśaya), misconception (viparyaya), indefinite cognition (anadhyavasāya), and dream (svapna). Śivāditya reduces these four to two, doubt and error, and brings under the former conjecture (ūha), indeterminate knowledge and indirect reasoning.[1] Śrīdhara justifies the separate mention of dreams on the ground that " it occurs only in a particular condition of the body."[2]

IV

The Categories

For some centuries, as we have already seen, the Buddhist standpoint, which defined things by their consequences, interpreted everything by its contexts, and denied self-sufficiency everywhere, dominated the mind of the country. Everything has being through mutual connections, and nothing exists in and for itself. As relations are the stuff of life, soul and matter are simply sets of relations. The Vaiśeṣika protests against this view and attempts to expound a more satisfactory plan, which reality seems to offer and justify. It takes its stand on the deliverance of the empirical consciousness, which deals first and last with real and separate things. The simplest and the widest spread of the characters of reality is that of things and relations between them. When we open our eyes we see spread out before us a material world with its different things and arrangements, on which thought can exercise itself ; when we look within we find a non-material one with its terms and relations. Sound philosophy requires us to confine our attention to the things of experience, the objects of knowledge, and accept only such hypotheses as are found to be indispensable for the explanation of the order of experience. An analytic survey is the first need of an accurate philosophy, and the results of the Vaiśeṣika analysis are found set forth in the doctrine of the padārthas.

Padārtha means literally the meaning of a word. A padārtha is an object which can be thought (artha) and named (pada). All things which exist, which can be cognised

[1] *Saptapadārthī*, 32. [2] *Nyāyakandalī*, p. 185.

and named,[1] in short, all objects of experience,[2] and not merely the things of the physical world, are padārthas. The sixteen padārthas of the Nyāya are not an analysis of existing things, but are a list of the central topics of the logical science. But the categories of the Vaiśeṣika attempt a complete analysis of the objects of knowledge.

The Vaiśeṣika categories include not only things predicable of another, but also subjects capable of having things predicated of them. Aristotle's categories are a logical classification of predicates only, and not a metaphysical classification of all thinkable objects. The Vaiśeṣika thinkers, as much as Aristotle, seem to have been aware of the intimate relation between name and thing. Though Aristotle classifies words, it happens to be a classification of things as well, for whatever receives a separate name is a thing. "Of words expressed without syntax (*i.e.* single words), each signifies either substance, or quantity, or quality, or relation, or place, or time, or disposition (*i.e.* attitude or internal arrangement), or appurtenance, or action (doing), or suffering (being done to)." [3] Of these ten categories the last nine are predicable of something else, while the first substance is *ens*, and cannot be predicated of anything, not even of itself, for then it is no more a substance but becomes an attribute. But Aristotle is not very strict in his usage. The forms of common speech determined his classification, and among words we have those which signify the substance of a concrete individual. When the substance is a concrete individual, we ask, What is it? and answer, a horse or a cow, which Aristotle calls a substance, though it is really a quality.[4] He distinguishes first and second substances, and holds that the first are not properly used as predicates. The inclusion of the logical subject in a classification of predicates shows that Aristotle intended his categories to be also a list of existences or "kinds of being." We have in Aristotle's list substances and qualities which are either permanent or temporary. Almost all the commentators

[1] Astitva, abhidheyatva, jñeyatva (P.P., p. 16).
[2] Pramitiviṣayāḥ padārthāḥ (*Saptapadārthī*, p. 2).
[3] Aristotle's *Categories*, ii. 6; Minto's *Logic*, p. 113.
[4] Cp. Johnson: "A substantive proper cannot characterise, but is necessarily characterised" (*Logic*, part ii, p. xii).

agree that the category of relation should be taken as including the last six of his scheme. We may therefore take substance, quality, temporary or permanent, and relation as exhausting all significations.

The Vaiśeṣika adopts a sixfold classification of padārthas into substance (dravya), quality (guṇa), activity (karma), generality (sāmānya), particularity (viśeṣa), and inherence (samavāya), to which a seventh non-existence (abhāva) was added by the later Vaiśeṣikas, Śrīdhara, Udayana and Śivāditya.[1] The inclusion of non-existence under padārthas suggests the transformation of an ontological into an epistemological scheme. Our beliefs are positive or negative, and not things which exist. In its initial stages, the Vaiśeṣika endeavoured to determine the general characteristics which apply to existence as a whole, but soon turned its attention to the nature of beliefs and inquired what sorts of beliefs were true and what not. That something is, that something exists, is the first proposition of the Vaiśeṣika philosophy. But nothing can simply be. If we stop with bare existence and refuse to go further, then, as Hegel has taught us, we are left with a mere blank, and even the first principle that something exists has to be given up. So we must push forward and assert that a thing *is* because it possesses certain properties besides mere existence. Whatever exists does so because it has certain qualities. Substances exist and have qualities. We have two kinds of qualities, those which reside in a plurality of objects and those which are confined to individuals. The former are the general qualities (sāmānya), while the latter are distinguished as permanent (guṇa) and transitory (karma). Inherence is a special kind of relation.[2]

[1] Praśastapāda mentions only the six categories. The sevenfold scheme became established by the time of Śivāditya, as is evident from the title of his work, *Saptapadārthī*. Saṁkara and Haribhadra (*Ṣaḍdarśanasamuccaya*, 60) attribute to the Vaiśeṣika only six categories. See S.B., ii. 2. 17; and Ui: *Vaiśeṣika Philosophy*, p. 126.

[2] Dravya and guṇa of the Vaiśeṣika correspond to Aristotle's substance and quality. Aristotle's quantity is brought under guṇa. Relations are of two kinds: external, like conjunction (saṁyoga), or internal, like inherence (samavāya). The first is regarded as a quality and the second is made a separate category. The remaining categories fall under relation, while space and time are taken as independent substances. Activity is

The first three categories of substance, quality and action possess a real objective existence.[1] Kaṇāda calls them artha, and declares, in treating of yogic insight, that we can have an intuition of them.[2] The other three, generality, particularity and inherence, are products of intellectual discrimination (buddhyapekṣam).[3] They are logical categories. Praśastapāda observes: "they have their sole being within themselves (svātmasattvam), have the intellect as their indicator (buddhi-lakṣaṇatvam), they are not effects (akāryatvam), not causes (akāraṇatvam), have no generality or particularity (asāmānyaviśeṣavattvam), are eternal (nityatvam), and are not expressible by the word 'thing' (arthaśabdānabhidheyatvam)."[4] The proof of the reality of the last three categories is said to be logical,[5] the implication being that these are not capable of direct apprehension, a view which was modified when the Nyāya and the Vaiśeṣika principles got mixed up. In early Vaiśeṣika, while all categories are said to possess the feature of existence in general (astitva),[6] a distinction is made between two kinds of being, sattāsaṁbandha, ascribed to substances, qualities and actions, and svātmasattva, or the being of generality, particularity and inherence.[7] Udayana in his *Kiraṇāvali* defines the former as subsistence of being by the

karma, while passivity is only the absence of activity. Property may be either general or particular. Disposition is a quality. If Aristotle had proceeded on a definite principle, he would have argued thus: Things possessing qualities, either permanent or temporary, exist in relations of time and space bound together with other things in a network of reciprocal relations, and in that case substance, quality, action and relation would be the main heads. The defective character of Aristotle's analysis was noticed by the Stoics and the Neo-platonists, Kant, who thinks that Aristotle simply jotted down the categories as they occurred to him, and Hegel, who observes that Aristotle threw them together anyhow. Mill rather contemptuously remarks that Aristotle's list "is like a division of animals into men, quadrupeds, horses, asses and ponies." Cp. with the Vaiśeṣika scheme the Jaina classification of all things into substances, qualities and modifications (I.P., pp. 312 ff., and *Uttarādhyayana*, I., S.B.E., vol. xlv). The earlier Mīmāṁsakas accept the categories of power (śakti) and similarity (sādṛśya). Udayana rejects these, as well as number (saṁkhyā). See *Kiraṇāvali*, p. 6; *Saptapadārthī*, p. 10; *Nyāyakandalī*, pp. 7, 15, 144 ff.

[1] V.S., i. 2. 7; viii. 2. 3; P.P., p. 17.

[2] V.S., ix. 1. 14.

[3] i. 2. 3.

[4] P.P., p. 19; V.S., i. 2. 3–10, 12, 14, 16; vii. 2. 26.

[5] Buddhir eva lakṣaṇam pramāṇam. *Nyāyakandalī*, p. 19.

[6] P.P., p. 11.

[7] P.P., p. 19.

relation of inherence, and the latter as self-sufficient existence independent of all being. Śaṁkara Miśra is more helpful, for in his *Upaskāra* he defines sattāsaṁbandha as liability to destruction and capacity to produce effects from out of its nature. This seems to have been the technical way of stating existence in space and time. Svātmasattva, or self-sufficient existence, is independent of space and time, and therefore something which belongs to the timeless categories. Though the latter are products of abstraction, they are regarded as more real than the things themselves from which they are abstracted. The Vaiśeṣika insists on the timeless and non-causal character of the categories of generality, particularity and inherence, and warns us against the natural tendency to attribute existence in space and time to the results of abstraction.

V

Substance

The category by which the Vaiśeṣika pits itself definitely against all idealistic systems is that of substance. Even the unthinking admit that substances are. Objects in the external world come to us as real, in and for themselves, present actualities with a subsistence of their own. Substance denotes the feature of the self-subsistence of things out there. What we vaguely call being is nothing more than a series of things variously conditioned in time and space and distinguished from one another by different properties. The Buddhist view that there is no substance apart from its qualities, or a whole apart from its parts, contradicts the testimony of experience.[1] Reality presents us with substances marked by the possession of qualities and parts. We are able to recognise the jar we saw yesterday, which would be impossible if the jar were a string of sensations.[2] It is a matter of common experience that qualities occur in groups, which are invariable in character and sufficiently marked off from others. An apple always consists of the same group of qualities and invariably grows on the same kind of tree. The unbroken continuity

[1] N.V., i. 1. 13.

[2] N.S., ii. 1. 30–36.

of the mummy or the mountain which has a continued existence for several millenniums is unintelligible apart from the assumption of substances in which qualities inhere. "That which contains in it action and qualities and is a co-existent cause"[1] is a substance. It is the substrate of qualities.[2] The other categories are devoid of qualities.

The Vaiśeṣika believes that a substance is something over and above the qualities. At the moment the substances are produced they are devoid of qualities.[3] For if qualities arise simultaneously with substances, there cannot be any distinction between them. If they do not arise, then substances would be free from qualities, and then the definition of substance as that which possesses qualities seems to be violated. To meet this difficulty, it is said that substance is the substrate of qualities either in the relation of intimate union (samavāyasaṁbandha) or antecedent negation (prāgabhāva), *i.e.* future existence. In other words, a substance is the basis of qualities, actual or potential, present or future.[4] The Vaiśeṣika is anxious to assert the existence of something which has qualities without being itself a quality, for we predicate qualities of substances and not qualities of qualities. Nor can it be said that we predicate one quality of a group of qualities. But since a substance cannot be conceived apart from qualities, it is defined as possessing qualities.

A distinction is made between eternal and non-eternal substances. Whatever depends on something else is not eternal. Compound substances (avayavidravyas) are dependent and transitory. Simple substances have the characteristics of eternity, independence and ultimate individuality.[5] They are neither caused nor destroyed. Non-eternal substances are caused and destroyed not by themselves but by something different from themselves.[6]

Earth, water, light, air, ākāśa, time, space, soul and manas are the nine substances intended to comprise all corporeal

[1] i. 1. 15.
[2] Guṇāśrayo dravyam.
[3] Ādye kṣaṇe nirguṇaṁ dravyaṁ tiṣṭhati.
[4] *Siddhāntamuktāvali*, 3.
[5] Nityatva, anāśritatva, antyaviśeṣavatva (P.P., pp. 20–21).
[6] P.P., p. 20; *Nyāyakandalī*, p. 20. See V.S., i. 1. 9–10, 12, 15, 18; x. 2. 1–2.

and incorporeal things.[1] The Vaiśeṣika is not a materialism, though a realistic scheme, since it admits non-material substances like souls, and regards as real not the gross material substances but their minima. Of the nine substances, earth, water, light, air, soul and manas have many individuals.[2] These, with the exception of soul, are extended, have relations of distance and proximity, are capable of action and possess speed.[3] Ākāśa, time and space are all-pervading, have the largest dimensions and are the common receptacles of all corporeal things.[4] Soul and manas, ākāśa, time and space, air and ultimate atoms are not ordinarily perceptible.[5] A distinction is made between corporeal (mūrta) and elemental (bhūta) substances. The former have definite dimensions,[6] act and move. Elemental substances, singly or in combination, become the material causes of the products of the world. Manas, though atomic, does not produce anything else, while ākāśa, though all-pervading, produces sound. Earth, water, light and air are both corporeal and productive.[7]

The Vaiśeṣika theory of the soul is practically identical with that of the Nyāya, though a direct perception of the self where the self is both the perceiver and the perceived is not admitted.[8] Comparison does not help us. Āgama, or revelation and inference, are our only sources of knowledge.[9] The existence of the self is inferred from the fact that consciousness cannot be a property of the body, sense-organs or the manas.[10] In addition to the qualities of pleasure, pain, desire, aversion, volition, and knowledge, the facts of expiration and inspiration, the closing and the opening of the eyelids, the healing

[1] An interesting question about the nature of darkness (tamas) is raised by Śrīdhara (*Nyāyakandalī*, p. 9; V.S., v. 2. 19–20). Kumārila regards it as a distinct substance with the quality of colour, *i.e.* blackness, and the action of motion (S.V., p. xliii). The Prābhākaras hold that darkness is the absence of light (Jhā: P.M., p. 93). Annaṁ Bhaṭṭa is of this view (*Tarkasaṁgraha dīpikā*, 3). Darkness is not ranked as a substance by the Vaiśeṣika, since it is destitute of qualities. It is said to possess the black colour figuratively, even as the colourless sky is spoken of as blue. It is a variety of non-existence, being merely the negation of light (V.S., v. 2. 19; S.D.S., x).

[2] Anekatvam pratyekaṁ vyaktibhedaḥ (*Nyāyakandalī*, p. 21).

[3] P.P., p. 21.

[4] p. 22.

[5] V.S., viii. 1. 2.

[6] Paricchinnaparimānatvam.

[7] *Tarkadīpikā*, p. 14.

[8] V.S., iii. 2. 6.

[9] V.S., iii. 2. 8 and 18.

[10] P.P., p. 69; V.S., iii. 1. 19.

up of bodily injuries, the movement of the mind and the affections of the senses are urged as evidence for the existence of the self.[1] In its natural state the self is devoid of intelligence, as in pralaya. It has cognitions of things when it is connected with the body.[2] Consciousness is sustained by the ātman, though it is not an essential or inalienable characteristic of it. By means of manas the soul knows not only external things but also its own qualities. Though the soul is all-pervading, its life of knowing, feeling and activity resides only where the body is.

The plurality of souls is inferred from differences in status, the variety of conditions.[3] The scriptural injunctions assume the distinctness of souls.[4] Each soul undergoes the consequences of its own deeds.[5] It remains one throughout the series of its experiences.[6] Śrīdhara repudiates the view of the oneness of self.[7] There would be no risk of the absolute dissolution of the world by the emancipation of the souls from it, since their number is infinite. The pluralistic bias of the Vaiśeṣika leads its followers to look upon plurality as ultimate. The freed souls are conceived as eternally existing with specific differences.[8] Though each soul is supposed to be distinguished by a peculiarity (viśeṣa), it is impossible for us to

[1] V.S., iii. 2. 4–13.

[2] Aśarīriṇām ātmanām na viṣayāvabodhaḥ (*Nyāyakandalī*, p. 57; see also p. 279).

[3] Vyavasthāto nānā (V.S., iii. 2. 20).

[4] Śāstrasāmarthyāt (V.S., iii. 2. 21).

[5] V.S., vi. 1. 5.

[6] *Nyāyakandalī*, p. 86.

[7] "If the self were one, the contact of manas would be common to all persons. . . . For one, however, who admits of many selves, even though all selves, being omnipresent, would be present in all bodies, yet his experiences would not be common to all of them, as each of them would experience only such pleasures, etc., as would appear in connection with the particular body that will have been brought about by the previous karma of that self, and not those belonging to the other bodies. And the karma also belongs to that self by whose body it has been done. Hence the restriction of the body is due to the restriction of the karma and *vice versa*, the mutual interdependence going on endlessly" (*Nyāyakandalī*, pp. 87–88).

[8] It is difficult to accept Dr. Das Gupta's suggestion that the Vaiśeṣika held that the "self was one, though, for the sake of many limitations, and also because of the need for the performance of acts enjoined by the scriptures, they are regarded as many" (*History of Indian Philosophy*, p. 290, n. 1). The Vaiśeṣika is interested in the empirical variety and not in ultimate truth, and the view of plurality, based as it is on the doctrine of viśeṣa, is accepted by it as final.

know what it is. The differences among souls are due to their connections with bodies. Even in rebirth the manas accompanies the soul and gives it individuality. For all practical purposes the distinctiveness of the soul is determined by the distinctiveness of the manas, which accompanies it throughout its career. There are as many of them as there are souls. As the same manas accompanies the soul throughout its career, there is the possibility of the continuity as well as the survival of character.[1] A distinction is made between the individual soul and the supreme soul, jīva and Īśvara.[2] The two are similar but not identical.

Ākāśa, space and time have no lower species and are names of individuals.[3] To account for the variety of experience, these comprehensive unities are assumed. All phenomena take place in them. Space and time are the instrumental causes of all produced things.[4] Reality is a process or a passage, and is therefore both spatial and temporal.

In the case of physical changes we require a whole in which they occur. All atomists ascribe reality to empty space. If there were more than one space, then atoms which whirl about in different spaces cannot have anything to do with one another. Space is the basis of the notions of east and west, of far and near.[5] The apparent diversity of space is determined by its effects.[6] Things maintain their relative positions which they could not do apart from space.

The form of time is essential to the concrete changes of nature, such as production, destruction and persistence of things. It is the force which brings about changes in non-eternal substances. It is not the cosmic power which causes the movements, but is the condition of all movement.[7] All perceptible things are perceived as moving, changing, coming into existence and as passing out of it. Discrete things have no power of self-origination or self-movement. If they had, there would not be that mutual relation of things, which

[1] P.P., p. 89; V.S., vii. 2. 21; iii. 2. 22.
[2] *Kiraṇāvali*, p. 7. See also *Upaskāra*, iii. 2. 18.
[3] P.P., p. 58.
[4] P.P., p 25.
[5] *Tarkasaṁgraha*, 16; *Bhāṣāpariccheda*, pp. 46–47.
[6] V.S., ii. 2. 13.
[7] ii. 2. 9; v. 2. 26. This view is not to be confused with the kālavāda, which deifies time.

persists in spite of all change. The movement is ordered, which means that there must be a reality which has a general relation to all changes. Time is regarded as the independent real pervading the whole universe and making the ordered movement of things possible. It is the basis of the relations of priority and posteriority, simultaneity and non-simultaneity, and of the notion of soon and late.[1] There is only one time which is omnipresent in dimension,[2] individual in character, and has the qualities of conjunction and disjunction. Conventional notions, as moment, minute, hour, year, etc., are derived by abstraction from concrete time. According to the Vaiśeṣika time is an eternal substance,[3] and the basis of all experience.[4] We do not know what time is in itself, but our experience is cast in the form of time. It is the formal cause of the relations of priority and posteriority, while their material cause is the nature of objects, as jar, cloth and the like. Time which is one appears as many on account of its association with the changes that are related to it.[5]

The distinction between time and space is noticed in the Vaiśeṣika treatises. Space deals with coexistence, time with successions, or more accurately, space deals with visible objects, while time deals with things produced and destroyed.[6] Śaṁkara Miśra holds that the relations of time are constant or irreversible (niyata), while those of space are not irreversible (aniyata).[7] Things move by virtue of time and hold together by virtue of space. While space and time cover the most comprehensive kinds of relations, transition from place to place, or state to state, spatial locomotion and temporal alternation, they are only formal and imply real things which move and change.

Ākāśa is a simple, continuous, infinite substance, and is the substratum of sound. The qualities of colour, taste, smell and tangibility do not belong to it. By the process of

[1] V.S., ii. 2. 6. [2] vii. 1. 25. [3] ii. 2. 7.

[4] Atītādivyavahārahetuḥ (*Tarkasaṁgraha*, 15; *Bhāṣāpariccheda*, 45).

[5] *Nyāyamañjari*, p. 136.

[6] *Siddhāntacandrodaya* says: "Janyamātraṁ kriyāmātraṁ vā kālopādhiḥ, mūrtamātraṁ digupādhiḥ."

[7] *Upaskāra*, ii. 2. 10. Cp. with this Kant's Second and Third Analogies of Experience.

elimination sound is proved to be the distinguishing quality of ākāśa.[1] It is inactive (niṣkriya). All corporeal objects are found conjoined with it.[2] The atoms which are infinitely small cannot make up a magnitude by coming together or touching each other. If they stand apart from one another and yet are joined somehow so as to constitute a system, it can only be through the medium of ākāśa. The atoms unite, but not continuously. That which binds together the atoms, though not itself atomic, is the ākāśa. If ākāśa were also discrete, *i.e.* capable of being analysed into atoms, then we shall have to assume some other connecting tissue which is not atomic. Ākāśa is eternal, omnipresent, supersensible, and has the qualities of individuality, conjunction and disjunction. Ākāśa fills all space, though it is not space itself, since it cannot affect or operate on things without entering into special relations with them and thereby having sound produced in it. That which sustains the positional relations and order of discrete things is called dik, though it is not space itself, if the latter means room or place, which is ākāśa. The distinction between ākāśa and space is admitted in view of the fact that while ākāśa is regarded as the material cause of the special quality of sound, space is the general cause of all effects.

The physical theory of the Vaiśeṣika is developed in connection with the five substances of earth, water, light, air and ākāśa. Matter, as we meet with it, is a mixture of five elements, containing one or the other in a predominant degree. The five phenomenal products (bhūtas) are the five states of matter, solid (earth), liquid (water), gaseous (air), luminous (light), etheric (ākāśa). The earth possesses the four qualities of smell, taste, colour and tangibility, water the three qualities of taste, colour and tangibility, light the two of colour and tangibility, while air has the quality of tangibility and ākāśa that of sound.[3] Though earth contains a number of qualities, we yet say it has smell on account of the predominance of this quality.[4] If water and other substances besides earth possess smell, it is because particles of earth are mixed up with them. We cannot think of earth without smell, though

[1] V.S., ii. 1. 27, 29–31.
[2] N.S., iv. 2. 21–22.
[3] N.S., iii. 1. 60–61.
[4] N.S., iii. 1 66.

we can so think of air and water. Things made of earth are of three kinds, bodies, sense-organs and objects of perception.[1] The special quality of water is taste. Light has for its special property luminosity. Air is invisible, though limited in extent and made up of parts. The discrete nature of air is inferred from the movements in the air, which would not be possible were air an absolute continuum devoid of parts.[2] Its existence is inferred from touch,[3] and it is said to be a substance, since it possesses quality and action. Temperature is the special quality of air. The ultimate constituents of the concrete things of earth, air, light and water are called atoms.

VI

The Atomic Theory

The atomic theory is so natural to the human mind that early attempts at the explanation of the physical world assume this form. Traces of the theory are to be found in the Upaniṣads, which generally regarded all material things as made up of the four elements of light, water, air and earth. Ākāśa is left out, since it has a peculiar character of its own and does not enter into combination with the other elements. But the four elements of light, water, air and earth are themselves changeable and divisible, while the real is regarded as unchangeable and eternal. The question naturally arises as to what the unchangeable, indivisible, eternal particles are. In the ferment of thought which produced the great systems of Jainism and Buddhism, there were some who held the atomic hypothesis, for example, the Ajīvakas and the Jainas.[4] Kaṇāda formulated the theory on purely metaphysical grounds, and tried through it to simplify the world to thought. It was

[1] P.P., p. 27.

[2] V.S., ii. 1. 14.

[3] The ancient Vaiśeṣikas and Annaṁ Bhaṭṭa hold that air is not perceived, but only known by inference. They argue that air has no colour and so cannot be seen. The modern Naiyāyikas say that a thing need not be seen for being perceived. We may perceive things by touch.

[4] I.P., pp. 317–319. Though not the canonical works of Buddhism, northern Buddhist literature contains many references to the atomic theory. The Vaibhāṣikas and the Sautrāntikas accept it. See Ui: *Vaiśeṣika Philosophy*, pp. 26–28.

the same with Leucippus and Democritus, for the atomic theory never acquired a serious scientific status until the time of Dalton.

All things consisting of parts originate from the parts with which they are connected by the relation of inherence, conjunction co-operating. The things that we experience are all products, *i.e.* discrete or made up of parts. They are therefore non-eternal. Non-eternal has no meaning apart from eternal.[1] Earth, water, fire and air are both eternal and non-eternal, while ākāśa is eternal only. The compounds which are produced are non-eternal, while the component particles which are not produced are eternal.[2] The invisible eternal atoms are incapable of division into parts.[3] The atom marks the limit of division. If it is endlessly divisible into parts, then all material things would be the products of an equally endless number of constituent parts, so that differences in the dimensions of things cannot be accounted for.[4] If matter were infinitely divisible, then we should have to reduce it to nothing, and admit the paradoxical position that magnitudes are built up of what has no magnitude, bodies out of the bodyless.[5] The changes in the volumes of bodies are determined by the accession and withdrawal of the atoms composing them. Infinite greatness and infinite smallness are not realised magnitudes. They are the upper and the lower limits, and what we know is intermediate between the two. By a continual addition we reach the infinitely great, and by a continual splitting up we reach the infinitely small. The atoms are the material causes of effects. Though they are supersensible, they can be classified, though not from the standpoint of size, shape, weight and density. The qualities which they produce in the different forms of sensible things help us in the classification of atoms. If we leave aside the

[1] iv. 1. 4.
[2] iv. 1. 1; ii. 3, 4–5; vii. 1. 20–21.
[3] Paraṁ vā truṭeḥ (N.B., iv. 2. 17–25).
[4] Sarveṣām anavasthitāvayavatve merusarṣapayos tulyaparimāṇatvāpattiḥ. See *Nyāyakandalī*, p. 31.
[5] Herbart considers the diversity and changes of experience to be intelligible only if the things themselves which are simple and unchangeable furnish some reasons for them. These unknowable realities have to be conceived in certain relations by means of which we may understand the variety of their apparent properties and changes.

general properties of sensible things, such as impenetrability, which are perceived by more senses than one, the special qualities are odour, flavour, luminosity and temperature. These differ in kind and not merely in degree. It is assumed that there are four classes of paramāṇus, answering to the four great classes of material objects, earth, water, light and air. These four classes of paramāṇus are said to produce the four senses of touch, taste, sight and smell, and this is why each special sense reveals a single quality, however excited. Though the qualities of earthly things, as colour, taste, smell and tangibility, vanish on the destruction of the thing itself, they are always found in their respective atoms, though in earth and atoms of earth some qualities are produced by heat (pākaja).[1] Water, light and air do not suffer a similar change.

The Vaiśeṣika adopts the theory of pīlupāka. When the jar is baked the old one is destroyed, *i.e.* resolved into atoms. The application of the heat produces the red colour in the atoms, which are again brought together and a new jar is produced. On this view we have first the disintegration of the whole into its atoms, and then a reintegration of them into a whole. All this complicated process is imperceptible, since it takes place with extreme rapidity in an interval of nine moments.[2] The Naiyāyika advocates the theory of piṭharapāka, by which the change of colour is effected in both the atoms and the products simultaneously. This view seems to be more reasonable. The Naiyāyika objects to the Vaiśeṣika theory on the following grounds. If the first jar be destroyed and a new one substituted for it, we shall not be able to identify it as the old jar. We see the same jar as before except for the difference in colour. Moreover, the Vaiśeṣika view seems to make even the odour of the earth atoms non-eternal. The fact that sensible things are operated on by heat shows that they are not absolutely solid but are porous.[3]

The paramāṇus are said to be globular (parimāṇḍalya), though it does not follow that they have parts. Certain objections on the assumption that they have parts were urged. When three atoms are in juxtaposition, the middle one touches the atoms on the sides. When the atom is surrounded on all sides we distinguish six sides of the atoms, which we may speak of as its parts, and if the six sides are reduced to a point, then it would follow that any number of atoms would take up no more space than a single atom, and things of the world could be reduced to the size of an atom and they would be invisible. All this

---

[1] vii. 1. 1–6.
[2] S.D.S., x.
[3] N.V.T.T., p. 355; *Nyāyamañjari*, p. 438.

difficulty is met by the answer that the division of atoms into parts is empirical and not real.[1] The atoms have no inside or outside[2] and are non-spatial.[3]

The atoms are naturally passive, and their movement is due to external impact. During the dissolution of the world (pralaya) the atoms subsist without producing any effects. They then remain isolated and motionless. According to Vaiśeṣika, the movement of the ultimate atoms arises from a peculiar dharma.[4] Praśastapāda says: "Actions which we find appearing in the rudimentary elements (mahābhūteṣu), and for which we cannot find any cause either by sense-perception or by inference, and which are yet found to be useful or harmful to us, must be regarded as produced by these unseen agencies (adṛṣṭakāritam)."[5]

The qualities of all products are due to the atoms of which they are composed. These atoms possess the five general qualities of all substances, as also those of priority and posteriority. In addition to these, earth has the special quality of odour and the other qualities of taste, colour, touch or temperature, heaviness, velocity and fluidity. Water has the special quality of viscosity and the other qualities of earth except smell. Light has the usual seven, and temperature, colour, fluidity and velocity, while air has only touch and velocity in addition to the seven common qualities. These qualities are eternal in the atoms but transient in the products.

There can never come a time when there will be an utter annihilation of things. Though the structures built are perishable, the stones of which they are built are eternal.[6] The components which unite to form a whole, and therefore were previously able to exist apart from such combination, possess the capacity for independent existence and return to it. Fabric after fabric in the visible world up to the terrestrial mass itself may be dissolved, but the atoms will abide ever new and fresh, ready to form other structures in the ages yet to come. The individual atoms combine with others and continue in that co-operative existence for some time and

[1] N.B., iv. 2. 20.

[2] The question is raised whether ākāśa, which is a simple all-pervading substance, penetrates the atoms or not. If it does, then the atoms have parts; if it does not, then atoms have no parts, but ākāśa is not all-pervading. It is said in reply that the conception of within and without is inapplicable to an eternal entity, and the omnipresence of ākāśa need not imply the existence of parts in the atom.

[3] N.V., iv. 2. 25. The atoms are said to be of a minute size as opposed to largeness. They possess some sort of magnitude. For a different view see Chatterji: *Hindu Realism*, pp. 19–34, 149–153, and 164.

[4] Dharmaviśeṣāt, iv. 2. 7. [5] p. 309. [6] N.B., iv. 2. 16.

again disintegrate into their original solitary being to form new combinations. This process of grouping and separation goes on endlessly. According to the Vaiśeṣika, atoms do not exist in an uncombined state in creation.[1] During creation they are said to possess a vibratory motion (parispanda). Singly the atoms are not productive. Śrīdhara argues that if an eternal thing were singly productive, there would be an unceasing production, and this would necessitate the admission of the indestructibility of the products also. Nor can triads be productive, since a gross material object is the product of parts of smaller dimension than the object itself. The triad, which is of a gross dimension, must be regarded as a product of something that is itself a product. So dyads alone produce things.[2] Even the dyads composed of two primary atoms are minute, and three of these produce the triad,[3] which has a dimension not too small for apprehension. Both single atoms and dyads are invisible, and the least magnitude required for visibility is a triad said to be of the size of a mote in the sunbeam. Apparently, this is an exception to the general rule that the qualities of the causes produce corresponding qualities in the effects. When two atoms of white colour combine to produce a dyad, the latter will also have the corresponding white colour. But the atoms are parimāṇḍalya and the dyads are minute,[4] and yet they produce a visible magnitude. That is why it has been said that the magnitude of the product depends on the magnitude of the parts or their number or arrangement.[5] As the number of the dyads increases, there is a corresponding increase in the dimension of the product. The things produced by the union of atoms are not mere aggregates but wholes. If we deny the whole, we have only the parts, which may be subdivided

[1] Atmospheric air is, however, an exception to this rule, since it is said to consist of masses of atoms in a loose, uncombined state. The Naiyāyika is not satisfied with this account.

[2] *Nyāyakandalī*, p. 32.

[3] Some later Vaiśeṣika thinkers are of opinion that a triad consists of three single atoms (*Siddhāntamuktāvali*, p. 37; Ui: *Vaiśeṣika System*, pp. 130–131).

[4] Mahādeva Bhaṭṭa holds that dyads are not supersensuous. It is also the view of *Daśapadārthī*. See Ui: *Vaiśeṣika Philosophy*, and *Nyāyakośa*, p. 350.

[5] V.S., vii. 1. 9

further and further until we reach the ultimate parts of the imperceptible atoms. If we deny the whole, we cannot admit anything beyond imperceptible atoms. If it is said that the atoms by themselves are imperceptible, while collections of atoms are perceptible, even as a single soldier or a single tree cannot be seen, though an army or a forest can, the Nyāya says in reply, that the analogy is unsound, since soldiers and trees possess bulk and are perceptible, while atoms are not.[1] The whole is something different (arthāntara) from the parts, even as a melody is something more than a sum of its notes.[2] Besides, if there were no whole, there is no meaning in saying "that is a chair," "this is a man." The whole and the parts are related by way of inherence.[3]

No school of Hindu thought cares to leave the groove already worn so deeply of the theory of cycles or alternating cosmic periods of creation and destruction. These processes are described by Praśastapāda.[4] When a hundred years by the measure of Brahmā are at an end, the time for his deliverance arises. To secure rest for all the living beings worried by their wanderings, the supreme Lord, who is not to be confused with Brahmā, desires to reabsorb all creation. The rise of this desire means the cessation of the operations of the unseen tendencies (adṛṣṭa) of all souls that are the causes of their bodies, sense-organs and gross elements. Then out of the Lord's desire and from the conjunction of the souls and the material atoms, disruptions of the atoms constituting the bodies and the sense-organs occur. When the groupings of atoms are destroyed, things made of them are also destroyed. There ensues a successive disruption or reabsorption of the ultimate material substances—earth, water, fire and air, one after the other. The atoms remain isolated, as also the souls permeated with the potencies of their past virtue and vice. Again, for the sake of experience to be gained by living beings the supreme Lord desires creation. By the will of God, motion is set up in the atoms of air due to their conjunction under the influence of the unseen tendencies that begin to operate in all souls. The atoms of air unite to form dyads and triads, and finally the great air, and soon appear the great water, then the great earth, and then the great fire. By the mere thought of God (abhidhyānamātrāt), the cosmic egg is produced out of the fire and the earth atoms, and in it the Lord produces the world and the Brahmā, who is assigned the future work of creation. Brahmā is the highest in the hierarchy of selves, and he holds the post as long as his

---

1 N.B., iv. 2. 14.
2 N.S., ii. 1. 35–36.
3 N.B. and N.V., iv. 2. 12.
4 P.P., pp. 48 ff.

merit requires. The world as a whole is not the creation of Brahmā, nor is its destruction the automatic result of the exhaustion of his merit. The supreme Lord is responsible for it. Brahmā, endowed with the highest degrees of knowledge, dispassion and power, creates his mind-born sons, the Prajāpatis, the Manus, gods, fathers, seers and the four castes, and all other living beings in accord with their respective impressional potencies.[1] According to Śrīdhara, the three infinitely great unchanging substances, space, time and ākāśa, are unaffected by the processes of creation and destruction. There is no such thing as a new creation of the universe. Any one universe is one of a beginningless series. The world is brought into being to enable conscious spirits to obtain their share of experience according to their respective worths. The universe is the actualisation of the potential worths of beings, and is created by their acts and for their experiences. The highest being at any time in the universe is Brahmā, and the whole universe is said to exist for his experience. But as all worth is something acquired and so has a beginning as well as an end, even Brahmā's worth is not unlimited. When it ends, the universe is said to come to an end. There will, however, remain the unenjoyed remnants of other peoples' experiences. If one Brahmā's worth ends, another Brahmā will step into the throne and will fill the highest place in the hierarchy. So every universe has its predecessor and successor, and the flow will go on for ever.[2]

The atoms which are the material causes of the dyads are eternal and cannot be destroyed. The dyads are destroyed, not by the destruction of the primary atoms, but by the destruction of the conjunction of the primary atoms.[3] The ancient Naiyāyikas believed that the destruction of the effects is immediately brought about by the destruction of their causes, except in the case of dyads, where the conjunction is destroyed and not their material causes. Later Naiyāyikas, however, are of the opinion that in all cases the conjunction is destroyed. This is more satisfactory, since destruction is viewed as a gradual dissolution of things into their components. If the process of destruction repeats but does not reverse the process of creation, and if the destruction of the effects follows that of the parts, then there must be an interval when the parts have vanished and the effect remains, and it is impossible to conceive where the effect could reside in the interval. It cannot

---

[1] Faddegon notices an important difference between the order of creation and that of destruction. Fire, instead of being created immediately after air, is formed last. "The author's reason for changing the order was to place the creation of the fire immediately before the formation of the mundane egg, the Hiraṇyagarbha, which, being of gold, consisted of a mixture of fire and earth. The harmony of the system was thus broken for the purpose of complying with current mythological ideas" (*Vaiśeṣika System*, p. 164).

[2] Udayana: *Ātmatattvaviveka*.

[3] Paramāṇudravyasaṁyoganāśa.

be in the parts which are extinct nor in the atoms, since they are not directly connected with the effects.[1]

Śaṁkara criticises the Vaiśeṣika theory of atomism on several grounds. The beginning of motion in the state of dissolution (pralaya) is inconceivable. Human effort cannot account for it, since it does not yet exist. If the unseen principle of adṛṣṭa is regarded as the source, where does it reside? If it abides in the souls, it cannot affect the atoms; if it abides in the atoms, then as unintelligent it cannot start motion. If the soul is supposed to inhere in the atoms and the unseen principle to be combined with it, then there would be eternal activity, which is opposed to the existence of the state of dissolution. Besides, the unseen principle is said to bring about reward and punishment for souls, and it has little to do with the origin and the dissolution of the universe. Śaṁkara raises difficulties about atomic combination. If the atoms combine as wholes, then there is complete interpenetration, and so there is no increase of bulk, and the production of things is not possible. If the atoms combine in parts, then the atom must be regarded as possessing parts. Besides, how atomic compounds acquire spatial properties which the atomic units do not possess is hardly intelligible. By a combination of atoms we get properties which were not in the atoms themselves. Nor is it easy to understand how minute and indestructible atoms can be regarded as possessing colour and like properties. Again, among gross elements, fire, air, earth, water and ether, some possess more attributes than others; while water has colour, taste and touch, air has touch only. These properties must be possessed in some form by the atoms themselves. So atoms of water must have more properties than those of air. But an increase of properties means an increase in size, which is hardly consistent with the view that all atoms are of the same size. There is the further difficulty about the conjunction (saṁyoga) of the soul and manas and the atoms which are all partless. Again, the atoms must be either ever active or ever inactive, or both or neither. If they are ever active, dissolution is impossible; if they are ever inactive, creation is impossible; if they are both, it is self-contradictory; if they are neither, then activity and inactivity would require operative causes, and these latter, like the unseen principle being in permanent connection with the atoms, would produce permanent activity or permanent inactivity.[2]

Modern thought is suspicious of the atomic hypothesis. The Vaiśeṣika view that the contiguous or the extended is

[1] The Vaiśeṣika conceives of two kinds of destruction, an avāṁtarapralaya, or intermediate dissolution, where only tangible products are destroyed, and a mahāpralaya, or a universal destruction, where all things, material and immaterial, are resolved into the atoms. Sṛṣṭi (creation) and pralaya (destruction) are the phases of potentiality and explication of the eternal substances. Cp. *Mahānārāyaṇa Upaniṣad*, v; Keith: I.L.A. p. 216.

[2] S.B., ii. 2. 14

composed of an infinite number of non-contiguous, unextended units is but a hypothesis, since nothing actual is confined to any of these units. The smallest event has duration, and contains an infinite number of such mathematical units.

The atomic theory of the Vaiśeṣika, it has been alleged, owes its inspiration to Greek thought, and arose possibly at a period when India was in contact with the Western world, where the doctrine was widespread.[1] In the present state of our knowledge it is difficult to say anything definite on this question. Apart, however, from the general conception of the atom as the imperceptible unit, there is practically nothing in common between the Greek and the Indian versions of the atomic theory. According to Democritus, atoms have only quantitative differences and not qualitative ones. He believed in an indefinite multitude of atoms, destitute of quality and divisibility, but differing in figure, size, weight, position and arrangement. For Kaṇāda the atoms are different in kind, each possessing its one distinct individuality (viśeṣa). As a result, the qualitative differences of objects are reduced to quantitative ones with the Greek thinker, while it is otherwise with the Vaiśeṣika. It follows that the Indian thinker does not accept the Greek view that secondary qualities are not inherent in the atoms. For Democritus and Epicurus, the atoms are by nature in motion, while for Kaṇāda they are primarily at rest. Another fundamental difference between the two lies in the fact that while Democritus believed it possible for atoms to constitute souls, the Vaiśeṣikas distinguish souls from atoms and regard them as co-eternal existences. The Greek atomists developed a mechanical view of the universe, God being banished from the world. The atoms, infinite in number and diversified in form, fall through boundless space, and in so doing dash against each other, since the larger ones are moved more rapidly than the smaller. Thus falling into vortices they form aggregates and worlds. The changes in the motions of the atoms are said to occur in an incalculable way.[2] Though the early Vaiśeṣikas did not openly admit the hypothesis of God, they made the principle

[1] Keith: I.L.A., pp. 17–18.
[2] Wallace: *Epicureanism*, p. 100.

of the moral law or dharma (adṛṣṭa) central to their whole system. The atomistic view of the Vaiśeṣika is thus coloured by a spiritual tendency which is lacking in the Greek counterpart of it. There are thus distinctive features of the Vaiśeṣika atomism which cannot be due to Greek influence, and it is easy to find the anticipations of the atomic theory in early Indian thought.

Till the other day the atomic theory held the field even in physics. Recent advances are, however, unfavourable to it. Mass is no longer an unalterable quantity, but is said to vary with velocity. It is resolved into infinitesimal centres of electric energy, with no bodily support, scattered at relatively wide intervals and flying to and fro at incredible velocities. Heat, light and motion are found to have weight quite apart from matter. The atom has now become a system of electrons, which are units deriving their character from ether. The atom is a miniature solar system, with a central sun of one revolving mass round which tiny electrons are flying in obedience to the law of gravity which binds the earth to the sun. The old atomic theory is unable to explain the new facts. Yet it was a fruitful theory judged by its triumphs in science. Atomism displaced animism, which is smitten with sterility so far as science goes. But in Greece, as well as in India, the hypothesis was put forward as a metaphysical one, and not a scientifically verified principle. In the nature of the case, empirical verification is not possible.[1] It is a conceptual scheme adopted to explain the facts of nature. It is not a matter of observation but a question of principle. Since it bases its claim for acceptance on the ground of the order and harmony which it introduces into our conception of the universe, there is nothing to prevent us from rejecting the hypothesis if we find that it ceases to have explanatory value.

[1] "The atomic theory has never properly been proved either in ancient or in modern times. It was, it is, and it remains, not a theory in the strict sense of the word, but merely an hypothesis, though an hypothesis, it is true, of unparalleled vitality and endurance, which has yielded a splendid harvest to physical and chemical research down to our own day. Still it is an hypothesis, and its assumption of facts that lie far beyond the limits of human perception deprives it for all time of direct verification" (Gomperz: *Greek Thinkers*, vol. i. p. 353.

VII

Quality

While substance is capable of existing independently by itself, quality or guṇa [1] cannot so exist. It abides in substance and has itself no qualities. Kaṇāda defines it as "that which has substance for its substratum, has no further qualities, and is not a cause of, nor has any concern with, conjunction or disjunction." [2] The Sūtra mentions seventeen qualities: colour (rūpa), taste (rasa), smell (gandha), touch (sparśa), number (saṁkhyā), size (parimāṇa), individuality (pṛthaktva), conjunction (saṁyoga), disjunction (vibhāga), priority (paratva), posteriority (aparatva), knowledge (buddhi), pleasure (sukha), pain (duḥkha), desire (icchā), aversion (dveṣa), and effort (prayatna).[3] To these Praśastapāda adds seven more, which are heaviness (gurutva), fluidity (dravatva), viscidity (sneha), merit (dharma), demerit (adharma), sound (śabda), and faculty (saṁskāra).[4] Attempts were made to add lightness (laghutva), softness (mṛdutva), hardness (kaṭhinatva) to the qualities, but they did not succeed, since lightness is only the absence of heaviness, and softness and hardness were regarded as representing different degrees of conjunction.[5] Modern Naiyāyikas drop priority, posteriority and individuality, since the two former are dependent on space and time, while individuality is mutual non-existence (anyonyābhāva). Qualities include both mental and material properties.

The qualities that belong to eternal substances are called eternal, and those of transient ones non-eternal. Those that subsist in two or more substances are said to be general, while those residing in only one substance are said to be specific. Colour, taste, smell, touch, viscidity, natural fluidity, knowledge, pleasure, pain, desire, aversion, effort, merit, demerit, faculty and sound are special qualities which help to distinguish objects which possess them from others, while qualities like number, dimension, individuality, conjunction, disjunction, priority, posteriority, heaviness, caused fluidity, velocity are general qualities.[6] These belong to substances in general, and are

---

[1] The term guṇa has a distinct sense in the Sāṁkhya system.

[2] i. 1. 16. See P.P., p. 94.

[3] i. 1. 6.

[4] P.P., p. 10.

[5] *Tarkasaṁgrahadīpikā*, 4.

[6] P.P., pp. 95–96.

notional in their character. They are not as objective as the other qualities. Number, for example, is regarded as subjective. The same object may be viewed as either one or many. Number, dimension, individuality, conjunction, and disjunction belong to all substances. While time and space possess no other qualities, ākāśa has sound also. Manas, which is regarded as corporeal (mūrta) has the seven qualities of the atomic substances together with velocity. The self has the five general qualities and the nine special ones of knowledge, pleasure, pain, desire, aversion, effort, merit and demerit, and capacity in the sense of mental impressibility. God has the five general qualities, and in addition, knowledge, desire and effort.[1] Qualities are also distinguished into those open to perception and those that are not. Merit and demerit, heaviness and capacity are not open to perception. A distinction is also made into qualities like colour, taste, smell and tangibility, and sound which are apprehended only by one sense-organ, and others like number, size, individuality, conjunction, disjunction, priority and posteriority, fluidity, viscidity and speed, which are apprehended by two senses. The qualities of self, such as knowledge, pleasure, pain, desire, aversion, effort are perceptible by manas.[2]

Colour (rūpa) is what is apprehended only by the eye and is found in earth, water and light, though in the two latter the colour is permanent. In earth it varies when heat is applied. Seven different colours are admitted, such as white, blue, yellow, red, green, brown and variegated (citra). Taste (rasa) is the quality of things apprehended only by the tongue. Earth and water have taste. Five different tastes are admitted, which are sweet, sour, pungent (kaṭu), astringent (kaṣāya) and bitter (tikta). Odour (gandha) is the specific quality which can be apprehended only by the organ of smell. It is fragrant or the reverse, and belongs to earth. Touch (sparśa) is the quality which is apprehended only by the skin. The admission of three kinds of touch, cold, hot, neither hot nor cold, makes us feel that touch is really temperature. It belongs to earth, water, light and air. Sometimes touch is made to cover qualities, as roughness, hardness, smoothness and softness.[3] Sound (śabda) is the quality of ākāśa.

Number (saṁkhyā) is that quality of things by virtue of which we use the terms one, two, three. Of these numbers, unity (ekatva) is eternal, as well as non-eternal, while other numbers are non-eternal only. When we see a jar we have

[1] *Bhāṣāpariccheda*, pp. 25–34.
[2] P.P., p. 96.
[3] Athalye: *Tarkasaṁgraha*, pp. 155–156.

a knowledge of the unity or singleness of the object seen. If we see another jar, it is also apprehended as one, and there is no duality (dvitva) in it. By thinking together the unities of the two objects we produce duality. The conception of all numbers beyond the first is due to the activity of thought (apekṣābuddhi).[1]

Dimension (parimiti) is that quality of things by virtue of which we are able to measure things and apprehend them as great or small, long or short. Dimension is eternal in eternal substances and transient in non-eternal ones. Ākāśa has extreme greatness (paramamahattvam), an atom extreme smallness (parimāṇḍalya). The dimension of non-eternal substances is determined by the number, magnitude and arrangement of the parts composing them.[2] Dyads are minute, while the rest are of limited magnitude.

Individuality (pṛthaktva) is the basis of distinctions among things.[3] It is real and not conceptual in character. It is eternal or transient according to the nature of the substance in which it resides. While individuality is applied to non-eternal things also, viśeṣa, or particularity, applies to the eternal substances. Individuality refers to the numerical differences of things, while particularity deals with the qualitative peculiarities of things.

Conjunction (saṁyoga) and disjunction[4] (vibhāga) refer respectively to the union of things which were separate and separation of things which were in union. Conjunction is brought about by motion of one thing, as when a flying kite comes into contact with a fixed post, or of both the things, as when two fighting rams butt against each other. Conjunction is also brought about by another conjunction. When we write with a pen, the conjunction of pen and paper brings about the conjunction of the hand with the paper. Since the two things that are conjoined must first have been separate, there cannot be conjunction between two all-

[1] *Nyāyakandalī*, pp. 118–119; *Upaskāra*, vii. 2. 8. While the Nyāya is of opinion that duality, etc., are real, like unity, though revealed by cognition, the Vaiśeṣika holds that these numbers are not simply revealed by intelligence but created by it. In this account the Vaiśeṣika forgets that even the idea of oneness cannot arise so long as there is only one object. As much as the idea of duality it requires the exercise of thought.

[2] V.S., vii. 1. 8–9. [3] V.S., vii. 2. 2. [4] P.P., pp. 139 ff., 151 ff.

pervading things which are never apart from each other. Disjunction is also caused by the motion of one of the two things, or both, or by another disjunction. Conjunction and disjunction account for the changes of things.

Priority (paratva) and posteriority (aparatva) [1] are the bases of the notions of remote and near in time and space alike. These are not so much qualities as relations of corporeal things. That these relations are not absolute is admitted by Praśastapāda.[2]

Pleasure, pain, desire, hatred and effort, as well as knowledge, are qualities of the soul. Heaviness (gurutva) is the quality of things by which they tend, when let fall, to reach the ground.[3] The heaviness of the atoms of earth and of water is eternal, while that of products is non-eternal. Fluidity, which is the cause of the action of flowing, is either self-existent (sāṁsiddhika) or caused (naimittika). Water is naturally fluid, while earth is so for extraneous reasons.[4] Viscidity (sneha) belongs to water, and is the cause of cohesion, smoothness, etc.[5] Dharma and adharma are qualities of the soul by virtue of which it enjoys happiness or suffers misery. Adṛṣṭa is the unseen power produced by souls and things, which brings about the cosmic order and enables the selves to reap the harvest of their past experiences. In the Vaiśeṣika it serves as the general panacea for all logical difficulties. Whatever cannot be accounted for is traced to adṛṣṭa. The movement of the needle towards the magnet, the circulation of moisture in plants, the upward motion of fire, the motion of air and the original movement of the atoms, are all assigned to adṛṣṭa.[6] The demand for an explanation is satisfied by the reference of an event to a power regarded as sufficient to produce it. Adṛṣṭa in the scheme of the Vaiśeṣika is the *deus ex machina* of the dramatists, whose function it is to descend from heaven and cut the tragic knot when other means to disentangle the confusion is not available. The limitations of the Vaiśeṣika philosophy are just the points

[1] P.P., pp. 164 ff.
[2] P.P., p. 99.
[3] V.S., v. 1. 7–18; v. 2. 3; P.P., p. 263.
[4] P.P., p. 264.
[5] P.P., p. 266.
[6] v. 1. 15; v. 2. 7, 13; iv. 2. 7. Kepler explained planetary motions by attributing them to celestial spirits (Whewell: *History of the Inductive Sciences*, 3rd. ed., vol. i, p. 315.)

where adṛṣṭa is said to operate. The beginnings of the universe, the order and beauty of it, the linking together of things as means to ends, are traced to adṛṣṭa. When the later thinkers accepted the reality of God, adṛṣṭa became the vehicle through which God's will operates. Faculty (saṁskāra) is of three different kinds: velocity (vega), which keeps a thing in motion; mental impressibility (bhāvanā), by which the soul is able to remember and recognise things already experienced, and elasticity (sthitisthāpaka), by virtue of which a thing reverts to its original state even when it is disturbed. Velocity is produced in the five corporeal substances by action or motion, and is counteracted by the conjunction of tangible solid substances. Elasticity subsists in substances which contract and expand.

VIII

Karma or Activity

Karma, or movement,[1] is regarded as an irreducible element of the universe. It is neither substance nor quality, but an independent category by itself. All movements belong to substances as much as qualities. Only while a quality is a permanent feature of the substance, activity is a transitory one. The heaviness of the body is a quality, while its falling is an accident. Qualities which continue to exist are called guṇa, while those that cease to exist are called karma. It is a distinction between continuant and occurrent qualities.[2] Kaṇāda defines activity as that which resides only in one substance, is devoid of qualities, and is the direct and immediate cause of conjunction and disjunction.[3] Five kinds of movement are distinguished, which are upward, downward, contraction, expansion, and movement in general. Karma is instantaneous in its simplest form, while velocity is a persistent tendency and implies a series of motions. Karma in all its forms is transient, and comes to an end either by a subsequent conjunction or destruction of its basic substance.

[1] Karma here signifies movement, and not voluntary action or the law of moral causation.

[2] Cp. W. E. Johnson: *Logic*, vol. i, p. xxxvii.

[3] V.S., i. 1. 7.

Ākāśa, time, space, soul, though substances, are devoid of action, since they are incorporeal.[1]

IX

Sāmānya or Generality

When we admit a plurality of substances, it is evident there will be relations among them. The substances will be similar to one another, since they are all substances; they will be diverse from one another, since they are separate substances. When we find a property residing in many things we call it sāmānya, or general; but if we regard it as distinguishing these objects from others, we call it viśeṣa, or particular. Kaṇāda seems to regard the generality as a conceptual product.[2] When we come to Praśastapāda, the conceptual view gives place to the more popular realist doctrine, which regards the generality as eternal, one, and residing in many things belonging to the group of substance, quality or action. Conjunction and duality are intimately related to many things, but are not eternal. Ākāśa is eternal, but is not related to many things. Absolute non-existence is eternal, and is also a quality of many things, but is not intimately related to, *i.e.* is not a constituent element of, many things. Similarly, particularity is not sāmānya, since then it would lose its nature and become confused with the latter. Intimate relation (samavāya) cannot be confused with sāmānya, since then it will require intimate relation with intimate relation, and so on *ad infinitum*. Sāmānya, or the generality, by the possession of which different individuals are referred to one class, is an independent category. It is eternal (nityam), one (ekam), residing in many (anekānugatam).[3] It is present

[1] V.S., v. 2. 21; ii. 1. 21. It is doubtful whether Kaṇāda regards the soul as without action.

[2] ii. 1. 3 ff. See vi. 2. 16. Praśastapāda limits movements to physical bodies, atoms and the manas.

[3] Udayana says that there is no jāti, or generality, where only one individual exists as ākāśa (abheda), where there is no difference of individuality as, say, between ghaṭa and kalaśa (tulyatvam), where there is confusion of objects belonging to different classes (saṁkara), where there is infinite

in all objects of its class (svaviṣayasarvagatam), with an identical nature (abhinnātmakam) and cause of the notion of concordance (anuvṛttipratyayakāraṇam).[1] While substance, quality and action have the generality: generality, particularity, inherence and non-existence have no generality. Generality cannot exist in another generality. Treeness (vṛkṣattva) and jarness (ghaṭatva) are themselves generals, and cannot have another common to them all, since that would land us in infinite regress.

There are two kinds of generality, higher and lower. The highest generality is that of being (sattā).[2] It covers the largest number of things. It includes all, and is not included in anything. It is not a species of any higher genus. While being is the only true universal, the true particulars are the individuals themselves (antyaviśeṣa) and between the two we have universal-particulars, such as substance and the rest, which cover a limited number of things. These latter serve as bases of inclusive as well as exclusive cognitions, since they are both species and genera.[3] The extension determines the grade of generality.

regress (anavasthā), where there is a violation of essence (rūpahāni), where there is no relation (asaṁbandha). See *Siddhāntamuktāvali*, p. 8.

The Advaita refuses to admit jāti. While admitting that jarness (ghaṭatva) constitutes the jar as such, it refuses to allow that jāti is a thing in itself. See *Vedāntaparibhāṣā*, i.

[1] Cp. Clarke's definition: " The essence of an object is the true nature of the object which it shares with all other objects belonging to the same class and called by the same name; a nature which is perfectly alike in all, and as conceived by us, is not only alike in all, but the same in all; a nature which is the source of the common qualities of the objects, causing them to resemble one another and to make on us similar impressions . . . a nature which can be reached by the intellect and by the intellect alone, in virtue of its immaterial and supersensible character " (*Logic*).

The Jains regard the universal as multiform, non-eternal, limited, *i.e.* non-ubiquitous. It is the common character of the members of the class. The Nyāya-Vaiśeṣika and Pūrva Mīmāṁsā hold that the universal has its objective counterpart in a real essence in the world different from the individuals, one, eternal, ubiquitous. According to the Jains, the universal has its reality in the common character or similarity of individuals, which is not one but many, existing in many individuals, non-eternal, *i.e.* being produced and destroyed along with the individual in which it exists, and not all-pervading, but confined only to the individual in which it exists.

[2] V.S., i. 2. 4, 7–10, 17; P.P., p. 311.

[3] P.P., p. 11. See Ui: *The Vaiśeṣika Philosophy*, pp. 99–100. Cp. *Saptapadārthī*, p. 5: " Sāmānyam param aparam parāparaṁ ceti trividham."

A distinction is also made into akhaṇḍa and sakhaṇḍa, jāti and upādhi. The jāti of a thing is inborn, natural and eternal, while the upādhi is adventitious and transitory. Every common characteristic is not a jāti. Since some persons are blind, we cannot have a jāti of blindness. The classification of men as human beings is a jāti, while their grouping according to their nationality or language is an upādhi. Humanity distinguishes human beings from other animals, but blackness does not differentiate black men from black sheep or black stones.[1] The former is a natural classification, while the latter is an artificial one.

Praśastapāda gives to sāmānya a reality independent of individual objects. The later Vaiśeṣikas adopt the realist view of the independent existence of the universals, which are said to subsist even in the state of pralaya, or the destruction of the world. The universals, on this view, answer to the separate, suprasensual arch-typal forms of Plato's poetical fancy.[2] While Kaṇāda insisted more on the activity of thought and therefore the inseparable relation between the universal and the individual, Praśastapāda shifts the stress to the *eternal nature* of the universals. He is thus compelled to the view that in creation universals enter into the individuals and make for themselves temporary manifestations.[3] The crux of such a position is the relation of the universal and the particular, the essence and the existence. Praśastapāda's view is akin to Plato's realism, according to which sensible things are what they are by participation in the universal forms of

---

[1] N.S., ii. 2. 71. The Jainas classify generality into crosswise and vertical. The crosswise is a similar development in several instances, while the vertical is the identity which persists in the prior and posterior states of an object. The former is the static universal and the latter is the dynamic identity. See *Pramāṇanayatattvālokālaṁkāra*, v. 3–5.

[2] The following quotations from Aristotle help us to understand the difficulties of the problem. In his *Metaphysics* Aristotle says: "Two things may be fairly ascribed to Socrates—inductive arguments and universal definition, both of which are concerned with the starting-point of science. But Socrates did not make the universals or the definitions exist apart; his successors, however, gave them separate existence, and this was the kind of thing they called Ideas" (E.T., by Ross, 1078*b*. 28). Agreeing with Socrates, Aristotle criticises the Platonists: "They at the same time treat the Ideas as universal substances, and as separable and individual. That this is not possible has been shown before. The reason why those who say the Ideas are universal combined those two views in one is that they did not make the Ideal substances identical with sensible things. They thought that the sensible particulars were in a state of flux and none of them remained, but that the universal was apart from these and different. And Socrates gave the impulse to this theory . . . by means of his definitions, but he did not separate them from the particulars; and in this he thought rightly in not separating them" (*Metaphysics*, 1086*a*. 32, E.T., by Ross).

[3] Cp. with this the view of Duns Scotus, that general notions are not only in objects potential, but active, and generality is not only formed by the understanding, but it exists previous to mental conception as a reality indifferent to general or individual existence.

Ideas which are eternal and self-subsistent. All the objections urged against Plato's view,[1] that it is difficult to conceive how without division or multiplication Ideas can participate in the individuals and the individuals in the Ideas, that a still higher universal is necessary to connect the Idea with its corresponding individuals, as well as the so-called third man argument, apply here also.

The question of the ontological status of universals was as hotly debated in the schools of India as in those of medieval Europe. The Vaiśeṣika has obviously no sympathy with the Buddhist view that the general notion is but a name. According to the Buddhists, universality attaches to names[2] and has no objective existence. Different individuals do not possess any common features called sāmānya. If the specific individuality of a cow requires some common factor, then the latter requires another, and so on *ad infinitum*. Sāmānya is not perceived. We frame the notion of generality as the result of past experiences and erroneously extend it to outward objects.[3]

---

[1] See Plato's *Parmenides*.

[2] Cp. Hobbes: "There is nothing universal but names" (*Human Nature*, v. 6).

[3] See *Sāmānyadūṣaṇadikprasāritā*, in *Six Buddhist Nyāya Tracts*. Jayanta argues against the Buddhist view of the identity of the universal and the individual. The objection that the universal is not different from the individual, since it does not occupy a different portion of space from the individual, is met by the consideration that the universal exists in the individual. The next question is whether the universal is entirely or partly present in the individual. If the universal has parts, then it is liable to destruction and cannot be eternal, and so it must be entirely present in the individual and must be exhausted in one individual. But Jayanta contends that experience testifies to the fact that the universal, though entirely present in each individual, is yet present in ever so many individuals. The Buddhist urges that a universal should be either all-pervading (sarvagata) or limited to certain individuals (piṇḍagata) belonging to the same class, and neither is possible. If the universal is found in all objects, then cowness must be found in horses, stones, etc., in which case we shall have an intermixture of genera (sāṁkarya). If the universal exists only in a select group of individuals (svavyaktisarvagata), then how does it happen that we perceive cowness in a newly born cow if it did not exist there before the cow was born? We cannot say that the universal was born along with the individual, since the former is eternal; nor can it be said to be transmitted from some other individual, since the universal is formless (amūrta) and incapable of movement, and we do not perceive its coming from any individual. Does the universal disappear when the individual is destroyed? Jayanta answers that it exists everywhere, *i.e.* in all individuals, though it is not manifested in all and is not perceived in all individuals, and though it must be said that the manifestation is the only proof of its presence. It is wrong, therefore, to assume that the universal "cow" did not exist in the particular cow just born before its birth, and it comes to it when it is born, since the universal is incapable of movement. It is admitted that a universal exists only in its proper subjects. When a particular individual enters into existence, it comes to be related to the

Śrīdhara repudiates this view. "As a matter of fact we are cognisant of something that exists in all individual cows and serves to distinguish them from all other animals, such as the horse and the like. If there were no such common character possessed by all the various kinds of cows, then one individual cow would be cognised to be as different from another individual cow as it would be from an individual horse; or conversely, the cow and the horse would be regarded as being like each other as two individual cows, since there would be no difference in the two cases. As a matter of fact, however, we find that all individual cows are perceived to be alike; and this distinctly points to a certain factor which is present in all cows and is not present in horses and other animals." [1] Śrīdhara contends that the denotation of words assumes the reality of general features.[2] So sāmānya is not a mere name.

Kaṇāda suggests that generality and particularity are relative to thought (buddhyapekṣam),[3] intellectual devices by which we classify the variety of phenomena. His view that sattā, or existence, is a different object (arthāntaram) from substance, quality and action does not contradict this position. He tells us that a quality is regarded as sāmānya, or general,

universal. Though the universal is eternal, its relation to a particular individual comes into existence only at the moment when the individual comes into being (*Nyāyamañjari*, pp. 311 ff., 299–300). A different view, attributed to the Śrotriyas, called Rūparūpilakṣaṇasaṁbandha, is mentioned by Jayanta. The universal is the rūpa of the individual, which is the rūpin in relation to the former. The word "rūpa" is ambiguous. It cannot mean colour, since even colourless substances, like air, manas, qualities and actions, possess universality; nor can it mean form (ākāra), since formless qualities have also universality. If it means essential nature (svabhāva), then the universal is not different from the individual except in name. The rūpa is not a different substance (vastvantaram) from the rūpin, since it is not perceived as such, nor is it the same (vastv eva), since then there cannot be any talk of a relation between them; nor can rūpa be a property (vastudharma) of the rūpin, since then it should be perceived as distinct from the individual, which is not the case (*Nyāyamañjari*, p. 299).

[1] *Nyāyakandalī*, p. 317.

[2] Prabhācandra, in his *Prameyakamalamārtāṇḍa* (pp. 136–137), criticises the Buddhist view. The universal is an object of perception as the individual, and not a mere fancy of imagination, and we feel the difference between the cognition of the universal and that of the particular. Simply because we perceive in the same object and at the same time both the universal and the particular, we cannot confuse the two. The cognition of universals is inclusive in nature (anugatākāra), while that of particulars is exclusive in character (vyāvṛttākāra). The cognition of the universals implies the existence of the universals. No number of individuals can generate the idea of a universal.

[3] i. 2. 3

when it is conceived as residing in many individuals, and viśeṣa, or particular, when it is used to differentiate the objects. Jarness is sāmānya when it is regarded as residing in many objects, and viśeṣa when used to distinguish jars from other things.[1] The distinction of qualities into general and particular is one of intellectual analysis. The implication is that universals, particulars and relations do not exist in the sense in which substances, qualities and actions do.[2] They, however, are positive (bhāva) and not non-existent (abhāva). We cannot class Kaṇāda as a conceptualist, since he admits sāmānya as an element of the real. Extreme conceptualism holds that universals exist only in the mind. The general qualities signified by the sāmānya are as real as the individual peculiarities, though our thought discriminates the common qualities and gathers them into the universal notion. Kaṇāda is careful to note that the points of resemblance are as much independent of us and our thinking as the individuals themselves. We do not make all dogs alike, but we find them to be so. In this sense the Aristotelian view of *universalia in re* is supported. It is also true that the universal is eternal and one, since the type abides, while the individuals come and go. Men are born and die, but man remains. Universals have a more enduring reality than the individuals. Thus the Platonic doctrine of *universalia ante rem* is also true. This latter view comes to the foreground in Praśastapāda. The distinction between the universal and the particular is real, since the relation is said to be one of intimate union (samavāya).[3]

[1] Cp. this view with that of Duns Scotus, who believes in an Essence or Form in itself which is subject to no individuating conditions. He distinguishes between the unity of an individual and the unity of a universal nature. The universal appears in the particular individual things, though it is apprehended as the universal by the understanding. In itself it is neither particular nor universal, but just what it is, something antecedent to universality and particularity.

[2] i. 2. 7.

[3] Pārthasārathi objects to this view of the relation between the universal and the particular. When we perceive a cow, our perception is to the effect " This is a cow " (iyaṁ gauḥ), and not " Here is the class essence of cow in the individual cow " (iha gavi gotvam). The universal is not, therefore, different from the individual. The two are said to be inseparable. Separability (yutasiddhi) means either the capacity for separate or independent movements (pṛthaggatimattva) or subsistence in different substrata (pṛthagāśrayāśrayitva). In either case, there would be no relation between

X

Viśeṣa or Particularity

By means of viśeṣa, or particularity, we are able to perceive things as different from one another.[1] It is the basis of exclusion. Whatever is individual is unique and single. Kaṇāda makes particularity as much dependent on thought as generality.[2] Praśastapāda makes it an independent reality residing in eternal substances distinguishing them from one another. We distinguish empirical objects by means of the parts of which they are composed, and when, in the course of analysis, we reach simple substances which have no parts by means of which we can distinguish them, we must assume that each simple substance has a quality which makes it distinct from all others. Atoms, time, space, ākāśa, souls and manas all have their particularities, which are not qualities of classes but only of individuals. These distinctive particularities are the final facts beyond which we cannot go. As the ultimate atoms are innumerable, so are the particularities.[3] Praśasta-

the composite whole and its component parts, since there can be a movement in the parts without a movement in the whole, and since the whole and its parts inhere in different substrata, the whole in the parts and the parts in their component atoms. Likewise, the universal and the individual have different substrata, since the substratum of the universal is the individual and that of the latter the parts composing it. So Pārthasārathi Miśra defines inherence as a relation between the container and the contained, such that the latter produces a corresponding cognition in the former. "Yena saṁbandhenādheyam ādhāre svānurūpām buddhim janayati sa saṁbandhaḥ samavāya iti" (*Śāstradīpikā*, pp. 283–4). To say that the universal inheres in the individual means that the universal (cowness) produces an apprehension of it in the individual (cow). Since the universal is perceived in the individual, they are not different from each other. If the universal is absolutely different from the individual, then we can never say "This is a cow." According to Kumārila and Pārthasārathi Miśra, the relation of the universal and the particular is one of identity and difference. Ibid., pp. 283 ff.

[1] P.P., p. 13. [2] i. 2. 3 ff.

[3] Viśeṣās tu yāvan nityadravyavṛttitvād anantā eva (*Saptapadārthī*, p. 12). Cp. with this Leibniz's doctrine of the Identity of Indiscernibles. In his lecture on the *Nature of Universals and Propositions*, Professor Stout maintains that the unity of a class or kind as including its members or instances is an ultimate one. He differs from Bergson and Russell, who hold that qualities and relations are as such universal, and contends that a character characterising a concrete thing or individual is as particular as the thing

pāda believes that the yogis are able to perceive the ultimate particularity of the simple substances.[1]

Some modern Naiyāyikas do not find any justification for the assumption of particularities. If these are necessary to distinguish individual atoms, how are the particularities themselves distinguished from one another? We must say that the viśeṣas, or particularities, have a unique essence or inherent power which serves to differentiate them. But then this same power may be ascribed to the atoms without introducing the conception of particularity. The followers of Kumārila, Prabhākara and the Vedānta refuse to accept the doctrine of viśeṣa. If things are fundamentally different, then it is impossible to find a common character in them.

XI

Samavāya or Inherence

Kaṇāda means by inherence the relation between cause and effect.[2] Praśastapāda defines it as the relationship subsisting among things that are inseparable, standing to one another in the relation of the container and the contained, and being the basis of the idea, "this is in that." [3] Virtue and pleasure, Śrīdhara says, are not related by inherence, though they reside in the self, since they are not related as the container and the contained. The relationship between the word and the thing signified is not one of inherence, since one is not contained in the other. The fruit may be on the ground, but as the two are not inseparable, they cannot be

or the individual which it characterises. Each of two billiard balls has its own particular roundness, distinct and separate from that of the other, even as the billiard balls themselves are distinct and separate. To say that many things share in a common character really means that each is characterised by a particular instance of a general kind or class of characters. Professor Stout holds that a substance is a complex unity including within it all characters truly predicable of it, and the unity of such a complex is a concrete unity, while its characters, though particular, are not concrete.

[1] P.P., pp. 321, 322. See *Tarkasaṁgraha*, 7 and 8.

[2] vii. 2. 26.

[3] Ayutasiddhānām, ādhāryādhārabhūtānāṁ yaḥ saṁbandha ihapratyayahetuḥ sa samavāyaḥ (P.P., p. 14). See also p. 324; V.S., vii. 2. 26–28; v. 2. 23.

said to be related by way of inherence. Ayutasiddhi, or inseparability, is not identity, since the two things are not one in reality. The form of fire and the ball of iron are distinct from each other. While Kaṇāda includes only causal ties in the relation of samavāya, Praśastapāda brings non-causal ones also under it. Generally the relation which binds a substance and its qualities, a whole and its parts, motion and the object in motion, individual and universe, cause and effect, is that of samavāya, or inherence. The members related are so unified as to represent one whole or one identical real.

Samavāya, or necessary connection, is distinguished from saṁyoga, or accidental conjunction, which is a quality of things. While objects conjoined have a separate existence prior to conjunction, the members related by samavāya are inseparably connected. The relationship of samavāya is not caused by the action of one of the members related. Conjunction terminates as soon as there is a disjunction of the members conjoined, while connection is indestructible. Again, conjunction takes place between two independent substances, while the members related by way of inherence stand in the relation of the container and the contained.[1] Two things in the relation of samavāya cannot be separated without at least one of them being destroyed. Saṁyoga takes place between two things of the same nature which exist disconnectedly and are for a time brought into conjunction. It is external relation, while samavāya is internal relation.[2] In saṁyoga two differents are joined together without forming a real whole which enters into each. Samavāya is a real coherence.

Inherence is said to be eternal, since to be produced would involve infinite regress. Śrīdhara says that it cannot appear before, or after, or along with the thing related to it. If the inherence of the cloth were possible before the cloth appears, it is inconceivable where the inherence could reside, since one member of the relationship is non-existent. If it is produced along with the cloth, then the cloth would lose the character of being the substrate of the relationship of inherence. If it appeared after the cloth is formed, then, too, the cloth could

[1] P.P., p. 326.

[2] Cp. with this Johnson's distinction between a characterising tie and a coupling tie.

not be its substrate. Nor is it possible for the effect to be its substrate. Samavāya is eternal in the sense that it cannot be produced or destroyed without producing or destroying the product. Its eternity is thus relative. The relation of samavāya is not perceptible, but only inferrible from the inseparable connection of things.[1]

While the first five categories have the character of inherence (samavāyitvam) and plurality (anekatvan), or possession of forms differentiating them from one another, samavāya is one only and has no plurality.[2] It does not reside in anything by the relation of inherence, since such residence would involve infinite regress. There is no difference in our various notions of inherence, even as there is no difference in our various notions of being. The kind of relationship is the same though the members related may differ.[3]

Strictly speaking, the notion of inherence is the result of intellectual discrimination, though an objective existence is granted to it. It has its origin in abstraction, and has no existence apart from substances. Śaṁkara criticises the theory of samavāya. He argues that conjunction such as that which subsists between the atoms and ākāśa is eternal as much as inherence. Inherence, in so far as it is a relation, is not identical with what it relates. The relation of inherence falls outside the terms to be related, and itself requires a relation to relate it to the terms, and so on *ad infinitum*. Again, we have always to assume a relationship by which the samavāya would reside in the samavāyi, or the things related by samavāya relationship. If the samavāya does not rest in the samavāyi by another samavāya, but is identical with it, then even saṁyoga (conjunction) may be regarded as identical with the things conjoined.[4] It is useless to assert that inherence can exist without a third thing to unite it with the things in which it exists, while conjunction needs inherence to hold it to things which are in conjunction. The difficulty is not removed by calling one a category and the other a quality. There is no doubt that the relation of a binary atomic compound to its constituent elements, or of a species to the individuals constituting it, is not the same as the relation of the tablecloth to the table. But the difficulty in both the cases seems to be the same, that a relation, however intimate, cannot be identical

[1] The ancient Naiyāyikas thought that it was open to perception.

[2] *Tarkasaṁgraha*, 8.

[3] P.P., p. 326.

[4] Kumārila observes: "If samavāya is something different from the class and the individual that resides in the class by samavāya, then it (the samavāya) could not exist in them as a relation; on the other hand, if it be identical with them, then these two would be identical—by the law that the things that are identical with the same thing are identical with themselves." S.V., Pratyakṣa Sūtra, 150.

with the terms related. The argument that there must be this relation between cause and effect cannot be accepted. If cause and effect are inseparably connected, as the Vaiśeṣika admits, then it is far simpler to assume that there is identity of essence between the two. Moreover, the conception of inseparable connection contradicts the idea that the cause precedes the effect, which is an essential feature of the Nyāya-Vaiśeṣika theory of causality.[1] The cause is capable of separate existence. If samavāya is the connection with the cause of the effect which is incapable of separate existence, then, since a connection requires two terms, and the effect as long as it does not exist cannot be connected with the cause, there can be no samavāya relation between the two. It is equally unavailing to say that the effect enters into the connection after it has begun to exist, for, if the Vaiśeṣika admits that the effect may exist previous to its connection with the cause, then it is not incapable of separate existence. The principle that between effect and cause conjunction and disjunction do not take place is violated. If the effect can exist before entering into connection with the cause, then the subsequent connection of the two is no longer samavāya, but only saṁyoga. Just as conjunction and not inherence is the connection in which every substance as soon as it has been produced stands with the all-pervading substances as ākāśa, etc.—although no motion has taken place on the part of the said substance—so also the connection of the effect with the cause will be conjunction, and not inherence.

XII

Abhāva or Non-existence

Kaṇāda did not admit abhāva, or non-existence, as an independent category. For him, absolute non-existence has no meaning, and all other kinds of non-existence—antecedent non-existence (prāgabhāva), or the state of the cause before it produces the effect, subsequent non-existence (pradhvaṁsābhāva), or the state of the effect when resolved into its elements, and mutual non-existence (anyonyābhāva), or the relation between things possessing identities of their own—are related to positive being (bhāva).[2] Though an empirical classification of existent things has no need for an independent category of abhāva, still the dialectical representation of the universe requires the conception of negation. When the Vaiśeṣika enlarged its scope and attempted to give a coherent

[1] S.B., ii. 2. 13–17. [2] ix. 1. 1 ff.

account of experience as a whole, it developed the category of abhāva. In all systems of thought, relations play a large part. A relation carries us from one thing to another, and this transition is not a mere negation. Otherness is the basis of negation, and what is called contradiction is the perverse form of negation. Every relation is a kind of negation which does not transgress the law of contradiction. A thing and its relations are closely connected. When we speak of a thing, the fact of its being or affirmation is emphasised; when we speak of a relation, the fact of its non-being or negation is emphasised. A thing is position without contradiction; a relation is op-position without contradiction.

Though abhāva is more a logical category than an ontological one, there is a tendency to regard non-being as something existent equally with being.[1] Thus negation and non-existence became mixed up. Viśvanātha says that non-being arises on account of the reciprocal negation of the six categories.[2] Negation can be applied to all kinds of relations, and not merely to those of identity and existence, as Śrīdhara supposes. The followers of the Vedānta and Prabhākara refuse to regard it as a category at all. They look upon it as simple substratum and nothing more.[3] If abhāva is a separate category, then there will be infinite regress, since absence of the jar (ghaṭābhāva) is different from the jar (ghaṭa), and the absence of the absence of the jar (ghaṭābhavābhāva) is different from the latter. To obviate this difficulty, the ancient Naiyāyikas regarded the absence of the absence of the jar as identical with the presence of the jar. The negative of the negative is the positive. This view is not, however, accepted by all. Modern Naiyāyikas hold that a negative can never be equivalent to a positive, though the negation of the negation of the first negation is equivalent to the first negation.[4]

Vātsyāyana admits two kinds of non-existence, prior, or the non-existence of a thing prior to its production and posterior, or non-existence of a thing after its destruction. Till the son is born he is non-existent, in the first way. When the jar is broken it is non-existent in the second way.[5] Vācaspati[6] divides non-existence into: (1) tādātmyābhāva, or negation of identity; and (2) saṁsargābhāva, or negation of correlation, and the latter is divided into prior, posterior and absolute non-existence, or atyantābhāva. The last is also called

---

[1] N.B. and N.V., ii. 2. 12. See *Nyāyakandalī*, pp. 225–230.

[2] Abhāvatvaṁ dravyādiṣaṭkānyonyābhāvavattvam (*Siddhāntamuktāvalī*, 12).

[3] Adhikaraṇakaivalyamātram.

[4] *Tarkasaṁgrahadīpikā*, 80.

[5] N.B., ii. 2. 12.

[6] N.V.T.T., ii. 2. 9.

samavāyābhāva. Self-contradictory notions, such as a barren woman's son or the horns of the hare, are said to be absolutely non-existent. In absolute non-existence there is the affirmation of something actual and the negation of a relation in regard to it. In reciprocal or mutual non-existence the objects between which the relation of identity is said to be non-existent need not be actual. In reciprocal negation we deny the identity of the two objects, cloth and jar; in absolute negation what is denied is a relation other than identity. The reciprocal negation in the judgment "a jar is not a cloth" has for its opposite "a jar is a cloth." The absolute non-existence of colour in the air is asserted in the judgment "there is no colour in the air," and it has for its opposite a proposition which connects the two, colour and air, and says, "there is colour in the air." The opposite of reciprocal non-existence is an identity, while that of absolute non-existence is a connection. Śivāditya holds that reciprocal non-existence is non-eternal, since it ceases to exist as soon as the cloth is destroyed.[1] Śrīdhara admits four kinds of non-existence: prior, posterior, mutual and absolute.[2] Viśvanātha develops a similar view.[3] When the jar is on the ground, its existence is perceived, and its non-existence is perceived when it is removed from the ground. Viśvanātha says that the non-existence was there all the time, though it was hidden when the jar was on the ground. The absolute non-existence of everything is at all times present everywhere, though it is hidden for the time and in the place the thing happens to be. Thus universal non-existence is limited in some direction or not limited at all. The latter is unlimited or absolute non-existence, or atyantābhāva. Limited non-existence may have either a definite beginning or a definite ending. Prior non-existence of the jar has no beginning though it has an end; posterior non-existence has a beginning but no end. The logicians of modern Nyāya develop different varieties of abhāva with great subtlety.[4]

We see that the whole view of abhāva is based on the metaphysical conception of the Vaiśeṣika. If things simply exist and do not become, *i.e.* non-exist, then all things would be eternal. If antecedent non-existence is denied, then all things and their movements should be regarded as beginningless; if subsequent non-existence is denied, then things and their activities will be unceasing and endless; if mutual non-existence is denied, then things will be indistinguishable; and if absolute non-existence is denied, then things should be regarded as existing always and everywhere.

1 *Saptapadārthī*, 189.

2 *Nyāyakandalī*, p. 230. See also Samantabhadra's *Āptamīmāṁsā* and *Tarkasaṁgraha*, p. 80.

3 *Siddhāntamuktāvali*, pp. 12–13.

4 See Bhīmācārya's *Nyāyakośa*, under Atyantābhāva, Anyonyābhāva and Abhāva.

XIII

Ethics

The Vaiśeṣika makes a distinction between voluntary and involuntary activities, and holds that moral distinctions apply only to the former.[1] Acts due to organic life (jīvanapūrvaka) are involuntary, while those which spring from desire and aversion (icchādveṣapūrvaka) are voluntary. The former have organic ends in view, while the latter aim at the realisation of human values (hitaprāpti).[2] Pleasure, or the state of agreeableness, gives rise to an affection for the objects which yield pleasure. Pain, which is of the nature of uneasiness, produces an aversion for the object causing it. Desire (icchā) and aversion (dveṣa) are the volitional reactions to pleasurable and painful objects,[3] resulting in action for attaining the desired object or avoiding the hated one. Dharma, according to the Vaiśeṣika, treats of the attainment of worldly prosperity (abhyudaya) as well as spiritual good (niḥśreyasa). While the former is the product of ceremonial piety, the latter is the result of spiritual insight (tattvajñāna).[4] The highest kind of pleasure, according to Praśastapāda, is the pleasure of the wise, which is "independent of all such agencies as the remembrance of the object, desire, reflection, and is due to their knowledge, peacefulness of mind, contentment, and the peculiar character of their virtues."[5]

The programme of duties is to be inferred from the scriptures. A distinction is drawn between duties which are universally obligatory, *i.e.* regardless of distinctions of castes and conditions of life, and those which are obligatory for particular conditions of life.

The universal duties are: (1) faith (śraddhā); (2) non-violence (ahiṁsā), or the determination never to do any harm to any living being[6]; (3) kindly feeling for all beings (bhūtahitatva); (4) truthfulness (satyavacana); (5) integrity (asteya); (6) sexual purity (brahmacarya); (7) purity of mind (anupadhā-bhāvaśuddhi); (8) renunciation of anger (krodhavarjana); (9) personal cleanliness

---

[1] v. 1. 11. [2] P.P., p. 263. [3] P.P., pp. 259 ff.
[4] i. 1. 1–2 and 4. [5] P.P., p. 259.
[6] Bhūtānām anabhidrohasaṁkalpaḥ (*Nyāyakandalī*, p. 275).

through bathing (abhiṣecana); (10) and use of purifying substances (śucidravyasevana); (11) devotion to the deity (viśiṣṭadevatābhakti); (12) fasting (upavāsa); and (13) non-neglect of duties (apramāda). The specific duties of the four castes and the four āśramas are laid down in the usual way.[1] According to Śrīdhara, one can become a recluse without passing through the stage of the householder.[2] It is admitted that the sannyāsin is not one who gives up the world to itself, but one who takes the vow of universal benevolence.[3] After detailing the nature of duties, Praśastapāda concludes that the observance of duties results in virtue (dharma) when they are done, without a desire for gaining thereby any visible results (as wealth, etc.), and with the utmost purity of motive.[4] Spiritual growth requires suppression of self. It is said: "To the unrestrained (ayatasya), exaltation, or abhyudaya, does not accrue from eating what is pure, since there is no self-restraint."[5] Yoga as a means to self-control is allowed.[6] It is not mechanical conformity to the rules but inner goodness that counts.

Broadly speaking, dharma is ahiṁsā alone, and adharma is hiṁsā, or hatred for creation. The Vaiśeṣika allows exceptions to scriptural injunctions in certain contingencies, which fact has led some thinkers to suspect that the system had its origin in heterodox speculations.[7]

Dharma in the Vaiśeṣika refers nor merely to the content of morality, but also the power or quality which resides in the human being and not in the action performed. It is super-sensuous in nature, and is destroyed when the individual undergoes its results. True knowledge puts an end to it. If dharma were absolutely indestructible, there can be no final deliverance. Dharma counts for progress, but must be abolished before there can be final release. So long as we observe the rules laid down with the self-regarding motive of furthering our progress towards perfection or rising in the scale of existence, we may get our reward, but the place we win is not abiding. Not even Brahmā has abiding joy.[8] Whatever be our dharma, it cannot be unlimited, and cannot therefore give us abiding peace. Only a selfless insight into the truth of things can secure final release.[9] So long as we are dominated by desire and aversion, we store up dharma

1 P.P., p. 273; V.S., vi. 2. 3.

2 *Nyāyakandalī*, p. 277.

3 Sarvabhūtebhyo nityam abhayaṁ dattvā. . . . (P.P., p. 273). See also V.S., ii. 30.

4 P.P., p. 273. See also V.S., vi. 2. 1–2, 4–6, 8.

5 V.S., vi. 2. 8.

6 V.S., v. 2. 16–18.

7 Ui: *Vaiśeṣika Philosophy*, p. 31.

8 *Nyāyakandalī*, p. 281.

9 *Ibid*. p. 6.

and adharma or adṛṣṭa, and the results of our deeds force on us an embodied existence.[1] The body is the seat of enjoyment (bhogāyatanam). Union with adṛṣṭa and its effect of body is saṁsāra ; separation from it is mokṣa.[2]

Activity motived by the feeling of separate self-existence is based on ignorance of the truth of things. When we realise that the objects which look so attractive and repulsive are only temporary compounds of atoms, they cease to have power over us. Similarly, when we realise the true nature of the ātman, which is distinct from this or that form of its existence, we shall know that all souls are alike. When true knowledge dispels the motive of self-interest, selfish activities cease, no potential worth is produced, and there will be no more rebirth. When the system became theistic, the bliss of deliverance was regarded as the result of divine grace, and the rules of dharma as the expression of the will of God.[3]

All the time the soul is in saṁsāra, it is incarnate in some body or other, which is subtle in pralaya and gross in creation, and there is never a state when the ātman is devoid of adṛṣṭa, since there is no beginning for the series of incarnations.[4] The time, place, and circumstances of birth, family and parentage, the period of life are all determined by the adṛṣṭa.[5] Each soul is allowed the chance to reap the harvest of its past deeds. It is not necessary, however, that the present life should be the result of the immediately preceding one, since all our potent qualities cannot be actualised in all cases in one life.[6] Though the saṁskāras (potential tendencies) are not lost, some of them may have to wait for a future life. It is held that we can remember our past lives by suitable discipline.[7] Like other systems of Hindu thought, the Vaiśeṣika admits that it is possible for us to rise to a superior order of existence or fall into a subhuman one.[8] All beings occupy their respective places according to their merit.

The Vaiśeṣika theory of mokṣa, or release, is slightly different

[1] Saṁsāramūlakāraṇayor dharmādharmayor. . . .
[2] v. 2. 18. See also N.S., iv. 1. 47.
[3] Īśvaracodanābhivyaktāt. P.P., p. 7.
[4] N.B., i. 1. 19; N.V., iv. 1. 10; iii. 1. 19, 22. 25–27.
[5] *Vivṛti*, vi. 2. 15.
[6] *Nyāyakandalī*, p. 53, 281, and *Upaskāra*, vi. 2. 16.
[7] *Upaskāra*, v. 2. 18; vi. 2. 16.
[8] P.P., pp. 280–1.

from that set forth in the Nyāya. Mādhava in his *Saṁkara-vijaya* says that, according to the school of Kaṇāda, the soul in the state of liberation is absolutely free from all connection with qualities, and subsists like the sky free from all conditions and attributes, while according to the Naiyāyikas, the state of freedom is one of bliss and wisdom.[1] According to the Vaiśeṣika, the state of freedom cannot be regarded as one of pleasure, and though such an end may not be attractive, it is in conformity with the logical implications of the system. When the soul is rid of the qualities produced by contact with names and body,[2] it regains its independence. Maṇḍana's criticism that the destruction of the qualities of suffering, pain and the like, is not different from destruction of the self is not without force.[3] Śrīdhara contends that the self in such a condition enjoys its own natural state.[4] While annihilation is impossible for the self which is eternal, the state of freedom comes perilously near the unconscious condition of a stone.[5] Śrīdhara quotes texts from the Upaniṣads in support of his view.[6]

XIV

God

Kaṇāda's Sūtra does not openly refer to God. He traces the primal activities of the atoms and souls to the principle of adṛṣṭa.[7] While he seemed to have been satisfied with the explanation of the universe by the principle of adṛṣṭa his

1 Atyantanāśo guṇasaṅgater yā sthitir nabhovat kaṇabhakṣapakṣe
Muktis tadīye caraṇākṣapakṣe sānandasaṁvitsahitā vimuktiḥ.

2 Ātmaviśeṣaguṇānām atyantocchedaḥ.

3 Viśeṣaguṇanivṛttilakṣaṇā muktir ucchedapakṣaṁ na bhidyate.

4 Ātmanaḥ svarūpeṇāvasthānam.

5 S.S.S.S., v. 36.

6 *Nyāyakandalī*, pp. 282–7.

7 Sometimes V.S., ii. 1. 18–19, are said to contain the proofs for the existence of God, though it is difficult to accept this view. In ii. 1. 9–14, the existence of invisible eternal air is established, and in ii. 1. 15–17, an objection is raised that its existence is not a matter of perception or inference, but only of revelation, and ii. 1. 18–19, state that some of our notions have their origin in the perceptions of our ancestors and are handed down to us, and these constitute the logical ground for the existence of the corresponding objects (see Ui: *Vaiśeṣika Philosophy*, pp. 164–166). In iii. 2. 4–9, we find a similar treatment of the problem of self.

followers felt that the principle of adṛṣṭa was too nebulous and unspiritual and made it dependent on God's will. God is the efficient cause of the world, while the atoms are the material cause. It is, however, hard to concede that Kaṇāda himself felt the need of a divine being. The famous passage [1] which occurs twice, and has been made to support theism by the later commentators, has no reference to God. Apparently Kaṇāda felt that the Vedas were the work of the seers, and not God. Praśastapāda does not make God central to his system, though he regards Īśvara as the cause of the world in the opening verse of his *Padārthadharmasaṁgraha.*[2] Śaṁkara's criticism [3] in his commentary on the *Vedānta Sūtra* assumes that the system has no place for God, and that it believes in the eternal and uncreated nature of souls and atoms, and accounts for their varying states by the principle of adṛṣṭa.

The criticisms of rival schools clearly brought out the unsatisfactory character of the non-theistic Vaiśeṣika. Countless millions of unthinking atoms cannot produce the marvellous unity in variety of the world. They are incapable of taking counsel together or carrying out a common plan of evolving a spiritual commonwealth. The logical minds of the Vaiśeṣika thinkers were not favourable to the hypothesis of mere chance. They soon realised that the atoms, however immutable and eternal were of no avail unless their activities were regulated by a presiding mind. God perceives the atoms, and in his intellect, first, arises the notion of duality and then the dyads are formed. Inference and scripture both require us to admit God.[4] The four great elementary substances (mahābhūtas) are preceded by someone having a knowledge of them, since they are effects.[5] The conventions of the meanings of words are established by God. Again, the Vedas are a collection of sentences which imply authorship of intelligent beings,[6] and since the contents of the Vedas are free from error, inadvertence and the desire to deceive on the part of their authors, they must be due to an eternal omniscient, all-holy spirit

[1] Tadvacanād āmnāyasya prāmāṇyam (i. 1. 3; x. 2. 9).

[2] See the opening and the concluding portions of P.P. and pp. 48–49.

[3] S.B., ii. 3. 14.

[4] Keith: I.L.A., pp. 265–6; *Nyāyakandalī*, p. 54.

[5] ii. 1. 18–19.

[6] Buddhipūrvavākyakṛtir vede. See *Upaskāra*, vi. 1. 1.

(nirdoṣapuruṣa).[1] Again, souls in the praḷaya state are devoid of intelligence, and so they cannot control the activity of the atoms, and within the world of atoms there is not to be perceived any source of motion. If we are to avoid infinite regress, we are thrown back on a first Mover as the origin and starting-point.[2] There need be only one such Mover. To admit a number is unnecessary. A plurality of gods may produce discord, and so there is one creator, and he is God.

The question whether God has a body is considered by Śrīdhara. It is not necessary for God to be embodied. Even a bodyless being can act. The immaterial soul operates towards the moving of the body. Though the body belongs to the soul, it does not supply the force impelling itself. The object impelled is the body, and God has such an object in the atoms. If it is argued that a body is necessary for the production of desire and effort, Śrīdhara replies, that it is the case only where desire and effort are adventitious (āgantukam), and not when they are natural (svabhāvikam). God's intelligence, desire and effort, are eternal.[3] Śrīdhara deals with a number of objections to the creation of the world by God. If it is said that God has no unsatisfied desires and so cannot possess the impetus to creation, he says that he has no selfish desires, but acts for the benefit of others. In conformity with the principle of karma, he allows pain in the world, and pain is, after all, not a great evil, since it helps us to realise the variety of all existence. It is no limitation of his independence that he reckons with the law of character.

The Vaiśeṣika view of God is practically the same as that of the Naiyāyika [4] and is open to the same criticism. The world was originally regarded as a piece of mechanism, complete and self-sufficient, with atoms and souls held together in their place by the principle of adṛṣṭa. The difficulties relentlessly pressed by the critics of the Vaiśeṣika, that an unintelligent principle could not keep together the *disjecta membra* of the world, forced the later Vaiśeṣikas to accept a divine principle as a way out of the difficulties. God is not the creator of the world, since souls and atoms are co-eternal with him. God

[1] *Upaskāra*, x. 2. 9. The whole argument rests on the acceptance of the authoritativeness of the Vedas. If we deny it, as the Buddhists do, the argument loses its force.

[2] Cp. Aristotle's theory of God as the First Mover, who starts all heavenly and earthly motions.

[3] *Nyāyakandalī*, pp. 55–8.

[4] Devatāviṣaye bhedo nāsti naiyāyikaiḥ samam (Haribhadra's *Ṣaḍdarśanasamuccaya*, p. 59).

is distinguished from human souls by his omniscience and omnipotence, which qualify him for the government of the universe. He is never entangled in the cycle of existence. He sets the world under certain laws and lets it go, but he does not interfere with its course. The world is a gigantic piece of clockwork set in motion by its maker and guaranteed to go without any further interference. But a non-interfering God does not help the actual life of the world, while an interfering God runs the risk of upsetting his own laws. God and the world exclude each other, but if we do not revise the original premises, even " God " cannot help us. If we start with a plurality of entities unrelated to one another, we cannot correct their isolation by the mechanical device of a God who arranges things from outside. The world held together by the mechanical expedient of a foreign medium is a mere aggregate of things, and not an organic whole. The souls cannot even know one another. Each real thing will be a little world to itself shut up within the closed circle of its own internal content. Souls and their objects are essentially disparate, and their relation is an externally imposed harmony. Before we can arrive at a more satisfactory view, the starting-point must be surrendered. If there is a God, he could produce the ultimate elements of matter as well, and there is no need for maintaining the eternal and self-existent character of atoms and souls. If there is a God, the heavens and the earth hang on him, and the inconceivably small particles of matter moving through boundless realms of space are his creation as well.

XV

General Estimate of the Vaiśeṣika Philosophy

A critical consideration of the general principles of the Vaiśeṣika will help us to understand the central features as well as the limitations of the system. A philosophic theory should order and organise the manifold characters which reality reveals into a coherent and intelligible whole. The Vaiśeṣika attempts " to exhibit in one system the characters and interrelations of all that is observed." [1] It will be useful

[1] Whitehead : *The Concept of Nature*, p. 185.

for us to distinguish, as Professor Whitehead does, sense-data, the world of perception and scientific objects. Sense-data are the actual colours, tastes, sounds, temperatures that we perceive. We build on these data the world of experience, and to account for these sense-data and the world of experience we postulate a number of scientific objects which are not objects of perception, though they account for all perception. In the Vaiśeṣika, also, we have sense-data, or the objects of perception, with which all experience starts. When we think together these objects by the categories of substance, quality and relations, we rise to the world of experience. As we have more than once urged, when we speak of a thing and its qualities, we are not stating facts, but interpreting them. When the Vaiśeṣika distinguishes eternal from non-eternal substances, qualities, etc., it emphasises the transient character of our experience and postulates a number of scientific objects as atoms and souls, and space and time, and ākāśa and manas. The theory may be regarded as satisfactory, if sense-data lead to the experienced world and the latter leads to the scientific objects, but, as we shall see, there is no such logical connection discernible.

The emphasis on the principle of negation marks the distinctive pluralistic tendency of the Vaiśeṣika. Reality is not a substance or an aggregate of substances which are the subjects of qualities, but an essential relatedness, where we find need for analysis and comparison, distinction and identification. The changing world of experience consists of a plurality of existent things standing in a complicated network of relations of all kinds with one another. The Vaiśeṣika has for its aim the representation of the universe as a systematic whole, a harmony of varying members. So long as we are not able to harmonise the jarring elements, we have not reached our logical ideal. The self-contradictory is the unthinkable, and yet there are members of the system which we are not able to think together as parts of one whole.

The Vaiśeṣika admits the relative character of negation. The content which it denies is never excluded absolutely. Before we deny, the idea denied must be entertained. Again, the attempted suggestion which the negation refutes, rests on a positive identity which proves to be incompatible with the suggested content. We look for the jar on the ground and fail to find it, and we negate it. The real excludes because it is qualified incompatibly. Negation implies at its base a disjunction which is real. The aim of negation is to set before us reality conceived as a system. The simple affirmative is a one-sided abstraction as much as the simple negative. Mere "being" is the abstraction of an empty object, while mere "nothing" goes beyond mere emptiness. Mere "nothing" is the idea of a "that," or an entity which excludes and is excluded by any and every "what" or qualification. It is the abstraction of an object which negates all qualifications and is forced to reject even itself. Insistence on negation commits the Vaiśeṣika to the ideal of the world as harmony of elements, though, strictly speaking, such an ideal falls short, in principle, of ultimate truth and reality. Diversity, distinction and plurality have a meaning only within a whole. What the Vaiśeṣika regards as an independent individual is a factor discerned within the nature of the real. It confuses distincts and opposites. What is different need not be discrepant. Differents do not exclude one another, they only exclude the denial of their difference. There are incompatibles, but they are not final and absolute. Within limits they are found, but the logical view of identity demands that the real is the individual, the harmonious and the self-consistent. By postulating for all things a self-identity, the Vaiśeṣika is not able to rise to the conception of a true spiritual whole, where the reciprocal exclusiveness of parts is overcome. Though it makes both unity and plurality original to the world, the two are left side by side, and not worked into a whole. The Vaiśeṣika is not loyal to the conception of knowledge as an organised whole implied by its view of negation.

The Vaiśeṣika points out, however, that experience has things and relations. Substance, quality and action exist in themselves as also one in the other, and these are bound by a number of relations called sāmānya or generic nature, viśeṣa or specific marks, and samavāya or inseparable connection. Every substance has a generic quality, a specific difference, and with these latter it is bound up by the relation of samavāya. The affirmation of the reality of relations is a fundamental necessity for any satisfactory pluralistic metaphysics. If the relations are unreal, then there can be only one substance in the world called the Absolute; or the world is composed of monads, independent absolutes, which are unrelated and which can never be related.

The theory of samavāya is a weak link in the Vaiśeṣika system. We cannot look upon samavāya as a connection between two distinct things and yet regard it as of a different kind from saṁyoga, or conjunction. If samavāya is distinct from saṁyoga, then the whole is something over and above the parts. The conception of the world as a systematic whole with interrelated elements is the implication of the Vaiśeṣika view of samavāya as of its view of negation. Its pluralism, therefore, is not final.

The distinction of sāmānya (general) and viśeṣa (particular) is a distinction of the qualities of substances. What is the nature of viśeṣa, or particularity? It is quite true that we accept unique individuals at the common-sense level of life. But we cannot give a satisfactory account of what this particularity is. What is it that makes a thing the particular thing it is? All that we know of a thing is a number of its qualities and the way it behaves. The uniqueness cannot be defined: yet it seems to be inexhaustible. Individuality seems to be a mere assumption as good as non-existent. Take the individual soul. Is there anything which it cannot alter? If its individuality is something which changes with its historical life, it is then capable of alteration. If it is an unchangeable essence, then we do not know what it is. If we appeal to facts, we are given not "blue," but always "a blue," a "blue" of a certain sort, neither the universal by itself, nor the specification which makes the particular blue. We do not know how these unite to make a unique particular. Ultimately we cannot define what we mean by uniqueness. Though the theory of viśeṣa, or particularity, is not borne out by logical evidence, an obstinate empirical prejudice inclines us to grant unique indestructible essences to individuals. The individuality of the innumerable elements and souls is destructive of the individuality of the whole, and so, if the conception of an organised whole implied by the Vaiśeṣika view of negation and samavāya is to be sustained, the doctrine of individuals will have to be modified.[1]

The general notion is a common property said to exist, independent of the intelligence which conceives it, in substances, qualities and actions, and regarded as eternal in eternal substances and non-eternal in non-eternal ones. If the individuals and the universals are equally real, and if our scientific generalisations are regarded as dealing with these entities eternally fixed in the order of nature, then there ought to be universals corresponding to all conceivable entities, good, bad and indifferent. Besides, there are no universals which are eternal. Under the influence of formal logic which tends to make thought static, the Nyāya-Vaiśeṣika emphasises essences and their qualities and their differences. Nothing can at the same time exist and not exist. Such is the law of contradiction, and under its influence things were divided into classes that were supposed to have been the same ever since the world began, and to continue to be so till the world comes to an end. Darwin's theory of evolution discredits belief in the fixity of species. One species develops into another by the accumulation of individual differences under natural selection. The classes are what they are as a result of the process of evolution carried on through millions of years. The classes are mutable in the highest degree, and tend to shade off into one another even to-day. Mendelian heredity may transform the nature of the horse beyond identification. The so-called universals are not immutable self-existent types, but represent stages of growth and development adapted to the changing conditions of the environment. When classes tend to melt away, the

[1] Cp. Bradley: "The natures of the many are therefore not each merely self-contained, because if you extirpate from each every reference beyond itself, you have no manyness left. 'And' has no signification except as the expression of a containing whole, and diversity apart from identity has lost its sense. The required particulars, therefore, are self-contradictory. And you cannot escape by drawing a distinction within each of separate aspects: for such a road leads to a division into fresh particulars, with regard to each of which the same dilemma results. If the many are not each itself beyond itself, they have ceased to be many; and, on the other hand, whatever fails to be self-contained is not individual and unique. Hence the particular beings, which, if they were possible, would each be unique, prove to be mere abstractions. And these because in principle self-discrepant are unreal, and in the end are senseless" (*Logic*, vol. ii, p. 651). See also Gentile: *Theory of Mind as Pure Act*, E-T., p. 113.

logician who plays with types and essences has his ground cut from under his feet. At any one stage the class character is denoted by the sāmānya, or generality, though this character is by no means stereotyped. When universals are said to be eternal, what is meant is not existence through endless time, but independence of time relations. The Jaina logicians argue that even the Nyāya-Vaiśeṣika does not admit the universal notion of negation said to be common to antecedent negation, subsequent negation, etc.; nor does it admit the universal notion of universals. If the universal of the different universals or of the different kinds of negation is simply their common character, we can say that there is no other kind of universal than that of common character. The theory of sāmānya, or generality, is motived by the desire to distinguish the unchanging from the changing. If we assign the universals to a supersensible world of superior reality, it becomes difficult to bring them into relation with the particular individuals which embody them. It is not easy to relate the one eternal ubiquitous general essence with the many, non-eternal, discrete, isolated individuals. If the universal does not so much underlie the individual as coexist with it, we are brought to a position similar to Plato's theory of Ideas and the *Universalia ante Res* doctrine. Two utterly disparate things, as the universal and the individual, cannot be unified. We must dismiss the world of individuals as a vain show standing in no intelligible relation to reality. The Nyāya-Vaiśeṣika admits that the universal and the individual are inseparable, since they are bound by the tie of samavāya. In other words, the distinction between the universal and the particular is a distinction in thought, but not a division in reality, and yet, inconsistently, the universals are given an independent existence. They are supposed to survive the destruction of the world, and during pralaya they have for their substratum, time, which is conceived as a real thing (kālikasaṁbandha).

Substance, quality and action are regarded as objective, while the relations are products of logical analysis, which we have no right to transform into facts of the cosmos. The first three categories are said to partake of the character of sattā, a fiction endowed with existence, and supposed to confer the same property on the three categories. The different relations, causal and reciprocal and mere togetherness of compresence, are not existents, since all existents are individual. Guṇa (quality) and karma (action) are different kinds or adjectives of substantives.[1] Whatever temporal alterations and spatial movements may happen, the guṇas may be looked upon as the continuant factors of causation, while the alterable states are the karma referring to the "occurrent, or in accordance with the scholastic usage, the occasional causal factor." A complete conception of substance includes both guṇa and karma, continuant and occurrent factors, neither being conceivable apart from the other.[2] Every substance has its unique essence (viśeṣa), its qualities (guṇa), and its modes of behaviour (karma). Common sense regards the occurrences of the world as the attributes of certain substances. The conception of a thing and its qualities is so familiar to us all that it enters into all our experience. The Vaiśeṣika takes it for a simple unambiguous axiom, which does not stand in need of much discussion or proof. Everything real is either a substance or an attribute of it. The attributes are dependent aspects of reality incapable of existing on their own account, and they imply a more ultimate form of living substance, to which they belong. The existence of a plurality of substances, each complete in itself and independent of all the rest, is accepted as a dictate of common sense, though we cannot form a satisfactory idea of what a substance is in itself.

The naïve theory of substance and quality conceals a bottomless abyss of unsolved problems. Substance is defined as the substratum of qualities.[3] So qualities have no independent existence. We distinguish in thought substance and quality, but there is no need to assume that qualities and actions possess a higher degree of reality than generality, particularity, etc. The Vaiśeṣika, however, assumes that there can be substance apart from any qualities. At the first moment of creation the substance is said to be without any

[1] W. E. Johnson distinguishes adjectives into transitive and intransitive; transitive adjectives are the relations. See *Logic*, vol. i, p. xxxv.

[2] W. E. Johnson: *Logic*, vol. i, p. xxxvii.

[3] While substance was defined by the ancient Nyāya as the substratum of qualities and actions, modern Nyāya defines it as the substratum of qualities alone.

qualities, the suggestion being that the metaphysical identity of a substance is not the same as the permanent identity of its properties. The essence of a substance, which makes it what it is, has little to do with the permanent qualities which are characteristic of and peculiar to it. The permanence of the qualities is not essential to its remaining what it is. The special qualities of substances are regarded as effects, *i.e.* qualities are derived from substances; but how can a substance become a cause, *i.e.* produce something different from itself? What is above all positive and concrete qualities is for our thought destitute of any content. It is an unknown X, a supposed I-know-not-what, lying behind all qualities. An inveterate habit of thought inclines us to give greater reality to substance than to qualities. The Vaiśeṣika substances are unknown substrata to account for the qualities of experience, the results of possible speculation, and not scientific observation. But the Vaiśeṣika believes also that a thing would lose its nature if it loses its qualities. The relation between substance and qualities is said to be one of samavāya, *i.e.* one cannot exist without the other.[1]

Śaṁkara criticises this view of the relation between substance and quality. If the two are inseparably related, the inseparability must refer to place, time or nature. The two are not inseparable in place, since the cloth originating from the threads occupies the place of the threads only and not that of the cloth, while the qualities of the cloth, such as its colour, occupy the place of the cloth only and not that of the threads.[2] If inseparability in time is the essence of the samavāya relation, then the right and the left horns of a cow would be related in that way. If it is inseparability in nature or character, then it would be impossible to make any further distinction between substance and quality, since the two are one.[3]

If the substance depends on its qualities, then it is not really independent. Substance is not only united with its qualities by the relation of samavāya, but all substances are united with the general notion of substantiality, and single substances are united in the same way with the notion of their own class.[4] We do not perceive a substance apart from

[1] See Śaṁkara on Gauḍapāda's *Kārikā*, iii. 5.

[2] V.S., i. 1. 10.

[3] S.B., ii. 2. 17.

[4] Śrī Harṣa asks as to why qualities which possess other qualities, like number, should not be included under substances. If qualities are defined

qualities, and the assumption of something which remains unchanged though the qualities change is an illogical one.[1] If we take our stand on the qualities which change, then there cannot be any permanent substance. The leaf which is verdant and full of sap to-day is sere and yellow to-morrow, and brown and shrivelled the day after. We cannot know what the permanent quality of the leaf is. The whole history of philosophy proves that the underlying core of a thing is an impenetrable mystery.[2] What a substance is, apart from its qualities and behaviour, we cannot hope to know. In the world of experience we are obliged to use the categories of substance and quality, though existence cannot be reduced to qualities, and yet substance, the Vaiśeṣika admits, is nothing apart from its qualities. We can define a substance only by its qualities. We can distinguish things by their different properties. We speak of a substance as the same at different times only so long as it has the same properties. When we find different qualitative groupings, we say that we deal with different things. Substance refers to the stable elements of our experience. Souls and atoms, space, time, akāśā and manas refer to the constant factors in our experience.

The Vaiśeṣika endeavours to take in all aspects of experience and fit them into a general scheme. The sensible world has a real basis independent of the percipient. The relations are real in the sense that they are not fabricated by the mind of man. The Vaiśeṣika does not think that experience comes to us as a mere manifold. It is grounded in laws which are not simply imposed on it. The categories of quality, action, generality, particularity and inherence are dependent (āśrita), while substance is the independent entity on which they all depend (āśraya). Substances are absolutely independent. Non-eternal substances which are caused are not truly sub-

as the substrata of sāmānya, he asks whether they are not the substrata of positive entities like upādhis (*Khaṇḍana*, iv. 3). Alexander refuses to call quality a category.

[1] See, however, N.V., i. 1. 13, where "pṛthivyādiguṇāḥ" is taken as a dvandva compound, meaning earth, etc., *and* the qualities, suggesting that substances as well as qualities are apprehended by the senses.

[2] The Sāṁkhya regards substance and quality as possessing the same reality; the Advaita Vedānta looks upon the conception of substance as an illogical one, representing a mode of thought. Cp. Locke: *Essay on the Human Understanding*.

stances. The theory of the nine eternal substances becomes the central thesis of the Vaiśeṣika pluralism. These nine eternal substances are what Professor Whitehead calls scientific objects as distinct from perceptual objects and sense-data. Their value lies in their power to explain and order the data of perception, to make nature as perceived by the senses more intelligible. A naturalistic bias led the Vaiśeṣika thinkers to regard experience as an ever shifting phantasmagoria demanding explanation from outside. They regard objects of experience as shadows on the screen cast by substances behind. That shadows are cast on the screen of our minds by substances lurking behind, is a metaphysical assumption for which there is no warrant. We need not go behind experience and assume mysterious things in themselves. The Vaiśeṣika asks us to be loyal to the deliverances of the empirical consciousness, which is said to deal first and last with real and separate things, but it is itself going beyond the testimony of consciousness when it looks upon the world of experience as a sort of screen that stands between us and the imperceptible reals. The Vaiśeṣika sets to itself the task of simplifying or unifying phenomena, but adopts a false metaphysics when it assumes that the multiplicity of the world is the phenomenon of a noumenal multiplicity. When it once breaks up the unity of experience into a number of distinct elements, it is unable to reunite them into the whole. A scattered and dissociated diversity cannot engender unity unless it be through the instrumentality of a divine Providence. These substances both in their eternal self-identity and non-eternal manifestations do not form a coherent whole. There is no string by which we can tie them all together.

The idea of the interconnection of substances is not well developed. While the Vaiśeṣika makes relatedness a central feature of the world of experience, still, in conceiving unrelated atoms and souls as the scientific objects, it makes all relations external and arbitrary. The world of true being, the nine eternal substances, remain for ever unaffected by change, and the ground of phenomenal change is not to be sought in any mark of the real itself. Relatedness thus becomes an external accident of the reals. Unrelated atoms cannot account for the phenomenal world. To generate the phenomenal things they must meet and clash. If the atoms are endowed with the property of motion, they are not rigidly unrelated, for even a movement of atoms is a negation of their unrelatedness. To accept adṛṣṭa is to surrender all possibility of philosophical explanation. If the Vaiśeṣika wishes to be faithful to its principle of the reality of relations, which it accepts in its account of padārthas, or the world of experience, it must give up its theory of the eternal non-changing substances, which are the scientific objects, and make relatedness also real. Real relatedness is inconsistent with the absolute independence of the related elements. The so-called eternal substances cannot therefore be the simple, changeless permanent elements, but only the relatively fixed points of one continuously altering system. If change and relatedness belong to the very essence of reality, then reality is not an aggregate of simple reals. The truly scientific object is not the eternal substance, but the ever-changing identity of the world itself.

When the Vaiśeṣika posits eternal atoms, it means to suggest that in the vast reaches of space-time we have a host of supersensible particles too small singly to meet the edge of human vision, though they become visible when they enter into combinations which are more or less lasting, though by no means everlasting. The application of the causal principle, that out of nothing nothing comes, requires it to posit these eternal atoms. The Vaiśeṣika rightly argues that while latitude, longitude, shape, date and motion are space-time properties, smell, taste, colour, temperature and sound are space-time filling properties. Leaving aside sound for the present, the Vaiśeṣika traces smell, taste, colour and temperature, which are the contents of our experience to the atoms. Since these characters of our experience are permanent, it attempts to account for them on the hypothesis of eternal atoms. The changing aspects of experience are traced to non-eternal substances and permanent aspects to eternal ones. The ultimate data from which the Vaiśeṣika starts, and which it seeks to explain, are our sense-experiences. The atoms are frankly acknowledged to be inaccessible in themselves to our perception, though they are supposed to be indispensable for the occurrence of phenomena which we can and do observe.

We perceive a series of colours, sounds, tastes and temperatures. These sense-data are perceived as a part of nature and not, as the Buddhists believed, as a part of mind ; but need we assume atoms as the imperceptible causes of these sense-data ? If we perceive colours and sounds, touches and tastes serially, one detached from the other, there may be some justification for regarding nature as composed of atomic bits. But the Vaiśeṣika rightly emphasises that nature as perceived is a togetherness, a mass of sense-data which melt into one another, a continuously flowing stream. From out of these sense-data we build our view of experience as consisting of things and their qualities and relations, but the atoms assumed are not integral factors of the world of experience. The atomic hypothesis only creates fresh difficulties and leads the Vaiśeṣika system into the dangers of subjectivism. We are not conscious of atoms, and yet they are imagined to be the only reality producing the experienced objects. The manner of the causation is mechanical, and what we perceive is divorced from what is—the atoms, the hypothetical and unverifiable causes of experience. These abstract foundations are not adequate to the concrete experience built on them. Our experience comes to us in a series of events which are in space and time. Every event has a spatial position, *i.e.* is somewhere ; has a history, *i.e.* occurs at some time ; but these properties of space and time do not exhaust the nature of the event. We do not know anything about the material points or atoms. All that we know is that bodies occupy several positions simultaneously, and so we say that they possess spatial extension and figure. Strictly speaking, we know neither a universal matter nor invisible atoms, but only bodies. A body is ordinarily regarded as that which moves. It is a portion of matter which maintains the natural position of its parts unchanged, while their relations to other positions are changed. An extended unit has fixed boundaries, and its identity is said to be unaltered so long as this independence of internal and external relations continues. What we call a thing or a body is a region of space which is marked by some distinguishing character that remains unchanged through time. In the complex given to us in experience we distinguish that which occupies space and time from space and time themselves. Matter is that something which fills the space-time framework.[1] The Vaiśeṣika has no sympathy with the Buddhist attempts, comparable to those of some Neorealists, as Alexander and Russell, to derive the individual from the universal, real things from their connections, terms from their relations, and matter from the union of space and time. We cannot have motion without things that move. The Vaiśeṣika regards the atom as a real entity and not a mere limiting conception. The atoms, according to the Vaiśeṣika, are said to possess the qualities of colour, etc.; and Śaṁkara argues that what has colour, etc., cannot be minute (aṇu) and eternal (nitya). Judging from experience, things possessing colour, etc., are gross and impermanent.[2] If non-perception is indicative of permanence, then even dyads which are too small for perception must be regarded as permanent.[3] If something eternal is required as the basis of the universe, it cannot certainly be the atoms.[4] The determinateness of the world is sought to be accounted for by the diversity of atoms. But altogether external and accidental relations cannot account for the determinate character of the world. The theory of transmutation of matter in its various states goes against the hypothesis of immutable atoms. While ordinary unreflective experience breaks the world into fragments, where everything is distinct if not separate, a little reflection tells us that things pass into one another. There is such a thing as becoming, evolution or development. The truth of things is not a plurality of types but one universal nature. The empirical tendency of the Vaiśeṣika should have led it to supersede the idea of being by that of becoming. If we are impressed by one thing more than another, it is the oneness of nature and the fundamental unity of origin of all classes of "atoms." The idea of development implies that a principle is more than any of the forms through which it passes. The real as presented to us is not atomic in character, but seems to be one stuff where qualitatively different aspects melt into one

[1] More accurately, events are the concrete stuff from which space and time are derived. Mere extension and pure serial process are both abstractions. If anything may be looked upon as the fundamental units of the universe, they are space-time-matter, or the events of Professor Whitehead. The static stuff of objects, space and time are all adjuncts of events.

[2] V.S., iv. 1. 1. [3] iv. 1. 5 [4] S.B., ii. 2. 15.

another. Śaṁkara says that the different elements are different conditions of one stuff, the earth is gross, the water fine, light finer, and air is the finest of all.[1] The atoms answering to the four elements cannot be assumed to have a greater and smaller number of qualities simply because earth has the four qualities of smell, taste, colour and touch, and water the three of colour, taste and touch, and so on. Again, all atoms cannot be said to have all the qualities. If they have only one quality, then we cannot perceive taste in earth, or colour in water, since the qualities of the effects have for their antecedents the qualities of the causes.[2] An immensity of distinct atoms cannot produce a harmonious universe. The mysterious relation of samavāya is invented to cover this difficulty. Dyads which originate from two atoms are said to be different from them, though related to them by way of inherence.

Atoms represent the permanent factors of the flux of events. There is that in nature which does not pass. There are some constants in our experience which we correlate with substances. Substance, as we have already seen, is the name for a way in which things behave. Our experience has some permanent characteristics in spite of its changing character. The conclusion that may be regarded as forced on us by experience is that the principle of nature is something which is eternally changing, though it remains for ever constant. The only helpful suggestion for philosophy which we get from the atomic theory is that the real is that which exists in and for itself. In concrete idealism the whole alone has such reality, for the individuality of the parts would mean the destruction of the individuality of the whole. But the relation of whole and parts is not free from difficulties, so that the real can be identified only with consciousness.

When the Vaiśeṣika asserts the universal and real character of space and time, what it means is that the universe as it appears to us is an endless expanse, an immeasurable extent, an abyss in which there are no bounds, no bottom, no end Every event has spatial and temporal properties. If the

[1] Modern science is reducing atoms to electrical emanations, and matter is becoming almost as ethereal as spirit.

[2] S.B., ii. 2. 16.

spatial position of a thing remains the same while the temporal varies, we say that the body is at rest; if it varies continuously as the time varies continuously, we speak of motion. Since our experience has a spatio-temporal character, the Vaiseṣika infers that space and time stand there outside us, as empty receptacles waiting for things and events to fill them. The truth seems to be that spatial and temporal relations are constituted out of spatial and temporal perceptions. If the spatial and temporal characters of our experience demand the assumption of the universal substances of space and time, there is no reason why we should not have one vast intelligence in the vast heaven, one vast light and one vast darkness, vast cosmic reservoirs of all properties, good, bad and indifferent, which characterise our actual experiences. Space and time cannot be regarded as derivatives from experience, which presupposes them. That space and time are universal, all-pervading substances, is their way of saying that whatever is, is in space, and whatever happens, happens in time. Things of the world are in motion, *i.e.* occupy space and change their behaviour in time. The space void of bodies and the time void of events are called substances. To account for our experiences, which have the features of spatiality and temporality, the Vaiśeṣika assumes an immensity or infinite space that refuses to submit to bounds and a duration that cannot be completed. But these infinite space and time are metaphysical hypotheses and not descriptions of facts.

Though space without time changes does not seem to be absurd, time is nothing without changes or events, even as a relation is nothing without terms that are related. Time is interpenetrated by real stuff. Time does not involve a plurality of things. It might occur in a single substance. A person may change his character, a flower may change its colour. Space, dealing as it does with properties of position, distance, etc., requires various real things. Time alone of itself does not imply such a variety of coexistence. It no more involves coexistence than one real thing involves others.

The argument by which atoms are assumed is not applied to space and time. The Vaiśeṣika does not say that the continuance of time arises out of the separate indivisible instants of time or the continuance of space out of separate points or spatial units. If the difficulty of the crumbling of matter into nothing is to be avoided only by the assumption of indivisible atoms, the continuity of space and time can only be accounted for on an analogous theory of points and instants. If in the latter the assumption of one universal space or time is feasible, the assumption of one universal matter is quite a legitimate hypothesis even for the explanation of the physical universe. We have things in certain relations to each other which we call spatial and events in certain relations which we call temporal. Time and space represent the relations of the objects for our experience. These spatial and temporal relations are facts for immediate experience, and the theory that events occur in a given space and a given time, involving changes in the given persistent atomic stuff, is the result of metaphysical reflection. A universal space, a universal time and persistent atoms are all hypothetical explanations and not given facts.[1] The defective definition of substance as the substratum of qualities leads the Vaiśeṣika to regard space, time, etc., as substances. Matter is the stuff which fills space and time, and if we wish to be accurate we must say that the fundamental concept by which the universe can be explained is space-time-matter stuff, a conclusion of which some Vaiśeṣikas had a dim apprehension. Śivāditya says that ākāśa, space and time are one in reality, though conceived as threefold on account of the diverse effects,[2] a view confirmed by Candrakānta Tarkālaṁkāra, who argues that, according to Kaṇāda, space, time and ākāśa are one substance only, though variously called space, or time, or ākāśa, according to the effects produced by it and the variety of external conditions attending it.[3] Space and time are

[1] Cp. Whitehead: "We must not conceive of events as in a given time, a given space, and consisting of changes in given persistent material. Time, space and material are adjuncts of events. On the old theory of relativity, time and space are relations between materials; on our theory they are relations between events" (*Enquiry*, p. 26).

[2] Ākāśāditrayaṁ tu vastuta ekam eva upādhibhedān nānābhūtam (*Saptapadārthī*, 17). S.P.B., i. 61.

[3] See App. B, p. iv, to V.S., in *Sacred Books of the Hindus* series. See also S.P.S., ii. 12.

abstractions from nature. Later Naiyāyikas described space and time as the modes of God.[1]

Consciousness is an activity, the property of a thing confronted in relations of extension and succession by another thing, the non-conscious world. The relation between the soul and its qualities is one of samavāya. Śaṁkara raises the question of the relations of the ātman to the qualities of knowledge, etc., and contends that the Vaiśeṣika cannot allow the two equal rank, since the self is permanent and the qualities impermanent. If it allows them equal rank, then there cannot be a condition of ātman when it is free from the qualities. In short, ātman must be impermanent as much as the qualities.[2] The narrowness of mental life is accounted for by the assumption of the atomic manas, but it is difficult to conceive satisfactorily the relation between soul and manas. When the Vaiśeṣika distinguishes the soul substance from the quality of consciousness, it is adopting a mechanical view. The conception of experience as the resultant of the interaction of something outside our mind with it, we have already seen, makes all experience unintelligible. We do not know what the innermost essence of the soul is. Its different qualities of pleasure, pain, knowledge, etc., arise through the interaction of unintelligent selves with unintelligent atoms. When the soul is freed, the qualities disappear, and the released soul, rid of all qualities, is a unit devoid of any internal variety, and is therefore not real at all. The object swallows the subject. Man is a creative centre co-operating in the making of the world which he knows. Experience, which is the problem for philosophy, is neither nature closed to mind nor mind isolated from nature. Psychical and physical reality are everywhere in closest alliance The basis of all is consciousness and not externality. Physicists, with their atoms and forces, and psychologists, with their souls and faculties, have again and again fallen into the temptation of hypostatising abstractions. There is a good deal to be said for the theory adopted by the Advaita Vedānta and the Sāṁkhya that everything other than the transcendental self arises in the course of cosmic evolution.

[1] Athalye: *Tarkasaṁgraha*, 15.

[2] See S.B. on Gauḍapāda's *Kārikā*, iii. 5.

If we accept the doctrine of the plurality of souls, for which we did not find any metaphysical justification in the examination of the Nyāya Philosophy, we now have souls on the one side and space-time-matter on the other. The characteristic feature of the latter is movement or passage, and so it is called in the Sāṁkhya Philosophy prakṛti. The Sāṁkhya, with its doctrine of puruṣas or souls and prakṛti or nature, marks an advance on the Nyāya-Vaiśeṣika conception.

Closer analysis reveals to us that relations, attributes and qualities are all subordinate to existents, which are of two different kinds, matter and non-matter or souls, prakṛti and puruṣa; and we may profit by the suggestion of the Ṛg-Veda, which is also found in the first chapter of Genesis, that the brooding spirit of order elicits out of an original chaos a hierarchy of living beings and the natural world. Only that can be called a substance which has existence as a whole. Nowhere in the world do we come across a whole confined to a here and a now. We cannot mark off the limits of things from one another. We have of course degrees of oneness or individuality. The highest kind of individuality we come across is that of the finite individual, but even that is not self-contained. The true substance is that which includes finite minds and the world of nature. The fundamental reality of the world is the Absolute Spirit expressed in the dissolving view of the universe, forming and transforming itself as it passes along. Experience is one continuous "passage" or interrelatedness. Space can be broken into points, time into instants, and matter into atoms; but we have seen that the universe cannot be regarded as space and time and matter, but space-time-matter, so that prakṛti, or that which changes, forms the fundamental stuff of the universe, and its fractional elements are to be looked upon not so much as things but as events.

The categories of the Vaiśeṣika are defective, whatever standpoint we may adopt. If we take them as distinctions which have a meaning on the plane of ordinary life, then we may point to certain distinctions in common use which do not find a place in the list of categories, such as the conceptions of values and ends. If we take them as a philosophical interpretation of experience, then all the variety and change of the world can be reduced to a single concept. The finite souls and the world of nature are aspects of the continuous advance adapted to each other. The Vaiśeṣika view that the soul is another strand of the real, between which and matter there is a good deal of difference, is sound.

If the whole nature of object-experience may be assigned to prakṛti, which is an ever-advancing growth of events, what is the place of soul in this scheme? This is the problem of theory of knowledge, and we have already seen how the Nyāya theory adopted by the Vaiśeṣika, that the individual soul has a passive mind into which, as into an empty receptacle, the world outside conveys ideas of its nature, is inadequate. The study of inanimate objects determines the whole philosophical attitude of the Vaiśeṣika. The shadow of materialism darkens the background, and souls are regarded as substances of the same nature as the atoms, unintelligent in themselves.

Atoms and souls, space and time, are mere sounds and symbols which have no meaning apart from experience. The Vaiśeṣika makes them serve as dummies on which it could hang its theories. These are merely names for the different aspects of our experience. As we have seen in our criticism of the Nyāya, both the psychological and the physical orders are rooted in a universal consciousness which is not to be confused with the psychological consciousness. It underlies the distinction of subject and object. Until this view is accepted, the Vaiśeṣika will have no explanation for the genetic order, the objective reality and the ever-changing character of cosmic evolution with its members of plants, animals and men. To indent upon adṛṣṭa is arbitrary, and God cannot take the place of adṛṣṭa until he is transformed into an absolute Consciousness. If the unity of substance is compatible with the variety of its states, then there does not seem to be any special difficulty in the way of our envisaging the whole wealth of varied existence in the world as the qualitative aspects of a fundamental Being. The defect of the Vaiśeṣika is that it does not piece together its results into a single coherently articulated structure. It is not a philosophy in the sense implied by the famous saying of the *Republic* that he who sees things together is the true dialectician or the philosopher. A catalogue of items is not a systematic philosophy. The many-sided context of human life is ignored by the Vaiśeṣika, and its physical philosophy and moral and religious values are not worked into a unified interpretation. An atomistic pluralism is not the final answer to the intellectual demand for a rational interpretation of the universe. But we agree with the Vaiśeṣika in thinking that the refined analysis of the mere logician gives no more than a science of the possible, an abstract formalism dissociated from the real world. Philosophy may criticise but cannot cut itself loose from common sense. Common sense may not be all, but it is certainly the first condition of all fruitful philosophy. Only the method of philosophy is different from that of common sense. It tries to press as far beyond and above the facts presented to the senses as possible. Creative logic, which is the instrument of philosophic genius, seeks to ground the world in a higher principle. The same facts noticed by the Nyāya-Vaiśeṣika thinkers are capable of a more satisfactory interpretation; and, as we shall see, the Sāṁkhya and the Vedānta arrive at more satisfactory philosophical constructions justifying the faith in "one God, one law, one element."

REFERENCES.

CHATTERJEE: Hindu Realism.
COWELL and GOUGH: Sarvadarśanasaṁgraha, x.
GANGĀNĀTH JHĀ: Praśastapāda's Padārthadharmasaṁgraha with Śrīdhara's Nyāyakandalī.
FADDEGON: The Vaiśeṣika System.
KEITH: Indian Logic and Atomism.
NANDALAL SINHA: The Vaiśeṣika Sūtras of Kaṇāda.
ROER: Bhāsāpariccheda and Siddhāntamuktāvali of Viśvanātha.
UI: The Vaiśeṣika Philosophy.

CHAPTER IV

THE SĀMKHYA SYSTEM

Introduction—Antecedents—Literature—Causality—Prakṛti—Guṇas—Cosmic evolution—Puruṣa—The relation between Puruṣa and Prakṛti—The problem of knowledge—Jīva—Ethics—Release—God—Is Sāṁkhya atheistic ?—General estimate.

I

Introduction

THE Sāṁkhya system represents a notable departure in thought from what may be called the formalistic habit of mind. By its emphasis on the principle of continuity, it marks, in some degree, the abandonment of the tendency to view the universe as tied up in neat parcels. Its rejection of the rigid categories of the Nyāya-Vaiśeṣika as inadequate instruments for describing the complex and fluid universe, makes it a real advance on the theory of atomistic pluralism. It undermines the foundations of supernatural religion by substituting evolution for creation The world is not the act of a creator God, who summoned up by a single fiat of his will a world entirely distinct from himself, but is the product of the interaction between the infinite number of spirits and the ever-active prakṛti, or the potentiality of nature—what Plato calls "the receptacle and nurse of all generation." [1]

The Sāṁkhya philosophy assumes the reality of puruṣas and prakṛti from the fact of knowledge with its distinction between the subject and the object. No explanation of experience is possible if we do not assume the reality of a knowing self and an object known. The Sāṁkhya endeavours to give an intelligible account of all experience, why we have

[1] See also *Enneads*, iii. 6. 13; E.T. by McKenna, vol. ii, p. 86.

it and how we acquire it. Richard Garbe, who has made a special study of this school, says: "In Kapila's doctrine, for the first time in the history of the world, the complete independence and freedom of the human mind, its full confidence in its own powers, were exhibited."[1] It is "the most significant system of philosophy that India has produced."[2] Even those who regard this estimate as exaggerated will concede that the Sāṁkhya is a notable attempt in the realm of pure philosophy.

The system takes its name from the fact that it arrives at its conclusions by means of theoretical investigation. The word "Sāṁkhya" is said by some to be derived from saṁkhyā, or number,[3] and the name is justified as being appropriate to a system which gives an analytical enumeration of the principles of the cosmos. But this tendency to enumeration is common to all Hindu systems of thought. In the early texts, "Saṁkhyā" is used in the sense of philosophical reflection and not numerical reckoning.[4] This particular system, which expounds by careful reflection the nature of puruṣa or spirit,[5] and the other entities, acquired its significant title.[6]

II

Antecedents

In the history of thought there is nothing altogether new. No system of thought issues forth in all its fulness from the head of any one man. There must have existed philosophical ideas and doctrines

---

[1] *Philosophy of Ancient India*, p. 30. See also Davies: S.K., p. v.

[2] S.P.B., p. xiv.

[3] Garbe: *Philosophy of Ancient India*, p. 44. M.B. associates Sāṁkhya with parisaṁkhyāna, or exhaustive enumeration. See xii. 11393; xii. 11409, 11410. Winternitz says: "It seems to me to be proved that Pythagoras was influenced by the Indian Sāṁkhya" (*Calcutta Review*, 1924, p. 21).

[4] See I.P., p. 527. Cp. M.B., xii. 11934.

Doṣāṇāṁ ca guṇānāṁ ca pramāṇam pravibhāgataḥ
Kaṁcid artham abhipretya sā saṁkhyety upadhāryatām.

The weighing of the defects and the merits severally, as one attempts some interpretation, should be understood as saṁkhyā. Sāṁkhya has not always a numerical reference. In his commentary on *Viṣṇusahasranāma*, Śaṁkara quotes a passage where Sāṁkhya means knowledge of the nature of pure spirit: "Śuddhātmatattvavijñānaṁ sāṁkhyam ity abhidhīyate." See Hall: *Sāṁkhyasāra*, p. 5.

[5] Cp. Samyagvivekenātmakathanam.

[6] It is also suggested that the system derived its name from its first founder Sankha, though there is little evidence for this surmise. See Hall: *Sāṁkhyasāra*, p. 3.

affording the necessary material for the founder to work upon. In our account of the cosmology of the Ṛg-Veda,[1] we referred to certain vague anticipations of the Sāṁkhya theory of puruṣa and prakṛti. When we pass to the Upaniṣads, we find, in their varied teachings, the leading conceptions of the Sāṁkhya philosophy.[2] The authors of the Upaniṣads did not all think alike. Some of them threw out suggestions capable of being worked into the Sāṁkhya system, though they did not themselves reach it. When the Sāṁkhya claims to be a system based on the Upaniṣads, there is some justification for it, though the main tendency of the Upaniṣads is radically opposed to its dualism. The realistic tendencies of the Upaniṣads receive emphasis in the Sāṁkhya conception of the universe. The first mention of the Sāṁkhya is in the *Śvetāśvatara Upaniṣad*,[3] though the elements co-ordinated into the system are to be met with in the earlier Upaniṣads. Not only the notions of rebirth and the unsatisfactoriness of the world but also such central principles as that knowledge is the means to release, and puruṣa is the pure subject, are taken from the Upaniṣads.[4] In the *Kaṭha Upaniṣad*,[5] the unmanifested (avyakta) stands at the top of an evolution series on the plane of matter, from which the great self (mahān-ātmā), intellect, mind, objects and senses spring in succession. Self-sense (ahaṁkāra) is not mentioned and the supreme spirit is admitted. Yet this is the earliest account of cosmic evolution which seems to have been utilised by the Sāṁkhya thinkers. The first product of prakṛti is called mahat, the great one; and the natural source of this idea is the Upaniṣad conception that the supreme spirit reappears as the first-born of creation, after producing primitive matter.[6] The classification of the psychical functions may have been suggested by the account of the *Praśna Upaniṣad* regarding the states of sleep, dream, etc.[7] The *Śvetāśvatara Upaniṣad*[8] contains a more developed account of the Sāṁkhya principles of the cosmos, the three guṇas, though the Sāṁkhya elements are subordinated to its main doctrine of theism. It identifies pradhāna and māyā as well as Brahman and puruṣa.[9] The *Maitrāyaṇī Upaniṣad*, which seems to be a post-Buddhist one,[10] is familiar with a developed Sāṁkhya and refers to tanmātras,[11] the three guṇas,[12] and the distinction of spirit and

---

[1] I.P., pp. 100–105. [2] See I.P., pp. 259–260. [3] vi. 13.

[4] Bṛh. Up., ii. 4. 14; iii. 4. 2; iv. 3. 15. See also *Muṇḍaka*, iii. 1. 1.

[5] iii. 10–11. See also vi. 7–11. Cp. Chān., vi. 8. 6.

[6] R.V., x. 12. 1. Cp. M.B., xii. 311. 3.

[7] iv. Cp. the subtle body of the Sāṁkhya with the being of sixteen elements of this Upaniṣad.

[8] I.P., 510–515. See Śvet. Up., i. 4; iv. 5.

[9] i. 10; iv. 10; iii. 12; and iv. 1.

[10] See I.P., p. 142 n.; Keith: *Sāṁkhya*, pp. 14–15. The *Nṛsiṁhatāpanīya*, *Garbha*, *Cūlikā* are much influenced by the Sāṁkhya doctrines.

[11] iii. 2. See also Chān. Up., vi. 3.

[12] ii. 5; v. 2. Some trace the conception of three guṇas to the three colours mentioned in the *Chāndogya Upaniṣad* and repeated in the *Śvetāśvatara Upaniṣad*.

nature.[1] The Upaniṣads make use in a general and indeterminate way of these terms, which later systems have stamped with a special significance.

Jacobi's attempt to regard the Sāṁkhya as the development of an early materialist school has little to support it. By its insistence on the absolute reality and independence of spirit, the Sāṁkhya set itself against all materialist views of mental phenomena. We do not come across any stage of the development of the Sāṁkhya at which it can be identified with materialism.

The relation of the Sāṁkhya to early Buddhism has given rise to much speculation as to mutual borrowing.[2] Though the Sāṁkhya works, which have come down to us, are later than the origin of Buddhism, and may have been influenced by Buddhist theories, the Sāṁkhya ideas themselves preceded Buddha,[3] and it is impossible to regard Buddhism as the source of the Sāṁkhya. Insistence on suffering, the subordination of Vedic sacrifices and denunciation of ascetic extravagances, indifference to theism and the belief in the constant becoming of the world (pariṇāminityatva) are common to Buddhism and the Sāṁkhya. These casual coincidences are not enough to justify the theory of mutual borrowing, especially in view of the marked divergences between the two. Buddhism does not accept any of the central principles of the Sāṁkhya, an inactive puruṣa, an ultimate prakṛti and the theory of the guṇas. If the Buddhist chain of causation resembles, in some respects, the Sāṁkhya theory of evolution, it is because both of them have for their common source the Upaniṣads. Whether the Sāṁkhya at the time of Buddha was atheistic in character is more than we can say.

In the *Mahābhārata* evidently we find a definite movement of thought identical with the Sāṁkhya.[4] Anugītā explains the distinction of puruṣa and prakṛti.[5] The puruṣa is the subject of knowledge,

---

[1] vi. 10. Cp. Keith: "There is, in detail, in the Sāṁkhya little that cannot be found in the Upaniṣads in some place or other" (*Sāṁkhya*, p. 60).

[2] See I.P., pp. 472–473.

[3] "There is abundant evidence, both in Hindu and Buddhist works, of unquestionable antiquity and authenticity of the Sāṁkhya and the Yoga systems having been current before the time of Buddha" (Rājendra Lāl Mitra: Y.S., p. xvi). Buddhistic legends mention Kapila as one of the predecessors of Buddha. See Garbe's S.P.S., Vṛtti, p. 3. Cp. *Brahmajāla Sūtra*: "There are brethren, some recluses and Brahmins who are eternalists, and who on four grounds proclaim that both the soul and the world are. They are addicted to logic and reasoning, and give utterance to the following conclusions of their own, beaten out by their argumentations and based on their sophistry. Eternal is the soul; and the world, giving birth to nothing new, is steadfast as a mountain peak, as a pillar firmly fixed; and these living creatures, though they pass from birth to birth, fall from one state of existence and spring up in another, yet they are for ever and ever."

[4] I.P., pp. 501–504.

[5] xiv 50. 8 ff.

the twenty-fifth principle set over against the other twenty-four principles of nature which are the objects of knowledge.[1] Final release is effected by a recognition of the fundamental distinction between spirit and nature.[2] The plurality of spirits is empirical. The souls are many—so long as they are in union with nature; but when they realise their distinction from it they return to the twenty-sixth principle of God.[3] The Epic philosophy is decidedly theistic in character and whatever elements of the Sāṁkhya are present in it are pressed into the service of theism. The self is said to send out from itself the guṇas even as a spider emits a web.[4] Prakṛti works under the control of puruṣa.[5] It is said to be a product of puruṣa into which it is resolved from time to time.[6] Mahat, ahaṁhāra and manas are cosmic functions of the supreme spirit. Kapila, the founder of the system according to the tradition, is referred to as a great sage of revered memory. It is clear that the Sāṁkhya did not assume its later distinctive shape even in the Epics, which, for one thing, do not mention tanmātras. Different views of the order and development of the principles are to be met with. The nearest approach on this point to the classical Sāṁkhya is found in the *Anugītā*.[7] The views of Pañcaśikha,[8] and Asita Devala[9] are mentioned. Āsuri is said to have taught the Sāṁkhya to Pañcaśikha, and the *Sāṁkhya Kārikā* repeats this suggestion of the Epic. Both Āsuri and Pañcaśikha adhere to a theistic Sāṁkhya and believe in the supremacy of Brahman. The independence of the individual soul is only relative. There are important differences in details between the Sāṁkhya views and those of Pañcaśikha.[10]

Though Manu[11] does not mention the Sāṁkhya by name, the account of creation given in the first chapter, the acceptance of the three sources of knowledge,[12] the detailed description of the three

---

[1] M.B., xii. 306. 39–40.
[2] xii. 307. 20.
[3] xii. 350. 25–26; xii. 351. 2–4.
[4] xii. 285. 40.
[5] xii. 314. 12; xii. 315. 8.
[6] xii. 303. 31 ff.
[7] xiv. 40–42.
[8] xii. 219; xii. 321. 96–112.
[9] xii. 274.
[10] Corresponding to mind, which he regards as the sixth organ of perception, Pañcaśikha looks upon power as the sixth organ of action. The account of xii. 219 differs from that in xii. 318. 96–112, where Pañcaśikha is said to have recognised thirty principles. It is sometimes said that this latter view is an early form of the Pañcaśikha cult. It is difficult to decide whether the Pañcaśikha of the school tradition is the same as the Pañcaśikha referred to in the Epic, since there is a divergence between the views attributed to him in the M.B. and those to be gathered from the Sāṁkhya and the Yoga works. Professor Dās Gupta gives a long summary of a more or less similar view from Caraka's medical treatise, *History of Indian Philosophy*, pp. 213 ff., but there is no mention of the tanmātras, and puruṣa and prakṛti are both regarded as avyakta; nor is the puruṣa regarded as passive and passionless. Release is said to be the attainment of the state of Brahman. The account is influenced by the views of the Vedānta, the Nyāya-Vaiśeṣika and Buddhism as much as the Sāṁkhya.
[11] I.P., pp. 516–517.
[12] xii. 105.

guṇas,[1] show the strong influence of the Sāṁkhya. The Purāṇas[2] and the later Vedānta writings use Sāṁkhya theories, though they give no quarter to its atheistic metaphysics, and are of little use in deciding the question of the antiquity of the system.

The Sāṁkhya views, as we meet with them in the Upaniṣads, the *Mahābhārata*, including the *Bhagavadgītā* and *Manu*, lean to theism.[3] Puruṣa and prakṛti were not independent realities but only the modes of God. In Aśvaghoṣa's *Buddhacarita* we have an account of a meeting between Buddha and his former teacher Arāḍa, who holds the Sāṁkhya views, though in a theistic setting. It seems to be very probable that the earliest form of the Sāṁkhya was a sort of realistic theism, approaching the Viśiṣṭādvaita view of the Upaniṣads. While this type of Sāṁkhya may be regarded as a legitimate development of the teaching of the Upaniṣads, the dualistic Sāṁkhya, which insists on the plurality of puruṣas and the independence of prakṛti and drops all account of the Absolute, can hardly be said to be in line with the teaching of the Upaniṣads. The question is, how did it happen that the Sāṁkhya rejected the idea of the Absolute which alone could make the system satisfactory? The Sāṁkhya did not become a well co-ordinated system until after the rise of Buddhism. When Buddhism offered a challenge to realism, the Sāṁkhya accepted the challenge and argued on strictly rational grounds for the reality of selves and objects. When it developed on a purely rationalistic soil, it was obliged to concede that there was no proof for the existence of God.

III

Literature

Tradition unanimously ascribes the authorship of the system to Kapila.[4] Some say that he is the son of Brahmā,[5] others that he is

---

[1] xii. 24–25

[2] See *Bhāgavata*, iii. 5; *Matsya*, iii; *Agni*, xvii; *Mārkaṇḍeya*, xlv.

[3] " A study of the Epic and other early materials has convinced me that there is not a single passage in which disbelief in Brahman or God is attributed to the Sāṁkhya" (Franklin Edgerton: *American Journal of Philology*, xlv. 1. p. 8). M.B., xii. 11039, is usually regarded as emphasising the vital distinction between the Sāṁkhya, which denies God, and the Yoga, which does not. Edgerton combats this opinion, but it is difficult to explain away those passages of the M.B. which distinguish the Sāṁkhya of twenty-six principles from that of twenty-five principles. The latter type of Sāṁkhya is indifferent to the Absolute or God (xii. 300). It is, however, true that the M.B. does not support the latter view.

[4] Śvet. Up., v. 2. Cp. M.B., *Mokṣadharma*.

Sāṁkhyasya vaktā kapilaḥ paramarṣiḥ purātanaḥ
Hiraṇyagarbho yogasya vaktā nānyaḥ purātanaḥ.

[5] M.B., xii. 340. 67; *Rāmāyaṇa*, i. 40–41.

an avatār of Viṣṇu,[1] still others identify him with an incarnation of Agni.[2] While these accounts are mythical, it may be accepted that a historical individual of the name of Kapila was responsible for the Sāṁkhya tendency of thought. We shall not be wrong if we place him in the century preceding Buddha.[3] There is no evidence to show that the *Sāṁkhyapravacana Sūtra* and the *Tattvasamāsa* generally attributed to Kapila were composed by him. Īśvarakṛṣṇa in his *Kārikā* describes himself as being in the succession of disciples from Kapila through Āsuri and Pañcaśikha.[4] Āsuri probably lived before 600 B.C., if he be one with the Āsuri of the *Śatapatha Brāhmaṇa*. Garbe thinks that Pañcaśikha may be assigned to the first century A.D. From the few fragmentary passages that have come down to us, Pañcaśikha held the theory of the three guṇas. He regarded the puruṣas[5] as atomic in size,[6] and attributed the connection of puruṣa and prakṛti to want of discrimination rather than to works.[7]

The *Sāṁkhya Kārikā* of Īśvarakṛṣṇa is the earliest available as well as the most popular textbook of the school. From its name it is clear that it is not the first work of the system. A Chinese tradition ascribes to Vindhyavāsa the rewriting of a work by Vārṣagaṇa. If Vindhyavāsa is the same as the author of the *Kārikā*,[8] it follows that the *Kārikā* was based on an earlier work of which we have no information.[9] It is a work of the third

---

[1] *Bhāgavata*, iii. 24. 36; ii. 7. 3.

[2] S.P.B., vi. 70.

[3] Weber holds that the Sāṁkhya is the oldest of the existing systems (*History of Indian Literature*, p. 235). M.B. mentions the Sāṁkhya and the Yoga as very ancient systems, sanātane dve. xii. 13711.

[4] S.K., 70. According to the M.B. (xii. 218. 14–15), the successors of Kapila are Āsuri, Pañcaśikha, Gārgya and Ulūka. The Chinese tradition regards one Pañcaśikhī as the disciple of Kaṇāda. Evidently he is different from Pañcaśikha. See Ui: *Vaiśeṣika Philosophy*, pp. 7–8. There is in the M.B. a section on "Janakapañcaśikhasaṁvāda," and some of his opinions are quoted in Y.B.

[5] S.P.B., i. 127.

[6] Y.B., *Tattvavaiśāradi*, i. 36.

[7] S.P.B., vi. 68.

[8] Takakusu thinks that Vindhyavāsin was a title of Īśvarakṛṣṇa (J.R.A.S., 1905). Guṇaratna regards them as different (*Tarkarahasyadīpikā*, pp. 102, 104).

[9] The *Bhāgavata* tells us that only a portion of the Sāṁkhya works has come down to us, while a large part is said to be lost by time (kālavipluta). i. 3. 10. Vijñānabhikṣu holds that many works have been devoured by time (kālārkabhakṣitaṁ) (S.P.B., Introduction). The last verse of the *Sāṁkhya Kārikā* reads: "The subjects treated in the seventy verses are those of the entire *Ṣaṣṭitantra*, exclusive of the illustrative tales, and omitting also controversial questions." It is admitted that the verse is an interpolation, since Gauḍapāda, the earliest commentator of the *Kārikā*, does not mention it. Guṇaratna refers to *Ṣaṣṭitantroddhāra*. It is said that Āsuri popularised it, and Pañcaśikha made it atheistic and attributed it to Kapila. It is, however, difficult to be definite about all this. Vācaspati and Nārāyaṇa are of opinion that *Ṣaṣṭitantra* refers not to a work but only to a scheme of sixty topics. The same explanation may perhaps be true

century A.D.[1] Gauḍapāda wrote a commentary on the *Kārikā*. Whether this commentator is the same as the author of the *Kārikā* on the *Māṇḍūkyopaniṣad* cannot be decided, in view of the diversity of thought between the two works. As he is earlier than Vācaspati, he may be assigned to the eighth century A.D.[2] Vācaspati's *Sāṁkhyatattvakaumudī* (ninth century A.D.) is a popular work. Nārāyaṇa's *Sāṁkhyacandrikā* is a treatise on the *Kārikā*.

The *Sāṁkhyapravacana Sūtra*, attributed to Kapila,[3] has six chapters, of which the first three are devoted to an exposition of the Sāṁkhya principles, the fourth gives some illustrative stories, the fifth refutes rival views, and the sixth winds up with a recapitulation. The work is assigned to the fourteenth century A.D., chiefly on the ground that Mādhava's *Sarvadarśanasaṁgraha* does not refer to it, but bases its account of the Sāṁkhya on the *Kārikā*.[4] While the *Kārikā* develops

---

of the *Ṣaṣṭitantra* mentioned in the Jaina *Anuyogadvāra Sūtra*. According to the *Ahirbudhnyasaṁhitā* (xii), the Sāṁkhya is a theistic system of sixty divisions of two parts of thirty-two (prakṛti) and twenty-eight (vikṛti) sections. Vācaspati quotes a passage from *Rājavārttika* in his *Tattvakaumudī* (72) to the effect that *Ṣaṣṭitantra* is so called since it dealt with the sixty topics of prakṛti, its oneness, its difference from puruṣas, etc. A Chinese tradition ascribes the authorship of *Ṣaṣṭitantra* to Pañcaśikha, while Vārṣagaṇya sometimes gets the credit for it. See *Bhāmatī*, ii. 1. 3.

1 The Buddhist monk Paramārtha (sixth century A.D.) translated it into Chinese and also wrote a commentary on it. The Chinese tradition places Vindhyavāsa before Vasubandhu, who quotes the second verse from the *Kārikā*. See Ui: *Vaiśeṣika Philosophy*. Whether Vindhyavāsa be the author of the *Kārikā*, as Keith suggests (*Sāmkhya*, p. 79; I.L.A., p. 248; *Karmamīmāṁsā*, p. 59), or a commentator on it, as Belvalkar holds (*Bhandārkar Commemoration Volume*, pp. 175–178), Īśvarakṛṣṇa is earlier than Vasubandhu, who is now assigned to the fourth century A.D. Svapneśvara identifies Īśvarakṛṣṇa with Kālidāsa. "Īśvarakṛṣṇanāmnā kālidāsena kṛtaḥ kārikāḥ." See Hall's *Sāṁkhyasāra*, p. 29. Īśvarakṛṣṇa seems to have been definitely atheistic. Though the *Kārikā* is said to contain seventy verses, only sixty-nine have come down to us. B. G. Tilak tried to reconstruct from Gauḍapāda's commentary on S.K., 61, the missing verse thus:—

Kāraṇam īśvaram eke bruvate kālam pare svabhāvaṁ vā,
Prajāḥ kathaṁ nirguṇato vyaktaḥ kālasvabhāvaś ca.

Gauḍapāda's commentary seems to have in view such a verse, and later it was perhaps suppressed, since it was inconveniently atheistic.

2 *Māṭharavṛtti* is a work of the Sāṁkhya philosophy, of which Gauḍapāda's *Bhāṣya* is reported to be an abridgment. But, as a rule, vṛttis come later than the bhāṣyas, and the fact that the *Māṭharavṛtti* comments on the last three verses of the S.K. makes for its later date. See *Bhandārkar Commemoration Volume*.

3 Svapneśvara, in his *Kaumudīprabhā*, assigns the S.P.S. to Pañcaśikha. and traces its attribution to Kapila to the fact that the latter initiated the tradition. See Hall's *Sāṁkhyasāra*, p. 8.

4 Guṇaratna (fourteenth century A.D.) does not refer to this work. Besides, the *Bhāṣya* on it appeared in the sixteenth century, and if the

a strict dualism, the *Sutra* shows a more conciliatory attitude towards theistic monism.[1] Aniruddha's *Sāṁkhyasūtravṛtti* belongs to the fifteenth century, while Mahādeva's *Sāṁkhyasūtravṛttisāra* is said to have been written about A.D. 1600. Nāgeśa's *Laghusāṁkhyasūtravṛtti* is not of much value. The most important work on the *Sāṁkhyapravacana Sūtra* is Vijñānabhikṣu's *Sāṁkhyapravacanabhāṣya* (sixteenth century). This author endeavours to minimise the distinction between the Sāṁkhya and the theistic Vedānta, which he regards as the genuine Vedānta, while the Advaita Vedānta is its modern falsification. Vijñānabhikṣu wrote also *Sāṁkhyasāra*, *Yogavārttika*, *Yogasārasaṁgraha* as well as a commentary on the *Brahma Śūtra* called *Vijñānāmṛta*.

IV

Causality

We may now consider the arguments by which the Sāṁkhya system arrives at its dualism of prakṛti and puruṣa. The Sāṁkhya argues to the existence of prakṛti, through the application of the principle of causality.

The theory that the effect really exists beforehand in its cause is one of the central features of the Sāṁkhya system. The Sāṁkhya defines cause as the entity in which the effect subsists in a latent form, and gives the following grounds in support of it[2]: (1) The non-existent cannot be the object of any activity. The sky-flower cannot be produced. What is non-existent can never be made existent. Blue cannot

Sūtra was of an earlier date, it is difficult to know why no bhāṣya was composed earlier. It refers to all other systems. Vācaspati is not aware of it. Alberuni, who wrote his account in the first half of the eleventh century, is familiar with the works of Īśvarakṛṣṇa and Gauḍapāda, but does not seem to know of the *Sūtra*.

[1] Cp. Garbe: "In particular, the author of the Sūtras is at great pains to furnish proof of the utterly impossible thesis that the teachings of the Sāṁkhya system are not in irreconcilable contradiction with the doctrine of a personal God, with the doctrine of the all-embracing unity of Brahman, with the doctrine of the nature of Brahman as bliss (ānanda), and with the doctrine of the attainment of the highest aim in the heavenly world" (see i. 95, 154; v. 64, 68, 110; vi. 51, 58, 59). Indeed, the *Sāṁkhya Sūtra* shows easily recognisable results of Vedāntic influence in many places; most plainly perhaps at iv. 3, which is a word for word repetition of the *Vedānta Sūtra*, iv. 1. 11, and at v. 116, where the Vedānta technical term *brahmarūpatā* is used instead of the proper Sāṁkhya expression" (Garbe's ed. of S.B.P., p. xi).

[2] S.K., 9.

be made into yellow even by a thousand artists.[1] (2) The product is not different from the material of which it is composed. (3) It exists before it comes into being in the shape of the material. If this is not admitted, then anything can come out of anything. (4) Causal efficiency belongs to that which has the necessary potency. (5) The effect is of the same nature as the cause. The cloth is not different from the threads in its essence. The causal relation cannot subsist between objects essentially different from one another.[2] Development is the coming to light of what is latent and hidden, or, as Aristotle would say, it is the transition from potential being to actual being, or, in Hegel's words, it is the passage from the implicit to the explicit. This view has also the support of scripture.[3] According to this doctrine of satkāryavāda, the cause and the effect are the undeveloped and the developed states of one and the same substance. All production is development (udbhāva), and all destruction is envelopment (anudbhāva) or disappearance into the cause.[4] There is no such thing as utter annihilation. The past and the future states are not destroyed, since they are perceived by the Yogis.[5] The Sāṁkhya adopts the theory of evolution (āvirbhāva) and involution (tirobhāva).

Cause and effect are different states, and so are distinct from each other,[6] though this distinction is based on our practical interests. While a jar can hold water, clay cannot. While the material cause and the effect are fundamentally one, they are practically different, since they serve different purposes. Identity is fundamental, while difference is only practical. The Sāṁkhya distinguishes two kinds of causes, efficient and material. While the material cause enters into the effect, the efficient cause exerts influence from outside. Though the effect is contained in the cause, something else is necessary to liberate it from the causal state. We have to press the seeds to get the oil, beat the paddy to get the grain. When this concomitant activity (sahakāriśakti) is

[1] Nahi nīlaṁ śilpisahasreṇāpi pītaṁ kartuṁ śakyate (*Tattvakaumudī*, p. 9).
[2] See *Tattvakaumudī*, p. 9.
[3] Chān., vi. 2. 2. See also B.G., ii. 16.
[4] S.P.S., i. 120–1.
[5] S.P.B., i. 121.
[6] Kāraṇakāryavibhāgāt (S.K., 15).

wanting, the effect does not arise.[1] Though the effect is potentially contained in the cause, this potentiality is not actualised all at once. The removal of the barriers is the concomitant cause required to actualise the potentiality. These concomitant conditions are, according to Vyāsa, place (deśa), time (kāla), and form and constitution of a thing (ākāra).[2] From a piece of stone a plant cannot spring.[3] Two kinds of effects are distinguished. When cream is produced from milk, we have a case of simple manifestation. When a jewel is made of gold, we have an instance of reproduction. When the quality of a thing changes, we have a case of dharmapariṇāma; when the potential becomes actual and the change is only external, we have a case of lakṣaṇapariṇāma. The change of state due to mere lapse of time is avasthāpariṇāma.[4] Change is taking place everywhere and at every moment. We cannot twice step into the same stream, since the waters do not remain identical for two moments together. It is also true that the same individual does not twice step into the same river, for he has meanwhile changed even as the river has done. All things and states, outward and inward, are subject to this law of change.[5] From out of this changing process the mind of man constructs the rule of causality,[6] by means of the relation of antecedents and consequents.

[1] Vyāsa illustrates the working of these concomitant causes thus: "As the owner of many fields can irrigate from a field which is already flooded, others of the same or a lower level without forcing the waters thereto with his hand, and merely by making an opening in the barrier or dyke, on which the waters rush in by their own force; or, further, as the same person cannot force these waters, or the earthly matters held in solution therein, into the roots of the rice plants, but only removes the obstructive grasses and weeds, on which the fluids of their own power enter the roots; such is the action of an effectuating condition (nimitta) added to a sum of material causes or conditions." (Y.B., iv. 3.)

[2] Y.B., iii. 14.

[3] But according to the Sāṁkhya philosophy, any cause can produce any effect (since all things are modifications of prakṛti) if only the obstructing barriers of that particular effect are removed. Vijñānabhikṣu admits that if by the will of God the arrangement of particles in the stone serving as a barrier to the potential tendencies to develop into the shoot of a plant is removed, then a plant may spring from a stone.

[4] Y.B., iii. 13. [5] S.P.S., i. 121 [6] Buddhinirmāṇa.

V

Prakṛti

The Sāṁkhya attempts an explanation of nature as an immense complexity of elements which is ever changing. The hierarchy of forms from physical matter, which is itself a product of submaterial elements, is represented as an unfolding of the resources of nature. If all effects are latent in their causes, and if infinite regress is to be avoided, there must be an uncaused cause. From the principle of causality it is deduced that the ultimate basis of the empirical universe is the unmanifested (avyaktam) prakṛti. The *Sāṁkhya Kārikā* argues for the existence of prakṛti on the following grounds[1]: (1) Individual things are limited in magnitude. Whatever is limited is dependent on something more enduring and pervasive than itself. The finite as finite, therefore, cannot be the source of the universe. (2) All individual things possess certain pervasive characteristics, thus implying a common source from which they all issue. The Sāṁkhya does not believe that the different elements are completely distinct from one another. (3) There is an active principle manifesting itself in the development of things. Evolution implies a principle which cannot be equated with any one of its stages. It is something larger than its products, though immanent in them. (4) The effect differs from the cause, and we cannot, therefore, say that the finite and conditioned world is its own cause. (5) There is the obvious unity of the universe, suggesting a single cause. The Sāṁkhya assumes the continuity of the world from the lowest to the highest. The products evolve and dissolve in a definite order. The world is said to be the pariṇāma, or transformation, of prakṛti, which is its cause Everything is the effect of a producing cause; for from nothing nothing comes. If less should be contained in the cause than in the effect, then this excess would have to be produced by nothing. It follows that the cause must contain more reality than, or at least as much reality as, the effect. The natural light of reason, to use Descartes's words, tells us that the

[1] 15 and 16.

ultimate cause must contain eminently all the reality, meaning and value of the effect. Nothing can be evolved which is not in kind originally involved.[1] While every effect is caused, prakṛti has no cause,[2] but is the cause of all effects, from which it is inferred.[3] It is called pradhāna. since all effects are founded on it,[4] Brahmā, or that which grows,[5] māyā, or that which measures or limits. It is the primary form of being from which different orders of existences issue. The Sāṁkhya recognises the impossibility of deducing puruṣa or the self, from prakṛti or the not-self.

The products are caused, while prakṛti is uncaused; the products are dependent, while prakṛti is independent; the products are many in number, limited in space and time, while prakṛti is one, all-pervading and eternal.[6] The products are the signs from which we infer the source. Prakṛti can never perish, and so it could never have been created. An intelligent principle cannot be the material out of which the inanimate world is formed, for spirit cannot be transformed into matter. Besides, agency belongs not to the puruṣa or the soul, but to the ahaṁkāra or self-sense, which is itself a product.[7]

The difficulty that prakṛti is not perceived is not of much moment. There are ever so many things which are accepted as real, though they are not open to perception. Perception cannot succeed with regard to objects too near or too remote. Defects of senses or manas, obstruction of another object, or presence of more attractive stimuli, render perception useless. The fineness of prakṛti renders it imperceptible.[8] Vyāsa describes prakṛti as "that which never is nor is not, that which exists and does not exist, that in which there is no non-existence, the unmanifested, without any specific mark,

[1] Cp. with this Descartes's distinction of eminent and formal causes.

[2] S.P.S., i. 67.

[3] S.P.S., i. 110, 136.

[4] Pradhīyate (S.P.B., i. 125). Lokācārya writes that it is called prakṛti, since it is the source of all change, avidyā, since it is opposed to all knowledge, māyā, since it is the cause of the varied creation Prakṛtir ity ucyate vikārotpādakatvāt, avidyā jñānavirodhitvāt, māyā vicitrasṛṣṭikaratvāt (*Tattvatraya*, p. 48). Plato had a similar idea of a universal invisible source of all material forms. See *Timæus*, p. 24.

[5] B.G., xiv. 3.

[6] S.K., 10; S.P.S., i. 124. See also Y.B., iv. 12; S.P.B., i. 76.

[7] S.P.S., vi. 54.

[8] S.K., 8.

the central background of all."[1] If what serves the ends of self is the existent, then prakṛti is non-existent, though it is not non-existent as a square circle. Again, nothing that exists can be destroyed, and the products exist in prakṛti, though in an unmanifested state. In it all determinate existence is implicit. The different guṇas do not annul themselves, but are in a state of equipoise, which is not inactivity but a kind of tension. Prakṛti is not so much being as force. As the equilibrium of the three guṇas,[2] it is the ground of all modifications, physical and psychical. It is pure potentiality.[3] We do not know the real nature of prakṛti or the guṇas, since our knowledge is confined to phenomena.[4] It is devoid of sound and touch,[5] practically the limit beyond which we cannot go. It is empirically an abstraction, a mere name.[6] But it must be assumed to exist as the prius of all creation.[7]

The Sāṁkhya description of the world in terms of one homogeneous substance, of which all things are but different configurations resulting from the different combinations of its ultimate constituents, has some resemblance to the materialist theory. Both the Sāṁkhya and materialism attempt to attain a more rational conception of the universe than the somewhat chaotic view which surface appearances leave on our minds. Both of them assert the ultimate reality of a primary substance which they regard as eternal, indestructible and ubiquitous. The multiplicity of heterogeneous things which we come across in our ordinary experience is traced to this single substance. But the prakṛti of the Sāṁkhya cannot be compared with matter pure and simple. The Sāṁkhya thinkers are aware of the incapacity of prakṛti

1 Niḥsattāsattaṁ niḥsadasan nirasad avyaktam aliṅgam pradhānaṁ (Y.B., ii. 19; S.P.B., i. 61).

2 Sāmyāvastha (S.P.B., i. 61).

3 Cp. R.V., x. 92.

4 Vyāsa quotes a verse from the *Ṣaṣṭitantra* to the effect:
Guṇānāṁ paramaṁ rūpaṁ na dṛṣṭipatham ṛcchati
Yat tu dṛṣṭipathaṁ prāptaṁ tan māyeva sutucchakam. (Y.B., iv. 13.)
Vācaspati, commenting on it. observes that prakṛti is not māyā, but is like māyā, māyeva na tu māyā.

5 S.P.B., i. 128; *Viṣṇu Purāṇa*, i. 2. 20–21.

6 Saṁjñāmātram (S.P.B., i. 68).

7 Pra = before, krti = creation, or pra = forth, kṛ = to make.

to produce puruṣa as well as the incapacity of puruṣa to produce prakṛti. They admit, while the materialists do not, that the evolution of prakṛti is purposive, "an arch where through gleams the untravelled world." The prakṛti of the Sāṁkhya is not a material substance, nor is it a conscious entity, since puruṣa is carefully distinguished from it. It gives rise not only to the five elements of the material universe, but also to the psychical. It is the basis of all objective existence. The Sāṁkhya arrives at the conception, not from the side of science, but from that of metaphysics. The real in its fulness is distinguished into the unchanging subject, and the changing object and prakṛti is the basis of the latter, the world of becoming. It is the symbol of the never-resting, active world stress. It goes on acting unconsciously, without regard to any thought-out plan, working for ends which it does not understand.

VI

THE GUṆAS

The development of prakṛti arises by means of its three constituent powers, or guṇas,[1] which are postulated in view of the character of the effects of prakṛti. Prakṛti is a string of three strands. Buddhi, which is an effect, has the properties of pleasure, pain and bewilderment, and so its cause, prakṛti, must have answering properties. The guṇas are not perceived, but are inferred from their effects. The first of these is called sattva. It is potential consciousness, and therefore tends to conscious manifestation and causes pleasure to the individual. Etymologically, the word sattva is derived from "sat," or that which is real or existent. Since consciousness (caitanya) is generally granted such existence, sattva is said to be potential consciousness. In a secondary sense, "sat" also means perfection, and so the sattva element is what produces goodness and happiness. It is said to be buoyant or light.[2] The second, rajas, is the source of all activity and produces pain. Rajas leads to a life of feverish

[1] S.K., 16. [2] Sukhaprakāśalāghava. (Tattvakaumudi, 13.)

enjoyment and restless effort.[1] The third is tamas, that which resists activity and produces the state of apathy or indifference. It leads to ignorance and sloth. The respective functions of sattva, rajas and tamas are manifestations (prakāśa), activity (pravṛtti), and restraint (niyamana),[2] producing pleasure, pain and sloth. The three guṇas are never separate. They support one another and intermingle with one another. They are closely related as the flame, the oil and the wick of a lamp.[3] They constitute the very substance of prakṛti. All things are composed of the three guṇas,[4] and the differences of the world are traced to the predominance of the different guṇas. The origin of this conception is undoubtedly psychological, since the kinds of feeling tone are made the basis of the distinction, but even so early as the period of the *Sāṁkhya Kārikā* the guṇas signified factors or constituents of prakṛti.[5] They are called guṇas (or qualities), since prakṛti alone is substantive, and these are merely elements in it. They may be regarded as representing the different stages of the evolution of any particular product. The sattva signifies the essence or the form which is to be realised, the tamas the obstacles to its realisation, and the rajas represents the force by which the obstacles are overcome and the essential form is manifested. A thing is always produced, never created, according to the Sāṁkhya theory of satkāryavāda. Production is manifestation and destruction is non-manifestation. These two depend on the absence and presence of counteracting forces. A thing is manifested when the impediments are removed. It

1 Duḥkhopaṣṭambhakatva, pravartakatva, while tamas is characterised by mohagurutvāvaraṇaiḥ (*Tattvakaumudī*, 13).

2 Prakāśakriyāsthitiśīlam . . . (Y.S., ii. 18).

3 S.K., 13.

4 Triguṇātmaka.

5 Cp. Śvet. Up., iv. 5. "Ajām ekāṁ lohitaśuklakṛṣṇām . . ." Śaṁkara sees in it a reference to the three colours mentioned in the *Chāndogya Upaniṣad* (vi. 4). Śaṁkara makes an adherent of the Sāṁkhya school interpret it thus: "In this verse, by the words 'red, white and black' are to be understood rajas, sattvam and tamas. The red is rajas (emotion), because it naturally makes red, produces unrest, rañjayati; the white is sattvam (essentially good), because it naturally makes bright; the black is tamas (darkness), since it naturally darkens. As the three guṇas belong to the primal prakṛti, they are called ajā, unborn." (S.B., i. 4. 9.) The guṇas are so called because they bind the spirit (guṇa = rope) (S.P.B., i. 61).

is sattva or the form of a thing that is manifested; it is rajas that brings about the manifestation; tamas is the resistance to be overcome, the obstacle to the manifestation of sattva.[1] While sattva and tamas answer to the affirmative being and negative non-being, rajas refers to the struggle between the two. Everything has its ideal essence, which it strives after, and actual setting, which it tries to get rid of. The latter is its tāmasa state, the former its sattva state, while the process of striving represents the rājasa condition. Sattva, finally, is that by which a thing manifests itself to consciousness. Since these moments are found in all existence, they are attributed to the original prakṛti.[2]

The guṇas are not qualities in the Vaiśeṣika sense, since they possess the properties of lightness, activity, etc.[3] Vijñānabhikṣu makes them types of reals,[4] while in the early Upaniṣads [5] they stand for psychic states which produce physical and mental evil. The guṇas are said to be extremely fine in texture. They are always changing. Even in what is regarded as the state of equilibrium the guṇas are continually changing into one another.[6] These changes in themselves do not produce objective results, so long as the equil-

[1] Dr. Seal writes: "Every phenomenon consists of a threefold arché: intelligible essence, energy and mass. In intimate union these enter into things as essential constitutive factors. The essence of a thing (sattva) is that by which it manifests itself to intelligence, and nothing exists without such manifestation in the universe of consciousness (samaṣṭibuddhi). But the essence is only one of three moments. It does not possess mass or gravity, it neither offers resistance nor does work. Next, there is the element of tamas, mass, inertia, matter-stuff, which offers resistance to motion as well as to conscious reflection. But the intelligence-stuff and the matter-stuff cannot do any work, and are devoid of productive activity in themselves. All work comes from rajas, the principle of energy, which overcomes the resistance of matter and supplies even intelligence with the energy which it requires for its own work of conscious regulation and adaptation" (*The Positive Sciences of the Hindus*, p. 4). To some Dr. Seal's clever attempt would seem not so much interpreting the Sāmkhya as rewriting it.

[2] Sometimes it is said that activity, which characterises the whole universe, has no meaning apart from something that resists activity. Thus rajas, or the active phase, implies tamas, or the passive aspect. Without it there will be perpetual activity of all things. The activity itself serves rational ends, and so the sattva aspect also is present (*Tattvakaumudī*, 13).

[3] S.P.B., i. 61.

[4] Vācaspati and *Sāṁkhyakārikā* do not give this interpretation.

[5] *Śvetāsvatara* and *Maitrāyaṇī Upaniṣads.*

[6] Sārūpapariṇāma.

ibrium is undisturbed. If there is a disturbance of the equilibrium (guṇakṣobha), then the guṇas act on one another and evolution takes place. The varied interaction of the guṇas accounts for the variety of the world. Whichever guṇa is preponderant in any phenomenon, it becomes manifest in it, though the others are not absent. In material things at rest, tamas is preponderant, while sattva and rajas are subordinate; in things in motion, rajas is preponderant, while the others are latent. So the terms "sattva, rajas and tamas" are employed to mark predominant aspects rather than exclusive characters. Though the guṇas work together for the production of the world of effects, still they never coalesce. They are modified by mutual influence on one another or by their proximity. They evolve, join and separate. No one loses its power, though the others may be actively at work.[1] Prakṛti and its products possess the guṇas and so are unconscious. They are devoid of the power of discriminating between themselves and puruṣa. They are always objective, while puruṣa alone is subject.

A different view of guṇas is found in Vijñānabhikṣu, who regards them as subtle entities, infinite in number according to the diversity of individuals. It is not correct, according to this view, to say that the universal guṇas produce a diversity of effects on account of their varying combinations, since such a view cannot account for the appearance of minor differences.[2] Though the manifestations of the guṇas are innumerable, still on account of the possession of certain features in common, as lightness, they are classified into three kinds.[3] Each of the three "causal substances, sattva, etc., has manifold individual manifestations."[4] The guṇas cannot be created or destroyed. While the concrete phenomenal modes are subject to addition and subtraction, growth and decay, which changes are brought about by collocations and alterations from potential to actual, still the potential and the actual together are ever the same. It is just as in a game of dice: they are ever the same dice, but as they fall in various ways, they mean to us different things. All change relates to the position, order, grouping, mixing, separation of the eternally existing essentials, which are always integrating and disintegrating.[5]

---

1 Y.B., ii. 18.
2 S.P.B., i. 127.
3 S.P.B., i. 128.
4 *Ibid.*
5 *Tattvakaumudī*, 13–16; *Tattvavaiśāradī*, ii. 20; iv. 13–14; and *Yogavārttika*, iv. 13–14.

VII

Evolution

Prakṛti is the fundamental substance out of which the world evolves. In the unmanifested condition, prakṛti is but the union of opposites. When they are all held together in a state of equilibrium (sāmyāvastha), there is no action. The state of rest is said to be the natural condition of prakṛti.[1] Yet the absence of outer activity does not mean the absence of any tendency to act. The tendencies to manifestation (sattva) and activity (rajas) are held in check by the tendency to non-manifestation and non-activity (tamas). The Sāṁkhya conceives the supreme principle of the world as a unity with a real opposition of elements. An abstract unit can be either perpetually active or perpetually inactive. Prakṛti is not, by nature, unstable, and need not differentiate itself of necessity.[2] When there is a disturbance of the equilibrium of the guṇas, we have the destruction of prakṛti,[3] the relieving of the tension by the overweighting of one side, and the setting in of the process of becoming. Prakṛti evolves under the influence of puruṣa. The fulfilment of the ends of the puruṣa is the cause of the manifestation of prakṛti in the three specialised states.[4] Since prakṛti is one and ubiquitous, all things have prakṛti for their basis, and, in a sense, everything shares the characters of everything else. But, as a matter of fact, the things do not manifest all effects at once. The cause of development follows a definite law of succession in space, time, mode and causality.[5] We cannot say why this development happens. We have only to accept it. Prakṛti, which contains within itself the possibilities of all things, develops into the apparatus of thought as well as the objects of thought.

Mahat, or the Great, the cause of the whole universe, is the first product of the evolution of prakṛti. It is the basis

[1] Y.B., ii 18

[2] See Spencer : *First Principles*, p. xix.

[3] Prakṛtināśa.

[4] Trayāṇāṁ tv avasthāviśeṣāṇām ādau puruṣārthatā kāraṇam bhavati (Y.B., ii. 19). See also Vācaspati on it.

[5] Pariṇāmakramaniyama.

of the intelligence of the individual. While the term "mahat" brings out the cosmic aspect, buddhi, which is used as a synonym for it, refers to the psychological counterpart appertaining to each individual. In the Sāṁkhya, stress is laid on the psychological aspect of "mahat." From the synonyms of buddhi,[1] and its attributes of virtue (dharma), knowledge (jñāna), equanimity (vairāgya), and lordship (aiśvarya), and their opposites, it is clear that buddhi is to be taken in the psychological sense. But the designations of "mahat," the Great, Brahmā, etc., imply that it is used in the cosmic sense also.[2] Buddhi is not to be confused with the incorporeal puruṣa. It is regarded as the subtle substance of all mental processes. It is the faculty by which we distinguish objects and perceive what they are. The functions of buddhi are ascertainment and decision. All other organs function for the intellect (buddhi), which works directly for the puruṣa, enabling the latter to experience all existence and discriminate between itself and prakṛti.

Like the other products of prakṛti, buddhi has the three guṇas. In its sattva aspect, buddhi is distinguished by the observance of duty, knowledge, freedom from desire and divine powers; in its aspect as rajas it produces desires; and in its tamas aspect, it produces negligence, ignorance, etc. Vijñānabhikṣu says that all souls are divine,[3] though their "innate lordliness suffers obscuration by rajas and tamas."[4] The elemental creation is distinguished from pratyayasarga or the creation of buddhi, which is fourfold, ignorance (viparyaya), incapacity (aśakti), contentment (tuṣṭi), and perfection (siddhi). There are fifty subdivisions of these.[5] Five kinds of ignorance are admitted which are avidyā and asmitā (or egotism), each of which is eightfold; rāga (desire), tenfold; dveṣa (hatred), and abhiniveśa (or fear), which are eighteenfold. There are twenty-eight varieties of incapacity and nine kinds of contentment and eight forms of perfection.

Buddhi is both eternal and non-eternal. It exists in germ as seed-force in the causal condition of prakṛti when its functions are not manifested. When it is transformed into the condition of effect it is called buddhi. Vijñānabhikṣu

[1] Mati, khyāti, prajñā, jñāna.

[2] In later Vedānta, buddhi is taken collectively, as the upādhi of Hiraṇyagarbha.

[3] Sarva eva puruṣā īśvara iti.

[4] S.P.B., ii. 15. See also Y.B., i. 2.

[5] S.K., 46.

regards it as never-failing and as containing all saṁskāras.[1] The memories are stored in buddhi, and not in ahaṁkāra or manas. "Even after the dissolution of ahaṁkāra and manas by means of the knowledge of the truth, there remains recollection."[2]

Apparently, the functions assigned to intellect by the *Kārikā* can be performed by it only if it is posterior to the self-sense or ahaṁkāra, and of the manas and the senses, as well as something knowable as the gross elements; but the Sāṁkhya holds that all these are not present at the first stage when buddhi is present. We have, therefore, to take it in a cosmic sense, as the basis of the distinction between the subject and the object, the perceiving and the perceived; but then we shall have to assume a world-spirit, which the Sāṁkhya does not allow. The status of mahat or buddhi is left in an uncertain condition. Buddhi, as the product of prakṛti and the generator of ahaṁkāra, is different from buddhi which controls the processes of the senses, mind and ahaṁkāra. If the former is identified with the latter, the whole evolution of prakṛti must be regarded as subjective, since the ego and the non-ego are both the products of buddhi. This ambiguity is found in the other products of prakṛti also.

Ahaṁkāra (self-sense), or the principle of individuation, arises after buddhi. Through its action the different spirits become endowed each with a separate mental background. We have here also to distinguish the cosmic and the psychological aspects. Psychologically, the sense of selfhood is impossible without a non-ego or an object. But the development of the objective comes after the rise of ahaṁkāra in the Sāṁkhya theory of evolution. We have to admit the possibility of a cosmic ahaṁkāra out of which individual subjects and objects arise. Ahaṁkāra is conceived as material, and while buddhi is more cognitive in function, ahaṁkāra seems to be more practical. Psychologically, the function of ahaṁkāra is abhimāna or self-love. Agency belongs to it, and not to the self or puruṣa.[3] Mahat stands to ahaṁkāra

[1] S.P.B., ii. 41–42. [2] S.P.B., ii. 42.

[3] S.P.S., vi. 54. Vijñānabhikṣu quotes the Chāndogya passage "bahu syām prajāyeya" (let me multiply myself, let me procreate), and comments: "The creation of the elements and all the rest is preceded by abhimāna, and so it is said to be the cause of creation" (S.P.B., i 63).

as consciousness to self-consciousness. The former is the logical presupposition of the latter. We infer the existence of ahaṁkāra from its effects.[1] It is regarded as a substance, since it is the material cause of other substances. The puruṣa identifies itself with the acts of prakṛti through ahaṁkāra. It passes to the self the sensations and suggestions of action communicated to it through manas. It thus helps in the formation of concepts and decisions. Ahaṁkāra is not what individualises the universal consciousness, since the individuality is already there according to the Sāṁkhya. It individualises the impressions that come from the outer world. When the ahaṁkāra is dominated by the aspect of sattva, we do good work ; when by rajas, evil ones ; and when by tamas, indifferent ones. In dreamless sleep the function of ahaṁkāra may be absent, but the desires and the tendencies are all there.[2] It is difficult to know how the self-sense is derived from the intellect, or mahat.

The guṇas take three different courses of development from ahaṁkāra according to which the latter is said to be sāttvika, rājasa or tāmasa. From ahaṁkāra in its sattva aspect (vaikārika) are derived the manas and the five organs of perception and the five of action, and from the same in its tāmasa aspect (bhūtādi) the five fine elements. The rājasa aspect (taijasa) plays its part in both and is present in the results.[3] From the tanmātras, or the five fine elements by a preponderance of tamas, the five gross elements arise. In all these developments, though one of the guṇas may be predominant, the others are also present, perform their functions, and help indirectly the evolution of the products.

Manas is the organ which has the important function of synthesising the sense-data into percepts, suggesting alternative courses of action and carrying out the decrees of the

[1] S.P.S., i. 63.

[2] S.P.B., i. 63.

[3] S.K., 24–25. Vijñānabhikṣu holds that the sāttvika ahaṁkāra gives rise to manas, the rājasa to the ten organs, and the tāmasa to the five tanmātras (S.P.B., ii. 18). Aniruddha accepts the usual view that rajas is a condition precedent to all evolution, while the other guṇas determine the character of the constituents. While Vācaspati holds that from mahat arises ahaṁkāra and from ahaṁkāra the tanmātras, Vijñānabhikṣu is of opinion that the separation of ahaṁkāra and the evolution of the tanmātras take place in the mahat.

will through the organs of action. As in the case of the intellect and the self-sense, so also in the case of manas no distinction is made between the organ and its function. Manas is said to be the doorkeeper, while the senses are regarded as the doors.[1] The co-operation of manas is necessary for both perception and action.[2] It assumes manifold forms in connection with different senses.[3] Manas is not all-pervading, since it is an instrument possessing movement and action.[4] It is made up of parts, since it is connected with the senses. Buddhi and the other organs are not eternal in the sense that there is an eternal subject or Īśvara possessing them.[5]

The five organs of perception are the functions of sight, hearing, smell, taste and touch. The need creates the function. Since we have the desire, we create the functions and the objects to satisfy them.[6] The senses are not formed of the elements, since the sense and the elements arise out of ahaṁkāra.[7] The senses are not eternal, since their rise and lapse are seen. Each sense grasps one quality. The senses are not the organs of sight, etc., as the functions of manas.[8] They are the means of observing the fine and the gross elements.[9] The organs of action are the functions of the tongue, feet, hands, and the organs of evacuation and reproduction. Maṇas, with the organs, is said to produce by their action the five vital airs,[10] which are given an independent place in the Vedānta system. According to the Sūtra, prāṇa (life) is a modification of the senses and does not subsist in their absence.[11]

The world as the object of perception has the five tan-

[1] S.K., 35. Buddhi, ahaṁkāra and manas are not always carefully distinguished. They are taken as the inner organ (antaḥkaraṇa). "Antaḥkaraṇa is one and one only according to the threefold distinction of mere states; as in the case of the seed, the sprout, and the huge tree, etc., it falls under the relation of effect and cause." Vijñānabhikṣu quotes a verse from *Vāyu Purāṇa* to the effect: "Mano mahān matir brahmā pūr buddhiḥ khyātir, Īśvaraḥ" (S.P.B., ii. 16). See also S.P.B., ii. 40.

[2] S.P.S., ii. 26.

[3] S.P.S., ii. 27.

[4] S.P.S., v. 69–70.

[5] S.P.S., v. 127.

[6] Cp. M.B. Rūparāgād abhūc cakṣuḥ. From attachment to form the eye was produced. See M.B., Śāntiparva, 213. 16.

[7] S.P.S., ii. 20.

[8] S.P.S., ii. 23.

[9] S.K., 34.

[10] S.P.S., ii. 31.

[11] v. 113.

mātras,[1] corresponding to the five sense-organs. These are the essences of sound, touch, colour, taste and smell conceived as physical principles, imperceptible to ordinary beings. Each of them is exclusively concerned with one sense, while the gross elements appeal to more than one sense. These invisible essences are inferred from visible objects, though they are said to be open to the perception of the yogis.[2] The fine elements are said to be devoid of difference (viśeṣa), while the gross elements arising from them have a definite quality.[3] The tanmātras cannot act as sense stimuli until they combine to form atoms. Bhūtādi, or ahaṁkāra, dominated by tamas, is absolutely homogeneous, inert and devoid of all characters except quantum or mass. With the co-operation of rajas it is transformed into subtle matter, vibratory, radiant and instinct with energy, and the tanmātras of sound, touch, colour, taste and smell arise Ākāśa forms the transition link between bhūtādi and the tanmātras. A distinction is made between kāraṇākāśa, non-atomic and all-pervasive, and kāryākāśa, or atomic ākāśa, formed by the combination of bhūtādi, or mass, units with the sound essences. The latter are found held up in the original kāraṇākāśa as the medium for the development of the atoms of air.[4] According to the *Vyāsabhāṣya*, the tanmātra of sound is produced from ahaṁkāra, and from the tanmātra of sound accompanied by ahaṁkāra is produced the tanmātra of touch with the attributes of sound and touch, and so on ; the others are produced by the addition of one attribute at each step.

According to Gauḍapāda and Vācaspati, the gross elements arise from the compounding of the fine elements by the process of accumulation. There is, of course, the difficulty that on this view ether, which has but one quality, audibility, cannot be contrasted as a gross element with the corresponding fine element.[5] Vācaspati holds that

[1] That only. See *Praśna Upaniṣad*, iv. 8. Cp. the theory of the elements of elements of Empedocles.

[2] *Tattvakaumudī*, 5.

[3] Cp. this with the Chāndogya view (vi. 4) of the production of the gross elements by the intermingling of the three elements, where the former receive their special name from the presence in them of a greater proportion of one element. According to one view of the Vedānta, each element consists of a half of one element and one-eighth of each of the other four.

[4] See Seal: *Positive Sciences of the Ancient Hindus*.

[5] See Tait. Up., ii. 1.

the ether atom is generated from the other essence, the air atom from the two essences of sound and touch, of which that of touch is the chief, the light atom from the tanmātras of sound, touch and form, of which that of form is the chief, the water atom from the four tanmātras, and the earth atom from the five tanmātras, of which those of taste and smell are the chief ones respectively.[1] Vijñānabhikṣu holds a slightly different opinion. The ether atom is produced from the ether tanmātra through the help of bhūtādi.[2]

When the gross atoms combine, their properties are found in their products, so that they do not give rise to a new kind of existence (tattvāntara).[3] The ākāśa atom possesses penetrability, the air atom impact or mechanical pressure, the light atom radiant heat and light, the water atom has viscous attraction and earth cohesive attraction. By a combination of the gross atoms the element of earth arises. The capacity of the tanmātras to produce the feeling of pleasure or of pain is not perceived while they subsist as tanmātras. Since it is discernible in the state of the gross atoms, the gross elements are distinguished as soothing (śānta), terrific (ghora), and dull (mūḍha). The atoms of earth, etc., by various changes of quality, appear as the manifold variety of cosmic existence. There are not any intrinsic differences between things which are of the same stuff. As the potentiality of everything is in everything,[4] there is always change for the sake of puruṣa. The gross atoms[5] constitute the inorganic as well as the organic bodies, and in the development from the one to the other there is no breach of continuity. Inorganic, vegetable and animal kingdoms are the three stages in the process of development, marked only by changes in the qualities of the constituents[6] and not in the constituents themselves. The

[1] *Tattvavaiśaradī*, i. 44.

[2] *Yogavārttikā*, i. 45. Nāgeśa extends to all atoms this co-operation of bhūtādi. Sarvatra tanmātrais tattatbhūtotpādane 'haṁkārasya sahakāritvam bodhyam.

[3] The evolution of the specific (viśeṣa) from the unspecific (aviśeṣa) is called tattvāntarapariṇāma, as distinct from a mere change of qualities, dharmapariṇāma.

[4] Y.B., iii. 14.

[5] Since they contain tanmātras of different kinds as their constituents, the gross atoms cannot be identified with the Vaiśeṣika atoms. The tanmātras, which have no parts, are invisible compared to the Vaiśeṣika atoms.

[6] Dharmapariṇāma.

appearance of the different qualities is brought about by the different arrangements of the atoms. To the four kinds of bodies usually admitted, the Sāṁkhya adds two, *viz.* those born of will (sāṁkalpikam) and artificial ones (sāṁsiddhikam). Earth is the material cause of all these bodies,[1] though the other elements are present as auxiliary to it. The gross body is composed of the five elements, though there are some who think that ether is not necessary, and others who hold that earth alone will do. It is also said that, while the element of earth predominates in the body of man, that of light predominates in the world of the sun.[2]

Prakṛti and its effects, constituted by the three guṇas, are said to be non-discriminating (aviveki), object (viṣayaḥ), common to many puruṣas (sāmānyam), non-intelligent (acetanam), and productive (prasavadharmi).[3] Each evolute is finer than the one succeeding it and grosser than the one preceding it. The series from prakṛti to the five gross elements numbers twenty-four, and puruṣa is said to be the twenty-fifth principle of the Sāṁkhya system.[4] The twenty-three principles derived from prakṛti are effects, since they are different from prakṛti and puruṣa, are of limited magnitude, and possess the attributes of pradhāna, such as growth and assimilation, and serve as instruments of puruṣa.[5] All the things of the world are said to be the vikṛtis of prakṛti. Prakṛti stands to vikṛtis in the relation of an original substance to its modifications. Mahat, ahaṁkāra, and the five tanmātras are the effects of some and causes of others. The five gross elements and the eleven organs are only effects and not causes of others. While prakṛti is only cause, the

[1] v. 112. [2] iii. 17–19. S.P.B., iii. 19. [3] S.K., 11

[4]
1. Puruṣa.
|
2. Prakṛti (unmanifested) = manifested.

3. Buddhi, or intellect.
4. Ahaṁkāra, or self-sense.
5–9. Five tanmātras of sound, touch, smell, form or colour and taste.

10. Manas.
11–15. Five senses.
16–20. Five organs of action.
21–25. Five gross elements of ether, air, light, water and earth.

[5] S.P.S., i. 129–134; S.K., 15.

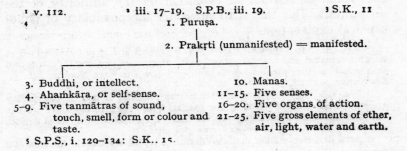

eleven products are simply effects. Seven of the products are both causes and effects, while the puruṣa is neither cause nor effect.[1]

These products of the evolution, which are capable of originating other products like themselves, are said to be non-specialised (aviśeṣa), while those which cannot originate other existences like themselves are said to be completely specialised (viśeṣa). When ahaṁkāra gives rise to tanmātras, we cannot easily trace the presence of ahaṁkāra in the fine elements. What is derived from ahaṁkāra seems to be a different existence altogether, and this transformation is a case of tattvāntarapariṇāma. The senses and the gross elements cannot give rise to an altogether different kind of existence. So, while ahaṁkāra is non-specialised (aviśeṣa), the senses, etc., are highly specialised (viśeṣa).[2]

Development is only the unfolding of what has already potential existence. The beginning and the end are alike determined. In spite of the things to which prakṛti gives rise, its substance is in no way diminished. The source of becoming is not exhausted by the things produced. No material thing can act without exhausting some of its latent energy. It is thus difficult to regard prakṛti as purely material in nature.

It is difficult to understand the precise significance of the Sāṁkhya account of evolution, and we have not seen any satisfactory explanation as to why the different steps of evolution are what they are.

The different principles of the Sāṁkhya system cannot be logically deduced from prakṛti, and they seem to be set down as its products, thanks to historical accidents. There is no deductive development of the products from the one prakṛti. Vijñānabhikṣu is aware of this defect, and so asks us to accept the Sāṁkhya account of evolution on the authority of the scriptures.[3] But this is to surrender the possibility of philosophical explanation.

[1] S.K., 3. Cp. Erigena: "That which creates and is not created; that which is created and creates; that which is created and creates not; and that which neither creates nor is created" (*De Divisione Naturæ*, Lib. 5). See Garbhopaniṣad, 3.

[2] See Y.B., ii. 19, where the tanmātras and the feeling of personality are said to be aviśeṣa forms of the mahat, while the five elements are the viśeṣa forms of the tanmātras, and the five senses, the five organs of action, and manas are said to be viśeṣa forms of asmitā.

[3] Atra prakṛter mahān mahato 'haṁkāra ityādi sṛṣṭikrame śāstram eva pramāṇam (*Sāṁkhyasāra*). See also Jayanta's *Nyāyamañjari*, pp. 452–466.

Buddhi, ahaṁkāra, manas and the rest need not be taken as a series of chronologically successive stages of evolution. They are the results of the logical analysis of evolved selves. Vācaspati writes: "Every man uses first his external senses, then he considers (with the manas), then he refers the various objects to his ego (ahaṁkāra), and lastly he decides with his buddhi what to do."[1] While this analysis gives an explanation of the recognition of the different factors on the subject side, it does not help us towards understanding the precise functions of these factors when enlarged to a cosmic plane. The cosmic scheme is framed on the analogy of the human self, since man is a microcosm in which all the factors of reality are repeated, as it were, on a reduced scale. Answering to the alternations of waking, sleeping, we have creation and destruction of the world. In the state of dreamless sleep the self is present, though it does not apprehend the world. So, in the state of world-absorption (pralaya), the selves are not destroyed, though prakṛti is not perceived. When a man wakes up from sound sleep and says, "I slept well, I knew nothing," this nothing is the not-self, or avyakta prakṛti, from which arises the cognition of something. The state of prakṛti, when its activity sinks into rest, corresponds to the state of suṣupti or dreamless sleep of the individual soul. When one wakes up from it, there is first the dawning of consciousness, followed immediately by the rise of the sense of selfhood and the restlessness of desire. The senses and the five elements of sound, touch, etc., come next into activity. It is only when the man wakes up that the gross elements are apprehended by him. Consciousness or buddhi, is the first glow in the vacant sky that arises when the self is confronted by the not-self. The self becomes aware that there is something. It next becomes conscious of its individuality through distinction from the not-self. It has the feeling that "I perceive the object." Then we discover that the object is a series of mental states synthesised by mind and made up of elements.[2] The whole scheme of the Sāṁkhya

[1] *Tattvakaumudī*, 23.

[2] Sir R. G. Bhāndārkar gives a Fichtean interpretation of the Sāṁkhya theory of evolution. The individual who knows directly what passes in his consciousness is aware of certain sensations of which he is not the generator. He therefore assumes an external nature. Its reality is evidenced

evolution seems to be based on the psychological experience of the individual. But the transition from the psychological to the metaphysical was mediated by the historical fact that in the Upaniṣads the self-conscious Brahmā is said to be the first offshoot of the absolute consciousness. The conception of mahat as the first product of prakṛti can be traced to the derivation of the great soul from the unmanifested (avyakta) in the *Kaṭha Upaniṣad.*[1] Mahat is prakṛti (non-being) illuminated by consciousness (being). We have in the Upaniṣads the idea of Hiraṇyagarbha or Brahmā, the world soul, who is said to be derived from the impersonal Brahman. The only way in which the conception of the rise of mahat from prakṛti can be made intelligible is through the acceptance of the Vedānta position. There is the supreme Brahman beyond both the subject and the object. The moment it is related to the object it becomes a subject with an object set over against it.[2] While the nature of the supreme is pure consciousness, that of prakṛti is unconsciousness; and when the two intermingle we have consciousness-unconsciousness, or subject-object, and that is mahat. Even non-being is potential being or potential consciousness. Immediately the subject contrasts itself with the object, it develops the sense of selfhood. There is first intelligence and then selfhood. Creation is preceded by a sense of selfhood. "I shall be

by the limitations of the free activity of consciousness. "In the state of consciousness when the 'me' feels itself limited, then intellect first of all posits or affirms the 'me' and then opposes to itself the 'not me.' The limitation of the 'me' implies its previous freedom or unlimitedness." We thus get the finite ego, the non-ego, the limitation, and the absolute self. The ahaṁkāra of the Sāṁkhya belongs to the finite ego. The subtle and the gross elements, as well as their counterparts, the senses, said to be produced by the ego, correspond to the non-ego. The free, unlimited absolute self is the puruṣa and its limitations by the non-ego bondage. But since the absolutely free puruṣa cannot be the source of limitations, the Sāṁkhya admits the existence of a distinct cause, which in its nature is infinite, and whose finiteness, from its intimate connection with the infinite ego, the ego attributes to itself from ignorance. See *Indian Philosophical Review*, ii. pp. 200 ff.

[1] iii. 11.

[2] Cp. Bṛh. Up., i. 4. 2: Īkṣāncakre (He looked round); Chān. Up., vi. 2. 2: Tad aikṣata (That he saw). Cp. *Bhāgavata*: "What they declare to be the citta, or mind, called Vāsudeva, *i.e.* Viṣṇu, that consists of mahat," yad āhur vāsudevākhyaṁ cittaṁ tan mahadātmakam (iii. 26. 21). See S.P.B., vi. 66.

many; I shall procreate."[1] The obscurity of the Sāṁkhya theory is due to the fact that a psychological report is mixed up with a metaphysical statement. The order of psychological presentation need not be the order of real evolution unless the subject is the ultimate and supreme one. The Sāṁkhya combines with its own presuppositions ideas essentially alien to it taken from the Upaniṣads.

VIII

Space and Time

Every phenomenon of cosmic evolution is characterised by activity, change or motion (parispanda).[2] All things undergo infinitesimal changes of growth and decay. In the smallest instant of time (kṣaṇa) the whole universe undergoes a change. In the empirical world, space and time appear as limited, and are said to arise from ākāśa, when it is conditioned by coexistent things in space and moving bodies in time.

Vijñānabhikṣu says: "Eternal space and time are of the form of prakṛti, or the root-cause of ākāśa, and are only the specific modifications of prakṛti. Hence the universality of space and time is established. . . . But these, space and time, which are limited, are produced from ākāśa through the conjunction of this or that limiting object (upādhi)."[3] Limited space and time are ākāśa itself particularised by this or that limiting object, though they are said to be its effects. Space and time are by themselves abstractions. They are not substances, as the Nyāya-Vaiśeṣika thought, but relations binding the events of the development of prakṛti. Events stand in relations of time and space. We have no perception of infinite time or infinite space, and so they are said to be constructed by the understanding. From the limited objects of perception which stand to one another in the relation of antecedence and sequence, we construct an infinite time order to represent the course of evolution. Vyāsa says: "Just as the atom is the minimal limit of matter, so the moment (kṣaṇa) is the minimal limit of time, or the time taken by an atom in motion in order to leave one point and reach the next point is a moment. But the continuous flow of these is a sequence (krama). Moments and the sequences of these cannot be combined into a real (vastu). Thus, time, being of

---

[1] Chān. Up., vi. 2. 3.

[2] Vyaktam sakriyam parispandavat *Tattvakaumudī*, 10. See also Y.B., iii. 13.

[3] S.P.B., ii. 12; ii. 10.

[4] Y.B., iii. 52.

this nature, does not correspond to anything real, but is a product of mind, and follows as a result of perceptions or of words "[1]; but the moment is objective and rests on the sequence.[2] The sequence (krama) has for its essence an uninterrupted succession of moments which is called time (kāla) by experts. Two moments cannot occur simultaneously, since it is impossible that there be a sequence of two things that occur simultaneously. When a later moment succeeds an earlier, there is a sequence. Thus in the present there is a single moment and there are no earlier or later moments. Therefore, there is no combination of them. But those moments which are past and future are to be explained as inherent in the changes (pariṇāma). Accordingly, the whole world passes through change in any single moment;[3] so all those external aspects of the world are relative to this present moment.[4]

The world is neither real nor unreal. It is not unreal, like a man's horn, nor real, since it passes away.[5] It is not, however, to be regarded as indescribable, since such a thing cannot exist.[6] The Sāṁkhya repudiates the view that regards the world as a reflection of what is not,[7] nor is the world a mere idea.[8] The world exists in its eternal form of prakṛti and passes away in its transitory manifestations.[9] The world has phenomenal reality as undergoing transformations.[10] Cosmic process is twofold in character, creative as well as destructive. Creation is the unfolding of the different orders from the original prakṛti, and destruction is the dissolution of them into the original prakṛti. As a result of the disturbance of the condition of equilibrium, the universe is evolved with its different elements, and at the close of the world-period the products return by a reverse movement into the preceding stage of development, and so finally into prakṛti. Prakṛti remains in this condition until the time arrives for the development of a new universe. This cycle of evolution and reabsorption has never had a beginning and will never have an end The play of prakṛti does not cease when this

[1] Sa khalv ayaṁ kālo vastuśūnyo 'pi buddhinirmāṇaḥ śabdajñānānupātī.

[2] Kṣaṇastu vastu patitah kramāvalaṁbī. [Y.B.

[3] Tenaikena kṣaṇena kṛtsno lokaḥ pariṇāmam anubhavati.

[4] So the Yogis can perceive directly both the moments and their sequence (Y.B., iii. 52).

[5] S.P.S., v. 52–53.

[6] S.P.S., v. 54.

[7] S.P.S., v. 55.

[8] S.P.S., i. 42.

[9] Sadasatkhyātir bādhābādhāt (S.P.S., v. 56).

[10] S.P.B., i. 26.

or that individual attains release,[1] though the emancipated are unaffected by the action of prakṛti. Though prakṛti is one only, and common to all puruṣas, it manifests itself in many ways: to the souls in bondage it evolves into many a form from the subtlest to the grossest; and to the freed it retraces its steps and becomes resolved into its own primeval form. So long as there are spectators, the play of prakṛti goes on. When all souls are set free, the play is over and the actors retire.[2] But as there will be always souls struggling to escape out of entanglement in prakṛti, the continuous rhythm of prakṛti's activity will be maintained for ever. Saṁsāra will never reach its end.[3] Since the state of dissolution is the normal condition, in the state of evolution there is a tendency to lapse into dissolution. When the desires of all puruṣas require that there should be a temporary cessation of all experience, prakṛti returns to its quiescent state. The guṇas are so finely opposed that no one becomes predominant. There is therefore no generation of new things and qualities. Even the state of pralaya is intended to serve the interests of puruṣas. In the state of pralaya, prakṛti is not inactive, though its changes are homogeneous.

IX

Puruṣa

All organic beings have a principle of self-determination, to which the name of "soul" is generally given. In the strict sense of the word, "soul" belongs to every being that has life in it, and the different souls are fundamentally identical in nature. The differences are due to the physical organisations that obscure and thwart the life of the soul. The nature of the bodies in which the souls are incorporated accounts for their various degrees of obscuration. The souls cannot be referred to the same principle from which physical organisations spring. So the Sāṁkhya asserts the existence of puruṣas freed from all the accidents of finite life and lifted

[1] S.P.S., iii. 66.
[2] S.K., 58–59; S.P.S., iii. 63.
[3] Y.S., ii. 22; S.P.B., ii. 4; S.P.B., i. 159; i. 67; vi. 68. 69.

above time and change. There is the testimony of consciousness that, though the individual is in one aspect a particular finite being subject to all the accidents and changes of mortality, there is something in him which lifts him above them all. He is not the mind, life or body, but the informing and sustaining soul, silent, peaceful, eternal, that possesses them. When the facts of the world are viewed from the epistemological point of view, we get a classification into subjects on the one side and objects on the other. The relation between any subject and any object is that of cognition or, more broadly, experience. The Sāṁkhya regards the knower as puruṣa and the known as prakṛti.

The Sāṁkhya puts forward several arguments to establish the existence of puruṣas [1]: (1) The aggregate of things must exist for the sake of another. Gauḍapāda says that even as a bed, which is an assemblage of different parts, is for the use of the man who sleeps upon it, so "this world, which is an assemblage of the five elements, is for another's use; there is a self for whose enjoyment this enjoyable body, consisting of intellect and the rest, has been produced." (2) All knowable objects have the three guṇas, and they presuppose a self who is their seer devoid of the guṇas. (3) There must be a presiding power, a pure consciousness which co-ordinates all experiences. (4) Since prakṛti is non-intelligent, there must be someone to experience the products of prakṛti. (5) There is the striving for liberation (kaivalya), which implies the existence of a puruṣa with qualities opposed to those of prakṛti. The longing for escape from the conditions of existence means the reality of one that can effect the escape.

What is the nature of the self or the subject consciousness? It is not the body. Consciousness is not a product of the elements, since it is not present in them separately, and so cannot be present in them all together.[2] It is different from the senses,[3] since the latter are the instruments of seeing and not the seer. The senses bring about modifications in buddhi. Puruṣa is different from buddhi, since the latter is non-conscious. The consolidation of our experiences into a

[1] S.K., 17; S.P.S., i. 66; Y.S., iv. 24.

[2] S.P.S., v. 129; iii. 20–21.

[3] S.P.S., ii. 29.

systematic whole is due to the presence of the self, which holds the different conscious states together. The self is defined as pure spirit, different from the body, or prakṛti.[1] If it were liable to change, knowledge would be impossible. As its character is consciousness, it helps to bring the products of the evolutionary chain into self-consciousness. It illuminates the whole sphere of thought and feeling. If puruṣa underwent transformation, then it would lapse at times, and there would be no security that the states of prakṛti, as pleasure and pain, will be experienced. Puruṣa's nature as unfailing light (sadāprakāśasvarūpa) does not change.[2] It is present in dreamless sleep,[3] as well as in states of waking and dreaming, which are all the modifications of buddhi.[4] So purusa exists, though it is neither cause nor effect.[5] It is the light by which we see that there is such a thing as prakṛti. It does not depend on anything else for illuminating objects. Prakṛti and its products are not self-manifested, but depend for their manifestation on the light of puruṣa. Consciousness, though physically mediated, is not physically explained. Buddhi, manas, and the like, are the instruments or the means; they cannot explain the end of consciousness which they subserve. Puruṣa is only consciousness and not bliss, for happiness is due to the sattva guṇa, which belongs to the side of prakṛti. The duality of subject-object is involved in pleasurable experiences as much as in painful ones. Pleasure and pain belong to the buddhi.[6] Moreover, the presence of bliss in addition to consciousness would introduce duality into the nature of puruṣa.[7] If pain constitutes the nature of puruṣa, no liberation is possible. Puruṣa is incapable of movement, and on attaining release it does not go anywhere.[8] It is not of limited size, since then it would be made up of parts and so be destructible.[9] It is not of atomic size, for then it is not possible to account for its cognition of all bodily states. It does not participate in any activity. The Sāṁkhya denies the puruṣa all qualities, since otherwise it would not be capable of emancipation. The nature of a thing is

[1] S.P.S., vi. 1–2.
[2] S.P.B., i. 75; Y.S., iv. 18; S.P.S., i. 146.
[3] S.P.S., i. 148.
[4] S.P.B., i. 148.
[5] S.P.S., i. 61.
[6] S.P.S., vi. 11.
[7] v. 66.
[8] S.P.S., i. 49. S.K., 3.
[9] i. 50.

inalienable, and happiness and misery cannot belong to the soul.

There are many selves, since experience shows that men are differently endowed physically, morally and intellectually. There are many conscious beings in the world, each regarding the world in his own way, and with an independent experience of its subjective and objective processes. The differences of outlook cannot be due to the operations of prakṛti, and so it is argued that there are different witnessing consciousnesses. These have different organs and actions and undergo separate birth and death.[1] One goes to heaven, the other goes to hell. The Sāṁkhya lays stress on the numerical distinctness of the streams of consciousness as well as the individual unity of the separate streams. While we cannot account for the organised unity of the individual's experiences apart from the assumption of an individual subject, the distinctness of the different unities makes for a plurality of selves. If the self were one, all should become free if any one attained freedom.[2] If the self is opposed in nature to prakṛti, which is one and common to all, the plurality of selves follows. The passages of the scriptures which support monism are interpreted as referring to the non-difference of essential properties.[3] They imply non-difference in kind and not homogeneity.[4] Freedom is not coalescence with an absolute spirit, but isolation from prakṛti. The selves lodged in the several individuals have the common property of being the silent spectators of the proceedings of the products of prakṛti with which they are temporarily connected.

The Sāṁkhya view of puruṣa is determined by the conception of Ātman in the Upaniṣads.[5] It is without beginning or end, without any qualities, subtle and omnipresent, an eternal seer, beyond the senses, beyond the mind, beyond the sweep of intellect, beyond the range of time, space and causality, which form the warp and woof of the mosaic of the empirical world. It is unproduced and unproducing. Its eternity is not merely everlastingness, but immutability and

[1] S P.S., vi. 45 ; i 149 and 150.
[2] S.K., 18.
[3] S.P.S., v. 61 ; S.P.B., i. 154
[4] Vaidharmyaviraha, and not akhaṇḍatā
[5] Bṛh. Up., iv. 3. 16 ; Śvet., vi. 11 and 19 ; *Amṛtabindu*, v. 10.

perfection. It is of the form of consciousness (cidrūpa), though it does not know all things in the empirical sense, for empirical cognition is possible only through the limitations of body. When the self is set free from these limits, it has no cognition of modifications, but remains in its own nature.[1] Puruṣa is unrelated to prakṛti.[2] It is mere witness, a solitary, indifferent, passive spectator.[3] The characteristics of prakṛti and puruṣa are opposed in nature. Prakṛti is non-consciousness (acetanam), while puruṣa is consciousness (sacetanam). Prakṛti is active and ever-revolving, while puruṣa is inactive (akartā). Puruṣa is unalterably constant, while prakṛti is so alterably. Prakṛti is characterised by the three guṇas, while puruṣa is devoid of the guṇas; prakṛti is the object, while puruṣa is the subject.

X

The Empirical Individual

The Jīva is the self distinguished by the conjunction of the senses and limited by the body.[4] Vijñānabhikṣu says that puruṣa with ahaṁkāra is the jīva, and not puruṣa in itself.[5] While the pure self remains beyond buddhi, the reflection of puruṣa in buddhi appears as the ego, the cogniser of all our states, pleasures and pains included. We have the notion of self in buddhi when we do not know that the self is beyond buddhi and different from it in character and knowledge.[6] Each buddhi, with its grasp of senses and the like, is an isolated organism determined by its past karma,[7] and has its own peculiarly associated ignorance (avidyā). The ego is the psychological unity of that stream of conscious experiencing which constitutes what we know as the inner life of an empirical self. This unity is a temporal one, which is ever changing, and not the puruṣa, which is timelessly

[1] S.P.S., Vṛtti, vi. 59.

[2] Bṛh. Up., iv. 3. 15.

[3] S.K., 19. Cp. Maṇibhadra on Haribhadra's *Ṣaḍdarśanasamuccaya*. 41.

Amūrtaś cetano bhogī nityaḥ sarvagato 'kriyaḥ
Akartā nirguṇaḥ sūkṣma ātmā kāpiladarśane.

[4] S.P.S., Vṛtti, vi. 63.

[5] S.P.B., vi. 63.

[6] Y.S., ii. 6.

[7] S.P.B., ii. 46.

present as the presupposition of the temporal unity. While the puruṣa is the self which is eternally one with itself, the jīva is an item in the natural world. The egos are existences in a world of existences and alongside of them, and are no more ultimately real than material things. The egos may be experienced by us as other existences are, though differently from them. Every ego possesses within the gross material body, which suffers dissolution at death, a subtle body formed of the psychical apparatus, including the senses. This subtle body is the basis of rebirth,[1] as well as the principle of personal identity in the various existences. The subtle body, which retains the traces of all our experiences, is called the liṅga, or the mark distinguishing the puruṣa. The liṅgas are the empirical characteristics without which the different puruṣas cannot be distinguished. As products of prakṛti, they have the three guṇas. The specific character of the liṅga depends on the combination of the guṇas. Each life-history has its own liṅga. So long as the subtle body is present, there will be embodied existence and rebirth. In the lowest animal stage the tamas predominates, since we notice that the life of an animal is characterised by ignorance and stupidity. The faculties of memory and imagination are but imperfectly developed, so that the pleasure or pain experienced by the animals is neither long nor intense. Since the sattva nature is very low, the knowledge of animals is but a means to present action. When rajas becomes more predominant, the puruṣa enters the human world. The human beings are restless, and strive for liberation and freedom from pain. When sattva predominates, the saving knowledge is obtained, and prakṛti no longer binds the ego to the misery of existence. The released soul is a disinterested spectator of the world show. At death, the bond between puruṣa and prakṛti is dissolved, and the released soul is freed absolutely. The changes, *i.e.* release and bondage, belong to the subtle body attached to the puruṣa, which ever remains pure consciousness, though it forgets its true nature so long as the subtle body abounds in rajas and tamas. The puruṣas in all the subtle bodies are of the same kind, and the subtle bodies themselves which differentiate them belong to one continuous

[1] S.P.S., iii. 16.

evolution in prakṛti. The evolution hypothesis links man in blood relationship with every other form of life, animal as well as vegetable.

The empirical self is the mixture of free spirit and mechanism, of puruṣa and prakṛti. Through the union of puruṣa and prakṛti, the subtle body, which is a product of prakṛti, becomes conscious, though it is in itself non-conscious. It is subject to pleasure and pain, action and its fruits, and rotates in the round of rebirth. The ātman or the puruṣa is quite indifferent to worldly concerns. Activity belongs to the buddhi, one of the products of prakṛti; nevertheless, on account of its union with puruṣa, the indifferent puruṣa appears as an actor. Actual agency belongs to antaḥkaraṇa, or the inner organ, which is lighted up by puruṣa.[1] The unconscious antaḥkaraṇa cannot by itself be the agent, but it is invested with consciousness. This investment or illumination of antaḥkaraṇa consists in a particular conjunction of it with consciousness, which is eternally shining; consciousness does not pass into the antaḥkaraṇa, but is only reflected in it. This conjunction of puruṣa with prakṛti is of course not a permanent one. Puruṣa allies itself with prakṛti in order that the nature of the latter may be revealed to itself and that it may attain freedom from association with prakṛti. Prakṛti underlies both psychical and physical phenomena. Its constituents behave in the one case as the subject or the perceiver, and in the other as the object or the perceived. The two represent different orders of development.[2] Prakṛti acts and puruṣa enjoys the fruits of action. Happiness and misery belong to the modes of prakṛti, and puruṣa is said to experience them through its ignorance.[3] The light of consciousness is attributed to the workings of prakṛti; and puruṣa, passively observing the workings of prakṛti, forgets its true nature, and is deluded into the belief that it thinks, feels and acts. It identifies itself with a particular finite form of existence, animal body, and is thus shut out from

[1] S.P.S., i. 99.

[2] Cp. Vācaspati: "Guṇānāṁ dvairūpyaṁ vyavaseyātmakatvam, vyavasāyātmakatvaṁ ca. Tatra vyavaseyātmakatāṁ grāhyatām āsthāya pañcatanmātrāṇi bhūtabhautikāni . . . vyavasāyātmakatvaṁ tu grahaṇasvarūpam āsthāya sāhaṁkārāṇīndriyāṇi" (*Tattvavaiśāradī*, iii. 47).

[3] *Tattvakaumudī*, 5.

the true life. Losing the peace of eternity, it enters the unrest of time. Puruṣa does not move, though the body which invests it moves from place to place. Puruṣa, which is passive and supposed to give consent or withdrawal, is but a name for a movement which takes place in prakṛti. Though not an agent, the puruṣa appears as an agent, through confusion with the agency of prakṛti, even as prakṛti through proximity to puruṣa appears to be conscious.[1] The experience of pain (duḥkhasākṣātkāra) is only in the form of reflection, which is of the modification (vṛtti) of the upādhi.[2] The real bondage is of the citta, while only its shadow falls on the puruṣa.

The narrow and limited existence of the jīva is not due to the essential nature of the soul as puruṣa ; it is the result of a fall from its original estate. The experience of puruṣa means only the reception of the reflections of objects.[3] When prakṛti acts, the puruṣa experiences the fruits, since the activity of prakṛti is intended for the experience of puruṣa.[4] Strictly speaking, even this experiencing is due to abhimāna (sense of selfhood), born of aviveka (non-discrimination).[5] When the truth is known, there is neither pleasure nor pain, neither agency nor enjoyment.[6]

The Sāṁkhya account of puruṣa and jīva resembles in many respects the Advaita Vedānta account of the ātman and the individual ego. The ātman, according to the Advaita Vedānta, is free from action, from the encumbrances of body and mind which involve us in action. The ātman seems to act on account of its accidents. The unconditioned puruṣa or ātman is regarded as jīva, when it is confused with the narrow bounds of individuality. Strictly speaking, individuality belongs to the sūkṣmaśarīra in the Advaita and the liṅgaśarīra in the Sāṁkhya. Vijñānabhikṣu speaks of a mutual reflection, which is to some extent akin to the pratibimbavāda of the Advaita Vedānta, which holds that the ātman is reflected in the antaḥkaraṇa, or the inner organ. This cidābhāsa, or appearance of cit, is the individual self or jīva.

The Sāṁkhya theory is evidently a compromise between the empirical view of the soul struggling for release and the

[1] S.K., 20 and 22 ; S.P.S., i. 162–3 ; Y.S., ii 17 ; B.G., viii. 21 ; Kaṭha Up., iii. 4.

[2] S.P.B., i. 17.

[3] Puruṣasya viṣayabhogaḥ pratibimbādānamātram (S.P.B., i. 104).

[4] S.P.S., i. 105 [5] S.P.S., i. 106. [6] S.P.S., i. 107.

metaphysical view of the Advaita Vedānta, that the infinite and passionless soul is incapable of submitting to bondage. So, it is said, that though the puruṣa remains in its essence eternally unchanged, still it experiences the reflection of the suffering which goes on. Even as a crystal allows a red flower to be seen through it without itself becoming red, the soul remains unchanged, though the illusion of its suffering or joy may be present in consciousness. Vijñānabhikṣu quotes a verse from the *Sūrya Purāna* to the effect: "As a pure crystal is observed by people to be red on account of the superimposition of some red-coloured stuff, so is the great puruṣa."[1] Śaṁkara uses the analogy of the crystal vase which appears red on account of the red flowers in it, though it is itself devoid of any taint or tinge.[2] If the puruṣa appears affected or disturbed, this appearance is due to the mind with which it is for a time associated. The association does not leave any permanent or temporary impression on the self. Since there is no real contact, there are no traces left behind.

XI

Puruṣa and Prakṛti

The most perplexing point of the Sāṁkhya system is the problem of the relation between puruṣa and prakṛti. We have already seen that the evolution of prakṛti has not only a certain glamour, but has also a design in its adaptation to the realisation of spiritual ends.[3] Prakṛti evolves a world full of woe and desolation to raise the soul from its slumber. The unrolling of the tragedy of the world is said to be necessary for the self, which remains inactive, though it sees all that is presented to it. Serviceability to puruṣa is acknowledged

[1] Yathā hi kevalo raktaḥ sphaṭiko lakṣyate janaiḥ
Rañjakādyupadhānena tadvat paramapūruṣaḥ. (S.P.B., i. 19.)

The puruṣa, passively indifferent, appears as if he were an agent owing to the influence of the three guṇas. Cp.

Prakṛteḥ kāryaṁ nityaikā prakṛtir jaḍā
Prakṛtes triguṇāveśād udāsīno 'pi kartṛvad. (S.S.S.S., ix. 15.)

[2] *Ātmabodha.*

[3] S.P S., ii. 1; iii. 58.

to be the end of the activities of prakṛti,[1] though parkṛti is not conscious of this end. While the Sāṁkhya eliminates mythological miracle-working, it admits an immanent teleology. It is a sublime thought to trace the grandeur of the cosmos and the marvellous arrangement of the world to the activity of prakṛti, which, though mechanical, effects results which suggest strongly the wisest computation of sagacity. But the Sāṁkhya is clear that the activity of prakṛti is not due to conscious reflection.[2] The analogies employed by the Sāṁkhya do not carry us very far. The non-intelligent prakṛti is said to act even as the non-intelligent trees grow fruits,[3] or even as the milk of the cow is secreted for the purpose of nourishing the calf. Mechanism does not explain itself, nor can the products of prakṛti be regarded as the mechanical results of the lower conditions. If prakṛti were spontaneously active, then there can be no liberation, since its activity will be unceasing; if it were spontaneously inactive, then the course of mundane existence would at once cease to go on. The Sāṁkhya admits that the activity of prakṛti implies a mover not itself in motion, though it produces movement. The evolution of prakṛti implies spiritual agency. But the spiritual centres admitted by the Sāṁkhya are incapable of exerting any direct influence on prakṛti; the Sāṁkhya says that the mere presence of the puruṣas excites prakṛti to activity and development. Though puruṣa is not endowed with creative might, prakṛti, which produces the manifold universe, is so on account of its union with puruṣa. Prakṛti is blind, but with the guidance of puruṣa it produces the manifold world. The union of the two is compared to a lame man of good vision mounted on the shoulders of a blind man of sure foot.[4] The collective

[1] S.K., 56. The Sāṁkhya view of prakṛti is different from the view of nature popularised by Huxley in his Romanes Lecture or by Hardy's lines:—

> " . . . Some Vast Imbecility,
> Mighty to build and blend,
> But Impotent to tend.
> . . An Automaton,
> Unconscious of our pains."

[2] S.P.S., iii. 61.

[3] S.P.S., Vṛtti, ii. 1.

[4] S.K., 21. Gauḍapāda says: "As a lame man and a blind man, deserted by their fellow travellers, who, in making their way with difficulty

influence of the innumerable selves which contemplate the movement of prakṛti is responsible for the evolution of the latter. The disturbance of the equilibrium of the guṇas which sets up the process of evolution is due to the action of the puruṣas on prakṛti.[1] The presence of the puruṣas disturbs the balance of the forces which keep each other at rest. At the beginning of the evolutionary process we have prakṛti in a state of quiescence and numberless puruṣas equally quiescent, but exerting on prakṛti a mechanical force. This upsets the equilibrium of prakṛti and initiates a movement which, at first, takes the form of development and, later, of decay and collapse. Prakṛti, again, returns to its quiescent condition, to be again excited by the puruṣas. The process will continue until all the selves are freed. So the first cause, as well as the final cause, of the cosmic process is puruṣa. But the causation of puruṣa is purely mechanical, being due not to its volition but to its mere proximity. Puruṣa moves the world by a kind of action which is not movement. It is compared to the attraction of a magnet for iron.[2] The puruṣa of the Sāṁkhya is not unlike the God of Aristotle. Though Aristotle affirms a transcendant God as the origin of the motion of the world, he denies to his God any activity within the world. God, according to Aristotle, is a purely contem-

through a forest, had been dispersed by robbers, happening to encounter each other, and entering into conversation so as to inspire mutual confidence, agreed to divide between them the duties of walking and of seeing. Accordingly, the lame man was mounted on the blind man's shoulders, and was thus carried on his journey, whilst the blind man was enabled to pursue his route by the directions of his companion. In the same manner the faculty of seeing is in the soul, though not that of moving—it is like the lame man; the faculty of moving is in prakṛti, but not of seeing, which resembles, therefore, the blind man. Further, as a separation takes place between the lame man and the blind man, when their mutual object is accomplished and when they have reached the end of the journey, so prakṛti, having effected the liberation of the puruṣa, ceases to act; and puruṣa, having contemplated prakṛti, obtains freedom; and so, their respective purposes being effected, the connection between them is dissolved" (*Bhāṣya* on *Kārikā*, p. 21).

[1] Any system of constructive evolutionary philosophy needs an organising principle, a nisus or an elan. Alexander, who gets down at the base of the pyramid to a kind of space-time, makes time the energising factor. Hobhouse, in his preface to the second edition of *Mind in Evolution*, urges that mind in some form is the driving force of all evolution. Lloyd Morgan attributes this function to God in his *Emergent Evolution*.

[2] S.K., 57; S.P.S., i. 96.

plative being shut up within himself, so that he can neither act upon the universe nor take cognisance of it. God, the first mover, is said to move the world by being the object after which the whole creation strives, and not as if it were in any way determined by his action. Concern with the affairs of the world would destroy the completeness of God's life. So God, who is pure intelligence, though himself unmoved, moves the world by his mere being. The further development of things arises from their own nature. But puruṣa is said to be outside prakṛti, and its influence on prakṛti, though real, is unintelligible. The relation between the two is a mystery which encompasses us, though we cannot penetrate it.[1] We cannot say that prakṛti acts with reference to the end of the puruṣas, since the latter are eternally free and are incapable of enjoying the activities of prakṛti. It follows that the activities of prakṛti are meant for the consumption of the jīvas, who, on account of imperfect insight, identify themselves with their liṅgaśarīras, or subtle bodies, possess desires and stand in need of discriminative knowledge. So prakṛti produces beings who are bound to suffer in order to give them an opportunity of extricating themselves.[2]

The real puruṣa has relations with a real world on account of a fancied relation between the two. So long as this fancied relation subsists, prakṛti acts towards it. When the puruṣa recognises its distinction from the ever-evolving and dissolving

[1] Cp. S.B., ii. 2. 6. Śaṁkara, discussing the question of the purpose of the activities of prakṛti, whether it is the enjoyment (bhoga) or release (mokṣa) of souls, says: "If enjoyment, what enjoyment can belong to the soul incapable of any accretion (of pleasure or pain)? Moreover, there would in that case be no opportunity for release (since the soul as inactive cannot aim at release, while pradhāna aims only at the soul's undergoing varied experience). If the object were release, the activity of pradhāna would be purposeless, since even antecedent to it the soul is in the state of release. If both enjoyment and release, then, on account of the infinite number of the objects of pradhāna to be enjoyed by the soul, there would be no opportunity for final release. Nor can the satisfaction of a desire be regarded as the purpose of the activity of pradhāna, since neither the non-intelligent pradhāna nor the essentially pure soul can feel any desire. If, finally, you assume that the pradhāna is active, since otherwise the power of sight (belonging to the soul as intelligence) and the creative power (of the pradhāna) would be purposeless, it would follow that, since the two do not cease at any time, the apparent world would never come to an end, so that final release of the soul is impossible."

[2] S.P.S., Vṛtti, ii. 1.

world of prakṛti, the latter ceases to operate towards it.[1] The efficient cause of prakṛti's development is not the mere presence of the puruṣas, for they are always present, but their non-discrimination.

Prior to the transformation of prakṛti into mahat, etc., there is only non-discrimination. Adṛṣṭa, or unseen merit or demerit, is as yet unproduced, since it is a product of mahat and appears subsequent to the initial action of prakṛti. Adṛṣṭa, acquired in the previous creation, is of no help, since it is different for different individuals, and at the moment of creation the different adṛṣṭas are not distributed to the different selves. In the last analysis, the cause of the activity of prakṛti is non-discrimination,[2] since the connection with karma is only an effect of non-discrimination.[3] This non-discrimination brings about a temporary union between puruṣa and prakṛti; the union, however, is not real, since it dissolves on the rise of true knowledge.

Prakṛti has caught puruṣas somehow in her web. No cause is assigned to account for the original entanglement of the eternal souls, once free, in the equally eternal prakṛti. Only the fact is noticed that the puruṣas are caught in the meshes of prakṛti apparently without their consent. It is due to non-discrimination which has no beginning. If it had a beginning, then, prior to it, the souls would have been in release and after it, in bondage. This would mean the bondage of the released.

We cannot say by what avidyā is caused. So it is regarded as beginningless, though it may have an end.[4] Aviveka is said to be the cause of the conjunction (saṁyoga) between puruṣa and prakṛti.[5] The former, which is the cause, exists even in pralaya or dissolution, though not the latter. This conjunction is not a real change (pariṇāma), since no new properties are produced in the puruṣa. The relation between the two is sometimes viewed as that of the enjoyer and the enjoyable.[6]

XII

Puruṣa and Buddhi

Of all the evolutes of prakṛti, buddhi is the most important. The senses present their objects to buddhi, which exhibits them to puruṣa. It is buddhi that discriminates the difference

[1] S.K., 61; S.P.S., iii. 70.
[2] Y.S., ii. 24.
[3] S.P.S., iii. 67.
[4] See S.P.S., vi. 12–15.
[5] S.P.B., i. 19; Y.S., ii. 23–24.
[6] S.P.B., i. 19. Vijñānabhikṣu disputes it on the ground that if the relation is eternal, it cannot be terminated by knowledge, and if it is non-eternal, it may as well be called conjunction (saṁyoga).

between puruṣa and prakṛti and accomplishes, for puruṣa, the fruition of all that is to be experienced.[1] Buddhi, by means of the reflection of puruṣa, which is adjacent to it, becomes verily of its form and accomplishes its experience of all objects. Though buddhi is a product of prakṛti and so non-conscious in character, still it appears as if intelligent.[2] Puruṣa does not transfer its characteristics of consciousness to buddhi. "Because of the transparency of prakṛti in her sattva part, the puruṣa reflected therein mistakes the sense of selfhood and agency (abhimāna) of prakṛti as belonging to itself. This misconception is in the self also as reflected in prakṛti and not in the self as such; even as the motionless moon reflected in water moves through the motion of water."[3] Vācaspati holds that there can be no contact (saṁyoga) between puruṣa and the state of buddhi, since they belong to two different orders of reality; and so it is said that there is a reflection of puruṣa in buddhi which makes the latter conscious. The ego is the seeming unity of buddhi and puruṣa. When puruṣa sees there is a modification of buddhi simultaneous with it. When buddhi suffers modification, it catches a glimpse of puruṣa, so that the contact (saṁyoga) of puruṣa and prakṛti is simultaneous with the unity of the reflecting puruṣa and the particular transformation of buddhi. The relation between puruṣa and prakṛti associated with it is such that whatever mental phenomena happen in the mind are interpreted as the experiences of the puruṣa. Even non-discrimination belongs to buddhi, and in bondage it is reflected in puruṣa.[4]

Puruṣa is said to be immediately connected with the buddhi pertaining to it, and indirectly with the rest. So Vijñānabhikṣu says that while puruṣa is the sākṣin of buddhi, *i.e.* the witness of the states of buddhi without any intermediary, it is the beholder (draṣṭā) of others through the aid of buddhi. The free and indifferent puruṣa becomes the sākṣin when connected with buddhi.[5] If a real connection

[1] S.K., 37; S.P.B., i. 161.

[2] Cetanāvad iva (S.K, 20). See also S.K., 60.

[3] S.P.S., Vṛtti, vi. 59.

[4] Cp. S.P.B., i. 19. "Birth means conjunction with an individual buddhi. It is by reason of the conjunction of buddhi as an upādhi that conjunction of pain takes place in the puruṣa."

[5] S.P.S., vi. 50.

between soul and body is asserted, then the imperfections of the latter will have to be attributed to the former. This will prejudice the Sāṁkhya theory of the essential purity of the soul. Bondage is the reflection in puruṣa of the impurities of buddhi. Release is the removal of this reflection consequent on the recovery by buddhi of its original purity, *i.e.* dissolution into prakṛti. To say that the activity of prakṛti is for the benefit of puruṣa is a figurative way of saying that it is for the purification of buddhi. While buddhi is in itself sāttvika, in any individual it is rājasa or tāmasa, on account of the contaminating influences of its past life. The feeling of pain or pleasure which we experience arises from the interaction of buddhi and the objective world with puruṣa as the onlooker. While buddhi should give rise only to pleasure, on account of the play of its acquired influences, it brings about painful results. This is why the same thing affects different persons differently. Every object apprehended is viewed through the distracting medium of individual purpose. Thus, what is pleasant to one is unpleasant to another, or to the same person at a different time. We generally live in worlds of our own, where we over-estimate our particular needs and purposes and set a conventional value on our preferences. Our ordinary lives are bound up with our selfish desires and give rise to pain mixed with some amount of uncertain pleasure. If we purify our buddhi, get rid of our past tendencies, then we shall be in a position to look at things, not as related to us, but as related among themselves, *i.e.* absolutely. When buddhi is dominated by sattva, it gives rise to true knowledge; by rajas, to desire; and by tamas, to false knowledge and the like.[1]

XIII

THE MECHANISM OF KNOWLEDGE

In all knowledge, three factors are involved: the object known, the subject knowing, and the process of knowledge. In the Sāṁkhya philosophy "the pure consciousness is the

[1] Sattvaṁ yathārthajñānahetuḥ, rajo rāgahetuḥ, tamo viparītajñānādihetuḥ.

knower (pramātṛ); the modification (vṛtti) is the pramāṇa; pramā is the reflection in consciousness of the modifications in the form of the objects. The knowable is the subject matter of the reflected modifications." [1] Experience belongs to puruṣa.[2] Buddhi (intellect), ahaṁkāra (self-sense), manas (mind), and the senses constitute the apparatus by means of which the external object is apprehended by the subject. When an object excites the senses, the manas [3] arranges the sense-impressions into a percept, the self-sense refers it to the self, and the buddhi forms the concept.[4] Buddhi, spread over the whole body, contains the impressions (saṁskāras) and tendencies (vāsanās) of past lives, which are revived under suitable conditions. "By means of the contact with objects through the channels of the senses, or by means of the knowledge of the inferential mark and the like, is first produced a modification of buddhi in the form of the object to be cognised. This modification, tinged with the object, enters on (the field of union of) the puruṣa by the form of a reflection and shines there, since puruṣa, who is not liable to transformation, cannot possibly be modified into the form of the object." If apprehension of the object means the assumption of the form of the object, such a transformation is not possible with the puruṣa; so buddhi is said to be modified. For the modification to be manifested, there must be the reflection of buddhi in consciousness.[5] This reflection is determined by the modification of the buddhi. The reflection in puruṣa lasts only so long as that which is reflected is present. The reflection in puruṣa of the modification of buddhi is not subsequent to but simultaneous with the modification. When,

[1] S.P.B., i. 87.

[2] S.P.S., i. 143.

[3] Manas is recognised as an eleventh sense for several reasons. If the eternal puruṣa were itself associated with the objects of pleasure and pain, then there could be no liberation. If the connection with objects took place in dependence on prakṛti, then there could be no liberation, since prakṛti is eternal. If the non-eternal objects, jars, etc., were associated with the eternal intelligence of puruṣa, then there could be no such distinction as seen and unseen, since all things now existing would necessarily be seen at one and the same moment. If the association of objects with intelligence depended only on the external organs, we could not account for the non-simultaneous character of our perceptions.

[4] *Tattvakaumudī*, 36. For a criticism of the Sāṁkhya theory of knowledge, see N.V. and N.V.T.T., iii. 2. 8–9.

[5] S.P.B., i. 99.

through the sense-organs, buddhi comes into contact with the external object and is affected by it, it assumes the form of that object. The force of consciousness (cetanāśakti), reflected in the buddhi thus modified, imitates the modification of buddhi; and it is the imitation (tadvṛttyanukāra) that is known as apprehension (upalabdhi). The reflection of the puruṣa is not an actual intercourse, but is only apparent, being due to the failure to perceive the distinction between the puruṣa and buddhi. The connection of the puruṣa, as reflected in the buddhi, with the object is called knowledge, and the connection of the puruṣa with this knowledge is seen in the resulting determination that "I act,"[1] whereas in reality the "I," or puruṣa, cannot act, and what acts, *i.e.* buddhi, cannot think.[2]

No movement of buddhi will be conscious apprehension until it attracts the attention of some puruṣa. This view is intended to bring out the unconscious nature of buddhi, manas and the senses.[3]

The action of the different functions is successive, though, in some, the succession is so rapid as to escape attention. When one sees a tiger in a dark night, one's senses are excited, manas reflects, ahaṁkāra identifies, and the buddhi determines the nature of the object, and one runs away for dear life. Here the different acts take place so quickly that they seem to occur simultaneously. When one sees an object in a dim light, suspects it to be a thief, and slowly makes up one's mind and moves away in an opposite direction, the different stages are discernible.[4]

---

[1] Buddhāv āropitacaitanyasya viṣayeṇa saṁbandho jñānam, jñānena saṁbandhaś cetano'haṁ karomīty upalabdhiḥ (Haridāsa Bhaṭṭācārya on Udayana's *Kusumāñjali*, i. 14).

[2] While Vācaspati thinks that the self knows the object through the mental modification on which it casts its reflection, Vijñānabhikṣu holds that the mental modification which takes in the reflection of the self and assumes its form is reflected back on the self, and it is through this reflection that the self knows the object. *Yogavārttika*, i. 4. *Tattvavaiśāradī*, p. 13.

[3] But in the Sāṁkhya theory there cannot arise buddhi, ahaṁkāra, etc., until there is the pervading influence of puruṣa over prakṛti. It is therefore unnecessary for us to think that buddhi is simply non-conscious. The development of buddhi is itself due to the influence of puruṣa. We need not regard buddhi, ahaṁkāra, etc., as mere instruments ready made for the use of puruṣa, but remaining unconscious and inert, until puruṣas look through them as through a telescope; for this would be to ignore the central principle of the Sāṁkhya that prakṛti cannot give rise to buddhi, etc., until puruṣa disturbs the equilibrium of prakṛti.

[4] S.K., 30; *Tattvakaumudī*, 30

The psychic functions of perception and thought, desire and choice, are, strictly speaking, mechanical processes of the products of prakṛti, which constitute the inner organs.[1] They would remain unconscious but for the puruṣa which illuminates them, *i.e.* makes them conscious. This is the sole function of puruṣa, since all activity belongs to prakṛti. Puruṣa is a passive mirror in which the inner organ is reflected. The purely immaterial self bathes the processes of the inner organ in its own consciousness, so that they do not remain unconscious. The Sāṁkhya assumes not only the proximity of the puruṣa to buddhi, but also the reflection of puruṣa in buddhi. We cognise the conscious occurrence even as we see the face reflected in a mirror. Only in this way can consciousness have a vision of itself.[2]

The relation between the incorporeal puruṣa and the corporeal buddhi is hard to conceive. According to Vācaspati, there can be no contact between the two on the plane of space and time. He therefore interprets proximity (sannidhi) as fitness (yogyatā). The puruṣa, though it remains aloof from the states of buddhi, falls into the misconception of identifying itself with buddhi and ascribing the states of the latter to itself. Vijñānabhikṣu contends that if such a special kind of fitness is admitted, there is no reason why the puruṣa should lose it at the time of deliverance. In other words, there can be no deliverance, since the puruṣa will continue to experience the states of buddhi for ever. So he holds that there is a real contact of the puruṣa with the modifications of buddhi in any cognitive occurrence. Such a contact need not involve any change in the puruṣa, for change means the rise of new qualities. Buddhi suffers changes, and when these are reflected in the puruṣa there arises the notion of a person or experiencer in the puruṣa, and when the puruṣa is reflected back in the buddhi the state of the latter appears as a conscious occurrence. But even Vijñānabhikṣu allows that the relation between the puruṣa and the buddhi is like

[1] The three inner organs, buddhi, ahaṁkāra and manas, are frequently treated as one, since they are closely related to one another. Cp. Garbe: "This combined material inner organ exactly corresponds as regards its unspiritual nature, and all the functions that the Sāṁkhya doctrine ascribes to it to the nervous system" (E.R.E., vol. ii, p. 191).

[2] Citcchāyāpatti, or the falling of the shadow of consciousness (S.D.S., xv).

that of a crystal to a rose reflected in it; there is no actual transference (uparāga), but only the assumption of such transference (abhimāna).[1]

The puruṣas, though innumerable and universal and of the form of consciousness, do not illumine all things at all times, since they are free from attachment (asaṅga) and cannot by themselves be modified into the form of the objects. The puruṣas reflect the modifications of their respective buddhis and not those of others. That object by which the buddhi is affected is known, while that by which it is not affected is not known.[2]

The different states of waking, dreaming, sleep and death are distinguished. In the waking state, buddhi is modified in the form of objects through the channels of senses; in dreams the modifications of buddhi are the results of the saṁskāras, or the impressions of previous experiences. Dreamless sleep is twofold according as the withdrawal (laya) is partial or complete. In the former condition buddhi is not modified in the form of objects, though it assumes the forms of pleasure, pain and dulness inherent in it. This is why, when one wakes from sleep, one has memory of the kind of sleep one had. In death we have a case of complete laya.[3]

XIV

THE SOURCES OF KNOWLEDGE

Cognitive consciousness is of five different kinds: pramāṇa, or valid knowledge, viparyaya, or unreal cognition resting on a form not possessed by that which is its object,[4] vikalpa, or cognitive consciousness, induced by conventional expressions though devoid of any object (vastuśūnya),[5] nidrā (sleep), or cognition supported on tamas,[6] and smṛti or remembrance.

The Sāṁkhya accepts the three pramāṇas of perception, inference and scriptural testimony.[7] Knowledge produced through sense-activity is perception. When a thing like a jar comes within the range of vision, buddhi, or the intellect,

[1] S.P.B., vi. 28; Y.S., i. 4, 7. See also Y.B., ii. 20; iv. 22.
[2] S.D.S., xv.
[3] S.P.B., i. 148.
[4] Y.S., i. 8.
[5] Y.S., i. 9.
[6] Y.S., i. 10.
[7] S.K., 4.

is so modified as to assume the form[1] of the jar; and the soul becomes aware of the existence of the jar.[2] The two kinds of perception, indeterminate (nirvikalpaka) and determinate (savikalpaka), are admitted. According to Vācaspati, buddhi comes into touch with external objects through the senses. At the first moment of the contact there is an indeterminate consciousness in which the particular features of the object are not noticed, and we have only indeterminate perception. At the second moment, through the exercise of mental analysis (vikalpa) and synthesis (saṁkalpa), the object is perceived as possessing a definite nature,[3] and we have determinate perception. While Vācaspati thinks that the activity of manas is necessary for perception, Vijñānabhikṣu denies it, and holds that buddhi directly comes into touch with the objects through the senses. Vācaspati assigns to manas the function of arranging the sense-data and ordering them into determinate perceptions, while Vijñānabhikṣu thinks that the determinate character of things is directly perceived by the senses and that manas is only the faculty of desire, doubt and imagination. Yogic perception is admitted by the Sāṁkhya, which holds that all things exist involved or evolved at all times. The mind of the yogin can come into connection with the past and the future objects which exist at present in a latent condition by virtue of certain powers produced by meditation.[4] Yogic perception produced by the powers of mind is unlike ordinary sense-perception. In memory—knowledge, the manas, the self-sense and the intellect alone are active, though their activity presupposes the results of previous perceptions—such as a memory image. While the outer organs of perception can operate only on objects presented to them, manas can deal with the past and the future as well. In the case of internal perception, the co-operation of the sense-organs is lacking. Buddhi perceives the states of pleasure and the like.[5]

[1] Tadākārollekhi.

[2] S.P.S., i. 89.

[3] Cp. Vyāsa: Sāmānyaviśeṣasamudāyo dravyam (Y.B., iii. 44).

[4] S.P.B., i. 91.

[5] "What is manifested in dreamless sleep, when there is no contact with objects, as the sāttvika pleasure of tranquillity (śāntisukham), the same is the property of buddhi, the pleasure of the self (ātmasukham)" (S.P.B., i. 65).

Even if puruṣa is knowable, it is because puruṣa is reflected in buddhi. The eye cannot see itself except as it is reflected in a mirror. All cognitions are modifications of the internal organ. A primary cognition such as "This is a jar" is a modification of that organ. When its reflection falls on puruṣa, it is apprehended. The cognition, "I cognise the jar," is a modification of the internal organ. Puruṣa, along with the reflection of the modification of the internal organ, such as "This is a jar," is reflected in the internal organ. This second reflection is the modification of the internal organ. Even the cognition "I am distinct from prakṛti" is a modification of the internal organ.[1] Buddhi changes according to the objects offered to it.

The notion of self, which is connected with all our mental phenomena and which illumines them, is due to the reflection of the self in buddhi. So puruṣa may be said to see again that which was perceived by the buddhi, and so impart consciousness by transferring its illumination to the buddhi as the ego. The puruṣa can know itself only through its reflection in the buddhi, modified into the form of the object. According to Vācaspati, the self can know itself only when attention is entirely withdrawn from the mental function in which the self is reflected, and is wholly concentrated on the reflection of the self in the sattva nature of buddhi. In this act the subject of self-apprehension is said to be buddhi in its sattva nature, rendered conscious by receiving the reflection of puruṣa in it; and the object is the self in its purity.[2] Vyāsa[3] holds that the self cannot be known by the buddhi in which it is reflected, but it is the self which knows itself through its reflection in the pure nature of buddhi. Vijñānabhikṣu thinks that the self knows itself through the reflection in itself of the mental modification, which takes in the reflection of the self and is modified into its form, even as it knows an external object through the reflection in itself of the mental modification which assumes the form of the object.[4] Since the self is essentially self-luminous, it can know itself through the reflection in itself of the mental mode which assumes the form of the self. Vijñānabhikṣu regards the self as determined by the mental mode which is modified into the form of the self as the subject, and the self in its pure essence as the object.

Pratyabhijñā or recognition, is brought under perception. It is possible because buddhi is eternal, and quite different from the momentary cognitions of individuals. The eternal buddhi undergoes modifications, by virtue of which it becomes connected with the different cognitions involved in recognition. This would not be possible of the self which is unmodifiable.[5]

[1] Y.S., ii. 20, reads: "The self as seer is absolute in its purity, yet is capable of being perceived in experience" (pratyayānupaśyah).

[2] *Tattvavaiśāradī*, iii. 35. [3] Y.B., iii. 35. [4] *Yogavārttika*, iii. 35.

[5] For a criticism of the theory, see N.S., iii. 2. 1–9.

According to the Sāṁkhya, a cognition is not perceived by another cognition, but is perceived by the self. For cognition is regarded as a function of the buddhi, which is unconscious, and so it cannot be its own object, but can only be apprehended by the self.[1]

Negation (abhāva) is also mentioned under perception. The Sāṁkhya does not admit negation as such, but interprets it in terms of the positive. Mere non-perception cannot prove non-existence, since it may be due to other causes, such as long distance, exces ive nearness, extreme subtlety, or disturbance of sense-organs, inattention, concealment of the object, and mixture with other things.[2] Internal perception, self-consciousness, recognition and knowledge of non-existence are treated as falling under perception.

Inference is said to be of two kinds: affirmative (vīta) and negative (avīta). The former is based on affirmative concomitance and the latter on negative concomitance.[3] The five-membered form of the syllogism is admitted.[4] Generalisation is the result of the observation of the accompaniment attended with the non-observation of non-accompaniment.[5] Vyāpti, which is constant concomitance, is not a separate principle.[6] It is a relation of things, but not itself a thing.[7] Arthāpatti or implication, and saṁbhava or subsumption, are included under inference.

Āptavacana or trustworthy assertion, is also a source of valid knowledge. A word is related to its object as a sign to the thing signified. This is evident from the instruction of the trustworthy, the law of use and wont, conventions and the fact of their possessing the same denotation.[8] The Vedas are not said to be the composition of persons, since there are not any persons who can be their authors.[9] The released have no concern with the Vedas, and the unreleased are not

[1] Y.B., iv. 9. [2] See also *Tattvavaiśāradī*, i. 9. S.K., 7; S.P.S., i. 108–9.

[3] Vācaspati brings the pūrvavat and sāmānyatodṛṣṭa kinds under the former and śeṣavat under the latter. See *Tattvakaumudī*, 5.

[4] S.P.S., v. 27.

[5] S.P.S., Vṛtti, v. 28. Constant coexistence of both the sādhya and sādhana or of one is vyāpti (S.P.S., v. 29). All produced objects are non-eternal is a case of the former, while "all smoky things are fiery" is a case of the latter.

[6] Tattvāntaram, v. 30. Pañcaśikha is of opinion that vyāpti is the possession of the power of that which is sustained (*Ādheyaśaktiyoga*, v. 32).

[7] v. 33–35. [8] S.P.S., Vṛtti, v. 38. [9] S.P.S., v. 46.

competent for the work.[1] Nor are the Vedas eternal, since they possess the character of effects. Letters perish after they are pronounced. When we say " It is the same letter," we mean that it belongs to the same genus.[2] Simply because the Vedas are not of personal origin, we cannot infer that they are eternal, since a sprout is not eternal, though it has not a personal origin.[3] Their objects are supersensuous, yet " there can be intuition even in the case of supersensuous objects, by means of the universal forms which determine the character of being a padārtha, or an object denoted by a word." [4] Though the Vedas are not of personal authorship, their natural power to denote objects is communicated by āptas to their disciples.[5] The Veda, on account of its non-personal authorship, is free from doubts and discrepancies, and is regarded as of self-evident validity. If the validity of the Vedas depended on something else, they would not be authoritative for us.[6] Kapila, at the beginning of the kalpa, only remembered it. The scriptural statements are tested and lived by the muktas or the liberated, who pass them on to others. If those who teach us the śāstras are not inspired seers, but have accepted them at second-hand, then it would be a case of the blind leading the blind.[7] We accept the utterances of the āptas as valid, since their authority is established by the tested validity of their sayings in other branches of knowledge as āyurveda.[8]

The Sāṁkhya is aware that there are other systems which profess to be revealed, and so argues that reason will have to be employed in finding out which codes of revelation are true and which not. Vācaspati says: " The invalidity of these systems is due to their making unreasonable assertions, to the lack of sufficient support, to their making statements opposed to the canons of logic, to their acceptance by the mlecchas and such other low classes." [9] Aniruddha quotes a

[1] S.P.S., v. 47.

[2] S.P.S., Vṛtti, v. 45. The sphoṭavāda is refuted in v. 57, and sound, on account of its character as effect, is said to be non-eternal (v. 58).

[3] S.P.S., v. 48.

[4] Atīndriyeṣv api padārthatā'vacchedakena sāmānyarūpeṇa pratīter vakṣyamāṇatvād (S.P.B., v. 42).

[5] S.P.B., v. 43.

[6] S.P.S., v. 51.

[7] S.P.S., iii. 81.

[8] S.P.B., i. 98., iv. 51.

[9] *Tattvakaumudī*, 5.

verse in his *Vṛtti* to the effect: "Huge giants do not drop from heaven simply because an āpta, or competent person, says so. Only sayings which are supported by reason should be accepted by me and others like yourselves."[1]

The Sāṁkhya avoids the appearance of being an innovation by its acceptance of the Veda as a means of knowledge. But, as we shall see, it discards many an old dogma and silently ignores others. It, however, never openly opposes the Vedas, but adopts the more deadly process of sapping their foundations.

The modification of buddhi is the pramāṇa, and the validity or the invalidity of these modifications can be tested by the later modifications, and not by any reference to external objects. The object of illusory cognition is not a non-existent object, but an existent one. Water is the object of the illusion of water, and when this illusory cognition is contradicted by the cognition of the rays of the sun, the latter cognition has for its object the rays of the sun.[2] Validity, as well as invalidity, belongs to the cognition itself.[3] Sometimes it is said that only the śruti is of self-evident validity (svataḥpramāṇam), while perception and inference are liable to error and require confirmation.[4] The test of reality is workability (arthakriyākāritva). Our apprehension, moreover, is relative to our ahaṁkāra, or individual purpose. It is difficult to have a disinterested knowledge of the world independent of us. The jīva is imprisoned in its own isolated consciousness, and cannot attain to the knowledge of reality beyond it. It follows that all empirical knowledge is vitiated by a central flaw. Every cognition implicating the puruṣa confuses it with the internal organ. It is when the shadow of buddhi falls on puruṣa that the latter appears as though possessed of cognition.[5]

[1] Na hy āptavacanān nabhaso nipatanti mahāsurāḥ
Yuktimad vacanam grāhyam mayānyaiśca bhavadvidhaiḥ.
(i. 26.)

[2] Prabhācandra criticises this view on the ground that it abolishes the distinction between valid and invalid cognitions.

[3] The Naiyāyika criticises this view on the ground that if cognitions were inherently invalid, we cannot act; and if they were inherently valid we cannot account for erroneous cognitions which are facts.

[4] S.P.S., i. 147; also i. 36, 77, 83, 154; ii. 20, 22; iii. 15, 80; iv. 22.

[5] *Tattvakaumudī*, 5.

XV

Some Critical Considerations on the Sāṁkhya Theory of Knowledge

Postponing to a later section a critical estimate of the Sāṁkhya metaphysics, we may briefly notice here some of the striking defects of the Sāṁkhya theory of knowledge.[1] From the fact that in the world of experience the individual deals with a datum or something given, the Sāṁkhya argues to the independent existence of subjects and objects. As we have seen, in the discussion of the Nyāya theory of knowledge, pure subjects and pure objects are false abstractions which have no meaning apart from the concrete experience in which they function. When the Sāṁkhya breaks up the concrete unity of experience into the two elements of subject and object and makes them fictitiously absolute, it cannot account for the fact of experience. When puruṣa is viewed as pure consciousness, the permanent light which illuminates all objects of knowledge, and prakṛti as something opposed to consciousness and utterly foreign to it, the latter can never become the object of the former. The Sāṁkhya cannot get across the ditch which it has dug between the subject and the object. The metaphors of proximity, reflection, and the like, are artificial remedies intended to cure imaginary diseases. Puruṣa can never know prakṛti, if the two are what the Sāṁkhya takes them to be. The puruṣa cannot say in what way the changes in its consciousness, said to be the reflections of the modifications of buddhi, are brought about. The Sāṁkhya says, when buddhi is modified, this modification is reflected in the consciousness of puruṣa. Granting for argument's sake the validity of this theory of reflection, are we not in the grip of psychological subjectivism? To receive a reflection is not the same thing as to perceive a reality that

[1] There is some similarity between the Sāṁkhya and the Kantian theories of knowledge. The phenomenal world is constituted in both by the co-operation of the transcendental subjects (puruṣas) and objects (prakṛti). Both assert the autonomy of the selves in the trans-empirical world and admit the existence of matter in view of the passivity of the subjects which cannot produce their own sensations. Both hold that the existence of God cannot be proved. In other respects there are vital differences.

is not merely mental. What is the relation between the external object and the internal idea? If the two things are related causally, what becomes of the radical opposition between the two? Is perception at any time a mere change of consciousness? Is it not always an awareness of an object? Are we not going beyond the verified experience when we regard the awareness and the object as two distinct realities? If the puruṣa and the prakṛti are absolutely unrelated to each other, then we cannot account for a conscious occurrence or even a material process. This is evidently a *reductio ad absurdum.* But the Sāṁkhya hides from itself the unsatisfactoriness of its position by a number of metaphors and inconsistencies. When subject and object approach one another, there is said to be a mutual reflection of qualities and transfer of properties. Unless the subject and the object are akin to each other, how can the one reflect the other? How can buddhi, which is non-intelligent, reflect puruṣa? How can the formless puruṣa which is the constant seer be reflected in buddhi which is changing? The two cannot, therefore, be absolutely opposed in nature. The last sūtra of the Vibhūtipāda of the *Yoga Sūtra* states that when buddhi becomes as pure as puruṣa, freedom is attained.[1] A purified buddhi does not bind the puruṣa; and, before the abolition of buddhi, we have the reflection of puruṣa in the purified buddhi. Buddhi makes possible complete knowledge of puruṣa and prakṛti and their distinction. So long as buddhi is tinged with selfish aims and particular purposes the truth cannot be known by us.

The Sāṁkhya theory does not account for the fact of knowledge which is a subject-object relation. It admits that the object depends on the subject to be known, and the subject requires an object to know. In other words, there is no knowledge without the synthesis of the two. The subject cannot know itself fully until it knows the object fully. It cannot know the object until the latter is manifested by the subject. Is not the relation between the two essential? The two cannot be external to each other. The appearance of externality arises on account of our going beyond the fact of experience to account for it.

[1] Sattvapuruṣayoḥ śuddhisāmye kaivalyam.

The principle of consciousness is never perceived in itself. It is inferred from knowledge. It is said to be pure awareness. The universal element of knowledge is abstracted and set down as the puruṣa or the consciousness which has no form, no quality, no movement. It is called the pure subject. The contents of consciousness which are ever fluctuating are traced to the object world, which is regarded as a fundamental unity whose character is variableness. All objects are material, including sense-data and mental states which are limited in their nature. They come and go and are copies of outer things, though made of subtler stuff. Though the modifications of buddhi belong to the same group as the things of the world, the puruṣa illuminates the former, since buddhi is of a far subtler nature and possesses the quality of sattva in a preponderant degree. Buddhi is better adapted for the reflection of the light of puruṣa than the other products of prakṛti.[1] So far as knowledge is concerned, we get to know other things through the modifications of buddhi or mind-stuff. Each act of knowledge is broken up into the principle of consciousness, which illumines it, and a modification of buddhi which is in itself non-conscious, though it becomes a content of consciousness the moment it is illumined by the puruṣa. The movements of buddhi are in themselves unconscious, but through their connection with puruṣa they are interpreted as the coherent experiences of an individual. Since experience has in it two elements, one constant and the other variable, we cannot isolate the two and argue that the two exist separately and happen to come together in experience. To assume that the subject and the object of knowledge are complete in themselves is to rend the seamless garment of truth by setting up its different elements against the whole to which they essentially belong. If puruṣa is self and prakṛti selfless, then they are, by definition, reciprocally

[1] In gross matter, mass and energy answering to tamas and rajas are the dominant features. In buddhi, tamas is at its lowest and sattva at its highest, and so it has the power of translucence. If buddhi had only sattva and rajas elements, it would give rise to a simultaneous revelation of all objects. It does not do so because of the element of tamas in it. The light of consciousness is reflected wherever tamas is removed. In a sense buddhi hides within it all knowledge potentially. What becomes actual depends on the lifting of the veil of darkness.

exclusive, and there can be no communion between them; and rightly the Sāṁkhya views the relation between the two as a mechanical one. A mechanical relation implies that the subject and the object of consciousness are not only numerically different, but are also, *per se*, wholly independent of and separate from each other. The mechanical modifications of buddhi become illuminated, as if by magic, with the light of consciousness. We have not here any explanation of conscious knowledge.[1] The rise of consciousness on the occasion of a mechanical modification is a baffling mystery. But the problem is of our own creation. We first of all assume the existence of a pure subject and a pure object, which lie wholly without the range of experience, and then struggle to bring them together into experience. A truer philosophy tells us that subject and object are distinguished within consciousness or knowledge, and not simply outside of it. Subject and object do not happen to come together, but are really inseparable from each other. If experience is allowed to speak for itself, it will tell us that subject and object are presented as one. Knowledge becomes intelligible when we recognise that the fundamental relation in all conscious experience is a relation of members which are in an organic unity, which exist as terms in a living process, in and through each other, or in and through a universal which transcends them both, though it does not exclude them. The fundamental fact of a universal consciousness is the presupposition of all knowledge. The Sāṁkhya puruṣa should be really this one universal self, though it is regarded as many on account of the confusion between the psychological and the metaphysical self. Of course, every jīva has the universal self operating in it. In one sense, our knowledge is the manifestation of a universal principle; while, from another point of view, it is dependent on a sensible process, which must be stimulated from without by its appropriate objects. Intelligence is the same in all in whom it is

[1] Cp. "That the non-intelligent ahaṁkāra should manifest the self-luminous self has no more sense than to say that a spent coal manifests the sun."

Śāntāṅgāra ivādityam ahaṁkāro jaḍātmakaḥ
Svayaṁjyotiṣam ātmānaṁ vyanaktīti na yuktimad.

Yāmunācārya: *Ātmasiddhi*, quoted in R.B., ii. 1. 1).

developed, and is everywhere struggling to free itself from individual limitations and regards things, not from the point of view of a particular organism, but from that of a pure subject. While in one sense our knowledge is our own, in another it is independent of us who possess it.

XVI

Ethics

The Sāṁkhya starts with the idea of the universality of suffering,[1] which is of three kinds: ādhyātmika, *i.e.* arising from the psychophysical nature of man; ādhibhautika, *i.e.* arising from the external world; and the ādhidaivika, *i.e.* arising from the supernatural agencies. The pain caused by the disorders of the body or mental unrest is of the first kind; the second type is due to men, beasts and birds; while the third owes its existence to the influence of planets and the elemental agencies.[2] Every individual strives to alleviate and if possible get rid of pain. But pain cannot be rooted out by the remedies prescribed by the science of medicine or the scriptures.[3] Liberation is not attainable by the observance of Vedic rites. Like Buddhism and Jainism, the Sāṁkhya urges that the Vedic rites involve a violation of the great moral principles. The law of ahiṁsā is set aside when we kill an animal for the Agniṣṭoma sacrifice. Killing is productive of sin, even though it be in a sacrifice. Besides, the kind of heaven we get to by the performance of the sacrifice is a temporary one. Life in heaven (svarga) is not exempt from the influence of the three guṇas. By the practice of virtue and the performance of sacrifices we simply postpone the evil but do not get rid of it. We cannot escape from evils by death, since the same fate pursues us life after life. If the miseries are natural to the soul, there is no help for us; if they are only accidental and arise from something else, we can escape suffering by separating ourselves from the source of suffering.

Bondage belongs to prakṛti and is attributed to puruṣa.

1 S.P.S., vi. 6–8; Y.S., ii. 15.
2 *Tattvakaumudī*, 1.
3 S.K., 2.

"Although bondage in the form of the cognition of pain, and discrimination and non-discrimination in the form of functions belong to the citta or the inner organ, still puruṣa's enjoyment or suffering consists in the mere reflection of pain in him."[1] Puruṣa's bondage is a fiction,[2] due to its proximity to citta. It is therefore said to be adventitious (aupādhika). If puruṣa's connection with pain were real, it could not be cut off. Vijñānabhikṣu quotes a verse from the *Kūrma Purāṇa*[3] to the effect: "Were the self by nature impure, unclean, mutable, verily release would not be possible for it even by hundreds of rebirths."[4] Bondage is not due to time or space, embodiment or karma.[5] All these belong to the not-self. The property of one thing cannot produce change in another, for then all would enjoy pleasure or suffer pain.[6] Bondage arises through the conjunction of prakṛti with puruṣa, which is by nature eternal and pure, enlightened and unconfined.[7] Nor is the mere presence of prakṛti the cause of experience, since on such a view the released soul might have experience; but its cause is "the object of experience, which does not exist in the state of release."[8] Non-discrimination (aviveka) is the cause of bondage (bandhahetu). This aviveka belongs to buddhi, though it has the puruṣa for its object. It follows that our misery will terminate only when our aviveka ends. Knowledge and ignorance are the sole determinants of release and bondage.[9]

Puruṣa is eternally free. It does not desire or hate, govern or obey, impel or restrain. The moral life is vested in the subtle body which accompanies the puruṣa from birth to birth; pain is the essence of bodily existence.[10] When the

[1] S.P.B., i. 58.

[2] Vāṅmātram. S.P.S., Vṛtti, i. 58.

[3] ii. 2. 12.

[4] Yady ātmā malino 'svaccho vikārī syāt svabhāvataḥ
Na hi tasya bhaven muktir janmāntaraśatair api. (S.P.B., i. 7.)

Were pain natural to puruṣa, there would be no point in the injunction to get rid of it (S.P.S., i. 8–11).

[5] S.P.S., i. 12–16.

[6] S.P.S., Vṛtti, i. 17.

[7] i. 19.

[8] S.P.S., Vṛtti, vi. 44.

[9] S.P.S., ii. 7. Aniruddha quotes a verse in his S.P.S., Vṛtti, to the effect: "There is no bondage in the nature of things (vastusthityā), nor does release follow from its non-existence. Both these constituted by error have no real existence" (i. 7).

[10] S.K., 55.

soul is left alone, it is said to be purified. The supreme good, which the jīva aims at and strives for, is to realise the perfection of the puruṣa. All ethical activity is for the fuller realisation of the puruṣa in us. The circuit of saṁsāra is one of conflict and change, made up of parts that are indifferent and external to each other. The jīva, in its endless revolutions, is ever seeking and ever failing to attain to unity with itself, *i.e.* attain to the status of puruṣa, which is eternally one with itself and complete in itself, having no necessary relation with anything external to it. Every jīva has in it the higher puruṣa, and to realise its true nature has no need to go out of itself, but only to become conscious of its real nature. The ethical process is not the development of something new, but a re-discovery of what we have forgotten. Release is a return into one's true self and deliverance from a yoke to which the jīva has subjected itself. It is the removal of an illusion which hides our true nature from our eyes. The knowledge that " I am not " (nāsmi), that " naught is mine " (na me), and that " the ego exists not " (nāham), leads to release.[1]

While freedom is brought about by knowledge, this knowledge is not merely theoretical. It is what results from the practice of virtue, yoga, etc.[2] While bondage is traced to wrong knowledge (viparyaya), this wrong knowledge includes not only avidyā, or unreal cognition, but also asmitā, or egoism, rāga or desire, dveṣa or hatred, and abhiniveśa or fear.[3] These are brought about by aśakti, or incapacity, which is of twenty-eight kinds, of which eleven belong to the senses and seventeen to buddhi.[4] Unselfish activity is an indirect means to salvation.[5] By itself it does not lead us to freedom. It may yield birth in the divine regions, which is not to be confused with mokṣa.[6] Vairāgya, which follows the rise of discriminative knowledge, is different from that which precedes it.[7] Through vairāgya, or unattachment, absorption into prakṛti takes place.[8] This dissolution into prakṛti is not

[1] S.K., 64.
[2] S.P.B., iii. 77 and 78.
[3] S.P.S. and S.P.B., iii. 37.
[4] S.P.S., iii. 38; S.K., 49.
[5] i. 82, 85.
[6] S.P.S., iii. 52–53.
[7] Four kinds of vairāgya are distinguished in *Tattvakaumudī*, 23.
[8] Vairāgyāt prakṛtilayaḥ (S.K., 45; S.P.S., iii. 54).

ultimate freedom; for the souls thus absorbed in prakṛti reappear as Īśvaras, or Lords, since their error is not consumed by knowledge. "He who in a previous creation was absorbed into the cause (prakṛti) becomes in another creation the ādipuruṣa, having the character of Īśvara, or Lord, all-knowing and all-doing." [1] Ethical virtues help us to realise the deeper consciousness, while vices involve a darkening of this consciousness. By indulging in vices the soul immerses itself more and more completely in the material body.

The method of yoga occupies a prominent place in the *Sāṁkhya Sūtra*, though not in the *Kārikā*. We can obtain discriminative knowledge only when our emotional stirrings are subdued and intellectual activities are controlled. When the senses are regulated and the mind acquires calm, buddhi becomes transparent, and reflects the pure light of puruṣa. While buddhi is in its intrinsic nature sāttvika, on account of its acquired impulses and tendencies (vāsanās), it has lapsed from its innate purity. By dhyāna (meditation), the taints of citta caused by the external objects are removed.[2] When the citta regains its pristine condition and rids itself of its desires, the objects no longer excite love or hatred. We have to gain spiritual calm and composure, when the objects do not excite our egoistic interests but reveal their true nature. Since this absolute detachment is beyond the reach of ordinary men, they attempt to develop the impersonal outlook by resorting to art. Works of art offer a temporary release from the natural world.

The doctrine of the guṇas [3] has great ethical significance. The beings of the world are classified according to the preponderance of the different guṇas in them. In the devas the sattva element predominates, while the rajas and the tamas are reduced. In man the tamas element is reduced to

[1] S.P.B., iii. 56. Different kinds of bondage are distinguished by Vācaspati as natural (prākṛtika), incidental (vaikṛtika), and personal (dākṣiṇaka). While the first look upon prakṛti as the absolute spirit, the second look upon the products of prakṛti as the absolute spirit. The third neglect the true nature of spirit in wordly activities indulged in for the gaining of personal ends (iṣṭāpūrta) (*Tattvakaumudī*, 44; *Tattvasamāsa*, p. 19).

[2] S.P.S., iii. 30; S.P.B., iii. 30.

[3] While in the Sāṁkhya the guṇas are purely non-intelligent, in the Vedānta they reflect the character of intelligence.

a less extent than in the devas. In the animal world the sattva is reduced considerably. In the vegetable kingdom tamas is more predominant than in the others. The upward ascent consists in the gradual increase of the sattva element and diminution of the tamas, since pain is a particular modification of the quality of rajas.[1] Strictly speaking, the guṇas mingle, combine and strive in every fibre of our being. Their relative strength determines our mental character. We have men of elevated spirituality, passionate force and depressing apathy. Tamas, if predominant, brings in inertia, ignorance, weakness, incapacity, want of faith and disinclination to act. It produces the coarse, dull, ignorant type of human nature. The individuals in whom the rajas is predominant are intrepid, restless and active. Sattva develops the critical, balanced, thoughtful nature. While the three guṇas are present in different proportions in all men, the seer, the saint and the sage have sattva highly developed in them; the warrior, the statesman and the forceful man of action have rajas highly developed in them. Again, though the guṇas affect every part of our natural being, relatively speaking, the three guṇas have their strongest hold in the three different members of it, namely, mind, life and body. The Sāṁkhya recognises no merit in sacrifices. It does not exclude the śūdras from higher studies. The teacher is not necessarily a Brahmin, but he who has freed himself. The winning of a good teacher depends on our previous conduct.

XVII

RELEASE

Salvation in the Sāṁkhya system is only phenomenal, since bondage does not belong to puruṣa. Bondage and release refer to the conjunction and the disjunction of puruṣa and prakṛti resulting from non-discrimination and discrimination.[2] Prakṛti does not bind the puruṣa but itself in various shapes.[3] Puruṣa is entirely free from the oppositions of merit and demerit.[4] While bondage is the activity of prakṛti

[1] Duḥkhaṁ rajaḥpariṇāmaviśeṣaḥ.
[2] S.P.S., iii. 72.
[3] S.K., 62.
[4] S.P.S., iii. 64; Y.S., ii. 22.

towards one not possessing discrimination, release is its inactivity towards one possessing discrimination.[1] When prakṛti is active, it catches the reflection of puruṣa and casts its shadow on the puruṣa. Yet the change appearing in puruṣa is unreal and fictitious.[2] The union of puruṣa with the subtle body is the cause of saṁsāra, and salvation is attained through the breaking of the union by means of the knowledge of the distinction between puruṣa and prakṛti. When prakṛti withdraws itself from puruṣa, the latter realises the absurdity of attributing the adventures of prakṛti to itself. Puruṣa remains in eternal isolation and prakṛti relapses into inactivity. So long as there are objects concealing the real natue of the soul, liberation cannot be attained. When prakṛti ceases to act, the modifications of buddhi cease, and the puruṣa assumes its natural form.[3] "The cessation of the creation by the pradhāna in regard to the released one is nothing but this, *viz.* the non-production of the cause of the experience thereof, *i.e.* the particular transformation of one's own upādhi called birth."[4] When freed, the puruṣa keeps no company, looks to nothing without itself, and entertains no alien thoughts.[5] It is no longer at the mercy of prakṛti or its products, but stands as a star apart, undisturbed by the earthly cares. There is in reality no distinction between the bound and the released, for freedom consists in the removal of obstacles which hinder the full manifestation of the glory of puruṣa.[6] In samādhi or ecstatic consciousness, suṣupti or dreamless sleep and release, the puruṣa rests in its own form of Brahman (brahmarūpatā) through the dissolution of the modifications of buddhi.[7] In dreamless sleep and ecstatic consciousness the traces of past experiences are present, while they are absent in release.[8] The discriminative knowledge itself disappears when release is attained, for it is like a medicine which purges itself out as well as the disease. While deliverance is an escape from suffering, it is not an escape from all existence. The Sāṁkhya has firm faith in

[1] S.K., 61. [2] S.P.S., ii., 8. Cp. also S.P.B., i. 164. [3] S.P.S., ii. 34; Y.S., ii. 3.

[4] Muktam prati pradhānasṛṣṭyuparamo yat tadbhogahetoḥ svopādhi pariṇāmaviśeṣasya janmākhyasyānutpādanam (S.P.B., vi. 44).

[5] Prakṛtiviyogo mokṣaḥ: Haribhadra.

[6] S.P.S., vi. 20. [7] Y.S., i. 4. [8] S.P.S., v. 117.

the continuance of puruṣa, and so cannot be regarded as pessimistic. When the play of prakṛti ceases, its developments will lapse into the undeveloped. The puruṣas will be seers with nothing to look at, mirrors with nothing to reflect, and will subsist in lasting freedom from prakṛti and its defilements as pure intelligences in the timeless void. On release, "the puruṣa, unmoved and self-collected, as a spectator contemplates prakṛti which has ceased to produce."[1] The Sāṁkhya ideal of freedom is not to be confused with the Buddhist goal of voidness or extinction of self,[2] or the Advaita absorption into Brahman,[3] or the Yogic acquisition of supernatural powers.[4] Nor is mukti the manifestation of bliss (ānanda), since puruṣa is free from all attributes.[5] The scriptural passages which speak of bliss mean to convey that the state of release is one of freedom from pain.[6] So long as the puruṣa has attributes, it is not free.[7]

When discrimination arises, prakṛti does not forthwith free the puruṣa, for, on account of the momentum of past habits, its work continues for some little time[8]; only the body is no more an obstacle to it. By virtue of the force of prārabdhakarma, the body continues, though no fresh karma is accumulated. Though the jīvanmukta has no aviveka, yet his past saṁskāras compel him to possess a body.[9] Release from bondage and continuance of body are compatible with each other, since they are determined by different causes. At death the jīvanmukta attains complete liberation, or disembodied isolation (videhakaivalya).[10] The jīvanmuktas teach us about the nature of freedom and the means of attaining it.[11]

If the play of prakṛti ceases, the puruṣa is no more the spectator, since there is nothing to see; yet it is said that the freed soul has knowledge of the whole universe.[12] We do not know whether the released souls hold social intercourse among themselves. The goal seems to be an extinction of individuality, and not an enhancement of personality. The

1 See also S.K., 65.
2 S.P.S., v. 77–79.
3 S.P.S., v. 81.
4 S.P.S., v. 82.
5 v. 74.
6 v. 67.
7 The Sāṁkhya view of freedom is not unlike Aristotle's view of blessedness as eternal thinking free from all activity.
8 S.K., 67.
9 S.P.S., iii. 82–83.
10 Chān. Up., viii. 12. 1.
11 iii. 79.
12 S.P.S., Vṛtti, vi. 59.

highest state of isolation from prakṛti and other souls is one of passivity, which no breath of emotion or stir of action disturbs. It is likely to be confused with a state of unconscious existence. Praśastapāda objects to the Sāṁkhya theory of freedom, on the ground that prakṛti, which is by its very nature active, cannot rest idle. If prakṛti is unintelligent, how can it know whether the puruṣa has perceived the truth or not ?[1] If, according to the Sāṁkhya, there is only disappearance and not destruction of things, there is no possibility of a complete destruction of ignorance, passion, etc. ; in other words, there is every chance that they may burst out again in the released soul.[2]

XVIII

Future Life

The Sāṁkhya guarantees the endless existence of the soul in both directions. If the soul does not exist from all eternity, then there is no reason why it should exist to all eternity. The soul is not, therefore, created. The more we recognise the eternity of souls the less need do we find for a creator God.[3] According to the Sāṁkhya, the failure to discriminate between puruṣa and prakṛti is the cause of saṁsāra. This non-discrimination leaves an impression on the internal organ which produces in the next birth the same fatal defect. The liṅgadeha, or subtle body, which migrates from one gross body to another in successive births, is composed of buddhi, ahaṁkāra and manas, the five organs of perception and the five of action, the five tanmātras as well as the rudiments of the gross elements, which serve as the seed whence the physical body grows. These subtle portions of the gross

[1] ' In fact, we find that even when it has duly brought about a certain perception of sound, for instance, it still goes on functioning towards the same perception ; and in the same way, even after it will have brought about discriminative knowledge, it would go on with its functioning towards the same end, as its active nature will not have been set aside (by the said knowledge) " (P.P., p. 7).

[2] Udayana's *Pariśuddhi*, ii. 2. 13 ; *Śāstradīpikā*, pp. 323 ff.

[3] Some thinkers like McTaggart argue for a non-omnipotent and non-creative God.

elements are as necessary to the psychic apparatus as the canvas to a picture.[1] This subtle body, incorporeal in character, receives the impressions made by deeds performed in the course of its various migrations. The form of the new embodiment is determined by it. It is the real seat of pleasure and pain.[2] The liṅga, though distinct from puruṣa, constitutes the character and essential being of the person. In it are contained the saṁskāras or predispositions. The liṅga is compared to an actor who plays various parts. It has this power, because it shares in the property of all-pervadingness which belongs to prakṛti. The conjunction of puruṣa with the liṅga is the cause, as well as the symptom, of misery, and persists until the attainment of true insight. While the subtle bodies are continuant, those produced from father and mother perish at death.[3] The union of the liṅga with the gross body constitutes birth, and its separation from it death. Except in the case of those who have attained freedom, the existence and rebirth of liṅga last for a whole world-period, at the end of which come quiescence and equilibrium. But, when creation is renewed, it starts out again on its career.

The investiture in successive frames is determined by the dispositions (bhāvas), which are the results of acts which are impossible without bodies subtle and gross.[4] This mutual dependence, like that of seed and sprout, is beginningless, and need not be regarded as a defect.[5] The evolution of buddhi,

1 S.K., 41. We cannot therefore say that mere buddhi, ahaṁkāra, manas will do, since these require the support of a subtle body. Some construe this passage as demanding the existence of a gross body, but this interpretation is not satisfactory in view of the obvious fact that during the transition from one life to another the subtle body subsists without the gross. Vijñānabhikṣu suggests that there is a third kind of body called adhiṣṭhānaśarīra formed of a finer form of the gross elements and serving as the receptacle of the subtle body (S.P.B., iii. 12).

2 S.P.S., iii. 8.

3 S.K., 39.

4 S.K., 52. While Vācaspati and Nārāyaṇa interpret the relation of liṅga and bhāva as one of experiencing and the objects experienced, Vijñānabhikṣu takes it to refer to the relation of intellect and its conditions.

5 Thus there are three kinds of creation : corporeal creation (bhautikasarga), consisting of souls with gross bodies, comprising eight orders of superior beings and five of inferior, which, together with the human kind, which forms a class apart, constitute the fourteen orders of being distributed in the three worlds, the creation of the subtle bodies (tanmātrasarga), and

ahaṁkāra, the subtle body and the gross body, is a physical process, and the result is also a physical one, though some of these products are of so fine a structure that they cannot be perceived by the ordinary senses. The physical organisation becomes a living being, a god, man or animal, when it is connected with a puruṣa.

Dharma and adharma are the products of prakṛti and attributes of the inner organ,[1] which help the formation of particular bodies and senses suited to the living beings, according to their place in the scale of development. The law of karma operates through the bhāvas or dispositions of buddhi.[2] Each soul is relative to its organism, and, according to its merit, can pass through all the grades of being from the lowest to the highest,[3] which are fourteen in number. We may get a bodily organism where our life is confined to the obscure sensations, and instincts of the animal or the unconscious movements of the plants. The plant world is also a field of experience.[4] All these products of prakṛti can only stunt, but not kill, the puruṣa within.

XIX

Is Sāṁkhya Atheistic?

We have seen how the elements of the Sāṁkhya were subordinated in the Upaniṣads and the *Bhagavadgītā* to an idealistic theism. While the Epic philosophy borrowed the cosmogony and the theory of the absolute passivity of puruṣa from the Sāṁkhya, it did not regard puruṣa and prakṛti as self-sufficient realities, but represented them as modes of one ultimate Brahman. In its classical form, however, the Sāṁkhya does not uphold theism. In its indifference to the supremacy of an absolute spirit, as well as in its doctrine

intellectual creation (pratyayasarga or bhāvasarga), consisting of the affections of intellect, its sentiments and faculties classified into four groups according as they obstruct, disable, satisfy and perfect the understanding (S.K., 53; S.P.S., iii. 46).

[1] S.P.S., v. 25; S.K., 43.

[2] S.K., 40, 43, 55; B.G., vii. 12; x. 4. 5. For the three kinds of bodies see S.P.S., v. 124.

[3] S.K., 44.

[4] S.P.S., v. 12.

of the relation of avidyā and the soul's entanglement in saṁsāra, the Sāṁkhya reminds us of Buddhism. It may well be that the attempt of the Sāṁkhya in its systematic form was to declare that a strict adoption of the rationalistic method did not lead us to the repudiation of the reality of selves.

The difficulties of creation are noticed. All actions are motived by self-interest or benevolence. God, who has all his interests fulfilled, can have no more selfish interests. If God is affected by selfish motives or desires, then he is not free; if he is free, then he would not involve himself in the act of creation.[1] To say that God is neither free nor fettered is to remove all basis for argument. The creation of the world cannot be regarded as an act of kindness, since the souls, prior to creation, have no pain from which they require to be released. If God were moved by goodwill, he would have created only happy creatures. If it is said that differences of conduct require God to deal with men in accordance with these differences, the answer is that the law of karma is the operative principle and the aid of God is unnecessary.[2] Again, material things cannot issue from an immaterial spirit. The eternal existence of the puruṣas is inconsistent with the infinity and creatorship of God. Theism seems to weaken belief in immortality, for if we have a creator of souls, then souls have a beginning and need not be immortal. The Sāṁkhya, which is anxious to abide within the strict limits of knowledge, holds that the reality of God cannot be established by logical proofs.[3] There is no sensible evidence or inferential knowledge or scriptural testimony of Īśvara. The Sāṁkhya is not atheistic in the sense that it establishes that there is no God. It only shows that there is no reason for supposing there is one.[4] The passages which are apparently theistic in the scriptures are really eulogies of freed souls.[5]

The old gods of the Vedic hymns manage to live under the ægis of the rationalistic Sāṁkhya. They are, however, not eternal in nature. The Sāṁkhya accepts the theory of a

[1] S.P.S., i. 93–94. [2] S.P.S., v. 1. See *Tattvakaumudī*, 57.

[3] S.P.S., v. 12. Cp. Darwin: "The mystery of the beginning of all things is insoluble by us, and I for one must be content to remain an agnostic" (*Life and Letters of Charles Darwin*).

[4] It does not say Īśvarābhāvāt, but only "Īśvarāsiddheḥ."

[5] S.P.S., i. 95; iii. 54–6.

Vyavasthāpaka Īśvara, who, at the time of creation, arranges the successive developments of prakṛti. Śiva, Viṣṇu, etc., are regarded as phenomenal.[1] The Sāṁkhya admits the existence of an emergent Īśvara previously absorbed in prakṛti.[2] The souls, who, through the practice of unattachment to mahat, etc., become absorbed in prakṛti, are said to be all-knowers and all-doers.[3] These are the characteristics we generally attribute to God, but, as the Sāṁkhya holds that prakṛti is always under the rule of another,[4] these gods are not independent.

The unconscious but immanent teleology of prakṛti, which reminds us of Leibniz's doctrine of pre-established harmony, is a crux in the Sāṁkhya philosophy. How does it happen that the evolution of prakṛti is adapted to the needs of spirits? Prakṛti without puruṣa is helpless, nor can puruṣa gain freedom without the aid of prakṛti. It is difficult to regard the two as entirely distinct. The analogy of the lame and the blind is unsound, since both are conscious and can take counsel together. But prakṛti is not conscious.[5] Again, in the end only the puruṣa is said to be liberated and not prakṛti. The metaphor of the magnet and the piece of iron is unavailing, since the permanence of the proximity of the puruṣa to prakṛti would involve an unceasing evolution. "The pradhāna being non-intelligent and the puruṣa indifferent, and there being no third principle to connect them, there can be no connection of the two."[6] The simile of the actress, who desists from the dance after exhibiting herself to the spectators, does not seem to be rightly conceived. Puruṣa falls by error into a confusion with prakṛti, and the remedy seems to be to make the confusion worse confounded. The evil is said to be removed by a full enjoyment thereof. The puruṣa is liberated when it gets disgusted with prakṛti's doings.

The later thinkers found it impossible to account for this harmony between the needs of puruṣa and the acts of prakṛti, and so attribute the function of guiding the development of

[1] S.P.S., iii. 57.

[2] Prakṛtilīnasya janyeśvarasya siddhiḥ (S.P.B., iii. 57).

[3] Sarvavit, sarvakartā (S.P.S., iii. 56).

[4] S.P.S. Vṛtti and S.P.B., iii. 55, and Y.S., iv. 3.

[5] S.B., ii. 2. 7.

[6] S.B., ii. 2. 7.

prakṛti, by removing the barriers, to God.[1] They thus improve on the original plan of the system. The Sāṁkhya requires a comprehensive life, which allots to different puruṣas their respective organisations. Vācaspati holds that the evolution of prakṛti is directed by an omniscient spirit. Vijñānabhikṣu thinks that Kapila's denial of Īśvara is a regulative principle, which he insisted on to induce men to withdraw themselves from the excessive contemplation of an eternal god, which would impede the rise of true discriminative knowledge. He also regards atheism as an unnecessarily extravagant claim (prauḍhivāda) to show that the system does not stand in need of a theistic hypothesis. He sometimes explains the atheism of the Sāṁkhya as a concession to popular views,[2] and suggests also very naïvely that it is propounded with the set object of misleading evil men and preventing them from attaining true knowledge.[3] He attempts to explain away the Sāṁkhya attitude to God. In several places[4] Vijñānabhikṣu tries to reconcile the Sāṁkhya views with those of the Vedānta.[5] He admits the reality of a universal puruṣa. "He, the supreme, *i.e.* the generic universal, collective puruṣa, possesses the power of knowing all and doing all, being like the lodestone, the mover to activity by means of mere proximity."[6] The Sāṁkhya, however, overlooks the fundamental problem of metaphysics by not being sufficiently thorough. It has had a misleading idea that the inquiry was irrelevant for its purpose.

XX

General Estimate

The student of the history of philosophic thought finds a constant recurrence of the fundamental problems, however

[1] Vācaspati, Vijñānabhikṣu and Nāgeśa. Cp. Vācaspati: "Īśvarasyāpi dharmādhiṣṭhānārtham pratibandhāpanaya eva vyāpāraḥ." *Tattvavaiśāradī*, iv. 3.

[2] Abhyupagamavāda (S.P.B., Introduction).

[3] Pāpinām jñānapratibandhārtham.

[4] S.P.B., i. 122; v. 61, 65; vi. 52, 66.

[5] Prakṛti, the material cause of the world, is said to be undivided (avibhakta) from Brahman, which is different from the souls (S.P.B., i. 69; iii. 66).

[6] Sa hi paraḥ puruṣasāmānyaṁ sarvajñānaśaktimat sarvakartṛtāśaktimac ca (S.P.B., iii. 57). See also S.P.B., v. 12.

varied their statements and however widely separated in time and place their authors may be. The problems do not alter, nor even the answers, so much in themselves as in their application. When the scientific theory of evolution discovers an orderly process of development from the crudest germ of life to the fullest flower of man, it is not the hypothesis that is new, for that is as old as the Upaniṣads in India or Anaximander, Heraclitus and Empedocles in Greece; but what is new is the experimental study of details and verification of the theory by modern science. The Sāṁkhya theory, which offers some satisfaction to a need which the mind of man experiences, is a philosophical conception arrived at more under the moulding influence of metaphysical tendencies than under the scientific impulse of the observation of objective existence. But the philosophical view of the Sāṁkhya, with its dualism of puruṣa and prakṛti and a plurality of infinite puruṣas, each unlimited and yet not interfering with the unlimitedness of the others, though existing out of and independent of them, cannot be regarded as a satisfactory solution of the main problem of philosophy. The dualistic realism is the result of a false metaphysics. It will be well for us to understand at the outset that the puruṣa and the prakṛti are not facts of experience, but abstractions set up beyond experience to account for it.

The fundamental truth intended by the Sāṁkhya theory of puruṣa is that consciousness is not a form of energy like motion, heat and electricity. The most advanced science has only established a relation in which certain nervous processes are co-ordinated with certain conscious occurrences. While we cannot derive consciousness from material existence, the former, in its empirical form, is always mediated by the latter. To overlook this essential relation is a mistake. The puruṣa is said to be something over and above the continuum of mental states. Such a puruṣa is never experienced and does not enter into the view of an empirical metaphysics. If we separate from puruṣa everything that is material, remove from it every attribute of empirical objects, we lose hold of everything by which we could positively characterise it. The puruṣa is defined negatively as eternal and indivisible, "without variableness or shadow of turning," as resting ever in its own pure self-identity. It is deprived even of ideal activity, and it becomes just the possibility of a pure consciousness. It is postulated as an element in our personality to illumine the mental processes, which are the outcome of the physical organisation. It does not figure among the *dramatis personæ* of the play it witnesses. The spirit which the art of prakṛti serves is never on the stage, though it is said to be an implication of all experience. What we observe is the jīva, which is not pure puruṣa, but puruṣa qualified by prakṛti. Every soul known to us is an embodied soul. We are breaking up the unity of the jīva when we regard it as a juxtaposition of a puruṣa complete in itself, and standing only in accidental relations to the things and beings without, which are simply organisations of the products of prakṛti. If we are loyal to the facts of experience, we shall have to admit that a pure self, emptied of all contents, is a fiction of the imagination.

The Sāṁkhya arguments for the existence of the puruṣa turn out to be proofs for the existence of the empirical individuals and not transcendental subjects. This fact comes out more clearly in the Sāṁkhya theory of the plurality of puruṣas. The chief argument for the plurality of puruṣas is that, if there were only one puruṣa, when its buddhi returns from its delusion the cosmic process would cease. But nothing of the kind happens. The cosmic play continues for the infinite number of bound souls, even when a few are released The argument that if the puruṣas were not many but only one, then all individual souls existing in bodies would have to die at the same time and be born at the same time, assumes that birth and death apply to the eternal puruṣa, which is not allowed by the Sāṁkhya system. We can only infer that the embodied souls are many and different, since they do not rise or die together. If one man sees a particular object, others do not see it at the same time, simply because each jīva has its own separate organism and interests.[1] There does not seem to be any need to pass from the manyness of empirical souls, which all philosophers admit, to the manyness of eternal selves which the Sāṁkhya upholds. The Sāṁkhya puruṣa is altogether distinct from prakṛti. We cannot ascribe to it any features such as personality or creative force. All

[1] S.S.S.S., xii. 68–69.

definite characterisation of puruṣas is due to confusion. The self is without attributes or qualities, without parts, imperishable, motionless, absolutely inactive and impassive, unaffected by pleasure or pain or any other emotion. All change, all character belong to prakṛti. There does not seem to be any basis for the attribution of distinctness to puruṣas. If each puruṣa has the same features of consciousness, all-pervadingness, if there is not the slightest difference between one puruṣa and another, since they are free from all variety, then there is nothing to lead us to assume a plurality of puruṣas. Multiplicity without distinction is impossible. That is why even the Sāṁkhya commentators like Gauḍapāda are inclined to the theory of one puruṣa.[1] That there must be an enjoyer of things shows that there is an enjoying soul and not a passive puruṣa. The separate allotments of form, birth, death, abode and fortune lead only to the empirical multiplicity of jīvas. From the different conditions of the three modes we cannot infer a radical pluralism, since they are only the modifications of prakṛti. The Sāṁkhya view of prakṛti as moving for the sake of the enjoyment and release of puruṣas, it is said, requires that there should be many puruṣas. If there were only one puruṣa there would be only one buddhi. But let us remember that the pure puruṣa is immortal and indifferent and has no longing for anything. The play of prakṛti is not for the sake of the ever-free puruṣas, but only for the sake of the reflected egos. There is no dispute about the manyness of the latter. Superintendence and yearning for release hold good of selves which suffer from want of discrimination. The different arguments prove the plurality of actual souls in relation to prakṛti and not of the puruṣa we reach by way of abstraction. Plurality would involve limitations, and an absolute immortal, eternal and unconditioned puruṣa cannot be more than one. If the being of puruṣa were necessary for the play of prakṛti, one puruṣa will do.[2] Apparently, the Sāṁkhya is compelled to concede the

[1] See Gauḍapāda on S.K., 11 and 44.

[2] Regarding the plurality of all-pervading selves, whose nature is pure intelligence devoid of qualities and of unsurpassable excellence, Śaṁkara says: " The doctrine that all selves are of the nature of intelligence, and that there is no difference between them in the point of proximity (to prakṛti), etc. (and non-activity, or audāsīnya, of the selves), implies that if

reality of puruṣa on account of its explanatory value. Every conscious state belongs to a conscious individual. We have never a feeling but that of the self feeling in a certain way. But how can we distinguish the self of puruṣa from its experiences? While we cannot describe mental facts without assuming a mental subject, we cannot describe them adequately if we make the subject an empty focus of an immaterial substance or an unchanging principle of universality utterly unrelated to the particular facts which it is said to relate. To explain the coherence of our conscious experiences by the presence of puruṣa is to restate the characteristic nature of the fact and hypostatise it as a causal prius of its own existence. Puruṣa is not a sort of supernatural hold-all to take in all conscious experiences. Throughout the Sāṁkhya there is a confusion between the puruṣa and the jīva. If puruṣa is eternally unchanging, inactive and isolated, then it cannot be the cogniser or the enjoyer subject to error resting on superposition.[1] But these qualities cannot belong to prakṛti, since they are attributes of intelligent beings. Superposition (adhyāsa) means the attribution by an intelligent being of the qualities of one object to another. So the conception of jīva is developed. Jīvas exist as individuals, but we cannot conclude that puruṣas have a separate existence of their own in another world beyond space and time. Puruṣa is the perfect spirit, not to be confused with the particular human spirit. The puruṣa is certainly in me, this individual me, as my very core and substance; and the jīva, or the individual, with all his irrational caprices and selfish aims, is but a distortion of puruṣa. To say that every jīva is striving to realise its puruṣa means that every jīva is potentially puruṣa, every man is potentially divine.

Prakṛti is also an abstraction from experience. It is the limiting concept on the object side, the name for the unknown and hypothetical cause of the object world. If the real is the experienced, then prakṛti is the unrealisable abstraction

one self is connected with pleasure and pain, all selves will be so connected" (S.B., ii. 3. 50). "It is impossible to maintain that there exist many all-pervading selves, since there are no parallel instances" (S.B., ii. 3. 53). The selves, if equally omnipresent, would all occupy the same place.

1 S.K., 20–21.

of pure object. This character of prakṛti is admitted when it is denoted by the word "avyakta," or the unmanifested. It is mere emptiness, being the formless substrate of things. The most general features of the object world are summed up in the conception of prakṛti. Every part of physical and mental nature symbolises the tension [1] between a quality and its opposite, giving rise to activity. If change is a passage from the potential to the actual, it may be regarded as a struggle of the form to realise itself by overcoming the obstacles to its realisation. The three guṇas represent the three moments of all being; and prakṛti, said to be the equilibrium of the three guṇas, is but the framework of all existence. As Mahādeva says, it is not something which underlies the guṇas, but is the triad of the guṇas.[2] The guṇas are the forms (rūpa) of prakṛti and not its attributes (dharma). What is really a conceptual abstraction becomes, when viewed empirically, an undifferentiated manifold containing the potentialities of all things.

The Sāṁkhya account of prakṛti and the guṇas inclines one to the view that prakṛti and its development are not real in the ultimate sense of the term. The three guṇas imply the necessary conditions of all existence. Every stage of the evolution of prakṛti involves an ideal or purpose (sattva), a striving to realise it (rajas), and a materiality (tamas) which are not abstractions but definite positive existents, at any rate in the opinion of Vijñānabhikṣu. Nothing can exist without these. They are, according to the Sāṁkhya, in a natural state of conflict. Prakṛti possesses contrary capacities. It has not only the tendency to activity, but also the contrary tendency to oppose activity. Tamas is the restraining force. As offering resistance to activity, it becomes the basis of activity also. The existent, or that which has the three guṇas, represents at best a situation and not reality. To look upon sattva, rajas and tamas as subsisting in a state of contradiction and, at the same time, as constituents of the object, is possible only if we admit that every object in which the guṇas participate is nothing but a conflict, an unreal

[1] Viṣamatva. See *Maitrāyaṇī Up.*, v. 2.

[2] S.P.S., Vṛttisāra, i. 61. See also vi. 39. Cp. Guṇā eva prakṛtiśabdavācyā na tu tadatiriktā prakṛtir asti (*Yogavārttika*, ii. 18).

existent trying to transcend itself. In the world of prakṛti there is no individual which is entire and harmonious, for it is always a question of one guṇa keeping in subjection the others. Even when sattva prevails tamas is there, though in bondage to sattva. Evolution is nothing more than the domination of the one or the other, or the suppression of the one or the other. But suppression is not supersession. No one guṇa can extirpate the others. We cannot conceive of a state where sattva, rajas and tamas exist in themselves, having overcome the others, or exist in harmony. In pralaya they seem to be in absolute harmony, but it is only seeming; for prakṛti in pralaya is said to be in a state of tension. It has the three guṇas; but since they are equally strong, no evolution takes place. We have evolution when one of these guṇas becomes more dominating. Evolution is unceasing so long as harmony does not prevail. The Sāṁkhya philosophy does not contemplate a state of perfection, where the three guṇas will be in harmony. The original state of prakṛti cannot be said to be a harmony; it is really a suspense, a condition in which prakṛti may be said to be neither active nor inactive. The incompatibles seem to stand in absolute opposition. It is not so much possibility but its limit, the impossibility, where possibilities are sharply divided into contraries. Prakṛti cannot, in any sense, be regarded as a unity or a harmony. It is not the concrete universal which binds together the different existences, or the bare unity of being which characterises them all. It is a state of tension of the guṇas. Puruṣa is necessary to introduce some order and meaning into the region of prakṛti. The influence of puruṣa makes the suspense disappear; one or the other guṇa becomes supreme, holding the others in restraint. There can never be a state of perfection. Harmony is an impossibility with the guṇas. Where there is not a state of perfection, change, evolution or involution is bound to appear. The world of prakṛti is not the real in itself. Its possession of the three guṇas brings out its self-contradictory character. Since perfection or reality is that in which the opposition of the three guṇas is overcome and transcended, and such is not the character of prakṛti; it is not the real. The very endlessness of the process of prakṛti marks it off as unreal and relative.

The Advaita Vedānta faces this conclusion and regards the world of prakṛti as māyā.

If we admit the Sāṁkhya view of prakṛti and its complete independence of puruṣa, then it will be impossible to account for the evolution of prakṛti. We do not know how latent potentialities become fruitful without any consciousness to direct them. As Sāṁkhya says, there can be no activity where an intelligent principle is not present. "The three guṇas of the Sāṁkhyas, when in a state of equipoise, form the pradhāna. Beyond the pradhāna there exists no external principle which could either impel the pradhāna to activity or restrain it from activity. The puruṣa is indifferent, neither moves to nor restrains from action. As therefore the pradhāna stands in no relation, it is impossible to see why it should sometimes modify itself into mahat and sometimes not."[1] "Nor can we say that pradhāna transforms itself into mahat, etc., even as grass does into milk, for grass requires other causes which are present only in a cow and not in a bull."[2] The argument that from limited effects an unlimited cause can be inferred does not necessarily prove the reality of prakṛti composed of the three guṇas. The guṇas limit one another and are therefore effects. If the guṇas are unlimited, no inequality can arise, and so no effects can originate.[3] If the three guṇas in equipoise form pradhāna, and if they do not stand in the relation of mutual superiority or inferiority, they will not enter into a relation of mutual subserviency, since then they would forfeit their absolute independence. Since there is no extraneous principle to stir up the guṇas into an unstable state, activity is impossible.[4] Unintelligent prakṛti cannot spontaneously produce effects which serve the

[1] S.B., ii. 2. 4. See also S.B., *Praśna Up.*, vi. 3.

[2] S.B., ii. 2. 5.

[3] R.B., ii. 2. 1.

[4] S.B., ii. 2. 8. Rāmānuja says: "If the Sāṁkhyas maintain that the origination of the world results from a certain relation between principal and subordinate entities (aṅgāṅgibhāva) which depends on the relative inferiority and superiority of the guṇas according to the difference of the abodes of the several guṇas (S.K., 16), then, as in the pralaya state, the three guṇas are in a state of equipoise, none of them being superior or inferior to the others, that relation of superiority and subordination cannot then exist, and therefore the world cannot originate. If it be maintained that, even in the pralaya state, there is a certain inequality, it would follow therefrom that creation is eternal" (R.B., ii. 2. 6).

purposes of puruṣas. Intelligence cannot be attributed to prakṛti, for that would be to contradict the central feature of the Sāṁkhya.[1] The scriptures do not tell us of a prakṛti undirected by intelligence as the cause of world evolution. The Sāṁkhya theory admits the presence of design in the evolution, for the final cause of the activity of prakṛti is to enable the puruṣas to gain their freedom. Both the efficient and the final causation attributed to prakṛti is inconceivable on the hypothesis of a non-intelligent prakṛti. It is sometimes suggested that the activity of prakṛti may be automatic or habitual. The horse drags the carriage by habit, while the driver does nothing but watch the movement of the horse. But habit presupposes past acts. The horses are trained by intelligent men. But the guidance of puruṣa is disallowed on the Sāṁkhya theory. The analogy of the unconscious rise of milk for the nourishment of the calf is ineffective, since a distinction is to be made between proximate and ultimate causes.[2] To state a fact is not to remove the mystery. We find certain laws to which things conform, but unless we posit the ultimate source of all these laws the explanation is incomplete. The simile of the blind and the lame man is misleading, since both of them are intelligent and active agents who can devise plans to realise their common purpose. Prakṛti and puruṣa have no common purpose. Unconscious prakṛti cannot suffer; inactive puruṣa cannot experience suffering. How can the two co-operate for the redemption of the world? The question cannot be answered so long as the Sāṁkhya declines to admit a higher unity.[3]

Subject and object are aspects of a higher unity, distinctions within a whole. If we are at the empirical level, even then we shall have to say that all consciousness is consciousness

[1] S.B., ii. 2. 9.

[2] S.B., ii. 2. 3. Again: "The cow, which is an intelligent being, loves her calf, makes her milk flow by her wish to do so, and the milk is in addition drawn forth by the sucking of the calf."

[3] Vijñānabhikṣu, who is a theist, is able to account for the conjoint action of puruṣa and prakṛti. He writes: "Prakṛtisvātantryavādibhyām, sāṁkhyayogibhyām puruṣārthaprayuktā pravṛttiḥ, svayam eva puruṣeṇa ādyajīvena saṁyujyate . . . ayaskāntena lohavat . . . asmābhis tu prakṛtipuruṣasaṁyoga Īśvareṇa kriyate" (*Vijñānāmṛta*, i. 1. 2).

of an object and all reality is the object of consciousness. It is only in distinguishing ourselves from and relating ourselves to an objective world that we know the self at all. We deepen our consciousness of self in widening our experience of the world. If we assume the essential unrelatedness of subject and object, it would be impossible to pass from the one to the other. The unity of the two terms is the presupposition of their difference. It is simply due to our avidyā, our ignorance or want of reflection on the nature and conditions of experience, that we fail to recognise the ultimate oneness of subject and object. It is quite true that the dualistic conception of mind and object is natural to our minds, but a little reflection tells us that if the two are independent we require a *tertium quid* to connect the two. The moment we realise the utter unsatisfactoriness of this *tertium quid* hypothesis, we are left with the view that the two are aspects of one ultimate consciousness, which is the basis of all knowledge as well as existence. Failure to recognise this ultimate unity is the fundamental mistake of the Sāṁkhya theory.

All evidence that we have shows that dualism is not absolute, that puruṣa and prakṛti are not accidentally related. We may set down here a few details of the Sāṁkhya in support of this view. Prakṛti gives rise in the puruṣa to a knowledge of the true being at once of itself and of the world which it inhabits. Does this not bear witness to the unity which underlies the difference between the two ? Prakṛti becomes manifested only when it is related to the subject. It is unmanifested when it is unrelated to the subject.[1] If prakṛti is what it does,[2] then it is informed by puruṣa. In other words, the conception of prakṛti independent of puruṣa is an unthinkable, self-contradictory one. The Sāṁkhya says that prakṛti is equally primordial with puruṣa, being underived and independent. If we are to be accurate, we have to say that the puruṣa and the prakṛti are antagonistic, though mutually dependent articulations within the real. They are the necessary presuppositions of the creative evolution. If the womb of the eternal ground of prakṛti is not impregnated by the puruṣa, there can be no experience. The dust of

[1] S.P.S., i. 79.

[2] Prakarotīti prakṛtiḥ.

prakṛti must be enchanted by puruṣa if it is to evolve into its products. Again, the immanent teleology of prakṛti's evolution is traced to the influence of puruṣa. The development of prakṛti is regarded as the means for the realisation of the freedom of spirit. While the Sāṁkhya does not admit that prakṛti consciously designs and executes any plan, it still holds that the development of prakṛti is the execution of a plan designed to meet the ends of spirit. What prakṛti, the bare potentiality of objects, becomes, depends upon what form or end of puruṣa is impressed upon it. Prakṛti, which is potentially everything, becomes this or that thing by the acquisition of form determined by the puruṣas. Though puruṣa is not anywhere in the chain of prakṛti, it is equally related to all its links. Its influence not only starts the evolution of prakṛti, but continually maintains it. If an error of judgment had not thrust the puruṣa into the playhouse, and if our deluded minds had not watched the performance of prakṛti, there would be no action of prakṛti at all.

While the dualism of puruṣa and prakṛti involves a division of the consciousness of man from the other elements of his nature, which makes knowledge, life and morality baffling mysteries, the latter are rendered intelligible by the Sāṁkhya, simply because it assumes the exact opposite of what it avows to itself, *viz.* the unity of human nature. We have already seen that if buddhi were unspiritual and unconscious, it could not even reflect consciousness. Things belonging to two different planes of existence cannot act as original and reflection. Puruṣa cannot be said to experience the states of buddhi, since its reflection in buddhi is unreal. The Sāṁkhya account of the relation of puruṣa to buddhi suggests the kinship between the two, and not their utter opposition. The most intimate point of contact between puruṣa and prakṛti is in buddhi, which discriminates and co-ordinates the operations of cosmic energy and, by the aid of ahaṁkāra, identifies the witnessing self with these activities of thought, sense and action. It is buddhi in its sattva aspect that has to strive for the discriminative knowledge. When buddhi realises that the identification is a mistake, and perceives that all is mere disturbance of the equilibrium of the guṇas, buddhi turns away from the false show which it has been supporting. Puruṣa ceases to associate itself with the cosmic dance, and prakṛti loses her power to reflect herself in the puruṣa; for the effects of ahaṁkāra are destroyed, buddhi becomes indifferent, and the guṇas fall into equilibrium. If buddhi is caught in the confusion, the puruṣa is said to be in trouble; if buddhi clears up the confusion, the puruṣa is said to be saved. Buddhi seems to function practically as puruṣa. It is, therefore, more akin to the subject than to the object.[1]

The ethical consequences of the view are equally significant. If prakṛti be completely mechanical, then freedom of the will is an illusion, since the will is a product of prakṛti. Ethical distinctions become meaningless, since vice and virtue are products like vitriol or sugar. But the Sāṁkhya will not admit that a human being cannot be blamed for killing any more than the stone for destroying. There is something in man which is absent in the stone or the plant. There is something more than mechanism in prakṛti, otherwise it cannot gain for us freedom. The Sāṁkhya asserts that the knowledge which saves is a gift of prakṛti.

The imagined connection between puruṣa and prakṛti, traced to aviveka or non-discrimination, will not be possible if the two are not related to each other. It is difficult to conceive how the false conception of a connection between two entities, which refuse to have anything to do with each other, arises. The connection must be real enough to further the development of prakṛti; it must be real enough to enable the puruṣa to recognise its purity and isolation through the instrumentality of prakṛti. That by which the puruṣa is helped cannot be simply external to it. The Sāṁkhya is obliged to bring the two, puruṣa and prakṛti, nearer to each other than its insistence on dualism would make us believe. The mutual adaptation of puruṣa and prakṛti is simply mar-

[1] Vidyāraṇya, in his *Vivaraṇaprameyasaṁgraha* (p. 63) says: "Were things as the Sāṁkhyas represent them, ahaṁkāra (the self-sense) and all that depends on it, all action, all enjoyment, and so on, would present themselves to consciousness in a purely objective form, 'This is a doer,' 'This is an enjoyer,' and not as something superimposed on the self; so that the actual forms of consciousness, 'I am a doer,' 'I am an enjoyer,' would never arise" (*Indian Thought*, vol. i. p. 376).

vellous. To give an example, by the stress of what we may call its unconscious desire, prakṛti develops little mechanical toys through which puruṣa could see the spectacle of the world. Conscious spirit and unconscious nature are two stages of one development. It is the jīva that strives for liberation ; for the finite consciousness presupposes an infinite consciousness, finitised by the nature of prakṛti ; and the finite spirit realises its true being by discovering the infinite consciousness within it.

When the Sāṁkhya breaks up the process of reality into its two articulations of the mechanism of matter and the freedom of spirit, it is to be noted that these reals are conceptual and not historical. They tell us that in the world of experience we have two different tendencies inseparably related. Prakṛti and puruṣa are the two aspects of all experience. If puruṣa is of the nature of consciousness, prakṛti is non-conscious, being opposed in character to puruṣa. These two, consciousness and non-consciousness, are the two aspects of the one becoming. The real is neither mere puruṣa nor mere prakṛti. These are non-existent, since whatever exists has name and form. Matterless form and formless matter are the upper and the lower limits of the scale of beings, though neither of them exists. The first existent is mahat, from which the rest is said to evolve. This mahat is not pure matter, but formed matter. Mahat is the determinate manifestation of the indeterminate prakṛti. If both puruṣa and prakṛti do not co-operate, we cannot have mahat. It is the first product, or empirical existence, which arises when prakṛti is informed by puruṣa. The God whom the Sāṁkhya admits is not pure subject, but has in him the potentiality of object. If we trace back the products of the world to their highest category, we get an all-conscious soul containing the potentiality of all things, *i.e.* a subject-object. All things that constitute the universe are subject-object. Both in God and in the lowest matter we have the two tendencies of puruṣa and prakṛti. Those in which matter predominates come lower down, and those in which form is predominant come higher up. In proportion to the success of spirit does the resultant being stand high in the scale of creation. In the lowest stage of matter we have the pure externality of things to things, though even this realm of nature serves the ends of spirit. We have a gradual ascent in plants, animals and men. While the plant stands low in the scale of organic life, the animal with its sensitive part comes higher up ; man is higher still with his rational-volitional nature. All things continually strive to rise higher and higher. The theory of development regards the individual, not as a permanent result, but as a transitory phase leading up to the revelation of the perfect puruṣa. These opposites are mutually dependent, through antagonistic movements of the one concrete becoming. If we separate the puruṣa from prakṛti, it becomes unreal ; so also prakṛti separated from puruṣa. All things combine puruṣa and prakṛti and struggle to reveal the puruṣa more and more, and this struggle is the process of the world.

When the Sāṁkhya thinkers hold that the highest product of experience is not ultimate, they mean that the world of experience, in which the two tendencies struggle for the domination of the one on the other, requires some other principle as its logical basis. Their suggestion that what is behind and beyond this world of strife is puruṣa on the one side and prakṛti on the other, possible subjects and possible objects eternally opposed to one another, does not do justice either to the facts of experience or to the principles of the Sāṁkhya. If the cosmic spirit (mahat) gives rise to the plurality of individual subjects (ahaṁkāra) and individual objects (tanmātrāṇi), it is unnecessary to postulate, behind mahat, a plurality of subjects and objects. If all the objects are reduced to one prakṛti, the subjects may also be reduced to one universal spirit, which in the empirical individuals of the world has to contend with the manifold impediments of matter. If the impassive consciousness of puruṣa and the incessant movement of prakṛti are regarded as independent of each other, the problem of philosophy is insoluble. But the Sāṁkhya philosophy becomes plausible, simply because it describes their different relations as if they were the different aspects of the single eternal energy of spirit. The wonderful way in which they help each other shows that the opposites fall within a whole. The transparent duality rests upon some unity above itself. If anything may be regarded as the presupposition of all experience, it is a universal spirit on which both the tendencies of puruṣa and prakṛti rest, for the two, puruṣa and prakṛti, do not stand confronting and contradicting each other. In the becoming of the world, the contradiction is resolved. It shows that the two things rest on a fundamental identity. The Sāṁkhya insistence on puruṣa, when it is not confused with the jīva, amounts to nothing more than the recognition of a pure and perfect presence, not divided by the divisions of things, not affected by the stress and struggle of the cosmic manifestation, within it all, while superior to it all. The absolute self is too great to be limited by the movement in time and space which it supports. But the world hangs on it. Prakṛti represents, in Hegel's phrase, "the portentous power of the negative," which brings the world into being. If we start with an original unbridgeable chasm, the unity of the world cannot be rendered intelligible. The moment it becomes conscious of an object the absolute spirit becomes the supreme subject acting on the object which is called mahat.[1] Vijñānabhikṣu quotes from the *Mahābhārata*[2] a verse which declares that prakṛti, which changes, is called avidyā and puruṣa, which is free from all change, is vidyā.[3] The Sāṁkhya is anxious to make out that prakṛti is not something subjective or unreal, since an unreal entity cannot give rise to real bondage.[4] However that be, prakṛti is the negative of puruṣa, the not-self of the self. The witnessing by the self of the not-self[5] is the affirmation by the self of the not-self or prakṛti. This affirmation gives to it all the existence which it has. The rise of the object is correlated with the rise of the subject. This self-conscious spirit, correlated with the rise of mahat,

[1] *Matsya Purāṇa* says that Brahmā, Viṣṇu and Maheśvara are produced from the principle of mahat according as it is dominated by the guṇas of rajas, sattva and tamas respectively.

Savikārāt pradhānāt tu mahat tattvam prajāyate
Mahān ity yataḥ khyātir lokānāṁ jāyate sadā.
Guṇebhyaḥ kṣobhyamāṇebhyas trayo devā vijajñire
Ekamūrtis trayo bhāgā brahmaviṣṇumaheśvarāḥ.

See *Indian Philosophical Review*, vol. ii. fn. to p. 200; also *Bhāgavata*, i. iii. 223.

[2] 12. 11419.

[3] S.P.B., i. 69.

[4] Cp. Na hi svāpnarajjvā bandhanaṁ dṛṣṭam (S.P.B., i. 20).

[5] Prakṛtim paśyati puruṣaḥ (S.K., 65).

is not this or that jīva, since it continues to force prakṛti into activity, however many jīvas might obtain release. Through the control of the supreme Lord, prakṛti is progressively pluralised, even as a single throb of Bergson's *élan vital* is broken into its manifold reverberations in nature. Vijñānabhikṣu refers to a supreme person produced at the beginning of creation with the principle of mahat as his upādhi, or external investment.[1] This supreme personality combines within himself the peace and bliss, the calm and silence of puruṣa, on the one hand, and the jarring multiplicity, the strife and suffering of prakṛti, on the other. The supreme contains within itself all lives and bodies,[2] and each separate individual being is nothing more than a wave of this boundless surge, a fragment of the world-soul. Īśvara-mahat is the unity at the start, in which the two different tendencies are fused into one. So the Vedānta, as well as the Purāṇas, looks upon prakṛti as dependent on the supreme reality.[3] Only such a view can make the Sāṁkhya philosophy more consistent. The Sāṁkhya does not rise to the truth of monistic idealism, but is content to remain at the level of mere understanding, which insists upon the distinction between being and non-being, and regards the opposition between the two as real and their identity as unreal. It was not able to realise all that is involved in the questions it raised—questions the difficulty and importance of which have been brought to light by ages of conflict and controversy—still less to reach a satisfactory solution of them. Yet withal it is a great effort of the human mind to reach a comprehensive view of the universe in which no element of reality is suppressed or mutilated. The different aspects of things must be clearly defined and distinguished ere their true relations can be seen, and the Sāṁkhya analysis of experience prepared the ground for a more adequate philosophy.

[1] S.P.B., v. 12.

[2] The mahat of the Sāṁkhya is identified in the fourth chapter of the *Vāyu Purāṇa* with Īśvara or Brahmā. Cp. *Viṣṇu Purāṇa*: "Avijñeyam brahmāgre samavartata." It is the divine mind in the creative mood, the source of the universe (jagadyoni).

[3] In the *Viṣṇu Purāṇa* (i. 2) it is described as Kāryakāraṇaśaktiyukta. It is the effect of the supreme Lord and the cause of the rest of the universe. *Cūlikā Up.* speaks of prakṛti as "Vikārajananīm māyām aṣṭarūpām ajām dhruvām." See also S.P.B., i. 26.

REFERENCES.

S. C. Banerjee : Sāṁkhya Philosophy.
Garbe : Sāṁkhyapravacanabhāṣya.
Garbe : Sāṁkhyasūtravṛtti.
Keith : Sāṁkhya System.
Nandalal Sinha : The Sāṁkhya Philosophy.
S.D.S., xiv and xv.
Seal : Positive Sciences of the Ancient Hindus.

CHAPTER V

THE YOGA SYSTEM OF PATAÑJALI

Introduction—Antecedents of the Yoga system—Date and literature—The Sāṁkhya and the Yoga—Psychology—The means of knowledge—The art of Yoga—Ethical preparation—The discipline of the body—Regulation of breath—Sense-control—Contemplation—Concentration—Freedom—Karma—Supernormal powers—Theism of the Yoga—Conclusion.

I

Introduction

The investigations of the Psychical Research Society into what are called "spiritualistic" phenomena have begun to shake the hardiest faith in the truths hitherto accepted in the name of science, that intelligence and memory are functions dependent on the integrity of the cerebral mechanism, which will disappear when that mechanism decays. Some thinkers are now beginning to believe that the brain is by no means indispensable for conscious activities. Psychologists tell us that the human mind has other perceptive faculties than those served by the five senses, and philosophers are slowly accepting the view that we have mental powers other than those of ratiocination and a memory conditioned by the brain. The ancient thinkers of India had a good working knowledge of what may be called the science of metapsychics, and were quite familiar with cryptesthesia and other kindred powers. They tell us that we can acquire the power of seeing and knowing without the help of the outer senses, and can become independent of the activity which we exercise through the physical senses and the brain. They assume that there is a wider world about us than we are normally able to apprehend.

When some day our eyes open to it, we may have an extension of our perception as stupendous as a blind man has when he first acquires sight. There are laws governing the acquisition of this larger vision and manifestation of latent powers. By following the principles of the Yoga, such as heightening the power of concentration, arresting the vagaries of mind by fixing one's attention on the deepest sources of strength, one can master one's soul even as an athlete masters his body. The Yoga helps us to reach a higher level of consciousness, through a transformation of the psychic organism, which enables it to get beyond the limits set to ordinary human experience. We discern in the Yoga those cardinal conceptions of Hindu thought, such as the supremacy of the psychic over the physical, the exaltation of silence and solitude, meditation and ecstasy, and the indifference to outer conditions, which make the traditional Hindu attitude to life appear so strange and fantastic to the modern mind. It is, however, conceded, by many who are acquainted with it, that it is a necessary corrective to our present mentality, overburdened with external things and estranged from the true life of spirit by humdrum toil, material greed and sensual excitement.

The word Yoga is used in a variety of senses.[1] It may simply mean "method."[2] It is often used in the sense of yoking.[3] In the Upaniṣads and the *Bhagavadgītā*, the soul in its worldly and sinful condition is said to live separate and estranged from the supreme soul. The root of all sin and suffering is separation, disunion, estrangement. To be rid of sorrow and sin, we must attain spiritual unification, the consciousness of two in one, or Yoga. In Patañjali, Yoga does not mean union, but only effort, or, as Bhoja says, separation (viyoga) between puruṣa and prakṛti. It is the search for what Novalis called "our transcendental me," the divine and eternal part of our being. It also signifies exertion, strenuous endeavour, and so came to be used for the system

[1] See I.P., p. 532.

[2] B.G., iii. 3.

[3] See I.P., p. 532. See R.V., i. 34. 9; vii. 67. 8; iii. 27. 11; x. 30. 11; x. 114. 9; iv. 24. 4; i. 5. 3; i. 30. 7; Śat. Brāh., xiv. 7. 1, 11. According to Yājñavalkya, the conjunction of the individual and the supreme souls is called Yoga. Saṁyogo yoga ity ukto jīvātmaparamātmanor iti (S.D.S., xv).

of the restraint of the senses and the mind.[1] Though it is sometimes used as a synonym for the end of samādhi, it is more often employed to indicate the way of reaching it. Passages are not wanting where it signifies the supreme power possessed by God.[2] Yoga, according to Patañjali, is a methodical effort to attain perfection, through the control of the different elements of human nature, physical and psychical. The physical body, the active will and the understanding mind are to be brought under control. Patañjali insists on certain practices which are intended to cure the body of its restlessness and free it from its impurities. When we secure through these practices increased vitality, prolonged youth and longevity, these are to be employed in the interests of spiritual freedom. The other methods are employed to purify and tranquillise citta. The main interest of Patañjali is not metaphysical theorising, but the practical motive of indicating how salvation can be attained by disciplined activity.[3]

II

Antecedents

That we can secure many physical and mental powers which are not found in ordinary men, by means of discipline, that restraint of bodily and mental activities helps us to gain release from suffering, is an old view in India. Crude conceptions of the value of ecstasy and hypnotic trance are to be met with in the *Ṛg-Veda*, which also

---

[1] Y.S., i. 1.

[2] B.G., ix. 5. See also Baladeva's *Prameyaratnāvali*, p. 14.

[3] The *Yogatattva Up*. speaks of four kinds of Yoga: Mantrayoga, Layayoga, Haṭhayoga and Rājayoga. Patañjali's Yoga is of the last kind, since it deals at length with the process of stilling the mind and attaining samādhi. Haṭhayoga holds that bodily activities can be mastered. Bodily control is a part of Patañjali's Yoga. Mantrayoga is based on faith-healing. While the Christian thinkers who practise this method attribute the influence to the Christian faith and ministry, there is evidence that faith-cure is not confined to any one form of religion. M. Coué reminds us of the ancient medicine man. Cure by faith is not interference with the order of nature by the direct hand of God or penetration of some secondary supernatural essence. Cure by mantras or incantations is possible only in cases where the disease is nervous and the mind is deranged under a baffled will or an overpowering conviction or some obsession or dislocation born of a mental shock. The scoffer who says, "Show me a broken leg re-set by faith and I will listen to your pretensions," is not altogether impertinent.

mentions the word "muni."[1] According to it, the meditation on the divine light is a sacred act of devotion.[2] In the *Atharva Veda* the idea is very common that supernatural powers can be obtained through the practice of austerities.[3] Soon the conception of tapas appears, giving a more ethical character to the discipline. One has to give up all worldly enjoyments to fix one's mind on the eternal. The Upaniṣads assume the Yoga practice in the sense of a conscious inward search or striving after a true knowledge of reality. Meditation and concentration are insisted on,[4] since a direct knowledge of the self as subject is not possible. The Upaniṣads regard tapas and brahmacarya as virtues productive of great power.[5] Those Upaniṣads which speak of the Sāṁkhya theories refer to the Yoga practices as well. The *Kaṭha*, the *Śvetāśvatara* and the *Maitrāyaṇī* refer to the practical side of religious realisation, as distinct from the theoretical investigation of the Sāṁkhya. Yoga, as a technical term, occurs in the *Kaṭha*, the *Taittirīya*, the *Maitrāyaṇī*[6] Upaniṣads, but it cannot be said that the Yoga mentioned in them is identical with the Yoga of Patañjali. The idea of samādhi may have developed out of the Upaniṣad doctrine that compares the realisation of the Absolute or freedom from the things of empirical life to the deep dreamless sleep. The *Kaṭha Upaniṣad* speaks of the highest condition of Yoga as a state in which the senses, with mind and intellect, are brought to a standstill.[7] Not unnaturally, there were people who tried to induce artifically such states of trance. The *Maitrī Upaniṣad* speaks of a sixfold Yoga, and mentions the technical terms of Patañjali's system.[8] Apparently the Yoga of Patañjali was not perfected at the time of the early Upaniṣads, though we see its gradual growth in the later ones.

Buddha practised Yoga in both its senses. He underwent ascetic austerities and practised the highest contemplation. According to *Lalitavistara*, numberless forms of ascetic austerities were in vogue in Buddha's time.[9] Some of the teachers of Buddha, like Ālāra, were adepts in Yoga. The Buddhist Suttas are familiar with the Yoga methods of concentration. The four states of dhyāna of Buddhism correspond roughly to the four stages of conscious concentration in the classical Yoga.[10] According to Buddhism, the possession of the five qualities of faith, energy, thought, concentration and wisdom, enables one to attain the end of Yoga[11]; and the Yoga accepts this

---

[1] x. 136. 4-5. See I.P., p. 111.

[2] The Gayatrī is mentioned in the R.V., iii. 3. 9, 10. See also *Śukla Yajur Veda*, iii. 35; *Sāma Veda*, ii. 8. 12.

[3] I.P., p. 121.

[4] Bṛh. Up., iv. 14; iii. 5; iv. 4; Tait., i; Kaṭha, iii. 12; Praśna, v. 5.

[5] Chān. Up., iii. 17. 4; Bṛh., i. 2. 6; iii. 8. 10; Tait., i. 9. 1; iii. 2. 1; iii. 3. 1; Tait. Brāh., ii. 2. 3. 3; Śat. Brāh., xi. 5. 8. 1.

[6] vi. 10.

[7] See also Chān., vi. 8. 6.

[8] vi. 18.

[9] I.P., p. 355, n. 3.

[10] Y.S., i. 17. See I.P., p. 426.

[11] *Majjhima Nikāya*, i. 16.

view.[1] The Yogācāra school of Buddhism openly combines Buddhist doctrine with the Yoga details. The later Buddhistic works assume a developed Yoga technique.[2]

In the *Mahābhārata*, the Sāṁkhya and the Yoga are used as complementary aspects of one whole, signifying theory and practice, philosophy and religion. It is said that the Yoga admits a twenty-sixth principle of God. Besides, salvation, which was originally looked upon as identification with the Absolute, becomes isolation of spirit from prakṛti, when the Absolute ceased to be the all-comprehensive being from which the individual souls sprang and became the Īśvara, or helper. There are references to dhāraṇa, prāṇāyāma in the *Mahābhārata*.[3] Many of the ascetics of the Epic resort to Yoga as a means to the attainment of magical powers,[4] which are frequently mentioned in the *Mahābhārata*.[5]

The Upaniṣads, the *Mahābhārata*, including the *Bhagavadgītā*, Jainism and Buddhism accept Yogic practices. The Yoga doctrine is said to be as old as Brahmā. Patañjali's Yoga is the crystallisation of ideas on asceticism and contemplation extant at his time in a more or less hazy and undefined way. He codified the nebulous tradition evolved under the pressure of life and experience. His system bears the marks of the age in which it was produced. While we have in it the most refined mysticism, we have also mixed with it many beliefs derived from the prevailing religions of the time.

Vātsyāyana refers to an earlier form of Yoga which held the doctrine of the creation of the world by the karma of the spirit, which is also responsible for the evils of love and hatred and the impulse for activity and the coming into being of the non-existent and the passing away of the existent.[6] This Yoga insists on the importance of human activity, and is more closely related to the Karma Mīmāṁsā than to the Sāṁkhya, which adopts the satkāryavāda, the ultimateness of soul and the rise of conscious occurrences on account of connection with the body, the senses, mind and material qualities. So, according to Vātsyāyana, there are sharp differences between the Sāṁkhya and the Yoga even on such fundamental questions as the nature of the soul, activity and causation. When insistence on activity is attached to the Sāṁkhya philosophy, we get the classical type of Yoga.

---

[1] Y.S., i. 33.

[2] For a detailed account, see Hopkins: *Yoga Technique in the Great Epic*, J.A.O.S., xxii.

[3] xii. 11683–4.

[4] xii. 326. 8.

[5] xii. 340–55; xii. 303. 163; xiii. 14. 420.

[6] Puruṣakarmā dinimitto bhūtasargaḥ, karmahetavo doṣāḥ pravṛttiś ca, svaguṇaviśiṣṭāś cetanā, asad utpadyata utpannaṁ nirudhyata iti yogānām (N.B., i. 1. 29). Uddyotakara adds that, according to this Yoga, the organs of senses were made of elements (bhūtas).

III

Date and Literature

The *Yoga Sūtra* of Patañjali is the oldest textbook of the Yoga school. It has four parts, of which the first treats of the nature and aim of samādhi, or meditative absorption (samādhipāda), the second explains the means of attaining this end (sādhanapāda), the third gives an account of the supernormal powers that can be attained through the Yoga practices (vibhūtipāda), and the fourth sets forth the nature of liberation (kaivalyapāda).[1] According to *Yājñavalkya Smṛti*, Hiraṇyagarbha is the founder of the Yoga system, and Mādhava points out that this does not contradict Patañjali's authorship of the *Yoga Sūtra*, since Patañjali calls his work "Anuśāsana," where the preposition "anu" implies that his statement follows a primary revelation, and is not itself the first formulation of the system.[2] Patañjali, the grammarian, is assigned to the middle of the second century B.C.,[3] though his identity with the author of the *Yoga Sūtra* is not proved.[4] Vyāsa's

---

[1] Since the criticisms of the other schools occur in the fourth part of the Y.S., and since the word "iti," denoting the conclusion of a work, occurs at the end of the third, it is suggested that the fourth part is a later addition. See Das Gupta: *Hist. of Ind. Ph.*, p. 230.

[2] S.D.S., xv.

[3] Patañjali's Y.S. is assigned to the second century B.C., though some are of opinion that it is so late as the fourth century A.D. The atomic theory (i. 40), the Sautrāntika theory of time as a series of moments (iii. 52), the sphoṭavāda (see Y.B., iii. 17), the Buddhist idealism (iv. 15–17) are referred to in the Y.S. Assuming that Vasubandhu's idealism is criticised in the V.S., Professor Woods puts the earlier limit of the Y.S. at the fourth century A.D. His opinion seems to be supported by the fact that Nāgārjuna does not mention the Yoga in his *Kārikā*. This argument does not take us far, in view of the admitted fact that the Chinese translation of Nāgārjuna's *Upāyakauśalyahṛdayaśāstra* mentions the Yoga as one of the eight schools of philosophy, and Buddhist idealism may be regarded as earlier than Vasubandhu and Asaṅga. Jacobi thinks that the Yoga system was in existence as early as 300 B.C. Umāsvāti's *Tattvārtha Sūtra*, ii. 52, refers to the Y.S., iii. 22. Umāsvāti, who must precede his commentator Siddhasena (fifth century) is generally assigned to the third century A.D. So Patañjali cannot be later than A.D. 300.

[4] Bhoja, in his commentary on the Y.S., called *Rājamārtaṇḍa* (Introduction, p. 5), says that he wrote works on grammar, Yoga and medicine, and so, "like Patañjali, removed the defilements from our speech, minds and bodies." He thereby suggests that Patañjali wrote works on grammar (speech), Yoga (mind), and medicine (body). This is the earliest reference. It is, however, open to doubt whether Bhoja wrote the Introduction. Woods, in his *Introduction to the Yoga System* (Harvard Oriental Series), makes out a case against the identification of the grammarian Patañjali, the author of the *Mahābhāṣya*, with Patañjali, the author of the Y.S. There are no special coincidences in language or doctrine between the two works. The great grammarians, Bhartṛhari, Kaiyaṭa, Vāmana and Nāgeśa, do not refer to the identity of the author of the Y.S. with the grammarian.

commentary on the *Yoga Sūtra* (fourth century A.D.) gives the standard exposition of the Yoga principles. Vācaspati wrote a glossary on Vyāsa's Bhāṣya called *Tattvavaiśāradī* (ninth century). Bhoja's *Rājamārtāṇḍa* is a work of considerable value. Vijñānabhikṣu's *Yogavārttika*, a running commentary on *Yoga bhāṣya* and *Yogasāra-saṁgraha* are useful manuals. The author criticises Vācaspati's views on some points and attempts to bring the Yoga system nearer the philosophy of the Upaniṣads.[1] Every system of thought utilises the methods of Yoga in its own interests. Some of the later Upaniṣads, such as *Maitrī*, *Śāndilya*, *Yogatattva*, *Dhyānabindu*, *Haṁsa*, *Varāha*, and *Nādabindu*, attach great importance to the principles of the Yoga.

IV

The Sāṁkhya and the Yoga

Patañjali systematised the conceptions of the Yoga and set them forth on the background of the metaphysics of the Sāṁkhya, which he assumes with slight variations. In the early works the Yoga principles appear along with the Sāṁkhya ideas.[2] The twenty-five principles are accepted by the Yoga, which does not care to argue about them. The universe is uncreated and eternal. It undergoes changes. In its noumenal state it is called prakṛti, which is associated with the guṇas, and is always the same. There are countless individual souls which animate living beings and are by nature pure, eternal and immutable. But, through the association with the universe, they become indirectly the experiencers of joys and sorrows, and assume innumerable embodied forms in the course of saṁsāra. Regarding the development of prakṛti, the Yoga holds that there are two parallel lines of evolution, starting from mahat, which, on the one side, develops into ahaṁkāra, manas, the five senses of cognition and the five of action, and, on the other, develops into the five gross elements through the five tanmātras. According to Vyāsa, the gross elements are derived from the five essences, and the eleven senses from ahaṁkāra or asmitā. The tan-

[1] The other works on the Yoga systems, such as those by Nāgoji Bhaṭṭa (Nāgeśa Bhaṭṭa), Nārāyaṇabhikṣu and Mahādeva, modify Patañjali's views so as to suit their own preconceptions.

[2] See *Kaṭha Up.* Vyāsa's commentary on the Y.S. is also called *Sāṁkhya-pravacanabhāṣya*, which brings out the intimate relation between the Sāṁkhya and the Yoga.

mātras are not derived from the latter, but they, together with asmitā, are said to be the six slightly specialised ones (aviśeṣa) due to mahat. Vijñānabhikṣu thinks that Vyāsa is simply describing the modifications of buddhi in two classes, but does not mean to suggest that the rise of tanmātras from mahat is independent of ahaṁkāra.[1] In the Sāṁkhya, ahaṁkāra, as sāttvikā, gives rise to the senses, and, as tāmasa, to the tanmātras, and both these are held up in the mahat; and so this distinction between the Sāṁkhya and the Yoga accounts of evolution is not a serious one. We find that the Yoga brings the three internal organs of the Sāṁkhya under citta. It does not recognise ahaṁkāra and manas as separate from buddhi. It also looks upon the sense-organs as material in character, and so finds no need for a subtle body.

Ignorance of the true nature of things causes desires and the like, which are the basis of pain and suffering in the world. The question of the origin of ignorance is meaningless in view of the beginninglessness of the world. Even in pralaya the individual cittas of puruṣas return to prakṛti and lie within it, together with their own avidyās, and at the time of each new creation or evolution of the world these are created anew, with such changes as are due to the individual avidyās. These latter manifest themselves in the cittas as the kleśas, or afflictions, which again lead to the kaṛmāśaya, jāti, āyuṣ and bhoga. The Yoga accounts for creation by the two agencies of God and avidyā. Through the force of the latter, the ever-revolving energy of prakṛtī transforms itself into modifications as the mental and the material world, while God, though remaining outside the pale of prakṛti, removes the obstructions offered by the latter. Avidyā is unintelligent and so is not conscious of the desires of the innumerable puruṣas; God is the intelligence adjusting the modifications of prakṛti to the ends of puruṣas. The jīva is found to be involved in matter, and this constitutes his fall from his purity and innocence. The individual, in the Yoga, is not so much at the mercy of prakṛti as in the Sāṁkhya. He has greater freedom, and, with the help of God, he can effect his deliverance. As in the Sāṁkhya, so in the Yoga, the round of rebirths, with its many pains, is that which is to be escaped

[1] *Yogavārttika*, i. 45.

from; the conjunction of pradhāna and self is the cause of this saṁsāra; the destruction of this conjunction is the escape, and perfect insight is the means of escape.[1] The self is the seer and pradhāna is the object of knowledge,[2] and their conjunction is the cause of saṁsāra.

The end of liberation is the isolation of puruṣa from prakṛti, to be attained by a discrimination between the two. While the Sāṁkhya holds that knowledge is the means of liberation, the Yoga insists on the methods of concentration and active striving.[3] As we have seen, in the *Bhagavadgītā*, as in the *Śvetāśvatara Upaniṣad*, Sāṁkhya is the way of salvation by knowledge, while Yoga is that of active striving or dutiful action in a spirit of disinterestedness.[4] So while the Sāṁkhya is busy with logical investigations, the Yoga discusses the nature of devotional exercises and mental discipline. Hence the latter was obliged to introduce the conception of God, thus meriting the title of Seśvara Sāṁkhya as distinct from Kapila's Nirīśvara Sāṁkhya. The aim of the Yoga is to free the individual from the clutches of matter. The highest form of matter is citta, and the Yoga lays down the course by which a man can free himself from the fetters of citta. By withdrawing the citta from its natural functions, we overcome the pain of the world and escape from saṁsāra.

[1] Duḥkhabahulaḥ saṁsāro heyaḥ, pradhānapuruṣayoḥ saṁyogo heyahetuḥ. Saṁyogasyātyantikī nivṛttir hānaṁ hānopāyaḥ samyagdarśanam (Y.B., ii. 15).

[2] ii. 18.

[3] Madhusūdana Sarasvatī speaks of jñāna and Yoga as two different methods for attaining liberation, and quotes from *Yogavāśiṣṭha* in his commentary on B.G., vi. 29: "To suppress mind with its egoism, etc., yoga and jñāna are the two means. Yoga is the suppression of mental activity; jñāna is true comprehension. For some yoga is not possible; for some jñāna is not possible."

> Dvau kramau cittanāśasya yogo jñānaṁ ca rāghava
> Yogo vṛttinirodho hi jñānaṁ samyagavekṣaṇam
> Asādhyaḥ kasyacid yogaḥ kasyacit tattvaniścayaḥ.

Cp. *Bhāgavata*: Nirvāṇānāṁ jñānayogo nyāsinām iha karmasu (B.G., v. 5; *Yogasārasaṁgraha*, i. 7). It all depends on the psychological type to which we belong. Perhaps an introvert will take to the Yoga, while an extrovert will turn rather to the Sāṁkhya.

[4] B.G., xiii. 24. See also M.B., xii. 11679–11707. See also S.S.S.S., x. 4–6, where mere knowledge is declared to be inadequate according to the Yoga system.

V

Psychology

What the Sāṁkhya calls "mahat" the Yoga calls "citta."[1] It is the first product of prakṛti, though it is taken in a comprehensive sense, so as to include intellect, self-consciousness and mind.[2] It is subject to the three guṇas, and undergoes various modifications according to the predominance of the guṇas. It is essentially unconscious, though it becomes conscious by the reflection of the self which abides by it. It undergoes modifications when it is affected by the objects through the senses. The consciousness of puruṣa reflected in it leads to the impression that it is the experiencer. Citta is really the spectacle of which the self is by reflection the spectator. Citta, as cause, is all-pervading like ākāśa, and we have as many cittas as there are puruṣas, since each puruṣa has a citta connected with it. The citta contracts or expands in the various kinds of abodes in the successive lives. It appears contracted when the puruṣa assumes an animal body and expanded relatively when it assumes a human body. This contracted or expanded citta is called kāryacitta, which manifests itself in the states of consciousness. At death the kāraṇacitta, always connected with the puruṣas, manifests itself as kāryacitta in the new body formed by the apūra, or the filling in of prakṛti, on account of past merit or demerit. The Yoga does not admit a separate subtle body in which the citta is encased.[3] While kāraṇacitta always remains vibhu or all-pervading, the kāryacitta appears contracted or expanded according to the body which it occupies.[4] It is the aim of the Yoga discipline to turn back the citta to its original status of all-pervading kāraṇacitta, by the suppression of

[1] Citta in the Vedānta is used as a synonym for buddhi or its modification See *Vedāntasāra*.

[2] Cittaśabdena antaḥkaraṇam buddhim upalakṣayati (Vācaspati) on Y.S., i. 1.

[3] See *Tattvavaiśāradī*, iv. 10.

[4] The Sāṁkhya, however, does not regard the citta as essentially all-pervading. See Vyāsa and Vācaspati on Y.S., iv. 10. Cp. Nāgeśa: Sāṁkhyāḥ pratipuruṣaṁ sarvaśarīrasādhāraṇam ekaikam eva cittam. Kiṁ tu ghaṭaprasādarūpam, svalpamahadāśrayabhedena, pradīpavat svalpamahaccharīrabhedena, saṁkocavikāsacālitayā svalpamahatparimāṇaṁ ca, na tu vibhu, iv. 10).

rajas and tamas. The Yogin acquires omniscience when the all-pervading state of citta is restored. When it becomes as pure as the puruṣa itself, the latter is liberated. It is by means of citta that the self (puruṣa) becomes aware of objects and enters into relation with the world.[1] Citta exists for the sake of the puruṣa, who is deeper than thought, feeling and will.[2] In knowledge the nature of puruṣa or self is not altered, though it is said to be the seat of knowledge.[3] Knowledge results when the intelligence (caitanya) is reflected in the mirror of the thinking substance (citta), and assumes its form in so far as the latter has the form of the object. Citta may undergo modifications and assume the form of the objects presented to it; but it cannot perceive what it sees, since it is unconscious in its nature.[4] It is the reflection of the self acting on it that makes it perceive what is presented to it. In the case of all objective knowledge, the citta is affected by the subject as well as the object. Even though citta is ever changing, our knowledge is constant, since the self, which is the real knower, is constant. Again, since citta can undergo only one modification at a time, the self knows only one object at a time. So we cannot have a cognition of the citta as well as the object at the same time.[5] The objects perceived are independent of our perception. What causes the knowledge of a thing does not cause the thing itself.[6] Two different ideas cannot arise simultaneously.[7] Impressions produced in the citta leave behind certain residua which are the causes of interests and desires, new births and further experiences. The functionings of citta produce potencies, which, in their turn, cause potencies; and so the wheel of saṁsāra goes on perpetually.[8] From these relations passions and desires arise, and the sense of personality is produced. Life in saṁsāra is the outcome of desires and passions. The

[1] i. 2; ii. 6, 17 and 20.

[2] Citta is not in connection with the self, but is only near it. This nearness does not result from a spatial or temporal correlation of the self with it. The distinguishing feature is that the self stands to citta in a condition of natural harmony (yogyatā). The self can experience and the citta can be experienced. Citta is described as an object of experience when it undergoes changes which have the forms of various kinds of things (Vācaspati, i. 4).

[3] ii. 20.

[4] iv. 17–19.

[5] iv. 20.

[6] iv. 16.

[7] iv. 19.

[8] Evaṁ vṛttisaṁskāracakram aniśam āvartate (Y.B., i. 5).

subject is distinguished from the ego dependent on the experience of the world. The life of the ego is restless and unsatisfied, subject as it is to the five afflictions of avidyā, or mistaking the non-eternal for the eternal, the impure for the pure, the unpleasant for the pleasant, and the non-self for the self,[1] asmitā, or the erroneous identification of oneself with the instruments of body and mind,[2] rāga, or attachment to pleasant things, dveṣa, or hatred of unpleasant things, and abhiniveśa, or the instinctive love of life and the dread of death.[3] Deliverance consists in severing the relation of self and citta. When the self is freed from citta, it withdraws itself into its ground, becomes passionless, purposeless and depersonalised. The puruṣa in its true nature is merely the spectator of the mind's activity. When the mind (citta) is active, the self appears to experience various conditions, and when the mind becomes calm in meditation the self abides in its own true form.

While the Yoga allows for the Sāṁkhya theory of liberation through discrimination, the main emphasis is on the other means of achieving freedom, the suppression of mental activities. The suppression of mental activities is not to be identified with the state of deep sleep. By yoga or concentration, we exclude the superficial layers and get at the inner spirit. Concentration is a quality of the citta in all its five stages.[4] The citta is called kṣipta, or restless, when it has an excess of rajas and is tossed about by objects. We might fix our attention on objects due to our passions and interests, but this kind of concentration does not help us to our real freedom. It is mūḍha, or blinded, when it has an excess of tamas and is possessed by the modification of sleep. It is vikṣipta, or distracted, when, as more often, it is unstable on account of natural defects or accidental troubles. The ordinary mind is in this condition pursuing the pleasant and

[1] ii. 5. Avidyā is not merely the non-perception (akhyāti) of the difference between puruṣa and buddhi, but a false perception (anyathākhyāti), by which we mistake buddhi for self and regard it as pure and permanent and a source of pleasure. Avidyā is the root of the unbroken series (santāna), of hindrances (kleśa), and of latent impressions of karma (karmāśaya), together with its fruition (Y.B., ii. 5).

[2] ii. 6.

[3] ii. 7–9

[4] Sa ca sārvabhaumaś cittasya dharmaḥ (Y.B., i. 1).

avoiding the unpleasant. These three are said to be imperfect, since they are associated with the three guṇas The mind is said to be ekāgra or single-pointed, when it is devoted to one object of meditation and is entirely filled with sattva. This prepares the mind for its greatest efforts. It is niruddha or restricted, when its developments are checked. Though their latent impressions remain,[1] the flow of mental modifications is arrested. The Yoga psychologists admit that concentration is a general characteristic of all states of mind, though it is found in its intensest form in the state of samādhi. Every mental modification (vṛtti) leaves behind a saṁskāra, or latent tendency, which may manifest itself as a conscious state when the occasion arises. Similar vṛttis strengthen similar dispositions. The Yogi should not only arrest the modifications but also destroy the dispositions, otherwise they may shoot forth again. When the mind is rid of its modifications, it is said to be in a balanced state (samāpatti), and to assume the form of whatever object is presented to it, the knower, the known or the act of knowledge.[2] It assumes the nature of the object as it is in itself.

There are lower forms of this balanced state. In savitarkasamāpatti, or the balanced state with deliberation, words, objects and meanings (śabdārthajñāna) are mixed up.[3] When words and meanings drop out, *i.e.* when the memory is rid of them, then the object makes its appearance in the mind in its own distinct nature, and we have nirvitarkasamāpatti, or non-deliberative balanced state.[4] Vyāsa says: "When the memory is purified from the remembrances of the conventional use of words, and when the concentrated insight (samādhiprajña) is free from relations (vikalpa) of ideas of inference or of what has been heard, the intended object remains as it is in itself and nothing more, and is specifically characterised as having just that form which it has in itself and as nothing more."[5] This is higher perception (param pratyakṣam) and the basis of all inferential and verbal knowledge. From it these have their being.[6] This knowledge is not accompanied by an idea either of inference or of verbal knowledge.[7]

---

[1] These two correspond to the saṁprajñāta and asaṁprajñāta samādhi. The first three are also brought under Yoga, since concentration in some degree is present even in the waking state. Yatkiṁcic cittavṛttnirodham (*Yogasārasaṁgraha*, v).

[2] i. 41. [3] i. 42. [4] i. 43. [5] Y.B., i. 43.

[6] Tac ca śrutānumānayor bījam. Tataḥ śrutānumāne prabhavataḥ (Y.B., i. 43).

[7] Na ca śrutānumānajñānasahabhūtaṁ tad darśanam. Y.B., i. 43.

We have also the reflective (savicāra) and the non-reflective balanced states. The former refers to subtle elements whose forms have been manifested and are characterised by an experience of space, time and cause. In it a subtle element capable of being apprehended by one idea and particularised by the manifested (udita) forms serves as the object of insight. The latter non-reflective samāpatti refers in all ways and by all means to the subtle elements that are free from characterisations by forms latent or manifested or indeterminable (avyapadeśya) and which yet corresponds to all forms and is the essence of them all. In the non-reflective samāpatti the insight becomes the intended object and nothing more.[1] The reflective and the non-reflective deal with subtle objects, while the deliberative and the non-deliberative deal with gross ones; and all these are said to be forms of sabīja samādhi, since they provide objects for concentration. Puruṣa, though subtle, is not the object of these forms of concentration.

Our mind is an arena of conflicting forces which require to be subdued to some unity. There are some desires that seek satisfaction, some vital urges of life, such as those of self-preservation and self-reproduction, which refuse to be easily controlled. The obstacles to concentration are said to be the different forms of misconception,[2] namely, ignorance (avidyā), egoism (asmitā), attachment (rāga), aversion (dveṣa), and clinging to life (abhiniveśa). Others are sickness, languor, doubt, heedlessness, laziness, worldliness, erroneous perception, failure to attain concentration, and instability in it when attained.[3] While the forms of misconception state the general attitude to life unfavourable to concentration, the other list mentions the detailed incidents which obstruct the process of concentration.

VI

The Pramāṇas

Perception, inference and scripture are accepted as the three means of knowledge.[4] When the citta is affected by some external object, through the sense-organs, we have a case of perception. The mental modification is directly related to the object. Though the latter has in it both generic and specific features, we are concerned more with the

[1] Y.B., i. 44.
[2] i. 30.
[3] Y.B., ii. 3. See also Y.B., i. 8.
[4] Y.S., i. 7.

latter in perception. The reality of external objects is accepted by the Yoga. Like the universe, all sensible objects have their eternal archetypes or noumena, which undergo phenomenal changes, but are never absolutely destroyed. When an object changes into another, only its form is modified, and when all forms are destroyed, the object ultimately reverts to its primary or noumenal state. The forms are, however, not phantasmal. Sensations occur whenever there are sensible objects exciting the senses. It is, however, true that though the presented object is the same, the resulting sensations may be different. For the citta receives the impressions of the presented objects under the influence of one or other of the three guṇas.[1]

Inference is the mental modification through which we cognise the generic nature of objects. The cognition of invariable concomitance is the basis of inference. Of two things invariably connected with each other, the perception of the one serves to establish the existence of the other.

The knowledge of an object seen or inferred by a trustworthy person may be communicated to others by means of words. This is the third means of knowledge.

Valid cognition is distinguished from four other kinds of mental modifications. Misconception (viparyaya) is an erroneous idea which is not true to the nature of the object.[2] Imagination (vikalpa) is a form of words which has no positive fact corresponding to it.[3] Sleep (nidrā) is that mental modification which is supported by the negation of the waking and dreaming modifications.[4] It is said to be a mental modification (vṛtti), since we have on awakening a memory of the kind of sleep we had. So Vyāsa says: "The man, just after awakening, would of course not have this connecting memory had there not been during sleep experience of a cause; nor would he have the memories based upon it and corresponding with it at the time of waking."[5] So sleep is a particular kind of presented idea (pratyaya), and in samādhi even this modification has to be restrained. Memory (smṛti) is the recollection of the object through the impressions left behind by the previous experience of it.

[1] iv. 15–17. [2] i. 8. [3] i. 9.
[4] Abhāvapratyayāvalambanā vṛttir nidrā (i. 10). [5] Y.B., i. 10.

The Yoga holds that the knowledge gained through perception, inference and scriptural testimony is not absolutely valid, since it assumes, with the Sāṁkhya, that empirical knowledge is the product of the erroneous confusion between puruṣa and buddhi. Truth of things as they are can be gained only through the practice of yoga. Vyāsa quotes a verse to the effect: "By the scriptures, by inference and by the eager desire for practice in contemplation, in three ways he furthers his insight and gains the highest yoga."[1]

VII

The Art of Yoga

The reality of the self is to be found not by means of an objective use of the mind, but by a suppression of its activities and penetration beneath the mental strata with which our ordinary life and activity conceal our diviner nature. Though the seed of spirit is present in each one of us, it is not realised by our consciousness, which is too busily engaged with other things. We must undergo a severe discipline before we can achieve the redirection of our consciousness. The Yoga philosophy urges that the necessary inhibition of mental states is brought about by practice and conquest of desire.[2] While the latter is the result of a life of virtue, the former refers to the effort towards steadiness of thought,[3] which is gained by purificatory action, continence, knowledge and faith.[4] Vairāgya or passionlessness, is the consciousness of mastery possessed by one who has rid himself of thirst for either seen or revealed objects.[5] Such a one is supremely indifferent to the pleasures of heaven or of earth. In the highest form of vairāgya, where the discernment of the self arises, there is no danger of any subjection to the desire for objects or their qualities.[6] This leads to ultimate freedom, while the lower

[1] Āgamenānumānena dhyānābhyāsarasena ca
Tridhā prakalpayan prajñāṁ labhate yogam uttamam (Y.B., i. 48).

Vācaspati refers to the correspondence between these three and śravaṇa, manana and nididhyāsana.

[2] i. 12.

[3] i. 13–14.

[4] Y.B., i. 14.

[5] i. 15.

[6] i. 16.

form of vairāgya, which has a trace of rajas (and so pravṛtti) in it, results in the condition of absorption in prakṛti (prakṛtilaya).

In the human organism we find the physical body, the vital dynamism, the psychic principles, in addition to the puruṣa.[1] The puruṣa is hidden behind veils of corruptible flesh and restless mind, all of which offer hindrances to the method of Yoga. The close connection of body and mind is insisted on, for " pain, despondency, unsteadiness of the body, and inspiration and expiration are the accompaniments of distractions."[2] Though physical health is not the end of human life, it is still one of its essential conditions. We cannot look upon man as a physical machine to which spiritual life is attached from outside. The body is the instrument for the expression of spiritual life. So, instead of renouncing the material basis, the Yoga accepts it as part of the spiritual problem. To overcome the hindrances, the Yoga gives us the eightfold method, consisting of yama (abstention), niyama (observance), āsana (posture), prāṇāyāma (regulation of breath), pratyāhāra (withdrawal of the senses), dhyāna (fixed attention), dhāraṇa (contemplation), and samādhi (concentration).[3] The last three are direct or internal

[1] The Yoga has developed a system of physiology which relates to nādis, or infinitely small nerves, which traverse the body, more than 700 million in number, psychic centres or cakras, a hidden energy known as kuṇḍalinī, said to reside at the base of the spine, which, when aroused, stimulates the cakras to activity. The human body has two main parts, the upper and the lower. The head, trunk and limbs form the upper and the legs and feet the lower part. The centre of the body, in human beings especially, lies at the base of the cerebro-spinal column, which supports and controls the two parts of the body. The nerves and ganglionic masses of nervous matter are arranged in the two great systems, the sympathetic and the cerebro-spinal. The brain and the spinal cord contained within the bony cavity of the skull and the spinal column are the great centres of the cerebro-spinal system. Brahmadaṇḍa or Merudaṇḍa of Hindu physiology is the spinal column. It is the seat of the nāḍīsuṣumṇā, which extends from the Mūlādhāra, or root support at the base of the vertebral column to the Sahasrāra lying within the cerebral region. The other four cakras (plexuses) are Svādhiṣṭhāna, Maṇipura, Anāhata and Viśuddha. The spinal column contains three yoganādis of special significance, namely, iḍā, piṅgalā and suṣumṇā. The last is the chief of them. To the right of it is piṅgalā, and to its left iḍā. This nāḍī has six subtle centres called padmas or cakras, invisible to our senses, that could be experienced through the eyes of Yoga.

[2] i. 31.

[3] ii. 29.

(antaranga) aids, while the first five are indirect or external (bahiranga).[1]

VIII

The Ethical Preparation

The first two, yama and niyama, abstentions and observances, lay stress on the ethical preparation necessary for the practice of Yoga. We should practise ahiṁsā, or non-violence, truthfulness, honesty, continence and non-acceptance of gifts, *i.e.* we should abstain from the inflicting of injury, from falsehood, theft, incontinence and avarice.[2] The chief of them all is ahiṁsā, or non-violence, and all other virtues are said to be rooted in it. Ahiṁsā is interpreted broadly as abstinence from malice towards all living creatures in every way and at all times.[3] It is not merely non-violence but non-hatred (vairatyāgaḥ).[4] The cultivation of friendliness, sympathy, cheerfulness and imperturbability with regard to things, pleasant and painful, good and bad, produces serenity of mind (cittaprasādanam). We must be free from jealousy and not be callous to the suffering of others. While hating sin, we must be gentle to the sinner. No exceptions are allowed to these principles, which are absolute in their character. " Kill not " is a categorical imperative, and we cannot compromise its absoluteness by holding that we can kill the enemies of our country, or the deserters from the army, or the renegades of religion, or the blasphemers of the Brahmins. Not even self-defence can justify murder. The yamas are of universal validity regardless of differences of caste and country, age and condition.[5] They are to be acquired

[1] While Patañjali's Yoga included all these in one scheme, in later works distinctions arose. Karma Yoga is the system of salvation by work. Bhaktiyoga insists on attaining perfection through devotion to God, Jñānayoga speaks of perfection through wisdom, while Rājayoga deals with the training of the mind and its psychic powers. Haṭhayoga discusses the methods of bodily control, breath regulation and mantras. An extreme development of the idea that physical processes can produce spiritual results is found in the Raseśvara darśana (S.D.S., ix).

[2] ii. 30.

[3] Sarvathā sarvadā sarvabhūtānām anabhidrohaḥ (Y.B., ii. 30).

[4] ii. 35.

[5] ii. 31.

by all, though all may not be chosen for the higher life of contemplation. The observances (niyama) are purification, external and internal, contentment, austerity (tapas), and devotion to God.[1] These are optional, though all who resort to yoga are required to practise them regularly. A practice of these two favours the development of vairāgya, or passionlessness or freedom from desire, either for things of the world or the pleasures of heaven.[2]

Whenever we are tempted to violate the ethical precepts, the Yoga asks us to think of their opposites (pratipakṣabhāvanā).[3] The psycho-analysts speak to us of three ways by which the primary instincts may be controlled, which are defence-reaction, substitution and sublimation. According to the first, the mind takes up an attitude directly contrary to the impulse and tries to shut it out. Where there is a strong current of a particular impulse subconsciously, the mind takes up consciously a counteracting opposite impulse. The ultimate aim of the Yoga is to bring about a complete transmutation of the substance of our nature.

The stream of mind flows in both directions towards good and towards evil. When it makes for freedom and knowledge, it is said to be flowing towards the good; when it is borne onward to the whirlpool of existence, downward towards non-discrimination, it is then flowing unto evil.[4]

The acts of karma are either bāhya or outer, and mānasa or inner. They are classified into four types. The black (kṛṣṇa) are wicked acts, either outer, such as speaking ill of others, or inner, as want of faith (aśraddhā). The white (śukla) are the deeds of virtue, and they are internal, as faith, wisdom, etc. The white and black (śukla-kṛṣṇa) are those external actions which, however good, are not devoid of elements of evil. Even Vedic karmas entail some injury to other beings. The neither-white-nor-black (aśukla-akṛṣṇa) are the acts of those who have renounced everything.[5] The highest kind of activity belongs to the last type.

IX

The Discipline of the Body

The Yoga realises that our body has a dignity of its own, as much as the mind. Āsana, or posture, is a physical help

[1] ii. 32. [2] i. 15. [3] ii. 33.
[4] Y.B.. i. 12. [5] iv. 7

to concentration.[1] We cannot fix our attention on an object when we are running or sleeping. We must settle ourselves down in a convenient posture before we begin to meditate. Patañjali simply mentions that the posture must be firm, pleasant and easy. The commentators have elaborated details about the different kinds of postures. When a recent critic of Indian culture assured his readers that Indian philosophers think that sitting cross-legged and contemplating one's navel are the best way of sounding the depths of the universe, he had in view one of the postures of the Yoga.

The body can be made the basis of either animal incontinence or divine strength. We are asked to be careful about our food. We should not eat and drink things which set our nerves on edge, driving them into fever or stupor. The lower satisfactions of life generally strangle the true joy of spirit. If intellectual life and moral activity are the true ends of man, then the bodily needs should be subordinated to them. The later stages of the Yoga demand great powers of physical endurance, and cases are not wanting where the strenuous spiritual life strains the earthen vessel to the breaking-point, and so the body has to be first brought under control. Haṭha Yoga aims at perfecting the bodily instrument, freeing it from its liability to fatigue and arresting its tendency to decay and age.

The Yoga asks us to control the body and not kill it. Abstinence from sensual indulgences is not the same as the crucifixion of the body, but the two have sometimes been confused in Hindu India as well as Christian Europe.[2] The

[1] See B.G., vi. 10 ff.; ii. 46–48.

[2] Cp. the passage from the Autobiography of Suso, where he relates his experiences in the third person: "He was in his youth of a temperament full of fire and life, and when this began to make itself felt it was very grievous to him, and he sought in many devices how he might bring his body into subjection. He wore for a long time a hair shirt and an iron chain, until the blood ran from him, so that he was obliged to leave them off. He secretly caused an under-garment to be made for him, and in the undergarment he had strips of leather fixed into which a hundred and fifty brass nails, pointed and filed sharp, were driven, and the points of the nails were always turned towards the flesh. He had this garment made very tight, and so arranged to go round him and fasten in front, in order that it might fit closer to his body and the pointed nails might be driven into his flesh; and it was high enough to reach upwards towards his navel. In this he used to sleep at night" (*Life of the Blessed Henry Suso by Himself*.)

Yoga says that the perfection of the body consists in beauty, grace, strength and adamantine hardness.[1]

X

Breath-Control

The regulation of breath receives considerable emphasis, though Patañjali mentions it as an optional measure.[2] Serenity of mind may be attained by the cultivation of virtues or regulation of breath.[3] So it is a concession to the people who have faith in it. Breath-control is regarded as a steadying influence on the mind, and plays an important part in Haṭha Yoga, where it is esteemed for its great efficiency in producing occult powers. Respiratory exercises are even at the present day looked upon as highly beneficial to health.[4] Monotony in breathing sometimes brings about hypnosis. When the physically weak take to some of these practices, there is great danger. This is why the Yogavidyā, or the science of concentration, is required to be kept very secret.[5]

translated by T. F. Knox). This book mentions many tormenting exercises of a more heart-rending description. There are other cases of Christian saints who tried to emulate the sorrows of the crucified Jesus, whose beloved companions were poverty, suffering and contempt. St. Bernard scourging his body to the point of death, St. Teresa crying out in the grip of her fierce infatuation with pain " Let me suffer or not live," St. John of the Cross, whose bodily severities are indescribable, are some of the noteworthy instances.

[1] Rūpalāvaṇyabalavajrasaṁhananatvāni kāyasampat (iii. 46).

[2] i. 34.

[3] i. 33–39.

[4] The following extract from Dr. Weber's lecture on ' The Means for the Prolongation of Life " has some interesting observations on this point: " The remarkable improvement in the heart's nutrition and action is, I think, to a great degree caused by the deep inspirations which are necessitated by the act of climbing, especially steady and prolonged climbing. This consideration has led me to pay particular attention to respiratory exercises, which since then have been very useful to myself and many others, especially persons with weak heart muscles. . . . I have mostly commenced with moderately deep inspirations and expirations continued during three to five minutes, once or twice a day, and have gradually increased the exercises to ten minutes or a quarter of an hour. . . ." (*British Medical Journal*, December 5, 1903).

[5] See Cintāmani's *Haṭhapradīpikā*.

XI

Sense-Control

The Chinese philosopher, Lao Tze, asked, "Who is there who can make muddy water clear?" and answered, "If you leave it alone, it will become clear of itself."[1] Pratyāhāra or the withdrawal of the senses from their natural outward functioning, answers to the process of introversion in modern psychology.[2] The mind is to be resolutely shut against all impressions from outside. The psalmist said, "Be still and know." The discipline requires us to drive away the vagrant impulses and insistent thoughts. We have to reach the condition described by St. John of the Cross as the Night of Sense. Every seeker after truth is called upon to make a monastic cell in his own heart and retire into it every day.

Ethical preparation (yama and niyama), bodily posture (āsana), breath-control (prāṇāyāma), and abstraction of the senses from their natural functions (pratyāhāra) are accessories to the Yoga, and not themselves elements in it.[3]

XII

Contemplation

To the roving, restless mind of man that would probe the secrets of earth and analyse the mysteries of heaven, the Yoga says that the truth can be known by a persistent withdrawal of consciousness from outward acts as well as inward changes. Dhāraṇa is fixing the mind (citta) in a particular spot. It is steadfastness of mind. In normal life ideas come and go, but do not stay long. Concentration is normally sustained at its fullest for a very short time only. Dhyāna is the

[1] Tao-Teh-King.

[2] "And thought is best when the mind is gathered into herself, and none of these things trouble her—neither sounds nor sights nor pain, nor any pleasure—when she has as little as possible to do with the body and has no bodily sense or feeling, but is aspiring after being" (Plato: *Phædo*, Jowett's E.T.).

[3] These represent the stage of purgation, while dhyāna and dhāraṇa illumination, and samādhi union.

resulting state of an even current of thought undisturbed by others. It is meditation. Dhyāna culminates in samādhi, where the sense of identity is lost; body and mind become dead to all external impressions, and only the object of meditation, whatever it be, remains shining out. When these three are directed to a single object, we are said to have saṁyama.[1] When this saṁyama is directed to objects, external or internal, extraordinary powers, such as seeing through closed doors, disappearing from sight, reading other people's thoughts, result. The seeker for liberation runs the risk of missing his end if he succumbs to the temptation of these powers. One has to resist it, to move upward.[2]

XIII

Samādhi or Concentration

Samādhi is the name of the condition to be passed through before reaching deliverance. Since the Yoga insists on attaining freedom through samādhi, it is defined as samādhi, *Yogaḥ samādhiḥ*.[3] It is the ecstatic condition in which the connection with the outer world is broken. It is the goal of the Yoga discipline, since it lifts the soul from its temporal, conditioned, changing existence into a simple, eternal and perfect life.[4] The puruṣa regains through it the eternal status. There are degrees of concentration or samādhi; samprajñāta or conscious, and asaṁprajñāta or superconscious. In the former the mind remains conscious of the object. That state where the citta is single in intent and fully illumines a distinct and real object, removes the afflictions and slackens the bonds of karma, and has for its goal the restraint of all

[1] iii. 4. [2] iii. 51. [3] Y.B., i. 1.

[4] "A kind of waking trance I have often had, quite from boyhood, when I have been all alone. This has generally come upon me through repeating my own name two or three times to myself silently, till all at once, out of the intensity of the consciousness of individuality, the individual itself seemed to dissolve and fade away into boundless being; and this not a confused state, but the clearest of the clearest and the surest of the surest, the weirdest of weirdest, utterly beyond words, where death was an almost laughable impossibility, the loss of personality (if so it were) seeming not extinction, but the only true life" (*Life of Tennyson*, vol. i, p. 320). See his *The Ancient Sage*.

modifications, is called saṁprajñātasamādhi.[1] In it there is a union between the knower and the known, in which the knower may be said to know the object simply because he is it. The thought and the object of thought are the same This state is accompanied by deliberation (vitarka), reflection (vicāra), joy (ānanda), and sense of personality (asmitā).[2] These are forms of concentration which have definite objects on which they rest. Different names are assigned to the various shades which the forms of saṁprajñātasamādhi assume, such as savitarka, savicāra, sānanda and sāsmita. We have conscious ecstasy (saṁprajñātasamādhi) as long as we argue about what is good or bad, what is present or absent, as long as we feel a sense of joy and have a sense of individuality. When the feeling of joy passes away and is lost in a higher equanimity, there occurs the state called dharmamegha, in which the isolation of the soul and its complete distinction from matter are realised and karma operates no more. According to the Vedānta, it is the state in which ideas flow in the clearest manner.

He who has gained internal calm has an intuitive insight into the truth of things. As Vyāsa remarks: "The sattva of buddhi, the essence of which is light (prakāśa), when freed from obscuration by impurity, has a pellucid steady flow which is not dominated by rajas and tamas. When in the super-reflective (nirvicāra) samādhi, this clearness (vaiśāradya) arises, the yogin gains inner calm (adhyātmaprasāda), and the vision by the flash (sphuṭa) of insight, which does not pass successively through the serial order (of the usual discursive knowledge of experience), and which has as its intended object the thing as it really is."[3] This insight is filled with truth, is truth-bearing.[4] There is not a trace of misconception. Patañjali distinguishes this insight from the knowledge derived through inference and scriptural testimony by holding that its object is a concrete reality and not merely a general notion.[5] In so far as it has a specific entity (viśeṣārtha) for its object, it has closer relation to perception;

[1] Y.B., i. 1.

[2] Since we do not have concentration on a real clear object (sadbhūtam artham) in sleep, sleep is not a state of concentration. See Vācaspati, i. 1.

[3] Y.B., i. 47. See also ii. 45; iii. 54.

[4] Ṛtaṁbharā tatra prajñā (i. 48).

[5] i. 49.

only the intuited objects are too subtle for gross perception.[1] It is higher perception (param pratyakṣam).[2] So the individual object, whether it belongs to the subtle elements or to the self, is apprehended only by this concentrated insight. It is seeing with the soul when our bodily eyes are shut. When once this intuition arises, its impression rules out all other impressions, so that their ideas no more recur.[3] When we gain the highest kind of intuitive knowledge, which simultaneously embraces the past, present and future, with all their states in one whole, it leads us to final perfection.[4]

Samādhi is not a simple experience uniform as long as it lasts. On the contrary, it is a succession of mental states which grow more and more simple until they end in unconsciousness. Asaṁprajñāta samādhi is concentration where there is no mental mode (cittavṛtti), though the latent impressions may remain.[5] In saṁprajñāta samādhi there is a clear consciousness of the object reflected upon as distinct from the subject, whereas this distinction disappears in the asaṁprajñāta.[6]

A distinction is made between the state of samādhi possessing the seed of future life (sabījasamādhi) and that in which it is absent (nirbījasamādhi). Bīja, or seed, according to Vācaspati, is "the latent deposit (āśaya) of karma which corresponds to the hindrances

[1] Y.B., i. 49. [2] Y.B., i. 43. [3] i. 50.
[4] iii. 54. [5] i. 18.
[6] "The soul is no longer conscious of the body or of the mind, but knows that she has what she desired, that she is where no deception can come, and that she would not exchange her bliss for all the heaven of heavens" (Plotinus: *Enneads*, vi. 7. 34). Schelling, in his *Philosophical Letters upon Dogmatism and Criticism*, says: "In all of us there dwells a secret marvellous power of freeing ourselves from the changes of time, of withdrawing to our secret selves away from external things, and of so discovering to ourselves the eternal in us in the form of unchangeability. This presentation of ourselves to ourselves is the most truly personal experience upon which depends everything that we know of the supersensual world. This presentation shows us for the first time what real existence is, whilst all else only appears to be. It differs from every presentation of the sense in its perfect freedom, whilst all other presentations are bound, being overweighted by the burden of the object. This intellectual presentation occurs when we cease to be our own object, when, withdrawing into ourselves, the perceiving image merges in the self-perceived. At that time we annihilate time and duration of time; we are no longer in time, but time, or rather eternity itself, is in us. The external world is no longer an object for us, but is lost in us." Evidently it is not correct to hold that only the Oriental mind feels at home in this type of "emotional" thinking which culminates in a supersensuous object of æsthetic contemplation.

of birth, length of life and kinds of enjoyment."[1] That which has this basis is sabīja, and that which is exempt from it is nirbīja. Like all products of prakṛti, citta has the three sides of sattva, rajas and tamas. According to Vyāsa, "its aspect of sattva, which is illumination, when commingled with rajas and tamas, loves power and objects of sense; the same, when dominated by tamas, tends towards vice, ignorance, absence of detachment and failure to realise its lordliness; the same, when the covering of error is removed, illumines all round, and since it is pervaded only slightly by rajas, tends towards merit, knowledge, detachment and lordliness. The same sattva, when the last vestige of rajas is removed, becomes grounded in itself (svarūpapratiṣṭham), and being nothing but the discernment of the difference between the sattva and the self (sattvapuruṣānyatākhyātimātram), tends towards the contemplation of the cloud of virtue (dharmameghadhyānopagam bhavati). It is called dharmamegha, or the cloud of dharma, since it is full of dharma, or truth, and rains blessings on the lower planes, while the man himself is basking in the light of the eternal sun of truth, raised above all afflictions and karmas. The contemplators (dhyāyinaḥ) call this the highest intellection (prasaṁkhyānam). But the energy of intelligence (citiśakti) is immutable and does not unite with objects; it has objects shown to it, and is undefiled and unending, while the knowledge of discrimination (vivekakhyāti), whose essence is sattva, is the opposite." Though this is the highest kind of knowledge possible, even that has to be suppressed.[2] "So the citta being disgusted with this also restrains this insight. In this state it has residual potencies (saṁskāra). . . . The sabīja samādhi, which gives great powers of understanding, is to be used as a stepping-stone to nirbīja samādhi. Since there is no consciousness of any objects in the state, it is also called asaṁprajñātaḥ." Though some residual potencies remain, their roots are cut off. Bhoja is, however, of opinion that in perfect asaṁprajñāta saṁadhi all residual impressions are destroyed.[3] Vyāsa and Vācaspati hold that residual impressions remain in that state.[4] They require, however, to be removed

---

[1] *Tattvavaiśāradī*, i. 2.

[2] Vyāsa (i. 4) quotes from Pañcaśikha to the effect: "Knowledge is but one, discrimination alone is knowledge." "Ekam eva darśanam khyātir eva darśanam."

[3] *Bhojavṛtti*, i. 18.

[4] Rājendra Lāl Mitra writes: "This contradiction may be explained by supposing that the Pātañjala Bhāṣya has in view a meditation from which there is awaking, while Bhoja describes the final meditation from which there is no further waking; for he admits that in the earlier stages of the unconscious meditation there are residua peculiar to it. Yogis admit that people do wake from unconscious meditation, and that that meditation is often practised, and in such cases the saṁskāras must remain in latent state, to be revived by proper stimuli on waking. It is difficult satisfactorily to describe to what condition Patañjali himself referred. The way in which he has used the word śeṣa would suggest the idea that he has been correctly interpreted in the Pātañjala Bhāṣya" (Y.S., p. 23).

for ultimate salvation, for the *Yoga Sūtra* says, when even the subliminal impression of insight is suppressed, since all is suppressed, the Yogin gains nirbīja samādhi or seedless concentration.[1]

Until we reach the stage of samādhi our effort is the negative one of discriminating puruṣa from prakṛti. When the distinction is realised, the positive nature of spirit manifests itself. This manifestation of the nature of spirit on its own plane, above all confusion with prakṛti, is the highest form of samādhi. In this superconscious samādhi the seer abides in himself.[2] All possibility of confusion between the self and the activity of citta ceases.[3] The Yoga believes that the citta of man is like a millstone. If we put wheat under it, it grinds it into flour; if we put nothing under it, it grinds on until it grinds itself away. When we strip the citta of its fluctuations, its workings cease, and it is reduced to a condition of absolute passivity. We then enter into a silence which is untouched by the ceaseless noises of the outer world. The citta has become desolate, but the self is quite at home. It is the mystical state which occurs as a sequel to intense concentration. We cannot give an adequate description of it. For, as Vyāsa quotes, "through yoga must yoga be known, and yoga becomes manifest through yoga, and he who is earnest about yoga rests in it for evermore."[4] Samādhi is a condition which few can attain and almost none can possess long, since it is broken in upon by the calls of life. So it is said that final liberation is not possible until the body is cast off.

That ecstatic states occur cannot be doubted. Plato regards "this divine madness" as "the source of the chiefest blessings granted to man." The highest intuitions are revealed in such moments. Moses at Mount Horeb heard the "I am" of the Eternal Spirit. Isaiah perceived the mystery of the reality in the words "Holy, Holy, Holy." St. Peter knew, from the vision of the street, that God was the God of all peoples and nations. St. Paul is reported to have fallen into a trance at his conversion. The mediæval mystics speak of

[1] i. 51. Tasyāpi nirodhe sarvanirodhānnirbījaḥ samādhiḥ.

[2] i. 3.

[3] i. 3–4.

[4] Yogena yogo jñātavyo yogo yogāt pravartate
Yo'pramattas tu yogena sa yoge ramate ciram. (Y.B., iii. 6.)

visions and voices as quite common. Wordsworth and Tennyson among modern poets refer to ecstatic conditions. These visions and voices are generally represented as the visitations of God, intended to help the struggling saint and strengthen him in his hour of need; so that, to the believers in God, ecstasy is another name for deification.[1] The Yoga, however, does not accept this view. Every soul is potentially divine, and its divinity is manifested when nature, external and internal, is controlled.[2] The visions and the voices are, in Yoga, regarded as the revelations of the creative spirit in man. Whether they are authentic or not is to be judged by the light of reason.

XIV

Freedom

Freedom in the Yoga is kaivalya, or absolute independence. It is not a mere negation, but is the eternal life of the puruṣa, when it is freed from the fetters of prakṛti. It is defined as the relapse of the qualities (guṇāḥ) in view of the absence of any purpose of the self or the energy of intelligence grounded in itself.[3] The puruṣa is in his true form (svarūpa). As in the case of other Hindu systems of thought, so also in the Yoga, the cause of all desire is ignorance of the true nature of things. The effect of this ignorance is the body, its support is citta, and its object is worldly enjoyment. So long as avidyā remains, the individual does not shake off his burden. Avidyā can be removed by discriminative knowledge (vivekakhyāti).[4] When the individual acquires knowledge, all

[1] " A condition of automatic activity, referred to Christ or God as the cause, is spoken of by some of the great Christian mystics as deification " (J. H. Leuba : *Journal of Philosophy*, xxi. p. 702).

[2] See the illuminating preface in Bernard Shaw's *Saint Joan*.

[3] Puruṣārthaśūnyānāṁ guṇānām pratiprasavaḥ kaivalyaṁ svarūpapratiṣṭhā vā citiśaktir iti (Y.S., iv. 34).

[4] It is said to have seven stages, as follows: (1) The thing to be escaped from has been known, and so need not be known again. (2) The reasons for the thing to be escaped from have dwindled away, and so need not dwindle away again. (3) The escape is directly perceived by the concentration of restriction (nirodhasamādhinā). (4) The means of escape in the form of discriminative discernment has been cultivated. While these four belong to the fourfold release from external phenomena (kāryavimukti),

false notions disappear. The self is purified and remains untouched by the conditions of citta. The guṇas retire to rest and the self abides in its own essence.[1]

The goal of jīva is detachment and independence. It is not compatible with the human relationships of family life, society, etc., and accordingly the Yoga is said to be an unethical system. Ethical considerations cannot have any place in a system that aims at the breaking of all bonds connecting the individual to the world.[2] The criticism is one which we have frequently met. The ethical pathway alone helps us to reach the goal of perfection, though the latter takes us to a region beyond good and evil. Salvation is the realisation of the true nature of the self which is obscured by so many impurities. We can get rid of them only by effort and discipline. The Yoga is much more emphatic than many other systems in holding that philosophy cannot save us. What we stand in need of is not subtleties of disquisition but control of will. We must subdue the inner turmoil of emotion and passion. The true philosopher is a physician of the soul, one who helps us to save ourselves from the bondage of desire.

The Yoga recognises that all men are not capable of the discipline it insists on. There are some who are called in modern psychology extraverts, and for them the Yoga of action (kriyāyoga), consisting of austerities (tapas), study (svādhyāya), and devotion to God (Īśvarapraṇidhāna), are prescribed.[3] Tapas or austerity is that which burns up the impurities mixed up with the subconscious impressions resulting from afflictions and karma. The Yoga psychology assumes that, besides the conscious mind, there is an unconscious but

the other three refer to the final release (cittavimukti), and they are: (1) the authority of buddhi is ended; (2) the guṇas come to rest; (3) the self that has severed its connection with the guṇas is enlightened by himself and nothing more, and is stainless and isolated. (Guṇasaṁbandhātītaḥ svarūpamātrajyotir amalaḥ kevalī puruṣa iti.) (Y.B., ii. 27.)

[1] iii. 24–33.

[2] "An ethical purpose and practice is not logically demanded by the goal of Yoga; for honesty, friendliness, etc., are irrelevant to one who seeks utter detachment and isolation. The coupling of a concern for moral values with a desire for the suppression of personality is one of the incongruities that betray the confusion of thought from which this system suffers" (*Journal of Philosophy*, xvi, No. 8, p. 200).

[3] ii. 1.

psychically active region, and tapas aims at the control of the contents of this unconscious region.[1]

A Yogi who has attained the power of samādhi sets about destroying karma, which is of three kinds: (1) deeds done in the past whose consequences have begun to operate in the present life (prārabdha); (2) those done in the past whose consequences have to be expiated in some future life or the stored (saṁcita) karma; and (3) those produced in the present life which require to be expiated in the present life or in some future one (āgāmi). The last can be checked through devotion to God and social service. The ripe karmas are exhausted in this life, and about the unripe ones, which demand a future life, it is said, the Yogi can create all the bodies necessary to pay off the old debts. Each of the bodies has a citta or mind, of its own, called the nirmāṇa citta or the artificial mind. The artificial bodies with their cittas are distinguished from the ordinary ones, since they are perfectly methodical in all their acts. The consciousness of the Yogi controls these different automatisms. As soon as the automaton, which has a particular destiny, a particular portion of the stored-up karma to exhaust, fulfils its aim, the Yogi withdraws his control from it, and the "man" dies a sudden death. Unlike the natural mind, the experiences of the artificial mind leave no traces behind.[2]

XV

Karma

So long as avidyā is not overcome, there will be life in saṁsāra. The law of karma is assumed as valid, and our life, its character and length, are all determined by it.[3] Though we do not remember our past lives, we can infer particulars about them from the tendencies of the present[4]; and these tendencies will cease to exist on the disappearance of their cause (hetu), motive (phala), substratum (āśraya), and object (ālaṁbana). The root cause is avidyā, though we may have other proximate causes; the motive refers to the purpose with reference to which any conation becomes operative in

[1] What happens above the threshold of consciousness is symbolic of the play of the forces underneath it. Adepts in Yoga explore, in cases of nervous disease and "possession," what is normally hidden in the unconscious being by letting it come to the surface through hypnotic trance or otherwise. Belief in such cures, which remind us of modern psycho-analysis, is wide in India.

[2] iv. 4–5.

[3] ii. 12–14.

[4] iv. 9.

the present; citta is the substratum of the residual potencies, and the object is that which excites the potencies.[1]

XVI

SUPERNORMAL POWERS

The popular cult of magic is mixed up with the religious scheme of salvation in the Yoga. That certain magical powers are acquired during the course of the yogic sādhana is recognised in early Buddhistic works, though Buddha himself set aside the pursuit of those powers as unfavourable to perfection. The Hindu scriptures speak to us of men who, through dint of hard tapas, acquired marvellous powers. The acquisition of these powers is subordinated to the chief end of samādhi in the Yoga system. Though the highest goal may not be attained, the lower stages are not without their value. Each stage brings its own reward. Control of the body through postures results in an indifference to the extremes of heat and cold.[2] We obtain a full intuitive knowledge of whatever we concentrate on. Saṁyama, or concentration, is the means by which we acquire a knowledge of supersensuous objects. Through it we know the inmost core of things and reach the great light of wisdom (prajñāloka). By means of constraint on friendliness, compassion and joy, these qualities increase.[3] If we concentrate on muscular powers, we will have a giant's strength.[4] Heightened powers of the senses (hyperæsthesia), by which the yogin can see and hear at a distance, follow as a result of concentration.[5] We can also acquire a direct knowledge of subliminal impressions, and, through them, of our past lives.[6] As the result of saṁyama on a presented idea, knowledge of another's mind (paracittajñānam) arises.[7] Transmission of thought from one individual to another without the intervention of the normal communicating mechanisms is quite possible. Through concentration on the threefold modifications which all objects constantly undergo, we acquire the power to know the past, present and the future.[8] The yogi can make his body

[1] Y.B. iv. 11. [2] ii. 48. [3] iii. 23. [4] iii. 24.
[5] iii. 35. [6] iii. 18. [7] iii. 19. [8] iii. 16.

invisible.[1] By means of saṁyama on the twofold karma, on the potencies which will soon be exhausted and those which will take a long time, he knows when he will die. He can know the fine, the concealed and the obscure, the cosmic spaces, the starry system, the pole star, the bodily constitution, by practising the relevant saṁyamas. According to Patañjali, he who discerns the distinction between the self and objective existence gains authority over all states of existence and omniscience.[2] Before we gain full knowledge we sometimes have a kind of prior intuition of the truth, and this is called pratibhā.[3]

The supernormal powers are really obstacles to samādhi, though they are regarded as perfections when one acquires them.[4] They are by-products of the higher life. They are the flowers which we chance to pick on the road, though the true seeker does not set out on his travels to gather them. Only through the disregard of these perfections can freedom be gained.[5] In Bunyan's allegory the pilgrims to the celestial city find, even at the very gateway of heaven, a little wicket that admits to a path leading down to hell. He who falls a victim to the magical powers rapidly goes downward.

These supernormal powers are not considered by the Yoga philosophy to be miraculous interferences with the laws of nature. The world open to the senses is not the whole world of nature. What appears to be a contravention of the principles of the physical world is only a supplementing of it by the principles of another part of the cosmic order. The world beyond the physical has its own science and laws. The attractions of unlimited physical and intellectual power were perhaps employed to induce the worldly to take to the higher life. The foolish always seek after signs.

"The perfections (siddhis) are attained through birth, drugs (oṣadhi), spells (mantras), austerity (tapas), or concentration (samādhi)."[6] Some are born with the powers,

[1] Y.S., iii. 21. "The great work of Gorres, in five volumes, is divided into Divine, Natural and Diabolical mysticism. The first contains stories of the miraculous enhancement of sight, hearing, smell and so forth, which results from extreme holiness, and tells us how one saint had the power of becoming invisible, another of walking through closed doors, and a third of flying through the air" (Dean Inge; *Christian Mysticism*, pp. 264–5).

[2] iii. 49.

[3] Y.B., iii. 33. iii. 37.

[4] iii. 37.

[5] iii. 50–51.

[6] iv. 1.

since they had practised yoga in their past lives. These born psychics turn into developed yogis with a little training. Sometimes psychic powers are also attained by the use of drugs and anæsthetics. Narcotic intoxication and ecstatic state are confused by the popular mind. The use of drugs is not recommended in Patañjali's Yoga, though it is mentioned as one of the ways of obtaining perfections.[1] Thus, the habit of drug intoxication prevalent in primitive tribes was mixed up with the higher mysticism of the Yoga. Spells[2] and austerities also help us in acquiring these powers. The insistence, however, is on concentration and not on the others. The visions due to drugs or disordered nerves are condemned. The system did not feel prepared to cut off all connection with its surroundings, and so incorporated elements which did not belong to its inmost being. This spirit of accommodation is responsible for the miscellaneous character of the Yoga system, which exhibits a medley of low naturalism and high idealism. There is such a thing as unconscious suggestion from the environment, and so the Yoga exhibits features determined by the conditions of the age in which it arose. But it is easy for us to separate these secondary accidental characteristics from the primary and the integral. The *Yoga Sūtra* does not take any further notice of drugs and spells, thus suggesting its considered conviction that the signs and wonders which the uncultured seek after, even if well authenticated, possess no spiritual value.

XVII

God

Patañjali makes devotion to God one of the aids to Yoga.[3] God is not only the object of meditation, but is also said to

[1] Nitrous oxide stimulates ecstatic consciousness. According to William James, alcohol "brings its votary from the chill periphery of things to the radiant core. It makes him for the moment one with truth" (*Varieties of Religious Experience*, p. 387).

[2] American New Thought recommends concentration on a carefully selected word or rhythmical formula, and this method answers to the recitation of mantras.

[3] i. 23.

help the realisation of the goal by the removal of obstacles. Theism is not, however, an integral part of Patañjali's creed. A personal God serves the practical purposes of Patañjali, who does not concern himself much with the speculative interests of theism. An argument which reminds us of the classical ontological argument is given by Vyāsa.[1] God has a perfect nature (prakṛṣṭasattva). "His pre-eminence is altogether without anything equal to it or excelling it. For, to begin with, it cannot be excelled by any other pre-eminence, since whatever might seem to excel it would itself prove to be that very pre-eminence. Therefore, that is the Īśvara wherein we reach this uttermost limit of pre-eminence." Nor, again, is there any pre-eminence equal to his. "Because, when one thing is simultaneously desired by two equals, the one saying, 'Let this be new,' and the other saying, 'Let this be old,' if the one wins his way, the other fails in his wish and becomes inferior. And two equals cannot obtain the same desired thing simultaneously, since that would be a contradiction in terms. Therefore we maintain that in whomsoever there is a pre-eminence that is neither equalled nor excelled, he is the Īśvara." [2] Patañjali proves the omniscience of God by means of the law of continuity, which must have an upper limit. Where there are a great and a greater, there must be a greatest. Whatever admits of degrees of excellence is capable of reaching the highest limit. Omniscience admits of degrees of excellence. It gradually increases in proportion to the degree to which the matter-stuff (tamas) which covers the pure essence (sattva) is removed. When the germ of omniscience reaches its height of perfection we get the omniscient God. "In him becomes perfect the germ of all-knowingness." [3] The blind tendency of non-intelligent prakṛti cannot bring forth the order and the harmony of the universe where men suffer according to their karmas. God is the guide of the evolution of prakṛti. He is ever solicitous that the development of prakṛti may serve the interests of puruṣas. God is not, however, the creator of the world, since a world full of pain could not have been created by a being of boundless

[1] Y.B., i. 24. [2] Y.B., i. 24.

[3] Tatra niratiśayaṁ sarvajñatvabījam (i. 25). See also Y.B. and *Yoga-vārttika* on it.

mercy. Scripture seeks to prove the existence of God. But this proof is a case of circular reasoning, since the Vedas are said to be authoritative on the ground that Īśvara composed them. They are said to be valid, since their declarations correspond to facts.[1] While the Sāṁkhya assumes the validity of the Vedas, it does not justify it. The Yoga offers some justification in making Īśvara the source of the Vedas.

The God of Patañjali is not easy to describe. He is said to be a special kind of self, untouched by the taint of imperfection and above the law of karma.[2] Being free from all entanglement in worldly existence, God lives in eternal bliss, without merit or demerit, unaffected by the weight of suffering with which living beings are burdened. He is omniscient, the teacher of the ancient ṛṣis. If God is to help toiling souls on the upward way to freedom and light, he must in some degree subject himself to the experience of saṁsāra. So Patañjali is inclined to regard him as the teacher of truth. God as the teacher has found an echo in the heart of every great thinker from Plato downwards. He is unlimited by time,[3] all-merciful, and though he has no desires to satisfy, yet, for the sake of those in saṁsāra, he dictates the scriptures at each world-epoch. His sattva nature of perfect quality, which is devoid of any imperfection due to rajas or tamas, is the means of his self-expression and it is completely under his control.[4] God is ever free, and so cannot be confused with freed souls who were once bound, or those absorbed in prakṛti (prakṛtilayas), who may incur bondage in the future. Unlike the liberated souls, who have no further relation with the world, God is everlastingly in connection with it. It is assumed that God stands in an eternal and indissoluble connection with the purest side of matter, sattva, and so God is for ever endowed with supreme power, wisdom and goodness. He in his mercy enters into the scene of change by assuming the quality of sattva. Since he does so voluntarily for the sake of the struggling puruṣas, he is not bound by the law of karma. At the great dissolution, when prakṛti relapses into its unmanifested state, this assumed form is set aside, though it is taken up again at the next development. As an

[1] *Tattvavaiśāradī*, i. 24.
[2] i. 24.
[3] i. 25–26.
[4] Y.B., i. 25.

individual resolves overnight to wake up at a certain hour next morning and does so through the force of the impression left behind by his determination, even so Īśvara resolves to resume the character of the great teacher when prakṛti begins a fresh evolution and the puruṣas emerge. The mystic syllable "Aum" represents God, and by meditating on it the mind rests in the true vision of God.[1]

The personal God of Yoga philosophy is very loosely connected with the rest of the system. The goal of human aspiration is not union with God, but the absolute separation of puruṣa from prakṛti. Devotion to God is one of several other ways of reaching ultimate freedom. God is only a particular self (puruṣaviśeṣa), and not the creator and preserver of the universe. He does not reward or punish the actions of men. But some work had to be devised for him when once he was on the scene. He is said to aid those who are devoted to him in removing the obstacles to their upward progress. By praṇidhāna, or disinterested devotion or bhakti, we become eligible for the grace of God. Īśvara facilitates the attainment of liberation, but does not directly grant it. Such a conception of Īśvara is, of course, unsatisfactory,[2] and we cannot help saying that the Yoga philosophy introduced the conception of God just to be in the fashion and catch the mind of the public.[3] Those who were anxious to propagate the Sāṁkhya theory of the universe and the Yoga method of discipline perhaps found it difficult to spread their ideas without satisfying the theistic instincts of man. In the later Yoga, the universal needs of the human heart prove stronger, and God begins to occupy a more central place. The reality of God is seen in the purified life of man. The witness of God is the religious experience of man. The over-soul speaks to the soul, and those who seek for truth find the answer in

[1] i. 27–28.

[2] See S.B., ii. 2. 38 and 41.

[3] Cp. Garbe: "The insertion of the personal God, which subsequently decisively determined the character of the Yoga system, was, to judge from the Y.S., the textbook of Patañjali, at first accomplished in a very loose and superficial manner, so that the contents and purpose of the system were not at all affected by it. We can even say that the Y.S., i. 23–27; ii. 1. 45, which treat of the person of God, are unconnected with the other parts of the textbook—nay, even contradict the foundations of the system" (*The Philosophy of Ancient India*, p. 15).

their hearts. The severe discipline of the Yoga, with its strenuous physical hardships and grave moral perils, demands a guide and help, a deliverer from darkness and pain, the teacher of truth and the inspirer of strength. Soon, union with God becomes the goal of human endeavour. In the *Bhagavadgītā*, for example, the deistic Yoga is replaced by theistic bhakti. In samādhi the soul sees and possesses God. By the separation of the self from every object of sense and thought, by the suppression of all desire and passion and the elimination of all personal sense, we become reunited with God. The end may be gained as the result of intense contemplation of God. Vijñānabhikṣu says: "Of all kinds of conscious meditation, the meditation of the supreme Godhead is the highest."[1]

XVIII

Conclusion

To the modern mind, in East or West, the whole Yoga scheme of attaining perfection appears to be only an elaborate process of self-hypnotisation. Intense and solitary meditations, accompanied by physical exercises and postures, help to make our minds run into particular moulds. Such a view gains some support from the popular confusion of the Yoga system with some of the repulsive practices of the Tantra cult and later adaptations of Patañjali's Yoga by fanatical mendicants. It is, however, necessary to bear in mind the fact that Patañjali's Yoga, in its original form, is free from these vagaries. It assumes that we have all reservoirs of life to draw upon of which we do not dream. It formulates the methods of getting at our deeper functional levels. The Yoga discipline is nothing more than the purification of the body, mind and soul, and preparing them for the beatific vision.[2] Since the life of man depends on the nature of the citta, it is always within our reach to transform our nature by controlling our citta. With faith and concentration, we can even rid

[1] *Yogasārasaṁgraha*, i.

[2] "Prepare thyself as a bride to receive her bridegroom," says Markos the Gnostic (*Irenæus*, i. 13. 3).

ourselves of our ills.[1] The normal limits of the human vision are not the limits of the universe. There are other worlds than that which our senses reveal to us, other senses than those which we share with the lower animals, other forces than those of material nature. If we have faith in the soul, then the supernatural is also a part of the natural. Most of us go through life with eyes half shut and with dull minds and heavy hearts, and even the few who have had those rare moments of vision and awakening fall back quickly into somnolence. It is good to know that the ancient thinkers required us to realise the possibilities of the soul in solitude and silence and transform the flashing and fading moments of vision into a steady light which could illumine the long years of life.

REFERENCES.

DĀS GUPTA: Yoga as Philosophy and Religion.

Patañjali's Yoga Sūtra with the commentary of Vyāsa and the gloss of Vācaspati. S.B.H.

RĀJENDRA LĀL MITRA: Yoga Aphorisms with the commentary of Bhoja. Asiatic Society of Bengal.

WOODS: The Yoga System of Patañjali. Harvard Oriental Series, xvii.

---

[1] As M. Coué says in his little work on *Self-Mastery*: "Be sure you will obtain what you want, and you will obtain it so long as it is within reason." Only when there is doubt is there no result.

CHAPTER VI

THE PŪRVA MĪMĀṀSĀ

Introduction—Date and literature—The sources of knowledge—Perception—Inference—Scriptural testimony—Comparison—Implication—Non-apprehension—Theory of knowledge: Prabhākara, Kumārila—The self: Prabhākara, Kumārila—Nature of reality—Ethics—Apūrva—Mokṣa—God—Conclusion.

I

INTRODUCTION

THE Pūrva Mīmāṁsā is so called because it is earlier (pūrva) than the Uttara Mīmāṁsā, not so much in the chronological as in the logical sense. Its central problem is ritual, even as that of the Uttara Mīmāṁsā is knowledge of the truth of things. The entire Veda, excluding the Upaniṣads, is said to deal with dharma or acts of duty, of which the chief are sacrifices. The performance of sacred rites is normally the prelude to the pursuit of wisdom. Even Śaṁkara, who insists on the radical opposition between karma and jñāna, allows that good karma, in this or in an earlier life, is the cause of the desire for truth.

The beginnings of the Mīmāṁsā may be traced to the Veda itself, where it is used to denote doubt and discussion regarding the rules of ritual and doctrine. The due performance of the sacrifices depended on the correct interpretation of the Vedic texts. Doubtful cases led to the elaboration of rules which helped to a knowledge of the way in which the sacrifice was to be performed. The many problems about interpretation were discussed and decided as they arose, and these decisions are found scattered in the Brāhmaṇas. The accounts in the Brāhmaṇas are so disjointed, obscure and incomplete, that one could not understand them without other help, which was then found in the oral tradition. Vedic text and oral tradition continued for long to be the two authorities on the performance of religious duty. When the various Vedic śākhas (schools) began to form themselves, great importance was attached to the authority of the sacred books handed down by unbroken tradition. After the rise of Buddhism, the followers of the Vedic dharma were called upon to review and recast all the knowledge they possessed, prove its soundness and embody it in the form of the sūtras. Jaimini attempts the work of systematising the rules of Mīmāṁsā and establishing their validity in his work.

The avowed aim of the Pūrva Mīmāṁsā is to examine the nature of dharma. Its interest is more practical than speculative. The philosophical speculations found in it are subordinate to the ritualistic purpose. For the sake of the integrity of dharma, it is obliged to affirm the reality of the soul and regard it as a permanent being possessing a body, to whom the results of acts accrue. The Veda enjoins the acts of duty, specifying at the same time the beneficial results which follow from their performance. The authority for the character of these acts as dharma and for their capacity to produce beneficial results is the eternal Veda, which needs no other basis to rest on. But such a dogmatic attitude is not enough when other thinkers disparage the importance of the Vedic texts, of which we cannot see the practical value. So elaborate discussions, theological and philosophical, arise. The Mīmāṁsā welcomes all philosophical views so long as they do not injure its central theme, *viz.* the transcendent importance of dharma interpreted in the ritualistic sense. This looseness of philosophic texture has enabled different thinkers to interpret the philosophical views of the Mīmāṁsā in different ways, even though they all agree about the supreme importance of dharma. The Veda is acknowledged as authoritative, and its validity is established against the Buddhists, who dispute it, and the seekers after knowledge, who subordinate karma to jñāna. The Mīmāṁsā is frankly polytheistic, though by implication atheistic. It accepts a realistic view of the world as against the Buddhists.

Its importance for the Hindu religion is great. The scriptures which govern the daily life of the Hindu require to be interpreted in accordance with the Mīmāṁsā rules. Modern Hindu law is considerably influenced by the Mīmāṁsā system.

II

Date and Literature

The *Mīmāṁsā Sūtra* of Jaimini presupposes a long history of Vedic interpretation, since it sums up the general rules (nyāyas) which were in use. It describes the different sacrifices and their purposes, the theory of apūrva as well as some philosophical propositions. It has twelve chapters, of which the first is of philosophical value, since it discusses the sources of knowledge and the validity of the Vedas. Jaimini tries to justify every part of the Vedas. His *Saṁkarṣaṇakāṇḍa*, otherwise known as *Devatākāṇḍa*, belongs to the Pūrva Mīmāṁsā, since it bears upon upāsana (worship), which is also enjoined in the Vedas.

The fourth century B.C. is the earliest period we can assign for Jaimini's work, which is familiar with the Nyāya and the Yoga Sūtras.[1] Śabara is the author of the chief commentary on the work of Jaimini. He lived about the first century B.C.[2] Evidently there were commentators on Jaimini's work prior to Śabara, such as Bhartṛmitra,[3] Bhavadāsa,[4] Hari,[5] and Upavarṣa,[6] but their works are not

---

[1] If we accept Kumārila's view that the M.S. criticises many of the Buddhist views (see S.V., i. 1. 3, 5 and 6), it may belong to the period immediately after the rise of Buddhism. From the absence of any reference to Jaimini's work in the M.B., nothing definite can be gathered. Jaimini's work, which mentions the name of Bādarāyaṇa in five places (i. 1. 5; v. 2. 19; vi. 1. 8; x. 8. 44; xi. 1. 64), belongs to the same period as the B.S. The latter refers to Jaimini as an authority on the Vedānta in ten different sūtras (i. 2. 28; i. 2. 31; i. 3. 31; i. 4. 18; iii. 2. 40; iii. 4. 2; iii. 4. 18; iii. 4. 40; iv. 3. 12, iv. 4. 5). Since nine of them cannot be traced to the M.S., it is sometimes urged that the Jaimini referred to in the B.S. is different from the author of the M.S. Others hold that some of Jaimini's works are lost. Jaimini in places assumes a knowledge of B.S. He adopts Bādarāyaṇa's view of ātman as non-corporeal, though he does not set forth any arguments in defence of it. The commentators suggest that he accepts Bādarāyaṇa's arguments (xi. 1. 64, and B.S., iii. 3. 53; see also M.S., ix. 1., and B.S., iii. 2. 40) and so does not re-state them.

[2] Jhā: *Prabhākara School*, pp. 6–7. Śabara's refutations of Vijñānavāda and Śūnyavāda do not commit us to a later date. Jacobi thinks that the Vṛtti quoted by Śabara belongs to the period between 200 and 500 A.D., to which Śabara may also be assigned. Keith holds that 400 A.D. is the earliest date for him.

[3] *Nyāyaratnākara*, 10. See also *Kāśikā*, p. 10.

[4] S.V., i. 63.

[5] *Śāstradīpikā*, x. 2. 59–60.

[6] Śabara, in his commentary on i. 1. 5, transcribes a long passage from a Vṛtti (see also Śabara on ii. 3. 16 and iii. 1. 6). Kumārila refers to the

available. Śabara's work is the main basis of all later Mīmāṁsā writings.

Kumārila,[1] the vigorous exponent of Brahmanical orthodoxy which assumes the authoritativeness of the Vedas and the supremacy of the priest, commented on the *Sūtra* and the *Bhāṣya*, and his work is in three parts. The first *Ślokavārttika* deals with the first part of the first chapter. The second *Tantravārttika* takes us to the end of Chapter III, and *Ṭupṭīkā* covers the rest. Kumārila is earlier than Śaṁkara, and may be assigned to the seventh century A.D.[2] Maṇḍana Miśra, the author of *Vidhiviveka* and *Mīmāṁsānukramaṇī*, is a follower of Kumārila. He is earlier than Vācaspati (A.D. 850), who expounds the views of *Vidhiviveka* in his *Nyāyakaṇikā*. Kumārila's work has had several commentators: Sucarita Miśra, author of the *Kāśikā*, a commentary on the *Slokavārttika*; Someśvara Bhaṭṭa, author of *Nyāyasudhā*, also known as *Rāṇaka*, a commentary on the *Tantravārttika*, and Pārthasārathi Miśra (A.D. 1300), author of *Nyāyaratnākara*, a commentary on the *Ślokavārttika*, as well as *Śāstradīpikā*, an independent manual of Mīmāṁsā system on the lines of Kumārila, and *Tantraratna*. Veṅkaṭa Dīkṣita's *Vārttikābharaṇa* is a commentary on *Ṭupṭīkā*.[3]

Prabhākara[4] wrote his commentary *Bṛhatī* on the *Bhāṣya* of Śabara, which it closely follows. Kumārila rejects now and then Śabara's views. From the fact that Prabhākara does not take notice of Kumārila's views, while Kumārila refers to views similar to those set forth in the *Bṛhatī*,[5] it is sometimes urged that Prabhākara preceded

---

author as Vṛttikāra. Dr. Jhā identifies him with Bhavadāsa. Pārthasārathi does not mention his name in this connection. See, however p. 48. Jacobi thinks that Bodhāyana wrote Vṛttis on both the Mīmāṁsās, even as Upavarṣa, his predecessor, did (J.A.O.S., 1911).

[1] Kumārila, reputed to be a great champion of Hinduism, is said to be a Brahmin of Behar converted from Buddhism to Hinduism. See Eliot: *Hinduism and Buddhism*, vol. ii, pp. 110, 207. Tāranatha makes him a native of South India. According to the tradition, Kumārila wanted to commit himself to the flames for two sins, which are the destruction of his Buddhist guru and the practical denial of God in his anxiety to prove the eternal character of the Vedas and the exclusive efficiency of Vedic ceremonialism to salvation. See Mādhava's *Śaṁkaradigvijaya*.

[2] According to Mr. Paṇḍit, Kumārila was the guru of Bhavabhūti (A.D. 620–680), and so is assigned to A.D. 590–650. This agrees with the admitted fact that the fame of Kumārila was well established in the later days of Harṣa.

[3] Rāmakṛṣṇa Bhaṭṭa (author of *Yuktisnehaprapūraṇī*), Somanātha (author of *Mayūkhamālikā*), Bhaṭṭa Śaṁkara, Bhaṭṭa Dinakara, Kamalākara are followers of this school.

[4] According to the tradition, Prabhākara and Maṇḍana were the pupils of Kumārila, who gave Prabhākara the title of "guru" in recognition of his brilliant powers.

[5] i. 2. 31; i. 3. 2; i. 4. 1.

Kumārila. The style of *Bṛhatī* is said to indicate it earlier date.[1] Śālikanātha's *Ṛjuvimalā* is a commentary on *Bṛhatī*. His *Prakaraṇa-pañcikā* is a popular manual of the Prabhākara system. His *Pariśiṣṭa* is a brief annotation on Śabara's work. Bhavanātha's *Nayaviveka* deals at length with Prabhākara's views. Śālikanātha, the disciple of Prabhākara, refers to Dharmakīrti.[2] Vācaspati, in his *Nyāyakaṇikā*, distinguishes between the two schools of the followers of Prabhākara.[3] The third school of Mīmāṁsā, associated with the name of Murāri,[4] is referred to in Hindu philosophical literature, though the works belonging to it have not come down to us. Mādhava's *Jaiminīya Nyāyamālāvistara* is an exposition of the Mīmāṁsā system in verse accompanied by a commentary in prose. Appaya Dīkṣita (1552–1624) attacks Kumārila in his *Vidhirasāyana*. Āpadeva (seventeenth century) wrote an elementary manual, the *Mīmāṁsānyāyaprakāśā*, which is also called *Āpadevī*, and it is a very popular work. Laugākṣi Bhāskara's *Arthasaṁgraha*, which is also popular, is based on Āpadeva's work. Khaṇḍadeva (seventeenth century) wrote a work, *Bhāṭṭadīpikā*, which is well known for its logic. His *Mīmāṃsākaustubha* deals with the *Sūtra*.[5]

III

Pramāṇas

Jaimini accepts the three pramāṇas of perception, inference and śabda, or testimony. Prabhākara admits upamāna (com-

[1] Jhā: *Prabhākara School*; Keith: *Karma Mīmāṁsā*. Professor Kuppuswāmi Śāstri supports the traditional view, and argues at some length against the position taken up by Jhā and Keith. See his paper on *The Prabhākara School of Pūrva Mīmāṁsā*, Proceedings of the Second Oriental Conference, Calcutta. An old South Indian tradition states that Uṁveka was a pupil of Kumārila.

Uṁvekaḥ kārikāṁ vetti, campūṁ vetti prabhākaraḥ
Maṇḍanas tūbhayaṁ vetti nobhayaṁ vetti revaṇaḥ.

Mr. Paṇḍit, in his Introduction to *Gauḍavaho* (Bombay Skt. Series), quotes the verse with the words Tantra and Vāmana in the places of Campū and Maṇḍana. See also Guṇaratna's *Ṣaḍdarśanasamuccaya Vṛtti* (1409). Uṁveka is identified with Bhavabhūti and regarded as one of the pupils of Kumārila. See also Citsukha's *Advaita Pradīpikā*, p. 265.

[2] See *Prakaraṇapañcikā*, i.

[3] Jaratprābhākarāḥ and navyaprābhākarāḥ.

[4] Murāres tṛtīyaḥ panthāḥ.

[5] Rāghavānanda's *Mīmāṁsāsūtradīdhiti*, Rāmeśvara's *Subodhinī*, a commentary on M.S., and Viśveśvara's (or Gāgā Bhaṭṭa) *Bhāṭṭacintāmaṇi* are works of some value. Vedānta Deśika's *Seśvara-Mīmāṁsā* is an attempt to combine the views of the Mīmāṁsā and the Vedānta. The author is a follower of Rāmānuja, who holds that the two Mīmāṁsās are parts of one whole.

parison) and arthāpatti (implication). Kumārila adds anupalabdhi (non-apprehension). Aitihya (rumour) is rejected, because there can be no certainty about the validity of the resulting cognition in the absence of definite information about the source of the rumour, whether it is trustworthy or not. Recollection (smṛti) is excluded from the scope of pramāṇas, since it tells us only of things previously perceived.

Prabhākara describes how we infer the existence of the manas and the senses. Our cognitions are ephemeral in character, and have both material (samavāyikāraṇa) and immaterial causes (asamavāyikāraṇa).[1] The material cause of cognitions is the self, and its immaterial cause cannot subsist in the cause of the self, since the self is uncaused. It must therefore subsist in the self itself. What inheres in a substance is a quality, and so the immaterial cause of cognition is a quality. If temporary qualities arise in an eternal substance, it must be due to contact with other substances. Since there is no evidence that the other substances inhere in still others, they are to be regarded as eternal. Perception, which is a positive kind of cognition, is a specific quality of the self. For such a quality to belong to eternal substances, the immaterial cause must be in the form of contact with some other substances. Such substances are either all-pervading, as space and time, or atomic. Contact with all-pervading substances cannot account for the varied nature of our cognitions. So the immaterial cause of cognition is contact with atomic substances, which is brought about by the action of motion of the atoms themselves. The atomic substance which resides in the body ensouled by the cognising self is manas, and none other could contain the substratum of the immaterial cause of the cognition of which the self is the material cause. The action of the atomic substance in the body which helps to bring about the contact is due to its contact with the self, which, in every act of cognition, puts forth an effort towards it. But, while manas can bring about such effects as pleasure, pain, it cannot give rise to qualities like colour, smell, etc. For the apprehension of these, it stands in need of other organs.[2] Through the contact of the external objects with the sense-organs mediated by the manas, the soul gets to know the outer world. The relation between the soul and the manas is brought about by merit and demerit, but the soul is not regarded as simply passive in its attitude to manas. Manas is included among the senses, since it perceives mental states like pleasure, pain, desire and aversion.[3] It is argued that we would have a simultaneous cognition of all things at once, if we were not dependent on manas and the sense-organs.

---

[1] Cp. *Prakaraṇapañcikā*: "Cognition of objects is temporary. Ātman is the constituent cause, and contact of ātman with manas is the auxiliary cause" (pp. 52 ff.).

[2] *Śāstradīpikā*, p. 100.

[3] *Ibid.*, p. 98.

The soul brings about cognitions when it is in contact with manas. This contact is due to the action of the manas determined by the effort of the soul or the unseen destiny set in action by the previous karma of the soul. The soul is the experiencer or the enjoyer, the body is the abode of experiences, the senses are the instruments of experience. The objects of experience are of two kinds: internal, like pleasure and pain, and external, like jars and the like. Prabhākara says that our saṁvit, or consciousness, connects itself at one time with one object and not two.

IV

Perception

Perception (pratyakṣa) is direct apprehension (sākṣāt pratītiḥ).[1] It proceeds directly from sense-contact. In perception we have the contact of the object and the sense-organ, of the distinctive qualities of the object with the sense-organ, manas and the sense-organ, and the self and manas. Kumārila explains contact of the sense with the object as mere relevancy or the capacity to reveal the object, which we infer from its effect.[2] Perception relates to objects that exist, *i.e.* are perceptible by the senses. It cannot apprehend supersensuous objects. According to Prabhākara, objects apprehended may be substances, classes or qualities.

The Mīmāṁsaka[3] accepts generally the Nyāya theory of the senses except in regard to the auditory sense. Spatial proximity and remoteness are perceived directly, not only through vision and touch, but also through hearing. Space is distinguished into deśa, or locus, and dik, or direction, and both these are directly perceived as qualifying adjuncts (viśeṣaṇas) of sounds. The auditory organ is prāpyakāri, *i.e.* comes into contact with the object, sound. The ear does not go out to the object, *viz.* sound at a distance, but the sound is propagated to the ear-drum through the air waves. This view accounts for the fact that persons near at hand apprehend sounds, while those at a distance do not. It also explains the different degrees of the intensity of sounds.[4] If the ear could apprehend sounds, without coming into direct contact with them, as the Buddhists imagine, then all sounds,

---

[1] *Prakaraṇapañcikā: Pratyakṣa.*

[2] S.V., *Pratyakṣasūtra*, 42–43.

[3] *Śāstradīpikā*, pp. 400 ff., *Ślokavārttika*, 760 ff.

[4] Tīvramandādivyavasthā.

far and near, would be simultaneously perceived through the ear, which is not the case. The ear contains a layer of air on which the current of air issuing from the speaker impinges, producing the condition under which sound is heard. The ear does not come into contact with the locus of the sound, but only with the sound which has its locus in the ear-drum. But sounds are always perceived as having their loci in different points of space, and not in the ear-drum. They reach the ear, not as mere sounds, but as coloured by the different directions from which they spring. So, sounds as well as their directions are directly perceived. Even distance is perceived through the ear, since sounds coming from a proximate point are more intense (tīvra) than those coming from a distance. So the perception of the feeble or intense character of sounds helps us to know the distance from which they issue.

Both Prabhākara and Kumārila adopt the distinction of determinate and indeterminate perceptions, and accept them as valid. According to Kumārila, indeterminate perception apprehends the individual, which is the substrate of its generic and specific characters, though there is no apprehension of the object as having specific or generic features.[1] Indeterminate perception is said to be due to the object itself.[2] In determinate perception the generic and the specific qualities are distinctly noticed.[3] Pārthasārathi argues further in support of this view. On the contact of an object with the sense-organs, we have the apprehension of an object devoid of all relations. We do not as yet discriminate between the qualified and the qualifications and the generic and the specific features. If there were not indeterminate perception, there would not be determinate perception,[4] for determinate perception is the apprehension of the relation between the qualified object and its qualities. The apprehension of such a relation depends on the previous apprehension of the terms of the relation. Unless these are implicitly known in indeterminate perception, they cannot be explicitly known in determinate perception. In the determinate perception of an object we remember the class to which it belongs and the name which it bears, and refer them to the object perceived. If the class and the name are not perceived at all, they cannot

1 S.V., *Pratyakṣasūtra*, v. 113.

2 Śuddhavastuja, or undiscriminated object, 112.

3 S.V., *Pratyakṣasūtra*, v. 120.

4 *Śāstradīpikā*, pp. 109–110. For a criticism of this view, see Jayanta's *Nyāyamañjari*, p. 98.

be remembered. So, the existence of indeterminate perception, where the genus, the name and the qualifying properties are implicitly apprehended, must be admitted.

Kumārila holds that the cognition of objects is independent of verbal expressions.[1] The class "cow" is not cognised always in the form of the word "cow," though we use the word in describing the object cognised.[2] While Kumārila thinks that indeterminate perception is non-determined perception, mere observation (ālocana) comparable to the apprehension of the new-born infant, where only the individual is presented to us, but not the generic or the specific features, Prabhākara believes that indeterminate perception apprehends both the class characters and the specific features; but, since other objects have not as yet entered into the apprehension, the object is not apprehended as actually belonging to a definite class. An object is apprehended as an individual only in comparison with other objects from which it is marked off; it is apprehended as belonging to a class when it is found to possess certain features in common with the other members of the class. Even though what is apprehended is actually an individual belonging to a class, its real nature cannot be cognised until it is compared with other objects of the same class.[3] While class characters and specific features are present in indeterminate perception, they are not recognised as such in it. In determinate perception the self remembers other objects of the same class and notes their resemblances and differences. Prabhākara believes that determinate perception is of a mixed character, and includes in it the element of remembrance, since the other members of the class present themselves to the self by virtue of the impressions which it has had of them. But the element of remembrance does not pertain to the object perceived, but to the others with which it is compared, and so does not affect the validity of the cognition of the object itself.

Both Prabhākara and Kumārila accept the reality of universals and regard them as objects of perception. The Buddhist, on the other hand, holds that specific individuality alone is real and univer-

---

[1] S.V., *Pratyakṣasūtra*, 176 [2] *Ibid.*, 180, 182.

[3] Vastvantarānusaṁdhānaśūnyatayā sāmānyaviśeṣarūpatā na pratīyate. See *Prakaraṇapañcikā*, pp. 54-55.

sality is a product of imagination.[1] The Buddhist view is criticised by Kumārila and Pārthasārathi. The universal is an object of perception, since whenever we perceive an object, we perceive it as belonging to a particular class. The act of perception involves both assimilation and discrimination. Perception is inclusive (anuvṛtta) as well as exclusive (vyāvṛtta). Inclusion depends on the reality of the universal. The act of inference is also based on it. Nor can the Buddhist contend that the universal is not real, since it is not perceived as different from the individual. For the argument that what is, must be either different or non-different,[2] assumes the universal being (vastutva). Nor is it correct to ask whether generality is present in its entirety in each individual or collectively in all, since such a distinction is relevant to individuals, and not to generality, which is partless. The Jaina view of the universal is also rejected.[3] If universality is one with similarity, we must say "this is like a cow," and not "this is a cow." Besides, similarity is not possible apart from universality. Things are similar, if they possess properties in common. The universal, according to Kumārila, is not different from the individual.[4] The relation between the two is one of identity in difference. Whether we cognise the universal or the individual depends on our interest. The universal, called also ākṛti (form) does not mean shape, but identity of character, for, ākṛti is said to belong to immaterial objects like the self. The shape of objects is destructible, but not so the class nature.[5] "The class itself is called ākṛti, which signifies that by which the individual is characterised. It is that which is common to all the individual objects and the means of a collective idea of all these as forming one composite whole."[6] Pārthasārathi argues that the universal is not absolutely different from the individual. Were it so, we would not be able to perceive the universal in the individual. In the perception "this is a cow," we have a cognition of this (iyambuddhi) as well as that of the cow (gobuddhi). The former has an individual for its object and the latter the universal. The cognitions of "this" and "cow" are different, and yet they inhere in

---

1 Vikalpākāramātraṁ sāmānyam. *Śāstradīpikā*, p. 381.

2 Yad vastu tad bhinnam abhinnaṁ vā bhavati, p. 382.

3 Na ca sādṛśyam eva sāmānyam, p. 394.

4 S.V., *Pratyakṣasūtra*, 141. Commenting on it, the *Nyāyaratnākara* says: "Class, etc., are not altogether different from the individual. It is a fact of common experience that the individual cow is recognised as such only when it is found to be identical with the class 'cow.' This could not be if the individual were totally different from the class. Such recognition of the identity of the individual with the class is the only means of knowing the class; hence there must be an identity between the individual and the class." See also *Ākṛtivāda*, 8, 10, 18, 25.

5 *Tantravārttika*, i. 3. 30.

6 Jātim evākṛtim prāhur vyaktir ākriyate yayā
Sāmānyaṁ tac ca piṇḍānām ekabuddhinibandhanam.
(S.V., *Ākṛtivāda*. v 3.

the same object. This twofold character of perception points to the nature of the object as both universal and individual. The two are not naturally inconsistent, since both identity and difference are perceived in a single act of perception. The identity and the difference do not contradict each other, as the cognitions "this is silver" and "this is not silver" do. The identity and the difference relate to different aspects of the object.[1]

The followers of Prabhākara do not agree with this view. One and the same act of cognition cannot apprehend both the difference and the identity between the universal and the individual. When we perceive the difference between the universal and the individual, we must perceive the universal and the individual as distinct; when we perceive the identity between them, we should perceive only one of them, the universal or the individual. In this case a single object, the universal or the individual, would give rise to two cognitions of both the universal and the individual and their identity. But it is not possible for the universal to produce a cognition of its identity with the individual any more than for the individual to produce a cognition of its identity with the universal. It cannot therefore be said that both difference and identity are apprehended by one and the same act of cognition. Pārthasārathi contends that this argument is invalid. The cognition of two objects does not necessarily involve the cognition of their difference. When an individual member of a class is perceived for the first time, both the individual and the universal are perceived, but not the difference between them. When another individual belonging to the same class is perceived, it is assimilated to the first individual as belonging to the same class and differentiated from it as being a different individual. The cognition of two objects does not therefore involve the cognition of their difference. The cognition of a single object does not necessarily involve the cognition of its identity, as when one perceives an object at a distance and feels a doubt whether it is a post or a man.[2]

The followers of Prabhākara plead that the universal and the individual cannot be identical, since the universal is eternal and common to many individuals, while the individual is non-eternal and specific. Were the universal identical with the individual, then the universal would be non-eternal and different in different individuals, and the individuals would be eternal and common to many. Pārthasārathi argues, in reply, that a complex or multiform object may be eternal in some respects and non-eternal in others, identical with others in some features and different from them in others.[3]

Regarding the question of whole (avayavi) and part (avayava), Prabhākara believes that the whole is an object of perception. Objects

---

[1] *Śāstradīpikā*, p. 284.

[2] Na vastudvayapratītir eva bhedapratītiḥ; nāpy ekavastupratītir evābhedapratītiḥ (*Śāstradīpikā*, p. 287).

[3] *Śāstradīpikā*, p. 288.

as wholes exist. It is not necessary for us to perceive all the parts before the whole is perceived. If we take any physical object, atoms are the material cause of it, and their conjunction is the immaterial cause which gives the whole its uniqueness. Kumārila believes that the whole and the parts are identical, and it depends on our standpoint whether we regard an object as a whole or a number of parts.[1]

Kumārila agrees with the Naiyāyika in regarding recognition as a presentative cognition, since it is present where there is sense-activity and absent where it is not. Simply because recognition is preceded by an act of recollection, we cannot treat it as non-perceptual. Wherever we have the contact of a sense-organ with a present object we have a case of perception.[2]

The Mīmāṁsakas do not support the theory of Yogic intuition, by which the Yogis are said to apprehend objects which are past and future, imperceptible and distant. This intuition is either sensuous or non-sensuous. If the former, then, since the senses cannot come into contact with past, future and distant objects, there can be no cognition of them. Even the internal sense of manas can produce only cognitions of the mental states of pleasure and pain. It is meaningless to argue that the senses can comprehend objects without coming into contact with them when they attain a high degree of development, for no amount of development can change the nature of the sense-organs. If the Yogic intuition apprehends things perceived in the past, then it is a case of memory. If it apprehends objects that have not been previously apprehended, then its validity is doubtful. A knowledge of past, distant and future objects can be got only through the Vedas.[3]

Mental perception by which we become cognisant of pleasure, pain, and the like, is admitted by the Mīmāṁsā. A cognition, however, cannot be the object of introspection. Mental perception is restricted to non-cognitive activities. Even in dreams, what the cognition renders cognisable is some object of the external world.[4] Though the object is not actually present at the time of dreaming, still it is some-

[1] S.V., *Vanavāda*. [2] S.V., *Pratyakṣasūtra*, 234–237.

[3] *Śāstradīpikā*, p. 52. See Yāmunācārya's *Siddhitraya*, p. 71.

[4] S.V., *Nirālambanavāda*, 107–8; *Śāstradīpikā*, pp. 162–3 and 165.

thing previously perceived and now revived through the impressions. The cognition that we have in dreams is of the nature of remembrance brought about by the arousing of certain impressions. Only that part of the past experience is revived in dreams which would cause happiness or unhappiness to the agent and for which he is ripe at that moment. Dreams are possible only in that form of sleep where the self is in contact with the manas, though the latter may not be in contact with the sense-organs. In deep dreamless sleep the contact of the self with the manas ceases. While this is Prabhākara's view, Kumārila is of opinion that in deep sleep the self regains its form of pure consciousness where no dreams are possible.[1]

V

Inference

According to Śabara, when a certain fixed relation has been known to subsist between two things, so that if we perceive any one of these things we have an idea of the other thing, this latter cognition is called inferential.[2] Śabara divides inference into two kinds: pratyakṣatodṛṣṭa, where the invariable relation holds between objects which are perceptible, as smoke and fire, and sāmānyatodṛṣṭa, where the relation is not apprehended by the senses, but known only in the abstract, as in the case of the sun's motion and its changing position in the sky.[3] According to Prabhākara, the relation must be unfailing, true and permanent, such as that which subsists between the cause and its effect, whole and part, substance and quality, class and individuals. The general principle is not derived from perception, since the latter operates only with regard to things in the present and in contact with sense-organs. It is not due to inference or implication, since these assume it. The general principle is

[1] Jhā: *Prabhākara School*, ii.

[2] Jñātasaṁbandhasyaikadeśadarśanād ekadeśāntare 'sannikṛṣṭe 'rthe buddhiḥ. See also *Prakaraṇapañcikā*, p. 64.

[3] The sāmānyatodṛṣṭa of Śabara is identical with Vātsyāyana's first explanation of it, while Vātsyāyana's pūrvavat and śeṣavat answer to Śabara's pratyakṣatodṛṣṭa.

established on the basis of experience. We observe cases where fire and smoke are present together as well as cases where they are not so present, and then infer a general principle which covers all the cases. When a permanent relation of coexistence, identity or causal nexus is fixed up in the mind, one term of it reminds us of the other.

Inferential argument, according to Prabhākara and Kumārila, has only three members: pratijñā, or statement of the case; the major premise, which gives the general rule with the corroborative instance; and the minor premise. These three members may be stated in any order. The Mīmāṁsakas admit the distinction between inference for oneself and inference for others. The object of inferential cognition is of two kinds: dṛṣṭasvalakṣaṇa, or that which has its specific character perceived, as the inference of fire from smoke; and adṛṣṭasvalakṣaṇa, or that which has its specific character unperceived, as the inference of the burning capacity of fire. Prabhākara holds that inference involves a previous knowledge of the general relation and refers to things already known. Kumārila makes novelty an essential feature of inference. Though it is true that the smoke is seen and the perception of smoke carries with it the generic idea of fire as related to the smoke, the object of the inferential cognition is something that is not already known, *i.e.* the subject as qualified by the predicate, the hill as possessing fire in the usual example.[1]

VI

VEDIC TESTIMONY

The aim of the Mīmāṁsā is to ascertain the nature of dharma. Dharma is not a physical existent, and so it cannot be apprehended through the senses. The other pramāṇas are of no use, since they all presuppose the work of perception. Perception, inference and such other sources of knowledge have nothing to say on the point that the performer of the Agniṣṭoma sacrifice will go to heaven. This knowledge is

[1] S.V., *Anumānapariccheda*, 50. Prabhākara accepts the four fallacies of asādhāraṇa, bādhita, sādhāraṇa and asiddha, while Kumārila's analysis, which accepts anaikāntika and asiddha, resembles closely the Nyāya scheme.

derived only from the Vedas. Though the pramāṇa of the Veda is the only source of our knowledge of dharma, the others are considered, since it is necessary to show that they cannot give rise to a knowledge of dharma. They are also found useful in repudiating wrong views.

The kernel of the Veda consist of those declarations in injunctive form which prompt men towards certain modes of action by declaring that such action leads to beneficial results. Accepting that ritual is all in all in the Vedas, Jaimini holds that parts apparently unconnected with it are useless,[1] and so they have to be interpreted as bearing on ritual injunctions. Other texts are authoritative only in so far as they help the individual to action.[2] The Mīmāṁsakas attempt to prove that every part of the sacred text refers to acts of duty. The broad division of the Veda is into the Mantras and the Brāhmaṇas. The contents of the Veda are also classified into (1) injunctions (vidhi), (2) hymns (mantras), (3) names (nāmadheya), (4) prohibitions (niṣedha), and (5) explanatory passages (arthavāda).[3]

Verbal cognition is defined as the cognition of something not present to the senses, produced by the knowledge of words. These words may be uttered by men or may belong to the Vedas.[4] The former are valid if we are certain that their authors are not untrustworthy. The latter are valid in themselves. That cognition is invalid which is contradicted

[1] This view is hardly just to those portions of the Veda which deal with the ultimate problems of the universe.

[2] i. 2. 1. The Vedānta admits the authority of non-injunctive Vedic texts also.

[3] Injunctions which impel one to action in expectation of certain results, such as "One who is desirous of heaven is to sacrifice" (svargakāmo yajeta), are the most important. There are subsidiary injunctions which describe the details of the sacrifice, the order in which the several parts of it are to be carried out, as well as the persons who are entitled to perform them. The mantras are largely useful in reminding the sacrificer of the different matters connected with the sacrifice, such as the deities to whom oblations are to be made. Some of the mantras are said to possess a mystical or supersensuous effect and to contribute directly to the transcendental result, apūrva. Names indicate the results to be obtained by the sacrifices. Niṣedhas are only vidhis in disguise. Arthavādas comprise the sentences which contain either praise of the things enjoined (praśaṁsa), or a censure of things prohibited (nindā), as well as description of the doings of others (parakṛti) and instances from history (purākalpa) (*Arthasaṁgraha*).

[4] Apauruṣeyaṁ vākyaṁ vedaḥ (*Arthasaṁgraha*, p. 3).

by a subsequent one. But the cognitions brought about by Vedic injunctions cannot be set aside at any time or place or under any conditions.[1] It is a self-contradiction to assert that the injunction expresses something which is not true. The Vedas manifest their own validity. Words used by us denote things that can be cognised by other means of knowledge; and, if we cannot know them through other means, then those who utter them must be of unquestionable authority. So non-Vedic utterances do not possess any inherent validity.[2] Prabhākara holds that non-Vedic verbal cognition is of the nature of inference. Only the verbal cognition afforded by the Veda is strictly verbal,[3] but it is not in consistency with the other theory of the self-validity of all cognitions. Since there is no author of Vedic texts, there is no possibility of defects, and so the non-authoritativeness of the Vedas is inconceivable.[4] As the utterances of human beings are valid, if their authors are trustworthy, Kumārila considers them also to be śabdapramāṇa.

The Vedas are eternal, since the words of which they are composed are eternal. The relationship between the word and its meaning is natural and not created by convention. That there is such a relationship between the word and its meaning is directly cognisable. If one does not recognise it, when one hears the word for the first time, it only means that the accessories are absent, but that does not make the relationship non-existent. If the eye cannot see without light, it does not mean that the eye is incapable of seeing altogether. The accessory is the knowledge that such-and-such a word denotes such-and-such an object, which is gained from experience. The expressiveness of the word belongs to it by its very nature. This is absolutely true of common names like jar and the like, where the relation of the words to their meanings is independent of any convention.[5] Words and objects denoted by them are both eternal, and men have

1 Śabara on i. 1. 2.

2 *Sāstradīpikā*, p. 53.

3 *Prakaraṇapañcikā*, pp. 88 ff. Cp. *Kusumāñjali*, iii. 16.

4 S.V., ii. See also ii. 62–69.

5 In the case of proper names, where names are applied to things and persons after they come into existence, Prabhākara admits that the relationship between the word and the meaning is due to convention.

from time immemorial applied the same names to the same objects.

According to Prabhākara, there is no such thing as mere dhvani or indistinct sound. All sounds are heard in the shape of some letter or other. The word is not different from the letters composing it. Letters are perceived by the ear, and the order in which they are perceived determines what words are cognised. There are as many perceptions as there are letters in the word, and, on account of the close proximity of the perceptions, we imagine that the perception of the word is one only. The perception of each letter vanishes as soon as it appears, and each leaves behind an impression. Impressions left by the different letters combine with that of the last and bring about the idea of the whole word which has the power to denote the meaning.[1] Since the potency of the word originates from the separate potencies of the letters, the latter are said to be the direct cause of verbal cognition. The cognition of the meaning of the word is not obtained through sense-perception. The senses present the letters which possess the power to bring about the apprehension of the thing denoted by the word composed of the letters. So Prabhākara holds that the letters are the means of verbal cognition. Words have naturally denotative powers by which they refer to objects whether we understand their meanings or not.[2]

Kumārila as well as Prabhākara argues that significance belongs to the letters themselves and not to any special sphoṭa, and therefore denies the theory according to which, apart from the momentary sounds of letters composing a word, there is a complete word-form manifestested (spota) but not produced by the passing sounds.

Several objections against the eternal character of words in general and the Veda in particular are considered. (1) It is a fact of common experience that all verbal utterance is brought about by human effort, and so it has a beginning, and cannot be regarded as eternal. Jaimini replies that the utterance helps to make the already existing word perceptible, but it does not create it for the first time. (2) It is said that the word exists for a brief time, since it is destroyed as soon as it is uttered. The word, says Jaimini, is not destroyed, but simply

---

[1] Cp. *Śāstradīpikā*, pp. 266 ff.

[2] According to Prabhākara, who accepts the theory of Anvitābhidhānavāda, the meanings of words can be known only when they occur in a sentence enjoining some duty, and so words denote objects only as related to the other factors of such a sentence. If they are not related to an injunction, but simply remind us of meanings, it is a case of remembrance, which is not valid cognition. According to the abhihitānvayavāda accepted by Kumārila's followers, the knowledge of meanings is due to words; but this knowledge is not due to recollection or apprehension, but to denotation. Words denote meanings which, when combined, give rise to a knowledge of the sentence.

reverts to its original unmanifested condition. There are many things in the world which exist unperceived. If people speak of "making" words, Jaimini holds that this "making" refers to sounds that manifest the word. (3) The same word is uttered at one and the same time by different persons at different places, and this would not be possible if the word were an eternal omnipresent entity. Jaimini replies that, as many people at different places simultaneously perceive the same sun, so do they utter the same word. (4) Words undergo modifications which cannot be the case if they were eternal. Jaimini contends that words are not modified, but others take their place. (5) The volume of the word decreases or increases according as it is uttered by one or more men, and what increases and decreases cannot be eternal. Jaimini asserts that the volume of the word never undergoes increase or decrease, though the sound proceeding from men increases or decreases.[1]

Jaimini sets forth positive considerations in support of his view. The word is ever present, since the utterance of it is only for the purpose of manifesting it to others. There cannot be any effort to manifest a non-existing thing. Again, when the word "cow" is uttered, it is always recognised to be the same word. People speak of uttering the word "cow" three or four times and not of uttering three or four such words. This points to the oneness or eternal nature of the word. For non-eternal things, causes of destruction are found, but we do not find such causes for the destruction of words. The sound produced from air is distinct from the word which it serves to manifest. Besides, we have many Vedic texts insisting on the eternal nature of words.[2]

Words denote classes and not individuals. When we say "bring a cow," we do not mean a particular cow, but any animal possessing the features of a cow. The word denotes the class or form, since it has action for its object.[3] If individuals are denoted by words, a generic idea like "cow" would be impossible. Again, a word cannot denote all the individuals, since then it would possess as many potencies as there are individuals. It cannot denote a collection of individuals, since then it would be undergoing changes, as some individuals die out and others get in. Again, if the word means a single individual only, there cannot be an eternal connection between word and meaning, and action would be impossible, as it would be difficult to decide which individual is meant. If individuals are objects denoted, then since they are not omnipresent, there cannot be a relation between a word and its meaning. Ākṛti is eternal, and is therefore capable of relationship with the eternal word. While words and their significations are eternal, there is a chance of our having mistaken notions of both, and human utterances may turn out erroneous, while there is no such possibility with regard to Vedic utterances.

---

[1] i. 1. 6–17.

[2] i. 18–23.

[3] Ākṛtis tu kriyārthatvāt (i. 3. 33).

The Mīmāṁsakas protest against the view which regards the Vedas as the work of God. They hold that the Vedas exist for ever in their own right. God, who is incorporeal, has no organs of speech, and cannot therefore utter the words of the Veda. If it is said that he assumes a human form for the purpose of revelation, then he will be subject to all the limitations of material existence, and his utterances will not carry any authority. Besides, there is no tradition of divine or human authorship. Even on the theory of the creation of the world, the Vedas may be regarded as eternal in the sense that the creator at the beginning of any world-epoch reproduces from memory the Vedas of the last and teaches them.[1] It is sometimes contended that the Vedas are human compositions, since the names of their authors, the ṛṣis, are prefixed to them. It is said in reply that the ṛṣis made a special study of them and taught them to others. The Vedas are uncreated in the sense that they are not controlled by God or the inspired seers, who, at best, apprehend the truths and transmit them.[2] The authoritativeness of the Vedas is criticised on the ground that they contain references to historical names. It is said, in reply, that the hymns deal with the eternal phenomena of nature. The names occurring in them are of universal applicability and do not have any historical reference. Viśvāmitra means the all-friendly and not any historical character.

[1] Evaṁ sraṣṭur vedapūrvatvaṁ sādhayatāṁ na kiṁcid uttaram bhavati, tena saty api sarge, suptaprabuddhanyāyena anādir eva vedavyavahāraḥ (*Nyāyaratnākara*). The Naiyāyikas dispute the Mīmāṁsā view. (1) Any tradition about the personal authorship of the Veda might have been interrupted at the last dissolution of the universe. (2) It would be impossible to prove that no one had ever recollected such an author. (3) The sentences of the Veda have the same character as other sentences. (4) The inference —drawn from the present mode of transmitting the Vedas from teacher to pupil—that the same mode of transmission must have gone on from eternity breaks down, since it is equally applicable to any other book. (5) The Veda is, as a matter of fact, ascribed to a personal author. (6) Sound is not eternal, and when we recognise letters as the same we have heard before it does not prove identity or eternality, but only that they belong to the same species as the letters we have heard before. See S.D.S., xii.

[2] See M.S., i. 1. 24–31. The views on the apauruṣeyatva of the Vedas are practically the same in the Pūrva Mīmāṁsā and the Vedānta. Cp. *Bhāmatī*: Puruṣāsvātantryamātram apauruṣeyatvaṁ rocayante jaiminīyā api tac cā' smākam api samānam. . . . (i. 1. 3.)

VII

Comparison

Judgments of similarity are due to comparison. When we see a certain object and remember another, the cognition that we have of the similarity of the remembered object to the seen one is said to be due to comparison. The cow that I had seen in the city is similar to the gavaya that I see now.[1] Knowledge by comparison is distinct from that by perception, since we cognise something which is not in contact with the senses by remembrance, since at the time the gavaya was seen the cow was not seen, from inference, since none of the factors necessary for inference is present.

VIII

Implication

Where the perception of a thing (artha) cannot be explained without the assumption of another thing, this assumption is a case of arthāpatti, or implication. It differs from inference, since an element of doubt enters into the facts observed, which can be removed only by the assumption of something else. The facts observed remain inconsistent or doubtful until the assumption is made. In inference there is no room for any element of doubt. While this is the view of Prabhākara, Kumārila believes that arthāpatti helps us to reconcile two apparently inconsistent facts. There is no such inconsistency between well-ascertained facts in inference. Kumārila's view is sounder, since any doubt about the observed fact will prejudice the validity of the argument by arthāpatti. Unless we are certain that a person is alive and he is not at home, we cannot presume that he is somewhere else.

[1] *Śāstradīpikā*, p. 208.

IX

Non-apprehension

Kumārila, after the Vṛttikāra, admits non-apprehension (anupalabdhi) as an independent source of knowledge.[1] Dissimilarity is only want of similarity, and it is accounted for by the principle of non-apprehension. When we say "There is no jar in this place," we cognise the absence of the jar. Absence (abhāva) cannot be apprehended by perception, which stands in need of sense-contact with a present object, which is not possible in the case,[2] nor can non-existence be apprehended by the other pramānas. Non-apprehension is a means of knowledge (mānam) with reference to the object negated. We perceive the vacant space and think of the absence of the jar. We may say that the non-existence of the jar is as much perceived as the vacant space, yet, since perception involves contact of an actual object with the senses, we cannot identify the act of non-apprehension with perception. We perceive the vacant space, remember the jar that is absent, and then we have the knowledge of the absence of the jar, which has no reference to the act of perception. Apprehension of non-existence is through anupalabdhi.[3] Abhāva is said to be a positive object of knowledge.[4] What we call emptiness is the locus unoccupied by any object.[5]

Prabhākara does not accept non-apprehension as an independent source of knowledge. The cognition of non-existence is inferred from the non-perception of something that would have been perceived if it were present. When we perceive the mere space and no jar in it, we say that there is no jar. The cognition of the substratum by itself (tanmātradhī) is what answers to non-apprehension.[6] Kumārila disputes this view. We may perceive not merely empty space, but space filled by books and paper, but that will also give us a knowledge of the non-existence of the jar. If we say that we apprehend space as not qualified by the jar, we are admitting

[1] See Śabara on i. 1. 5.
[2] S.V., *Abhāvaparicchеda*.
[3] *Śāstradīpikā*, pp. 234 ff.
[4] S.V., *Nirālambanavāda*, 40.
[5] Vastvantaraikasaṁsṛṣṭaḥ padārthaḥ śūnyatādhiyaḥ (112).
[6] This view of Prabhākara is criticised in *Khaṇḍanakhaṇḍakhādya*, iv. 21.

negative knowledge. For, the mere perception of the ground cannot give rise to a knowledge of the non-existence of the jar, since even where there is the jar the ground is perceived. So the ground must be perceived as negatively qualified, and this means that we have already the notion of negation.

X

Prabhākara's Theory of Knowledge

Prabhākara is an advocate of tripuṭīsaṁvit, according to which the knower, the known and the knowledge are given simultaneously in every act of cognition. Knowledge reveals itself as well as the knower and the known. In the consciousness, "I know this" (aham idaṁ jānāmi), we have the three presentations of the "I" or the subject (ahaṁvitti), this or the object (viṣayavitti), and the conscious awareness (svasaṁvitti).[1] All consciousness is at the same time self-consciousness as well as object-consciousness.[2] In all cognitions, whether inferential or verbal, the self is known directly through the agency and the contact of the manas. While there is always a direct and immediate knowledge of self in every act of cognition, there is not always a direct and immediate knowledge of the not-self or the object. In recollection and inference the object is not directly presented to consciousness. Though in indirect knowledge the object is not directly presented to consciousness, yet the indirect knowledge itself is directly presented to consciousness.[3] Cognition is also self-cognised by direct apprehension. The

[1] Some Western thinkers are also inclined to this view. According to Hamilton, "an act of knowledge may be expressed by the formula 'I know'; an act of consciousness by the formula 'I know that I know'; but, as it is impossible for us to know without at the same time knowing that we know, so it is impossible to know that we know without our actually knowing." Cp. also Varisco: "That I may know, it is necessary that I should be conscious of my consciousness, that I should know that I know." "It follows that the act of consciousness proves the reality of itself and of the thinking subject" (*Know Thyself*, p. 5).

[2] Since we have no knowledge of objects in deep sleep, we have no knowledge of self, though it exists. If the self did not exist in deep sleep, we could not have the recognition of personal identity on waking from sleep (*Prakaraṇapañcikā*, p. 59).

[3] *Ibid.*, p. 56.

cognition which is of the nature of light or illumination does not stand in need of any other thing to manifest it. Therefore, the cognition is said to be self-apprehended. The cognising self and the cognised object are not of the nature of light, and so they require for their manifestation the aid of something different from themselves which is of the nature of light. Cognitions are self-illumined, and not perceived as objects.[1] They are not cognised by other cognitions. They are never objects, and so cannot be cognised, as pleasure and pain are cognised. They are cognised as cognitions, but not as objects.[2] If cognitions are cognised as objects, then each individual cognition may require another cognition to cognise it, and so on *ad infinitum*. Prabhākara feels that his theory is not evidently consistent with Śabara's observation that we perceive objects in apprehension and not cognitions, and so argues that, though cognitions are self-cognised, their presence is known through inference. Inference tells us that there is a cognition from the fact that we have the apprehension of the object. This cognition is a prameya, or the object of right knowledge, but it is not saṁvedya, or apprehended in its fulness. According to Prabhākara, we have a case of saṁvedya only when the form of the object is manifested, and this is possible with the objects perceived by the senses. As cognitions have no form, they cannot be perceived. Their presence is only inferred. Inference does not apprehend the form or content of the object, but only its existence.[3] Both Prabhākara and Kumārila admit that cognitions, which are products (pariṇāma) of ātman, are objects of inference.

The validity of knowledge is not determined by anything external to it. There is no question of reproducing external objects. The validity of cognition is signified by the force with which all direct apprehension prompts us to action in the external world. All knowledge generates in us this specific attitude, and does not wait for the mediation of any later experience. A cognition which apprehends an object cannot be invalid. If cognitions were not valid in themselves,

[1] Cp. with this Alexander's distinction of enjoyment and contemplation (*Space, Time and Deity*, vol. i. pp. 12–13).

[2] Saṁvittayaiva hi saṁvit saṁvedyā na saṁvedyatayā.

[3] Nāpy anumānā rūpagrahaṇaṁ sanmātragrāhy anumānam bhavati.

we cannot have any confidence in our cognitions. The notion of validity is original and underived. While knowledge is self-evident, this validity is derived from the instruments of knowledge. The conditions of knowledge also produce the consciousness of its validity.[1]

Prabhākara distinguishes knowledge into valid and invalid. Anubhūti or direct apprehension, is valid, while smṛti, or remembrance is invalid. "Valid cognition or apprehension is different from remembrance, since the latter stands in need of a previous cognition."[2] The dependence on a previous apprehension is the cause of the invalidity of the remembrance. Cognitions that bear indirectly on the object are invalid. Previous non-apprehension of the object is made the test of valid knowledge by both Prabhākara and Kumārila, though the latter insists also on absence of discrepancies. All knowledge is valid and prompts us to activity.

What is called viparyaya is not false knowledge. If all cognition is self-luminous (svaprakāśa) and therefore true (yathārtha), the consciousness expressed in the judgment "This is silver" cannot be erroneous. When we mistake a piece of shell for silver, the error is due to the failure to distinguish the two different elements in it, the idea of silver and the impression of "this." We mix up the perceived and the remembered elements in one single psychosis. The object of a cognition is the thing which is presented to consciousness. In the "This is silver," what is presented to consciousness is "silver," and not "shell." We do not cognise the shell as silver, for the shell never enters into consciousness. The idea which is remembered does not agree with the fact, since the judgment "This is silver" is superseded by the judgment "This is only a piece of shell" when the knower picks up the piece. The error is due to akhyāti, or non-apprehension, of the difference between the given and the remembered

[1] Gaṅgeśa, in his *Tattvacintāmaṇi*, criticises this view on the ground that, if the validity of knowledge were derived from the general conditions of knowledge, then invalid knowledge would be one with valid knowledge, since both have the same conditions. Again, were knowledge self-evident, it would be difficult to account for doubtful cognition.

[2] Pramāṇam anubhūtiḥ sā smṛter anyā na pramāṇaṁ smṛtiḥ pūrvapratipattivyapekṣanāt (*Prakaraṇapañcikā*, p. 42; Jhā: *Prabhākara Mīmāṁsā*, ii).

elements. The perceived element, "this," and the remembered element, "silver," are true; only there is non-discrimination (akhyāti) of the two factors as distinct. This non-discrimination is due to certain defects of the sense-organs and to the suggestion of the similarity between shell and silver, which rouses the mental residuum (saṁskāra) of the silver previously cognised. This unconsciousness of the distinction between the given and the remembered elements leads to action. In actual experience there is no difference between the valid and the invalid cognitions of silver, since both give rise to the same kind of activity on the part of the agent.[1]

This theory is criticised by the other schools. "Do the two apprehensions, the perceived and the remembered ones, appear in consciousness or not? If they do not, they do not exist. . . . If they do, then non-perception of the difference between them is impossible."[2] The theory fails to account for the fact that, as long as the error lasts, there is the actual presentation to consciousness and not a mere memory image. It is difficult to account for the obscuration of memory (smṛtipramoṣa), which breeds the illusion of a direct presentation.[3] Gaṅgeśa argues that unconsciousness of the distinction cannot account for the activity to which the person is prompted. The knowledge of the given element, the shell, for which the person has no desire, will lead to counter-activity, the knowledge of the remembered silver to activity, and the unconsciousness of the distinction between the two should result in non-activity. It is difficult to understand how unconsciousness can prompt one to activity.[4]

Prabhākara's view that, in every act of knowledge, the object, the subject, and the knowledge of the object are manifested, is not in conformity with the evidence of psychology. When we know an object, there is no need whatever that the content of knowledge should at the same time include a reference to myself. Unless the individual is in a sophisticated mood, the probability is that it will not include the reference to self. Prabhākara mistakes the evidence of later reflection for that of perception. When one thinks of his knowledge

[1] When we judge "the shell is yellow," there is no element of remembrance involved in it. If we perceive the yellowness in the shell, even if it be due to the defect of the eye, the judgment is valid until it is sublated by a further cognition.

[2] See *Paṇḍit*, N.S., vol. xii, p. 109.

[3] *Vivaraṇaprameyasaṁgraha*, i. 1.

[4] *Tattvacintāmaṇi*.

of an object, subject and object are present in this thought. We cannot think of a thing as known without reference to the correlative knower. But there is no reason why one should not think of things without thinking of them as known. The act of reflection, which represents a higher stage in thought than the mere observation of objects, tells us about the implications of knowledge. Prabhākara believes that we cannot know without knowing that we know.[1] He does not seem to admit the distinction between "I know" and "I know that I know." Again, if cognition be self-luminous, the objects will appear as manifestations of cognition and not as real objects, and so we are landed in subjectivism.[2] To escape from subjectivism, Prabhākara holds that self-illumined cognitions are also inferred. Commenting on Śabara's remark that objects are perceived and not cognitions, he says that it follows that cognitions are only inferred.[3] But this contradicts the self-illumined character of cognitions. Śālikanātha suggests that the cognition inferred is the contact of the manas with the ātman, which produces the consciousness.[4] If this is all that is inferred, then it is wrong to say that cognitions are inferred; so long as cognitions are said to be self-illumined the danger of subjectivism remains. Prabhākara does not tell us what the nature of knowledge is, apart from its self-revealing character. He emphasises the ultimateness of knowledge, and incidentally brings out how the meaning of subject and object lies within knowledge itself. If he had developed the implications of this theory, he would have been led to abandon his dualistic presuppositions.

XI

Kumārila's Theory of Knowledge

Knowledge is a movement brought about by the activity of the self, which results in producing consciousness of

[1] Bonatelli, the Italian thinker, is also of opinion that in the knowledge of any fact there are given together the knowledge of the fact and the fact of knowledge.

[2] S.V., *Śūnyavāda*, 233.

[3] Ataḥsiddham ānumānikatvam buddheḥ.

[4] *Prakaraṇapañcikā*, p. 63.

objective things. Cognition of a certain object ends not in a further cognition of that cognition, but in the cognisedness (prakaṭatā) of the object.[1] An act of knowledge has four elements in it: (1) the knower (jñātā); (2) the object of knowledge (jñeya); (3) the instrument of knowledge (jñāna-karaṇa); and (4) the result of knowledge, or the cognisedness of the object (jñātatā). According to Kumārila, a cognition is not directly perceived, but is inferred from the cognisedness (jñātatā, prākaṭya) of the object produced by the cognition.[2] Every act of cognition implies a certain relationship between the perceiver and the perceived, which involves some activity on the part of the perceiver. The presence of the relationship enables us to infer the action of the agent, which is cognition, in the case of knowledge. The cognition is inferred from the relation between the knower and the known, which is apprehended by internal perception (mānasapratyakṣa). Were it not for this other factor intervening between the knower and the known, the self could not become related to the object. From the specific relation involved in knowledge between the subject and the object the existence of cognition is inferred. Consciousness is here regarded as a sort of *tertium quid* relating the self and not-self. Even those who hold that all cognitions are self-luminous (svaprakāśa) admit that the relation between the self and the not-self involved in knowledge is an object of internal perception. We cannot say "The jar is cognised by me" unless we know the relation between the cognising self and the cognised object, as well as the relation between the cognition and the object of cognition.[3] If cognition or consciousness is self-luminous, and if the object is manifested by consciousness, by what is the relation between consciousness and its object manifested? The relation between the two cannot be manifested by the same cognition, since it has not come into existence at the time the cognition is produced. When a cognition is produced it manifests its object, and so the relation between the two

[1] Cp. Rosmini, the Italian thinker, who says that though every act of the understanding makes us know the object in which it terminates, no act makes us know itself. See *Philosophical Review*, July, 1922, p. 400.

[2] Jñātatānumeyaṁ jñānam. See also Śabara on i. 1, 1.

[3] Anyathā jñāto mayā ghaṭa iti jñānajñeyasaṁbandho, jñātṛjñeya saṁbandho vā na vyavahartuṁ śakyate. *Śāstradīpikā*, p. 158.

cannot be the object of that cognition. Since the cognition is momentary, we cannot say that it first manifests the object and then its relation to the object. Nor can it be said that the relation between the cognition and the object is self-luminous, since there is no proof of it. The followers of Kumārila accordingly contend that the relation between the self and the object is an object of internal perception which proves the existence of cognition.[1]

The existence of a cognition may be proved by the peculiarity (atiśaya) produced by the cognition in its object.[2] This peculiarity must be admitted even by those who hold that the cogniser, the cognised object and the cognition are manifested by consciousness (tritayapratibhāsavādibhiḥ). Kumārila denies the self-luminosity of cognition in order that he may preserve the independent existence of external objects. The followers of the Nyāya-Vaiśeṣika protest against the view by which we are said to infer the cognition from the peculiarity produced by it in the object. Cognition should not be regarded as transforming what it cognises. To be cognised is not a quality of the object, but only a relation *sui generis* (svarūpasaṁbandha) existing between the object and the cognition.[3]

[1] *Śāstradīpikā*, pp. 158–159.

[2] Arthagato vā jñānajanyo 'tiśayaḥ kalpayati jñānam (*Śāstradīpikā*, p. 159).

[3] Apprehendedness (jñatatā) is nothing but the character of being the object of cognition. The nature of objectivity is hard to define. If objectivity means that a cognition is produced by the object, then even sense-organs and other conditions producing the cognition have to be regarded as objects. Again, it is not possible for a property to be produced in an object' at a time when the object does not exist. Apprehendedness is a property of the objects, though it cannot be produced in past and future ones, which are also apprehended. The argument that the object acquires the new property of apprehendedness after the cognition is produced, even as the act of cooking produces in the rice the condition of cookedness, is untenable, since we distinctly perceive cookedness in rice which changes from taṇḍula (uncooked rice) to odana (cooked rice), while we do not perceive the property of cognisedness in the object. Besides, when an object is cognised, there is said to be produced in it a peculiar property called cognisedness, and so, when this cognisedness is known, there will be produced another cognisedness in that cognisedness, and so on *ad infinitum*. If cognisedness be regarded as self-luminous, to avoid infinite regress, we may as well admit that the cognition itself is self-luminous. It may be argued that an object has existence extending over the past, present and the future, and when it is cognised it is cognised as belonging to the present. Cognisedness is just the condition of the object determined by the present time, and from the possession of this mark we infer the cognition. But it

The followers of Kumārila argue that, if cognition be regarded as perceptible, it has to be viewed as an object which would require another cognition to apprehend it, and so on *ad infinitum*. So, they regard cognitions as imperceptible, though capable of manifesting their objects of cognition.[1] Cognition itself is inferred, while objects are known through cognitions.

is not so, since determination by the present time belongs to the object and is not produced by the cognition, but only apprehended by it. If it is argued that the cognition is inferred from the cognition of objects (viṣayasaṁvedanānumeyam jñānam), we may ask whether the cognition inheres in the self or the object. It cannot reside in the object, which is unconscious. If it is in the self, what is the cognition which is inferred from the cognition of objects? If it is argued that what is inferred from the cognition of objects is its cause in the shape of the action of the cogniser (jñātṛvyāpāra), then we may ask whether this cause is eternal or transitory. If the latter, what is the cause for it? If it is due to the contact of the manas with the self, which aids the contact of the sense-organ with the object, then let all this be taken as the cause of the cognition. There is no need to assume an intermediate cause in the form of the self's activity. If it is held that the action is eternal and the occasional appearance of cognitions is due to accessory causes, then, since these are sufficient to bring about the cognition, it is unnecessary to postulate the action of the self (Śrīdhara. *Nyāyakandalī*, pp. 96–98). Prabhācandra asks whether this apprehendedness is a property of the object (arthadharma) or of cognition (jñānadharma). It cannot be the former, since it does not persist in the object at any other time than when it is cognised, and it appears also as the private possession of the cognising self. It cannot belong to cognitions, since the cognition, of which it may be said to be the property, is not, according to Kumārila, perceptible, and what is imperceptible cannot be the substratum of cognisedness. On the other hand, if the cognisedness, which is of the nature of knowledge (jñānasvabhāva), is perceptible, then even the cognition may be allowed to be perceptible. If cognisedness is of the nature of the object (arthasvabhāva), it only means the manifestation of the object (arthaprākaṭya). The object cannot be manifested if the cognition, by which it is manifested, is itself unmanifested (*Prameyakamalamārtaṇḍa*, pp. 31–32). According to Kumārila, the cognition of the jar produces in the jar the quality of cognisedness, which becomes an object of perception in the form "This jar is cognised by me." From this the existence of the cognition as well as its validity is inferred. While the Nyāya holds that knowledge, consciousness of knowledge (anuvyavasāya), and knowledge of validity are successive, Kumārila thinks that the last two are simultaneous.

[1] Prabhācandra criticises this view in his *Prameyakamalamārtaṇḍa* (p. 31). The cogniser (pramātṛ), cognitive act (pramāṇa), the resulting cognition (pramiti), are as perceptible as the object of cognition (pramēya). We distinctly perceive the different factors of knowledge in our experience. Nor is there any necessity why what is perceived must be perceived always as an object of perception. The self is perceived as a cognition, and not as an object of cognition. So, the cognition may also be perceived as an instrument of perception. When the followers of Kumārila recognise the

The Mīmāṁsakas accept the view of the self-validity of knowledge.[1] "Intrinsic validity belongs to all sources of right knowledge," says Kumārila, "for a power by itself non-existent cannot be brought into being by another."[2] Knowledge may be mediated by the senses, inferential marks, and the like, but it reveals objects by itself [3] and gives rise to a sense of its own validity. If we are to wait till we ascertain the purity of the causes, we have to wait for the origination of another cognition due to other causes, and so

perceptibility of the self, which is only the agent of cognition, they may admit the perceptibility of the cognition, which is the means for the manifestation of the object. If the self is perceptible, it can cognise an external object by itself without the aid of an imperceptible cognition. If it is said that an agent cannot produce an action without an instrument, the internal and the external organs may serve as the instruments of the cognition. Besides, if no action is possible without an instrument, what is the instrument in the cognition of self by itself? If the self is the instrument in the cognition of self, it may serve as the instrument in the cognition of objects also. If it is admitted that the self and the resultant cognition (phalajñāna) are perceived, though they do not appear in consciousness as the object of cognition, it may also be admitted that the instrument of cognition is also perceived not as an object of cognition but as an instrument. Again, the instrumental cognition (karaṇajñāna) is not entirely different from the cogniser (kartṛ) and the resultant cognition (phalajñāna), and so it cannot be imperceptible while the other two are perceptible. Moreover, the self and the cognition through which it knows an object are directly revealed in our experience, and so they should be regarded as objects of consciousness (pratīyamānatvaṁ hi grāhyatvam, tad eva karmatvam). Whatever is revealed in consciousness is an object thereof. In the cognition "I know the jar," the subject is conscious of himself as qualified by the cognition of the jar. The subject's cognition of the jar is as much an object of perception as the self and the jar. Again, if the cognitive act is imperceptible, it cannot be established to be real at all by any pramāṇa.

[1] Tatra gurūṇām mate jñānasya svaprakāśarūpatvāt tajjñānaprāmāṇyaṁ tenaiva gṛhyate. Bhāṭṭānām mate jñānam atīndriyam, jñānajanya jñātatā pratyakṣā, tayā ca jñānam anumīyate. Murārimiśrāṇām mate anuvyavasāyena jñānaṁ gṛhyate. Sarveṣām api mate tajjñānaviṣayakajñānena tajjñānaprāmāṇyaṁ gṛhyate (*Siddhāntamuktāvali*, 135).

[2] See also *Nyāyaratnākara*, ii. 47.

[3] "It is only for their origination that positive entities require a cause. When they once have originated they by themselves energise with regard to their various effects" (ii. 48). A jar may require clay, etc., for its production, but it performs the function of holding water by itself. A cognition may require a cause for its production, but it does not depend on the causes for its function of ascertaining the true nature of things. Thus the Mīmāṁsaka argues that there is no contradiction between svataḥprāmāṇya and dependence on causes like sense-contact, etc. The sense-contact, etc., are generally inferred after the rise of knowledge. Only in the case of memory is dependence on previous experience obvious.

on *ad infinitum.*[1] The doctrine of self-evidence (svataḥprāmāṇya) holds that cognitions by themselves are valid, and their validity can be set aside only by the contrary nature of their objects or by the recognition of discrepancies in their causes.[2] When we mistake a rope for a snake and find later that it is a rope and not a snake, our first cognition is set aside as invalid. When we recognise defects in the instruments of cognition, we suspect the validity of the cognition. One suffering from jaundice thinks that the shell is yellow. When he recognises the disorder in the eye, he attributes the yellowness to the eye and admits that the shell is white. So long as we do not cognise discrepancies there is no reasonable ground for doubt. Cognitions are externally invalidated either by the discovery through other means of the real character of the object, or by the discovery of the defects in the instruments of cognition. Every cognition due to one of the recognised modes of knowledge is to be regarded as valid so long as there are not any special reasons for doubt. The invalidity of a conception is never inherent, and is always arrived at by extraneous means.[3] Even when we are in doubt, say, as to the true nature of a thing perceived at a distance or in faint light, we can resolve the doubt by a second cognition springing from improved conditions. It may be that, in some cases, the second has to be corrected by a third, and sometimes the third may have to be corrected by a fourth; but, in most cases, it is unnecessary to go beyond a small number.[4] According to Kumārila, a series of cognitions carried on for three or four stages results in a cognition which is absolutely true.[5]

[1] S.V., ii. 49–51.

[2] S.V., ii. 53.

[3] S.V., ii. 85 and 87. Yatra kāraṇadoṣajñānam bādhakajñānaṁ vā tatra mithyātvam (*Śāstradīpikā*, p. 142). Jñānasya prāmāṇyaṁ svataḥ, aprāmāṇyam parataḥ.

[4] S.V., ii. 61.

[5] Pārthasārathi says: "The well-known causes of the falsity of cognition are certain defects connected with place, time, circumstance, sense-organs, the object of cognition, and so on. Where the existence of such defects is excluded—as, *e.g.*, when a man fully awake and in full possession of his faculties perceives, in bright daylight, a jar placed close to him—no suspicion of defects can arise, and hence no idea of the perception not being valid. In other cases there may be the possibility of a defect—the object, *e.g.*, may be at a distance—and hence suspicion of the invalidity of the perception may arise; but generally, by one further step, by walking up

Kumārila believes that even a cognition of shell as silver is valid as cognition. The cogniser at the time has the cognition. That it is rejected by subsequent experience is another matter. Even in the cognition of the shell as yellow there is a real yellowness belonging to the bile of the eye which is perceived. Doubtful cognition, as when we are uncertain whether a tall object we perceive at a distance is a man or a post, is a valid one, since we perceive tallness and remember two different objects which are both tall. Erroneous cognition is simply due to incomplete apprehension or non-apprehension. It is not due to positive misapprehension, but to negative non-apprehension.[1] Pārthasārathi defines valid cognition as that which, being free from discrepancies, apprehends things not already apprehended.[2] The self-evident character of knowledge is not compromised by this view.[3] It merely restates the character of apprehension, which is of its own nature valid. Validity is a property of knowledge, though we may and do *test* the truth of our knowledge by finding out whether it coheres with other knowledge or is in conflict with it. All this, however, is but the external test of truth; it does not give us its inner nature.

If coherence is the nature of truth and not merely its test, then it will be difficult to get at truth, for we cannot escape from the vicious circle. Kumārila and Pārthasārathi may tell us that it will not be necessary to go beyond three or

to the thing, one of the two alternatives—to the simultaneous presence of which doubt is due—may be determined as true, and the question settled in this simple way. . . . As soon as it appears that a suspected defect has no real existence, the cognition, the validity of which that defect appeared to threaten, asserts itself in its svataḥprāmāṇya (intrinsic validity)" (*Nyāyaratnākara* on S.V., ii. 58 and 60–61).

1 The non-authoritativeness of cognitions is of three different kinds: false cognition, non-cognition (ajñāna), and doubt. Doubtful and false cognitions are positive entities due to defective causes, and in non-cognition we have simply the absence of causes (S.V., ii. 54–55).

2 Kāraṇadoṣabādhakajñānarahitam agṛhītagrāhijñānam pramāṇam (*Śāstradīpikā*, p. 123).

3 But see Jhā: *Prabhākara Mīmāṁsā*, ii. In this difficulty it is suggested that the term "validity" is used in two different senses. Every cognition as cognition is valid, and in this sense error, remembrance, etc., are also valid. But for practical purposes a distinction is made between valid cognitions which stand the test of action and invalid cognitions which do not. See P. Sastri: *Pūrva Mīmāṁsā*, ch. ii.

four cognitions. If we once allow that validity is mediate, then we cannot be sure of the absolute validity of any cognition.[1]

The critics of the Mīmāṁsā theory urge that it will not be possible for us to distinguish cognitions, if they do not have forms. Since the only thing that distinguishes one cognition from another is the object, the cognition is said to assume the form of the object. It is asserted that there is an identity between the cognition and the thing cognised. The Mīmāṁsaka points out that, if there were an identity between the cognising self and the thing cognised, the latter cannot be said to be apprehended by the former. Nor is the form the only basis of distinction among cognitions. There is such a thing as saṁvedanā, or knowledge of a person, which is the manifestation of a special kind of merit (dharma), which favours his active operation towards a certain object. That object with regard to which it favours the activity of the cogniser is cognised. Since each cognition tends to active operation towards a distinct object, there is a basis for distinction.

The Naiyāyika does not accept the doctrine of the self-validity of knowledge. Knowledge does not testify to its own truth. There is no security that our cognitions always correspond with reality. When we act on our ideas, we are sometimes successful and sometimes not. In the former case we infer validity, in the latter invalidity.[2]

The Mīmāṁsā theory of self-validity points out that validity is a quality of all knowing inseparable from it. Correspondence and coherence test the validity, but do not produce it. They do not describe to us the nature of valid cognition. The function of knowledge is the cognitive one of knowing objects. It always involves the relation of mind to reality. The mind, moreover, works in accordance with the laws of thought, which, in a sense, are inviolable. When we say, " This is bread," what we call bread may not really be bread, but at the moment of judgment we accept it as bread and cannot resist the force of the idea. No doubt

[1] This is perhaps what Professor Stout has in view when he observes: " In the end, truth cannot be recognised merely through its coherence with other truth. In the absence of immediate cognition the principle of coherence would be like a lever without a fulcrum. . . . To affirm that all cognition is mediate in this sense leads inevitably to a vicious circle. If mediate cognition could only be mediated by cognitions which are themselves merely mediate, knowledge could never get a start. It is as if one should say that, in building a wall, every brick must be laid on the top of another brick and none directly on the ground " (*Mind*, 1908, p. 33).

[2] *Nyāyamañjari*, pp. 160–173.

disturbs our consciousness, and so the content of the idea at the moment of judgment is absolutely true for us. All judgments, whether true or false, have this element of necessity about them. This does not, however, mean that judgment is a mere game with ideas. There is something given in our consciousness that we must accept. There is a control exercised by reality over our mental process. In every judgment there is an assertion that the datum stands for more than itself, that there is something else, not now given, which is represented by it. Every judgment involves, moreover, an element of mental activity which amplifies the datum. It interprets the datum, gives significance to it, and asserts that it is a part of a whole not contained within itself. Though the Mīmāṁsakas are realists, still Kumārila's statement that a judgment is ascertained to be valid if it is confirmed by other judgments suggests the theory of coherence rather than of correspondence. The different judgments must fit together. But this inner coherence is not all. It holds simply because reality which is experienced is itself coherent.

The ultimate problem of the relation of mind to reality which it experiences is not raised by the Mīmāṁsā; it acquiesces in the common-sense view that reality as an existent world is external to our thinking. The difficulties of the correspondence notion of truth which results from this position are evaded by means of the theory of the self-validity of all cognitions.

XII

The Self

The Vedic injunctions hold out promises of rewards to be enjoyed in another world. They would be pointless if some real self did not survive the destruction of the body. The performer of a sacrifice is said to go to heaven, and what goes to heaven is not the body of flesh and blood, but non-corporeal ātman.[1] Jaimini does not offer any detailed proof of the reality of ātman, but seems to accept the argu-

[1] i. 1. 5.

ments of the Vedānta on the question.[1] He distinguishes the self (puruṣa) from the understanding (buddhi) and the senses (indriyas).[2] Śabara accepts the reality of a permanent cogniser which is "known by itself and incapable of being seen or shown by others."[3] Śabara's view implies that the ātman is one with consciousness. In refuting the Vijñānavāda, he says that there is a subject of cognitions,[4] and that subject is known by itself.

The Mīmāṁsaka thinkers regard the self as distinct from the body, the senses and the understanding. The self is present when buddhi is absent, as in sleep. Even if buddhi were concomitant with the self, we could not say that the one is identical with the other. The self is not the senses, since it persists even when the sense-organs are injured or destroyed. There is some entity which synthesises the different sense-data. The body is material, and in all cognitions we are aware of the cogniser as distinct from the body. The elements of the body are not intelligent, and a combination of them cannot give rise to consciousness. The body is a means to an end beyond itself, and so is said to serve the soul which directs it. The facts of memory prove the reality of self. It is admitted that the soul suffers change, but through all the changes the soul endures. Cognition, which is an activity (Kriyā), belongs to the substance called the soul.[5] It is no argument against the eternal character of the soul that it undergoes modifications.[6] Nor is it a serious objection that, when we reap the results, we forget the actions which bring them about. Refuting the Buddhist conception of the soul as a series of ideas, each of which gathers from its prede-

[1] Upavarṣa, the Vṛttikāra of the two Mīmāṁsās, says (i. 1. 5) that the question of ātman will be considered in the Uttara Mīmāṁsā. Śabara seems to have been of the same view, for Kumārila says in the last verse of his Ātmavāda (S.V.):—

Ity āha nāstikyanirākariṣṇur ātmāstitām bhāṣyakṛd atra yuktyā
Dṛḍhatvam etad viṣayaś ca bodhaḥ prayāti vedāntaniṣevaṇena.

"Thus the commentator (Sabara), with a view to refute atheism, has established the existence of the soul by means of reasoning, and this idea is strengthened by a study of the Vedānta." See S.B., iii. 3. 53.

[2] i. 1. 4.

[3] Svasaṁvedyaḥ sa bhavati, nāsāv anyena śakyate draṣṭuṁ darśayituṁ vā.

[4] Jñānātiriktaḥ sthāyī jñātā vartate.

[5] S.V., *Ātmavāda*, 100.

[6] S.V., *Ātmavāda*, 22 and 23.

cessors the impressions of its past, Kumārila urges that, if the law of karma is to have any meaning, there must be a common substrate. The Buddhist is not able to account for the law of retribution or the possibility of rebirth. The hypothesis of a subtle body is not of much help, since the relation of an idea to it is a mystery. The phenomena of self-consciousness, desire, memory, pleasure, pain are unintelligible on the Buddhist view of a series of ideas. So there must be something which possesses the potentiality of ideas, is eternal and capable of rebirth. The soul cannot be atomic, since it apprehends changes in different parts of the body It is regarded as vibhu or all-pervading, and as able to connect itself with one body after another. The soul directs the body, with which it is connected, until release. An omnipresent soul can act, since action is not merely atomic movement. The energy of the soul causes the movement of the body.

The Mīmāṁsakas adopt the theory of the plurality of selves [1] to account for the varieties of experiences. We infer the presence of the soul from the activities of the bodies, which are inexplicable without such a hypothesis. As my actions are due to my soul, other activities are traced to other souls. The differences of dharma and adharma, which are qualities of souls, require the existence of different souls. The analogy that as the one sun, reflected in different substances, becomes endowed with distinct properties, the one soul reflected in different bodies becomes endowed with different qualities, will not hold, since the qualities that appear different belong to the reflecting medium and not the sun. If the analogy were true, the diverse qualities appearing in connection with the souls would belong to the bodies and not the soul. But pleasure, pain, etc., are qualities of the soul and not of the body.[2]

Prabhākara understands by the self something non-intelligent which is the substrate of qualities like knowledge, activity and experience, or enjoyment and suffering.[3] There

[1] Buddhīndriyaśarīrebhyo bhinnā' tmā vibhur dhruvaḥ
Nānābhūtaḥ pratikṣetram arthajñāneṣu bhāsate. (S.S.S.S., vi. 206.)
See also S.V., *Ātmavāda*, pp. 5–7.

[2] Jhā's *prābhākara Mīmāṁsā*.

[3] Kartā bhoktā jaḍo vibhur iti prābhākarāḥ. Madhusūdana Sarasvatī's *Siddhāntabindu*, *Nyāyaratnāvali*, explains jaḍa thus: Sa ca jñānasvarūpabhinnatvāj jaḍaḥ; jānāmī'ti jñānāśrayatvena sa bhāti, na jñānarūpatvena.

is no direct knowledge of a permanent identical self. The latter is proved indirectly from the fact of the recognition of permanent objects of thought.[1] In the phenomenon of recognition we have the two elements of recollection (smṛti) and previous perception (pūrvānubhava) of the object. The fact that we are able to remember a past cognition means the existence of a permanent self which is the substrate (āśraya) of the past perception and the present recollection. So, according to Prabhākara, the permanent self or personal identity is not the object of recognition but the substrate thereof.[2] It is all-pervading and unchanging. It is not self-illumined, for then we should have knowledge even in deep sleep, which we do not have, though the self evidently exists in deep sleep. The self-luminous cognition, "I know the jar," manifests the jar as the object and the self as the substrate of the cognition. The self is immediately known as the substrate of the cognition, even as the jar is known as the object of the cognition. What appears as the "I" is the self, free from all objective elements. Since the self is manifested to us in all cognitions, even in those in which there is no cognition of the body, the self is regarded as distinct from the body. The self is not perceptible in itself, but is always known as the agent (kartā) of the cognition and not the object (karma). The act of cognition does not produce its result (svaphala) in the self, so that the self is never an object of perception, external or internal. There is no such thing as self-consciousness apart from object-consciousness. The self cannot be the subject as well as the object of consciousness.[3] It is the agent, the enjoyer, and is omnipresent, though non-conscious. It is thus entirely distinct from the body, senses and understanding, is manifested

[1] *Vivaraṇaprameyasaṁgrata.* Thibaut's E.T., p. 405 (*Indian Thought*, vol. i.).

[2] The Advaita disputes this view. In the act of recollection there is the present self; in the previous perception there was the past self; and the gulf between the two cannot be bridged, unless it be through an act of recognition, which would require another, and so on *ad infinitum*. It cannot be argued that the present recollection and the previous perception jointly apprehend the continued existence of the self, since the two, one past and the other present, cannot come together.

[3] *Śāstradīpikā*, pp. 348–349.

in all cognitions, and is eternal. Prabhākara denies that the soul is of the size of an atom or of the body which it informs. Though it is omnipresent, it cannot experience what is going on in another body, since it can experience only that which goes on in the bodily organism brought about by the past karma of the soul. There are many souls, one in each body. In its liberated state the soul continues to exist as a mere *esse* (sat), serving as the substratum of the collective cognition of all things taken together, but not of feeling, since the properties of pleasure and pain cannot manifest themselves except in a body. It is imperishable, since it is not brought into existence by any cause.[1]

Pārthasārathi argues that there is no contradiction in holding that the self is both the subject and the object of perception. When Prabhākara says that the self is manifested by the act of cognition, he means that the self is also an object of consciousness. In the phenomena of recognition and recollection the object appears in consciousness and not the subject. It is the self apprehended as the object of perception that is represented in consciousness as the object of present recollection and recognition. If, in the recognition of the self, the self were not an object, then the act would be objectless, but there can be no consciousness without an object. So the self must be regarded as the object of self-consciousness.[2] The self is cognised by the same process of valid cognition as the objects themselves, but even then the self is the subject of cognition and not the object, even as a person who walks, though he has the action of walking as his own, is regarded only as the agent of walking and not its object.

According to the followers of Kumārila, the self is not manifested in every cognitive act. The object-consciousness is not always appropriated by the self. One sometimes knows the object " this is a jar," but one does not know that he knows the jar. While the self is not manifested as the subject or the object of the object-consciousness (viṣayavitti), sometimes there occurs along with the object-consciousness another distinct consciousness, *viz.* self-consciousness (ahaṁpratyaya), of which the self is the object. Prabhākara is right in holding that the subject is always involved in the consciousness of not-self,

[1] Jhā's *Prābhākara Mīmāṁsā*.

[2] Pp. 344 ff.

but it is not always explicitly manifested. Between the presence of the self and the consciousness of the presence, there is a difference and it is not necessary for us to be aware of the self whenever we apprehend an object. The self is manifested only in self-consciousness, which cannot be identified with object-consciousness. Self-consciousness marks a higher degree of conscious life than the mere consciousness of the object.[1] There is a distinction between direct or primary experience as the apprehension of the object and reflective or secondary experience as the return of the mind on itself.

Prabhākara does not admit that the ātman is the same as saṁvit, or consciousness, and is therefore obliged to say that the ātman is not self-illumined. But it is difficult to defend this view. The ātman is the pramātṛ or the knower, and Prabhākara describes saṁvit or consciousness, as the knower, and sometimes as cognition.[2] In refuting the theory of Kumārila that the self is an object of mental perception, Śālikanātha admits that the self is self-illumined and also involved in the cognition of external objects,[3] so that it is not the unconscious substrate of consciousness. Saṁvit is self-illumined, though it is not cognised as an object of consciousness. Again, cognitions are said to be pariṇāmas (modifications) of the self, and so the nature of the self must be consciousness, otherwise it cannot be modified into cognitions. The self or consciousness can never the the object of consciousness, but this does not mean that it is non-conscious. It is the basis of all knowledge. In knowledge itself it appears as the subject or the ego. The ego is neither more nor less than the self, of which we are immediately conscious as the subject or substrate of cognition. The self is neither a substance, nor a quality, nor an action. It is mere consciousness. As the Advaita Vedānta would put it, it becomes an ego when illusorily associated with the organ of egoity. The " ego-form " is absent in deep sleep, when the self is freed from all shackles of egoity. In the cognition of objects, the all-pervading ātman or consciousness, appears as qualified by its relation to the object. Prabhākara seems to be aware that his theory leads him to the position associated with the Advaita Vedānta, but is anxious that it should not be stressed, since his main objective is to emphasise the distinctions of persons and their individual responsibility. Prabhākara says: " The statement that the expressions ' I ' and ' mine ' indicate a misconception of ātman should be made to those who have subdued their attachment to worldly objects, and not to those who stick to karma."[4]

According to Kumārila, the soul is different from the body, eternal and omnipresent. The ātman is consciousness itself,

[1] *Śāstradīpikā*, pp. 344–352.

[2] Saṁvit is used as meaning consciousness. Saṁvid utpattikāraṇam ātmamanassannikarṣākhyam (*Prakaraṇapañcika*, p. 63).

[3] Svayaṁprakāsatvena, viṣayapratītigocaratvena (*Prakaraṇapañcikā*, p. 151).

[4] *Bṛhatī*, p. 32. MS. in the Asiatic Society of Bengal.

though the souls are many.[1] Since all souls are of the nature of consciousness, the Upaniṣads speak of them as one.[2] The ātman is consciousness as well as the substrate of cognition, which is a product of the ātman.[3] The existence of the self is inferred through the notion of "I." The self is manifested by itself, though imperceptible to others.[4] The self is an object of cognition, since it is directly perceived as the jar is. It is the object of mental perception (mānasa-pratyakṣa). The self is both the object and the subject of knowledge,[5] and this is no contradiction, since we distinguish in the self a substantial (dravya) element, which is the object of cognition, and an element of consciousness (bodha), which is the subject of cognition.[6] The followers of Prabhākara object to this view. If the substantive element of the self is non-intelligent, then it is not self at all. What remains is the conscious element only, and it cannot serve as both subject and object. It is partless, and therefore incapable of undergoing changes so as to have simultaneously the character of both subject and object. If substantiality constitutes the object of consciousness, then the self cannot be the subject or the knower, since it is as much a substance as a jar is. If Kumārila urges that the pure form of consciousness is the subject, while the same consciousness empirically modified is the object,[7] then we seem to have three types, *viz.* consciousness of an object in itself (śuddhaviṣayagrahaṇam), pure subject (śuddhajñātṛtā) and the subject modified by an object like a jar (ghaṭāvacchinnajñātṛtā). Besides, since the self is directly revealed in every cognition of an object as its cogniser, it is unnecessary to assume another cognition like

[1] S.V., *Ātmavāda*, 74–75.

[2] *Tantravārttika*, ii. 1, 5.

[3] Rāmānuja, who accepts a similar view, regards cognition as an eternal quality of the ātman, capable of expansion and contraction, while Kumārila thinks that cognition is an evolution (pariṇāma) of ātman which arises through the pramāṇas.

[4] S.V., *Ātmavāda*, 142–3.

[5] S.V., *Ātmavāda*, 107.

[6] Cp. *Nyāyaratnāvali*. "Ātmano' sti aṁśadvayam, cidaṁśo' cidaṁśaś ca; cidaṁśena draṣṭṛtvam acidaṁśena jñānasukhādipariṇāmitvam 'māṁ ahaṁ jānāmi' iti jñeyatvaṁ ca" (P. Sastri: *Pūrva Mīmāṁsā*, p. 95). See also *Vivaranapraneyasaṁgraha*, Thibaut's E.T., *Indian Thought*, vol. i., p. 357.

[7] Ghaṭāvacchinnā hi jñātṛtā grāhyā, śuddhaiva jñātṛtā grāhikā (*Nyāyamañjari*, 430).

internal perception, which is said to reveal directly the self as its object.

If knowledge belongs to the self, then the self cannot be non-sentient. If the self is consciousness, then it is self-established, for all proof assumes its reality.[1] In Kumārila objects seem to be connected with consciousness by means of vṛtti. The unconscious element (acidaṁśa) of the ātman is, perhaps, the antaḥkaraṇa (the inner organ), through which the self is evolved into the form of the vṛtti. Simply because the ātman is both subject and object in the phenomenon of self-consciousness, it does not follow that it has elements of consciousness and unconsciousness. In fact, we see that both Prabhākara and Kumārila are struggling towards a more adequate conception of the self which they are unable to reach on account of their practical interests.

XIII

The Nature of Reality

The Mīmāṁsaka theory of perception assumes the reality of objects, for perception arises only when there is contact with real objects.[2] When we perceive, we perceive objects and not our cognitions.[3] We infer the cognition, but do not perceive it. The doctrine of the self-validity of knowledge implies the reality of objects which are apprehended. Kumārila refutes the theory that ideas have no foundation (nirālambanavāda) as well as the theory that the external reality is a mere void (śūnyavāda). The reality of the external world is the only foundation of experience and life. If there were nothing but ideas, all our judgments, which rest on the belief in external reality, would be false. That cognitions have real substrata in the external world is not contradicted by further knowledge. If it is said that the unreality of waking cognitions follows from the insight of the Yogis, Kumārila answers by denying the validity of yogic insight,

[1] See Sureśvara's *Saṁbandhavārttika*, 1066.

[2] Satsaṁprayoga, M.S., i. 1. 4.

[3] Arthaviṣayā pratyakṣabuddhir na buddhiviṣayā. Śabara on i. 1. 4.

and cites other yogic intuitions which confirm the reality of the world. The Mīmāṁsā thinkers do not support the theory of the phenomenality of the world. "If it be the conclusion of those who know Brahman that all that is known is false, and that what is not known is true, I beg to part from them with a bow." [1] The universe is real and is independent of the mind which perceives it.

Prabhākara admits eight categories of substance (dravya), quality (guṇa), action (karma), generality (sāmānya), inherence (paratantratā), force (śakti), similarity (sādṛśya), and number (saṁkhyā). Substance, quality and action are explained practically on the lines of the Nyāya theory. Sāmānya is, according to Prabhākara, real. It exists in each individual entirely and is an object of sense-perception. It has not a separate existence apart from individuals. Prabhākara does not admit the existence of the highest genus, on the ground that we have no consciousness of it. We do not perceive a number of objects as merely existing. When we speak of an individual object as existent (sat), we mean that the individual has its specific existence (svarūpasattā). We do not perceive a thing apart from its qualities. The universal and the particular are related by way of samavāya, or inherence. When a new individual is born, a new relation of inherence is generated by which the individual is brought into relation with the class character that exists in the other individuals. When an individual is destroyed, the relation of inherence between the individual and the universal is destroyed. Inherence is not eternal (nitya), since it subsists in perishable things as well. It is not one, but is as many as there are things. It is both produced and unproduced, perceptible and imperceptible, in accordance with the nature of the things to which it belongs. Force is the common name given to the potency by which substances, qualities, actions and generalities happen to be the causes of things.[2] The potency which is inferred from the effects is eternal in eternal things and non-eternal in others. According to Prabhākara, similarity must

[1] *Bṛhatī*, p. 30. See also *Śāstradīpikā: Advaitamatanirāsa.*

[2] The view, that an unseen power resides in the cause which produces the effect, is criticised by the Naiyāyika on the ground that this power is not a matter of observation or inference. See *Kusumāñjali*, i.

not be confused with substance, quality or action, since it abides in qualities by internal relation. Substance cannot abide in qualities, nor can a quality or action abide in another quality or action. Similarity is not identical with generic nature, since it depends on its correlative. It belongs to genera also, as when we say that the genus of a cow is like that of a horse. It cannot be identified with non-existence, since it is not cognised in relation to its counter-entity. We have already seen that similarity cannot be known through perception; inference or testimony and upamāṇa or comparison, give us a knowledge of it.[1] Force, similarity and number are regarded as independent categories, since they cannot be reduced to others. Viśeṣa of the Naiyāyika is not recognised, since it denotes a particular kind of quality. Abhāva, or non-existence, is nothing apart from its basis in space where it is supposed to exist.

Kumārila divides all categories into positive (bhāva) and negative (abhāva). The latter are of four kinds: prior, posterior, absolute and mutual. The positive categories are of four kinds: substance, quality, action and generality. Force (śakti) and similarity (sādṛśya) are brought under substance. Potency is a property of objects which we infer but do not perceive. It is brought into existence along with things. Number is a quality. Force is natural (sahaja) or produced (ādheya). Similarity is only a quality consisting in the fact that more than one object has the same set of features. It cannot be a distinct category in view of the fact that we are cognisant of different degrees of similarity in our ordinary experience. Inherence is not, for Kumārila, something distinct from the things themselves in which it exists.[2] Like Prabhākara, Kumārila holds that generic nature is perceptible.[3] Relation subsists between things which are distinct, but inherence is said to be a relation between things which are inseparable, like the class and the individual, and so it is an impossible conception.

Substance is that in which qualities reside, and there are nine substances: earth, water, air, fire, ākāśa, self, mind, time

[1] *Prakaraṅapañcikā*, pp. 110 ff. [2] S.V., *Pratyakṣasūtra*, pp. 146–150.
[3] Indriyagocara, S.V., *Vanavāda*, 24.

and space. Kumārila adds darkness and sound to this list.[1] Earth, water, air and fire possess colour and tangibility, and so are the objects of the senses of sight and touch when they are not in their atomic state. The other substances are not perceptible but only inferred. The apparent whiteness of ākāśa is due to the particles of fire in it. Ākāśa is inferred as the substratum of sound. Air, in Prabhākara's view, is neither hot nor cold. The heat or coldness of it is due to the fire or water particles diffused in it. It is perceptible, according to Kumārila, through touch.

In the statement of qualities, and their assignment to substances, Prabhākara and Kumārila are indebted to the Vaiśeṣika. Kumārila enumerates the twenty-four qualities after Praśastapāda, only substituting tone (dhvani) for sound, and manifestation and potency for merit and demerit. While Prabhākara asserts that individuality applies to eternal things alone, Kumārila holds that it applies to products as well as eternal things.

Action is of the five kinds mentioned in the Vaiśesika. While Prabhākara holds that it is only an object of inference, Kumārila maintains that it is perceived. According to Prabhākara, we say we see motion when we see conjunction and disjunction with points of space. These contacts are in space while motion is in the object. Kumārila holds that if motion is inferred, it can only be inferred as the immaterial cause of the conjunction and disjunction of an object with points in space, and this would imply that it subsists both in the object and in space, whereas it exists only in the object. So he argues that we see motion which is in the object and which brings about conjunction and disjunction in space. While Kumārila admits the existence of generalities of substance, quality and action, Prabhākara does not accept the last two. The Pūrva Mīmāṁsā does not accept the doctrine of original creation or utter dissolution.[2]

XIV

Ethics

Dharma is the scheme of right living. Jaimini defines dharma as an ordinance or command.[3] Codanā, or injunction,

[1] Darkness, according to Prabhākara, is mere absence of light. If it were a substance or a quality, it must be perceptible by day also. Kumārila argues that darkness is a substance, since it has the quality of blueness and is capable of motion.

[2] S.V., *Saṁbandhākṣepaparihāra*, 113.

[3] Codanālakṣano 'rtho dharmaḥ (i. 1. 2).

is the lakṣaṇa or sign of dharma. It is the jurist's definition of law. According to Śabara, codanā denotes utterances which impel men to action.[1] The "ought" has an external source, since duties are revealed to us by a power not ourselves. The word "codanā" has another meaning, namely, inspiration or impulsion from within. What appeals to the heart within agrees with what is commanded from without. The individual's will and the verdict of the race agree. The commentators make out that what is enjoined has the capacity to produce more pleasure than pain; so the courses of conduct prescribed lead to desirable ends. Happiness is the goal recognised by the Pūrva Mīmāṁsā, though it is not happiness in this world. For the sake of happiness hereafter we have to practise self-denial here. Activities which result in loss or pain (anartha) are not dharma. Dharma is what is enjoined, and it leads to happiness.[2] If we do not observe the commands, we not only miss our happiness but become subject to suffering.

The ethics of the Pūrva Mīmāṁsā is founded on revelation.[3] The Vedic injunctions lay down the details of dharma. Good action, according to the Mīmāṁsaka, is what is prescribed by the Veda. The smṛti texts, according to the orthodox theory, have corresponding Vedic texts, though some of them may be lost. If the smṛtis are in conflict with the śruti, the former are to be disregarded.[4] When we find that the smṛtis are laid down with a selfish interest, they must be thrown out.[5] Next to the smṛtis is the practice of good men or custom.[6] The duties which have no scriptural sanction are explained on principles of utility. If we perform any acts in response to natural instincts, we are not virtuous.[7] The life of the Hindu is governed by the rules of the Vedas, so that Mīmāṁsā rules are very important for the interpretation of the Hindu law.

To gain salvation, we have to observe nitya karmas like sandhyā, etc., and naimittika karmas when the proper occasion

[1] Codaneti kriyāyāḥ pravartakaṁ vacanam āhuḥ (Sabara on i. 1. 2).

[2] Command corresponds to vidhi, duty to dharma, and sanction to phala.

[3] Cp. Paley's definition of Virtue as "the doing good to mankind in obedience to the will of God and for the sake of everlasting happiness."

[4] i. 3. 3. [5] i. 3. 4. [6] i. 3. 8–9. [7] iv. 1. 3.

arises. These are unconditional obligations. If we do not fulfil them we incur sin (pratyavāya). To gain special ends, we perform kāmya karmas. We need not perform them if we do not care for the ends. By avoiding forbidden (niṣiddha) courses of conduct we avoid hell, and if we keep clear of kāmya (optional) karmas we will free ourselves from selfish ends, and if we keep up the unconditional duties we attain salvation.

According to Jaimini, only the three upper classes are entitled to the performance of sacrifices. He has the support of Ātreya. But even then there were thinkers like Bādari who held that all castes were equally entitled to their performance. Jaimini takes his stand on the fact that the Śūdras cannot study the Vedas, and so holds that they cannot perform sacrifices.[1]

The followers of Prabhākara enter into an elaborate analysis of volition. In the *Siddhāntamuktāvali*, Prabhākara's view of voluntary action is set forth as consisting of the following steps: The consciousness of something to be done (kāryatājñāna), or the feeling of the sense of duty; the desire to do it (cikīrṣā), which implies the consciousness that it can be done (kṛtisādhyatājñāna); the volition (pravṛtti); the motor reaction (ceṣṭā); and the act (kriyā). Prabhākara lays more stress on the sense of duty than on the consciousness of good, which is, however, present in kāmya karmas. In the Vedic sacrifices, the injunction by its verbal power (śābdībhāvanā) tends to produce action in the agent towards the end indicated in the injunction. The Mīmāṁsā assumes human freedom, otherwise the human individuals cannot be held responsible for their acts.

The law of karma, when rightly understood, is not inconsistent with freedom. We can refrain from taking the first step, but when once we take it we are led on easily to the second by the operation of the law of habit.[2]

The Vedas represent the wisdom of the race, and if they are

[1] vi. 1. 25–38. Jaimini is opposed by certain facts which he tries hard to explain away. In vi. 1. 44–50, the right of the chariot-builder (rathakāra), who is outside the four castes, to the performance of Agnyādhāna sacrifice is admitted. Niṣādas are entitled to perform Raudrayajña (vi. i. 51–52).

[2] The ghost of Darius moralises on the Persian downfall: "When of our own free will we rush into sin, God himself becomes our ally."

found to conflict with enlightened social opinion, a suspicion of their validity naturally arises. Kumārila argues that Vedic injunctions have intrinsic validity, since they are acceptable to most people. In his opinion, the social consciousness confirms the authoritativeness of the Vedic rules. He, however, asks us to accept the guidance of the Veda in the matter of duty, and not rely on such uncertain guides as the social good or the happiness of others.[1] The conduct of the great men also indicates to us the nature of dharma. But Kumārila is afraid of supporting the principles of Buddhism on account of their opposition to the authoritativeness of the Vedas. He has the honesty to admit that the Buddhist code of conduct emphasising ahiṁsā is a noble one, though its repudiation of the Vedas is ignoble. The truth of Buddhism is mixed up with much that is false, and so he compares it to the milk put in the dog's skin.[2]

The Vedānta protests against the doctrine of mechanical ceremonialism in the same spirit in which Jesus protested against the Pharisees and Luther against the doctrine of justification by works. Every work, however holy it may seem, may be done in a mechanical way without any feeling whatever, and cannot therefore by itself be of much avail for salvation. Rituation is rather injurious on account of the false trust reposed in it. We may perform any number of sacrifices, though they may not effect much change in the inner spirit. If virtue consists in moral regeneration or transformation of the heart, what is necessary is not the ceremonial sacrifice, but the sacrifice of selfishness. The Vedas speak of śraddhā or faith, bhakti or devotion, and tapas or austerity,[3] which are only remotely connected with sacrifices. The theistic views which declare that all work should be performed as a sacrifice to God are in conformity with the spirit of the Veda. Some later Mīmāṁsakas hold this view. Laugākṣi Bhāskara tells us that when duty is performed in a spirit of dedication to God it becomes the cause of emancipation.[4] The scene

[1] S.V., ii. 242–47.

[2] Śvacarmanikṣiptakṣīravad (*Tantravārttika*, i. 3. 6, p. 127).

[3] Śraddhāṁ devā yajamānā . . . upāsate (R.V., x. 151–4). See also R.V., x. 167.

[4] Īśvarārpaṇabuddhyā kriyamāṇas tu niḥśreyasahetuḥ (*Arthasaṁgraha*).

of rewards in this world or hereafter suppresses the spirit of disinterestedness and self-sacrifice. The Mīmāṁsakas, moreover, speak to us mainly of sacrifices,[1] and thus fail to cover the major part of human life.

XV

Apūrva

Acts are enjoined with a view to their fruits. There is a necessary connection between the act and its result. An act performed to-day cannot effect a result at some future date unless it gives rise before passing away to some unseen result. Jaimini assumes the existence of such an unseen force, which he calls apūrva,[2] which may be regarded either as the imperceptible antecedent of the fruit, or as the after-state of the act. Since sacrifices and the like are laid down for the purpose of definite results to follow after a long time, the deferred fruition of the action is not possible unless it be through the medium of apūrva.[3] Apūrva is the metaphysical link between work and its result.[4] The Mīmāṁsakas are unwilling to trace the results of actions to God's will, since a uniform cause cannot account for the variety of effects.[5]

According to Kumārila, apūrva is a capability in the principal action or in the agent, which did not exist prior to the performance of the action and whose existence is proved by the authority of the scriptures. The positive force created by the act and leading to the attainment of the result is the apūrva. Arthāpatti, or implication, proves the existence of apūrva. If we do not assume its existence, many Vedic passages become inexplicable. A sacrifice performed by an agent produces directly a certain potency in the agent which resides in him like many other powers throughout life, at the end of which it gains for him the promised reward. According to Prabhākara, apūrva cannot be in the self, since by its very omnipresence the self is inactive. He does not accept the view that the action tends to produce in the agent a certain faculty, which is the immediate cause

[1] Yāgādir eva dharmaḥ, tallakṣaṇaṁ vedapratipādyaḥ prayojanavad artho dharmaḥ (*Arthasaṁgraha*, p. 1).

[2] Something new, not known before.

[3] P.M.S., ii. 1. 5.

[4] Cp. Bhīmācārya's definition: Yāgādijanyaḥ svargādijanakaḥ kaścana guṇaviśeṣaḥ (*Nyāyakośa*).

[5] S.B., iii. 2. 40.

of the final result. That the sacrifice produces such a faculty is not proved either by perception, inference or scripture. Action is brought out by the exertion of the agent, and causal potency must reside in this exertion. So we must assume the faculty in the action and not the agent. Again in iii. 1. 3, it is established that the kārya is the direct cause of the production of the result desired by the prompted (niyojya) person. This kārya cannot be the act, since the act is not the direct cause of the final result. The kārya is brought about by the act (kṛti) or the exertion of the agent, which is due to the prompting (niyoga).[1] The exertion produces in the agent a result (kārya), to which also Prabhākara gives the name of niyoga, since this acts as an incentive to the agent to put forth exertion towards the performance of the action. But this niyoga cannot produce the result unless it is aided by fate, as Śālikanātha expresses it. Prabhākara's[2] view is not easy to follow, and does not seem to be an improvement on Kumārila's.

Uddyotakara criticises the doctrine of apūrva.[3] It cannot be eternal, since, on such a view, there would be no possibility of death, as merit and demerit would be eternal. If apūrva is one, then the happiness and the misery of all persons should be alike. We cannot say that, though apūrva is one, the manifesting agencies are many, since we do not know what the manifesting agency is, whether it is the capacity to bring about the result or a property belonging to apūrva. We cannot say whether the apūrva is one with the capacity or different from it. If we say that the hidden apūrva is made manifest, we must explain how it is first hidden. Even if the eternal apūrva be different for different persons, the difficulties of manifestation are not avoided. Śaṁkara criticises the theory of apūrva on the ground that it is non-spiritual and cannot act unless it is moved by something spiritual. The results of actions cannot be explained by the principle of apūrva alone. If it is said that God acts in accordance with the principle of apūrva, it is just the view of the Vedānta that God acts with reference to the law of karma.[4]

XVI

MOKṢA

Jaimini and Śabara did not face the problem of ultimate release. They pointed the way to a life in heaven, but not to freedom from saṁsāra. But the later writers could not avoid the problem, since it occupied the attention of the

[1] iii. 1. 3. [2] *Prakaraṇapañcikā*, pp. 185 ff.
[3] N.V., i. 1. 7.
[4] Karmāpekṣād apūrvāpekṣād vā yathāstu tathāstu Īśvarāt phalam (S.B., iii. 2. 41).

thinkers of the other schools. According to Prabhākara, liberation consists in the total disappearance of dharma and adharma, whose operation is the cause of rebirth. It is defined as "the absolute cessation of the body, caused by the disappearance of all dharma and adharma."[1] The individual, finding that in saṁsāra pleasures are mixed up with pain, turns his attention to liberation. He tries to avoid the forbidden acts as well as the prescribed ones which lead to some sort of happiness here or hereafter. He undergoes the necessary expiations for exhausting the previously accumulated karma, and gradually, by a true knowledge of the soul aided by contentment and self-control, gets rid of his bodily existence.[2] Mere knowledge cannot give us freedom from bondage, which can be attained only by the exhaustion of action. Knowledge prevents further accumulation of merit and demerit.[3] Evidently the followers of Prabhākara do not regard karma by itself as sufficient for effecting release. Karma, in expectation of reward, leads to further birth. Our likes and dislikes determine our future existences. We must break through the circle if we want to attain release. Liberation is the cessation of pleasure as well as of pain. It is not a state of bliss, since the attributeless soul cannot have even bliss. Mokṣa is simply the natural form of the soul.[4]

According to Kumārila, mokṣa is the state of ātman in itself, free from all pain.[5] Some regard mokṣa as experience of the bliss of ātman.[6] This, however, is against the view of Kumārila, who asserts that liberation cannot be eternal unless it is of a negative character.[7] Pārthasārathi also holds that the state of release is one of freedom from pain, and not enjoyment of bliss. The self is the potency of knowledge (jñānaśakti). Cognitions of objects are due to the

1 Ātyantikas tu dehocchedo niśśeṣadharmādharmaparikṣayanibandhano mokṣa iti siddham. Dharmādharmavaśīkṛto jīvas tāsu tāsu yoniṣu saṁsarati (*Prakaraṇapañcikā*, *Tattvāloka*, p. 156).

2 Śamadamabrahmacaryādikāṅgopabṛṁhitenā'tmajñānena, p. 157.

3 For a different view, see *Bhāṭṭacintāmaṇi*, Benares ed., p. 57.

4 Svātmasphuraṇarūpah (*Prakaraṇapañcikā*, p. 157).

5 Paramātmaprāptyavasthāmātram.

6 Cittena svātmasaukhyānubhūti.

7 S.V., *Saṁbandhākṣepaparihāra*, p. 107.

activities of the manas and the senses. Since these have no existence in mokṣa, the self exists in its pure essence without any kind of manifestation. It is a state devoid of characteristic qualities like pleasure, pain and the like. It may be regarded as a state of consciousness devoid of objective cognition or feeling of any sort. Kumārila, however, regards mokṣa as a positive state, the realisation of the ātman, and this comes very near to the Advaita view. He thinks that knowledge is not enough for liberation. He believes that release can be attained through karma combined with jñāna.

XVII

God

The Pūrva Mīmāṁsā posits a number of deities in order that prescribed offerings may be made to them. It does not go beyond these gods, since the observance of Vedic dharma does not require the postulation of any supreme power. Jaimini does not so much deny God as ignore him. No detail of the Vedic religion requires the assistance of God. The dharma is laid down by an eternal self-existent Veda, and we have already seen how attempts to regard the Veda as the work of God are rejected. The rewards of sacrifices are not due to any beneficent God. Even when the results do not appear at once, the supersensuous principle of apūrva is produced, and in time it helps the sacrificer to his reward. There is no reliable evidence to prove the existence of an omniscient being. Perception, inference and scripture are all unavailing. The passages of the scripture, which declare "he knows all," "he knows the world," extol the merits of the sacrificer. The succession of works and the consequent effects go on from eternity to eternity like seed and plant. The Mīmāṁsā declines to accept the belief in the periodic creation and dissolution of all things. The process of becoming and passing away is constant. It is idle to assume that the supreme Lord brings to a stand at one time the potencies of all the souls and then awakens them all when a new creation starts. While Prabhākara admits that the universe has constituent parts which have a beginning and an end, he holds that the universe as a whole has neither beginning nor end. We do not see the interference of any divine being in the production of the bodies of men and animals, which owe their existence to their parents. We cannot say that the atoms act under the will of God, since in our experience each soul acts on the body which belongs to it. But atoms are not the body of God. Even if we grant a bodily organism to God, the activity of the latter must be due to the effort of God. If the effort is eternal, the atoms would be incessantly active. Nor can we say that there is a divine superviser of dharma and adharma, since they belong to intelligent individuals. One being, however great, cannot know the dharma and the adharma of another. God cannot perceive the imperceptible dharma of others through his senses or by his mind, since it is outside his body. It is difficult to understand the nature of God's control over dharma and adharma. The control is not a case of conjunction (saṁyoga), since dharma and adharma are qualities and conjunction is possible only for substances. It is not a case of samavāya, since dharma and adharma inhere in other souls and cannot inhere in God.[1]

Kumārila criticises the Nyāya view that establishes the existence of God by reasoning, and declares that the Vedas are composed by God. If the Vedas, considered to be the work of God, say that God is the creator of the world, no value need be attached to such a statement.[2] If the creator created the world, who can testify to it? Again, how does he create the world? If he has no material body, he cannot have any desire towards creation. If he has one, it cannot be due to himself, and so we require another creator of it. If his body be regarded as eternal, of what constituents is it made, since earth and the other elements are yet unproduced? If matter exists prior to his creative activity, there is no reason to deny the existence of other objects. What is the purpose of God in creating a world fraught with misery? The explanation of past karma is not available, since there is no creation

[1] Jhā: *Prābhākaramīmāṁsā*, pp. 80–7.
[2] S.V., *Saṁbandhākṣepaparihāra*, 114; *Codanāsūtra*, 142.

prior to it. He cannot create out of pity, since there are no beings to whom compassion can be shown. Besides, on such a view, only happy beings should have been created. We cannot say that no creation is possible without an element of pain, since nothing is impossible for God. But if he is limited by other considerations, then he is not omnipotent. If creation is said to be for the amusement of God, then it contradicts the theory that he is perfectly happy and would involve God in much wearisome toil. Nor would his desire to destroy the world be intelligible. Why should we trust his words? for, though he may not have created the world, he might say so to show off his great power.[1] If the creator differs from others in the amount of his dharma, the latter is possible only through the Vedas, and so they are prior to creation.[2] If it be said that the atoms act under the will of God, how does God's will arise? If it is impelled by a cause like adṛṣṭa, that may as well be the cause of the world.[3] If God depends on other things, then his independence is compromised. If we introduce the will of God, that is enough to account for the world, and karma will sink into insignificance.

As to the corporeal nature of the deities, Śabara thinks that the Vedas speak of such a nature by way of praise. To say that "we have taken hold of your hand" means that we have come under your protection.[4] Both Prabhākara and Kumārila deny the possession of bodies by gods. We do not derive the fruits of our actions through the favour of gods, and so they need not have any physical forms. Though the deities were taken as possessing some sort of reality by the founders of the Mīmāṁsā, the later Mīmāṁsakas, anxious to emphasise the importance of mantras, argue that the sacrificer has nothing to do with the person of the gods, but should confine his attention to the mantras. They are inclined to regard the deities as imaginary, and yet persist in urging that making offerings to them will ensure reward, though they may not have any existence beyond the mantras addressed to them.[5]

[1] Asṛṣṭvāpi hy asau brūyād ātmaiśvaryaprakāśanāt, 60.

[2] S.V., *Saṁbandhākṣepaparihāra*, 44–72, 114–116.

[3] *Ibid.*, 72–73.

[4] See Śabara on ix. 1. 9.

[5] See Āpadeva: *Devatāsvarūpavicāra*.

In a recent work on the Pūrva Mīmāṁsā, an ingenious attempt is made to reconcile the Mīmāṁsā view on this question with that of the Vedānta.[1] It is argued that while Jaimini repudiates the conception of God as the distributor of rewards, he does not deny the existence of God as the creator of the world. While the other systems hold that God is the creator of the world as well as the apportioner of the fruits, Jaimini contends that God is not the latter. Any object is called a "fruit" when it gives pleasure or pain to a person. So long as it is not related to an individual by way of enjoyment or suffering, it is not to be regarded as a "fruit."[2] When karma is said to be the cause of the "fruit," it means that it causes the enjoyment of the object and not its simple creation. Since Bādarāyaṇa takes up Jaimini's view in the third chapter of his work, he is attacking the view of Jaimini that apūrva and not God is the cause of the apportionment of the rewards. If Jaimini had denied the creatorship of God, Bādarāyaṇa would certainly have taken up its refutation in the second chapter, which is devoted to the criticism of the rival hypotheses. Jaimini felt that, if God had the sole responsibility for the inequalities of the world, he could not be freed from the charge of partiality and cruelty, and for this reason traced the varying fortunes of men to their past conduct. The explanation is not convincing, for things should first exist before we can derive happiness or misery from them. If apūrva is the apportioner of our happiness and misery, then it must also be the creator of things. If God is necessary for creation, then apūrva must be simply the principle of karma which God takes into account in the creation of the world. Directly or indirectly, God becomes the creator as well as the apportioner of the fruits.

The lacuna in the Pūrva Mīmāṁsā was so unsatisfactory that the later writers slowly smuggled in God. The force of the criticism that the unconscious principle of apūrva cannot achieve the harmonious results attributed to it was felt.[3] Slowly the divine principle was introduced. But this superintending Lord need not be regarded as bound by the law of karma, for no one is bound by his own nature. The law of karma expresses the constancy of God. When Kumārila admits that both karma (work) and upāsana (worship) are necessary for effecting liberation, he is positing the existence of God, though, of course, it is argued that upāsana is a kind of karma which of itself produces its proper fruit. Evidently it was felt very early that the Mīmāṁsā system could not satisfy the thoughtful if it did not ally itself with theism.

[1] P. Śāstri: *Pūrva Mīmāṁsā*, p. iii. [2] S.B., iii. 2. 38.
[3] *Bhāmatī*, iii. 2. 41.

So Āpadeva and Laugākṣi Bhāskara declare that if the sacrifice is performed in honour of the supreme Lord, it will lead to the highest good. The tendency is carried out to its fullest extent in Vedānta Deśika's *Seśvara Mīmāṁsā.*

In the Pūrva Mīmāṁsā the emphasis is on the ethical side. The ultimate reality of the world is looked upon as the constant principle of karma. God is righteousness, or dharma. The contents of dharma are embodied in the Vedas, and the Vedas simply reveal the mind of God. Kumārila says: "This śāstra called the Veda, which is Brahman in the form of sounds, is established by the one supreme spirit."[1] Kumārila opens his treatise with a prayer to Śiva: "Reverence to him whose body is made of pure knowledge, whose divine eyes are the three Vedas, who is the cause of the attainment of bliss, and who wears the crescent moon."[2] The Vedas are the revelation of the mind of God. While the sacrificial works may be the special causes of bliss, God is the general cause. This view is also in consistency with the avowed purpose of Kumārila to reinterpret the Mīmāṁsā doctrine so as to bring it into agreement with the non-naturalistic tendencies of the time.[3]

It is unnecessary to say much about the unsatisfactory character of the Pūrva Mīmāṁsā as a system of philosophy. As a philosophical view of the universe it is strikingly incom-

[1] Sabdabrahmeti yac cedaṁ śāstraṁ vedākhyam ucyate
Tad apy adhiṣṭhitaṁ sarvam ekena paramātmanā.
(*Tantravārttika*, p. 719.)

[2] Viśuddhajñānadehāya trivedīdivyacakṣuṣe
Śreyaḥprāptinimittāya namaḥ somārdhadhārine. (S.V., i. 1.)

Pārthasārathi, in his *Nyāyaratnākara*, interprets this verse in a different sense, so as not to commit Kumārila to a theistic position. He makes the verse refer to the sacrificial ceremony. Viśuddham mīmāṁsayā saṁśodhitaṁ jñānam eva deho yasya (that whose body is the knowledge purified by the Mīmāṁsā science); trivedy eva divyaṁ cakṣuḥ prakāśakaṁ yasya (that which is manifested by the three Vedas); somasya ardham sthānaṁ graha-camasādi tad dhārine (that which is equipped with the vessels of soma); iti yajñapakṣe'pi saṁgacchate. He allows, however, that Kumārila referred to the personal God "Siva": viśveśvaram mahādevaṁ stutipūrvaṁ namasyati. From S.S.S.S. (viii. 37) we find that Kumārila believed that Ātman is one as well as many, bhinnābhinnātmakatvātmā. This work, as a few others on the Vedānta, tries to make out that Kumārila was a Vedāntin.

[3] Prāyeṇaiva hi mīmāṁsā loke lokāyatīkṛtā
Tām āstikapathe kartum ayaṁ yatnaḥ kṛto mayā. (S.V., i. 10.)

plete. It did not concern itself with the problems of ultimate reality and its relation to the world of souls and matter. Its ethics was purely mechanical and its religion was unsound. The performance of the sacrifice was regarded as the most essential thing, and the devatās disappeared from the sight of the sacrificers. The later Mīmāṁsakas openly tell us that the deity is that whose name is inflected in the dative case. In the formula " Indrāya svāha," Indra is the deity. There is little in such a religion to touch the heart and make it glow. No wonder a reaction occurred in favour of a monotheism, Vaiṣṇava, Śaiva, or Tāntrika, which gave man a supreme God on whom he could depend and to whom he could surrender himself in sorrow and suffering.

REFERENCES.

GAṄGĀNĀTH JHĀ: **Ślokavārttika.**
GAṄGĀNĀTH JHĀ: **Prabhākara School of Pūrva Mīmāṁsā.**
KEITH: **Karma Mīmāṁsā.**
P. ŚĀSTRI: **Introduction to Pūrva Mīmāṁsā.**
SIRKAR: **The Mīmāṁsā Rules of Interpretation.**

CHAPTER VII

THE VEDĀNTA SŪTRA

The Vedānta and its interpretations—Authorship and date of the *Sūtra* —Relation to other schools—Brahman—The world—The individual self—Mokṣa—Conclusion.

I

Introduction

THE Vedānta philosophy deserves closer attention not only on account of its philosophical value, but also because it is closely bound up with the religion of India and is much more alive in that continent than any other system of thought. In one or the other of its forms the Vedānta determines the world view of the Hindu thinkers of the present time.

The term "Vedānta" means literally "the end of the Veda," or the doctrines set forth in the closing chapter of the Vedas, which are the Upaniṣads. The views of the Upaniṣads also constitute "the final aim of the Veda," or the essence of the Vedas.[1] The *Vedānta Sūtra* is called *Brahma Sūtra,* because it is an exposition of the doctrine of Brahman, and also *Śārīraka Sūtra,*[2] because it deals with the embodiment of the unconditioned self. While the *Karma Mīmāṁsā* of Jaimini investigates the duties (dharma) enjoined by the Veda, together with the rewards attached thereto, the *Uttara Mīmāṁsā* of Bādarāyaṇa describes the philosophico-theological views of the Upaniṣads.[3] Together, the two form a systematic investigation of the contents of the whole Veda. The Upani-

[1] "Tileṣu tailavad vede vedāntas supratiṣṭhitaḥ" (*Muktikopaniṣad*). Gautama distinguishes between the Upaniṣads and the Vedānta (xxii. 9), but the tradition has always held that the Aupaniṣadas are the followers of the Vedānta.

[2] Śarīra, body.

[3] Cp. Vedāntavākyakusumagrathanārthatvāt sūtrāṇām (S.B., i. 1. 1).

ṣads are but a series of glances at truth from various points of view, and not an attempt to think out the great questions consecutively. Yet those who look upon them as revealed truth are under an obligation to show that their teaching forms a consistent whole, and Bādarāyaṇa attempts this work of systematisation. His work is not so much systematic philosophy as theological interpretation. "The work of Bādarāyaṇa stands to the Upaniṣads in the same relation as the Christian Dogmatics to the New Testament; it investigates their teaching about God, the world, the soul in its conditions of wandering and of deliverance, removes apparent contradictions in the doctrines, binds them systematically together, and is especially concerned to defend them against the attacks of opponents." [1] In five hundred and fifty-five sūtras, which consist mostly of two or three words each, the whole of the system is developed. The sūtras are unintelligible by themselves, and leave everything to the interpreter. They refuse, Proteus-like, to be caught in any definite shape. Their teaching is interpreted sometimes in the bright hues of personal theism, sometimes in the grey abstractions of absolutism. In different theological schools different traditions became established very early, which thinkers like Śaṁkara and Rāmānuja reduced to writing. The commentators, of whom the chief are Śaṁkara, Bhāskara, Yādavaprakāśa, Rāmānuja, Keśava, Nīlakaṇṭha, Madhva, Baladeva, Vallabha, and Vijñānabhikṣu,[2] do not all develop the same view, and it is not an easy question to settle which of them can be accepted as a guide to the right understanding of the Sūtra, for their commentaries were written at a time when the tenets had become matters of grave doubt and serious discussion. They develop their interpretations in the light of their own preconceived opinions, and sometimes overlook the literal and the obvious sense of the words in the effort to force the texts

[1] D.S., v. p. 21.

[2] Indian tradition also makes Śuka one of the earliest commentators. Śabara, in his P.M.B., called the Vṛttikāra Upavarṣa. It is the view of Śaṁkara also (iii. 3. 53). Rāmānuja and his followers call him Bodhāyana. Vedāntadeśika declares that the same man is called by both the names. The commentaries of Drāmiḍa, Ṭaṅka, Bhartṛprapañca, Bhāruci, Kapardi, Brahmānanda and Guhadeva do not seem to be available. See S.B., i. 1. 4; i. 2. 23; i. 3. 19; i. 4. 12; iv. 3. 14.

to bear testimony to the truth of their own philosophic theories. The *Sūtra* is one of those rare books where each, in accordance with his merits, finds his reward.

References to the other teachers of the Vedānta in Bādarāyaṇa's work clearly make out that independent interpretations of the Upaniṣads different from Bādarāyaṇa's were also in vogue.[1] Even when Bādarāyaṇa formulated his *Sūtra*, there were differences of opinion about such central topics as the characteristics of the released soul[2] and the relation of the individual soul to Brahman.[3] Āśmarathya holds the bhedābheda view of the relation of the soul to Brahman, that it is neither absolutely different nor absolutely non-different from it.[4] Auḍulomi is of opinion that the soul is altogether different from Brahman up to the time of final release, when it becomes merged in it,[5] and Kāśakṛtsna thinks that the soul is absolutely identical with Brahman, which, in some way or other, presents itself as the individual soul.[6] The later interpreters accept one or more of these views. The Upaniṣads obviously were subjects of considerable discussion and Bādarāyaṇa's view of the Vedānta seems to be the outcome of a very prominent school of thought, though other schools of considerable repute also flourished.

II

Authorship and Date

Tradition from Śaṁkara downwards attributes the *Sūtra* to Bādarāyaṇa. The fact that the name of the latter is mentioned in several places in the third person[7] inclines one to think that Bādarāyaṇa is not its author.[8] Such a use of the third person is not, however, an uncommon practice in ancient India, and it need not imply a different authorship. Indian tradition identifies Bādarāyaṇa, the author of the *Sūtra*, with Vyāsa. Śaṁkara's followers, Govindānanda, Vācaspati

[1] Bādari (i. 2. 30; iii. 1. 11; iv. 3. 7; iv. 4. 10), Auḍulomi (i. 4. 21; iii. 4. 45; iv. 4. 6), Āśmarathya (i. 2. 29; i. 4. 20), Kāśakṛtsna (i. 4. 22), Kārṣṇājini (iii. 1. 9), Ātreya (iii. 4. 44), and Jaimini. Even the M.B. does not state their views.

[2] iv. 3. 7–14; iv. 4. 5–7.

[3] i. 4. 20–22.

[4] i. 4. 20.

[5] i. 4. 21.

[6] i. 4. 22.

[7] i. 3. 26; i. 3. 33; iii. 2. 41; iii. 4. 1; iii. 4. 8; iii. 4. 19; iv. 3. 15; iv. 4. 7; iv. 4. 12.

[8] Deussen, for example, argues that the works of Jaimini and Bādarāyaṇa, each of whom quotes both himself and the other, were compiled by a later editor into one work, which was commented upon by Upavarṣa, and that the last work was the basis of the Śabarabhāṣya on the P.M. and the Śaṁkarabhāṣya on the B.S. (D.S.V., p. 24, fn. 17).

and Ānandagiri identify Vyāsa with Bādarāyaṇa; Rāmānuja, Madhva, Vallabha and Baladeva ascribe the *Sūtra* to Vyāsa. Sometimes this view is contested on the ground that Jaimini, whom Bādarāyaṇa quotes a number of times, is a pupil of Vyāsa, if we believe the *Mahābhārata*, *Viṣṇu Purāṇa* and the *Bhāgavata*, and so the cross references in the works of Jaimini and Bādarāyaṇa are not consistent with the relation of disciple and master. Śabara, Govindānanda and Ānandagiri hold that there is nothing inconsistent.[1] It is not, however, clear what opinion Śaṁkara himself held.[2]

The *Sūtra* alludes to the views of the Sāṁkhya and the Vaiśeṣika schools and the Jains and the Buddhists. Śaṁkara, Rāmānuja, Madhva and Vallabha are unanimous in understanding references to the Gītā (xv. 7; viii. 24), in ii. 3. 45 and iv. i. 10 respectively, and the first three see a similar reference to the Gītā (vii. 11) in iv. 1. 10. Many of the names mentioned in the *Sūtra* are also found in the *Śrauta Sūtra*, Āśmarathya in the *Āśvalāyana*, Bādari, Kārṣṇājini and Kāśakṛtsna in the *Kātyāyana*, Ātreya in the *Taittirīya Prātisākhya Sūtra*. Ātreya, Kāśakṛtsna, Bādari are mentioned in Bodhāyana's *Gṛhya Sūtra* and Ātreya in *Bhāradvāja Gṛhya Sūtra* as well. Kāśakṛtsna is a very old Vedic commentator. Auḍulomi is referred to in the *Mahābhāṣya* on Pāṇini.[3] *Garuḍa Purāṇa*, *Padma Purāṇa* and *Manu* refer to the *Vedānta Sūtra* and *Harivaṁśa*, assigned by Hopkins to A.D. 200, contains clear references to it. Keith holds that Bādarāyaṇa cannot be dated later than A.D. 200.[4] Indian scholars are of opinion that the *Sūtra* was composed in the period from 500 to 200 B.C. Fraser assigns it to 400 B.C.[5] Max Müller says: "Whatever the date of the *Bhagavadgītā* is, and it is a part of the *Mahābhārata*, the age of the *Vedānta Sūtra* and of Bādarāyaṇa must have been earlier."[6]

---

[1] See Belvālkar, "Multiple Authorship of the Vedānta Sūtras," *Indian Philosophical Review*, October 1918, and Abhay Kumar Guha's *Jīvātman in Brahma Sūtras*, p. 8.

[2] In one passage of his commentary on the B.S., Śaṁkara states that at the time of the transition from the Dvāpara to the Kali age, an ancient sage and Vedic teacher named Apāntaratamas was born as Kṛṣṇa Dvaipāyana by direction of Viṣṇu. Since Śaṁkara does not say that this Kṛṣṇa Dvaipāyana is the author of the B.S., Windischmann, and after him Telang, conclude that in Śaṁkara's eyes the two personages were distinct ("A Note on Bādarāyaṇa," J.A.S., Bombay, vol. xvi, 1883, p. 190). Wherever Śaṁkara quotes Vyāsa, he does so without implying that Vyāsa is the author of the *Sūtra* (ii. 1. 12; ii. 3. 47). There are many references to the B.G. and *Śāntiparva* of the M.B. in the B.S., if we accept the testimony of the commentators, which cannot be easily understood if the author of the *Sūtra* and the writer of the M.B. were one.

[3] iv. 1. 14.

[4] *Karma-Mīmāṁsā*, pp. 5–6. Jacobi, however, believes that the *Sūtra* was composed between A.D. 200 and 450 (J.A.O.S., 1911).

[5] *Literary History of India*, p. 196.

[6] S.S., p. 113; Guha: *Jīvātman in the Brahma Sūtra.*

III

Relation to Other Schools

The exact relation of Bādarāyaṇa's *Vedānta* to Jaimini's *Mīmāṁsa* is interpreted in different ways by the different commentators.[1] Rāmānuja, after Vṛttikāra, holds that the two *Mīmāṁsās* belong to one work, while Śaṁkara is of a different opinion. It may be that the two originally formed parts of the same treatise.[2] The two *Mīmāṁsās* are pre-eminently orthodox systems, and were originally and primarily exegeses of Śruti or Veda or revelation. Bādarāyaṇa does not mention the Nyāya anywhere. The Yoga is linked with the Sāṁkhya, and the criticisms against the Sāṁkhya are said to hold good against the Yoga as well.[3] The Sāṁkhya receives elaborate refutation,[4] and is mentioned in many places.[5] It is the one system which is treated with great respect, partly because some of its doctrines are acceptable to Bādarāyaṇa and partly because it is supported by sages like Manu and Vyāsa.[6] The Vaiśeṣika doctrines are criticised,[7] and we gather that, in Bādarāyaṇa's time, the Vaiśeṣika system was not in great repute. The several schools of Buddhism, the Lokāyata and the Bhāgavata doctrines are also discussed.[8] The author of the *Sūtra* is considerably influenced by the theism of the *Bhagavadgītā* and the Bhāgavatas.

IV

Metaphysical Views

The *Vedānta Sūtra* has four chapters. The first deals with the theory of Brahman as the central reality. Its purpose is samanvaya or reconciliation of the different Vedic statements on this subject. Any interpretation of religion, any explanation of God, soul and the world is bound to take

[1] Bādarāyaṇa refers to Jaimini in several places: i. 2. 28; i. 2. 31; i. 3. 31; i. 4. 18; iii. 2. 40; iii. 4. 2; iii. 4. 18; iii. 4. 40; iv. 3. 12; iv. 4. 5; iv. 4. 11.

[2] See R.B., i. 1. 1; Jacobi: J.A.O.S., 1910. Deussen has suggested an analogy in the sequence of the N.T. upon the old, when life under the law passes into life in spirit (D.S.V., p. 20).

[3] ii. 1. 3.

[4] i. 1. 5–11; i. 4. 1–13; ii. 1. 1–12; ii. 2. 1–10.

[5] i. 1. 18; i. 2. 19; i. 2. 22; i. 3. 3; i. 3. 11; i. 4. 28; ii. 1. 29; ii. 3. 51; iv. 2. 21.

[6] See S.B., i. 4. 28.

[7] ii. 2. 11–17.

[8] See ii. 2. 1–45; i. 4. 28; iii. 3. 53–54.

account of the religious experiences of those who declare that they have seen the eternal, and all conflicts among the recorded experiences of the sages of the past require to be reconciled if the theory put forward is to be looked upon as a satisfactory one. We have, in the first chapter, an account of the nature of Brahman, its relation to the world and the individual soul. The second (avirodha) meets objections brought against this view and criticises rival theories. It also gives an account of the nature of the dependence of the world on God and the gradual evolution from and reabsorption into him, and in the latter part [1] there are interesting psychological discussions about the nature of the soul, its attributes, its relation to God, body and its own deeds. The third discusses the ways and means (sādhana) of attaining Brahma-vidyā. We have in it an account of rebirth and minor psychological [2] and theological [3] discussions, together with many exegetical comments. The fourth deals with the fruits (phala) of Brahma-vidyā. It also describes in some detail the theory of the departure of the soul after death along the two paths of the gods and the fathers and the nature of the release from which there is no return. Each chapter has four parts (pādas), and the sūtras in each part fall into certain groups called adhikaraṇas. Some textual differences in the readings adopted by the different commentators are found, though they are not all of great importance.[4]

For Bādarāyaṇa the Veda is eternal [5] and the śāstra is the great authority.[6] He declares openly that there is no possibility of discovering metaphysical truth by means of tarka or reflection.[7] He admits that there are two sources of knowledge, śruti and smṛti, and calls them pratyakṣam (perception) and anumānam (inference)[8] possibly because the latter, as Śaṁkara suggests, requires a basis of knowledge (prāmāṇyam), and the former not. The revealed śruti, which is self-evident, is called pratyakṣam. By śruti Bādarāyaṇa understands the Upaniṣads, and by smṛti he means the

[1] ii. 3. 15 onwards. [2] iii. 2. 1. 10. [3] iii. 2. 11–41.

[4] See Belvālkar: *The Multiple Authorship of the Vedānta Sūtras*, pp. 144–145, I.P.R.

[5] i. 3. 29. [6] i. 1. 3. [7] ii. 1. 11.

[8] i. 3. 28; iii. 2. 24; iv. 4. 20.

Bhagavadgītā, the *Mahābhārata*, the *Code of Manu*. As in the world of secular knowledge, inference rests on perception, so is smṛti dependent on śruti. Bādarāyaṇa admits of no other pramāṇas. He makes a distinction between two spheres of existence, the thinkable, which is the region of prakṛti, with the elements, mind, intellect and egoity and the unthinkable, which is Brahman. In the latter, śāstras are our only guide.[1] Any reasoning which is not in conformity with the Veda is useless for Bādarāyaṇa. Reasoning proceeds from characteristic marks. But of Brahman we cannot say that it is characterised by this or that to the exclusion of other attributes. Reasoning, therefore, is subordinate to intuitional knowledge,[2] which can be obtained by devotion and meditation.[3]

According to the *Vedānta Sūtra*, the puruṣa and prakṛti of the Sāṁkhya are not independent substances, but modifications of a single reality. A plurality of true infinites is not possible. The one infinite substance, Brahman, is identified with the highest reality set forth in the Upaniṣads. In the first chapter we have a discussion of the several descriptions of Brahman given in the Upaniṣads.[4] He is the origin, support and end of the world,[5] the efficient and the material cause of the universe. He creates without implements.[6] A psychological proof of the reality of Brahman is offered on the evidence of dreamless sleep.[7] Brahman is not to be confused with the unintelligent pradhāna, or the individual soul. He is possessed of all dharmas,[8] and is the inner law and guide.[9] He has the qualities of purity, truth of purpose, omniscience, omnipotence, etc.[10] His cosmic aspects are also brought out. He is the cosmic light, the golden person in the Sun, the cosmic space or ākāśa, and the cosmic breath or air or prāṇa.[11] He is also the light in the soul.[12] He is to be contemplated as residing in the heart of man,[13] and we are allowed to look upon the omnipresent God as occupying a limited space. The ultimate ground of things is a single

[1] i. 1. 3; ii. 1. 27.
[2] ii. 1. 6; ii. 1. 11.
[3] iii. 2. 24.
[4] i. 2 and 3.
[5] i. 1. 2.
[6] ii. 1. 23–27
[7] i. 1. 9.
[8] ii. 1. 37.
[9] i. 1. 20.
[10] i. 2. 1–2; ii. 1. 30.
[11] i. 1. 20–23.
[12] i. 1. 24.
[13] i. 2. 7.

supreme spirit, which is the source of everything, and an adequate object of unqualified adoration and worship.[1]

How are unintelligent things and intelligent souls to be related to the one supreme ? Are we to regard them, as the *Gītā* does, as the higher and the lower manifestations of the one reality ? The *Sūtra* does not give a clear lead. The vagueness of the Upaniṣad view of creation remains in it. Brahman, itself uncreated and eternal,[2] is the cause of the whole universe.[3] Every material element is created by Brahman.[4] If, through the activity of the primary elements, the evolution of the world takes place, even then it is Brahman that confers the power through the exercise of which the evolution takes place. As it is said, Brahman, after creating the elements, enters them; and it is Brahman dwelling in the elements that effects the production of other things.[5]

It has already been said that Brahman is the material cause as well as the instrumental cause of the world.[6] Brahman is the creator of all things, and transforms himself into all things, as clay or gold becomes things of clay or of gold. In the *Sūtra* [7] the nature of the relation between the cause and the effect, Brahman and the world, is discussed. The identity of cause and effect is brought out by two illustrations. Just as a piece of cloth, when rolled up, does not show its nature properly, but shows its nature fully when spread out, though the same piece of cloth is present in the two cases, so cause and effect are the same though their qualities differ.[8] Just as, when breath is held up, the individual is not able to perform any action, though he continues to live, and, when the breath is let loose, he is able to move the limbs, the breath remaining the same throughout, similarly cause and effect produce different actions, though they really are the same.[9] Brahman and the world are not different (ananya),[10] even as the clay pot is not different from clay.[11] While the

[1] i. 1. 7.
[2] ii. 3. 9.
[3] i. 1. 5 ; i. 2. 1 ; ii. 1. 22 ; i. 1. 22.
[4] ii. 3. 7.
[5] ii. 3 .13.
[6] i. 4. 23–27.
[7] ii. 1. 14–20.
[8] ii. 1. 19, S.B.
[9] ii. 1. 20, S.B. The effect, according to Rāmānuja, is a transformed condition of the cause. Even Śaṁkara owns that the world is only an avasthāntara of Brahman as cloth of threads.
[10] ii. 1. 14.
[11] i. 1. 4 ; i. 4. 22.

commentators agree that the cause is not different from the effect, the nature of the identity of Brahman and the world is differently explained by them. To Bādarāyaṇa, ananya does not mean absence of difference or change. For the explanation of this change Śaṁkara postulates avidyā. The world exists only for those who are under the influence of avidyā, even as the imagined serpent exists only for the man who has the wrong view of the rope. The other commentators hold to the theory of pariṇāma or transformation. The instances of cause and effect given in the *Chāndogya Upaniṣad* are earth, gold and iron, and things made of them, and not rope and snake or shell and silver. Finite things are real as determinations of Brahman. The statement that Brahman is the material cause of the world suggests that the world is a modification of the substance of Brahman.[1] The world is not an illusion or a dream-like structure, but a real, positive something which has its origination, existence and absorption in Brahman.[2] Bādarāyaṇa believes that the power of creation belongs to the pure, stainless Brahman, even as heat belongs to fire.[3] Brahman for its own sport [4] develops [5] itself into the world without undergoing the least change [6] and without ceasing to be itself. Bādarāyaṇa does not care to explain how this is possible. He does not even say, as Rāmānuja and others urge, that Brahman has wonderful powers by which even the inconceivable might be achieved. He invites our attention to the apparently contradictory statements contained in the śruti, and warns us that we have no right to question the authority of the śruti. From a philosophical point of view this answer is unsatisfactory. Śaṁkara explains the situation and shifts the contradiction from the śruti to the individual mind, and contends that Brahman is not transformed into the world. We, the victims of the confusion, believe that the one changes into the other. He holds that the ultimate reality is Brahman, the indeterminate spirit, and argues that the world of knower, known and knowledge is somehow in Brahman. Rāmānuja is of a different opinion. He resorts to śruti when he is confronted by the difficulty of a pure, secondless Brahman having the

[1] i. 1. 26. See also ii. 3. 7. [2] iii. 2. 3.
[3] i. 3. 1. [4] ii. 1. 33. [5] i. 4. 26. [6] ii. 1. 27.

beginningless (anādi) course of the world (jagatpravāha) for its second. The impossible is possible with God,[1] who has wonderful powers.[2]

Bādarāyaṇa[3] says that the soul is jña, which Śaṁkara interprets as intelligence, while Rāmānuja takes it as an intelligent knower. Vallabha agrees with Śaṁkara, while Keśava thinks that the soul is both intelligence and knower. The individual soul is an agent (kartā).[4] Birth and death refer to the body and not the soul,[5] which has no beginning. It is eternal.[6] The jīvātman is said to be aṇu, of the size of an atom. Rāmānuja, Madhva, Keśava, Nimbārka, Vallabha and Śrīkaṇṭha accept this view. Śaṁkara is of opinion that the soul is all-pervading or vibhu, though it is considered to be atomic in the worldly condition.[7] Bādarāyaṇa holds that Brahman is in the individual soul, though the nature of Brahman is not touched by the character of the soul.[8] As the jīva and Brahman are different as the light of the sun and the sun, and as when the light is covered by clouds the sun is not affected, even so, when the jīva is subject to pain, Brahman is not.[9] The embodied self acts and enjoys, acquires merit and demerit, and is affected by pleasure and pain, while the highest self has an opposite nature and is free from all evil.[10] The statements "That art thou" and "This ātman is Brahman" attempt to show that the two, Brahman and ātman, God and man, are in reality one. If Brahman be the cause of everything, it must be the cause of the individual soul as well. The absolute divine essence is present in all its manifestations. Every individual shares in the spirit of God. It is not clear, from Bādarāyaṇa's account, in what exact manner the individual is related to Brahman, as a part (aṁśa) or reflection (ābhāsa) of the universal self.[11] Bādarāyaṇa points out that Āśmarathya, Auḍulomi, and Kāśakṛtsna take up different positions with regard to the relation of the individual soul to Brahman. Āśmarathya thinks that the soul is a part of Brahman, even in a spatial sense. Auḍulomi holds that, in deep sleep, the soul is temporarily in union with Brahman. Kāśakṛtsna, whose opinion Śaṁkara upholds, believes that Brahman

---

[1] See R.B., ii. 1. 27.

[2] According to the B.S. (iii. 2. 3), the world is not māyā as dreams are. The word "māyā" is, as is clear from the later Vedānta, highly ambiguous. We may take it to mean arthapratyayaśūnyatva with Bhāskara, or dṛṣṭanaṣṭasvarūpatva with Śaṁkara, or āścaryātmakatva with Rāmānuja, or sarvabhāvanāsāmarthya with Vallabha.

[3] ii. 3. 18. [4] ii. 3. 33–39. [5] ii. 3. 16. [6] ii. 3. 18.

[7] See ii. 2. 19–28. The jīvas, according to the B.S., are of four classes: those born of uterus (jarāyuja), of eggs (aṇḍaja), or moisture (śvedaja), and of plants (udbhijja). All of them are considered to be conscious, though in different degrees. The plants are not able to express their consciousness on account of the predominance of *tamas*.

[8] i. 2–8. [9] ii. 3. 46. See Keśava on it.

[10] i. 1. 17. See also ii. 1. 22. [11] ii. 2. 43 and 50.

exists, whole and undivided, in the form of the individual soul, and Bādarāyaṇa simply mentions these different opinions, but does not say which view he supports.[1] The passage that the jīva is a part (aṁśa) of the highest reality is taken by Śaṁkara to mean "a part as it were" (aṁśa iva).[2] Since Brahman, who is not composed of parts, cannot have parts in the literal sense, Bhāskara and Vallabha assert that the jīva is a part of the Lord because there is difference as well as identity between them. Rāmānuja, Nimbārka, Baladeva and Śrīkaṇṭha think that the jīva is a real part of Brahman, even as the light issuing from a luminous object like the fire or the sun is a part of that object. The view that the jīva is both different and not different from the supreme, even as a serpent is both different and not different from its folds,[3] is refuted. Rāmānuja, however, takes the sūtra as dealing with the relation of Brahman to matter, and disputes the view that matter is only a different posture of Brahman and not different from it, even as the folds of the serpent are only a different position of and not different from the serpent. Rāmānuja contends that both jīva and matter are parts of Brahman. Keśava argues that matter is both different from and one with Brahman, even as the serpent and its hood are different and also not different when the serpent is viewed as a whole. Matter is identical with Brahman inasmuch as its very existence depends on Brahman, and it is different from Brahman since it has name and form. The jīva is also different and not different from Brahman, and the difference is certainly real.[4] There is strong support for the view that Bādarāyaṇa looks upon the difference between Brahman and the individual soul as ultimate, *i.e.* something which persists even when the soul is released. The jīva, though minute in size, pervades the whole body even as a little sandal ointment refreshes the whole body.[5]

The world is due to the will (saṁkalpa) of God. It is his līlā, or play. It does not, however, mean that he created sin and suffering for his joy or, as it is sometimes put in some religious schemes, that there may be inferior creatures who will praise and glorify him for his eternal greatness. A God all blissful, who delights in the suffering of creatures, is no

[1] i. 4. 19–22. [2] ii. 3. 43, S.B. [3] iii. 2. 27.

[4] Keśava on iii. 2. 27–28.

[5] ii. 3. 23. According to the *Sūtra*, the jīva has its seat in the hṛdaya or the hṛtpadma, which is a subtle centre of the spinal cord of the nervous system, where different nerves, 101 in number, meet. Of them all, the suṣumṇā passes up to the cranium. At the approach of death, the knowing soul, through the grace of the Lord, breaks open the knot of the hṛdaya and enters the path suṣumṇā, and passes out of the body, piercing the skull (iv. 2. 17). When the jīva passes out of the body, it does so enveloped by the subtle senses, mind (manas), and the chief prāṇa (iii. 1. 1–7; iv. 2. 3–21). It takes rebirth along with them.

God at all. The diversity of mankind is determined by the karma of the individuals.[1] God is limited by the necessity of taking into account the previous lives of men. The unequal distribution of happiness is the expression of the moral order of which God's will is the embodiment. So Brahman is neither partial nor pitiless, and has not the delightful freedom and irresponsibility which some theologians would like to attribute to him. If God's inexorable impartiality is saved by the doctrine that he renders unto every man according to his work, the other view that God himself is the causal agent of right and wrong conduct[2] remains unexplained. If God pulls the strings for every kind of action, then he is the agent as well as the patient. He seems to be inextricably involved in the endless succession, and is also the giver to himself of the fruits of good and evil. Here again the *Sūtra* resorts to śruti, but does not attempt to remove the contradiction.

In chapter iii of the *Sūtra* it is pointed out how ethical discipline can secure for the individual a body fit for the acquirement of absolute knowledge or Brahmajñāna. The general rules of the Upaniṣads regarding the purification of the instruments in our possession are accepted.[3] The three upper classes are, as a rule, allowed the right to perform sacrifices, etc., and even śūdras and women attain salvation through the grace of the Lord.[4] The author finds that active service and renunciation of the world get equal support from the scriptures,[5] and is himself inclined towards the combining of the spirit of renunciation with strenuous life.[6] Action done out of ignorance, but not all action, impedes the rise of spiritual perception or jñāna.[7] Whatever freedom we might have after attaining release, on earth, even in the jīvanmukta condition, action is enjoined.[8] Following the Upaniṣads, the *Sūtra* allows worship of gods who grant blessings to their devotees, though even these are governed by the supreme.[9] The reality is beyond and not contained in the pratīkas, or symbols, which are permitted in view of the weakness of man.[10] The absolute is avyakta or unmanifested,

[1] ii. 1. 34.
[2] iii. 2. 41; *Kauṣītaki Up.*, iii. 8.
[3] ii. 3. 40–42.
[4] i. 3. 34–38; iii. 4. 38.
[5] iii. 4. 9.
[6] iii. 4. 32–35.
[7] iii. 4. 26.
[8] iii. 4. 32.
[9] iii. 2. 38–41.
[10] iv. 1. 4.

though he is seen in the state of *saṁrādhana*.[1] The highest kind of religion is the possession of God-vision. Those who are incapable of developing this spiritual intuition rely on the *śāstras*. The ultimate end of the individual is the attainment of the self.[2] We cannot say whether this union with the self is of the nature of identity or communion and fellowship. Bādarāyaṇa believes in jīvanmukti or liberation in life. Knowledge of Brahman puts an end to the karmas which have not begun to operate,[3] though the body lasts until the karmas which have started to operate (ārabdha) are exhausted.[4]

In chapter iv we have an account of how the individual soul reaches Brahman through the devayāna, whence there is no return. In iv. 4. 5–7, the characteristics of the released soul come up for discussion. According to Auḍulomi, its chief feature is thought. Jaimini maintains that it has a number of exalted qualities, and the author of the *Sūtra* declares himself in favour of a combination of these two views. After mentioning the almost infinite power and knowledge which will come to the liberated soul on attaining mokṣa, the author remarks that none, however, will get the power of creating, ruling and dissolving the universe,[5] since that belongs to God alone. Madhva and Rāmānuja easily explain this passage, since it is in line with their doctrine of the eternal distinction of soul and God.[6] Bādarāyaṇa, however, is not explicit on this question. While some passages declare the difference to be permanent,[7] others explain it away.[8]

V

Conclusion

Bādarāyaṇa affirms a monistic view of the world. He will have nothing to do with polytheism or a plurality of independent and equally ultimate reals or unoriginate souls or a dualism between God and the Evil One. He accepts the two views of Brahman as the indeterminate intelligence (nirviśeṣa

[1] iii. 2. 23–24. [2] i. 1. 9. [3] iv. 1. 13–15.
[4] iv. 1. 19. [5] iv. 4. 17. [6] i. 1. 17.
[7] iv. 4. 17 and 21. [8] iv. 2. 13 and 16.

cinmātra) held by Bādari, Kāśakrtsna and Auḍulomi, and determinate personal Lord (saviśeṣa) held by Āśmarathya and Jaimini. From the nature of the *Sūtra*, it is not possible to set forth the way in which these two accounts are reconciled in the mind of the author. The Upaniṣads declare that Brahman is avikāri or changeless, nityam or eternal. The world is changing and impermanent. How can such an effect issue from such a cause? The *Sūtra* simply asserts on the basis of śruti that Brahman develops itself into the universe and remains transcendent.[1]

The attempt at a more adequate definition of the causality of Brahman (brahmakāraṇatā) leads to divergent views. Śaṁkara argues that Brahman produces the world without undergoing any substantial change, Rāmānuja and Vallabha believe that the world is the actual product of Brahman, *i.e.* Brahman is really transformed into the world. Again, Bādarāyaṇa says, though Brahman is in the individual soul, still, there is no pollution of Brahman by the defects of the individual on account of the difference in nature between the two.[2] He asserts both identity and difference between Brahman and the individual soul. There is no logical statement of this position. Śaṁkara finds it impossible to make the Sūtrakāra's ideas of Brahman applicable to the nirguṇa, nirviśeṣa Brahman of the Upaniṣads, while the other commentators are willing to take the Sūtrakāra's definitions as relevant to the highest Brahman. The latter argue that the Sūtrakāra is unaware of the theory of a twofold Brahman or of the unreality of the world. The author of the *Sūtra* could not have refuted the Sāṁkhya and discussed the theories of creation so seriously, if he had held that the world was an appearance, in which case its creatorship was out of the question. It may well be that Bādarāyaṇa believes in a really changing aspect of the Divine nature, a svagatabheda, which enables Brahman to manifest itself in various objects and under the limitations of individual life. A clear statement is, however, lacking.

The state of the released soul is one of non-separation (avibhāga) from Brahman. This simple formula of non-separation is capable of varied interpretations which it gets from the later commentators. Śaṁkara takes it to mean a complete identification with the universal self, while Rāmānuja interprets it as a partial assimilation to God. Room is found for both in Śaṁkara's system. On the question of ethics, Bādarāyaṇa does not discuss the relation of renunciation to action and the efficacy of these to the attainment of the end. In religion, he looks upon Brahman as unmanifested (avyakta), and yet as an object of spiritual perception. The two require to be reconciled.

---

[1] i. 4. 27.

[2] i. 2. 8.

The *Sūtra* of Bādarāyaṇa reflects the indecision and vagueness characteristic of the Upaniṣads, whose teachings it attempts to set forth, and harbours within it many seeds of doubt and discussion. Any attempt at a more precise characterisation of the views of the sūtras is bound to contain many rocks of offence and sources of spiritual disturbance. We shall see in the sequel how identical formulas give rise to various interpretations through the differences of spiritual setting into which they are received.

CHAPTER VIII

THE ADVAITA VEDĀNTA OF ŚAMKARA

Introduction—Date—Life and personality of Śaṁkara—Literature—Gauḍapāda's *Kārikā*—Buddhist influence—Analysis of experience—Causation—Creation—Ethics and religion—Relation to Buddhism—General estimate of Gauḍapāda's position—Bhartṛhari—Bhartṛprapañca—Śaṁkara's relation to the Upaniṣads and the *Brahma Sūtra*—Relation to Buddhism and other systems of philosophy—The reality of Ātman—Its nature—Theory of knowledge—Mechanism of knowledge—Perception, its nature and varieties—Inference—Scriptural testimony—Refutation of subjectivism—Criterion of truth—Inadequacy of logical knowledge — Self-consciousness — Adhyāsa — Anubhava — Scriptural authority—Higher wisdom and lower knowledge—Śaṁkara and Kant, Bergson and Bradley—The objective approach—Reality and existence—Space, time and cause—The world of phenomena—Brahman—Saguṇa and Nirguṇa—Īśvara—Proofs for the existence of God—Brahman and Īśvara—Personality—Creation—The phenomenal character of Īśvara—Being, not-being and becoming—The phenomenality of the world—The doctrine of māyā—Avidyā—Is the world an illusion ?—Avidyā and māyā—The world of nature—The individual self—Sākṣin and jīva—Brahman and jīva—Avacchedavāda—Bimbapratibimbavāda—Īśvara and jīva—Ekajīvavāda and Anekajīvavāda—Ethics—Charges of intellectualism and asceticism considered—Jñāna and Karma—Karma and freedom—Mokṣa—Future life—Religion—Conclusion.

I

INTRODUCTION

THE Advaitism of Śaṁkara is a system of great speculative daring and logical subtlety. Its austere intellectualism, its remorseless logic, which marches on indifferent to the hopes and beliefs of man, its relative freedom from theological obsessions, make it a great example of a purely philosophical scheme. Thibaut, who cannot be charged with any partiality for Śaṁkara, speaks of his philosophy in these words : " The doctrine advocated by Śaṁkara is, from a purely philosophical point of view, and apart from all theological considerations, the most important and interesting one which has arisen on Indian soil ; neither those forms of the Vedānta which diverge from the view represented by Śaṁkara, nor any of the non-Vedāntic systems can be compared with the so-called orthodox Vedānta in boldness, depth and subtlety of speculation." [1] It is impossible to read Śaṁkara's writings, packed as they are with serious and subtle thinking, without being conscious that one is in contact with a mind of a very fine penetration and profound spirituality. With his acute feeling of the immeasurable world, his stirring gaze into the abysmal mysteries of spirit, his unswerving resolve to say neither more nor less than what could be proved, Śaṁkara stands out as a heroic figure of the first rank in the somewhat motley crowd of the religious thinkers of mediæval India. His philosophy stands forth complete, needing neither a before nor an after. It has a self-justifying wholeness characteristic of works of art. It expounds its own presuppositions, is ruled by its own end, and holds all its elements in a stable, reasoned equipoise. The list of qualifications [2] which Śaṁkara lays down for a student of philosophy brings out how, for him, philosophy is not an intellectual pursuit but a dedicated life. The first, "discrimination between things eternal and non-eternal," demands of the student the power of thought, which helps him to distinguish between the unchanging reality and the changing world. For those who possess this power, it is impossible to desist from the enterprise of metaphysics. "Renunciation of the enjoyment of the reward here and in the other world" is the second requirement. In the empirical world and man's temporal life within it there is little to satisfy the aspirations of spirit. Philosophy gets its chance, as well as its justification, through the disillusionment which life brings. The seeker after truth must refuse to abase himself before things as they are and develop an austere detachment characteristic of the superior mind. Moral preparation is insisted on as the third requisite,[3] and, lastly, longing for liberation (mumukṣutvam) is mentioned. We

[1] Introduction to B.S., p. xiv. The system of Śaṁkara, according to Sir Charles Eliot, "in consistency, thoroughness and profundity, holds the first place in Indian philosophy" (*Hinduism and Buddhism*, vol. ii, p. 208).

[2] S.B., Introduction.

[3] S.B., ii. 1.1.

must have a mind disposed, as St. Luke expresses it, "for eternal life."[1] Śaṁkara presents to us the true ideal of philosophy, which is not so much knowledge as wisdom, not so much logical learning as spiritual freedom. For Śaṁkara, as for some of the greatest thinkers of the world, Plato and Plotinus, Spinoza and Hegel, philosophy is the austere vision of eternal truth, majestic in its freedom from the petty cares of man's paltry life. Through the massive and at the same time subtle dialectic of Śaṁkara there shows forth a vivid, emotional temperament, without which philosophy tends to become a mere game of logic. A master of the strictest logic, he is also master of a noble and animated poetry which belongs to another order. The rays of his genius have illumined the dark places of thought and soothed the sorrows of the most forlorn heart. While his philosophy fortifies and consoles many, there are, of course, those to whom it seems to be an abyss of contradiction and darkness. But whether we agree or differ, the penetrating light of his mind never leaves us where we were.

II

Date and Life of Śaṁkara

According to Telang, Śaṁkara flourished about the middle or the end of the sixth century A.D.[2] Sir R. G. Bhāndārkar proposes A.D. 680 as the date of Śaṁkara's birth, and is even inclined to go a few years earlier.[3] Max Müller and Professor Macdonell hold that he was born in A.D. 788, and died in A.D. 820. That he flourished in the first quarter of the ninth century is also the opinion of Professor Keith.[4]

The picture of a solitary ascetic thinker, at home in austere meditation as well as in practical work, touches our imagination. Some of Śaṁkara's disciples compiled biographical accounts of which the chief

---

1 *Acts*, xiii. 48. See I.P., pp. 45–46.

2 His argument is that Pūrṇavarman referred to in Śaṁkara's commentary on the B.S. was a Buddhist king of Magadha about that time.

3 See the *Report on the Search for Sanskrit MSS.*, 1882, p. 15.

4 I.L.A., p. 30. In the Nāndiśloka of *Prabodhacandrodaya* of Kṛṣṇa Miśra (eleventh century A.D. *circa*), the most popular illustrations of the conception of māyā as those of the mirage and the snake-rope are given.

are Mādhava's *Śaṁkaradigvijaya* and Ānandagiri's *Śaṁkaravijaya.*[1] Śaṁkara belonged to the simple, learned and hardworking Nambūdri sect of Brahmins of Malabar, and is generally supposed to have been born at Kāladi, on the West Coast of the peninsula.[2] Though there is a tradition that Śiva was the family deity of Śaṁkara, it is also held that he was by birth a Śākta. Early in his youth he went to a Vedic school, presided over by Govinda, the pupil of Gauḍapāda. In all his works, Śaṁkara subscribes himself as the pupil of Govinda, who evidently taught him the main principles of the Advaita system. Even while a young boy of eight he is said to have devoured with avidity and delight all the Vedas. Apparently he was a youthful prodigy of Vedic learning and free intelligence. He was impressed with the mystery and importance of life, and had an early vision of the beauty of holiness. Before he learned the ways of the world, he rejected them and became a saññyāsin. But he was no passionless recluse. The pure flame of truth burned within him. He wandered as a teacher from place to place, engaging in discussions with the leaders of other schools of thought. According to the traditional accounts, he met, in the course of these tours, Kumārila [3] and Maṇḍana Miśra, who later became his disciple under the name of Sureśvarācārya.[4] The story of his entering the dead body of Amaruka shows that Śaṁkara was an adept in yogic practices. He established four mutts or monasteries, of which the chief is the one at Śringeri in the Mysore Province. The others are those at Pūri in the East, Dvārakā in the West, and Badarināth in the Himalayas. A touching incident, about which tradition is unanimous, shows how full of the milk of human kindness and filial affection Śaṁkara was. In open defiance of the rules which govern the order of Saññyāsins, Śaṁkara performed the funeral rites of his mother, and thus incurred the serious opposition of his community. He died at Kedārnāth in the Himalayas at the age of thirty-two, according to the tradition. To us, men of life and feeling, there seems to be a certain bareness in the life of Śaṁkara lacking the colour and joy of cheerful fellowship and social amusement, but this is generally the case with those who pursue the higher life and feel called to exalt God's righteousness and the claims of spirit. He was a prophet commissioned to lead a people along the paths of virtue, and nobody in India can undertake

---

[1] Cidvilāsa and Sadānanda wrote some accounts. *Skanda Purāṇa* gives a few facts (see ix). A Madhva writer, Nārāyaṇācārya, relates some details in his *Madhvavijaya* and *Maṇimañjari*. But many of the facts mentioned in these are legendary and of doubtful historical value. See *Life and Times of Śaṁkara*, by C. N. Kṛiṣṇaswāmi Aiyar, Madras.

[2] Ānandagiri holds that Śaṁkara was born at Cidambaram in 44 B.C. and died in 12 B.C. His views have not received much support.

[3] A South Indian tradition states that Śaṁkara was a disciple of Kumārila.

[4] Professor Hiriyanna of Mysore has urged cogent arguments against the identification of Sureśvara with Maṇḍana Miśra. See J.R.A.S., April 1923, and January 1924.

this task if he does not back his message with a life of detachment from the cares of the world.

In a few years Śaṁkara practised several careers, each enough to satisfy an ordinary man. His great achievement in the field of speculation is the Advaita system which he developed by means of commentaries on the ancient texts. He found it the best way to reconcile contemporary standards of knowledge and belief with the ancient texts and traditions. The sixth and the seventh centuries saw the rise of popular Hinduism. In the South, Buddhism had begun to decline [1] and Jainism was at its zenith. The Vedic rites were falling into disrepute. Śaivite bhaktas (adiyārs) and Vaiṣṇavite devotees (āḷvārs) were popularising the way of devotion to God. Festivals and temple worship connected with Purāṇic Hinduism were spreading everywhere. In South India the Pallava sovereignty was supreme, and in the freedom and peace afforded by a central government, Brahmanism was being transformed into Hinduism. The religious persuasions of the Pallava kings give a clear indication of the reconstruction then taking place. While the earliest rulers of the Pallava dynasty were Buddhists, those next in order were Vaiṣṇavites, while the latest were Śaivites. As a reaction against the ascetic tendency of Buddhism and the devotional one of theism, the Mīmāṁsakas were exaggerating the importance of Vedic rites. Kumārila and Maṇḍana Miśra denounced the value of jñāna and saññyāsa, and insisted on the value of karma and the stage of the householder. Śaṁkara appeared, at one and the same time, as an eager champion of the orthodox faith and a spiritual reformer. He tried to bring back the age from the brilliant luxury of the Purāṇas to the mystic truth of the Upaniṣads. The power of the faith to lead the soul to the higher life became for him the test of its strength. He felt impelled to attempt the spiritual direction of his age by formulating a philosophy and religion which could satisfy the ethical and spiritual needs of the people better than the systems of Buddhism, Mīmāṁsā and Bhakti. The theists were veiling the truth in a mist of sentiment. With their genius for mystical experience, they were indifferent to the practical concerns of life. The Mīmāṁsaka emphasis on karma developed ritualism devoid of spirit. Virtue can face the dark perils of life and survive only if it be the fine flower of thought. The Advaita philosophy alone, in the opinion of Śaṁkara, could do justice to the truth of the conflicting creeds, and so he wrote all his works with the one purpose of helping the individual to a realisation of the identity of his soul with Brahman, which is the means of liberation from saṁsāra.[2] In his wanderings from his birthplace in Malabar to the Himālayas in the north he came across many phases of worship, and

[1] While Fahian saw Buddhism flourishing in the fifth century, Yuan-Chwang, who came later, *i.e.* in the sixth and seventh centuries, witnessed evident signs of decline. Bāṇa's *Harṣacarita* confirms this impression.

[2] "Saṁsārahetunivṛttisādhanabrahmātmaikatvavidyāpratipattaye." See S.B., i. 1. 1.

accepted all those which had in them the power to elevate man and refine his life. He did not preach a single exclusive method of salvation, but composed hymns of unmistakable grandeur addressed to the different gods of popular Hinduism—Viṣṇu, Śiva, Śakti, Sūrya. All this affords a striking testimony to the universality of his sympathies and the wealth of natural endowment. While revivifying the popular religion, he also purified it. He put down the grosser manifestations of the Śākta worship in South India, and it is a pity that his influence is not perceptible in the great temple of Kālī in Calcutta. In the Deccan, it is said that he suppressed the unclean worship of Śiva as a dog under the name of Mallāri, and the pernicious practices of Kāpālikas whose god Bhairava desired human victims. He condemned branding or marking the body with hot metallic designs. He learned from the Buddhist church that discipline, freedom from superstition and ecclesiastical organisations help to preserve the faith clean and strong, and himself established ten religious orders of which four retain their prestige till to-day.

The life of Śaṁkara makes a strong impression of contraries. He is a philosopher and a poet, a savant and a saint, a mystic and a religious reformer. Such diverse gifts did he possess that different images present themselves, if we try to recall his personality. One sees him in youth, on fire with intellectual ambition, a stiff and intrepid debater; another regards him as a shrewd political genius, attempting to impress on the people a sense of unity; for a third, he is a calm philosopher engaged in the single effort to expose the contradictions of life and thought with an unmatched incisiveness; for a fourth, he is the mystic who declares that we are all greater than we know. There have been few minds more universal than his.

III

Literature

The central texts of the school are Śaṁkara's commentaries on the principal Upaniṣads,[1] the *Bhagavadgītā* and the *Vedānta Sūtra*. *Upadeśasahasrī* and *Vivekacūdāmaṇi* reflect his general position. His popular hymns to the different forms of Godhead, such as *Dakṣiṇāmūrti Stotra, Harimīḍe Stotra, Ānandalaharī* and *Saundaryalaharī*, explain to us his faith in life and justify his love of it. Other works attributed to him are *Āptavajrasūcī, Ātmabodha, Mohamudgara, Daśaślokī, Aparokṣānubhūti* and commentaries on *Viṣṇusahasranāma* and *Sanatsujātīya*. The many strands of the complex texture of his

[1] The *Chāndogya*, the *Bṛhadāraṇyaka*, the *Taittirīya*, the *Aitareya*, the *Śvetāśvatara*, the *Kena*, the *Kaṭha*, the *Īśa*, the *Praśna*, the *Muṇḍaka*, and the *Māṇḍūkya*. He is also said to have written commentaries on the *Atharvaśikhā*, *Atharvaśiras* and *Nṛsiṁhatāpanīya* Upaniṣads.

personality found their expression in his writings. The great point about his style is the way in which it mirrors the qualities of his mind, its force, its logic, its feeling and its sense of humour. The philosophy set forth by Śaṁkara has a long history which is yet in progress. The upholders of other views generally support their positions by refuting those of Śaṁkara. This has rendered necessary a defence of Śaṁkara's position in every age. It is not possible for us to trace adequately the fortunes of his system in times later than his own.[1]

---

[1] Sureśvarācārya's *Vārttikas* and *Naiṣkarmyasiddhi*, Vācaspati's *Bhāmatī*, Padmapāda's *Pañcapādikā*, and Ānandagiri's *Nyāyanirṇaya* are well-known Advaita treatises, which were composed immediately after Śaṁkara's time. Amalānanda's *Kalpataru* (middle of the thirteenth century) is a commentary on *Bhāmatī*. Appayadīkṣita (sixteenth century) wrote his *Kalpatarupari-mala*, a voluminous treatise on the *Kalpataru*. His *Siddhāntaleśa* is an important summary of the divergent developments of Advaita. Padma-pāda's *Pañcapādikā*, which is an elaborate gloss on the first four sūtras, was commented on by Prakāśātman (A.D. 1200) in his *Pañcapādikāvivaraṇa*. Vidyāraṇya (fourteenth century), generally identified with Mādhava, wrote his *Vivaraṇaprameyasaṁgraha* as a gloss on Prakāśātman's work. While his *Pañcadaśī* is a classic of later Advaita, his *Jīvanmuktiviveka* is also of considerable value. Tradition is divided as to the authorship of the *Pañcadaśī*. Vidyāraṇya is said to have written the first six chapters and Bhāratītīrtha the other nine (see Pītāmbarasvāmin's ed., p. 6). Niścaladāsa, in his *Vṛttiprabhākara* (p. 424), assigns the first ten to Vidyāraṇya and the other five to Bhāratītīrtha. Sarvajñātmamuni (A.D. 900) made a general survey of Śaṁkara's position in his *Saṁkṣepaśārīraka*, which was commented on by Rāmatīrtha. Śrī Harṣa's *Khaṇḍanakhaṇḍakhādya* (A.D. 1190) is the greatest work of Advaita dialectics. It is one long dissertation on the vanity of philosophy, setting forth the inability of the human mind to compass those exalted objects which its speculative ingenuity suggests as worthy of its pursuit. In the spirit of Nāgārjuna, he analyses the common categories with minuteness and accuracy and takes the reader through a long and arduous process of dissection to establish the simple truth that nothing can be conclusively proved to be either true or false. Everything is doubtful except universal consciousness. His belief in the ultimate reality of spirit marks him off from Buddhist nihilism (i. 5). He discusses at great length the pramāṇas of the Nyāya, its theory of causation, and argues that the Nyāya is busy with apparent existence and not reality. The diversity of things is not ultimate (i. 9), while the absolute *is*, though never known. Citsukha wrote a commentary on it in addition to an independent work on the same lines known as *Tattvadīpikā*. *Citsukhīyam* is criticised in *Nyāyāmṛtam*. Madhusūdana Sarasvatī (sixteehth century) criticises the latter work in his *Advaitasiddhi*. Rāmācārya criticises *Advaita-siddhi* in his *Taraṅgiṇī*. *Gauḍabrahmānandīyam*, or *Gurucandrikā*, a work by Brahmānanda, is a defence of *Advaitasiddhi* against the criticism of *Taraṅgiṇī*. Śaṁkara Miśra and Raghunātha wrote independent works on the *Khaṇḍana*. Dharmarāja's *Vedāntaparibhāṣā* (sixteenth century) is an excellent manual of logical metaphysics. Rāmakṛṣṇa, the son of Dharmarāja, wrote his *Śikhāmaṇī* on it. Amaradāsa's *Maṇiprabhā* is a useful gloss on it. Vijñānabhikṣu's *Vijñānāmṛta* (sixteenth century) attempts to prove that the duality of the Sāṁkhya persists within the Vedānta. Advaitānanda's

IV

GAUḌAPĀDA

Gauḍapāda[1] is the first systematic exponent of the Advaita Vedānta. He is reputed to be the teacher of Śaṁkara's teacher, Govinda, and is said to have lived about the beginning of the eighth century or the end of the seventh.[2] It is said that Gauḍapāda also wrote a commentary on the *Uttaragītā*. The central principles of the Advaita philosophy, such as the orders of reality, the identity of Brahman and Ātman, Māyā, the inapplicability of causation to ultimate reality, jñāna or wisdom, as the direct means to mokṣa or

Brahmavidyābharaṇa (fifteenth century), Govindānanda's *Ratnaprabhā*, Sadānanda's *Vedāntasāra* (fifteenth century), with its commentaries, *Subodhinī* and *Vidvanmanorañjanī*, Prakāśānanda's *Siddhāntamuktāvali*, Sadānanda's *Advaitabrahmasiddhi*, Lakṣmīdhara's *Advaitamakaranda* are other works of considerable importance. Many of the later Upaniṣads, such as *Mahopaniṣad* and religious works like *Yogavāśiṣṭha* and *Adhyātmarāmāyaṇa*, advocate advaitism. *Yogavāśiṣṭha* is coloured by the Buddhist views. Cp.

Yad idaṁ dṛśyate kiñcit tan nāsti kim api dhruvam
Yathā gandharvanagaraṁ yathā vāri marusthale (ii).

Many other works on Advaita Vedānta have been written which do not add to the depth and solidity of Śaṁkara's utterances. Sureśvara, Vācaspati, Padmapāda, Śrī Harṣa, Vidyāraṇya, Citsukha, Sarvajñātmamuni, Madhusūdana Sarasvatī, Appayadīkṣita, though they all belong to the same general type of thinking, have something fresh to say, and reflect some facet of the meaning of absolute idealism not seen before with the same intensity. While they employ the same method and expound the same view, they yet manage to maintain their own individualities.

[1] He is, perhaps, not the same as the author of the commentary on the Sāṁkhya system.

[2] He must be much earlier, since Walleser states that the *Kārikā* is quoted in the Tibetan translation of Bhavaviveka's *Tarkajvālā*. The latter author is earlier than Yuan Chwang, and Gauḍapāda must be therefore about A.D. 550 or so (see Jacobi, J.A.O.S., April 1913). Jacobi believes that the *Kārikā* is later than the B.S. This view is not affected by the absence of any references to the B.S. in the ancient Buddhist works, for the "enigmatical character" of the B.S. makes it impossible for outsiders to quote it to illustrate points of the Vedānta philosophy. "Besides, the Buddhists may have ignored the old Vedānta of Bādarāyaṇa, as the Jainas did so late as the ninth century A.D.; but they could not well have ignored the Gauḍapādī, since that work taught a philosophy which resembled their own in many regards" (J.A.O.S., April 1913). Many Indian scholars are inclined to Jacobi's opinion, though not for his reasons, as against that of Walleser.

freedom, and the inconceivability of absolute nothing, are set forth in the *Kārikā*. This work is divided into four chapters. The first, called the Āgama, explains the text of the *Māṇḍūkyopaniṣad*. Gauḍapāda tries to show that his view of reality is sanctioned by śruti and supported by reason.[1] The second chapter, called Vaitathya, explains by means of arguments the phenomenal nature of the world, characterised as it is by duality and opposition. The third part establishes the Advaita theory. In the last part, called Alātaśānti or Quenching the Firebrand, there is a further development of the Advaita position regarding the sole reality of the Ātman and the relative character of our ordinary experience. As a stick burning at one end, when waved round, quickly produces an illusion of a circle of fire (alātacakra), so is it with the multiplicity of the world.[2] It refers to the Yogācāra views, and mentions the name of Buddha half a dozen times.

Gauḍapāda lived at a time when Buddhism was widely prevalent. Naturally he was familiar with Buddhistic doctrines, which he accepted when they were not in conflict with his own Advaita. To the Buddhists he appealed on the ground that his view did not depend on any theological text or revelation. To the orthodox Hindu he said that it had the sanction of authority also. His liberal views enabled him to accept doctrines associated with Buddhism and adjust them to the Advaita design.

V

Analysis of Experience

We have referred, in another place, to the theory of the grades or kinds of consciousness sketched in the *Māṇḍūkyopaniṣad*.[3] Gauḍapāda takes his stand on this analysis and

[1] iii. 23.

[2] See also *Maitrāyaṇī Upaniṣad*, vi. 24. The simile is frequently employed in Buddhist writings. Indeed, in language and thought the *Kārikā* of Gauḍapāda bears a striking resemblance to the Mādhyamika writings, and contains many illustrations used in them. Cp. especially ii. 32; iv. 59. See J.R.A.S., 1910, pp. 136 ff.

[3] See vol. i, pp. 32–33, 159 ff. Cp. Bradley: *Truth and Reality*, pp. 462–4.

urges that dream experiences are on a par with the waking ones. If the dream states do not fit into the context of the general experience of our fellow men or of our own normal experience,[1] it must be understood that it is not because they fall short of absolute reality, but because they do not conform to our conventional standards. They constitute a separate class of experiences, and, within their order, they are coherent. The water in the dream can quench the thirst in the dream, and to say that it does not quench the real thirst is irrelevant. To say so is to assume that waking experience is real in itself and is the only real. The two, waking and dream states, are equally real within their own orders or equally unreal in an absolute sense.[2] Gauḍapāda recognises that the objects of waking experience are common to us all, while those of dreams are the private property of the dreamer.[3] Yet he says: "As in dream, so in waking, the objects seen are unreal."[4] His contention is that whatever is presented as an object is unreal. The argument that all objects are unreal and only the subject that is the constant witness self is real, is suggested in some Upaniṣads and developed with negative results in Buddhistic thought. It is now employed by Gauḍapāda to prove that life is a waking dream.[5] We accept the waking world as objective, not because we experience other people's mental states, but because we accept their testimony. The relations of space, time and cause, which govern the objects of the waking world, need not be considered to be ultimate. According to Gauḍapāda, "By the nature of a thing is understood that which is complete in itself, that which is its very condition,

[1] ii. 203.

[2] "When I consider the matter carefully, I do not find a single characteristic by means of which I can certainly determine whether I am awake or whether I dream. The visions of a dream and the experiences of my waking state are so much alike that I am completely puzzled, and I do not really know that I am not dreaming at this moment" (Descartes: *Meditations*, p. i). Pascal is right when he asserts that if the same dream came to us every night we should be just as much occupied by it as by the things which we see every day. To quote his words: "If an artisan were certain that he would dream every night for fully twelve hours that he was a king, I believe that he would be just as happy as a king who dreams every night for twelve hours that he is an artisan."

[3] ii. 14. [4] ii. 4. [5] ii. 31.

that which is inborn, that which is not accidental, or that which does not cease to be itself." [1] When we apply such a test, we find that both the souls and the world are nothing by themselves and are Ātman only.[2]

The phenomena of experience present themselves to our mind as obeying certain laws and bound by certain relations, of which the chief is cause. What is the order in which the cause and the effect succeed each other? If they are simultaneous, like the two horns of an animal, they cannot be related as cause and effect. The analogy of the seed and the tree is not more helpful. We cannot call anything an effect if we do not know its cause.[3] In the nature of the case, the causal explanation cannot be complete. We regard any given state of things as conditioned and ask for its conditions, and when the latter are found we have to go behind them. Such a process has no finality about it.[4] If, however, we believe that there are beginningless eternal causes which are themselves uncaused and yet produce effects, then how, Gauḍapāda asks, can that which produces itself be unproduced (ajā)? How can a thing which changes be also eternal? Where can we find unproduced things producing things? Cause and effect are obviously relative, sustaining each other and falling together.[5] Causality is not of the nature of reality, but only a condition of knowledge. Gauḍapāda says: "Neither the unreal nor the real can have the unreal as their cause; nor can the real have the real as its cause . . . and how could the real be a cause of the unreal?" [6] The difficulties of causation lead Gauḍapāda to say that "nothing is produced either by itself or by another, nor is anything in fact produced, whether it be being, or non-being, or either." [7] Causation is an impossibility. We cannot say either that God is the cause of the world or that the waking

[1] iv. 9.
[2] iv. 10. 28, 61.
[3] iv. 16–21.
[4] Ch. iv. 11–13, 21, 23, 25.
[5] iv. 14–15.
[6] iv. 40.
[7] iv. 22. Śaṁkara comments on this thus: "In fact, the being produced by something is impossible to establish in any manner. Nothing is born of itself, *i.e.* from its own form. Nothing can reproduce itself, as a jar a jar. Nor is anything produced from something else, as cloth from a jar; and another cloth from the first; and nothing can be born both of itself and of another for obvious reasons; for a jar and a cloth cannot together produce either the one or the other."

experience is the cause of the dream states.[1] The various things, subjective and objective, the individual souls and the world, are all unreal.[2] They only seem to be real so long as we accept the principle of causality.[3] "Everything is produced by the power of saṁvṛti (or relative truth), and nothing is therefore eternal; everything, again, is unborn, being inseparable from *sat*, and there is nothing therefore like destruction."[4] Production and destruction are only phenomena, and in reality there is nothing produced or destroyed.[5] We have to negate causality and other relations to reach the real, which transcends the phenomenal.[6]

It is necessary to note that the distinction of subjective and objective in the Advaita is not identical with the usual one. The mental world is as much objective or unreal as the material, for the only subject or reality is the Ātman. While both Gauḍapāda and Śaṁkara advocate this view, Śaṁkara takes special care to distinguish the dream world from the waking one. While Śaṁkara insists that the two worlds, mental and material, are not of the same kind or order, though they are in essence Brahman, Gauḍapāda is liable to the charge of subjectivism in the traditional sense, since he uses the arguments which the Buddhist Vijñānavāda employs to prove the unreality of external objects of perception and traces them to ideas of mind.[7] It is the movement of consciousness (vijñānaspanditam) that produces the appearance of the perceiving and the perceived, and we imagine a variety where it is not.[8] The world exists only in the mind of man.[9] Gauḍapāda reduces all reality to mental impressions, and declares that the latter have no objective causes. "Arguments drawn from the nature of the things points to

[1] iv. 39. [2] iv. 51–52, 67. [3] iv. 55–56; iv. 42.
[4] iv. 57. [5] ii. 32. [6] Prapañcopaśamam, ii. 35.

[7] Jacobi puts Gauḍapāda's argument in the following syllogistic form: "Things seen in the waking state are not true: this is the proposition (pratijñā); because they are seen, this is the reason (hetu); just like things seen in a dream, this is the instance (dṛṣṭānta): as things seen in a dream are not true, so the property of being seen belongs in like manner to things seen in the waking state; this is the application of the reason (hetūpanaya); therefore things seen in the waking state are also untrue; this is the conclusion (nigamana)" (J.A.O.S., vol. xxxiii, part i, April 1913). See also ii. 29, 31; iv. 61–66, 72–73.

[8] ii. 15 and 17, and iv. 47. [9] iv. 45–48, 72; iv. 77; i. 17.

the causelessness of the cause."[1] "The citta (or thought) does not relate itself to objects, nor does it allow them to reflect themselves in itself; for objects are unreal and their reflection is not apart from it (citta)."[2]

The realist contends that ideas and feelings would not arise if external things did not cause them. Gauḍapāda shows the unreasonableness of assuming objects existing beside and independent of ideas, and Śaṁkara is obliged to admit that this refutation is "the argument of the Buddhists of the Vijñānavāda school who combat the opinion of the realists (bāhyārthavādins), and the teacher agrees with them thus far."[3]

But even the theory of a real flow of ideas is repugnant to Gauḍapāda. He refutes the central position of the Vijñānavāda, *viz.* the reality of citta. "Therefore mind (citta) does not originate, nor do objects cognised by the mind originate. Those who pretend to recognise the origination of them seem to see only marks in the air."[4] If the whole experience is only apparent, what is the distinction between true and false perception? From the standpoint of the absolute, there is none at all. The perception of the rope as rope is as vicious as the perception of the rope as snake. The consciousness of objects present in waking and dream experiences is not a constant factor. We have dreamless sleep in which there is no cognition of external and internal objects. We have only a unity where all things seem to melt into one indiscriminate mass of sentiency.[5] The existence of this state is a clear evidence that knowledge, with its distinctions of knower and known, is not ultimate. Dreams are real so long as we dream; waking experiences so long as we do not dream or sleep. Dreamless sleep from which we pass into waking or dream is as unreal as the other states, and all the three disclose their relative character when the individual wakes up "from the sleep of delusion, which has

[1] iv. 25. Śaṁkara, commenting on it, writes: "Jars, etc., which you take as the objective causes of subjective impressions, have themselves no cause, nothing to rest upon; they are therefore not the cause of subjective impressions."

[2] iv. 26. [3] iv. 21, 25–27. [4] iv. 28.

[5] Yathā rātrau naiśena tamasā'vibhajyamānaṁ sarvaṁ ghanam iva, tadvat prajñānaghana eva. S.B. Māṇḍ, Up. 5.

no beginning, and realises the unborn, ever awake, dreamless, one, without a second." [1]

Another reason assigned for the unreality of the world is that "anything which is naught at the beginning and is so also at the end, necessarily does not exist in the middle." [2] In other words, whatever has beginning or end is unreal.[3] The test of reality is not objectivity or practical efficiency, but persistence for all time or absolute self-existence. Objects of waking experience come to naught in dreams, and *vice versa*. Gauḍapāda thus establishes the unreal character of the world of experience (1) by its similarity to dream states; (2) by its presented or objective character; (3) by the unintelligibility of the relations which organise it; and (4) by its non-persistence for all time.

Admitting that relativity is the all-absorbing power governing things in the realm of experience, he posits the reality of something which transcends experience and relativity. The possibility of the relative implies the reality of the absolute. If we deny the real, we deny the relative also.[4] The Upaniṣads declare that, beyond the three states, as the basis of them all, is the Ātman.[5] It alone *is*. It is indivisible, for were there parts in it there would be plurality. There can be no differences or distinctions in being, for what is different from being is non-being, and non-being is not. "That which is cannot not be, as that which is not cannot also be." [6] Being is identical with thought, for if it were not, it could not otherwise be absolutely one. Thought is the same thing as being; but this thought is not human thought, which needs an object. Such a conception would involve relations and therefore dualism. Thought here means simple self-luminousness, which renders possible all relative knowledge. "The ever unborn, awake, dreamless, illumines itself of itself. It is ever illumined by its very nature." [7] The absolute is not to be confused with a negative blank

[1] i. 16. [2] ii. 6. [3] ii. 7. [4] iii. 28.

[5] i. 1. Eka eva tridhā smṛtaḥ. Cp.

Sattvāj jāgaraṇaṁ vidyād, rajasā svapnam ādiśet,
Prasvāpanaṁ tu tamasā turīyaṁ triṣu saṁtatam.

See S.P.B., i. 91.

[6] iv. 4. [7] iv. 81. See also iii. 33, 35–36.

such as we have in sound sleep. In the latter we have non-cognition, while in Brahman we have pure cognition.[1] The three states of waking, dreaming and sleep are the three modes in which the one unconditioned Ātman reveals itself when it is limited by different upādhis (limitations).[2]

VI

Creation

Gauḍapāda raises the question of the relation between the supreme principle Ātman and the phenomenal world. If we are earnest students of truth (paramārthacintakāḥ) and not mere speculators about creation (sṛṣṭicintakāḥ), we shall see that there is no such thing as creation at all. The real cannot be subject to change. If it be, then "the immortal would become mortal."[3] "In no way is it possible that a thing can be changed into something quite the opposite."[4] All becoming is unreal, valid only in the empirical world. In reality, there is nothing like distinction (nāsti bhedaḥ kathaṁcana).[5] The Ātman, which is the one unconditioned reality, is cognisant of nothing beside itself. As Śaṁkara says: "Objects are cognised by a subject in action, not by one in simple subsistence." How this adhyāsa, or confusion of self with not-self, arises, how the one appears as manifold, since the indivisible Ātman cannot be really divided, is unaccountable, though the fact of the confusion cannot be gainsaid, and sometimes it is argued that it is necessary to seek for an explanation of the world even though it is not real.[6] Gauḍapāda considers the different alternatives suggested to account for creation. "Some regard it as the manifestation of God (vibhūti), while others regard it as of

[1] iii. 34. See also i. 26–29; iii. 26; iv. 9.

[2] The Ātman associated with the gross body, the subtle body and the causal body is called Viśva, Taijasa and Prājña. Cp. with this the Hegelian idea that the successive steps by which the human mind gradually passes from less adequate to more adequate conceptions of reality correspond to the stages of the process by which reality itself is manifested with ever-increasing adequacy in an ascending order of phenomena.

[3] iii. 19.

[4] iii. 21.

[5] iii. 15, 9 and 24.

[6] i. 17–18.

the nature of dream or illusion (svapnamāyā); others maintain that it is the will of God, while those who believe in time declare that everything proceeds from time (kāla). Some say that creation is for the sake of enjoyment (bhoga), while others hold that it is for sport (krīḍā)." Gauḍapāda rejects all these views and declares that "it is the inherent nature of the shining one (devasyaiṣa svabhāvo yam). What desire can he have who has attained all?"[1] Rejecting, therefore, the view that the world is comparable to a dream or an illusion, Gauḍapāda contends that it is the manifestation of the very nature of God, the expression of his power. A realistic conception of the world also comes out in other passages. "The Ātman imagines himself by himself through the power of his māyā (svamāyayā). He alone cognises the objects so sent forth. This is the last word of the Vedānta on the subject."[2] Here Gauḍapāda uses the word "māyā" in the sense of wondrous power; it becomes the svabhāva, or the nature of the Ātman, "inseparable from the ever-luminous who is hidden by it."[3] Māyā is also said to be the beginningless cosmic principle which hides reality from the vision of man.[4] The absolute, together with this principle of māyā or svabhāva, which is the unmanifested (avyākṛtam), is the Īśvara, "who sends forth all the centres of consciousness."[5]

The illustrations of earth, iron and sparks of fire used in the Upaniṣads are meant only to help us to a realisation of the absolute.[6] In later Vedānta this position is elaborated into the view of adhyāropāpavāda, or an illusory attribution to be followed by withdrawal.[7] The metaphysical truth contained in these statements is that the empirical world has for its substratum the Ātman, which, in reality, is a non-cognition of all duality (dvaitasyāgrahaṇam).[8] "The world of duality is mere māyā, the real being the non-dual."[9] Śaṁkara says: "The variety of experience subsists in the Ātman, as the snake does in the rope."[10] We should not say

[1] i. 7–9. [2] ii. 12. See also iii. 10. [3] ii. 19.
[4] i. 16. [5] i. 6. [6] iii. 15.
[7] *Vedāntasāra*, ii. [8] i. 13, 17.
[9] Māyāmātram idaṁ dvaitam advaitam paramārthataḥ (ii. 17).
[10] S.B. on ii. 12, 19.

that the Ātman converts itself into the world. It gives birth to things as a rope does to a snake, and not in reality.[1] It appears to become many only through māyā, and not of itself (na tattvataḥ).[2] "The existence of the variety of experience cannot be said to be identical with the Ātman, nor in any way standing independently by itself, and nothing is different or identical."[3] The world is neither one with the Ātman nor different from it. When Gauḍapāda has his attention fixed on the supreme reality, he declares that the world is only a dream or an illusion, and that the differences are only apparent.[4]

The word māyā is not used by Gauḍapāda with any strictness. It is used to indicate (1) the inexplicability of the relation between the Ātman and the world; (2) the nature or power of Īśvara; (3) the apparent dreamlike character of the world. The first is brought into greater prominence by Śaṁkara, who is indifferent to the third, which makes Gauḍapāda's position more akin to the saṁvṛti-satya or untruth, of the Mādhyamikas rather than to the vyāvahārikasatya or practical truth.[5]

If the world is the objectivisation of the mind (cittadṛśyam) imposed on the absolute Ātman, so is the jīva. The individuation of the Ātman into the many jīvas is only apparent. Ātman is compared to universal space, and the jīva to the same enclosed in a jar; and when the enclosure is destroyed, the limited space (ghaṭākāśa) merges into the universal space (mahākāśa). The differences are only in such accidents as form, capacity and name, but not in the universal space itself. Even as we cannot say that the limited space is either a part (avayava) or an effect (vikāra) of universal space, we cannot say that the jīva is either a part or an effect of the Ātman. The two are one, and the differences are apparent, though for practical purposes we have to treat the two as distinct.[6]

[1] iii. 27; ii. 17. [2] iii. 27. [3] ii. 34.
[4] iii. 19, 24; iv. 45. See also ii. 18.
[5] Gauḍapāda regards the empirical world of things (dharmas) as a mere illusion like the sky (gaganopama). Knowledge is said to be as imaginary as the sky and non-different from the objects (jñeyābhinna).
[6] iii. 3–14.

VII

ETHICS AND RELIGION

The supreme good for man consists in the breaking down of the fetters that shut him out from the reality which he is. Freedom consists in the realisation of the Ātman in the individual soul.[1] The freed soul "is never born, being beyond the range of causality."[2] When one realises the truth, he will live in the world with a sublime unconcern comparable to the perfect indifference of inanimate nature (jaḍavat).[3] He is not bound by the conventional rules and regulations.[4]

The ethical endeavour consists in a progressive approximation to the highest good. The distinctions of good and evil are relevant to the world of experience, where the jīvas possess the sense of individuality. Since avidyā is something which affects man's personality as a whole, in order to get rid of it not only right knowledge but good conduct and devotion to God are necessary. Religion helps us to the attainment of the supreme good. Full liberty of worship is allowed to the finite soul, who can image the infinite in any way he chooses, since all forms rest on the one absolute.[5] The form of religion, resting on the distinction between the human soul and God, is a relative one, adopted on account of its instrumental value.[6] Gauḍapāda accepts the Yogic method as a means. "When the mind ceases from imagining, by a knowledge of the truth of the Ātman, it becomes naught, and remains at rest for want of things to cognise."[7] The state is not to be identified with sleep, for it is knowledge which has for its object Brahman.[8] It is beyond conceptual description, beyond all duality, in a region where jñāna is centred in the Ātman.[9] The method of Yoga is a hard one, involving as it does the control of mind (manonigraha), so hard that Gauḍapāda compares it to the effort of the individual

[1] ii. 18, 38. [2] iv. 75; iii. 38. [3] ii. 36.
[4] ii. 37. [5] ii. 29–30. [6] iii. 1.
[7] iii. 32. [8] iii. 33–34. [9] iii. 35–38.

who is engaged in emptying the ocean drop by drop with the tip of a straw of kuśa grass.[1] The mind, however, should not stop in the enterprise until the ultimate bliss is attained.

VIII

Gauḍapāda and Buddhism

The general idea pervading Gauḍapāda's work, that bondage and liberation, the individual soul and the world, are all unreal, makes the caustic critic observe that the theory which has nothing better to say than that an unreal soul is trying to escape from an unreal bondage in an unreal world to accomplish an unreal supreme good, may itself be an unreality. It is one thing to say that the secret of existence, how the unchangeable reality expresses itself in the changing universe without forfeiting its nature, is a mystery, and another to dismiss the whole changing universe as a mere mirage. If we have to play the game of life, we cannot do so with the conviction that the play is a show and all the prizes in it mere blanks. No philosophy can consistently hold such a view and be at rest with itself. The greatest condemnation of such a theory is that we are obliged to occupy ourselves with objects, the existence and value of which we are continually denying in theory. The fact of the world may be mysterious and inexplicable. It only shows that there is something else which includes and transcends the world; but it does not imply that the world is a dream. Later Buddhism is responsible for this exaggeration in Gauḍapāda's theory. He seems to have been conscious of the similarity of his system to some phases of Buddhist thought. He therefore protests—rather overmuch—that his view is not Buddhism. Towards the end of his book he says: "This was not spoken by Buddha."[2] Commenting on this, Śaṁkara writes: "The theory (of Buddhism) wears a semblance to the Advaita, but is not that absolutism which is the pivot of the Vedānta philosophy."

[1] iii 40–41.

[2] Naitad buddhena bhāṣitam (iv. 99).

Gauḍapāda's work bears traces of Buddhist influence,[1] especially of the Vijñānavāda and the Mādhyamika schools. Gauḍapāda uses the very same arguments as the Vijñānavādins do to prove the unreality of the external objects of perception. Both Bādarāyaṇa and Śaṁkara strongly urge that there is a genuine difference between dream impressions and waking ones,[2] and that the latter are not independent of existing objects. Gauḍapāda, however, links the two, waking and dreaming, experiences together.[3] While Śaṁkara is anxious to free his system from the subjectivism associated with Vijñānavāda, Gauḍapāda welcomes it.[4] Unwilling to accept the Vijñānavāda as final, he declares that even the subject is as unreal as the object, and thus comes perilously near the nihilist position. In common with Nāgārjuna, he denies the validity of causation [5] and the possibility of change. "There is no destruction, no creation, none in bondage, none endeavouring (for release), none desirous of liberation, none liberated; this is the absolute truth."[6] The empirical world is traced to avidyā or, in Nāgārjuna's phrase, saṁvṛti. "From a magical seed is born a magical sprout; this sprout is neither permanent nor perishing. Such are things and for the same reason."[7] The highest state beyond the distinctions of knowledge cannot be characterised by the predicates of existence, non-existence, both or neither. Gauḍapāda and Nāgārjuna regard it as something which transcends the phenomenal.[8] In addition to these points of doctrine, there are affinities in phraseology which point unmistakably to the influence of Buddhism. The use of the word "dharma" for

[1] There are some who believe that Gauḍapāda was himself a Buddhist and wrote a commentary on the *Mādhyamika Kārikā*, since, in his opinion Buddhism tallied with the system of the Upaniṣads. See Dasgupta: *History of Indian Philosophy*, pp. 423–428.

[2] ii. 2. 28–32. [3] ii. 4. [4] iv. 24–28.

[5] ii. 32; iv. 4, 7, 22, 59.

[6] ii. 32; *Mādhyamika Kārikā*, i. 1. See also *Yogavāśiṣṭha*, iv. 38. 22.

Na bandho 'sti na mokṣo 'sti nābandho 'sti na bandhanam
Aprabodhād idaṁ duḥkham prabodhāt pravilīyate.

[7] iv. 59. This is a paraphrase of the Buddhistic doctrine that "from void things are born."

[8] Prapañcopaśamam, ii. 35. Cp. *Mādhyamika Kārikā*, i. 1; also xx. 25.

Sarvopalambhopaśamaḥ prapañcopaśamaḥ śivaḥ
Na kvacit kasyacit kaścid dharmo buddhena deśitaḥ.

a thing or entity, "saṁvṛti" for relative knowledge, and "saṁghāta" for objective existence, is peculiarly Buddhistic.[1] The simile of the firebrand circle is often used in Buddhist writings as a symbol for unreality.[2]

The *Kārikā* of Gauḍapāda is an attempt to combine in one whole the negative logic of the Mādhyamikas with the positive idealism of the Upaniṣads. In Gauḍapāda the negative tendency is more prominent than the positive. In Śaṁkara we have a more balanced outlook.

IX

Bhartṛhari

Another predecessor of Śaṁkara, whose views were akin to his, is Bhartṛhari, the famous logician and grammarian.[3] According to Max Müller,[4] he died about A.D. 650. His great philosophical work is *Vākyapadīya*, which is more or less Buddhist in its tendencies. I-Tsing relates that Bhartṛhari became several times a Buddhist monk and as often lapsed. His teachings are not inconsistent with this story. His insistence on the phenomenality of the world and detachment from things is strongly Buddhist in tone. "All things are attended with fear to men; detachment alone is safe."[5] The world, with all its distinctions, is imagined (kālpanikam). Things of the world are soulless (nairātmya), though words give them individuality. Bhartṛhari is, however, unlike the Buddhists when he posits the reality of Brahman and views the whole world as a vivarta, or a phenomenon based upon it. He identifies Brahman with speech. "Brahman without beginning or end, which is the eternal essence of speech, is changed into the form of things like the evolution of the world."[6] "The

---

[1] iii. 10; iv. 72.

[2] *Laṅkāvatāra*, B.T.S. ed., p. 95. That Gauḍapāda gives us a Vedāntic adaptation of the Buddhist śūnyavāda is supported by many scholars, such as Jacobi, Poussin, Sukhtankar, and Vidhuśekhara Bhaṭṭācārya. Unfortunately Śaṁkara explains away all obvious references to Buddhism. See S.B. on iv. 1, 2, 19, 42, 90, where striking references to Buddha and his doctrine are explained away.

[3] Dr. Winternitz doubts the identity of Bhartṛhari, the poet, with Bhartṛhari, the logician and grammarian. Perhaps in this the learned doctor is a little over-cautious.

[4] S.S., p. 90.

[5] Sarvaṁ vastu bhayānvitam bhuvi nṛṇām, vairāgyam evābhayam.

[6] Anādinidhanam brahma śabdatattvaṁ yad akṣaram
Vivartate 'rthabhāvena prakriyā jagato yataḥ.
Vākyapadīya i. 1.

eternal word, which is called sphoṭa, and does not consist of parts, is indeed Brahman."[1] The ambiguity of the Greek term "logos," which means both reason and word, points to the affinity of the Divine reason and the Divine word.

X

Bhartṛprapañca

In his commentary on the Bṛhadāraṇyaka Upaniṣad,[2] Śaṁkara refers to the dvaitādvaita (or bhedābheda) of Bhartṛprapañca, according to which Brahman is, at once, one and dual. The causal Brahman is different from the effect Brahman, though identical with the latter, when the world returns into the original Brahman. Śaṁkara observes that two contradictory attributes, duality and non-duality, cannot both be true of the same subject. An identity in difference is possible with regard to phenomenal objects, but not with regard to the noumenon. Duality may be true for the individual encased in the upādhis, but it disappears when he is freed from them.

XI

Saṁkara's Relation to the Upaniṣads and the *Brahma Sūtra*

Philosophy is the self-expression of the growing spirit of mankind, and the philosophers are its voice. Great thinkers appear in all great ages, and are as much the creatures as the creators of their era. Their genius lies in the power to seize the opportunity of the hour and give voice to the inarticulate yearnings that have been for long struggling in the hearts of men for expression. A creative thinker of the first rank, Śaṁkara entered into the philosophic inheritance of his age, and reinterpreted it with special reference to its needs. Though Hindu thought had practically triumphed over Buddhism, the latter had instilled its secret strength into the people. The shadow of distrust which Buddhism threw over cherished beliefs did not completely vanish. The Mīmāṁsakas were not able to satisfy the reason of all regarding

[1] Sphoṭākhyo niravayavo nityaśabdo brahmaiveti. (S.D.S., p. 140.)

[2] S.B., Bṛh. Up., v. 1. See also Sureśvara's Vārttika on Bṛh. Up. and Ānandajñāna's gloss on it.

the spiritual value of Vedic ritualism. The different theistic sects were practising rites in support of which they could cite some text or other. It was a critical period in the history of the Hindu nation, when there was a general sense of weariness with the wrangling sects. The age needed a religious genius who was unwilling to break with the past and yet open to the good influences of the new creeds, one who could stretch the old moulds without breaking them and synthesise the warring sects on a broad basis of truth, which would have room for all men of all grades of intelligence and culture. Śaṁkara " set to music " the tune which had been haunting millions of ears, and announced his Advaita Vedānta as offering a common basis for religious unity.

Śaṁkara's modesty makes him say that the doctrine he is expounding is nothing more than what is contained in the Vedas. He thinks that he is voicing an old and weighty tradition which has been handed down to us by an unbroken series of teachers.[1] He is aware that the *Vedānta Sūtra* is commented on by other thinkers in a different way. He frequently refers to one other commentator from whom he differs.[2] It is indeed difficult to decide whether Śaṁkara's philosophy is a continuation or reinterpretation of, or an addition to, the old teaching. We cannot distinguish the old from the new, for in the living the old is new and the new is old.

So far as the classical Upaniṣads are concerned, it must be said that Śaṁkara's view is representative of their main tendency. The Upaniṣads, as we have seen, do not yield any consistent view of the universe. Their authors were many, and not all of them belonged to the same period, and it is doubtful whether they all intended to set forth a single view of the universe ; but Śaṁkara insists on interpreting

[1] Śaṁkara refers to previous teachers of the Advaita in opposition to the Vṛttikāra. See Daharādhikaraṇa, where the expression " asmadīyāś ca " occurs. There are frequent references to " saṁpradāyavidbhir ācāryaiḥ." See the opening verse of S.B. Tait. Up.

[2] S.B., iv. 3. 7; i. 3. 19. Liṅgeśa Mahābhagavat thinks that the Vṛttikāra refuted by Śaṁkara is not Bodhāyana, and the Draviḍa referred to by Śaṁkara as " saṁpradāyavid " in the commentary on the Bṛh. Up. is different from Drāmiḍa of the Viśiṣṭādvaita school. See the *Indian Philosophical Review*, vol. iv, p. 112. The name of Bhagavān Upavarṣa occurs twice in S.B., i. 3. 28 ; iii. 3. 53.

the Upaniṣads in a single coherent manner. According to him, the knowledge of Brahman which we gain from the Upaniṣads must be uniform throughout and without contradiction.[1] Śaṁkara attempts to harmonise such of the assertions of the Upaniṣads as seem most opposed.

There are descriptions in the Upaniṣads of the ultimate reality, as both nirguṇa (devoid of qualities) and saguṇa (possessing qualities), and Śaṁkara reconciles them by means of his distinction between parāvidyā (higher knowledge) and aparā vidyā (lower knowledge). This latter distinction can be traced to the Upaniṣads.[2] Though the distinction as stated in the Upaniṣads is not identical with that which Śaṁkara adopts, still, it lends itself to the latter interpretation. Only through the acceptance of the distinction between higher metaphysics and lower common sense can we reconcile the pure idealism of Yājñavalkya with the less advanced views setting forth the reality of the world and its creation by a personal God. This distinction helps Śaṁkara to get over a number of difficulties. For example, in the *Īśa Upaniṣad*,[3] contradictory predicates are attributed to Brahman, such as, " It is motionless and yet swifter than the mind." Śaṁkara says, " This is no contradiction." It is possible with reference to its being thought of as unconditioned and conditioned."[4] Regarding the descriptions of Brahman as nirviśeṣa (non-determinate) and saviśeṣa (determinate), Śaṁkara says: " From two different standpoints Brahman may be conditioned and unconditioned at the same time. From the standpoint of the liberated soul he is unconditioned; from that of one in bondage Brahman appears to be the cause of the universe endowed with omniscience and with other attributes." The two sets of passages describing mokṣa as identity or equality with Brahman are easily explained by Śaṁkara. Though the māyā doctrine is not found in the early Upaniṣads, still it is an intelligible development of the Upaniṣad view.[5] The word avidyā (ignorance) occurs in the *Kaṭha Upaniṣad*,[6] though it is used in the ordinary sense of ignorance of the true end of man. In Śaṁkara's scheme, the concept of avidyā plays a great part. Other interpreters of the Upaniṣads find it extremely difficult to account for all those passages which regard Brahman as indeterminate and mokṣa as oneness with Brahman. There are of course passages which Śaṁkara passes over as unim-

---

[1] D.S.V., p. 95.

[2] See I.P., p. 149; *Muṇḍaka*, i. 1. 4–5; *Maitrāyaṇī*, vi. 22.

[3] Naiṣa doṣaḥ, nirupādyupādhimattvopapatteḥ.

[4] See also Chān., viii. 1. 5; Bṛh., iv. 5. 13.

[5] *Kaṭha Up.*, ii. 4. 2; Chān., viii. 3. 1–3; i. 1. 10; *Praśna*, i. 16. The prayer of the Bṛh. Up. to " lead us from non-being to being, from darkness to light, from death to immortality," suggests the māyā theory.

[6] ii. 4 and 5; Muṇḍ., ii. 1. 10.

portant.[1] Yet his interpretation of the Upaniṣad is more satisfactory than any other.[2]

The matter is not quite so simple when we take up the question of the *Vedānta Sūtra.* It is difficult to make out the intentions of the author if we leave aside the commentaries. There are six well-known tests, according to the Hindu theory of interpretation, by which we can ascertain the teaching of a work, which are: (1) upakrama (commencement) and upasaṁhāra (conclusion); (2) abhyāsa (reiteration); (3) apūrvatā (novelty); (4) phala (fruit); (5) arthavāda (explanatory statements); and (6) upapatti (illustration). In view of these tests, Śaṁkara believes that Bādarāyaṇa had in view Advaitism of the type advocated by himself.[3] This is in accord with the accepted position that the *Vedānta Sūtra* sums up the teachings of the Upaniṣads. Many students of the Vedānta, notably Thibaut, favour the view that Rāmānuja is more faithful to the intentions of the author.[4]

[1] See D.S.V., p. 95.

[2] Thibaut, Gough and Jacob are also of this opinion. "The task of reducing the teaching of the whole of the Upaniṣads to a system consistent and free from contradiction is an intrinsically impossible one. But the task once given, we are quite ready to admit that Śaṁkara's system is most probably the best that can be devised" (Introduction to S. B. Thibaut). "The teaching of Śaṁkara is the natural and legitimate interpretation of the doctrines of the Upaniṣads" (Gough: *Philosophy of the Upaniṣads,* p. viii). Colonel Jacob says: "It may be admitted that if the impossible task of reconciling the contradictions of the Upaniṣads and reducing them to a harmonious and consistent whole is to be attempted at all, Śaṁkara's system is about the only one that could do it" (Introduction to the *Vedāntasāra*).

[3] S.B., i. 1. 4.

[4] "They do not set forth the distinction of a higher and lower knowledge of Brahman; they do not acknowledge the distinction of Brahman and Īśvara in Śaṁkara's sense; they do not with Śaṁkara proclaim the absolute identity of the individual and the highest self" (Introduction to S.B.). His chief arguments may be briefly stated: (1) The last three parts of the fourth chapter refer to the successive steps by which the soul of him who knows the Lord reaches the world of Brahmā and lives there without returning to the cycle of rebirth. Besides the concluding sūtra of the whole work, "of them there is no returning according to scripture," is the upasaṁhāra, and must be taken as describing absolute freedom from rebirth and not a mere stage on the road to it, as Śaṁkara takes it. According to Śaṁkara, iv. 2. 12–14, and iv. 4. 1–7, describe the state of him who had attained the knowledge of the highest or unconditioned Brahman. It is said in reply to this charge that the upakrama, or the introduction, is more decisive on this question than the upasaṁhāra or the conclusion. Appaya

Every Indian commentator believes that his own view is that of the author of the *Sūtra*, and that every other view is different from it.[1]

XII

Śaṁkara and Other Schools

It is said, not without truth, that Brahmanism killed Buddhism by a fraternal embrace. We have seen already how Brahmanism silently assimilated many Buddhist practices, condemned animal sacrifices, accepted Buddha as an avatār of Viṣṇu, and thus absorbed the best elements of the

Dīkṣita refers to the superior value of the introduction (upakramaparākramaḥ) in a work of that name. The same reply holds against Thibaut's view regarding iv. 3. 7–16, containing the opinions of Bādari, Jaimini and Bādarāyaṇa, where he urges that what occurs first is the pūrvapakṣa, and what comes last the siddhānta. (2) The definition of Brahman given in i. 1. 2 cannot be taken as a definition of Īśvara. " It certainly is as improbable that the sūtras should open with a definition of that inferior principle from whose cognition there can accrue no permanent benefit, as it is unlikely that they should conclude with a description of the state of those who know the lower Brahman only and thus are debarred from attaining true release." The Advaitins contend that, though Brahman in its true nature is indefinable (anirdeśya) and unknowable (agrāhya), still we have to give some provisional definitions. They mention some attributes (viśeṣaṇas) or characteristics (lakṣaṇas) to mark off from Brahman objects possessing other attributes, and thus help us to concentrate on the object in question. These characteristics are either essential (svarūpalakṣaṇas), as sat, cit and ānanda, or accidental (taṭasthalakṣaṇas), as creatorship of the universe, etc. The definition of the second sūtra helps us to a knowledge of Brahman. (3) The argument that the *Sūtra* does not contain the doctrine of māyā, as Śaṁkara understands it, is too complicated to be discussed in a footnote. This, at any rate, is true, that Śaṁkara's view of the world is a legitimate development of the teaching of the *Sūtra*. The question of the identity of the individual soul and Brahman is a specific application of the general principle of māyā. One cannot be certain on the point whether or not Śaṁkara is a faithful interpreter of Bādarāyaṇa's work. See Thibaut: S.B., Introduction; Jacob: *Vedāntasāra*, Introduction; Sundararaman: *Vedantasāra*, Introduction; Apte: *The Doctrine of Māyā*; and Lingeśa Mahābhagavat's article on this subject in the *Indian Philosophical Review*, vol. iv. Deussen admits that there are great differences between Bādarāyaṇa and Śaṁkara. See D.S.V., p. 319.

[1] Cp. *Bhāskarabhāṣya*, 2. Suppressing the intentions of the sūtras and developing their own views, many commentaries are written and new commentaries must be written.

Sūtrābhiprāyasaṁvṛtyā svābhiprāyaprakāśanāt
Vyākhyātaṁ yair idaṁ śāstraṁ vyākhyeyaṁ tan nivṛttaye.

Buddhist faith. Though the accidents of its first immediate form disappeared, Buddhism became, partly through Śaṁkara's influence, a vital force in the life of the country. Buddhism created in the region of thought a certain atmosphere from which no mind could escape, and it undoubtedly exercised a far-reaching influence on Śaṁkara's mind. An Indian tradition opposed to Śaṁkara holds that he is a Buddhist in disguise and his māyāvāda but crypto-Buddhism. In the *Padma Purāṇa*, Īśvara is said to have declared to Pārvatī: "The theory of māyā is a false doctrine, a disguised form of Buddhism; I, myself, O goddess, propounded this theory in the Kaliyuga in the form of a Brahmin." [1] Yāmunācārya, the spiritual grandfather of Rāmānuja, is of the same opinion, which Rāmānuja repeats.[2] Vijñānabhikṣu, commenting on the Sāṁkhya system, observes: "There is not a single Brahmasūtra in which our bondage is declared to be due to mere ignorance. As to the novel theory of māyā propounded by persons calling themselves Vedāntists, it is only a species of the subjective idealism (of the Buddhists) That theory is not a tenet of the Vedānta." [3] Apparently, shortly after Śaṁkara had established the orthodoxy of the māyāvāda, opponents of the view maintained that it was nothing more than a *réchauffé* of Buddhism, and so not in conformity with the Vedas. The words of Siva in the *Padma Purāṇa* later in the same chapter are to the effect that "that great system, the māyā theory, is not supported by the Veda, though it contains the truths of the Veda."[4] All these estimates imply that Śaṁkara incorporated certain Buddhistic elements such as the doctrine of māyā and monasticism into the Vedānta philosophy. It is held that, in an endeavour to preserve the continuity of thought, he attempted to combine logically incompatible ideas. However creditable this may be to the elasticity of Śaṁkara's mind or his spirit of genuine

[1] Māyāvādam asac chāstram pracchannam bauddham eva ca
Mayaiva kathitaṁdevi, kalau brāhmaṇarūpiṇā (Uttara Khanda, ch. 236). See also S.D.S.

[2] In his *Siddhitraya*, Yāmunācārya remarks that, for both the Buddhists and the Advaitins, the distinctions of knower, known and knowledge are unreal. The Advaita traces them to māyā, while Buddhist subjectivism traces them to buddhi (J.R.A.S., 1910, p. 132).

[3] S.P.B., i. 22.

[4] Vedārthavan mahāśāstram māyāvādam avaidikam.

toleration, it cannot but affect the logical rigour of his thought; and the theory of māyā serves as a cloak to cover the inner rifts of his system. However that be, there is no doubt that Śaṁkara develops his whole system from the Upaniṣads and the *Vedānta Sūtra* without reference to Buddhism.[1] A persistent misreading of India's religious history is responsible for the prevalent view that Buddha's faith is an alien one opposed to the Vedas. In our discussion of Buddhism we have repeatedly urged that Buddha developed certain views of the Upaniṣads. The inclusion of Buddha among the avatārs of Viṣṇu means that he appeared for the establishment of the Vedic dharma, and not for the undermining of it. There are no doubt similarities between the views of Buddhism and Advaita Vedānta, and this is not surprising in view of the fact that both these systems had for their background the Upaniṣads.

Śaṁkara was clearly conscious of this fact, while Buddha did not seem to be so. While Śaṁkara had the Buddhist's love of free thought, he had much respect for tradition. Philosophically, he became convinced that no movement could thrive on a spirit of negation, and so asserted the reality of Brahman on the basis of śruti. The phenomenalism of the Buddhists is akin to the doctrine of māyā. Śaṁkara declares that the world of experience neither is nor is not. It has an intermediate existence which both is and is not. Buddha repudiates the two extreme views that everything is and everything is not, and holds that there exists only a becoming.[2] Śaṁkara admits the distinction between absolute truth (paramārtha) and empirical truth (vyavahāra), which answers to the Buddhistic distinction between paramārtha and saṁvṛti.[3] Early Buddhism was positivist in its outlook and confined its attention to what we perceive. Some of the

[1] Many followers of the Advaita adopt the dialectical method of the Mādhyamikas so far as the refutation of opposed views is concerned. Śrī Harṣa believes that for criticising other systems we need not assume any views, but simply adopt the Mādhyamika logic. Vitāṇḍākathām ālambya khaṇḍanānāṁ vaktavyatvāt. Madhusūdana Sarasvatī adopts vāda, jalpa and vitaṇḍā in his criticism of the other theories.

[2] See I.P., p. 369; *Saṁyutta Nikāya*, xxii. 90. 16.

[3] Dve satye samupāśritya buddhānām dharmadeśanā
Loke saṁvṛtisatyaṁ ca, satyaṁ ca paramārthataḥ.
See *Nyāyaratnākara* on S.V., *Niralambanavāda*.

early Buddhists even went the length of saying that there was nothing behind appearances, not only nothing for us but nothing at all. Śaṁkara, as a Hindu, claims that, beyond the unsatisfactoriness of its phenomena, in its deepest depths, there is the real spirit which embodies all values. Yet Śaṁkara's conception of mokṣa (freedom) is not much different from the Buddhist view of nirvāṇa.[1] If we introduce the reality of an absolute Brahman into early Buddhism, we find the Advaita Vedānta again. Śaṁkara had a firm grasp of the real significance as well as the limitations of Buddhist thought, and if at times we are tempted to quarrel with his treatment of the Buddhist schools, we must remember that he wrote in reply to the prevalent views of Buddhism and not the teachings of Buddha.

Every system of thought is determined not only by the positive content which it attempts to express, but also by the views which it wishes to oppose. The controversy with Maṇḍana Miśra shows that Śaṁkara was opposed to the exclusive supremacy of Vedic ritualism. He emphasised jñāna, or knowledge of the supreme spirit, as the chief end of man's endeavour. He had the fear that a ceremonial cult led to mere pharisaism. As Jesus denounced the Pharisees and Paul protested against the law, Śaṁkara declared that ceremonial piety by itself was not the end of religion and was often its deadly enemy. He did not, however, dismiss the Vedic code as useless. While only true philosophers can get beyond the Vedic rule of life, others were called upon to conform to the Vedic regulations, not in the expectation of good things here or hereafter, but out of a sense of duty and as a help for the development of the moral competency for the study of the Vedānta. Vedic piety helps us by turning our minds towards the inner soul, and thus leads us to the realisation of the eternal goal of mankind.

According to Śaṁkara, the contents and aims of the Pūrva and the Uttara Mīmāṁsās are independent. The former investigates the question of man's duty and holds before our

[1] Vāsanātyantavirāmaḥ. The realisation of the identity of the individual soul with Brahman (so'ham or aham brahmāsmi) answers to the ' I am nullity " (śūnyataivāham) of the Mādhyamikas, though the emphasis is on the different aspects of the one fact.

vision a future world dependent on our conduct here on earth. The highest happiness it presents is but transitory. The Vedānta, on the other hand, helps us to the realisation of the truth. Its goal is not happiness on earth or heaven (abhyudaya), but freedom from rebirth (niḥśreyasa). This cannot be had so long as we pin our faith to the future. The investigation of Brahman relates to a reality which has always existed and is not dependent on our actions.[1]

As a rule, Śaṁkara attacks the philosophical views of the rival schools and not their religious tenets. Regarding the Bhāgavata system, Śaṁkara agrees that its religious conception is based on the authority of śruti and smṛti, but he objects to the view that the individual souls are born from God.[2] He admits the supremacy of a personal Īśvara, who is the cause of the freedom and the bondage of the individual. In the difficulty as to how the knowledge of Brahman arises in the mind of man, which cannot be due to logical investigations, which belong to the realm of avidyā, Śaṁkara brings in the will of God.[3]

[1] Normally, however, inquiry into dharma prepares the mind for the inquiry into Brahman. Those who take straight away to Brahma knowledge must have performed the necessary duties in the previous life.

[2] The Bhāgavatas say that the Lord Vāsudeva divides himself into soul, mind and self-sense. Śaṁkara argues that if the soul is produced from the Lord, then it can be destroyed, and there can be no final release for it. The Bhāgavatas also hold that just as the soul is produced from the Lord, so also mind is produced from the soul and the self-sense from the mind. This, says Śaṁkara, is inconceivable, since it is not a matter of experience. The soul cannot produce out of itself its instruments any more than the farm labourer can produce from himself the spade he works with. If it is said that all the four have the same powers and status and are equally real, then they are all one. If each of these forms results from the preceding, in the order Lord, soul, mind, self-sense, then the effects suffer from the defect of impermanency. If all four are permanent, then there is no reason why the Lord should produce the soul and not the soul the Lord. If all the four are forms in which the one reality manifests itself, the Advaitin retorts that Brahman is present in forms too numerous to mention and not merely in four forms (S.B., ii. 2. 42–44).

[3] "For the individual soul, which is impotent, in the condition of ignorance, to distinguish the Ātman from the aggregate of the organs of activity (appearing as the body), and is blind through the darkness of avidyā, from the highest soul, the overseer of the work, the onlooker dwelling in all being, the Lord who is the cause of spirit, from him, by his permission, comes the saṁsāra, consisting in the states of doing and enjoying, and through his grace is caused knowledge and, through this, liberation." Again, although the truth of the identity of God and the soul is hidden,

Śaṁkara, as we have seen, criticised the loose and hasty speculations of the Sāṁkhya thinkers, as well as the empirical tendencies of the Nyāya-Vaiśeṣika. He broke away from the common-sense method of the Naiyāyikas, and substituted for it a logical criticism quite as subtle and penetrating as that of the Buddhist thinkers.

XIII

The Ātman

Metaphysics is a consideration of what is implied in the fact of experience. Its problem is not one of observing and tabulating the facts of consciousness; it is concerned with what the existence of facts implies regarding the nature of reality. Śaṁkara does not question the facts of psychology any more than the facts of physical science, but raises the further question of the presupposition of these facts, and he approaches the problem from the subjective and the objective sides, which do not ultimately diverge. In the Introduction to his commentary on the *Vedānta Sūtra*, he asks whether there is anything in experience which may be regarded as foundational, and discusses the claims of all the factors of experience to such a title. Our senses may deceive us and our memory may be an illusion. The past and the future may be abstractions. The forms of the world may be pure fancy, and all our life may be a tragic illusion. Nothing prevents us from regarding the waking tracts of experience as analogous to dream-worlds, where also we visit places, handle shadows and do battle with ghosts, and remember, too, all our adventures in the fairy land. If dreams are facts, facts may well be dreams. Though all objects of knowledge may be matters of belief and so open to doubt, there seems to be still something in experience transcending it. If one finds within oneself something not made by one's

"yet, when a creature thinks on and strives towards the highest God, just as the faculty of sight in one who has become blind, after the darkness is shaken off by the power of remedies, in him in whom the grace of God perfects it, does it become manifest, but not naturally in any being whatsoever. Why? Because through him, through God as cause, the binding and the loosing of the soul are accomplished, binding when it does not recognise the essence of God, and loosing when it does" (D.S.V., pp. 86–87)

environment but making it and moulding it, if in the very possibility of one's knowledge and evaluation of the sense-world there is implied that which cannot be derived from the sense-world, then logic requires that one should affirm the reality of that transcendent presence within oneself. The note of scepticism finds its limit in regard to the self, of which we are immediately conscious. Everyone is conscious of the existence of his own self, and no one thinks "I am not."[1] Like Descartes, Šaṁkara finds the basis of truth in the immediate self certainty which is untouched by any of the doubts cast on other things.[2] If the existence of self were not known, then everyone would think "I am not," which, however, is not true. The self is prior to the stream of consciousness, prior to truth and falsehood, prior to reality and illusion, good and evil. "All means of knowledge (pramāṇas) exist only as dependent on self-experience, and since such experience is its own proof, there is no necessity for proving the existence of self." "The very existence of understanding and its functions presupposes an intelligence known as the self, which is different from them, which is self-established, and which they subserve."[3] Each function and faculty, the gross body and the vital breath, the senses and the internal organ, the empirical "me," appear only on the basis of and in relation to the Ātman. They all serve an end beyond themselves, and depend on some deeper ground of existence. Ātman cannot be doubted, "for it is the essential nature of him who denies it."[4]

Šaṁkara argues that it is impossible for us to know the self by means of thought, since thought itself is a part of the flux belonging to the region of the not-self. If we grasp it by inducing a sort of sleep on all our critical and interpretative powers, then we do fail to have knowledge of the type we desire. Yet we cannot think away the self, for there is no consciousness or experience possible apart from it. Though it escapes our knowledge, it does not entirely escape us. It is the

[1] Sarvo hy ātmāstitvam pratyeti na nāham asmīti (S.B., i. 1. 1).
[2] Cp. Descartes: *Discourse on Method.*
[3] Sureśvara's *Vārttika*, pp. 189 and 542, 791–795. See also S.B., ii. 3. 7; i. 3. 22.
[4] Ya eva hi nirākartā tad eva tasya svarūpam (S.B., ii. 3. 7).

object of the notion of self,[1] and is known to exist on account of its immediate presentation.[2] It cannot be proved, since it is the basis of all proof and is established prior to all proof.[3] Logically it is a postulate. We have to take it for granted.[4]

Śaṁkara tries to distinguish the true self from the object, and declares that subject and object are opposed like light and darkness, so that what is truly subject can never become an object. Metaphysically, the conception of self-existence involves the ideas of eternity, immutability and completeness. What is truly real is what has being in itself and for itself,[5] so that to affirm the reality of Ātman or the permanent self is to affirm the reality of an eternal Brahman. Ātma ca Brahma.[6] The proof of the reality of Brahman is that it is the ground of the self of everyone.[7]

Though we know that the self is, we do not know what it is, whether finite or infinite, knowledge or bliss, one only or one among others like itself, a mere witness or an enjoyer, or neither. As there are conflicting opinions about the nature of the self, Śaṁkara says that it is both known and unknown. The "I" must be distinguished from the "not I," which includes not only the outer world, the body and its organs, but also the whole apparatus of understanding and the senses. In ordinary usage we regard mental states as subjective, and physical states as objective. But from the metaphysical point of view both orders of phenomena, material and mental, are equally objective.[8] The materialists identify the self with

1 Asmatpratyayaviṣaya. Cp. Kena., ii. Pratibodhaviditam.

2 Aparokṣatvāc ca pratyagātma-prasiddheḥ (S.B., i. 1. 1).

3 Ātmā tu pramāṇādivyavahārāśrayatvāt prāg eva pramāṇādivyavahārāt siddhyati (S.B., ii. 3. 7; S.B.G., xviii. 50).

4 Śaṁkara says: "The eternal spirit different from the agent, which is the object of the presentation of I (ahaṁpratyayaviṣaya) dwelling as witness (sākṣin) in all being, uniform (sama), one, the highest is not apprehended by anyone from the Veda (vidhikāṇḍa) or any book based on reflection (tarka). He is the soul of all (sarvasyātmā) . . . and therefore none can deny him, for he is even the self of him who denies" (i. 1. 4).

5 See Hegel: *Æsthetics*, E.T., chap. i.

6 S.B., i. 1. 1.

7 Sarvasyātmatvāc ca brahmāstitvaprasiddhiḥ. S.B., i. 1. 1.

8 "As one is accustomed when it goes ill or well with his son or wife and the like to say, 'It goes ill or well with me,' and thus transfers the qualities of outer things to the self, in just the same way he transfers the qualities of the body when he says, 'I am fat, I am thin, I am white, I stand, I go, I leap,' and similarly the qualities of the sense-organs when he says,

the body or the senses. But consciousness and matter represent different kinds of reality, and one cannot be reduced to the other. Nor can we identify the self with the senses. For then there would be as many selves as there are senses, and this would make the recognition of personal identity a problem. Besides, if the different senses constitute the self, there should be the simultaneous enjoyment of sight, sound, taste, etc. According to the Yogācāra theory, the self is nothing more than a series of impermanent mental states.[1] But we cannot, on this theory, account for the facts of memory and recognition. The Śūnyavāda, which declares that there is no permanent self at all, comes into conflict with the first principle of Śaṁkara's philosophy, that the existence of the self cannot be doubted. Even if we declare the whole world to be a mere void, this void presupposes a cogniser of itself.[2] Even in dreamless sleep there is the self, for when one rises from it one is aware that one had good sleep undisturbed by dreams. This he knows from memory. Since memory is only of presentations, the bliss of sleep and the consciousness of nothing must have been presented during the sleeping state. If it is said that the absence during sleep of disquiet and knowledge is only inferred from the memory of the state before sleep and the perception of the state after it, then it

'I am dumb, impotent, deaf, one-eyed, blind,' and similarly the qualities of the internal organ (antaḥkaraṇa), desire, wish, doubt, resolution, and the like. Thus also he transfers the subject presenting the 'I' (ahaṁpratyayin) to the inner self present solely as witness (sākṣin) of the personal tendencies, and, conversely, the witness of all, the inner self to the internal organ and the rest" (S.B., i. 1. 1). See D.S.V., p. 54, n.; *Ātmabodha*, p. 18; S.S.S.S., xii. 49–62, 72–77. Cp. Descartes: "I am not the assemblage of members called the human body; I am not a thin and penetrating air diffused through all these members, or wind, or flame, or vapour, or breath, or any of all the things I can imagine, for I supposed that all these were not, and without changing the supposition I find that I still feel assured of my existence" (*Meditations*, p. ii). See also Chān. Up., viii. 7–12; Tait. Up., ii. 1. 7; Māṇḍūkya Up. Felt-masses and content-complexes do not explain but demand explanation. Kant made an effective contribution to logical theory when he asked us to shift our attention from the contents of consciousness to the consciousness which apperceives or is aware of the contents. But he was not fully aware of the implications of his theory that there could be only one universal consciousness. He knew that the distinction o objects into inanimate and animate, sentient and conscious, were distinctions in the world of contents. But he illegitimately inferred from the plurality of the content world the plurality of things in themselves.

[1] Kṣaṇikavijñānadhārā.

[2] Śūnyasyāpi svasākṣitvāt.

is replied that we cannot infer anything the like of which was not presented. If it is said that a negative concept cannot have any percept answering to it, and therefore the absence of knowledge and disquiet is only inferred, it is said in reply that absence of knowledge, etc., to be inferred must be conceivable, *i.e.* must have been directly perceived during their absence. So we have during dreamless sleep direct consciousness of the absence of knowledge and disquiet. In that state the empirical mind is inactive, and pure consciousness alone is present.[1] The self is not to be identified with the inner feeling which accompanies the continual changes of our mental attitudes or the empirical "me," consisting of a number of mental contents developing in time.[2] It is true that self-consciousness (ahaṁkāra) precedes activity, but it is not the self, since it is not antecedent to knowledge, as it is itself an object of knowledge.[3] To equate the self with a flux of states, a presentation continuum, or a stream of consciousness, would be to confuse the principle of consciousness with portions of its contents. The felt-masses and

[1] The inner organ is inactive and the pure consciousness is only in relation to avidyā. Any activity in suṣupti is traced to avidyā by the author of *Vivaraṇa*, while Sureśvara contends that there is no activity at all in suṣupti.

[2] M. Bergson has made us familiar with the conception of a growing self which goes on gathering its past experience through memory and pressing forward to its future ends (*Creative Evolution*, p. 210). If the basis of personality is only the consciousness of the past, as some Buddhists believe, then there can never be the same self at two different moments of time. While the connecting-link of memory may give some force and significance to the notion of selfhood, the sense of timelessness inherent in the consciousness of self remains unexplained. Bergson is aware of the unsatisfactory nature of an endlessly growing self, and so tells us that the true self is to be defined by a reference to pure duration which is unconscious of a forward movement or a past history. It is the undivided present where all the temporal categories are absent. Bergson thus tries to satisfy the instinct for eternity by making short work of time and developing a theory of duration or non-temporal growth. But the self that endures does so in dependence on external factors. It is not self-dependent. When Bergson admits the reality of memory, whole and complete, even in deep dreamless sleep, and employs it to account for the unity and continuity of consciousness, he comes very near Śaṁkara. He admits that the spiritual in memory persists even when every form is extinguished in the universal flux of things. While it serves as a binding link of the successive experiences, it can exist even when all experiences vanish.

[3] Ahaṁkārapūrvakam api kartṛtvaṁ nopalabdhir bhavitum arhati, ahaṁkārasyāpy upalabhyamānatvāt (S.B., ii. 3. 40).

conscious streams rise and fall, appear and vanish. If all these varying contents are to be connected, we require a universal consciousness which ever accompanies them. "When it is said, It is I who now know what at present exists, it is I who knew the past and what was before the past, it is I who shall know the future and what is after the future, it is implied in these words that, even when the object of knowledge alters, the knower does not alter, for he is in the past, present and the future, as his essence is eternally present."[1] We can know a temporal series of events as a series only if the facts are held together through something present alike to each of them and itself therefore out of time.[2] The self is not a creature of the natural world, for the simple reason that there would not be any natural world were not the principle of self presupposed. Śaṁkara holds that we get the notion of the Ātman if we divest it of all that surrounds it, discriminate it from the bodily frame with which it is encompassed, strip it of all contents of experience.[3] To our logical minds it may appear that we have reduced it to a bare potentiality of thought, if not mere nothing, but it is better to regard it this way than as a whole of parts or a thing with qualities or a substance with attributes. It is undifferenced consciousness alone (nirviśeṣacinmātram) which is unaffected even when the body is reduced to ashes and the mind perishes.[4]

[1] Sarvadā vartamānasvabhāvatvāt (S.B., ii. 3. 7, and S.B.G., ii. 18). See *Advaitamakaranda*, pp. 11 and 13.

[2] Śaṁkara would endorse Lotze's argument that the simplest comparison of two ideas and the recognition of them as like or unlike presupposes "the indivisible unity of that which compares them," an Ātman external to the content with which it deals (*Metaphysics*, p. 241).

[3] Understanding, senses, etc., are unconscious and objects of a subject. Cp. *Bhāmati*: "Citsvabhāvātmā viṣayī, jaḍasvabhāvā buddhīndriyadeha-viṣayā viṣayaḥ."

[4] S.S.S.S., xii. 8. 41. Cp. Augustine: "Step by step was I led upwards from bodies to the soul which perceives by means of the bodily senses; and thence to the soul's inward faculty, to which the bodily senses report external things, which is the limit of the intelligence of animals; and thence again to the reasoning faculty, to whose judgment is referred the knowledge received by the bodily senses. And when this power also within me found itself changeable, it lifted itself up to its own intelligence and withdrew its thoughts from experience, abstracting itself from the contradictory throng of sense-images, that it might find what that light was wherein it was bathed, when it cried out that beyond all doubt the unchangeable is

The crux of all philosophy is this, that the sense-organs and the neural processes of the body, which is in space and time, seem to produce consciousness. Surely the non-conscious cannot be the cause of the conscious. If anything, the conscious must be the cause of the non-conscious. The senses, the mind and the understanding are not self-sufficient. "The activity of these organs demands in addition upalabdhi, which belongs to the Ātman . . . whose very nature is eternal knowledge."[1] But this consciousness, which is the cause of the non-conscious, is not the finite consciousness but the ultimate one, for ever so many objects and events that do not exist in this or that finite consciousness still exist in reality. So we must assume an ultimate consciousness of which the finite is only a fragment. The fundamental consciousness, which is the basis of all reality, is not to be confused with the human consciousness, which appears rather late in the cosmic evolution. Presentations are subject to origin and decay, and are not self-luminous, and they are known only through the light of Ātman,[2] whose essential nature is self-luminosity.[3] It is pure consciousness (caitanyam) or mere awareness, "the supreme principle in which there is no differentiation of knower, knowledge and known, infinite, transcendent, the essence of absolute knowledge."[4] It is of

to be preferred to the changeable; whence also it knew that Unchangeable; and thus with the flash of one trembling glance it arrived at *That which is*" (*Confessions*, vii. 23).

[1] Nityopalabdhi svarūpatvāt (S.B., ii. 3. 40). Cp. *Citsukhī*, i. 7.

Cid rūpatvād akarmatvāt svayaṁjyotir ity śruteḥ
Ātmanaḥ svaprakāśatvaṁ ko nivārayituṁ kṣamaḥ.

[2] S.B., ii. 2. 28. Cp. with this Aristotle's Nous, which helps understanding, etc., which are potentially intelligent, to realise their potencies.

[3] Svayaṁjyotis svarūpatvāt (S.B., i. 3. 22). See also S.B. on *Praśna Up.*, vi. 3.

[4] *Vivekacūḍāmaṇi*, p. 239.

The Naiyāyika (*Nyāyamañjari*, p. 432) objects to this theory on the following grounds: Nobody has experienced pure consciousness, since our empirical consciousness is always conditioned by the mind and the senses. To say that it is known by intuitive consciousness (aparokṣajñāna) is self-contradictory. If it is argued that the self as self-luminous is known immediately, it may be said that a shining lamp is manifested to a blind man though unperceived by him. If the lamp manifests itself only to one who apprehends it, then even the self is known only when it is apprehended, *i.e.* when it becomes an object of consciousness, and then it ceases to be pure and undefiled. Kumārila asks, if the self as being of the nature of consciousness is self-the nature of non-objective consciousness.[1] "The Ātman is throughout nothing but intelligence; intelligence is its exclusive nature, as the salt taste is of the lump of salt."[2] Spirit cannot have an unspiritual nature. By the law of its being, it is ever shining. As the sun shines when there is nothing for it to shine on, so the Ātman has consciousness even when there is no object.[3] It is pure light, clear radiance, not merely the foundation of all our knowledge, but the light of all our seeing.

Śaṁkara sets aside the view of Nyāya and the Viśiṣṭādvaita that the self is an intelligent substance and the relation of self to consciousness is one of substance and attribute (dharmi and dharma).[4] The relation between intelligence and self must be one of identity or difference, or identity and difference. If intelligence be different in nature from the self, then there can be no relation of substance and attribute between them.[5] Besides, in the case of different objects, the relation may be either external conjunction (saṁyoga) or internal relation (samavāya). The former holds between two corporeal things, but self and intelligence are not corporeal. If there be the internal relation of samavāya between self and intelligence, then this relation must itself be related to the self, and the second relation must also be related to the self, and so on *ad infinitum*. So if self and intelligence are different from each other, it is impossible to conceive of the relation of substance and attribute between them. If the two are identical, then there is no meaning in saying that the one is an attribute of the other. It would be contradictory to hold that one thing is both identical with and different from another. So the self must be regarded as identical with intelligence.[6]

The caitanya or Ātman is not to be confused with logical apprehension, where it ceases to be the ultimate real that

luminous, are pleasure and pain to be regarded as self-luminous? On this view we cannot account for its suspension in sleep. If it is said that the self alone is manifested in dreamless sleep, but not the body or the senses or the objects, which are all manifested in waking life, Kumārila denies it on the ground that we have a consciousness that we apprehended nothing during deep sleep when we awake from it. He contends that the self is an object of internal perception (mānasapratyakṣagamyam). See also *Śāstradīpikā*, pp. 347–350.

[1] Nirviṣayajñānamayam. Cp. Śaṁkara's *Hymn to Hari*, p. 4.

[2] S.B., iii. 2. 16. See also S.B., i. 3. 19, 22.

[3] S.B., ii. 3. 18.

[4] Ciddharma ātmā na tu citsvabhāvaḥ. Cp. Jñānabhinno nityātmeti siddham (Viśvanātha's *Muktāvali*, p. 49).

[5] Atmaghaṭādivad dharmadharmitvānupapatteḥ.

[6] See *Hastāmalaka*. See Haldane: *Reign of Relativity*, p. 196.

can be rendered in its own terms, but becomes an effect of, the interaction of subject and object. If knowledge is conceived as at a level where it is creative of its object, there is yet implicit in it a distinction between subject and object, and this limitation is not the less a limitation simply because knowledge itself has produced it. True existence and intelligence go together. Ātman cannot be existence without intelligence or intelligence without existence.[1] It is also of the nature of bliss (ānanda).[2] Ānanda is freedom from all suffering.[3] Ātman has nothing to cast off and nothing to acquire, nothing dark or disorderly. Śaṁkara denies activity to Ātman, since activity by its nature is non-eternal.[4] "The self cannot be the abode of any action, since an action cannot exist without modifying that in which it abides."[5] All activity presupposes the self-sense, and, so far as we are aware, it is of the form of pain[6] and motived by desire.[7] Activity and enjoyment are dependent on a dualistic vision, which is not the highest truth.[8] There can be no agency without the limitation of the Ātman by a body, etc., and every limitation is unreal.[9] The Ātman by itself has no agency.[10] Śaṁkara attributes to the Ātman truth, dependence on its own greatness, omnipresence, and the character of being the self of all.[11] He regards the Ātman as one, universal and infinite, for the same reason for which Hegel calls his idea infinite. It is at no point limited by its antitheses or opposites, by something else which it is not but which yet sets bounds to it. It is always in his own sphere. Consciousness has no limit, since the consciousness of limits shows that the consciousness is

[1] Sattā eva bodhaḥ bodha eva ca sattā.

[2] Tait. Up., ii. Ātman is (asti), shines (bhāti), and pleases (prīṇāti).

[3] Cp. Bṛh. Up., iii. 5. [4] Adhruva. [5] S.B., i. 1. 4.

[6] Kartṛtvasya duḥkharūpatvāt (S.B., ii. 3. 40).

[7] Karmahetuḥ kāmah syāt, pravartakatvāt (Śaṁkara's Introduction to the Tait. Up).

[8] Avidyāpratyupasthāpitatvāt kartṛbhoktṛtvayoh. S.B., ii. 3. 40. Cp. also Bṛh. Up., iv. 5. 15.

[9] Cp. Sureśvara: "The existence of the Ātman in its natural state (svarūpa) is spoken of by the wise as liberation (niḥśreyasa), and the contact of the Ātman with any other condition is the result of ajñāna" (*Vārttika*, p. 109).

[10] Svataḥ anadhikāriṇah. See Sureśvara's *Vārttikas*, pp. 110–113.

[11] Satyatvam, svamahimapratiṣṭhitatvam, sarvagatatvam, sarvātmatvam (S.B., i. 3. 9).

greater than the limit. If there were a limit to it, then consciousness as limited by other things cannot be conscious of limits. Consciousness and limit are opposed in nature. Limit is the nature of a thing and consciousness is no thing.

It is urged against Descartes that he tried to abstract the self totally from the not-self and established the reality of the former independently in its own right. We must be clear that Śaṁkara's self is not the individual knowing subject. If Śaṁkara tried to establish the reality of the individual knowing subject in abstraction from or as opposed to the not-self, he would get a plurality of finite contentless selves or an abstract universal self. The Ātman of Śaṁkara is neither the individual self nor a collection of such selves. These latter are dependent on the universal self. Śaṁkara says that it is "not a thing in the empirical sense which we may indicate by words; nor is it an object like a cow which can be known by the ordinary means of knowledge. It cannot even be described by its generic properties or specific marks; we cannot say that it acts in this or that manner, since it is always known to be actionless. It cannot, therefore, be positively described." Śaṁkara's self is different from the transcendental ego of Kant, which is purely a form which attaches to all objects of experience. Though it is said to transcend empirical consciousness, it is still individualised, since it becomes the practical will. Kant's account of its difference from the empirical ego, which is a product of conditions, applies to Śaṁkara's Ātman. Only Śaṁkara would say that the ever-present light of consciousness is something perfect and not in process of growth.[1] The practical will of Kant is the empirical self, for which there is always the indefinable sense of the beyond. Fichte's absolute ego is not different in essence from the empirical self, since the activity by which it becomes actually what it is potentially is determined by the non-ego. It is because Śaṁkara finds the essence of personality in its distinction from other existences that he contends that the Ātman which has no other existences independent of it is not a person. It is true, however, that the empirical self is the only reality

[1] Cp. Gentile's theory of the pure subject which cannot be made an object (*Theory of Mind as Pure Act*, pp. 6–7).

from the logical point of view and the pure self but a shadow. But when we rise to intuition, where the subject and the object coincide, we realise the truth of the ultimate consciousness.[1] It is the absolute vision that is its own visibility. It is the essence of everyone who, having thought "I am who I am," thus knows himself. It is the absolutely real which no experience will ever alter. It has no dimensions. We cannot think of it as extended or capable of division. It is always and everywhere the same. There is in it no plurality. It is as much in one as in another. It is incapable of particularisation. We live because we share the universal life; we think because we share the universal thought. Our experience is possible because of the universal Ātman in us.[2]

XIV

The Mechanism of Knowledge

Scepticism about the preconceptions of common sense and the first principles of thought is what Śaṁkara inherited from the Buddhist thinkers. It became clear to him that no attempt at philosophical construction can take for granted a system of first principles. So he undertook a critical analysis of knowledge and man's cognitive mechanism. Deep within us our self lives a life of which it does not speak. The ultimate reality is the non-dual spirit. But all determinate knowledge

[1] Cp. Caird: "If knowledge is the relation of an object to a conscious subject, it is the more complete the more intimate the relation, and it becomes perfect when the duality becomes transparent, when subject and object are identified, and when the duality is seen to be simply the necessary expression of the unity—in short, when consciousness passes into self-consciousness" (*Critical Philosophy of Kant*, p. 46).

[2] S.B. on Māṇḍūkya Up., ii. 7. Cp. Eckhart: "There is something in the soul which is above the soul, divine, simple, an absolute nothing; rather unnamed than named; unknown than known. . . . It is higher than knowledge, higher than love, higher than grace, for in all these there is still distinction. This light is satisfied only with the supra-essential essence. It is bent on entering into the simple ground, the still waste wherein is no distinction, neither Father nor Son nor Holy Ghost; into the unity where no man dwelleth. Then is it satisfied in the light, then it is one; then it is one in itself—as this ground is a simple stillness, in itself immovable, and yet by this immovability are all things moved" (quoted in Hunt's *Essay on Pantheism*, p. 180).

presupposes the modification of the ultimate consciousness into (1) a subject who knows (pramātṛcaitanya), the cognising consciousness which is determined by the internal organ; (2) the process of knowledge (pramāṇacaitanya), the cognitive consciousness determined by the vṛtti, or the modification of the internal organ; and (3) the object known (viṣaya-caitanya), the consciousness determined by the object cognised. The ultimate consciousness is one only (ekam eva), pervading all things (sarvavyāpi), enlightening all, the internal organ, its modification and the object.[1] The arguments for the existence of antaḥkaraṇa (internal organ),[2] besides the senses, are already familiar to us.[3] The internal organ is so called because it is the seat of the functions of the sense as distinct from their outer organs. It receives and arranges what is conveyed to it through the senses. It is not itself regarded as a sense, since, if it were a sense, it could not have a direct perception of itself or its modifications. It is said to consist of parts and to be of medium size, neither atomic nor infinite in magnitude. It has transparency, by which it reflects objects, even as the mirror has the lustre to reflect our faces. The power to reflect objects, *i.e.* to become conscious of them, is not innate in the internal organ, but is acquired by it from its relation to the Ātman. Though the internal organ is said to shed its lustre on the objects and reflect them, it is still the Ātman that reflects in it.[4] Ātman is the illuminator, and by means of it the internal organ perceives.[5] The internal organ

1 Cp. *Pañcadaśi*, vii. 91.

2 Vācaspati regards manas as a sense.

3 Between the Ātman and the organs of sense a connecting-link is necessary. If we do not admit the internal organ, there would result either perpetual perception or perpetual non-perception, the former when there is the conjunction of the Ātman, the sense (indriya), and the object (viṣaya), the three constituting the instruments of perception. If, on the conjunction of these three causes, the effect did not follow, there would take place perpetual non-perception. But neither is the fact. We have therefore to acknowledge the existence of an internal organ on whose attention (avadhāna) and non-attention (anavadhāna) perception and non-perception take place (S.B., ii. 3. 32).

4 See *Manīṣāpañcakam*. Śaṁkara here follows the Sāṁkhya view that buddhi, manas, etc., are in themselves unintelligent, though they derive the power of intelligence from their proximity to puruṣa. In the Advaita, the ātman, which is mere self-luminousness, takes the place of puruṣa.

5 *Upadeśasāhasri*, xviii. 33–54. See S.B. on Tait. Up., ii. 1; *Vārttika* on Tait. Up., ii. 1.

undergoes changes or modifications of form. The modification which reveals objects (viṣaya) is called the vṛtti.[1] The vṛttis or modes of the internal organ are of four different kinds: indetermination (saṁśaya); determination (niścaya); self-consciousness (garva); and remembrance (smaraṇa). The one internal organ (antaḥkarana) is called mind (manas) when it has the mode of indetermination; buddhi, or understanding, when it has the mode of determination; self-sense (ahaṁkāra) when it has the mode of self-consciousness; and attention (citta) when it has the mode of concentration and remembrance.[2] The cause of cognition is not the ultimate consciousness alone, but this consciousness as qualified by the internal organ. This internal organ differs with each individual, and so the cognition by one man does not mean cognition by all. As the internal organ is a limited entity, it cannot apply itself to all things in the world. It functions within varying limits, which are defined by the past conduct of the individual to whom it belongs.[3]

[1] It has other modifications in experiencing emotions, etc., which are not called vṛttis.

[2] The object of buddhi has but three moments in which it is born, exists and dies, while citta endures. The function of citta is important from the point of view of worship, where contemplation and concentration are essential. Śaṁkara draws a distinction between manas, which has doubt for its function, and buddhi, which has determination for its province (ii. 3. 32). Manas includes saṁkalpa or conation, vikalpa or negation of conation, sense-perception, memory, desires and emotions. Buddhi is the higher power responsible for conception, judgment, reasoning and self-consciousness. The Sāṁkhya, as we saw, admitted ahaṁkāra in addition to buddhi, though it merged citta in buddhi. The *Paribhāṣā* gives all the four. Other Vedānta works, as *Vedāntasāra* and *Vedāntasiddhāntasārasaṁgraha*, reconcile these divisions by identifying manas with citta and buddhi with ahaṁkāra. Later Advaita does not distinguish mental states so much into feeling, knowledge and will, as into conceptual and perceptual levels of mind's activity with regard to all its modes of consciousness, affective, cognitive and volitional.

[3] The jīva cannot illumine objects by its own essential nature of intelligence without the aid of the modes of antaḥkaraṇa, as Īśvara does, since the jīva has avidyā as its limiting condition, while the absolute consciousness is identical with all things as their material cause and so illumines them only in relation to itself. By the very constitution of the jīva, it is not in relation with the external objects, but only with the internal organ. See *Siddhāntaleśa*.

XV

Perception

Śaṁkara refers to three sources of knowledge: perception, inference and scriptural testimony.[1] Later writers add comparison, implication and negation.[2] Memory (smṛti) is not included under right knowledge, since novelty is said to be a feature of all knowledge.[3]

Since Śaṁkara does not discuss the psychology of perception and inference, we are not able to state his views. We have to be content with the account in the *Vedāntaparibhāṣā* which is evidently unsatisfactory. According to it, perception is the direct consciousness of objects obtained generally through the exercise of the senses. In sense-perception there is actual contact between the percipient and the object of perception.[4] When the eye is fixed on a jar, the internal organ is supposed to go out towards it, illuminate it by its own light, assume its shape and cognise it. This inner activity is assumed to account for the transformation of the physical vibrations into mental states. If we simply stare at the blue sky, we do not perceive anything. The internal organ functions like light, its vṛtti moves outwards in the form of an elongated ray of light. This vṛtti, like the ray of light, extends only up to a certain distance. This accounts for the non-perception of remote objects. The vṛtti identifies itself with the object, and its identification might spread over the whole surrounding scene. What we perceive depends on the nature of the mode. If the mode takes the form of the weight of the object, we perceive weight; if of colour, we perceive colour. In inferring fire from smoke, the vṛtti does not move up to the fire for the simple reason that fire is not in contact with the organ of vision which is in contact with

---

[1] Sureśvara, in his *Naiṣkarmyasiddhi*, draws a distinction between scriptural means of knowledge (āgamika pramāṇas) and worldly (laukika). See also *Saṁkṣepaśāriraka*, ii. 21.

[2] See *Vedāntaparibhāṣā*.

[3] Anadhigatābādhitārthaviṣayajñānatvam pramātvam (*ibid.*, i). This definition applies also to the persistent cognition of the same object (dhārāvāhikabuddhi), since it changes from moment to moment.

[4] Six different kinds of contact are admitted, *viz.* saṁyoga, or conjunction of the object jar and the sense-organ eye; saṁyuktatādātmya, or contact with the jarness of the jar; saṁyuktābhinnatādātmya, or contact with the colouredness of the colour of the jar; tādātmya, or contact with the sound, which is a property of ākāśa, not distinct from it; tādātmyāvadabhinna, or contact with the soundness of the sound; and viśeṣyaviśeṣaṇabhāva, or the relation of the qualified and the qualification. See *Vedāntaparibhāṣā* and *Śikhāmaṇi*.

smoke. In the case of the perception of the jar, the consciousness determined by the jar is found to be unified with that determined by the vṛtti of the internal organ falling on that jar, even as the space (ākāśa) enclosed within a vessel in the room is unified with that enclosed within the room itself. The two limiting conditions of ultimate consciousness, the modification and the object, do not produce a difference, since they are in the same spot. This unification makes the cognition of the jar perceptual in character,[1] and marks off perception from inference. The implication is that in perception the given element and its interpretation are welded together in a unity, while the given and the inferred elements are kept distinct in the act of inference. In inference the mind only thinks the object but does not go out to meet it. Perception is distinct from memory, since only past events are recollected. A further qualification is mentioned, that the object and the mental mode must belong to the present time.[2]

Different kinds of perception are admitted. Perceptions caused by the exercise of the senses (indriyajanyam) are distinguished from those which are not caused by sense-activity (indriyājanyam). Inner perceptions of desire, etc., are of the latter type. The defining feature of perception is not the mediation of a sense-organ, but the identity between the consciousness particularised by the object and that belonging to the pramāṇa.[3] When we perceive pleasure and such like inner states, the two limiting conditions of the pleasure and the mental mode of pleasure are necessarily situated in the same place. It is, however, admitted that dharma and adharma (virtue and vice), though they are attributes of the internal organ, are not objects of perception. No better explanation is given than that they are not fit objects of perception. Fitness is an essential requirement.[4] Experience is our only guide on the question of what objects are fit and what not. From verbal communication perceptual cognition may result when the object perceived is in contact with the mental mode, as in the assertion "thou art the tenth."[5] The knowledge conveyed through the pro-

---

[1] While the senses of smell, taste and touch produce a knowledge of their respective qualities without moving beyond their quarters, those of sight and hearing move towards their objects. The wave theory of sound is not supported.

[2] Vartamānatvam.

[3] Pramāṇacaitanyasya viṣayāvacchinnacaitanyābheda iti.

[4] Yogyatva. When the internal organ and its attributes are said to be objects of perception by the witnessing consciousness (sākṣin), even then the cognising subject (pramātṛ) is associated with the vṛtti or the mode, in the form of the internal organ and its attributes. Cognition by the witness-self does not mean cognisability without a mode, but only the absence of sense-mediation or inference, and such other means of knowledge. When the mode of the internal organ is cognised, the cogniser need not be associated with a second vṛtti or mode, and so on *ad infinitum*, since the first vṛtti becomes its own object. Vṛtteḥ svaviṣayatvābhyupagamena.

[5] See *Pañcadaśi*, vii. 23 ff.

position " I see the sweet sandal-wood " is perceptual as regards the sandal-wood and non-perceptual with regard to the sweet smell which is not an object for sight. Perception is therefore defined as " the identity between the ultimate consciousness particularised by an object which exists in the present time and is fit to be perceived by the senses and the ultimate consciousness particularised by the mode (vṛtti) which has taken the form of the object." [1]

The distinction between determinate (savikalpaka) and indeterminate (nirvikalpaka) perception is admitted. In determinate perception we have the distinction between the thing determined, the jar, and the determining attribute, jarness.[2] In indeterminate perception all determining attributes are left out of view. No distinction exists between S and P as in the propositions, " that art thou," " this is that Devadatta." In " that art thou," since the cogniser is the object, there is no difference between the consciousness of the cogniser and the consciousness of the mode in the form of the cogniser.[3] We grasp the meaning of the proposition without apprehending the relation between its different parts.

Another distinction is made on the basis of the cogniser, whether it is jīvasākṣi or Īśvarasākṣi. While the jīva is the ultimate consciousness particularised by the internal organ, the jīvasākṣi is that same consciousness conditioned or limited by the internal organ. The internal organ enters into the constitution of the jīva while it remains outside screening the jīvasākṣi. In the former case, it is an attribute (viśeṣaṇa), in the latter case a limitation (upādhi).[4] With regard to Īśvara and Īśvarasākṣi, māyā takes the place of the internal organ. While the ultimate consciousness particularised by māyā is the Īśvara, the same consciousness conditioned by māyā is Īśvarasākṣi. Īśvara as a personal centre has the same relation to the world as the jīva to the organism.

The psychology of erroneous perception, such as mistaking a piece of shell for silver, is also studied. When there is the contact of the eye affected by some disorder, such as cataract or the like, with the

---

[1] " Tattadindriyayogyavartamānaviṣayāvacchinnacaitanyābhinnatvam, tattadākāravṛttyavacchinnajñānasya tattad aṁśe pratyakṣatvam." See also *Vivaraṇaprameyasaṁgraha*, i. 1.

[2] Ghaṭaghaṭatvayor vaiśiṣṭyam.

[3] It is said that in indeterminate perception mere being exclusive of all predicates is apprehended. It is the *summum genus*, " mahāsāmānyam anye tu sattām " (*Nyāyamañjari*, p. 98). Jayanta criticises this view on the ground that if indeterminate perception gives us only " being," then particular features cannot be perceived in determinate perception. Besides, the existence of an object cannot be perceived apart from its different qualities. Na ca bhedaṁ vinā sattā grahītum api śakyate (*Nyāyamañjari*, p. 98).

[4] An attribute is an invariable distinguishing feature, as blueness in a lotus. A limitation is a separable, distinguishable feature, as the red flower standing in the vicinity of a crystal which seems to be red owing to its presence.

presented object, there arises a modification of the internal organ in the form of this object and its glitter. The illusory silver is presented to the cogniser through the force of avidyā [1] aided by the residual traces of the past cognition of the silver, which are revived by the perception of the quality of brightness common to the shell and the silver. Silver as a modification of avidyā resides in the consciousness particularised by the object (idam). The substratum of the illusory silver is not the ultimate consciousness in itself, but the same particularised by the object. In the case of illusory perception, we have two modes, one of thisness (idam) and the other of apparent silver. The former is correct presentation and the latter has memory for one of its causes. The "silver" is supposed to be out there for the time being as śuktyavidyāparināma. The same consciousness unifies the two modes, one true and the other false, and so error arises. Even an illusory object is not simply nothing at all, else there were no illusion. When we call an object illusory we admit that it is something, but call it illusory since it has not the status in the world that it claims to have.[2] Though even real silver is not absolutely real according to Śaṁkara's metaphysics, there is a difference between the empirically real silver and apparent silver. The perception of apparent silver is purely personal. This apparent silver is cognised by the witness self alone,[3] and, like pleasure and pain, closed to other selves.[4]

According to the Advaita, recognition (pratyabhijñā) is a perceptual process modified by the residua of past experiences. The Advaita lays stress not only on the identity of the object but on the identity of the self recognising.

Śaṁkara distinguishes the empirical world, which is logically established, from dreams and illusions.[5] The tests of logical reality are

---

[1] The author of *Nyāyāmṛta* asks whether the avidyā operative when we mistake a rope for a snake is also without beginning. Our particular errors are concrete expressions of the primary avidyā. Cp. the distinction between mūla or primary, and tūla or secondary forms of avidyā.

[2] On this view the production of silver in the place of the shell is as real as the production of anything in the world, for every effect subsists in the substratum of that avidyā out of which it is produced. The Naiyāyikas hold that there is no need to posit the production of an apparent silver. Silver perceived elsewhere is the object of the erroneous apprehension, and illusion is a case of erroneous judgment. The Advaitin replies that the object of apprehension, though illusory, is immediately present, and therefore a piece of silver perceived elsewhere at a different time cannot be the object of the present perception. To get over the difficulty, the Naiyāyika says that there is no direct sense-contact with the object, but only mediated non-sensuous contact (pratyāsatti). But if we admit it, then even inference would cease to be an independent pramāṇa. The objection that if the illusory silver is superimposed on the self, like pleasure and pain, then we must say "I am silver," even as we say "I am happy or miserable," is set aside on the ground that "I" and "silver" cannot be felt together.

[3] Kevalasākṣivedya.

[4] Sukhādivad ananyavedya.

[5] S.B., iii. 2. 1, 3.

the fulfilment of the conditions of place, time, cause, and non-contradiction.[1] The objects of dream do not conform to these tests.

The dream world, if it has any claim to reality, must hang together, even if it hangs on nothing; but the dream experiences are contradicted not only by waking ones but also in the same dream. Śaṁkara allows that dream states which have a prophetic significance are existent, though their objects are unreal. So the dream world is not real in the same sense as the waking one.[2] Illusorily surmised objects seen in a dream continue until an intuition of the reality underlying it arises. The objection is put forward that the dream objects must persist in the waking condition, since an intuition of ultimate consciousness which is the only reality does not arise in waking experience. The Advaitin draws a distinction between sublation (bādha) and cessation (nivṛtti). In the former the effect is destroyed together with its material cause; in the latter the cause persists, though the effect is nullified. Only an intuition of reality is capable of destroying avidyā, which is the material cause of the world of appearance. Cessation happens whenever a new mental mode arises or some original defect disappears. Dream objects disappear on waking, not because there is an intuition of reality, but because other modes arise and the defects of sleep disappear. The knowledge of the shell removes the illusion of silver. Dream consciousness is a form of memory, and therefore essentially different from perceptual states.[3]

The theory of perception adopted by the Advaita Vedānta is rather crude on the scientific side, though its metaphysical

[1] Deśakālanimittasampattir abādhaś ca.

[2] Pāramārthikas tu nāyaṁ saṁdhyāśrayaḥ sargo viyadādisargavad (S.B., iii. 2. 4).

[3] S.B., ii. 2. 29. It is held by later commentators that Śaṁkara here refers to the view of another school (S.B., i. 1. 9). See also iii. 2. 1–10. Śaṁkara believes that even dreams excite joy and fear in accordance with one's past good and evil (S.B., ii. 3. 18). Regarding the basis of dream experience, it is sometimes said that the pure universal consciousness (anavacchinnacaitanya) is the basis of dreams, but on this view dreams must occur even outside the consciousness associated with the ego, which cannot be admitted. The witnessing soul can illumine only those phenomena with which it coexists. If, on the other hand, the basis of dreams is the consciousness limited by the ego (ahaṁkārādyavacchinnacaitanya), then the dreamer should perceive dreams as one with him or residing in him. The proposed substratum and the dream perception should be in identical relation (tādātmyasaṁbandha), or the relation of location and thing located (ādhārādheyasaṁbandha). Then the dream perception should take the form "I am an elephant" or "I am possessed of an elephant," whereas the dreamer perceives that he sees an elephant on a mountain, and that it is different from him or belonging to someone else. Yet unless the latter view is accepted, the variety of dreams cannot be accounted for, since the universal consciousness is common to all egos, and, if it were the basis of dreams, then the dreams of all egos should be the same.

insight is valuable. The whole question of the internal organ and its modifications which take the form of the objects is dealt with in a dogmatic way. There is no reference to the place and significance of images which, together with sense-presentations, constitute the percept. Primitive consciousness is not a duality but one mass of sentiency, and all knowledge grows by dissociation within it. The merit of this theory of perception, as of the Sāṁkhya, is its open admission of the impossibility of reducing consciousness to a mere material change. Consciousness must be assumed as the primal fact, and not explained in terms of non-conscious factors. When the Advaita says that the immediately perceived object has no existence distinct from that of the knower, it only means that the substratum which maintains the object is not different from that of the subject.[1] Since all perceived objects must have an individuality, eternal consciousness and mere negation are not objects of perception.

XVI

Inference

Inference is produced by a knowledge of invariable concomitance (vyāptijñāna) which is its instrumental cause. " When there is the knowledge that the minor term possesses the attribute as in the proposition ' the hill is smoky,' and also an awakening of the mental impression due to previous presentative knowledge in the form ' smoke is invariably accompanied by fire,' there results the inference ' the hill is on fire.' " A vyāpti is defined as the community of reference existing between the middle term (hetu) and the major (sādhya), which resides in all the substrata of the middle term, *i.e.* the minor term. It is reached through the observation of the concomitance of the major and the middle and non-observation of non-concomitance.[2] Positive instances lead to the generalisation which is confirmed by the negative evidence. According to the Advaita, inference, strictly speaking, follows only from the knowledge of a concomitance expressed in a universal affirmative proposition as " where there is smoke, there is fire." Knowledge of a concomitance expressed in a universal negative, as in " where there is no fire, there is no smoke," leads to

---

[1] Pramātṛsattātiriktasattākatvābhāvaḥ.

[2] *Vedāntaparibhāṣā*, ii. Sā ca vyabhicārājñāne sati sahacāra darśanena gṛhyate.

arthāpatti, or argument by implication. Strictly speaking, there is no such thing as a mere negative, and all determinate things have an element of negativity in them. Exclusively affirmative relations (kevalānvayi), where the middle and the major are invariably found together in every minor term, and never absent as in the proposition "this is nameable because it is knowable," are not allowed as major premises, since in regard to them dissimilar instances (vipakṣa) are non-existent. Besides, since every attribute is the counter-entity of its own negation, and all negations reside in the ultimate reality of Brahman, which is destitute of attributes, there can be no such attribute as the merely affirmative with regard to Brahman. Since Brahman is the constant ground of all differences, the negation of all things is existent. Barbara represents the true syllogistic form. The Advaitin admits the distinction between inference for one's own sake (svārtha) and inference for the sake of others (parārtha). The latter has three members, which may be either proposition, reason and example, or example, application and conclusion.

XVII

Scriptural Testimony

Āgama or scriptural testimony, is accepted by the Advaitin as an independent source of knowledge. A sentence is valid if the relation implied by its meaning is not falsified by any other means of knowledge.[1]

Śaṁkara criticises the sphoṭa theory of words, and agrees with Upavarṣa that the letters only are the word. These letters do not pass away, "since they are recognised as the same letters each time they are produced anew."[2] Words denote the class (jāti or ākṛti) and not the individuals (vyakti), which are infinite in number. Since it is only the individuals that have origin and destruction and not the classes, the relation between the words and the classes denoted by them is said to be relatively eternal. The meaning of a word is twofold, direct (śakya) and implied (lakṣya). The universals are admitted by

[1] Yasya vākyasya tātparyaviṣayībhūtasaṁsargo mānāntareṇa na bādhyate tad vākyam pramāṇam.

[2] "The letters of which a word consists, assisted by a certain order and number, have through traditional use entered into a connection with a definite sense. At the time when they are employed they present themselves as such to the understanding, which, after having apprehended the several letters in succession, finally comprehends the entire aggregate, and they thus unerringly intimate to the understanding their definite sense" (S.B., i. 3. 28).

Śaṁkara, and are said to be unborn while the individuals are.[1] The universals live below and behind what is seen and felt. They are the originals in heaven of things on earth. They represent the norms according to which God has been moulding the universe.

The Veda is eternal wisdom, and contains the timeless rules of all created existence. The Vedas are of superhuman origin (apauruṣeya) and express the mind of God.[2] While the significance of the Vedas (vedārtha) is eternal, the texts themselves are not so, since they are re-uttered by Īśvara in each world-age. The Advaitin admits that the Vedas are collections of letters, words and sentences, and begin to exist at the creation and cease to exist at the universal dissolution of things, even as ākāśa and other elements rise and fall out. "In spite of the constantly repeated interruption of the course of the world, a necessary determination (niyatatvam) exists in the beginningless saṁsāra."[3] The Vedas are said to embody the ideal form of the universe, and since the latter is constant, the Vedas are said to be eternal. Since the successive worlds have their constant form (niyatākṛti), the authoritativeness of the Vedas is not impaired at any successive world-epoch.[4] The archetypal forms are not eternal in the sense in which the ultimate reality is eternal, since they are

[1] Later Advaitins do not admit the existence of universals, since they are neither perceived nor inferred. The perception of the same form in different individuals is not a proof of the existence of the universals (na tāvat gau gaur ity abhinnākāragrāhi pratyakṣaṁ jātau pramāṇam). To apprehend the cow in different instances is not indicative of the existence of the universal "cow," since the apprehension of the moon in different vessels in which it is reflected does not mean the reality of a universal moon. To say that we apprehend the same nature of "cow" in all individual cows is not true. Even if it be true, it only means that there are common qualities, and not universals in the realist sense. We do not perceive an individual cow as possessing the universal essence. We perceive the same configuration or arrangement of parts, which is not the same as universal essence. See *Tattvapradīpikā*, p. 303. The Buddhist arguments against the reality of universals are repeated in *Citsukhī*.

[2] S.B., i. 1. 3. Cp. Plato: "God's mind is the rational order of the universe" (713, E. Jowett's version).

[3] D.S.V., p. 70.

[4] "The great being which, according to scripture (Bṛh., ii. 4. 10), brought forth unwearying in sport, like the outbreathing of a man, the Ṛg-Veda and the rest, as a mine of all knowledge, which is the basis of the division into gods, animals, men, castes, stages of life and the like, this being must possess an unsurpassable omniscience and omnipotence" (S.B., i. 1. 3).

all the products of avidyā. The origination of the world from the word (śabda) does not mean that the word constitutes the material cause of the world as Brahman does. Śaṁkara says: "While there exist the everlasting words, whose essence is the power of denotation in connection with their eternal significations (*i.e.* the forms denoted), the creation of such individual things as are capable of having those words applied to them is called the origination from those words."[1] Īśvara, who is eternally free in intelligence and volition, remembers these and manifests them in every cycle. Creation is the actualisation of the same words, or the objective reason, which is timeless. The authoritativeness of the Vedas is defended on grounds other than those urged by the Nyāya and the Mīmāṁsā thinkers. The Vedas are eternal and self-luminous, since they reveal the character of God, whose ideas they embody. Their validity is self-evident and direct, even as the light of the sun is the direct means of our knowledge of form.[2]

Smṛti or tradition, has not absolute validity. It is to be accepted when its teaching conforms to śruti,[3] which gives us knowledge which is not open to the senses or thought.[4] Even śruti cannot supersede science on the question of matter and its properties.[5] It is, however, the sole authority on questions of virtue and vice (dharma-adharma). Regarding the nature of reality, inference and intuition may also be employed.[6]

XVIII

Refutation of Subjectivism

The relatively enduring framework of the external world is not expunged from Śaṁkara's picture of reality. He does not believe that the perception of a chair or a table is the perception of a mental state, for that would be to fly in the face of all evidence and dissolve the material universe into

[1] S.B., i. 3. 28.
[2] Vedasya hy nirapekṣaṁ svārthe prāmāṇyaṁ raver iva rūpaviṣaye.
[3] S.B., ii. 1. 1.
[4] S.B.G., iii. 66.
[5] S.B., i. 1. 4; i. 3. 7.
[6] S.B., i. 1. 2.

an unsubstantial dream. "We are compelled to admit objects outside our knowledge (upalabdhi). For no one knows the column or a wall as a mere form of knowledge, but everyone knows the column and the wall as objects of knowledge. And that everyone knows this is shown by the fact that those who deny outward objects bear witness to this when they say the form perceived internally seems as if it were outside." "Knowledge and object are different." The variety of knowledge is determined by the variety of objects. We perceive objects, we do not merely contemplate apparitions. The mental activity of perception is not the explanation of the object, but the nature of the object is the cause of the mental activity. Mere presence to an individual consciousness is not the *esse* of a thing. Even when we perceive pain, it is not a mere mental affection. It is as objective and existent as any object of consciousness. We perceive things as they are, and they are what they appear to be. Even metaphysically, as we shall see, Śaṁkara is obliged to posit an object, for consciousness is mere knowing or awareness. It has no content, no states. It is a pure, featureless transparency. The colour, the richness, the movement and the tumult are all on the object side. We distinguish between sensing, perceiving, remembering, imagining, reflecting, judging, reasoning, believing, because the objects of consciousness are different. Pure consciousness neither gives nor receives. Even in erroneous perception there is some object. That is why for Śaṁkara, as for Bradley, there are no absolute truths, as there are no mere errors.[1] Only, while true ideas answer to our needs and fit into our conception of reality as a systematic whole, erroneous ideas refuse to do so. The world, seen, felt, tasted and touched, is as real as the being of the man who sees, feels, tastes and touches.[2] The mind with its categories, on the one side,

[1] "Subject to a further explanation, all truth and all error on my view may be called relative, and the difference between them in the end is one of degree" (*Truth and Reality*, p. 252). For Śaṁkara's criticism of Buddhist subjectivism, see I.P., pp. 632–634.

[2] Commenting on the *Praśna Upaniṣad*, Śaṁkara says: "It cannot be said that there exists an object, but it cannot be known. It is like saying that a visible object is seen, but there is no eye. Where there is no knowledge, there is no knowable" (vi. 2).

and the world which it construes through them, on the other, hang together. The essential correlativity of subject and object, which is the central truth of all idealism, is accepted by Śaṁkara, who sets aside both mentalism and realism as inadequate to the facts of experience. Not only does Śaṁkara distinguish his position from that of subjective idealism, but he also emphasises the distinction between the states of waking and dream. While dream experiences conflict with those of waking life, the latter are not sublated in any other state (of empiricality).[1]

While Śaṁkara repudiates the view that the things of the world are phantoms of our creation, he upholds a metaphysical idealism in the sense that even the objects of knowledge are phases of spirit (viṣayacaitanya). The contents of knowledge are ultimately irreducible to matter or motion or energy or mind-stuff, for these themselves are concepts of thought. Objects have no existence for themselves, and if they are not the contents of my or your consciousness, they are the contents of the divine consciousness.[2] To the divine consciousness world-systems are present, full of contents and selves that are aware of their contents. The continuous divine percipient accounts for the permanent world-order. He is superior to the finite selves and objects in his infinity of content and complete presence to himself. He is the universal spirit who creates and is aware of the contents of the universe. As we deal with our private contents, so does God deal with the world-systems. This larger world and the divine consciousness for which it is are both contracted into subordinate centres which are only partially free. All contents are sustained by the divine consciousness, and were the latter known intensely enough it would be a veritable sea of consciousness. When the individual awakes to life, breaks down the contracting upādhis which limit his vision, he will realise that the whole world is filled with Ātman inside and out, even as the water of the sea is filled with salt. Strictly speaking, all

[1] Naivaṁ jāgaritopalabdhaṁ vastu stambhādikaṁ kasyāṁcid api avasthāyām bādhyate (S.B., ii. 2. 29).

[2] Even Berkeley, who is generally charged with subjectivism, postulates a God who perceives the system of the universe, thus offering a home for all those ideas which have no place in the minds of individual thinkers.

contents of the universe are spiritual in their character.[1] Ātman thus is the final fact transcending both the subject apprehending and the object apprehended, the ultimate reality outside of which there is nothing existent. When once we have the subject-object opposition, the Ātman appears as the supreme subject for whom all that exists is the object, and we all are subordinate subjects with portions of the object-world belonging to us. It is a hopeless method of attacking Śaṁkara's theory that Ātman is all to say that the physical facts and mental forms stare us in the face. He does not deny it. An ultimate metaphysical question cannot be answered by an appeal to empirical facts.

Śaṁkara's theory of truth is, strictly speaking, a radical realism. Logical truth is independent of psychological processes. Against the Mīmāṁsakas, Śaṁkara argues that, while the pursuit of the ideal of truth or the process of psychological valuation may depend on the free choice of the individual,[2] the object of valuation is independent of all these.[3] We may or may not engage in the activity of seeking the true. This choice rests with us ; but if we do take up the enterprise, the nature of truth will have only to be accepted by us.[4] Knowledge is never created or produced, but is always manifested or revealed. While the manifestation may be a temporal process, what is manifested is out of time. Knowledge has no history, while our mental life has one. Perception and inference serve as vehicles for the revelation of knowledge under the limitations of empirical life.

XIX

The Criterion of Truth

According to the Advaita, a mental mode (vṛtti) must have an object (viṣaya). The latter may be either the mode itself or something else. It may apprehend an external object when it is modified in the form of the latter or appre-

1 S.B. on Tait. Up., ii. 1.

2 Puruṣacittavyāpārādhīnā. S.B., i. 2. 4.

3 Na vastuyāthātmyajñānam puruṣabuddhyapekṣam.

4 S.B., i. 1. 4.

hend itself.[1] There is no such thing as a cognition of cognition, since all cognitions are self-luminous. There is no intervening mental mode between a cognitive process and the cognition of this latter. There is direct and immediate consciousness of a cognition. In the apprehension of a mental mode there is a direct intellectual intuition.[2] Cognitions are said to be self-luminous (svaprakāśa) in the sense that they are objects of their own apprehension.[3] Knowledge is known to be valid directly, *i.e.* by the same instrument by which it is known as knowledge. All knowledge is true knowledge.

We cannot think what is not true. If we can, then truth will be unattainable, for any standard of truth we can adopt will be unable to supply the intrinsic deficiency of thought itself, since the apprehension of the standard will itself be an act of thought and thus suffer from the natural uncertainty of thought. Therefore we must grant that there is no thought which is not a true thought, and error is only privation due to the passions and interests of men which cloud the intellect. Even the acceptance of śruti does not compromise the individual and intrinsic character of truth, for śruti refers only to a kind of experience (anubhava) which may be accepted as provisionally true.

While thus all knowledge bears immediate witness to its own validity, this self-evident character is hidden by our psychological prejudices, and to know that empirical knowledge is free from flaws, empirical tests like correspondence, practical efficiency and coherence are also employed. "The question of the reality of a thing does not depend on human notions. It depends on the thing itself. To say of a post that it is either a post or a man or something else is not to give its truth. That it is a post is alone the truth, since it answers to the nature of the thing." The test of truth

[1] Svaviṣayavṛtti.

[2] Kevalasākṣivedyatva.

[3] The Bhāṭṭa theory that a cognition which is itself unperceived can apprehend an object is declared to be defective. Nor can a cognition be the object of another cognition, since cognitions are not of the nature of unconscious objects. This is also the view of Prabhākara. Some Buddhists hold that a cognition cognises itself and manifests itself. The Advaita contends that a cognition is not apprehended or manifested by another. If a cognition can make itself an object of cognition, then it can as well be the object of another cognition.

regarding things is their correspondence with the nature of things.[1] Śaṁkara allows that truth and error both have reference to objects. But in the ultimate sense there is only one reality (vastu), Brahman, and no idea corresponds to it, and so all our judgments are imperfect.

The principle of non-contradiction (abādha) is, in Śaṁkara, the test of truth. Knowledge which is not contradicted is truth.[2] The straight stick appears bent in the water. Its crookedness in water is as real to the eye as its straightness to the touch. Touch corrects the judging of the eye and reveals a more constant relation. This definition emphasises the systematic character or harmonious nature of truth. But can we succeed in comprehending all things in a unity? Does anyone lay claim to wholeness of knowledge about life and the universe? We know little of the past and nothing of the future, and the present is so immense that it exceeds our range of experience. Whatever undergoes a radical transformation by the experience of something else is not itself or is not its own truth. Dream states are contradicted by waking experiences, which latter are contradicted by insight into reality (brahmānubhava). This is the highest, since there is no other knowledge that can contradict it.[3] Let us be clear that these tests are at best empirical. Highest knowledge, according to Śaṁkara, is the immediate witness of reality to itself, and this is rendered possible by the fact that the knower and the known are ultimately one real. Logical proof arises only in the empirical world, where this ultimate oneness of the observer and the observed is obscured by the clogging psychological hindrances which are summed up in the word avidyā. Logical proof enables us to break down the obstructing veils and reveal the self-evident character

[1] Evam bhūtavastuviṣayāṇām prāmāṇyaṁ vastutantram (S.B., i. 1. 2).

[2] Cp. *Bhāmatī*: Abādhitānadhigatāsaṁdigdhabodhajanakatvaṁ hi pramāṇatvam pramāṇānām (i. 1. 4). See also *Vedāntaparibhāṣā*. Abādhitārthaviṣayajñānatvam. "A cognition is not valid simply because it represents a thing as it actually is, nor is it invalid because it represents it otherwise; but it is valid only when its object is such as is not subsequently rejected (as unreal), and it is invalid when its object is thus rejected; and as a matter of fact this validity can belong only to the knowledge of Brahman obtained by means of the scriptures and not by any other cognitions" (*Advaitasiddhi*, i. 12).

[3] Bādhakajñānāntarābhāvāt (S.B., ii. 1. 14).

of truth. Logical rules are working tools, serving as negative checks by which we break down our prejudices.

XX

The Inadequacy of Empirical Knowledge

Empirical knowledge revels in the distinctions of knower, knowledge and the known,[1] while the real is free from all these distinctions.[2] If the real excludes relations, then relational thought is imperfect. It is avidyā, since it does not yield the true nature of things (vastusvarūpam). The real self, which is pure consciousness, is not an object of knowledge. The self can never be the subject and the object of the knowing process. In true self-consciousness the subject must be all out there in the object, so that there is nothing more left in the subject. In no state of mind is the subject before itself as an object.[3] Anything becomes an object only when we think of it as having a place in space and time; but these latter, as well as the objects that fall within them, are there only in relation to the self that holds them together. So the universal witness of all knowledge is unmanifest and imperceptible.[4] The impossibility of grasping the real as an object of knowledge is the cause of the sense of the beyond in all knowledge. While the process of knowledge is nothing more than a manifestation of the ultimate reality, it is impossible to catch the real in a process of self-consciousness. As the Ātman is the condition of time and space and all objectivity, it involves a hysteron-proteron to confine Ātman within the limits of its own offspring. "How shall I know you?" is as absurd a question as Crito's to Socrates, "How shall I bury you?"[5] Self-consciousness

[1] Avidyākalpitaṁ vedyaveditṛvedanābhedam (S.B., i. 1. 4).

[2] S.S.S.S., xii. 47. See also *Advaitamakaranda*, p. 19. See S.B. or Gauḍapāda's *Kārikā*, iv. 67.

[3] See S.B. on Tait. Up., ii. 1.

[4] Avyaktam anindriyagrāhyaṁ sarvadṛśyasākṣitvāt (iii. 2. 23).

[5] Socrates chaffs Crito for asking the question immediately after Crito had admitted the validity of arguments tending to show that Socrates was neither temporal nor spatial and so could not be buried.

is possible only with regard to the self qualified by the internal organ.[1]

Śaṁkara supports the inadequacy of all empirical knowledge by pointing out its affinity to the kind of knowledge possessed by animals.[2] "For just as the animals, when, for instance, a sound strikes their ears, in case the perception of sound is disagreeable to them, move away from it, and in case it is agreeable, move towards it—as, when they see a man with a stick raised before them, thinking 'He will strike me,' they try to escape, and when they see one with a handful of fresh grass, approach him—so men also whose knowledge is more developed (vyutpannacittāḥ), when they perceive strong men of terrible aspect, with drawn swords in their hands, turn away from them and turn towards the contrary. Thus with reference to the means and objects of knowledge, the process in men and animals is alike. Of course, in the case of animals, perception and similar processes go on without previous judgment (avivekapūrvakaḥ); but, as can be seen by the resemblance even in the case of developed men (vyutpattimatām), they are for the time being the same."[3]

[1] Of this self there can also be recognition. While the recognising agent is the self qualified by the internal organ, the object of recognition is the empirical self qualified by the earlier and the later temporal experiences. The difference in the conditioning adjuncts renders it possible for the self to be at the same time agent and object of action. Immediate consciousness vouches for acts of recognition in the form "I am now the same person I was." Cp. with this Kant's theory: "Through this 'I' or 'He' or 'It' (the thing) which thinks, nothing is set before our consciousness except a transcendental subject = X, which is known only through the thoughts that are its predicates (or more properly which it attaches as predicates to other things), and of which, if it is separated from other things, we cannot have the smallest conception. In attempting to grasp it, in fact, we turn round it in a continual circle, since we must always make use of it in order to make any judgment regarding it. Here, therefore, we are brought into an awkward pass, out of which there is no escape, because the consciousness in question is not an idea which marks out for us a particular object, but a form which attaches to all ideas in so far as they are referred to objects, *i.e.* in so far as anything is thought through them" (Caird: *Critical Philosophy of Kant*, vol. ii, p. 25). Descartes thought that since it was possible to abstract the subject in thought and free it from all determination, it existed as an object among objects. A logical possibility was transformed into an actually existent substance.

[2] Paśvādibhiś cāviśeṣāt (S.B., Introduction). See D.S.V., p. 57 n.

[3] Cp. Darwin: "The difference in mind between man and the higher animals, great as it is, is certainly one of degree and not of kind" (*Descent of Man*).

In all this Śaṁkara has in view the selective nature of mental activity. Our practical interests determine our whole thought procedure. The internal organ helps us to concentrate consciousness on a narrow range, like a bull's-eye lantern which restricts the illumination to a particular spot. We take note of those features of the "what" of things which have a significance for our purposes. Even our general laws are established with a view to our plans and interests.

Śaṁkara emphasises the point that discursive thinking, however extended, cannot lead us to an apprehension of reality. The philosophical imagination of Voltaire has conceived of beings with nearly a thousand senses, who could yet come no nearer to the apprehension of what reality is than those apparently less fortunate creatures who have only the five senses. It is difficult to know precisely how far our knowledge of the external world which science investigates is objective. The more we reflect on the matter the more impossible it seems to assert that the world known to us under the conditions of empirical knowledge is the real in itself. The man with five senses knows more than the blind man. May not the real exceed the empirical conception of it, even as the world known to sight exceeds that known to touch? May not a state like that of brahmānubhava, or what Tennyson has called a "last and largest sense," enlarge our own knowledge of reality, as the gift of sight would enlarge that of a race of blind men? This view does not involve any scepticism with regard to the world of science and common sense. So long as we do not reach a higher plane attainable only by higher intelligences, our conclusions are quite valid, except that they remain on the same plane as their premises.

Śaṁkara, as we shall see, enforces his conclusion, that all thought is vitiated by a central flaw, by a mass of subtle dialectic, which aims at showing the unintelligibility of every concept which the human mind employs. Though we talk freely about experience, it is impossible for us to understand the true relation between consciousness (dṛk) and the objects of consciousness (dṛśya). Consciousness must be admitted to have some kind of connection with the object which it illumines Were it not so, there could be any kind of knowledge at any time regardless of the nature of the objects. The kind of connection between consciousness and its objects is neither contact (saṁyoga) nor inherence (samavāya), *i.e.* neither external nor internal.

Objectivity does not consist in the fact that jñātatā (knownness) is produced in the object as the Kaumārila holds, for this effect is not admissible. To say that objects are those which are practically useful is not permissible, for there are many useless things like the sky which are objects of consciousness. Objectivity cannot mean that the thing is the object of the function of thought (jñānakaraṇa), since it applies only to perceived objects and not those remembered or inferred. Again, while in perception the conscious mode is moulded after the nature of the object, this is not the case with inferred objects. We do not understand the exact nature of the relation between consciousness and the objects of which we are conscious. Strictly speaking, all the life and movement belong to the object side, with which, we can only say, consciousness is compresent, in Alexander's phrase, and this compresence is assumed as intelligible, since subject and object are not opposed to each other but fall within the universal consciousness.

All thought struggles to know the real, to seek the truth, but, unfortunately, it can attempt to know the real only by relating the real to something other than itself. The real is neither true nor false. It simply *is*. But in our knowledge we refer this or that characteristic to it. All knowledge, whether perceptual or conceptual, attempts to reveal reality or the ultimate spirit.[1] While perception is an event in time, non-existent both before it happens and after, it is still the manifestation of a reality which is not in time, though it falls short of the real which it attempts to manifest. So far as inadequacy to the grasp of the real is concerned, all means of knowledge are on the same level. All judgments are false in the sense that no predicate which we can attribute to the subject is adequate to it. We have either to say Reality is Reality, or say that Reality is X, Y or Z. The former is useless for thought, but the latter is what thought actually does. It equates the real with something else, *i.e.* the non-real. To attribute to the real what is different from it is what Śaṁkara calls adhyāsa, or attributing to one thing what is different from it.[2] Adhyāsa is defined as the appearance of a thing where it is not.[3] When the light appears double, or when the rope appears as a snake, we have adhyāsa. All knowledge of finite things is in a sense the negation of pure being, since objects are imposed (adhyasta)

[1] Pratyakṣapramā cātra caitanyam eva (*Vedāntaparibhāṣā*, i).
[2] Adhyāso nāma atasmiṁs tadbuddhiḥ. S.B., Introduction.
[3] Smṛtirūpah paratraparāvabhāsaḥ.

on the one eternal consciousness. The most striking instance of this adhyāsa is the confusion [1] of subject with object where we attribute to the Ātman activity, agency and enjoyment. Strictly speaking, there is nothing different from the subject, for the subject of reality includes all that we can possibly predicate of it. What we attribute to the subject is something less than the real, an appearance thereof. "Object (viṣaya) and subject (viṣayin), having as their province the presentation of the 'thou' (yuṣmat) and the 'I' (asmat), are of a nature as opposed as darkness and light. The transfer of the object which has as its province the 'thou' (or the not-self) and its qualities to the pure spiritual subject which has for its province the idea of the 'I' (or the self), and, conversely, the transfer of the subject and its qualities to the object, is logically false. Yet in mankind this procedure, resting on false knowledge (mithyājñānanimitta), of pairing together the true and the untrue (the subject and the object) is natural (naisargika), so that they transfer the being and qualities of the one to the other." [2] Adhyāsa leading to avidyā is "the presupposition of all practical distinctions—made in ordinary life and the Vedas—between means of knowledge, objects of knowledge (and knowers) and all spiritual texts, whether they belong to karma or jñāna." [3] All the sources of knowledge are valid only until the ultimate truth is gained,[4] and thus have relative value for the finite understanding. All our knowledge is, strictly speaking, non-knowledge (avidyā), and

[1] Ātmani kriyākārakaphalādyāropalakṣaṇam. Kant's transcendental illusion, by which we apply to the thinking self conceptions which it makes and applies to phenomena given under conditions of space-time and regard the thinking self as a substance with things outside it, is a case of adhyāsa.

[2] S.B., Introduction. Dehādiṣv anātmasu aham asmīty ātmabuddhir avidyā (S.B., i. 3. 2).

[3] "Without the delusion that 'I' and 'mine' consist in the body, sense-organs and the like, no knower can exist; and consequently no use of the means of knowledge is possible. For without calling in the aid of the sense-organs there can be no perception; but the action of the sense-organs is not possible without a resting-place (the body), and no action at all is possible without transferring the being of self (ātman) to the body, and without all this taking place no knowledge is possible for the soul, which is independent of embodied existence. But without the action of knowing, no knowing is possible. Consequently, the means of knowledge, perception and the rest belong to the province of avidyā" S.B., Introduction). See D.S.V., p. 56 n.; S.S.S.S., xii. 85–86.

[4] S.B., i. 1. 4.

the ascertainment of the ultimate consciousness by the exclusion of all that is imposed on it is vidyā, or wisdom.[1]

What Śaṁkara means by subject and object, Ātman and non-Ātman, is the transcendental reality and the empirical existence. The "object" includes the individual agents, bodily organs and material world, etc. The subject is the ultimate consciousness[2] on which the whole object world depends. It is the characteristic of all objects of consciousness that they cannot reveal themselves apart from being manifested as objects of consciousness through a mental state (vṛtti). Even when we comprehend the nature of the ultimate Ātman from the scriptural texts, we do not comprehend its true nature. The true knowledge of Ātman is devoid of any form or mode.[3]

That particular application of adhyāsa which inclines us to break up the nature of the one absolute consciousness into a subject-object relation results from the very constitution of the human mind. This adhyāsa, which gives rise to the world of subjects and objects, is said to be beginningless (anādi), endless (ananta), natural (naisargika), possessed of the form of wrong knowledge (mithyāpratyayarūpaḥ), the cause of the agency, enjoyment and activity of the individual souls,[4] and patent to all.[5]

Śaṁkara's analysis of erroneous perception gives us a clue to his view of knowledge. When we mistake a rope for a snake and judge "This is a snake," we have two elements: the "this," or what is present to the senses, and the "snake," which we attribute to the "this." The latter describes the mode or form in which we happen to cognise the presented datum. The error of the judgment is due to the element of interpretation or what our thought superimposes on the ground. The "this" element, or what is actually present before us, persists even after the disillusionment. Śaṁkara argues that, even in normal perception, we have the two elements of a

[1] S.B., i. 1. 1.

[2] S.B., i. 1. 1.

[3] To the objection that Ātman is not an object, and so the attributes of other objects cannot be imposed on it, Śaṁkara replies that it is the object of the notion of self; nor is it necessary that the object should be in contact with our sense-organs, since the ignorant attribute dark-blue colour to ākāśa, which is not an object of sense-perception.

[4] Kartṛtvabhoktṛtvapravartakaḥ.

[5] Sarvalokapratyakṣaḥ.

datum and an interpretation, and asks, What is it that is common as the substratum of all objects of our consciousness? Is there anything which is held in common by everything we perceive, normal and abnormal, true and false? Śaṁkara answers that it is being. Everything we perceive is perceived as existent. Whatever be the nature of our interpretations, the substratum persists and is real. In the words of the Upaniṣads, it is like clay in things made of clay, or gold in ornaments made of gold. It endures, however much the forms impressed on it may change. The cause of avidyā is ignorance of the fundamental basis.[1]

Avidyā, or the natural tendency to adhyāsa, is involved in the very roots of our being, and is another name for our finitude. The real is its own explanation. It always remains in its own nature. It is the unreal that does not remain in its own nature that calls for some explanation. When avidyā is known, our bondage is broken. Avidyā is not inevitable, though quite natural. If it were inevitable, there is no point in asking us to get rid of it. We cannot strive against the inevitable. We cannot know what cannot be known. It is possible for us to check the course of avidyā, and it shows that we are really greater than our habits.

The finite consciousness, bound up with the pramāṇas, is limited to a certain kind and order of experience in which bodily states play an exceedingly important part. Our intellect is so made that it demands order and regularity in things. It resents accident and disorder. The world of objects is rational through and through, and answers to the demand of reason for law and order in all things. This is the faith of common sense and science. Śaṁkara does not sever thought from things. The principles of our mind, expressing themselves through the categories of space, time and cause, are at once the forms of combination which make up the nature of the thinking subject and also the forms that are to be met with in the realm of objective fact. The categories of intelligence apply to the things presented to it. This space-time-cause world, with all its contents, exists for the knowing subject. The two depend on each other, the empirical self and the world. This fact of the response of

[1] Adhiṣṭhānaviṣaya.

nature to the demand of reason proves the reality of a universal mind, which on the one hand ensouls nature and on the other is the cause of the reason in us, participating in and co-operating with the universal mind. The reality of an ordered world exists only for mind and in terms of mind. The world of an animal presupposes the mind of an animal; that of man, the mind of man. The whole world reality in its fulness and complexity postulates a universal and perfect mind, Īśvara, who sustains those parts of the universe which are unperceived by us. Our phenomenal knowledge suggests the noumenal as a necessity of thought, but not as something known through the empirical pramāṇas. Being men, we think in a human fashion. The universal reality is viewed as a central personality or subject with the whole world as object. This is the synthesis arrived at through logic, but there is no necessity about it. It is not an immediate object of thought. It is assumed as the highest synthesis of our experience, and so long as other experience is of the same texture, it will hold.[1] The subject-object relation applies to the animal world, the human and the divine alike. But these two constituents of experience are relative to each other and subject to the same laws of change and development. That fully constructed view of reality in which every element, subject and object, mind and body, present, past and future, shall have fallen into its proper place, is not an object of human experience, though the ideal goal of all thinking. But all knowledge, whether of God or man, involves the subject-object relation, and cannot therefore be regarded as the highest. All determinate knowledge is a self-abnegation, involving, as it does, a modalisation of the ultimate consciousness into the subject, mode and object. Except in ecstatic intuition, there is the given element distinct from the cognising subject reaching to it through a mode. Thinking and logic belong to the level of finite life, while ultimate reality transcends thought. The real is present to itself and has therefore no need to think itself.

[1] ii. 1. 11.

XXI

Anubhava or Integral Experience

An object is established to be real, an idea proved to be true, when the denial of it brings consequences which are recognised as self-contradictory and so untenable. This seems to be the final test for fallible intelligence. Logically, there is no higher proof of the existence of the Ātman possible. To ask whether the Ātman is real or not is to raise a meaningless question, for all life, all thought, all experience is the abiding though unformulated affirmative answer to this question. But any attempt to grasp the real by the tools of mind lands us in a hopeless maze of contradictions. If mind is to avert this tragic destiny, it must try to suppress itself, and then the veil will be lifted. The dissatisfaction which we feel with our logical categories is a sign that we are greater than we know, that we can pass beyond our mental confines to a region of truth, though it is a mere beyond to our intellect, which seeks to transcend what it can and will never transcend. The limits which seem to be inevitable and impassable for intellect point to a limitless ground in us higher than logical mind. If thought becomes one with reality, and the individual subject shakes off its individuality and is lifted up into its universal essence, the goal of thought is reached, but it is no more thought. Thought expires in experience. Knowledge is lifted up into wisdom when it knows itself as identical with the known, where only the Ātman as eternal knowledge (nityajñāna) shines.[1] This absolute knowledge is at the same time knowledge of the absolute. The word "jñāna" is rather unfortunate on account of its empirical associations.[2] Integral experience or anubhava, brings out the sense better.

Śaṁkara admits the reality of an intuitional consciousness, anubhava,[3] where the distinctions of subject and object are

[1] "To understand, much more to know, spiritual reality is to assimilate it with ourselves who know it" (Gentile: *Theory of Mind as Pure Act*, p. 10).

[2] Madhva declares that it is not knowledge, since there is no object to be known. "Jñeyābhāve jñānasyāpy abhāvād." Bṛh. Up., S.B.H., p. 460.

[3] See S.B., i. 1. 2; ii. 1 4; iii. 3. 32; iii. 4. 15.

superseded and the truth of the supreme self realised.[1] It is the ineffable experience beyond thought and speech, which transforms our whole life and yields the certainty of a divine presence. It is the state of consciousness which is induced when the individual strips himself of all finite conditions, including his intelligence. It is accompanied by what Mr. Russell calls " the true spirit of delight, the exaltation, the sense of being more than man."[2] Foretastes of such bliss we have in moments of selfless contemplation and æsthetic enjoyment.[3] It is sākṣātkāra or direct perception, which is manifested when the avidyā is destroyed and the individual knows that the Ātman and the jīva are one. It is also called saṁyagjñāna (perfect knowledge)[4] or samyag-darśana (perfect intuition).[5] While saṁyagjñāna insists on the reflective preparation necessary for it, saṁyagdarśana points to the immediacy of intuition, where the ultimate reality is the object of direct apprehension (īkṣaṇa) as well as meditation (dhyāna).[6] Śaṁkara explains that it is possible for us to meditate on unreal objects but not to experience them ; so that his anubhava is different from idealised fancy. The Yogin is said to see God in the state of saṁrādhana, which Śaṁkara explains as sinking oneself in pious meditation.[7] Śaṁkara admits ārṣajñāna, by which Indra and Vāmadeva realised identity with Brahman.[8] Psychologically it is of the nature of perception,[9] since it is direct awareness

1 See *Ātmabodha*, p. 41.

2 *Philosophical Essays*, p. 73.

3 Plotinus says : " It is that union of which the union of earthly lovers who wish to bind their being with each other is a copy " (*Enneads*, vi. 7. 34). Cp. Bṛh. Up., vi. 3. 21.

4 S.B., i. 2. 8.

5 S.B., i. 3. 13.

6 S.B., i. 3. 13.

7 S.B., iii. 2. 24. See also Kaṭha Up., iv. 1. To the objection whether such an act of meditation does not involve a distinction between the subject and object of meditation, Śaṁkara answers : " As light, ether, the sun, and so on appear differentiated, as it were, through their objects, such as fingers, vessels, water, and so on, which constitute the limiting adjuncts, while in reality they preserve their essential non-differentiatedness, so the distinction of different selves is due to limiting adjuncts only, while the unity of all selves is natural and original " (S.B., iii. 2. 25).

8 It is explained in *Ratnaprabhā* as " the spontaneous intuition of truth rendered possible through the hearing, etc., acquired in former existences." Janmāntarakṛtaśravaṇādinā asmiñ janmani, svatassiddham, darśanam ārṣam (i. 1. 30). See S.B. on Tait. Up., i. 10.

9 S.B., i. 4. 14.

of reality; only the latter is not of the nature of an existent in space and time. Anubhava is not consciousness of this or that thing, but it is to know and see in oneself the being of all beings, the Ground and the Abyss. As direct experience or anubhava, in the Nyāya sense of the word, is the sole means of knowledge of the external world, anubhava of non-dual existence is the innermost experience on which whatever we know and believe of the supersensual world depends. The object of intuition is not a private fancy or a subjective abstraction in the mind of the knower. It is a *real object*,[1] which is unaffected by our apprehension or non-apprehension of it, though its reality is of a higher kind than that of particular objects of space and time which are involved in a perpetual flux and cannot therefore be regarded strictly as real.[2] The subtleties of the schools are all silenced before the protest of the soul that it has seen reality. "How can one contest the fact of another possessing the knowledge of Brahman, though still in the body, vouched as it is by his heart's conviction?"[3] All faith and devotion, all study and meditation, are intended to train us for this experience.[4] Intuition of self, however, comes only to a mind prepared for it. It does not come out of the blue. It is the noblest blossoming of man's reason. It is not a mere fancy which refuses to make an appeal to man's intelligence. What is true is true for every intelligence that can apprehend it. There is no such thing as a private truth, any more than a private sun or a private science. Truth has an intrinsic and universal character, which depends on no individual, not even on God. The process of apprehending reality may be private or singular, but not the object apprehended. The real cannot be real now and then, here and there, but always and everywhere.

Kant spoke of an intellectual intuition to indicate the

[1] Anubhavāvasānatvād bhūtavastuviṣayatvāc ca (S.B., i. 1. 2).

[2] Cp. with this, Plato's realism, where reason discloses the world of reality lifted altogether out of space and time, "a reality colourless, formless and intangible . . . visible to the mind alone who is lord of the soul" (Phædrus). While Plato recognises a plurality of essences, Śaṁkara has only one essence.

[3] Kathaṁ hy ekasya, svahṛdayapratyayam brahmavedanam, deha-dhāraṇaṁ cāpareṇa pratikṣeptuṁ śakyate? (iv. 1. 15, S.B.).

[4] S.B., ii. 1. 6. Anubhavāvasānam brahmavijñānam (D.S.V., p. 89 n.). Anubhavārūḍham eva ca vidyāphalam (iii. 4. 15). The fruit of knowledge is manifest to intuition (S.B.G., ii. 21; Bṛh. Up., iv. 4. 19).

mode of consciousness by which a knowledge of things in themselves might be obtained in a non-logical way. According to Fichte, intellectual intuition enables us to get at self-consciousness, which is the basis of all knowledge in his philosophy. Schelling employs the same term to denote the consciousness of the absolute, the identity between subject and object. But, according to Śaṁkara, the object of intuition is not the many things in themselves of Kant, or the self of Fichte, or the neutruum of Schelling, but the Ātman or the universal consciousness. As for Plotinus, so for Śaṁkara, the absolute is not presented as an object, but in an immediate contact which is above knowledge.[1] Since the intuitional knowledge is not contradicted by anything else, it is the highest truth.[2]

Anubhava is not the immediacy of an uninterpreted sensation, where the existence and the content of what is apprehended are not separated. It has kinship with artistic insight rather than animal perception. It is immediacy which is higher and not lower than mediate reflective knowledge. The real is, no doubt, problematic from the point of view of demonstrable knowledge, and our ideas of God, freedom and immortality are only names and symbols of the deepest of human values, which we may strive after but never attain until we transcend the never-ending struggle of mind with its antinomies. Anubhava and adhyāsa, intuition and intellect, point to a fissure between the infinite reality and the finite mind.

Śaṁkara admits that, while this anubhava is open to all, few attain to it.[3] But the important point is, that it is open to all. Reality is there, objective, ever-present, waiting to be seen by the individual minds that can seize it. Apparently

[1] *Enneads*, vi. 9. 4.

[2] Bādhakajñānāntarābhāvāc ca (S.B., ii. 1. 14). In the *Śataślokī* it is said: "Scripture speaks of the knowledge of Brahman as twofold, *viz.* experience relating to oneself (svānubhūti) and conclusive certainty (upapatti). The former arises in relation to the body (dehānubandhāt), while the latter arises with reference to the universe (sarvātmakatvāt). First arises the experience that 'I am Brahman' (brahmāham asmīty anubhava), and then that 'All this is Brahman' (Sarvam khalvidam brahma)."

[3] Cp. Dean Inge: "Complete knowledge is the complete unity of the knower and known, for we can in the last resort only know ourselves. The process of divine knowledge therefore consists in calling into activity a faculty which, as Plotinus says, all possess but few use, the gift which the Cambridge Platonists called the seed of the deiform nature in the human soul" (*Outspoken Essays*, Second Series, p. 14).

Śaṁkara has no sympathy with the view that the real reveals itself to a few elect souls in moments of illumination through doubtful dreams and mystic voices. A God who reveals himself to some and not to others is a fiction of pious imagination. Insight or spiritual experience is, as a matter of fact, confined to some individuals, though it is a universal possession, while reason is common to the greater mass of thinking humanity. While some powers are well developed in all men, others are not equally developed. In the present state of evolution, anubhava may be subjective and its evidence worthy of credence only when it is in conformity with the dictates of reason.

XXII

Intuition (Anubhava), Intellect (Tarka), and Scripture (Śruti)

While intuitional experience carries with it the highest degree of certitude, it has only a low degree of conceptual clearness. This is why interpretation is necessary, and these interpretations are fallible and so require endless revision. Śruti attempts to say things which are not fully to be said. Men of vidyā, or vision, say what language and logic were not invented to say. Those who have had no direct insight into reality are obliged to take on trust the Vedic views which record the highest experiences of some of the greatest minds who have wrestled with this problem of apprehending reality. For the ordinary man the central truth of the ultimate consciousness is essentially revealed, and not ascertained by any human evidence like that of perception or inference. These latter give us strong suggestions of the beyond, but not positive proofs. Śaṁkara admits that truth has to be investigated,[1] and himself adopts the principle of non-contradiction in criticising rival systems. His objection to the other philosophical conceptions, notably those of Buddhism, is not so much that they are open to criticism, but that they have not realised the inadequacy of the dialectical method. He holds that the Vedic testimony

[1] Satyaṁ vijijñāsitavyam (S.B., i. 3. 8).

is superior to the evidence of the senses or the conclusions of reason, though, of course, it is useless in the regions open to perception and inference. A hundred texts cannot make fire cold.[1] It is the aim of the Scriptures to impart such knowledge as cannot be reached through the ordinary means.[2]

It is the purpose of the Vedas to teach the oneness of the Ātman.[3] Śaṁkara says that this investigation of the Vedānta is not the cause of our freedom from avidyā, for all investigation as well as all knowledge, involving as it does the duality of subject and object, is a hindrance to the recognition of Brahman. It helps us to unmask folly rather than achieve wisdom.[4] To remove avidyā is to realise the truth even as the realisation of the rope means the removal of the misconception of the snake.[5] No additional instrument or fresh act of knowledge is necessary to realise the truth.[6] "Knowledge does not wait even for the moment immediately next the annihilation of duality, for if it did there would be an infinite regress, and duality will never be annihilated. The two are simultaneous."[7] We reach the real when the wrong view is cleared up.[8] If the question is asked as to how we are helped out of avidyā to vidyā—an illegitimate question, since, when error is destroyed, truth, which is self-sufficient, is revealed—no better answer than assigning it to the grace of God is possible.[9] The pure soul is like a blind man whose lost sight is restored as by the grace of God.

1 Jñānaṁ tu pramāṇajanyaṁ yathābhūtaviṣayaṁ ca. Na tanniyogaśatenāpi kārayituṁ śakyate, na ca pratiṣedhaśatenāpi vārayituṁ śakyate (S.B., iii. 2. 21 ; S.B.G., xviii. 66).

2 Pratyakṣādipramāṇānupalabdhe hy viṣaye śrutiḥ prāmāṇyaṁ na pratyakṣādiviṣaye (S.B.G., xviii. 66). Ajñātajñāpanaṁ hy śāstram.

3 Ātmaikatvavidyāpratipattaye sarve vedāntā ārabhyante (S.B., Introduction).

4 Avidyākalpitabhedanivṛtti (S.B., i. 1. 4). See S.B.G., ii. 18. Cp. Plotinus : "God is neither to be expressed in speech nor in written discourse ; but we speak and write in order to direct the soul to him and to stimulate it to rise from thought to vision, like one who points the upward road which they who would behold him have to traverse. Our teaching reaches so far only as to indicate the way in which they should go, but the vision itself must be their own achievement" (*Enneads*, vi. 9. 4 ; Caird : *Greek Theology*, vol. ii, p. 237).

5 S.B. on Māṇḍ. Up., ii. 7.

6 *Ibid.*

7 *Ibid.*

8 Ātmaiva ajñānahāniḥ.

9 S.B., ii. 3. 41. See Kaṭha Up., ii. 22. Deussen has this in view when he charges Śaṁkara with theological bias. See D.S.V., pp. 86–87.

To accept śruti is to accept the witness of the saints and sages. To ignore śruti is to ignore the most vital part of the experience of the human race. In matters of physical science we accept what the greatest investigators in those departments declare for truth; in music we attend to what the accredited great composers have written, and endeavour thereby to improve our natural appreciation of musical beauty. In matters of religious truth we should listen with respect to what the great religious geniuses, who strove by faith and devotion to attain their spiritual eminence, have given out. There is no use of pitting against the last the opinion of the first. "Mere reflection must not be quoted against a matter which is to be known by sacred tradition; for reflections which, without basis in traditions, rest only on the speculation (utprekṣā) of men are untenable, since such speculation is unbridled."[1] If we depend on thought, we have to doubt the world, doubt our being, doubt the future, and end our life in doubt. But since we must either react on our environment or be destroyed by it, the force of the life within drives us irresistibly to faith. There are spiritual impulses which refuse to be set aside at the bidding of logic. No one can live on negation. Śaṁkara's philosophical undertaking is intended to disillusion us with systematic philosophy and make out that logic by itself leads to scepticism. We assume that the world is a rational one and a righteous one. We believe in the wholeness of the world without any acquaintance with its significant details. We call it an assumption, since we cannot hope to discover the eternal order underlying the apparent disorder. By accepting the reality of a divine mind, Īśvara, our lives gain in richness and security.[2] Besides, truth[3] must be identical,[4] uncontradictable,[5] and universally accepted; but the results of

[1] S.B., ii. 1. 11. That is why opinions of even such recognised thinkers like Kapila and Kaṇāda often contradict each other. Cp. Kumārila: "A thing inferred with ever so great a care by logicians, however expert, is quite otherwise explained by other and greater experts."

[2] "Neither by direct knowledge nor by inference can men have any idea as to their relation with another birth or as to the existence of the self after death. Hence the need for the revelation of the scriptures" (S.B. on Bṛh. Up., Introduction).

[3] Samyagjñāna.

[4] Ekarūpam.

[5] Puruṣāṇāṁ vipratipattir anupapannā.

reflection are not so accepted. But "the Veda as a source of knowledge is eternal, its subject stands fast, the full knowledge of it formed thereform cannot be turned aside by all the speculations of the past, present and future." Mere reasoning is a formal process. The conclusions at which it arrives depend on the premises with which it starts, and Śaṁkara insists that the religious experience as recorded in the scriptures ought to be the basis for reason in the matter of the philosophy of religion. By tarka, Śaṁkara means reason that has not been restrained by the lessons of history. Such individualistic reasoning cannot lead to the establishment of truth on account of the endless diversity in the power of apprehension.[1] The śruti embodies the truths of spirit which have satisfied the spiritual instincts of a large portion of humanity. It contains the traditional convictions of the race which embody not so much thought as the life of spirit, and for those of us who do not share the life these recorded experiences are of great value.[2]

Śaṁkara recognises the need of reason for testing scriptural views. Wherever he has an opportunity, he tries to confirm scriptural statements by rational argument.[3] Reasoning (tarka), which works as an auxiliary of intuition (anubhava), is commended by him.[4] Reason with him is a critical weapon against untested assumptions and a creative principle which selects and emphasises the facts of truth.[5] "Even those destitute of the power of judgment do not attach themselves to particular traditions without any reason."[6]

Anubhava is the vital spiritual experience which can be

[1] Kasyacit kvacit pakṣapāte sati puruṣamativairūpyeṇa tattvāvyavasthānaprasaṅgāt (S.B., ii. 1. 1).

[2] S.B., ii. 1. 11; ii. 3. 1; i. 1. 2.

[3] See S.B. on Gauḍapāda's *Kārikā*, iii. 27. In commenting on iii. 1 of Gauḍapāda's *Kārikā*, Śaṁkara says: "It is asked whether the Advaita is to be taken as proved only on the evidence of śruti and whether reason cannot possibly demonstrate it, and this chapter shows how the Advaita can be demonstrated by reason." For a fuller discussion of the relation of reason to revelation in Śaṁkara's philosophy, see two articles by Mr. V. Subrahmanya Aiyar in *Sanskrit Research* for July 1915, and *Indian Philosophical Review* for April 1918, and Mr. S. Suryanarayanan's paper on "Critical Idealism and the Advaita Vedānta" in the *Mysore University Magazine* for November 1919.

[4] S.B., ii. 1. 6; ii. 1. 11.

[5] S.B., ii. 1. 4, 37; ii. 2. 41; ii. 4. 12.

[6] S.B., ii. 1. 1.

communicated only through the language of imagination, and śruti is the written code embodying it Without the background of the experience the statement of the śruti is mere sound without sense.[1] Texts which contain censure or praise (arthavāda) and which have not any independent import help to strengthen injunctions (vidhivākyas), and they are not superior to perception. The texts which describe the nature of reality are authoritative.[2] Śruti, of course, has to conform to experience and cannot override it. Vācaspati says: "A thousand scriptures cannot make a jar into a cloth."[3] So also in religious discussions scriptural statements have to conform to the intuited facts. The highest evidence is perception, whether it is spiritual or sensuous, and is capable of being experienced by us on compliance with certain conditions. The authoritativeness of the śruti is derived from the fact that it is but the expression of experience, and since experience is of a self-certifying character, the Vedas are said to be their own proof, requiring no support from elsewhere.[4] The Vedas, therefore, contain truths which man could by the exercise of his own faculties discover, though it is to our advantage that they are revealed, seeing that not all men have the courage, time and equipment to face such an enterprise.

XXIII

Higher Wisdom and Lower Knowledge

Parā vidyā is absolute truth. Its content is the oneness of Ātman and the sole reality thereof. If by means of the logical resources we try to describe the ultimate reality, we

[1] Mere śruti is not superior to the evidence of perception, but śruti which has a definite import. Tātparyavatī śrutiḥ pratyakṣād balavati, na śrutimātram (*Bhāmatī*). S.L.S.

[2] The author of *Vivaraṇa* disputes this view of *Bhāmatī* on the ground that the existence of independent import is not a safe criterion, and śruti as such is superior to the testimony of other means of knowledge on account of its infallibility (nirdoṣatvāt) and its nature as the final court of appeal for the ascertainment of truth (paratvāc ca).

[3] Na hy āgamāḥ sahasram api ghaṭam paṭayitum īṣate (*Bhāmatī*, Introduction).

[4] Prāmāṇyam nirapekṣam.

have perforce to employ myth and symbol. The Vedas give us the highest logical approximation to the truth. Empirical truth, or aparā vidyā, is not absolutely untrue. It is truth seen from the standpoint of the empirical consciousness.[1] The world extended in space and time and causality is not final, but is relative to the degree of our enlightenment. It is due to our partial vision, and to the extent to which our vision is partial its object is abstract. The higher monistic and the lower pluralistic views cannot be true in the same sense. Śaṁkara cuts the Gordian knot by attributing the latter to a fall from the higher.

Lower knowledge is not illusory or deceptive, but is only relative. If not, Śaṁkara's elaborate and even passionate discussion of the lower knowledge will border on the grotesque. He admits that the lower knowledge leads us eventually to the higher wisdom. "This scriptural account of creation admitted by avidyā . . . has, for its highest aim, the teachings that Brahman is the true self. This must not be forgotten."[2] Transcendental absolutism becomes when it passes through the mill of man's mind an empirical theism, which is true until true knowledge arises, even as dream states are true until awakening occurs.[3]

Avidyā, or finite thought, bears its witness to the real which transcends thought. It leads us to the conclusion that its truth is relative and that it cannot directly grasp the nature of reality.[4] While the ordinary mystic strives to

[1] Cp. Deussen: "Strictly viewed, this aparā vidyā is nothing but metaphysics in an empiric dress, *i.e.* vidyā as it appears considered from the standpoint of avidyā, the realism innate in us" (D.S.V., p. 100).

[2] D.S.V., p. 106.

[3] S.B., ii. 1. 14.

[4] Cp. Dr. McTaggart: "A mysticism which ignores the claims of the understanding would no doubt be doomed. None ever went about to break logic, but in the end logic broke him. But there is a mysticism which starts from the standpoint of the understanding and only departs from it in so far as that standpoint shows itself not to be ultimate, but to postulate something beyond itself. To transcend the lower is not to ignore it" (*Hegelian Cosmology*, p. 292). Spinoza draws a distinction between Ratio and Scientia Intuitiva. He believes in three kinds of knowledge: (1) That due to imagination which gives mere opinion. To it belong all inadequate and confused ideas. It is also the source of erroneous knowledge. (2) Reason which gives us common notions and the knowledge of science, which tries to "understand the agreements, differences and contrasts of things" (*Ethics*, vol. ii, p. 29, Scholium). While Imagination accounts for the content of the average uninstructed man's thinking, Reason is responsible for the

rise above differences and lose himself and the object of his quest in a cloud of unknowing, Śaṁkara presents to us certain philosophical difficulties, and tells us that these indicate the possibility of a superior insight to which all that is divine and dark to intellect is radiant. The Vedas, which are regarded as authoritative, contain, according to Śaṁkara, both higher wisdom and lower knowledge. They give descriptions of the one non-dual Brahman and the unreality of the pluralistic universe.

We have, in Śaṁkara's philosophy, three kinds of existence: (1) pāramārthika, or ultimate reality; (2) vyāvahārika, or empirical existence; and (3) prātibhāsika, or illusory existence. Brahman is of the first kind, the world of space-time-cause of the second, while imagined objects, like silver in the shell, are of the third kind.[1] Illusory existence has no universality about it. It arises on occasions. It has not any practical efficiency. The erroneous notion of apparent existence ceases when its substratum of experience is perceived; the mistake in respect to empirical existence ceases when its substratum of Brahman is realised. The empirical world possesses a higher degree of truth than the world of fiction and dreams. It is the world of souls, their environment and their Lord, but strictly speaking it is rooted in the one Brahman.[2] Let it be clearly understood that the empirical self and the empirical world are both of the same rank of reality. The external world is not an illusion due to the projection of the ideas of the empirical ego. There is an external world in space independent of the empirical self and its ideas. These two empirical spheres of selves and things stand in a causal relation to each other. What we as empirical egos find in the world, we ourselves as transcendental subjects have placed there.

---

systematic knowledge of the man of science. (3) Intuition involves the exercise of philosophic genius, artistic insight and creation. Its object is individual. However, Śaṁkara reminds us most among European thinkers of Plato. Both were great spiritual realists who synthesised the main tendencies of the past in their own thoughts. Both distinguished knowledge into two kinds, higher and lower, the former referring to the ultimate truth or the ideal good, the latter to the world of shadows. Admitting that reality lies far behind the surface appearances, both tell us that it can be grasped by a complete withdrawal of the soul into its own self. Both believe in intuition which gives us the transcendent vision of reality.

[1] *Vedāntaparibhāṣā.* In some later Advaita treatises this distinction is applied to the jīva also. In the *Dṛgdṛśyaviveka,* it is said that the impersonal consciousness limited by the adjuncts is the real self; when it assigns to itself agency and activity and is limited by the senses and the antaḥkaraṇa, it is the empirical self; the apparent jīva believes that its dream body and consciousness all belong to it (S.L.S., i).

[2] Cp. Ānandagiri on S.B. on Māṇḍūkya Up. Brahmaṇy eva jīvo jagad īśvaraś ceti sarvaṁ kālpanikaṁ saṁbhavati.

XXIV

ŚAṀKARA'S THEORY AND SOME WESTERN VIEWS COMPARED

Śaṁkara's theory of knowledge is often compared with that of Kant.[1] While there are striking similarities, there are far-reaching differences. Like Kant, Śaṁkara formulates the problem of the possibility of knowledge—even knowledge of self—and puts it in the forefront of philosophical inquiry. Both of them look upon the world of experience as phenomenal, and trace the root of this limitation to the structure of the human mind. By an examination of man's cognitive mechanism, Kant arrives at the conclusion that it is impossible for man to have a knowledge of transcendent objects, for whatever becomes an object of knowledge is enveloped in the forms of space, time and the categories of the understanding, the chief of which is causality. The being of reality is not apprehended by us; what we grasp is an appearance thereof. According to Śaṁkara, it is some monstrous deformity of our vision that makes us see what is really one as if it were many. Paradoxically enough, our logical activity forces on us a phenomenal world which for ever insinuates itself between us and the reality. Both Śaṁkara and Kant attempt to solve the question of the conditions of knowledge by the critical rather than the empirical method. Śaṁkara avoided the error of Kant, who sought not so much the logical implications of experience as the *a priori* conditions of experience, and thus asserted the reality of an extra-empirical world of things in themselves. Śaṁkara's object was to discover the immanent principle within experience, and not a world beyond it. Both, however, agree that if the logical intellect sets itself up as constitutive of reality, it forfeits its title to truth and becomes, as Kant says, a faculty of illusion. Śaṁkara and Kant repudiate mentalism. As against Descartes, who distinguishes between our knowledge of our own existence, which is immediate and indubitable, and that of external objects, which is

[1] The mystic idealism of Plotinus is said to owe much of its content to Indian thought. We know that Plotinus accompanied the Emperor Gordian in his campaign in the East, and he may have then come into contact with the representatives of Indian idealism.

only inferential and problematic, Kant contends that our knowledge of the external world is quite as direct and certain as our knowledge of self. He repudiates Berkeleyan subjectivism in the famous section on the "Refutation of Idealism" in the second edition of the *Critique of Pure Reason.* "The simple but empirically determined consciousness of my own existence proves the existence of external objects in space." But if by real we understand that which is thought of as existing independent of consciousness and out of all relation to any knowledge, then, according to Śaṁkara, neither the empirical self as we are acquainted with it nor the external world as it is known to us is real; and Kant says that all objects of experience are phenomena and not noumena.[1] If, on the other hand, we mean by the real, dependable matter of experience, then both the empirical self and the external world are real, and the two stand on the same footing. The finite self and the world are real or unreal according to the meaning assigned to reality. While Kant believes in a plurality of things in themselves, Śaṁkara declares that there is only one fundamental reality. In this matter Śaṁkara is certainly more philosophical than Kant, who illegitimately imports the distinctions of the world into the region of things-in-themselves.

Śaṁkara does not draw a hard-and-fast line of distinction between sense and understanding, as Kant does, nor does he believe that the principles of our intelligence have no power to represent concrete fact. According to Kant, the rhapsody of perceptions which is not knowledge is what is given to us; what we make of it by means of our categories, which add necessity and universality from outside, is knowledge. In Śaṁkara, there is no contrast between the mental construction and the presented fact. The two are adapted to each other. This is also the difference between Śaṁkara and Bradley. Śaṁkara would not say that in actual feeling we have the "that," and that thought rests on the vicious abstraction of separating the "what" from the "that," the result being that we are unable to recapture the "that" through mere ideal representation. Nor would Śaṁkara endorse the objection of Aristotle against Plato, that if the

[1] See Kant's *Prolegomena.* See 13, Remark II.

sensible is not the intelligible, then ideas cannot help us to understand the sensible world. The sensible, for Śaṁkara, is less than the intelligible, and the latter helps us to comprehend the former, though he believes that even the intelligible falls short of the real. He distinguishes the real from the sensible as well as the intelligible, and holds that the latter is a greater approximation to reality than the former.

Sometimes Śaṁkara's theory is compared with that of M. Bergson, which argues that there has been a growth of consciousness in man. The upward ascent from the amœba has been a long one. Many kinds of awareness or consciousness implicit in those beings have been suppressed in the development of man. We have paid an enormous price for being what we are. While our logical minds are useful for practical purposes, it is unreasonable to suppose that the whole of us is exhausted by what we are now. Even in this world we come across men of genius or insight, in whom the slumbering powers are stirred to life. Śaṁkara would not agree with Bergson's view that the intellect breaks up the flow of life, that the unending dynamic process is reduced by intellect to a static or geometrical presentation. Intellect not only dissects reality, but attempts to reconstitute it. It is both analytic and synthetic in its functions. Thought displaces contingency by law. It does not merely sunder reality into parts, but holds these in the bonds of unity by means of space, time and causality. To the concrete life of experience our intellects are quite adequate. Nay, they are made for each other, practically the parallel manifestations of one process. If Śaṁkara regards intellect as not the highest mode of man's consciousness, it is because the completed world of intellect still leaves us with a riddle. The completed world of logic is not the complete world of life and experience. That is why Śaṁkara does not regard it as final. For him it is not only mathematics that is abstract, but all knowledge —history, art, moral theory, and religion too ; for all these assume the dualistic standpoint. Śaṁkara does not condemn the intellect on the ground that it employs analysis and abstraction. He accepts its concreteness and yet finds it to be unsatisfactory. When we pass from the simple elements to complex categories and arrive logically at the conception of a supreme personality (Īśvara), whose life is expressed in the universe, Śaṁkara feels that our logic has grown in concreteness. The triumph of thought is the triumph of the concrete, but the most concrete thought is abstract in the sense that it is incapable of apprehending reality as it is. The higher we think the better we know; yet even the highest thought is not complete truth. In pressing forward and upward in the quest of reality with the aid of intelligence, we reach a reality seemingly full, rich and profound, that of Īśvara, the only way in which Brahman can be envisaged at the level of finite thought. But Īśvara is not the highest Brahman, since the unity of God is not an intelligible one.

Among Western thinkers Bradley comes nearest to Śaṁkara, though there are fundamental differences between the two. In the first part of his *Appearance and Reality* Bradley develops the doctrine of the limitations of human knowledge by an acute and penetrating criticism of the distinction of primary and secondary qualities, substance and attribute, qualities and relations. It is his considered conviction that thought can never do justice to reality. By sundering the "what" and the "that," it is incapable of reaching the goal, *i.e.* recapturing the secret of reality. According to Bradley, when we have, say, the sensation of blue colour, we have a *that* which is actually present and a *what*, or the peculiar quality by which it is distinguished. In immediate apprehension we are not conscious of the distinction between the two aspects. It is a "this-what," a process-content where the distinction of the "this" from the "what" does not enter into consciousness. In judgment we distinguish the two, the predicate from the subject, and attribute the former to the latter. This is true of all judgments. Life or reality is feeling in which the "that" and the "what" are inseparable, while logical reflection is always abstract in the sense that its very essence lies in the mental separation of the content from the process. Śaṁkara does not regard the separation of the *that* from the *what* as the essential defect of logic in the sense in which Bradley takes it; nor does he say that the reality which constitutes the subject of judgment is presented to us in the feeling fact itself. Granting that in knowledge the idea is not the psychical image, but an ideal content, granting also that the ideal content is referred in the judgment to the real world, Śaṁkara would say that the real which the ideal content tends to characterise is not the feeling experience of a private individual but the independent reality. Knowledge attempts to characterise by objective qualities, not any feeling or any extension of it, but the permanent reality out there, whatever may happen to me or my feeling. So long as we are investigating the nature of a private experience, we are engaged in a psychological quest and not a logical endeavour. The ambiguity due to Bradley's use of the word "feeling" is absent in Śaṁkara. He would, however, admit that the true subject of all judgment is reality as it is, and the predicate is a quality which we attribute to it, though it falls short of it. In this way subject and predicate correspond to reality and appearance. "In every judgment the genuine subject is reality, which goes beyond the predicate and of which the predicate is an adjective." Until the "what" coincides with the "that," we have not truth; when it coincides we have not thought. As Bradley says: "If you predicate what is different, you ascribe to the subject what it is *not*; and if you predicate what is *not* different, you say nothing at *all*." So long as we think, the predicate is less than the subject, the appearance less than reality. All judgment, according to Śaṁkara, is invalid, not because it separates the "that" from the "what," but because the predicate is other than the subject which is the reality. Without difference there is no thought; with difference there is no reality. Bradley believes that the real is the harmonious, and truth must therefore be a harmony. Self-completeness and consistency are the marks of reality. Śaṁkara adopts these in the evaluation of possible predicates. Space, time and cause, etc., are neither self-complete nor consistent. They are self-discrepant and stretch beyond themselves. From the stricter point of view of Śaṁkara, even harmonious truth is not reality. We cannot say that reality is a harmony, for the latter means a number of parts interrel ted in a whole. This distinction of parts and whole is an empirical one, which we are attributing to the transcendental reality. Truth, as harmony, requires us to postulate an absolute experience of Īśvara, which includes all finite subjects and all finite objects in a systematic unity. Śaṁkara holds that as the unity we assume is an unintelligible one, it has also the mark of appearance or unreality. Bradley is clear on this point. In all our thought the "that" and the "what" fall out and are at strife. To restore the unity is an impossibility. Logic piously assumes that all aspects of the world belong to one whole, that the discrepancies are apparent, and that the predicates are all one with the subject, appearances one with reality. Bradley assumes that in the world of logic there is nothing so imperfect that it cannot be taken into reality with sufficient modification. But he does not clearly tell us what the extent of the modification is. When he says that no judgment can possibly be true so long as the subject of judgment is reality, he is perfectly logical, and Śaṁkara would endorse his view. Bradley observes: "The conclusion to which I am brought is that a relational way of thought—anyone that moves by the machinery of terms and relations—must give appearance and not truth. It is a makeshift, a device, a mere practical compromise, most necessary, but in the end most indefensible." From this it follows that even the representation of reality as a harmony is a "device, a practical compromise most necessary, but in the end most indefensible." For Śaṁkara, as for Bradley, the weakness of logic is in its assumption of the distinction between the knower and the known. All duality is mental.[1]

The logic of Śaṁkara has in it elements of both agnosticism and mysticism. The absolute is the unattainable goal towards which the finite intellect strives, and when it reaches its consummation thought ceases to be what it is in our empirical life, and passes into a higher and more direct form of apprehension in which it and its object can no longer be distinguished. Logical dialectic helps us to overcome the errors into which thought of necessity falls. The inconsistencies and the incompleteness in which Śaṁkara's theory of knowledge is content to remain are not due to any defects in his reasoning, but are the inevitable imperfections of a philosophy which tries to go to the depth of things. For him knowledge is so vital and error so fatal that he will not admit anything as true unless it stands the scrutiny of logic.

[1] Dvaitaṁ sarvam manas.

XXV

The Objective Approach: Space, Time and Cause

Dissatisfaction with the first view of things is the mother of all metaphysics. While common sense accepts the surface phenomena as real, reflection asks whether the first view is to be regarded as the final one. To discriminate the real from the unreal, the eternal from the transitory, is the chief function of philosophy. At a time when the problem of religion was formulated in terms of the question whether God exists, Śaṁkara said that the chief problem related to the *real* as opposed to the *existent*. That which does not *exist* may be real, while that which does may not be so; for the real it is impossible to exist. This distinction is the justification of *metaphysics* as distinct from physics, and pervades all philosophical thinking, Eastern as well as Western. The "matter" of the Milesians, the "elements" of Empedocles and Anaxagoras, the "numbers" of Pythagoras, the "atoms" of Leucippus and Democritus, the "ideas" of Plato, and the "entelechies" of Aristotle, represent the results of the search for the real behind the appearances. The Middle Ages were busy with the problem of essence *versus* existence. Descartes and Spinoza were obsessed by it. Wolff and Kant changed the terms and opposed the noumenon to the phenomenon. Hegel distinguished being from existence. Modern scientists consider that the things we perceive are phenomena of the real, which is electric energy. Though there are far-reaching differences among these thinkers, the persistent common element is the distinction of reality into a true self-existent and an apparent derived one.

For Śaṁkara, philosophy is an exposition of the eternal nature of reality or the innermost essence of the world. It is *Brahmavidyā*. For him the existent is not the real. The happening of an event is one thing; the attribution of value to it another. The fact that we perceive a thing does not mean that it is true. If all that occurs or that we perceive were true, then there could not be a false experience. Even deceptive dreams are events of an inner life. As mere happenings, all experiences are on the same level, are neither true nor false.[1] Logic regards those things as true which are open to the observation of every intelligence, and those as false which are purely private. Śaṁkara takes up the central principles of experience, and declares that whatever is bound by space, time and cause cannot be real. Our experience has space for its general form, but the real is non-spatial and indivisible. For whatever is spatial is divisible, and the latter is always a produced effect and not a reality which is unproduced and indivisible and therefore non-spatial.[2] The universality (vibhutva) of space is only relative. Whatever is limited in space is limited in time also.[3] Time has an inherent tendency to pass beyond itself, though it can never do so. It is real in the world of experience.[4] Within the world of experience time has universal scope. But the unending duration of the world is not self-sufficient. The temporal is not the real.

Since causality is the central category of experience, Śaṁkara subjects it to a penetrating criticism intended to show the thoroughly unsatisfactory nature of the concept. That events are interconnected in a system is the assumption of common sense and science.

Śaṁkara criticises the Nyāya-Vaiśeṣika view that the effect is something not contained in the cause He argues that the effect must exist before its manifestation as the cause; for where a thing is not already present, it cannot arise. Oil cannot be pressed out of sand. If the effect were not prefigured in the cause, no amount of activity could bring it forth from the cause. All that the agent does is to transform the cause into the form of the effect. If the effect were not in existence before its manifestation, then the activity of the agent respecting it would be without an object. If we regard the

---

[1] Cp. Bradley: "That I find something in existence, in the world or in myself, *shows* that this something exists, and it cannot show more. . . . The given, of course, is given; it must be recognised and it cannot be ignored. But between recognising a datum and receiving blindly its content as reality is a very wide interval" (*Appearance and Reality*, pp. 206–207).

[2] See S.B., ii. 3. 7.

[3] Yad dhi loka iyattāparicchinnaṁ vastu ghaṭādi tad antavad dṛṣṭaṁ (S.B., ii. 2. 41).

[4] Some of the Purāṇas regard time as eternal, Prakṛtiḥ puruṣaś caiva nityau kālaś ca sattama (*Viṣṇu Purāṇa*); but, as Vidyāraṇya observes, the viewpoint of the Purāṇas is that of the empirical world. Purāṇasyāvidyā dṛṣṭiḥ.

effect as an extension beyond itself of the cause which is inherent in it, then it means that the effect is there already and is not freshly brought out. To the objection that if the effect exists in the cause, the activity of the causal agent is purposeless, Śaṁkara says in reply that the activity of the agent "may be looked upon as having a purpose in so far as it arranges the causal substance in the form of the effect." Cause and effect are continuous, *i.e.* there is no lapse of time in which the cause persists unchanged. For if the cause could persist like this for some time unchanged and then suddenly change, there must be a reason for this sudden change which we do not know. The cause, therefore, is said to change continuously into the effect. If causation is continuous, then cause and effect are not two distinct things, and we cannot speak of one becoming the other. It is said that the cause has in it a certain reaching forth [1] (atiśaya) towards the effect, a power by which it brings the effect into manifestation. Śaṁkara says: "If by atiśaya you understand the antecedent condition of the effect, you abandon the doctrine that the effect does not exist in the cause. If by it you mean a certain power of the cause assumed with the object of accounting for the fact, that only one determined effect springs from the cause, you must admit that the power can determine the particular effect only if it is neither other (than cause and effect) nor non-existent; for if it were either, it would not be different from anything else which is either non-existent or other than cause and effect (and then it will not be able to produce the particular effect). It follows that that power is identical with the self of the cause and the effect is identical with the self of that power." Again, the cause does not merely precede the effect but makes it occur. Unless the cause persists in the effect, the latter cannot be perceived. Clay continues in the vessel and the threads in the cloth. Cause and effect are not two different things which can be seen independent of each other like horse and cow. The difference between the effect before manifestation and after is a relative one. The cause and the effect represent two phases of one thing and are really of one nature.[2] It is said that two things cannot be of the same nature, when their forms are altered by manifestation and dissolution. Śaṁkara says that this contention is absurd. "Manifestation, like the springing of plants from seeds, is only a becoming visible of what was already existent, conditioned by the accumulation of like particles; and in the same way dissolution is a becoming invisible, caused by the disappearance of these same particles. If we were to recognise a transition from non-existence to existence in them and from existence to non-existence, then the embryo would be other than the subsequently born man, the youth would be other than the greybeard he becomes, and the father of the one would not be the father of the other." [3] A thing is not changed by a change in outward appearance. Devadatta is the same

---

[1] S.B., ii. 1. 18.

[2] S.B., ii. 1. 17.

[3] S.B., ii. 1. 18; D.S.V., pp. 258–259.

whether he opens his arms or folds them. "Substances themselves persist, *e.g.* milk through its existence as sour milk, etc. They take the name of effect, and we cannot think of the effect as different from the cause even if we tried for a hundred years. As it is the original cause which, up to the last effect, appears in the form of this or that effect like an actor in all possible parts, it is thereby logically proved that the effect exists before its manifestation and is identical with the cause."[1] Śaṁkara illustrates his view by the example of the cloth, and argues that so long as the cloth is rolled up, we cannot see whether it is a cloth or something else, and even if it be seen its length and breadth are unknown, and when it is unrolled we see what it is as well as its length and breadth. Since the rolled up and the unrolled cloths are not different, so are cause and effect not different.[2] A substance does not forfeit its nature and become another substance by appearing under a different aspect. All change is change of and in something. A mere succession of disconnected contents held together by no common nature is no change at all. All that happens is a change of form. The continuity of the substance of milk in the curds, of the seed in the tree, is to be allowed whether it is visible as in the former instance or invisible as in the latter case. It may even be said that the cause is the only reality and the effects are mere appearances.[3] Śaṁkara adopts the theory that cause and effect are not different.[4] He reduces the transitions from causes to effects, which underlie the entire dynamic evolution of reality to a static relation of sequence characteristic of certain types of logical and theoretic connection.[5]

Causal explanation cannot be complete. There is an indefinite number of terms before and after any given member of the series. Every event points back to the conditions out of which it has arisen. To say that A is the cause of B is not to explain B.[6] To postulate a first cause is arbitrary, since it would be to assume a beginning for the causal series, a beginning for time. Either the first cause has a previous cause or else the whole causal scheme is illogical. But if there is no first cause, the causal explanation is inadequate. We are obliged to break up the continuity of nature into past, present and future. What comes to us as an unbroken

[1] S.B., ii. 1. 18. [2] S.B., ii. 1. 19. [3] *Ibid.*

[4] Kāryakāraṇābheda, or tādātmya, or ananyatva. See S.B., ii. 1. 14; i. 4. 14; and Gauḍapāda's *Kārikā*, iii. 15. Sureśvara's *Vārttika*, p. 258.

[5] Some scientists of the present day dispense with dynamic concepts like force and energy, and are content with descriptive formulæ devoid of any implication of ultimate causal explanation.

[6] Cp. Campbell: "The use of the causal relation in a law is a confession of incomplete knowledge" (*Physics. The Elements*, p. 67).

stream is made into a discontinuous series. We begin with one event A, followed by another B, between which we try to institute a causal connection. At best the category of causality can explain phenomena only so long as we look upon them as completely determined by their relations to each other, without reference to the ultimate principle which is not itself one of the phenomena determined. To this is to be added that causality is a relation and all relations are ultimately unintelligible. If the causal rule were ultimate, then the causal chain could not be abruptly snapped at any stage. But the scriptures assure us that we can get out of its sway.[1]

Gauḍapāda's arguments[2] are approved by Śaṁkara. Since cause and effect are identical, change and causation are only appearances. Since cause is rooted in the very organisation of our intellect, we are obliged to use the causal category of the determination of events by antecedent ones. "The reason for assuming the non-difference of cause and effect is

[1] Śaṁkara raises the question as to how the effect, which is a substance consisting of parts, is said to abide in its cause, *i.e.* the material parts of which it consists. Does it abide in all the parts taken together or in each particular part? "If you say that it abides in all the parts together, it follows that the whole as such cannot be perceived, since it is impossible that all the parts should be in contact with the organs of perception. . . . Nor can it be said that the whole is apprehended through some of the parts only, since manyness, which abides in all its substrates together, is not apprehended so long as only some of these substrates are apprehended. If it is assumed that the whole abides in all the parts by the mediation of intervening aggregates of parts, then we should have to assume other parts in addition to the primary originative parts of the whole in order that, by means of those other parts, the whole could abide in the primary parts. . . . The sword, for example, pervades the sheath by means of parts different from the parts of the sheath. This leads to infinite regress, since in order to explain how the whole abides in certain given parts we should always have to assume further parts. If we adopt the second alternative of the whole abiding in each particular part . . . several wholes would result. If the opponent rejoins that the whole may be fully present in each part, as the generic character of the cow is fully present in each individual cow, we say that the generic attributes of the cow are visibly perceived in each individual cow, but the whole is not thus perceived in each particular part. If the whole were fully present in each part, the result would be that the whole would produce its effects indifferently with any of its parts. A cow, for instance, would give milk from her horns or her tail. But such things are not seen to take place." For a criticism of the samavāya relation binding cause and effect see S.B., ii. 1. 18.

[2] See S.B. on *Kārikā*, iv. 11–20; iv. 40.

the fact that the understanding is affected by cause and effect jointly."[1] Commenting on it, Ānandagiri says: "We assume the ground of cause and effect not merely on the ground of the actual existence of one thing depending on that of another, but on the additional ground of the mental existence, the consciousness of the one not being possible without the consciousness of another." If we state the causal principle in such a way as to avoid self-contradiction, we find that it has to be modified until it becomes one with the principle of identity, when it is no longer of any service for the purposes of science and common sense. When it is formulated truly, it is useless; when it is useful, it is not true.

Every finite thing presents the contradiction that it is not only finite, *i.e.* confined within itself, but is also relative in the sense that it hangs on another. No object of experience is self-determined and self-contained. Every object is tending to pass away from itself to something else. The finite as such is transitory being, ever trying to transcend itself. This character of the world is enough to indicate its nature as appearance, or māyā. Change is unreal, since it implies instability, deficiency and incompleteness. Change is othering, alteration, *i.e.* contention and conflict. Whatever changes has parts which assert themselves and make life a scene of division and discord. Plato regards change as mere lapse, and Aristotle as a tendency to realisation, but both view the real as changeless. It is true that Aristotle regards God as activity or energy, but this activity knows no change and the energy does nothing. For Śaṁkara the real is changeless, unalterable, so full of being that it always is and for ever maintains itself in rest and repose. It has no lack, no need, and so knows no change or strife. For Bradley, "nothing that is perfectly real moves."

Our experience is self-contradictory and not real, since reality should at least be self-consistent. In Śaṁkara's phrase, reality must be one, non-dual, but our experience is varied and discordant. The real is not what is open to the senses. It is not the content of right knowledge, since knowledge cannot be understood as valid apart from the conception of reality. It is the unalterable and the absolute, what

[1] S.B., ii. 1. 15, and Ānandagiri on it.

remains identical with itself in all its manifestations in experience, the basis and ground of all appearances. The world of experience consists of names and forms,[1] and is bound by the relations of space, time and cause, which endlessly dissipate themselves. Take any event, it has an endless past and an endless future, it is never-ending and nowhere-ending. This tantalising endlessness which marks it as unreal invites the soul to press on to the absolute.

XXVI

BRAHMAN

"Time spins fast, life fleets, and all is change." Nothing is; everything flows. The struggle to go beyond, to seek the real, know the truth, means that this flowing stream is not all. The logical, the cosmological and the moral arguments all point to something larger than the finite. The effort to escape from the limits of the finite implies the consciousness that the finite in itself is not the real. A felt necessity of thought obliges us to admit an absolute reality. As Descartes contends, the conception of an infinitely perfect being is assumed in the admission of one's own finitude.[2] No truly negative judgment is simply negative. "Wherever we deny something as unreal, we do so with reference to something real."[3] We exclude the negative because of a positive. Something is *not*, means something is. If we exclude the real as well as the unreal, we get nihilism. While Śaṁkara agrees with the Buddhist view that all things change, he demands a supersensible reality which is not within the world of change. We require the reality of something which does not need the support or help of anything else. Even if we regard the whole universe as merely imagined, there must be something which is the basis of all imagination.[4] Even imagined entities cannot float unsupported in mid-air. If there is no such reality, *i.e.* if even what we regard as reality is a produced effect, then there can be nothing real at all in

[1] S.B., i. 3. 41.
[2] *Meditations*, p. iv.
[3] S.B., iii. 2. 22.
[4] Sarvakalpanāmūlatvāt (iii. 2. 22).

this world or out of it.[1] Religious experience as registered in the Vedas guarantees at least some reality which does not come to be or cease to be. Deussen's statement "that the Indians were never ensnared into an ontological proof"[2] is hardly correct. So far as any logical proof of Brahman is available in Śaṁkara's writings, it is undoubtedly the ontological proof. We are obliged to posit an absolute reality; otherwise our whole structure of knowledge and experience tumbles to pieces. In the method of procedure Śaṁkara shows great originality and freshness. He does not start, as theological philosophers do, with a discussion of God's attributes. He is indifferent to, and even critical of, the arguments which are adduced in favour of a great First Cause and Creator of the world. For him integral experience, or anubhava, is the basal fact. It is the highest religious insight. It supplies the proof—if proof be the name for it—of man's awareness of a spiritual reality. Brahman is present to every man and is the universal fact of life. If any logical proof were necessary, Śaṁkara points to the inability of the mind to rest in the relative, *i.e.* the impossibility of accounting for experience except on the hypothesis of Brahman.

In his account of causality Śaṁkara makes the causal nature the svabhāva, or the sāmānya or the universal, while the effect is regarded as a condition, avasthā, or viśeṣa.[3] "There are in the world many sāmānyas with their viśeṣas—both conscious and unconscious. All these sāmānyas in their graduated series are included and comprehended in one great sāmānya, *i.e.* in Brahman's nature as a mass of intelligence."[4] To understand the nature of this universal reality is to know all the particulars involved in it.[5]

To say that Brahman is reality is to say that it is different from the phenomenal, the spatial, the temporal and the sensible.[6] Brahman is what is assumed as foundational,

[1] S.B., ii. 3. 7. [2] D.S.V., p. 123. [3] S.B., ii. 3. 9.

[4] Anekā hi vilakṣaṇāś cetanācetanarūpāḥ sāmānyaviśeṣāḥ; teṣām pāramparyagatyā ekasmin mahāsāmānye antarbhāvaḥ prajñānaghane . . . (S.B., Bṛh. Up., ii. 4. 9). Cp. Plato's Idea of the Good as the ground of all other Ideas.

[5] Sāmānyasya grahaṇenaiva tadgatā viśeṣā gṛhītā bhavanti (S.B., Bṛh. Up., ii. 4. 7).

[6] S.B., iv. 3. 14.

though it is in no sense substance.[1] It is not in any point of space, though it may be said to be everywhere, since all things imply and depend on it. Since it is not a thing, it cannot have spatial relations to anything else, and is therefore nowhere. It is not a cause, for that would be to introduce time relations.[2] Its nature is inexpressible, for when we say anything of it we make it into a particular thing. We may speak about it, though we cannot describe it adequately or have any logical knowledge of it.[3] If the finite man can comprehend Brahman, then either our understanding must be infinite or Brahman finite. " Every word employed to denote a thing denotes that thing as associated with a certain *genus*, or act, or quality, or mode of relation."[4] Brahman has no *genus*, possesses no qualities, does not act, and is related to nothing else. It is devoid of anything of a like kind or of a different kind, and has no internal variety.[5] A tree, for example, has the internal variety of leaves, flowers and fruits, has the relation of likeness to other trees and of unlikeness to objects of a different kind like stones.[6] Brahman has nothing similar to it, nothing different from it, and no internal differentiation, since all these are empirical distinctions. As it is opposed to all empirical existence, it is given to us as the negative of everything that is positively known. Śaṁkara declines to characterise it even as one except in the sense of secondless, but calls it non-dual, advaitam. It is the " wholly other," but not non-being.[7] Though the words used are negative, what is meant

[1] *Vedāntaparibhāṣā*, i.

[2] Cp. Kāryakāraṇavyatiriktasyātmanaḥ sadbhāvaḥ . . . aśanāyādi-saṁsāradharmātītatvaṁ viśeṣaḥ (S.B., iii. 3. 36).

[3] S.B., iii. 2. 23.

[4] S.B.G., xiii. 12.

[5] Sajātīyavijātīyasvagatabhedarahitam.

[6] See S.B., i. 3. 1; ii. 1. 14. *Pañcadaśi*, ii. 20. Rudolf Otto: *The Idea of the Holy*, E.T., p. 25. Plato mounts beyond the worlds of being and becoming to the good. Plotinus seeks to apprehend the Absolute as yet undivided between subject and object and so above all diversity. " This absolute is none of the things of which it is the source; its nature is that nothing can be affirmed of it—not existence, not essence, not life—since it is That which transcends all these. . . ." " Once you have uttered the 'Good,' add no further thought to it; by any addition, and in proportion to that addition, you introduce a deficiency. Do not even say that it has Intellection; you would be dividing it " (*Enneads*, iii. 8. 10, E.T., McKenna, vol. ii, pp. 134, 135). Clement of Alexandria reaches a point where the Supreme could be recognised not by what it is, but by what it is not.

[7] Vāṅmanasātītatvam api brahmaṇo nābhāvābhiprāyenābhidhīyate (S.B., iii. 2. 22).

is intensely positive. A negation is only an affirmation of absence. It is non-being, since it is not the being which we attribute to the world of experience. It does not follow that it is pure nothing, since the negative has its meaning only in relation to the positive. The Upaniṣads as well as Śaṁkara,[1] deny of Brahman both being and non-being of the type with which we are familiar in the world of experience. We can at best say what Brahman is not, and not what it is. It transcends the opposition of permanence and change, whole and part, relative and absolute, finite and infinite, which are all based on the oppositions of experience. The finite is always passing beyond itself, but there is nothing which the infinite can pass into. If it did so, it would no longer be the infinite. If we call it infinite, it is not to be equated with a mere negation of the finite. We cannot understand the nature of Brahman until we let go the formal and the finite. Since personality cannot be realised except under the limiting condition of a non-ego, the absolute is not a person. If we use the term personality in a different sense, in which it does not demand any dependence on another, then it is an illegitimate use. When the Absolute is said to be nirguṇa, this only means that it is trans-empirical, since guṇas are products of prakṛti and the Absolute is superior to it. The guṇas qualify the objective as such, and God is not an object. The objects come and go, but the real persists as the permanent in the midst of all changes. So it transcends the guṇas or phenomenal being. The Absolute is not on that account to be regarded as a mere blank. So the Upaniṣad says "nirguṇo guṇi." Brahman is of the nature of ultimate consciousness and yet knows nothing, since empirical cognition is a modification of the internal organ.[2] Knowledge, again, is its essence and not its property.[3] It is not eternal in the sense

[1] S.B., *Praśna Up.*, iv. 1.

[2] As Spinoza says: "The intellect which would constitute the essence of God must differ *toto cœlo* from our will and intellect, nor can they agree in anything save in name, nor any more than the Dog as a celestial constellation and the dog as a barking animal agree" (*Ethics*, i. 17, Scholium).

[3] Rāmānuja and the Naiyāyikas interpret jñānam in "satyaṁ jñānam anantam Brahma" as the basis of knowledge. Cp. Nityaṁ vijñānam ānandam Brahma ityādau vijñānapadena jñānāśraya evoktaḥ (Viśvanātha's *Siddhāntamuktāvali*, p. 49).

of persisting changelessly through time like the motionless being of Parmenides, the "mindless, unmoving fixture," which Plato derides in the *Sophist*,[1] but in the sense of absolute timelessness and incorruptibility. It is eternal because its completeness and perfection are unrelated to time.[2] The sequence which binds things and events in the time order has no meaning for it. It is eternal perdurance, to which all time relations are irrelevant. It can only be negatively described as the other of its own otherness. It is sat (real), meaning that it is not asat (unreal). It is cit (consciousness), meaning that it is not acit (unconsciousness).[3] It is ānanda (bliss), meaning that it is not of the nature of pain (duḥkha-svarūpa). It is real, having authentic being. It never fails to be, since it depends on nothing to preserve it in being. It does not take in anything from outside itself, for then being would include non-being. There is no first or last in it. It does not unfold, express, develop, manifest, grow and change, for it is self-identical throughout. It cannot be regarded as a whole including parts, for it is uniform in nature (ekarasa).[4] It is real and yet devoid of the nature of the world.[5] Such a being cannot of course be physical and quantitative and fragmentary. The everlasting being devoid of any deficiency is of the nature of consciousness, cit. Such a fulness of authentic being and ideality perforce is free delight, ananda.[6] All human bliss is a phase of the bliss of Brahman.[7] It is highest truth, perfect being and fullest freedom.

Ātman and Brahman have the same characteristics of being, consciousness, all-pervadingness and bliss. Ātman is Brahman. The purely subjective is also the purely objective. Brahman

[1] P. 249.

[2] Cp. Spinoza: "Eternity cannot be defined in terms of time nor can it have any relation to time" (*Ethics*, v. 1, Scholium). Nicholas of Cusa distinguishes between the *infinitum* of God and the *interminatum* of the world. As infinity is to boundlessness, so is eternity to perpetuity.

[3] Jaḍatvarāhityam. Deussen defines caitanyam as "a potency which lies at the root of all motion and change in nature, which is therefore also ascribed, for example, to plants, and means thus rather the capacity of *reaction to outer influences*, a potency which in its highest development reveals itself as human intellect, as spirit" (D.S.V., p. 59).

[4] S.B., i. 3. 1.

[5] Niṣprapañcasadātmakatvam (S.B., ii. 1. 6).

[6] S.B., i. 1. 12; iii. 3. 11–13; Tait. Up., ii. 7.

[7] Bṛh., iv. 3. 32.

seems to be mere abstract being, even as Ātman seems to be mere abstract subjectivity to the eyes of intellect. When we strip the Absolute of all its veils, we find that it is being refined away, evaporated into almost nothing. How can we assume this residuum, this nonentity, to be the supreme reality of the world? "Is Brahman then non-being? No, since even imagined things must have something to stand upon."[1] If anything exists, Brahman must be real. It is our human conception of Brahman that seems to be empty and not Brahman in itself, which is the fullest reality. The differenceless Brahman which we reach by an everlasting No, "not coarse, not fine, not short, not long,"[2] "not to be heard, not to be felt,"[3] is likely to be confused with an indeterminate blank, an uncomfortable night of nothing. Hegel has declared that pure being devoid of all predicates is not different from non-being. Rāmānuja and the Naiyāyikas agree with Hegel in thinking that such an undifferenced Brahman is not a reality capable of being known.[4] Śaṁkara knows it as much as his critics, for he says: "Brahman, free from space, attributes, motion, fruition and difference, being in the highest sense and without a second, seems to the slow of mind no more than non-being."[5] We seem to get a Brahman in which all is lost, though the mystic might explain that everything is found. The upward flight of thought which is afraid of making God determinate seems to us, the worldly minded, to end in making God nothing. Yet all the great religious seers deny conceptual designations to the Absolute.[6] For the sake of the mass of mankind, the scripture

[1] "Śūnyam eva tarhi tat, na, mithyāvikalpasya nirnimittatvānupapatteḥ" (S.B. on Gauḍapāda's *Kārikā*).

[2] Bṛh., iii. 8. 8. Cp. Augustine: "We can know what God is not, but not what He is" (*Trinity*, viii. 2).

[3] Kaṭha, iii. 15.

[4] Nirviṣayasya jñānatve mānābhāvāt (Viśvanātha's *Siddhāntamuktāvali*, p. 49).

[5] Digdeśaguṇagatiphalabhedaśūnyaṁ hi paramārthasad advayam brahma mandabuddhīnām asad iva pratibhāti (S.B., Chān. Up., viii. 1. 1).

[6] Cp. Rudolf Otto: "This negative theology does not mean that faith and feeling are dissipated and reduced to nothing; on the contrary, it contains within it the loftiest spirit of devotion, and it is out of such negative attributes that Chrysostom fashions the most solemn confessions and prayers. . . . A conception negative in form may often become the symbol for a content of meaning which, if absolutely unutterable, is none the less

defines Brahman in positive terms,[1] for "the scripture thinks, Let them first find themselves on the path of the existent, then I shall gradually bring them also to an understanding of the existent in the highest sense."[2] As an interpreter of the Upaniṣads, Śaṁkara was obliged to offer a reconciliation between the negative and the positive descriptions of Brahman.[3] Commenting on the spatial conception of Brahman, Śaṁkara says that it is meant to convey our ideas to others[4] or serve the purposes of worship.[5] We rise to the highest in itself, Brahman, through the highest in relation to us or Īśvara, the creator and governor of the universe. While Brahman is devoid of attributes, still those of being, consciousness and bliss may be said to be its essential features (svarūpalakṣaṇas), while those of creatorship, etc., are accidental ones (taṭasthalakṣaṇas).[6] Śaṁkara knows that even the definition of Brahman as *saccidānanda*[7] is imperfect though it expresses the reality in the best way possible. The power of the human mind is great enough to recognise its own limitations. Brahmānubhava gives the highest insight into Brahman, and he who has it answers every question of the nature of Brahman by silence or negative marks. Vidyā gives the highest positive conceptual account of Brahman by equating it with the attributes of being, consciousness and bliss, which are self-sufficient. Avidyā, or lower knowledge, applies attributes which imply relation,

in the highest degree positive. . . . A negative theology can and indeed must arise . . . from purely and genuinely religious roots, the experience of the luminous" (*The Idea of the Holy*, p. 189).

[1] Chān. Up., i. 6. 6; iii. 14. 2.

[2] Sanmārgasthās tāvad bhavantu, tataḥ śanaiḥ paramārthasad api grāhayiṣyāmīti manyate śrutiḥ (S.B., Chan. Up., viii. 1. 1).

Sadānanda, in his *Vedāntasāra* (ii), describes the method of adhyāropāpavāda by which we first attribute certain qualities to Brahman and then withdraw them. See S.B.G., xiii. 13.

[3] See S.B., i. 1. 1–31; i. 2 *passim*; i. 3. 1–18, 22–25, 39–43; i. 4. 14–22; iii. 3. 35–36. See D.S.V., p. 102, pp. 206–210.

[4] Upalabdhyartham.

[5] Upāsanārtham. S.B., Chān. Up., viii. 1. 1; S.B., i. 1. 20, 24, 31; i. 2. 11, 14; iii. 2. 12, 33.

[6] When we define Devadatta's house as that on which a crow is perched, we do not define its essence but state a feature which applies to it accidentally. It is an indirect definition of Devadatta's house. Even so is the definition of Brahman as the Creator and the cause of the universe.

[7] *Nṛsiṁhatāpanī Up.*

such as creatorship and rulership of the universe.[1] There are thus two views of the ultimate, higher and lower. "Where, by discarding the differences of name, form, and the like, ascribed by avidyā, Brahman is indicated by negative expressions, as not gross, etc.,[2] it is the higher (param). But where, on the contrary, exactly the same reality is described, for purposes of worship, as distinguished by some difference or other, it is the lower (aparam)."[3] Brahman cast through the moulds of logic is Īśvara. It is not the highest reality, since it has no meaning for the highest experience where existence and content are no longer separated. Yet it is the best image of the truth possible under our present conditions of knowledge. The saguṇa Brahman is not the mere self-projection of the yearning spirit or a floating air-bubble. The gleaming ideal is the way in which the everlasting real appears to our human mind.[4] A demand for theoretic con-

[1] Cp. *Ratnaprabhā*: "Vidyāviṣayo jñeyaṁ nirguṇaṁ satyam avidyā-viṣaya upāsyaṁ saguṇaṁ kalpitam" (i. 1. 11). Cp. with this the analogical knowledge of Schoolmen, the knowledge that knows its deficiency and by the very acknowledgment of it corrects it. Cp. Plotinus: "If we call it the Good, we do not intend any formal affirmation of a quality within itself; we mean only that it is the Goal or Term to which all aspire. When we affirm existence of it, we mean no more than that it does not fall within the realm of non-existents; it transcends even the quality of being" (McKenna's E.T., vol. i, p. 118).

[2] Bṛh., iii. 8. 8.

[3] S.B., i. 31; iv. 3. 14.

[4] D.S.V., p. 103. Cp. Eckhart, who draws a distinction between Godhead who is incomprehensible and God who works and creates. "In himself he is not God, in the creature only doth he become God. I ask to be rid of God, *i.e.* that God by his grace would bring me into the essence; that essence which is above God and above distinction. I would enter into that eternal unity which was mine before all time, and when I was what I would and would what I was; into that state which is above all addition or diminution, into the immobility whereby all is moved" (quoted in Hunt's *Essay on Pantheism*, p. 179). Plotinus says: "We form a conception of its Authentic Being from its image playing upon the Intellectual Principle. This image of itself it has communicated to the Intellect that contemplates it; thus all the striving is on the side of the Intellect, which is the eternal striver and eternally the attainer. The Being beyond neither strives, since it feels no lack, nor attain, since it has no striving" (*Enneads*: McKenna's E.T., vol. ii, p. 135). Cp. Bradley: "Fully to realise the existence of the Absolute is for finite beings impossible. . . But to gain an idea of its main features—an idea true so far as it goes, though abstract and incomplete—is a different endeavour. . . . And surely no more than this is wanted for a knowledge of the Absolute. It is a knowledge which of course differs enormously from the fact. But it is true for all that, while it respects its own limits; and it seems fully attainable by the finite intellect" (*Appearance and Reality*, p. 159).

sistency requires us to describe the Absolute by a set of negations, "neither personal nor moral, nor beautiful nor true," as Bradley does. The inevitable effect of the negative account is to make us believe that the Absolute has nothing to do with or is indifferent to the higher aspects of experience. When these negative formulas of an exact metaphysics defeat their object, we are inclined, in the interests of our religious needs, to lay a different emphasis.[1]

But Brahman cannot be both determinate (saguṇa) and indeterminate (nirguṇa).[2] A reality that has two sides or can be experienced in two ways is not the highest reality. The sides are dissolved the moment we touch the fountain of being. We catch aspects of the Absolute when we look at it from outside. In itself the Absolute is without sides, without forms, and without any element of duality or guṇas. These characters of form and personality have meaning in the world of vidyā, or experience. In the supreme Brahman there is a natural dissolution of all relativities. It is not a system or a whole which can be achieved by an endless process of reconciling opposites.[3] The infinite is not an object constructed by philosophy; it is an ever-present fact. Śaṁkara is opposed to all attempts to think the Absolute. The moment we think it, it becomes a part of the world of experience.[4]

[1] Cp. Bradley: *Truth and Reality*, p. 431.

[2] "One and the same thing cannot in itself be affected by differences such as form, etc., and not be affected by them, for this is a contradiction. . . . And by being connected with limitations a thing of one kind cannot assume another nature; for when rock crystal is transparent it does not become opaque by being connected with limitations such as red colour and the like; on the contrary, it is a misconception (bhrama) that opaqueness permeates it. . . . Whatever character is assumed, Brahman must be regarded as unchangeably free from all differences and not the reverse" (D.S.V., pp. 102–3).

[3] While strict logic requires Bradley to adopt a similar position, he yet wavers and has certain ultimate doubts. Strictly speaking, the Absolute excludes all positive and negative features, and we cannot reach it through logic, for we cannot go out of the relative by the relative. Our logical understanding, proceeding from limit to limit, cannot arrive at the unlimited. When we transcend our finiteness, we have nothing else than an absolute in which all that is formal and finite is dissolved.

[4] Ramānuja holds that the divine is the human view enlarged. The difference between the human understanding and the divine is one of range and not character; while the human view takes in some relations, the divine takes in all of them. But Śaṁkara is of a different opinion. If we are lost in the world of relatives, it is not possible to exhaust the relative.

XXVII

Īśvara or Personal God

Īśvara, according to Śaṁkara, is the determinate (saguṇa) Brahman regarded as the supreme personality. Śaṁkara believes that the question of God's existence is an absurd one. If God exists, then he must exist as other objects do, which would be to reduce God to the level of the finite, making him simply a unit in the indefinite multiplicity of objects, distinct from them all, even as they are distinct from each other, or merging him in the totality of existence in a pantheism which will be practically indistinguishable from atheism. To state the question of God in terms of existence removes in advance all possibility of solving it. If the rigidity of reason is any security for the attainment of truth, we should have arrived at it long ago. As a matter of fact we find different schools, each pretending to be logical, in conflict with the rest. Śaṁkara takes up the so-called proofs for the existence of God, the epistemological, the cosmological and the physico-theological, and shows their futility, as Kant did at a much later day.

The ideal of logic compels us to assume the reality of a perfect subject, to whom all existence is related as an object. Truth as systematic harmony means the reality of a divine experience. That events are interconnected in a system is the assumption of common sense and science, which is increasingly confirmed by experience, though never realised in its entirety. For there is much in the world which never directly enters into our experience. We seem to know much, though even in this limited region our knowledge is imperfect. Only a complete apprehension of reality as a whole can justify the hypothesis that God is and he is the creator of all. Our human experience is incapable of apprehending the world in its entirety, achieve a harmony of pure being with restless

When the terms are capable of endless subdivisions, and when their relations are capable of infinite permutations, a whole view of terms and relations is impossible. The putting together of the appearances does not lead us to truth. The real is beyond appearances and truth is beyond thought.

infinitude.[1] However much we might simplify and order our experience and reduce its complexity to the single prakṛti, the puruṣa, or the subject, would still remain the outside observer of its lonely flight through space and history. If the universe is small enough for our little minds to explore, if we can tell whence it comes and whither it goes, can understand its origin, nature and destiny, then we are not finite and we do not demand an infinite. The logical belief that all facts belong to a system and express the mind of God is only an idea.

The cosmological argument employs the concept of cause, which is not adequate even in the empirical world, and turns out altogether useless when we try to relate the world of experience to the ultimate reality, which is said to manifest itself through it. The different lines in the phenomenal series cannot explain one another. We cannot admit within the world of phenomena an uncaused cause. The question of an absolute beginning of the phenomenal series, saṁsāra, is a self-contradictory one. To seek for it is to seek in time for that which is the condition of the very being of time. It is the essence of saṁsāra that it has no beginning. The infinite to which we rise by the mere negation of the finite is another idea requiring explanation. When the argument from causality, which has its validity confined to the world of changing phenomena, is applied to the real, the latter is misconceived, since it is made an object of knowledge, and that which we infer as the cause of the world belongs also to the world of experience. We can infer only a finite creator from a finite world, even if we assume the universality of the principle that every effect has a cause.[2] The first cause must be a unity of the same order of being as the objects of experience, since the latter are brought into relation with it. If Īśvara is the cause of the world, he must be within the space-time framework, a vastly magnified man whose self-consciousness is defined by the instrumentality of a body and a mind analogous to our own. If such a being exists, no foreseeable extension of our knowledge could enable us to

[1] Cp. " For God alone sits high enough above
To speculate so largely."

[2] Yat kāryaṁ tat sakartṛkam.

determine his nature and existence. Such a God, moreover, working through instruments analogous to the human ones, is neither infinite nor omnipotent.

The moral argument that the context of things is adapted to the soul of man and shows the workmanship of a benevolent God is quite unsatisfactory. However the matter be turned, in a real world the responsibility for sin and evil falls on God.[1] If, to relieve him of the authorship of evil, we accept something like the mythology of Persia and make Satan responsible for it, then the oneness of God disappears and we reinstate a dualism between God and Satan. Again, if the soul is a part of God, God must feel the pain of the soul also, even as, when one member of the body suffers, the whole body suffers with it. It follows that the sufferings of God are much greater than those of the individual souls, and it is better for us to remain self-enclosed individuals with our limited sufferings than rise to the level of God and take upon ourselves the burden of the whole world.

A perfect God does not require the world for his satisfaction. If it is said that the world is for his enjoyment, then God is no God but only a saṁsārin. If we say that God has determinations, guṇas, like personality, perfection, etc., it is difficult to conceive how these can coexist with absoluteness. The attempt to conserve the characters of personality (guṇa) and absoluteness (Brahman) seems to be wellnigh impossible for logic.

The lesson which Śaṁkara derives from these inadequate proofs for the existence of God is that the question has no meaning in reality and arises only within the world of experience. When we realise the relative character of the world, we shall see that the problem of creation and the answer to it both belong to our logical world and not to reality as it is. To set aside the logical proofs is not to deny the existence of Īśvara. Śaṁkara's point is that no purely rational argu-

[1] The solution suggested by the Hebrew prophet, "I form the light and create darkness, I make peace and create evil, I the Lord do all these things," finds an echo in some passages of the Upaniṣads. "For he makes those do good works whom he will guide out from this world, and he makes those do evil whom he will guide downwards; he is the guardian of the world, he is the ruler of the world, he is the lord of the world" (*Kauṣītaki Up.*, iii. 8).

ment for the existence of God as a personal supreme being is finally acceptable. At best the "proofs" only tell us that God is a possibility. The reality of God transcends our rational powers of conceiving as well as comprehending[1]; only if we resort to the spiritual insight of seers as recorded in the scriptures can we be certain of God. The reality of Īśvara, in Śaṁkara's philosophy, is not a self-evident axiom, is not a logical truth, but an empirical postulate which is practically useful. Śruti is the basis for it.[2] Īśvara is the supreme spirit, all-knowing (sarvajña), and possessed of all powers (sarvaśaktisamanvitam). He is the soul of nature, the principle of the universe, its animating breath and actuating spring, the source and end of all existent modes. What is based on scriptural testimony is not necessarily opposed to reason. To accept śruti is to accept belief for which there are no disproofs, though there are not adequate proofs. In the logical account we render to ourselves of the world we reach a point where we require help from another source. Before we rise to intuition, we resort to śruti. Regarding the creatorship of Īśvara, scripture is our only means of knowledge.[3] It declares that "the cause from which (proceeds) the origin, substance and dissolution of the world, which is extended in names and forms, which includes many agents and enjoyers, which contains the fruit of works, specially determined according to space, time and cause, a world which is formed after an arrangement inconceivable even for the mind—this omniscient and omnipotent cause is Brahman (*i.e.* Īśvara)."[4] All the perfections, metaphysical and moral,

[1] Cp. Schweitzer: "If we take the world as it is, it is impossible to explain it in any way which will give meaning to the ends and aims of the activities of men and of humanity. We can discover no trace in the world of any purposive development which might lend significance to our actions" (Preface, xii, *Civilisation and Ethics*, pt. ii).

[2] Though Kant is regarded as the first philosophical thinker in Europe who sought to establish the futility of logical proofs, it must be said in fairness to Plato that he recognised it. "Therefore is it an impossible task to discover the Creator and father of this whole universe and publish the discovery of him in words for all to understand" (*Timæus*, 28, C.). Cp. Bishop Gore: "I acknowledge that human reason could never by its unassisted efforts have arrived at this conception of God the Creator" (*Belief in God*, p. 152), and so he asks us to turn to Revelation. So St. Thomas Aquinas. Cp. S.B. on *Kena Up*., i. 4.

[3] B.S., i. 1. 3.

[4] S.B., i. 1. 2.

are ascribed to him. He is said to be raised above all evil.[1] He is the immanent spirit (antaryāmin) pervading the object and the subject worlds, seen in the interior of the sun (object) as well as in the interior of the eye (subject).[2] He is the creator, ruler and destroyer of the universe.[3]

Śaṁkara takes great pains to prove that the reality of Īśvara, when once it is ascertained from the scripture, can be reconciled with the demands of reason. We only perceive the effect, so that it cannot be decided whether the world is connected with Īśvara as its cause or with something else, since the same effect can have different causes. So we must accept the statement of the scriptures that Īśvara is the cause of the world. Īśvara is the first cause, since he has no origin (asambhava). Īśvara as pure being (sanmātram) cannot have sprung from pure being, since the relation of cause and effect cannot exist without a certain superiority in the cause.[4] Īśvara cannot have sprung from differentiated being, since experience tells us that differences arise from the non-differenced, and not *vice versa*. He cannot have sprung from non-being, since it is essenceless (nirātmaka). Scripture also rejects this view, for it asks, How can being come out of non-being? Nor can Īśvara be a modification, since this would land us in infinite regress.[5] Īśvara is unproduced, has no cause, and is no effect. If Īśvara were an effect, then every effect from ākāśa downwards would be essenceless and we should embrace nihilism.[6] That which gives reality to all modifications is Īśvara.

Admitting the principle that every effect has a cause, may not the cause be the atoms, or the prakṛti, or non-being, or an individual agent, or spontaneity?[7] Śaṁkara refutes all these possibilities. Nature is not dead, but is alive and animated from within. The scene of nature is well adapted for the drama of the soul-life. "In the world, no non-intelligent object without being guided by an intelligence brings forth from itself the products which serve to further given aims of man. For example, houses, palaces, beds, seats, pleasure-gardens

[1] Chān., i. 6; S.B., i. 1. 20.

[2] S.B., i. 1. 20; Bṛh. Up., iii. 7. 9.

[3] See S.B., i. 1. 18–20, 22; i. 3. 39, 41; i. 2. 9–10.

[4] Since nothing superior to Īśvara can be conceived, therefore Īśvara exists uncaused. Cp. with this Descartes's ontological argument.

[5] S.B., ii. 3. 9.

[6] S B ii. 3. 7.

[7] S.B., i. 1. 2.

and the like are contrived in life by intelligent artists in due time for the purpose of obtaining pleasure and averting pain. It is exactly the same with this whole world. For when one sees how, for example, the earth serves the end of the enjoyment of the fruit of the manifold works, and how, again, the body within and without by possessing a given arrangement of parts suitable to the different species and determined in detail that it may form the place of enjoyment of the fruit of the manifold works . . . how should this arrangement proceed from the non-intelligent pradhāna ? . . . Clay, also, for example, is formed, as experience teaches, to different shapes only so long as it is guided by the potter, and exactly in the same way must matter be guided by another intelligent power." [1] The purpose of creation is to serve as the stage for the reward of the deeds of earlier existences which stretch back for each individual *ad infinitum*. Unconscious prakṛti is not the explanation of nature or the subjective aspect of the world and the working of the law of karma. Consciousness and activity must belong to the cause of the world.[2] The regularity and adaptation (racana) of the world indicate a conscious director. The same is implied by the co-operation of several means for one end.[3] Śaṁkara notices the theory of the Pūrva Mīmāṁsā that not God but apūrva accounts for the ordered way in which men reap the fruits of their deeds. He criticises it on the ground that apūrva is unspiritual and cannot operate unless it is moved by something spiritual. The extra-cosmic God of the Nyāya-Vaiśeṣika is inadequate, since he is not the material cause of the universe. Were the individual the creator, he would have produced what is beneficial to himself, and not things of a contrary nature such as birth, death, old age, disease, etc. For "we know that no free person will build a prison for himself and take up his abode in it." [4] Chance, atoms, prakṛti and the Nyāya God are larger and more impossible demands than what the scripture makes. So the omniscient, all-powerful, eternal, all-pervading Īśvara is the cause of the world.[5]

Īśvara is said to be the material as well as the efficient cause of the world. To the objection that in experience material causes do not possess knowledge, Śaṁkara answers : "It is not necessary that it should be here the same as in experience ; for this subject is known

[1] S.B., ii. 2. 1.

[2] If the mere presence of Brahman is enough to move the world as a magnet does iron, will not the mere vicinity of puruṣas suffice for the activity of prakṛti ? Again, avidyā naturally tends to creation and is in need of no purpose. "Avidyā ca svabhāvata eva, kāryonmukhī na prayojanam apekṣate" (*Bhāmatī*, ii. 1. 33).

[3] S.B., i. 3. 39.

[4] Na hi kaścid aparatantro bandhanāgāram ātmanaḥ kṛtvā'nupraviśati (ii. 1. 21). Cp. Descartes : "If I were myself the author of my being, I should have bestowed on myself every perfection of which I possess the idea, and I should thus be God" (*Meditations*, p. iii).

[5] See S.B., ii. 1. 22 ; iv. 1. 23 and 24.

by revelation and not inference." When we rely on scriptural statements, it is not necessary for us to conform to experience.[1] An efficient cause, according to the Nyāya philosophy, is that whose knowledge, desire and effort are necessary to bring about the product. The Vedāntin admits only knowledge which is self-sufficient and not desire and effort which assume a prior desire and a prior effort *ad infinitum*. It is argued that Īśvara cannot be the cause of the world since there is a difference of nature (vilakṣaṇatvam) between the cause and the effect. A piece of gold cannot be the cause of a vessel of clay; so Īśvara pure and spiritual cannot be the cause of the world, which is impure and unspiritual.[2] Śaṁkara replies that unconscious objects frequently take their rise from conscious beings, such as hairs and nails from men. From the inanimate dung, the animate dung-beetle comes forth. If it is urged that in these cases, in spite of apparent diversity, there is fundamental identity, since both of these spring from the earth, Śaṁkara replies that Īśvara and the world have the common characteristic of being, or sattā. The two are not totally different, and if Īśvara has a certain superiority (atiśaya), it is not surprising, since the cause everywhere has this feature.[3]

Another objection states that if the world issues from and returns to Īśvara, then, on its return, the qualities of the world such as materiality, compositeness, non-intelligence, limitedness, impurity, etc., must defile Īśvara.[4] Śaṁkara says in reply that when the effects return to their causes, they lose their specific qualities and merge in their cause, as when gold ornaments return to gold. It is not a true return, if the effect retains its qualities, even when withdrawn into the cause.[5] If it is said that, as the world loses its special qualities and gets absorbed into Īśvara, there is then no reason for it to go forth again, differentiated into the enjoyers and the enjoyed which we have in every new world-period, Śaṁkara answers this objection by an analogy. "As the soul in deep sleep and meditation returns (temporarily) into its original unity, but on waking from these states returns to its individual existence so long as it is not free from avidyā, so also is it with the return into Īśvara."[6] The force of differentiation continues in Īśvara, though it is not manifested, when the world is withdrawn into him. The basis of the recurring return of the world into existence is in the works performed in former lives which require to be atoned for. The liberated do not return since the condition of rebirth, *viz.*, false knowledge, is absent in their case.[7] Strictly speaking, there is no creation at all since saṁsāra is beginningless and endless. Creation and destruction are stages in the process of saṁsāra which is from eternity to eternity. At the beginning of every kalpa

---

[1] Na avaśyaṁ tasya yathādṛṣṭam eva sarvam abhyupagantavyam. See also D.S.V., pp. 92–93.

[2] S.B., ii. 1. 4.

[3] S.B., ii. 1. 6.

[4] Sthaulya, sāvayavatva, acetanatva, paricchinnatvāśuddhyādi.

[5] S.B., ii. 1. 9.

[6] S.B., ii. 1. 9.

[7] S.B., ii. 1. 9.

(world period) we have the unpacking of the original complex which contains within itself the whole range of diversity. There is continuity between the past and the present, between the state of destruction and the state of creation which succeeds it. If the supreme Īśvara and the individual jīva are related as whole and part, the former should be subject to pain, whenever the jīva suffers. To get over this difficulty, the relation of whole and part is interpreted as one of original and reflection. Any injury to the reflection does not affect the original.

It is said that God cannot be the cause of the world where some are treated well and some ill, and he who inflicts such varying lots on his creatures is unjust and cruel.[1] The difficulty is overcome by the recognition of the law of karma. God does not act arbitrarily, but acts with reference to the good and evil works of each creature in its earlier births. God brings about a creation suited to the deeds of men. Since the world is only a scene of atonement for the works of an earlier existence, the rôle of God as creator is a secondary one. We cannot attribute to the gardener what is due to the vital forces of the plant. Śaṁkara compares God to rain which helps the plants to grow, while what they grow into depends not on the rain but on the nature of the seed. Each individual's new life is determined by the moral quality of his acts.[2] But it may be asked, Why did not God create a world free from suffering, misery, at the very beginning, when there was neither merit nor demerit in the individuals to determine his action. This leads to circular reasoning. Śaṁkara says: "Without merit and demerit, no one can come into existence; again, without an individual no merit and demerit can exist, so that on the doctrine of the world having a beginning we are led into a logical see-saw."[3] The world is beginningless (anādi).[4] Each existence in it owes its nature to some prior existence. Even in periodical creations and returns the law of karma is observed, and saṁsāra in a subtle or gross form subsists in the nature of God. Prakṛti, or the principle of the world, which is itself no effect and is therefore superior to all effects,[5] exists in him. The spring has no source outside Īśvara, and so māyā or prakṛti is made a part of the nature of God. Īśvara, *i.e.* Brahman associated with prakṛti, is the efficient and the material cause of the world. The world as the effect of Īśvara persists even before it is created in the form of the causal self (kāraṇātmanā), even as it persists through his power in creation.[6] Even prior to creation the nāmarūpa (name and form) is the object of Īśvara's knowledge.[7]

The Upaniṣads believe in the immanence of God. They declare that God is not separated from the individual soul, but, by means of

---

1 S.B., ii. 1. 34. 2 S.B., i. 3. 39. 3 S.B., ii. 1. 36.
4 S.B., ii. 3. 42.
5 Sarvasmād vikārāt paro yo 'vikāraḥ (S.B., i. 2. 22).
6 S.B., ii. 1. 6. See S.B. on Kaṭha Up., iii. 11; Chān., viii. 14. 1.
7 S.B., i. 1. 5

it, he himself has entered into nature. "As the absolutely pure he would not enter the impure body with his own self, and even if he had done so, he would leave it remembering that he himself had made it. Without any trouble, the soul in whose form God entered the world would put an end to the world, even as the magician does to the glamour produced by himself. Since this does not occur, it follows that the world is not created by a spiritual being who knows what is good for himself."[1] Śaṁkara answers this objection by pointing to the production of different kinds of effects from one cause. The same earth brings forth many kinds of stones, costly jewels as well as ordinary stones. So also from one God a variety of souls and effects follow.[2]

Īśvara creates without implements. He is able to transform himself into manifold effects by his great powers.[3] No outside co-operation is necessary for God who possesses all the necessary powers perfect within himself. It is said that God and the ṛṣis can create many things through the sheer force of meditation, without the aid of anything external.[4] His work of creation is not like human acts.[5] By the specific quality of his nature, God transforms himself into the world even as milk is changed into curd.[6] Since the manifold world arises from Īśvara, the latter is assigned a multiplicity of powers.[7] If Īśvara is essentially free, he cannot be under any compulsion to create. God has no imperfections, no unfulfilled desires. The attribution of any motive (prayojana) to God conflicts with his all-sufficiency.[8] If the world issued for some purpose or expressed some desire or fulfilled some want, then it would betray a sense of need and incompleteness in the Supreme. If he created with no definite aim, then his acts would be no better than a child's. If God were the sole cause, the whole effect should have been present at once; but, as a matter of fact, we have a slowly unfolding growth which seems to indicate different causes for different stages. It is said in reply that action is not necessarily determined from without. It may be determined by motives intrinsic to the activity itself. So it is said that "the activity of the Lord may be supposed to be mere sport (līlā) proceeding from his own nature, without reference to any purpose."[9] The creative activity of Īśvara is the undesired overflow of his perfection, which cannot rest sterilely in itself. The conception of līlā conveys a number of suggestions. The act of creation is not motived

---

1 S.B., ii. 1. 21.

2 S.B., ii. 1. 23.

3 Paripūrṇaśaktikam (S.B., ii. 1. 24).

4 ii. 1. 25, 31.

5 S.B., i. 4. 27.

6 Kṣīravad dravyasvabhāvaviśeṣāt (S.B., ii. 1. 24). The analogy of milk is unsound, since the change of milk into curds requires the association of warmth.

7 S.B., ii. 1. 30.

8 Nityaparitṛptatvam (S.B., ii. 1. 32–33). Brahmaṇ is prāptakāmaḥ of realised purpose, and so the teleology of finite consciousness cannot apply to him.

9 S.B., ii. 1. 33.

by any selfish interest. It is the spontaneous overflow of God's nature (svabhāva), even as it is the nature of man to breathe in and out.[1] God cannot help creating. The work of the world is not the result of chance or thoughtlessness, but is simply the outcome of God's nature. Out of the fulness of his joy, God scatters abroad life and power.[2] Śaṁkara does not regard the infinite as something which exists in itself first and then feels itself under a necessity to go out into the finite. He creates out of the abundance of his joy and for the fulfilment of the demands of morality. By looking upon creation as the cosmic game in which the Supreme indulges, Śaṁkara brings out the purposiveness, rationality, ease and effortlessness with which the creation is sustained. The liberated are called upon to share the joy of Īśvara. The finite centres are distinguishable not from but within the whole, and the whole is also the ideal for the selves to attain to. Even things that seem to be unspiritual and unreasonable belong to the whole. The life of Īśvara throbs in all parts unifying and containing all. "All living creatures from Brahmā down to plants are regarded as my body."[3] Īśvara and the world, the cause and the effect, are identical. They are not identical as forms or modifications, but are identical in their fundamental nature of Brahman. The world in creation is developed in name and form, while it is in an undeveloped state in dissolution. Creation is the expression in the plane of space-time of what exists already in God.[4] At the end of each of the world periods (kalpas) Īśvara takes back the whole world, *i.e.* the material world becomes merged in non-distinct prakṛti, while the individual souls, free for the time being from actual connection with upādhis, lie in deep slumber as it were. But as the consequences of their deeds are not yet exhausted, they have again to enter an embodied existence as soon as Īśvara sends forth a new material world. Then the old round of birth, action and death, etc., begins anew.[5]

The individual souls which are different from one another are regarded as parts of Īśvara, which are, however, not confused. The

---

1 S.B., ii. 1. 33.

2 Cp. with this the Plotinian conception of Spirit as overflowing perfection.

3 *Upadeśasāhasrī*, ix. 4; *Dakṣiṇāmūrti Stotra*, p. 9.

4 Cp. Emily Brontë:

"Though earth and man were gone,
And suns and universes ceased to be,
And Thou wert left alone,
Every existence would exist in Thee."

5 The one supreme Lord is called Brahmā, Viṣṇu and Śiva according as he is creating, preserving and withdrawing the whole universe. Creation (sṛṣṭi) is the function of Īśvara enveloped in sattva or Brahmā. Withdrawal (pralaya) is the function of Īśvara enveloped in tamas or Śiva, while subsistence (sthiti), with its upward and downward tendencies, is the function of Īśvara enveloped in rajas or Viṣṇu.

works and fruits of different souls, which at death return to their source and proceed out again to a new existence,[1] do not intermingle.[2] The individual soul as identified with the material body is the jīva, or the dehin, or the embodied. The unity of all these jīvas, the collective or cosmic self in the waking state, is Virāj or Vaiśvānara. As identified with the subtle body as in the dream state, the individual is the liṅgin, or the taijasa. The unity of all the taijasas or subtle selves is Hiraṇyagarbha or Sūtrātman.[3] Lastly, as identified with the kāraṇa-śarīra, the individual is called prājña, and the unity of all prājñas is Īśvara. The individual in the state of dreamless sleep has still the element of duality. He has buddhi, the spring of thought and volition. Īśvara, in the state of withdrawal, is like the jīva in suṣupti, connected with the principle of duality, though it is not manifested. Īśvara is Brahman enclosed in pure buddhi. He has the three guṇas, and is also said to transcend them. He is said to be invested with a transparent body of pure sattva. From Īśvara to Virāj, from dreamless sleep to waking, from prājña to dehin is the order of sṛṣṭi (creation), or progressive materialisation, the reverse being that of pralaya, or progressive idealisation. Śaṁkara admits actual transformation (pariṇāma) in the phenomenal world, though he employs the conception of appearance (vivarta) to indicate the relation of the world to Brahman.

A material cause is that which brings about a product not different from the cause.[4] The world is not different from Brahman, which as the existent (sadrūpeṇa) appears to undergo change; it is also different from avidyā, which as the non-intelligent (jaḍena) undergoes change. The world thus is a mixture of Brahman and māyā. While Śaṁkara is explicit that Īśvara is the efficient as well as the material cause of the universe,[5] in later Advaita differences arise. According to the *Vedāntaparibhāṣā*, the cause of the evolution of the world is māyā and not Brahman.[6] Vācaspati holds that while Brahman is the cause, māyā is the auxiliary (sahakāri). Brahman looked at as an object by the individuals affected by māyā is the non-intelligent world, and is said to be the cause of it.[7] But this view takes for granted the māyā which affects the jīvas. The insentience (jaḍatā) of the world must be due to something else than Brahman pure and simple, and it is perhaps better to say that the world with its finite-infinite nature is to be traced to Brahman-māyā; and since we are not in a position to account for the relation of the world to Brahman, we may say that Brahman is the substratum of the world which is a product of

[1] Chān. Up., vi. 10. [2] S.B., ii. 3. 49. [3] S.B., ii. 3. 15.

[4] Svābhinnakāryajanakatvam upādānatvam.

[5] A view which is supported by *Vivaraṇa*.

[6] Prapañcasya pariṇāmy upādānam māyā na brahmety, siddhāntaḥ.

[7] Vācaspatimiśrās tu, jīvāśṛtamāyāviṣayīkṛtam brahma svata eva jāḍyāśrayaprapañcākāreṇa vivartamānatayopādānam iti māyāsahakārimātram (S.L.S., i).

māyā. This view is adopted by *Padārthatattvanirṇaya*.[1] The author of *Siddhāntamuktāvali* feels strongly against subjecting Brahman to any kind of relation, and so holds that māyā alone is the cause of the world. The author of *Saṁkṣepaśārīraka* regards the absolute Brahman as the material cause of the world, since all that is must belong to the one reality. Others who decline to attribute any kind of relation to Brahman, look upon Īśvara, *i.e.* Brahman as related to māyā, as the material cause.[2] If material causality is attributed to the absolute Brahman, it is only accidentally (taṭasthatayā). Vidyāraṇya holds that the cause which changes into the world is māyā,[3] while that which is the basis of the world is the pure consciousness limited by māyā.[4] There are thinkers who believe that the gross objective world is the effect of Īśvara's māyā, while the subtle world of mind, sense, etc., is the product of the individual jīva, aided by the māyā of God.[5] There are others who attribute the subjective world to the force of avidyā, and do not find any necessity for the co-operation of Īśvara's māyā, assigning to the latter only the elemental universe. When we look at the question from the two different points of view, objective and subjective, Brahman is the basis on which the objective world is imposed, while Ātman is the basis on which the subjective is imposed. While the ultimate reality is the material cause of the entire practical world of sense and activity, the jīva is the material cause of the world of apparent things and of the dream world. While all these views refuse to make the world the product of the individual subject or the jīva, there are some thinkers who are of opinion that the jīva is the material cause of all, projecting within itself the whole order of things from Īśvara downwards, even as it projects a dream world.[6]

XXVIII

The Phenomenal Character of Īśvara

It is indifferent whether we say that Brahman, cast in the moulds of logic, is the world of experience or that it is Īśvara.

1 Prapañce ubhayor api māyā brahmaṇor upādānatvam; tatra ca pariṇāmitayā māyayā upādānatvam; adhiṣṭhānatayā ca brahmaṇa upādānatvam. Brahmavivartamānatayā, avidyāpariṇāmamānatayā upādānam (Commentary on S.L.S., i).

2 *Vivaraṇa*, which takes its stand on S.B., i. 1. 20; i. 2. 1.

3 Pariṇāmyupādānatā.

4 Vivartopādānatā is attributed to māyopahitacaitanyam.

5 Viyadādiprapañca īśvarasṛṣṭamāyāpariṇāma iti; tatra īśvara upādānam; antaḥkaraṇādikaṁ tu, īśvarāśṛtamāyāpariṇāma mahābhūtopaśṛṣṭajīvāvidyākṛtabhūtasūkṣmā kāryam iti, tatrobhayor upādānatvam (S.L.S., i).

6 Appayadīkṣita describes their position thus: "Jīva eva svapnadraṣṭṛvat svasminn īśvarādisarvakalpakatvena sarvakāraṇam ity api kecit."

Īśvara is all-comprehensive and contains within himself all that exists, potentially in pralaya and actually in creation. There does not seem to be much point in Deussen's observation, that Śaṁkara did not carefully distinguish Brahman, the undifferentiated, from the phenomenal world on the one hand, and Īśvara on the other. He says: "This undifferentiated Brahman has two contraries: first the *forms of the phenomenal world,* as Brahman, conditioned by upādhis, appears; then the imperfect *figurative ideas,* which we form of the Godhead, in order to bring it nearer to our understanding and our worship. It is strange that between these two contraries of the undifferentiated Brahman, however wide apart they naturally are, Śaṁkara draws no sharp distinction, and even if, according to one passage, it seems as if he saw in the *phenomenal forms* the basis (ālambanam) of the *presentation forms,* yet from the continual intermingling of the two . . . it follows that our author never became clearly conscious of the difference between them." [1] Deussen agrees that Śaṁkara referred to this distinction in one passage [2] and dismissed it as meaningless (vyartha). The whole phenomenal world is the appearance of Brahman. Brahman, on which all rests, becomes Īśvara, which includes all, when shaped by the phenomenal forms. The distinction between the infinite Īśvara on the one side and the individual souls on the other is a distinction of different members of a whole, analogous to that between the kingdoms of Magadha and Vaideha, which belong to the same world.[3] When Brahman the real is conceived as Brahman the saṁsāra, God, man and the world (Īśvara, jīva, prapañca) become the chief elements.

Theoretical philosophy, interested in deducing the world of being from the first principle of an absolute self which has nothing contingent about it, is obliged, whether in East or West, to accept some principle of self-expression (māyā), of objectivity (prakṛti). In European thought Kant contended that there was no experience apart from the transcendental unity of apperception, and yet he made this purely formal, and so failed to derive the whole of experience from it. By regarding experience as an interaction between the trans-

[1] D.S.V., pp. 205–206. [2] S.B., iii. 2. 21. [3] S.B., iii. 2. 31.

cendental unity of apperception and the things in themselves, he introduced into his system an element of irrational contingency. Fichte accepts from Kant the central truth that all experience is only for a subject, and attempts to develop the whole of experience from it. He holds that in the development of the subject there is no intrusion of a foreign factor, but every step is determined from within. The absolute subject gives itself an " other " in the very act of self-positing. The self cannot affirm or posit itself except by oppositing or distinguishing from itself a not-self. The element of otherness is brought about within the very being of the self. Gradually we have the differentiation of the absolute self into a multiplicity of finite egos at once other than itself and modes of itself. The self of Fichte has thus to throw up from itself a check or an impediment, a not-self, as the very condition of its becoming aware of its activity. The self limitation of the primal consciousness, or the rise of the obstacle against which the self breaks itself, has to be assumed, however incomprehensible it may be. Similarly in the conception of Īśvara we have, besides the absolute Brahman, the element of objectivity or prakṛti, self-expression or māyā.

When we start from the human end, we must offer some explanation of the world of becoming. It cannot be due to Brahman, which is immutable. If Brahman itself changes, it ceases to be Brahman. If it never ceases to be itself, *i.e.* never changes, the change we come across remains unexplained. The changing universe cannot be traced to prakṛti, which is unintelligent. While Brahman stands for being, prakṛti stands for becoming. But to posit prakṛti by the side of Brahman as an ultimate category would be to limit the nature of Brahman, which has no second, nothing outside ; but if no second is posited, the explanation of the world becomes difficult. The only way is through the recognition of a saguṇa Brahman or changing Brahman, an Īśvara who combines within himself the natures of both being and becoming, the unattached Brahman and the unconscious prakṛti. The indeterminate for thought becomes the self-determined. The primal unity goes out of itself and produces a manifestation relatively independent of it. The pure, simple, self-subsistent Absolute becomes the personal Lord, the principle of being in the universe binding all things to each other in binding them to himself Brahman is what is beyond both subject and object. When it becomes subject dealing with an object, we have Īśvara, the Logos, the one-many. The blank objectivity or prakṛti, develops the whole world through the power of the subject, God. By itself prakṛti or the object, has no existence or meaning. It is unintelligent, and so cannot cause anything without the aid of an intelligent spirit. It is merely the other of the subject and the world is the heterisation or the othering of Īśvara, the self-conscious Brahman. Īśvara combines the two principles of Brahman and prakṛti. He is not pure consciousness (caitanya) but a self-conscious personality. "He designed (aikṣata), I will become many, I will procreate."[1] Knowledge, self-consciousness and personality are possible only if there are objects. Omniscience (sarvajñatva) characterises God, though its possibility is explained in different ways.[2] The nature of Brahman is jñāna, or knowledge. This takes the shape of an effect when it is limited by an object to be known. Then in relation to that object is Brahman known as Vijñātṛ, or the subject of knowledge. In other words, Brahman, whose nature is knowledge, becomes a knower, when he is confronted with an object to be known.[3] Śaṁkara agrees with Rāmānuja and Hegel in thinking that a not-self remains an integral element of personality. Only, while they regard the conception of personality as the highest, Śaṁkara declares that we are in the world of phenomena, so long as we have the consciousness of not-self. To reach the real, we must transcend this distinction. When pure being becomes related being, its first relation must be to something different from being. That which is different from being is

[1] Chān., vi. 2. 3. See also Ait., i. 1. 1; Praśna, vi. 3. 4; Muṇḍ., i. 1. 9.

[2] Bhāratītīrtha makes out that Īśvara is conditioned by māyā, in which abide the subtle impressions of the minds of all creatures. The author of *Prakaṭārtha* agrees with this, and remarks that as māyā is coextensive with the phenomenal world, past, present and future, it enables its possessor to have all-comprehensive knowledge. The author of *Tattvaśuddhi* observes that God's knowledge need not always be direct. While the whole of the present world is directly cognised by God, he may remember the past and anticipate the future. The author of *Kaumudī* holds that God as having the characteristics of Brahman is the illuminator of all objects. See S.B., i. 4. 9, and *Siddhāntaleśa*, i.

[3] This is the view of Vācaspati also.

not-being.[1] Īśvara, who is different from Brahman, or the unbroken energy of light, is the light affirming itself in and through darkness. He is the principle of truth creating order of chaos, the spirit of God brooding on the face of the waters.[2] The darkness tries to overwhelm and eclipse the light and seeks to cover all, and the light is always busy overtaking the darkness. While there is an essential antagonism between Brahman and darkness, between Īśvara and darkness, there is struggle and ultimate victory of light over darkness. Īśvara is thus the mediating principle between Brahman and the world, sharing the natures of both. He is one with Brahman, and yet related to the object world. Śaṁkara holds that even before creation, the personal Īśvara has an object in " the names and forms which are neither to be defined as beings nor as their opposites, which are not evolved though striving towards evolution." [3] We have here the ultimate spirit viewed as ego contemplating the non-ego as its object. For Īśvara, changelessness and inactivity are impossible. As real in the empirical sense, he must be ever acting, losing himself to find himself, going out to the universe and returning to himself through the universe. He who does nothing and stands aloof from the world is not God, not at any rate a God of love. Love lives in the life of its objects, exhibiting the sorrow though not the guilt of wrong-doing and sin and the joy of righteous living. For Śaṁkara, as for many other philosophers, a self-conscious being which has no object, which does not possess its opposite and does not affirm its unity in terms of it, is impossible. It is through its manifestations or objects that a self-conscious personality lives, moves and has its being. Yet it is necessary to hold that it is in no way affected by the changes of its object, a thesis which it is difficult to maintain. The events of nature and the change of souls bring about alterations in the nature of Īśvara. The *Vedāntaparibhāṣā* openly admits that the activities of living beings produce various modifications of māyā

[1] Cp. " And the light shineth in darkness " (St. John i. 5). Bishop Westcott, commenting on it, writes : " Side by side with the light, the darkness appears suddenly and without preparation " (*The Gospel according to St. John*, p. 5).

[2] See Introduction, S.B.G.

[3] S.B., i. 1. 5. " Anirvacanīye, nāmarūpe avyākṛte vyācikīrṣite."

or prakṛti, which is the upādhi or the body of Īśvara.[1] The appearance and disappearance of the world shows that the Divine nature undergoes change, contraction and expansion. So long as creation and destruction are real movements in the life of God, the latter is not above time but is subject to time; so that, even as creation and destruction belong to the empirical world, Īśvara belongs to it. We employ the category of change which demands a permanence and argue that Īśvara is the permanent background, to whose body these changes pertain.[2] Īśvara assumes an undeveloped subtle body, forming the seed plot for names and forms, and serving as the groundwork for the Lord, and yet only as a limitation ascribed to himself.[3] The admission of a formless matter co-eternal with God clearly involves limitations on the infinity of God. To say that the limitations are not those of an external, more or less intractable material, does not help us much.

While the saguṇa Brahman changes, it is maintained that it still remains within its constitutive idea, so that the alterations are all in the accidents and not in the essentials. Īśvara's oneness is not impaired by self-expression in the many.[4] "As the magician is not affected by the māyā which he has himself created, since it is unreal, so also the Supreme is not affected by the māyā of saṁsāra."[5] Thus Śaṁkara attempts to combine the ideas of the negation of the finite and the presupposition of the finite in his conception of Īśvara. The charge against Spinoza that he reduces the Absolute to a mere blank of indeterminate being, which he inconsistently transforms into the self-determining God, has no force against Śaṁkara, who commits no such sublime inconsequence. He is clearly conscious that the negation of all the determinations of the finite can give us only an abstract being of which nothing can be said except that it is. So long as we

---

[1] Sṛjyamānaprāṇikarmavaśena parameśvaropādhibhūtamāyāyāṁ vṛttiviśeṣā idam idānīṁ sraṣṭavyam, idam idānīm pālayitavyam, idam idānīm saṁhartavyam ityādyākārā jāyante, tāsāṁ ca vṛttīnāṁ sāditvāt tatpratibimbitacaitanyam api sādīty ucyate (i).

[2] S.B., ii. 1. 4. In the *Dakṣiṇāmūrti Stotra* it is said: "All that is moving or unmoving in the universe—earth, water, air, fire, ether, the sun, the moon and the spirit—is but the eightfold form of Him, and there is nothing whatever which on reflection is other than the Supreme Lord."

[3] Avyākṛtaṁ nāmarūpabījaśaktirūpam, bhūtasūkṣmam īśvarāśrayam, tasyaivopādhibhūtam (S.B., i. 2. 22).

[4] Chān., viii. 14. 1; vi. 3. 2; Tait. Ar., iii. 12. 7; Śvet. Up., vi. 12.

[5] S.B., ii. 1. 9. Yathā svayaṁprasāritayā māyayā māyāvī triṣv api kāleṣu na saṁspṛśyate 'vastutvāt, evam paramātmāpi saṁsāramāyayā na saṁspṛśyata iti.

are employing the methods of logic, the highest reality is not the indeterminate Brahman but determinate Īśvara, who is the source of all the manifold changes of the universe. But there is throughout Śaṁkara's philosophy the pervading prejudice against the adequacy of logic and the finality of its ideal, and so we find that this conception of saguṇa Brahman, or concrete spirit, is, according to him, so riddled with self-contradictions and inconsistencies that it cannot be regarded as the highest reality.

That Īśvara is the home of all finite existence, the material and the efficient cause of the world, is an assumption. It is quite easy to say that the concrete universal combines the reality of the universal and the particular, but the how of it is a mystery. If the relation of identity and difference, permanence and change, is unintelligible in the world of experience, it cannot become intelligible when applied to Īśvara. Śaṁkara knows that his view is open to the charge of abstract identity, but he believes that identity and difference cannot be logically related. *How* the two can coexist he feels that he does not know.[1] The conception of Īśvara as a concrete whole is not so much an explanation of experience as a restatement of the problem. Our experience has in it the two features of identity and difference, or permanence and change. We ask how is the experience, which is a complex of souls and things and characterised by permanence and change, to be accounted for, and we answer that Īśvara is the explanation of experience, since he combines both these features and has the world of souls and things organically related to him. To say that they constitute his body is not to explain experience. We frame a generalised concept of experience and call it Īśvara. The explanation of the experienced world is that world itself, which in its general terms is called Īśvara. Rāmānuja and Hegel hold that the ultimate reality is a one containing many. For them the rational is the real: God and the world are both real. The indeterminateness of intuition and the mystery of reality do not appeal to them. They are interested not in the real in itself but the real for thought, which has an element of negativity in it. The process of thought consists in the continual absorbing and transcending by mind of its own discrepant and rebellious parts. So all spiritual life is an unceasing struggle with refractory elements. Divine life is regarded as an eternal activity. To think of the world as a logical unity or a single system is to think of it as the manifestation of one perfectly determinate principle in an

---

[1] Śaṁkara would not have found much help in the realist theory of the reality of the universals along with that of the particulars, for the universals of the realists do not claim infinity. They are finite reals, though of a different order from the particulars, and if God is a universal of this character, he can realise himself in various ways simply because he is finite. Were he infinite, he could only act in one way, or rather, Śaṁkara would say, he could not act at all. He could only *be* and not become, and there is then no question of his activity or manifestation.

infinity of details. But we should not overlook the difficulties attending this conception of the highest as the concrete universal or the union of the finite and the infinite.

Śaṁkara believes that the aim of the scriptural accounts of creation is to establish the identity of Brahman and the world.[1] If the world were not identical with God, and if he created it as a substance separate from himself, then he would be guilty of the charge of making efforts under the influence of motives. In other words, he is no God at all.[2] If he acts in obedience to the law of karma, then he is limited by it. We have referred to Fichte's conception of the self which comes to self-consciousness by breaking itself, so to speak, against some obstacle and by being reflected back, as it were, upon itself from this obstacle. Such a self is really dependent on its other, of which it is said to be the source and support. The self cannot precede the world nor can it survive it. If we succeed in abolishing the not-self, we at the same time succeed in abolishing the self. When Fichte becomes vaguely aware of these consequences, he rises to the conception of a reality which is "neither subject nor object but the ground of both." Śaṁkara recognises most clearly what Fichte was groping after, that subject and object are distinctions of logic which have no meaning when we speak of the source of all logic. The Absolute is neither the bearer of knowledge nor the object of knowledge, but knowledge itself (jñānam). If the whole world is regarded as an objectification of the thought of God, existing in order that he might perpetually maintain himself as self-conscious of the world as an object, then such a God is only relative and not absolute;[3] for "The Absolute does not want to make eyes at itself in a mirror or like a squirrel in a cage, to revolve the circle of its own perfections."[4] In short, personality is not the ultimate category of the universe. Plotinus observes: "All that has self-consciousness and self-intellection is derivative."[5] So beyond the

[1] Evam utpattyādiśrutinām aikātmyāvagamaparatvāt (S.B., iv. 3. 14). See also S.B., ii. 1. 33.

[2] S.B., ii. 2. 37.

[3] Māyopādhir jagadyoniḥ sarvajñatvādilakṣaṇaḥ (*Vākyavṛtti*, p. 45).

[4] *Appearance and Reality*, p. 172.

[5] *Enneads*, iii. 9. 3, McKenna's E.T., vol. ii, p. 141.

personal Īśvara is Brahman the Absolute, lifted above all self-divisions and holding together both absolute objectivity and subjectivity in the unbreakable bond of absolute consciousness.

There is a gap between the intuited Brahman which is devoid of logical determinations and the conceived Brahman which is the productive principle, which explains difference and at the same time overcomes it. The indeterminate Brahman in itself will seem to the logical intellect, as the dark in which all colours become grey. If it should serve as an explanation of the finite at all, it can only be through the introduction of the very form of the finite into the heart of the absolute. If we attempt to *think* pure being, we at the same time think *non-being*, and from the interaction of the two the becoming of the universe follows. Strictly speaking, even God *becomes*. The contradiction of being-non-being appears in his own inward nature. Perhaps Īśvara may not himself come to be, but still he makes his meaning explicit in an unending process of becoming. Being and non-being are aspects of one and the same reality, the positive substance and the negative shadow of the same reality. The criticism that Śaṁkara leaves us with an unbridgeable chasm at the summit of things, between the nirguṇa Brahman of which nothing can be said and the saguṇa Brahman which embraces and unifies all experience, is due to a confusion of standpoints. Thought can never overleap the distinction of subject and object, and so the highest for thought is the absolute subject with the object in it, but behind the subject and the object we have Brahman.

XXIX

The Phenomenality of the World

Both Brahman and the world, both unity and multiplicity, cannot be equally real. " Were both unity and multiplicity real, we could not say of one whose standpoint is that of worldly action that he is caught in untruth . . . it could not be said ' from knowledge comes deliverance ' ; moreover, in that case the knowledge of manifoldness cannot be transcended by the knowledge of unity."[1] Judged by the tests of reality, the world of experience reveals its phenomenal character. All particular facts and events as objects stand over against the knowing subject. Whatever is an object of knowledge is liable to destruction.[2] Śaṁkara holds that the distinction between reality and seeming, substance and show, is identical with that between subject and object. While the objects which are perceived are unreal, the Ātman which perceives but is not itself perceived is real.[3] While distinguishing waking objects from dream ones, Śaṁkara urges that the two, in so far as they are objects of consciousness, are unreal.[4] The real is what is free from self-contradiction, but the world is full of contradictions. The world of space, time and cause is not self-explanatory. There is no principle of reconciliation in the finite world by which its difficulties are dissolved. Space, time and cause, which are the forms of all experience, are not ultimates. The real is obscured by them. If we get beyond the distinctions of places, moments and events, it is said, the world of diversity will collapse into a single unit.[5] Experience cast in the moulds of space, time and cause is phenomenal only. The real is what is present in all times.[6] It is that which ever was, is and will be.[7] The real cannot be present to-day and absent to-morrow. The world of experience is not present at all times and is therefore not real. When insight into reality is gained, the world of experience is transcended. The world is said to be unreal since it is

[1] S.B., ii. 1. 14.

[2] Yad dṛśyaṁ tan naśyam.

[3] Cp. "The things which are seen are temporal, but the things which are not seen are eternal."

[4] Dṛśyatvam asatyatvaṁ ca aviśiṣṭam ubhayatra (S.B. on Gauḍapāda's *Kārikā*, ii. 4.

[5] Cp. Asti bhāti priyaṁ rūpaṁ nāma cety aṁśapañcakam
Ādyaṁ trayaṁ brahmarūpaṁ jagadrūpaṁ tato dvayam.
See Appaya Dīkṣita's *Siddhāntaleśa*, ii.

[6] Traikālikādyabādhyatvam.

[7] Kālatrayasattāvat. Cp. *Viṣṇu Purāṇa*:—

"Yat tu kālāntareṇāpi nānyasaṁjñām upaiti vai
Pariṇāmādisaṁbhūtaṁ tad vastu. . . ." (ii. 13. 95).

The real is that which even by the passage of time does not acquire a different designation derived from change of form and the like. Cp. the words of the Christian Liturgy: "As it was in the beginning, is now, and ever shall be, world without end."

sublated by true knowledge.[1] The recognition of a higher condemns the lower to the level of unreality. The objects of the world are changeable. They never are, but always become. Nothing that changes is real, which is eternal transcendent being. Says Śaṁkara: "What is eternal cannot have a beginning, and whatever has a beginning is not eternal."[2] Our understanding is not satisfied with objects that change, only those that do not change are real.[3] What is real cannot not be. If anything is real in saṁsāra, it cannot cease to be real in mokṣa. In this sense, the changing world is not real. The world is neither pure being nor pure non-being. Pure being is not an existence nor an item of the world process. Pure non-being is not a valid concept, for were it so, absolute nothingness would be an entity, and that which is by hypothesis the negation ot all existence will have to be granted existence. Nothing is not a thing. What exists is becoming, which is neither being nor non-being, since it produces effects.[4] At no point can the world reach being and stop becoming. The world is bound up in the historical process of struggling to become the infinite, though it never attains infinity. There is always something beyond the created universe.[5] The realisation of the Ātman is the final end (avasāna) of all worldly activities,[6] which is not reached so long as the world as world persists. The relation of Īśvara to the māyā world is beginningless (anādi). The relation of being and non-being is one of exclusion of contradiction, and the former tries to overcome non-being, negate it by transforming into being. This is the aim of the process of becoming presided over by Īśvara, who is ever active in pushing non-being out of existence and bringing

[1] Jñānaikanivartyatvam. "As soon as consciousness of non-duality arises in us, the transmigratory state of the individual soul and the creative quality of Īśvara vanish at once, the whole phenomenon of plurality which springs from wrong knowledge being sublated by perfect knowledge" (S.B., iii. 2. 4; *Ātmabodha*, vi and vii).

[2] Nahi nityaṁ kenacid ārabhyate, loke yad ārabdhaṁ tad anityam (S.B., Tait. Up., Introduction).

[3] Yadviṣayā buddhir na vyabhicarati tat sat; yadviṣayā buddhir vyabhicarati tad asat. See also S.B., i. 1. 4; Tait. Up., ii. 1.

[4] Arthakriyākāri. Cp. Sureśvara: "Mere nonentity is not amenable to proof, either as separate from or identical with entity. Hence entity alone can give rise to practice" (*Vārttika*, p. 927).

[5] S.B., iv. 3. 14.

[6] S.B.G., xviii. 50.

forward an eternal procession of existence out of it; but, at the logical level, it is an impossible feat to force non-being into the equivalence of being. The world process is engaged in this interminable task. From the beginning to the end of things it is always a question of light invading the realm of darkness. We may push it farther and farther. It only recedes, but never disappears. The relation of being to non-being in the finite world is not one of exclusion but one of polar opposition. The ideas are at once antithetic and correlative. Neither of them attains actuality except through its contrast with the other. However much the one may penetrate the other or be penetrated by it, the distinction and contrast are always there, so that everything in the world is unstable and doomed to be fugitive. Even the highest principle in the world process, the personal God, has in him the shadow of non-being. Brahman alone is pure being, possessing whatever there is of reality in all things, without their limitations or elements of non-being. Whatever is different from it is unreal.[1] The nature of saṁsāra is always to become what it is not, to transform itself by transcending itself. "The world neither is nor is not, and so its nature is indescribable."[2] While it is different from being and non-being,[3] it shares the characters of both.[4] All finite things, as Plato says, are made up of being and non-being.[5] The bewildering mass of phenomenal diversity must belong to reality, for there is nothing else in which it can be, and yet it is not reality. So it is said to be a phenomenon or appearance of reality.[6] All finite existence is, in the words of Bosanquet, "the great ultimate contradiction of the finite-infinite nature." Heaven and earth shall pass away, our body decays, our senses change and our empirical egos are built up before our eyes. None of these is ultimately real. The abstract expression of this phenomenality of the world is māyā.

[1] Brahmabhinnaṁ sarvam mithyā brahmabhinnatvāt (*Vedāntaparibhāṣā*)

[2] Tattvānyatvābhyām anirvacanīyā. . . . Cp. Plotinus, *Enneads*, iii. 6, 7. McKenna's E.T., vol. ii, p. 78.

[3] Sadasadvilakṣaṇa.

[4] Sadasadātmaka.

[5] Satyānṛte mithunīkṛtya (S.B., Introduction).

[6] Vikalpo na hi vastu (Śaṁkarānanda on B.G., iv. 18).

XXX

The Doctrine of Māyā

Let us now try to understand the significance of the doctrine of māyā,[1] which is the chief characteristic of the Advaita system. The world is regarded as māyā, since it cannot be accepted as real for reasons stated in the previous section. What is the relation between the real Brahman and the unreal world? For Śaṁkara, the question is an illegitimate one, and so impossible of answer. When we intuit the absolute Brahman, the question of the nature of the world and its relation to Brahman does not arise, for the truth which disarms all discussion is seen as a fact. If we take our stand on logic, then there is no pure Brahman which requires to be related to the world. It is because we shift our standpoint in the course of the argument that the problem arises. For an imaginary difficulty there cannot be any real solution. Again, a relation presupposes two distincts, and if Brahman and the world are to be related, they should be regarded as

[1] In the Ṛg-Veda the word māyā occurs frequently, and is used generally to indicate the supernatural power attributed to the gods, especially to Varuṇa, Mitra and Indra. In many ancient hymns, māyā is praised as a world-sustaining power (R.V., iii. 38. 7; ix. 83. 3; i. 159. 4; v. 85. 5). Māyā in the sense of deception and cunning is the special prerogative of the asuras, against whom the devas wage continual warfare. We come across a different signification in the famous verse of the R.V. (vi. 47. 18) where Indra, by his supernatural power, is said to assume various forms:

Rūpaṁ rūpam pratirūpo babhūva
Tad asya rūpam praticakṣaṇāya
Indro māyābhiḥ pururūpa īyate
Yuktā hyasya harayaḥ śatā daśa.

'In every form has he been imagined, and all these are only to be viewed as his form. In many forms Indra wanders through his māyā or wonderful powers; harnessed are his ten-times-hundred horses." Māyā here means the power to transform oneself or assume strange forms. R.V., x. 54. 2, reads: "When grown to fulness by bodily form thou didst wander among mankind proclaiming thy strength, O Indra. Then all thy battles, of which men tell, were but a product, a creation of māyā. For never hast thou yet, either to-day or in former times, found an enemy." The deeds of Indra were products of a sportive impulse. In the *Praśna Up.* (i. 16) the term māyā is used almost in the sense of illusion. In the Śvet. Up. (iv. 10) and the B.G. (iv. 5–7; xviii. 61) we have the conception of a personal God who has the power of māyā.

distinct, but the Advaita holds that the world is not other than Brahman. Śaṁkara distinguishes between the scientific principle of causality (kāryakāraṇatva) and the philosophical principle of non-difference (ananyatva). Brahman and the world are non-different,[1] and so the question of the relation between the two is an inadmissible one. The world has its basis in Brahman.[2] But Brahman is and is not identical with the world. It is, because the world is not apart from Brahman; it is not, because Brahman is not subject to the mutations of the world. Brahman is not the sum of the things of the world. If we separate Brahman and the world, we cannot bind them except loosely, artificially and externally. Brahman and the world are one and exist as reality and appearance. The finite is the infinite, hidden from our view through certain barriers. The world is Brahman since, if Brahman is known, all questions of the world disappear. These questions arise simply because the finite mind views the world of experience as a reality in and by itself. If we know the nature of the Absolute, all finite forms and limits fall away. The world is māyā, since it is not the essential truth of the infinite reality of Brahman.

Śaṁkara asserts that it is impossible to explain through logical categories the relation of Brahman and the world. "The real is never known to have any relation with the unreal."[3] The world somehow exists and its relation to Brahman is indefinable (anirvacanīyā). Śaṁkara takes up the different attempts at explanation and finds them all unsatisfactory. To say that the infinite Brahman is the cause of the finite world and creates it, is to admit that the infinite is subject to the limitations of time. The relation of cause and effect cannot be applied to the relation of Brahman and the world, since cause has meaning only in relation to the finite modes of being where there is succession. We

[1] Ataś ca kṛtsnasya jagato brahmakāryatvāt tad ananyatvāt (S.B., ii. 1. 20).

[2] Cp. with this Spinoza's theory of causality. By calling God the immanent cause of the totality of finite things in the world he reduces the causal relation to one of substance and attribute. The relation which *natura naturans* or God bears to *natura naturata* or the universe, is analogous to that which the idea of geometrical figure bears to the various inferences which can be drawn from it. To Spinoza God and the world are correlates as much as the equality of angles in a triangle and that of the sides.

[3] Na hi sadasatoḥ saṁbandhaḥ (S.B. on Māṇḍ. Up., ii. 7).

cannot say that Brahman is the cause and the world is the effect, for this would be to distinguish Brahman from the world and make it into a thing related to another thing. Again, the world is finite and conditioned, and how can the infinite unconditioned be its cause? If the finite is the limited and the transitory, then the infinite, as the limit of the finite, is itself finite and not infinite. It is difficult to conceive how the infinite comes out of itself into the finite. Does the infinite come out at a particular instant of time under the necessity to become finite? Śaṁkara supports Gauḍapāda's theory of ajāti, or non-evolution. The world is not evolved or produced, but seems to be so, on account of limited insight. The world is non-different from (ananya), non-independent (avyatirikta) of Brahman. "The effect is the manifested world beginning with ākāśa; the cause is the highest Brahman. With this cause, in the sense of the highest reality, the effect is identical, having no existence beyond it."[1] It is a case of identity, or, in empirical terms, eternal co-existence, and not temporal succession, where alone cause as a force determines the order of events. The inmost self of the world is Brahman. If it seems to be independent of Brahman, then we must say that it is not what it appears to be.[2] Nor can we ascribe action to the infinite, since all action implies an end to be realised, an object to be achieved. If it is said that the Absolute is manifesting itself in the finite, Śaṁkara would say that it is wrong to hold that the finite manifests the Absolute. Whether there is the finite or not, the Absolute is always manifesting itself even as the sun is always shining. If we sometimes do not see the light of the sun, it is no fault of the sun. The Absolute always abides in its own nature. We cannot draw a distinction between the being of the Absolute and its expression. The one is the other. The analogy of the seed manifesting itself in the form of the tree is inapplicable, since organic growth and development are temporal processes. To apply temporal categories to the eternal is to reduce it to the level of an empirical object

[1] "Kāryam ākāśādikam bahuprapañcaṁ jagat, kāraṇam paraṁ brahma, tasmāt kāraṇāt paramārthato 'nanyatvaṁ vyatirekeṇābhāvaḥ kāryasyāvagamyate" (S.B., ii. 1. 14).

[2] See S.B., ii. 1. 14; ii. 3. 30; ii. 3. 6.

or phenomenon. To represent God as dependent for self-expression on creation is to represent him as exclusively immanent. Śaṁkara does not accept the view of pariṇāma, or transformation. Does the whole or only a part of Brahman change into the world ? If it is the whole, then Brahman lies before our eyes as the world, and there is nothing transcendent which we have to seek. If it is a part that is transformed into the world, then Brahman is capable of being partitioned. If anything possesses parts, members or differences, then it is not eternal.[1] Scripture holds that Brahman is devoid of parts (niravayava).[2] When once Brahman becomes partially or totally the substance of the world, it is no longer its substance and no longer independent. If the Absolute grows and develops along with the evolution of the historical process of becoming, if some contributions are made to the life and growth of the Absolute by our actions, then the Absolute becomes relative. Yet if the Absolute abolishes all distinctions and swallows up the world of becoming, then the determinations of quality and quantity in the universe have no meaning for life. The relation of Brahman to the world is not analogous to that of a tree to its branches, or the sea to its waves, or clay to the vessels made of it, since all these employ intellectual categories of whole and part, substance and attribute. The relation between Brahman and the souls, which are both devoid of parts, cannot be either external (saṁyoga) or internal (samavāya). Do the souls inhere in Brahman or Brahman in the souls ? Every attempt to bring Brahman into connection with the world of becoming ends in failure. The relation of the finite world to the infinite spirit is a mystery for human understanding. Every religious system holds that the finite is rooted in the infinite, and there is no breach of continuity between the two, and yet no system till to-day has logically articulated the relation between the two.[3] We cannot construe to ourselves the way in which the realm of appearances is bound up with the Absolute.

[1] S.B., ii. 1. 26.

[2] Śvet. Up., vi. 19 ; Muṇḍ. Up., ii. 1–2 ; Bṛh., ii. 4. 12 ; iii. 8. 8.

[3] S.B., ii. 1. 24–26. " To show how and why the universe is, so that finite existence belongs to it, is utterly impossible. That would imply an understanding of the whole not practicable for a mere part." " That experience should take place in finite centres and should wear the forms

Progress in knowledge may enable us to describe the phenomena which make up the objective world with ever greater detail and more accuracy, but the rise of the finite world out of the bosom of the infinite, the explanation of the historical process of saṁsāra is quite beyond us. However long the chain of our reasoning may be, however many its links, we reach a point where elucidation stops and nothing is left for us but to admit a fact capable of no further deduction. The word "māyā" registers our finiteness and points to a gap in our knowledge. The magician produces a tree before us from out of nothing. The tree *is* there, though we cannot explain it, and so we call it māyā. The much abused analogy of the rope and the snake is employed by Śaṁkara to illustrate the difficulty of the world problem. The riddle of the rope is the riddle of the universe. Why does the rope appear as the snake, is a question which schoolboys raise and philosophers fail to answer. The larger question of the appearance of Brahman as the world is more difficult. We can only say that Brahman appears as the world, even as the rope appears as the snake.[1] The relation between Brahman and Īśvara is a special application of the general problem of the relation between Brahman and the world.

Śaṁkara brings out that the world, though it hangs on Brahman, does not affect Brahman, by distinguishing that kind of causality where the cause without undergoing any change produces the effect, as vivartopādāna from pariṇāmopādāna, where the cause is itself transformed in producing the effect. Vivarta literally means a turning round, a perversion.

of finite thisness is in the end inexplicable." "How there can be such a thing as appearance we do not understand" (*Appearance and Reality*, pp. 204, 226, 413). According to Green, there is an eternal consciousness which is essentially timeless and perfect, and other finite consciousnesses which are incomplete, imperfect and temporal. The relation between the two, Green admits, is incapable of explanation. To ask why a perfect consciousness should go on making innumerable imperfect copies of itself is to ask why reality is what it is—a question which in the nature of things cannot be answered. See also I.P., p. 186. Cp. Schiller: "It may reasonably be contended that the whole question (of creation) is invalid because it asks too much. It demands to know nothing less than how reality came to be at all, how fact is made absolutely. And this is more than any philosophy can accomplish or need attempt" (*Studies in Humanism*).

[1] Māyāmātraṁ hy etad yat paramātmano 'vasthātrayātmanāvabhāsanaṁ rajjvā iva sarpādibhāvena. . . . (S.B., ii. 1. 9).

Brahman is that of which the vivarta, or perversion, is the world of space, etc. Vivarta signifies the appearance of the absolute Brahman as the relative world of space and time. The original is, however, Brahman, of which the world may be regarded as a translation at the plane of space-time. As the translation is made for us, the original does not depend for its existence on the translation. The world of multiplicity is an aspect which reality takes for us, though not for itself. We have pariṇāma or transformation, when the milk is changed into curds, and vivarta or appearance, when the rope appears as the snake.[1] The different illustrations used by Śaṁkara of the rope and the snake, the shell and the silver, the desert and the mirage, are intended to indicate this one-sided dependence of the effect on the cause and the maintenance of the integrity of the cause. In the case of transformation, the cause and the effect belong to the same order of reality, while in that of appearance the effect is of a different order of being from the cause.[2] The world resides in Brahman even as the illusion of a snake is said to reside in the rope.

There are other interpretations of the doctrine of māyā to be met with in the Advaita treatises.[3] Māyā cannot be different from Brahman, which has no second. The universe is not due to any addition to Brahman from some other source of reality, for nothing can be added to that which is already perfect. It is therefore due to non-being. The process of the world is due to a gradual deprivation of reality. Māyā is used as the name of the dividing force, the finitising principle, that which measures out the immeasurable and creates forms in the formless.[4] This māyā is a feature of the central reality, neither identical with nor different from it. To give it an independent place would be to accept a fundamental

[1] S.B., ii. 1. 28.

[2] Pariṇāmo nāma upādānasamasattākakāryāpattiḥ; vivarto nāma upādānaviṣamasattākakāryāpattiḥ (*Vedāntaparibhāṣā*, i.)

[3] S.B., Tait. Up., ii. 6.

Nāsadrūpā na sadrūpā māyā naivobhayātmikā
Sadasadbhyām anirvācyā mithyābhūtā sanātanī.
(*Sūrya Purāṇa*, quoted in S.P.B., i. 26.)

[4] Eka eva parameśvaraḥ kūṭasthanityo vijñānadhātur avidyayā māyayā māyāvivad anekathā vibhāvyate, nānyo vijñānadhātur asti (S.B., i. 3. 19).

dualism. It is wrong to trace back to the eternal the schism of which we are conscious in the world of experience. The moment we try to link up māyā with Brahman, the latter becomes transformed into Īśvara, and māyā denotes the śakti, or the energy of Īśvara. Īśvara, however, is not in any manner affected by his māyā. If māyā exists, it will constitute a limit to Brahman; if it does not exist, even the appearance of the world cannot be accounted for. It is real enough to produce the world and not real enough to constitute a limit to Brahman. It is neither real as the Brahman nor unreal as the flower of the sky.[1] Whatever we may call it, illusive or real, it is necessary to account for life. It is an eternal power of God. The author of *Saṁkṣepaśārīraka* holds that Brahman is the material cause of the universe through the intervention of māyā, which is the essential operating condition. It is, however, regarded as a product of Brahman, a mode of Brahman's activity. It is essentially present in the world (anugata) and determines its existence (kāryasattāniyāmikā). Māyā is not a substance (dravyam), and so cannot be regarded as the material cause (upādānam). It is only a *modus operandi* (vyāpāra) which, coming itself from the material cause (Brahman), brings about the material product, *i.e.* the world.[2] According to this writer, māyā is the finitising process belonging to Brahman, and has the two properties of āvaraṇa or hiding the truth, and vikṣepa or misrepresenting it.[3] While the first is mere negation of knowledge, the second is positive generation of error. We not only do not perceive the Absolute but we apprehend something else in its place. Māyā evolves a variety of names and forms, which in their totality is the jagat or the universe. It also conceals the eternal Brahman under this aggregate of names and forms.

Māyā has the two functions of concealment of the real and the projection of the unreal. The world of variety screens us from the real.

> Some think Creation's meant to show him forth,
> I say it's meant to hide him all it can,[4]

---

[1] S.B., i. 4. 3.
[2] Tajjanyatve sati, tajjanyajanako vyāpāraḥ.
[3] See *Vedāntasāra*, iv.
[4] Browning: *Bishop Blougram's Apology.*

Since māyā is thus deceptive in character,[1] it is called avidyā or false knowledge. It is not mere absence of apprehension but positive error. When this activity is attributed to Brahman, the latter becomes Īśvara. "The one motionless, unconditioned, then became by its own power of māyā, that which is known as maker."[2]

Māyā is the energy of Īśvara, his inherent force, by which he transforms the potential into the actual world. His māyā, which is unthinkable, transforms itself into the two modes of desire (kāma) and determination (saṁkalpa). It is the creative power of the eternal God, and is therefore eternal; and by means of it the supreme Lord creates the world. Māyā has no separate dwelling-place. It is in Īśvara even as heat is in fire. Its presence is inferred from its effects.[3] Māyā is identified with the names and forms which, in their unevolved condition, inhere in Īśvara, and in their developed state constitute the world. In this sense it is synonymous with prakṛti.[4] Īśvara has less of reality than absolute being, and the other objects represent an increasing deprivation of reality. At the bottom of the scale we get something which has no positive qualities to be deprived of, that from which nothing more can be taken away, which, in a word, is there, but is there as not-being, a nothingness which rises like a blank wall where reality ends. It is not a part or a product of universal evolution, but is the unmanifested principle of multiplicity and deprivation, which is the basis of all evolution. The supreme Īśvara during creation imposes on the formless and the unqualified those forms and qualities which it possesses in itself. "This undeveloped principle is sometimes denoted by the term 'ākāśa,'[5] sometimes by the term akṣara,[6] or the indestructible, sometimes as māyā."[7] It is the material

[1] For māyā as deceit, see *Milanda*, iv. 8. 23.

[2] Aprāṇaṁ śuddham ekaṁ samabhavad atha tan māyayā kartṛsaṁjñam (*Śataślokī*, p. 24). Cp. *Pañcadaśī*, x. 1.

[3] Nistattvā kāryagamyāsya śaktir māyāgniśaktivat (*Pañcadaśī*).

[4] Cp. Īśvarasya māyāśaktiḥ prakṛtiḥ (S.B., ii. 1. 14). See also Śvet. Up., iv. 10; S.B.G., Introduction and vii. 4; S.P.B., i. 26.

[5] Bṛh. Up., iii. 8. 11.

[6] Muṇḍ., ii. 1. 2.

[7] Śvet., iv. 1. See S.B., i. 4. 3. "Avidyātmikā hi bījaśaktir avyaktaśabdanirdeśyā, tad etad avyaktaṁ kvacid ākāśaśabdanirdiṣṭaṁ kvacid akṣaraśabdoditaṁ kvacin māyeti sūcitam.

Avyaktanāmni parameśaśaktir anādyavidyā triguṇātmikā parā
Kāryānumeyā sudhiyaiva māyā yayā jagat sarvam idam prasūyate.

(*Vivekacūḍāmaṇi*, p. 108.)

substratum[1] in the creation of the world. It brings forth the universe in a natural order of sequence by undergoing mutations. It forms the causal body of Īśvara. Unlike the pradhāna of the Sāṁkhya, it is not independent of God.[2] It is a limitation which Īśvara imposes on himself. In prakṛti is centred the possibility of the world, even as the potentiality of the future tree is contained in the seed. This prakṛti, possessing the three guṇas,[3] cannot be described as either the self of Īśvara or different from it. It exists even in pralaya, dependent on the supreme Lord, as seed force (bījaśakti). Māyā or prakṛti becomes in the Purāṇas the loving consort of Īśvara and the principal instrument in the act of creation.[4] The world of māyā is the play of the mother of things ever eager to cast herself into infinite forms.[5] It follows that for Īśvara, or the subject, who is ever associated with the object, the universe is a necessity. God is in need of the universe, which is a necessary phase of the self-realisation of God, in Hegel's phrase.

We may bring together the different significations in which the term māyā is used in the Advaita Philosophy. (1) That the world is not self-explanatory shows its phenomenal character, which is signified by the word māyā. (2) The problem of the relation between Brahman and the world has meaning for us who admit the pure being of Brahman from the intuitive standpoint and demand an explanation of its relation to the world, which we see from the logical standpoint. We can never understand how the ultimate reality is related to the world of plurality, since the two are heterogeneous, and every attempt at explanation is bound to fail. This incomprehensibility is brought out by the term māyā. (3) If Brahman is to be viewed as the cause of the world, it is only in the sense that the world rests on Brahman, while the latter is in no way touched by it, and the world which rests on Brahman is

[1] Cp. with the *materia prima* of the Thomistic Philosophy.

[2] Na . . . svatantraṁ tattvam (S.B., i. 2. 22).

[3] From nāyā with tamas predominant in it the five elements are said to be produced; from the same with the sattva dominant in it arise the five organs of perception as well as the inner organ nāyā with rajas in it. From the five organs of action, and from their combination the five prānas. These together constitute the liṅga, or sūkṣma śarīra.

[4] Cp. also Bṛh. Up., i. 4. 3.

[5] Cp. Tvam asi parabrahmamahiṣi (*Ānandalaharī*).

called māyā. (4) The principle assumed to account for the appearance of Brahman as the world is also called māyā. (5) If we confine our attention to the empirical world and employ the dialectic of logic, we get the conception of a perfect personality, Īśvara, who has the power of self-expression. This power or energy is called māyā. (6) This energy of Īśvara becomes transformed into the upādhi, or limitation, the unmanifested matter (avyākṛta prakṛti), from which all existence issues. It is the object through which the supreme subject Īśvara develops the universe.[1]

XXXI

Avidyā

The concept of māyā is intimately related with that of avidyā. There are passages in Śaṁkara where the world of experience is traced to the force of avidyā. The cause of the appearance of the world is to be sought in the nature of the intellect, and not in that of Brahman. Brahman exists entire and undivided in the smallest object, and the appearance of plurality is due to the intellect which works according to the laws of space, time and causality. In the Introduction to his commentary on the *Brahma Sūtra* Śaṁkara points out how avidyā is the force that launches us into the dream of life. The tendency to confuse the transcendental and the empirical standpoints, or adhyāsa, however erroneous, is natural to the human mind. It is the result of our cognitive mechanism.[2] As we perceive by our senses sound and colour, while the reality is mere vibrations, even so we accept the variegated universe for the reality of Brahman, of which it is the effect. Through an examination of the subjective side of experience, Śaṁkara argues that we cannot attain to a knowledge of reality, so long as we are subject to avidyā, or the logical mode of thinking. Avidyā is the fall from intuition,

[1] Cp. Īśvarasyātmabhūte ivāvidyākalpite nāmarūpe tattvānyatvābhyām anirvacanīye saṁsāraprapañcabījabhūte . . . īśvarasya māyā śaktiḥ prakṛtir iti ca śrutismṛtyor abhilapyete (S.B., ii. 1. 14). See also S.B., i. 4. 3; ii. 2. 2.

[2] S.B., Introduction.

the mental deformity of the finite self that disintegrates the divine into a thousand different fragments. Darkness is the privation of light. Avidyā is what Deussen calls "the innate obscuration of our knowledge,"[1] the twist of the mind which makes it impossible for it to see things except through the texture of space-time-cause. It is not conscious dissimulation, but the unconscious tendency of the finite mind, which lives by the imperfect standards of the world. It is the negative power which shuts us from our godlike existence. The appearance of Brahman as the world is due to our avidyā, even as the appearance of the rope as the snake is due to defective senses. When we see the rope as it is, the snake becomes unreal. When we see the reality of Brahman, the appearance of the world will flee away. That which is proved to be an unreality by a higher experience cannot be connected with reality except through a confusion of standpoints. The appearances stand transfigured in the Absolute. If we are asked to connect the image of the snake with the reality of the rope, we say that no connection is possible between what is and what is not. We have only to blame the eye for the image. When we see the rope as rope, there is an end of the matter, and we say that the rope *appeared* as the snake. Relativity has no cause except defective insight. It operates no farther than the fact that we see things, while there is only caitanya, or pure consciousness. Avidyā is either absence of knowledge or doubtful and erroneous knowledge. It is not simply negative, but is also positive in character (bhāvarūpa). When Śaṁkara argues that the existence of avidyā is patent to all, he means only that there is the fact of finiteness. It is said that everybody has the feeling that he does not know everything.[2] The evidence for its existence is universal in scope, since all finite minds share the deficiency.

Avidyā in the Upaniṣads is only ignorance as distinct from knowledge possessed by the individual subject.[3] In Śaṁkara it becomes the logical way of thinking, which constitutes the finiteness of the human mind. It is not a nonentity like the son of a barren woman, since it appears and is experienced

[1] D.S.V.. p. 302.
[2] Aham ajña ityādyanubhavāt. See *Vedāntasāra*, p. iv.
[3] See Chān. Up., i. 1. 10; Bṛh. Up., iv. 3. 20; iv. 4. 3.

by all of us; nor is it an entity, real and absolute, since it is destroyed by intuitional knowledge. If it were non-being, it could not produce anything; if it were being, what it produces must also be real and not phenomenal. "It is neither real nor phenomenal, nor is it both."[1] Though its origin and explanation are beyond our reach, the conditions of its operation through the mental categories are discernible. Whence comes this avidyā, the source of all ignorance, sin and misery? Avidyā cannot be the cause of individuality, for it cannot exist unless there are individuals. If it is the cause of individuality, it must exist independen of that, *i.e.* must belong to the one ultimate reality, Brahman. But avidyā cannot belong to Brahman, whose nature is one of eternal light repugnant to avidyā.[2] It cannot reside in Brahman, as Sarvajñātmamuni thinks; it cannot reside in the individual, as Vācaspati believes.[3] To say that Brahman modified is the seat of avidyā is useless, for the question is, how can Brahman be modified apart from avidyā? Rāmānuja urges that we have to assume a different avidyā for each soul, since, otherwise, the release of one soul will mean the release of all. It follows that avidyā takes account of the distinction of the souls, which it does not cause and therefore cannot explain. We have here circular reasoning.[4] Śaṁkara escapes from

[1] *Vivekacūḍāmaṇi*, p. 3.

[2] "God is light, and in him is no darkness at all" (1 John v; 2 Cor. vi. 14).

[3] See Śrīdhara's *Nyāyakaṇdalī*, R.B., ii. 1. 15.

[4] R.B., ii. 1. 15; S.P.S., i. 21–24; v. 13–19, 54.

Pārthasārathi Miśra puts the objection thus: "Is this avidyā misapprehension or something else which causes misapprehension? If the former, whose (is this avidyā)? It cannot be Brahman's, whose nature is pure knowledge. In the sun there is no place for darkness. It cannot belong to the souls, since they are not distinct from Brahman. As avidyā cannot exist, no more can a second thing, the cause thereof. Besides, for those who regard misapprehension or cause of it as something additional to Brahman, non-duality vanishes. Whence arose Brahman's avidyā? There is no other, since Brahman is the sole entity. If it be said that it is natural to Brahman, how can ignorance be the nature of him whose nature is knowledge?" Kim bhrāntijñānam? kiṁ vā bhrāntijñānakāraṇabhūtaṁ vastvantaram? yadi bhrāntiḥ sā kasya? na brahmaṇas tasya svacchavidyārūpatvāt, na hi bhāskare timirasyāvakāśaḥ saṁbhavati; na jīvānām; teṣām brahmātirekeṇābhāvāt. Bhrāntyabhāvād eva ca, tatkāraṇabhūtaṁ vastvantaram apy anupapannam eva. Brahmātirekeṇa bhrāntijñānaṁ tatkāraṇaṁ cā'bhyupagacchatām advaitahāniḥ, kiṁkṛtā ca brahmaṇo 'vidyā, na hi kāraṇāntaram asti. Svābhāvikīti cet, katham

the difficulty by declaring avidyā to be inexplicable. The question is meaningless in Śaṁkara's metaphysics. We cannot make a transcendent use of an empirical category. We know that there is avidyā, and the question of its cause is meaningless, even as the question of the rise of finite spirits is. If we can understand the relation of Ātman to avidyā, we must be beyond the two.[1] Again, if avidyā were an essential property of the Ātman, the latter could never get rid of it; but the Ātman does not take in or part with anything whatsoever. It cannot belong to any finite being, whether he be God or man, since the latter must first be created in order that his avidyā may be possible. So his creation cannot be due to his or anyone else's avidyā. The individualisation of Brahman, the rise of finite spirits, cannot be due to the avidyā characteristic of finite life. It is an occurrence due to divine activity. But how avidyā and Brahman can coexist is just the problem for which we do not have any solution. Śaṁkara says: "We admit that Brahman is not the product of avidyā or is itself deluded, but we do not admit that there is another deluded conscious being (besides Brahman) which could be the producer of the ignorance."[2] According to *Saṁkṣepaśārīraka*, "Undifferenced absolute intelligence is the locus (āśraya) and object (viṣaya) of avidyā."[3] Deussen says: "In reality there is nothing else besides Brahman alone. If we

vidyāsvabhāvam avidyāsvabhāvaṁ syāt? (*Śāstradīpikā*, pp. 313–4; also p. 113).

Kumārila argues against the Advaita thus: "If Brahman is self-established and of pure form, there is nothing else beside it. What brings about the activity of avidyā which resembles a dream? If you say that some other causes it, or that it is different from Brahman, then non-dualism disappears; if it were its nature, then it can never be destroyed."

Svayaṁ ca śuddharūpatvād abhāvāc cānyavastunah
Svapnādivad avidyāyāḥ pravṛttis tasya kiṁkṛtā.
Anyenopaplave 'bhīṣte dvaitavādaḥ prasajyate
Svābhāvikīm avidyāṁ tu nocchettuṁ kiñcid arhati.
(S.V., *Saṁbandhākṣepaparihāra*, 84–85.)

1 S.B.G., xiii. 2.

2 S.B. on Bṛh., i. 4. 10. Lakṣmīdhara says in his *Advaitamakaranda*: "How should avidyā touch the self-illumined soul by whose light alone is caused the saying, 'I shine not'? Nevertheless, there does appear in the sky of consciousness some such mist as this, animated by absence of reflection and lasting till the sun of reflection arises" (16–17).

3 i. 319. Āśrayatvaviṣayatvabhāginī nirvibhāgacitir eva kevalā.

imagine that we perceive a transformation (vikāra) of him into the world, a division (bheda) of him into a plurality of individuals, this depends on avidyā. But how does this happen? How do we manage to deceive ourselves into seeing a transformation and a plurality, where in reality Brahman alone is? On this question our authors give no information."[1] They give us no information, simply because "no information" is possible. Critics are ready with the remark: "In this system which maintains that everything transcends explanation, unreasonableness is no objection."[2] It is true that no explanation is possible of the rise of the bewildering force of avidyā, creator of false values, which has somehow come into phenomenal being in spite of the eternal and inalienable purity of the original self-existent Brahman.[3]

XXXII

Is the World an Illusion?

The doctrine of avidyā with its subjective note suggests a misleading view of the nature of the phenomenal world, that it is an illusion, a creation of the mind. Śaṁkara frequently traces the whole plurality of appearances, including that of Īśvara, to avidyā.[4] But the nature of Brahman is

[1] D.S.V., p. 302.

[2] Pārthasārathi Miśra. "Atrānirvacanīyavāde nā'nupapattir dūṣaṇam."

[3] The authors of *Saṁkṣepaśārīraka, Vivaraṇa, Vedāntamuktāvali, Advaitasiddhi* and *Advaitadīpikā* hold that avidyā has Brahman for its basis (āśraya) and object (viṣaya), even as darkness is in the house which it conceals. Vācaspati thinks that avidyā has for its basis jīva and object Brahman. According to the latter view, even Īśvara is the product of jīvā'jñāna, and there must be as many Īśvaras as there are jīvas. There is besides the theory of mutual dependence; the jīva depends on avidyā and avidyā on jīva. So it is said that avidyā has its locus in Brahman, which is not opposed to avidyā. The author of *Vidvanmanorañjanī* discusses this question, especially in view of the Advaita doctrine, that in deep dreamless sleep the individual soul is merged in Brahman; and holds if avidyā admittedly exists, then it can only reside in Brahman. See *Paṇḍit*, September 1872. The śuddhacaitanya is not the contradictory of avidyā, but only vṛtticaitanya. As Vidyāraṇya puts it, through the modification of the inner organ, which assumes the form of Ātman, the avidyā in the Ātman is sublated.

[4] Ekatvam . . . pāramārthikam mithyājñānavijṛmbhitam ca nānātvam (S.B., ii. 1. 14).

not affected in any way, simply because our imperfect knowledge takes it to be so. The moon is not duplicated simply because those of defective vision see two moons. "The whole empirical reality, with its names and forms, which can be defined neither as being nor as non-being, rests upon avidyā; while in the sense of highest reality, Being persists without change or transformation. A change resting merely on words can alter nothing in the indivisibility of the real."[1] When confronted by the difficulties of creation and the finiteness of God, Śaṁkara says: "When by the teaching of non-separateness through sentences like 'That art thou,' the consciousness of non-separateness is awakened, then the wanderings of the soul and the creative function of God cease; for the whole tendency of the world to division springs from false knowledge and is removed by perfect knowledge. Whence then the creation? Whence the responsibility for not having brought forth the good only? For saṁsāra, which has as its characteristics the doing of good and evil, is a misconception produced by non-discrimination of the determination caused by avidyā, and consisting in the aggregate of the instruments of activity formed by names and forms; and this misconception, even like the attachment to division and separation by birth and death, does not exist in the absolute sense."[2] Again: "By that element of plurality which is the creation of avidyā characterised by name and form, which is evolved as well as non-evolved, which is not to be defined either as existing or non-existing, Brahman becomes the basis of this entire changing world, while in its true real nature it remains unchanged beyond the phenomenal universe."[3] This view, when exclusively emphasised, suggests that there is no plurality at all apart from the individual's avidyā. All change and motion, all growth and evolution, all science and speculation, are reduced to dreams, shadows and nothing more. The explanation of Brahman's causality of the world confirms the suspicion. In his anxiety to show that Brahman remains unaffected by the changes of the world,[4]

[1] Cp. S.B., ii. 1. 31; ii. 1. 14; ii. 3. 46; ii. 1. 27.

[2] Cp. also avidyākṛtaṁ kāryaprapañcam. The universe of effects is the product of avidyā (S.B., i. 3. 1).

[3] S.B., ii. 1. 27.

[4] S.B., ii. 1. 28; ii. 1. 9.

Saṁkara says that the world is attributed[1] to Brahman as the snake to the rope. "A man may in the dark mistake a piece of rope for a snake and run away from it, frightened and trembling. Thereon another man may tell him, 'Be not afraid, it is only a rope, not a snake,' and he may then dismiss the fear caused by the imagined snake and stop running. But all the while the presence and the subsequent absence of his erroneous notion as to the rope being a snake make no difference whatever to the rope itself."[2] The stars do not actually twinkle, though they appear to do so. The light they project is quite steady, though the disturbances in the earth's atmosphere through which the light passes so affect our vision as to give them a constantly flickering appearance. Even so the semblance of variableness in Brahman is a fancy occasioned by our distorted vision.[3] Some of the illustrations used by Śaṁkara, when literally interpreted, suggest that all distinction and difference are but a mirage produced by human imagination. Differences are a make-believe of human thought which, like a prism, breaks up the pure unity into difference, where, in truth, the variety and the mind which knows it are both unreal. But it is a mistake to stress metaphors beyond what they are able to bear, and Śaṁkara urges that the illustrations used are intended only to suggest some points of resemblance and not perfect identity.[4]

Many later Advaitins have adopted a subjectivist interpretation of the world. Vācaspati is of opinion that avidyā belongs to the knowing subject, and, like a film over the eye, conceals the nature of the object.[5] Madhusūdana Sarasvatī holds that ignorance is the cause of this illusory world, and, by virtue of this ignorance, we regard Brahman as its material cause.[6] "The apparent universe has its root in the mind (citta) and does not persist when the mind (citta) is abolished."[7] *Citsukhī*, *Advaitasiddhāntamuktāvali* and *Yogavāśiṣṭha*

---

[1] Adhyāropitam.

[2] S.B., i. 4. 6. See also S.B. on *Kaṭha Up.*, iii. 14; iv. 11.

[3] S.B., ii. 3. 46.

[4] S.B., iii. 21. 17–19.

[5] Jīvāśrayam brahmaviṣayam. He thinks that the different forms imposed on Brahman are due to the modifications of the inner organ, and thus has to admit the existence of modifications and their objects.

[6] Asya daityendrajālasya yad upādānakāraṇam
Ajñānaṁ tad upāśritya brahma kāraṇam ucyate.
(*Advaitasiddhi*, p. 238).

[7] Cittamūlo vikalpo 'yam cittābhāve na kaścana (*Vivekacūḍāmaṇi*, p. 407).

make out a strong case for solipsism, and declare that our consciousness gives birth to the world, which sinks into non-being with the cessation of subject-object consciousness.[1]

It is no wonder that the Western critics have adopted a similar view of the Advaita doctrine of the world. Edward Caird had in mind this interpretation of the world when he remarked: "The Brahman religion only rose to a pantheism which was an acosmism, to a unity which was no principle of order in the manifold differences of things, but merely a gulf in which all difference was lost."[2] As this view, which makes a tragic joke of life, renders meaningless many statements of Śaṁkara on the world of experience, and does violence to every canon of sound interpretation, we may here bring together certain considerations which support the phenomenal as against the illusory character of the world.

Avidyā by itself cannot be the cause of the world, since it is as dead as the pradhāna of the Sāṁkhya. Śaṁkara, who criticised the latter view, cannot be expected to support the theory of the creation of the world by avidyā. We have also to bear in mind Śaṁkara's criticism of the Buddhist chain of causation, which starts with avidyā. "Now avidyā is a mental fiction of a conscious subject. It is the first link in the twelve-linked chain of causation, which consequently must be regarded as taking for granted the aggregates of the mind and the body, without, however, showing how they come together."[3] Śaṁkara rejects the theory that nothing exists, neither matter nor mind (śūnyavāda),[4] as well as the

[1] See also S.S.S.S., xii. 17–19. Dṛṣṭisṛṣṭivāda, which holds that the world exists only so long as it is perceived, is upheld by *Yogavāśiṣṭha*.

> Manodṛśyam idaṁ sarvaṁ yat kiñcit sacarācaram,
> Manaso hy unmanībhāvād dvaitaṁ naivopalabhyate.

The whole world of movable and immovable things is the object of manas; by the suppression of it all duality ceases to be perceived. See the chapter on Jīvanmukti in *Yogavāśiṣṭhasāra*. Cp. also *Saṁkṣepaśārīraka*. "Tava cittam ātmatamasā janitam parikalpayaty akhilam eva jagat." *Nṛsiṁhatāpanī Up.*, "cid dhīdam sarvam" (ii. 1. 7).

Tasmād vijñānam evāsti na prapañco na saṁsṛtiḥ (*Liṅga Purāṇa*, quoted in S.P.B., i. 42). It is these that justify the remark of Vijñānabhikṣu: "Etenādhunikānāṁ vedāntibruvāṇām api mataṁ vijñānavādatulyayogakṣematayā nirastam" (S.P.B., i. 43).

[2] *Evolution of Religion*, vol. i, p. 263. For other similar criticisms of Western writers see Kirtikar: *Studies in Vedanta*, ch. ii.

[3] S.B., ii. 2. 19.

[4] S.B., ii. 2. 31.

theory that nothing exists for more moments than one (kṣaṇabhaṅgavāda).[1] The refutation of the Buddhist theory of subjectivism (vijñānavāda) is decisive on the question of the externality of the world to the thinking subject. Existence is not dependent on our mental modes: when the world is said to be of the form of knowledge (jñānasvarūpa), the metaphysical truth is described. Similarly Śaṁkara rejects all attempts to reduce waking experience to the level of dreams.[2] He does not admit that the world is a product of mere avidyā. Avidyā in Śaṁkara is not a mere subjective force, but has an objective reality.[3] It is the cause of the whole material world (pṛthivyādiprapañca) which is common to all (sarvasādhāraṇa). Avidyā is positive in character, an objective force, beginningless [4] and existing both in a gross and subtle form.[5] Practically avidyā, māyā and prakṛti are identified.[6]

Śaṁkara argues that the supreme reality of Brahman is the basis of the world. If Brahman were absolutely different from the world, if the Ātman were absolutely different from the states of waking, dreaming and sleeping, then the repudiation of the reality of the world or the three states cannot lead us to the attainment of truth. We shall then have to embrace nihilism and treat all teaching as purposeless.[7] The illusory snake does not spring out of nothing, nor does it pass into nothing when the illusion is corrected. The root

[1] S.B., ii. 2. 18–21 and 26.

[2] Later Advaitins write as if there were no distinction between the two. Svayamprakāśa, in his commentary on Lakṣmīdhara's *Advaitamakaranda*, says: "As the world of dreams in me is projected by illusion, so is the waking world in me projected by illusion." See *Paṇḍit*, October 1873, p. 128.

[3] A famous verse quoted in *Siddhāntaratnamālā* urges that "the soul, God, pure consciousness, the distinctness of the first two, avidyā and its connection with pure consciousness—these our six are said to be without beginning."

Jīva īśo viśuddhā cit vibhāgaś ca tayor dvayoḥ
Avidyā taccitor yogaḥ ṣaḍ asmākam anādayaḥ.

[4] Anādibhāvarūpam yad vijñānena vilīyate
Tad ajñānam iti prājñā lakṣaṇam saṁpracakṣate.
(*Citsukhī*, i. 13).

[5] Ātmany avidyā sānādiḥ sthūlasūkṣmātmanā sthitā (S.S.S.S., xii. 19).

[6] Cp. Lokācārya: *Tattvatraya*, p. 48, Chowkhaṁba ed.

[7] Yadi hi tryavasthātmavilakṣaṇaṁ turīyam anyat, tatpratipattidvārābhāvāt śāstropadeśānarthakyam śūnyatāpattir vā (S.B. on *Māṇḍ. Up.*, ii. 7).

of the illusion is logical and psychological, and not metaphysical. The pluralistic universe is an error of judgment. Correction of the error means change of opinion. The rope appears as a snake, and when the illusion is over, the snake returns to the rope. So does the world of experience become transfigured in the intuition of Brahman. The world is not so much negated as reinterpreted. The conception of jīvanmukti, the idea of kramamukti, the distinction of values, of truth and error, of virtue and vice, the possibility of attaining mokṣa through the world of experience, imply that there is Reality in appearances; Brahman is in the world, though not as the world. If the world of experience were illusory and unrelated to Brahman, love, wisdom and asceticism could not prepare us for the higher life. In so far as Śaṁkara allows that we can realise the Absolute through the practice of virtue, he allows a significance to it. Unreal the world is, illusory it is not. The jīva is not a mere nonentity, for release is effected through the sublation only of the false self which is opposed to the nature of Ātman. As Vidyāraṇya says: "If the entire individual self were annihilated, release would not be beneficial to men."

If there were not a Brahman, then we could have neither empirical being nor illusion. As Śaṁkara says: "A barren woman cannot be said to give birth to a child either in reality or in illusion." [1] If the world be regarded as baseless, as not rooted in any reality, as having its origin in non-being, then we shall have to repudiate all reality, even that of Brahman.[2] The world has the real for its basis (āspadam), for "not even the mirage can exist without a basis." [3] That kind of dream which God creates, and of which God is the substance, is no dream at all.[4] If we are able to penetrate to the real through

[1] S.B. on Gauḍapāda's *Kārikā*, i. 6. See also iii. 28.

[2] Yadi hyasatām eva janma syād brahmaṇo 'sattvaprasaṅgaḥ.

[3] Na hi mṛgatṛṣṇikādayo 'pi nirāspadā bhavanti (S.B.G., xiii. 14). See also S.B. on Chān. Up., vi. 2. 3; Māṇḍūkya Up., i. 7.

[4] In later Advaita, the comparison of the world to a dream has been stretched to the breaking-point. *Advaitamakaranda* says: "In this protracted dream which the world is, projected in that great sleep of ignorance regarding the self, flash forth the glimpses of paradise, emancipation and so forth."

Ātmājñānamahānidrā jṛmbhite 'smiñ jaganmaye
Dīrghasvapne sphuranty ete svargamokṣādivibhramāḥ (18).

this world, it is because the world of appearance bears within it traces of the eternal. If the two are opposed, it will be difficult to regard them even in the relation of the real and the apparent. The world is not the Absolute, though based on it. What is based on the real, and is not the real itself, can only be called the appearance or phenomenon of the real. While the world is not the essential truth of Brahman, it is its phenomenal truth, the manner in which we are compelled to regard the real as it presents itself within our finite experience. But all this does not touch the question of the practical reality of the world.[1]

Śaṁkara's views on mokṣa confirm this view of the world. He urges that mokṣa does not mean the disappearance of the world, since then the world should have disappeared when the first case of mokṣa occurred. If mokṣa should involve the annihilation of plurality, the right way to go about realising it is not to displace avidyā by vidyā but to destroy the world.[2] Śaṁkara distinguishes jīvanmukti, or the state of release, while one is alive, from videhamukti, or the release obtained when the liberated shakes off his body. The presence of the body makes no difference to the state of release, which is in essence one of freedom from worldly bonds. The state of release consists not in the persistence or annihilation of plurality, but in the incapacity of the pluralistic universe to mislead us. For the jīvanmukta obviously the world of plurality, including his own body, does not perish; only he has the right perspective regarding it. In the state of release the world of plurality does not disappear, but is lit up by another light. There is no more the blindness born of desire, which sets and keeps the unhappy victims hunting in vain for what is not to be found in the chain of samsāra. The false ideas of the independence of selves and objects and their

[1] What Berkeley says in another connection holds good of Śaṁkara. "What therefore becomes of the sun, moon and stars? What must we think of houses, rivers, mountains, trees, stones, nay, even of our own bodies? Are all these but so many chimeras and illusions of the fancy? . . . I answer, that by the principles premised we are not deprived of any one thing in nature. Whatever we see, feel, hear, or any wise conceive or understand remains as secure as ever, and is as real as ever. There is a *rerum natura*, and the distinction between realities and chimeras retains its full force" (*Principles of Human Knowledge*, p. 34).

[2] S.B., iii 2. 21.

activities are undermined when the truth of the oneness of self with Brahman is realised.[1] Avidyā is not so much imagination as failure to discriminate (aviveka) between reality and appearance. Śaṁkara does not dispute the obvious fact that we seem to ourselves to be knowing, feeling, willing individuals, but denies the theory founded on these facts that the finite selves are real subjects being actually what they purport to be. The real accepts the phenomenal. Appearances belong to reality. This is the truth suggested by the hypothesis of ananyatva or non-difference, advocated by the Advaita. Rāmānuja criticises it thus: "Those, however, who maintain the non-difference of an effect from its cause, on the ground that the effect is unreal, cannot establish the non-difference they seek to make out, for there can be no identity between what is true and what is false. If it were as they maintain, either Brahman would be unreal or the world would be real."[2] The Advaitin does not maintain that Brahman devoid of all changes is, as such, one with the changing world. Nor does he suggest that the Brahman which sustains the changing world is as unreal as the latter. He holds that the phenomenal world is unreal, *i.e.* has no real existence apart from Brahman. The non-difference (ananyatva) is interpreted by Śaṁkara to be non-existence, as something different from its cause.[3] Vācaspati makes the meaning clear by making out in his *Bhāmatī* that non-difference does not affirm identity, but only denies difference.[4] Discussing the question of causality and its metaphysical truth of identity, Śaṁkara says that the effect is identical with the cause, and not the cause with the effect.[5] While Monism (ekatvam) may swallow up all distinctions and differences, in Advaitism (non-dualism) the gulf between the relative and the absolute is bridged over in a comprehensive

1 Brahmātmadarśinam prati, samastasya kriyākārakaphalalakṣaṇasya vyavahārasyābhāvam (S.B., ii. 1. 14).

2 R.B., ii. 1. 15; 1. 19.

3 Tadvyatirekeṇābhāvaḥ (S.B., ii. 1. 14).

4 Na khalv ananyatvam ity abhedam brūmaḥ kiṁ tu bhedaṁ vyāsedhāma (*Bhāmatī*, ii. 1. 14). In the same spirit the Ṭīkākāra says: "The world is not identical with Brahman, only it has no separate being apart from or independent of its underlying cause." "Kāraṇāt pṛthak sattāśūnyatvaṁ sādhyate, na tv aikyābhiprāyeṇa."

5 S.B., ii. 1. 7.

affirmation. Śaṁkara's interpretation of the Upaniṣad passage, that the modifications of clay have for their reality clay, enforces the truth that the world is substantially Brahman and depends on it. Whenever he denies the reality of effects he qualifies his denial by some such phrase as "different from Brahman" or "different from the cause."[1] Nowhere does he say that our life is literally a dream and our knowledge a phantasm.

Since Śaṁkara repudiates the conception of a concrete universal as the ultimate category, it is thought that he dismisses the world as meaningless. Śaṁkara's Brahman, which has no other, nothing independent of it, seems to be an abstract unity, a sort of lion's den where all that enters is lost. Śaṁkara holds that we cannot construe the relation between Brahman and the world in any logical way, but he is as insistent as any advocate of the theory of the concrete universal that nothing is real apart from the ultimate reality. Though the world and Brahman are not regarded as complementary elements in a whole, they are not set in absolute antagonism. And yet great scholars have rushed to this conclusion.[2] Śaṁkara's view that the problem of the relation of reality and appearance remains for us finite souls a riddle, is the result of greater maturity of thought. We need not condemn human wisdom as illusory if it is unable to lift the veil which covers all ultimate beginnings.

The question is, are the appearances beyond which we have to penetrate to the truly real, actual states of the real, though possessing only a derivative and secondary sort of being, or are they simply the ideas with which the finite mind of man conceives the true reality in accordance with its own nature? In other words, is relative being a true modification of the original reality, or is it a distortion of the genuine being by the finite understanding of man? The former is the view of Rāmānuja, which is akin to the theory of Hegel, who regards

[1] Brahmavyatirekeṇa or Kāraṇavyatirekeṇa (S.B., ii. 2. 3, ii. 1. 14, and Gauḍapāda's *Kārikā*, i. 6).

[2] Deussen's interpretation is well known. Max Müller observes: "It must be clear to everyone who has once mastered the framework of the true Vedānta philosophy as I have here tried to explain it, that there is really but little room in it for psychology or cosmology, nay, even for ethics" (S.S.P., p. 170).

the relative world as a real self-expression of the Absolute. One view of Spinoza's philosophy admits the position.[1] The latter view is represented by the Yogācāra Buddhists, who, like Kant and more thoroughly Schopenhauer, regard the empirical world as a subjective appearance in consciousness, shaped according to the categories of space, time and causality among others. There are some passages in Śaṁkara which lead us to think that he tended to regard the world as a mere human presentation of the genuinely real, and others where he is inclined to make the world of experience objective and independent of the finite individual. To understand Śaṁkara's position, we should consider the relation of avidyā to māyā.

XXXIII

Māyā and Avidyā

When we look at the problem from the objective side, we speak of māyā, and when from the subjective side, we speak of avidyā.[2] Even as Brahman and Ātman are one, so are māyā and avidyā one. The tendency of the human mind to see what is really one as if it were many, is avidyā ; but this is common to all individuals. For when Śaṁkara speaks of avidyā, he means neither yours nor mine. It is an impersonal force which imparts itself to our individual consciousnesses, though it transcends them. For our knowing mechanism operates on things already created, which we perceive but do not make. The world is created by God in the order mentioned in the scriptures and noticed by us.[3] Māyā is both subjective and objective, individual and universal, that out of which the conditioned forms of intelligence and of

[1] Pandit Kokileśvar Śāstri attributes a similar view to Śaṁkara. See his *Advaita Philosophy*.

[2] "We speak of māyā when we have in view its power of producing extraordinary effects and its being subject to the will of the agent; of avidyā, on the other hand, we speak when having in mind its obscuring power and its independence" (*Vivaraṇaprameyasaṁgraha*, i. 1 : *Indian Thought*, vol. i, p. 280).

[3] Śrutidarśitena krameṇa parameśvareṇa sṛṣṭam, ajñātasattāyuktam eva viśvaṁ tadtadviṣayapramāṇāvataraṇe tasya tasya dṛṣṭisiddhiḥ (*Siddhānta-leśa*, ii).

objective existence arise. If that by reason of which the unreal world presents itself as real is purely subjective, then it is mere fancy and cannot be seriously treated as the material cause of the world. If, on the other hand, it is regarded as the material cause of the world, something like the prakṛti of the Sāṁkhya, then it is not mere individual ignorance. The two, the avidyā of the individual and the prakṛti of the Brahman, arise together; neither of them is thinkable apart from the other, so that even avidyā is dependent on the ultimate reality.[1] The phenomenal self and the phenomenal world are mutually implicated facts.[2] Avidyā and prakṛti are co-eternal and belong to the world of experience.[3] The space-time-cause world is the view of reality given to us through avidyā, which is adapted to the purpose of presenting us with such a world. Śaṁkara steers clear of mentalism as well as materialism. We cannot say that nature is a phenomenon of our consciousness, any more than the phenomenal self is a product of nature. The conditions of the possibility of objective experience are also the conditions of the possibility of logical selfhood or self-consciousness. Why do our minds work in this misleading way? Why is there avidyā? Why do we have the space-time-cause world? Why is there māyā? are different ways of stating the same insoluble problem. The Ātman, which is pure knowledge, somehow lapses into avidyā, just as Brahman, which is pure being, turns aside into the space-time-cause world. Through avidyā we reach vidyā, even as through the empirical world we reach Brahman. Why there is this universal and primeval turning aside or perversion, is more than we can say, yet we must hold that neither our logical minds nor the world which it apprehends is an illusion. A phenomenon is not a phantasm. Avidyā and māyā represent the subjective and the objective sides of the one fundamental fact of experience. It is called avidyā, since it is dissolvable by knowledge; but the objective series is called māyā, since it is coeternal with the supreme person-

[1] Cp. Kant, also Bergson's view that the materiality of matter comes into existence with the intellectuality of our consciousness. Intellect and the world as it appears are born together and involve each other.

[2] Cp. *Viṣṇu Purāṇa*: Avidyā pañcaparvaiṣā prādurbhūtā mahātmanaḥ (i. 5. 5).

[3] *Advaitasiddhi*, p. 595.

ality. Śaṁkara admits its existence even in the state of pralaya or destruction. Īśvara, the omniscient, who controls his māyā, has no avidyā, and if Śaṁkara here and there lends countenance to a different theory, it is in the figurative sense that Īśvara has the power which leads to avidyā in the individual. The Sāṁkhya thinkers did not admit the existence of an Īśvara, but the empirical world was traced to a primeval avidyā which is said to be beginningless. Avidyā is a quality of buddhi, and therefore must reside in buddhi, and logic requires that the beginningless nature of avidyā must be attributed to its locus in buddhi also. So buddhi becomes a manifestation of prakṛti, the fundamental object or root-substance. The objectivity of avidyā is thus safeguarded. *Vivaraṇaprameyasaṁgraha* says: "Avidyā no doubt constitutes a defect in consciousness in so far as it impedes the presentation of non-duality and gives rise to the presentation of duality; but, on the other hand, it constitutes an excellence since it forms the material cause, and thus renders possible the cognition of Brahman."[1] The finiteness is necessary before we can reach the infinite.

While Śaṁkara uses avidyā and māyā indiscriminately,[2] later Advaitins draw a distinction between the two. While māyā is the

---

[1] *Indian Thought*, vol. ii, p. 177. Cp. Īśā Up., where we are said to cross death by means of avidyā.

[2] Colonel Jacob is against identifying māyā with avidyā. See *Vedāntasāra*, v. The world of plurality is the product of avidyā. The central forms of the finite mind, space, time and cause, are also the basis (ālambanam) of the phenomenal world. Avidyā is said to produce the māyā names and forms through which the empirical world is produced. Avidyāpratyupasthāpitanāmarūpamāyāveśavaśena (S.B., ii. 2. 2). It is sometimes said that mūlaprakṛti is māyā, while its effect of concealment (āvaraṇa) and projection (vikṣepa) are avidyā. Others are of opinion that mūlaprakṛti with pure sattva is māyā, while that qualified by impure sattva is avidyā. Vikṣepaśaktipradhāna-mūlaprakṛti, or the root substance dominated by the power of projection, is māyā, while āvaraṇaśaktipradhāna-mūlaprakṛti, or the root-substance dominated by the power of concealment, is avidyā. In some works on Advaita, avidyā is said to consist of the three qualities of sattva, rajas and tamas, and is said to constitute the upādhi of Īśvara. This view is not quite satisfactory. If Īśvara has the qualities of rajas and tamas, it is difficult to discriminate him from the jīva. Cp. *Skanda Purāṇa*, where avidyā is regarded as the limiting adjunct of jīva and māyā as the limiting adjunct of the Supreme viewed as Brahmā, Viṣṇu and Maheśvara.

Avidyopādhiko jīvo na māyopādhikaḥ khalu
Māyākāryaguṇacchannā brahmaviṣṇumaheśvarāḥ.

upādhi of Īśvara, avidyā is the upādhi of the individual. According to Vidyāraṇya, the reflection of Brahman in māyā which is made of the pure sattva is Īśvara, while the reflection of Brahman in avidyā, in which rajas and tamas are also present, is the jīva or the individual.[1] Śaṁkara is of this view, since he says: " The highest Brahman becomes the lower Īśvara through association with a pure limitation, when one conceives of it."[2] The products of avidyā are also the powers of Īśvara. The world is the expression of the nature of God; it is also relative to the logical mind of man. The things of the world are said to be both ideas of the Divine mind and presentations of human knowledge. Īśvara is asserted to be the cause of the world,[3] and yet the world belonging to the very self of Īśvara is also said to be fashioned by avidyā.[4] Brahman and māyā are present in the universe and constitute the material cause of the world. The two are entwined together into one string as the real and the appearance based on it.

XXXIV

The World of Nature

Śaṁkara does not stop with a mere description of reality, but examines the realm of phenomena in the light of his theory, formulates the truth which inadequate conceptions contain, and arranges the various phenomena in the order of their varying approximations to truth. He attempts to show how each appearance endeavours to reveal the character of reality which is its ground. Since the inexhaustible Brahman stands at the root of all, continuously higher and higher expressions reveal themselves in the world.[5] " As in the series of beings which descends from man to blades of grass, a successive diminution of knowledge, power and so on is observed—although they have all the common attribute of being animated—so in the ascending series, extending from man up to Hiraṇyagarbha, a gradually increasing manifes-

[1] *Pañcadaśī*, . 16–17.

[2] S.B., Chān. Up., iii. 14. 2. " Viśuddhopādhisaṁbandhāt."

[3] i. 1. 2.

[4] Cp. Avidyātmikā hi sā bījaśaktir avyaktaśabdanirdeśyā parameśvarāśrayā māyā (S.B., i. 4. 3). See also S.B., ii. 1. 14; i. 3. 19. Avidyayā māyayā.

[5] Yady apy eka evātmā sarvabhūteṣu sthāvarajaṅgameṣu gūḍhas tathāpi cittopādhiviśeṣatāratamyād ātmanaḥ kūṭasthanityasyaikarūpasyāpy uttarottaram āviṣṭasya tāratamyam aiśvaryaśaktiviśeṣaiḥ śrūyate (S.B., i. 1. 11).

tation of knowledge, power, etc., takes place." [1] We can distinguish in the world of phenomena: (1) the Īśvara, the dispenser of retribution, (2) the extension of nature, the nāmarūpaprapañca, the name and form world which is the scene of retribution, and (3) the plurality of individual souls, subject to the limitations of individuality, which suffer retribution in each new existence for the works of the previous lives. The plurality of the world arises from the two factors of the enjoyer and the enjoyed, the actors and the stage. The material world is called kṣetra, since it is the environment where the individual souls can act, realising their desires and fruits of their past karma.[2] It is inorganic nature consisting of the five elements. Organic nature consists of bodies in which souls that have entered into the elements and wander as plants, animals, men and gods are housed.[3] The world of saṁsāra consists of various orders of beings with different modes of existence and different worlds answering to conditions necessary for the fulfilment of the experiences of beings. These beings form a graduated scale where the lowest limit is constituted by those whose experiences are most limited and the highest being the gods of the supersensible realm.[4]

The evolution of the universe obeys an order.[5] From prakṛti, the element of objectivity, arises first ākāśa, the prius of space and matter. "The entire world springs from Īśvara, ākāśa being produced first, and later on the other elements in due succession." [6] Ākāśa, one, infinite, imponderable, inert, all-pervasive, is the first product.[7] It stands for both space and an exceedingly fine matter filling all space. However attenuated a substance ākāśa may be, it is yet of the same order as the elements of air, fire, water and earth. Thus Śaṁkara disputes the Buddhist view that ākāśa is a

[1] S.B., i. 3. 30. Yathā hi prāṇitvāviśeṣe 'pi manuṣyādistambaparyanteṣu jñānaiśvaryādipratibandhaḥ pareṇa pareṇa bhūyān bhavan dṛśyate, tathā manuṣyādiṣv eva hiraṇyagarbhaparyanteṣu jñānaiśvaryābhivyaktir api pareṇa pareṇa bhūyasī bhavati. See also S.B., i. 1. 1.

[2] Phalopabhogārtham . . . sarvaprāṇikarmaphalāśrayaḥ (S.B., Muṇḍ. Up., iii. 1. 1).

[3] The Vedic deities also belong to the cosmic process (S.B., i. 2. 17; i. 3. 33).

[4] S.B., i. 3. 10; S.B. on Bṛh. Up., i. 4. 10.

[5] S.B., ii. 1. 24–25.

[6] S.B., ii. 3. 7.

[7] S.B., i. 1. 22; i. 3. 41. See Chān. Up., iii. 14. 3; viii. 14.

negative entity, the mere absence of hindrances.[1] He holds that the negative result is a consequence of its positive nature.[2] From ākāśa other subtle elements (sūkṣmabhūtas) arise in an ascending order.[3] Following the account of the Upaniṣads,[4] Śaṁkara declares that, from ākāśa, air arises. From air comes fire, from fire water, from water earth. Since these five elements are relatively more permanent than their modifications, they are figuratively called immortal, imperishable.[5] Ākāśa has the quality of sound, air of impact and pressure, light of luminosity and heat, water of taste and earth of smell. The relation of the properties to the elements is one of seed to plant. The śabdatanmātra, or the sound-essence, gives rise to ākāśa, which, in its turn, produces the outer form of sound. The tanmātra or the essence, contains in it both the element and its property. We have seen also that there is a graduated scale of the elements. All of them seem to be contained in the ākāśa tanmātra. The whole world takes its rise from ākāśa or sound.

The gross matter of the world (mahābhūtas) is made up of the varying combinations of these subtle rudiments (sūkṣmabhūtas).[6] The gross substance ākāśa manifests sound, air manifests sound and pressure, fire these and in addition light and heat, water has the qualities of taste in addition to the others, and earth has the qualities of other substances and its own special quality of smell. Every object has the properties of sound, tangibility, form, taste and smell. While the subtle rudiments are forms, homogeneous and continuous, of matter without any atomicity of structure, the gross substances are composite, though they are also said to be continuous and devoid of atomic structure.[7] The gross elements

[1] Āvaraṇābhāva (S.B., ii. 2. 22).

[2] Vastubhūtam.

[3] S.B., ii. 3. 8–13.

[4] Tait. Up., ii. 1 ; Chān. Up., vi. 2. 2–3.

[5] Chān. Up., iv. 3. 1 ; Bṛh. Up., i. 5. 22.

[6] In each gross substance all the five subtle elements are found, though in different proportions. Quintuplication (pañcīkaraṇa) is the name given to the process of the combination of the five subtle elements into the gross substances of the world. Śaṁkara does not speak of pañcīkaraṇa, which assumes great importance in later Advaita. See *Vedāntasāra*. He adopts the view of trivṛtkaraṇa, or the mingling of the three elements. This is also the view of Vācaspati.

[7] Atom or aṇu is in the Advaita Vedānta not an ultimate indivisible discrete constituent of matter, but is the smallest conceivable quantum of matter.

give rise by modifications (pariṇāma) to different kinds of things. Matter is constantly undergoing change of state. Changes may also be induced from without. Śaṁkara speaks of a cosmic vibratory motion.[1] All these elements are non-intelligent (acetana), and cannot of themselves bring about their development. The immanence of God in them all is assumed.[2] If the activities of the different elements are sometimes traced to the different Vedic deities, it makes little difference, since the latter only symbolise the functions of Īśvara.

The order of creation is reversed in the case of dissolution.[3] At the time of dissolution the earth becomes water again; water fire, fire air, air becomes ākāśa, and ākāśa re-enters Īśvara.

The psychic organs like manas (inner organ) are assumed by Śaṁkara to be of like nature with the physical elements. The human organism, like other things, is composed of the three elements of earth, water and fire.[4] Manas or the inner organ, prāṇa or the vital breath, and vāk or speech, correspond to earth, water and fire respectively.[5] Śaṁkara is aware that they are sometimes regarded as different in kind from the physical elements and produced before or after them. In any case they, as well as the elements, are in themselves lifeless and are produced as means to ends. Inorganic nature is parārtha, *i.e.* serves a purpose which lies beyond it.[6] There is uniformity of nature in the inorganic world.[7]

When we pass to organic nature, a new principle comes before us, the power of life immanent in certain things, by

[1] Sarvalokaparispandanam.

[2] Parameśvara eva tena tenātmanāvatiṣṭhamāno 'bhidhyāyaṁs taṁ taṁ vikāraṁ sṛjati (S.B., ii. 3. 13). Rāmānuja holds that God's saṁkalpa, or will, is not necessary on every occasion of change. It occurs only once before the rise of ākāśa.

[3] See S.B., ii. 3. 14. Cp. Deussen: "This view is likely to throw some light on the scientific motive of the teaching of the gradual evolution and absorption of the elements, as to which we have no other information; the observation that solids dissolve in water, that water turns into steam through heat, that the flames of fire flicker out into the air, air according to the altitude rarefies more and more into empty space, might lead us to the gradual progression of the dissolution of the world, and, by inversion into its opposite, the creation of the world" (D.S.V., p. 237).

[4] Chān. Up., vi. 2. 2–3.

[5] S.B., ii. 4. 20; iii. 1. 2.

[6] S.B.G., xiii. 22.

[7] S.B., Tait. Up., ii. 8.

which they are able to realise a state of greater perfection, the power of realising an ideal. A stone does not live, since it has no tendency to become perfect, no inward inclination or strength to turn itself into a pillar or a statue. A plant, however, lives. If placed in suitable conditions, it has the power to grow, put forth leaf and blossom, flower and fruit. The animal, again, is capable of a fuller life than the plant. It sees, hears and feels, and also knows vaguely what it is about. Not only does it thrive in favourable conditions, but it goes out to find those conditions. It moves on purpose, while the plant does not. The human being lives a much higher life. He is what Śaṁkara calls a vyutpannacitta, a reflective being, with understanding and will. He has the growing power of the plant, the moving and the sensing powers of the animal, as well as the power to pierce behind the veil, discriminate the eternal from the non-eternal, and choose between good and evil. Men who realise their ambition are the gods. Thus under organic nature we find four classes of beings, gods, men, animals and plants.[1] In the spirit of the Upaniṣads, Śaṁkara admits that plants are places of enjoyment and possess living souls,[2] which have entered into them in consequence of impure deeds. Though they are insensible of enjoyment and suffering, they are said to be atoning for the deeds of their past existence. For Śaṁkara generally recognises three kinds of embodied souls, gods to whom is assigned a condition of infinite enjoyment, men whose lot is a mixed one of happiness and misery, and animals whose share is infinite suffering.[3] In their embodied condition the souls exist together with the vital forces and subtle bodies, and, until they are liberated, these cling to them. The souls are said to be emanations from Brahman as the sparks are from fire; only they return into Brahman, while the sparks do not get back to fire.[4]

[1] S.B., iii. 1. 24. [2] *Ibid.* [3] S.B., ii. 1. 34.
[4] Muṇḍ. Up., ii. 1. 1; Kauṣītaki, iii. 3. 4. 20; Bṛh., ii. 1. 20. See S.B., iii. 1, 20–21; Ait. Up., iii. 3. See also Chān. Up., vi. 2. 2.

XXXV

The Individual Self

The aim of the Vedānta is to lead us from an analysis of the human self to the reality of the one absolute self. The passages of the Vedānta possess this dual application.[1] The individual self is a system of memories and associations, desires and dislikes, of preferences and purposes. Though it may not be possible for us to take in at a single glance this whole system, its general structure and predominant elements are open to our inspection. This system is the vijñānātman, which is subject to change, while the paramātman is free from all change.[2] The jīva is said to be in essence one with the Ātman. That art thou.[3] "Nor is there any force in the objection that things with contrary qualities cannot be identical; for the opposition of qualities can be shown to be false."[4] Śaṁkara distinguishes carefully the self that is implied in all experience from the self which is an observed fact of introspection, the metaphysical subject or the "I" and the psychological subject or the "me." The object of self-consciousness (ahampratyayaviṣaya) is not the pure self, the sākṣin, but the active and enjoying individual (kartṛ) endowed with objective qualities. When the psychologists speak of self, they treat it as an object of introspection. While the Ātman is purely cognitive,[5] our individual consciousness is essentially an active striving towards some end. The sense of activity is for each of us our most intimate experience. This empirical self is the agent of all activities.[6] If activity (kartṛtva) were the essential nature of the soul, there would be no delivery from it—any more than of fire from heat—and as long as man has not freed himself from activity, he has failed to attain his highest end, since activity is essentially painful. "The activity of the soul depends only

[1] S.B., ii. 3. 25.

[2] S.B., i. 3. 24. Cp. also Kaṭha Up., iii. 1; Muṇḍ., iii. 1. 1; Śvet. Up., iv. 6. 7.

[3] Cp. with this the well-known doctrine of the Quakers, according to which there is in every man's inmost being the Inner Light, the radiance by which all dogmas and doctrines are to be judged.

[4] S.B., iv. 1. 3. [5] S.B., ii. 3. 40. [6] S.B, i. 1. 4.

on the qualities of the upādhis being ascribed to it and not to its own nature." [1] The individual soul is essentially an agent; otherwise the Vedic injunctions, etc., would become purposeless. There are many passages in the Upaniṣads which attribute agency to the soul.[2] Agency really abides in the upādhi or limitation, of vijñāna or understanding. The jīva is subject-object, self and not-self, reality and appearance. It consists of the Ātman limited or individuated by the object.[3] It is the Ātman in association with ajñāna. In Emerson's language, "Every man is God playing the fool." [4] Avidyā or logical knowledge, causes the sense of individuality of the empirical self, which is "alike deceiving and deceived." The distinctive characteristic of the individual soul is its connection with buddhi or understanding, which endures as long as the state of saṁsāra is not terminated by perfect knowledge.[5] The soul's connection with buddhi continues even after death. It can be broken only by the attainment of freedom. During deep sleep and death this connection is potential, while it becomes actual on waking and rebirth respectively. If we do not assume a potential continuance of this kind, the law of causality will be violated, since nothing can arise without a given cause.[6]

The psychophysical organism consists of the organic body,[7] made up of the gross elements, which the soul casts off at

[1] S.B., ii. 3. 40. Tasmād upādhidharmādhyāsenaivātmanaḥ kartṛtvaṁ na svābhāvikam. See also S.B. on Kaṭha Up., iii. 4.

Both the Advaita and the Sāṁkhya regard the Ātman or puruṣa as unconditioned by the activities of the doer. It is regarded as the doer when confused with the limits of individuality. This confusion or non-discrimination is the work of avidyā in Advaita and prakṛti in Sāṁkhya.

[2] Bṛh. Up., iv. 3. 12; Tait., iii. 5. See also S.B., ii. 3. 33.

[3] S.B., ii. 3. 40.

[4] Sureśvara compares the jīva to a prince carried away by a cowherd and brought up in rural associations. When he became acquainted with his royal descent he gave up his other occupations and realised his kingly nature.

Rājasūnoḥ smṛtiprāptau vyādhabhāvo nivartate
Yathaivam ātmano 'jñasya tat tvam asy ādivākyataḥ.

(S.L.S.) See also S.B. Bṛh. Up., ii. 1. 20; Suresvara's *Vārttika* on Bṛh. Up., ii. 1. 507–516.

[5] S.B., ii. 3. 20.

[6] It is said that the souls connected with buddhi reside in Īśvara when the connection is potential, though it is also urged that the souls at death and deep sleep enter into Brahman itself (Chān. Up., vi. 8; S.B., ii. 3. 31).

[7] Deha, sthūlaśarīra, annamayakośa.

death, the life organs (prāṇas)[1] and the subtle body,[2] made up of the subtle portions of the elements which compose the seed of the body.[3] The subtle body[4] consists of the seventeen elements, *viz.*, five organs of perception, five of action, five vital forms, mind and intellect.[5] This subtle body, while material, is also transparent, and so is not seen when the jīva migrates. While the subtle body and the vital forms persist as permanent factors of the soul until liberation, there is the varying factor of moral determination (karmāśraya), which accompanies the soul in each life as a new form not previously existing.[6] The basis of individuality is to be found, not in the Ātman or the upādhis, but in moral determination, which is a complex of knowledge (vidyā), works (karma), and experience (prajñā).[7] The vital forces continue to exist, like the subtle body which carries them, as long as saṁsāra endures, and accompany the soul inseparably even if it should enter a plant, in which case the internal organ and the senses cannot naturally unfold themselves. As saṁsāra is beginningless, the soul must have been equipped with this apparatus of vital forms from eternity. A third, kāraṇa-śarīra, is sometimes mentioned and identified with the beginningless indefinable avidyā. The causal self (kāraṇa-ātmā) is the relatively permanent human self, which persists through successive rebirths determined by the law of karma. This account of the psychological organism is identical with that of the Sāṁkhya, except in the matter of the five vital forces.

The five organs of perception, the five of action and manas are created objects,[8] minute (aṇu or sūkṣma) and limited (paricchinna). They are not of atomic size (paramāṇutulya), since

1 The life organs are of two kinds: those of the conscious life, as the five organs of sense (buddhīndriyāṇi), five of action (karmendriyāṇi), and manas, which controls perception and action; those of the unconscious life. The mukhyaprāṇa, which is the chief breath of life, is divided into five different prāṇas, subserving the different functions of respiration, nutrition, etc. Though having a limited size, it is invisible (S.B., i. 4. 13).

2 Sūkṣmaśarīra, liṅgaśarīra, bhūtāśraya.

3 Dehabījāni, bhūtasūkṣmāṇi.

4 It corresponds to the liṅgaśarīra of the Sāṁkhya.

5 Kartṛtvabhoktṛtvaviśiṣṭajīvo manomayādipañcakośaviśiṣṭaḥ. Its elements are determined by mechanical causality. See S.B., Bṛh. Up. I. 4. 17.

6 S.B., ii. 4. 8–12; D.S.V., pp. 325–6.

7 See Bṛh. Up., iv. 4. 2.

8 S.B., ii. 4. 1–4.

their pervading the whole body would then be unintelligible. They are regarded as subtle, since, if they were gross, they could be seen passing at death. They are of limited size and not infinite, since in the latter case there can be no passing or going or returning for them. Śaṁkara, in this whole account, has in view the sense-functions and not their material counterparts. The senses are not all-pervading, but are of the same extent as the bodily regions where they function.[1] The several organs are, as usual, traced to the different elements,[2] and the gods who control the elements are said to control the organs as well. The mukhyaprāṇa is the supporting and animating principle of life. Even the psychical apparatus depends on it. The senses are sustained by the mukhyaprāṇa, and so are called prāṇas.[3] The Ātman clothed in the upādhis is the jīva, which enjoys and suffers (bhoktṛ) and acts (kartṛ), from both of which conditions the highest soul is free.[4]

The jīva rules the body and the senses, and is connected with the fruits of actions. Since its essence is the Ātman, it is said to be vibhu or all-pervading, and not aṇu or of atomic size. If it were the latter, it could not experience the sensations extending over the whole body.[5]

Those who hold that the soul is atomic argue that an infinite soul cannot move, whereas it is seen to leave one body and return to another. This passage, according to Śaṁkara, does not touch the soul as such but only its limitations.[6] The objection that if the soul be atomic, it can only be in one place in the body, and so cannot perceive throughout the body, is set aside by the example that even as a piece of sandal-wood refreshes the body all over, even though it touches the body only at one spot, so the atomic soul can feel throughout the body by means of the sense of touch which pervades the whole

---

[1] ii. 4. 8. 13.

[2] S.B., ii. 4. 14–16; Bṛh. Up., i. 3. 11; iii. 2. 13; Ait Up., i. 2. 4.

[3] ii. 4. 1–6.

[4] Param brahma . . . apahatapāpmatvādidharmakam, tad eva jīvasya paramārthikaṁ svarūpam . . . itarad upādhikalpitam (S.B., i. 3. 19). Plato has a similar view, which he illustrates by the striking simile of Glaucus plunging into the depths of the sea. If we see him there, we fail to recognise him, for he is so overgrown with seaweeds, mussels and other creatures of the deep. Each individual soul is a lost soul, and we cannot recognise its true nature until we recover it from the ocean of saṁsāra and strip it of its overgrowth of weeds, shells and slime.

[5] S.B., ii. 3. 29.

[6] *Ibid.*

body. Śaṁkara refutes the suggestion by urging that the thorn on which one treads is also connected with the whole sense of feeling, though the pain is felt only on the sole of the foot and not on the whole body. The advocates of the atomic view suggest that the atomic soul pervades the whole body by means of the quality of spirit or caitanya, even as the light of a lamp placed in one spot extends from there to the whole room. Śaṁkara declares that quality cannot extend beyond substance. The flame of a lamp and its light are not related as substance and quality. Both are fiery substances; only in the flame the parts are drawn closer together, while in the light they are more widely separated. If the quality of caitanya or spirit, pervades the whole body, then the soul cannot be atomic. The passages of the Upaniṣads which refer to the soul as aṇu [1] have in view not the Ātman but the nucleus of the qualities of understanding and mind. They are intended to show the subtlety of the Ātman which escapes perception.[2] It is admitted that the empirical self, bound down by manas, etc., is not infinite, while the supreme reality is infinite.[3] If it is said to be atomic, it is because empirically it is associated with buddhi.[4] All the statements about the soul's abiding in the heart are due to the theory of the location of the buddhi in it. Again, what is everywhere can certainly be in one place, though what is confined to a place cannot be everywhere.[5] In this way Śaṁkara explains all the passages of the Upaniṣads, which assert a spatial limitation of the soul.[6] The whole life of religious obligation is founded on the relative reality of the empirical ego. The entire field of practical existence, with its scheme of merit and guilt, its body of sacred law, with its commands and prohibitions, its prospects of happiness in heaven and suffering in hell, all assume the identification with the self of the body, the senses and the variety of conditions surrounding it. In all the successions of life it is not the Ātman, but the shadow of it, that grieves and complains and acts out the plot on the world-stage. The soul, until its separation from the upādhis, is subject to pleasure, pain and individual consciousness.[7]

Śaṁkara gives an account of the different states of the soul. In the waking condition, the whole perceptual mechanism is operative, and we apprehend objects by means of the mind and the senses. In dream states, the senses are at rest and only the manas is active. Through the impressions left on the senses by the waking condition, it knows objects. The dreaming self is not the ultimate spirit, but the same limited by adjuncts. That is why we are not able to create

[1] Muṇḍ. Up., iii. 19; Śvet., v. 8–9.
[2] S.B., ii. 3. 29.
[3] See S.B., ii. 3. 19–32.
[4] ii. 3. 29.
[5] S.B., ii. 1. 7; ii. 3. 49.
[6] See S.B., i. 3. 14–18 i. 2. 11–12.
[7] Viśeṣavijñāna.

at will in a dream. If we could do so, no one would have an unpleasant dream.[1] In the state of deep sleep, the mind and the senses are at rest, and the soul is, as it were, dissolved in its own self and regains its true nature. Śaṁkara mentions continuity of karma as an argument for the continuity of self. There is also remembrance. Consciousness of personal identity (ātmānusmaraṇa) proves that the same soul awakes as went to sleep. Scripture affirms it, and would lose its meaning if deep sleep disturbed the continuity of the self. If one goes to sleep as A and wakes up as B, there will be no continuity of acts. Even the liberated might awake. Evidently even in deep sleep, as at death, the nucleus of individuality is kept up. In spite of loose statements to the contrary, it is admitted that even in deep sleep the upādhi, which limits the jīva to samsāra, exists potentially. If, in deep sleep as in liberation, there is an entire absence of special cognition, how and in what does the sleeping person retain the seed of avidyā on account of which waking takes place? Śaṁkara draws a distinction between the temporary union with Brahman in deep sleep and the permanent one in mokṣa. "In the case of deep sleep, the limiting upādhi exists, so that when it starts up into being, the jīva must start up into existence."[2] In the state of mokṣa, the seeds of avidyā are all burnt up.[3]

The state of swoon is given a separate place, since it is different from waking, inasmuch as the senses no longer perceive objects. This indifference to the object world is not the result of concentration of attention on other objects. It is different from dreams since there is not any accompanying consciousness, from death since there is life in the body, and from dreamless sleep since there is unrest in the body. A fainting person cannot be roused so easily as a sleeping one. The state of swoon is said to be intermediate between deep sleep and death. "It belongs to death in so far as it is the door of death. If there remains any (unrequited) work of the soul, speech and mind return to the senseless person; if no work remains, breath and warmth depart from him."[4]

Each man is in essence the supreme reality, unchanging and unmodified and partless, and yet we speak of the rise

[1] S.B., iii. 2. 6.
[2] S.B., iii. 2. 9.
[3] See S.B. on Gauḍapāda's *Kārikā*, iii. 14.
[4] S.B., iii. 2. 10.

and growth of the soul. For when the adjuncts are produced or dissolved, the self is said to be produced or dissolved.[1] The limiting adjuncts give individuality to the different souls of the world.[2] They determine the nature of the body, the caste of the jīva, the duration of life, etc.[3] The souls are different on account of these adjuncts, and there is no confusion of actions or fruits of actions.[4] Even if the individual soul is regarded as an ābhāsa or reflection only, like that of the sun in water, the individuality of the souls is not prejudiced.[5]

XXXVI

Sākṣin and Jīva

In each individual self we have, besides the cognitive, emotional and conative experience, the witness self or sākṣin. The eternal consciousness is called the sākṣin when the internal organ serves as the limiting adjunct to it and when it illumines objects. The presence of this adjunct is enough to transform the ultimate consciousness into the witness self. Though this witnessing consciousness arises with the experience of objects, it is not due to the experience, but is presupposed by it. When the internal organ enters into the individual and becomes an organic constituent thereof, we have the jīva.

What is the relation between the witness self and the jīva? In the later Advaita treatises it has been variously defined. Vidyāraṇya defines the witness self as the unchanging consciousness, which is the substratum of the phenomena of gross and subtle bodies, observing their effects without being affected by them in any way.[6] When the action of the enjoying ego ceases, the illumination of the two bodies

---

1 S.B., ii. 3. 17.

2 S.B., iii. 2. 9.

3 Sureśvara's *Vārttika*, pp. 110–113.

4 S.B., ii. 3. 49.

5 "As when one reflected image of the sun trembles, another reflected image does not on that account tremble also, so when one soul is connected with actions and results of actions, another soul is not on that account connected likewise. There is therefore no confusion of actions and results" (S.B., ii. 3. 50).

6 *Pañcadaśī*, viii. *Siddhāntaleśa* (ch. i) describes Vidyāraṇya's view thus: "Dehadvayādhiṣṭhānabhūtaṁ kūṭasthacaitanyaṁ svāvacchedakasya dehadvayasya sākṣād īkṣaṇān nirvikāratvāt sākṣīty ucyate."

is due to this witness self. This witness self is immediately conscious of the two kinds of bodies which are present to it as its associates, even when the enjoying ego ceases to function. The constant presence of the witness self helps to maintain the identity of the seer in a series of mental ideas with respect to something other than the ego. Vidyāraṇya is clear that the witness self cannot be identified with the jīva which participates in life and affairs. The Upaniṣad declares it to be one without qualities, a mere looker on and not an enjoyer of fruits.[1] Vidyāraṇya compares it, in another place, to the lamp on the stage which illumines equally the stage manager, the actress and the audience, and shines of itself even in their absence.[2] This simile is to point out that the witness self illumines equally the empirical ego (jīva), the inner organ and the objects, and shines of its own accord in sound sleep where all these are absent.[3] Passivity distinguishes the sākṣin from Īśvara. In the *Tattvapradīpikā*, the witness self is defined as the pure Brahman, which is the universal self of all creatures, and which, being the substratum of each individual soul, seems to be as many as the jīvas. The witness self cannot be identified with the qualified Brahman or Īśvara, since it is defined as absolute, devoid of qualities; nor is the witness to be identified with the jīva, who is a doer and enjoyer of actions and their fruits.[4] The view advocated in *Pañcadaśī* and *Tattvapradīpikā* has the support of Śaṁkara.

Kaumudī teaches that the witness self is a special form of Īśvara. The author of this treatise takes his stand on the *Śvetāśvatara Upaniṣad* passage which makes Īśvara the witness. While he is conscious of the jīva's activity and cessation from activity, he is in no way moved by them.[5] He operates in the jīva, illumining his avidyā and all else pertaining to him. He is known as prājña, when all activities are withdrawn as in the state of dreamless sleep.[6] The author of *Tattva-śuddhi* agrees with this view. That Īśvara is the sākṣī, is the religious or empirical way of describing the first view. We find support for it in Śaṁkara's writings. Commenting on the famous passage[7] of the Upaniṣad which describes the two birds perched on the same tree, Śaṁkara writes: "Of these two so perched, one, the ksetrajña, occupying the subtle body, eats (*i.e.* tastes) from ignorance the fruits of karma marked as happiness and misery, palatable in many and diversified modes; the other, the Lord eternal, pure, intelligent and free in his nature, omniscient and conditioned by sattva, does not eat;

[1] Cp. "Sākṣī, cetā, kevalo, nirguṇaś ca" (Śvet. Up.).

[2] "Nṛtyaśālāsthito dīpaḥ prabhuṁ sabhyāṁś ca nartakīm
Dīpayed aviśeṣeṇa tadabhāve 'pi dīpyate." (*Pañcadaśi*, x. 11.)

[3] *Ibid.*, x. 12.

[4] Tattvapradīpikāyām api, māyāśabalite, saguṇe parameśvare, 'kevalo nirguṇa" iti viśeṣaṇānupapatteḥ sarvapratyagbhūtam, viśuddham brahma, jīvād bhedena, sākṣīti pratipādyata ity uditam (*Siddhāntaleśa*, i).

[5] Parameśvarasyaiva rūpabhedaḥ kaścit jīvapravṛttinivṛttyor anumantā svayam udāsīnaḥ sākṣī nāma (*Siddhāntaleśa*, i).

[6] See V.S., i. 3. 42.

[7] Muṇḍ. Up., iii. 1. 1.

for he is the director of both the eater and the eaten." 'His mere witnessing is as good as direction, as in the case of a king."[1]

Some others maintain that the jīva conditioned by avidyā is the witness self, since he is essentially a looker on and not a doer. It is only when he falsely identifies himself with the inner organ that he becomes the doer and the enjoyer.[2] Jīva has thus two aspects, one real and the other unreal, that of sākṣin or passive spectator, and abhimānin or active doer and enjoyer. It is objected to this view that if the all-pervading avidyā is to be regarded as the condition of the witnessing jīva, then the latter must be able to illumine not only one's own mind but the minds of other creatures also. But this is not confirmed by experience. So the jīva, with the antaḥkaraṇa or the inner organ, as its condition, is the witness self, and this is different in different individuals. In suṣupti (dreamless sleep) it is supposed to exist in a subtle form, and so is present in all the three states. The difference between the empirical ego and the witness self is that, while the inner organ is an attribute or property of the former, it is only a condition or limitation of the latter.[3] This is the view of the *Vedāntaparibhāṣā*, and is not in conflict with the other views set forth, since it points out that the ultimate consciousness, when it operates in an individual subject, is called sākṣin. The eternal consciousness or Ātman, is given the name of jīvasākṣi when it operates in the individual organism, as it is called Īśvarasākṣi when it operates in the universe as a whole. The limitations or upādhis in the two cases justify the different names. In the former, the upādhi is the internal organ, body, etc., in the latter the whole world of being. Īśvara is the world-soul, while the jīva is the individual soul.

XXXVII

Ātman and Jīva

We cannot attribute substantiality or simplicity to the individual ego. It is not an atomic unit, but a very complex structure. It is the systematic unity of the conscious experiences of a particular individual centre, which is itself defined or determined at the outset by the bodily organism and other conditions. The body, the senses, etc., enter into its experi-

1 Paśyaty eva kevalaṁ darśanamātreṇa hi tasya prerayitṛtvaṁ rājavat (S.B., Muṇḍ., iii. 1. 1).

2 Kecid avidyopādhiko jīva eva sākṣād draṣṭṛtvāt sākṣī; jīvasyāntaḥkaraṇatādātmyāpatyā kartṛtvādyāropabhāk tv epi svayam udāsīnatvāt (*Siddhāntaleśa*, i).

3 Antaḥkaraṇopadhānena jīvaḥ sākṣī . . . antaḥkaraṇaviśiṣṭaḥ pramātā (*Siddhāntaleśa*, i).

ence and introduce a sort of unity and continuity into it. The consciousness linked up with the organism is a purely finite one, which includes bodily states as part of the content of consciousness. As the body is built up gradually, so also is its conscious experience. The finite self is not the ultimate cause of its own consciousness. The ego is the felt unity of the empirical consciousness, which is evolving in time. It is an ideal construction or an object of conceptual thinking.[1] It is shifting in the same individual, and therefore cannot be identified with the unchanging and unchangeable essence. The Ātman, which is the underlying basis of empirical egos, suffers no change and experiences no emotions.

Inconceivable though it is, the Ātman has nothing to do with the individual's life history, which it so faithfully attends and accompanies. Assumed as the constant witness, the Ātman serves merely as the screen or the basis on which mental facts play. We cannot say that they grow out of it, for the real is not affected by what is confused with it. Things do not alter their nature simply because we do not rightly understand them. How does the unchanging Ātman appear as limited, how can the eternal light of intelligence be darkened by any agency whatever, since it is free from all relations? It is the old question How does the real become the phenomenal? It is the relation of Ātman to the upādhis of body, senses, mind and sense-objects that accounts for its phenomenal character; but this relation between the Ātman and the psychological self is inexplicable, māyā, or mysterious. If Ātman is eternal freedom and pure consciousness, and wants nothing and does nothing, how can it be the source of movement and desire in the embodied self? "A thing, it is answered, which is itself devoid of motion may nevertheless move other things. The magnet is itself devoid of motion, and yet it moves iron."[2] When we speak about the relation of the finite selves to the infinite Ātman, we are at the mercy of the finite categories, which do not strictly apply.

Saṁkara discusses the different views of the relation between the individual soul and Brahman, mentioned in the *Brahma Sūtra*, such

[1] Cp. Ward: *Psychological Principles*, pp. 361–382.
[2] S.B., ii. 2. 2.

as those of Āśmarathya, Auḍulomi and Kāśakṛtsna. Āśmarathya takes his stand on the Upaniṣad texts which compare the relation of individuals to the Absolute to that of sparks and fire. As the sparks issuing from a fire are not absolutely different from the fire, since they participate in the nature of fire and, on the other hand, are not absolutely non-different, since in that case they would not be distinguishable either from the fire or from each other; so the individual souls are neither different from the supreme reality, for that would mean they are not of the nature of intelligence, nor absolutely non-different from it, since, then, they would not be different from each other. So Āśmarathya concludes that the individuals are both different and non-different from Brahman.[1] Auḍulomi's view is that the individual soul, bound by the limiting adjuncts of body, senses, and mind, is different from Brahman, though, through knowledge and meditation, it passes out of the body and becomes one with the highest self. He admits the absolute distinction between the unfreed individual self and Brahman and the absolute identity of the freed with Brahman.[2] Śaṁkara accepts the view of Kāśakṛtsna.[3]

The individual ego cannot be a part of the absolute spirit, as Rāmānuja thinks, since the Absolute is without parts, being beyond space and time. It cannot be different from the Absolute, as Madhva supposes, since there is nothing different from the Absolute, which is one without a second.[4] It cannot be a modification of the Absolute, as Vallabha thinks, since the Absolute is unchangeable. We cannot regard the individual soul as the creation of God, since the Vedas which speak of the creation of fire and other elements do not speak of the creation of the soul. Jīva is neither different from nor a part of nor a modification of the absolute Ātman. It is the Ātman itself. We do not realise its nature, since it is covered by the upādhis.[5] Unless it were one with the supreme self, the statements of the scriptures proving immortality would become meaningless. Referring to the teaching of Āśmarathya, Śaṁkara says: "If the individual soul were different from the highest self, the knowledge of the highest self would not imply the knowledge of the individual soul, and thus the promise given in one of the Upaniṣads, that, through the knowledge of one reality, everything is known, would not be fulfilled."[6] Commenting on the *Taittirīya Upaniṣad*, Śaṁkara writes: "It is not possible that one can ever attain identity with another altogether distinct,"[7] and as the Upaniṣads speak of the knower of the Brahman becoming Brahman, the knower must be one with Brahman.

The metaphysical identity between the supreme Ātman and the individual jīva may be allowed; but it does not

[1] S.B., i. 4. 20. [2] S.B., i. 4. 21. [3] S.B., i. 4. 22.
[4] S.B., iv. 3. 14.
[5] See S.B. on Muṇḍ. Up., ii. 2. 1; Kaṭha Up., ii. 2. 1.
[6] S.B., i. 4. 20. [7] S.B. on Tait. Up., ii. 8. 15.

touch the question of the relation of the supreme to the latter, before it has arrived at a knowledge of its true nature. Our empirical egos move, weighted down by the burdens of the upādhis.[1] Knowing that the relation between the Absolute and the individual self is incapable of logical articulation, still Śaṁkara suggests certain analogies which have been developed into distinct theories in later Advaita.

It is told of an Irishman that, when asked to describe infinite space, he replied that "space is like a box wid the thop and the botthom and the sides knocked out of it." As the box with its limits and bounds is not space, even so lives bound by the mind and the senses are not Brahman. When we do away with the sides and the bottom of our finite individuality, we are one with Brahman. The theory of limitation[2] is employed in many places. Śaṁkara uses the simile of one cosmic space and parts of space, since it brings out well certain features of the relation of Brahman to the individuals. When the limitations caused by a jar, and the like, are removed, the limited spaces become merged in the one cosmic space. Even so, when the limitations of space, time and causality are removed, the jīvas become one with the absolute self. Again, when the space enclosed in one jar is associated with dust and smoke, the other parts of space are unaffected by them; so, too, when one jīva is affected by pleasure or pain, the others are not affected by it. The one space has different names given to it, owing to its upādhis, while the space itself is unchanged. When the Absolute is merged in these limitations (upādhi-antarbhāva), the nature of Brahman is hidden (svarūpatirobhāva), and the natural omniscience of the Absolute suffers a limitation (upādhiparicchinna). This contact of limitations (upādhisaṁparka) is akin to that of the crystal by the red colour with which it is associated.[3] Space does not burn with bodies or move with vessels.[4] The space in a jar cannot be said to be a part or a transformation of the one infinite space; so also the jīvas are not parts or modifications of Ātman. As space appears to be stained with dirt, etc., to children, even so the Ātman appears as bound or tainted with sin to the ignorant. When the jar is produced or destroyed, the space in it is not produced or destroyed; so also the Ātman is not born nor does it die. Some

[1] When it is said that the ahaṁkāra or self-sense, becomes the knower by its proximity to Ātman, which is reflected in the former, Rāmānuja asks: "Does consciousness become a reflection of the ahaṁkāra, or does the ahaṁkāra become a reflection of consciousness? The former alternative is inadmissible, since you will not allow to consciousness the quality of being a knower; and so is the latter, since the non-intelligent ahaṁkāra can never become a knower" (R.B., i. 1. 1).

[2] Avacchedyāvacchedaka. S.B., i. 3. 7; i. 2. 6; i. 3. 14–18; i. 2. 11–12; ii. 1. 14, 22; ii. 3. 17; iii. 2. 34.

[3] S.B., iii. 2. 15 *Ātmabodha*, p. 16.

[4] S.B., i. 2–8.

of the later followers of the Advaita adopt this view, and hold that the jīva is the universal spirit limited by the internal organ.

It is argued against the theory of limitation, that, when one jīva goes to heaven on account of its potency of merit, the intelligence limited by it in heaven is different from that which was limited by it while on earth. This will have unsatisfactory moral effects, such as the destruction of the rewards of our karma (kṛtanāśa) and attainment of the fruits of actions not performed by the agent (akṛtābhyāgama). We cannot say that the same limited intelligence goes to heaven, for that would be to attribute motion to what is all-pervading. Ether does not go with the jar, whenever we move the latter.

To secure the identity of the enjoying soul, the latter is looked upon not as the limited intelligence but as the reflected intelligence which is inseparably connected with the reflector, *i.e.* mind.[1] In the commentary of the *Bṛhadāraṇyaka Upaniṣad*,[2] Śaṁkara suggests the theory of reflection. As the appearance of sun and moon in water is a mere reflection and nothing real, or as the appearance of red colour in a white crystal is a mere reflection of the red flower and nothing real, since on removing the water, sun and moon only remain, and on removing the red flower the whiteness of the crystal remains unchanged, even so the elements and the individual souls are reflections of the one reality in avidyā and nothing real. On the abolition of avidyā, the reflections cease to exist and only the real remains. The Absolute is the original (bimba) and the world is the reflection (pratibimba). Again, the universe in its variety of forms is like an ocean reflecting the sun of Brahman in various ways, and Śaṁkara supports this view on account of its suggestive value, seeing that it brings out that the original really remains untarnished by the impurities of the reflection. As the differences of the reflections are traced to the mirrors, the Absolute, which is without a second, appears as different individuals through its reflections in different inner organs. When the water in which the reflection is cast is disturbed, the reflection itself appears as disturbed. While the supporters of the limitation theory hold that avidyā, as subtle matter in the form of the inner organ, is an avacchedaka or limitation, or viśeṣaṇa or an essential part of the jīva, without which the jīva as such could not exist, those who support the reflection theory regard the inner organ as an *upādhi*[3] merely, as the matter which receives the reflection of the pure intelligence, and is therefore *present* to it, but does not belong to jīva in its essential nature.

Some of the later followers of the Advaita adopt this view and

[1] S.B., ii. 3. 50; S.B. on Gauḍapāda's *Kārikā*, i. 6.

[2] S.B., Bṛh. Up., ii. 4. 12. See also *Brahmabindu Up.*, p. 12.

[3] While a viśeṣaṇa is an essential predicate which inheres in and is present with the product, *i.e.* the thing defined, an upādhi is not an essential property of the thing defined. Colour is the viśeṣaṇa of a coloured thing, while an earthen vessel is the upādhi of the space which it confines.

regard the jīva as a reflection of the universal spirit in the internal organ.[1] If the world is a shadow, then Brahman is the substance which casts the shadow. The theory of reflection is criticised on several grounds. A thing devoid of form cannot cast any reflection, much less in a formless reflector. Pure intelligence and avidyā are both formless. If the individual is a reflection, then that which is reflected must lie outside the reflector, and the reality which is the original must lie beyond the cosmos or the sum total of created objects. This is opposed to the "immanence" view of the system. The "reflection" hypothesis is not free from the difficulties of the limitation view. The reflection of each mind is due to the intelligence which is adjacent to it, and so it would follow that reflections in the same mind would vary at various places. This criticism forgets the uniform nature of intelligence. If the jīva is a reflection of Brahman, it is different from the latter and is therefore not real. The author of *Vivaraṇa* suggests a way out of this difficulty. The rays proceeding from the eyes are struck by the reflector, turn back and make the actual face perceptible. The reflection is thus the original itself. This view, called bimbapratibimbābheda vāda (or non-difference of the original and the reflection) is, however, not accepted. If the metaphor is taken literally, we require a luminous body, another on which the shadow is cast, and a third which intercepts the light. A reflection requires a really existing medium separate from the projection, but this contradicts the non-dualism of Brahman. Those who reject both the "limitation" and the "reflection" theories[2] declare that the jīva is the unchanging Brahman ignorant of its true nature. Śaṁkara is inclined to this view, as also Sureśvara. Personal consciousness is an inexplicable presentation of Brahman.[3] The jīva appears, but we do not know how.

XXXVIII

Īśvara and Jīva

If Īśvara is Brahman, if the jīva is also metaphysically one with Brahman, and if the two are subject to limitations, the difference between God and the individual seems to be minimised. Śaṁkara holds that, while Īśvara is omniscient, all-powerful and all-pervading, the jīva is ignorant, small and weak. "The Lord endowed with superior limiting adjuncts (niratiśayopādhi)[4] rules the souls with inferior limiting

[1] Antaḥkaraṇeṣu pratibimbaṁ jīvacaitanyam (*Vedāntaparibhāṣā*, i).
[2] For a criticism of these theories see S.P.B., i. 152 and 153.
[3] See S.B. on Bṛh. Up., ii. 1.
[4] S.B., ii. 3. 45.

adjuncts (nihīnopādhi).[1] Īśvara is ever free from avidyā.[2] The limitations of Īśvara do not affect his knowledge. Īśvara's māyā is subject to him, and so there is no concealment of his nature. It does not hide his qualities, even as glass which covers objects without concealing their properties. The māyā which is the limitation of Īśvara is made up of śuddhatattva, and does not produce avidyā or antaḥkaraṇa. It is subject to his control, and helps him in his task of creation and destruction. This māyā, or the force of self-expression, in Īśvara, resulting in the multiplicity of the world, deludes the individual soul into the false belief of the independence of the world and the souls in it. Avidyā is the result of māyā. The pure consciousness of Brahman, when associated with māyā in this sense, is called Īśvara, and when with avidyā, jīva. Since Īśvara has no selfish desires or interests in creating the world, he is called akartṛ or non-doer, while the jīva is kartṛ or doer. Īśvara is the worshipped, who distributes rewards according to karma, and he knows his oneness with Brahman, and so enjoys bliss for all time in his own mind. The jīva is the worshipper, who is ignorant of his divine origin, and is therefore subject to saṁsāra. In religion we have the relation of master and servant (svāmibhṛtyayoḥ).[3] Elsewhere the finite selves are said to be parts (aṁśa) of Īśvara, even as sparks are of fire.[4]

In later Advaita, different suggestions are put forward regarding the relation of Īśvara and jīva, which may be briefly noticed here. *Prakaṭārthavivaraṇa* says: "The reflection of Intelligence in māyā, which has no beginning, which is indescribable, which is the source of the inorganic world and which is connected with intelligence only, is Īśvara: the reflection in numerous small portions of that māyā which is possessed of the two powers of enveloping and projecting and known as avidyā is jīva."[5] According to this author, māyā and avidyā refer to the whole and the parts. Māyā is the adjunct of Īśvara and avidyā of jīva. The same view is adopted by *Saṁkṣepaśārīraka*, though the distinction of whole and parts is here said to be one of avidyā and antaḥkaraṇa, where avidyā is the cause and antaḥkaraṇa the effect.[6] Since this author supports the reflection

---

[1] S.B., ii. 3. 43.

[2] Nityanivṛttāvidyatvāt (S.B., iii. 2. 9).

[3] ii. 3. 43.

[4] S.B., ii. 3. 43.

[5] Anādir anirvācyā, bhūtaprakṛtiś cinmātrasaṁbandhinī māyā; tasyāṁ citpratibimba īśvaraḥ. Tasyā eva paricchinnānantapradeśeṣv āvaraṇavikṣepaśaktimatsvavidyābhidhāneṣu citpratibimbo jīva iti (*Siddhāntaleśa*, i).

[6] Avidyāyāṁ cit pratibimba īśvaraḥ; antaḥkaraṇe citpratibimbojīvaḥ. (S.L.S.)

theory, he does not approve of the division of whole and parts. *Pañcadaśī* adopts a distinction which is akin to it. The primitive non-intelligent principle of mūlaprakṛti, consisting of three guṇas, has two forms. That portion of it where sattva is not subordinate to rajas and tamas, but dominates the latter, is called māyā, and is the adjunct of Īśvara; that in which sattva is subordinate to the other two qualities is avidyā, which is the adjunct of jīva. The difference between māyā and avidyā is here not simply quantitative but qualitative. It comes out also in another passage of *Pañcadaśī*, where prakṛti, with its power of projection in prominence, is called māyā; the same, with the power of concealment dominating, is avidyā.[1] In *Pañcadaśī*,[2] Vidyāraṇya distinguishes ākāśa (1) limited by a jar (ghaṭākāśa); (2) that which is reflected together with clouds, storms, etc., in the water contained in the jar, or ākāśa, belonging to the water of the jar (jalākāśa); (3) the unlimited ākāśa (mahākāśa); and (4) that which is reflected in particles of water which resemble spray, which are inferrible as existing in the clouds of the sky, from the subsequent rain (meghākāśa). Even so there are four kinds of intelligence: (1) kūṭastha, or the unchanging intelligence limited by gross and subtle bodies; (2) the intelligence reflected in the manas, falsely superimposed on the unchanging intelligence (the jīva); (3) the unlimited intelligence; and (4) the intelligence reflected in the subtle impressions of mind[3] of all creatures which exist in the cloudlike māyā hanging in Brahman (Īśvara). From this account, it follows that while jīva is the intelligence reflected in manas, Īśvara is the intelligence reflected in māyā tinged with the subtle impressions of all creatures. The author of *Pañcapādikāvivaraṇa* regards the jīva as a reflection of Īśvara.[4] Sometimes jīva is said to be Īśvara under the influence of māyā.

XXXIX

Ekajīvavāda (Single Soul Theory) and Anekajīvavāda (Theory of Many Souls)

Śaṁkara does not support the view that the jīva, limited by avidyā, is one, as avidyā is one. For if all souls are one jīva, then when the first case of liberation occurred, mundane existence should have come to an end, which is not the case. Brahman, limited by the different inner organs born of avidyā, becomes divided, as it were, into many individual souls, but

[1] i. [2] vi. [3] Dhīvāsanā.

[4] These take their stand on the *Antaryami Brāhmaṇa* of the Bṛh. Up., vi. 7, and such passages of the B.G. as "Īśvaras sarvabhūtānāṁ hṛddeśe 'rjuna tiṣṭhati."

the difficulties of the relation of māyā and avidyā to Brahman led to the formulation of several theories in the later Advaita, of which the two chief are ekajīvavāda, single soul theory, and anekajīvavāda, or the theory of a plurality of souls.

There is but one jīva and one material body. This one personal consciousness is real, while other bodies like those seen in dreams lack personal consciousness. The manifold world is erroneously imagined by the avidyā of the one jīva, but this type of ekajīvavāda conflicts with B.S., ii. 1. 22; ii. 1. 33 and i. 2. 3. The creator of the world is not jīva, but Īśvara other than jīva, whose creative activity is due to mere sport; for since all his desires are fulfilled, he can have no motive in creating. So these writers maintain that there is one chief jīva, *viz.* Hiraṇyagarbha, who is a reflection of Brahman, and other jīvas are mere semblances of jīva, reflections of Hiraṇyagarbha, and to these semblances pertain bondage and final release. These writers admit the doctrine of the unity of jīva, with the qualification that many material bodies exist, each provided with an unreal jīva. A third variety of ekajīvavāda holds that there is one jīva residing in each of the many bodies. The individuality of consciousness depends on the numerical distinctness of the material bodies. The upholders of this view do not admit the force of the objection that just as the one person is variously conscious as the different parts of his body are affected, so the one jīva should at once be conscious of the pleasures and pains belonging to all the numerically distinct material bodies in which it resides. For, they say, the fact that we are not conscious of the pleasures and pains of a former state of existence proves that it is the numerical distinction of material bodies which hinders such a consciousness. They adopt the doctrine of the unity of jīva with a multiplicity of bodies.

There are varieties of anekajīvavāda, resulting from different conceptions of avidyā. (1) It is the presence of avidyā in the form of an inner organ that is essential to the jīva nature. If the inner organ, etc., are the conditions which constitute a jīva, and if these organs are many, it follows that the jīvas are many. (2) Others hold that though there is one avidyā which resides in Brahman as its substrate and conceals Brahman, though final release is nothing but the destruction of this avidyā, yet avidyā has parts, and some part of avidyā (otherwise termed its projecting power) must be admitted to exist in the case of the person who gains release while still living in this body; this avidyā ceases to exist in part, *i.e.* as regards some one limiting condition or other, when a knowledge of Brahman has arisen; and continues to exist as before in other parts, *i.e.* as regards the remaining limiting conditions. (In the jīvanmukta state the individual retains a consciousness of his body in the form of a saṁskāra, or mental *retentum*, which is a subtle form of avidyā; in the videhakaivalya state, the consciousness of body ceases to exist.) (3) A third variety, similar to the above, holds that bondage consists in the relation of avidyā and intelligence, and final release consists in the cessation of this relation. The inner organ or manas determines the relation of avidyā to intelligence. When the rise of the intuition of Brahman puts an end to the manas, then avidyā ceases to be in relation with that particular part of intelligence, though it continues as before in relation with the remaining parts of intelligence. (4) Avidyā is a whole and is completely present in each jīva, hiding Brahman from each jīva. Final release is when avidyā quits a jīva. (5) Avidyā consists of parts which are distributed to each jīva. Mokṣa of a jīva consists in the destruction of the avidyā belonging to it. The world as a whole has its origin in all the avidyās collectively. "As a piece of cloth has its origin in all the threads collectively, and ceases to exist when one of its threads is destroyed, and as a new piece of cloth is produced at that time out of the remaining threads; so this world originates from all the avidyās collectively, and it ceases to exist when one of the jīvas attains release . . . and a new world common to all the remaining jīvas is produced at that time out of the remaining avidyās." (6) Each part of avidyā gives rise to a separate and distinct world. The whole world of sense and activity is restricted to each person and produced by the avidyā residing in that particular person, even as the merely apparent silver (perceived in place of the shell) is different for each observer and is produced by the avidyā residing in each observer. . . . But that these many worlds should appear to be one, is a pure misapprehension similar to that expressed in the words, "I too saw the very same silver which you saw." (7) Others hold that there is but one world, whose material cause is māyā, residing in the Īśvara, which is different from the aggregate of avidyās as residing in the jīvas. These avidyās, on the other hand, have their function partly in concealing Brahman and partly in projecting merely apparent objects, as false silver observed in the shell and objects seen in dreams.[1]

XL

Ethics

Of all items of the universe, the human individual alone is the ethical subject. He knows that he has relations to the two worlds of the infinite and the finite. The operation of the infinite in the finite is not a mere poetic vision, but is the sober truth of philosophy. The infinite dwells in all finite, and man is conscious of this fact. Though he is bound up with an organism which is mechanically determined by the past, the infinite ideals of truth, beauty and goodness operate

[1] See *Siddhāntaleśa.*

in him and enable him to choose and strive for their greater expression It is because the infinite Brahman is revealed to a larger extent in human beings that they are entitled to ethical and logical activity.[1] So long as the individual strains after them and does not reach them, he is in bondage; the moment he reaches the infinite, the inner strain is relaxed and the freedom of joy fills his spirit. To realise Brahman is the end of all activities, for Brahman is not mere being or consciousness but also bliss (ānanda), and so is the object of all striving.[2] Brahmātmaikatva, or the realisation of the identity with the infinite reality, is the final end of life, "the proper food of every soul,"[3] and the only supreme value. Until it is reached the finite soul is at unrest with itself. "Every one in all the three worlds strives for the sources of happiness and not for those of misery."[4] All men seek the best, and, as Browning says, have

> All with a touch of nobleness despite
> Their error, upward tending all though weak—
> Like plants in mines which never saw the sun,
> But dream of him, and guess where he may be,
> And do their best to climb and get to him.

The best fruits which we can pluck from the tree of life (saṁsāra) turn to ashes in our mouth. The greatest pleasure palls and even life in heaven (svarga) is evanescent. A mere act of goodness or enjoyment of a sweet melody or contemplative insight may, for the moment, seem to lift us out of the narrowness of our individuality, but it cannot give us permanent satisfaction. The only object that can give us permanent satisfaction is the experience of Brahman (brahmānubhava). It is the supreme state of joy and peace and the perfection of individual development.[5] Unfortunately

[1] Prādhānyāt . . . karmajñānādhikāraḥ (S.B., Tait. Up., ii. 1).

[2] Prayojanasūcanārtham ānandagrahaṇam (*Śikhāmaṇi* on *Vedāntaparibhāṣā*, Introduction).

[3] *Phædrus*, p. 247.

[4] *Śataślokī*, p. 15.

[5] "The essence of mokṣa or release is boundless joy and utter removal of pain. As it is perfectly clear that men always desire both, there is always a desire for release" (*Saṁkṣepaśārīraka*, i. 67). Cp. Spinoza: "All our happiness or unhappiness depends solely on the quality of the object on which our love is fixed. . . . But love towards an object eternal and infinite feeds the mind with a joy that is pure with no tinge of sadness" (*De Intellectus Emendatione*, pp. 9 and 10).

our trouble arises because we cling to the world, cherish faith in its phantoms and feel disappointed when the mocking semblances of finite satisfactions vanish even as we reach them. "The individual sinks down in sin and grief so long as he believes that his body is the Ātman, but when he realises that he is one with the self of all things, his grief ceases."[1] We cannot manipulate reality into accord with any ideal of our mind, but have only to recognise it. Philosophy with Śaṁkara is not the production of what *ought to be*, but is the apprehension of what *is*. A spiritual perception of the infinite as the real leads to peace and joy.

All ethical goods, bound up as they are with the world of distinctions, are valuable as means to the end. While self-realisation is the absolute good, ethical goods are only relatively so. The ethically "good" is what helps the realisation of the infinite, and the ethically "bad" is its opposite.

Right action is what embodies truth, and wrong that which embodies untruth.[2] Whatever leads to a better future existence is good, and what brings about a worse form of existence evil. The individual tries to make good his infinite nature and become more and more godlike. In the empirical world, Īśvara is the highest reality and the world is his creation. The believer in God should love the whole universe, which is a product of God. True peace and excellence lie not in self-assertion, not in individual striving for one's own good, but in offering oneself as a contribution to the true being of the universe. Egoism is the greatest evil, and love and compassion are the greatest good. By identifying ourselves with the social good, we truly gain our real ends. Every individual must subdue his senses, which make for self-assertion; pride must give place to humility, resentment to forgiveness, narrow attachment to family to universal benevolence. It is not so much the deed that is valuable as the will to suppress one's selfish will and assert the will of society. Duties are the opportunities afforded to man to sink his separate self and grow out into the world. Śaṁkara accepts the standards of his age and exhorts us to avoid the

[1] S.B. on Muṇḍ. Up., iii. 1. 2.

[2] Cp. "Everyone that doeth evil hateth the light" (*St. John* iii. 19).

sins forbidden by the śāstras. The study of the Veda, sacrifices, gifts, penances and fasts are a means of knowledge.[1] They strengthen character, purify the spirit and deepen insight. Though rare spirits might grasp the truth at once, for the ordinary man time and effort are needed. Fulfilment of the daily obligations of life and the demands of household piety,[2] produce a frame of mind favourable to realisation.[3] Vedic rituals, when scrupulously observed, lead to abhyudaya (literally ascent or progress in the scale of saṁsāra), and not to niḥśreyasa or salvation.[4] While spiritual insight into the nature of ultimate reality has for its result mokṣa, the worship of God in this or that form leads to a variety of effects, though all these are confined to the world of saṁsāra.[5] They help us to escape from selfish desire, hatred and dullness, and attain calm, peace and patience in suffering. Devout meditation is a means to knowledge. Bhakti aids jñāna. True wisdom is won only by those whose minds are prepared by a rigorous discipline. It is not a question of pouring into the mind some kind of knowledge of which it is destitute. Truth is in the centre of the soul. To let it shine, the mind has to be turned from the perishing world. Our understanding must be made transparent like the glass of the lamp through which shines the light within. "Though the Ātman is at all times and in all things, it does not shine in all things. It shines only through understanding, just as reflection appears only in polished surfaces."[6] Śaṁkara attaches great importance to philosophical wisdom, which can be attained only through a practice of virtue. While jñāna leads to release, other means help its attainment indirectly.[7] "The desire to know Brahman springs only in the person whose mind is pure,

1 Bṛh. Up., iv. 4. 22.

2 S.B., iii. 4. 26.

3 iv. 1. 4.

4 S.B. on Muṇḍ. Up., Introduction.

5 S.B., i. 1. 24. See also iii. 2. 21.

6 Sadāsarvagato 'py ātmā, na sarvatrāvabhāsate.
Buddhyāvevāvabhāseta, svaccheṣu pratibimbavat. (*Ātmabodha*, p. 17.)

7 S.B., iv. 1. 1; S.B. on Tait. Up., i. 3. Plato recommends for philosophers the pursuit of wisdom, which has for its final fruit the vision of the idea of the Good, and for others true opinion, which is limited to one's station and its duties. See *Phædo* and *Republic*. Similarly, Aristotle recommends for the ordinary men "moral virtues," which are emphatically "human affairs," and for those who aim at immortality the exercise of reason, "which apprehends things noble and divine" (*Nichomachean Ethics*, x. 8).

who is free from desires, and who, free from deeds done in this birth or in previous ones, becomes disgusted with the external ephemeral medley of ends and means."[1] Śaṁkara accepts the principle of the yoga practice, which has for its chief end samādhi, what Śaṁkara calls saṁrādhana or complete satisfaction, which consists in withdrawing the senses from everything external and concentrating them on one's own nature. The Advaita accepts the yogic distinctions of yama, niyama, etc., as the outer means (bahiraṅgasādhanas) and dhāraṇa and dhyāna as the inner means (antaraṅgasādhanas).[2] The inner requirements are also stated to be the discrimination between the eternal and the non-eternal, detachment from all selfish endeavours for earthly or heavenly good, the development of the virtues of tranquillity (śama), restraint (dama), renunciation (uparati), resignation (titīkṣā), concentration (samādhi) and steadfastness of mind (śraddhā), and lastly an intense desire for freedom. These bring about the rise of true knowledge.[3]

A thinker who is reaching forward to a larger conception of truth does not break entirely from the common beliefs of his age. Though the efficacy of caste institutions has ceased to be vital for Śaṁkara, he allows room for belief in it. The traditional theory that birth in a particular caste is not a matter of chance, but is the necessary consequence of conduct in a former existence, inclines Śaṁkara to accept the claim of the upper classes, gods and ṛṣis, for the exclusive right to study the Veda.[4] While Śaṁkara holds that any man of any caste can attain the highest knowledge,[5] he allows that those who follow the Brahminical rule of life should observe the obligations of caste and the stages of life. While the Brahmin may study the Veda and acquire wisdom, others may resort to worship and the like and attain the same goal

[1] S.B., Kena Up., Introduction. See also S.B., Chān. Up., Introduction, and viii. 5. 1; Bṛh. Up., iv. 4. 22; Kaṭha, i. 2. 15.

[2] The Vedāntic śravaṇa and manana answer to dhāraṇa and steps to it, nididhyāsana to dhyāna, and darśana to samādhi.

[3] S.B., iii. 4. 27.

[4] The cases of Jānaśruti (Chān., iv. 1. 2), who was called a Śūdra by Raikva, who, however, taught him the Vedas, and Satyakāma Jābāla, are explained away on the ground that so long as a śūdra is not raised to a higher caste in the path of saṁsāra, he is not entitled to the saving knowledge.

[5] S.B., iii. 4. 38.

of brahmajñāna.[1] It is difficult to find support in Saṁkara for the claim that only through the study of the Veda can one acquire a knowledge of Brahman. As in his philosophy, so in his views of Hindu dharma, Śaṁkara tries to reconcile conflicting claims. By throwing open the highest knowledge or brahmajñāna to all who bear the human face divine (puruṣamātra), irrespective of caste or creed, he shows his fundamental humanity and his firm adherence to the logical implications of his Advaita philosophy. But he concedes to the Brahminical faith that the Śūdras, like Vidura, who attained the highest wisdom, did so as a result of their past conduct. If a Śūdra has capacity to understand the truth now, we may take it that he has studied the Veda in a previous life. Thus Śaṁkara undermined the belief of the exclusive right of the upper classes to salvation. He was willing to regard all who possess spiritual insight as his gurus, whether they were Brahmins or pariahs. " He who has learned to look upon the phenomenal world in the light of non-dualism is my true teacher, be he a caṇḍāla (pariah) or a dvija (twice-born). This is my conviction." [2]

The rules of āśramas or stages of life are insisted on. To gain salvation, one need not become a saññyāsin. In the *Bṛhadāraṇyaka* and the *Chāndogya Upaniṣads*, gṛhasthas, or householders, acquired and taught brahmavidyā. Saññyāsins, however, are best entitled to it, since it is easier for them to acquire it than for others, since they are not called upon to undertake active worship, household duties or vedic rites. Śaṁkara insists that those who follow the āśrama rules must become saññyāsins before they attain release, though there is no such obligation for those who do not adhere to the āśrama rules. The saññyāsins are grounded in Brahman (brahmasaṁsthā). " Such a state is impossible for those belonging to the three other stages of life, as scripture declares that they suffer loss through the non-performance of the works enjoined on their stage of life, while the saññyāsin can suffer no loss owing to non-performance." [3] Again, " Although

[1] Puruṣamātrasaṁbandhibhir japopavāsadevatārādhanādibhir dharmaviśeṣair anugraho vidyāyās saṁbhavati.

[2] *Manīṣapañcaka.* See also *Kaupīnapañcaka*, pp. 3 and 5.

[3] S.B., iii. 4. 20.

jñāna is permitted to all in any order of life, it is only that possessed by a saññyāsin that leads to freedom and not that combined with karma."[1] Śaṁkara felt in the practical religion of the Hindus the want of discipline and a common standard, and so rearranged the ascetic orders and thus tried to obtain for Hinduism the disciplinary advantages of the Buddhist organisation.[2] Obsessed by the lesson which the Buddhistic admission of women in the body of ordained ascetics had taught, Śaṁkara excluded women from his monasteries, which were mainly intended as seats of learning and asylums for those who courted poverty, austere purity of life and freedom from the thraldom of the world. Śaṁkara ignored caste distinctions in the monastic order he founded.

The rules of varṇāśrama are binding on the Hindus, since they express the higher mind of the community. These are not to be regarded as externally imposed on the individuals who do not exist simply for the community. The moral value of the individual does not depend entirely on his contribution to the community. Man is not like a piece of clay to be moulded from outside. He has to be persuaded from within. The śāstras do not compel a man to do this or that, but simply remind men of the collective experience of the race.[3] Apart from general principles, conventions alter from place to place.[4] Moral life deepens as we progress higher and higher.[5] Customary morality is something which is ever growing. The Vedic rule of life is not an indispensable aid to wisdom. Even those who are not entitled to it attained the highest goal. The poor and the outcast may by prayer and worship, fasting and sacrifice, attain the goal through the grace of God.[6]

He who realises the goal is the true Brahmin, the knower

[1] S.B., Introduction to Muṇḍaka Up. Sayññāsaniṣṭhaiva brahmavidyā mokṣasādhanam na karmasahiteti.

[2] Vidyāranya after Śaṁkara (see Introduction to Bhāsya on *Ait. Up.*) distinguishes vividiṣāsaññyāsa or the renunciation of the seeker from the vidvatsaññyāsa or the renunciation of the saved; while the first is optional, the second eventually follows the attainment of vidyā. The first, if adopted, is to be carried out in the orthodox way; the second has no regulations binding it. See *Jīvanmuktiviveka.*

[3] Jñāpakaṁ hi śāstraṁ, na kārakam. See also S.B., Bṛh. Up., ii. 1. 20.

[4] S.B., i. 1. 4.

[5] *Ibid.*

[6] S.B., iii. 4. 36–39.

of Brahman. The way in which he lives is described by Śaṁkara, who quotes the following passage :—

Whom no one knows as high nor lowly born,
No one as erudite, nor yet not erudite,
No one as of good deeds, nor of evil deeds,
He is a Brāhmaṇa in very truth.
Given up to hidden duties well fulfilled,
In secrecy let all his life be spent;
As he were blind and deaf, of sense bereft,
Thus let the truly wise pass through the world.[1]

It is life in the spirit full of meekness and peace, holiness and joy, and not sinking into a state of contemplative inertia. His activities do not bind him. His karma is not karma in the ordinary sense.[2] While some liberated undertake the minimum activity for sustaining life (jīvanamātrārtham), others throw themselves into the work of the world (lokasaṁgrahārtham).[3] This activity of the liberated is not centred in the individualistic standpoint [4] and so is not to be regarded as binding the individual to the circuit.[5] The freed souls,

1 Yaṁ na santam na cāsantam, nāśrutam na bahuśrutam
Na suvṛttaṁ na durvṛttaṁ veda kaścit sa brāhmaṇaḥ.
Gūḍhadharmāśrito vidvān ajñātacaritaṁ caret
Andhavaj jaḍavac cāpi mūkavac ca mahīṁ caret.
(S.B., iii. 4. 50 ; D.S.V., p. 144.)

2 Viduṣaḥ kriyamāṇam api karma paramārthato'karmeva (S.B.G., iv. 20).

3 S.B.G., iv. 19.

4 S.B., iv. 1. 13.

5 " He who, when awake, is as though in a sound sleep, and sees not duality, or, if seeing it, regards it as non-duality, who, though acting, is free from the results of actions, he, and he alone, is without doubt the knower of self " (*Upadeśasāhasrī*, p. 45). " He who, whether active or at rest, links not his ego with his act and allows not his mind to be affected, is said to be the real jīvanmukta." ' He who, though deep in intercourse with all things, is ever as cool and unconcerned as in attending to another's business, full of peace and contentment, is said to be the real jīvanmukta." Rāma asks Vaśiṣṭha : " Tell me which of the two is better than the other, he who is ever at rest though mixing in the world, even like one awakened from a prolonged trance, or he who rises to and remains in trance in some solitary corner ? " And his guru Vaśiṣṭha replies : " Trance is only that internal calm which comes of looking upon this world and the guṇas which create it as all not-self. Having gained this pleasant calm within from the conviction ' I have no touch with the objective,' the yogin may remain in the world or shut himself up in meditation. Both, O Rāma, are equally good if the fire of desire is entirely cooled down within " (*Yogavāśiṣṭha*, quoted in *Jīvanmuktiviveka*, i and iv).

who save themselves by their effort, save the world by their example.

While Vedic injunctions and moral rules are necessary for those involved in the circle of saṁsāra, they lose their point for the soul who leaves behind the whole sphere of desire and turns back on the differences of saṁsāra.[1] The question is raised whether the released soul can do what he will. Śaṁkara answers that, since selfish attachment that moves to action is absent in the case of the released soul, he does not act at all.[2] Action which arises from avidyā cannot coexist with a true knowledge of spirit.[3] While such explanations seem to deny all action whatsoever to the released soul, there are other passages in Śaṁkara which make out that the released soul, free from all selfish desire, acts in a disinterested way.[4] Evil action is psychologically impossible for him. Freedom from moral laws is mentioned as a glorification, alaṁkāra or ornament of the state of liberation and not an invitation to violate the moral laws. In no case is it to be regarded as encouraging the neglect of morality. The freed soul is lifted up into such a relationship with the absolute spirit that it is impossible for him to sin. He has verily died to sin. Śaṁkara's attitude is not to be confused with that taken sometimes by the Antinomians in the Christian Church. While it is true that the freed soul "has no longer any object to aim at, since he has achieved all," [5] still he works for the welfare of the world. Besides, while Śaṁkara holds that moral *obligation* has no meaning for the freed soul, he does not say that the moral virtues are abandoned by him.[6] Moral perfection leads to the death, not of morality, but of moralistic individualism. Rules of conduct have their force so long as we are struggling upward, working out the beast in us. They help to keep us straight when there is danger of our going

[1] Cp. Nistraiguṇye pathi vicaratāṁ ko vidhiḥ ko niśedhaḥ ?

[2] Na ca niyogābhāvāt saṁyagdarśino yatheṣṭaceṣṭāprasaṅgaḥ . . . sarvatrābhimānasyaiva pravartakatvāt, abhimānābhāvāc ca saṁyagdarśinaḥ (S.B., ii. 3. 48).

[3] See S.B., Introduction to Tait. Up.

[4] S.B.G., iv. 21.

[5] Introduction to S.B.G., v.

[6] Sureśvara says: 'To the person in whom the realisation of the supreme arises, non-hatred and other qualities will be a habit requiring no effort; they are no longer virtues to be acquired by conscious exertion" (*Naiṣkarmyasiddhi*, iv. 69).

wrong. As rules of murder, theft and the like do not worry the civilised man, so the spiritual man is not concerned with the conventional rules of morality.

XLI

Some Objections to Śaṁkara's Ethics Considered

The ethical views of Śaṁkara have been the subject of much criticism, and we may briefly consider the several charges.[1] If all that exists is Brahman, and if the world of plurality is a shadow, there cannot be any real distinction between good and evil. If the world is a shadow, sin is less than a shadow. Why should not a man play with sin and enjoy a crime, since they are only shadows? What shall it profit us if we fight wild beasts and sacrifice our interests in seeking virtue in this dream of life? If moral distinctions are valid, life is real; if life is unreal, then they are not valid. This objection falls to the ground if we do not accept the merely illusory nature of the world. Virtue and vice have moral weight for the supreme end.

On the view of the metaphysical identity of the individual and the Absolute, it is said, there is no warrant for ethics. If Brahman is all, there is no need for any moral endeavour. This objection rests upon a confusion between reality and existence, the eternal and the temporal. Śaṁkara does not say that the essentially imperfect and incomplete series of temporal events is the same as true timeless Brahman. The metaphysical truth of the oneness of Brahman does not in any way prejudice the validity of the ethical distinctions on the empirical level. Śaṁkara says: "Fire is one only, and yet we shun a fire which has consumed dead bodies, not any other fire; the sun is one only, yet we shun only that part of his light which shines on unholy places, not that part which falls on pure ground. Some things consisting of earth are desired, such as diamonds and beryls, other things likewise

[1] For an acute criticism of the ethics of the Advaita Vedānta and Deussen's reformulation of it, see Professor Hogg's article on "Advaita and Ethics" in the *Madras Christian College Magazine*, December 1916.

consisting of earth are shunned, dead bodies, etc." [1] Even so, though all things are Brahman ultimately, there are certain things to be avoided and others to be desired. The statement "I am Brahman" (aham brahmāsmi) does not mean direct identity [2] of the active self with the ultimate Brahman, but only identity of the real self when the false imposition is removed.[3] The ethical problem arises, because there is the constant struggle between the infinite character of the soul and the finite dress in which it has clothed itself. While the natural condition of man is one of integrity, the present state of corruption is due to a fall from it by the force of upādhis.[4] Our struggle with imperfection will have no meaning, if we rise to a point of view from which we behold the real. The struggle will go on until the isolation from the infinite is broken down. Until the finite soul realises that it is Brahman, it is at unrest with itself and feels homesick for its native country. We have duties and destinies as finite agents. Each individual is responsible for his work, and work done by one individual cannot be completed by another.[5]

The ethics of Śaṁkara is said to be intellectualistic, for avidyā or non-discrimination is the cause of our bondage.[6] Mithyājñāna of the jīva is the basis of all experience and activity; saṁyagjñāna or knowledge of oneness leads to freedom.[7] As the distinction between the highest self and the individual is one of false knowledge,[8] we get rid of it by true knowledge. All this leads one to believe that salvation is the result of metaphysical insight, and not moral perfection. Deussen regards this feature of the Advaita Vedānta as its "fundamental want." "Rightly," he says, "the Vedānta recognises as the sole source by which we may reach true knowledge, true apprehension of being in itself, our own 'I'; but it wrongly halts at the form in which it directly appeals

[1] S.B., ii. 3. 48.
[2] Mukhyasāmānādhikaraṇya.
[3] Bādhasāmānyādhikaraṇya.
[4] Eckhart asks: "What would it avail a man if he were king and knew it not?" The kingdom of heaven is a lost province.
[5] S.B., iii. 3. 53. See also iii. 2. 9.
[6] S.B., ii. 3. 48.
[7] S.B., i. 2–8. See also iii. 2. 25 and iv. 2. 8; S.B., i. 3. 19.
[8] Mithyājñānakṛta eva jīvaparameśvarayor bhedo na vastukṛtaḥ (S.B., i. 3. 19). See S.B. on Gauḍapāda's *Kārikā*, Introduction. Cp. jñānaṁ vinā mokṣo na siddhyati (*Ātmabodha*). Vivekāvivekamātreṇaiva (S.B., i. 3. 19). See also *Aparokṣānubhūti*, p. 14.

to our consciousness, as a knower, even after it has cut away the whole intellectual apparatus, and ascribed it to the not 'I,' the world of phenomena, just as it has also, very rightly, indicated as the dwelling of the highest soul, not as Descartes did the head, but the heart."[1] If the one and only existent Brahman is already perfect, and if all that we have to do is to assert its reality and deny the reality of everything else, there is no motive for ethical action. If the only way to escape the evils of finitude is simply to deny them, there is no room for any earnest ethics. We need not be serious about conquering hatred or changing our nature. But we have to remember that avidyā, though it is predominantly a logical concept, signifies, in the metaphysics of Śaṁkara, a whole attitude of life. "Avidyā is the conceit that the 'I' consists in the bodily nature; hence arise the worship of the body, which is passion, the despising of it, which is hate; thoughts of injury to it rouse fear, and so on."[2] False knowledge is the basis of all selfish desire and activity.[3] Avidyā is the finiteness of the finite individual impelling him to lead a life of desire and strife, consequent on the ignorance of his oneness with Brahman. Vices of character are not merely follies and errors, but perversions of will, and violations of the voice of God. Frequently Śaṁkara uses the one compound "avidyākāmakarma,"[4] where avidyā represents the cognitive error of looking upon the diversity of individuals as real,[5] kāma the emotional response towards the object and karma the practical act, to gain it or avoid it. It is this whole attitude of individualistic action that is rooted in a confusion between the real and the unreal, that leads to saṁsāra.[6] Kāma is born of avidyā, and karma is the result

[1] D.S.V., p. 59.

[2] Dehādiṣv anātmasv, aham asmīty ātmabuddhir avidyā; tatas tatpūjanādau rāgaḥ; tatparibhavādau dveṣaḥ; taducchedadarśanād bhayam, etc. (S.B., i. 3. 2).

[3] S.B., Kena Up., Introduction: Saṁsārabījam ajñānaṁ kāmakarma pravṛttikāraṇam. Again: "Avidyākāmakarmalakṣaṇaṁ saṁsārabījam" (S.B. on Kena Up., iv. 9).

[4] S.B. on Muṇḍ. Up., iii. 1. 1.

[5] Avidyākalpitaṁ lokaprasiddhaṁ jīvabhedam (S.B., ii. 1. 14; i. 3. 19).

[6] Anātmadarśino hy anātmaviṣayaḥ kāmaḥ; kāmayamānaś ca karoti karmāṇi; tatas tatphalopabhogāya śarīrād upādānalakṣaṇas saṁsāraḥ. (S.B., Tait. Up., i. 11.)

of kāma. The state of freedom is said to be the removal of the error, the restoration of the true desires and the suppression of all selfish endeavour.[1] The discipline of moral life includes the suppression of selfish activity, the development of true desires and the overcoming of empirical individualism. Until the last happens, we are not perfected in nature. We may suppress our kāma, we may act for the welfare of the world, but there is no security that we should not succumb to the temptation of a false desire or a selfish activity at another moment of our life; but until we cut the very roots of eager desire and petty egoism, until avidyā is abolished, we cannot be sure that we shall occupy the impersonal attitude of true enlightenment. The moral man is disinterested by chance; the saint is disinterested, thanks to his enlightenment.[2]

Śaṁkara distinguishes parokṣajñāna or logical learning, which we derive from books and teachers, that the supreme self and the individual are one, and aparokṣajñāna or anubhava, which is the experience of the seer who has surrendered his sense of separateness and realised his oneness with the Supreme.[3] Śaṁkara tells us that the former is incapable of releasing us from bondage. Commenting on the *Bṛhadāraṇyaka Upaniṣad*,[4] Śaṁkara says that one must raise oneself step by step from the state of mere learning (pāṇḍityam) to that of childlike simplicity (bālyam)[5] and from it to the state of the silent muni, and last of all to the state of the true Brahmin, who renounces in spirit all possessions and pleasures which are different from Brahman and so likely to bring subjection. The Advaita is both a philosophy and a religion.

[1] Sarvavāsanākṣayaṁ sarvakāmavināśaṁ sarvakarmapravilayam.

[2] See a very suggestive article by Professor Hiriyanna on this question in the *Proceedings of the Indian Oriental Conference*, Poona, vol. ii. Speaking of the distinction between true enlightenment and æsthetic delight, he says: ' To use Śaṁkara's words, the ever recurring series of kāma and karma, or interest and activity, constitutes life. The elimination of kāma and karma while their cause avidyā continues in a latent form marks the æsthetic attitude; the dismissal of avidyā even in this latent form marks the saintly attitude " (p. 241).

[3] Cp. *Varāhopaniṣad.*

Asti brahmeti ced veda parokṣajñānam eva tat
Aham brahmeti ced veda sākṣātkāras sa ucyate.

[4] iii. 8. 10. See also Chān. Up., iv. 1. 7.

[5] Cp. *St. Matthew*, xviii. 3

Enlightenment results in experience immediate and certain.[1] It is not the pursuit of a remote ideal.

In the same spirit it is maintained that cittaśuddhi or purification of the heart is a necessary prerequisite for spiritual realisation. This involves the increasing domination of the sattva quality and the suppression of rajas and tamas. It is brought about by disinterested work and practice of spiritual exercises. It does not supersede morality, but implies it. "When and to whomsoever the notion of the personal ego conveyed by 'I' (aham) and the notion of personal possession conveyed by 'mine' (mama) cease to be real, then he is the knower of Ātman."[2] Until selfish desire (kāma) is suppressed, avidyā cannot be rooted out. Jñāna has a larger sense than its English equivalent, knowledge. It is true wisdom, life at its highest stretch.[3] It is not the acceptance of a given dogma, but the living experience of which the intellectual apprehension is but the outward symbol. Śaṁkara has no great admiration for abstract intelligence. The highest intelligence, according to him, consists in the knowledge that intelligence alone is not enough. The end, it is true, is the destruction of avidyā, but we cannot get rid of avidyā by simply denying its reality. We are not said to know Brahman simply because we have a speculative notion of its being. Brahmajñāna is the spiritual realisation of our rootedness in the eternal, which remains an abiding possession, a part of our very being.

It is said that it is a weakness of Śaṁkara's system that he does not regard moral values as ultimately real. Moral distinctions have a meaning only so long as our ego is sharply marked off from whatever lies outside its body in space and beyond its experience in time. The moral world, which assumes the isolation and independence of its members, belongs to the world of appearances. The duties commanded and the claims that call for satisfaction are both alike the personal affairs of individuals. The command and the claim are based on the assumed independence of the finite individuals.

[1] Anubhavārūḍham eva ca vidyāphalaṁ na kriyāphalavat kālāntarabhāvi (S.B., iii. 4. 15).

[2] *Upadesasāhasrī*, xiv. 29. See also xiv. 141. See also S.B. on Kena Up., Introduction.

[3] See Plato's *Timæus*, p. 90; Aristotle's *Nichomachean Ethics*, x. 7.

So long as we occupy the standpoint of individualistic moralism, we are in the world of saṁsāra, with its hazards and hardships. Moral growth consists in a gradual correction of the individualistic point of view, and when the correction is complete, the moral as such ceases to exist. So long as the latter persists, the ideal is unrealised. The end of morality is to lift oneself up above one's individuality and become one with the impersonal spirit of the universe. But, so long as there is a trace of individuality clinging to the moral subject, this lifting up can only be partial. To attain oneness with the infinite, on the basis of the finite, is evidently an impossible task. To realise the ideal, we must pass beyond the moral life and rise to the spiritual realisation in which the life of finite struggle and endeavour is transcended. So Śaṁkara insists repeatedly on the inadequacy of moral goodness and finite striving, so far as the ideal of perfection is concerned. Karma cannot lead to mokṣa. The finite as finite must be transcended. Avidyā, which is the basis of all finite life, must be overcome. We must break through the circuit of saṁsāra, of ignorance, attachment and action (avidyākāmakarma), to recognise our oneness with the supreme spirit. However moral we may be, so long as mere goodness does not take us beyond the finite and break the barriers of avidyā, perfection is beyond us. So Śaṁkara argues that we cannot win mokṣa by any amount of striving; for all karma, whether it be observance of Vedic rites or devotion to God, leads only to a conservation of the finite as finite, and involves us in saṁsāra, or the struggle of the finite for the infinite, endlessly prolonged. Release from this revolving wheel comes through jñāna, or the insight which lifts us out of our individuality into the oneness with the infinite.[1] Morality is of the nature of development, and cannot lead to a realisation of the truth which is self-existent. If moral progress is the central feature

[1] The attitude of the late Professor Bosanquet on this question is analogous to that of Śaṁkara, and his interpretation of the justification by faith is similar to Śaṁkara's view of release through jñāna. Cp.: "We are one with the whole by faith, and not in works. Here our inadequacy is done away. This is the very meaning of 'saving experiences.' We throw ourselves upon the grace of the universe and find in oneness with it an adequacy which is self-contradictory for us as finite agents" (*The Meeting of Extremes in Contemporary Philosophy*, p. 173). See also *Mind*, N.S., vol. xxx. p. 98.

of man's life, there is no stage at which he can say that he has realised the goal and attained his nature. If God is the nature of man, there is no point in moral progress when the individual can say "I am God." He who conforms to moral rules cannot feel that he has realised his self If moral life were all, the most brilliant career is a futile thing, love a fleeting illusion and happiness an ever-receding goal. St. Paul [1] insists on the impossibility of redemption through the law. Whatever we may do, unless we surrender our selfishness, we cannot be saved. We may fulfil the law of morality from selfish motives, but it has not much moral value. To get rid of the sinfulness of our nature, our avidyā as Śaṁkara calls it, Paul demands faith and Śaṁkara jñāna, which alone lifts us above our finiteness and above the possibility of sin. Salvation is not a question of invention or construction, but of discovery or unveiling. Morality has always a reference to something beyond itself, but jñāna or pure beholding or realisation is complete in itself. It lacks nothing, has no aim or purpose. The śruti declares that the self-existent eternal freedom cannot be achieved by action.[2]

If we remember the sound canon of interpretation, that the best way to arrive at a true meaning of a religious formula is to consider the heresies it is intended to deny, we can appreciate what seems Śaṁkara's unnecessary emphasis on the futility of the karmamārga for the final end of perfection. He felt that the Mīmāṁsakas had bent the bow too much on the side of works by declaring that mere ritualistic formalism was adequate for gaining us freedom of spirit. His denial of the adequacy of works to salvation is a reaction against

[1] *Epistle to the Romans* iii, viii, x, xiii, and the *Epistle to the Galatians* ii and iii.

[2] Nāsty akṛtaḥ kṛtena. Śaṁkara comments akṛto mokṣaḥ kṛtena karmaṇā nāstīti. See also S.B. on Tait. Up., Introduction. Again: "An action is that which is enjoined as being independent of the nature of existing things and dependent on the energy of some person's mind . . . knowledge is the result of the pramāṇas (pramāṇajanyam) which have for their objects existing things and depends entirely on existing things (vastutantram), and not on vedic statements or the mind of man" (S.B., i. 1. 4). See also S.B., i. 4. 22. The Mādhyamikas regard the equipment of wisdom (jñānasaṁbhāra) as leading to absolute freedom (dharmakāya), while the equipment of merit (puṇyasaṁbhāra) leads to the body of bliss (saṁbhogakāya) (*Mādhyamikāvatāra*, iii. 12). See Keith's *Budd. Ph.*, p. 277.

the exaggerated emphasis which the Mīmāṁsakas place on Vedic ritualism. Ultimate freedom is nothing more than the removal of ajñāna. "The attainment of the highest is merely the removal of avidyā." [1] "On the removal of the ignorance of the nature of Brahman, one abides in one's own self and attains the supreme end." [2] To know Brahman is not to gain an object which we did not possess, but is realising our true nature of which we were unconscious. When avidyā is destroyed, vidyā shines of itself,[3] even as the piece of rope is known when the false notion that it is a snake is refuted.[4] Mere karma, which has for its effect transitory occurrences, cannot lead us to the eternal fact of freedom. Karma cannot dispel avidyā, since the two are not antagonistic. When knowledge is said to precede karma, it is not the highest spiritual insight, but external knowledge of this or that object. Karma is always undertaken for the fulfilment of desire. Mokṣa is incompatible with the presence of desire. Karma has no meaning unless the individual has faith in his own agency and distinguishes the object from himself [5]; but so long as these distinctions subsist, mokṣa is unattainable. "Mokṣa is impossible with a perception of difference, and karma is impossible without a perception of it." [6] The acts performed are expected to yield one of the following results: "Production of a new thing (utpatti), change of state (vikāra), consecration (saṁskāra) and acquisition (āpti)"; mokṣa is none of these.[7] Karma has preparatory value, but it is essentially based on a partial view, and so cannot lead us by itself to the ultimate goal. Jñāna or spiritual insight is the only means to freedom.[8] Śaṁkara insists on this fact sometimes with an unnecessary emphasis. "It is unreasonable to think that the knowledge of Brahman, before which all notions of distinctions of deed, doer, fruit, etc., vanish, can possibly require any extraneous thing as its complement or concomitant

[1] S.B., Muṇḍ. Up., i. 5. Avidyāpaya eva hi paraprāptiḥ. Avidyānivṛttir eva mokṣaḥ.

[2] S.B., Tait. Up., Introduction. "Avidyānivṛttau svātmany avasthānam paraprāptiḥ.

[3] S.B., iii. 2. 21.

[4] S.B., ii. 1. 14.

[5] S.B., Chān. Up., Introduction.

[6] S.B., Kena Up., Introduction.

[7] S.B., Tait. Up., ii. 11.

[8] *Ātmabodha*, p. 203.

aid in accomplishing it ; nor can its fruit of freedom require any such ; therefore jñāna cannot consistently with itself require karma as its concomitant help or complement."[1] Śaṁkara admits that the performance of obligatory acts (nityāni karmāṇi) helps us to undo the effects of our past sins, while those who desire specific objects may resort to acts intended to secure their fulfilment (kāmyāni karmāṇi). Both these satisfy the individual with cravings and desires for a time, but neither helps him to reach life eternal. The Mīmāṁsaka holds that, if we avoid interested and forbidden acts, exhaust by enjoyment the fruits of karmas which already have begun to operate, and ward off sins of omission by the performance of obligatory duties, without any other effort, mokṣa can be attained. Śaṁkara says in reply that there are ever so many karmas which have not begun to operate and whose effects cannot be exhausted in one birth ; these will involve us in other births, whereby fresh karma will go on accumulating. There is no hope for us until we get rid of the desires which give rise to karma. The desires are traced to avidyā, and so only vidyā, which annihilates avidyā, can take us out of the clutches of karma.[2] Brahmavidyā removes the very basis for these external observances.[3] What counts is not outer conduct but inner life. Its torturing problems cannot be solved by a reference to rules. Our secret hearts, our prayers and meditations help us to solve the problems of life. The highest morality therefore consists in developing the right spirit. The secret of moral genius lies in the spiritualising of our consciousness. Moral life is the necessary result of spiritual insight. Till the latter is gained, moral rules are obeyed in an external fashion.

In another sense, moral obligations are relative to the

[1] See S.B. on Kena Up.

[2] S.B., i. 1. 4. Cp. Plato: "Those who have practised the popular and social virtues which come from habit and practice without philosophy or reason are happiest in the round of transmigration ; for it is probable that they return into a mild and social nature like their own, such as that of bees or wasps or ants, or it may be into bodies of men, and that from them are made worthy citizens. But none except the philosopher or the lover of knowledge, who is wholly pure when he goes hence, is permitted to go to the race of the gods" (*Phædo*, p. 82).

[3] Idānīṁ karmopādānahetuparihārāya brahmavidyā prastūyate (S.B., Tait. Up., Introduction).

state of the individual. Morality, in the modern world, is confused with social values, but the latter are not the whole of values. Not only our views of society but our thoughts of God also count. A Robinson Crusoe on a desert island even without Friday can cherish values.

Śaṁkara holds that the knowledge of the inner self is antagonistic to karma, and cannot coexist with it even in a dream. If there are cases recorded in the scriptures where householders performing karma possessed the sacred wisdom and transmitted it to their disciples, Śaṁkara retorts that these statements cannot override an obvious fact, for " the coexistence of light and darkness cannot be brought about even by a hundred rules, much less by mere indications like these." [1] This whole discussion is permeated by the ambiguous usage of the word karma. If karma means activity undertaken by an individual for the fulfilment of this or that private end, it is inconsistent with spiritual insight. Impersonal action, on the other hand, undertaken by an individual after gaining insight for the sake of general ends, does not bind the doer, does not commit him to the life of saṁsāra. Karma, in the former sense, cannot coexist with spiritual insight.[2] If jñāna and karma are opposed as light and darkness, it is karma in the sense of selfish activity and jñāna in the sense of unselfish wisdom. According to Śaṁkara, what the released soul does is not to be called karma. The activity of the liberated soul for world-solidarity (lokasaṁgraha) is not karma strictly speaking. Commenting on the passage of the *Muṇḍaka Upaniṣad* which reads, " sporting in self, delighting in self and daily acts, he is the best of those who know Brahman," [3] Śaṁkara remarks that the view that the combination of karma and knowledge is allowed by this text is only " the prattle of the ignorant." [4] That some sort of activity is admitted cannot be denied. All that Śaṁkara affirms is that it is not activity which we ordinarily call karma,

[1] Vidyā karmavirodhāc ca na hibrahmātmaikatvadarśanena saha karma svapne 'pi saṁpādayituṁ śakyam . . . yat tu gṛhastheṣu brahmavidyā sampradāyakartṛtvādiliṅgam na tat sthitanyāyam bādhitum utsahate ; na hi vidhiśatenāpi tamaḥprakāśayor ekatrasaṁbhavas śakyate kartum. Kimuta liṅgaiḥ kevalair iti (S.B., Muṇḍ. Up., Introduction).

[2] See S.B., Īśa. Up., 18.

[3] iii. 1. 4.

[4] Asatpralapitam evaitat. See also S.B., Chān. Up., Introduction.

for karma is based on egoism.[1] In another passage he says: "To one who knows, no work will cling even if one performs works during his whole life—thanks to the greatness of knowledge."[2] Karma is the name for all activity which leads to continuance of existence in saṁsāra, and this is opposed to true knowledge. The other kind of activity is not to be called karma, since it is not due to kāma or selfish desire. The freed has suppressed his selfish desires (akāmayamāna). On the other hand, in certain passages where his interest is to insist on the freedom of the released soul from the trammels of saṁsāra, he declares that, since all activity is painful in effect, no activity is possible at all for the liberated.[3]

Asceticism is a charge that is frequently levelled against Śaṁkara's ethics. In a hundred ways Śaṁkara urges that there is never anything worthy of pursuit in empirical life.[4] Illness and death come, if not to-day then to-morrow, to ourselves and those whom we love, and nothing remains of all we love on earth but dust and ashes. Nothing on earth can offer a sure foothold for the soul of man. The futility of saṁsāra and attachment to it are indicated in the familiar story of the traveller who, to save himself from the wild beast that is pursuing him, gets into the dried-up well. But at the bottom of the well there is a dragon with its jaws wide open to devour him. He cannot get out for fear of the wild beast, he dare not descend for fear of the dragon, and so he catches hold of a branch of a wild plant growing out of a crevice of the well. He grows tired and feels that he must soon perish. Though death awaits him on either side, he still holds on, clinging fondly to the wild plant, but lo! there are two mice, one black and the other white, gnawing the trunk of the wild plant. It will soon give way and break off and the traveller cannot escape the jaws of death. Even so, we who are

[1] Karmahetuḥ kāma syāt (Tait. Up., S.B., Introduction).

[2] S.B., iii. 4. 14. See also S.B., Chān. Up., ii. 23. 1.

[3] S.B., ii. 3. 40.

[4] Cp. 1 *John* ii. 15–17 "Love not the world, nor yet what is in the world; if anyone loves the world, love for the Father is not in him. For all that is in the world, the desire of the flesh and the desire of the eyes and the proud glory of life, belongs not to the Father but to the world; and the world is passing away with its desire, while he who does the will of God remains for ever" (Moffatt's E.T.).

travelling on the circuit of saṁsāra know the pitfalls of our life, know that all things to which we cling will inevitably perish, but in spite of it all, we find some drops of honey on the leaves of some wild plant and are busy licking them. Though we know that the dragon of death awaits us, though we know that the white mouse and the black, day and night, are gnawing through the branches to which we cling, we still are tempted by the tree of life. The dragon is there, but that does not matter, the honey is sweet. We take the tree for the truth and do not want to face the terrible fact that nothing in saṁsāra can satisfy the infinite in man. Śaṁkara tells us that the supreme fulfilment is the result and reward of supreme renunciation. It is reached when desire is dead and pleasure and pain alike are cast away. The most perfect virtue and the loftiest intellectual vision are inadequate for the purpose of spiritual perfection. Śaṁkara insists on a life of self-sacrifice and asks us to free ourselves from attachment to the body. The enemy of the soul is not the body as such, but our bondage to the body and the sense of mineness.[1] The released soul before death is possessed of a body, but its presence is not inconsistent with the freedom of spirit. It is because the body in the ordinary individual offers a thousand hindrances to the free growth of the spirit that we find Śaṁkara arguing that the life of the spirit is repressed and hampered by union with the material body. The appearance of asceticism is due to the repeated exhortations to crucify the flesh with the passions and the lusts thereof.

It is said that there can be no sense of social life or civic duty in Śaṁkara's world-negating philosophy. There is no need for us to take any interest in the world if it is a lie. Śaṁkara, it is said, insists on redemption from the world and not of it. He does not demand a change of the world, but exhorts us to escape from it. There is no incentive to improve the existing social institutions. That the case is not so bad as it seems is evident from the life of Śaṁkara, which is a standing refutation of the charge that the existent world-order with its institutions is a thing to be escaped from. His whole philosophy refutes the assumption that individuality depends on separateness. Man has to purify himself from the defile-

[1] *Śataślokī*, p. 15.

ments of the world, strip off all clothing, leave behind everything unworthy. He must break away from the slavery of selfhood, passion and sense. A deliberate surrender of all personal feelings and preferences, a self-stripping to the point of apparent nothingness, a " flight of the alone to the alone," means eternal life. The emphasis in Śaṁkara is not on retirement from the world, but on renunciation of the self. It is easier to flee from the world than from the self. Śaṁkara asks us to suppress our selfishness, and, if that requires solitude and retirement, these are advised as means to an end. One who has completely shaken himself free from selfishness is at liberty to take upon himself the task of the world. His attitude will be not world-seeking or world-fleeing, but world-saving. The perfect man lives and dies, not for himself, but for mankind. It is, however, true that Śaṁkara asks us to be in the world but not of it, even as a drop of water is on the lotus leaf without getting mixed up with it. The part of wisdom is to dream with our eyes open, to be detached from the world without any hostility to it.[1]

The criticism that if we interpret mokṣa as the haven of peace, where all life is stilled, consciousness and personality are suppressed, then we can attain to it only by ceasing to be human, takes us beyond our present point to the larger question of the relation of the infinite to the finite, since morality belongs to the system of things finite. Logically, it is the question of the relation of intuition to intellect, spiritual insight to logical knowledge. While the latter depends on the former, we do not know how exactly the two are related. The empirical world depends on Brahman, and we cannot say how. Even so the moral life is related to the spiritual mokṣa ;

[1] Referring to Schopenhauer's statement that " the study of the Upaniṣads has been the solace of my life, it will be the solace of my death," Max Müller says : " Schopenhauer was the last man to write at random, or to allow himself to go into ecstasies over so-called mystic and inarticulate thought. And I am neither afraid nor ashamed to say that I share his enthusiasm for the Vedānta, and feel indebted to it for much that has been helpful to me in my passage through life. After all, it is not everybody who is called upon to take an active part in life, whether in defending or ruling a country, in amassing wealth or breaking stones ; and for fitting men to lead contemplative and quiet lives, I know no better preparation than the Vedānta. A man may be a Platonist and yet a good citizen and an honest Christian, and I should say the same of a Vedāntist ' (S.S., p. 193).

how, we cannot say. To divorce one from the other, intuition from intellect, Brahman from the world, religious realisation from moral life, is to justify the criticism that for Śaṁkara the world is an illusion, our knowledge a lie and our moral life a mockery. But Śaṁkara, again and again, declares that the world has its roots in Brahman. We have to pass through the world of phenomena to get beyond it. As the pathway to the real lies through the phenomenal, the pathway to perfection lies through moral life. Though the end is something in which the ethical as such is transcended, it does not follow that the spiritual has no relation to the ethical. The seeker is nowhere encouraged to give up the duties of the world or devotion to God. The unreality of the moral situation arises only when the function of morality is fulfilled. The final good is not a beyond, while the moral struggle here is a scene of error and failure. It can be realised here and now. To say that the moral effort is relative, is to recognise the element of the ideal in it. The consideration that the distinction of good and evil is relative to our finite level, does not invalidate its observance in the world of practice. The unreality of the distinction has no meaning for those who fetter themselves in chains of selfishness and prolong the misery of finite existence. Śaṁkara does not jettison law altogether, but holds that the approach to freedom lies through the gates of law. Intellect rests on intuition and moral life on spiritual freedom. It is the germ out of which the flower of perfection evolves.

XLII

Karma

The law of karma is assumed by Śaṁkara. Individuality is due to karma, which is a product of avidyā.[1] The kind of world into which we are born is just the return of the works on the doer.[2] The individual organism is the working machinery[3] intended to produce that requital in the form of actions and its results of suffering and happiness. Sometimes

[1] S.B., iii. 2. 9.

[2] Kriyākārakaphalam.

[3] Kāryakāraṇasaṁghāta.

the works of a single existence have to be atoned for in several succeeding ones. Even as the atonement for the past is completed, fresh karma accumulates, " so that the clockwork of atonement in running down always winds itself up again." [1] Moral life is an unremitting active energising, which is never exhausted. It takes endless forms, owing to the variety of the demands of the conditions of human life. This process goes on for ever, until perfect knowledge is gained, which consumes the seed of karma and makes rebirth impossible. Freedom from subjection to the law of karma is the end of human life. To get rid of avidyā is to be freed from the law of karma. But so long as the individual is finite, he is subject to the law of karma, *i.e.* he always strains after an ideal which he never reaches. Morality is a stepping-stone and not a stopping-place. All acts done with an expectation of reward yield their fruits in accordance with the law of karma, while those done with no selfish interest, in the spirit of dedication to God, purify the mind.

It does not, however, follow that we move like marionettes pulled by the strings of our past karma. It has already been said that the individual is responsible for his acts, and God is only the assisting medium, conserving the fruits of his deeds.[2] God does not compel anyone to do this or that. Even those tendencies with which we are bound can be overcome by strength of will.[3] Vaśiṣṭha asks Rāma in *Yogavāśiṣṭha* " to break the chain that holds us in bondage by free effort." [4] The individual has an impulsive nature by virtue of which he has likes and dislikes.[5] Man, if guided by the unformed nature with which he is born, is completely at the mercy of his impulses. So long as his activities are determined by these, they are not free. But man is not a mere sum-total of his impulses. There is the infinite in him. The self as causal power lies outside the empirical series and determines them. The history of man is not a puppet show. It is a creative evolution.

[1] D.S.V., p. 354.
[2] S.B., ii. 3. 42.
[3] S.B.G., iii. 3. 4.
[4] See *Jīvanmuktiviveka*. ch. i.
[5] S.B.G., viii. 18; iii. 33.

XLIII

Mokṣa

Mokṣa is a matter of direct realisation of something which is existent from eternity, though it is hidden from our view. When the limitations are removed, the soul is liberated. It remains where it is, what it is and eternally was, the first principle of all things. It is the peace that the world can never give, nor take away, the supreme and only blessedness. "That which is real in the absolute sense, immutable, eternal, all-penetrating like ākāśa, exempt from all change, all-satisfying, undivided, whose nature is to be its own light, in which neither good nor evil, nor effect, nor past nor present nor future has any place, this incorporeal is called liberation."[1] When avidyā vanishes, the true soul stands self-revealed, even as gold shines when freed from the impurities which affected it, or as the stars shine in a cloudless night, when the day which overpowers them disappears.[2] The enfranchisement of man from all his self-wrought bondages, the glory which is utterly beyond all grasp of thought, the peace that is the very purpose of all our striving, lies nearer to us than our nearest consciousness. Śaṁkara shows us not a heaven which is apart from, a different order of experience from, earth, but the heaven which is all the time here, could we but see it. It is not something in an imagined future, a continuance of existence in a world to come after the present life is ended, but a state of identification with the real here and now.[3]

The freed soul assumes the form of his true self (svātmanyavasthānam).[4] Freedom is not the abolition of self, but the realisation of its infinity and absoluteness by the expansion

[1] Idaṁ tu pāramārthikaṁ, kūṭasthaṁ, nityaṁ, vyomavat sarvavyāpi, sarvavikriyārahitaṁ, nityatṛptaṁ niravayavaṁ svayaṁjyotissvabhāvaṁ, yatra dharmādharmau sahakāryeṇa kālatrayaṁ ca nopāvartate tad aśarīram mokṣākhyam (S.B., i. 1. 4).

[2] S.B., i. 3. 19.

[3] Cp. with this Nāgārjuna's view that nirvāṇa is without origination or cessation, neither one nor many, without motion or absence of motion, neither eternal nor ceasing, and that it is one with saṁsāra (*Mādhyamika Kārikā*, xxv. 19).

[4] S.B., iv. 4. 1–3. Cp. *Advaitabrahmasiddhi*: Ātmany evāvidyānivṛttiḥ.

and illumination of consciousness. Citsukhācārya says that mokṣa is the realisation of all bliss.[1] The essential nature of self as bliss is concealed by pain, bred by ignorance; in the absence of ignorance, pain disappears and the nature of the self as unmixed bliss manifests itself. The realising of mokṣa is not an objective process by which we try to destroy the whole world. It is not "like annihilating the hardness of butter by putting it on the fire.[2] Such a huge undertaking as destroying the world is impossible for a mere man. If the significance of mokṣa be the destruction of the plurality of the world, then the whole world would have been destroyed when the first man attained liberation.[3] The realisation of the truth does not mean the abolition of plurality, but only the removal of the sense of plurality.[4] It is an insight which changes the face of the world and "makes all things new." This insight, this changed attitude to life and its happenings, is not so much a condition of mokṣa as mokṣa itself.[5] The unending procession of the world will go on through its ups and downs, but the liberated man's attachment to it is over.

The word avidyā is intended to bring out the essence of the position. On the attainment of freedom, nothing happens to the world but only our views of it alter. Its fleeting things, which have a bewildering fascination for the unwary, no more trouble the liberated The cause of pain is simply the error of false knowledge,[6] and with deliverance from error comes liberation from pain. Mokṣa is thus not the dissolution of the world but only the disappearance of a false outlook. In his anxiety to make out that the freed soul has no possibility of relapsing into the phenomenal world, Śaṁkara frequently suggests that freedom consists in an entire

[1] Anavacchinnānandaprāpti. S.L.S.

[2] S.B., iii. 2. 21. See also Bṛh. Up., iv. 5. 13.

[3] Ekena cādimuktena pṛthivyādipravilayaḥ kṛta itīdānīm pṛthivyādi śūnyaṁ jagad abhaviṣyat (S.B., iii. 2. 21).

[4] Jñāte dvaitaṁ na vidyate.

[5] Cp. Śuddhabrahmāśrayaviṣayam ekam eva jñānaṁ tannāśa eva ca mokṣaḥ. Kṛṣṇānanda, the commentator on *Siddhāntaleśa*, writes: Caitanyasyājñānasaṁbandho bandhas tadasaṁbandho mokṣo na tu tannivṛttiḥ. Padmapāda holds that mokṣa is the absence of false knowledge. Mithyājñānanivṛttimātram mokṣaḥ.

[6] Mithyābhimānabhramanimitta eva duḥkhānubhavaḥ (S.B., ii. 3. 46).

dissolution of all empirical categories and subject-object distinction.[1]

The criticism that the world is pure illusion finds its support in the view that the world of experience with its distinctions of souls, things and Īśvara, disappears for him who recognises the oneness of Brahman and the Ātman.[2] There are countless passages in Śaṁkara which declare that, as the misconception of the snake disappears on the perception of the rope, as the dream creations vanish on awakening, so also saṁsāra ceases to exist on attaining mukti. The form in which the world appears to our limited insight changes on the realisation of the identity of the soul with Brahman. The things we know as the contents of our environment in this practical life of ours are not present, as such, in the Absolute.[3] Śaṁkara, in different ways, emphasises the fact that the world does not exist for the Absolute in the way in which it exists for us. Bradley is as certain as Śaṁkara that the distinctive nature of appearances does not survive in the Absolute. To use his expression, the appearances are transmuted somehow in the Absolute. How all these are resolved into reality is a "somehow" in Bradley and anirvacanīya in Śaṁkara. Śaṁkara would object to Bradley's use of the word "transmutation." Even the amount of reaction on the imperfect which the word suggests, is inconsistent with the unchanging perfection of the Absolute. It is Śaṁkara's excessive attachment to logical precision that leads him into somewhat misleading statements, to the effect that the world is nought. We are employing intellectual categories when we speak of the "transmutation" of appearances in reality or the "blending" of notes in an eternal harmony. All these, in the opinion of Śaṁkara, attempt to introduce plurality and empirical distinctions into the heart of the Absolute, for which there is no metaphysical warrant. Reality is superior to all relations. The Absolute remains something which we cannot translate into our terms. The relative, as the relative, has no place

[1] Sureśvara says: "When the Infinite Light is intuitively realised, all creatures from Brahmā down to the lowest plant melt into an illusion like unto a dream" (*Mānasollāsa*, i).

[2] Gṛhīte tv ātmaikatve bandhamokṣādisarvavyavahāraparisamāptir eva syāt (S.B., i. 2. 6).

[3] S.B., i. 2. 12; i. 2. 20.

in the Absolute. When that which makes the Absolute into relative is destroyed, what remains is the Absolute. Commenting on the *Māṇḍūkya Upaniṣad*, Śaṁkara observes that the turīya or the fourth (integral experience) is realised by merging the three others (waking, dreaming and dreamless sleep) in it. The highest includes the rest, while transcending them.[1] The phrase used "prapañcopaśamam" means the sinking of the world in Brahman, and not its denial. We possess faculties capable of responding to orders of truth, the use of which would change the whole character of our universe. When we attain to the state of turīya, we shall have reality from another angle, lit by another light ; only this angle and this light are absolute. When we apprehend reality from this angle, we see that the reality of the world is the Brahman itself.[2] What we negate is the illusory framework, and what remains is the real in itself.[3] Māyā as concealment has no power over the liberated soul. When the certainty of the oneness of Brahman and the Ātman is reached by anubhava, the tie which binds us to forms is cut, and the forms cease to be attractive on their own account. They may remain and will remain, so long as the senses are alive and intellect operates, but there is no need to connect them with the intuited Brahman. When the illusion of the mirage is dissipated by scientific knowledge, the illusory appearance remains, though it no longer deceives us. We see the same appearance, but give a different value to it. When the illusoriness of the illusion is perceived, it ceases to be an illusion. Whether the forms dissolve themselves in the formless or show themselves to be mere appearances of Brahman, on either view the world is not a mere illusion.

Śaṁkara declares in many passages that the nature of liberation is a state of oneness with Brahman,[4] and even as the latter is lifted above all categories of experience, so the state of mokṣa cannot be described in terms of our knowledge. Since the latter deals with distinctions of space and time, cause and effect, persons and things, action and suffering, it

[1] Trayāṇāṁ viśvādīnām pūrvapūrvapravilāpanena turīyasya pratipattiḥ. Pravilaya suggests merging, and not nirākaraṇa or negation.

[2] S.B., i. 3. 1.

[3] S.B., Māṇḍūkya Up., ii. 7.

[4] Brahmaiva hi muktyavasthā.

is said that none of these distinctions applies to the state of freedom. It cannot be said that the liberated live in a geographical area called svarga or brahmaloka ; nor can it be said that they last for endless time. For, Śaṁkara agrees with Aristotle that " endless duration makes good no better, nor white any whiter." [1] We cannot regard the state of mokṣa as one of continuous activity. It is the highest experience where all intellectual activity is transcended and even self-consciousness is obliterated. The soul is lifted above the wheel of the world, the saṁsāracakra, with its perpetual rhythm of growth and decay, birth and rebirth, and achieves that experience of eternity which Boethius defines as " the total and perfect possession of unlimited life at a single moment." [2] Freedom consists in attaining to the state of universal spirit, sarvātmabhāva (literally all-selfness), or Brahman, which is lifted above all distinctions of the empirical world.[3] The state of mokṣa is " none other than one's own inherent nature as Brahman, and is not an acquired state like svarga (paradise) It has been taught in the scriptures (śruti), and even stands to reason, that Brahman is of one nature, and therefore liberation is of one sort, whether obtained by Brahmā or man. The sālokya (or being in the same world as Brahman) and other specific kinds of liberation mentioned, are acquired results, and therefore admit of degrees of excellence according to the quality of worship, but liberation (mukti) is not of that nature." [4] Since Brahman is " present everywhere, within everything and is the self of everything . . . it is altogether impossible that it ever should be the goal of the process of going. For we do not go to what is already reached ; experience tells us that a person goes to something different from him." [5] The worshippers of personal God may have to go to Brahmaloka, but not those who have attained mokṣa.[6]

Mokṣa is described negatively as the state of freedom where there is neither day nor night, where the stream of time has

[1] *Nichomachean Ethics*, i. 6.

[2] Quoted in Evelyn Underhill's *Jacopone de Todi*, p. 245.

[3] Sa sarvātmabhāvaḥ sarvasaṁsāradharmātītabrahmasvarūpatvam eva (S.B., Tait. Up., ii. 1).

[4] S.B., iii. 4. 52.

[5] S.B., iv. 3. 14. See also iii. 3. 31.

[6] S.B., iv. 3. 7–8.

stopped, where the sun and the stars are swept away from the sky. The distinctions of knowledge have no force in it.[1] It is like the heaven of the Christians, an inheritance incorruptible, undefiled, that fadeth not away. But it does not follow that it is a state of utter blankness. The freed soul does not see another, but sees himself in all.[2] Even as Brahman seems from our empirical point of view a mere nothing, so the state of mokṣa seems to be a dead loss, a fading into forgetfulness, a putting out the light and melting away into non-existence, of the type suggested by George Eliot in *The Legend of Jubal*:—

> Quitting mortality, a quenched sun-wave,
> The All-creating Presence for his grave.

As Śaṁkara protests that Brahman seems non-existent only to the feeble-minded, so he argues that, from our empirical point of view, this becoming one with the great All *seems* to be a sinking into death and not rising into life, but, strictly speaking, it is not that. There are even passages which make out that on the attainment of mokṣa there is consciousness. Taking one such, Śaṁkara argues that individual consciousness (viśeṣavijñāna) disappears in it and not all consciousness. The pure substance of Ātman (vijñānaghanātmā) remains.[3] Similarly, he holds that only limiting adjuncts are destroyed in mokṣa, and not the Ātman itself.[4] Mokṣa is not vanishing into a waste. To us, from our limited view-point, the soul with its outlook confined to the body, the senses, the mind and the understanding, is the real; and the liberated soul which has realised its oneness with the universal self, has conquered time, and reached life eternal, seems to be unreal. We demand an immortal life in the sense of continued personal existence. Śaṁkara grants it to the soul whose outlook does not go beyond the body, the senses and the mind. Only he regards such a soul as a mere particular, a phenomenon

[1] Darśanādivyahahārābhāva (S.B., i. 3. 9).

[2] Muktasyāpi sarvaikatvāt samāno dvitīyābhāvaḥ (S.B., Chān. Up., viii. 12. 3).

[3] S.B., i. 4. 22. He also quotes Bṛh. Up., iv. 3. 30, in S.B., i. 3. 19, and comments thus: "Viśeṣavijñānavināśābhiprāyam eva, na vijñātṛvināśābhiprāyam."

[4] Upādhipralayam evāyaṁ nātmapralayam (ii. 1. 14).

among phenomena that arise and pass away. But when everything that characterises the finite as finite vanishes, when the body which is the symbol of finitude is shaken off, *i.e.* when the finite is raised to the infinite level, we reach the true state of blessedness even here and now. What is positively its content it is difficult to describe. Of it, it is true, that eye hath not seen nor ear heard, neither hath it entered the heart of man, to conceive the glory that shall be revealed. Yet, if mokṣa is to have any significance for us, we must clothe the idea of immortality in the language of time and call it sarvātmabhāva, all-selfness.[1]

Similarly there are passages where Śaṁkara declares that the true nature of the individual is that of the highest lord, "The self of the highest Lord is the real nature of the embodied soul; and the state of embodiment is due to the limiting adjuncts."[2] "Even as the imagined serpent becomes a rope after the removal of avidyā, so the apparent individual soul which is stained by agency and experience, love and hate and other imperfections, and is subject to much that is evil, is transformed through wisdom to the sinless essence of the highest God, opposed to all these imperfections."[3] Appaya Dīkṣita quotes this passage and remarks that Śaṁkara evidently supports the view of mokṣa as oneness with Īśvara[4] which he himself adopts.[5]

The freed soul is said to be indistinguishable (avibhāga) from the highest.

This indistinguishableness is interpreted in various ways. Jaimini[6]

---

[1] Sarvātmabhāvo mokṣa uktaḥ (S.B., Bṛh. Up., iv. 4. 6).

[2] Pārameśvaram eva hi śarīrasya pāramārthikaṁ svarūpam, upādhikṛtaṁ tu śārīratvam (iii. 4. 8). Again: Evam mithyājñānakṛta eva jīvaparameśvarayor bhedo na vastukṛto vyomavad asaṁgatvāviśeṣāt (S.B., i. 3. 19). See also S.B., Īśa. Up., 14.

[3] Yad avidyāpratyupasthāpitam apāramārthikaṁ jaivaṁ rūpaṁ kartṛtvabhoktṛtvarāgadveṣādidoṣakaluṣitam anekānarthayogi tadvilayanena, tadviparītam, apahatapāpmatvādiguṇakam pārameśvaraṁ svarūpaṁ vidyayā pratipādyate, sarpādivilayaneneva rajjvādīn (S.B., i. 3. 19). See *Kalpataru* and *Parimala* on it.

[4] Bhāṣyakāro 'py atispaṣṭam muktasya saguṇeśvarabhāvāpattim āha.

[5] See *Siddhāntaleśa*, iv. It is suggested that, according to the anekajīvavāda, mukti is oneness with Īśvara until all are liberated, when it becomes identity with Brahman. See *Siddhāntaleśa*, iv, and Kṛṣṇānanda's *Vyākhyā* on it.

[6] S.B., iv. 4. 5. See also Chān. Up., viii. 1. 6; viii. 7. 1.

regards the released soul as possessing the many qualities of freedom from sin, truthfulness of conception down to omniscience and omnipotence. Auḍulomi takes exception to this view, and holds that the freed soul has only the one positive quality of spiritual energy (caitanyam) and the negative one of freedom from sin.[1] The other qualities which Jaimini attributes to the freed soul are due to the limitations (upādhis). Bādarāyaṇa sees no contradiction between the two views.[2] Śaṁkara agrees with Bādarāyaṇa. Auḍulomi gives us the metaphysical truth which refuses to be squeezed into the empirical categories, but if we insist on an empirical description, Jaimini's view will have to be accepted. So Jaimini and Auḍulomi give the intellectual and the intuitional accounts of the one state of freedom. Bādarāyaṇa, after stating the almost infinite power and knowledge which will come to the liberated soul after the attainment of release, makes the observation that, nevertheless, none will get the power of creating, ruling and destroying the universe, since that belongs to God alone.[3] This is consistent with the view of Madhva, who admits that it is impossible for the subordinate souls to acquire the infinite power and independence of God. Rāmānuja, with his view of internal differences in Brahman, and eternal differences between the liberated soul and God, has no difficulty. Śaṁkara finds the view inconsistent with the repeated declarations of the Upaniṣads that the liberated attains extreme "sameness with the pure One"; "He becomes the creator of the world," and yet Bādarāyaṇa says that he cannot rule the world. Śaṁkara explains that in the state of ultimate release there is neither subject nor object, neither self nor world, and so the question of rule and creation does not arise; but so long as we are at the stage of Īśvara and the souls and the world, mokṣa in the absolute sense is not attained, and so, in that state, it is true that the liberated soul has all the qualities of Īśvara, except the power of creation, etc.[4] According to Śaṁkara, he who has spiritual insight obtains oneness with Brahman, though the state can be described by us only as sameness with God. Those, however, who do not possess spiritual insight, but are worshippers of the personal Īśvara, are not completely rid of avidyā, and so obtain all powers in the brahmaloka excepting those of creatorship and rulership of the world. They retain their individuality independent of Īśvara, though they are filled with the spirit of God.

Is the state of mokṣa, or release from saṁsāra, consistent with work for the world? Śaṁkara is inclined to answer this question in the negative, since all activity, with which we are familiar, presupposes a sense of duality, and is not consistent

[1] S.B., iv. 4. 6. See also Bṛh. Up., iv. 5. 13.
[2] S.B., iv. 4. 7.
[3] V.S., iv. 4. 17.
[4] The apparent contradiction between Bādarāyaṇa and the Upaniṣads, as also between some sayings of Bādarāyaṇa (iv. 2. 13 and 16, and iv. 4. 17 and 21) is thus resolved by Śaṁkara.

with the realisation of the truth of non-duality. Still, so far as jīvanmuktas are concerned, activity is allowed. It follows that activity, as such, is not inconsistent with the truth of non-dualism. The liberated, even while alive, are lifted above the sense of egoity, and so above the sway of the law of karma, and they act, filled with the vision of the most high. There is not an essential antagonism between action and freedom.

In this connection the question of the possibility of a return of the liberated to earth in a new existence is discussed.[1] Sages like Apāntaratamas and others, though possessed of the highest wisdom, it is said, returned to bodily existence. Śaṁkara says that they do so in fulfilment of a mission (adhikāra) for the good of the world. When their mission is completed, their individual existence terminates, and there is no possibility of their return. It is, however, clear that, even after gaining insight into reality, we may take an interest in the world, though our return to it is of the nature of a visit and not habitation. Śaṁkara, however, insists that the state of liberation is opposed to that of saṁsāra; and since activity is a general characteristic of the latter, it is not present in the former.

In later Advaita, different views of mokṣa make themselves felt.[2] Those who hold to the theory of one jīva declare that mokṣa is absorption in Brahman and abolition of the phenomenal world, including God and man.[3] Those who accept the theory of the plurality of jīvas trace the phenomenal world to the avidyā of each soul. Though this world subsides on the cessation of avidyā, it continues to exist in the eye of the other unreleased souls. On the theory that God and the individuals are both reflections of Brahman, mokṣa means the breaking up of all reflecting mirrors and absorption into the original itself. It is also held that, while pure spirit underlies both Īśvara and jīva, the latter is a kind of reflection of Īśvara. On this view, liberation is not oneness with Brahman but oneness with Īśvara, so long as there are unliberated jīvas. When a single face is reflected in many mirrors, the removal of any one mirror causes the absorption so far of its reflection into the original; but the face will not get rid of its character as the original until all the mirrors are shattered. Accordingly, so long as there are unreleased souls, release means one-

---

[1] S.B., iii. 3. 32.

[2] *Siddhāntaleśa*, iv.

[3] Ekajīvavāde tadekājñānakalpitasya jīveśvaravibhāgādikṛtsnabhedaprapañcasya tadvidyodaye vilayān nirviśeṣacaitanyarūpeṇaivāvasthānam.

ness with Īśvara; but when all souls are released, Īśvara loses his character as the bimba, or the original, and sinks back into Brahman, thus securing for all released souls oneness with Brahman. But, since according to the orthodox Advaita, there is no end of saṁsāra, release means oneness with Īśvara.

An interesting question about the nature of saving knowledge is raised. So long as there is knowledge, mokṣa is not reached, but until we obtain knowledge of Brahman, there can be no mokṣa. Is not this latter knowledge, as knowledge, inconsistent with ultimate fruition? It is admitted that there is no knowledge in the ultimate state, and the abolition of the highest knowledge itself is brought out by a number of similes. As the powder of kataka fruit thrown into impure water carries down all its impurities and itself sinks to the bottom, as a drop of water thrown on a red-hot iron ball takes away a part of its heat and itself disappears, as fire after burning a heap of grass is extinguished of itself, so knowledge of Brahman destroys our ignorance and is itself destroyed.[1]

Śaṁkara admits the possibility of gradual liberation (kramamukti). Commenting on a passage of the *Praśna Upaniṣad*, regarding the meditation of Aum, he says that such meditation leads to brahmaloka, where we gradually attain perfect knowledge.[2] In another place, he argues that the worship of a personal Īśvara has for its aim purification from sin (duritakṣaya), attainment of lordship (aiśvaryaprāpti), or gradual liberation (kramamukti).[3] In brahmaloka the soul retains its separate personality. For Śaṁkara, as for all the mystics, the notion of a paradise where the soul is intent upon God and God alone, falls short of the ideal. It may be that the soul sees God face to face and is flooded with his presence, but there is still the distinction between the soul and its object. The soul is not the object of its vision, and its finite and created character withstands its becoming the object.

That life eternal is not a state of existence to follow upon physical death is clear from Śaṁkara's account of jīvanmukti. When insight dawns even here on earth, liberation is accomplished. The persistence of the body until death does not deceive. As the potter's wheel continues for a time to revolve even after the vessel has been completed, so also life continues after liberation, since it contains no cause to check the impetus already gained.[4] Śaṁkara also gives the analogy of the man

[1] See *Siddhāntaleśa*, iii.
[2] S.B., i. 3. 13.
[3] S.B., iii. 2. 21.
[4] S.B., iv. 1. 15.

who sees the moon double, on account of some defect in the eye, and cannot prevent himself from so doing even though he knows that there is really one moon.[1] All activities are understood by the released soul to take place in Brahman.[2]

XLIV

FUTURE LIFE

Only the knower of truth attains eternal life as distinct from survival, which is the lot of every other soul.[3] Until eternal life is gained, our lives are bound up with saṁsāra, or the weary wheel of endless becoming. Saṁsāra is the expression of the time process, and the jīvas are guaranteed future existence in this endless circuit, until they rise from time to eternal life by means of spiritual insight. The presence of the eternal shows itself in time as endless continuance. In the well-known words of Plato's *Timæus*, "Time is the moving image of eternity." No new arguments are advanced by Śaṁkara to prove the truth of future life. It is assumed that, when the physical body is annihilated, there is left behind a seed which brings forth a new organism according to its kind. Śaṁkara repudiates the materialist view that the individual soul is just the body, and with the dissolution of the latter, the soul perishes.[4] The soul is independent of the body, and

[1] S.B., iv. 1. 15.

[2] Different views are put forward in later Advaita, such as: (1) in the state of liberation during life primitive avidyā relaxes a little its power of projection, (2) the impression of avidyā survives its abolition for a little while, (3) the primitive avidyā exists lifeless like a burnt piece of cloth, and (4) the world, including the body, etc., ceases to exist for him. See *Siddhāntaleśa*, iv.

[3] S.B., Bṛh. Up., i. 1. 1. Sarvajñātmamuni does not accept mukti while on earth, though almost all other Advaitins support the conception of jīvanmukti.

[4] If from the fact that the qualities of the self persist as long as the body does, it is inferred that they are qualities of the body, it may be argued that they are not the qualities of the body, since they do not persist after death, even though the body does. We cannot say that, since perception in the dark requires a lamp for its existence, therefore it is a quality of the lamp. The body, like the lamp, is only a means. Moreover, the co-operation of the body is not always necessary, since we perceive many things even when the body is still in sleep. There is a difference between qualities of

its identity makes possible recollection etc.[1] Though our bodies may be shattered to dust, still there is something in us which survives; and it is this which determines our future life. The knowledge we have gained, the character we have formed will pursue us into other lives.[2] The moral and the pious rise, while the immoral and impious sink in the scale. The nature of the future life depends on the moral quality of the past life. Birth and death merely refer to the union of the individual soul with body and separation from it.[3]

Even the Vedic gods, according to Śaṁkara, are not immortal, for "the immortality of the gods means only existence for a long time, just as their lordship is not self-dependent but is the gift of Īśvara."[4]

Śaṁkara sketches in detail the departure of the soul after death. In the Ṛg-Veda the souls of the good pass after death into Yama's heaven of light, where they lead a blissful life in the company of the Fathers (pitaraḥ),[5] and the wicked who are shut out from it pass into the lower darkness.[6] In the Upaniṣads we read that the wise are carried higher and higher on the path of the gods (devayāna), onwards into Brahman, whence there is no return. The doers of works go upwards by the path of the Fathers (pitṛyāna) into the luminous region of the moon, enjoying there the fruit of their works, and then descend into a new birth determined by the character of the past life. Those who adhere neither to wisdom nor to works are assigned to a third place, and are born as lower animals and plants, which do not taste the bliss of the moon.[7] Śaṁkara recognises these three as different stages in the wheel of saṁsāra, while mokṣa is something by itself, different from all of them. While the path of the Fathers leads back to an earthly existence, that of the gods leads to brahmaloka, from which there is no return. In the account of the *Chāndogya*

---

the body like shape, etc., which are perceived by all, and those of the self, which are not so perceived. While it is true that from the existence of the body the presence of conscious qualities can be proved, nothing can be said about consciousness from the non-existence of the body. It may enter into another body and persist. If consciousness is a quality of the physical elements and their products, the latter cannot be objects of consciousness. Since the existence of the elements and their products is inferred from the fact that they are perceived, we must conclude that perception is different from them.

[1] S.B., iii. 3. 54.

[2] S.B., iii. 4. 11, and Bṛh. Up., iv. 4. 2. See also S.B., iii. 1. 5–6.

[3] S.B., ii 3. 16–17.

[4] S.B., i. 2. 17.

[5] x. 14. 10.

[6] x. 152. 4.

[7] Bṛh., vi. 2; Kaṭha Up.

Upaniṣad,[1] there are only two paths, devayāna and pitṛyana, and all those who are devoid of wisdom, good as well as bad, are destined to the latter. Śaṁkara adopts the theory of double retribution in the beyond and in the new existence, so as to reconcile the Vedic and the Upaniṣadic views.[2] There was some attempt to distinguish between Vedic ritual, as entitling to a reward in the beyond, and moral life to an experience on earth.[3] Those who follow customary morality, perform sacrifices, etc., without any true knowledge, follow the way of the Fathers through the smoky regions to the moon, and, after enjoying there some fruit of their karma, return to a new existence in the world; while others who worship the personal God and perform acts with knowledge, are led along the way of the gods higher and higher through the sun to the brahmaloka.[4] The worshipper of the personal God partakes of his powers and lordship, though "his darkness is not yet driven away," and his avidyā is not yet destroyed. Those who worship lower gods also receive their recompense, though it does not put them on the way to the highest mokṣa.[5] Those who lead immoral lives have a fall downwards,[6] but none of these is expelled from God's embrace and cast out into the desolate nothingness.[7]

At death the senses are absorbed in the manas, which merges into the vital spirit (mukhyaprāṇa), which in its turn is absorbed by the moral vehicle of the soul in the subtle body. The soul, which has for its limiting adjuncts avidyā, karma and previous experience with its sūkṣmaśarīra, leaves the body.[8] This subtle body is called subtle because it is said to depart through the veins. It has extension (tanutvam), renders possible locomotion (saṁcāra) and transparency (svacchatva), by which it meets with no obstacle in its way and is not seen by any.[9] This subtle body is not dissolved until liberation.

XLV

Religion

It is generally said that Śaṁkara's Advaita, though a masterpiece of intellect, cannot inspire religious piety. His

[1] v. 3. 10. See S.B., iii. 1. 12–21.

[2] S.B., iii. 1. 8.

[3] S.B., iii. 1. 9–11.

[4] S.B., iv. 3. 1–6.

[5] S.B., iv. 1. 4; iv. 3. 15–16.

[6] S.B. on Chān. Up., Introduction. See also iii. 1. 1–7, 18.

[7] An interesting question is raised about the condition of those who have entered into the brahmaloka through the path of the gods. Bādari holds that they have no bodies, while Jaimini maintains that they have; and Bādarāyaṇa reconciles the two by declaring that those possessed of lordship can subsist at pleasure either in bodily or bodiless form (S.B., iv. 4. 8–22).

[8] ii. 2. 1–5.

[9] iv. 2. 9–11.

Absolute cannot kindle passionate love and adoration in the soul. We cannot worship the Absolute whom no one hath seen or can see, who dwelleth in the light that no man can approach unto. The formless (nirākāram) Absolute is conceived as formed (ākāravat) for the purposes of worship. Worship of God is not a deliberate alliance with falsehood, since God is the form in which alone the Absolute can be pictured by the finite mind. The highest reality appears to the individual, who has not felt its oneness with his own nature, as possessing a number of perfections.[1] The conception of a personal God is the fusion of the highest logical truth with the deepest religious conviction. This personal God is an object of genuine worship and reverence, and not a non-ethical deity indifferent to man's needs and fears. He is regarded as creator, governor and judge of the universe, possessing the qualities of power and justice, righteousness and mercy, omnipresence, omnipotence and omniscience. Holiness of character and moral beauty are prominent aspects of Śaṁkara's God. He is set over against the human soul, who stands to him in the relation of a beloved to a lover, a servant to a master, a son to a father, and a friend to a friend. The severity of metaphysical abstraction relaxes when Śaṁkara dwells on the variety of the divine qualities by which the eternal draws to himself the spirits of the children he has made. Religion for Śaṁkara is not doctrine or ceremony, but life and experience. It starts with the soul's sense of the infinite and ends with its becoming the infinite. Sākṣātkāra, or intuition of reality, is the end of religion. True bhakti is seeking after one's own real nature.[2] There are many vidyās, or forms of contemplation advocated in the Upaniṣads,[3] and each individual has to select one of those, suited to his temper.[4] There is unity with regard to the object, though there is variety in the mode of approach. Religious worship is broadly of two kinds, that of a personal God, as Saguṇa Brahmā, and that of symbols (pratīka).[5] When the worshipper looks upon God as external to him, his worship is symbolic.

[1] S.B., iii. 3. 12.

[2] Svasvarūpānusaṁdhānam bhaktir ity abhidhīyate (*Vivekacūḍāmaṇi*, p. 31).

[3] iii. 3. 5. [4] S.B., iii. 3. 59. [5] S.B., iv. 1. 3.

The relation existing between the person worshipping and the object worshipped implies a difference between the two.[1] The highest worship takes us to brahmaloka, where the distinction between the individual and the Supreme still survives. Only gradually is mukti attained from that condition. Religion, in the popular sense, is something to be transcended. It is an imperfect experience, which exists only so long as we fail to rise to the true apprehension of reality. It is destined to be absorbed; for "when that which is perfect is come, then that which is in part shall be done away." Śaṁkara quotes passages from the highest religious seers declaring the identity of the soul and Ātman: "verily I am thou, O holy Godhead, and Thou art I."[2] Every philosophy of religion should offer some explanation of such declarations as "I am Brahman" (aham brahmāsmi), "That art Thou" (tat tvam asi), in which the difference between the creature and the creator is transcended. Śaṁkara accounts for these by declaring that religious consciousness with its distinctions comes to an end when the goal of it is reached. A "Personal God" has meaning only for the practical religious consciousness and not for the highest insight.[3] To the finite individual blinded by the veils, the Absolute seems to be determinate and exclusive of himself. Bondage and redemption possess a meaning for the finite individual, whose consciousness is fettered and repressed by his lower nature. If a personal God exclusive of the individual were the highest, then mystic experiences would become unintelligible, and we should have to remain content with a finite God. God is no God if he is not the All; if he be the All, then religious experience is not the highest.[4] If God's nature is perfect, it cannot be so, so long as man's imperfect nature stands over against it; if it is not

[1] Upāsyopāsakabhāvo 'pi bhedādhiṣṭhāna eva (S.B., i. 2. 4).

[2] Tvaṁ vā aham asmi bhagavo devate, aham vai tvam asi bhagavo devate (S.B., iv. 1. 3).

[3] Cp. Bradley: "For me the Absolute is not God. God for me has no meaning outside the religious consciousness, and that essentially is practical. The Absolute for me cannot be God, because in the end the Absolute is related to nothing, and there cannot be a practical relation between it and the finite will. When you begin to worship the Absolute or the universe, and make it the object of religion, you in that moment have transformed it" (*Truth and Reality*, p. 428).

[4] See Bradley: *Truth and Reality*, pp. 436 ff.

perfect, then it is not the nature of God. There is thus a fundamental contradiction in religious experience, clearly indicating that it belongs to the province of avidyā.

The acceptance of the karmakāṇḍa requires the recognition of the Vedic deities. They are regarded by Śaṁkara, who subscribes to the traditional view, as personifications of natural forces, and not simply natural elements. "The names of the gods like Āditya and so forth, even if they refer to light, etc., compel us, according to the scriptures, to assume spiritual beings corresponding (to the elements) and gifted with ruling power (aiśvarya); for they are used in the hymns and the Brāhmaṇas."[1] These deities act as presiding agents (adhiṣṭhātṛ) of different life functions.[2] Agni is said to aid speech, Vāyu breath, and Āditya eye. The deities are not affected by the experiences of the individual soul.[3] At death, the deities do not wander with the life organs, but simply withdraw their assisting power. The Supreme creates gods, men and beasts according to their merit and demerit. The immortality of the gods is, however, a relative (āpekṣikam) one, the deities are involved in saṁsāra and are subject to transitoriness.[4] They are in need of saving knowledge and are dependent on the supreme Lord. We have cases in the scriptures of gods learning brahmavidyā. The objection, that, if these deities are individuals, they are subject to birth and death, and this fact will affect the eternal character of the Vedas, is set aside on the ground that the words of the Veda do not refer to individuals but to general notions. The word "Indra" means not an individual, but a certain rank (sthānaviśeṣa) in the hierarchy of beings. Whoever occupies the position bears the name. To the objection that their individuality is neither real, since the gods are not seen at sacrifices, nor possible, since an individual cannot be at many places at the same time, as he should be for receiving sacrificial offerings, Śaṁkara replies that the gods are not seen because they have the power to make themselves invisible, and they can multiply their bodies a thousandfold even as the yogins do.

While Śaṁkara's spiritual faith needs no shrines and

[1] See D.S.V., pp. 65–66. [2] Ait. Up., i. 2. 4.
[3] Which alone is bhoktṛ, while the deities are bhogopakāraṇabhūta.
[4] S.B., i. 3. 28.

ritual, still, he had a sufficient sense of the historic to recommend them to those who were in want of them.[1] Unlike many other interpreters of the Vedānta, Śaṁkara adopts the philosophical, as distinct from the theological attitude in matters of religion. A theologian generally takes his stand on a particular denominational basis. As a member of a particular religious community, he sets himself to systematise, expand and defend the doctrines of his school. He accepts his creed as the truth with which his religion stands or falls. The philosopher, on the other hand, in so far as he is a philosopher, does not confine himself to any one religion, but takes religion as such for his province, without assuming that the religion in which he is born or which he accepts is the only true religion. In Śaṁkara we find one of the greatest expounders of the comprehensive and tolerant character of the Hindu religion, which is ever ready to assimilate alien faiths. This attitude of toleration was neither a survival of superstition nor a means of compromise, but an essential part of his practical philosophy. He recognised the limitations of all formulas and refused to compress the Almighty within them. No reasonable man can think that his sect has weighed and measured God and set forth the result of the process in its own infallible creed. Every creed is an adventure of faith, an approach to experience. It is the instrument which leads to the vital religious experience ; and if the reality of religious experience acquires a meaning for the individual who sincerely seeks after God in this or that particular form, it is impertinent for us to ask him to change his creed. Śaṁkara was not so fanatical as to question the religious experiences of those who claim to have direct contact with God through their respective tributes of faith and love. If men of radically different convictions are able to secure the same results of moral quickening, peace of mind and *rapport* with the central spiritual reality, he allowed them to have their own views. As one of the greatest religious geniuses of the world observed, " By their fruits " and not by their beliefs " ye shall know them." It does not matter by what names we worship God, so long as

[1] It is said that Śaṁkara on his death-bed prayed for forgiveness for having frequented temples, since by so doing he had seemed to deny the omnipresence of God.

we are filled with the spirit of God and fervour for service. The One reality is spoken of in various ways, according to the diversity of the human mind (matibhedāt).[1] When we seek to express that which lies beyond phenomena, we invent symbols bodying forth our needs as best we may. Śaṁkara's freedom from religious illusions and his deep-rooted humanism led him to take note of men's dreams, which seem to be the only things of value in the world of māyā. He refused to turn propagandist or lower his philosophical standards in order to widen his religious appeal. Hinduism, as Śaṁkara understood it, allowed room within its pale for all the different types of thought and temperament. He is called the Ṣaṇmatasthāpanācārya, or the teacher who established the six creeds.[2] In matters of religion it is easy to take the high-flying idealistic line, ignoring all the facts of the earth, as it is equally easy to take the crudely realistic line which repudiates all ideals; but it is difficult to combine a clear-eyed realism with a steadfast loyalty to the ideal, and this is what Śaṁkara attempted. It is a unique phenomenon for a religious teacher to justify six different religious systems, a phenomenon possible only in Hindu India. As Vidyāraṇya says, men have identified God with all sorts of objects, from the immanent spirit to stocks or trees.[3] While the followers of Vaiṣṇavism, Śaivism and Śāktaism, etc., were quarrelling one with another, Śaṁkara lifted these popular faiths from out of the dust of mere polemics into the lucid atmosphere of eternal truth. He gave a common basis to the prevalent forms and related them all to the central co-ordinating idea. He emphasised the religion of truth rooted in spiritual inwardness. The truth intended by all religions is the Ātman; and, until we recognise the oneness of our self with the reality that transcends all these imperfect characterisations, we shall revolve in the circle of saṁsāra. From his philosophical point of view he declares that, though the Absolute is visualised in many ways, the underlying reality is the same. There are no degrees of reality, though there are

[1] *Haristuti*, p. 18.

[2] The Saiva, the Vaiṣṇava, the Saura, the Śākta, the Gāṇapatya, and the Kāpāli creeds.

[3] Antaryāminaṃ ārabhya sthāvarānteśavādinaḥ (*Pañcadaśī*, vi. 121). See also vi. 206–209.

degrees of truth, *i.e.* our ways of comprehending the real. He did not jump to the conclusion that there is no God at all, for if there were, men would not differ in their ideas of him. The differences are due to men's limitations.[1] Thus he was singularly free from both scepticism and fanaticism. He showed his sincerity of conviction by composing hymns to the different deities, hymns which are hardly surpassed for their moving power. This does not, however, mean that he justified all forms of superstition and idolatry. He repudiated vehemently some pernicious practices which became associated with religion. By the inculcation of his Advaita doctrine, he helped men to interpret God in terms of spiritual value. He had faith in the power of the mind to grasp the truth, if we persist in acting up to our best lights. His attitude to the existing religions was both sympathetic and critical. Śaṁkara aims at interpreting Hinduism to the new age in such a manner as to conserve, and even assert more clearly than hitherto, its distinctive message. Within this larger intention we may possibly discern the idea of unifying the people of the country. But he did not seek to bring about this unity by insisting on strict outward organisation or inward beliefs. He tried to bring it about by a wider comprehension. By laying stress on the personal character of religious experience, he broadened and spiritualised Hinduism. In reinterpreting Hindu thought,

[1] S.B., i. 1. 20. There is a passage in Baron von Hügel's latest work which represents Śaṁkara's attitude in the matter. "It seems clear that the apparently endless variations which exist simultaneously between one entire religion and another entire religion, and even between single mind and single mind, or which show successively in one and the same religion, and even in one and the same mind, indeed that the crude childishness of much that most individuals and most religions think and represent their experience and its object to be, do not, of themselves, condemn the position that a great trans-subjective superhuman Reality is being thus variously and ever inadequately, yet none the less actually, apprehended by such groups or persons. The Reality extant and acting upon and within the world distinct from the human mind, and upon and within those human minds and spirits themselves, can indeed be taken as the determining occasion, object and cause of man's long search for and continuous refinding of God; of the gradual growth in depth and in delicacy of man's religious apprehensions; of man finding his full rest and abiding base in the religious experience and certainty alone; and of man simultaneously becoming ever more conscious both of the need of the best and of the inadequacy of all human categories and definitions to express this really experienced Reality" (*Philosophy of Religion*, pp. 44–45).

he sometimes found a place for those elements in it which are apparently inconsistent with his own views.

After the tumult and storm of the polemical period came the Advaita of Śaṁkara, with its elemental calm and persuasiveness of rational conviction. It does not dictate or dogmatise, and its stately and mature affirmations carry the weight of sincere endeavour and ripe reflection. It grounds religious reality in the centre of man's consciousness, from which it cannot be dislodged. The sole spiritual vocation of man consists in the discovery of reality, and not what serves our temporal ends. This discovery demands a complete abandonment of the egocentric and the anthropocentric points of view, in an absolute surrender of man's vain and inordinate pride in his own importance. We must relinquish all attempts to envisage God in terms of our limited knowledge and experience. God exists for himself, first and foremost, and not for us merely. Our logic and our ethics make God an instrument for the advancement of our ends. Such an instrumental view of God, formulated by the weak mind of man to advance his petty plans, may do honour to man, but it is not a compliment to God. Śaṁkara would in a manner endorse Spinoza's dictum that he who truly loves God cannot wish that God should love him in return.

If Śaṁkara's Advaita seems to us to be abstract, it is because we are content to dwell on a level lower than the highest that is possible for us. Śaṁkara's repugnance to anthropomorphism makes his religion appear a little cold. But if we deny will and knowledge to the absolute spirit, it is not so much a limitation of the Absolute as a consequence of its perfection. Religious feeling is by no means lacking in Śaṁkara. It finds frequent expression in his writings in a manner which is often affecting and sometimes rises to fervour. But our popular religious views are not exempted from his dialectical criticism, and our views of God are shown to be as unstable and fugitive as we ourselves.

When all is said, we find that Śaṁkara has combined a penetrating intellectual vision into things divine with a spirit of mystic contemplation. With Śaṁkara for our witness, it is impossible to say that a vigorous play of the intellect is an impediment to mystical contemplation. He also shows that freedom from external occupations is not a necessary characteristic of contemplative lives. He reconciles the personal or mystical, the institutional or authoritarian, the intellectual or philosophical elements of religion with one another.

XLVI

Conclusion

The Upaniṣads speak with the double voice of philosophy and religion. They represent the highest reality as Absolute and God, Brahman and Parameśvara. They speak of salvation as becoming one with Brahman as well as dwelling in the city of God. Negative descriptions of Brahman as well as positive characterisations, which are to be met with in the Upaniṣads, are also found in every great religious literature. The mystics, Jewish, Christian and Muslim, bring to us reports of the one darkness which is beyond what the tongue can tell; others relate to us the fullness of God. While the thinkers and mystics emphasise the illimitable character of God, the religious devotees look upon God as friend, helper and saviour. Every philosophy of religion has to take into account this dual nature of all religious experience and justify it. The problem which Śaṁkara set to himself, though it arises from the limited context of the religious experience as recorded in the Upaniṣads, has a universal interest, and the solution at which he has arrived seems a satisfying one, if all the elements are to preserve their equipoise. It is essentially a philosophical solution, since Śaṁkara lifts us, through the power of thought which alone can reconcile and ennoble the different sides of life, into the ideal of joy and peace. It is true that he admits that thought cannot solve all the problems, but stands in need of an intuitive grasp of reality. While Śaṁkara willingly bows before the mysteries of life, he does not hanker after mystery for its own sake. At the centre of Śaṁkara's system is the eternal mystery of creation, a mystery in which every movement of life and every atom of the world is implicated.

If instead of regarding the world as something for the rise

of which we cannot offer an adequate explanation, we at the same time, following the lead of some later Advaitins, dismiss it as a cosmic illusion which has somehow arisen to afflict us, deluded mortals of an evil dream, then the system becomes unsatisfactory. But such a view is hardly fair to Śaṁkara.

Śaṁkara's system is unmatched for its metaphysical depth and logical power. Thought follows thought naturally, until Advaitism is seen to complete and crown the edifice. It is a great example of monistic idealism which it is difficult to meet with an absolutely conclusive metaphysical refutation. Śaṁkara holds up a vision of life acceptable in the highest moments of poetry and religion, when we are inclined to sympathise with his preference for intuition to the light of the understanding. So long as he remains on this high ground, he is unanswerable. But a lingering doubt oppresses the large majority of mankind, who very rarely get into these exalted heights. They feel that it is unjust to leave in such high disdain the world in which they live, move and have their being, and relegate it to ajñāna or darkness, offering merely as a solace that all disagreeable appearances will quickly vanish in the eternal light. For them the all-transforming sunlight of the heights is spurious, and they declare that Śaṁkara's system is one of mystical indifference to fact. That human suffering will be healed, that the whole world will vanish like a pitiful mirage, that all our trouble is of our own making, and that in the world's finale all people will find that absolute oneness which will suffice for all hearts, compose all resentments and atone for all crimes, seem to many to be pious assumptions. The entranced self-absorption which arms itself with sanctity, involves a cruel indifference to practical life hardly acceptable to average intelligence. Śaṁkara knows all this, and so gives us a logical theism which does not slight the intellect, does not scorn the wisdom of ages, and is at the same time the highest intellectual account of the truth.[1] What

[1] Cp. Plato: "If then, amid the many opinions about the gods and the generation of the universe, we are not able in every respect to render all our ideas consistent with each other and precisely accurate, no one need be surprised. Enough if we are able to give an account which is no less likely than another; for we must remember that I who speak, and you who judge of what I say, are mortal men, so that on these subjects we should be satisfied with a likely story and demand nothing more" (*Timæus*, p, 27, E.).

is the relation between the absolutism of intuition and the empirical theism of logic, Śaṁkara does not tell us; for, as Goethe wisely observed, " man is born not to solve the problem of the universe, but to find out where the problem begins, and then to restrain himself within the limits of the comprehensible." Śaṁkara recognises that there is a region which we cannot penetrate, and a wise agnosticism is the only rational attitude. The greatness of Śaṁkara's achievement rests on the peculiar intensity and splendour of thought with which the search for reality is conducted, on the high idealism of spirit grappling with the difficult problems of life, regardless of theological consequences, and on the vision of a consummation which places a divine glory on human life.

Supreme as a philosopher and a dialectician, great as a man of calm judgment and wide toleration, Śaṁkara taught us to love truth, respect reason and realise the purpose of life. Twelve centuries have passed, and yet his influence is visible. He destroyed many an old dogma, not by violently attacking it, but by quietly suggesting something more reasonable, which was at the same time more spiritual too. He put into general circulation a vast body of important knowledge and formative ideas which, though contained in the Upaniṣads, were forgotten by the people, and thus recreated for us the distant past. He was not a dreaming idealist, but a practical visionary, a philosopher, and at the same time a man of action, what we may call a social idealist on the grand scale. Even those who do not agree with his general attitude to life will not be reluctant to allow him a place among the immortals.

REFERENCES.

CARPENTER: Theism in Mediæval India, Lect. VI.
DASGUPTA: History of Indian Philosophy, Ch. X.
DEUSSEN: The System of the Vedānta.
DVIVEDI: Māṇḍūkyopaniṣad with Gauḍapāda's Kārikā.
MAHĀDEVA ŚĀSTRI: Bhagavadgītā with Śaṁkara's Commentary.
MAX MÜLLER: Six Systems of Indian Philosophy, Ch. IV.
P. NARASIMHAM: The Vedāntic Absolute and the Vedāntic Good. *Mind*, N.S., 82 and 93.
THIBAUT: The Vedānta Sūtras with Śaṁkara's Commentary (S.B.E.).
Vidyāraṇya's Pañcadaśī. Ed. by Srinivasa Rao and Krishnasami Iyer.

CHAPTER IX

THE THEISM OF RĀMĀNUJA

Introduction—The Purāṇas—Life—History and literature—Bhāskara —Yādavaprakāśa—The Pramāṇas—Implications of Rāmānuja's theory of knowledge—God—The individual soul—Matter—Creation—Ethics and religion—Mokṣa—General estimate.

I

INTRODUCTION

PHILOSOPHY has its roots in man's practical needs. If a system of thought cannot justify fundamental human instincts and interpret the deeper spirit of religion, it cannot meet with general acceptance. The speculations of philosophers, which do not comfort us in our stress and suffering, are mere intellectual diversion and not serious thinking. The Absolute of Śaṁkara, rigid, motionless, and totally lacking in initiative or influence, cannot call forth our worship. Like the Taj Mahal, which is unconscious of the admiration it arouses, the Absolute remains indifferent to the fear and love of its worshippers, and for all those who regard the goal of religion as the goal of philosophy—to know God is to know the real—Śaṁkara's view seems to be a finished example of learned error. They feel that it is as unsatisfactory to natural instincts as to trained intelligence. The world is said to be an appearance and God a bloodless Absolute dark with the excess of light. The obvious fact of experience that, when weak and erring human beings call from the depths, the helping hand of grace is stretched out from the unknown, is ignored. Śaṁkara does not deal justly with the living sense of companionship which the devotees have in their difficult lives. He declares that to save oneself is to lose oneself in the sea of the unknown. Personal values are subordinated to impersonal ones, but the theist protests that truth, beauty and goodness have no reality as self-existent abstractions. An experience that is not owned by a subject is a contradiction in terms. Truth, beauty and perfection speak to us of a primal mind in whose experience they are eternally realised. God himself is the highest reality as well as supreme value. Moreover, the innermost being of God is not solely the realisation of eternal truth or the enjoyment of perfect beauty, but is perfect love which expends itself for others. The value of the finite world to the Spirit of the universe lies in the spirits to whom he has given the capacity to make themselves in his own image. The spirits themselves possess a value in the sight of God, and not merely their degrees of intelligence or virtue, abstractly considered, which they happen to realise. It follows that they are not made simply to be broken up and cast aside.

Rāmānuja concentrates his attention on the relation of the world to God, and argues that God is indeed real and independent ; but the souls of the world are real also, though their reality is utterly dependent on that of God. He believes in a spiritual principle at the basis of the world, which is not treated as an illusion. He insists on the continued individual existence of the released souls. Though the world of matter and the individual souls have a real existence of their own, still neither of them is essentially the same as Brahman. For, while Brahman is eternally free from all imperfection, matter is unconscious, and the individual souls are subject to ignorance and suffering. Yet they all form a unity, since matter and souls have existence only as the body of Brahman, *i.e.* they can exist and be what they are simply because Brahman is their soul and controlling power.[1] Apart from Brahman, they are nothing. The individual soul and inanimate nature are essentially different from him, though they have no existence or purpose to serve apart from him or his

[1] " Everything in this world, whether individual souls or material things, form the body of the supreme soul, and therefore the above can be said to possess a body unconditionally (nirupādhikaśarīra-ātmā). For this very reason competent persons call the body of teachings (śāstra), having Brahman for its subject-matter 'śārīraka.' "

service. So Rāmānuja's theory is an advaita or non-dualism, though with a qualification (viśeṣa), *viz.* that it admits plurality, since the supreme spirit subsists in a plurality of forms as souls and matter. It is therefore called *Viśiṣṭādvaita* or qualified non-dualism.

In ethics also there was a protest against the intellectualism favoured by the followers of Śaṁkara and the ritualism of the Mīmāṁsakas. Even as early as the age of the Ṛg-Veda we found that gods were sometimes entreated by prayer and at others compelled by ritual. The sacrificial cult had always to contend with the devotional worship of the Supreme through symbols, originally in groves and later in temples. In the sacrificial religion of the Vedas, the priest who officiates is more important than the deity. But the dative case offers no solace to the aching heart. Kumārila, moreover, the Brahmin architect who tried to build a stable society out of the chaotic conditions left by the disintegration of Buddhism, sought to strengthen the Brahmanical cult by laying the foundations of caste solid and strong in a system wherein only the three upper classes were allowed to perform sacrifices, while the people at large were left to their own devotional cults. Hence the reaction against the Mīmāṁsakas led to the development of the theistic religions of Vaiṣṇavism, Śaivism and Śāktaism, which laid little stress on considerations of caste, race or social status. Theism has implicit in it the social hope. As children of the common father or mother, we are all on the same footing. All men, high or low, are equally precious to the parental heart.

Though Śaṁkara did not mean by jñāna theoretical learning, there was a tendency among some of his disciples to make religion more an affair of the head than of the heart or will.[1] They shut out from eternal life the soul that is wrong, as well as the soul that is wicked. The mechanical repetition of the formula "I am Brahman" is a sorry substitute for intelligent devotion. Hence the emphasis on bhakti by the theistic systems, including the four Vaiṣṇava schools.[2] Despite doctrinal differences, these are all agreed

[1] Cp. Vākyārthajñānamātrād amṛtam iti (*Tattvamuktākalāpa*, ii. 45).

[2] Śrīsaṁpradāya of Rāmānuja, Brahmasaṁpradāya of Madhva, Rudrasaṁpradāya of Viṣṇusvāmin, and Sanakādisaṁpradāya of Nimbārka.

in rejecting the conception of māyā, in regarding God as personal, and the soul as possessed of inalienable individuality, finding its true being not in an absorption in the Supreme but in fellowship with him.

II

The Āgamas

As the native inhabitants of India came more and more completely under the Aryan influence, there was a great extension of the Hindu religion. The higher Dravidian and the lower aboriginal peoples both helped to modify the old Vedic sacrificial cult in favour of temple worship and public festivals. As new tribes were assimilated, new sects were formed, each with its own marks (tilaka), its mode of initiation (dīkṣā), its teacher (guru), its watchwords (mantras) and its scriptures (śāstras). Very early in its career Hinduism developed the important cults of Vaiṣṇavism, Śaivism and Śāktaism, with their distinctive scriptures, the *Pañcarātra Saṁhitā*, the *Śaiva Āgama* and the *Tantra*.

The Āgamas are generally divided into four parts, called jñāna or knowledge, yoga or concentration, kriyā or the acts relating to the founding of temples and the installing of idols, and carya or the method of worship.[1] It is clear that the Āgamas deal with religions which believe in image worship, since they lay down elaborate rules about the construction and the consecration of temples. The Śāktas were practically one with the Śaivas, except that they clung to certain primitive practices and worshipped Śakti, the consort of Śiva. The conception of God with wife and children is one of primitive thought, which is necessarily anthropomorphic. The Sāṁkhya theory of puruṣa and prakṛti offered a philosophical justification for Śakti, the principle of life and expression. As Śiva is unknowable, unapproachable and entirely inactive, Śakti, who is one with him, ever active, became the source of divine grace.

From the Tamil works of Nālaḍiyār, Śilappathikāram, Maṇimeghalai and Kural, it is obvious that the Buddhist and the Jaina religions had considerable influence in South India in the early centuries of the Christian era. According to Śilappathikāram (first century A.D.), there were Viṣṇu temples, Buddhist Vihāras and Jaina places of worship, in the city of Kāveripatnam. Aśoka sent his missionaries

[1] *Padma Saṁhitā*, i. 2. 6; ii. 1. 3; iii. 1. 6; iv. 1. 1.

in the third century B.C., and about the same time Bhadrabāhu, according to the tradition, led a migration of the Jains to the South with the Maurya King Candragupta. But Buddhism and Jainism could not satisfy the Draviḍian temperament, which longed for a God who could receive and reward passionate devotion. The monotheistic cults of Vaiṣṇavism and Śaivism developed, and the saints of the two schools were much influenced by the respective Āgamas.

III

THE PURĀṆAS

The Purāṇas are the religious poetry of the period of the schools, representing through myth and story, symbol and parable, the traditional view of God and man, cosmogony and social order. They were composed with the purpose of undermining, if possible, the heretical doctrines of the times. They are eclectic in their character, mixing up philosophical doctrines with popular beliefs. Vyāsa is reputed to be the author of the Purāṇas.[1] They regard themselves as continuing the tradition of the Vedas.[2] The Purāṇas,[3] though they refer to philosophical doctrines, do not aim at systematic development. Their main object is to convey the lessons of ancient thinkers, especially those of the Vedānta and the Sāṁkhya. Their name indicates that they are intended to preserve ancient (purāṇa) traditions. They are all theistic in

[1] Some of them trace their authorship to Viṣṇu. See *Padma P.*, i. 62. 18.

[2] *Vāyu P.*, i. 11. 194, 202.

[3] The principal Purāṇas are eighteen in number. Viṣṇu, Bhāgavata (Śrīmad Bhāgavata more than the Devī Bhāgavata), Nāradīya, Garuḍa, Padma, Varāha are Vaiṣṇava in character, while Śiva, Liṅga, Skanda, Agni (or Vāyu according to other accounts), Matsya, Kūrma are Śaiva in their emphasis. The others, Brahma (or Saura), Brahmāṇḍa, Brahmavaivarta (which extols Kṛṣṇa), Mārkaṇḍeya, Bhaviṣya and Vāmana deal with Brahmā. They are also called respectively Sāttvika, Tāmasa and Rājasa. See *Matsya P.*, 52. These are the Mahāpurāṇas, while there are other secondary ones called Upapurāṇas. Each Purāṇa is said to deal with sarga, pratisarga, vaṁśa, manvantara and vaṁśānucarita. The Purāṇas are later than the epics, and the earliest of them existed before the Christian era, though they were altered a good deal subsequently. They " must have existed at least as early as the beginning of the fifth century B.C., and this lower limit would be shifted 150 to 200 years earlier if a prior date is given to Āpastamba." (Pargiter: *Ancient Indian Historical Tradition*, p. 51). Chān. Up., iii. 4. 1; Śat. Brāh., xi. 5. 6. 8; *Arthaśāstra*, i. 5, among others, refer to the Purāṇas.

character, and recognise the distinctions of matter, soul and God. The conception of trimūrti comes into prominence, though each Purāṇa is interested in emphasising the supremacy of one particular aspect, Viṣṇu or Śiva. In a Purāṇa, which insists on the supremacy of Viṣṇu, Śiva and Brahmā worship Viṣṇu, and even declare that those who adore Viṣṇu are dear to themselves.[1] Śiva says to Pracetas, according to the *Bhāgavata Purāṇa*: "Dear to me is he who has resigned himself to Viṣṇu."[2] God is the sole source, support and termination of the world.[3] The Purāṇas give to the highest deity, whatever it be called, all conceivable perfections. "Who can describe him who is not to be apprehended by the sense, who is the best of all things, the supreme soul, the self-existent, who is devoid of all the distinguishing characteristics of complexion, caste or the like, who is exempt from birth, vicissitude, death, decay or increase, who is always and alone, who exists everywhere and in whom all things here exist, and who is therefore named Vāsudeva?"[4] The Sāṁkhya account of prakṛti and its development is accepted, with the reservation that prakṛti works in obedience to the will of the supreme spirit. Prakṛti is sometimes deified as the loving consort of the Father God. At the beginning of the third chapter in *Viṣṇu Purāṇa*, Maitreya asks Parāśara "how creative agency (sargādikartṛtvam) can be attributed to the pure Brahman," and the answer is given that the whole world is in him, even as heat is in fire.[5] The Purāṇas admit the reality of the world and refer to the conception of māyā only to condemn it.[6]

In religion we find a clear departure from the Vedic worship, consisting of prayer and sacrifice, to image-worship and bhakti. The ethics of the Purāṇas is not different from the traditional one. It accepts the doctrine of karma and rebirth and the possibility of release through virtue and wisdom. Devotion to God, and not assent to dogma, is the essence of bhakti, which is said to be the most effective means

[1] Cp. *Viṣṇu P.*, i. 2. 2. Śaktayo yasya caikasya brahmaviṣṇuśivātmikāḥ (i. 9). See also *Bhāgavata*, i. 2. 23.

[2] Bhagavantaṁ vāsudevam prapannaḥ sa priyo hi me (iv. 24. 28). See also iv. 24. 30.

[3] *Viṣṇu P.*, i. 2. 4.

[4] *Ibid.*, i. 2. 10.

[5] i. 3.

[6] *Padma P.*, vi. 263–70.

of salvation in this Kali age.[1] Bhakti can move mountains; nothing is impossible for it.[2] Dhruva is advised by his mother to be good, pious, friendly and eager to do good to living creation.[3] "Know him to be the devotee of Viṣṇu who never deviates from the duties of his caste, who looks with equal vision on friend and enemy, who takes nothing which is not his own, who hurts no being, and who is of unblemished mind."[4] The society decays when property confers rank, wealth becomes the only basis of virtue, passion the sole bond of union between man and woman, falsehood the source of success in life, sex the sole means of enjoyment, when the outer trappings are mistaken for the inner spirit.[5] Such a state of society calls for a redeemer. Mokṣa is equality with God (īśvarasādṛśyam).[6] Rāmānuja's faith was much influenced by the *Viṣṇu* and the *Bhāgavata Purāṇas.*

IV

Life of Rāmānuja

Rāmānuja was born in Śrīperuṁbudūr in the year A.D. 1027. He seems to have lost his father while young. After receiving the general training given to boys of his class, he had a course in the Vedānta under Yādavaprakāśa of Conjeevaram, but he could not support the interpretations of Yādava on all points. Āḷavandār, the famous head of the mutt at Śrīrangam, was impressed by Rāmānuja's learning, and thought of installing him in the apostolic seat at Śrīrangam. When Āḷavandār drew near his end, his disciples sent Perianaṁbi to bring Rāmānuja. By the time he arrived, the master was no more, and the tradition relates that, when Rāmānuja approached the body, he

---

[1] *Bhāgavata,* xii. 3. 52. The *Bhāgavata* distinguishes the different steps to bhakti.

Śravaṇaṁ kīrtanaṁ viṣṇoḥ smaraṇam pādasevanam
Arcanaṁ vandanaṁ dāsyaṁ sakhyam ātmanivedanam (vii. 5. 23).

[2] i. 12. [3] *Viṣṇu P.,* i. 11. [4] V.P., iii. 7.

[5] Artha evābhijanahetuḥ, dhanam eva aśeṣadharmahetuḥ, abhirucir eva dāṁpatyasaṁbandhahetuḥ, anṛtam eva vyavahārajayahetuḥ, strītvam evo'pabhoga hetuḥ. . . . brahmasūtram eva vipratvahetuḥ, liṅgadhāraṇam eva āśramahetuḥ. . . . (V.P., iv. 24. 21–22).

[6] In the *Āgamas* bhakti is emphasised. A larger freedom is given to the fulfilment of desires. Mantras, yantras and yogic exercises receive great attention.

saw three out of the five fingers of the right hand folded. The disciples explained this to mean that he had three unfulfilled desires, the chief of which was an easy commentary on the *Brahma Sūtra*. Rāmānuja returned to Conjeevaram and continued his usual devotions to God. One day, in great distress, he asked the priest of the temple to ascertain the divine will regarding his own future. The will of God was expressed in a verse to the effect, " I am the supreme reality, my view is distinction. Self-surrender is the unfailing cause of salvation, individual effort not being essential, release will come in the end. Perianaṁbi is the best of the teachers." [1] God spoke thus or Rāmānuja heard the voice and set his heart to obey. He met Perianaṁbi at Madhurāntakam, and was initiated by him into the mysteries of the Vedānta. Great men are often unable to find a woman suitable for them, and Rāmānuja was not blessed with a wife who would strive for his ideals and thus increase his powers. Incompatibility in marriage is difficult to conceal, and Rāmānuja soon felt, as Buddha and Śaṁkara, Plato and Paul did, that renunciation is a necessary condition for attaining the highest summits of human perfection or drawing near to God. When he became a saññyāsin, he grew very popular, and the admiring world called him the prince of ascetics (Yatirāja). Rāmānuja settled down at Śrīrangam and acquired a full knowledge of the Tiruvāymoyi. With the help of his disciple Kūrattāḷvār, who knew by heart the *Bodhāyanavṛtti*, Rāmānuja wrote *Vedāntasāra*, *Vedārthasaṁgraha* and *Vedāntadīpa*, and composed his great commentaries on the *Brahma Sūtra* and the *Bhagavadgītā*. The learned among the Vaiṣṇavas gave their approval to Rāmānuja's exposition of the *Brahma Sūtra*, and it became *the* commentary (Śrībhāṣya) for the Vaiṣṇavas. Rāmānuja toured round South India, restored many Vaiṣṇava temples and converted large numbers to Vaiṣṇavism.

The great thinker is the spokesman of his age, and re-lives in his own experience the ancient wisdom transmitted to him. The saints and the teachers in whose company Rāmānuja spent his days moved in the region of religious life and piety. The hymns of the Āḷvārs were outbursts of god-filled souls, for whom God was not merely the author of existence but an intimate personal friend and guide. The religious instinct of Rāmānuja seized on the concrete idea of God as a person. Both Śaṁkara and Rāmānuja were great exponents of the Vedānta. Their minds were driven to the same problems,

[1] Śrīmān paraṁ tattvam aham, matam me bhedaḥ, prapattir nirapāyahetuḥ
Nāvaśyakī ca smṛtir antyakāle mokṣo mahāpūrṇa ihāryavaryaḥ.

That all men attain salvation at the end of life is the central feature of the Pañcarātra religion. See Vedānta Deśika's *Pañcarātrarakṣā*.

their texts were practically the same, their methods were based on the same assumptions, and yet their results show striking differences. Their conclusions reveal their visions, their respective apprehensions of the truth. Rāmānuja trusts firmly to the religious instinct, and sets forth a deeply religious view which reveals God to man through creation, through the theophanies, through the prophets, through the incarnations. His study of the Āḷvārs and his training by the Ācāryas helped him to develop elements which otherwise would have remained latent in the Upaniṣads and the *Brahma Sūtra.* He did not for a moment feel that he was propounding a system of his own; he was but expounding the wisdom of the wise of all time.

V

History and Literature

The Vaiṣṇava movement has had a continuous history almost from the beginning of the Epic period. In the Ṛg-Veda, Viṣṇu is a solar deity regarded as the pervader, having his place in the supreme heaven.[1] The ideal of Varuṇa is strongly monotheistic in character. We have also in the Vedas the conception of the god Bhaga, who is a bestower of auspicious blessings. It soon came to stand for the power of goodness, and he who possessed the power was called Bhagavān. The religion in which Bhagavān (or Bhagavat) is the object of worship is Bhāgavatism. We have references in the *Mahābhārata* to the Bhāgavata religion. Vaiṣṇavism is the development of the Bhāgavata religion, which identifies Viṣṇu with Bhagavān. The distinctive features of Vaiṣṇavism are found in the Pañcarātra religion[2] mentioned in the *Mahābhārata.* In the Epic, however, Viṣṇu has for his rival Śiva, but in the *Viṣṇu Purāṇa* Viṣṇu's supremacy is unrivalled. *Harivaṁśa* strengthens the cult of Viṣṇu. The *Bhāgavata Purāṇa* (A.D. 900) emphasises the Bhāgavata cult centring round Kṛṣṇa. Its bhakti is of an emotional character, and the relation of God and soul is symbolised by that of man and maid. From the Nanaghat inscription, it is clear that Bhāgavatism found its way into South India some time before the first century of the Christian era. The *Bhāgavata* says that in the Kali age the worshippers of Nārāyaṇa will be numerous in Southern India.[3] The hymns of the poet-saints called Āḷvārs—twelve of whom obtained canonical recognition—are commonly known

---

[1] Viṣṇoḥ paramam padam. R.V., i. 22, 20. [2] I.P., pp. 490, 496–9.
[3] xi. 5. 38–40.

as Nālāyira Prabandham.[1] Among the Āḷvārs are a woman, several Śūdras and a prince. They are succeeded by the Ācāryas or the theologians, whose main objective was to establish a philosophical basis for the worship of a personal God and faith in the saving grace of that God. The chief of the teachers who preceded Rāmānuja are Nāthamuni and Āḷavandār or Yāmunācārya. Nāthamuni (tenth century), a disciple of the last of the Āḷvārs, is said to have arranged the hymns of the Āḷvārs. *Nyāyatattva* and *Yogarahasya* are attributed to him. Yāmunācārya struggled hard to defend the Vaiṣṇava Āgamas, and make out that they had the same purport as the Vedas. His chief works are: *Āgamaprāmāṇya, Mahāpuruṣanirṇaya, Siddhitrayam, Gītārthasaṁgraha, Catuśślokī* and *Stotraratna*. The sacred literature of the Vaiṣṇavas is often referred to as Ubhaya Vedānta, since it included the Sanskrit Prasthānatraya as well as the Tamil Prabandham. The tradition has long been current that the hymns of the Āḷvārs were in agreement with the Vedic scriptures. The uncompromising Advaitism of Śaṁkara made it necessary for Rāmānuja to reiterate the theistic view of the Vedas. He declares that he is only developing the views contained in the *Vṛtti* of Bodhāyana, and refers to other teachers of his way of thinking, Ṭaṅka, Dramiḍa,[2] Guhadeva, Kapardin and Bhāruci.[3] Śaṁkara admits the antiquity of the theistic tradition emphasised by Rāmānuja. Accordingly we may count as the antecedents of Rāmānuja's philosophy some of the theistic Upaniṣads, portions of the *Mahābhārata*, including the Nārāyaṇīya section, and the *Bhagavadgītā, Viṣṇu Purāṇa*, the Vaiṣṇava Āgamas, the works of the Āḷvārs and the Ācāryas. His own chief works attempt to reconcile the thought of the Upaniṣads, the *Gītā* and the *Brahma Sūtra* with the faith and belief of the Vaisṇava saints. Though it is not easy to decide the exact extent of his originality and independence, it must

---

[1] This collection, which consists of four thousand verses (nālāyiram), is arranged in four parts. The first, called Mudalāyiram, contains the utterances of various saints as Periāḷvār and the lady Āṇḍāḷ. The second, called Periatirumoyi, is the work of Tirumangai; and the third is the famous Tiruvāymoyi of Nammāḷvār. The fourth, Iyarpa, is a miscellany like the first. Nammaḷvar's *Tiruvāymoyi* is said to be the Tamil adaptation of the Vedas. Cp. "Vedam tamiy śeyda māran"; also

Krūre kaliyuge prāpte nāstikaiḥ kaluṣīkṛte
Viṣṇor aṁśāṁśasaṁbhūto vedavedārthatattvavit
Stotraṁ vedamayaṁ kartuṁ drāviḍyāpi ca bhāṣayā
Janiṣyati satāṁ śreṣṭho lokānāṁ hitakāmyayā. (*Bhaviṣya P.*)

Nāthamuni says of Tiruvāymoyi: "Sahasraśākhopaniṣatsamāgamam . . . drāviḍavedasāgaram." Tiruvāymoyi has for its central purpose the elucidation of the five topics (arthapañcakam) of the absolute reality, the individual soul, its relation to the Supreme, the destruction of the undesirable, and the realisation of the desirable.

[2] Śaṁkara, according to Ānandagiri, refers to this writer in his commentary on the Chān. Up., iii. 10. 4.

[3] *Vedārthasaṁgraha*.

be said that his attempt in the *Śrībhāṣya* "in substantial merit and completeness far outdid any previous effort to find in the *Brahma Sūtra* a basis for monotheism."[1] Rāmānuja's faith is more philosophical and restrained than that of some of his predecessors as well as successors. He did not show any anxiety to reject the ritual and the regulations of the Vedas, nor did he make much of the mythology of the Purāṇas. His chief aim was to proclaim the doctrine of salvation through bhakti, and make it out to be the central teaching of the Upaniṣads, the *Gītā* and the *Brahma Sūtra*. Sudarśana Bhaṭṭa's *Śrutaprakāśikā* is a celebrated gloss on Rāmānuja's *Bhāṣya*.

About the thirteenth century the distinctions between the Tengalais (Southern school) and the Vaḍagalais (Northern school) became accentuated. The former regard the Tamil Prabandham as canonical, and are indifferent to the Sanskrit tradition. The Vaḍagalais accept the two as equally authoritative. The Tengalais adopt the dangerous doctrine of doṣabhogya, namely, that God enjoys sin, since it gives a larger scope for the display of his grace.[2] The Vaḍagalais use more Sanskrit than Tamil, and adopt elements of Śākta theology in their conception of Lakṣmī.[3]

Piḷḷai Lokācārya is the chief representative of the Tengalai school. He teaches that the grace of God is irresistible and should be met not merely by active faith (bhakti) but by passive surrender (prapatti). Entire submission to the guidance of the spiritual preceptor (ācaryābhimāna) is emphasised by this school of thought. It must be said that this is not quite the same as the active and intelligent devotion taught by Rāmānuja. Lokācārya is the author of eighteen works called Rahasyas (secrets), of which the chief are *Arthapañcaka* and *Tattvatraya*. Maṇavāḷa Mahāmuni is the chief saint of the Tengalais.

Vedānta Deśika, or Veṇkaṭanātha (thirteenth century), one of the greatest of the successors of Rāmānuja, is the founder of the Vaḍagalai sect. Though a native of Conjeevaram, he spent much of his life at Śrīrangam. He was a prolific writer on many subjects, but his chief philosophical works are *Paramatabhaṅga* and *Rahasyatrayasāra*, in Tamil. His *Pañcarātrarakṣā* and *Saccaritrarakṣā* describe the principles and practices of the Pañcarātra school. He wrote a commentary on *Śrībhāṣya* called *Tattvaṭīkā*, and another called *Tātparyacandrikā* on Rāmānuja's commentary on the *Gītā*. His *Seśvara Mīmāṁsā* treats

---

1 Keith, in E.R.E., vol. x, p. 572.

2 See Oscar Wilde's *De Profundis*: "Christ, through some divine instinct in him, seems to have loved the sinner as being the nearest possible approach to perfection in man. . . . In a manner not yet understood of the world, he regarded sin and suffering as being in themselves beautiful, holy things and modes of perfection."

3 They believe that the consort of Viṣṇu is, like him, uncreated and is to be equally worshipped as the bestower of grace; while the Tengalais look upon her as created and, though divine, merely a mediatrix or channel of the Lord's grace. See *Aṣṭādaśabhedas*, by Govindācārya Svāmin, J.R.A.S. 1910.

the Pūrva and the Uttara Mīmāṁsās as parts of one whole, and argues that karma cannot produce its fruit, independent of divine agency. His *Nyāyasiddhāñjana* and *Tattvamuktākalāpa*, with its commentary *Sarvārthasiddhi*, are useful works. His polemical work, *Śatadūṣaṇī*, which is an attack on Advaita philosophy, had an equally tell-tale commentary called *Caṇḍamāruta* (seventeenth century). Śrīnivāsācārya's *Yatīndramatadīpikā* is a valuable work of the seventeenth century. Appaya Dīkṣita, though a follower of Śaivism, commented on several Vaiṣṇava treatises.[1] Raṅgarāmānuja (eighteenth century) wrote commentaries on the Upaniṣads in the interests of Rāmānuja's theism. The influence of Rāmānuja is visible throughout the later history of Hinduism. The movements of Madhva, Vallabha, Caitanya, Rāmānanda, Kabīr and Nānak, and the reform organisations of Brahmoism are largely indebted to Rāmānuja's theistic idealism.

VI

BHĀSKARA

Bhāskara wrote a commentary on the *Brahma Sūtra* called the *Bhāskarabhāṣya* about A.D. 900.[2] It is not a sectarian work, and does not favour either Śaṁkara's views or those of Pañcarātra Vaiṣṇavas. Bhāskara is an upholder of the bhedābhedavāda, or the doctrine that unity and multiplicity are equally real.[3] Brahman is not an undifferentiated mass of pure consciousness, but possesses all perfections. The causal state of Brahman is regarded as a unity, while its evolved condition is one of multiplicity.[4] Things are non-different in their causal and generic aspects and different as effects and individuals. Non-difference does not absorb difference as fire consumes grass. The two are equally real. Bhāskara believes in real evolution (pariṇāma).[5] He regards the illusion theory as unauthentic, and traces it to Buddhist influence.[6] He holds that the world of matter has real existence, though it is essentially of the same nature as Brahman. When matter acts on Brahman, it serves as a limiting

---

[1] At a meeting of the Pundits held at Conjeevaram, he said that he saw no distinction between Śiva and Viṣṇu, and so he clung to Śiva.

Māheśvare vā jagatām adhīśvare
Janārdane vā jagadantarātmani
Na vastubhedapratipattir asti me
Tathāpi bhaktis taruṇenduśekhare.

[2] His views are attacked by Udayana in his *Kusumāñjali* (A.D. 980).

[3] For a criticism of it, see R.B., i. 1. 4.

[4] Kāryarūpeṇa nānātvam, abhedaḥ kāraṇātmanā. Bhāskara on i. 1. 4.

[5] Bhāskarīyās tu cidacidaṁśavibhaktam brahmadravyam acidaṁśena vikriyate (*Sarvārthasiddhi*, iii. 27).

[6] Māhāyānikabauddhagāthitam māyāvādam. Bhāṣya on i. 4. 25.

adjunct in the form of body and senses and results in the rise of individual souls. He admits the reality of upādhis, and does not trace them to avidyā. The jīva is naturally one with Brahman, while its difference from Brahman is due to limitations.[1] The relation of jīvas to Brahman is illustrated by the analogy of sparks and fire. The life of saṁsāra is based on the confusion between Brahman and the upādhis. Through virtue and piety, we can discriminate between the two, and then we are saved. Bhāskara thinks that Brahman actually undergoes the suffering and the rebirth of the individual souls. Karma is, according to him, an essential means (aṅga) to knowledge which results in salvation. He adopts the view of Rāmānuja, or more accurately, jñānakarmasamuccaya or the combination of karma and jñāna.

VII

Yādavaprakāśa

Yādavaprakāśa, for some time the guru of Rāmānuja, who lived in the eleventh century A.D. at Conjeevaram, wrote an independent commentary leaning to the Advaita interpretation. He adopts the Brahmapariṇāmavāda, or the theory of the transformation of Brahman. He holds that Brahman is really changed into cit (spirit), acit (matter), and Īśvara (God). If Īśvara is brought under cit, both conscious and unconscious forms are only different states (avasthābheda) of one substance and not different substances themselves. His theory is called the bhedābhedavāda, or the doctrine of the simultaneous difference and non-difference. While Brahman undergoes changes, it does not forfeit its purity. Yādava does not find any contradiction in saying that a thing can be different and at the same time non-different from itself. He says that all things always present themselves under these two different aspects. They present non-difference so far as their causal substance (kāraṇa) and class characters (jāti) are concerned; they present difference so far as their effected conditions (kārya) and individual characteristics (vyakti) are concerned. Brahman and the world are thus both different and non-different.[2] While Bhāskara believes that Brahman undergoes in a way the experiences of the finite souls, Yādava contends that Brahman remains in its pristine exalted condition.[3] If we believe that the three, God, soul and matter, are ultimate realities and not transformations of Brahman, we are in the realm of misconception (bhrama). Brahman alone is real, and all else is produced from Brahman. For Yādava the distinctions are as real as the identity, while for Bhāskara the distinctions

---

[1] Jīvaparayoś ca svābhāviko 'bheda aupādhikas tu bhedaḥ. Bhāskara on iv. 4. 4. See also iv. 4. 15; ii. 3. 18.

[2] *Sarvārthasiddhi*, iii. 27.

[3] Bhāskara on i. 1. 17.

are due to upādhis, which are of course real, while the identity is the ultimate truth. Saṁsāra is nothing more than life based on the wrong knowledge that cit, acit and Īśvara are ultimately distinct. For removing this false knowledge, both karma and jñāna are useful.

Rāmānuja protests against Yādava's view on the ground that the distinction between Brahman and Īśvara is unauthorised. There is none else beyond Īśvara, and Īśvara is not to be regarded as a mere modification of Brahman. The relation of the śaktis, or powers of God, souls and matter to the basis of them (śaktyāśraya), Brahman, is not clear.[1]

VIII

The Sources of Knowledge

Rāmānuja accepts perception, inference and scripture as valid sources of knowledge, and is indifferent about the rest. His followers add one or two to this list. Perception has for its object what is distinguished by difference, possessing a general character which constitutes its form.[2]

Rāmānuja admits the distinction between determinate and indeterminate perception. Indeterminate perception is neither the apprehension of an absolutely undifferentiated object or pure being, nor the apprehension of a qualified object and its qualifications unrelated to one another. It is not the former, since it is impossible to apprehend objects devoid of all elements of distinction. The essential feature of consciousness is discrimination, and we cannot apprehend an object without apprehending some special features of it. All knowledge consists in the apprehension of an object qualified by some specific quality[3]; for, even in determinate perception, only those qualities which were apprehended in indeterminate perception are remembered and recognised. The difference between the two consists in this, that in indeterminate perception we perceive the individual for the first time, and, though we apprehend its class character, we are not aware that it is common to the individuals belonging to the class.[4]

[1] *Tattvamuktākalāpa*, iii. 28.

[2] The external properties are open to perception. When we hear a sound, the vṛtti of the ear goes out. Air is an object of the senses. Light is open to touch and sight, even though devoid of smell.

[3] Saviśeṣavastuviṣayatvāt sarvapramāṇānām (i. 1. 1).

[4] *Tattvamuktākalāpa*, iv. 32.

When we perceive the individual a second or a third time, we recognise the generic character as common to the whole class.

For Rāmānuja the individuals alone are real. There is no such thing as a class essence subsisting in them, though there is a resemblance (sādṛśya) among the individuals, such as the arrangement of parts (saṁsthāna). We frame the concept from the fact of resemblance. It is the resemblance that is the basis of the use of the same word.[1] Vedānta Deśika argues that difference in itself (bheda) is in no way relative to the fact which it distinguishes. Accordingly, perception can give us a knowledge of fact as well as its distinction.[2] These two do not determine each other and are not dependent on one another. They seem to determine each other when it is sought to unite them. But even if we assume all this, it is difficult to understand how there can be a difference which differentiates nothing.[3]

Yogic perception is not admitted as an independent source of knowledge by the followers of Rāmānuja. Each sense has its particular sphere of objects, and, even when well trained, cannot grasp objects belonging to other senses. The ear cannot see nor the eye hear. If the Yogic perception operates through the senses, then it is not different from sense-perception; if it is independent of all experience, then it is invalid.

Smṛti or remembrance is regarded as valid and given a separate place. We cannot bring it under perception simply because all remembered knowledge assumes perception; for in that case even inference, which presupposes perceptual knowledge, will have to be brought under perception.

Inference is knowledge derived from a general principle. As a matter of fact, a single instance suggests the general principle. A number of instances helps us in removing our doubts. By means of tarka or indirect proof, and the use of both positive and negative instances, we eliminate the non-essentials and establish the general rule.[4] The syllogism

[1] Cp. this with the Jaina view. [2] *Sarvārthasiddhi*, v. 14.

[3] Abhāva or non-existence is said to be an object of perception, since non-existence of a thing means its existence somewhere else. Through anupalabdhi or non-perception we know that consciousness has not always objects with which it is related (i. 1. 1).

[4] *Sarvārthasiddhi*, iv. 47.

has three members, the first three or the last three of the Nyāya five-membered syllogism. Comparison is not recognised as independent, since it is a case of either remembrance or inference. Implication (arthāpatti) and subsumption (saṁbhava) are also brought under inference.

Rāmānuja accepts the authority of scripture. The highest reality, which is the sole cause of the world, is not the object of the other means of knowledge, but is known only through the śāstras.[1] Brahman is not an object of perception.[2] No generalisation from experience can prove or disprove the reality of Brahman.[3] Its reality, to which intelligence points, lies in a region beyond that which can be actually observed or understood by finite intelligence. Scripture is our only source regarding supersensuous matters, though reason may be employed in support of scripture.[4] The Vedas are eternal, since at every world-epoch Īśvara only gives utterance to them. The smṛtis and the Epics expound the ideas contained in the Vedas, and so they are also authoritative. The *Pañcarātra Āgamas* may also be accepted as valid, since they owe their origin to the divine Vāsudeva.[5] Aitihya or tradition, when it is true, is a case of scriptural knowledge (āgama).[6]

Rāmānuja admits that thought by itself cannot bring us face to face with reality. Even the Vedas give us only indirect knowledge. Something more is needed than the mere understanding of the words of the scripture. Intuition (sākṣātkāra) of reality, which is not the logical knowledge of it, is possible only in meditation bearing the character of devotion.[7] Vāmadeva and others saw the one Brahman with the material and immaterial objects for its distinguishing modes.[8] This, the highest knowledge, involves the exercise of the non-cognitive elements of the soul. The mind has other ways of exploring the nature of reality, and all these ways are connected in their final purpose and first source. To realise

[1] i. 2. 1. [2] i. 1. 3. [3] i. 2. 23.

[4] ii. 1. 12. Yāmunācārya adopts a thoroughly rational view in dealing with rival dogmatisms. Declining to accept the assertion of his opponent, he remarks: "All this teaching may carry weight with believers; we are not credulous, and so we require logic to convince us" (*Siddhitraya*, p. 88).

[5] *Tattvamuktākalāpa*, iv. 121.

[6] When false, it is a case of āgamābhāsa.

[7] R.B., iii. 2. 23 [8] iii. 2. 24.

the truth the mind must exercise all its resources and act at the highest level of its life. Mind at its fullest stretch is suffused with reason as well as feeling. It is quite true that there are wrong feelings even as there are wrong cognitions. It is also true that, in the lower level, feelings stand isolated even as cognitions do. But as the cognitions are systematised, so are feelings transformed and disciplined, *i.e.* rationalised. Since the object intuited is not directly presented, the nature of intuition is said to be indirect or representative in character ; yet, so far as its immediacy and clearness go, it is not inferior to perceptual knowledge.[1] As we shall see, this knowledge arises through divine grace in response to acts of daily worship and prayer. This is religious experience or the immediate awareness of the infinite. The individual soul is *en rapport* with the ultimately real.

If all knowledge is of the real,[2] how does it happen that our knowledge sometimes does not correspond to things ? The object, appearing in false perception, is not illusory but real ; for, according to the doctrine of quintuplication (pañcīkaraṇa), all objects of the physical world are compound substances, containing the five elements in varying proportions. " That one thing is called ' silver ' and another ' shell ' has its reason in the relative preponderance of one or the other element. We observe that shells are similar to silver ; thus perception itself informs us that some elements of the latter actually exist in the former." Likeness in certain respects is the indication of a partial identity of substance. We perceive water in the mirage simply because water exists in connection with light and earth particles. When the white conch is seen as yellow by a person suffering from jaundiced eyes, the yellowness of the eye is transmitted to the conch along with the rays of the organ of sight, and the white colour of the conch is obscured. However unscientific this theory may be, it shows Rāmānuja's unwillingness to give up his view that knowledge is always of the real. Even in dreams, God creates objects for the enjoyment or suffering of the individual, in accordance with his merit or demerit.[3] God

[1] R.B., iii. 4. 26.
[2] Sarvaṁ vijñānajātaṁ yathārtham (i. 1. 1).
[3] See also R.B., iii. 2. 5 and 6.

"while producing the entire world as an object of fruition for the individual souls, in agreement with their respective good and evil deserts, creates certain things of such a nature as to become common objects of consciousness, while certain other things are created in such a way as to be perceived only by particular persons and to persist for a limited time only. It is this distinction of things that are objects of general consciousness and those that are not so which makes the difference between what is called 'things sublating' and 'things sublated.'"[1] It is a mistake to think that some cognitions have false things for their objects and others true ones.

Rāmānuja's view seems to explain away all error. While he maintains that all knowledge is of the real, he does not say that knowledge is of the whole of reality. Our knowledge is generally imperfect and partial. When we mistake a piece of shell for silver, we notice certain features and miss others. In the illusion of the "yellow" conch we fail to notice the whiteness of the conch. In dream experiences we overlook the fact that the objects are private and peculiar to the dreamer and not to others. Even in what is generally taken as true knowledge we ignore much that is unnecessary for practical purposes. While both true and erroneous knowledge are incomplete, the former takes note of the features necessary for the interests in view and serves our needs; the latter fails to achieve the end in view. True knowledge is useful in life. The mirage is an error, not because the element of water is not present in it, but because the water in it does not quench our thirst. The true is what represents the real (yathārtha) and what is practically useful (vyavahārānuguṇa).[2]

While all knowledge is representative of some aspects of reality, it is not complete and perfect until it takes in the whole of reality. The possibility of error is not removed until our knowledge becomes complete and comprehensive, and the individual knower is freed from all defects. In saṁsāra this is not possible, though the aspiration is there.

Rāmānuja believes in an immanent necessity operating in the nature of knowledge. It is this necessity which enables

[1] i. 1. 1.

[2] *Yatīndramatadīpikā.*

the indeterminate cognition to pass over into the determinate. Throughout, our judgments attempt to relate the subjects to the larger whole. When knowledge is at its highest, *i.e.* when it reaches its goal, we shall have a single organised experience including a number of parts with their specific functions. In such a whole each member would be characterised by its own place and function, and, though finite, would be none the less individual and unique. The jīva, when freed, attains the ideal of perfect knowledge.

Śaṁkara is quite right in thinking that a bare identity cannot be grasped by thought, but thought need not be blamed for not achieving the impossible. If the subject is a simple self-identity, then the judgment which asserts that S is P is not true, for we can only say S is S. Significant predication is false, and tautological judgment is useless. But Rāmānuja asserts that while the judgment affirms the identity of the subject with the predicate, there is another equally important factor, that the subject and the predicate are different. There can be no judgment unless there be an identity maintaining itself through the different aspects of things, but the identity must manifest itself in difference and overcome it. Identity is a relation, and every relation requires two terms. If the terms are not distinct, they cannot be related. The negation of all difference renders impossible even the relation of identity. In absolute self-sameness there cannot be any talk of identity. Even when we say S is S, we make such a proposition only in answer to a suggested difference. Śaṁkara argues that when we say "That art thou" there is the *apparent difference* between the two, and the judgment asserts the *real identity* between them. But Rāmānuja contends that identity and difference apply to terms which are on the same level of reality. All identity is an identity in and through difference, and every judgment is an illustration of it. In "the sky is blue," "the sky" and "blue" are not identical; nor are they completely different. The object and the property of blueness subsist together, though the two have different significations. The relational view of thought is best adapted to the exposition of the nature of reality, since the real is a perfect system determined by and determining its contents. It is a false standard of intelligibility that regards the rational nature of thought as a defect. Knowledge, to be knowledge, must unfold and develop the system of relations through which it asserts its own existence. The active living principle is what inwardly distinguishes itself and yet remains free in so doing. Śaṁkara holds that a system of relations leads to an infinite regress. A relation implies two terms which, with the relation itself, make three; and if we add to them the mutual relations of them to one another, we are forced to an infinite regress. Rāmānuja rejects this view in favour of a dynamic reality, which has in it the possibility of self-revelation. He does not believe that there are no relations where there is oneness, and where there are relations there is no oneness. The world for knowledge is an orderly whole, the detailed development or expression of a single principle. God and the world are equally real, and each must be real through the other; and this is possible only if we regard the system as a single experience of the personal type. Thought reaches the full apprehension of God as self-conscious intelligence. Reality is an individual of which the elements are the lesser individuals.

IX

Cause and Substance

Rāmānuja adopts the theory of satkāryavāda. Every effect implies a pre-existent material cause. Alteration of state is the meaning of causation.[1] Threads are the cause of cloth, for cloth is only a cross arrangement of threads.[2] Existence and non-existence are different states of a substance. Non-existence is only relative and not absolute.

Whatever has qualities is a substance or dravya. The basis (ādhāra) is the substance, and what depends on it (ādheya) is the non-substance (adravya). While things are dravyas, attributes and relations are adravyas. The lamp is a substance, so also the light (prabhā), though the latter is also a guṇa or a quality. Buddhi is a substance, as it has

[1] Avasthāntarāpattir eva hi kāryatā (R.B.G., xiii. 2).
[2] R.B., ii. 1. 19–20. See also ii. 1. 16.

the quality of being subject to expansion and contraction; it is also a quality of the self.[1] The whole world as the viśeṣaṇa (adjective) of God is non-substantial (adravya) from the standpoint of Īśvara though it contains dravya and adravya as elements and qualities. A viśeṣaṇa may be a substance like jñāna. While substances serve as the material cause, non-substances cannot do so.[2] The substances are prakṛti or matter, kāla or time, śuddhasattva or pure matter, dharmabhūtajñāna or attributive consciousness, jīva or the individual soul, and Īśvara or God.[3] While the first three are unconscious (jaḍa), God and the soul are conscious (ajaḍa), and jñāna has the features of both. It is unlike unconscious substances since it can manifest itself and external objects. Knowledge, however, is never for itself, but is always for another, the self. Knowledge is a unique adjunct of the self, and is called dharmabhūtajñāna. The self knows this or that object when the jñāna issues forth through this or that sense and comes into contact with an object. It is assumed that subjects and objects exist independently and are brought into relation with each other by means of knowledge.

The five qualities of sound, resistance, form, taste and smell, cohesion, quantity, number, magnitude, individuality, conjunction, distinction, as well as desire, aversion, pleasure, pain and will and understanding, are non-substances.

X

Self and Consciousness

Śaṁkara believes that the distinction between subject and object is a relative one, since the real is the one undifferenced Brahman. Rāmānuja disputes this view, and holds that the nature of consciousness testifies to the existence of a permanent thinking subject, as well as objects distinct from the self.[4] Knowledge involves the perception of difference. There is no source of knowledge enabling us to apprehend mere undifferenced being. Even if there were, it would place Brahman in the position of an object, and thus involve

[1] *Tattvamuktākalāpa*, iv. 7.

[2] *Ibid.*, v. 2.

[3] *Ibid.*, i. 6.

[4] Na ca nirviṣayā kācit saṁvid asti.

it in the sphere of the perishable. There cannot be such a thing as pure consciousness. This is either proved or not. If pure consciousness is proved to be real, it follows that it has attributes; if it is not, then it is non-existent, like a sky flower.[1] Even Śaṁkara attributes to consciousness qualities like eternity, self-luminousness. Knowledge, to be sure, is self-luminous (svayaṁprakāśa), but it is also an object of knowledge (vedya). It is not necessary that everything known must be a non-conscious (jaḍa) object.

If knowledge were unlimited, its objects also should be so, which is, however, not the case. It is a mistake to think that knowledge exists in deep sleep and similar states, as pure knowledge devoid of any objects. "For a person risen from deep sleep never represents to himself his state of consciousness during sleep in the form 'I was pure consciousness, free from all egoity and opposed in nature to everything else, witnessing nescience (ajñāna).' What he thinks is only 'I slept well.' From this form of reflection it appears that even during sleep the self, *i.e.* the 'I,' was a knowing subject and perceptive of pleasure. Even when the self says that it was 'conscious of nothing,' it means that the knowing 'I' persisted, and what is negated is the objects of knowledge."[2] Jñāna is not known except in relation to an object, and, in deep sleep, it does not function, since there is no object. The soul, in deep sleep, remains in its intrinsic state of self-consciousness along with the jñāna, which is not functioning at the moment. The self is always an ego and never pure knowledge. Śaṁkara admits as much when he says that the self exists in deep sleep as the witness (sākṣin) of the general nescience, though the organ of egoity (ahaṁkāra) is dissolved. But that which does not know cannot be a witness (sākṣin). Pure knowledge is not a witness. Sākṣin is a knower, *i.e.* a subject. This subject persists even in deep sleep, only we are not conscious of it, since it is overpowered by tamas. If it did not persist in deep sleep, we could not remember that we slept well on waking from sleep. But for this permanent self memory would be impossible, and we could not

[1] Saṁvit siddhyati vā na vā, siddhyati cet sadharmatā syāt, na cet tuccatā gaganakusumādivat (i. 1. 1).

[2] i. 1. 1. See also ii. 3. 31.

recognise anything to-day as something we had seen yesterday. Even if consciousness were identified with the conscious subject and acknowledged as permanent, the phenomenon of recognition would not be easily explained. For it implies a conscious subject persisting from the earlier to the later moment, and not merely consciousness.[1] The self is not self-luminous knowledge, but only the subject of it. We do not say "I am consciousness,"[2] but only "I am conscious."[3] The self-luminous character of knowledge is derived from the self or the knower. The existence of knowledge and its self-luminous character depend on its connection with a self.[4] To argue that the subject, thus established, belongs to the side of the object is "no better than to maintain that one's own mother is a barren woman." We cannot attribute to self-sense (ahaṁkāra), which is a non-intelligent effect of prakṛti, knowership any more than knowledge. The self is of the essence of knowledge, and has knowledge also for its quality.[5] It is a knower and not mere light.[6] We need not think that to be a knower is to be essentially changing. For to be a knower is to be the substrate of the quality of knowledge; and, since the knowing self is eternal, knowledge, which is its quality, is also eternal. Only this eternal knowledge does not manifest itself always. Knowledge, which is in itself unlimited (svayam aparicchinnam), is capable of contraction and expansion. Owing to the influence of karma, it becomes contracted when it adapts itself to work of different kinds and is variously determined by the different senses. With reference to these adaptations due to the senses, it is said to rise and vanish. It never ceases to be, though it functions, throughout life, in a more or less restricted manner. But since the quality of adaptation is not essential and is brought about by action, the self is regarded as essentially unchanging.[7]

[1] Pratisaṁdhānaṁ hi pūrvaparakālasthāyinam anubhavitāraṃ upasthāpayati, nānubhūtimātram (i. 1. 1).

[2] Anubhūtir aham.

[3] Anubhavāmy aham.

[4] i. 1. 1. See also ii. 3. 18.

[5] Cidrūpa . . . caitanyaguṇaka.

[6] Jñātaiva na prakāśamātram. See also Bṛh. Up., iv. 3. 7 and 14; iv. 5. 15; Chān., viii. 12. 3 and 4; viii. 26. 2; Praśna, iv. 9; vi. 5; Tait., ii. 4.

[7] i. 1. 1.

Rāmānuja disputes the view that consciousness is never an object. Though it is not an object when it illumines other things, it can and does frequently become an object. For common observation shows that the consciousness of one person becomes the object of the cognition of another, as when we infer something from the friendly or unfriendly appearance of another, or when one's past states of consciousness become the objects of his present cognition. Consciousness does not lose its nature simply because it becomes an object of consciousness. We cannot say that consciousness is self-proved. For Rāmānuja the essential nature of consciousness consists in its manifesting itself at the present moment through its own being to its substrate, or in being instrumental in proving its own object by its own being.[1] When unconscious things are revealed, they are not revealed to themselves. The other attributes of the self, such as atomic extension, eternity and so on, and the past states of consciousness, are revealed not through themselves, but through an act of knowledge different from them.[2]

XI

God

From Rāmānuja's theory of knowledge, it follows that the real cannot be a bare identity. It is a determinate whole, which maintains its identity in and through the differences. While Rāmānuja is clear that there exists an absolute self, he is equally clear that every finite reality is an expression of this self. To make reciprocal interaction among a plurality of existents possible, the constituent elements of the world-whole must have a common bond of unity and interdependence, which must be a spiritual principle. Not only logic, but religious experience, demands a conservation of the finite and an admission of the infinite as a personal being. The sense of personal communion with God involves a real fellowship with an "other," divine personality. The nirguṇa Brahman,

[1] Anubhūtitvaṁ nāma vartamānadaśāyāṁ svasattayaiva svāśrayam pratiprakāśamānatvaṁ, svasattayaiva svaviṣayasādhanatvaṁ vā (i. 1. 1).

[2] See *Śrutaprakāśikā*.

which stares at us with frozen eyes regardless of our selfless devotion and silent suffering, is not the god of religious insight. Śaṁkara's method, according to Rāmānuja, leads him to a void, which he tries to conceal by a futile play of concepts. His nirguṇa Brahman is a blank, suggesting to us the famous mare of Orlando, which had every perfection except the one small defect of being dead. Such a Brahman cannot be known by any means, perception, inference, or scripture.[1] If the sources of knowledge are all relative, they cannot tell us of something which transcends experience; if the scriptures are unreal, even so is the Brahman of which they relate. In the ultimate reality called God we have determination, limitation, difference, other-being which is at the same time dissolved, contained and gathered together in the one. Finitude is in the infinite itself. Brahman has internal difference (svagatabheda) and is a synthetic whole, with souls and matter as his moments (cidacidviśiṣṭa).[2] The qualities of being (sat), consciousness (cit), and bliss (ānanda) give to Brahman a character and a personality. Brahman's knowledge is immediate, and is not dependent on the organs of sense.[3] He is all-knowing and has direct intuition of all. Brahman is the supreme personality, while the individuals are personal in an imperfect way. Personality implies the power to plan and realise one's purposes. God is perfect personality, since he contains all experience within himself and is dependent on nothing external to him. The differences necessary for personality are contained within himself. The most prominent qualities of God are knowledge, power and love (karuṇa). Out of his love God has created the world, established laws, and helps constantly all who seek to attain perfection.[4] While each quality by itself is different from the others, they all belong to one identity and do not divide its integrity of being. The Lord's connection with them is natural (svābhāvika) and eternal (sanātana).[5] These attributes are said to be abstract, as distinct from matter and souls, which are also called the attributes of God. Īśvara is the support (ādhāra) of his own essential qualities, as well as

[1] i. 1. 2. [2] i. 1. 2; S.D.S., iv. [3] i. 2. 19.
[4] *Rahasyatrayasāra*, xxiii. [5] R.B., i. 1. 15.

those of the objects dependent on him.[1] The Supreme has "a divine form peculiar to itself, not of the stuff of prakṛti and not due to karma."[2] A body is not a mere combination of the elements or something which is sustained by prāṇa or life-breath. It is not the seat of the senses or the cause of pleasure-pain. It is, according to Rāmānuja, "any substance which a conscious soul is capable of completely controlling and supporting for its own purposes, and which stands to the soul in an entirely subordinate relation."[3] Though embodied, God does not suffer, seeing that karma, and not embodiedness, is the cause of suffering.[4] He is the Lord of karma, for the latter by itself cannot give rise to the consequences. Action, which is non-intelligent and transitory, is incapable of bringing about a result connected with a future time.[5] It is the supreme Lord that bestows the different forms of enjoyment in this and the heavenly world. We may say also that Brahman is devoid of form,[6] though connected with various forms, for "the individual soul is connected with the shape of the body in which it dwells, since it participates in the pleasures and pains to which the body gives rise ; but, since Brahman does not share these pleasures and pains, it has no form."[7] Brahman is not touched by the suffering of souls or the mutations of matter. All evil is the result of past wrong, the product of the soul's life in saṁsāra. God is in no way responsible for it. Above the endless succession of existences, he dwells in light, where no shadow can dim his glory.[8] Such a life is possible for the liberated spirits also ; much more therefore for God.[9]

Souls and matter are comprehended within the unity of the Lord's essence and are related to the Supreme as attributes to a substance, as parts to a whole, or as body to the soul[10] which animates it. They are also called prakāras or modes, śeṣas or accessories, niyāmya[11] or the controlled, while God

[1] *Rahasyatrayasāra*, iii. [2] i. 2. 1.
[3] ii. 1. 9. [4] i. 1. 21. [5] iii. 2. 37.
[6] Brahmarūparahitatulyam eva. [7] iii. 2. 14.
[8] i. 1. 21. [9] iii. 3. 27.
[10] Cp. Jagat sarvaṁ śarīram te. *Rāmāyaṇa* Yuddhakāṇḍa, i. 20. 26 ; *Tiruvāymoyi*, i. 1. 8 ; Bṛh. Up., v. 7.
[11] Niyāmyatvam is defined by Vedānta Deśika as "tatsaṁkalpādhina. sattāsthitipravṛttikatvam."

is the supporter (prakāri), controller (niyantā) and the principal (śeṣi).[1] They are real and permanent, though subject to the control of the one Brahman in all their modifications and evolutions. The relation of body to soul is said to bring out roughly the nature of the dependence of the world on God. Since the body (śarīra) decays when the soul departs, it has only derivative being; the movements of the body are subject to the will of the soul.[2] The world stands in the same relation to God, deriving its being from him and subject to his will.[3] Īśvara exists, with the jīva as his inner and the world as his outer body. If souls and matter are attributes of God, it does not mean that they are not in themselves substances possessing attributes, with their own distinct modes, energies and activities. The illustration of the soul and body points out that the body has its own qualities, though it qualifies the soul. This hypothesis enables Rāmānuja to account for the harmony of the universe and the interaction of the reals, so as to form one world. The world is one on account of the supreme mind which gives organic connection to the multiplicity of spiritual reals and a place and a function to each of them. Souls (bhoktā), matter (bhogya), and God (preritā)[4] are three, on account of their natural differences (svarūpabheda), but one on account of the identity (aikyam) of the modes and substance (prakāra and prakāri).[5] Identity means only inseparable existence (apṛthaksiddhi).

Rāmānuja's conception of God is not that of a merely last term in an ascending series of real reflective self-conscious individuals, nor that of a merely transcendental Absolute existing above and beyond the finite universe. While the conscious and the unconscious objects of the universe coexist with God they yet derive their existence from him and are sustained through him. The pluralistic universe is real in precisely the same sense as God is real. The universe, however, depends on God as its ground, its *ratio essendi*, but not as its cause. God is not to be regarded as simply the immanent ground, for then God will have to be conceived as wholly differentiated into the "many," or the "many" will have to

[1] iii; R.B., ii. 4. 14.
[2] Svarūpāśritam. Saṁkalpādhīnam.
[3] Īśvarasya rūpāśritam and icchādhīnam.
[4] Śvet. Up., i.
[5] Brahman is prakāraviśiṣṭaprakāri.

be conceived as wholly absorbed into the undifferentiated oneness of God. To Rāmānuja, God is both the transcendent and the immanent ground of the world. God is a person, and not a mere totality of other persons, and so he cannot be confused with the thinking individuals and the objects of their thought.

God, from within the cosmic order, sustains it as its ultimate ground and support, and receives it back on its dissolution.[1] Creation and dissolution are not to be taken as events in time, but are to be interpreted as signifying logical dependence on the one Supreme. Brahman alone is uncaused, while all the rest is caused.[2] Though he is responsible for the world, which is imperfect, he is not touched by its imperfections. The supreme spirit is identified with Viṣṇu by Rāmānuja, and the highest attributes are ascribed to him. Brahmā and Śiva are also Viṣṇu.[3]

The divine spirit can be envisaged in several ways. "Brahman" may denote the central unity when souls and matter are regarded as its attributes, or the combined whole when the real is said to be Brahman and Brahman alone. Brahman is the supreme reality, of which the world is the body or the attribute (viśeṣaṇa). This world may be manifest, as in creation, or unmanifest, as in pralaya. Even in the latter condition the attributes of souls and matter exist, though subtly. The condition of absolute liberation for all is the consummation of the world. It is the ideal aimed at by the process of the universe. When it is realised, the souls regain their innocence and exist in heaven facing God. Even nature displays its sattva form. This ideal world is inherent in God. It is a state already individualised. This condition cannot be identified with the state of souls and matter in pralaya. Apart from the world-body, Īśvara has an ideal materiality, a sort of plastic stuff, through which he displays his boundless power of appearing diverse and multiple, though he is inwardly one and the same. Yet his essence is to be distinguished from this nityavibhūti also.

[1] i. 1. Cp. *Tiruvāymoyi*, x. 5. 3. Rāmānuja's philosophy is called Viśiṣṭādvaitam for the reason, among others, that it insists on the non-duality of two different objects, viśiṣṭayor advaitam.

[2] ii. 3. 9.

[3] Cp. *Tiruvāymoyi*, x. 10. 1.

Rāmānuja supports his conception of reality from the scriptures. The Vedas declare that Brahman is full of auspicious qualities. "Truth, knowledge and infinite is Brahman," says the Upaniṣad. These several terms refer to the one supreme reality and declare that the absolute Brahman is unchangeable perfection, and possesses intelligence which is ever uncontracted, while the intelligence of released souls was for some time in a contracted condition. It is infinite (anantam), since its nature is free from all limitations of place, time and substance, and different in kind from all other things. Infinity characterises the qualities as well as the nature of Brahman, which is not the case with regard to the souls called eternal (nitya).[1] It is first without a second, since there is no other God than God. Rāmānuja admits that there are texts which deny all predicates to Brahman, but contends that they only deny finite and false attributes, and not all attributes whatsoever. When it is said that we cannot comprehend the nature of Brahman, it only means that the glory of Brahman is so vast that it eludes the grasp of the finite mind. The texts which deny plurality are explained as intended to deny the real existence of things apart from the supreme spirit which is identical with all things. The supreme spirit subsists in all forms as the soul of all (sarvasyātmatayā). In the highest intuition the Upaniṣads declare that "one sees nothing else, hears nothing else, and knows nothing else" than Brahman. Rāmānuja explains that "when the meditating devotee realises the intuition (anubhava) of Brahman, which consists of absolute bliss, he does not see anything apart from it, since the whole aggregate of things is contained within the essence (svarūpa) and outward manifestation (vibhūti) of Brahman.[2] Rāmānuja interprets the famous text, "Tat tvam asi," in accordance with his view of knowledge. Śaṁkara is of opinion that the passage, "That art thou," is intended to bring out the metaphysical identity between Brahman and the individual soul, when their special characteristics are ignored. In the judgment, "This is that Devadatta," the idea conveyed is of Devadatta and him alone. To understand the identity

[1] Deśakālavastuparicchedarahitam . . . sakaletaravastuvijātīyam (i. 1. 2).
[2] i. 3. 7.

between S and P we must eliminate thisness and thatness. Until we do so, S and P are never identical, and the sentence would be affirming a contradiction. So the text, "That art thou," means the absolute oneness of Brahman and the individual soul, which we should realise when we drop the imagined distinctions produced by avidyā. Rāmānuja argues against this contention and holds that every judgment is a synthesis of distincts. When Brahman and the individual soul are placed in the relation of subject and predicate (sāmānādhikaraṇya),[1] it follows that there is a difference between the two. Subject and predicate are *distinct* meanings referred to the *same* substance. If the two meanings cannot coinhere in the same substance, the judgment fails. We distinguish subject and predicate in their meaning or intension, but unite them in their application or extension. So the text, "That art thou," brings out the complex nature of the ultimate reality, which has individual souls inhering in it.[2] Brahman and the jīva are related as substance and attribute (viśeṣa and viśeṣaṇa), or soul and body.[3] If there were not a difference between the two, we could not say that the one is the other. There are statements recorded in the scripture where the mystic soul identifies himself with the supreme and calls on others to worship him. Indra's statement, "Meditate on me," and Vāmadeva's declaration, "I am Manu, I am Sūrya," are interpreted by Rāmānuja as affirming the view that Brahman is the inner self of all (sarvāntarātmatvam).[4] Since the infinite one dwells in all, he may be said to dwell in any individual, and so one can say with Prahlāda that as Brahman "constitutes my 'I' also, all is from me, I am all, within me is all."[5] All words, directly or indirectly, refer to Brahman.[6]

[1] Samānam = ekam, adhikaraṇam = viśeṣaṇānām ādhārabhūtaṁ viśeṣyam.

[2] See also ii. 1. 23.

[3] Jīvaparamātmanoḥ śarīrātmabhāvena tādātmyaṁ na viruddham. See *Vedārthasaṁgraha*, pp. 32, 35, 44 and 110.

[4] i. 1. 31.

[5] *Viṣṇu P.*, i. 19. 85, quoted in R.B., i. 1. 31.

Sarvagatvād anantasya sa evāham avasthitaḥ
Mattas sarvam ahaṁ sarvam mayi sarvaṁ sanātane.

[6] *Vedārthasaṁgraha*, p. 30.

The Vaiṣṇava theology is based on the Vedas and the Āgamas, the Purāṇas and the Prabandham. The Vedas speak of the Absolute in itself and the inner ruler. The Pañcarātra Āgamas accept the theory of Vyūhas or manifestations. The Purāṇas inculcate the worship of the avatārs, such as Rāma and Kṛṣṇa. The Drāviḍa Prabandham is full of devotional utterances addressed to the images in the shrines of South India. So it is said that the one Absolute identified with Viṣṇu exists in five different modes, images and the like (arcā), incarnations (vibhava), manifestations (vyūha) like Saṁkarṣaṇa, Vāsudeva, Pradyumna and Aniruddha, the subtle (sūkṣma) form of Vāsudeva or the supreme spirit and the inner ruler of all (antaryāmin). Sometimes the highest mode (para) is said to be Nārāyaṇa or Brahman living in Vaikuṇṭha,[1] where God is said to exist in a body made of pure sattva. God in his infinite fulness transcends his own manifestations. The perfect personality of God is not exhausted in its cosmical aspects. God has his own independent life, rendering possible personal relations with him. In Vaikuṇṭha, the Lord is seated on the serpent Śeṣa, supported by his consort Lakṣmī. Lakṣmī, the imaginative symbol of the creative energy of God, becomes in later Vaiṣṇavism the divine mother of the universe, who sometimes intercedes with God on behalf of weak and erring humanity. She is the power united eternally with the Lord. While Īśvara symbolises justice, Lakṣmī stands for mercy, and the two qualities are united in the godhead. Lakṣmī, the śakti of Viṣṇu, has the two forms of kriyā or the principle of regulation and control, and bhūti or the principle of becoming. These, answering to force and matter, enable Viṣṇu to become the efficient and the material causes of the universe. The Supreme has the six perfections of knowledge, energy, strength, lordship, vigour and brilliance.[2] While the highest spirit Vāsudeva possesses all the six perfections, the three other vyūhas possess only two of these. The vyūhas, according to Rāmānuja, are the forms which the highest Brahman assumes out of tenderness for his devotees. They are respectively the rulers of individual souls (Saṁkarṣaṇa), minds (Pradyumna) and egoity (Aniruddha).[3] The Vibhavarūpas are the incarnations of Viṣṇu. In his Introduction to the *Gītābhāṣya*, Rāmānuja says that God in his infinite mercy "assumed various forms without putting away his own essential godlike nature, and time after time incarnated himself . . . descending not only with the purpose of relieving the burden of the earth, but also to be accessible to men, even such as we are, so revealing himself to the world as to be visible to the sight of all, and doing such other marvellous deeds as to ravish the hearts and eyes of all beings, high and low." Rāmānuja's God is not an impassive absolute who looks down upon us from the height of heaven, but joins us in the experiences of our life, shares our ends and works for the

---

1 Parabrahmaparavāsudevādivācyo nārāyaṇaḥ (*Yatīndramatadīpikā*).

2 See also *Viṣṇu P.*, vi. 5. 79.

3 R.B., ii. 2. 40.

upbuilding of the world. The avatārs are literally the descents from the supernatural (aprākṛta) to the natural (prākṛta) order. They are principal (mukhya) or subordinate (gauṇa). When Viṣṇu himself interferes with the natural order, we have a case of the former; the inspired souls[1] are the subordinate incarnations. The avatārs are worshipped by the seeker for freedom, while the latter are resorted to by those who desire wealth, power and influence. God dwells in duly consecrated images (pratimā or vigraha). *Arthapañcaka* speaks of the suffering which the Lord out of his love for men undergoes in permitting himself to be embodied in an idol.[2] God, as the antaryāmin, dwells in all beings and accompanies the soul in all its wanderings through heaven and hell. The God in man is like a flash of lightning in the heart of a blue cloud.[3] God, as antaryāmin, is said to be the highest of all.[4]

XII

The Individual Soul

The absoluteness of God is qualified in Rāmānuja so as to admit of the existence, within the scope of his universal activity, of free spirits, who, though they draw all they are from God, yet possess such spontaneity and choice that they deserve to be called persons. Rāmānuja wages a vigorous and telling polemic against those who regard persons as vain variations of the self-same absolute. The individual soul, through a mode of the supreme, is real, unique, eternal, endowed with intelligence and self-consciousness, without parts, unchanging, imperceptible and atomic.[5] It is different from the body, the senses, vital breath, and even buddhi. It is the knower, the agent (kartā) and the enjoyer (bhoktā). It is attached, on the human plane, to the gross body, the vital

[1] Āveśāvatāras.

[2] "Though omniscient, he appears as ignorant, though spirit as non-spirit, though his own master as one who is in the power of men, though omnipotent as powerless, though entirely free from needs as having needs, though all-protecting as helpless, though lord like servant, though invisible as visible, though unseizable as seizable."

[3] Nīlatoyadamadhyasthā vidyullekheva bhāsvara (in *Vedārthasaṁgraha*).

[4] Cp. *Pañcarātrarahasya*.

Pūrvapūrvoditopāsti viseṣaksīṇakalmaṣaḥ.
Uttarottaramūrtīnām upāstyadhikṛto bhavet.

See S.D.S., iv.

[5] ii. 2. 19-32; ii. 3. 18. *Yatīndramatadīpikā*, viii.

breath, which is an instrument as much as the sense organs,[1] the five organs of action and manas. Manas reveals to the soul the inner states and, with the aid of the senses, conveys a knowledge of the outer states. The functions of manas are threefold : decision (adhyavasāya), self-love (abhimāna), and reflection (cintā).[2] The atomic jīva has its seat in the hṛtpadma. In deep sleep it rests in it and in the highest self.[3] Sleep is not a breach of the continuity of the self, as is evident from the continuity of work, from the fact of memory, from the statements of scripture, and from the adequacy of the hypothesis to ethical injunctions.[4] In spite of the atomic size of the jīva, through its attribute of knowledge which expands and contracts, it is able to feel pleasure and pain all over the body, even as the flame of the lamp, though tiny in itself, illumines many things by means of its light, which is capable of contraction and expansion.[5] It can apprehend objects far away in space and remote in time. The cognition of the souls, as in the case of God, is eternal in character, self-sustained, extends over all things, and is valid ; albeit its range is narrowed on account of defects, such as past karma and the like.[6] The plurality of souls is evident from the distribution of pleasures and pains.[7] Until liberation, they are bound to prakṛti, which serves as a vehicle (vāhana) to the jīva, even as a horse does to the rider. The bondage to the body, "this muddy vesture of decay," obstructs the vision of the eternal and prevents the soul from recognising its kinship with God.

The soul remains unchanged in its essential nature through all the processes of birth and death. It is born many times into the sensible world and departs from it again ; but throughout it maintains its identity. At each pralaya, or destruction of the world, the particular forms of the souls are destroyed, though the souls themselves are indestructible. They cannot

[1] ii. 4. 10.

[2] It is called buddhi, ahaṁkāra and citta according to these three functions.

[3] iii. 2. 9. [4] iii. 2. 7. [5] ii. 3. 24–26.

[6] Īśvarasyeva jīvānām api nityaṁ jñānaṁ svataś ca sarvaviṣayam pramātmakam ca, tattatkarmādidoṣavaśāt saṁkucitaviṣayam (Vedānta Deśika : *Seśvara Mīmāṁsā*).

[7] ii. 1. 15.

escape the consequences of their past lives, and they are again thrust into the world at the new creation with appropriate endowments. Association with or dissociation from bodies, resulting in the contraction or expansion of intelligence, is what is meant by birth or death, and, until release, the souls are attached of necessity to bodies, though in pralaya they are connected with subtle stuff which does not admit of differentiation by name and form.[1] The self cannot bear witness to its own past, since memory does not reach beyond the present embodiment.

The characteristic essence of the jīva is the consciousness of self (ahaṁbuddhi). It is not a mere attribute of the self, which might perish, leaving the essential nature of the self unaffected. Self-distinction constitutes the very being of the self. Were it not so, there would be no point in striving for liberation. In the states of bondage and release the soul retains its character of a knowing subject (jñātā). The self is also an active agent. It is because acts belong to the soul that it suffers the consequences of its acts. Simply because it has the power to act it does not, however, follow that it always acts. So long as the souls are attached to bodies due to karma, their acts are largely determined; but when freed from the bodies, they realise their wishes by their mere will (saṁkalpād eva).

The jīva is not one with God, since it differs in essential character from him. It is said to be a part (aṁśa) of Brahman. Though it cannot be a part cut out of the whole since Brahman admits of no divisions,[2] yet it is comprised within the universal self. Rāmānuja says that the souls are parts in the sense of viśeṣaṇas, qualified forms or modes of Brahman.[3] The souls are regarded as the effects of Brahman, since they cannot

[1] iii. 2. 5.

[2] ii. 3. 42.

[3] "The individual soul is a part (aṁśa) of the highest self, as the light issuing from a luminous thing, such as fire or the sun, is a part of that body, or as the generic characteristics of a cow or a horse, and the white or black colour of things so coloured, are attributes and hence parts of the things in which those attributes inhere, or as the body is part of an embodied being. For by a part is meant that which constitutes one place (ekadeśa) of something; a distinguishing attribute (viśeṣaṇa) is a part of the thing distinguished by that attribute (viśiṣṭavastu). Though the attribute and the substance stand to each other in the relation of part and whole, yet we observe them to differ in essential character" (ii. 3. 45).

exist apart from him, and yet they are not produced effects, as ether and the like. The essential nature of the soul does not alter. The change of state it undergoes relates to the contraction and expansion of intelligence, while the changes on which the production, *e.g.*, of ether depend are changes of essential nature.[1] Characteristics of the soul, such as liability to pain, do not belong to God. He alone is free from the changes of essential nature, characteristic of non-conscious objects, and of contraction and expansion, characteristic of the souls.

The indwelling of the supreme spirit does not deprive the jīva of its autonomy of will, though the mere effort of the individual soul is not enough for action. The co-operation of the supreme spirit is also necessary.[2] Though emphasising the autonomy of the individual soul in determining its future, and though admitting that a good man can transcend the merely natural laws of the universe, Rāmānuja declares that God alone is the supreme moral personality, free from all bondage to matter and karma.[3] God is called the śeṣi, or the sovereign lord, between whom and the individual souls exists the relation of lord and liege expressed by the phrase śeṣa-śeṣibhāva. Śeṣitva is the absolute power of God to deal with the soul.[4]

The questions of human freedom and divine sovereignty assume great importance in Rāmānuja's philosophy, since he is anxious to emphasise both. Individual souls depend entirely on God for their activity. God declares what is good and what is bad, supplies souls with bodies, gives them power to employ them, and is also the cause in an ultimate sense of the freedom and bondage of the souls. Yet, if the world has in it so much suffering and misery, it is not God that is responsible for it, but man, who has the power to work for good or evil. The will of man seems to constitute a limitation of the absoluteness of God. The souls, which have freedom of choice, may act so as to interfere with the

[1] Svarūpānyathābhāvalakṣaṇa, ii. 3. 18.

[2] ii. 3. 41.

[3] i. 1. 21.

[4] Cp. with this Lotze's theory that the soul is aware of its own unity and is a real individual distinct from God and from every other soul, though the soul derives its character from the creative and sustaining nature of God.

will of God. If the absolute God is obliged to take note of and act according to the law of karma, he is not absolute. Rāmānuja escapes from this difficulty by urging that God is ultimately the cause of the actions of all men. But this is not Calvinism, for God acts according to certain laws which are the expression of his nature. God does not make the soul do good or evil acts according to his caprice, but shows his constancy of nature by acting according to the law of karma. If the law of karma is independent of God, then God's absoluteness is compromised. The critic who declares that we cannot save the independence of God without sacrificing the doctrine of karma has not the right conception of the Hindu idea of God. The law of karma expresses the will of God. The order of karma is set up by God, who is the ruler of karma (karmādhyakṣaḥ). Since the law is dependent on God's nature, God himself may be regarded as rewarding the righteous and punishing the wicked.[1] To show that the law of karma is not independent of God, it is sometimes said that, though God can suspend the law of karma, still he does not will to do so.[2] Pledged to execute the moral law which is the eternal expression of his righteous will, he permits evil

[1] ii. 2. 3; iii. 2. 4.

[2] Lokācārya says: "Though, on account of his power to do as he likes, God can liberate at one and the same time all the souls by circumventing, *i.e.* removing, the karma of the soul, which depends on him for its essence, permanence, and the like, his decision that he will subject the souls to the restrictions of the scriptures, *i.e.* the law of karma, is due to his mere wish for the joy of the play." Yatthecchaṁ kartuṁ śaktatvāt sakalātmano 'pi yugapad eva muktān kartuṁ samarthatve 'pi svādhīnasvarūpasthityādinātmanaḥ karma vyājīkṛtya dūrīkṛtya śāstramaryādayā tān aṅgīkuryām ittham sthiti līlārasecchayaiva (*Tattvatraya*, p. 108). God is the first cause, while karma is the secondary one. "The divine being . . . having engaged in sport befitting his might and greatness (svamahātmyānuguṇalīlāpravṛttaḥ), and having settled that work (karma), is of a twofold nature (dvaividhyam), good and evil, and having bestowed on all individual souls bodies and sense-organs enabling them to enter on such work and the power to control their bodies and organs (tanniyamanaśakti), and having himself entered into their souls as their inner self, abides within them. . . . The souls endowed with all the powers imparted to them by the Lord . . . apply themselves on their own part and in accordance with their own wishes to work out good or evil (svayam eva svecchānuguṇyena puṇyāpuṇyarūpe karmaṇī upādadate). The Lord then recognising him who performs good acts as one who conforms to his commands, blesses him with piety and wealth, happiness and release, while he makes him who transgresses his commands experience the opposites of all these" (ii. 2. 3).

which he might otherwise arrest. The inner ruler has regard in all cases to the volitional effort which prompts a man's action.[1] He does not care to upset his own laws and interfere with the world-scheme. God, though immanent in the world, does not wish to be intrusive.

There are three classes of jīvas: eternal (nitya), or those who dwell in Vaikuṇṭha, enjoying bliss and free from karma and prakṛti; the freed (mukta), or those who achieve liberation through their wisdom, virtue and devotion; the bound (baddha), or those who wander in saṁsāra owing to their ignorance and selfishness.[2] While the soul can rise to the highest, it can also sink to the lowest, becoming more and more immersed in the body till the life of intelligence is lost, as it were, in the obscure animal movements of sensation and appetite.[3] The souls wandering in saṁsāra are distinguished into four classes: celestial or superhuman, human, animal, and stationary (sthāvara). While all souls are of one kind, their distinctions are due to the bodies with which they are associated. Even caste differences among the souls are due to their connection with different kinds of bodies. In themselves, the souls are neither human nor heavenly, neither Brahmin nor Śūdra. The souls in saṁsāra are grouped into those desirous of enjoyment and those desirous of deliverance. Until the soul attains release it has to be reborn to experience the fruits of karma. The soul, when moving towards another embodiment, is enveloped by the rudiments of the elements[4] which serve as the substrate of life.[5] The subtle body persists so long as the state of bondage lasts.[6] The released go by the devayāna, the good go by pitṛyāna, while the wicked return to earth immediately, without passing to the moon. There are agents of God who lead the soul on its upward way.[7] If souls are in any way sharers in the divine nature, they must have once possessed its freedom and purity. How did they lose these and transfer themselves to the rule of karma? Rāmānuja holds that neither reason nor scripture

[1] ii. 8. 41.

[2] See *Rahasyatrayasāra*, iv. There are some Viśiṣṭādvaitins who believe in those who are for ever bound to the wheel of saṁsāra (nityabaddhaḥ). See *Tattvamuktākalāpa*, ii. 27–28.

[3] i. 1. 4. [4] iii. 1. 1. [5] iii. 1. 3.

[6] iv. 2. 9, and iii. 3. 30. [7] iv. 3. 4.

can tell us how karma got the souls into its power because the cosmic process is beginningless (anādi).

XIII

MATTER

Prakṛti or matter, kāla or time, and śuddhatattva or pure matter, are the three non-conscious substances. They are objects of experience (bhogya), liable to changes and indifferent to the ends of man.[1] The existence of prakṛti is not an object of perception or of inference. It is accepted on the authority of the scripture.[2] Its three qualities of sattva, rajas and tamas are evolved in it at the time of the world-creation. In pralaya matter exists in an extremely subtle condition, without distinction of name and form, and is called tamas. Matter is uncreated (aja), though its forms appear and disappear.

At creation, from the tamas mahat appears; from mahat ahaṁkāra or bhūtādi. From sāttvika ahaṁkāra arise the eleven senses, from the tāmasa, the five tanmātras, or five elements, and rājasāhaṁkāra helps both these processes.[3] From ahaṁkāra comes the subtle element of sound and then ākāśa; from ākāśa comes the subtle element of touch, and then air and so on for the other elements also. From the qualities of sound, touch, etc., we infer corresponding substances. Sound is in all the elements. The feeling of touch is of three kinds, hot, cold and neutral. There are five colours, which are subject to changes under the action of heat. The Viśiṣṭādvaitins do not admit any real space independent of ākāśa, and argue that we fix certain points in it as east where the sun rises and west where it sets, and measure proximity and distance from these standpoints.[4] Prāṇa or vital breath, is not to be confused with the senses, but is only a peculiar condition (avasthāviśeṣa) of air.[5] Unlike the Sāṁkhya, the Viśiṣṭādvaita holds that the development of prakṛti is caused and controlled by Iśvara.[6]

Kāla or time is given an independent place. It is the form of all existence.[7] It is an object of perception. Dis-

[1] S.D.S., iv.
[2] *Tattvamuktākalāpa*, i. 11.
[3] *Sarvārthasiddhi*, i. 11.
[4] *Tattvamuktākalāpa*, i. 48.
[5] *Ibid.*, i. 53–54.
[6] *Sarvārthasiddhi*, i. 16.
[7] According to *Tattvatraya*, kāla is tattvaśūnyam.

tinctions of days, months, etc., are based on the relations of time.[1]

While prakṛti has the three guṇas of sattva, rajas and tamas, śuddhatattva has only sattva. It is the stuff of the body of God in his condition of nityavibhūti. It does not conceal the nature within. God reveals himself as a cosmic force through his *līlāvibhūti* with the aid of prakṛti, and in his transcendent existence through his *nityavibhūti* with the aid of śuddhatattva.

All these non-conscious entities work in obedience to the will of God.[2] They are not in themselves good or bad, but happen to please or pain the individuals according to their karma. It is God that determines their behaviour, for "if the effects of things depended on their own nature alone, everything would at all times be productive for all persons either of pleasure or of pain only. But this is not observed to be the case." "To the highest Brahman, which is subject to itself only, the same connection is the source of playful sport, consisting in this, that he guides and controls those things in various ways."[3] The world will appear to be essentially blissful to one who has freed himself from all bonds of karma and avidyā. While both souls and matter constitute the body or the attributes of God, he is directly connected with the souls and only indirectly with matter, which is controlled by the souls. Matter is more completely dependent on Brahman than the souls, which have freedom of choice. The latter can partake in the divine life, and thus be lifted above change and death.

XIV

Creation

According to Rāmānuja, every effect involves a material cause, and the effect of the world implies free existing souls and unevolved matter. Though souls and matter are the modes (prakāras) of God, they have enjoyed the kind of individual

[1] Upādhibhedaḥ (*Tattvamuktākalāpa*, i. 69). [2] ii. 2. 2.
[3] iii. 2. 12.

existence which is theirs from all eternity, and cannot be entirely resolved into Brahman. They have a sort of secondary subsistence, which is enough to enable them to develop on their own lines. They exist in two different conditions which periodically alternate, the first being a subtle state when they do not possess the qualities by which they are ordinarily known, when there is no distinction of individual name and form, when matter is unevolved (avyakta) and intelligence is contracted (saṁkucita). It is the state of pralaya when Brahman is said to be in a causal condition (kāraṇāvasthā). When creation takes place on account of the will of the Lord, subtle matter becomes gross and souls enter into connection with material bodies corresponding to the degree of merit or demerit acquired by them in previous forms of existence, and their intelligence undergoes a certain amount of expansion (vikāsa). Brahman, with souls and matter thus manifested, is said to be in the effect condition (kāryāvasthā). Creation and destruction are only relative and signify different states of the same causal substance, namely Brahman.[1] Souls and matter have a twofold existence, a causal existence and an effect existence. In their causal existence the souls are unmaterialised and nature is in equipoise; but when the time for creation comes, the souls, under the influence of their karma, disturb the equilibrium of the three guṇas, and prakṛti works out the fruits of their karma under divine providence. It is to enable the souls to undergo the experiences for which their deeds have entitled them that creation is brought about. God creates the world to suit the karma of the souls. In this sense God's creative act is not independent or absolute.[2]

According to the Pañcarātra account, a distinction is made between pure creation (śuddhasṛṣṭi) and gross creation. The former is not so much a creation as the everlasting expression of the inwardness of God's being, wherein the qualities of God, omniscience (jñāna), lordship centred in unimpeded activity (aiśvarya), power to originate the cosmos (śakti), strength to support all (bala), changelessness (vīrya) and the divine self-sufficiency and splendour (tejas) manifest themselves. These qualities form the body of Vāsudeva and Lakṣmī, or of Vāsudeva associated with Lakṣmī. The Vyūhas and the Vibhavas also belong to the pure creation. Vaikuṇṭha, which has for its

[1] See R.B.G., xiii. 2; ix. 7.

[2] ii. 1. 34–35.

material cause śuddhasattva belongs to the pure creation.[1] The gross creation takes place in the order already mentioned by means of prakṛti, composed of the three guṇas.[2] For God, the creation of the world is said to be mere līlā or sport.[3] The metaphor of līlā brings out the disinterestedness, freedom and joy underlying the act of creation. It enables Rāmānuja to insist on the absolute freedom and independence of God. Nature and souls are instruments of God's play, and cannot at any time offer any resistance to his will. The whole drama is undertaken by the Lord at his own sweet will.[4]

Śaṁkara's difficulty, that from Brahman, which is absolute perfection, the world of imperfection cannot be said to take its rise, at any rate that it is impossible for the finite mind to account for the rise of the finite from out of the infinite, does not trouble Rāmānuja, since he is willing to accept on the authority of the śruti that the finite springs from the infinite. What the śruti says must be capable of being logically determined. Does it or does it not depend on the will of God that there be unevolved matter and immaterial souls? It is quite true that these given elements, on which the divine will is dependent in creation, are not given from outside, as Madhva believes, but inhere in God as his modes. At any rate, the will of God is dependent on their pre-existence. It is theoretically possible to imagine that with a different kind of material the world could have been shaped better. God could not choose the best of all possible worlds, but was obliged to make the best of the given one. Brahman has absolutely non-conditioned existence,[5] which is not the case with non-intelligent matter, which is the abode of change and the souls implicated in matter. But it is difficult to conceive how Brahman could be supposed to be unchangeable in view of the changing conditions of his attributes, souls and matter.

1 The Bengal School of Vaiṣṇavism accepts this scheme, but substitutes for Viṣṇu and Lakṣmī, Kṛṣṇa and Rādhā.

2 The Pañcarātra Saṁhitās admit an intermediate creation also.

3 Cp. Krīḍā harer idam sarvam; again, hare viharasi krīḍā kantukair-iva jantubhiḥ; and also the Sūtra, lokavat tu līlā kaivalyam.

4 Svasaṁkalpakṛtam (R.B.G., i. 25). Cp.

"God tastes an infinite joy
In infinite ways." (Browning: *Paracelsus.*)

5 Nirupādhikasattā, i. 1. 2. Cp. *Śrutaprakāśikā*: Kenāpi pariṇāma-viśeṣeṇa tattadavasthasya sattā sopādhikasattā, ato nirupādhikasattā nirvikāratvam.

These modes (prakāras) change from a subtle to a gross condition and *vice versa,* and Rāmānuja is obliged to concede that Īśvara is also subject to change.[1] Rāmānuja makes the finite the attribute of the infinite. From this view it should follow that the infinite cannot exist without its attribute, and so the attribute is necessary to the infinite. Yet Rāmānuja is unable to concede it in view of the many opposed scriptural texts. Commenting on the passage, "These beings are not in me,"[2] Rāmānuja says: "By my will I am the supporter of all beings, and yet there is no help to me from any of these beings." "No kind of help whatever is contributed by these towards my existence."[3] The existence of the world is completely immaterial to the divine being. Such a view is hardly consistent with Rāmānuja's general position, that the world has its basis in the nature of God. Commenting on the passage of the *Gītā* that "I enjoy whatever is offered with devotion, be it a leaf or a flower," Rāmānuja observes: "Even though I remain in the enjoyment of my own natural, unbounded and inestimable bliss, I enjoy these as if I obtained a beloved object which lies far beyond the path of my desire."[4] God is ready to acquire some happiness through the willing devotion of his devotees, though he is not equally ready to be touched by the pain and the suffering of others. If the souls are parts of the Lord, then the latter must be afflicted by the pain caused to the soul in its experiences, even as the individual suffers from the pain affecting his hand or foot. So the supreme Lord would suffer more pain than the soul.[5] But Rāmānuja contends that the suffering of the souls does not pollute the nature of God. If the acts of creation, maintenance and destruction give God delight, are we to think that God's delight is capable of modifications, and is increased by these operations? God's nature as transcendent spirit is one of delight, and the modifications of his attributes also add to his joy. As the relation between soul and body is not logically determined, the relation between the transcendent delight which is perfect and incapable of

[1] Ubhayaprakāraviśiṣṭe niyantraṁśe tadavasthatadubhayaviśiṣṭatārūpavikāro bhavati (R.B., ii. 3. 18).

[2] B.G., ix. 4.

[3] Matsthitau tair na kaścid upakāraḥ (R.B.G., ix. 4).

[4] R.B.G., ix. 26.

[5] S.B., ii. 3. 45.

variation and that derived from the changes of his body is not intelligibly stated.

Rāmānuja protests vigorously against the doctrine of māyā and the phenomenality of the world. If the distinctions of the world are due to the imperfections of man's mind, then, for God, there should be no such distinctions; but scripture tells us that God creates the world, allots to different souls their rewards, thus indicating that God reckons with the world of distinction. It cannot be said that the multiplicity is unreal, even as a mirage is; for the latter is unreal because our activity prompted by it is unsuccessful; but not so the activity based on the perception of the world. Nor is it logical to urge that the reality of the world, testified by perception, is sublated by the testimony of the scripture; for the spheres of perception and scripture are quite different, and so they cannot contradict each other.[1] All knowledge reveals objects.[2] To say that objects do not exist, simply because they do not persist, is rather strange. The argument involves a confusion between opposites and distincts. Distinction is not denial. Where two cognitions are mutually contradictory, then both cannot be real. "But jars, pieces of cloth and the like do not contradict one another, since they are separate in place and time. If the non-existence of a thing is cognised at the same time and the same place where and when its existence is cognised, we have a mutual contradiction of two cognitions. But when of a thing that is perceived in connection with some place and time, the non-existence is perceived in connection with some other place and time, there arises no contradiction."[3] In the example of mistaking the rope for a snake, the cognition of non-existence arises in connection with the given place and time. So there is contradiction. But if an object perceived now does not exist at another time and place, we cannot rush to the conclusion that the thing is unreal. Both Śaṁkara

[1] Ākāśavāyvādibhūta . . . padārthagrāhi pratyakṣaṁ; śāstraṁ tu pratyakṣādyaparicchedya sarvāntarātmatvasatyatvādyanantaviśeṣaṇaviśiṣṭa brahmasvarūpa . . . viṣayam, iti śāstrapratyakṣayor na virodhaḥ (*Vedārthasaṁgraha*, p. 87).

[2] Arthaprakāśa.

[3] Deśāntarakālāntarasaṁbandhitayānubhūtasyānyadeśakālayor abhavāpratipattau na virodhaḥ (i. 1. 1).

and Rāmānuja lay stress on the logic of identity[1]; only Rāmānuja believes that a true identity implies distinction and determination, though not contradiction and denial.

Rāmānuja urges several objections against the Advaita doctrine of avidyā. What is the seat (āśraya) of avidyā? It cannot be Brahman, who is full of perfections. It cannot be the individual, who is the product of avidyā. Avidyā cannot conceal Brahman, whose nature is self-luminosity. If self-luminous consciousness, which is without object and without substrate, becomes through the influence of an imperfection residing within itself conscious of itself as connected with numberless objects, is that imperfection real or unreal? It is not real, according to Advaita; it cannot be unreal, according to Rāmānuja, since it is something permitted by God himself. In human knowledge, where something unmanifested becomes manifested, we may assume the existence of some entity which hindered the manifestation. But there is no need to attribute to Brahman any such defect. Again, if avidyā involves Brahman also in its meshes, then universal falsehood will alone be the reality, and we cannot escape from it. The nature (svarūpa) of avidyā cannot be logically determined. It is neither real nor unreal. To say that a thing is indefinable (anirvacanīya) is illogical. No means of knowledge (pramāṇa) testifies to the existence of avidyā. Neither perception nor inference nor revelation establishes it. In the scriptures māyā is used to indicate the wonderful power possessed by God, who has nothing to do with an eternal unreal avidyā. On the Advaita view, even the scriptures are a part of the world-error, and the whole foundation of knowledge is destroyed. If cessation (nivartana) of avidyā takes place by means of the knowledge of Brahman devoid of attributes and qualities, then it cannot take place, since such knowledge is impossible. The abolition (nivṛtti) of avidyā, which is a concrete reality, cannot be brought about by abstract knowledge. The world, forsooth, is too great and meaningful to be lightly dismissed as a mere product of avidyā. The real avidyā to which we are the victims is that power of illusion which makes us believe that we ourselves and the world are independent of Brahman.

[1] S.B., ii. 2. 33; R.B., ii. 2. 31.

XV

Ethical and Religious Life

The jīvas in saṁsāra, with their souls shrouded in bodies, are like islanders who live unconscious of the sea. They believe that they are not so much modes of God as products of nature. On account of its past deeds, the soul finds itself confined in a material body, its inner light obscured by the outer darkness. It mistakes the garment of nature for its true self, attributes to itself the qualities of the body, loves the fleeting pleasures of human existence as true bliss, and turns its face away from God. The downfall of the soul is due to karma and avidyā, which bring about its embodiment. The connection of soul, which is pure spirit, with matter is the degradation of the soul. Its sin is not merely a check to its own upward progress, but is also an offence against God. Avidyā has to be displaced by vidyā, or the intuition that God is the fundamental self of all.

Rāmānuja grants to the individual souls freedom to act according to their own will. So far as responsibility is concerned, each individual is an other to God, a different person. When the soul fails to recognise its dependence on God, God helps it to realise the truth by the machinery of karma, which inflicts punishments on the soul, thus reminding it of its sinful efforts. Through the operation of the indwelling God, the soul recognises its sinfulness and entreats God for help. In Rāmānuja's philosophy great emphasis is placed on the conviction of sin and man's responsibility for it. Yāmunācārya describes himself as " the vessel of a thousand sins " and implores the grace of God. The Vaiṣṇava faith does not encourage tapas or austerities.

As a theist, Rāmānuja believes that salvation is possible, not through jñāna and karma, but through bhakti and prasāda (grace). Jñāna, in the scriptures, stands for dhyāna, or meditation, and nididhyāsana or concentrated contemplation.[1] Bhakti is gained through concentration on the truth that

[1] iii. 4. 26.

God is our innermost self and that we are but modes of his substance. But such jñāna cannot be had unless the bad karma is destroyed. Work undertaken in a disinterested spirit helps to remove the past accumulations. So long as karma enjoined in the scriptures is undertaken with a selfish motive, the end cannot be gained. The results of ceremonial observances are transitory, while the result of the knowledge of God is indestructible (akṣaya); but if we perform work in the spirit of dedication to God it helps us in our effort after salvation.[1] Work performed in such a spirit develops the sattva nature and helps the soul to see the truth of things. The two, jñāna and karma, are means to bhakti, or the power which tears up our selfishness by the roots, gives new strength to the will, new eyes to the understanding and new peace to the soul.

Bhakti or devotion is a vague term extending from the lowest form of worship to the highest life of realisation. It has had a continuous history in India from the time of the Ṛg-Veda[2] to the present day. Bhakti, in Rāmānuja, is man's reaching out towards a fuller knowledge of God quietly and meditatively. He insists on an elaborate preparation for bhakti, which includes viveka, or discrimination of food[3]; vimoka, or freedom from all else and longing for God; abhyāsa, or continuous thinking of God; kriyā, or doing good to others[4]; kalyāṇa, or wishing well to all; satyam, or truthfulness; ārjavam, or integrity; dayā, or compassion; ahiṁsā, or non-violence; dāna, or charity; and anavasāda, or cheerfulness and hope.[5] Thus bhakti is not mere emotionalism,[6] but includes the

[1] Tadarpitākhilācāratā (Nārada: *Bhakti Sūtra*, p, 19).

[2] Cp. "All my thoughts, seeking happiness, extol Indra, longing for him; they embrace him as wives embrace a fair young bridegroom, him the divine giver of gifts, that he may help me. My mind is directed to thee, Indra, and does not turn from thee; on thee I rest my desire, O much invoked one" (R.V., x. 43. 1.)

[3] Śaṁkara's interpretation that we should not be attached to the things of sense is better.

[4] Five kinds are distinguished, which are study, worship of God, duties to forefathers, human society and animal creation.

[5] S.D.S., iv.

[6] Svapneśvara, commenting on the word "anurakti" used by Śāṇḍilya, says that anu means after, and rakti attachment, and so anurakti is attachment which comes after the knowledge of God. Blind attachment is not bhakti.

training of the will as well as the intellect.[1] It is knowledge of God as well as obedience to his will.[2] Bhakti is loving God with all our mind and with all our heart. It finds its culmination in an intuitive realisation of God.[3]

Bhakti and mokṣa are organically related, so that at every stage of bhakti we are perfecting ourselves. Bhakti is salvation in becoming, and is regarded as superior to the other methods, since it is its own reward (phalarūpatvāt).[4] The soul becomes through bhakti more and more vividly conscious of its relation to God, until at last it surrenders itself to God, who is the soul of its soul. Then there is no longer self-love or self-seeking, since God has taken the place of self and the whole life is transfigured. Nammāḷvār says: " In return for thy great and good gift—the mingling of my spirit with thine—I have entirely yielded up my spirit to thee." [5] Every drop of one's blood, every beat of one's heart, and every thought of one's brain are surrendered to God. It is a case of " I yet not I." Bhakti is distinguished into formal (vaidhī) and supreme (mukhyā). The formal is the lower phase, where we indulge in prayers, ceremonies and image-worship. All these help the soul onward, but cannot by themselves save the soul. We must worship the supreme; for nothing else, in the last analysis, can serve as the object of meditation.[6]

Prapatti is complete resignation to God,[7] and is, according

[1] Jñānakarmānugṛhītam bhaktiyogam (R.B.G., Introduction). Dhīprītirūpā bhaktiḥ (*Tattvamuktākalāpa*).

[2] In *Vedārthasaṁgraha*, Rāmānuja distinguishes between sādhana-bhakti and parā-bhakti. The former includes control of body, mind and speech, performance of one's duties, study, non-attachment, etc.

[3] i. 1. 1.

[4] Nārada: *Bhakti Sūtra*, p. 26.

[5] *Tiruvāymoyi*, ii. 3. 4.

[6] Rāmānuja quotes a teacher to the effect: " From Brahmā to a tuft of grass all things that live in the world are subject to saṁsāra due to karma, therefore they cannot be helpful as objects of meditation, since they are all in ignorance and subject to saṁsāra." i. 1. 1.

Ābrahmastambaparyantā jagadantarvyavasthitāḥ
Prāṇinaḥ karmajanitasaṁsāravaśavartinaḥ.
Yatas tato na te dhyāne dhyāninām upakārakāḥ
Avidyāntargatās sarve te hi saṁsāragocarāḥ.

[7] See R.B.G., Introduction to ch. vii and vii. 14. Six factors are distinguished in prapatti, which are: (1) acquisition of qualities which would make one a fit offering to God (ānukūlyasya saṁpattiḥ); (2) avoidance of conduct not acceptable to God (prātikūlyasya varjanam); (3) faith that

to the Bhāgavatas, the most effective means for gaining salvation. It is open to all, the learned as well as the ignorant, the high as well as the low, while the path of bhakti, involving as it does jñāna and karma, is confined to the three upper classes. But anyone, after taking instruction from a preceptor, may fling himself on the bosom of God and take refuge in him. According to the Southern school (Tengalais), which follows more closely the tradition of the Āḷvārs, prapatti is the only way to salvation, and no more effort on the part of the devotee is necessary. God saves the soul who has utterly surrendered himself to him. The Northern school (Vaḍagalais) holds that prapatti is one way of reaching the goal, and not the only way. For them human effort is an essential factor in salvation. The individual who has qualified himself by karma, jñāna, bhakti and prapatti wins the favour of the Lord. This school upholds the markaṭanyāya, or the monkey theory, since the young monkey is to exert and stick to the mother; while the Southern holds the mārjāranyāya or the cat theory, since the kitten is taken up by the cat with its mouth. This school holds that nothing depends on man's effort, for the grace of God selects the individuals to be freed. It also believes that the soul is seized by God in one supreme act, which need not be repeated, while the Northern section insists on the continuous offering of the soul to God.

In the *Bhāgavata Purāṇa* bhakti is less restrained in its character than in Rāmānuja. A certain tendency to extravagant enthusiasm marks the opening of the religious sense in men. The individual undergoing the conversion of the soul has the shudder of awe and delight. In the *Bhāgavata* bhakti is a surging emotion which thrills the whole frame, chokes speech, and leads to trance. The *Bhāgavata* is indifferent to sacrificial observances and declares that we must love God for his own sake and not for any reward. It admits that union with God is open to any individual, if he cares for it. He can obtain it through bhakti, but the soul who remains

God would protect him. (rakṣiṣyatīti viśvāsaḥ); (4) appeal for protection (goptṛtvavaraṇam); (5) a feeling of one's own littleness (kārpaṇyam); and (6) absolute surrender (ātmasamarpaṇam). The last is one with prapatti though the others are means to it.

ever distinct from God he worships is happier than one who becomes absorbed in God.[1] We find in the God of the *Bhāgavata* an intimately human feeling. He is not free (asvatantra), as he is subject to the will of his devotees (bhaktaparādhīna).[2] Without the church of his saints, God does not think much of himself.[3] A striking feature of the *Bhāgavata* is the idealisation of the story of Kṛṣṇa and the gopis. The legend is transformed into the ideal of bhakti and, as we shall see, the later sects of Vaiṣṇavism are influenced by it.

Vaiṣṇava devotion has used the most intimate human relations as symbols of the relation of man and God. God is viewed as the teacher, the friend, the father, the mother, the child, and even as the beloved. The last is stressed by the Āḷvārs, the *Bhāgavata Purāṇa* and the Bengal school of Vaiṣṇavism. In the best love, as in bhakti, to live in the presence of the beloved is the highest happiness and creative productivity; to live without him or her is pain and despair and barrenness. We think that the use of the symbolism of love is wrong because we assume that sensual attraction is all in all in love; but in true love there is little of sensual attraction. Many women, as well as some men, who in love are above the level of beasts, will protest that love is not a mere search after new sensations. In true love, the two souls trust each other more than all others they have met or known before. The lover is ready to fight the world, endure all privations and feel happy in poverty, exile and persecution, for the sake of the beloved. Even if he or she is sundered from the other through many difficulties, so that reunion seems remote, nay impossible, yet he or she cannot afford to lose the other and, at the risk of losing everything else, keeps alive the eternal link created by mutual love which cannot be broken even by death. The stories of Sīta and Sāvitrī, Damayanti and Śakuntalā have burnt this lesson into the heart of India. No wonder the Indian Vaiṣṇava looks upon God as his beloved,[4] and tries to redirect to God the passions, longings and transports of human love. The bhaktas feel helpless and restless when they lose the presence of God, for nothing else can satisfy them. In many of their hymns we find the cry of the heart for God, the sense

---

[1] *Bhāgavata*, iii. 25. 33.

[2] ix. 4. 67.

[3] Nāham ātmānam āśāste madbhaktair sādhubhir vinā (ix. 4. 6). Cp. Bhaktaprāṇo hi kṛṣṇaś ca kṛṣṇaprāṇā hi vaiṣṇavāḥ (*Nāradapañcarātra*, ii. 36).

[4] Cp. Sa eva vāsudevo 'sau sākṣāt puruṣa ucyate
Strīprāyam itarat sarvaṁ jagad brahmapurassaram.

The supreme Lord is the only man; all others, from Brahmā downwards are women, *i.e.* depend on him and long to be united with him. Cp. also
Svāmitvātmatvaśeṣitvapuṁstvādyas svāmino guṇāḥ
Svebhyo dāsatvadehatvaśeṣatvastrītvadāyinaḥ.

of devastating desolation in his absence, the anticipated joy in his fellowship and a sense, real though undefined, of the preciousness of his love. In the rapt utterances of the Vaiṣṇava saints, we feel the ecstatic joy of the mystic desirous of union with God in a spiritual sense. "Thou splendid light of heaven," cries Nammāḷvār, "thou art in my heart melting and consuming my spirit. When shall I become one with thee?"[1] Deep attachment to God results in an indifference to all else.[2]

The Hindu devotee does not seek to destroy desire, but attempts to lift it from earth to heaven, seeks to withdraw it from creation that he may centre it on the Creator. Maṇavāḷa says: "The pleasure which arises for the ignorant from sense-objects, the same is called bhakti when directed to God; in the case of Nammāḷvār, this bhakti has become love for the beautiful Lord, hence for Āḷvārs there arises the 'love' type of devotion."[3] While many of those who employ the symbolism of bridegroom and bride are free from all traces of eroticism and morally impeccable, it cannot be denied that there were abuses of it.[4] But such abuses were deviations from the normal path.

The distinctions of caste do not touch the nature of the soul. At best they belong to the bodies and determine the duties which the different individuals owe to society. But caste has nothing to do with the qualities of souls. Some of the Āḷvārs worshipped by the Brahmins were Śudras. Rāmānuja allows that no distinctions should be made among the lovers of God.[5] He admits that those outside the āśramas are eligible for the knowledge of Brahman.[6] Strictly speaking, the religion of bhakti or devotion, and prapatti or submission, requires no priest, for the offering of love does not need the

[1] *Tiruvāymoyi*, v. 10. 1.

[2] Anurāgād virāgaḥ. The way of bhakti has in it four movements: (1) The desire of the soul when it turns towards God and the straining of the emotions towards him; (2) the pain of love unrealised; (3) the delight of love possessed and the play of that delight; and (4) the eternal enjoyment of the divine lover which is the heart of divine bliss.

[3] Yā prītir asti viṣayeṣv avivekabhājām
Saivācyute bhavati bhaktipadābhidheyā.
Bhaktis tu kāma iha tatkamanīyarūpe
Tasmān muner ajani kāmukavākyabhaṅgī.
(*Dramiḍopaniṣadsaṁgati.*)

[4] I.P., pp. 495–496.

[5] Cp. Nāsti teṣu jātividyārūpakuladhanakriyādibhedaḥ (Nārada: *Bhakti Sūtra*, p. 72. Cp. also
Śvapaco 'pi mahīpāla viṣṇubhakto dvijādhikaḥ
Viṣṇubhaktivihīnas tu yatiś ca śvapacādhamaḥ. (*Bhāgavata.*)

[6] iii. 4. 36; i. 3. 32–39.

sanction of the scripture, and the grace of God is not in the keeping of any man. For one who is deep in devotion there is neither scripture nor rule.[1] Rāmānuja preaches equality in worship and proclaims that bhakti transcends all caste distinctions. He admitted the pariahs to the temple at Melkoṭe. But it is by no means clear that he was prepared for a wholesale defiance of the accepted order. Out of deference to tradition he concedes that freedom is open only to the three upper classes, and others will have to work their way up and wait for the next birth. We cannot, therefore, say that he was in full sympathy with the logical implications of his teaching. A later Vaiṣṇava teacher, Rāmānanda (thirteenth century), protested against caste distinctions. "Let no man," he says, "ask a man's caste or sect. Whoever adores God is God's own." His apostolate of about twelve included a Brahmin, a barber, a leather-worker, a Rajput and a woman. Caitanya preached the religion of devotion and love to all men irrespective of caste or class. In South India, on the other hand, Vedānta Deśika emphasised ritualistic religion.[2] Again and again, throughout the history of Indian civilisation, protests were made against the rigidity of caste; but all these protestant movements have not been able to check, in any considerable degree, its sway on the national mind.

XVI

Mokṣa

Salvation, according to Rāmānuja, is not the disappearance of the self, but its release from the limiting barriers. For disappearance of the self will be the destruction of the real self (satyātmanāśa).[3] One substance cannot pass over into another substance.[4] However high a man may rise, there will always be an almighty power, an eternal love for him

[1] Atyantabhaktiyuktānāṁ naiva śāstram na ca kramaḥ.

[2] Śrutismṛtir mamaivājñā yas tām ullaṅghya vartate
Ājñācchedī mama drohī madbhakto 'pi na vaiṣṇavaḥ.

See the chapter on Śāstraniyamanādhikāra in *Rahasyatrayasāra*.

[3] i. 1. 1.

[4] *Viṣṇu Purāṇa*, ii. 14. 27.

to reverence, worship and adore. Rāmānuja, who ranks religious experience as the highest open to us, contends that it implies an "other." The released soul attains the nature of God, though not identity with him.[1] It becomes omniscient and is ever having the intuition of God.[2] It desires nothing else, and so has no chance of returning to saṁsāra.[3] It is egoity that is opposed to salvation, and not individuality. The essential nature, though something eternally accomplished, is, in the state of saṁsāra, obscured by avidyā and karma. The state of release means the unimpeded manifestation of the natural qualities of intelligence and bliss. The released soul is said to be svarāṭ in the sense that he is not subject to the law of karma.[4] For Rāmānuja there is no jīvanmukti. One attains to fellowship with God after exhausting all karma and throwing off the physical body. In the state of release the souls are all of the same type. There are no distinctions there of gods, men, animals and plants. In the world of saṁsāra these distinctions have a meaning. It is the connection with matter that gives uniqueness to the soul. But the souls can get rid of this connection, which is not a natural one.[5] It follows that the individuality determined by bodily connections is not eternal. When it is shattered the soul is said to attain the nature of Brahman and manifest its own true nature. It does not develop any new character.[6]

In the released condition the souls have all the perfections of the Supreme except in two points. They are atomic in size, while the supreme spirit is all-pervading. Though of atomic size, the soul can enter into several bodies and experience different worlds created by the Lord[7]; but it has no power over the creative movements of the world, which belong exclusively to Brahman.[8]

1 Brahmaṇo bhāvaḥ na tu svarūpaikyam (i. 1. 1).

2 Paripūrṇaparabrahmānubhavam. Cp. " Sarvadeśa sarvakāla sarvāvasthaigaḷilum, sarveśvaranai, anantamgaḷāna, vigraha guṇa vibhūti ceṣṭitamgaḷil oṇrum kurayāmal, niratiśayabhogya māka, visayīkarittukoṇḍirukkum " (*Rahasyatrayasāra*, xxii).

3 R.B., iv. 4. 22.

4 *Śrutaprakāśikā*, i. 1. 1.

5 Karmarūpajñānamūlaḥ, na svarūpakṛtaḥ (i. 1. 1).

6 iv. 4. 1.

7 iv. 4. 13–15.

8 iv. 4. 17.

The city of God consists of a number of souls who do not simply repeat one another. The forms which they assume are due to the pure matter (viśuddhasattva). Through its aid the liberated souls give shape to their thoughts and wishes. At the end of the play—if such a thing can be conceived—each individual soul will have become perfect and yet be regarded as an adjective of the Absolute. The Absolute, which is one self, by virtue of its immanent principle, becomes an interrelated unity of selves without being the less one self. It has a social character about it. Each one of the society of selves aims at no selfish interest, but at the universal being.

The Viśiṣṭādvaita philosophy distinguishes two classes of the released: those who are intent on service to God on earth and so do it in heaven, and those (kevalins) who are altogether isolated from the rest, since they achieved their end by constant meditation on the real nature of their own soul.

The picture of the heaven where the redeemed souls dwell is not much different from the usual description.[1] It only differs in details of dress, custom and landscape from the paradise of the popular imagination. There are streams of living waters, trees laden with delicious fruits, gentle breezes and golden sunshine to cheer them. Amid these delights they sing and feast, listen to the music of the heavenly choirs, and enjoy at times philosophic converse with one another. But such a vision of paradise does not satisfy the mystic soul, who cries out against the loneliness of being imprisoned in a particular nature. He yearns to burst through the barriers of personality and merge himself in the life and essence of the universe. In his theory of mokṣa, Rāmānuja does not do justice to the mystics, who thus hunger for becoming one with the supreme reality. For them a heaven painted in terms of earthly experience, however idealised it be, is not essentially different from that experience itself. Though the soul sees God and God only, and is flooded with his presence, she retains her individuality and is still herself and not the object of her vision. A tendency to escape from oneself into God has been the central motive of some seers of the Upaniṣads, the Orphic brotherhood in ancient Greece,

[1] *Nāradapañcarātra*, vi.

and some Christian and Sufi mystics. They try to slough off not only their bodies but their personalities, and melt their souls in God. But there is no evidence that any mystic achieved such a goal. In the nature of things, Rāmānuja contends, evidence of such absorption into God is impossible. He who has become God cannot return to tell us of his experience; he who narrates his story has not become God.

XVII

General Estimate

While the philosophy of Śaṁkara may have some attraction for those superior minds which shy at sentimental solutions of difficulties and seek their internal satisfaction in the discipline of the will, which will enable them to bear with a Stoic calm the worst that circumstances will inflict on them, even Śaṁkara allows that the millions of humanity crave for a God who has some heart about him. Rāmānuja's view is the highest *expression* of the truth, though Śaṁkara would add that the real is something larger and better than our thinking has room for. We need not assume, Rāmānuja contends, that what comes through religion is not the highest reality.[1] Theism of the type advocated by Rāmānuja is what even Śaṁkara allows in life and religion. It is the faith of Hinduism, whether in its Vaiṣṇava, Smārta, Śaiva or Śākta form. It is strange that Western thinkers and critics should overlook this striking fact and persist in foisting on Hinduism as a whole the theory of abstract monism.[2] While Rāmānuja's statement is not in any way inferior to other forms of theism, it is not free from the difficulties incident to the theistic outlook.

By the theory of the relation of viśeṣya and viśeṣaṇa, or

[1] Cp. Bradley: "The man who demands a reality more solid than that of the religious consciousness knows not what he seeks."

[2] Hegel writes: "In the Eastern religions, the first condition is that only the one substance shall, as such, be the true, and that the individual neither can have within himself, nor can he attain to any true value in as far as he maintains himself as against the being in and for itself. He can have true value only through an identification with its substance in which he ceases to exist as subject and disappears into unconsciousness."

substance and attribute, Rāmānuja attempts to bring out the reality of one and one existence only[1] and assimilate the others to it. Taking up the relation of Brahman to the qualities of sat, cit and ānanda, Rāmānuja argues that the unity of these attributes is not an absolute unity but one of inherence, *i.e.* relation, wherein distinction subsists between the substance and the attributes as well as between the attributes themselves. God is the underlying substratum in which infinite attributes inhere. Rāmānuja cannot escape from this conclusion so long as he accepts logical judgment as providing the clue to the nature of ultimate reality. All judgment is a synthesis of subject and predicate or substance and attribute. But all affirmations deal with finite objects, whose unity does not exceed the relation of inherence; in finite experience we do not find the absolute unity. We are impelled to transcend the world of change and finitude in order to reach a reality where the subject and the predicate are absolute. The assumption of such a reality is the basis of all logical procedure. In judgment we try our best to bring out the full nature of reality by a series of predications. But a string of abstractions cannot do justice to the wealth of reality unless we assume that the ultimate reality is thought as such. It is this absolute judgment that is implicit in our mind from the first, that being and thought are one.

Beyond the fact that the Absolute characterised by sat, cit and ānanda is a concrete one possessing these distinctive attributes, Rāmānuja does not tell us how exactly these attributes are found organically related in the Absolute itself.

Between substance and attributes,[2] Brahman and the world, the relation is one of non-difference and not coinherence. For the latter denotes an inherent separateness.

Are the souls and the world also one with Brahman? If so, in what sense? The dependence of the viśeṣaṇas or attributes is eternal and is connected with his essential

[1] *Nyāyasiddhāñjana*, p. 06.

[2] The conception of the relation of substance and attributes is an unsatisfactory one. If the two are identical, the distinction is meaningless; if the two are different, then the relation becomes a purely external one. If the two are related internally by samavāya, this relation itself must be related to the terms, and so on *ad infinitum*.

nature.[1] The world is not merely a viseṣaṇa but has to do with the nature of the supreme as well. It is the manifestation of the inner determination of the real. The admission of individual souls as coeternal with Brahman constitutes a limit. The infinitude of Brahman is compromised by the unconditioned infinitude of its constituent factors. If Brahman and the soul exist coeternally what is the relation between them? An eternal relation between them, whether essential or accidental, will be an inexplicable mystery. The self of Brahman is distinct from its body, and we can call it the unconditioned self.

The finite centres of experience seem to be resolved, in Rāmānuja's scheme, into movements in the life of God. If the Absolute is a perfect personality including all selves and the world, it is difficult to know how the finite selves, with their respective consciousnesses, unique meanings and values, are sustained. One self cannot be a part of another. Rāmānuja's Brahman is not only a supreme self, but an eternal society of eternal selves. How can God both include and exclude the individual in the same ultimate sense? We may distinguish between God as distinct from the lesser spirits who derive their being from him and the Absolute which comprehends all conceivable existence. God, spirits and matter are the Absolute, and not God alone. Yet Rāmānuja identifies God with the Absolute, beside which and beyond which nothing exists. When he emphasises the monistic character of his system, he makes out that the supreme reality has the unity of self-consciousness, and matter and souls are but moments in the being of that supreme spirit. When he is anxious to preserve the independence of the individual, he argues that the individual souls are all centres of consciousness, knowing subjects possessing self-consciousness, though their selfhood is derived from God.

Brahman is the material and the efficient cause of the universe of souls and matter. The changes relate to the body of God, while the soul (dehi) remains unchanged (nirvikāra).[2] "Everything different from that highest self, whether conscious or non-conscious, constitutes its body, while the self

[1] Svarūpānubandhitvena niyatatvāt (ii. 4. 14).
[2] *Tattvamuktākalāpa*, iii. 25.

alone is the unconditioned embodied self."[1] The body of God is the material cause and the soul is the efficient cause, and so we can say that God is both the material and the efficient cause of the world. This distinction is to be maintained; for Rāmānuja believes that the changes of the body do not affect the soul of God, even as the changes of the jīva's body do not affect the essence of the jīva. What, then, is the essence of God which remains unchanged? Whether in a subtle condition, as in pralaya, or a gross condition, as in creation, or an individualised though not imperfect condition, as in the state of release, the essence of Īśvara differs from that of the world. It has also to be distinguished from the nityavibhūti of Īśvara. It is difficult to conceive the nature of the Absolute if we set aside the attributes of sat, cit and ānanda, which, after all, are only attributes. Yet if the attributes form the essential nature of God, then the process of change in them must also affect his nature. Does all this mean that God is not absolute actuality, but is himself in the making? The distinction, finally, that the soul of God is the efficient cause and his body the material cause is untenable. We cannot take half a fowl for cooking and leave the other to lay eggs.[2]

The crux of all monism is the relation of the finite to the infinite. A system of finite reals cannot itself be infinite We must have something over and above the finite. Rāmānuja comprehends all aspects of the world under the two categories of thought and matter, and finds that the two are well adapted to each other, and so concludes that there is a God who directs the world process. Logic suggests it, religious consciousness confirms it, and so most of us accept it. But it is not a solution of the problem. It is open to say that all explanation is within the reality and not of it. We can never say why the real is what it is. But even within the real the relations are not logically determined. If the finite is equated with thought and matter, such opposed factors cannot belong to the same reality. Either the unity of the whole or the distinction of the attributes requires to be modified. What Rāmānuja does is to combine the two

[1] Svavyatiriktaṁ cetanācetanavastujātaṁ svaśarīraṁ iti, sa eva nirupādhikaś śārīra ātmā (i. 1. 13).

[2] Ānandagiri on B.S., i. 2. 8.

into one Absolute, which is a concrete organic whole, all of whose parts and elements exist in and through a supreme principle which embodies itself in them. The criticism directed against Śaṁkara is that he elevates the Absolute to such a height that there is no path which leads down to the lowlands of humanity. Rāmānuja intends to give us a more satisfying unity which is neither an identity nor an aggregate of parts, but comprehends all differences and relations. One may well ask whether such an absolute experience is not an arbitrary fancy incapable of verification. We can combine words so as to make a plausible statement, but it is doubtful whether there is a corresponding reality. If the Absolute is supposed to be a transcendent changeless existence, it is a problem how such an Absolute, which has no history, includes the time process and the evolution of the world. Unless Rāmānuja is willing to explain away the immutable perfection of the Absolute, and substitute for it a perpetually changing process, a sort of progressing perfection, he cannot give us any satisfactory explanation of the relation of the soul of the Absolute to its body.

How, again, are the mechanism of nature and the sphere of souls combined in the unity? It is all very well to attempt to preserve the unity of the world as well as the distinctness of individuals. But if our sorrows and struggles, sins and imperfections are integral parts of the Absolute, and are eternally present to the divine mind as distinct constituents of his unruffled beatific consciousness, are not the souls simply certain permanent elements in God's mind? On the other hand, if we are separate individuals, God must be separate from us. The mere fact that we share in a common life does not lessen our individuality.[1] Rāmānuja uses the analogy of soul and body to indicate that the body cannot exist apart from the soul embodied in it. When the soul departs the body perishes. Again, body exists only to give pleasure and pain to the soul. The final cause of the body is the soul. But if the analogy is pressed, it will mean that God is all, and the souls and body are merely instrumental

[1] If we assume, says Bradley, that "individual men, yourself and myself, are real, each in his own right, to speak of God as having reality in the religious consciousness is nonsense" (*Truth and Reality*, pp. 434–5).

to the pleasure of God. The concrete universal of certain Hegelian thinkers is a word which does not solve the problem but restates it. The problem of philosophy is for them the relating in one whole of the eternal perfection of the Absolute and the endless process of the world.

Rāmānuja is anxious to conserve the permanent and independent reality of the individual souls, and vigorously protests against the view which reduces individuality to a delusive appearance. Within the one reality, which we may call the Absolute, a distinction is made between God, the individual souls and unconscious matter.[1] The Supreme is the soul of the individual jīva, since all things form the body of God.[2] What Rāmānuja takes for the soul is the empirical ego, which is something finite and has a before and an after. It is not much to the point to urge that all knowledge involves the distinction of subject and object. For this distinction is a relative one. In the case of vision, we distinguish the scene of sight as the object of vision and the eye as the subject. So also in conscious experiencing we distinguish the content of consciousness from its form and call the latter subject and the former object, though, strictly speaking, both these belong to the world of experience. What Rāmānuja calls the subject is not the subject truly conceived as subject, but is a subject which is itself objectified and reduced to one of the many finite objects contained in experience.[3]

Rāmānuja says that the individual soul is not affected by the changes of its body.[4] It is naturally pure. The dark shadows of materiality do but hide its glory, but do not destroy it. Materialisation is but an accident which can be shaken off. This materialisation is the product of sin, but the pure soul cannot sin. So sin cannot be without the

[1] Cp. with this Rashdall's view (*Theory of Good and Evil*, vol. ii, pp. 238 ff.).

[2] Sarvātmatvāt pratyagātmano 'py ātmā paramātmā.

[3] Cp. Gentile: "If then we would know the essence of the mind's transcendental activity, we must not present it as spectator and spectacle, the mind as an object of experience, the subject an outside onlooker. In so far as consciousness is an object of consciousness it is no longer consciousness. Strictly speaking, it is no longer a subject but an object, no longer an ego but a non-ego" (*Theory of Mind as Pure Act*, E.T., p. 6).

[4] Svaśarīragatabālatvayuvatvasthaviratvādayo dharmāḥ jīvaṁ na spṛśanti (i. 1. 13).

embodied soul, and there can be no embodied soul without sin. Rāmānuja, like other Hindu thinkers, gets over the difficulty by the conception of a beginningless saṁsāra. But this involves the pure spirituality of the soul. Sin and punishment both belong to the objective series and have nothing to do with the pure subject, which cannot sin; but if the soul can sin, then it means that it is already connected with matter, and it is not the pure soul but the empirical ego. When it is said that the object series is beginningless, we get the pure spirit on the one side and the object on the other, both being absolute existents, since they find no explanation outside themselves. The soul is pure in itself; the body hangs on to it. How does this happen?

What is the relation of the self to knowledge? Are they different or are they one? If they are different, then experience of pleasure or pain at a certain point in the body will belong to knowledge and not to self, and so the self will not be able to feel pleasure or pain. We cannot say that knowledge is a function (vyāpāra) of the self, for then it must be caused. But, in Rāmānuja, knowledge is eternal and independent, and not a product. If the self and knowledge are one, then even the self will be liable to expansion and contraction. But the atomic soul cannot expand and contract. The relation between the self, which is itself made up of consciousness,[1] and knowledge, is not clearly conceived. The self is filled with consciousness, and has also for its quality consciousness.[2] "Knowledge is distinct from the knowing subject whose quality it is, as smell which is perceived as a quality of earth is distinct from earth."[3] But Rāmānuja admits that in deep sleep there is consciousness, though it does not relate itself to objects.[4] The nature of self is not so much knowledge as pure consciousness, which, now and then, relates itself to objects.

The relation of the jīva to Brahman is not free from difficulties. Rāmānuja says: "The highest Brahman resolved to be many. It thereupon sent forth the entire world, consisting of fire, water, etc., introduced in this world so sent

[1] Vijñānamayo hi jīvo na buddhimātram (i. 1. 13).
[2] ii. 3. 29.
[3] ii. 3. 47.
[4] Jñānasya viṣayagocaratvaṁ jāgaryādāv upalabhyate (ii. 3. 31).

forth, the whole mass of individual souls (cetanam jīvavargam) into different bodies, divine, human, etc., corresponding to the desert of each soul, and finally itself entering according to its wish into these souls, so as to constitute their inner self (jīvāntarātmā), evolved in all these aggregates names and forms, *i.e.* rendered each aggregate something substantial (vastu) and capable of being denoted by a word." [1] The jīva is thus a reflex of the whole reality. Each jīva has (1) the antaryāmin Brahman, the light which lighteth every existence; (2) the soul, which is the knowing subject; and (3) the unconscious instruments through which the soul works. Each individual seems to be a trinity in unity, even as the supreme Brahman is.[2] Brahman is the prototype, of which the individual is the ectype; for each individual possesses in finite and material outlines the supreme perfection of God. Again, when the soul casts off the body and enters on the state of release, it seems to become a bare point of mere existence. It is not cut off from God, since the currents of divine life flow through it. Will there not be an overlapping of these souls? If not, what is it that distinguishes these souls from one another? Are they substances in their own right, or mere qualities housed in the Absolute? Rāmānuja believes that each of these souls has a centrality and has experiences which it organises into a unity, but the logic of it all seems to be rather weak.

Rāmānuja's conception of the individual self reminds us of the Scholastic theory of substance which Kant, in his *Refutation of Rational Psychology*, and Śaṁkara, in his commentary on the *Brahma Sūtra*, have attacked. Rāmānuja believes in a continuous self-identical entity which is eternal, while Śaṁkara maintains that the quality of continuous self-identity is true only of the ātman. On Rāmānuja's view, it is difficult to know the relation between the continuous development and the identical essence of the self. As in Hegel, we have here an identity of process, an identity which is said to persist in and through difference. If the identity of individual self is not affected by the passage from body to body, or by the periodic suspension of consciousness, it

[1] i. 1. 13. [2] Acijjīvaviśiṣṭaparamātmā (i. 1. 13).

follows that the bodily relation, memory and consciousness, are not fundamental to the nature of the self. We cannot understand what the permanent unchanging nature of the self is to which all the known experiences are irrelevant. We seem to be reduced to an abstract monadism where terms like personal identity, continuity of consciousness, immortality and pre-existence are meaningless. The abstract monad has little to do with the concrete living self of experience. It is an assumption to hold that the simple colourless unit called the self is different in each individual. We are obliged to admit that there is a fundamental ātman in each individual, which is somehow related to a fluid historical development.

Śaṁkara and Rāmānuja are the two great thinkers of the Vedānta, and the best qualities of each were the defects of the other. Śaṁkara's apparently arid logic made his system unattractive religiously; Rāmānuja's beautiful stories of the other world, which he narrates with the confidence of one who had personally assisted at the origination of the world, carry no conviction. Śaṁkara's devastating dialectic, which traces all—God, man and the world—to one ultimate consciousness, produces not a little curling of the lips in the followers of Rāmānuja. Śaṁkara's followers outdo the master, and bring his doctrine perilously near atheistic mentalism. The followers of Rāmānuja move with as much Olympian assurance through the chambers of the Divine mind as Milton through the halls of heaven. Yet Rāmānuja had the greatness of a religious genius. Ideas flowed in on him from various sources—the Upaniṣads and the Āgamas, the Purāṇas and the Prabandham—and he responded to them all with some side of his religious nature. All their different elements are held together in the indefinable unity of religious experience. The philosophic spirit was strong in Rāmānuja, so, too, was his religious need. He tries his best to reconcile the demands of the religious feeling with the claims of logical thinking. If he did not succeed in the attempt to give us a systematic and self-contained philosophy of religion, it should not surprise us. Much more remarkable is the deep earnestness and hard logic with which he conceived the problem and laboured to bridge the yawning gulf between the apparently conflicting claims of religion and philosophy. A thin intellect with no depth of soul may be blind to the wonders of God's ways, and may have offered us a seemingly simple solution. Not so Rāmānuja, who gives us the best type of monotheism conceivable, inset with touches of immanentism.[1]

REFERENCES.

Rāmānuja's commentary on the Brahma Sūtra: Thibaut's E.T. S.B.E., XLVIII.

Rāmānuja's commentary on the Brahma Sūtra: Rangācārya's E.T.

Rāmānuja's commentary on the Bhagavad Gītā: Govindācārya's E.T.

Yatīndramatadīpikā: Govindācārya's E.T.

S.D.S., Ch. IV.

[1] The Saguṇa Brahman of Śaṁkara and the brahmaloka answer to Rāmānuja's Viṣṇu and vaikuṇṭha. Śaṁkara presses the point that these conceptions, though the highest open to us, are not the highest in themselves. This reservation makes little difference so far as life is concerned.

CHAPTER X

THE ŚAIVA, THE ŚĀKTA, AND THE LATER VAIṢṆAVA THEISM

Śaiva Siddhānta—Literature—Metaphysics, ethics and religion—The Pratyabhijñā system of Kashmir—Śāktaism—The dualism of Madhva—Life and literature—Theory of knowledge—God—Soul—Nature—God and the world—Ethics and religion—General estimate—Nimbārka and Keśava—Vallabha—Caitanya, Jīva Gosvāmi and Baladeva.

I

Śaiva Siddhānta

FROM the beginning the cult of Vaiṣṇavism had for its chief rival Śaivism,[1] which is even to-day a very popular creed in South India. While it prevailed in South India even before the Christian era, it received a great access of strength from its opposition to Buddhism and Jainism, which it, along with Vaiṣṇavism, overcame about the fifth or the sixth century after Christ. It elaborated a distinctive philosophy called the Śaiva Siddhānta about the eleventh century A.D. Dr. Pope, who gave much thought to this system, regards it as "the most elaborate, influential, and undoubtedly the most intrinsically valuable of all the religions of India."[2] While there are striking similarities between the Siddhānta and the Śaivism of Kashmir, we cannot say that the former owes its general structure or essential doctrines to the latter. The earliest Tamil works, like *Tolkāppiam*, refer to the Arivars or

[1] Mādhava's S.D.S. refers to four schools of Śaivism: Nakulīśa-pāśupata, the Śaiva and the Pratyabhijñā, and the Raseśvara. The last is not of philosophical interest. For the central principles of the first, see I.P., pp. 488–489.

[2] *Tiruvāsagam*, p. lxxiv.

the seers, who chalked out the path to freedom and bliss. These latter were influenced by the Vedic conception of Rudra and the Rudra-Śiva cult of the Brāhmaṇas, the *Mahābhārata* and the *Śvetāśvatara Upaniṣad.*[1] Besides these, the twenty-eight Śaiva Āgamas, especially the parts dealing with jñāna or knowledge, the hymns of the Śaiva saints, and the works of the later theologians, form the chief sources of Southern Śaivism.

II

LITERATURE

Twenty-eight Āgamas are recognised,[2] of which the chief is Kāmika, including the section dealing with knowledge called Mṛgendra Āgama. The Tamil saints Māṇikkavāsagar (seventh century A.D.) and Sundarar refer to them. Śaiva devotional literature [3] belongs to the period from the fifth to the ninth centuries. The Śaiva hymns compiled by Nambi Āṇḍār Nambi (A.D. 1000) are collectively called Tirumurai. The first part, known as Devāram, contains the hymns of Sambandar, Appar and Sundarar ; of the others the most important is *Tiruvāsagam* of Māṇikkavāsagar. Sekkirar's *Periapurāṇam* (eleventh century), which describes the lives of the sixty-three Śaiva saints, contains some valuable information. Meykaṇḍer's *Sivajñānabodham* (thirteenth century), regarded as an expansion of twelve verses of the Raurava Āgama, is the standard exposition of the Śaiva Siddhānta views. Arulnandi Śivācārya, the first of the forty-nine disciples of Meykaṇḍer, is the author of the important work *Śivajñānasiddhiyar.* Of Umāpati's works (fourteenth century), *Śivaprakāśam, Tiru-arul-payan* are well known. The Śaiva Siddhānta rested on the twofold tradition of the Vedas and the Āgamas [4] and the systematic reconciliation of the two was undertaken by Nīlakaṇṭha [5] (fourteenth century

---

1 See I.P., pp. 88, 488–9, 510 ff.

2 In the Kailāsanātha temple of Conjeevaram we have the earliest inscriptional record of the twenty-eight Śaiva Āgamas in which the Pallava king Rājasimhavarman states his faith, and it is said to belong to the end of the fifth century A.D.

3 "No cult in the world has produced a richer devotional literature, or one more instinct with brilliance of imagination, fervour of feeling and grace of expression" (Barnett : *The Heart of India*, p. 82).

4 Tirumūlar, quoted in *Siddhānta Dīpikā,* November 1911, p. 205. Śivajñāna Siddhiyar says : "The only real books are the Vedas and the Śaivāgamas. . . . Of them the Vedas are general and given out for all. The Āgamas are special and revealed for the benefit of the blessed, and they contain the essential truths of the Veda and the Vedānta. Both are said to be given out by God" (i. 46). Cp. Nilakaṇṭha : vayaṁ tu vedaśivāgamayoḥ bhedam na paśyāmaḥ. *Brahmamīmāṁsā,* p. 156.

5 See Nīlakaṇṭha, i. 1. 3.

A.D.), who wrote a commentary on the *Brahma Sūtra*, interpreting that work in the light of the Śaiva system. He accepts generally the standpoint of Rāmānuja, and protests against the absolute identity or absolute distinction of God on the one side and the souls and the world on the other.[1] The supreme is Śiva, with his consort Aṁbā, having for his body the conscious and unconscious entities. Appaya Dīkṣita's commentary called *Śivārkamaṇidīpikā* is of great value.

III

Doctrines

The supreme reality is called Śiva, and is regarded as beginningless, uncaused, free from defects, the all-doer and the all-knower, who frees the individual soul from the bonds which fetter them. The formula of saccidānanda is interpreted as implying the eight attributes of self-existence, essential purity, intuitive wisdom, infinite intelligence, freedom from all bonds, infinite grace or love, omnipotence, and infinite bliss. Some proofs of the existence of God are mentioned. The world is undergoing change. Its material cause, prakṛti, is unconscious like clay, and cannot organise itself into the world. The development is not due to the elements, which are devoid of intelligence. Karma is equally unavailing. Kāla, or time, is, according to Meykaṇḍar, changeless, though it appears to the observer as changing.[2] It is a condition of all action, but is not by itself an active agent. But if God is directly the cause, his independence and perfection may perhaps be compromised. It is therefore said that God operates through his śakti as his instrumental cause. The principle of karma works in accordance with the spiritual ends of man. It does not frame the ends or make distinctions between good and evil. These are laid down by an infinite spirit, who also, with the aid of his śakti, sees to it that the souls get their proper rewards. As the jar has the potter for its first cause, the staff and the wheel for its instrumental cause, and clay for its material cause, even so the world has

[1] Many of the central passages are echoes of Rāmānuja's bhāṣya. Cp., *e.g.*, Sūkṣmacidacidviśiṣṭam brahma kāraṇam, sthūlacidacidviśiṣṭaṁ tat kāryam bhavati (i. 1. 2). But see Appaya Dīkṣita's *Ānandalaharī*.

[2] *Śivajñānabodham*, i. 4.

Śiva for its first cause, śakti for its instrumental cause, and māyā for its material cause. As sound fills all the notes of a tune, or flavour pervades the fruit, so God, by his śakti, pervades the whole world so fully that he does not appear to be different from it. God is the soul of which the universe of nature and man is the body. He is not identical with them, though he dwells in them and they in him. Non-dualism does not mean oneness (ekatva), but inseparability.

Śiva is everlasting, since he is not limited by time. He is omnipresent. He works through his śakti, which is not unconscious but conscious energy—the very body of God. This body is composed of the five mantras,[1] and subserves the five functions of creation, sustenance and destruction of the universe, obscuration or embodiment (tirodhāna) and liberation of the souls. His knowledge is ever-shining and immediate. According to the Pauṣkara Āgama, Śakti, called Kuṇḍalinī (the coiled), or śuddhamāyā, is that from which Śiva derives his functions and in which his being is grounded. Śakti is the intermediate link between Śiva pure consciousness and matter the unconscious. It is the upādhi, the cause of the differentiation of Śiva's functions.[2] It is the cause of the bondage of all beings from Ananta, who is next only to Śiva, downwards, and also of their release. Śakti, often called Umā, is but the reflex of Śiva, and not an independent existence. The Absolute in itself is called Śiva, and the Absolute in relation to objects is called Śakti. In the *Siddhānta*, Śiva is not only the Absolute of metaphysics, but the God of religion. He is the saviour and guru, and he assumes this form out of his great love for mankind. He is the God of love.[3]

To the Lord (pati) belong the paśu, literally cattle, the infinite host of souls. He is not their creator, since they are eternal. The soul is distinct from the body, which is an unconscious object of experience (bhogya). Its presence is evidenced from the facts of memory and recognition. It is an omnipresent, constant, conscious actor. It is the abode

[1] Sadyojāta, Vāmadeva, Aghora, Tatpuruṣa and Īśāna. Cp. Tait. Araṇ., x. 43. 47.

[2] *Pauṣkara Āgama*, ii. 1.

[3] *Sivaprakāśam*, i. 1; Nallasvāmi Piḷḷai: *Śaiva Siddhānta*, p. 277.

of the eternal and omnipresent citśakti.[1] It has consciousness (caitanyam), whose essence lies in the act of seeing (dṛkkriyārūpam). According to *Śivajñānasiddhiyar*, the soul is distinct from the gross body as well as the subtle, though united to them, and it has the functions of desire, thought and action (icchājñānakriyā).[2] It becomes one with the thing in which it dwells for the time being. In the world of saṁsāra it concentrates on worldly things, while in the state of release it centres its consciousness on God. During pralaya, the souls devoid of embodiment rest as powers and energies in the great Śiva. The number of souls cannot be increased or decreased. As more souls get released the embodied ones become reduced in number. Consciousness is perfectly manifested in the liberated, while it is obscured in the unliberated. The individual souls are of three classes, according as they are subject to the three, two or one of the impurities.[3] The earth and the rest are also the effects of God's creation. They are unconscious and serve the purposes of the souls.

The web of bonds (pāśajāla) is distinguished into avidyā, karma and māyā.[4] The first is called āṇavamala, or the taint due to the false notion of finiteness (aṇutva) which the soul has. The self, which is pure consciousness, imagines itself to be finite and confined to the body and of limited knowledge and power. It is ignorant of its nature as consciousness and also mistakes the body for its reality. This is the bondage (paśutva) of the soul (paśu). This avidyā is one in all beings, beginningless, dense, great and multiform. Creation, destruction, etc., take place with reference to the finite world, and so they are regarded as the modifications (pariṇāma) of avidyā.[5] Karma is the cause of the conjunction of the conscious soul with the unconscious body. It is an auxiliary of avidyā. It is called karma because it is produced by the activities of beings. It is as unseen (adṛṣṭa) as it is subtle. It prevails during creation and merges back into

[1] *Mṛgendra Āgama*, vii. 5.

[2] iii. 1.

[3] The highest (vijñānakala) are freed from māyā and karma, and have only the one impurity of āṇavam. The next (pralayakala) are those who are subject to the impurities of āṇavam and karma, which bind them to rebirth; and the last (sakala) include all beings subject to the three impurities.

[4] *Mṛgendra Āgama*, ii. 3–7.

[5] *Ibid.*, vii. 11.

māyā during pralaya. It cannot be destroyed, but must work out its results.[1] Māyā is the material cause of the world, unconscious in nature,[2] the seed of the universe, possessing many powers, omnipresent and imperishable. "As the trunk, the leaf and the fruit latent in the seed grow thereform, so the universe from kala to earth (kṣiti) develops from māyā." [3]

The process of creation receives great attention in the Śaiva system. While Śiva is pure consciousness, matter is pure unconsciousness, and Śakti is said to meditate between the two. She is not the material cause of the world, since she is of the nature of consciousness [caitanya). She is the external sound, the connecting-link between the gross and the subtle, the material and the spiritual, the word and the concept.[4] Śuddhamāyā, the mother of the universe, is Vāk, or Nāda, "the voice of the silence." The Śaiva Siddhānta analyses the universe into thirty-six tattvas as against the twenty-five of the Śāṁkhya. Above the puruṣa, we have the pañcakañcuka, or the fivefold envelope of niyati (order), kāla (time), rāga (interest), vidyā (knowledge), kala (power). Above kala there are māyā, Śuddhavidyā, Īśvara, Sadāśiva, Śakti and Śiva. Śivatattva is a class by itself; Sadāśiva, Īśvara and Śuddhavidyā form the Vidyātattvas, and the other thirty-two from māyā downwards are the Ātmatattvas. These are the different stages of evolution. Māyā first evolves into the subtle principles and then into the gross. Kalā, the first principle evolved from māyā, overcomes the impurities obstructing the manifestation of consciousness, and helps it to manifest itself in accordance with karma; by the next principle of vidyā, the soul derives the experience of pleasure and pain. "That instrument by which the active soul observes the operations of buddhi is vidyā."[5] Māyā is the desire on which all experience depends. Kāla or time regulates experiences as past, present and future. Time is not eternal, for eternity is independence of time. Niyati is the fixed order governing the distinction of bodies, organs and the like, for the different souls. The puruṣas are enveloped by these five. The Śaiva Siddhānta holds that the mūlaprakṛti of the Sāṁkhya is itself a product, and admits five subtle principles beyond it. Of these five, the first three serve to manifest the powers of knowledge, action and feeling, while the other two answer roughly to time and space. Prakṛti is the stuff of which the worlds which the puruṣa is to experience are made. It is the first gross development. From prakṛti evolve the guṇas, from the guṇas the buddhi; the rest of the evolution is on the lines of the Sāṁkhya.

---

[1] viii. 1–5. [2] ix. 2–4. [3] *Pauṣkara Āgama*, iii. 4.
[4] *Ibid.*, ii. 17. [5] *Ibid.*, v. 9.

Śivatattva is the niṣkala, or undifferentiated basis of all consciousness and action. "When śuddhamāyā, the śakti of Śiva, begins her life of activity, then Śiva becomes the experiencing (bhoga) Śiva; he is Sadāśiva, also called Sadākhya, not really separate from Śiva. When śuddhamāyā is actually active, the experiencing Śiva becomes the ruling (adhikāra) Śiva; he is then Īśvara, not really separate from Sadāśiva."[1] It is Sadāśiva that has the body of the five mantras, and not Śiva. Śuddhavidyā is the cause of true knowledge. Between world periods there are pauses of quiescence, at the end of which evolution sets in. The Lord helps the impurities to manifest themselves, and sustains the whole course of their development for the ultimate good of the souls dependent on his grace.[2] He takes note of the activities of the souls and helps them in their onward pursuit. Respect for the law of karma is not a limitation of God's independence, for the law of karma is the means he employs.[3]

The Śaiva Siddhānta does not support the illusory conception of the world. The beginningless saṁsāra is due to matter and souls which are also eternal. The world has a serious moral purpose, and cannot be dismissed as a mere error or jest. God is for ever engaged in the rescue of souls from the bondage of matter. The unceasing rhythm of the world, with the law of karma regulating it, continues for the one purpose of attracting man to the higher life. "Śiva desires that all should know him," says Meykaṇḍer.[4] It is not merely the ambition of the soul to know God, but it is the desire of the Lord as well.

Sin is the threefold bond from which we have to obtain emancipation. We must get rid of the āṇavam or the avidyā, or the defilement which darkens the light of the soul, neutralise the karma which produces rebirth, and shake off the māyā, which is the basis of all impurities. God helps us in our endeavours. A metaphysical absolute, unaffected by the pleasures and pains of the soul, is of no avail. But Śiva is full of grace and is waiting through successive æons to receive the recognition of the soul and his adoring love. A personal tie binds the soul to God. The grace of God is the road to freedom. It demands childlike trust in Śiva. "To those who draw not nigh he gives no boon; to those who draw nigh he vouchsafes all good; the great God knows no dis-

[1] *Pauṣkara Āgama*, i. 25–26.
[2] vii. 11–22.
[3] S.D.S., vii; *Śivajñānabodham*, ii. 5.
[4] *Śivajñānabodham*, xii. 3.

like."[1] The Śaiva saints yearn to see God. Māṇikkavāsagar sings :—

To cast quite off this sinful frame ; to enter Śiva's home
To see the wondrous Light, that so these eyes may gladness gain ;
O Infinite, without compare ! The assembly of Thy saints
Of old, to see, Behold, O Sire, Thy servant's soul hath yearned.[2]

The consciousness of sin is intensely felt, and some saints utter the cry that their sins are shutting them off from communion with God.[3] The devotion of the Śaivas is more virile and masculine than that of the Vaiṣṇavas.

Tiruvāsagam[4] depicts in beautiful hymns the progress of the soul from the bondage of ignorance and passion into the liberty of light and love, its first awakening, its joy and exaltation, waywardness and despondency, struggle and unrest, the peace and the joy of union. In the intuition of God, the distinction of knower, knowledge and known is said to disappear.[5] There was, at any rate, in the early form of Śaivism, a spirit of toleration. "Whatever God you worship, even as he Śiva will appear. He who is above all this will understand your true worship and show you grace."[6] The guru or the teacher plays an important part in the scheme of salvation. The true guru is one who is in his last birth ; and Śiva himself is said to live in the guru, looking lovingly on the disciple through the eyes of the guru.[7] There are no incarnations of Śiva, though he appears frequently to test

[1] *Tiru-aruḷ-payan*, i. 9. [2] Pope's Trans., *Tiruvāsagam*, xxv. 9.

[3] Cp. Appar :—

" Evil, all evil my race, evil my qualities all,
Great am I only in sin, evil is even my good.
Evil my innermost self, foolish, avoiding the pure,
Beast am I not, yet the ways of the beast I can never forsake.

. . . .

Ah ! wretched man that I am,
Whereunto came I to birth."

(Kingsbury and Philips : *Hymns of the Tamil Śaivite Saints*, p. 47.)

[4] Regarding the literature of the Śaiva Siddhānta, Sir Charles Eliot writes : " In no literature with which I am acquainted has the individual religious life—its struggles and dejections, its hopes and fears, its confidence and its triumph—received a delineation more frank and more profound " (*Hinduism and Buddhism*, vol. ii, p. 217).

[5] *Tiru-aruḷ-payan*, viii. 74. [6] *Śivajñānāsiddhiyar*.

[7] *Tiru-aruḷ-payan*, v.

the bhakti of the devotees or initiate them into truth. But Śiva is not born; nor has he any human career.

The ethical virtues are insisted on. Siddhiyar says: "They have no love for God who have no love for all mankind."[1] Though the law of karma is inviolable, the choice of the soul is not fettered. God is always ready to second the efforts of man. Karma and jñāna conjointly produce release.[2] The restrictions of caste lose their rigour in any true theism. Though Māṇikkavāsagar did not develop a defiant attitude towards the caste rules, the later Śaivas, Paṭṭaṇathu Piḷḷai, Kapilar, and the Telugu poet, Vemana, are critical of the caste restrictions. Tirumūlar held that there was only one caste, even as there was only one God.[3] The reform movement of Basava (middle of the twelfth century) is marked by its revolt against the supremacy of the Brahmin, though Basava himself was a Brahmin.[4] This sect does not accept the hypothesis of rebirth.

After the destruction of pāśa, the individual is said to become Śiva,[5] *i.e.* attain perfect resemblance to him, though the five functions of creation, etc., are reserved for God only.[6] Since the soul has no dust or darkness in it, the light of God shines through it. Deliverance is not becoming one with God, but enjoying the presence of the Lord. Meykaṇḍar says: "Did the soul perish on becoming united with Śiva, there would be no eternal being to be associated with God. If it does not perish, but remains a dissociated being, then there would be no union with God. But the impurities will cease to affect the soul, and then the soul, like the union of salt with water, will become united with Śiva as his servant and exist at his feet as one with him."[7] "On the removal of sin, the soul attains to the status of Śiva himself."[8] The

[1] xii. 2, quoted in *Siddhānta Dīpikā*, November 1912, p. 239.

[2] Nīlakaṇṭha, i. 1. 1.

[3] Onre kulamum oruvane devanum (*Tirumantram*).

[4] Though the Lingāyata reformation started with a vigorous protest against the caste system, the Lingāyats to-day observe caste divisions.

[5] *Mṛgendra Āgama*, vi. 7. "Nirantaraṁ śivo 'ham iti bhāvanā pravāheṇa, śithilitapāśatayā'pagatapaśubhāva upāsakaḥ śiva eva bhavati" (Nīlakaṇṭha on iv. 1. 3).

[6] Nīlakaṇṭha on iv. 4. 7.

[7] *Śivajñānabodham*, xi. 5 See also Pope's Note iii, *Tiruvāsagam*, p. xlii.

[8] Nīlakaṇṭha, iv. 4. 4.

freed souls may exist in an embodied or disembodied condition.[1] Some Śaivas believe that in emancipation the body itself is irradiated with the light of Śiva; others think that the souls acquire some miraculous powers. Before they attain union with the Supreme, the souls must consume the fruits of their deeds. The jīvanmukta, though in the body, is one in feeling and faculty with the Supreme. He does not engage in works which lead to further embodiments. He is filled with the presence of God.[2] He continues to be embodied until his past karma is exhausted, and the deeds of the interval are consumed by the grace of God.[3] All the deeds performed by the freed are due to the impulsion of God within them.[4]

IV

The Pratyabhijñā System

Though the Āgamas were also the basis of Kashmir Śaivism, the later works show a distinct leaning to Advaitism.

Vasugupta (eighth century A.D.) is said to have found the *Śiva Sūtra* and taught it to Kallaṭa. *Spanda Kārikā* composed by Vasugupta or Kallaṭa, Somānanda's *Śivadṛṣṭi* (A.D. 900), Utpala's *Pratyabhijñā Sūtra* (A.D. 930), Abhinavagupta's *Paramārthasāra* and *Pratyabhijñāvimarśini*, *Tantrāloka*, Kṣemarāja's *Śivasūtravimarśinī* and *Spandasandoha*, are some of the important works of this school. They accept the Śaiva Āgamas and the Siddhānta works as authoritative, and modify them in the direction of Śaṁkara's Advaita. These works, which show differences of opinion and are said to represent three distinct kinds of monistic idealism, are collectively called Trika.[5] *Śiva Sūtra* with Bhāskara's *Vārttika* and Kṣemarāja's *Vimarśinī* represents one tendency; Vasugupta's *Spanda Kārikā*, with Kallaṭa's *Vṛtti*, expound an idealism which is not much different from the first. Somānanda's *Śivadṛṣṭi* and Utpala's *Pratyabhijñā Sūtra* and Abhinava-

---

[1] Nīlakaṇṭha, iv. 4. 5.

[2] *Tiru-aruḷ-payan*, x. 93.

[3] *Ibid.*, x. 98.

[4] "The tongue itself that cries to thee,—all other powers
Of my whole being that cry out—all are Thyself!
Thou art my way of strength! The trembling thrill that runs
Through me is Thee! Myself the whole of ill and weal!
None other here! . . ."
(Pope's trans. of *Tiruvāśagam*, xxiii. 5.)

[5] They are so called since they treat of the ultimates, God, soul and matter.

gupta's works support non-dualism.[1] Of these the last seemed to Mādhava the most important, for he brings the other two under it,[2] and the supporters of the doctrine also held that all other systems were preparatory stages for it.[3]

The only reality of the universe is Śiva, who is infinite consciousness and unrestricted independence. He has many other features like omnipresence, eternality, formlessness, though independence (svacchanda) is peculiar to him. Śiva is the subject as well as the object, the experiencer as well as the experienced.[4] "As the consciousness on which all this resultant world is established, whence it issues, is free in its nature, it cannot be restricted anywhere. As it moves in the differentiated states of waking, sleeping, etc., identifying itself with them, it never falls from its true nature as the knower."[5] In the strain of Advaita Vedānta, it is said, "That in which there is no pleasure, no pain, no known or knower, nor again unconsciousness, alone really exists."[6] The reality of the subject does not require proof, since all proof assumes it.[7] A second to Śiva there is none. The world exists within consciousness, though it seems to be outside. "The Lord, of the form of cit (intelligence), being under the influence of desire, causes the totality of objects to shine, as if existing outside, though without a substratum, like a Yogi."[8] The existence of a prompting cause, like karma, or a material cause, like prakṛti, for the creation of the world is not admitted. Nor is māyā the principle which creates illusory forms. God is absolutely independent, and creates all that exists by the mere force of his will. He makes the world appear in himself as if it were distinct from himself, though not so really; even as objects appear in a mirror. God is as unaffected by the objects of his creation as the mirror is by the images reflected in it. By his own wonderful power (śakti) inherent in him, God appears in the form of

[1] See *Paramārthasāra*, pp. 34 and 36, 48–50, 54.

[2] S.D.S., viii.

[3] Tad bhūmikāḥ sarvadarśanasthitayaḥ (*Pratyabhijñāhṛdaya Sūtra*, p. 8).

[4] *Spandakārikā*, p. 29.

[5] *Ibid.*, pp. 2–4.

[6] *Ibid.*, p. 5.

[7] *Śivasūtravimarśini*, p. 5.

[8] *Īśvarapratyabhijñā Sūtra*, v. 6. *Paramārthasāra* says that the Lord, compact of thought and bliss, brings into being Śakti, māyā, prakṛti and the earth (see 4). The Lord assumes the semblance of gods, men, etc. (6).

souls and constitutes objects for their experiences.[1] The only reality is the unlimited pure self, the one and only substratum of the universe, whose activity (spanda, vibration) is the cause of all distinctions.

While Śiva is the changeless reality underlying the entire universe, his energy or śakti has an infinity of aspects, of which the chief are cit (intelligence), ānanda (bliss), icchā (will), jñāna (knowledge), and, kriyā (creative power). Thirty-six tattvas or principles, are recognised. When Śakti functions as cit, the Absolute becomes the pure experience called Śivatattva. So soon as life is introduced by the operation of the ānanda of Śakti, we get the second stage of Śaktitattva. The will to self-expression brings about the third stage of being. There is next the conscious experience (jñāna) of being, the Īśvaratattva with its power and will to create the universe. In the next stage there is the knower, as well as the object of knowledge, when action (kriyā) commences. It is the stage of *Śuddhavidyā*. Thus the five transcendental tattvas are the expression of the Śakti of Śiva with its five powers.

The phenomenal world arises through the force of māyā, from which the limitations of space (niyati), time (kāla), interest (rāga), knowledge (vidyā) and power (kala) arise. Through the force of māyā, the infinite experience manifests itself in a number of limited experiences or puruṣas. But all limitation implies a somewhat which limits. The distinction between puruṣa and prakṛti arises. Further evolution is on the lines of the Sāṁkhya scheme. All the stages of evolution are traced back to the one absolute Śiva. The cyclical appearance and disappearance of the world are admitted. The process of the manifestation (ābhāsa) of the universe does not stain the purity of the absolute Śiva, who transcends his own manifestations.

As the soul is of the nature of consciousness, and the individual soul is the same as the universal soul, the doctrine of an ultimate plurality of souls is denied. The pure consciousness dwells in each of us, though it is obscured by unreal upādhis. Our bondage is due to ignorance (ajñāna).[2] Kṣemarāja observes: "Being infinite consciousness, the soul thinks 'I am finite'; being independent, he thinks 'I am the body.'[3] It forgets that the world is wholly unreal apart from Śiva and that the soul is identical with Śiva."

Recognition (pratyabhijñā) of the reality is all that is needed for release. If the individual soul is one with the universal soul, it may be asked, why is the recognition of the fact necessary? Mādhava answers the question by an analogy. A love-sick woman is not consoled by the mere presence of the lover, she must recognise him to be so. The bondage of ignorance is overcome only by this recognition. When the soul recognises itself as God, it rests in the mystic bliss of

---

[1] *Paramārthasāra*, pp. 48–50.

[2] *Śiva Sūtra*, 2.

[3] Commenting on *Śiva Sūtra*, i. 2.

oneness with God. According to the Spanda school, the soul gains knowledge through intense yogic contemplation, realises the supremacy of Śiva in the universe and becomes absorbed in the mystic trance of peace and quietness. The three methods of gaining release mentioned in the *Śiva Sūtra* belong to the Śaiva, the Tantra and the Yoga.

According to Abhinavagupta, there are three classes of liberated souls : those assimilated to the Supreme (paramukta), those united to him in his manifested phase (aparamukta), and those still in the body (jīvanmukta). The delivered soul becomes one with the Supreme, since it is admitted that " there is nothing distinct from the redeemed to which he should offer praise or oblation." [1] " When thus the imagining of duality has vanished, the individual has surmounted the illusive māyā, he is merged in Brahman as water in water or milk in milk." [2]

V

Śāktaism

The cult of Śakti [3] finds its beginnings in the Ṛg-Veda. In one of the hymns Śakti is represented as the embodiment of power, " the supporter of the earth living in heaven." [4] She is the supreme power " by which the universe is upheld," [5] " the great mother of the devotees (suvratānām)," and soon became identified with " Umā of golden hue " of the *Kena Upaniṣad*. In the *Mahābhārata* she is the sister of Kṛṣṇa, and so became related to Vaiṣṇavism. The Śaivas made her the wife of Śiva. In the Purāṇas she appears as Caṇḍī, with a daily worship and an autumn festival. She soon came to be worshipped as Devī, who is one with Brahman, the absolute, whose nature is sat, cit and ānanda, and might be contemplated as male, female or attributeless.[6] Gradually the worship of Śakti as the world-mother displaced Vedic ritualism. The literature relating to this phase of Hinduism is called Tantra. It is famous for its reverence for women, who are regarded as forms of the divine mother.[7]

1 J.R.A.S., 1910.
2 *Paramārthasāra*, p. 51.
3 I.P., pp. 487–8.
4 i. 136. 3.
5 See Chān. Up., iii. 12; Bṛh. Up., v. 14.
6 Cp. Puṁrūpāṁ vā smared devīṁ strīrūpāṁ vā vicintayet
Athavā niṣkalām dhyāyet saccidānandalakṣaṇām.
7 Vidyāḥ samastās tava devi bhedāḥ.
Striyaḥ samastāḥ sakalā jagatsu.
Saptaśatī, xi. 5.

The seventy-seven Āgamas belonging to the Śākta cult are divided into five subhāgamas (or samaya), which teach practices leading to knowledge and liberation, sixty-four kaulāgamas which teach practices intended to develop magical powers, and eight miśrāgamas which aim at both. Bhāskararāya quotes nine sūtras in his *Lalitasahasranāma-bhāṣya* from a work called *Śakti Sūtra*. The latter work has not come down to us. The Tantras, which are in the form of dialogues between Śiva and Devī, themselves belong to the seventh century and onwards. Thanks to the loving labours of Sir John Woodroffe, the chief of the available Tantra texts are now published.

Śiva in this system is of the nature of omnipresent (akhilānugata), pure consciousness (prakāśa), impersonal and inactive. It is pure being devoid of any relativity. The active personal being, Śakti, includes all individual souls. The opening verse of *Saundaryalaharī* reads: "Śiva, when he is united with Śakti, is able to create; otherwise he is unable even to move."[1] Śiva and Śakti are related as prakāśa and vimarśa. Bhāskararāya defines vimarśa as the spontaneous vibration of the ultimate reality.[2] The first touch of relation in the pure absolute is Vimarśa, which gives rise to the world of distinctions. Vimarśa or Śakti is the power latent in the absolute or pure consciousness. It is the absolute personified, consciousness become a subject, and it passes over into its opposite, the not-self or the object. If Śiva is consciousness (cit), Śakti is the formative energy of consciousness, Cidrūpiṇī. Brahmā, Viṣṇu and Śiva perform their functions of creation, preservation and destruction in obedience to Śakti.[3] In the perfect experience of ānanda, Śiva and Śakti are indistinguishable. The two coalesce in one being. Śiva answers to the indeterminate Brahman in a state of quiescence; Śakti is determinate Brahman endowed with icchā (will), jñāna (knowledge), and kriyā (action), projecting the whole objective universe. Śiva and Śakti are one, since force is inherent in existence. The force may be at rest or in action, but it exists none the less in both the states. The potentiality of the whole object-world exists as the Śakti of Śiva.

[1] Śivaḥ śaktyā yukto yadi bhavati śaktaḥ prabhavitum
Na ced evaṁ devo na khalu kuśalaḥ spanditum api.

[2] See his commentary on *Lalitasahasranāma* under Vimarśarūpiṇī, p. 548.

[3] *Ānandalaharī*, pp. 2 and 24.

Śakti is differentiated as gross and subtle. She is the mother of all things. The five functions of illumination (ābhāsa), coloration (rakti), examination (vimarśana), sowing the seed (bījāvasthāna) and lamentation (vilāpanatā) are attributed to her. There is also the non-conscious matter which corresponds to the prakṛti of the Sāṁkhya system.

Prakṛti or māyā is looked upon as of the substance of Devī.[1] Within the womb of Śakti is māyā or prakṛti, the matrix of the universe, potential in pralaya and active in creation. The Sāṁkhya account of evolution from prakṛti is followed. Under Śakti's direction, māyā evolves into the several material elements and physical portions of all sentient beings. In all living beings, caitanya or consciousness is present, though it appears as broken up into a multiplicity of beings on account of the varying physical adjuncts. Instead of the twenty-five tattvas of the Sāṁkhya, we have thirty-six, which are classified into: (1) Śivatattva, the supreme; (2) Vidyātattva, or the subtle manifestations of Śakti; (3) Ātmatattva, or the material universe from māyā down to earth. These three answer to prakāśa (Śiva), vimarśa and the not-self. The supreme spirit of the Śākta scheme has inner differences, though frequently we meet with ideas of salvation and oneness of the world, which remind us of Śaṁkara's more rigorous non-dualism.[2] We have, first of all, the absolute Brahman; next, we have the determinate subject endowed with Śakti. Nāda issues immediately and from nāda bindu appears,[3] and then the Śuddhamāyā. These five answer to Śiva, Śakti, Sadākhya, Īśvara and the Śuddhamāyā of the Śaivas. The rest of the evolution is not different from the Śaiva scheme.

The jīva, under the influence of māyā, looks upon itself as an independent agent and enjoyer until release is gained. Knowledge of Śakti is the road to salvation,[4] which is dissolution in the blissful effulgence of the Supreme. It is said that "for him who realises that all things are Brahman, there is neither Yoga nor worship."[5] Jīvanmukti, or liberation in this life, is admitted.[6] Liberation depends on self-culture,

[1] Sāmyāvasthā guṇopādhikā brahmarūpiṇī devī.

[2] It is said to be a non-dualism. *Kulārṇava Tantra*, i. 108. Sir John Woodroffe, who has made a special study of the Tantra school, believes that its philosophy "occupies in some sense a middle place between the dualism of the Sāṁkhya and Śaṁkara's ultra-monistic interpretation of the Vedānta" (*Indian Philosophical Review*, vol. i, p. 122).

[3] *Śāradātilaka*, i.

[4] Śaktijñānaṁ vinā devi nirvāṇaṁ naiva jāyate (*Niruttara Tantra*).

[5] *Mahānirvāṇa Tantra*, xiv. 123. See also 124–127.

[6] *Ibid.*, xiv. 135.

which leads to spiritual insight. It " does not come from the recitation of hymns, sacrifices or a hundred fasts. Man is liberated by the knowledge that he is himself Brahman." [1] " The state of mind in which it is realised that Brahman alone is (brahmasadbhāva), is the highest ; that in which there is meditation on Brahman (dhyānabhāva) is the middle ; praise (stuti) and recitation (japa) of hymns is the next, and external worship is the lowest of all." [2] There is a protest against ritualistic religion. *Kulārṇava Tantra* says: " If the mere rubbing of the body with mud and ashes gains liberation, then the village dogs who roll in them have attained it." [3] The distinctions of castes are subordinated; and the discipline of the Tantras is open to all.[4] Bhakti is regarded as helpful to salvation. Freedom of worship is allowed. " As all streams flow into the ocean, so the worship offered to any God is received by Brahman." [5] The subordinate deities are however subject to the force of karma and time.[6]

The mystic side of the Yoga system plays a large part throughout. Mantras are sacred and are regarded as divine creations, in a sense, identical with Śakti, who is Śabda, or eternal word. Great emphasis is laid on the awakening of the forces within the organism. The perfected man will awaken the Kuṇḍalinī and pierce the six cakras.[7] The theories of karma, rebirth, gross and subtle bodies, are accepted by the Śākta thinkers.

VI

MADHVA

A leading form of reaction against Śaṁkara's Advaitism is the dualistic philosophy associated with the name of Madhva,

1 *Mahānirvāṇa Tantra*, xiv. 115, 116. 2 *Ibid.*, xiv. 122.

3 i.

4 Antyajā api ye bhaktā nāmajñānādhikāriṇaḥ
Strīśūdrabrahmabandhūnāṁ tantrajñāne 'dhikāritā.
(*Vyomasaṁhitā*).

5 *Mahānirvāṇa Tantra*, ii. 50.

6 Ye samastā jagatsṛṣtisthitisaṁhārakāriṇaḥ
Te' pi kāleṣu līyante kālo hi balavattaraḥ.

7 See Avalon : *The Serpent Power*. A cloud hangs over the sādhana of the Śāktas. Though much of the obloquy is undeserved, there is apparently something which can be improved.

which has many points in common with Rāmānuja's view of reality.[1] Madhva stands out for unqualified dualism and insists on the five great distinctions of God and the individual soul, God and matter, the individual soul and matter, one soul and another, and one part of matter and another. The doctrines of exclusive mediatorship through Vāyu, the son of Viṣṇu, eternal hell as well as the missionary fervour of Madhva's faith, suggest the influence of Christianity, though there is little evidence in support of it. In view of the fact that Madhva's commentary on the *Kena Upaniṣad* is taken from *Brahmasāra*, it is reasonable to think that there was the tradition of dualism even prior to Madhva. As we shall see, Madhva makes a clever use of the Sāṁkhya and the Nyāya-vaiśeṣika theories.

VII

Life and Literature

Madhva,[2] also known as Pūrṇaprajñā and Ānandatīrtha, was born in the year 1199 in a village near Udipi, of the South Canara district. He became early very proficient in Vedic learning and soon became a saññyāsin. He spent several years in prayer and meditation, study and discussion. He developed his dualistic philosophy in discussions with his preceptor Acyutaprekṣa, an adherent of Śaṁkara's school. He proclaimed the supreme godhead of Viṣṇu and admitted the validity of branding one's shoulders with the arms of Viṣṇu, a practice accepted by Rāmānuja. He made many converts to his faith in different parts of the country, founded a temple for Kṛṣṇa at Udipi, and made it the rallying centre for all his followers. Prohibition of bloodshed, in connection with sacrifices, is a salutary reform for which he is responsible. He died at the age of seventy-nine.

The standard treatises of this school of thought are, of course, the works of Madhva. He wrote a commentary on the *Brahma Sūtra*,

---

[1] The main differences are that while Rāmānuja thinks that the individual souls are similar in their natural essence, Madhva makes them different. Madhva denies that Brahman is the material cause, which Rāmānuja admits. For Madhva, the universe is not the body of God. In Rāmānuja there are no souls disqualified for salvation and there are no differences in the enjoyment of bliss for freed souls.

[2] Nārāyaṇācārya's *Madhvavijaya* and *Maṇimañjari* contain the orthodox account of Madhva's life and work. If we eliminate the miracles and supernatural incidents which the piety of his followers attributed to him, we may get the historical basis of Madhva's life and mission.

and justified his interpretation of it in another work called *Anuvyākhyāna*. His commentaries on the *Bhagavadgītā* and the Upaniṣads,[1] his epitome of the *Mahābhārata* called *Bhāratatātparyanirṇaya* and gloss on the *Bhāgavata Purāṇa* help to elucidate his philosophy. He also wrote a commentary on the first forty hymns of the Ṛg-Veda and discussed many philosophical and other themes in his *Prakaraṇas*. Throughout his works he gives the impression that he relies more on the Purāṇas than on the Prasthānatraya, the Upaniṣads, the *Bhagavadgītā* and the *Brahma Sūtra*. It is not quite easy for Madhva to interpret these authoritative works in the interests of his dualistic metaphysics. Jayatīrtha's commentary on Madhva's *Sūtrabhāṣya* and that on Madhva's *Anuvyākhyāna* called *Nyāyasudhā*, are works of great importance. Vyāsarāya wrote a gloss called *Candrikā* on Jayatīrtha's commentary on Madhva's *Sūtrabhāṣya*. Pūrṇānanda's *Tattvamuktāvali* [2] is a bitter attack on the Advaitavāda.

VIII

Theory of Knowledge

Madhva accepts the three sources of knowledge, perception, inference and scriptural testimony. Comparison (upamāna) is regarded as a variety of inference. Perception and inference by themselves cannot help us to solve the riddle of the universe. Perception is confined to the facts open to the senses. Inference is incapable of supplying us with new facts, though it helps us to test and systematise the facts obtained through other means. We have to depend on the Vedas for a true knowledge of reality. Madhva accepts the authoritativeness of the Vedas as a whole, and does not discriminate between the different parts of it. The Hymns and the Brāhmaṇas are as useful and valid as the Upaniṣads. Madhva distinguishes between testimony due to personal authority (pauruṣeya), which may be fallible, and that which is not the composition of any person (apauruṣeya). The latter is of absolute validity and infallible. The Vedas, of which Madhva's philosophy purports to be the right interpretation, are regarded by Madhva as apauruṣeya or uncreated by any personal author, and are therefore said to be authoritative in character.

[1] See S.B.H., vols. i, iii and xiv.

[2] Translated by Cowell. See J.R.A.S., vol. xv. pt. ii.

Apprehension, through whatever means, is the direct evidence of the thing that is apprehended. The instruments which mediate apprehension are not present in the apprehension itself. The relation between the knower and the known is direct and immediate. The pramāṇas of perception, inference, and Vedic testimony, are so called simply because they are instrumental in producing knowledge—which fact comes out when we study knowledge externally. Every apprehension of fact that we have is valid, and implies the existence of the fact, even though it may exist only for the moment of apprehension. If we repudiate it as invalid, it is because of some other apprehension whose validity we accept. Sunrise and sunset are occurrences, until we have the further knowledge that the sun neither rises nor sets. Madhva accepts the intrinsic validity of apprehension as such, and disputes every theory which regards our knowledge as a mere appearance. If our knowledge does not reveal the structure of reality and indicate objective existence, but simply gives us a wrong lead, then the unreal cannot even appear, cannot be the object of even erroneous apprehension, and cannot be related to knowledge as cause to effect. If all knowledge is erroneous, the distinction between true and false ideas disappears. An analysis of illusion tells us that there is an object presented to consciousness, though we mistake its nature, owing to some defect of the senses or other means of knowledge. The elements of false perception are not false. They are facts of experience. Through some defect, we do not take a full view of the object, but what we see of it recalls something like it in nature, though different from it, with which we confuse the given datum. Every case of illusion implies two positive entities, a given thing and a suggested object. The notion of the unreality of the world means that there is something real which we mistake for something else. It does not mean that there is nothing real at all.

Madhva takes his stand on experience or knowledge and argues that there can be no knowledge without a knower and a known. To speak of knowledge, independent of a knowing subject or a known object, is meaningless. Knowing subjects and known objects must exist. The world is not an unreality. If we do not admit distinctions of things, we cannot account for distinctions of ideas. Our knowledge tells us that differences exist. We cannot regard them as merely conventional, for convention does not produce the distinctions.

The fact of difference is generally traced to the force of space and time, which are considered to be mere forms of the subject's intelligence. If space and time were identical with the knowing self, it is difficult to see how the notion that they are identical with the subject could arise. If the self as knowledge is all-pervading, we cannot have distinctions of space and time. To attribute the latter to the force of avidyā does not help us, since the status of avidyā and its relation to the self cannot be explained satisfactorily. Every explanation of avidyā implies the presuppositions of space and time, and so the latter cannot be explained away as the products of avidyā. Space and time are regarded as real wholes having parts. If they have no parts, we cannot have distinctions of here and there, now and then. We are presented with parts of space, for it is incorrect to hold that everything presented to us occupies all space, unlimited and indivisible. We are conscious only of limited bodies occupying portions of space and resisting one another. We perceive parts of space and time, and so they must be regarded as existing. According to Madhva, they are objects of perception to the witnessing self (sākṣin).

Reality (padārtha) is of two kinds, according to Madhva, independent (svatantra) and dependent (paratantra). God, the supreme person, is the only independent reality. The dependent beings are of two kinds, positive (bhāva) and negative (abhāva). Of the positive we have two varieties, conscious (cetana) souls, and unconscious (acetana) entities, like matter and time. Unconscious existence is either eternal like the Vedas, eternal and non-eternal like prakṛti, time and space, or non-eternal like the products of prakṛti.[1]

IX

God

There are three entities existing from all eternity to all eternity, fundamentally different from one another, which are God, soul and the world. Though these are all real and

[1] According to *Madhvasiddhāntasāra* (2), there are ten padārthas. Dravyaguṇakarmasāmānyaviśeṣaviśiṣṭāṁśiśaktisādṛśyabhāvā daśa padārthāḥ.

eternal, the latter two are subordinate to God and dependent on him. Independent (svatantra) reality is Brahman, the absolute creator of the universe. We can know his nature through a study of the Vedas,[1] and so his nature is not indefinable. When the Supreme is said to be indefinable, all that is meant is that a complete knowledge of him is difficult to acquire.[2] The Supreme transcends all perception.[3] The form seen during meditation by imagination is not Brahman. Madhva has no sympathy with the view that the different parts of the scripture relate to different kinds of Brahman. Though the supreme being and his qualities are identical, they can be spoken of in different terms.[4] The famous passage that Brahman is one only without a second (ekam evādvitīyam brahma) means that Brahman is unsurpassed in excellence and without an equal, since it penetrates everywhere. The attributes of God are absolute in their character and so do not limit him. Brahman possesses every kind of perfection. He is identified with Viṣṇu and is said to direct by his will the world and all that is in it as an absolute ruler. He creates and destroys the world again and again. He is endowed with a supernatural body and is regarded as transcendent to the world as well as immanent, since he is the inner ruler (antaryāmin) of all souls.[5] He manifests himself in various forms (vyūhas), appears periodically in incarnations (avatāras), and is said to be mystically present in the sacred images. He creates, maintains and destroys the universe, imparts knowledge, manifests himself in several ways, condemns some and redeems others. By his side is Lakṣmī, capable of assuming various forms, but without a material body, coeternal with him and all-pervading. She witnesses the glory of God through eternity. Unlike the gods and goddesses who acquire release after many existences, Lakṣmī is eternally redeemed (nityamuktā). Lakṣmī is the personification of God's creative energy. She is intelligent prakṛti, though God is greater than she in point of subtlety and the extent of qualities.[6] God rules the souls and matter, though he does not create them

[1] M.B., iii. 3. 1. [2] M.B., i. 1. 5. [3] M.B., iii. 2. 23.

[4] See *Nyāyasudhā*, i. 1. 2; i. 1. 6. Cp. also *Madhvasiddhāntasāra*: Bhedābhāve 'pi bhedavyavahāranirvāhakā anantā eva viśeṣāḥ (21).

[5] i. 2. 13. [6] iv. 2. 9.

from nothing or reduce them to nothing. He is the efficient but not the material cause of the universe. An unintelligent world cannot be produced by a supreme intelligence. God's activity is the result of his overflowing perfection. Simply because God takes into account the karma of the individuals, it cannot be said that the Lord is dependent on karma, for, as Madhva says, "the very existence of karma and other things depends on the Lord."[1]

X

The Individual Soul

Everything on earth is, according to Madhva, a living organism. The universe is a vast expansion of animated nature with every atom of space filled up with jīvas. In his *Tattvanirṇaya*, he says, "Infinite are the souls dwelling in an atom of space."[2] Madhva regards the distinction between Brahman and jīva as real,[3] and holds that it is wrong to think that the jīva and Brahman are non-different in release and different in saṁsāra, since two different things cannot at any time become non-different or *vice versa*. Though absolutely dependent on Brahman, the jīvas are essentially active agents and have responsibilities to bear.[4] The soul is not an absolute agent, since it is of limited power, depending, as it does, on the guidance of the Lord.[5] The jīva is said to be of atomic size as distinct from Brahman who is all-pervading.[6] Though limited in size, it pervades the body on account of its quality of intelligence. The organ of knowledge is called sākṣin, to which the material manas presents its impressions. It is the cognising principle to which is due the consciousness of I-ness, which is the basis of individuality. The soul is by nature blissful, though it is subject to pain and suffering, on account of its connection with material bodies due to its past karma. So long as it is not freed from its impurities, it wanders about in changing forms of existence. The qualities

[1] ii. 1. 37; iii. 2. 39–42.
[2] Paramāṇupradeśeṣv anantāḥ prāṇirāśayaḥ.
[3] i. 2. 12.
[4] ii. 3. 33–42.
[5] ii. 3. 38; ii. 3. 28.
[6] ii. 3. 23.

like bliss become manifest at the time of release.[1] Though the souls are eternal, they are said to be born with reference to their embodied connection[2] No two jīvas are alike in character. Each has its own worth and place in the scale of existence. The jīvas are dependent on the Lord, who, however, impels them to action according to their previous conduct.[3]

The conscious souls are of three kinds: (1) those eternally free (nitya), like Lakṣmī; (2) those who have freed themselves from saṁsāra (mukta) devas and men, ṛṣis and fathers; and (3) the bound (baddha). The last class includes both those who are eligible for release (muktiyogya) and those who are not eligible for it. These latter are either those intended for hell or the blinding darkness (tamoyogya) or those who are bound to the circuit of saṁsāra for all time (nityasaṁsāriṇaḥ). While some are preordained for salvation by their inherent aptitude, others are destined for hell, while a third class keeps revolving on the wheels of saṁsāra from eternity to eternity, now enjoying, now suffering, in endless alternation. This threefold classification is based on the three guṇas. The sāttvika soul goes to heaven, the rājasa revolves in saṁsāra, while the tāmasa falls into hell. The living beings are divided into a number of classes, gods (devas), men, animals and plants. A fixed gradation dependent on distinctions (tāratamya) of souls is worked out on an elaborate scale. Even among the souls who are entitled to salvation, no two souls possess the same degree of eligibility. In the celestial hierarchy, Brahmā and Vāyu occupy the most prominent places. At Viṣṇu's command, Brahmā creates the world. He is also the greatest teacher and the first exponent of Madhva's philosophy, which is also called Brahmasaṁpradāya. Vāyu is the mediator between God and the souls. He helps the souls to gain saving knowledge and obtain release. He is also called the dearest image (pratimā preyasī) or the son of God (hareḥ sutaḥ).[4] It is not right to hold that the souls are Brahman. The perfect and the imperfect souls cannot merge together.

XI

The World of Nature

Material products are the objects of the inanimate world and form the bodies and organs of all beings. They all

[1] ii. 3. 31.

[2] Madhva on B.S., ii. 3. 19.

[3] ii. 3. 41–42. Even the rise of dreams is assigned to the will of God (iii. 2. 3 and 5).

[4] Madhva is regarded by his followers as the incarnation of Vāyu, who manifested himself in previous lives as Hanumān and Bhīma.

originate from the primary matter, prakṛti, and return to it in course of time. Though prakṛti appears to be homogeneous, it is really composed of different principles in a subtle state. It develops into the perceptible universe when worked up by God and the souls. God moulds forms out of prakṛti, which is the material cause and in which he exists himself in various forms.[1] Before we get from the unmanifested prakṛti to the well developed forms of creation, we have twenty-four transitional products of creation which are mahat, ahaṁkāra buddhi, manas, ten senses, five sense-objects and the five great elements. These exist in the primordial prakṛti in subtle forms before their evolution.

The three aspects of prakṛti are presided over by the three forms of Lakṣmī, Śrī, Bhū, and Durgā. Avidyā is a form of prakṛti of which there are two kinds, jīvācchādika, or that which obscures the spiritual powers of the jīva, and paramācchādika, or that which screens off the Supreme from the jīva's view. These two forms of avidyā are positive principles formed out of the substance of prakṛti.

XII

God and the World

Madhva rejects all attempts to reduce the world of souls and nature to a mere illusion or an emanation of God, and sets forth an absolute dualism. The individual soul is dependent (paratantra) on God, since it is unable to exist without the energising support of the universal spirit, even as the tree cannot live and thrive without its sap. Even Lakṣmī, the consort of Viṣṇu, though supreme and eternal, is dependent on God. She is the presiding deity over prakṛti, which is the material cause of the world. Īśvara somehow energises prakṛti, which forms no part of his being. Prakṛti somehow lends itself to the control of Īśvara.

Madhva comes into conflict with many scriptural passages, which he strains to make them yield a dualism. Taking the

[1] i. 4. 25.

great text, "Tat tvam asi" ("That art thou"). Madhva argues that it does not declare any identity between God and the soul. It only states that the soul has for its essence qualities similar to those of God.[1] This is also the meaning of passages which declare that the soul is a portion of the Lord.[2] He sometimes reads the passage in a different way. Sa ātmā tat tvam asi, is read as sa ātmā atat tvam asi. "That ātman, thou art not."[3] Regarding the text, "ayam ātmā Brahma," Madhva says that it is either a simple eulogy of the jīvātman or it is a subject for meditation. It is also suggested that it is a pūrvapakṣa to be overthrown. Madhva uses the etymological meanings of Ātman and Brahman to explain away the passages which identify the individual and the universal self. The Ātman is Brahman, since it grows (vardhanaśīlaḥ) or since it penetrates everywhere (atanaśīlaḥ).

The supremacy of God introduces order and unity into the universe, in spite of ultimate differences. Through the category of viśeṣa, which distinguishes a quality from a substance, a part from whole, the one and the many are brought into relation.[4] Viśesa or particularity is numerically infinite, since it abides in eternal and non-eternal things and belongs to positive and negative being. One kind of negative being is distinguished from another by means of viśeṣa. But how can one viśeṣa be distinguished from another? If it is through another viśeṣa, then we are faced with infinite regress. So viśeṣa is said to be self-determined. By means of the category of viśeṣa, it will be possible for us to account for the world of distinctions without assuming the latter as ultimate. It is through the functioning of viśeṣa that we have difference or bheda. If viśeṣa is different from the Supreme, it breaks the integrity of the Supreme; if it is non-different from it, we cannot call it viśeṣa.

[1] ii. 3. 29.

[2] B.G., xv. 7.

[3] S.B.H., Bṛh. Up., p. 114. See also Chān., vi. 8. 7 This passage is also regarded as equivalent to tvam tadīyo 'si, or tvam tasyāsi. See also *Tattvamuktāvali*, J.R.A.S., N.S., xv.

[4] *Nyāyāmṛta*, vol. iii, p. 137.

XIII

Ethics and Religion

It is knowledge that produces the feeling of absolute dependence on God and love for him.[1] A correct knowledge of all things, material and spiritual, leads to a knowledge of God, which naturally results in the love for God. Towards the close of his *Tattvaviveka*, Madhva says: "Surely *he* finds release from saṁsāra who understands that all this limited existence is ever under the control of Hari."

A sound moral life is a preliminary for salvation. The moral rules are to be obeyed and obligations fulfilled without any desire or claim for fruit. A virtuous life helps us to win insight into truth. We can gain true knowledge from a study of the Vedas, which must be carried out under the guidance of a proper teacher Each individual has in him the capacity for the perception of a particular aspect of Brahman. The wise teacher will have to take account of these differences, for it is said "by the perception for which one is fit, final release is obtained, not by any other means."[2] Only gods and men of the three upper classes are allowed to study the Vedas, while women and Śūdras may draw the requisite knowledge from the Purāṇas and the Smṛtis. Madhva allows to all who can understand it the right to study the Vedānta.[3] Meditation, or the act of absorbing oneself as often and as intensely as possible in the glory of God, is advised. In the act of meditation the soul can by divine grace arrive at a direct intuitive realisation of God (aparokṣajñāna). When the soul has this vision, as steady as the sun and not merely as swift as lightning, its fetters fall off and it is said to be redeemed.

God cannot be approached directly. Vāyu is the mediator. The theory of grace adopted by Madhva reminds us of the Augustinian view. A man can never deserve to be saved. It is only through grace that he can be redeemed. God is not forced by any considerations of merit. He simply elects some for salvation and others for the opposite state. The divine

[1] iii. 3. 49. [2] M.B. iii. 3. 53. [3] i. 1. 1.

will sets men free or casts them into bondage. But the Hindu tradition does not allow Madhva to hold that God's choice is arbitrary, unconditioned and groundless. Though, in a sense, the states of the soul are brought about by Brahman,[1] it is also admitted that the grace of the Lord is proportioned to the intensity of our devotion.[2] Our conduct cannot by itself lead us to freedom; God must co-operate. The Supreme who is non-manifested cannot be made manifested by the force of our efforts. He reveals himself when pleased with our devotion.[3] The grace of God responds to the faith of the worshipper. Different sects of the followers of Madhva emphasise, in different degrees, divine predestination and human freedom. Insight, devotion, performance of rites and ceremonies, are insisted on. Service of the Supreme consists in branding the body with Viṣṇu's symbols, giving the Lord's names to sons and others and worshipping him in word (veracity, sacred study), act (charity) and thought (mercy and faith). Worship of God is the indispensable, preliminary condition for obtaining divine grace. Works done with knowledge help us in the upward progress. Rites and sacrifices, as well as pilgrimages, are recommended. Animal sacrifices are forbidden, and those who undertake sacrifices are called upon to substitute animals made of flour for the living ones.

The soul may continue the bodily existence so long as its prārabdhakarma is operative, but when it departs from the body, it is freed absolutely. Absolute liberation and embodied life are not compatible. The author of the *Nyāyāmṛta* argues that he who has the vision of the truth but not the grace of God necessary to effect freedom, continues to live in the flesh. This is jīvanmukti. Complete freedom can be achieved only through the grace of God.

Release, according to the *Bhāgavata*, consists in a restoration to the pure spiritual existence (svarūpeṇa vyavasthitiḥ), after casting off the unessential forms (anyathārūpam).[4] It is fellowship with God, and not identification with him. If the distinction between the jīva and the Lord is not perceived, as in deep sleep or destruction of the world, it is not a state

[1] iii. 2. 9. [2] iii. 2. 20–21. [3] iii. 2. 23–27.

[4] i. 1. 17. According to Madhva, mukti is svasvayogyasvasvarūpānandābhivyakti.

of release.[1] The freed retain their consciousness of individuality both in pralaya and creation. In the state of release, we have the absence of pain as well as the presence of positive enjoyment. But the soul is not capable of rising into equality with God. It is entitled only to serve him. If salvation is said to be becoming one with Brahman, it is only in a qualified sense that it has a vision of Brahman. Absolute one-ness is not intended by the passages which declare that "he who sees Brahman becomes Brahman."[2] The released are all of one will and purpose.[3] They have, no doubt, real desires; but their desires are one with those of the supreme Lord. They perform meditation at their pleasure.[4] They realise their wishes without any effort.[5] They assume a body of pure matter (śuddhasattva) of their own accord, though this body is not the product of karma; nor do they develop any attachment to the bodies they assume. Even if they do not assume such a body, they can experience bliss as we do in the case of dreams.[6]

While those who attain release escape from the world of saṁsāra, others pass on at death to a different existence, which is determined by the law of karma. At death the coarse body dissolves into its component parts, while the soul, clad in a body of fine imperceptible matter, together with the senses, goes either to the celestial regions, temporary hells, or gets into the luminous regions of the moon, where it stays for a time in accordance with its merit. Then it gets into the womb of the mother, where the soul's new earthly body is produced.[7] Thus rebirth continues till the soul develops love or hatred for God to the fullest extent, when it is released or cast into hell.

XIV

Critical Reflections

The fact of knowledge leads us to an organic conception of the world, but does not justify the division of the world

[1] S.B.H., Bṛh. Up., p. 118. [2] *Tattvamuktāvali*, p. 55–56. [3] iv. 2. 16. [4] iii. 3. 27. [5] iv. 4. 8. [6] iv. 4. 10–16. [7] iii. 1. 29.

into God, souls and objects externally related to one another. Nor can we understand the relation of the so-called essence or the individual soul to the universal principles operating in it. If God creates, if the beginning of the world-process is the result of the desire of the divine self, we may, no doubt, be able to account for creation. But the difficulty remains that whatever feels a want or has a desire is imperfect and limited. God, on such a view, cannot be regarded as the supreme perfection. The nature of the dependence of the world on God is not clearly brought out. If God were really independent, then there must not be anything to limit him from without. A dualism makes the independence of God impossible. Madhva conceives the infinite in an abstract manner, and is therefore not able to see any unity between it and the finite. If Brahman is co-eternal with the world, what is the relation between the two ? If it is also a co-eternal relation, is the supreme spirit bound to objects other than itself ? We cannot say that it is the nature of the supreme spirit to stand related to the individual souls, since the former does not contain the reason of the latter's existence. It is difficult to believe that the essence of God involves a relation to objects whose existence it does not necessitate. It is equally difficult to hold that the relation is a non-essential or accidental one, for an eternal accident, which subjects unborn spirits to itself and binds down the Supreme also, cannot be a mere accident. If the souls and matter depend on the ultimate Brahman, they cannot be regarded as substances. In the highest sense, the term "substance" can be predicated only of a *res completa*, that which is complete in itself, determined by itself and capable of being explained entirely from itself. Madhva recognises that such a reality is possessed only by the supreme spirit. All else is produced from Viṣṇu, the supreme spirit, directly or indirectly. Even his consort Śrī and his son Vāyu are entirely dependent on him. But the admission of Viṣṇu as the supreme reality of the world does not involve the denial of derivative and dependent being to other objects.

Again, the theory of election is fraught with great danger to ethical life. The predestinarian scheme of thought puts an excessive strain on the other parts of Madhva's theology.

The moral character of God is much compromised and the qualities of divine justice and divine love are emptied of all meaning and value. Individual effort loses its point, since whether one believes oneself to be the elect or the non-elect, one is bound to lapse into indifferentism and apathy. If we do not know what we are destined for, we may work on to purify ourselves. In the absence of knowledge we may at least have hope. But this theory will overwhelm us in despair and raise the question : Is not God playing a practical joke on us, when he implants in us a desire for heaven while making us unfit for it ? Unless we are in a position to believe in the spiritual possibilities of every one who bears the human form divine, we cannot have a really useful ethics. In certain passages Madhva says that the individual soul is of the form of knowledge and bliss, though it is not conscious of this nature, while God is eternally conscious that he is of the nature of knowledge and bliss. The distinction, therefore, between God and man, however great, is not one of kind. The essence of each soul may perhaps represent its degree of obscuration, but it is difficult to prove that there are eternal essences persisting in souls even when they are released. In all this we are simply transferring the distinctions of experience to the kingdom of God.

XV

Nimbārka

Nimbārka was a Telugu Brahmin of the Vaiṣṇava faith who lived some time after Rāmānuja and prior to Madhva, about the eleventh century A.D. He wrote a short commentary on the *Brahma Sūtra* called *Vedāntapārijātasaurabha*, as well as ten verses, *Daśaślokī*, elucidating his view of the distinctness of Jīva, Īśvara and Jagat. His theory is called dvaitādvaita, or dualistic non-dualism. Keśavakāśmīrin wrote a commentary on the *Bhagavadgītā* called *Tattvaprakāśikā*, in defence of Nimbārka's general view. His commentary on the *Brahma Sūtra* develops the theory of the transformation (pariṇāma) of Brahman. A distinction is made between the independent reality of Puruṣottama and the dependent realities of jīva and prakṛti. While both jīva and Īśvara are self-conscious, the former is limited, while the latter is not. While the jīva is the enjoyer (bhoktṛ), the world is the enjoyed (bhogya), and Īśvara or God is the supreme controller (niyantṛ).

According to Nimbārka's teaching the jīva is of the form of knowledge (jñānasvarūpa), though not in Śaṁkara's sense. It is knowledge as well as the possessor of knowledge, even as the sun is light as well as the source of light. The relation of soul to its attribute is that of the dharmin (the qualified) to the dharma (the qualification). It is one of difference as well as non-difference. Between the qualification and the qualified there is no absolute identity, but only the non-perception of the difference. Though jīva is atomic in size, on account of its possession of the omnipresent quality of knowledge, it is able to experience the pleasures and the pains throughout the body.[1] The jīva is the agent of activity (kartṛ). The scriptural texts which deny activity are intended to bring out the dependent character of the activity of the jīva. The jīva has no independent (svatantra) knowledge or activity. Ānanda or delight pertains to the jīva in all its states. The jīva continues to exist in dreamless sleep and the state of release. As Īśvara is the governor, the jīva in all its states has the nature of being governed (niyāmyatva). The number of jīvas is infinite, though they are all sustained by the supreme spirit.

The inanimate world has three principal categories (tattvas), which are: (1) aprākṛta or what is not derived from the primordial prakṛti, such as the stuff of the divine body akin to Rāmānuja's śuddhasattva, which is the basis of the nitya-vibhūti of Īśvara; (2) prakṛti, or what is derived from prakṛti with its three guṇas; and (3) kāla, or time. Prakṛti and kāla are the basic principles of cosmic existence. These three categories are also eternal like the individual souls.

The eternal nature of Īśvara is to govern (niyantṛtva). Nimbārka and Keśava refute the predicateless character of Brahman and attribute to the latter good and auspicious qualities.[2] The supreme spirit is identified by Nimbārka with Kṛṣṇa, and is regarded as possessing all auspicious qualities and exempt from the faults of egoism, ignorance, passion and attachment. He has the four forms (vyūhas), and also mani-

[1] ii. 3. 25.

[2] Keśava says: 'Nāpi nirdharmakam brahma ᴄasya jñānakriyādīnāṁ svābhāvikaśaktīnāṁ śāstrasiddhatvāt" (i. 1. 5). Again; "Ānandamaya-śabdanirdista ātmā brahmaiva" (i. 1. 13).

fests himself in the avatāras, or incarnations. He is the material and the efficient cause of the universe. He is the material cause, since creation means the manifestation of his powers (śakti) of cit and acit in their subtle forms. He is the efficient cause of the universe, since he brings about the union of the individual souls with their respective karmas and their results and the proper instruments for experiencing them.

The universe cannot be dismissed as a mere illusion, since it is a manifestation (pariṇāma) of what is contained subtly in the nature of God. Nimbārka criticises the vivarta (illusion) theory of the world, and argues that, if the world were not real, it could not be superimposed on another.

The relation of the three principles of jīva, the world and God, is not one of absolute identity or non-distinction, since such a view would contradict numberless passages of the Upaniṣads which insist on difference and will also involve confusion between the natures and attributes of the different principles. Nor can it be said that the three principles are absolutely distinct, since this would be to fly in the face of the monistic evidence of the Upaniṣads. Were the supreme spirit absolutely distinct from the individual soul and the world, it could not be omnipresent. It would be as limited as the individual soul or the world, and could not, therefore, be regarded as their governor. The suggestion that non-difference is the reality while difference is due to upādhis or limitations cannot be accepted, since it would be to subject Brahman to conditions. On such a view, Brahman would cease to be pure and become subject to faults, and would experience pleasure, pain and the like, and all this would be contrary to the accepted nature of Brahman. So Nimbārka concludes that both difference and non-difference are real. The soul and the world are different from Brahman, since they possess natures and attributes different from those of Brahman. They are not different, since they cannot exist by themselves and depend absolutely on Brahman. The difference signifies distinct and dependent existence (paratantrasattābhāvaḥ), and non-difference signifies the impossibility of independent xistence (svatantrasattā'bhāvah). In the light of this ioctrine of difference-non-difference, the famous text, " Tat tvam asi," is interpreted. "Tat" signifies the eternal omnipresent Brahman; "tvam" refers to the individual soul, whose existence depends on Brahman; and "asi" brings out the relation between the two, which is one of difference compatible with non-difference. Such a relation subsists between the sun and its rays or the fire and its sparks. Though souls and matter are distinct from God, they are yet intimately connected with him, as waves with water or coils of a rope with the rope itself. They are both distinct and non-distinct from Brahman. We need not regard the distincts as mutually exclusive and absolutely cut off from each other. Difference and identity are both equally real, and what is different is also identical.

Yet the individual souls and the world are not self-sufficient, but are guided by Īśvara.[1] In pralaya, these two get absorbed into the nature of Īśvara, who contains the subtle forms of jīva and jagat. Between the periods of dissolution and re-creation, all existence, conscious and unconscious, dwells in him in a subtle state. Through Brahman's śakti, or energy, the world is produced where each separate soul finds fit embodiment.

Nimbārka does not accept the theory that the conscious and the unconscious worlds form, together with Brahman, a composite personality, which is the material cause of the world, so far as the body of that personality goes. According to him, the śakti of Brahman is the material cause of the world, and the changes of śakti do not touch the integrity of Brahman. What Rāmānuja calls the "body" of Brahman is the śakti of Nimbārka. God does not stand in need of materials to construct the world. He is all-powerful, and by his mere will he is able to create the world.[2] Brahman is thus both the efficient and the material cause of the world. The world is identical with Brahman, and depends on him for its becoming and its power to act; and yet, in a sense, it is distinct from Brahman. The usual theory which traces the evolution of nature to the three guṇas is accepted.[3]

The supreme spirit is conceived as free from all defects, a storehouse of all beneficent attributes, possessed of a

[1] *Daśaślokī*, 7. [2] i. I. 19. [3] *Daśaślokī*, 3.

heavenly body, full of beauty and tenderness, sweetness and charm.[1] Souls are infinite in number and are atomic is size. Each soul is a ray of Brahman individualised.[2] The theory attempts to avoid the affirmation of an absolute identity, where attributes are confused and distinctions abolished, and, at the same time, tries to escape from mere pluralism, which would impair the omnipresence of Brahman and limit his nature and sovereignty.

The pure nature of the jīva is obscured by its karma, which is the result of avidyā, which is beginningless, yet through the grace of God can be terminated. Prapatti, or complete submission to God, is the way to deliverance. Those who possess this attitude of prapannas are favoured by God, who engenders in them bhakti or devotion, which eventually results in brahmasākṣātkāra or realisation of God. Bhakti involves a knowledge of the supreme reality, the nature of the individual soul, the fruit of divine grace or mokṣa, which is an uninterrupted realisation of the nature and attributes of Brahman, resulting in the absolute destruction of all selfishness and ignorance, and the nature of the hindrances to God-realisation, such as the erroneous identification of the soul with the body, the senses or the mind, dependence on another than God, violation of or indifference to his commandments, and confusion of God with ordinary beings, the sense of freedom and joy born of true devotion. In Nimbārka Kṛṣṇa and Rādhā[3] take the place of Nārāyaṇa and his consort. Bhakti is not meditation (upāsana), but love and devotion. The grace of God is ever ready to lift up the helpless and make them see the truth of things. The worship of other gods is forbidden. Ethical rules, prescribed in the śāstras, are insisted on. Karma is said to be the means for the acquisition of brahmajñāna,[4] carrying with it devotion.[5]

While both Rāmānuja and Nimbārka regard difference and non-difference as necessary, and treat animate and inanimate existences as attributes of Brahman, Rāmānuja emphasises more the principle of identity. For Nimbārka the two are equally real and have the same importance. Again, Rāmānuja regards the individual souls (cit) and the

[1] *Daśaślokī*, 4.
[2] Commentary on the B.S., ii. 3. 42.
[3] *Daśaślokī*, 5 and 8.
[4] i. 1. 4.
[5] i. 1. 7.

world (acit) as the attributes (viśeṣaṇas or prakāras) of Brahman; and his view emphasises the non-duality of the supreme Lord, qualified by the individual souls and the world.[1] Nimbārka disputes this view on the ground that the presence of a body does not necessarily imply the possession of attributes; for an attribute has for its object the distinction of the thing which possesses it from others which do not possess it. If cit and acit are the attributes of Brahman, then, what is that reality from which Brahman is distinguished by the possession of these marks?

XVI

Vallabha

Vallabha (1401 A.D.) is a Telugu Brahmin of South India, who migrated to the north and developed the views of Viṣṇusvāmin, who belonged to the thirteenth century. He accepts the authority not only of the Upaniṣads, the *Bhagavadgītā* and the *Brahma Sūtra*, but also of the *Bhāgavata Purāṇa*. In his works, *Aṇubhāṣya*, *Siddhāntarahasya* and *Bhāgavata-ṭīkāsubodhini*,[2] he offers a theistic interpretation of the Vedānta, which differs from those of Śaṁkara and Rāmānuja. His view is called Śuddhādvaita, or pure non-dualism,[3] and declares that the whole world is real and is subtly Brahman. The individual souls and the inanimate world are in essence one with Brahman. Vallabha admits that jīva, kāla or time, and prakṛti or māyā, are eternal existences; they are referred to the being of Brahman and have no separate existence. Those who accept the force of māyā as the explanation of the world are not pure Advaitins, since they admit a second to Brahman.[4] While Śaṁkara traces the world to Brahman through the force of māyā, Vallabha holds that Brahman can create the world without any connection with such a principle as māyā. In his view the śāstra is the final authority, and our reason cannot protest against its dictates.[5] God is

[1] Cidacidviśiṣṭaparameśvarādvaita.

[2] Giridhara's *Śuddhādvaitamārtāṇḍa* and Bālakṛṣṇa's *Prameyaratnārṇava* belong to this sect.

[3] As distinct from Śaṁkara's Kevalādvaita.

[4] i. 1. 6.

[5] i. 1. 20.

saccidānanda, and has qualities; the śruti passages which declare that he has no qualities mean merely that he has not the ordinary qualities.[1] God is personified as Kṛṣṇa, when he is endowed with the qualities of wisdom (jñāna) and action (kriyā). He is the creator of the world, and we need not suppose that he should possess a physical body as worldly agents do, since what applies to us need not apply to the transcendent God. By the mere force of his will he creates the whole world. Not only is he kartā or agent, but also enjoyer or bhokta.[2] Though he has no need to assume a body, he appears in various forms to please his devotees.[3] The highest, when associated with action only, is yajñarūpa, who can be propitiated by karmas, as stated in the Brāhmaṇas; when associated with wisdom, it is Brahman, and can be approached through jñāna, as stated in the Upaniṣads. Kṛṣṇa the Supreme has to be worshipped according to the principles of the *Gītā* and the *Bhāgavata*.

In human and animal souls the quality of ānanda is suppressed, while in matter consciousness is also suppressed. Brahman becomes whatever it wills by the evolution (āvirbhāva) and involution (tirobhāva) of its qualities. The jīva is atomic in size,[4] is one with Brahman, and constitutes a part of it.[5] When the ānanda of Brahman is obscured, we have the jīva. Though its production is only a manifestation, it is as real and eternal as Brahman. Three kinds of jīvas are distinguished. The pure (śuddha) jīvas are those whose lordly qualities (aiśvarya) are not obscured by the force of ignorance (avidyā). The mundane (saṁsārin) jīvas are those which are caught in the meshes of avidyā, and experience birth and death by reason of their connection with gross and subtle bodies. The liberated (mukta) jīvas are those which are freed from the bonds of saṁsāra through insight into truth (vidyā). When the soul attains release, it recovers its suppressed qualities and becomes one with God. The inanimate world is also filled with Brahman (brahmātmaka). In it the two qualities of Brahman, knowledge and bliss, are obscured, and what remains is pure sattva or existence. Since it is Brahman that is manifested in the form of the world, the

[1] See his commentary on B.S., iii. 2. 22. [2] i. 1. 1.
[3] i. 1. 20–21. [4] ii. 3. 19. [5] ii. 3. 43.

latter is regarded as the effect of Brahman (brahmakārya). Creation and destruction of the world are only the manifestation and non-manifestation of the Supreme who puts on these forms. Brahman becomes a product and is apprehended in the state of creation, while in destruction the world returns to its original form, and ceases to be an object of perception. The world is therefore as eternal and real as Brahman himself, and its creation and destruction are due to the power (śakti) of Brahman. The world cannot be regarded as an illusory appearance; nor is it essentially different from Brahman. The relation of cause and effect is one of absolute identity.[1] The universe in truth is Brahman. Brahman manifests himself of his own will, as the individual souls and the world, without undergoing any change in his essential nature. He is the material as well as the efficient cause of the world.[2] The charges of partiality and cruelty cannot be urged against Brahman, since the difference of the jīvas from Brahman is admitted by Vallabha. He holds that the jīva, freed from the fetters of māyā, is one with Brahman.

Vallabha looks upon God as the whole and the individual as part; but, as the individual is of identical essence with God, there is no real difference between the two. The analogy of sparks to fire is employed to great purpose. The individual soul is not the Supreme clouded by the force of avidyā, but is itself Brahman, with one attribute rendered imperceptible. The soul is both a doer and an enjoyer. It is atomic in size, though pervading the whole body by its quality of intelligence, even as sandal-wood makes its presence felt where it does not exist, by its scent. For Rāmānuja, who accepts one ultimate substantive reality, the difference between God and soul is never destroyed. Rāmānuja relates God and the soul as whole and parts, where the parts are really different moments of the whole. His view of sāmānādhikaraṇya or viśeṣaṇaviśeṣyabhāva points to the coinherence of many parts in the same whole. Vallabha, on the other hand, gives us something like Schelling's *neutrum*, where the differences are abolished, while Rāmānuja's view is more like Hegel's.

[1] Prāgabhāva, or prior non-existence, is the causal condition; pradhvaṁsābhāva is but disappearance of the effect.

[2] i. 1. 4.

The world of māyā is not regarded as unreal,[1] since māyā is nothing else than a power which Īśvara of his free will produces. "Brahman is the efficient and the material cause of the universe. He is not only the creator of the universe but is the universe itself."[2] He accepts the *Bṛhadāraṇyaka* account,[3] that Brahman desired to become many, and himself became the multitude of individual souls and the world. A desire for self-expression is innate in Brahman. Māyā, according to Vallabha, is the power of Īśvara, through which he brings about the evolution and the dissolution of the world. Māyā is different from avidyā, which is responsible for the obscuration of the unity of things and the production of the consciousness of difference.[4] Vallabha does not admit an inert prakṛti which is energised by Brahman. Though Brahman in himself is not known, he is known when he manifests himself through the world.

Saṁsāra, however, is unreal. The soul is right in regarding the world as real, but is wrong when it ascribes to it plurality. The world is true, though our experience (pratīti) of it is wrong. We do not realise that the world is but a form of Brahman. The jīva is thus infected with a wrong view of the nature of the world. To those who have attained to the truth, the world appears as Brahman. To those who have learnt the truth from the scriptures, it appears as both Brahman and māyā, *i.e.* something other than Brahman, though they know that the former is real and the latter not. The ignorant make no distinction between the reality of Brahman and the unreality of the plural appearances which set themselves forth as objective and independent. Avidyā is located in the mind of man. Vallabha thus does not accept the view of the unreality of the world as such. If the world is unreal, we cannot even say that it is one with Brahman, since a relation of identity cannot exist between a real entity and an unreal appearance. There is a possibility of deception, though it is not divinely conditioned.

The jīva bound by māyā cannot attain salvation except through the grace of God. Bhakti is the chief means of salvation, though jñāna is also useful. All sins are put away

[1] *Aṇubhāṣya* on i. 1. 4.

[2] *Aṇubhāṣya*, i. 1. 4.

[3] i. 4. 3.

[4] See *Śuddhādvaitamārtāṇḍa*.

if we have true faith in God, a principle that was much exaggerated in practice. Vallabha deprecated all kinds of self-mortification. The body is the temple of God, and there is no meaning in attempting to destroy it. Karmas precede knowledge of the Supreme, and are present even when this knowledge is gained. The liberated perform all karmas.[1] The highest goal is not mukti or liberation, but rather eternal service of Kṛṣṇa and participation in his sports in the celestial Bṛndāvana. Vallabha distinguishes the transcendent consciousness of Brahman from Puruṣottama.[2] The souls, delivered from the trammels of life, are of different kinds. There are those who have freed themselves from previous subjection, like Sanaka, and those who dwell in the city of God, where they attain freedom through the grace of God. There are others who resort to bhakti and develop perfect love and become the associates of God. Vallabha lays great stress on a life of unqualified love to God.

The relation between Brahman on the one side and the individual souls (jīva) and the inanimate nature (jaḍa) on the other, is one of pure identity, even as the relation of whole (aṁśin) and part (aṁśa) is. While the difference is subordinated by Vallabha, non-difference alone is said to be real. He interprets " Tat tvam asi " (" That art thou ") as literally true, while Rāmānuja and Nimbārka take it in a figurative sense. When the soul attains bliss, and the inanimate world both consciousness and bliss, the difference between Brahman and these will lapse—a position which Rāmānuja does not accept.

XVII

The Caitanya Movement

The Vaiṣṇavism of South India did not pay much attention to the glorification of the Bṛndāvana līlā, though some of the Āḷvārs refer to Kṛṣṇa's sports with the gopis. In the north, however, the case was different. In Nimbārka, Rādhā, the beloved mistress, is not simply the chief of the gopis but is the eternal consort of Kṛṣṇa. The writings of Jayadeva, the author of *Gītagovinda*, Vidyāpati, Umāpati and Caṇḍi Dās (fourteenth century), show the growing influence of

[1] *Aṇubhāṣya*, i. 1. 1.

[2] *Ibid.*, iv. 3. 27.

the Rādhā-Kṛṣṇa cult in Bengal and Bihar, thanks to the influence of the Śākta system of thought and practice. Trained in such an atmosphere, Caitanya, the great Vaiṣṇava teacher (fifteenth century), was attracted by the account of Kṛṣṇa in the *Viṣṇu Purāṇa*, *Harivaṁśa*, the *Bhāgavata* and the *Brahmavaivarta Purāṇas*, and by his personality and character gave a new form to the Vaiṣṇava faith. His breadth of view and democratic sympathies gave him a large following, though the orthodox were much disturbed by his startling ways. He accepted converts from Islam freely, and one of the earliest of his disciples was a Moslem fakir, who attained to great fame and sanctity in the sect under the name of Haridās. His disciples, Rūpa and Sanātana, were renegade converts to Islam and outcasts from the Hindu society, whom Caitanya welcomed back into the fold. Jīva Gosvāmi (sixteenth century) and much later Baladeva, furnished the philosophical basis for the sect. The philosophical classics of the school are Jīva's *Satsandarbha* and his own commentary on it, *Sarvasaṁvādinī*, and Baladeva's *Govindabhāṣya* on the *Brahma Sūtra*. The latter's *Prameyaratnāvali* is also a popular work. These writers are influenced considerably by the views of Rāmānuja and Madhva.[1] They admit the five principles of God, souls, māyā or prakṛti, and svarūpaśakti, with its two elements of jñāna or knowledge, śuddhatattva or pure matter, and kāla, or time.

On the question of the theory of knowledge, there is not much that is peculiar to the school. The traditional account of the sources of knowledge, including Vedic testimony, is accepted. Jīva argues that there is such a state of consciousness as simple apprehension, which is later developed into determinate knowledge. Non-relational immediate experience precedes determinate cognition. The former is indeterminate (nirvikalpa) cognition. The determinate is contained potentially in it. It is the fact given in indeterminate perception that is analysed and understood in the determinate. It follows that indeterminate cognition is a fact of consciousness; and the intuition, where relations seem to be absent, is of this kind. Jīva does not believe in a universal which includes all differences.[2] We have first the knowledge of the universal as such and then the universal as qualified. The intuition of Brahman, pure and simple, is, for Jīva, an undoubted fact of consciousness, though it requires to be transcended.

The ultimate reality is Viṣṇu, the personal God of love and grace, possessing the usual attributes of sat, cit and ānanda. He is nirguṇa, in the sense that he is free from the

[1] *Prameyaratnāvali*, p. 8.
[2] *Bhāgavatsandarbha*, p. 55.

qualities of prakṛti and saguṇa, since he has the qualities of omniscience, omnipotence, etc. These qualities are bound to him by the relation of svarūpasaṁbandha. They express the nature of Brahman and inhere in him.[1] He is the source, support and end of the world, the material and the efficient cause of the universe.[2] He is the efficient cause through his higher energy (parā śakti),[3] and material cause through his other energies, called aparā śakti and avidyāśakti. His former nature is unchangeable, while his latter is subject to modifications. The chief character of God is love[4] and the power of joy. The incarnations are one with the Supreme and not parts, as the individuals are.[5] God assumes infinite forms, of which the chief is that of Kṛṣṇa, whose supreme delight is in love. Kṛṣṇa, when identified with the Supreme, has three chief powers, cit, māyā and jīva. By the first he maintains his nature as intelligence and will, by the second the whole creation is produced, and by the third the souls. The highest manifestation of the cit power of Kṛṣṇa is the power of delight (hlādinī). Rādhā is the essence of this delight-giving power.[6] According to Jīva, God is one without a second. He is Brahman when viewed in himself and Bhagavān when viewed as the creator of the world. The former is abstract and the latter concrete. Jīva holds that the latter is the more real. According to Baladeva, the Supreme is called Hari, his Majesty and magnificance are personified as Nārāyaṇa, and his beauty and ecstasy as Kṛṣṇa.

The universe and its creatures have come into being through the powers of God. They are dependent on him, though separate and distinct from him. They are neither one with God nor different from him. An incomprehensible difference-

[1] Baladeva, after Madhva, admits the doctrine of viśeṣa, though he confines it to the svarūpaśakti and its modification; since the distinctions of the world are established facts and do not require any viśeṣa to distinguish them.

[2] *Ibid.*, i. 4. 24.

[3] Identified with Śrī. See Baladeva, iii. 3. 40 and 42.

[4] Prītyātmā, iv. 1. 1.

[5] A distinction is made between svāṁśa, or a manifestation identical with the original, and vibhinnāṁśa, or a part separate from the original. See Baladeva, ii. 3. 47.

[6] Cp. "Kṛṣṇasvarūpiṇī paramānandarūpiṇī" (*Brahmavaivarta Purāṇa*, v. 4. 17).

non-difference [1] is the truth of things. The world is real and not illusory; it is called māyā on account of its nature, since it attracts men to itself and away from God. The servant of God becomes, through the power of māyā, the slave of the world.

The soul is different from the Lord, who is its ruler. God is omnipresent while the soul is of atomic size.[2] God's svarūpaśakti, according to Jīva, supports his jīva śakti (also called tatasthaśakti) by which the souls are created. This latter in its turn supports māyāśakti (or bahiraṅgaśakti). None of these can exist apart from God At the time of creation, the Supreme remembers the constitution of the world immediately preceding the pralaya and desires to "become manifold," *i.e.* give separate existence to the enjoying souls and the objects of enjoyment merged in him. He creates the entire world from the great principle of mahat down to the cosmic egg and Brahmā. He then manifests the Vedas in the same order and arrangement as they had had before, and communicates them mentally to Brahmā, to whom other stages of creation are assigned. Through the help of the Vedas, Brahmā remembers the archetypal forms, and creates objects as in the previous existence. It follows that the Vedas, when they refer to Indra, etc., refer to types which do not perish, though the individuals do.[3] While Rāmānuja regards the souls and matter as the adjectives (viśeṣaṇas) of God, Jīva and Baladeva regard them as the manifestations of God's energy. The latter are averse to making unconscious prakṛti a predicate of God, which may introduce an element of discord into his nature. So Jīva makes prakṛti the outer energy (śakti) of God, which is not directly related to him, though under his control. Baladeva identifies māyā with prakṛti, which is set in motion by the mere sight (īkṣaṇa) of God.

The souls become fettered by the bonds of the world through the power of māyā, which makes them forget their real nature. The force of karma can be overcome if we have bhakti.[4] By the development of love (ruci) for Kṛṣṇa, we

[1] Acintyabhedābheda.

[2] Baladeva, ii. 2. 41.

[3] Baladeva, i. 3. 30.

[4] Caitanya accepted the usual stages of bhakti: (1) śānta, or tranquil meditation on God; (2) dāsya, or active service of God; (3) sakhya, or friendship; (4) vātsalya, or parental tenderness; (5) mādhurya, or sweetness

can have intuition of the divine. God's affection for his creatures is said to be brought out in his love for Rādhā. It is the desire of the creator that his creatures should cleave to him only in the hope of salvation. Kāma or sexual love is distinguished from prema or spiritual love. Bhakti is the way to salvation. Study of the Vedas, the *Bhāgavata Purāṇa* and the like, is inculcated. Reverence for the guru is a cardinal feature. In matters of religion it is said that reason is not to be depended upon. The distinctions of caste are ignored. No man or woman is too low for the grace of God. Ethical virtues of mercy towards all creatures, humility, tranquillity, freedom from worldly desires and purity of heart, are emphasised.

Salvation consists in the eternal experience of love (prīti).[1] Souls in heaven realise their status as the servants of God, and are utterly devoted to him. Love is release. Bhakti is the true mukti. Through it bondage to rebirth is broken, and the soul attains to a status of equality with God, though it is never absorbed in God.[2] The intuition of Brahman, as the abstract universal of all existence, is, according to Jīva, the prelude to the intuition of Bhagavān, who is the concrete reality of all existence and life. The former, due to knowledge, is not ultimate. The latter, due to bhakti, can be had only when the body is cast off. Though jīvanmukti is possible regarding the intuition of Brahman, it is of no avail for the love of the Bhagavān.

Jīva attempts to displace the theory of attributes (viśeṣaṇa) advocated by Rāmānuja, by his own theory of energy (śakti). But if God cannot possess an attribute opposed in nature to his being, how can he possess a power or energy which equally contradicts his being? Though some of the writers belonging to this school call themselves the followers of Madhva, in their thought they are really nearer Rāmānuja, since they emphasise identity, even while they admit differences. The latter are traced to the śaktis, which belong to God in an inconceivable

symptomatic of conjugal love. Each stage includes the preceding, so that the last is the most complete. Bhakti literature of Bengal is full of acute analysis of feelings. See Rūpa's *Ujjvalanīlamaṇi*.

[1] Saccidānandaikarase bhaktiyoge tiṣṭhati (*Gopālatāpanī*). See Baladeva, iii. 3. 12.

[2] Baladeva on i. 1. 17.

(acintya) manner. Jīva admits in his *Sarvasaṁvādinī* that we cannot regard God and his powers as either identical or as different.

REFERENCES.

AVALON: Mahānirvāṇa Tantra.
AVALON: Śakti and Śākta.
BARNETT: The Heart of India.
CARPENTER: Mediæval Theism in India.
CHATTERJI: Kashmir Saivism.
MĀDHAVA: S.D.S., V, IX.
MADHVA: Commentaries on the Bhagavadgītā, Brahma Sūtra. Subba Rao's E.T.
NALLASVĀMI PIḶḶAI: Studies in Śaiva Siddhānta.
PADMANĀBHĀCĀRYA: Life and Teachings of Śrī Madhva.
POPE: Tiruvāśagam.
SRINIVASA IYENGAR: Outlines of Indian Philosophy, Chs. II and III.
Śivasūtravimarśinī.

CHAPTER XI

CONCLUSION

The course of Hindu philosophic development—The unity of the different systems—The decline of the philosophic spirit in recent times—Contact with the West—The present situation—Conservatism and radicalism—The future.

I

Philosophical Development

Throughout the history of Indian thought, the ideal of a world behind the ordinary world of human strivings, more real and more intangible, which is the true home of the spirit, has been haunting the Indian race. Man's never-ceasing effort to read the riddle of the sphinx and raise himself above the level of the beast to a moral and spiritual height finds a striking illustration in India. We can watch the struggle for four millenniums (or longer, if the recent archæological finds in Sind and the Punjab, which are withdrawing the shroud that hid the remote past, are to be taken into account). The naïve belief that the world is ruled by the gods of Sun and Sky, who watch from on high the conduct of men, whether it is straight or crooked; the faith that the gods who can be persuaded by prayer or compelled by rites to grant our requests, are only the forms of the one Supreme; the firm conviction that the pure stainless spirit, to know whom is life eternal, is one with the innermost soul of man; the rise of materialism, scepticism and fatalism, and their supersession by the ethical systems of Buddhism and Jainism, with their central doctrine that one can free one-self from all ill only by refraining from all evil, in thought, word and deed—God or no God; the liberal theism of the *Bhagavadgītā*, which endows the all-soul with ethical in addition to metaphysical perfections; the logical scheme of the Nyāya, which furnishes the principal categories of the world of knowledge which are in use even to-day; the Vaiśeṣika interpretation of nature; the Sāṁkhya speculations in science and psychology; the Yoga scheme of the pathway to perfection; the ethical and social regulations of the Mīmāṁsā and the religious interpretations of the Supreme reality, as put forward by Śaṁkara, Rāmānuja, Madhva and Nimbārka, Vallabha and Jīva Gosvāmi—form a remarkable record of philosophical development in the history of the human race. Type succeeds type, school follows on school, in logical sequence. The life of the Indian was ever on the move, shaping itself as it grew, and changing from time to time in relation to its physical, social and cultural contexts. In the early stages the ancient Indians were doing everything for the first time. They had practically no wisdom of the past to fall back upon. They had, moreover, enormous difficulties to contend with, which are now almost things of the past. In spite of these, their achievement in the realm of thought and practice is a considerable one. But the cycle is not complete, and the range of possible forms is not exhausted; for the sphinx still smiles. Philosophy is yet in its infancy.

The survey of Indian thought, as of all thought, impresses one with the mystery and the immensity of existence as well as the beauty and the persistence of the human effort to understand it. The long procession of thinkers struggled hard to add some small piece to the temple of human wisdom, some fresh fragment to the ever incomplete sum of human knowledge. But human speculation falls short of the ideal, which it can neither abandon nor attain. We are far more conscious of the depth of the surrounding darkness than of the power to dispel it possessed by the flickering torches that we have the privilege to carry as the inheritors of a great past. After all the attempts of philosophers, we stand to-day in relation to the ultimate problems very near where we stood far away in the ages—where perhaps we shall ever stand as long as we are human, bound Prometheus-like to the rock of mystery by the chains of our finite mind.[1] The pursuit of

[1] "No one," exclaims Xenophanes, "has attained complete certainty in respect to the gods and to that which I call universal nature, will nor

philosophy is not, however, a vain endeavour. It helps us to feel the grip and the clanging of the chains. It sharpens the consciousness of human imperfection, and thus deepens the sense of perfection in us, which reveals the imperfection of our passing lives. That the world is not so transparent to our intellects as we could wish is not to be wondered at, for the philosopher is only the lover of wisdom and not its possessor. It is not the end of the voyage that matters, but the voyage itself. To travel is a better thing than to arrive.

At the end of our course, we may ask whether the known facts of history support a belief in progress. Is the march of human thought a forward movement, or is it one of retrogression? The sequence is not capricious and unmeaning. India believes in progress, for, as we have already said, the cycles are bound together by an organic tie. The inner thread of continuity is never cut. Even the revolutions that threaten to engulf the past help to restore it. Backward eddies serve rather to strengthen than retard the current. Epochs of decadence, like the recent past of this country, are in truth periods of transition from an old life to a new. The two currents of progress and decline are intermingled. At one stage the forces of progress press forward with a persistent sweep, at another the line sways to and fro, and sometimes the forces of retrogression seem to overwhelm those of progress, but on the whole the record is one of advance. It would be idle to deny that much has perished in the process. But few things are more futile than to rail against the course which the historical past has taken or weep over it. In any case, some other kind of development would have been worse. The more important thing is the future. We are able to see further than our predecessors, since we can climb on their shoulders. Instead of resting content with the foundations nobly laid in the past, we must build a greater edifice in harmony with ancient endeavour as well as the modern outlook.

anyone ever attain it. Nay, even if a man happened to light on the truth, he would not know that he did so, for appearance is spread over all things" (Gomperz: *Greek Thinkers*, vol. i, p. 164).

II

The Unity of all Systems

The twin strands which in one shape or another run through all the efforts of the Indian thinkers are loyalty to tradition and devotion to truth. Every thinker recognises that the principles of his predecessors are stones built into the spiritual fabric, and, if they are traduced, one's own culture is defamed. A progressive people with a rich tradition cannot afford to neglect it, though it may contain elements which are not edifying. The thinkers try hard to explain, allegorise, alter and expurgate the traditional lore, since men's emotions are centred round it. The later Indian thinkers justify the different philosophical interpretations of the universe advanced by the earlier ones, and regard them as varying approximations to the truth as a whole. The different views are not looked upon as unrelated adventures of the human mind into the realm of the unknown or a collection of philosophical curiosities. They are regarded as the expression of a single mind, which has built up the great temple, though it is divided into numerous walls and vestibules, passages and pillars.

Logic and science, philosophy and religion are related organically. Every fresh epoch in the progress of thought has been inaugurated by a reform in logic. The problem of method, involving as it does an insight into the nature of human thought, is of great value. The Nyāya points out that no stable philosophy can be built except on the foundations of logic. The Vaiśeṣika warns us that all fruitful philosophy must take into account the constitution of physical nature. We cannot build in the clouds. Though physics and metaphysics are clearly distinct and cannot be blended, still a philosophic scheme must be in harmony with the results of natural science. But to extend to the universe at large what is true of the physical world would be to commit the fallacy of scientific metaphysics, and the Sāṁkhya asks us to beware of that danger. The resources of nature cannot generate consciousness. We cannot reduce nature and consciousness the one to the other, as scientific and psychological metaphysics attempt to do. Reality appears not only in science and in human life, but in religious experience, which is the subject matter of the Yoga system. The Pūrva Mīmāṁsā and the Vedānta lay stress on ethics and religion. The relation between nature and mind is the supreme problem of philosophy which the Vedānta takes up. The saying, that the saints do not contradict one another, is true of philosophies also. The Nyāya-Vaiśeṣika realism, the Sāṁkhya-Yoga dualism and the Vedānta monism do not differ as true and false but as more or less true.[1] They are adapted to the needs of the slow-witted (mandādhikāri), the average intellect (madhyamādhikāri) and the strong-minded (uttamādhikāri) respectively. The different views are hewn out of one stone and belong to one whole, integral, entire and self-contained. No scheme of the universe can be regarded as complete, if it has not the different sides of logic and physics, psychology and ethics, metaphysics and religion. Every system of thought developed in India offered its own theory of knowledge, interpretation of nature and mind, ethics and religion. Our knowledge of the universe has grown enormously under the guidance of the natural sciences, and we cannot afford to be satisfied with any restricted outlook on life. The future attempts at philosophic construction will have to relate themselves to the recent advances of natural science and psychology.

III

Philosophy and Life

Philosophy has for its function the ordering of life and the guidance of action. It sits at the helm and directs our course through the changes and chances of the world. When philosophy is alive, it cannot be remote from the life of the people. The ideas of thinkers are evolved in the process of their life history. We must learn not only to reverence them,

[1] Mādhava S.D.S.; Madhusūdana Sarasvatī's *Prasthānabheda*; Vijñānabhikṣu's Introduction to S.P.B. Cp. Kant: " We are in a way maintaining the honour of human reason when we reconcile it with itself in the different persons of acute thinkers and discover the truth, which is never entirely missed by men of such thoroughness, even if they directly contradict each other " (quoted in J. Ward: *A Study of Kant*, p. 11, n. 1).

but to acquire their spirit. The names of Vaśiṣṭha and Viśvāmitra, Yājñavalkya and Gārgī, Buddha and Mahāvīra, Gautama and Kaṇāda, Kapila and Patañjali, Bādarāyaṇa and Jaimini, Śaṁkara and Rāmānuja, are not merely themes for the historian but types of personality. With them philosophy is a world-view based on reflection and experience. Thought, when it thinks itself out to the end, becomes religion by being lived and tested by the supreme test of life. The discipline of philosophy is at the same time the fulfilment of a religious vocation.

IV

The Decline of Philosophy in the Recent Past

The evidence brought together in this work does not support the general criticism that the Indian mind has a fear of thinking. We cannot dismiss the whole progress of Indian thought with a sapient reference to the oriental mind, which is not sufficiently dry and virile to rise above grotesque imagination and puerile mythology. Yet there is much in the thought history of the last three or four centuries to lend countenance to this charge. India is no longer playing her historic rôle as the vanguard of higher knowledge in Asia.[1] It seems to some that the river that has flowed down the centuries so strong and full is likely to end in a stagnant waste of waters. The philosophers, or rather the writers on philosophy of this period of decadence, profess to be votaries

[1] Regarding China's debt to India, Professor Liang Chi Cho says: "India taught us to embrace the idea of absolute freedom, that fundamental freedom of mind, which enables it to shake off all the fetters of past tradition and habit as well as the present customs of a particular age—that spiritual freedom which casts off the enslaving forces of material existence. . . . India also taught us the idea of absolute love, that pure love towards all living beings which eliminates all obsessions of jealousy, anger, impatience, disgust and emulation, which expresses itself in deep pity and sympathy for the foolish, the wicked and the sinful—that absolute love which recognises the inseparability between all beings." He goes on to explain the contributions of India to Chinese literature and art, music and architecture, painting and sculpture, drama, poetry and fiction, astronomy and medicine, educational method and social organisations. See *Viśvabhārati Quarterly*, October 1924. The influence of India on Burma and Ceylon, Japan and Corea, is well known.

of truth, though they understand by it merely the pious sophistries or the sacrosanct hair-splittings of this or that school of dogmatics. These professional dialecticians imagine that the small brook by their side, trickling away in the sand or evaporating in the fog, is the broad river of Indian philosophy.

A variety of causes have contributed to this result. The political changes brought about by the establishment of the Mohammadan supremacy turned men's minds into conservative moulds. In an age when individual self-assertion and private judgment threatened at every point to dissolve into anarchy the old social order and all stable conviction, the need for authoritative control was urgently felt. The Mohammadan conquest, with its propagandist work, and later the Christian missionary movement, attempted to shake the stability of Hindu society, and in an age deeply conscious of instability, authority naturally became the rock on which alone it seemed that social safety and ethical order could be reared. The Hindu, in the face of the clash of cultures, fortified himself with conventions and barred all entry to invading ideas. His society, mistrusting reason and weary of argument, flung itself passionately into the arms of an authority which stamped all free questioning as sin. Since then it has failed in loyalty to its mission. There were no longer any thinkers, but only scholars who refused to strike new notes, and were content to raise echoes of the old call. For some centuries they succeeded in deceiving themselves with a supposedly final theory. Philosophy became confused with the history of philosophy when the creative spirit had left her. It abdicated its function and remained wrapped up in its illusions. When it ceased to be the guide and the guardian of the general reason, it did a great wrong to itself. Many believed that their race had travelled long and far towards a goal at which it had at length arrived. They felt rather tired and inclined to rest. Even those who knew that they had not arrived, and saw the large tract of the country stretching into the future, were afraid of the unknown and its ordeals. The silences and the eternities cannot be questioned without peril by the weak of heart. The dizziness of the inquiry into the infinite is a vertigo which even mighty minds try to avoid, if they can. The strongest of human forces are subject to intervals of lethargy, and the philosophic impulse has had in these three or four centuries an attack of lethargy.

V

The Present Situation

To-day the great religions of the world and the different currents of thought have met on Indian soil. The contact with the spirit of the West has disturbed the placid contentment of recent times. The assimilation of a different culture has led to the impression that there are no official answers to ultimate problems. It has shaken the faith in the traditional solutions, and has, in some degree, helped to a larger freedom and flexibility of thought. Tradition has become fluid again, and while some thinkers are busy rebuilding the house on ancient foundations, others want to remove the foundations altogether. The present age of transition is as full of interest as of anxiety.

During the recent past, India was comfortably moored in a backwater outside the full current of contemporary thought, but she is no longer isolated from the rest of the world. The historian of three or four centuries hence may have much to say on the issues of the intercourse between India and Europe, but as yet they lie hidden from our view. So far as India is concerned, we notice the broadening of men's range of experience, the growth of the critical temper and a sort of distaste for mere speculation.

But there is another side to the picture. In the field of thought, as well as in that of action, the spirit of man is doomed to decay as much in anarchy as in bondage. There is not much to choose between the two, so far as culture and civilisation are concerned Anarchy may mean material discomfort, economic ruin and social danger and bondage material comfort, economic stability and social peace. But it would be incorrect to confuse the standards of civilisation with economic welfare and maintenance of social order. It is easy to understand the feeling of the Indians of the beginning of the nineteenth century, who after generations of public strife and private suffering welcomed the British rule as the dawn of a golden age; but it should be equally easy to sympathise with the Indian feeling of the present day that the spirit of man craves, not comfort, but happiness, not peace and order, but life and liberty, not economic stability or equitable administration, but the right to work out one's own salvation even at the cost of infinite toil and tribulation. Even non-political virtues do not thrive in the absence of political autonomy. British rule has given India peace and security, but they are not ends in themselves. If we are to put first things first, then we must admit that economic stability and political security are only means, however valuable and necessary, to spiritual freedom. A bureaucratic despotism which forgets the spiritual ends, for all its integrity and enlightenment, cannot invigorate the peoples beneath her sway, and cannot therefore evoke any living response in them. When the founts of life are drying up, when the ideals for which the race stood for millenniums, the glow of consciousness, the free exercise of faculty, the play of life, the pleasure of mind and the fulness of peace, prāṇārāmam, mana-ānandam, śānti-samṛddham, are decaying, it is no wonder that the Indian is conscious only of the crushing burden and not of the lifted weight. It is no use speaking to him of the magnitude of Britain's work, for the verdict of history is passed on the spiritual quality of the achievement. If the leaders of recent generations have been content to be mere echoes of the past and not independent voices, if they have been intellectual middlemen and not original thinkers, this sterility is to no small extent due to the shock of the Western spirit and the shame of subjection. The British are aware of the deep-rooted causes of the present attitude of India, whatever it may be called, unrest, revolt or challenge. They tried to bring their civilisation, which they naturally regard as higher, to touch the Indians, and they felt that they should press on in the task of enlightenment and education, good in themselves, without any hesitation or cessation of effort. But India has no sympathy with this policy of cultural imperialism. She tenaciously clings to her ancient customs which helped her to check the swell of passion, the blindness of temper and the thrust of desire One who is acquainted with the history of her past can sympathise with her anxiety to dwell in her own spiritual house, for "each man is the master of his own house."[1] Political subjection which interferes with this inner freedom is felt as a gross humiliation. The cry for swarāj is the outer expression of the anxiety to preserve the provinces of the soul.

Yet the future is full of promise. If India gains freedom within, then the Western spirit will be a great help to the Indian mind. Hindu thought never developed a Monroe doctrine in matters of culture. Even in the ancient times when India grew enough spiritual food to satisfy her own people, there is no recorded age when she was not ready and eager to appreciate the products of other people's imagination. In her great days India conformed to the wisdom of the Athenians, of whom Pericles said: "We listen gladly to the opinions of others and do not turn sour faces on those who disagree with us." Our fear of outside influence is proportioned to our own weakness and want of faith in ourselves. To-day, it is true, we bear lines of sorrow in our face and our hair is grey with age. The thoughtful among us have a brooding uneasiness of soul, some are even steeped in pessimism, and so have become intellectual hermits. The non-co-operation with Western culture is a passing episode due to unnatural circumstances. In spite of it, there are attempts to understand and appreciate the spirit of Western culture. If India assimilates the valuable elements in the Western civilisation, it will be only a repetition of parallel processes which happened a number of times in the history of Indian thought.

Those who are untouched by the Western influence are for a large part intellectual and moral aristocrats, who are indifferent to political issues, and adopt a gospel not of confident hope but of resignation and detachment. They think that they have little to learn or to unlearn, and that they do their duty with their gaze fixed on the eternal dharma of the past. They realise that other forces are at work, which they cannot check or control, and ask us to face the storms and disillusionment of life with the unruffled calm of self-respect. This was the class which in better times was more elastic and was ever renewing the attempts to reconcile rational philosophy with revealed religion. It had always explained and

[1] Sarvas sve sve gṛhe rājā. Every man is the lord in his own house.

defended the faith in the face of heretics and unbelievers, and had recourse to the allegorical method as the instrument of theological interpretation. Religion, for it, embraced within its scope the whole nature of man, his intelligence as much as his practical and emotional aspirations. If to-day the representatives of the ancient learning had the inspiration of the past, they would, instead of non-co-operating with other forces, build a fresh scheme with originality and freedom and in the strength of the legacy of ancient wisdom. But they have an exaggerated respect for authority in thought and action, in things spiritual and things secular, and have thus exposed themselves to the charges of mental servility and obscurantism. While, in pre-Mohammadan times, appeal to authority was no bar to intellectual independence, and while men were able and ready to offer rational grounds for allegiance to the authorities of their choice, be they the Vedas or the Āgamas, and while authority was made to speak in the voice of reason by means of a critical selection and philosophical interpretation, now reverence for authority has become the imprisonment of the human spirit. To question the belief of the scriptures is to question the authority of the great dead. To accept them is a sign of loyalty. Inquiry and doubt are silenced by the citation of ancient texts, scientific truths are slighted, if they cannot be fitted into the procrustean bed of established belief. Passivity, docility and acquiescence become the primary intellectual virtues. No wonder the philosophical writings of recent times are far below the level of the best work of the past ages. If thought had been less strained, it would have been more spacious.

The thinkers of India are the inheritors of the great tradition of faith in reason. The ancient seers desired not to copy but to create. They were ever anxious to win fresh fields for truth and answer the riddles of experience, which is ever changing and therefore new. The richness of the inheritance never served to enslave their minds. We cannot simply copy the solutions of the past, for history never repeats itself. What they did in their generation need not be done over again. We have to keep our eyes open, find out our problems and seek the inspiration of the past in solving them. The spirit of truth never clings to its forms but ever renews them.

Even the old phrases are used in a new way. The philosophy of the present will be relevant to the present and not to the past. It will be as original in its form and its content as the life which it interprets. As the present is continuous with the past, so there will be no breach of continuity with the past.

One of the arguments of the conservatives is that truth is not affected by time. It cannot be superseded, any more than the beauty of the sunset or a mother's love for a child. Truth may be immutable, but the form in which it is embodied consists of elements which admit of change. We may take our spirit from the past, for the germinal ideas are yet vital, but the body and the pulse must be from the present. It is forgotten that religion, as it is to-day, is itself the product of ages of change; and there is no reason why its forms should not undergo fresh changes so long as the spirit demands it. It is possible to remain faithful to the letter and yet pervert the whole spirit. If the Hindu leaders of two thousand years ago, who had less learning and more light, could come on earth again after all these centuries, they would seldom find their true followers among those who have never deviated from the most literal interpretations of their views.[1] To-day a great mass of accretions have accumulated, which are choking up the stream and the free life of spirit. To say that the dead forms, which have no vital truth to support them, are too ancient and venerable to be tampered with, only prolongs the suffering of the patient who is ailing from the poison generated by the putrid waste of the past. The conservative mind must open itself to the necessity of change. Since it is not sufficiently alive to this need, we find in the realm of philosophy a strange mixture of penetrating sagacity and unphilosophical confusion. The chief energies of the thinking Indians should be thrown into the problems of how to disentangle the old faith from its temporary accretions, how to bring religion into line with the spirit of science, how

[1] Cp. Aurobindo Ghosh: "If an ancient Indian of the time of the Upaniṣad, of the Buddha, or the later classical age were to be set down in modern India . . . he would see his race clinging to forms and shells and rags of the past and missing nine-tenths of its nobler meaning . . . he would be amazed by the extent of the mental poverty, the immobility, the static repetition, the cessation of science, the long sterility of art, the comparative feebleness of the creative intuition" (*Ārya*, v. p. 424).

to meet and interpret the claims of temperament and individuality, how to organise the divergent influences on the basis of the ancient faith. But, unfortunately, some of the pariṣads are engaged not with these problems but those suited for the society of Antiquarians. It has become the tilting-ground of the specialists. The religious education of the nation is not undertaken on broad lines. It is not seen that the spiritual inheritance cannot be any longer the monopoly of a favoured few. Ideas are forces, and they must be broadcasted, if the present ageing to death is to be averted. It would be indeed strange if the spirit of the Upaniṣads, the Gītā and the Dialogues of Buddha, that could touch the mind to such fine issues, should have lost its power over man. If, before it is too late, there is a reorganisation of national life, there is a future for Indian thought; and one cannot tell what flowers may yet bloom, what fruits may yet ripen on the hardy old trees.

While those who have not yet been subjected to the influence of Western culture are conservatives in all matters of thought and practice, there are some among those educated in Western ways of thinking who adopt a despairing philosophy of naturalistic rationalism and ask us to get rid of the weight of the past. These are intolerant of tradition and suspicious of the alleged wisdom of age. This attitude of the "progressives" is easily understood. The spiritual heritage of the race has not protected India from the invader and the spoiler. It seems to have played her false and betrayed her into the present state of subjection. These patriots are eager to imitate the material achievements of Western states, and tear up the roots of the ancient civilisation, so as to make room for the novelties imported from the West. Till the other day Indian thought was not a subject of study in the Indian Universities, and even now its place in the philosophical curricula of the Universities is insignificant. Suggestions of the inferiority of Indian culture permeate the whole educational atmosphere. The policy inaugurated by Macaulay, with all its cultural value, is loaded on one side. While it is so careful as not to make us forget the force and vitality of Western culture, it has not helped us to love our own culture and refine it where necessary.

In some cases, Macaulay's wish is fulfilled, and we have educated Indians who are "more English than the English themselves," to quote his well-known words. Naturally some of these are not behind the hostile foreign critic in their estimate of the history of Indian culture. They look upon India's cultural evolution as one dreary scene of discord, folly and superstition. One of their number recently declared that, if India is to thrive and flourish, England must be her "spiritual mother" and Greece her "spiritual grandmother." Albeit, since he has no faith in religion, he does not propose the displacement of Hinduism by Christianity. These victims of the present age of disillusion and defeat tell us that the love of Indian thought is a nationalist foible, if not a pose of the highbrows.

It is a bewildering phenomenon that, just when India is ceasing to appear grotesque to Western eyes, she is beginning to appear so to the eyes of some of her own sons. The West tried its best to persuade India that its philosophy is absurd, its art puerile, its poetry uninspired, its religion grotesque and its ethics barbarous. Now that the West is feeling that its judgment is not quite correct, some of us are insisting that it was wholly right. While it is true that it is difficult in an age of reflection to push men back into an earlier stage of culture and save them from the dangers of doubt and the disturbing power of dialectic, we should not forget that we can build better on foundations already laid than by attempting to substitute a completely new structure of morality, of life and of ethics. We cannot cut ourselves off from the springs of our life. Philosophical schemes, unlike geometrical constructions, are the products of life. The heritage of our history is the food that we have to absorb on pain of inanition.

The conservatives are convinced of the glory of the ancient heritage and the godlessness of modern culture; the radicals are equally certain of the futility of the ancient heritage and the value of naturalistic rationalism. There is much to be said for these views; but the history of Indian thought, when rightly studied, will lead us to regard the two as equally defective. Those who condemn Indian culture as useless are ignorant of it, while those who commend it as perfect are ignorant of any other. The radicals and the conservatives, who stand for the new hope and the old learning, must come closer and understand each other. We cannot live by ourselves in a world where aircraft and steamships, railways and telegraphs are linking all men together into a living whole Our system of thought must act and react on the world progress. Stagnant systems, like pools, breed obnoxious growths, while flowing rivers constantly renew their waters from fresh springs of inspiration. There is nothing wrong in absorbing the culture of other peoples; only we must enhance, raise and purify the elements we take over, fuse them with the best in our own. The right procedure regarding the fusing together of the different elements tossed from outside into the national crucible, is indicated roughly in the writings of Gandhi and Tagore, Aurobindo Ghosh and Bhagavan Das. In them we see the faint promise of a great future, some signs of a triumph over scholasticism, as well as a response to the discovery of a great culture. While drawing upon the fountains of humanist idealism in India's past, they show a keen appreciation of Western thought. They are anxious to reseek the ancient fountain-head and direct its waters to irrigate, through pure and uncontaminated conduits, lands which hunger and thirst. But the future which we wish to see is practically non-existent. With the slackening of the political excitement, which is absorbing the energies of some of the best minds of India, with the increasing insistence on the study of Indian thought in the new Universities, which the old ones are following most reluctantly, the dawn may break. The forces of the conservatism, which prefers the life that was to the life that will be, are not likely to gain any strength in the days to come.

The problem facing Indian Philosophy to-day is whether it is to be reduced to a cult, restricted in scope and with no application to the present facts, or whether it is to be made alive and real, so as to become what it should be, one of the great formative elements in human progress, by relating the immensely increased knowledge of modern science to the ancient ideals of India's philosophers. All signs indicate that the future is bound up with the latter alternative. Loyalty to the spirit of the previous systems of thought, as well as the mission of philosophy, requires us to possess an outlook that always broadens. Indian philosophy acquires a meaning and a justification for the present only if it advances and ennobles life. The past course of Indian philosophic development encourages us in our hope. The great thinkers, Yājñavalkya and Gārgī, Buddha and Mahāvīra, Gautama and Kapila, Śaṁkara and Rāmānuja, Madhva and Vallabha, and scores of others are India's grandest title to existence, a clear testimony of her dignity as a nation with a soul, the proof that she may yet rise above herself and the pledge of this supreme possibility.

NOTES

CHAPTER I

Page 17.—Pāṇini derives the words āstika, nāstika and daiṣṭika in the sūtra astināsti diṣṭam matih. An āstika is one who believes in a transcendent world (astiparalokah); a nāstika is one who disbelieves in it (nāstiparalokah). A sort of fatalist is a daiṣṭika.

Page 18, Note 2.—See *Nyāyakośa.*

Page 20, Note 4.—In the Tamil work *Maṇimekhalai*, Lokāyata, Bauddha, Sāṁkhya, Nyāya, Vaiśeṣika and Mīmāṁsā are regarded as orthodox. See S. Krishnaswamy Aiyangar: *Maṇimekhalai*, p. xxi.

Page 25, Line, 20.—The Vaiśeṣika accepts only perception and inference.

CHAPTER II

Page 34, Note 5.—Akṣapādāt pūrvam krito vedaprāmāṇya niścaya āsīt; jaimineh pūrvam kena vedārtho vyākhyātaḥ; pāṇineh pūrvam kena padāni vyutpāditāni; piṅgalāt pūrvam kena cchandāṁsi racitāni. *Nyāyamañjari*, p. 5.

Page 39.—For a short account of Buddhist logic before Dignāga, see Professor Tucci's article on the subject, *J.R.A.S.*, July 1929.

See also *J.R.A.S.*, January 1928, *Is Nyāyapraveśa by Dignāga?*

Page 40.—Paṇḍit Gopinath Kaviraj argues that Bhāsavarjña's rejection of upamāna (comparison) as a pramāṇa or means of knowledge is due to the influence of the Yoga system. His acceptance of kriyāyoga consisting of tapas, svādhyāya and other typical yogic sādhanas as yama, niyama, etc., supports this opinion. The classification of prameyas into heya, tannivartaka, ātyantikahāna and hānopāya suggests Y.S., ii. 16–17, 25–26. While the early Nyāya writers Gautama, Vātsyāyana, Uddyotakara do not recognise yogipratyakṣa, Bhāsarvajña admits it. Yogipratyakṣam deśakālasvabhāva vipra kṛṣṭārthagrāhakam. Bhāsarvajña's view of Īśvara (God) is strikingly similar to the yogic view.

Bhāsarvajña wrote also a commentary on *Nyāyasāra* called *Nyāyabhūṣaṇa.*

Bhāsarvajña's *Nyāyasāra* with Vāsudeva's *Nyāyasārapadapañcikā* is edited by M. M. Vāsudeva Śāstri Abhyankar and Professor Devādhar. Poona, 1922.

Page 43.—The terms pramāna, prameya, etc., are used ordinarily with reference to valid knowledge and not all knowledge. In the latter case jñāna and jñeya seem to be better.

Page 48.—Pratyakṣa derived from prati and akṣa or akṣi, present to the sense organ or the eye, is opposed to parokṣa or away from the sense organ or the eye. The former is immediate and the latter mediate.

Page 48, Note.—See *Tarkasaṁgrahadīpikā*, p. 7. Bombay Skt. Series.

Page 50.—There is no contact of the manas directly with the object except when the object is an internal state like pleasure, pain and such like.

Page 55.—For the Buddhists, the senses are the sense orifices; for the Mīmāṁsakas the senses are the peculiar power; others hold that it is neither the visible organ nor the peculiar power, but is a different substance which has its locus in the visible sense organ. Golakamātraṇiti sugatāḥ, tacchaktya iti mimāṁsakāh, tadvyatiriktāni dravyāntarāṇity anye sarve vādinaḥ. *Vivaraṇaprameyasaṁgraha*, p. 185. Snakes hear, though they have no visible sense organs. The sense consists of a subtle substance the quality of which is sensed by it. The eye which senses form is composed of the same substance as light whose form it perceives. The nose which senses smell is composed of earth even as smell is a quality of earth. (*Ibid.*, pp. 185–7.)

According to the Advaita Vedānta, the senses are prāpyakāri, i.e. come into actual contact with the objects (see *Vivaraṇaprameya-saṁgraha*, p. 187). If senses could perceive objects without coming into contact with them, we should be able to perceive the taste of distant objects. If it is said that the visual and the auditory senses at any rate can apprehend objects without coming into actual contact with them, we should then be able to apprehend sights and sounds after they have vanished. So it is argued that the senses act only by coming into contact with their objects.

The senses are not the visible organs, but subtle material substances which are able to travel outwards with lightning rapidity. Sounds do not travel to the ear as the Nyāya holds, but the imperceptible sense goes out to the object producing the sound. Śabdasya ca vīcīsantānavat paramparayā śrotrasamavāyaḥ prāptir iti yat tārkikair ucyate tad asat; tathā satīha śrotra śabda iti pratīyeta, pratiyate tu tatrā śabda iti (*ibid.*). That is why we perceive distant sounds and not auditory impressions. Our organs approach the objects and not the objects the organs.

Page 57, Note 3.

Trilocanagurūn nītamārgānugamanonmukhaih
yathāmānam yathāvastu vyākhyātam idam idṛśam.

N.V.T.T., i. i. 4.

Page 59.—Nāmajātyādiyojanārahitam vaiśiṣṭyānavagāhi niṣprakārakam pratyakṣam nirvikalpakam. Gangeśa in *Cintāmaṇi*. Bhīmācārya's *Nyāyakośa*.

Viśeṣaṇaviśeṣyasambandhānavagāhi jñānam. Annam Bhaṭṭa's *Tarkasaṁgrahadīpikā*.

Page 67.—According to Buddhist idealism, cognition and its object are known together. " As blue and the consciousness of blue are invariably known together, one is not different from the other." S.D.S.

For the Advaita criticism of the Nyāya view, see *Vivaraṇaprameyasaṁgraha*, p. 55.

Page 69.—Locanagocare'pi kundakusume tadaviṣayagandhaviśeṣite jñānam evam bāhyendriyadvārakagrahaṇam aghaṭamānam iti mānasam eva surabhikusumam iti jñānam. *Nyāyamañjari*, p. 461.

For yogajadharmalakṣaṇa, see *Prameyakamalamārtāṇḍa*, p. 67.

Pratigatā abhijñām iti pratyabhijñā.

Atikrāntakālaviśeṣita pūrvavarti sthambhādipadārthaviṣayam indriyādi sannikarṣotpannam evedam pratyabhijñā jñānam iti siddham. *Nyāyamañjari*, p. 461.

Page 70.—Atītāvacchinnavastu grahanam pratyabhijñānam (*Saptapadārthī*, 167). Recognition is the apprehension of a thing qualified by the idea of being past.

According to *Tarkabhāṣā* (50), pūrvāvasthānubhavajanitasaṁskārasahakṛtendriyaprabhavā pratyabhijñā.

Page 71.—The earlier Naiyāyikas regarded dreams as presentations (anubhava) and not remembrance (smṛti). See N.S., iii. 1. 14; iv. 2. 34–35; N.B., i. 1. 16; and N.V., p. 79, Kaṇāda and later Naiyāyikas, like Bhāsarvajña and Jayanta, look upon dreams as representative. Udayana does not identify dream states with recollections. See Kiraṇāvali, p. 275. Śaṁkara refers to the view that the dreams produced by spells, deities, and particular kinds of substances possess some truth. Mantra devatā dravya viśeṣanimittāś ca kecit svapnās satyārthagandhino bhavanti. S.B., iii. 2. 4.

Page 72.—See *Dream Theory in Indian Thought*, by Umeṣa Miśra. Allahabad Univ. Studies, Vol. V.

Page 95.—The material cause (upādānakāraṇa) is one with the inherent cause (samavāyi kāraṇa), when we refer to things as produced, but in the case of guṇa or quality and karma or activity the inherent cause is not the material one. In the case of a white cloth, the inherent cause of whiteness is the cloth, which is not, however, its material cause.

Page 122.—In the persistent knowledge of the same object (dhārāvāhikajñāna), as when we notice a table for a few moments continuously, is one's knowledge of the second moment the same as one's knowledge of the first? It is argued by some that the two are not the same. Knowledge varies each moment even as the object varies its character each moment in its space-time setting. The Naiyāyika objects to this on the ground that the moments of our experience are not distinguished by our consciousness. What we perceive is not an atomic moment but a stretch of time. Kṣaṇānām atīndriyatvāt sthūlopādhim ādāya vartamānatvagrahaṇāt (*Tattvacintāmaṇi*, p. 380). The moments are products of logical analysis and not facts of observation. While persistent knowledge depends on objective conditions, memory knowledge depends on previous experience.

Page 127.—When we apprehend the colour blue, there does not follow an apprehension of the validity of the cognition of " blue."

Na hi nīlasaṁvitprasavasamanantaram yathārtheyam nīlasaṁvitiriti saṁvedanāntaramutpādayamānam anubhūyate. *Nyāyamañjari*, p. 168.

Page 128.—The Buddhists who hold that both knowledge and its objects are momentary cannot adopt the realist criterion of conformity to the nature of the object, since the object vanishes as soon as it is known.

Page 131, Note 2.—Cf. Plato's *Theaetetus*.

Page 132.—Śuktitvaprakārikāvidyā cākacakyādi sādṛśya samdarśana samudbodhita rajatasaṁskāra saddhricīnā kācādidoṣa samavahitā rajatarūpārthākāreṇa rajatajñānābhāsākāreṇa ca pariṇamate. *Vedāntaparibhāṣā*, I.

Page 148.—Souls are active only in a secondary sense in the Nyāya. There can be no parināma and even parispanda is inadmissible for an all-pervading soul.

Page 164, Note 2.—See also *Syādvādamañjari* and Rājaśekhara's *Saḍdarśanasamuccaya*, 23.

CHAPTER III

Page 181.—Paṇḍit Miśra thinks that *Līlāvatī* belongs to the twelfth century A.D. See *J.B.O.R.S.*, p. 158.

Page 189.—While the Nyāya regards the soul as the object of mental perception (mānasapratyakṣa viṣaya. *Bhāṣāpariccheda*, 50–51), the Vaiśeṣika makes it an object of inference (anumānagamya. V.S., viii. 1. 2).

Page 199.—The Mīmāṅsakas do not believe in the theory of cycles.

Page 209, Note 3.

Vyakter abhedas tulyatvam saṁkarothānavasthitih
Rūpahānir asambandho jātibādhaka samgrahaḥ.

Page 216, Note 3.—Five kinds of ayutasiddhi are admitted: Avayavāvayavinau, guṇaguṇinau, kriyākriyāvantau, jātivyaktī, viśeṣanityadravyeceti. See *Nyāyakośa*.

Page 230.—Kāla, ākāśa and dik have no generic quality.

Page 254.—An excellent edition of S.K., with Introduction, English Translation, and Notes by S. S. Sūryanārāyaṇa Śāstri, is published by the University of Madras.

CHAPTER IV

Page 258.—Dharmapāriṇāma is the name applied to a mode. A ghaṭa (jar or ghaṭākāra as it is called) is a dharmapāriṇāma of clay, even as clay is of pṛthivī (earth).

Page 271, Note 3.—The *Chāndogya Upaniṣad* refers to three bhūtas, and Śaṁkara in his commentary on vi. 4 speaks of trivṛtkaraṇa. Pañcīkaraṇa is not known to the older Upaniṣads, though the Taittirīya speaks of five bhūtas. It is not mentioned by Bādarāyaṇa or Śaṁkara, though later commentators like Ānandajñāna refer to it. See his gloss on B.S., ii. 4. 20.

Page 277.—Parispanda is change of place as distinguished from pariṇāma or change of form. The former applies only to manifested (vyakta) tattvas.

Page 294.—Arthākāreṇa pariṇatāyā buddhivṛtteś cetane pratibimbanād viṣayaprakāśa rūpam jñānam. *Nyāyakośa.*

Page 298.

Sāṁkhyavṛddhāḥ saṁmugdham vástumātram tu prāggṛhṇātyavikalpitam

Tatsāmānyaviśeśābhyām kalpayanti manīṣinaḥ.

Sāṁkhyatattvakaumudī, 27.

CHAPTER V

Page 360.—The all-comprehensive knowledge is, however, a siddhi, which naturally includes discrimination between prakṛti and puruṣa, which is the real cause of kaivalya or liberation.

Page 371.—The followers of the Sāṁkhya worshipped Nārāyaṇa (nārāyaṇaparāḥ), while those of the Yoga worshipped Īśvara (īśvaradevatāḥ), or Siva, who is the Yogin *par excellence*. See Rājaśekhara on Haribhadra's *Ṣaḍdarśanasamuccaya*, pp. 34, 42–43.

Page 377.—Regarding the differences between the two schools of the Prābhākaras, see Professor Hiriyanna's article on " Prābhākaras: Old and New," *Journal of Oriental Research*, Madras, April–June 1930.

CHAPTER VI

Page 378.—Tantrarahasya of Rāmānujācārya seems to have been an extensive work of which the first five chapters are published in the *Gaekwad's Oriental Series*, 1923.

Mānameyodaya contains two sections on māna and meya, written by Nārāyaṇa Bhaṭṭa and Nārāyaṇa Paṇḍit respectively It gives a lucid exposition of the doctrines of the school of Kumārila. The work is published in the *Trivandrum Skt. Series* by T. Gaṇapati Śāstri, 1912.

Page 381.—Taccendriyasannikarṣajam jñānam dvividham, nirvikalpakam savikalpakam ceti. Tatra indriyasannikarṣānantaram eva dravyādisvarūpamātrāvagāhi śabdānugamaśūnyam yat sammugdha jñānam jāyate, tad viśiṣṭakalpanā bhāvād nirvikalpakam ity ucyate. Yat tu tad anantaram śabdasmaraṇa sahakṛtam jātyādiviśiṣṭavastu viṣayam raktoyam ghaṭoyam ityādi vyaktavijñānam, tat savikalpakam. *Mānameyodava*, p. 8.

Pages 381–2.

Jātih sarvagatā nityā pratyakṣajñāna gocarā
Bhinnābhinnāca sā vyakteḥ kumārila matematā.

Mānameyodaya, p. 85.

Page 391.—Ākṛti for Kumārila means jāti.

Jātim eva ākṛtim prāhuh. i. 3. 3.

Page 395.—For the views of the different schools of Mīmāṁsā on the validity of knowledge, see Pramātvam in *Nyāyakośa*.

Sarvair eva jñānahetubhir ātmani sākṣātkāravatī dhīr upajanyate . . . sarvatra prameyasya aparokṣaniyamābhāvāt. Smṛtiṣu anumānāntareṣu ca na prameyam aparokṣam. Sarvāśca pratītayaḥ svayam pratyakṣāh prakāśante. *Prakaraṇapañcikā*, p. 56.

While all knowledge is immediately known, it is distinguished into immediate and mediate, according as the object is apprehended immediately or mediately.

Page 396.—Na hi pradīpaḥ svagatavyavahārarūpe kārye pradīpāntaram apekṣate; tasmād na buddhir api buddhyantaram. *Mānameyodaya*, p. 103.

Buddhiḥ svayamprakāśeti guruśaṁkarayor matam. *Ibid.*

Page 403, Note 1.—Commenting on Murāri Miśra's view, *Śithikaṇṭhīyam* on *Nyāyasiddhāntamañjari* says: Ghaṭoyam iti vyavasāyaḥ; tataś ca ghaṭam aham jānāmi iti anuvyavasāyaḥ, tena prāmāṇyam gṛhyate.

Page 406.—The Mīnāṁṣaka contends that if validity and invalidity are both external to cognitions, cognitions by themselves should be held to be neutral or characterless, which is not the case.

Na hi prāmāṇyāprāmāṇyavyatiriktam kiñcid api svarūpam asti vijñānasya. *Mānameyodaya*, p. 76.

If it is argued that all cognitions are cases of doubt until they are verified, the Nyāya, which regards doubt as a form of invalid cognition, seems to imply the view of intrinsic invalidity, which is opposed to the doctrine of parataḥ prāmāṇya.

Page 408.

Sa ca dehendriyajñānasukhebhyo vyatiricyate
Nānābhūto vibhur nityo bhogas svargāpavargabhāk.

Mānamenodaya, p. 82.

Page 411.—Mānameyodaya contrasts the position of Prabhākara with that of Kumārila and defends the latter.

For the followers of Prabhākara, the form " I know the jar " represents the general feature of all cognitions. Such knowledge is impossible if the self and the cognition are not manifested. So the self and the cognition must be admitted to be revealed as subject and cognitive activity. (Ātmasvātmanor kartṛtayā vittitayā ca pratīyamānatvam abhyupagacchanti.) The followers of Kumārila object to the very premise that all cognitions are of the form " I know the object." Śālikanātha contends that if the subject is not manifested in all cognitions, it would be impossible to distinguish between the object of one's own cognition and that of another (svapara vedyayor anatiśaya iti). Those who follow Kumārila reply that knowledge appropriated by the self is revealed as such. If it is argued that self-appropriation should also be manifested, it is said in reply that the effect may be present without conscious manifestation, even as sense knowledge may be imparted without a knowledge of the sense that operates.

Murāri Miśra's view is nearer the Bhāṭṭa position. Miśramate ayam ghaṭah ity ākārakajñānānantaram ghaṭatvena ghaṭam aham jānāmi ity jñānavisayakalaukika mānasam utpadyate. Nīlakaṇṭha on *Tarkasaṁgrahadīpikā* (Nirṇayasāgar ed., p. 167).

We first have the knowledge "This is a jar," and then the direct presentation that I know the jar as jar. Only, according to Kumārila, the latter knowledge is inferred, while, according to Murāri Miśra, it is perceived. Both, however, dispute Prabhākara's view that all knowledge is of the form "I know a jar," sarvam eva jñānam ghaṭam aham jānāmi ity ākārakam. *Nyāyasiddhāntamañjari*, p. 341.

Āloka on *Tattvacintāmaṇi* says: Vyavasāyotpattyavyavahitottarakṣanotpanna anuvyavasāyavyakter eva bhāttaiḥ jñātatālingaka anumititvena miśrādibhiśca sākṣātkāratvenābhyupagamāt (*Pratyakṣakhaṇḍa*, p. 158, Asiatic Society of Bengal ed.).

Page 429.—See also *Pūrva Mīmāṁsā Sūtra*, English translation by Paṇḍit Mohan Lal Sandal, S.B.H. Series.

CHAPTER VII

Page 430, Note 1.—Brahmavidyāpratipādakam vedaśiro bhāgarūpam vedāntaśāstram. S.B. on Bṛh. Up., i. 1. 1.

CHAPTER VIII

Page 451.—Dr. Jhā has translated into English *Khaṇḍanakhaṇḍa Khādya* and Mr. S. V. Aiyar, Sureśvara's *Sambandhavārttika*.

Page 466.—Bhartṛprapanca's dvaitādvaita view is described by Śaṁkara in his Commentary on Bṛh. Up., v. 1.

Pūrṇād kāraṇād pūrṇam kāryam udricyate. Udriktam kāryam vartamānakālepi pūrṇam eva paramārtha vastu rūpam dvaitarūpeṇa. Punaḥ pralayakāle pūrṇasya kāryasya pūrṇatām ādāya 'tmani dhitvā pūrṇam evāvaśiṣyate kāraṇarūpam. Evam utpattisthiti pralayeṣu triṣvapikāleṣu kāryakāraṇayoh pūrṇataiva. Sa caikaiva pūrṇatā kārya kāraṇayor bhedena vyapadiśyate. Evam ca dvaitādvaitātmakam ekam brahma yathākila samudro jalatarangaphenabudbudādyātmaka eva. Yathā ca jalam satyam tad udbhavāś ca tarangaphenabudbudādayaḥ samudrātmabhūtā evāvirbhāvatirobhāvadharmiṇaḥ paramārtha satyā eva. Evam sarvam idam dvaitam paramārthasatyam eva jalataraṅgādisthānīyam, samudrajalasthānīyam tu param brahma. S.B. Bṛh. Up., v. 1.

Page 469.

Upakramopasaṁhārāv abhyāso'pūrvatā phalam
Arthavādopapattī ca hetus tātparyanirṇaye.

Page 482.—Cf. with Śaṁkara's account of absolute consciousness as supreme witness (sākṣī) the following verse attributed to the text of *Tarkabhāṣā*:

Samvid bhagavatī devī smṛtyanubhava vedikā
Anubhūtir smṛter anyā smṛtih saṁskāramātrajā.

Page 488.—Immediacy is the essential mark of pratyakṣa, and not sense activity. God's knowledge is not sensuous but immediate.

Page 490.—Some Advaitins hold that indeterminate perception gives us knowledge of pure being (sanmātram) and not knowledge of distinct objects which are the products of imagination (kalpanā). S.L.S.

Page 494.—In Advaita Vedānta, Brahman alone is eternal, and so even the significance of the Vedas is eternal only in a relative sense.

Page 495.—Īśvara in reuttering the Vedas in each world age preserves intact the previous ānupūrvī or order of words.

Page 499, Note 3.—Jñānam tu vastutantratvān na deśa kāla nimittādy apekṣate, yathā agniruṣ ṇa ākāśo'mūrta iti tathā ātmavijñānam api. S.B. Bṛh. Up., iv. 5. 15.

Page 501.—Truth for Advaita Vedānta consists in its non-contradictedness. The Buddhist criterion of successful activity is accepted by the Nyāya with the qualification that it constitutes the test and not the content of truth. Truth is constituted by correspondence with the object. The Advaita contends that correspondence cannot be directly observed; it is only inferred from coherence (samvāda) or harmony of experience. On this view all empirical truth is relative. The true is what is yet uncontradicted. It is possible that some further experience may contradict even the most probable empirical truth. We can never be certain that any empirical truth is absolutely true. *Nyāyamañjari*, pp. 62 ff.

Page 507.—Under the stress of ajñāna, the distinction between self and not-self is set up in the absolute caitanya. The ātman behaves as the aham (the limited ego) that has accepted the limitations of antaḥkaraṇa. Limitation means the presence and the possible ignorance of an other. The struggle to know the other results.

Page 512, Note 4.—Brahmadarśane sādhanam ucyate. Manasaiva paramārtha jñāna saṁskṛtenā 'cāryopadeśa pūrvakam cānudraṣṭavyam. S.B. Bṛh. Up., iv. 4. 19.

Page 519.—Lower knowledge is deceptive only in the sense that it veils reality.

Page 557. From the standpoint of Brahman there is no avidyā at all. But Brahman as sākṣin reveals avidyā. So far as Īśvara is concerned, he sees through avidyā or māyā, which is distinct from him since there is no āvaraṇa for him.

Page 575.
Anādi bhāvarūpam yad vijñānena vilīyate
Tad ajñānam iti prājñā lakṣaṇam sampracakṣatā.
S.D.S., xiii.

Page 585.—Cf. S.B. Bṛh. Up., ii. 1. 20. Parabrahma vyatirekena saṁsārīnāma nānyad vastvantaram asti.

Page 597.—Bhīmācārya, quoting Vācaspati, says: Māyāvādimate trayo hi jīvasyopādhayah; tatra suṣuptau buddhyādi saṁskāravāsitam ajñānamātram, svapne jāgradvāsanāmayam liṅgaśarīram, jāgradavasthāyām sūkṣma śarīra samsṛṣṭam sthūlaśarīram upādhir iti.

Page 607.—Śaṁkara mentions the following similes: Yathā'dbhyah sūryacandrādipratibimbo, yathāvā svacchasya spnaṭikasyā laktakādy upādhibhyo raktādibhāva evam . . . yathodakā laktakādi hetva panaye sūryacandrasphaṭikādi pratibimbo vinaśyati candrādi svarūpam eva paramārthato vyavaṭiṣṭhate; tadvad prajñānaghanam anantam apāram svaccham avatiṣṭhate.

CHAPTER IX

Page 672.—Nirvikalpakam ekajātīyadravyeṣu prathama piṇḍagrahaṇam; dvitīyādi piṇḍagrahaṇam savikalpakam. . . . Prathama pratīty anusaṁhitavastu saṁsthāna rūpagotvāder anuvṛttidharma viśiṣṭatvam dvitīyādipiṇḍagrahaṇāvaseyam iti dvitīyādigrahaṇasya savikalpakatvam. R.B., i. 1. 1.

Page 696.—Śuddhatattva is also called Śuddhasattva.

CHAPTER X

Page 765.—See also:—
Baladeva's *Govindabhāsya* and *Prameyaratnāvali*. E.T. by S C. Basu. S.B.H. Series.
The *Śivādvaita of Śrīkaṇṭha* by S. S. Sūryanārāyaṇa Śāstri.

CHAPTER XI

Page 770, Note.—See also Udayana's *Ātmatattvaviveka* and Sarvajñātmamuni's *Saṁkṣepaśārīraka*.

INDEX

Abhidharmamahāvibhāṣāśāstra, 179 n.
Abhinavagupta's *Paramārthasāra*, 731, 732, 733, 734; his *Pratyabhijñāvimarśinī*, 731
Ādheyaśaktiyoga, 300 n.
Advaitadīpikā, 578 n.
Advaitānanda's *Brahmavidyābharaṇa*, 452 n.
Advaitasiddhāntamuktāvali, 553, 578 n., 580
Āgamas, 674
Agni Purāṇa, 253 n., 663 n.
Ahirbudhnyasaṁhitā, 255 n.
Aitareya Brāhmaṇa, 35 n.
Ājīvakas, 194
Ālambanaparīkṣā, 39
Alexander, Professor, 101, 135 n., 236 n., 240 n., 289 n., 505; his *Space, Time and Deity*, 396 n.
Āloka, 41, 789
Amalānanda's *Kalpataru*, 642 n.
Amṛtabindu Upaniṣad, 282 n.
Ānandagiri, 433, 520 n., 532, 668, 715 n.; his *Nyāyanirṇaya*, 451 n.; his *Śaṁkaravijaya*, 448
Ānandalaharī, 450, 573 n., 735
Anantavīrya, 81 n.
Anaxagoras, 527
Anaximander, 320
Āṇḍāḷ, 668
Aniruddha, 131 n., 146 n.
Annam Bhaṭṭa, 31 n., 41, 57, 59, 76, 79, 110 n.; his *Tarkasaṁgraha*, Chaps. II and III, *passim*; his *Tarkasaṁgrahadīpikā*, 31 n., 41, 50 n., 59 n., 67, 95 n., 148 n.
Anumāna Sutta, 35
Anuyogadvāra Sūtra, 35, 255 n.
Ānvīkṣikī, 18, 23, 30, 33, 38 n., 42, 179
Āpadeva, 33 n., 426 n.; his *Mīmāṁsānyāyaprakāśa*, 378
Aparokṣānubhūti, 450, 622 n.
Āpastamba's *Dharma Sūtra*, 33 n.
Apohasiddhi, 57 n., 108 n.
Appar, 723
Appaya Dīkṣita, 642, 670; his *Ānandalaharī*, 724 n.; his *Kalpataruparimala*, 451 n., 642 n.; his *Siddhāntaleśa*, 451 n., 487 n., 552 n., 553 n., 556 n., 562 n., 587 n., 603 n., 609 n., 612 n., 637 n., 642 n., 644 n., 645 n., 646 n.; his *Śivārkamaṇidīpikā*, 724; his *Vidhirasāyana*, 378
Āptavajrasūcī, 450
Apte's *The Doctrine of Māyā*, 470
Aquinas, Thomas, 545 n.
Areopagitica, 33 n.
Aristotle, 33 n., 34, 71, 77, 84, 85, 89, 96, 214, 227, 313 n., 527, 532; his *Categories*, 184; his *Metaphysics*, 211 n.; his *Nichomachean Ethics*, 615, 625 n., 640 n.; his *Politics*, 33 n.
Ārya, 777 n.
Āryadeva, 31 n., 39 n., 179 n
Aryarakṣita, 35
Asaṅga, 36 n., 341 n.
Āśmarathya, 432, 433, 439, 443, 605

Aśoka, 23
Aṣṭasāhasrī of Vidyānanda, 108 n.
Aṣṭāvakra, 34 n.
Aśvaghoṣa, 37 n.; his *Buddhacarita*, 253; his *Sūtrālaṁkāra*, 178 n.
Āśvalāyana Gṛhya Sūtra, 433
Athalye, 166 n.
Atharvaśikha Upaniṣad, 450
Atharvaśiras Upaniṣad, 450
Ātmabodha, 287 n., 450, 478 n., 511, 563, 606 n., 615 n., 622 n., 628 n.
Ātmopaniṣad, 32 n.
Ātreya, 418, 433
Ātreya Punarvasu, 34 n.
Auḍulomi, 432, 439, 442, 443, 605, 643
Augustine, 538 n.; his *Confessions*, 480–1 n.
Āvaśyaka, 178
Avayavanirākaraṇa, 144 n.

Bādarāyaṇa, 20, 37 n., 376 n., Chaps. VII–IX, *passim*
Bādari, 418, 433, 443, 648 n.
Baladeva, 431, 440; his *Govindabhāṣya*, 761, 762, 763; his *Prameyaratnāvali*, 338 n., 761
Bālakṛṣṇa's *Prameyaratnārṇava*, 756 n.
Bāṇa, 39; his *Harṣacarita*, 39 n., 449 n.
Barnett's *The Heart of India*, 723
Basava, 730
Belvalkar, Professor, 255 n., 433 n., 435 n.
Bergson, M., 215 n., 334, 588 n.; his *Creative Evolution*, 479 n.
Berkeley, 498 n.; his *Principles of Human Knowledge*, 91 n., 584 n.
Bernard, St., 356 n.
Bhagavadgītā, 18, Chaps. VII–X, *passim*
Bhagavan Das, 780
Bhāvagata Purāṇa, 18 n., 253 n., 276 n., 333 n., 344 n., 433, 663 n., 664, 665, 667, 706–8, 748, 757, 761
Bhagavatī Sūtra, 35
Bhagavatsandarbha, 761 n.
Bhāndārkar, Sir R. G., 275 n., 447 n.
Bhāndārkar Commemoration Volume, 37 n., 255 n.
Bhāradvāja Gṛhya Sūtra, 433
Bhāradvāja Vṛtti, 180
Bharata Śāstra, 85
Bhāratītīrtha, 451 n., 556 n.
Bhartṛhari, 57 n., 341 n., 465; his *Vākyapadī*, 465–6
Bhartṛmitra, 376
Bhartṛprapañca, 431 n., 466, 789
Bhāruci, 431 n., 668
Bhāsa, 38 n.
Bhāsarvajña, 40, 57, 68 n., 73, 82 n., 104, 119 n., 783
Bhāskara, 431, 439, 440, 670–1
Bhāskararāya's *Lalitāsahasranāmabhāṣya*, 735
Bhāṭṭacintāmaṇi, 423 n.
Bhavadāsa, 376
Bhavanātha's *Nayaviveka*, 378
Bhavaviveka's *Tarkajvāla*, 452 n.
Bhaviṣya Purāṇa, 663 n.
Bhikṣu Sūtra, 23
Bhīmācārya's *Nyāyakośa*, 20 n., 124, 421 n., 783
Bhoja's *Rājamārtaṇḍa*, 221 n., Chap. V, *passim*
Bodas, 37 n., 39 n., 43 n.
Bodhāyana, 377 n., 431 n.
Bodhāyana Gṛhya Sūtra, 433
Boethius, 640
Bonatelli, 399 n.
Bosanquet, 564; his *Meeting of Extremes in Contemporary Philosophy*, 626 n.
Bradley, 522, 532, 541, 712; his *Appearance and Reality*, 524, 528 n., 540 n., 560, 569 n.; his *Logic*, 99 n., 141 n., 232 n.;

his *Truth and Reality*, 453 n., 497 n., 541 n., 650 n., 716n.
Brahmabindu Upaniṣad, 607 n.
Brahmajāla Sutta, 35, 251 n.
Brahmānanda, 431 n.
Brahmāṇḍa Purāṇa, 663 n.
Brahma Purāṇa, 663 n.
Brahmasāra, 738
Brahmavaivarta Purāṇa, 663, 761, 762
Bṛhadāraṇyaka Upaniṣad, 34 n., 50 n., Chaps. VII–XI, *passim*
Bṛhadvāśiṣṭha, 26
Bṛhaspati Sūtra, 23
British Medical Journal, 356 n.
Broad's *Scientific Thought*, 136 n.
Bronte, Emily, 551 n.
Browning, 613; his *Bishop Blougram's Apology*, 571 n.; his *Paracelsus*, 699
Buddha, 17, 23, 35, 178
Buddhism, 17, 19, 20, 25, 28, 29, 39, 41, 194; theory of cause, 94–5; negation, 55; perception, 60 ff.; phenomenalism, 177; truth, 125–8; universals, 91–2, 383–4; and words, 108
Bunyan, 367

Caird's *Critical Philosophy of Kant*, 485 n., 503 n.; his *Evolution of Religion*, 581; his *Greek Theology*, 515 n.
Caitanya, 41, 670, 760–5
Campbell's *Physics*, 530 n.
Caṇḍamāruta, 670
Caṇḍi Dās, 760
Candra's *Daśapadārthaśāstra*, 180
Candrakīrti, 36 n.
Caraka, 46, 49 n., 179 n.
Carakasaṁhitā, 23 n., 34 n., 37 n.
Cārvākas, 91, 170 n.
Chāndogya Upaniṣad, 34 n., 35, 263 n., Chaps. VII–X, *passim*
Chatterji's *Hindu Realism*, 197 n.
Cidvilāsa, 448
Cintāmaṇi's *Haṭhapradīpikā*, 356 n.
Citsukha, 580, 582, 637; his *Advaitapradīpikā*, 378 n., 481 n., 495 n.; his *Tattvadīpikā*, 451 n., 495 n.
Clarke's *Logic*, 210 n.
Clement of Alexandria, 535 n.
Coué, 338 n.; his *Self-Mastery*, 373 n.
Critical Realism, 125 n.
Cūlikā Upaniṣad, 334 n.

Dakṣiṇāmūrti Stotra, 450, 551 n., 558 n.
Dalton, 195
Darwin, 232; his *Descent of Man*, 503 n.; his *Life and Letters*, 319 n.
Das Gupta, Professor, his *History of Indian Philosophy*, 179 n., 180 n., 190 n., 252 n., 341 n., 464 n.
Daśaślokī, 450
Daśavaikālikaniryukti, 40, 81 n.
Dattātreya, 34 n.
Democritus, 49, 195, 202, 527
Descartes, 55 n., 134, 155, 259, 260 n., 623; his *Discourse on Method*, 476 n.; his *Meditations*, 454 n., 478 n., 533 n., 547 n.
Deussen, vii, 106 n., 431, 434 n., 534, 554, 593 n., 619 n.; his *System of Vedānta*, 73 n., 515 n., 519 n., 541 n., 593 n., 619 n.
Devasūri, 40, 81, 82 n.
Dharmakīrti, 27 n., 39, 60 n., 61, 62, 66, 78, 79, 82 n., 83 n.
Dharmapāla, 180
Dharmarāja's *Vedāntaparibhāṣā*, 43 n., 69, 77, 79, 83 n., 110, 113 n., 133 n., 210 n., 451 n., 487 n., 488, 494, 501 n., 505 n., 520 n., 535 n., 552, 557, 570 n., 603, 608, 613 n.

Dharmottara, 39, 61, 66, 79 n., 128 n.
Dhruva, Professor, 73 n.
Dīdhiti, 41
Dignāga, 39, 61, 62, 76, 78, 82 n., 83, 85, 91, 104, 111 n., 119 n.
Drake, 125 n.
Drāmiḍa, 431 n., 668
Drāmiḍopaniṣatsaṁgati, 708 n.
Dṛgdṛśyaviveka, 520 n.
Duns Scotus, 211, 214 n.

Eckhart, 485 n., 540 n., 622 n.
Edgerton, Franklin, in *American Journal of Philology*, 253 n.
Eliot, Sir Charles, his *Hinduism and Buddhism*, 377 n., 446, 729 n.
Eliot, George, her *Legend of Jubal*, 641
Emerson, 596
Empedocles, 271 n., 320, 527
Encyclopædia of Religion and Ethics, 31 n., 296 n.
Epicurus, 202
Epistle to the Galatians, 627 n.
Epistle to the Romans, 627 n.
Erigena, 274 n.
Essays in Critical Realism, 124 n., 128
European Thought in the Nineteenth Century, 21 n.

Faddegon's *Vaiśeṣika System*, 179 n., 180 n., 200 n.
Fahian, 449 n.
Fichte, 275 n., 513, 555, 560
Fraser's *Literary History of India*, 433 n.

Gadādha a, 41, 124 n.
Gandhi, 780.
Gaṅgādhara, 180 n.
Gaṅgeśa, 40, 41, 42, 48, 58, 67, 68, 73, 79, 82, 89 n., 112 n., 181 n.; his *Tattvacintāmaṇi*, 41, 73 n., 82 n., 83 n., 87 n., 128, 397, 398 n., 784
Garbe, viii, 31 n., 37 n., 254; his *Philosophy of Ancient India*, 31 n., 165 n., 177, 249, 371 n.
Garuḍa Purāṇa, 433, 633 n.
Gauḍabrahmānandīyam, 451 n.
Gauḍapāda, 531, 567; and Buddhism, 453–65; theory of creation, 459–61; ethics, 461–3; his *Kārikā* on *Māṇḍūkya Upaniṣad*, 452, 502 n., 517 n., 530 n., 531, 562 n., 583 n., 600 n., 607 n., 622 n.
Gautama, 19, Chap. II, *passim*
Gautama's *Dharma Sūtra*, 18 n., 33 n.
Gentile's *Theory of Mind as Pure Act*, 232 n., 484 n., 510 n., 717 n.
Ghosh, Aurobindo, 777 n.
Giridhara's *Śuddhādvaitamārtaṇḍa*, 756, 759
Goethe, 21 n.
Goldstücker, 31 n.
Gomperz's *Greek Thinkers*, 71 n., 84 n., 768 n.
Gopālatāpanī Upaniṣad, 764 n.
Gopināth Kavirāj pandit, 783
Gore, Bishop, his *Belief in God*, 545 n.
Gough's *Philosophy of the Upaniṣads*, 469 n.
Govardhana's *Nyāyabodhinī*, 156
Govindācārya, 669
Govindānanda, 432; his *Ratnaprabhā*, 49 n., 180 n., 452 n., 511 n.
Green, 175 n., 569 n.
Guha Abhay Kumar, his *Jīvātman in Brahma Sūtra*, 433 n.
Guhadeva, 668
Guṇaratna's *Ṣaḍdarśanasamuccayavṛtti*, 117, 164 n., 170 n., 378 n.; his *Tarkarahasyadīpikā*, 164 n., 254 n.

Guyau, 101

Haldane, Lord, his *Reign of Relativity*, 482 n.
Hamilton, 395 n.
Hara Prasad Sastri, M. M., 37 n., 39 n., 57 n.
Hardy, Thomas, 288 n.
Hari, 376
Haribhadra, 20 n., 185, 312 n.; his *Ṣaḍdarśanasanuccaya*, 20 n. 102 n., 170 n., 227 n., 283 n., 787
Haridāsa Bhaṭṭācārya, 295 n.
Harimīḍe Stotra, 450
Haristuti, 653 n.
Harivaṁśa, 433, 761,
Harivarman, 31 n., 37 n., 179 n.
Harṣa, 39 n., 41 n.
Hastāmalaka, 482 n.
Hegel, 185, 447, 527, 538, 556, 559, 586, 712 n.; his *Æsthetics*, 477 n.
Heraclitus, 320
Herbart, 195 n.
Hindu Logic as preserved in China and Japan, 41 n., 81 n.
Hiriyanna, Professor, 448 n., 624 n., 787
History of Buddhism, 39 n.
History of Indian Logic, 34 n., 35 n., 38 n., 39 n., 40 n., 41 n., 43 n., 81 n., 85 n., 87 n., 126 n.
Hobbes's *Human Nature*, 212
Hobhouse's *Mind in Evolution*, 289 n.
Hogg, Professor A. G., 621 n.
Hopkins, 433; his *Yoga Technique in the Great Epic*, 340 n.
Hügel, Baron von, his *Philosophy of Religion*, 654 n.
Hume, 134
Hunt's *Essay on Pantheism*, 485 n., 540 n.
Huxley, 288 n.

Indian Philosophical Review, 276 n., 333 n., 736 n.
Indian Thought, 40 n.
Inge, Dean, his *Christian Mysticism*, 367 n.; his *Outspoken Essays*, 513 n.
Irenæus, 372 n.
Isaiah, 362
I-Tsing, 39 n.

Jacob, 469 n., 589 n.
Jacobi, 31, 36 n., 37 n., 251, 341 n., 433 n., 434 n., 452 n., 456 n., 465 n.
Jagadīśa, 31 n., 41
Jaimini, 19, 20 n., 34 n., 37 n., 432 n., 442, Chap. VI, *passim*, 642–3, 648 n.
Jainism, 17, 20 n., 28, 35, 41, 58, 67 n., 70, 79 n., 81, 194, 210 n., 383
James, William, 60; his *Principles of Psychology*, 60; his *Varieties of Religious Experience*, 368 n.
Jayadeva's *Gītagovinda*, 760
Jayanārāyaṇa, 56; his *Vivṛti*, 56, 187, 224
Jayanta, 34 n., 38 n., 40, 44, 57, 61, 63, 69, 94; his *Nyāyamañjari*, Chap. II, *passim*, 192 n., 196 n., 274 n., 381 n., 406, 413 n., 490 n., 790
Jayasiṁhasūri, 133
Jayatīrtha, 29 n.; his *Nyāyasudhā*, 739, 742
Jha, Dr. Ganganath, viii, 40 n.; his *Prabhākara School*, 110 n., 189 n., 377 n., 378 n., 397 n., 405 n.
Jinadatta, 20 n.
Jinavardhana, 156
Jīva, 761–5, 767; and Madhva, 764; Rāmānuja, 764; his *Sarvasaṁvādinī*, 761, 765
John, 631 n.
John, St., 614 n.
John, St., of the Cross, 356 n., 357

Johnson, W. E., his *Logic*, 45 n., 123 n., 184 n., 208 n., 217 n., 234 n.
Journal of the Asiatic Society of Bengal, 37 n., 39 n.
Journal of Philosophy, 363, 364 n.

Kabīr, 670
Kaiyaṭa, 341 n.
Kālāgnirudropaniṣad, 35 n.
Kālidāsa, 39 n.
Kallaṭa, 731
Kaṇāda, 19, 71, 77, 82, 85, 97 n., Chap. III, *passim*
Kant, 61, 134, 192 n., 303 n., 506, 512, 513, 520–3, 527, 545 n., 554–5, 588 n., 717; his *Prolegomena*, 61 n.
Kapardi, 431 n., 668
Kapila, 19
Kārṣṇājini, 432 n., 433
Kāśakṛtsna, 432, 433, 439, 443, 605
Kaṭha Upaniṣad, 35 n., 276, Chaps. VII–X, *passim*
Kathāvattu, 35
Kātyāyana, 37 n., 46 n.
Kātyāyana Sūtra, 433
Kaupīnapañcaka, 617 n.
Kauṣītaki Upaniṣad, 544 n.
Kauṭilya, 18 n., 23, 32 n., 38, 79; his *Arthaśāstra*, 23, 38, 663 n.
Keith, Professor Berriedale, viii, 21, 31–2, 39 n., 43 n., 54, 74, 85, 433, 447, 669; his *Buddhist Philosophy*, 91 n., 627 n.; his *Classical Sanskrit Literature*, 39 n.; his *Indian Logic and Atomism*, 21 n., 37 n., 39 n., 43 n., 54 n., 74 n., 85, 180 n., 201–2 n.; his *Karma-Mīmāṁsā*, 376 n., 378 n.; his *Sāṁkhya, System* 255 n.
Kepler, 207
Keśava, 431, 439, 440, 752; his *Tattvaprakāśikā*, 751
Keśava Miśra, 31 n., 40, 57, 93, 96
Khaṇḍadeva's *Bhāṭṭadīpikā*, 378; his *Mīmāṁsākaustubha*, 378
Khaṇḍanakhaṇḍakhādya, 70, 126 n., 130 n., 235–6 n., 394 n., 451 n., 472 n.
Kingsbury and Philips, their *Hymns of the Tamil Śaivite Saints*, 729
Kirtikar's *Studies in Vedanta*, 581 n.
Kokileśvar Śāstri's *Advaita Philosophy*, 587 n.
Krishnaswami Aiyar, C. N., his *Life and Times of Śaṁkara*, 448 n.
Kṛṣṇānanda, 41, 642 n.
Kṣaṇabhaṅgasiddhi, 57 n.
Kṣemarāja's *Śivasūtravimarśinī*, 731; his *Spandasandoha*, 731
Kulārṇava Tantra, 736, 737
Kumārila, 20, 21 n., 54, 56 n., 58, 131, 214 n., 215 n., 216, 218 n., 399–407, 449, 505, 506 n.; his *Ślokavārttika*, 79 n., 109 n., 189 n., Chap. VI, *passim*, 577 n.; his *Tantravārttika*, 20 n., 21 n., 110 n., 377, 427 n.; his *Ṭupṭīkā*, 377
Kuppuswāmi Śāstri, Professor, 378 n.
Kural, 662
Kūrma Purāṇa, 308, 663 n.

Lakṣmīdhara's *Advaitamakaranda*, 452 n., 480 n., 502 n., 577 n., 582 n., 583 n.
Lalitavistara, 23 n., 35, 178, 339 n.
Laṅkāvatāra Sūtra, 36 n., 178, 465 n.
Lao Tze, 357
Laugākṣi Bhāskara, 31 n., 68 n.; his *Arthasaṁgraha*, 378
Leibniz, 215 n., 318
Leuba, 363 n.
Leucippus, 195, 527

Liang Chi Cho, Professor, 771 n.
Liṅga Purāṇa, 581 n., 663 n.
Liṅgeśa Mahābhagavat, 467 n., 470 n.
Lloyd Morgan, Professor, his *Emergent Evolution*, 289 n.
Locke, 51, 134; his *Essay on the Human Understanding*, 51 n., 236 n.
Lokācārya's *Tattvatraya*, 260 n., 582 n.
Lokāyata, 23 n.
Lotze's *Metaphysics*, 480 n.
Luke, St., 447

Macdonell, Professor, 447
Mādhava, 18 n., 28, 33 n., 37 n., 43 n.; his *Śaṁkaravijaya*, 225, 377 n., 448, 605, 670
Madhusūdana Sarasvatī, 344 n., 472 n., 580; his *Advaitasiddhi*, 137, 451 n., 501, 578, 580 n., 588 n., 770 n.; his *Siddhānta-bindu*, 409 n.
Madhva, 22 n., 28, 431, 439, 442, 510 n., 516, 643, 663, 761, 767; his *Anuvyākhyāna*, 739; his *Bhāratatātparyanirṇaya*, 739; his *Tattvanirṇaya*, 743; his life and work, 737–9; his theory of ethics and religion, 747–9, 750–1; God, 741–3; reality, 741, 744–6, 749–50; soul. 743–4; and Rāmānuja, 738
Mādhyamika Kārikāvṛtti, 36 n.
Mādhyamika philosophy, 120–2, 131, 142
Mādhyamikāvatāra, 627 n.
Madras Christian College Magazine, 621 n.
Mahābhārata, 18, 23 n., 33 n., 35, 38 n., 42, 46, 249 n., 253 n., 270 n., 333 n., 433, 667, 723, 734
Mahābhāṣya, 22 n., 36, 38, 341 n., 433
Mahādeva Bhaṭṭa, 198 n., 324, 342 n.
Mahānārāyaṇa Upaniṣad, 201 n.
Mahānirvāṇa Tantra, 736 n., 737 n.
Mahopaniṣad, 452 n.
Maitrāyaṇī Upaniṣad, 264 n., 453 n.
Maitrī Upaniṣad, 35 n.
Makaranda, 40
Manameyodaya, 787
Maṇḍana Miśra, 449; his *Mīmāṁsānukramaṇī*, 377; his *Vidhiviveka*, 377
Maṇibhadra, 283 n.
Māṇikkavāsagar, 723
Māṇikyanandi, 40, 73 n., 81, 82 n.
Maṇimeghalai, 662, 783
Manīṣāpañcaka, 486 n., 617 n.
Manu, 18 n., 20 n., 32, 33 n., 34 n., 35 n., 46 n., 433.
Mārkaṇḍeya Purāṇa, 253 n., 663 n.
Markos, 372
Māṭharavṛtti, 81 n., 255 n.
Mathurānātha's *Tattvacintāmaṇi-rahasya*, 43 n.
Matsya Purāṇa, 253 n., 333 n., 663 n.
McTaggart, 314 n.; his *Hegelian Cosmology*, 519 n.; his *Nature of Existence*, 48 n., 127 n.
Medhātithi, 38 n.
Meghadūta, 39 n.
Mendel, 232
Meykaṇḍar's *Śivajñānabodham*, 723, 724, 728, 730
Milesians, 527
Mill, J. S., 33 n., 46 n., 78, 82; his *Essay on Liberty*, 33 n.; his *System of Logic*, 46
Milton, 33 n., 720
Mind, 84 n., 406 n., 626 n.
Minto's *Logic*, 184
Mitabhāṣiṇī, 70 n., 117 n.
Mitra, Rajendra Lal, 361 n.
Mohamudgara, 450
Moses, 362
Mṛgendra Āgama, 726, 730
Muir's *Original Sanskrit Text*, 165 n.

Muktikopaniṣad, 35 n., 431 n.
Müller, Max, 23, 24 n., 85, 433, 447, 586 n., 633 n.
Murāri, 378
Mysore University Magazine, 517 n.

Nāgārjuna, 36 n., 38, 39 n., 81, 451 n.; his *Mādhyamika Kārikā*, 36 n., 126 n., 464 n., 636 n.; his *Prajñāpāramitāśāstra*, 179 n.; his *Upāyakauśalya Sūtra*, 38, 81, 341 n.; his *Vigrahavyāvartanī Kārikā*, 38, 126 n.
Nāgeśa, 341 n., 342 n., 345 n.; his *Laghusāṁkhyasūtravṛtti*, 256, 272 n.
Nāgeśa Bhaṭṭa's *Mañjūṣā*, 106 n.
Nāgoji Bhaṭṭa, 342 n.
Nālaḍiyār, 662
Nallasvāmi Piḷḷai's *Śaiva Siddhānta*, 725
Nambi Āṇḍār Nambi, 723
Nammāḷvār, 668
Nānak, 670
Nārada, 35; his *Bhakti Sūtra*, 704 n., 705 n., 708 n.
Nāradapañcarātra, 707 n., 711
Nāradīya Purāṇa, 663 n.
Nārāyaṇa, 315 n., 342 n.
Nārāyaṇācārya's *Madhvavijaya*, 448, 738 n.; his *Maṇimañjari*, 448
Nāthamuni, 668
Nettipakaraṇa, 35
Nicholas of Cusa, 537 n.
Nīlakaṇṭha, 96, 431, 439, 440, 723, 730
Nimbārka, 439, 440, 751–6, 767; his *Daśaślokī*, 751, 754, 755; his *Vedāntapārijātasaurabha*, 75; and Rāmānuja, 753, 754, 756, 760
Niruttara Tantra, 736 n.
Niścaladāsa, 451 n.
Novalis, 337
Nṛsiṁhottaratāpanī Upaniṣad, 35 n., 450 n., 539 n., 581 n.
Nyāya, 19, 20, 21 n., 28, Chaps. II and III, *passim*, 769; and Advaita Vedānta, 538; Pūrva Mīmāṁsā, 33 ff.; Vaiśeṣika, 29 ff.; history and literature, 36 ff.; theory of causation, 92–102; comparison, 102–4; definition, 47–8; doubt, 116–8; dreams, 71–2; error, 130; ethics, 160–5; fallacies, 118–20; God, 165; implication, 112; individual self, 144–60; induction, 86–92; inference, 72–5; karma, 164; memory, 115–16; mokṣa, 151 ff.; nature, 142–4; non-existence, 53–4, 112–14; perception, 48–72; rebirth, 150–1; recognition, 69 ff.; syllogism, 75–86; truth, 120–30
Nyāyabindu, 27 n., 39, 55 n., 62 n., 91 n., 128 n., 136
Nyāyabinduṭīkā, 39, 48 n., 62 n., 66 n., 68 n., 71 n., 79 n., 82 n., 106 n., 128 n., 136 n., 178 n.
Nyāyamālāvistara, 33 n.
Nyāyāmṛta, 451 n., 491 n., 746, 748
Nyāyanibandhaprakāśa, 40
Nyāyapariśiṣṭa, 40
Nyāyaprakāśa, 33 n.
Nyāyapraveśa, 39, 81
Nyāyaratnākara, 33 n., 472 n.
Nyāyaratnāvali, 409 n., 413
Nyāyasāra, 40, 59 n.
Nyāyasiddhāntamañjari of Jānakīnātha, 83 n.
Nyāyasūcī, 37 n., 40, 43 n.
Nyāya Sūtra, Chaps. II and III, *passim*
Nyāyasūtravṛtti, 18 n., 35 n., 41, 43 n., 57 n., 73, 116 n., 119 n., 122 n., 124 n., 152 n., 164 n., 170 n.

Nyāyasūtroddhāra, 37 n., 40
Nyāyatattva, 668
Nyāyāvatāra, 40, 81 n.

Otto, Rudolf, his *Idea of the Holy*, 535 n., 538 n.

Padārthakhaṇḍana, 41
Padārthatattvanirṇaya, 553
Padmapāda, 637 n.; his *Pañcapādikā*, 451 n.
Padma Purāṇa, 38 n., 433, 471, 663 n., 664 n.
Paley, 418 n.
Pañcarātra, 21 n.
Pañcarātrarahasya, 690
Pañcarātrasaṁhitā, 662
Pañcaśikha, 37 n.
Paṇḍit, 398 n.
Paṇḍit, Mr., 377 n., 378 n.
Pāṇini, 28, 34 n., 35 n., 46 n., 106 n., 783
Paramārtha, 180 n., 255 n.
Parāśara, 34 n.
Pargiter's *Ancient Indian Historical Tradition*, 663 n.
Parīkṣāmukhasūtra, 40, 73 n.
Parivāra, 34 n.
Parmenides, 537
Pārthasārathi Miśra, 33 n., 58 n., 60, 64, 578; his *Nyāyaratnākara*, 108 n., Chap. VI, *passim*; his *Śāstradīpikā*, 61 n., 64 n., 113 n., 215 n., 314 n., 482 n., Chap. VI, *passim*, 576 n.
Pascal, 454 n.
Patañjali, 19, Chap. V, *passim*
Patañjali, the grammarian, 22 n., 36, 37 n., 38, 46 n., 341
Paṭisambhidāmagga, 35
Paul, St., 362
Pauṣkara Āgama, 725, 728
Periāḷvār, 668
Peter, St., 362
Philosophical Review, 101 n.
Piḷḷai Lakācārya, 669; his *Arthapañcaka*, 6, 9, 690; his *Tattvatraya*, 669, 694, 696
Plato, 33 n., 34, 211–12, 214, 233, 362, 372, 447, 495, 522, 527, 532, 534, 564, 598 n.; his *Parmenides*, 212; *Phædo*, 357 n., 615 n., 629 n.; *Phædrus*, 512 n., 613 n.; *Republic*, 615 n.; *Sophist*, 537; *Theaetetus*, 786; *Timæus*, 260 n., 545 n., 625 n., 646, 657 n.
Plotinus, 447, 513, 521 n., 551, 560; his *Enneads*, 248 n., 360 n., 511 n., 515 n., 535 n., 540 n., 564 n.
Pope, Dr., 722
Poussin, M., 465 n.
Prabhācandra, 41, 64 n., 216, 302 n.; his *Prameyakamalamārtaṇḍa*, 41, 68 n., 108 n., 109 n., 132 n., 133 n., 213 n., 402 n., 785
Prabhākara, 58, 70, 72; his *Bṛhatī*, Chap. VI, *passim*; theory of error, 132; knowledge, 395–9
Prabodhacandrodaya, 447
Prakāśānanda's *Siddhāntamuktāvali*, 452 n.
Prakāśātman's *Pañcapādikāvivaraṇa*, 451 n., 518 n., 552 n., 553 n., 610
Prakaṭārtha, 556 n.
Prakaṭārthavivaraṇa, 609
Pramāṇanayatattvālokālaṁkāra, 41, 211 n.
Pramāṇasamuccaya, 39
Pramāṇaśāstrapraveśa, 39
Praśastapāda, 39, 71, 72, 75 n., 77, 78, 82, 92, 117, 119 n., 314; his *Padārthadharmasaṁgraha*, 76 n., 77, 78 n., 118 n.
Praśna Upaniṣad, 34 n., 271 n., Chaps. VII–X, *passim*

Pratimānāṭaka, 38 n.
Pratyabhijñā system, 722 n., 731–4; and Advaita Vedānta, 731–4
Proceedings of the Oriental Conference, Poona, 73 n.
Pūrṇānanda's *Tattvamuktāvali*, 739, 746, 791
Pūrva Mīmāṁsā, 19, 20, 23, 26, 28, 73 n., Chap. VI, *passim*, 770; and Buddhism, 375, 376 n.; Nyāya-Vaiśeṣika, 33, 34, 37 n., 56, 70, 81, 104 n., 401, 406, 415–16, 417, 425–6; Vedānta, 374–6, 408, 412, 420, 421, 426; theory of apūrva, 420–2; comparison, 393; ethics, 417–20; God, 392, 424–8; implication, 393; inference, 386–7; nature, 414–17; non-apprehension, 394–5; non-existence, 54, 220; perception, 380–6; pramāṇas, 378–80; self, 407–14; truth, 125; universals, 210 n.; Vedas, 110 ff., 387–93; words, 391–2
Pythagoras, 144 n., 527

Quakers, 595 n.
Questions of Milinda, 35, 46 n.

Rabindranath Tagore, 140 n., 780
Radhakrishnan's *Indian Philosophy*, Vol. I, Chaps. I–XI, *passim*; his *Philosophy of the Upaniṣads*, 140 n.
Rāghavānanda's *Mīmāṁsāsūtradīdhiti*, 378 n.
Raghunandana, 41
Raghunātha, 41, 451 n.
Rājaśekhara, 20 n.; his *Ṣaḍdarśanasamuccaya*, 170 n., 786
Rājavārttika, 255 n.
Rāmakṛṣṇa's *Śikhāmaṇi*, 142, 451 n., 488 n., 613 n.
Rāmakṛṣṇa Bhaṭṭa's *Yuktisnehaprapūraṇī*, 377 n.
Rāmānuja, 24, 28, 131, 132 n., 172, 175, 326 n., Chaps. VII–X, *passim*; and Śaṁkara, 658–62, 676–8, 683 ff., 701–2, 714–21; life, 665–7; theory of cause, 678; comparison, 674; consciousness, 679–82; empirical ego, 690–6, 713–14; ethics and religion, 703–9; God, 682–90; inference, 673–4; karma and freedom, 693–5; matter, 696–7; memory, 673; mokṣa, 709–12; perception, 672–3; scripture, 674; self, 679–82; substance, 679, 712–13
Rāmānanda, 670, 709
Rāmatīrtha's *Taraṅgiṇī*, 451 n.
Rāmāyaṇa, 18 n., 33 n., 35 n., 38 n., 253 n.
Randle, Mr. H. N., 84 n.
Raṅgarāmānuja, 670
Raseśvara, 722 n.
Rashdall's *Theory of Good and Evil*, 717 n.
Ratnakīrti, 40, 57 n.
Raurava Āgama, 723
Rāvaṇabhāṣya, 180
Ṛg-Veda, 250, 261 n., 565 n.
Rosmini, 400 n.
Rucidatta, 40
Rūpa, 761; his *Ujjvalanīlamaṇi*, 764
Russell, Mr. Bertrand, 215 n., 240; his *Philosophical Essays*, 511

Śabara, 37 n., Chap. VI, *passim*
Śābdikas, 57 n.
Sadānanda, 448; his *Advaitabrahmasiddhi*, 452 n., 636 n.; his *Vedāntasāra*, 345 n., 452 n., 460 n., 487 n., 539 n., 571 n., 575 n., 592 n.

Śaiva Āgama, 662
Śaiva Siddhānta, 722 ; literature, 723–4 ; metaphysics, 724–8 ; religion and ethics, 728–31
Śāktaism, 734–7
Śālikanātha's *Pariśiṣṭa*, 378 ; his *Prakaraṇapañcikā*, Chap. VI, *passim* ; his *Ṛjuvimalā*, 378
Samantabhadra's *Āptamīmāṁsā*, 221 n.
Sāmānyadūṣaṇadikprasāritā, 91, 212 n.
Sāma Veda, 339 n.
Sambandar, 723
Śaṁkara, 24, 35, 73, 99, 153–4, 171, 174, 177, 185, 218–19, 226, 235, 240, 241, 244, 290 n., 322 n., 422 n., 431, 433, 434, Chaps. VII–X, *passim*, 767 ; and Bergson, 523–4 ; Bradley, 502–9, 522–3, 524–6, 638 ; Bhāgavata school, 474 ; *Brahma Sūtra*, 469–70 ; Buddhism, 470–3, 496–7 ; Kant, 521–3 ; Nyāya, 482, 528–30, 547 ; Plato, 520 n. ; Pūrva Mīmāṁsā, 473–4, 499, 500 n., 547, 562 ; Sāṁkhya, 546–8, 581, 590 ; Upaniṣads, 466–9 ; life, 447–50 ; theory of Ātman, 475–85 ; avidyā, 574–8 ; Brahman, 533–4, 553–6 ; cause, 528–32 ; error, 132 ; ethics, 612–34 ; God, 542–53 ; individual self, 595–612 ; inference, 83, 493–4 ; intuition, 510–11 ; Karma, 634–5 ; knowledge, 486–8 ; mokṣa, 636–46 ; perception, 488–93 ; rebirth, 646–8 ; religion, 648–56 ; substance, 236 ; truth, 499–502 ; Vedas, 494–6, 515–18 ; world and its status, 561–9, 590–4
Śaṁkara Miśra, 451 n. ; his *Upaskāra*, 68 n., 72 n., 104 n., 181, 187, 191 n., 192 n., 224 n., 226 n.
Sāṁkhya, 19, 20, 23, 28, 49, 58, 67, 106 n., 154, 175, Chap. IV, *passim*, 769 ; and *Bhagavadgītā*, 316 ; Buddhism, 251, 253, 291–3, 317 ; Kant, 303 n. ; *Mahābhārata*, 251–2 ; Nyāya Vaiśeṣika, 248–9 ; Upaniṣads, 250–1, 253, 282–3, 286–7, 302 n., 316 ; Vedānta, 270, 276, 326, 334 ; theory of cause, 95 n., 97–8, 256–8 ; comparison, 104 ; ethics, 307–11 ; evolution, 266–7 ; guṇas, 262–6, 310–11 ; God, 316–19 ; individual self, 283–7 ; inference, 300 ; knowledge, 293–302 ; mokṣa, 152, 308–10, 311–14 ; negation, 300 ; perception, 297–300 ; prakṛti, 259–62, 287–91, 323–34 ; puruṣa, 279–83, 287–91, 320–3 ; rebirth, 314–16 ; space and time, 277–9 ; substance, 236 n. ; truth, 125, 302 ; Vedas, 300–2
Sāṁkhya Kārikā, 97, Chap. IV, *passim*, 786
Sāṁkhyapravacana Sūtra, 146 n., Chap. IV, *passim*
Sāṁkhyasūtravṛtti of Aniruddha, Chap. IV, *passim*
Sāṁkhyasūtravṛttisāra of Mahādeva, Chap. IV, *passim*
Sāṁkhyatattvakaumudī, 40, Chap. IV, *passim*
Sanātana, 761
Sanatsujātīya, 450
Śāṇḍilya, 704 n.
Sanskrit Research, 517 n.
Śāradātilaka, 736
Sarvadarśanasaṁgraha, 18 n., 28, 43 n., 106 n., 151 n., 297 n., 722 n.
Sarvajñātmamuni, 576, 646 n. ; his *Saṁkṣepaśārīraka*, 451 n., 488 n., 553, 577, 578 n., 581 n., 609, 613 n., 791

Sarvasiddhāntasārasaṁgraha, 182, 225 n., 287 n., 321 n., 344 n., 409 n., 428 n., 480 n., 506 n., 581 n., 582 n.
Sarvopaniṣadsāra, 35 n.
Ṣaṣṭitantra, 23 n., 254 n.
Śāstri, P., his *Introduction to Pūrva Mīmāṁsā*, 405 n., 413 n., 426–7
Śatapatha Brāhmaṇa, 254
Śataślokī, 513 n., 572 n.
Saundaryalaharī, 450, 735
Sautrāntikas, 131, 194 n.
Schelling, 513; his *Philosophical Letters on Dogmatism and Criticism*, 360 n.
Schiller's *Studies in Humanism*, 569 n.
Schopenhauer, 633 n.
Schweitzer's *Civilisation and Ethics*, 545 n.
Seal, Dr. B. N., 78; his *Positive Sciences of the Ancient Hindus*, 78 n., 88 n., 264 n., 271 n.
Sekkirar's *Periapurāṇam*, 723
Semon, Richard, his *Mnemic Psychology*, 66 n.
Sen, Dr. Śaileśvar, 43 n.
Siddhāntacandrodaya, 192 n.
Siddhānta Dīpikā, 723 n., 730 n.
Siddhāntaratnamālā, 582 n.
Siddhasena Divākara, 40, 78, 79, 82 n., 341 n.
Śilappathikāram, 662
Śivācārya Arulnandi, 723; his *Sivajñānasiddhiyār*, 726, 729
Śivāditya, 37 n., 41 n., 44, 73, 117, 156; his *Saptapadārthī*, 31 n., 44 n., 73 n., 82 n., 117 n., 181, 221, 243 n.
Śiva Purāṇa, 663 n.
Six Buddhist Tracts, 57 n.
Skanda Purāṇa, 38 n., 589 n., 663 n.
Socrates, 33 n., 34, 502
Somānanda's *Śivadṛṣṭi*, 731
Somanātha's *Mayūkhamālikā*, 377
Someśvara Bhaṭṭa's *Nyāyasudhā*, 377
Sophistical Refutations, 34
Spencer, Herbert, his *First Principles*, 266 n.
Sphoṭa, 106
Spinoza, 447, 527, 558, 566, 587; his *De Intellectus Emendatione*, 613 n.; his *Ethics*, 519 n., 536 n., 537 n.
Śrīdhara, 58, 69, 72; his *Nyāyakandalī*, 53 n., 64 n., 68 n., 69 n., 72 n., 91 n., 114 n., 145 n., 146 n., 151 n., 159, 162, 170 n., Chap. III, *passim*, 403–4, 576 n.
Śrīnivāsācārya's *Yatīndramatadīpikā*, 670, 676, 689, 690
Śrīvatsa's *Līlāvatī*, 181
Stout, Professor, 215–16 n., 406 n.
Suali, 37 n.
Subālopaniṣad, 35 n.
Subandhu, 39 n.
Subodhinī, 452 n.
Subrahmanya Aiyar, Mr. V., 517 n.
Sucarita Miśra's *Kāśikā*, 376 n., 377
Sudarśana Bhaṭṭa's *Śrutaprakāśikā*, 669, 682, 699, 710
Suguira, 41 n.
Sukhtankar, 465 n.
Sulabhā, 34 n.
Sundaranāman, Professor K., 470
Sundarar, 723
Sureśvara, 596 n., 608 n.; his *Mānasollāsa*, 638 n.; his *Naiṣkarmyasiddhi*, 451 n., 488, 620; *Vārttika*, 413 n., 451 n., 466 n., 486 n., 530 n., 563, 601 n.
Sūryanārayanan, Mr. S. S., 517 n., 786, 791
Sūrya Purāṇa, 287, 570 n.
Suso's *Life of the Blessed Henry Suso by Himself*, 355 n.
Suśrutasaṁhitā, 34 n.
Svapneśvara, 704 n.; his *Kaumudīprabhā*, 255 n.
Svayamprakāśa, 582 n.
Śvetāśvatara Upaniṣad, 179 n. 263 n., 264 n.

Taittirīya Āraṇyaka, 35 n.
Taittirīya Prātiśākhya Sūtra, 433
Takakusu, 39 n., 254 n.
Ṭaṅka, 431 n., 668
Tantra, 662
Tantrāloka, 731
Tao-Teh-King, 357 n.
Tāranātha, 39 n.
Tarkabhāṣā, 31 n., 40, 58 n., 91 n., 93 n., 95 n., 126 n.
Tarkadīpikā, 189 n.
Tarkakaumudī, 31 n., 68 n., 79 n., 110 n., 116 n., 117 n., 187
Tarkāmṛta, 31 n., 181
Tarkasaṁgrahdīpikāprakāśa, 60 n.
Tātparyapariśuddhi, 40, 122
Tattvacintāmaṇivyākhyā, 41
Tattvakaumudī, 104 n.
Tattvapradīpikā, 602
Tattvasamāsa, 254
Tattvaśuddhi, 586 n., 602
Tattvaviveka, 610 n., 747
Tennyson, 363 ; his *Ancient Sage*, 358 n. ; *Life of Tennyson*, 358 n.
Teresa, St., 356 n.
Thibaut, viii, 23 n., 106 n., 445
Thomas, St., 64 n.
Tilak, B. G., 255 n.
Tirumantram, 730
Tirumūlar, 723, 730
Tiruvāsagam, 722–3, 729, 730, 731
Tiruvāymoyi, 668 n., 684, 686, 705, 708 n.
Tolkāppiam, 722
Topics, 34
Trilocana, 57

Udāna, 35 n.
Udayana, 40, 41 n., 56, 72, 87 n., 93, 110 n., 117, 130, 137, 149 n., 165, 181 n., 185, 209 ; his *Ātmatattvaviveka*, 40, 108 n., 200 n., 791 ; his *Kiraṇāvali*, 40, 156, 181, 186, 191 n. ; his *Kusumāñjali*, 40, 93, 98 n., 113 n., 114 n., 127 n., 166 ff., 170, 295 n., 415 n., 670 ; his *Pariśuddhi*, 314 n.
Uddyotakara's *Nyāyavārttika*, Chap. II, *passim*, 422
Ui, 31 n., 36 n., 37 n., 62 n. ; his *Vaiśeṣika Philosophy*, 31 n., 36 n., 37 n., 62 n., 81 n., Chap. III, *passim*, 254 n.
Umāpati's *Śivaprakāśam*, 723, 725 ; his *Tiru-aruḷ-payan*, 723, 729, 731
Underhill, Miss Evelyn, her *Jacopone de Todi*, 640 n.
Upadeśasāhasrī, 486 n., 551 n., 619 n., 625 n.
Upavarṣa, 376, 377 n.
Utpala's *Pratyabhijñā Sūtra*, 731, 732
Uttarādhyayana, 186 n.

Vācaspati, 5, 7, 8, 576, 580, 592 ; his *Bhāmatī*, 22 n., 40, 49 n., 131 n., 392 n., 427 n., 451 n., 480 n., 501 n., 513 n., 547 n., 585 ; his *Nyāyakaṇikā*, 371 ; his *Nyāyavārttikatātparyaṭīkā*, Chap. II, *passim* ; his *Tattvavaiśāradī*, 265 n., 272 n., 285 n., Chap. V, *passim*
Vaibhāṣikas, 194 n.
Vaikhānasa Sūtra, 23
Vaiśeṣika, 19, 20, 21 n., 23 n., 28, 31–2, 35, 38, 54, 58, 71 n., 75 n., 76 n., 98 n., 101 n., 105 n., 115 n., 155, 165, Chap. III, *passim*, 769 ; and Aristotle, 184–6 ; Buddhism, 177–8 ; Jainism, 177–8 ; Nyāya, 177–8, 196, 245–7 ; Pūrva Mīmāṁsā, 179, 182 ; Sāṁkhya, 180 n., 245–7 ; theory of atomism, 194–203, 238–41 ; categories, 183–7 ; ethics, 222 ff. ; generality,

209–14, 231–3; God, 225–8; inherence, 216–19, 234 ff.; karma, 208–9, 233–6; knowledge, 181–3, 244 ff.; mokṣa, 224–5; nature, 193–203, 241–4; negation, 219–21, 229–30; quality, 204–8, 233–6; particularity, 215–16, 231–3; rebirth, 224; self, 145; substance, 187–94, 233–6
Vallabha, 41, 431, 439, 440, 443, 605, 670, 756–60, 767; his *Aṇubhāṣya*, 756, 759, 760; his *Bhāgavataṭīkāsubodhinī*, 756; his *Siddhāntarahasya*, 756; and Nimbārka, 760; Śaṁkara, 756; Rāmānuja, 758–60
Vāmana, 341 n.
Vāmana Purāṇa, 663 n.
Varadarāja, 31, 40, 78; his *Tārkikarakṣā*, 31 n., 34 n., 40, 81 n., 87 n., 103 n.
Varāha Purāṇa, 663 n.
Varāhopaniṣad, 624 n.
Varisco's *Know Thyself*, 395 n.
Vāsavadattā, 39 n.
Vasubandhu, 36 n., 39 n., 341 n.
Vāsudeva Sarvabhauma, 41
Vasugupta, 731; his *Śiva Sūtra*, 731, 733, 734; his *Spandakārikā*, 731–2
Vātsyāyana's *Nyāyabhāṣya*, Chap. II, *passim*, 340 n.
Vāyu Purāṇa, 270 n., 334 n., 663 n.
Vedānta, 20, 23, 24, 28, 37 n., 56, 67, 70, 81, 95 n., 104 n., 106, 175, 216, 220, 271 n., Chaps. VII–X, *passim*, 770; and Bhāgavata school, 434; materialism, 434; Nyāya-Vaiśeṣika, 434; Pūrva Mīmāṁsā, 430–1, 434, 439; Sāṁkhya, 434, 663; Yoga, 434; theory of cause, 97–8; God, 165; mokṣa, 152; non-existence, 54–5
Vedānta Deśika's *Nyāyasiddhāñjana*, 670, 713 n.; his *Pañcarātrarakṣā*, 666 n., 669; his *Paramatabhaṅga*, 669; his *Saccaritrarakṣā*, 669; his *Rahasyatrayasāra*, 669, 683, 684, 695, 709, 710 n.; his *Tātparyacandrikā*, 669; his *Tattvamuktākalāpa*, 661 n., 670, 672, 674, 679, 695, 696, 697, 705; his *Tattvaṭīkā*, 669; his *Sarvārthasiddhi*, 670, 671, 696; his *Śatadūṣaṇī*, 670; his *Seśvara Mīmāṁsā*, 378 n., 427, 431 n., 669, 691
Vedāntasiddhāntasārasaṁgraha, 487 n.
Vedārthasaṁgraha, 668, 688, 690, 701, 705 n.
Veṅkaṭa Dīkṣita's *Vārttikābharaṇa*, 377
Vibhaṅga, 35 n.
Vidhuśekhara Bhaṭṭācārya, 465 n.
Vidvanmanorañjanī, 452 n., 578 n.
Vidyābhūṣaṇ, Dr., viii, 34 n., 37 n., 38 n., 85
Vidyāpati, 760
Vidyāraṇya, 528 n., 553, 578 n.; his *Jīvanmuktiviveka*, 451 n., 618, 619, 635 n.; his *Pañcadaśī*, 106, 451 n., 486 n., 490 n., 535 n., 572 n., 590 n., 601 n., 602, 610, 653; his *Vivaraṇaprameyasaṁgraha*, 133 n., 330 n., 398 n., 451 n., 490 n., 578, 587 n., 589, 784–5
Vijñānabhikṣu, 26 n., 106 n., 146 n., 431; his *Sāṁkhyapravacanabhāṣya*, Chap. IV, *passim*, 471 n.; his *Sāṁkhyasāra*, Chap. IV, *passim*; *Vijñānāmṛta*, 451 n.; his *Yogasārasaṁgraha*, 256, 327 n., Chap. V, *passim*; his *Yogavārttika*, 26, 256, 265 n., 272 n., Chap. V, *passim*
Viṣṇu Purāṇa, 32 n., 261, 334 n., 528 n., 562 n., 588 n., 663 n.,

664, 665, 667, 688, 689, 709 n., 761
Viṣṇusahasranāma, 249 n., 450
Viṣṇusvāmin, 663 n.
Visuddimagga, 162 n.
Viśvabhārati Quarterly, 771
Viśvanātha's *Bhāṣāpariccheda*, Chap. II, *passim*, 181, 191 n., 192 n., 205 n.; his *Siddhāntamuktāvali*, Chap. II, *passim*, 181, 188, 210 n., 403 n., 419, 482 n. 536 n., 538 n.
Viśveśvara's *Bhāṭṭacintāmaṇi*, 378 n.
Vivekacūḍāmaṇi, 481 n., 572 n., 576 n., 580 n., 649 n.
Voltaire, 504
Vyāsa, 18 n., 24, 37 n.; his *Yogabhāṣya*, 258, Chaps. IV and V, *passim*
Vyāsarāya's *Candrikā*, 739
Vyomasaṁhitā, 737 n.
Vyomaśekhara's *Vyomavatī*, 181

Wallace's *Epicureanism*, 202
Walleser, 452 n.
Ward's *Study of Kant*, 770 n.; his *Psychological Principles*, 604 n.
Weber, 23 n.; his *History of Indian Literature*, 254 n., 356 n.
Westcott, Bishop, his *Gospel according to St. John*, 557 n.
Whewell's *History of the Inductive Sciences*, 207 n.
Whitehead, Professor A. N., 229, 237, 240 n.; his *Concept of Nature*, 228 n.; his *Enquiry*, 243 n., his *Principle of Relativity*, 143 n.
Wilde, Oscar, his *De Profundis*, 669 n.
Windischmann, 433 n.
Winternitz, 249 n., 465 n.
Wolff, 527
Woodroffe, Sir John, 735–6; his *Serpent Power*, 737 n.
Woods, Professor, 341 n.
Wordsworth, 363

Xenophanes, 767

Yādavaprakāśa, 431, 671–2
Yājñavalkya, 32, 337 n.; his *Smṛti*, 32, 34 n., 341
Yajur Veda, 339
Yamaka, 35
Yāmunācārya, 668; his *Āgamaprāmāṇya*, 668; his *Ātmasiddhi*, 306 n.; his *Catuśślokī*, 668; his *Gītārthasaṁgraha*, 668; *Mahāpuruṣanirṇaya*, 668; his *Siddhitraya*, 385 n., 471 n., 668, 674; his *Stotraratna*, 668
Yoga, 19, 20, 23, 28, 173; and Advaita Vedānta, 339; *Bhagavadgītā*, 337, 340, 344; Buddhism, 339–40, 341; *Mahābhārata*, 340; psychical research, 336–7; psychoanalysis, 354; Pūrva Mīmāṁsā, 340; Sāṁkhya, 340, 342–4, 380; Upaniṣads, 337, 339, 342, 344; theory of concentration, 358–63; contemplation, 357–8; ethics, 353–4; God, 368–72; inference, 350; karma, 365–6; mokṣa, 344, 363–5; perception, 349–50; psychology, 345–9; supernormal powers, 366–8; truth, 350–1; Vedas, 370
Yogarahasya, 668
Yoga Sūtra, 251, Chaps. IV and V, *passim*
Yogatattva Upaniṣad, 338 n.
Yogavāśiṣṭha, 344 n., 457 n., 464 n., 580, 581 n., 635
Yuan Chwang, 39 n., 449 n.